SOCIAL RESEARCH
IN THE JUDICIAL PROCESS
Cases, Readings, and Text

SOCIAL RESEARCH
IN THE JUDICIAL PROCESS
Cases, Readings, and Text

WALLACE D. LOH

Russell Sage Foundation   New York

The Russell Sage Foundation

The Russell Sage Foundation, one of the oldest of America's general purpose foundations, was established in 1907 by Mrs. Margaret Olivia Sage for "the improvement of social and living conditions in the United States." The Foundation seeks to fulfill this mandate by fostering the development and dissemination of knowledge about the political, social, and economic problems of America. It conducts research in the social sciences and public policy, and publishes books and pamphlets that derive from this research.

The Foundation provides support for individual scholars and collaborates with other granting agencies and academic institutions in studies of social problems. It maintains a professional staff of social scientists who engage in their own research as well as advise on Foundation programs and projects. The Foundation also conducts a Visiting Scholar Program, under which established scholars working in areas of current interest to the Foundation join the staff for a year to consult and to continue their own research and writing. Finally, a Postdoctoral Fellowship Program enables promising young scholars to devote full time to their research while in residence for a year at the Foundation.

The Board of Trustees is responsible for the general policies and oversight of the Foundation, while the immediate administrative direction of the program and staff is vested in the President, assisted by the officers and staff. The President bears final responsibility for the decision to publish a manuscript as a Russell Sage Foundation book. In reaching a judgment on the competence, accuracy, and objectivity of each study, the President is advised by the staff and a panel of special readers.

The conclusions and interpretations in Russell Sage Foundation publications are those of the authors and not of the Foundation, its Trustees, or its staff. Publication by the Foundation, therefore, does not imply endorsement of the contents of the study. It does signify that the manuscript has been reviewed by competent scholars in the field and that the Foundation finds it worthy of public consideration.

Cover and text design: Huguette Franco

Library of Congress Catalog Number: 84-60263
Standard Book Number: 0-87154-551-9
10 9 8 7 6 5 4 3 2 1

To my parents,
S. Y. and Lily

PREFACE

Interdisciplinary study is flourishing. Since the mid-sixties, research in law and the social sciences generally has grown steadily in quantity and in quality. Particularly in law and psychology, since the mid-seventies, the rate of publications has soared and various institutional developments—for example, the establishment of new journals, joint degree programs, and professional organizations—auger the coming of age of this field. The formation of a critical mass of specialists makes laboring at the boundaries of two disciplines less lonely. In the law school world, "law and" movements took hold at about the same time. Calls for empirical legal studies were sounded as early as the turn of the century by the proponents of sociological jurisprudence and again in the 1930s by the advocates of legal realism. However, it was really not until the turbulent era of the mid-sixties, when the courts spearheaded far-reaching changes in criminal justice and civil rights and student activists sought (in the parlance of the day) "social relevance" in higher learning, that interdisciplinary and clinical offerings were integrated into the standard curriculum of major law schools. These academic changes enriched scholarship and teaching; in the ensuing years, they spread to virtually every law school.

However, realities being what they are, academic boundaries cannot be wholly disregarded. For the most part, courses are taught, degrees awarded, and papers published in disciplinary contexts. Professional socialization also creates mind sets that may inhibit rapprochement. Social scientists are trained in the scientific method. They are socialized to think in terms of generating and testing theories. Lawyers are trained in the dialectical method. They are skilled in working with precedents and analogy in light of principles and policies in order to arrive at authoritative settlements of disputes. They are applied social scientists: they think in terms of regulating—rather than understanding—behavior. Thus, it is a natural tendency to frame problems in ways that require for their analysis those methods and concepts with which one is most familiar. A trained incapacity to view things the way another discipline sees them is inevitable, yet to overcome it is necessary to interdisciplinary endeavor.

This is a book of empirical legal studies. The subject matter is legal and the method of analysis involves an intermeshing of scientific inquiry and dialectical reasoning. The focus is on the application of social research in the judicial process. The contents cover three areas. First, issues of substantive justice: what courts do and should do, and how judges reason and should reason, in creating, implementing, expanding, and abolishing case law. These processes of judicial decision-making, and the use or misuse of social science therein, are exemplified by the landmark opinions on southern and northern school desegregation, capital punishment, and the regulation of the police. Second, issues of procedural justice: what courts do and should do in safeguarding the fairness, reliability, and efficiency of fact-finding processes at trial. These processes, which have been the subject of empirical study, include the selection and functioning of the jury, the prophylactic measures against pretrial influences, and the web of evidentiary and procedural rules that govern the presentation of information in court. And third, issues in the jurisprudence of law and social science: the philosophical conceptions of law which underlie different styles of judicial decision-making and of legal scholarship and how these conceptions, in turn, affect the uses and limits of social science in law.

The thrust of this book is on bridging the domain of social facts (which the social scientist systematically gathers) and the domain of social judgments (which is the stock-in-trade of the lawyer). Decisions which embody moral values need not, of course, be grounded on factual proof. But this is not to say that data may not have an indirect effect on shaping legal outcomes. Even normative conclusions are generated by an awareness of the facts; social research can illuminate and sharpen the factual predicates of decision-making. Law initially defines the facts that are relevant to adjudication, but newly uncovered facts can also help create new law. The main purpose of the book is to expose students to the reciprocal relationship between facts and law that permits the applications of social research in judicial decision-making. It is a process-oriented book—it seeks to cultivate an informed appreciation for the liberating possibilities of empirical inquiry in law.

This book also serves derivative purposes. Social science students will find that it offers a basic introduction to law. Law, as used here, does not mean primarily a body of doctrinal rules to be learned, but a technique of practical reasoning and problem-solving that implicates normative choices. Both social science students and law students will gain some insights into the uses of social research in law and lawyering. Although this book is not a primer for law students on how to do social research, it should help them become intelligent consumers of the work of professional social scientists. Exposure to legal reasoning and to the methods of social science is an unavoidable by-product of a book on judicial applications of social research.

Since my concern is to involve students with process rather than substance, I opted to prepare a casebook (which is the standard mode of law school teaching) rather than a textbook (which is more commonly used in the arts and sciences). A casebook has an open texture quality which lends itself to the task at hand. I have juxtaposed judicial opinions, empirical research studies, text, and questions. The opinions have been edited to highlight the factual dimensions of legal issues, without giving short shrift to doctrinal and policy considerations. The studies have been selected and edited to explore the relevance of research data to the issues raised in the opinions. In both opinions and studies, I have routinely excised all footnotes and all citations to other cases and publications, except for those that have special significance. The text provides background and context for the opinions and the research studies. The questions are intended to push the student to read aggressively. The whole—which I hope is more than the sum of its parts—should impart analytical perspectives on the interrelationships between law and social science.

At this time, I believe it may be the only available casebook of its kind in law and social research (where social research includes, primarily, psychological and social psychological studies and, secondarily, sociological studies). Since not all social scientists are accustomed to the casebook format, I have described in greater detail the organization, content, objectives, and themes of this book in Chapter 1, which is essentially an expanded preface. I shall not recapitulate further what is presented there, except to indicate the intended readership.

Ideally, the book is suited for use in mixed classes of advanced social science students and law students. This mix may not always be available on every campus. In addition, the realities of the marketplace are such that interest in and demand for courses in law and social science are usually greater in academic departments than in law schools. Most law schools and law students see their main mission not in terms of contributing to scholarship, but in more workaday terms of training for the bar. Consequently, I have prepared this casebook in the anticipation that it will find greater—but not exclusive—use in academic departments. As to the "legal" component of the book, it is largely self-contained. It presupposes no background in law. The text amply supplements the judicial opinions so that social science students, inexperienced in reading cases, can grasp the legal rulings and critically evaluate their ramifications. The "social research" component of the book, however, may require supplementation by the instructor depending upon the level of expertise of the students in empirical research methodology and the technical depth to which the research studies are pursued. The text also addresses methodological issues, but does so less extensively than the legal and policy issues. The student is presumed to have some background in social research, equivalent to that attained in an undergraduate course on research methods. I have tried to keep the statistical and methodological presentations spare and simple. Law students who lack the requisite background will not be overwhelmed by numerology—they should still be able to evaluate the thinking that lies behind the figures. Melding the concepts and tools of law and of social science is not without challenge. But that, of course, is part of the allure of interdisciplinary study.

ACKNOWLEDGMENTS

I am indebted to many institutions and individuals for helping make possible the publication of this book. My foremost thanks go to the Russell Sage Foundation. During the late sixties and most of the seventies, it operated a Law and Social Science Program under the direction of Professor Stan Wheeler. This program provided fellowships to social scientists to study law and to lawyers to study social science, at a time when such support was virtually unavailable elsewhere. The critical mass of social-legal specialists that exists today is due in no small measure to the largesse of this program. In my case, the Russell Sage Foundation funded my legal education and later the initial preparation of this book. From the time I first applied for a fellowship to the time I completed the book, and especially through the intervening years of law school, Stan was present as adviser, colleague, and cheerleader.

In law school, I met Neil Vidmar, another Russell Sage Fellow, who was on leave from the University of Western Ontario. Since we were both social psychologists and shared common research interests, we decided to prepare a casebook jointly. We presented the idea to the Russell Sage Foundation, which promptly supported it, and for the next couple of years we burned the midnight oil as we struggled with the content and organization of the book. Such collaborative undertakings, as no doubt others can attest to, are not necessarily less demanding than solo efforts and collaborating by long distance simply adds another complicating dimension. I eventually assumed the task of completing it, but the imprint of Neil's contribution remains. He helped write and edit Chapter 5 on capital punishment, a subject in which he has made important contributions to the empirical literature. He also critiqued preliminary drafts of other chapters.

At the University of Washington, a succession of very able students have assisted me. Laurence Severance was my alter ego during his law school years. The final structure of the book emerged from our brainstorming sessions. The first draft was used and evaluated by him in teaching an undergraduate class on law and psychology. Larry, who was a psychology professor and is now an attorney, is one of the few practitioners who is also engaged in social-legal research. Chapter 9 includes one of his articles. Edith Green and Barbara Critchlow were enrolled in my law and social science class when they offered their assistance. Edith, who has since received her Ph.D. in cognitive psychology, collaborated in the preparation of Chapter 10 and Barbara, a Ph.D. candidate in social psychology, helped write Chapter 5. I have also benefited from discussions with many other students whose thoughtful comments have informed my thinking. They include Larry Johnson, Catherine Martinson, Noella Hashimoto (all of the University of Washington Law School) and Marcia Bansley (of Emory Law School).

Different drafts of different chapters were reviewed by several colleagues. Their detailed and incisive criticisms improved the final product. I want to thank Professor Richard Lempert of Michigan Law School, Professor Stewart Macaulay of Wisconsin Law School, Professor Arval Morris of the University of Washington Law School, Professor Lawrence Friedman of Stanford Law School, Mr. Herbert Morton (editorial consultant to the Russell Sage Foundation), and the anonymous reviewers retained by the Russell Sage Foundation. The failings that remain are my responsibility alone. Professor Richard Katzev of Reed College, also a former Russell Sage Fellow, used drafts of the book in his course on law and psychology. His students provided critical commentaries on the manuscript and many of their suggestions were taken into account in the final draft.

Bibliographic, editorial, and administrative tasks were performed with Job-like sufferance and indefatigable good humor by Mark Emory, now a student at McGeorge Law School, and Barbara Kurtz, then a student at the University of Houston Law Center. I was carefree about making endless changes in the manuscript because of the access to outstanding word processing services. Our word processing staff, composed of April Low and Jeri Miles, and my secretary, Karen Walton, have earned my appreciation.

Skill, patience, helpfulness, sympathy, and efficiency—these are the endowments of an ideal editor. These, and more, were displayed by Priscilla Lewis, publications director of the Russell Sage Foundation, as she shepherded the manuscript through the publication process. The final draft was much enhanced by the copyediting of Sylvia Newman.

I thank the publishers and authors of articles that are quoted or reproduced in this casebook for granting copyright permission.

Most of the casebook was completed at Condon Hall. For me, it is a special place. It is very satisfying to have deans (past and present) and fellow faculty members who are highly supportive of my research and teaching interests. And it uplifts the spirit to look out my office window and see—on those rare days when it isn't overcast and raining—Mount Rainier soaring 14,408 feet above Lake Union. The colleagueship, the (occasional) view, and the continuous flow of classical music on KING-FM radio help ease the burden of writing. For these blessings, I'm thankful.

Wallace D. Loh
Professor of Law and
Adjunct Professor of Psychology
University of Washington
Seattle, Summer 1984

SUMMARY OF CONTENTS

PART I
FOREWORD: DEFINING THE FOCUS

Chapter 1. Introduction to the Book   3
Chapter 2. Introduction to Law and the Judicial
            Process   23

PART II
SOCIAL RESEARCH AND SUBSTANTIVE JUSTICE:
LAWMAKING IN THE APPELLATE PROCESS

Chapter 3. Creation of Law: Case Study of Southern
            School Desegregation   43
Chapter 4. Implementation and Expansion of Law:
            Case Study of Southern and Northern
            School Desegregation   107
Chapter 5. Contraction and Abolition of Law: Case
            Study of the Death Penalty   193
Chapter 6. Impact of Law: Case Study of Regulating
            Police Conduct   273

PART III
SOCIAL RESEARCH AND PROCEDURAL JUSTICE:
FACT-FINDING IN THE TRIAL PROCESS

Chapter 7. Selection of the Jury: Case Study of Jury
            Impartiality   353
Chapter 8. Functioning of the Jury: Case Study of
            Jury Size, Verdict, and Litigation
            Complexity   425

Chapter 9.   Presentations to the Jury: Case Study of
              Evidence Rules   477
Chapter 10.   Extrajudicial Influences on the Jury Before
              Trial: Case Study of Eyewitness
              Identification   549

PART IV
AFTERWORD: PERSPECTIVES ON THE FOCUS

Chapter 11.   Historical and Conceptual Perspectives on
              Psycholegal Research   607
Chapter 12.   Jurisprudential Perspectives on the Judicial
              Process   637
Chapter 13.   Conceptual and Jurisprudential
              Perspectives on the Uses of Social
              Research in the Judicial Process   695

TABLE OF CONTENTS

PART I
FOREWORD: DEFINING THE FOCUS

Chapter 1.   Introduction to the Book   3

1.1   Focus   3
    The Judicial Process   4
    The Interface of the Judicial Process and
      Social Research   5
    Social Research   6

1.2   Objectives   7
    Introduction to Applied Social-Legal Research   8
    Introduction to Legal Reasoning   10
    Intended Readership   13

1.3   Method   14
    Casebook Format   14
    Case Method of Study   15

1.4   Content   17

References   20

Chapter 2.   Introduction to Law and the Judicial Process   23

2.1   Law as a System of Rules   24

2.2   Law as a Process of Solving Disputes   26

2.3   Some Functions of Law   28

2.4   Structure of the Courts   29
    Overview   29
    State Courts   31
    Federal Courts   31

2.5   Procedure of the Courts   33
    The Adversary System   33
    Trial Process   34
    Appellate Process   37

2.6   Selected Provisions of the United States Constitution   38

References   39

PART II
SOCIAL RESEARCH AND SUBSTANTIVE JUSTICE:
LAWMAKING IN THE APPELLATE PROCESS

Chapter 3.   Creation of Law: Case Study of Southern School
             Desegregation   43

3.1   Introduction and Overview   43

3.2   Historical and Legal Background   45
    The Civil War Amendments and Reconstruction
      Legislation   45
    Dismantling the Federal Protection   46
    The Rise of Jim Crow Legislation   47
    Challenging School Segregation   48

3.3   Doctrines of Equality and the Social Science Context   50
    The "Separate-But-Equal" Doctrine   50
      Plessy v. *Ferguson*   50
    NOTES AND QUESTIONS   54
    The Social Science Context   56
      Biological Perspectives on Social Behavior   56
      Environmental Perspectives on Social
        Behavior   57
      The Effects of Segregation and the Consequences of
        Desegregation: A Social Science Statement (Appendix
        to Appellants' Briefs)   59
    The "Separate-Is-Inherently-Unequal" Doctrine   62
      Brown v. *Board of Education of Topeka*   62
    NOTES AND QUESTIONS   66

3.4   Social Science at Trial: Expert Testimony   69
    Expert Testimony in South Carolina   70
    Expert Testimony in Virginia   72
    Expert Testimony in Kansas   75
    Impact of the Social Science Testimony
      on the Trial Courts   76
    NOTES AND QUESTIONS   77

3.5 Evaluating the Role of Social Science in Law Creation   78

   Jurisprudence (Edmond Cahn)   *78*
   The Desegregation Cases: Criticism of the
    Social Scientist's Role (Kenneth B. Clark)   *81*
   NOTES AND QUESTIONS   *83*

3.6 Social Science on Appeal: The Brandeis Brief   84

   Due Process and the Brandeis Brief   *84*
    Muller v. *Oregon*   *85*
    The Brandeis Brief (Marion E. Doro)   *87*
   A Note on Due Process and Judicial Review   *90*
    Meanings of Due Process   *90*
    Standards for Judicial Review   *93*
   NOTES AND QUESTIONS   *95*

3.7 Reading Judicial Opinions   97

   Structure and Analysis of a Case   *98*
    Statement of Facts   *98*
    The Legal Issue(s) or Question(s)   *99*
    The Decision or Holding   *100*
    The Reasoning   *101*
    Role of Social Science   *101*
   Synthesis of Cases: Building the Apperceptive
    Mass   *101*

References   *103*

Chapter 4.   Implementation and Expansion of Law:
     Case Study of Southern and Northern
     School Desegregation   *107*

4.1 Introduction and Overview   *107*

4.2 Implementation of *Brown*   *109*

   Amicus Curiae Brief of the Attorney General of Florida:
    Appendix A   *111*
   Brown v. *Board of Education of Topeka*
    [Brown II]   *113*
   NOTES AND QUESTIONS   *114*

4.3 Post-*Brown* Southern School Desegregation   *115*

   Token Desegregation   *115*
   Massive Desegregation   *116*
    Swann v. *Charlotte-Mecklenburg Board of*
    Education   *117*
   NOTES AND QUESTIONS   *120*

4.4 Expansion of School Desegregation to the North   *121*

   Milliken v. *Bradley*   *123*

Social Science and the Courts: The Detroit Schools Case
(Eleanor P. Wolf)   *126*
NOTES AND QUESTIONS   *131*

4.5   Social Science in Post-*Brown* School Desegregation   *133*
Residential Segregation and School
Segregation   *134*
NOTES AND QUESTIONS   *135*
White Flight   *137*
The Social Science Debate on White Flight   *137*
Judicial Responses to White Flight   *139*
Academic Achievement, Self-Concept,
and Race Relations   *141*
A Brief Summary of the Coleman Report (James S.
Coleman)   *141*
The Evidence on Busing (David J. Armor)   *143*
Busing: A Review of "the Evidence" (Thomas F.
Pettigrew, Elizabeth L. Useem, Clarence
Normand, and Marshall S. Smith)   *147*
NOTES AND QUESTIONS   *149*
Unconstitutional Practices of School
Authorities   *154*
NOTES AND QUESTIONS   *155*

4.6   Reinterpretation of *Brown*   *157*
Evolving Interpretations of *Brown*: Input and
Output Perspectives   *157*
The Detroit Case: Throughput Perspective   *158*
Implications for Social Research   *159*

4.7   Second-Generation Problems in Schools:
Intelligence Testing   *160*
Larry P. v. *Riles*   *162*
NOTES AND QUESTIONS   *170*

4.8   Second-Generation Problems in the Marketplace:
Employment Testing   *175*
Title VII   *175*
Griggs v. *Duke Power Co.* (1971)   *176*
Albemarle Paper Co. v. *Moody* (1975)   *177*
Washington v. *Davis* (1976)   *178*
NOTES AND QUESTIONS   *179*

4.9   Social Science in Law Creation and Expansion:
Perspectives and Overview   *181*
From Consensus to Dissensus   *181*
Lawmaking and Fact Determination   *183*

References   *186*

Chapter 5.   Contraction and Abolition of Law: Case Study of
             the Death Penalty   *193*

5.1   Introduction   *193*
         The Historical Scope of Capital Offenses   *194*
         Statutory Reform and Repeal   *195*
         The Start of Judicial Challenges   *197*
         Overview   *199*

5.2   Equal Protection Challenges   *200*
         *Statement of Professor Marvin E. Wolfgang
            of the University of Pennsylvania Center for
            Studies in Criminology and Criminal
            Law*   *201*
         Maxwell v. *Bishop*   *205*
         NOTES AND QUESTIONS   *209*

5.3   Due Process Challenges   *211*
         Witherspoon v. *Illinois*   *211*
         NOTES AND QUESTIONS   *214*
         Hovey v. *The Superior Court of Alameda
            County*   *217*
         NOTES AND QUESTIONS   *227*

5.4   Eighth Amendment Challenges: Round One   *230*
         The Social-Political Climate and the Evolution
            of Death Penalty Litigation   *230*
         Early Adjudication on the Eighth Amendment   *232*
         Round One   *234*
         Furman v. *Georgia*   *234*
         NOTES AND QUESTIONS   *241*
         Social Research on "Evolving Standards of
            Decency"   *244*
         Public Opinion on the Death Penalty (Neil Vidmar and
            Phoebe Ellsworth)   *244*
         NOTES AND QUESTIONS   *246*
         *Public Opinion, the Death Penalty, and the Eighth
            Amendment: Testing the Marshall Hypothesis* (Austin
            Sarat and Neil Vidmar)   *247*
         NOTES AND QUESTIONS   *250*

5.5   Eighth Amendment Challenges: Round Two   *251*
         Gregg v. *Georgia*   *251*
         NOTES AND QUESTIONS   *254*
         The Deterrent Effect of Capital Punishment   *256*
         The Companion Cases   *260*
         NOTES AND QUESTIONS   *261*

5.6   The Jurisprudence of Death in Perspective   265
          The Politics and Dialectics of Adjudication   265
          The Death Sentence: A Compromise
              Sanction?   268

References   269

Chapter 6.   Impact of Law: Case Study of Regulating
              Police Conduct   273

6.1   Introduction   273
          The Police Function in a Democratic Society   273
              Balancing Law and Order   273
              The Exclusionary Rule   275
          A Brief History of the Police   276
          Overview   277

6.2   Judicial Regulation of Police Interrogation   279
          The Role of Police Interrogation   279
          A Historical Sketch of Judicial Regulation of
              Interrogations   280
          Miranda v. Arizona   282
          NOTES AND QUESTIONS   286

6.3   Impact of *Miranda* on Police Interrogation   289
          *Interrogations in New Haven: The Impact of
              Miranda*   289
          NOTES AND QUESTIONS   295

6.4   Judicial Regulation of Police Enforcement Practices   301
          The Fourth Amendment Exclusionary Rule   301
              Historical Background   301
              Procedure of Exclusion   301
          The Purpose and Impact of the Exclusionary
              Rule   302
              The Exclusionary Rule: Why Suppress Valid Evidence?
              (Malcolm R. Wilkey)   302
              *The Exclusionary Rule in Historical Perspective: The
              Struggle to Make the Fourth Amendment More Than
              "an Empty Blessing"* (Yale Kamisar)   306
          NOTES AND QUESTIONS   310

6.5   Impact of the Exclusionary Rule on Police Enforcement
          Practices   312
              Studying the Exclusionary Rule in Search and Seizure
              (Dallin H. Oaks)   312
          NOTES AND QUESTIONS   318

6.6   Social Psychological and Legal Perspectives
        on the Police   *321*
            Levels of Analysis   *321*
            Individual and Organizational Characteristics
                of the Police   *322*
                Social-Economic Background   *322*
                Socialization and Training   *322*
                Organization and Functions   *323*
                Personal Characteristics   *324*
                Social and Organizational Norms   *326*
                Attitudes Toward, and Compliance With,
                    Legality   *328*
            Institutional Relationships in the Criminal
                Justice System   *330*
                Educative Effect of the Suppression
                    Hearing   *330*
                Clarity and Communication of Legal Norms   *331*

6.7   Self-Regulation of the Police by Rule-Making   *332*
            Law Enforcement Policy: The Police Role (President's
                Commission on Law Enforcement and the
                Administration of Justice)   *332*
            NOTES AND QUESTIONS   *335*

6.8   A Jurisprudence of Impact   *342*
            Deductive Syllogistic Method   *342*
            Impact Analysis Method   *343*
            NOTES AND QUESTIONS   *345*

References   *345*

PART III
SOCIAL RESEARCH AND PROCEDURAL JUSTICE:
FACT-FINDING IN THE TRIAL PROCESS

Chapter 7.   Selection of the Jury: Case Study of Jury
                Impartiality   *353*

7.1   Introduction   *353*
            Origins of the Jury   *353*
            The Sixth Amendment Jury and the Seventh
                Amendment Jury   *355*
            Overview   *356*

7.2   Discrimination in Jury Selection   *357*
            Swain v. *Alabama*   *357*
            Mechanics of Jury Selection   *359*
            Grounds for Challenging Jury Selection   *360*

NOTES AND QUESTIONS   *361*
Post-*Swain* Underrepresentation Cases   *363*

7.3   Legal and Statistical Proof of Discrimination   *364*
Proof in Jury Cases   *364*
Castaneda v. *Partida*   *364*
NOTES AND QUESTIONS   *368*
People v. *Powell*   *371*
NOTES AND QUESTIONS   *373*
Proof in Other Contexts   *375*
Hazelwood School District v. *United States*   *376*
NOTES AND QUESTIONS   *378*
Gay v. *Waiters' and Dairy Lunchmen's Union,*
Local 30   *379*
NOTES AND QUESTIONS   *383*

7.4   Discrimination in Peremptory Challenges   *385*
Swain v. *Alabama*   *385*
Objectives of Voir Dire   *386*
Procedure of Voir Dire   *387*
NOTES AND QUESTIONS   *389*

7.5   Juror Partiality and Personal Characteristics: Methods
of Selection   *392*
The Uses of Social Science in Trials with Political and
Racial Overtones: The Trial of Joan Little (John B.
McConahay, Courtney J. Mullin, and Jeffrey
Frederick)   *392*
NOTES AND QUESTIONS   *399*

7.6   Juror Partiality and Pretrial Publicity: Remedial and
Preventive Safeguards   *407*
Remedying Pretrial Publicity: Change of
Venue   *407*
NOTES AND QUESTIONS   *409*
The Free Press/Fair Trial Controversy   *412*
The First Amendment   *413*
The Social-Legal Background   *413*
Preventing Pretrial Publicity: Prior Restraint   *415*
Nebraska Press Association v. *Stuart*   *415*
NOTES AND QUESTIONS   *418*
Research on Pretrial Publicity   *418*
The ABA Report   *418*
Experimental Studies   *419*

References   *420*

Chapter 8.   Functioning of the Jury: Case Study of Jury Size,
Verdict, and Litigation Complexity   *425*

8.1   Introduction   425
        Jury Competence   426
        Jury Sovereignty   427
        Constitutional Dimensions of Jury Functioning   430
        Overview   431

8.2   Effects of Size on Jury Functioning   432
        Williams v. *Florida*   432
        NOTES AND QUESTIONS   434
        Ballew v. *Georgia*   437
        NOTES AND QUESTIONS   441

8.3   Effects of Decision Rules on Jury Functioning   442
        Apodaca v. *Oregon*   442
        NOTES AND QUESTIONS   444
        United States v. *Dougherty*   447
        NOTES AND QUESTIONS   450
        Political Policy and the Jury Cases   451

8.4   Methodological Issues in Jury Research   453
        "Convincing Empirical Evidence" on the Six Member Jury
          (Hans Zeisel and Shari Seidman
          Diamond)   453
        *Uncovering "Nondiscernible" Differences: Empirical
          Research and the Jury Size Cases* (Richard O.
          Lempert)   456
        NOTES AND QUESTIONS   460

8.5   Effects of Case Complexity on Jury Functioning   462
        Complexity and the Seventh Amendment   462
        Historical and Functional Approaches   464
        Fifth Amendment Due Process Approach   466
        *In Re Japanese Electronic Products Antitrust
          Litigation*   466
        NOTES AND QUESTIONS   469
        Schematic Overview of the Jury Process and
          Jury Research   473

References   473

Chapter 9.   Presentations to the Jury: Case Study of Evidence
             Rules   477

9.1   Introduction   477
        The Structure of Evidence Law   477
        The Rationale of Evidence Law   478
        Overview   480

9.2   Order of Presentation of Evidence   481
        Stages in the Presentation of Evidence   481

Gross Order and Internal Order of Presentation   *484*
  Brooks v. *Tennessee*   *485*
  NOTES AND QUESTIONS   *487*
Social Research on Order of Communications   *488*
  Prior Familiarity with the Communication   *489*
  Delay Between Opposing Communications   *490*
  Anticipation of Opposing Communications   *490*
  A Summing Up   *491*
  Order of Presentation at Trial (Laurens Walker, John
      Thibaut, and Virginia Andreoli)   *492*
  NOTES AND QUESTIONS   *495*
Methods of Proof   *497*
  Inquisitorial and Adversarial Methods   *497*
  Study of Judicial Bias in Inquisitorial and
      Adversarial Methods   *499*
  NOTES AND QUESTIONS   *500*

9.3 Mode of Presentation of Evidence   *501*
  Applications to the Judicial Process   *502*
  Technical Aspects   *503*
  Economies and Efficiencies   *503*
  Behavioral Impact on the Jury   *504*
    *The Effects of Videotape Testimony in Jury Trials: Studies
      on Juror Decision Making, Information Retention, and
      Emotional Arousal* (Gerald R. Miller, David C.
      Bender, Frank Boster, B. Thomas Florence,
      Norman Fontes, John Hocking, and Henry
      Nicholson)   *504*
    NOTES AND QUESTIONS   *507*
  Television Cameras in the Courtroom   *508*

9.4 Admissibility of Evidence   *509*
  The Basic Policy and Principle of Evidence Law   *509*
  The "Other Crimes Evidence" Rule   *510*
  Effectiveness of Limiting Instructions   *511*
    *Section 12 of the Canada Evidence Act and the
      Deliberations of Simulated Juries* (Valerie P. Hans
      and Anthony N. Doob)   *512*
    NOTES AND QUESTIONS   *514*
  Empirical and Normative Justifications of
      Instructions   *518*

9.5 Sufficiency of Evidence   *520*
  Burden of Production and Burden of Persuasion   *521*
    Standard of Proof in Criminal Cases   *522*
    Standard of Proof in Civil Cases   *522*
    Quantification of Evidence and of Standards of
      Proof   *523*

Using Objective Probability Estimates at Trial   *524*
    People v. *Collins*   *524*
    NOTES AND QUESTIONS   *527*
Using Subjective Probability Estimates at Trial   *530*
    Objective and Subjective Probability   *530*
    Bayes' Theorem   *531*
    Application of the Theorem to School
        Admissions   *531*
    Application of the Theorem to Identification
        Evidence   *532*
    Systematic Biases in Decision-Making   *534*
    NOTES AND QUESTIONS   *535*

9.6   Comprehensibility of Instructions on Evaluating
       Evidence   *537*
    Historical Background   *537*
    Research on Comprehensibility   *538*
        *Improving the Ability of Jurors to Comprehend and Apply
        Criminal Jury Instructions* (Laurence J. Severance
        and Elizabeth F. Loftus)   *539*
    NOTES AND QUESTIONS   *543*

References   *544*

Chapter 10.   Extrajudicial Influences on the Jury Before
               Trial: Case Study of Eyewitness Identification   *549*

10.1   Introduction   *549*
    The Relationship Between Pretrial and In-Court
        Identification   *550*
    Parameters of the Problem   *551*
    Overview   *553*

10.2   Safeguards Against Suggestive Police Identification
        Procedures   *554*
    Presence of Counsel   *554*
        United States v. *Wade*   *554*
    NOTES AND QUESTIONS   *557*
    Reliability of Identifications   *559*
        Manson v. *Brathwaite*   *559*
    NOTES AND QUESTIONS   *561*
    Research on Lineup Identifications   *563*
        Lineup Instructions   *563*
        Lineup Size   *564*
        Lineup Similarity   *565*
        Witness Confidence   *567*
        Further Research   *567*

10.3   Psychology of Eyewitness Identification   568
      Did Your Eyes Deceive You? Expert Psychological
      Testimony on the Unreliability of Eyewitness
      Identification (Frederic D. Woocher)   *569*
      Note: Did Your Psychologist Deceive You?   *574*

10.4   Safeguards Against Fallible Eyewitness Identification:
      Expert Testimony   581
      Example of Expert Testimony   *582*
        The Physiology of Eyewitness Testimony: Eyewitness
        Identification (Marshall Houts)   *582*
      NOTES AND QUESTIONS   *588*
      Admissibility of Expert Testimony on Eyewitness
      Identifications   *589*
        United States v. *Amaral*   *589*
      NOTES AND QUESTIONS   *590*

10.5   Safeguards Against Fallible Eyewitness Identification:
      Cautionary Instructions   596
      United States v. *Telfaire*   *596*
      NOTES AND QUESTIONS   *599*

References   600

PART IV
AFTERWORD: PERSPECTIVES ON THE FOCUS

Chapter 11.   Historical and Conceptual Perspectives on
             Psycholegal Research   607

11.1   Introduction and Overview   607

11.2   A Look at the Past   608
      Pioneering Stage (1900s): "Yellow Psychology"   *608*
      Legal Realist Stage (1930s): Psychologism in
        the Law   *610*
        The Context of Legal Realism   *612*
      Forensic Stage (1950s): Psychologists on the
        Stand   *614*
      Coming of Age Stage (1970s and 1980s):
        New Research on Procedural Justice   *617*

11.3   An Overview of the Present   618
      Psychology of Eyewitness Identification   *618*
        Level of Analysis in Eyewitness
        Identification   *620*
        The Methods of Experimental Psychology and
        of Law   *622*
        Social Psychology of the Criminal Trial
        Process   *623*

Presentations of Evidence and Law to the
    Jury   *623*
Assessment of the Legal Impact of Social
    Psychological Research on the Criminal Trial
    Process   *624*
Conclusion   *625*

11.4 Reflections on the Future   627
    [Conference Presentation on] *The Future of Law and
        Social Sciences Research* (Marc Galanter)   *627*
    NOTES AND QUESTIONS   *629*

References   630

Chapter 12. Jurisprudential Perspectives on the
              Judicial Process   637

12.1 Introduction   637
    Classical Theories of Law   *638*
        Natural Law   *638*
        Legal Positivism   *639*
        Historical and Sociological Jurisprudence   *640*
    Styles of Judicial Reasoning   *641*
    The Place of Jurisprudence in Social-Legal
        Inquiry   *643*
    Overview   *644*

12.2 Sources of Law   645
    The Case of the Speluncean Explorers
        (Lon L. Fuller)   *645*
    NOTES AND QUESTIONS   *650*

12.3 Formalist Reasoning   653
    The Path of the Law (Oliver W. Holmes)   *653*
    NOTES AND QUESTIONS   *656*
    Formalism: Deductive Reasoning and Inductive
        Science   *657*
    The Social-Intellectual Context of Formalism   *659*
        A Scientific (or Scientistic) Era   *659*
        Laissez Faire and Social Darwinism   *660*
        The Decline of Formalism   *662*

12.4 Realist Reasoning   662
    A Realistic Jurisprudence—The Next Step (Karl N.
        Llewellyn)   *662*
    NOTES AND QUESTIONS   *666*
    The Social-Intellectual Context of Realism   *669*
    NOTES AND QUESTIONS   *672*
    The Decline of Realism and the Rise of Purposive
        Jurisprudence   *674*

12.5   Purposive Reasoning   676
         *The Evolution of Reasoned Elaboration: Jurisprudential
           Criticism and Social Change* (G. Edward
           White)   *676*
         NOTES AND QUESTIONS   *681*
         Other Postrealist Models of Adjudication   *684*
         Hart's Positivist Model   *684*
         Dworkin's Natural Law Model   *685*
         NOTES AND QUESTIONS   *688*

12.6   A Summing Up   689
         Jurisprudential Theories and Psychological
           Theories   *689*
         Law: A House with Many Mansions   *690*

References   691

Chapter 13.   Conceptual and Jurisprudential Perspectives
                on the Uses of Social Research in the Judicial
                Process   695

13.1   Introduction and Overview   695

13.2   Whether and How to Use Social Research   697
         Framing the Issues   *697*
           *Social Science Evidence and the Courts: Reaching
             Beyond the Adversary Process* (Peter W.
             Sperlich)   *697*
           *Social Science and the Courts: The Seduction of the
             Judiciary* (David M. O'Brien)   *701*
         NOTES AND QUESTIONS   *706*
         Presenting Social Science Evidence   *709*
         Communication and Evaluation of the
           Evidence   *709*
         Facts, Values, and the Adversary Process   *710*
         The Role of Experts and the "Science
           Court"   *712*
         Judicial Notice   *713*

13.3   When to Use Social Research   714
         *The Quest for the Middle Range: Empirical Inquiry and
           Legal Policy* (Harry Kalven, Jr.)   *714*
         NOTES AND QUESTIONS   *716*

13.4   Limits to Rapprochement: Differences in Methodology   716
         *Psychology and Legal Change: On the Limits of a Factual
           Jurisprudence* (Craig Haney)   *717*
         NOTES AND QUESTIONS   *721*

13.5   Limits to Rapprochement: Differences in Professional
       Socialization and Culture   723
           Partnership with the Social Sciences (Lloyd E.
               Ohlin)   723
           Social Science (and Economics) in Law
               Schools   725
           Law Schools and Formalism   726
           Law Schools and Realism   726
           Law Schools and Postrealism   728
           Implications for Rapprochement   732

13.6   A Summing Up: Mapping the Role of Social Research
       in Law   739
           Judicial Adjudication   739
           Judicial Legislation   740
           Judicial Rationalization   742
           Conclusion   743

References   744

Index of Cases   749
Name Index   755
Subject Index   767

SOCIAL RESEARCH IN THE JUDICIAL PROCESS
Cases, Readings, and Text

PART I
FOREWORD: DEFINING THE FOCUS

CHAPTER 1

Introduction to the Book

1.1. FOCUS

During oral argument in the School Desegregation Cases, Justice Frankfurter remarked to counsel, "How to inform the judicial mind, you know, is one of the most complicated problems" (in Friedman 1969, p. 63). On the one side are the legal and policy issues posed by the case, on the other side are the sources of information (including social science) introduced to help inform judicial deliberation, and in between is the complex process of evaluating and using the materials presented. These three interrelated components of the judicial process, which merge in the judgment, form the triptych of this volume.

Issues of law and social policy set the parameters for judicial reliance on empirical inquiry. These parameters may differ according to the nature of the problem being adjudicated, so the subject of the role of social research in the courts cannot be discussed in the abstract. It has to be delineated in the context of particular substantive issues, just as the contours of a visually perceived figure take shape against the ground in which the figure appears. Consequently, one must begin by understanding the legal context of a given problem before turning to the empirical analysis. Without this initial understanding, one risks doing research which, notwithstanding its methodological rigor, may have no special importance or relevance to the policy concerns of law (Elwork, Sales, and Suggs 1981, p. 49).

The need to "intellectualize fact-finding" goes hand in hand with the need to "empiricize jurisprudence" (Kalven 1968, p. 70). Courts have a proclivity for making factual assertions with "a cavalier sense of certainty without empirical support" (Rosenblum 1971, p. 459). Lawyers say it is important to get a "feel" for the law. Likewise, it is important that the legal profession "develop a *taste* in empirical inquiry. It needs to develop an understanding of and an appreciation for the kind of informed guess social science can offer it today" (Kalven 1968, p. 70). Legal rules define the range of relevant facts for purposes of adjudication. But social research might call attention to new or additional facts which, if taken into account, could alter the character of the legal issue itself. Questions of law are conditioned upon constituent questions of fact: *ex facto jus oritur* (from facts arises the law). Social research can inform and illuminate the factual predicates of judicial decision-making.

The third component—the evaluation and use of empirical research—lies at the interface of law and social science. This is a "no man's land" that neither side fully cultivates (Kalven 1968, p. 63). For those interested in social-legal inquiry, it is not only a matter of knowing something about law and something about social research. It is also a matter of knowing how to bring the two together. The application of empirical data in the judicial process is part of the broader subject of how information about social reality ("what has already become") contributes to shaping the way society should be ordered ("what is in the process of becoming"; Mannheim 1936, p. 112). It deals with the integration of the objectively true with the morally right.

The focus of this book, then, is on (1) the application of (2) social research to (3) the judicial process. Before describing in the next section the rationale for this focus, we shall begin by expanding briefly on this tripartite focus.

The Judicial Process

In applying social research to law one must first specify the context of "law." Empirical information may be more or less apt depending on whether it is directed toward legislatures, administrative agencies, or courts. Each institution performs different functions. In crude terms, legislatures look to the future and promulgate rules to govern subsequent actions. Agencies look to the present and monitor ongoing activities in their areas of regulation. Courts look to the past and resolve disputes arising from prior conduct. Reliance on research methods and data is, in principle, most suitable in the first two institutional settings. Legislatures, unlike courts, are open to all kinds of information in making policy. They are not restricted to evidence presented by the litigants and filtered through layers of evidentiary sieves. Legislative research staffs have more time, resources, and expertise to conduct or evaluate scientific studies than judges and their clerks. Independent agencies or bureaus within executive departments are also more promising forums for the use of social research. Administrative regulation involves a continuing, long-term relationship between the agency and an affected party. There is the opportunity to relitigate issues and introduce new information as it develops. Agencies also have technically competent staffs. The same potential for learning and reconsideration is absent in the adversarial atmosphere of the courtroom. Judges and juries are under time constraints to reach a final decision notwithstanding incomplete information.

The fact that the courts, relative to the other organs of government, do not provide as congenial a setting for the use of social research has not, however, dissuaded lawyers from presenting and judges from considering such extralegal information at trial and appellate proceedings. This book concentrates on the judicial process and elides the legislative and administrative processes. The latter sources of lawmaking are touched upon only insofar as they intersect with the judicial materials under discussion. By judicial process is meant (1) substantive justice in the appellate process (what appellate courts do and should do, and how appellate judges reason and should reason, in deciding particular cases and in creating new law via adjudication) and (2) procedural justice in the trial process (what trial courts do and should do to safeguard the fairness, reliability, and efficiency of fact-finding procedures). There are several reasons for this focus.

The use of extralegal information in adjudication implicates evidentiary and procedural issues unique to the courts. No such constraints govern the reception of research data in the coordinate branches of the legal system. The result is that the points of contact and divergence between the methods of scientific and legal fact-finding are cast in sharpest relief in the judicial arena. Since this book deals with the intermeshing of these two modes of inquiry in addressing policy issues, our pedagogical aims are best served by narrowing the scope of coverage to adjudication.

The temper of the times also accounts for why much of the research literature deals with the judiciary. Social-legal research flowered during the tidal social changes of the 1960s, when activist courts were the principal and most visible agents of reform. The establishment of civil rights for racial minorities and procedural rights for the criminally accused was spearheaded by judicial action and then followed by legislative and administrative implementation. Empirical research, therefore, centered on the social impact of judicial decisions.

American jurisprudence as a whole, an English legal philosopher has observed, "is marked by a concentration, almost to the point of obsession, on the judicial process" (Hart 1977, p. 969). This preoccupation with the nature and function of the courts arises in part because of the centrality of the judiciary in the American scheme of government. Scarcely any major social issue is not translated, sooner or later, into a judicial one (Tocqueville 1969, p. 280). American courts develop the common law and have the power and duty to nullify state and federal statutes and regulations which infringe upon the Constitution. This kind of broad judicial legislation, infrequent or nonexistent in other countries (including England), partly explains the "obsession." In areas where the judiciary's legislative or policy-making function has been most pronounced, such as in constitutional interpretation, its reliance on social science has been more common and less vulnerable to institutional criticisms. Consequently, a large part of the American literature on "social science and law" is composed of "social science and *constitutional* law." The contents of this book mirror this orientation.

The Interface of the Judicial Process and Social Research

This volume examines specific instances of the use, nonuse, and misuse of empirical data in the appellate and trial processes. The application of social research in judicial decision-making is the leitmotif of the various chapters. Questions regarding whether courts should rely on such information, and, if so, when and how to rely on it and for what purposes, comprise the analytical hub that holds together the substantive spokes of the book.

There is no single, graceful, consensual bridge between social research (the realm of social facts) and judicial decision-making (the realm of social values). There are no established standards for informing the judicial mind of extralegal information. The relationship between scientific and normative inquiry is often uncertain and oblique, rendering it difficult to formulate any generalized account. Nonetheless, it is important to provide more than a gallimaufry of particular situations in which social research and law have commingled. One must attempt to construct a conceptual bridge. Like any other intellectual scheme, this book might yield only partial answers or simply raise further questions. But it should, at least, provide reference points to guide one's thinking.

There are three identifiable but overlapping approaches to social-legal study. One is "social science *and* law," which consists of collating available research information with a legal problem. For example, in some of the studies on witness testimony or on the psychological premises of evidence rules, social scientists and lawyers would comb through the inventory of psychology to see what could be extracted and generalized to the legal setting. The limitation to this collating strategy is that psychology does not always possess a corpus of learning that can be directly and validly transposed to particular legal concerns. The research may have been gathered in ways and for purposes other than those which are of relevance to law. Even when it has a direct bearing on law, its applicability may not be sensed in advance (Kalven 1968, p. 62). In this approach to social-legal research, the two disciplines are on parallel rather than integrated tracks.

A second approach is "social science *in* law," or what might be termed a strategy of "de novo research." Instead of merely extrapolating from existing knowledge, social scientists engage in new studies specifically tailored to given legal issues. Research on, say, the social impact of certain legal rules or on the reliability of police lineup procedures exemplifies this approach. Because the research is organized and written mainly to address practical applications rather than to test theories, it is more likely to have legal utility.

"Social science *of* law" represents a third approach. Empirical inquiry need not be linked to the policy concerns of law. Instead of complementing and illuminating legal learning by adding an empirical dimension, social research could be geared to formulating and testing new theories about legal institutions and their relationship to other social institutions. Some scholars have called for "autonomous inquiry" designed to establish scientific generalizations about the role of law in society rather than to solve pressing problems of the day (Galanter 1974, p. 1065). In this view, research on police compliance with legal rules, for example, can and should be justified on scientific grounds of contributing to the development of a general theory of legal compliance rather than on practical grounds of improving the lawfulness of police conduct. The case for "basic" social research on law rests ultimately on its theoretical interest.

A clear separation between these approaches to social-legal research is, of course, somewhat artificial. A study designed to test a scientific hypothesis may also provide a basis for social action. However, an emphasis on one or another approach serves to limit the scope of study and sharpen its focus. Our main attention is on social research *in* the judicial process—that is, on empirical analysis of factual issues upon which substantive and procedural law are predicated.

Social Research

Since the 1930s, when the social sciences became differentiated and institutionalized in separate university departments (for example, sociology split off from political science and psychology from philosophy; Haskell 1977), social scientists have usually insisted on maintaining their own professional turfs and identities. They write in terms of, say, the "sociology of . . ." or a "social psychological analysis of . . . ," which suggests that they examine a given problem from a distinctive disciplinary viewpoint. It also highlights their concern with theory-testing in lieu of or in addition to practical problem-solving. Hans Zeisel (1974), a sociologist-lawyer, tells of a conversation he once had with a graduate student in sociology. After discussing possible topics for social-legal research, the student called back with regrets because his thesis adviser thought none of the topics was "sociologically interesting." "We should cease asking," said Zeisel, "whether a question is a psychological one or a sociological one. What should matter is whether the answer will be legally interesting" (p. 981).

An atheoretical, policy orientation to research also colors this book. In an applied endeavor, it is of higher priority to produce answers that are meaningful to the subject under investigation than to ask questions which advance a disciplinary perspective. As two social psychologists propose, "[T]he task of using psychological methods to gain a comprehensive understanding of the operation of the legal system should take precedence . . . over the testing and application of the currently popular psychological theories in legal or quasi-legal contexts" (Konečni and Ebbesen 1982, p. 27). The demands of the problem rather than academic boundaries should channel the inquiry.

However, boundaries cannot be entirely disregarded since studies are designed and published in disciplinary contexts. The research presented in this book has been drawn mainly from psychology and social psychology and, where appropriate, from sociology as well. These branches of social science implicate different but complementary ways of looking at problems in law and human behavior. There is the individual or psychological level (for example, perception, motivation), the interpersonal or social psychological level (for example, small group dynamics, social attitudes), and the system or sociological level (for example, organizational norms, cultural values). The three disciplines differ mainly in terms of their conceptualizations and explanations of human action. Their methods of research (field surveys, laboratory experiments, and so forth) and the kinds of data they gather are essentially the same. Since our interest is in legal applications, we shall attend more to the methodology and findings of the studies, whatever their disciplinary origin, rather than to their implications for advancing theory. Therefore, in our nomenclature, these studies are all lumped together under the common rubric of "social research" or "empirical research." The legal community, as the consumer of this research, is hardly fastidious anyway about these intramural distinctions.

1.2. OBJECTIVES

The needs and expectations of social science students and law students in a course on law and social science are, naturally, different. The former often seek a panoramic overview. "I'm familiar with the studies on this or that topic," they say, "but how do they fit into the broader scheme of legal things?" They also wonder how empirical research can be made more relevant to law. They appear perplexed by the mixed reaction from the legal community—which varies from (usually) indifference to (occasionally) uncritical acceptance or outright rejection—to the fruits of such research. On the other hand, law students are mainly interested in applications to their craft. They want to know what there is in social science that is of practical use in lawyering. This book attempts to address these felt needs for a broader picture and for legal applicability.

Introduction to Applied Social-Legal Research

The primary objective is to develop an informed sensitivity to the possibilities and limitations of empirical inquiry in trial and appellate litigation. To this end, this is not mainly a content-oriented book. It does not merely transmit scholarly knowledge. It is a process-oriented book. Obviously, there needs to be content, but the contents—policy issues of substantive and procedural law—have been selected and arranged to present certain ways of thinking about law and the role of social research in law. The doctrinal and empirical information is incidental to the aim of imparting analytical perspectives on the field.

For the social science student, this book offers an introduction to the research literature, particularly to psycholegal research, in its legal context. The 1960s and 1970s were the heyday of "sociology and law," and there are many textbooks and casebooks that organize the literature on society and the legal order (for example, Schwartz and Skolnick 1970; Friedman and Macaulay 1977; Vago 1981). Since the mid-seventies and into the eighties, research on law and human behavior has become one of the "growth stocks" of law and the social sciences generally (Friedman 1974, p. 1071). More books have been written in the past dozen years than in the preceding three-quarters of a century since Münsterberg (1908) published the first English language text on psychology and law. The following topics, covered in some of the recent books, illustrate the diversity:

- legal socialization (Tapp and Levine 1977)
- courtroom process, including jury functioning (Thibaut and Walker 1975; Saks and Hastie 1978; Baldwin and McConville 1979; Sales 1981; Kerr and Bray 1982; Hastie, Penrod, and Pennington 1983)
- eyewitness testimony (Clifford and Bull 1978; Yarmey 1979; Loftus 1979; Parker 1980)
- criminal justice processes (Sales 1977; Toch 1979; Cohn and Udolf 1979; Konečni and Ebbesen 1982; Ellison and Buckhout 1981; Greenberg and Ruback 1982)
- discretionary justice (Abt and Stuart 1979)
- forensic psychology (Brodsky 1973; Monahan 1980; Cooke 1980)
- legal aspects of psychological practice (Schwitzgebel and Schwitzgebel 1980)
- courtroom applications (Saks and Baron 1980)
- insanity defense and civil commitment (Robinson 1980)
- and other assorted issues (see collected papers in Bermant, Nemeth, and Vidmar 1976; and Lipsitt and Sales 1980)

For purposes of learning and teaching, some sort of intellectual framework has to be created and imposed upon a field that is as wide-ranging as the foregoing list suggests. Most of the available books are original monographs or collections of research reports in particular areas. Even those that are general textbooks concentrate on a relatively narrow range of subject matter (for example, Ellison and Buckhout 1981 and Greenberg and Ruback 1982 on the psychology of the criminal justice system; however, Bartol 1983 and Horowitz and Willging 1984 include more expansive coverage). The student who seeks an introduction to the literature by reading these books will be richly informed in specialized areas, but will still have the burden of transcending the details to acquire a vision of the whole.

This book complements the psycholegal research literature. It identifies some of the parameters of inquiry, develops connective legal tissue among empirical studies, and suggests directions for new policy-oriented research. It does not attempt a comprehensive review, nor is it necessary to do so given its purpose. It places relatively greater emphasis on ideas than on data, skills than on information, thinking than on knowing, action than on theory, research possibilities than on existing accomplishments. It is essentially a *teaching book*—one that exposes the student to analytical viewpoints, different points of reference, for harmonizing the legal and empirical materials so that these can be read with an appreciation of their bearings.

For the law student, a derivative benefit from immersion in the empirical literature is the possibility of gaining a conceptual understanding of social science methodology. An ancillary objective of this book is to enable the law student to become a knowledgeable consumer (not producer) of social research so that he* would be capable of using these empirical means, in conjunction with legal skills, as intellectual tools for analyzing issues of legal policy. As Justice Holmes (1897) wrote long ago with prophetic authority, "For the rational study of the law the black-letter man may be the man of the present, but the man of the future is the man of statistics and the master of economics" (p. 469, these disciplines being the "social sciences" of the day). Some contemporary legal scholars are of the same view: "The law student of the future will be . . . out-of-place without an education of increasingly greater sophistication in social science" (Priest 1983, p. 441).

Today, a working familiarity with scientific and statistical reasoning is needed in certain areas of litigation and law reform. It is "a basic responsibility which [lawyers] have not completely met," Judge Skelly Wright noted reprovingly. When they "hire their respective social science experts, [lawyers should know] . . . how to put the [results] into language which serious and concerned laymen could, with effort, understand" (*Hobson* v. *Hansen*, 1967, p. 859). The law student will not learn in this book, and normally would not need to acquire later in law practice, the technical know-how to engage in research. An expert consultant can be retained for that task. Our goal is to provide literacy, not expertise, in social research. As a result, he should be able to determine whether and how empirical data are useful for the solution of legal problems and to communicate with the consultant from the standpoint of an informed lay person. He should also be able to read research reports critically, evaluate the assumptions inherent in different methods, and know how to challenge (if necessary) the inferences drawn from the results. Too often, lawyers accept social science "as a kind of magic practiced by experts" (Friedman and Macaulay 1977, p. xv).

There is no dearth of textbooks on social science methods, but generally they are not tailored to the requirements of law students. Likewise, methodology courses in social science departments are not designed with legal applications in mind. This book provides a relatively efficient way to expose law students to the logic (as well as

---

*Here and throughout the book the masculine pronoun is used in a generic rather than literal sense unless the context indicates otherwise.

the substance) of social research. Although some of the materials presented here can be translated immediately to lawyering, our chief goal is not to convey practical information. This is not a primer on how to practice law using social science techniques. If good pedagogy in doctrinal courses involves more than learning black-letter law, then so does the teaching and learning of empirical inquiry in law. Our hope is to start students on the road toward developing competencies that are more generic and of more long-lasting value than that provided by a "cookbook recipe" approach. The test of this learning will come when the student begins to perceive the usefulness of social research in areas of law that heretofore have not been subject to it.

Introduction to Legal Reasoning

The concern of social scientists with the applicability of their work to law is long-standing. Since the beginning, both sides have maintained an uneasy partnership (Katz and Burchard 1971) or conducted their affairs "most of the time as though the other did not exist" (Fahr 1961, p. 161). The first book in this country on psycholegal research (Münsterberg 1908) was roundly criticized by legal scholars (Wigmore 1909) because of the oversimplified conception of law underlying the research and the nonmateriality of the data to the practical concerns of lawyers. Since then, the history of relations between psychology and law has been marked by alternating cycles of optimism, skepticism, and mutual neglect.

One reason for the nonuse of empirical research by the courts has to do with its legal relevance. (Other factors, related to social values and the purposes of the judicial process, also limit its applicability notwithstanding its germaneness, but these will be dealt with later in the book.) The point to be made here is that "without some guiding idea for determining what is [legally] relevant and what is not, the advancement of our knowledge will be severely restricted" (Bartol 1983, p. 323). In recent years, some researchers have "jump[ed] on the 'relevance bandwagon'" of law-related inquiry, but "they have often failed to take the additional step of learning the realities . . . of the law and the legal system. . . . This has commonly resulted in their doing research . . . that applied to legally irrelevant questions" (Elwork, Sales, and Suggs 1981, p. 49). Legal psychology has often reflected the operation of the "law of the hammer": If all you have is a hammer, the whole world looks like a nail. It is a natural tendency to frame new problems in ways that require for their analysis those methods and concepts with which one is most familiar. The objection is not to pushing one's discipline to the utmost, but that in so doing the legal dimensions of the problem are ignored. A trained incapacity to view things the way the other discipline sees them is inevitable, yet to overcome it is indispensable to interdisciplinary endeavor.

Over a generation ago, some psychologists were already noting the importance of conducting studies within a legally sophisticated framework. Powers (1937) analyzed the undercurrent of discord between psychologists and lawyers, despite their mutual professions of interest in collaboration. "The lawyer is not convinced that the psychologist has any comprehension of legal problems; the psychologist sees the lawyer fumbling blindly . . . and rebukes him for not drawing freely upon the body of knowledge he has so carefully and laboriously built up." He placed the responsibility for failing to reach a meeting of the minds on both sides: on the lawyer for his ignorance of and hostility toward the social sciences; on the psychologist for his "insensitivity to the lawyer's point of view" (p. 258). As an initial step toward rapprochement, he urged that each side seek to understand the other's viewpoint.

For the social scientist this means acquiring a working grasp of what might be called the intellectual culture of the law. Some acquaintance with the manner in which lawyers define, analyze, and solve problems—that is, with legal reasoning—is needed in undertaking empirical research on issues of legal policy. By training and professional orientation, social scientists are generally not accustomed to thinking in terms of social action. As students, they are socialized in the scientific method. They are trained to think in terms of the establishment of general principles from specific instances. Early on, students realize that the profession rewards those who are adept at devising conceptual models and inventive empirical studies to verify them. Recognition in the social sciences is seldom gained by attending to policy or practical implications of theory and research (Ohlin 1970). It is not surprising, then, that the law-related investigations of social scientists, especially psychologists, are not usually adapted to practical decision-making.

On the other hand, lawyers can be seen as applied social scientists. They are trained in those intellectual skills and sensitivities that are geared toward problem-solving. Law schools place an inordinate emphasis on developing the capacity to analyze facts and rules. To learn to "think like a lawyer" means to learn to engage in a method of reasoning that is designed for making decisions for action. The legal profession prizes skill in this ratiocination process. Early in their legal education, they are taught to think in terms of regulating—rather than understanding—human conduct. Their impatience with the theorizing interests of social scientists and their indifference to the niceties of research methodology bespeak habits of mind rooted in their professional socialization.

If what social researchers do is to matter to the law, they need to take into account the problem-solving perspective of lawyers. Some have acknowledged that "social scientists with clear applied interests need training in the law and legal realities . . ." (Bray and Kerr 1982, p. 318). This means plunging into the legal thickets and acquiring some familiarity with legal reasoning. An ancillary purpose of this volume is to develop in the social science student, who might be uninitiated in law, a basic understanding of the legal viewpoint. The aim is not for the student to "learn law" in the sense of learning a body of legal rules, but to learn something about the technique of legal (including judicial) thinking—the intellectual processes of analysis and decision-making in solving problems via the instrumentality of law. The application of law is an exercise in practical reasoning. It is a method of using precedents and analogies in the light of broader principles and social ends in order to reach authoritative settlements of disputes. One could acquire this perspective by venturing into the lion's den and enrolling in regular law school courses. However, this may be a hapless prospect for those who do not seek technical training and are interested only in selected aspects of the law for purposes of research. An integrated set of teaching materials on law and social research can accomplish this objective as effectively and perhaps more painlessly. Professional legal education dwells primarily on doctrinal learning. The nonprofessional student should not have to master the black arts of a particular body of legal rules in order to gain a nontechnical, but informed, appreciation of the analytical processes that underlie the substantive law. This is possible in the same way that a law student, for example, could grasp the logic of statistical reasoning without having to memorize the formulas for statistical tests of significance or to study the mathematics upon which they are predicated. Of course, exposure to some legal rules or to statistical formulas is unavoidable in learning, but one should bear in mind what is focus and what is background.

The insularity of legal education and legal scholarship in this country is a prime reason why educated laypersons are generally unlettered in the law. Until the early nineteenth century, aspiring lawyers were trained in law offices in a sort of apprenticeship system. Law courses offered in universities were usually part of the liberal arts curriculum and were made available to and taken by the entire student body. Law in the early years of the Republic followed a two-track approach, as a vocation and as an intellectual pursuit. With the founding and flourishing of professional university law schools, there began the shift from law teaching as part of liberal education to specialized training for the bar. By the middle of the last century, these schools had effectively replaced apprenticeship training. The result was an improvement in the quality of the formation of new lawyers, but the price paid was high: the sacrifice of general education in law for students in the arts and sciences.

Once the study of law became a professional monopoly, it was assumed that it was beyond the ken or interest of the nonspecialist. In contrast, law is taught as part of an undergraduate, liberal arts curriculum in European universities; the professional side is taken care of subsequently by apprenticeship. To this day, there is no direct counterpart in England or on the Continent to the American law school (Merryman 1975). Thus, European social scientists, who usually have had exposure to law as part of their university education, have been traditionally more interested in and perhaps better equipped to do research on law than their American counterparts. Max Weber and Emile Durkheim were trained in law as well as in sociology. The early work on psychology and law reviewed by Münsterberg (1908) was pioneered by German psychologists.

An introduction to legal thinking can provide the social science student with more than a foundation for action-oriented research. It can also provide an introduction to what Berman and Greiner (1980) call "responsible social thought": "the kind of thinking . . . which persons in positions of social responsibility use to reach decisions requiring action" (p. 14)—or what, in a finer time, used to be called right reason. In a society as law-dominated as ours, a critical understanding of what law is about is important to effective citizenship. By studying case opinions and analyzing how judges articulate the reasons for their actions, the student begins to sharpen, gradually and unconsciously, his own analytical capacity for social judgment. For those who have been educated mainly in scientific thinking, the perspective on law here provided may well unveil for them a different way of looking at social reality.

For the law student, the emphasis on legal reasoning will not (or should not) be new learning, since this is a skill which presumably is cultivated in every law school class. Some of the cases included here also may not be new to those in law school, since they are mostly well-known ones culled from the areas of civil rights, criminal law and procedure, evidence, and civil procedure. The doctrinal materials, which provide the legal propaedeutics for the empirical studies, will generally be less technical and comprehensive than those customarily found in traditional casebooks. Nonetheless, the legal half of this volume on social-legal research can still be read with profit by the law student. Law school courses and casebooks typically concentrate on legal doctrine. They approach the study of law from the inside, attending to its cognitive workings or *elegantia juris*. We approach it from the outside as well, examining the social context and consequences of the law as revealed by empirical inquiry. An external perspective could highlight aspects of the discipline that may not have been fully appreciated by its daily practitioners. The social sciences can help illuminate the symbiotic relationship between law and the larger society. "The vast bulk of this [social research on law]," says law professor Lawrence Friedman, "is not done by law professors, not understood by law professors, not even treated in class by law professors" (in Margolick 1983, p. 30). Derek Bok (1983), the president of Harvard and former dean of its law school (the school that originated the traditional case method of legal training), has urged that law faculties incorporate social science tools in their research and teaching, warning that "we ignore the social sciences at our peril . . ." (p. 45). "The narrowing of this gap [between the work of social scientists and lawyers] is an urgent task of American scholarship" (Hughes 1983, p. 430). This book may risk superficial treatment of law from a doctrinal angle, but it offers a broader scholarship on law than is usually found in conventional law school offerings. The attention on judicial process rather than judicial doctrine could aid the law student in focusing—with the spectacles of social science—on the forest rather than the trees.

Intended Readership

Ideally, this book is intended for use by mixed classes of (graduate and advanced undergraduate) social science students and law students. Their different skills would intermesh as the group dealt with common problems. The give-and-take that would arise from their respective viewpoints would enrich the discussions. Practically, we recognize that social science students will probably compose the main readership. The interest in and demand for courses in law and social science have always been greater in academic departments. Law schools treat such offerings as curricular luxuries which are peripheral to the demands of professional training. Friedman (1974) likens them to expensive rugs in faculty offices. They add intellectual status to the law schools which offer them, but no one is deceived as to which are the frills and which is the main show.

Consequently, this book was designed primarily but not exclusively with the social science student in mind. This relative emphasis allows us to sidestep the formidable hurdle of how to give equal attention to the different needs of social science students and law students within the confines of a single volume. Everybody touts interdisciplinary study but it is honored more often in the breach. One reason is the difficulty of preparing teaching materials appropriate for use at the same time by both groups. One worries, for example, whether the legal materials are too technical for social science students and too elementary for law students, and vice versa for the empirical materials.

We have devoted somewhat greater attention to the "legal" side of social-legal scholarship—or, more precisely, to the legal context and legal applications of social research. We felt that a small but carefully chosen sample of studies would be sufficient to expose students to the empirical literature. This book is not intended to be an overview of the field. It is best read as a sampler, intended to whet the appetite and to illustrate some research possibilities. We concentrated on how existing studies fit into the legal landscape and on directions for future research. We wanted to provide a road map for social scientists who might not feel sure-footed enough on the paths of the law. Our assumption was that the gaps and imbalances in the empirical coverage can be redressed in class and by supplementary readings. After the student has been led through part of the research maze and knows the general layout, he should be able later to make his own way through the rest. We have provided citations to other studies for those who wish to pursue them in tandem with this book. Insofar as the legal materials are concerned, the book is largely self-contained. There is enough here to keep a student busy in a regular, one-semester course.

Some acquaintance with research methodology—at a level equivalent to that attained in, say, a basic undergraduate course—is desirable but not essential for using this book. We know that lawyers are wary of social science vocabulary and some have been known to turn pale when faced with simple statistics. It was not practical to include an introductory chapter or an appendix on "research methods for lawyers." It was also not necessary since lawyers are more interested in legal uses of social research than in undertaking such research. For this purpose, those without any social science background should still be able to cope with the empirical materials as they are presented here. We have kept the methodology spare and simple. When some of the studies were unavoidably technical, we added explanatory comments. On the whole, both the "social" and "legal" halves of this book were intended to be accessible to informed "amateurs" in one discipline or the other. This is part of the charm and challenge of interdisciplinary study.

1.3.   METHOD

Casebook Format

The format of this book, although it partakes of the law school casebook, the social science "reader," and the conventional textbook, is patterned principally after the casebook. It consists of judicial cases, empirical studies, jurisprudential essays, scholarly debates, original text, and editorial questions. These are the raw materials from which the student is expected to build a structure; in the process of building, the student should gain some analytical skills and perspectives. Unlike textbooks and readers, the main ideas are not always neatly summarized and conveniently packaged for passive reading.

The format for the chapters of this book is as follows. Each chapter begins with a short introduction that sets forth the legal background and social context for the readings to be presented. The legal and research questions of the chapter are high-lighted at the outset.

After the introduction, there are one or more case opinions. By presenting the issues through these decisions, the student vicariously learns how litigants and courts approach them. The manner in which the cases were selected and edited was dictated by our teaching purpose. We emphasized those opinions, or portions of an opinion, that contained the court's empirical analysis. We gave relatively less coverage and attention to the exposition of legal doctrine.

The opinions are followed by theoretical and/or empirical research studies that address the factual issues raised in the cases. The selection of these studies was not necessarily governed by the criterion of the best or most representative research. Although most of them are sound and serve as springboards for discussion on policy-relevant research, some have flaws and were included for teaching reasons. Case-books frequently present poorly justified decisions in order that students learn skills of critical analysis. Likewise, there are advantages in having students read some studies that are weak in their procedure, interpretation of results, or legal relevance. How well a study fitted into our organizational structure was another criterion for selection.

Interspersed between the cases and research studies are text and "Notes and Questions." They constitute the connective tissue, so to speak, between the readings. The text and notes provide information to fill the gaps in the readings. They explain certain points and expand or critique others. They also include brief summaries of other cases and research studies that supplement the main selections.

The questions are designed to encourage an active and probing attitude toward the readings. The student is expected to think about the questions that we pose and to argue alternative responses back and forth, in class or in his own mind when studying. By tackling queries about, for example, the logical weakness in an opinion, or the kinds of empirical data that need to be mobilized in support of a policy alternative, the student begins to enhance his own analytical capacities for action. He begins to acquire a sense for what to attend to in reading opinions and how social science can be brought to bear in the decision-making. The text and "Notes and Questions" are road maps to help the student navigate through unfamiliar territory.

The coverage of this casebook stresses depth over breadth. We prefer to treat in detail a limited number of topics rather than to survey broadly the subject matter. This approach stems from our emphasis on analytical skills and perspectives. Each of the chosen social-legal topics, presented in a separate chapter, can be viewed—like a cubist painting—from multiple angles. We have paired opposing research findings and juxtaposed competing policy arguments. Confrontation of ideas and controversy run throughout the book. Some overlap in exposition, therefore, is inevitable and purposeful. Frank Knight, the economist, once said that "only through varied iteration can alien concepts be forced on reluctant minds" (in Barnes 1983, p. 3). The concepts of a different discipline are often alien and student minds may be unwilling. At times, then, certain concepts and themes will be developed iteratively, using the cases and materials of different chapters. Ideas that are strangers at first should become, by the end of the book, life-long friends.

Case Method of Study

As used in law schools, the main purpose of the case method is to teach students the skill of legal reasoning via the analysis of appellate opinions. These opinions are selected, abridged, and organized in a systematic fashion. The task of the student is to analyze and synthesize the cases. Guided by questions presented in the casebook or by the instructor, the student learns to dissect an opinion and analyze its constituent parts. In addition, he learns to relate one case to another, to harmonize the outcomes of seemingly inconsistent cases so that they are made to stand together. By taking apart and putting together different cases, the student acquires a way of thinking and working with cases that constitutes the fundamentals of legal reasoning, as well as knowledge of a body of doctrinal rules presented by these cases.

Law schools rely on casebooks rather than textbooks because the teaching of legal reasoning is not susceptible to simple exposition. As an intellectual process, it is "an art, capable only to a limited extent of routinization or (to date) of accurate and satisfying description" (Llewellyn 1930, p. 451). It is by immersion in case-by-case reading that one best acquires a sense for judge-made law.

For the social science student the case method is also a useful means to obtain an exposure to what law is and how lawyers think. After reading this book, he should have enough background to converse as an informed lay person with lawyers about the legal aspects of empirical research. He should have gained a vicarious feel for the dynamics of the lawyering process, which is the interplay of issues of law (values) and issues of fact (data). These are insights about law which are difficult to achieve except by firsthand experience with cases. The analysis of appellate decisions "develops a sensitivity to how legal rules play out in particular fact situations" (Hegland 1983, p. 16).

The typical law casebook usually does not state explicitly the basis for the selection and organization of the cases. The editorial comments rarely restate the decisions of the cases. The burden is placed almost entirely on the student (and the instructor) to make sense out of the decisions. By dint of effort and imagination, the student is expected to uncover the underlying conceptual organization of the cases and, beyond that, to restructure the materials according to his own framework. The open-texture quality of the case method lends itself to this kind of creative manipulation of the raw materials. There is no single correct way of analyzing or synthesizing opinions. In the case method of study, it is the process, not the outcome, that counts.

In this book, we have avoided a strict adherence to the traditional case method. It is not, after all, a common learning style for most social science students. A modification in format was needed to suit their needs. Consequently, we include far more textual material than the typical casebook. Our notes, for instance, describe how the cases and research readings are organized, and why. We identify the key issues so that the student is not left floundering about aimlessly in a sea of cases—the common lot of many first-year law students, as their perennial ululations attest.

On the other hand, we retained the essentials of the case method that have teaching value. The materials always raise more questions than they provide answers, especially since clear-cut answers are unavailing for many of the problems presented. The student has to integrate the readings, not only within a chapter but between chapters. There are guidelines to be sure, but there is still enough of an open-texture quality to the book that invites aggressive and reflective reading. At the heart of any process-oriented method of study is the interrelatedness of the parts. A case or research study standing alone provides little guidance. It must be read in relation to other cases and studies. It is still mostly up to the reader to put together the various ideas and concepts that make up the mosaic of this book.

Notwithstanding this "de-tuned" case method, we know from experience that it can still be a difficult and initially unsettling approach to learning. It is not unusual to find some social science students feeling at a loss and frustrated with the materials during the first one-half or three-fourths of the course. This is the same reaction that law school students have when they are first exposed to the case method, regardless of the particular subject matter. Students will read a case two or three times and still feel that they have not grasped the meaning behind the words. They may be unable to see any connection between different cases. Feelings of anxiety begin to surface when other students, or the instructor, bring out issues that they missed in their own reading. It may be no consolation that other students, or even the instructor, may have missed points that they were able to see. The materials of the casebook appear like the pieces of a jigsaw puzzle. They have to put it together but the pieces do not seem to fit. At times they may not even be sure what the whole picture looks like.

One reason the case method can be mildly traumatic at first is its novelty. The student is not only learning a new subject matter—"the law." He is also learning, consciously or not, a new way of thinking. This method of legal thinking takes some time to adapt to, especially if one's prior learning has emphasized scientific reasoning rather than other modes of dialectical thinking. And if one is interested in empirical research on law, there is still another new learning component that is involved: the application of one discipline to the other.

But happily, in the end, the case method does work. It cultivates the desired intellectual capacities. In our experience, if a student diligently works through the materials—reads each case two or three times before class discussion, and again afterward; analyzes the research studies critically in light of the cases; wrestles with the editorial questions—he will likely have what we call the "Damascus experience." About three-fourths of the way through the course, most students will "see the light," as Saul of Tarsus did on the road to Damascus. It will dawn on the student—sometimes suddenly, sometimes gradually—that he is understanding the cases better. He becomes more adept at criticizing them and seeing how social research fits into law. The contours of a pattern begin to emerge; the pieces of the jigsaw puzzle begin to fall into place. It may be only a flicker of a light, hardly enough to blind. But it is usually enough to restore confidence and inject a new sense of vitality and purpose to the study. For those who keep the faith, the result will justify the means.

1.4.   CONTENT

The choice of content was shaped by the teaching purposes. We opted to analyze in depth selected aspects of the judicial process and social research rather than try to survey broadly the field. Part I introduces the book and the legal system. Part II deals with the application of social research in the lawmaking process on appeal, and Part III deals with the uses of social research in the fact-finding process at trial. Part IV pulls together the thematic concerns of the book and, by way of overview, presents different perspectives (jurisprudential, conceptual, historical) on the relationships between law and social research.

Lawmaking in appellate adjudication comprises the processes of creation of new law, the implementation and expansion of existing law, the contraction and eventual abolition of law, and the evaluation of the probable impact of law on conduct. These processes provide the analytical pegs on which to hang the substantive materials. Each chapter of Part II concentrates on one topic which is used as a "case study" to illuminate the particular process. These topics are of current interest but the underlying issues that they reflect are long-lived. The topic of southern school desegregation, for example, may someday fade from memory but the issues of social change through law and the influence of social science in that change are likely to be enduring ones in any democratic society.

Chapter 3 deals with the creation of new law and uses the problem of southern school segregation as a vehicle for analysis. It begins by juxtaposing two cases, one establishing the principle of "separate but equal" treatment of the races in railway carriages and the other (almost one century later) overruling it and creating the new rule of equal educational opportunity in public schools. The social psychological theories and data relied upon in litigation are examined.

Chapter 4 examines the expansion of school desegregation law from its early, rural, southern beginnings to its present, urban, northern manifestation. Consequently, the legal issues are more subtle and the kinds of social research needed more sophisticated. The materials of these two chapters set the tone and direction for the whole book. They introduce basic questions concerning the role of social science in constitutional adjudication that will be explored in subsequent chapters.

Chapter 5 looks at the opposite of law expansion, namely, the processes of restriction and attempted abolition of law in the instance of capital punishment. The jurisprudence of death is a rich tapestry of social science ideas, doctrinal concepts, and litigation strategies. The materials show how empirical analysis is woven into the fabric of judicial decisions. Judicial assumptions about public knowledge and attitudes undergird in part the determination of the constitutionality of the death penalty. The examination of this topic also shows how procedural and substantive justice are intertwined in adjudication.

Chapters 3–5 look at the internal dynamic of the decision-making process, the determination of facts and rules. In Chapter 6 we turn to the external dimension of law, its impact on social behavior. It is not the substantive rules but "the area of contact between judicial (or official) behavior and the behavior of laymen" that is at the core of law (Llewellyn 1930, pp. 442–43). The jurisprudence of consequences is the subject of Chapter 6. Our attention centers on one area of legal impact and compliance. This is the impact of the judicial exclusionary rule—that renders inadmissible at trial any evidence illegally obtained—on the regulation of police conduct. The cases and empirical studies consider the justifications and effectiveness of this rule in checking improper police intrusions and interrogations. This chapter raises questions about the limits of judicial control of behavior and casts in sharp relief the effectiveness of legal rules—compared with social and organizational norms—in regulating conduct.

Fact-finding procedures at trial constitute the analytical backbone of Part III. As in the earlier chapters, the cases are drawn mostly (but not solely) from the appellate courts. The difference is that in Part III more attention is given to the making of procedural and evidentiary rules than to substantive rules.

The fact-finding process can be divided into three stages: the investigation and gathering of evidence before trial, the presentation of evidence and law during the trial, and the decision-making on the evidence by the jury at the end of the trial. Each stage involves rules that safeguard and promote the values of fairness, reliability, and administrative efficiency in fact-finding.

For example, all three values are present with respect to the jury. Fairness in the jury exists when it is composed of a representative cross section of the community. Only then can the jury be said to represent the conscience of the community. The jury's fact-finding is reliable (error-free) when its decision procedures are not systematically tilted toward one type of verdict rather than another. Finally, efficiency is ensured if the procedures for selection and deliberation of the jury do not result in undue delay or cost in disposing of cases. At different times and in different circumstances, each value may have a different priority, and one may be in conflict with another. A smaller jury, for instance, may be quicker and less expensive to impanel, but if its judgments are more variable than those of a larger jury, the value of reliability is imperiled. The balancing of these different values is an essential part in the fashioning of procedural rules.

These values make up what we call procedural justice. In our legal system, *how* a dispute is handled by the courts is as important as, and is inextricably tied to, *what* the final disposition is. Law is procedure. It is a way of settling controversies. Procedural justice and substantive justice cannot be divorced in thinking about law.

The chapters of Part III are organized in terms of three stages. We begin the study of procedural justice by examining the selection and functioning of the jury because it is "the nerve center of the fact-finding process" (*Estes* v. *Texas*, 1965, p. 545). We then go to presentations of evidence to the jury at trial, and conclude with pretrial (extrajudicial) influences on the jury.

The Constitution guarantees in every criminal trial the right to an impartial jury. The first two chapters of Part III deal with the rules that define impartiality. Chapter 7 looks at discrimination in jury selection. If minority members or women are excluded or substantially underrepresented, it cannot be said that cross-sectional fairness is observed. The problem of underrepresentation arising from facially neutral procedures can be a subtle form of invisible discrimination. It can be found in other contexts as well, such as employment, housing, and schooling. The focus of the materials is on legal and statistical proof of discrimination in jury venires and, for comparison purposes, in the labor market. This chapter also examines scientific jury selection and raises legal, ethical, and methodological questions about it.

Chapter 8 considers some determinants of criminal and civil jury functioning. Jury size (fewer than twelve members) and verdict criteria (unanimous or majority) are relevant to the guarantee of impartiality: If smaller and nonunanimous juries affect adversely the quality of group deliberation and the eventual outcome, the reliability of their decision-making—and hence their impartiality—are called into question. Another determinant of constitutional status is case complexity. Social research on whether jurors are capable of deciding rationally when faced with complicated issues and massive information may determine whether there is an exception to the right to a civil jury trial.

Chapter 9 focuses on the procedural rules that govern the presentation of evidence and of law in the trial itself. Several interrelated issues are examined, such as the order of presentations and its effect on the jury, the quantification of standards of persuasion, and the efficacy of judicial instructions. We also look at some research and policy issues occasioned by recent technological advances that permit videotaped trials.

Chapter 10 deals with extrajudicial influences on the jury before trial. Ideally, the jury decides solely on the basis of what transpires within the courtroom walls; in practice, the trial outcome is often influenced or even determined in advance by events at the pretrial stage. One such biasing event is eyewitness identification. Our attention is on the nature and extent of the bias influences and on the procedural safeguards that can be erected at the trial stage to prevent or mitigate its impact. Prophylactic and remedial measures include presence of counsel at police lineups, cautionary jury instructions on the fallibility of human observation, and expert witness testimony by psychologists. The legal and policy justifications for these safeguards, and the empirical research on their purported effectiveness, are analyzed.

The last three chapters, which compose the Afterword, attempt a conceptual integration of the various themes that are present throughout the book. Our expectation is that after working through Parts II and III, a student will begin to acquire a "feel" for the law. In Part IV, we articulate more systematically what this "feel" is and how social science intermeshes with legal reasoning.

Despite the explosive growth of the psycholegal literature in recent years, there has been little historical analysis or theoretical assessment of the field as a whole. Chapter 11 presents an intellectual history of the relations between psychology and law and thereby places in expanded perspective the various empirical studies presented in Parts II and III. It tries to capture the mood, difficulties, and prospects of contemporary social-legal research.

Chapter 12 explores one aspect of jurisprudential thought central to our focus, namely, the nature of judicial decision-making. An allegorical case and classical essays in legal philosophy are relied upon to illustrate three models or styles of adjudication, applicable to common law and constitutional cases, whereby judges create, expand, abolish, and interpret legal rules for the governance of human conduct. They are formalism, realism, and purposivism. They are generalized mind sets which find parallels in the methods of decision-making in public administration and organizational behavior. Each has had a profound influence on American law and on social-legal scholarship.

Finally, Chapter 13 offers different views on when, whether, and how the courts use social research in the decision-making process. A debate between two social scientists—one representing a latter-day realist viewpoint and the other a purposive jurisprudence—helps to identify some of the key issues. Other theoretical papers on differences in the methods of reasoning in law and in science, and differences in the professional socialization of lawyers and social scientists, offer insights into the difficulties of interdisciplinary endeavors. The chapter concludes with a discussion of paradigmatic uses of empirical evidence by the courts, which reflect the influence of jurisprudential models of decision-making.

The learning and teaching of a subject from a dual perspective is always an exciting one. For us, the materials in these chapters work well as an advanced-level introduction to the application of social research in law, the melding of empirical analysis and normative judgment. We trust it will for others, too.

REFERENCES

Abt, L., and Stuart, I., eds. *Social Psychology and Discretionary Law*. New York: Van Nostrand Reinhold, 1979.

Baldwin, J., and McConville, M. *Jury Trials*. Oxford: Oxford University Press, 1979.

Barnes, D. W. *Statistics as Proof: Fundamentals of Quantitative Evidence*. Boston: Little, Brown, 1983.

Bartol, C. R. *Psychology and American Law*. Belmont, Ca.: Wadsworth, 1983.

Berman, H., and Greiner, W. R. *The Nature and Functions of Law*, 3rd ed. Mineola, N.Y.: Foundation Press, 1980.

Bermant, G.; Nemeth, C.; and Vidmar, N., eds. *Psychology and the Law*. Lexington, Mass.: Heath, 1976.

Bok, D. C. "A Flawed System." *Harvard Magazine*, May–June 1983, p. 38.

Bray, R. M., and Kerr, N. L. "Methodological Considerations in the Study of the Psychology of the Courtroom." In *The Psychology of the Courtroom*, edited by N. L. Kerr and R. M. Bray. New York: Academic Press, 1982.

Brodsky, S. L. *Psychologists in the Criminal Justice System*. Urbana: University of Illinois Press, 1973.

Clifford, B. R., and Bull, R. *The Psychology of Person Identification*. London: Routledge & Kegan Paul, 1978.

Cohn, A., and Udolf, R., eds. *The Criminal Justice System and Its Psychology*. New York: Van Nostrand Reinhold, 1979.

Cooke, G., ed. *The Role of the Forensic Psychologist*. Springfield, Ill.: Thomas, 1980.

Ellison, K. W., and Buckhout, R. *Psychology and Criminal Justice*. New York: Harper & Row, 1981.

Elwork, A.; Sales, B. D.; and Suggs, D. "The Trial: A Research Review." In *The Trial Process*, edited by B. D. Sales. New York: Plenum Press, 1981.

Estes v. Texas, 381 U.S. 532 (1965).

Fahr, S. M. "Why Lawyers Are Dissatisfied with the Social Sciences." *Washburn Law Journal* 1 (1961): 161–74.

Frank, J. *Law and the Modern Mind*. New York: Tudor, 1930.

Friedman, L., ed. *Argument: The Oral Argument Before the Supreme Court in Brown v. Board of Education of Topeka, 1952–55.* New York: Chelsea House, 1969.

Friedman, L. [Conference presentation on] "The Future of Law and Social Sciences Research." *North Carolina Law Review* 52 (1974): 1068–73.

———, and Macaulay, S. *Law and the Behavioral Sciences*, 2nd ed. Indianapolis: Bobbs-Merrill, 1977.

Galanter, M. [Conference presentation on] "The Future of Law and Social Sciences Research." *North Carolina Law Review* 52 (1974): 1060–67.

Greenberg, M., and Ruback, B. *Social Psychology of the Criminal Justice System*. Monterey, Ca.: Brooks/Cole, 1982.

Hart, H. L. A. "American Jurisprudence Through English Eyes: The Nightmare and the Noble Dream." *Georgia Law Review* 11 (1977): 969–89.

Hart, H. M., and McNaughton, J. T. "Evidence and Inference in the Law." In *Evidence and Inference*, edited by D. Lerner. Glencoe, Ill.: Free Press, 1959.

Haskell, T. *The Emergence of Professional Social Science: The American Social Science Association and the Nineteenth Century Crisis of Authority*. Urbana: University of Illinois Press, 1977.

Hastie, R., Penrod, S. D., and Pennington, N. *Inside the Jury*. Cambridge, Mass.: Harvard University Press, 1983.

Hegland, K. *Introduction to the Study and Practice of Law*. St. Paul: West, 1983.

Hobson v. Hansen, 269 F. Supp. 401 (D. D.C. 1967).

Holmes, V. W. "The Path of the Law." *Harvard Law Review* 10 (1897): 457–78.

Horowitz, I. A. and Willgang, T. E. *The Psychology of Law: Integrations and Applications*. Boston: Little, Brown, 1984.

Hughes, G. "The Great American Legal Scholarship Bazaar." *Journal of Legal Education* 33 (1983): 424–31.

Jones, H. W. "Legal Inquiry and the Methods of Science." In *Law and the Social Role of Science*, edited by H. W. Jones. New York: Rockefeller University Press, 1967.

Kalven, H., Jr. "The Quest for the Middle Range: Empirical Inquiry and Legal Policy." In *Law in a Changing America*, edited by G. C. Hazard. Englewood Cliffs, N.J.: Prentice-Hall, 1968.

Katz, M., and Burchard, J. D. "Psychology and the Legal Enterprise." *Kansas Law Review* 19 (1971): 197–210.

Kerr, N. L., and Bray, R. M., eds. *The Psychology of the Courtroom*. New York: Academic Press, 1982.

Konečni, V. J., and Ebbesen, E. B. "Social Psychology and the Law: The Choice of Research Problems, Settings, and Methodology." In *The Criminal Justice System: A Social Psychological Analysis*, edited by V. J. Konečni and E. B. Ebbesen. San Francisco: Freeman, 1982.

Konečni, V. J., and Ebbesen, E. B., eds. *The Criminal Justice System: A Social Psychological Analysis*. San Francisco: Freeman, 1982.

Lipsitt P., and Sales, B., eds. *New Directions in Psycholegal Research*. New York: Van Nostrand Reinhold, 1980.

Llewellyn, K. "A Realistic Jurisprudence: The Next Step." *Columbia Law Review* 30 (1930): 431–65.

Loftus, E. F. *Eyewitness Testimony.* Cambridge, Mass.: Harvard University Press, 1979.

Mannheim, K. *Ideology and Utopia: An Introduction to the Sociology of Knowledge.* New York: Harcourt, Brace, 1936.

Margolick, D. "The Trouble with America's Law Schools." *New York Times Magazine,* May 22, 1983, p. 21.

Merryman, J. H. "Legal Education There and Here: A Comparison." *Stanford Law Review* 27 (1975): 859–78.

Monahan, J., ed. *Who is the Client? The Ethics of Psychological Intervention in the Criminal Justice System.* Washington, D.C.: American Psychological Association, 1980.

Münsterberg, H. *On the Witness Stand: Essays on Psychology and Crime.* New York: Clark Boardman, 1908.

Ohlin, L. "Partnership with the Social Sciences." *Journal of Legal Education* 23 (1970): 204–8.

Parker, L. C. *Legal Psychology: Eyewitness Testimony—Jury Behavior.* Springfield, Ill.: Thomas, 1980.

Powers, E. "Psychology and the Law." *Journal of Abnormal and Social Psychology* 32 (1937): 258–74.

Priest, G. L. "Social Science Theory and Legal Education: The Law School as University." *Journal of Legal Education* 33 (1983): 437–41.

Robinson, D. N. *Psychology and Law: Can Justice Survive the Social Sciences?* New York: Oxford University Press, 1980.

Rosenblum, V. G. "A Place for Social Science Along the Judiciary's Constitutional Law Frontier." *Northwestern University Law Review* 66 (1971): 455–80.

Saks, M. J., and Hastie, R. H. *Social Psychology in Court.* New York: Van Nostrand Reinhold, 1978.

Saks, M. J., and Baron, C. H., eds. *The Use/Nonuse/Misuse of Applied Social Research in the Courts.* Cambridge, Mass.: Abt Books, 1980.

Sales, B. D., ed. *Perspectives in Law and Psychology,* vol. 1. *The Criminal Justice System.* New York: Plenum Press, 1977.

———. *Perspectives in Law and Psychology,* vol. 2. *The Trial Process.* New York: Plenum Press, 1981.

Schwartz, R. D., and Skolnick, J. H., eds. *Society and the Legal Order: Cases and Materials in the Sociology of Law.* New York: Basic Books, 1970.

Schwitzgebel, R. L., and Schwitzgebel, R. K. *Law and Psychological Practice.* New York: Wiley, 1980.

Tapp, J., and Levine, F., eds. *Law, Justice, and the Individual in Society.* New York: Holt, Rinehart & Winston, 1977.

Thibaut, J., and Walker, L. *Procedural Justice: A Psychological Analysis.* Hillsdale, N.J.: Laurence Erlbaum, 1975.

Toch, H., ed. *Psychology of Crime and Criminal Justice.* New York: Holt, Rinehart & Winston, 1979.

Tocqueville, A. de *Democracy in America,* vol. 1. Garden City, N.Y.: Doubleday, 1969.

Vago, S. *Law and Society.* Englewood Cliffs, N.J.: Prentice-Hall, 1981.

Wigmore, J. "Professor Münsterberg and the Psychology of Testimony: Being a Report of the Case of Cokestone v. Münsterberg." *Illinois Law Review* 3 (1909): 399–445.

Yarmey, A. D. *The Psychology of Eyewitness Testimony.* New York: Free Press, 1979.

Zeisel, H. [Conference presentation on] "The Selection of Topics and Methods for Law and Social Sciences Research." *University of North Carolina Law Review* 52 (1974): 974–81.

CHAPTER 2

Introduction to Law and
the Judicial Process

The term "law" in the United States evokes almost limitless associations: with institutions of the legal system (courts, legislatures, administrative agencies, arbitration boards, police departments, and so forth); with substantive sources of law (statutes, regulations, case opinions, memoranda of understanding, and so forth); with the administration of justice (court management, videotapes at trial, rules of procedure, and so forth); with actors in the legal system (legislators, judges, attorneys, sheriffs, and so forth). The subject is obviously too large and complex to be canvassed in a few pages, or in a few volumes for that matter. To try to portray the whole of the law risks oversimplifications. Yet, boundaries must be drawn if one is to define the focus.

Lawyers and judges themselves have no generally agreed upon definition of law. Arguably, though, they do not need to articulate one. For them, it is simply what they practice and what courts do. A person intuitively knows from everyday experience what is meant by the notion of "time," despite being hard-pressed to say what it is. Likewise, as a result of the socialization processes of legal education and everyday professional work, law persons tend to acquire a "feel" for what law is all about, even though they might not be able to verbalize it.

Social scientists, however, who come to law from the outside and are not steeped in its professional culture and intellectual perspective, need some kind of conception of law to guide their investigation. If they are to deal with issues which are of central importance to law, their contributions must be marshaled and organized around problems which confront lawyers. To do this requires some notion of law as it is understood by lawyers.

We begin with a tentative concept or working hypothesis of law. It serves as a thinking tool. It does not encompass all of law, but it does highlight what is at the core and what is in the penumbra. As Berman and Greiner (1980) caution, "Without a concept of what law is, however tentative, there is no assurance that the particular aspect of the subject being studied at a given time has any special importance, or even relevance, to the ultimate inquiry" (p. 16).

A concept of law is also needed because it establishes the method of analysis. "Every [legal] decision," according to Justice Frankfurter, "is a function of some juristic philosophy" (in Berman and Greiner 1980, p. 37). If, for example, law is viewed as a logical, deductive system of rules of conduct, then the appropriate method is formal analysis: a comparison of the concepts and rules according to semantic and logical analysis. There is no role in this system for contributions of empirically based disciplines because law is understood in a social vacuum. Legal rules are studied separately from the facts that gave rise to them.

However, "if the Law of the State be seen as in the first essence not a 'code' nor a body of Rules, but as in first essence a going institution," wrote Llewellyn (1940), "it opens itself at once to inquiry by the non-technician" (p. 1355). This approach sees rules not only as logical deductions from other rules, but as the product of human judgments shaped by social attitudes, values, and experience. To view law as a social process for managing human affairs, rather than solely as an autonomous logical system, is to invite the insights that the social sciences have to offer to law. Indeed, "it is accepted today . . . that the legal system can be best understood·with the methods and theories of the social sciences" (Priest 1983, p. 437).

2.1. LAW AS A SYSTEM OF RULES

It is useful to think of law as comprising a set of authoritative and prescriptive rules for conduct. Some rules instruct persons in what they must or must not do (for example, "pay your income taxes"; "do not segregate public school pupils on the basis of race"); others tell people how to do what they wish to do so that their actions are legally enforceable, that is, are backed by the power of the state (for example, "this is how to make a valid contract"; "follow these steps in setting up a partnership"). Some rules compel conduct; others serve to facilitate voluntary action by providing guidelines for them. Law, of course, is not the only institution in society that helps create and maintain order by setting forth standards of conduct. The family, religious organizations, schools, work associations—each, too, shapes ways of acting and thinking and feeling. But legal rules are not the same as informal social controls and group norms. They possess certain characteristics that distinguish them from standards that come from social institutions.

First, unlike customary or moral standards, legal rules have an authoritative character because they are enforced by the state. "They speak with the power and prestige of the community behind them," because at stake in their implementation is "the good name as well as the good order of the community" (Hart and McNaughton 1959, p. 49).

A second attribute, though not unique to them, is their prescriptive or normative quality. Legal rules embody the values and purposes of society. The rule against racial segregation in public schools expresses the collective aspiration that government should be colorblind in its treatment of all citizens. Law is a means for symbolizing and implementing social ends. Other languages use two different words to denote these two dimensions of law: the dimension of justice (*derecho* in Spanish, *Recht* in German) and the dimension of specific standards of conduct (*ley, Gesetz*). The former "is much more long lived than particular rules of law, and the ideals are much more far-reaching in their effects" (Pound 1933, p. 477).

Third, rules consist of patterns of facts to which certain legal (authoritative) consequences attach. Hazard (1967) points out that "most, if not all, questions of [law] can be reduced to a series of constituent questions of fact" (p. 76). This attribute is critical to the understanding of law.

Legal rules can be cast in the form "If X, then Y." If fact pattern $X_1, X_2 \ldots X_n$ occurs, then legal consequence Y follows. For example, an antisegregation rule in public schools may consist of the following proposition: If there is substantial racial disproportion in a school which is the result of intentional action by school officials, then there is wrongful discrimination. Thus, if the fact of racial imbalance is present but the fact of official intent is not, the law does not recognize it as an instance of discrimination for which there is a legal remedy. This combination of facts and the consequence that flows from these facts are what constitute a rule of law. It is only when school segregation is deemed wrong (a value judgment embodied in the rule) that we need to inquire whether there is racial imbalance and whether officials purposely sought to create this condition. But at the same time, it is only when the evidence shows there is statistical disproportion and improper motives that the legal question of wrongfulness is presented. This example illustrates in elementary form the dynamic of the law—how legal rules are applied and how they grow. "The issues of fact arise out of the law, but at the point of application of law, the issues of law also arise out of the facts" (Hart and McNaughton 1959, p. 60). There is, in their words, a "chicken-and-egg relationship" between facts and legal rules.

The dialectical relationship between facts and law has significance for interdisciplinary collaboration between lawyers and social scientists. Suppose there is a school desegregation lawsuit and the aforementioned rule is the governing law in the jurisdiction. The lawyer bringing the suit may ask a social scientist for aid in collecting evidence about the case. This evidence would consist, principally, of a statistical showing of racial imbalance in the school system and some kind of objective proof of the discriminatory motives of school officials.

Here is an instance of using empirical research in law application. The social scientist makes available to the lawyer evidence of facts to which the legal rule will be applied in resolving the dispute. Notice that this existing rule defines and limits the types of facts that need to be proven. This is a source of the difficulties in communication which sometimes arise between members of different disciplines. Social scientists criticize lawyers for not taking into account information which, from their own professional viewpoint, is relevant to the problem. The social scientist may believe, for example, that the attitudes and perceptions of the discriminated school children should be considered in this case. One reason the lawyer might ignore this fact and seem possessed of tunnel vision in analyzing the problem is that "issues of fact arise out of law." It is the prevailing legal rule that renders facts relevant or not for adjudication.

Thus, knowing the legal rule, the lawyer indicates to the social scientist the kinds of empirical data that are needed. Although the initial factual questions for investigation are posed by the lawyer, the social scientist does not remain in a handmaiden's role. He may call attention to other facts which the lawyer had not initially considered, facts which could alter the character of the legal problem itself. He might point out research that shows that segregated schooling produces detrimental personality and educational effects on minority children and that these effects occur whether the segregation came about by deliberate action or fortuitous circumstances.

These findings, if they are of proven reliability and validity, have significance for legal policy. The reform-minded lawyer could rely on these data to challenge the existing rule. He would argue that racial imbalance and negative effects on personality and education are sufficient to find unlawful discrimination, without any further showing of improper motive. He would want to establish this new rule because proof of motive is difficult and, under the present rule, he cannot win without proving this fact.

If a court accepts the argument and finds that segregation exists, the lawyer and his social science colleague would have helped make new law. Here is an instance of using empirical research in law creation. The facts established by the research and accepted by the court result in the formulation of a new legal rule. In this respect, "the issues of law also arise out of the facts."

A fourth characteristic of legal rules is their general and indeterminate character. Each dispute that is presented for legal resolution is treated in the same manner as other similar disputes. This means that a dispute is placed in a general class, and all members of that class are attended to according to the same standards. A dispute about school segregation, for instance, is treated the same way regardless of whether it arises in Detroit or New York. But human experience is variable and no two segregation disputes are identical. Rules created for a specific circumstance cannot be applied mechanically to other "like" cases. To frame a rule that resolves a present issue and also anticipates and encompasses all possible variations of this issue as may arise in the future is impossible and unwise. "The difficulties of discerning what the past has to say to the present are great. The difficulties of deciding what the present can wisely try to say to the future are even greater" (Hart and McNaughton 1959, p. 49).

For this reason, legal rules are sometimes purposefully indeterminate. Rules that govern school segregation disputes—"separate but equal educational facilities are inherently unequal" (*Brown* v. *Board of Education,* 1954); desegregation must proceed "with all deliberate speed" (*Brown* v. *Board of Education,* 1955)—use sweeping language that artfully dodges and postpones issues of policy that must be confronted when these rules are applied in the future. All words, Justice Frankfurter (1961) noted, "are symbols of meaning." If "individual words are inexact symbols, with shifting variables, their configuration can hardly achieve invariant meaning or assure definiteness" (p. 75). The process of rule formulation and application is not only an exercise of logical reasoning but is, ultimately, a political craft.

2.2. LAW AS A PROCESS OF SOLVING DISPUTES

Law, however, is more than a system of rules for conduct. Rules are the substantive component of law, but "rules alone, mere forms of words, are worthless"; they are "the shell and not the substance" (Llewellyn 1930, p. 12). Rules, after all, do not rule themselves. They are made and implemented by judges in the course of adjudicating disputes. There is a process or procedural component to law: the method by which disputes are settled via the instrumentality of rules. In this view, law is an activity designed to create and maintain order in society. Disputes that disrupt social order are the raw stuff of the law. Legal rules are the tools for resolving disputes. And the sequence of steps involved in the process of resolution constitutes the dynamic of the law.

The takeoff point in adjudication is a case at law, that is, a dispute brought before a judicial tribunal. In an imperfect society, disputes are bound to arise. Some are actual disputes; others are potential controversies. Some are between private individuals; others are between individuals and the state. The overwhelming majority of them are mediated informally or, if formally, without litigation. When it is not settled, it reaches the point of a contested trial. Although formal adjudication plays a small role in terms of the total number of disputes in society that it processes, it is nonetheless symbolically and practically important because it is usually the last peaceful recourse left.

In Llewellyn's view (1930), "The doing of something about disputes, the doing of it reasonably, is the business of law. . . . What officials [judges, lawyers, sheriffs, and so forth] do about disputes is, to my mind, the law itself" (p. 12). Society expects judges to follow rules when they straighten out things that go awry. It disapproves of idiosyncratic or purely discretionary judgments in resolving conflicts. But these rules are not the law. According to Judge Frank (1930),* "The law . . . consists of decisions, not of rules. If so, whenever a judge decides a case he is making law" (p. 128). "Rules, whether stated by judges or others, whether in statutes, opinions, or textbooks by learned authors, are not the law, but are only some among many of the sources to which judges go in making the law of the cases tried before them" (p. 127).

Legal reasoning consists, in essence, of the application of a legal rule (major premise) to the facts (minor premise) of a given dispute in order to reach a decision (conclusion). Judgment and choice are also involved in reasoning. Law "cannot be dealt with as if it contained only the axioms and corollaries of a book of mathematics" (Holmes 1881, p. 1). The process of judgment can be divided into several steps.

There is, first, the identification of the legally significant facts from the mass of raw facts that surrounds the dispute. In a school desegregation case, the racial imbalance is such a fact. The particular minority race that is involved or the grade level of the affected pupils are not legally relevant facts. The judge sifts through the facts (evidence) initially presented by counsel at trial and selects the few that are deemed to have a legal bearing on the outcome. "The facts" of a case, then, are those that the judge adopts as the grounds for decision—a highly distilled, abstract version of the raw events of real life. The task of opposing counsel is to persuade the judge as to what facts ought to be considered as relevant from their respective points of view—relevant in the sense that those facts will help one side to win.

Fact determination depends partly on the second step in the decisional process, the choice of the appropriate rule to apply to the facts. There is a circular relationship between law and facts. As Judge Frank (1930)* describes it, "[A]lthough decisions are governed rather by one's beliefs about the facts than by abstract rules, yet the act of deciding can be divided into two parts, the determination of the facts and the determination of what rules are to be applied to those facts. But these two parts of judging are usually not separated but intertwined" (p. 134). He goes on to quote Edmund Burke, "No rational man ever did govern himself by abstractions and universals. The major (premise)[legal rule] makes a pompous figure in the battle, but victory depends upon the little minor of circumstances [facts]" (p. 134).

Issues of fact arise out of law. The factual issue of racial imbalance is important

---

*Reprinted by permission of the publisher. Copyright ©1930 by the Tudor Publishing Company.

because a legal rule calls it into play. But just as there is a sifting of facts, there is also a choosing of the governing rule. In a given dispute, there might be two conflicting rules, each of which could lead to a different result if applied. The determination of which rule to apply depends partly on the facts, since issues of law can arise out of facts. This determination of the facts is an entry point for social research.

Policy judgments are a third step in the decision-making. The application of a specific rule (for example, prohibiting school segregation) may involve the invocation of a higher-order legal principle (for example, equal treatment before the law). One can think of a hierarchy of legal rules, from specific rules to principles or super-rules. These principles are the reasons or justifications that underlie the black-letter law of rules. "The letter of the Law," said Sergeant Plowden, "is the body of the Law, but the sense and reason of it is the soul" (in Wigmore 1935, p. 5). The legal principle or the rule-behind-the-rules reflects broad, social policy judgments which affect the determination of both facts and rules. A judge must often weigh competing social policies in adjudicating a case. The principle of equal treatment for all might have to be balanced against, for example, the principle of preferential treatment for some who have suffered inequality in the past. Discerning the policies of the rules, which are often buried from sight, is to be halfway toward understanding the rules derived therefrom.

The final step is the decision itself that settles the dispute. It is announced in the opinion of the court, a statement written by the judge whose name it bears, that presents a justification for the decision. The opinion contains a summary of "the facts," the question(s) presented by the case, the decision of the court, and the reasons for that decision. These opinions constitute "the cases" one reads and are the corpus of judge-made law.

In sum, to say that law is a process for settling disputes is to say that it is a method for thinking about and acting upon social problems. It is a form of reasoning that consists of fact analysis, rule analysis, and policy analysis in order to reach an informed judgment on how a dispute can be resolved. An understanding of this process helps place in perspective the roles of legal scholars, advocates, and social researchers. Legal scholars seek to analyze and synthesize the rules in a given area of law into a coherent, logical system. They also assess and critique the policies underlying the rules. The role of judges and attorneys is to prevent or solve disputes via case-by-case adjudication. They use legal rules to fit them to the facts of a case to reach a solution. The social scientist interested in policy-oriented research investigates the empirical dimensions of legal issues, in order to provide a factual basis for applying or creating law.

2.3. SOME FUNCTIONS OF LAW

The foregoing conceptualization of law is a utilitarian one. It stresses the purpose of law as a means for establishing order. Berman and Greiner (1980) have identified three components to this purpose: the restoration of social equilibrium, the facilitation of voluntary social conduct, and the molding of social values (p. 36).

By settling disputes via an authoritative allocation of legal rights and obligations, the law provides an alternative to other means of conflict resolution. It serves a peacemaking function in that it pre-empts forcible self-help measures. This is perhaps most evident in a criminal case. The victim of crime has an alternative to private vengeance. A criminal act is deemed by law to be directed at society as a whole, so that it is "the People" or "the State"—not the individual victim—who is, formally, the aggrieved party demanding justice.

As a problem-solving method, law enables reasonably reliable prediction of the legal consequences of human conduct. In addition to settling disputes, it serves to permit and protect voluntary action. By the rules of contract law, two parties can create a structure for social relationships (as in a marriage contract) and economic transactions (business contract) to be carried into the future. By adhering to these rules, the parties voluntarily bind themselves to the agreement that the state will enforce. There are sanctions that induce performance or compensate nonperformance. The law protects the expectations of the parties in entering into the agreement and their reliance on it. It thereby assures stability, predictability, and efficiency in relationships, characteristics which are important for societal order. The law has many other such vehicles by which people can do what they want to do and make it legally enforceable: corporations, tax shelters, wills, trusts, and partnerships, to name a few.

Law, then, becomes a tool for forecasting. As Justice Holmes (1897) declared, "The prophecies of what the courts will do in fact, and nothing more pretentious, are what I mean by the law" (p. 461). When a lawyer tenders advice on, say, the breach of a contract or the liability in an automobile accident, he is essentially predicting how that problem will be resolved in court should it end up in litigation. Of course, prediction alone is not all there is to the lawyering task. Once the probable outcome is determined, other legal activities need to be undertaken such as negotiation, drafting, litigation, and lobbying. But making judgments of the likely legal effects of human action is basic to the function of law.

Finally, law has a teaching component. It serves a "moral or socio-pedagogic" purpose to reflect and shape the values and beliefs of society (Andenaes 1966, p. 949). It complements and enhances the moral learning initially acquired through nonlegal (such as family and religious) sources. For example, a study of the impact of reform rape legislation on prosecution found few of the effects expected by reform proponents. Despite major revisions in the substantive law designed to enhance prosecutorial effectiveness, there was no increase in overall charging and conviction rates. Nonetheless, the new rape law served as a catalyst for attitude change among criminal justice officials. It symbolized and reinforced emerging conceptions about the crime and the right of women to self-determination in sexual conduct. This educative effect may be more important in the long run than any immediately observable effects on prosecution (Loh 1980). Procedural law, too, helps mold social values. Thus, the process of trial itself can be a "series of object lessons and examples." "It is the way in which society is trained in right ways of thought and action, not by compulsion, but by parables which it interprets and follows voluntarily" (Arnold 1935, p. 129).

2.4.   STRUCTURE OF THE COURTS

Overview

The American court system may appear like a legal maze. There are numerous separate court systems, one for each state established under the authority of state governments, and one for the United States organized under the authority of the

Constitution by the Congress. An elementary description of the structure and procedure will provide the background needed to facilitate the reading of cases.

There are two principal types of judicial tribunals: trial courts (also called lower courts or courts of first instance) and appellate courts (or upper courts or courts of review). A case does not reach an appellate court unless it first goes through trial, since otherwise there is nothing to review. There are exceptional circumstances when this is not so in the United States Supreme Court, but they need not concern us for purposes of an overview. The cases or opinions for study are drawn principally from the appellate courts.

Trial courts are those in which lawsuits are initiated, the disputed issues framed, the evidence or proof presented, and the decision handed down by the fact-finder (judge or jury). The disposition of the trial court is final unless timely application for appellate review is made. The losing party at trial usually has the right of appeal. When review is granted, the function of the appellate court is to review the appellant's claims of mistakes of law made by the trial judge.

In reading appellate opinions, it is helpful to bear in mind the basic idea of appellate review. An upper court's task is only to hear complaints of the losing party that a trial judge has made an error of law—that he has not applied a rule of law in correct fashion (correct according to the appellant's view). If the appellate court decides that the trial judge indeed made a mistake of law that affected the outcome, in contrast to a merely "harmless error," it will reverse the judgment and order a new trial. For example, in a criminal case, if a defendant is convicted by a jury on the basis of a confession he made to the police, and the trial judge failed to exclude it from evidence because the confession was illegally extracted by torture, an appellate court can reverse the conviction because the rule forbidding the use at trial of wrongfully obtained evidence was not applied. (The defendant does not go free; he only gets a new trial.) However, an appellate court does not receive new evidence for making factual determinations again. It does not review the findings of fact made at trial regarding the guilt of the defendant, the credibility of the witnesses, the truthfulness of the testimony given, or any other kind of evidence. It will do so only in the uncommon instances when the findings of fact are totally without evidentiary basis. Then the erroneous fact determinations will be considered as errors of law. Otherwise, the appellate court does not reopen the facts of the case. It does not inquire whether a more just result could have been reached by the jury. In short, an appeal is not a trial de novo, a readjudication of the dispute.

In addition to providing an opportunity to correct legal errors, appeals are recognized in order to ensure certainty and finality in the law. Different trial judges may decide like cases differently because they interpret the rules differently. Predictability and consistency in the law is an ideal that bends to the reality of individual differences in ability, knowledge, bias, and values. The State of Georgia, for example, struggled along for nearly half a century with only trial courts. Trial judges had to meet in periodic conferences to work out their differences in construing the law. Eventually, an appellate court of last resort had to be established. This tribunal reduced the discrepancies in law by pronouncing the one "right answer" to any dispute in the territory. It simply laid down "the rule" to be followed by all of the trial courts.

There is, then, a division of functions between the two types of courts. All of this is according to the theory of how courts are expected to function. In practice, as we shall see when we examine the cases, there is no neat and simple separation between facts (the province of trial courts) and law (the province of appellate courts). The appellate courts feel the pressure of the particular case and sometimes consider the facts and strain to reach a "just" decision. Although they are confined to rulings as to law, their interpretations of the rules may be rooted in unstated assumptions or interpretations of the facts. They are not, in practice, courts of review of "pure" law.

State Courts

State trial courts are generally divided into two types according to their jurisdiction, that is to say, their power over the persons and subject matters involved in the particular dispute. There are trial courts of limited jurisdiction—known as justice courts, municipal courts, district courts, or recorder's court, in different states—that have authority to hear civil cases involving small monetary claims or criminal cases involving minor misdemeanor offenses. There are trial courts of general jurisdiction, unlimited by amount in controversy or subject matter. Organized usually along county lines, they are variously denominated superior court or county court. There is right to appeal from a justice court to a superior court, with trial de novo in the latter. Specialized "courts" such as "probate court" or "criminal court" typically do not refer to separate tribunals staffed by separate judges, but to specialized procedures used for these types of disputes in the superior courts. In both types of trial courts, the hearing of cases is conducted by a single trial judge.

In underpopulated states, there is usually only one appellate court known as the supreme court of that state. It consists of five to nine judges, all of whom sit together to hear the cases. In more populous states, there are intermediate appellate courts organized along geographical lines of groups of counties. They are usually called state courts of appeals.

Federal Courts

The structure of the federal court system substantially parallels that of the states. They differ primarily in their authority to hear certain types of controversies. State courts have general power to decide almost every type of case, subject only to limitations of state law. Most of the legal business of the nation is conducted in state courts. Those are the tribunals with which most citizens come into contact. The limited kinds of cases cognizable in United States courts are set forth in the Constitution (Article III, Section 2) and in implementing statutes enacted by Congress (28 U.S.C. §§1251–57, §3731). The question of jurisdiction of the federal courts is a highly complex and technical matter, to which lawyers devote as much time and effort as the substantive issue of the dispute itself. It is not one that we need to go into.

There are nearly one hundred federal trial courts called United States District Courts organized around geographical areas called districts. Each district consists of a state or part of a state. Thus, there is an Eastern District and a Western District for the U.S.D.C. in Washington State. California is divided into four districts. There are one to twenty-seven judges per district depending on the volume of cases it processes, and they normally sit individually in hearing each case. They have jurisdiction over three basic types of disputes. "Diversity jurisdiction" includes lawsuits between citizens of different states where the amount in controversy exceeds $10,000. "Federal question jurisdiction" includes actions by private individuals arising under federal law. Finally, there is jurisdiction over "controversies to which the United States shall be a party" (Article III, Section 2, of the Constitution); that is, lawsuits by or against the federal government. The criminal and civil (excluding bankruptcy) cases received each year in all of the district courts total about 150,000.

The intermediate appellate court of the federal system is the United States Court of Appeals. It is organized along twelve geographical circuits, consisting of groups of three or more states plus the District of Columbia. The Court of Appeals for the Second Circuit, for example, hears appeals from the district courts located in New York, Connecticut, and Vermont. Each court consists of three to fifteen judges, depending on the workload. Appeals are usually heard by panels of three judges. Sometimes they are heard in banc (with the entire membership sitting). The courts receive about 17,000 appeals per year.

The highest court in the federal system is the United States Supreme Court. It consists of nine justices appointed for life by the President with the advice and consent of the Senate. Its yearly term begins on the first Monday of October and continues until June. During this session, it receives some 4,000 cases, of which roughly 10% (or less) are deemed of sufficient importance to warrant full Court review. About one-half of the reviewed cases are disposed of by full written opinions, some as long as 50 to 100 pages or more.

The Court has original jurisdiction (that is, the power to be both trial and appellate court) in only limited types of cases, mostly in disputes between different states, and it is infrequently exercised. Usually it reviews cases originating from lower federal courts and certain types of cases coming from state supreme courts.

There are three methods of seeking review. Most cases, regardless of state or federal origin, reach the Supreme Court by applying for a "writ of certiorari." This is a method of discretionary appellate review authorized by Congress in 1925. It serves two related aims. One is to allow the screening of only those cases that present substantial constitutional or federal questions. The other is administrative economy. The Court does not have the resources to review all of the applications. Only a small percentage of all cases filed with the Court are granted certiorari. Four justices must agree to review before the writ is granted. A denial of the writ lets the decision of the last lower court stand. It is not a decision based on the merits of the dismissed case; it means only that there were not at least four justices willing to review it.

The second and less frequent type of review is by direct appeal from lower federal courts and state supreme courts. In these instances, appellate review is a matter of right made mandatory by federal legislation. This "mandatory review" is actually as discretionary as review by writ of certiorari, because a substantial federal question must be presented as concurred in by at least four justices. In practice, both types of review are quite similar.

The final and least frequent method is by certification. A federal appellate court (and not the party litigants) can request that the Supreme Court review a case in which a point of law is unclear, thereby by-passing the intermediate appellate stage. The granting of review on certificate is also, in practice, discretionary.

Figure 2.1 summarizes the various courts and the different routes of appeal. Excluded from this summary are specialized federal courts (for example, Court of

FIGURE 2.1

The Structure of the Courts and the Appeals Process

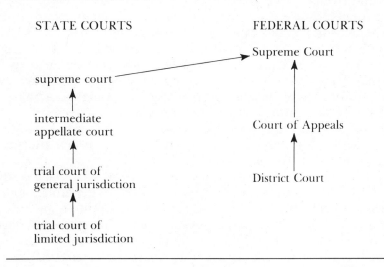

STATE COURTS   FEDERAL COURTS

Supreme Court

supreme court

intermediate
appellate court   Court of Appeals

trial court of
general jurisdiction   District Court

trial court of
limited jurisdiction

Claims, Tax Court, Court of Military Appeals). Cases from these courts can also be reviewed ultimately by the Supreme Court.

2.5. PROCEDURE OF THE COURTS

The judicial opinions reproduced in this book are drawn primarily from the appellate courts. Informed reading of opinions requires at least a rudimentary view of the procedure that precedes and leads to the appellate decisions. Procedure in this context is the engine that powers the court system. It consists of intellectual activities by which disputes are adjudicated. These activities encompass (1) the initial determination by the lawyers of the issues of fact and of law in the given dispute; (2) the trial of the issues of fact by evidence and the decision about the facts by the lower courts; (3) the review of the issues of law by argumentation as to the applicable rules and social policies and the decision about the appropriate rule by the appellate courts; and (4) the prediction of the impact of the decision on future conduct.

The Adversary System

The adversary system lies at the bottom of Anglo-American judicial procedure. This system lets the parties fight their own battles, so long as legal rules of evidence and procedure designed to ensure that the fight is within bounds of fairness and reasonableness are observed. Its origins are said to hark back to the time of the Norman Conquest when common means of dispute resolution included trial by ordeal and combat, although hard evidence for this claim is wanting (Richard Lempert, 1981, personal communication). Today, the fight is by use of reasoned argumentation, but the backdrop of adversarial clash remains.

The premise is that each side will exert effort to present its case in the strongest possible light, and from this partisan confrontation, truth will eventually emerge and justice will be served. The societal interest in the proper resolution of disputes is entrusted to the self-interest and abilities of the opposing parties. It is the duty of the parties to initiate the litigation, investigate the facts, present proof of their claims, and argue the applicable law. The litigants themselves move and shape the contour of the lawsuit. The judge, in turn, sits solely to rule on issues presented by each side. He assumes a neutral and relatively detached role as decision-maker. The parties come to him with all the necessary information so that he can make a decision. It is not his task to go out and find out what the row is all about. Thus, presentation and prosecution of the case by the litigants and division of functions between the judge and the litigants are the main features of the adversary system.

Under the continental civil law approach (that is, where legal rules are fully codified and adjudication consists of application of or generalizations from pre-established codes, in contrast to the Anglo-American common law approach where the rules are made by judges on a case-by-case basis), the judicial procedure is an inquisitorial one. The lower court judge is the prime mover of the case, spurring the parties to present additional evidence, helping them to sharpen their respective positions, applying the case law without relying on the parties to call it to his attention, calling and questioning witnesses on his own initiative, operating without a jury, constantly striving to reach a settlement of the dispute—in short, the civil law judge is far more vigorous and has greater freedom of action than his common law counterpart. However, the lawyers are noticeably lacking in adversarial fervor. On appeal, the parties are entitled to a retrial of the case. They can bring in new evidence and make new legal arguments to supplement the record of the proceedings of the court below.

The inquisitorial system puts its trust in a nonadversary system dominated by a judge who is specifically trained for that function. The adversary system relies on a free-wheeling duel between counsel before a detached judge who, though legally educated, is not trained for this task and is either elected or appointed to that position. These two systems have emerged over the centuries partly by design and partly by historical stresses and accidents (Kaplan 1960).

We present a quick sketch of the stages of a typical lawsuit. A civil lawsuit or action is one in which the complaining party (plaintiff) seeks a personal remedy from the defendant in the form of money or other property, or seeks a court order to enforce a legal right. A criminal prosecution is one in which the state seeks to convict a person accused of committing a crime. The outline of a trial and an appeal presented below is that of a civil proceeding.

Trial Process

Suppose pedestrian A is hit by B's car. A consults an attorney who advises him, based on the facts reported by A and the precedent of past cases, that B is obligated to compensate him for his injury. If there is no informal settlement of the dispute, A may ask his attorney to initiate a suit.

After deciding on the trial court that has jurisdiction over this matter, A's attorney files a written "complaint" with the court, thereby commencing the action. A becomes a plaintiff. The complaint contains allegations of the facts of the incident and prays for a damage award. It must state a "cause of action," that is, "it must describe a particular situation that falls within the general class of situations to which the substantive law rule refers" (Louisell and Hazard 1979, p. 5). Given facts X (B's car crossed a red light and hit A), then legal conclusion Y ensues (B is negligent and must compensate A).

Upon being notified of the complaint, B, now a defendant, also retains a lawyer. A written defense called an "answer" is filed in court. It may admit some of the factual allegations of the plaintiff (for example, that B drove the car), deny others (for example, that B did not cross a red light), and allege other facts (for example, that A was drunk and stumbled into the street). The complaint and the answer are collectively known as "pleadings." They serve to inform the court what the quarrel is about. Plaintiff's allegations that are denied and defendant's own allegations define the facts at issue—the facts that are in dispute and must be resolved in favor of one side or the other by the court.

While the pleadings are being prepared and processed, the parties probe the merits of each other's case. This is the stage of "discovery." Up to this point, the lawyer for each side has gotten an account of the incident mainly from his own client. In discovery, he tries to find out directly what the other party has to say. The most common discovery tool is the deposition, an interrogation of a party or a witness by the opposing lawyer before a court reporter. Written interrogatories or question-naires are also used.

Prior to trial, there may also be a pretrial conference. This is a meeting in the judge's chambers between opposing lawyers in an attempt to settle the case or, failing that, at least to clarify the factual and legal issues that will be litigated.

At any time after the complaint is filed and before the trial starts, defendant can make a motion for summary judgment to the court. This is a request by affidavit, often accompanied by oral argument, that the complaint be dismissed summarily because there really is no factual issue (for example, twenty bishops swear they saw A drunk and stumble into the street) or because, even if plaintiff's allegations are true, there is no legal basis for recovery under existing rules. Let us assume the motion is denied and the case goes to trial.

Plaintiff can elect to have a trial before a jury or before the judge alone. The first stage at trial is the selection of the jury. By voir dire examination, lawyers and/or the judge question prospective jurors (called venirepersons) to determine if they are qualified for jury service and if they are unbiased with respect to this case. A lawyer can challenge for cause an unqualified or biased juror, or excuse a juror without any articulated reason by exercising one of his limited number of peremptory (that is, discretionary) challenges. After the jury is seated, the lawyers make their opening statements.

First in order is the plaintiff. His lawyer introduces evidence (documents, testimony of witnesses, and so forth) to prove the allegations of fact made in the complaint. He also presents arguments regarding the appropriate legal rule that should govern this case. The witnesses are questioned by plaintiff's lawyer on direct examination. After each direct testimony, defendant's lawyer may cross-examine the witness to bring out weaknesses and mistakes or to discredit him. When the plaintiff believes he has proved enough to persuade the judge or jury in his favor, he rests. He is done with his case in chief.

Defendant then proceeds with his case in chief. He also calls witnesses who are subject to direct examination and cross-examination, and finally rests.

All of the proof presented by both sides is screened through an intricate sieve of evidentiary rules designed to further certain procedural values, including reliability, fairness, and administrative efficiency. For example, hearsay evidence (witness X tells in court what he heard from person Y, and person Y is not in court) is excluded because secondhand information, unsworn and untested by cross-examination, is deemed unreliable notwithstanding its possible relevance to the case. And like all rules, this one has some two dozen exceptions, more or less. There is a rule against opinion evidence. Unless a duly qualified expert, a witness can only describe his perceptions and leave inferences and conclusions from that testimony to the fact-finder. And so on, with rules upon rules and exceptions upon exceptions, and the crafty trial lawyer is the one who knows how to use and get around these rules for the purpose of admitting as much evidence as possible that favors his side and excluding as much as possible that is to his adversary's benefit.

A reason for this elaborate web of rules is to be found in the jury. This is an important point in understanding procedural and evidentiary rules. The jury is entrusted to decide disputed issues of fact. It alone weighs the evidence. On the one hand, the jury is an essential institution in our system of justice. Having a representative body of lay persons from the community resolve the dispute lends a certain legitimacy and democratic color to the decision. On the other hand, there is always a lingering distrust of the judgment of lay persons inexperienced in legal niceties and unskilled in evaluating evidence. To keep the jury as fact-finder and also protect it from being misled by cunning advocates, our legal system has devised these elaborate rules that define what the jury can or cannot hear. It should be added that these rules apply in theory, though less in practice, in bench trials (before a judge, not a jury) as well.

These rules often prevent a party from proving certain key facts. When a party challenges the other side's attempt to admit evidence at trial, the judge rules on the question of its admissibility. The losing party on this issue can note his "exception" to the ruling. Each exception can become the basis for a claimed error of law in requesting appellate review.

At the end of the presentation of the evidence, defendant's lawyer might move for a dismissal of the case or a directed verdict. It is a request that the judge order the jury to return a verdict in favor of defendant because plaintiff has clearly not made out his case. Plaintiff too might move for a directed verdict in his own favor.

If the motions are denied, the case goes to the jury. Plaintiff opens his concluding argument. It is a review of the evidence that stresses the most persuasive facts in his favor and the most damaging facts for the other side. Then defendant makes his concluding argument. Finally, plaintiff finishes with his concluding argument. Thus, the plaintiff has the first and last say at trial.

This tactical advantage for the plaintiff is offset by a procedural handicap: He bears the burden of proof. He has to come forward with enough evidence to persuade the fact-finder that a (hypothetical) reasonable person would agree with his version of the facts and that therefore he should prevail. How this omnipresent "reasonable person" would decide disputed facts is the standard that the laws asks the fact-finder to use. The amount of proof needed by the plaintiff to persuade the fact-finder, using this reasonableness standard, is "by a preponderance of the evidence," typically operationalized as .50 +. This standard is not so high that it should discourage lawsuits. (In criminal cases, more proof is needed: It must be "beyond a reasonable doubt," a criterion which is deliberately not quantified.) The fact-finder must decide that it is "more likely than not"—another way of stating the preponderance criterion—that the events occurred as claimed by plaintiff in order for him to win. As a rough analogy, this criterion of proof serves to weigh legal evidence in the same manner that statistical levels of significance are used to weigh scientific data.

To carry the burden of proof is to carry the risk of nonpersuasion. If after hearing the evidence from both parties the fact-finder remains in equipoise, unpersuaded by either side, the plaintiff loses because he has not met the burden. It is up to the plaintiff to prove his case and not to the defendant to clear himself. This handicap on the plaintiff reflects a policy to discourage unfounded lawsuits.

Finally, the judge charges the jury. He instructs the jury as to the applicable rule of law in this dispute (for example, no liability without driver's negligence) and the facts they must find in order to render a verdict (for example, was defendant negligent in driving? was plaintiff drunk?). There is a separation of functions in the trial court. The judge determines the applicable law and the jury decides the contested facts. It then deliberates in private and renders a decision based on a unanimous or majority vote, depending on the procedural rules of the jurisdiction. The jury usually returns a general verdict (for example, "We find for the plaintiff in the sum of $8,000"). Unlike the judge, the lay fact-finder need not give any reason or justification for its decision. The jury simply states a naked result. The judge then renders a judgment based on the jury verdict. It is a formal statement of the outcome of the lawsuit (for example, "Judgment of the court is hereby entered in favor of A against B in the sum of $8,000"). Except for any posttrial motions which need not concern us here, the trial phase of the lawsuit is over.

We have sketched in some detail the trial process because the ultimate appellate court decision is shaped by these preceding transactions. In Part III we shall look in closer detail at selected aspects of this trial procedure in light of empirical studies.

Appellate Process

After final judgment by the trial court, either or both parties may be unsatisfied with the result and appeal to a review court for a hearing on claimed errors of law. Usually the losing party is the appellant (also called petitioner or plaintiff in error). Appellate judges usually defer to the findings of fact of the lower tribunal because, not having been directly exposed to the evidence, they are reluctant to second-guess factual judgments. The decision of the appellate court is based only on its reading of the evidence as contained in a verbatim transcript of the trial proceeding, the legal arguments of the attorneys at the appellate hearing, and its own analysis of the applicable law.

The legal arguments are presented in written and oral form. Appellant's "brief" states the facts of the case as he understands them, the legal questions for review (that is, the legal issues he is complaining that the trial judge erred on), and how he believes these questions should be decided. Appellee (also called respondent or defendant in error) prepares a rebuttal brief. The briefs are exchanged and submitted to the court. Depending on local practice, there may or may not be opportunity for oral argument before a panel of judges or before the entire bench. This gives the lawyers a chance to address the judges face to face and attempt to persuade them as to the correct law. It also gives the judges an occasion to probe counsel's arguments and to inform themselves over and above the contents of the briefs.

The court then recesses to engage in group deliberation and decision-making in private conference. A decision to affirm or reverse the lower court judgment is made by majority vote. This ruling is announced and justified in an opinion. Appellate opinions (and trial court opinions that are affirmed on review) constitute the common law—the end products of the long course of trial and appellate adjudication, the subject matter of casebooks read by students. How to read and analyze opinions will be discussed at the end of Chapter 3, after some opinions have been presented.

2.6. SELECTED PROVISIONS OF THE UNITED STATES CONSTITUTION

Reproduced below are those provisions of the Constitution—namely, selections from the Bill of Rights (the first ten amendments, ratified in 1791) and the Civil War Amendments—that will be alluded to in subsequent chapters.

AMENDMENT I

Congress shall make no law respecting an establishment of religion, or prohibiting the free exercise thereof; or abridging the freedom of speech, or of the press; or the right of the people peaceably to assemble, and to petition the Government for a redress of grievances.

. . .

AMENDMENT IV

The right of the people to be secure in their persons, houses, papers, and effects, against unreasonable searches and seizures, shall not be violated, and no Warrants shall issue, but upon probable cause, supported by Oath or affirmation, and particularly describing the place to be searched, and the persons or things to be seized.

AMENDMENT V

No person shall be held to answer for a capital, or otherwise infamous crime, unless on a presentment or indictment of a Grand Jury, except in cases arising in the land or naval forces, or in the Militia, when in actual service in time of War or public danger; nor shall any person be subject for the same offence to be twice put in jeopardy of life or limb; nor shall be compelled in any criminal case to be a witness against himself, nor be deprived of life, liberty, or property, without due process of law; nor shall private property be taken for public use, without just compensation.

AMENDMENT VI

In all criminal prosecutions, the accused shall enjoy the right to a speedy and public trial, by an impartial jury of the

State and district wherein the crime shall have been committed, which district shall have been previously ascertained by law, and to be informed of the nature and cause of the accusation; to be confronted with the witnesses against him; to have compulsory process for obtaining witnesses in his favor, and to have the Assistance of Counsel for his defence.

AMENDMENT VII

In suits at common law, where the value in controversy shall exceed twenty dollars, the right of trial by jury shall be preserved, and no fact tried by a jury, shall be otherwise re-examined in any Court of the United States, than according to the rules of the common law.

AMENDMENT VIII

Excessive bail shall not be required, nor excessive fines imposed, nor cruel and unusual punishments inflicted.

. . .

AMENDMENT XIII [1865]

Section 1. Neither slavery nor involuntary servitude, except as a punishment for crime whereof the party shall have been duly convicted, shall exist within the United States, or any place subject to their jurisdiction.

Section 2. Congress shall have the power to enforce this article by appropriate legislation.

AMENDMENT XIV [1868]

Section 1. All persons born or naturalized in the United States, and subject to the jurisdiction thereof, are citizens of the United States and of the State wherein they reside. No State shall make or enforce any law which shall abridge the privileges or immunities of citizens of the United States; nor shall any State deprive any person of life, liberty, or property, without due process of law; nor deny to any person within its jurisdiction the equal protection of the laws.

. . .

Section 5. The Congress shall have the power to enforce, by appropriate legislation, the provisions of this article.

AMENDMENT XV [1870]

Section 1. The right of citizens of the United States to vote shall not be denied or abridged by the United States or by any State on account of race, color, or previous condition of servitude.

Section 2. The Congress shall have power to enforce this article by appropriate legislation.

. . .

REFERENCES

Andenaes, J. "The General Preventive Effects of Punishment." *University of Pennsylvania Law Review* 114 (1966): 949–83.

Arnold, T. *The Symbols of Government.* New Haven: Yale University Press, 1935.

Berman, H. J., and Greiner, W. R. *The Nature and Functions of Law,* 3rd ed. Mineola, N.Y.: Foundation Press, 1980.

Brown v. Board of Education of Topeka, 347 U.S. 483 (1954).

Brown v. Board of Education of Topeka, 349 U.S. 294 (1955).

Frank, J. *Law and the Modern Mind.* New York: Tudor, 1930.

Frankfurter, F. "Reflections on Reading Statutes." In *The Supreme Court: Views from*

Inside, edited by A. Westin. New York: W. W. Norton, 1961.

Hart, H. M., and McNaughton, J. T. "Evidence and Inference in Law." In *Evidence and Inference,* edited by D. Lerner. Glencoe, Ill.: Free Press, 1959.

Hazard, G. "Limitations on the Uses of Behavioral Science in Law." *Case Western Reserve Law Review* 19 (1967): 71–76.

Holmes, O. W. *The Common Law.* Boston: Little, Brown, 1881.

————. "The Path of the Law." *Harvard Law Review* 10 (1897): 457–78.

Kaplan, A. "Civil Procedure: Reflections on the Comparison of Systems." *Buffalo Law Review* 9 (1960): 409–32.

Llewellyn, K. N. *The Bramble Bush: On Our Law and Its Study.* Dobbs Ferry, N.Y.: Oceana, 1930.

————. "The Normative, the Legal, and the Law-Jobs: The Problem of Juristic Method." *Yale Law Journal* 49 (1940): 1355–1400.

Loh, W. D. "The Impact of Common Law and Reform Rape Statutes on Prosecution: An Empirical Case Study." *University of Washington Law Review* 55 (1980): 543–652.

Louisell, D. W., and Hazard, G. C., Jr. *Cases on Pleading and Procedure,* 4th ed. Mineola, N.Y.: Foundation Press, 1979.

Pound, R. "Hierarchy of Sources and Forms in Different Systems of Law." *Tulane Law Review* 7 (1933): 475–87.

Priest, G. L. "Social Science Theory and Legal Education: The Law School as University." *Journal of Legal Education* 33 (1983): 437–41.

Wigmore, J. H. *A Students' Textbook of the Law of Evidence.* Brooklyn, N.Y.: Foundation Press, 1935.

PART II

SOCIAL RESEARCH AND SUBSTANTIVE JUSTICE: LAWMAKING IN THE APPELLATE PROCESS

CHAPTER 3

Creation of Law: Case Study of Southern School Desegregation

3.1. INTRODUCTION AND OVERVIEW

Equality, Alexis de Tocqueville said in *Democracy in America* (1969, pp. 473–76), is the prerequisite for a democratic society. Of all the values that compose the American Creed, none perhaps is more honored than the notion that "all men are created equal"—that the law deals equitably with all persons, respecting the dignity of each and denying opportunities to none.

Since the founding of the Republic, however, the practice of this ideal has fallen short of its profession, particularly with respect to equal treatment of persons of different races. The glowingly asserted "self-evident" truth of the Declaration of Independence was simply ignored eleven years later during the drafting of the Constitution. No egalitarian rights were guaranteed in the very framework of the new government. Instead, the 1787 Constitutional Convention, in arriving at a compromise formula for the representation of the states in the federal government, institutionalized racial inequality by defining a black slave as three-fifths of a free white male. As Madison explained it in *The Federalist*, No. 54: "[L]et the compromising expedient of the Constitution be mutually adopted, which regards them [slaves] as inhabitants, but as debased by servitude below the equal level of free inhabitants, which regards the slave as divested of two-fifths of the man" (Hamilton, Jay, and Madison 1938, p. 357). A few years after the Nation was conceived in liberty, equality was interpreted to mean equality for all white men.

The passage of time failed to narrow the rift between principle and reality. Even after slavery was abolished by a fratricidal war and the country entered the new century in the midst of unparalleled growth and prosperity, legally enforced racial discrimination in many areas of social and public life became widespread and harsh. No office of the national government was fully mobilized to address this wrong. It was not until 1954 that the first major step since Reconstruction was taken to save the tarnished ideal, and it was taken by the Supreme Court of the United States. In the landmark decision of *Brown* v. *Board of Education* (1954), the nine appointed, life-tenured Justices—who are said to constitute the least democratic branch of government, and who have to decide some of the most vexing social policy problems of the day ostensibly above the prejudices and passions of the electorate—unanimously declared that racial separation in one of the nation's most basic institutions, the public school, is "inherently unequal." Few opinions in the history of the Court have had more far-reaching symbolic and practical significance. In the literature on equality, it occupies a special place because it marks "the turning point in America's willingness to face the consequences of centuries of racial discrimination" (Kluger 1977, p. x).*

An additional reason makes *Brown* a singularly appropriate starting point for the study of social-legal research. The application of social science to law began in Europe at the turn of the century, when experimental psychologists served as experts in court testifying on the reliability of the perception, memory, and recall of witnesses (Münsterberg 1908). In this country, it was not "until 1950 that psychologists began to make an appreciable contribution in this role" (Anastasi 1957, p. 548). The era of forensic—and especially constitutional—applications was ushered in by social psychologists testifying in school segregation litigation. *Brown* saw their most visible and controversial role to date. The Court, in holding that segregation of school children "solely because of their race generates a feeling of inferiority" and "[retards their] educational and mental development," cited as "modern authority" for these findings the writings of social scientists in the now celebrated footnote 11 (*Brown*, pp. 494–95). Social researchers read the opinion as an acknowledgment of their impact on constitutional decision-making. "Proof [of the wrongfulness of segregation]," said Kenneth Clark (1953), the plaintiff's chief social science consultant, "had to come from the social psychologists" (p. 3).

This chapter, then, begins with *Brown* and its predecessors. They illustrate how the law of equality develops and how social science theories and data can be used in the processes of law creation.

To apprehend the applications and utility of social research to law, it is necessary to start with an understanding of the legal issues involved. After a short overview of the historical and legal background in section 3.2, the two principal cases of this chapter, *Plessy* v. *Ferguson* (1896) and *Brown*, are presented in section 3.3. These cases are examined in light of the social ideology and social science contexts in which they arose.

The foregoing materials serve as a kind of legal compass. In section 3.4, we present the expert social science testimony given in the desegregation lawsuits pursued in the various lower federal courts. The introduction of social science and its apparent reliance by the Supreme Court in reaching its decision provoked sharp criticism in political, legal, and scientific circles, even among those who were otherwise wholly in sympathy with the ultimate outcome. Part of the debate between two distinguished scholars—a lawyer and a social psychologist—is reproduced in section 3.5 to serve as a springboard for evaluating the role of empirical research in law creation.

In the appellate courts, social science evidence is normally introduced by brief of counsel. The first "social science brief" was submitted by (later Justice) Brandeis in

---

arguing for the constitutionality of a social welfare statute in *Muller* v. *Oregon* (1908). After first considering the legal issues posed by the case and the social-economic context in which it occurs, we turn to the empirical dimension. In section 3.6, we examine the content, form, and purpose of the Brandeis brief in *Muller* and compare it with the like brief in *Brown*. The materials are designed to raise questions on how social science interrelates with elements of procedural law (such as burden of proof and presumption of constitutionality) in order to shape the substantive law outcome (such as the legality of segregated schools).

The chapter ends with a note in section 3.7 on the structure and analysis of judicial opinions. We thought it helpful to social science students to include some comments on the reading of cases. We deliberately placed this note at the end because it will be more meaningful to the student after he has been exposed to a few cases and has tried to work through them on his own.

3.2.   HISTORICAL AND LEGAL BACKGROUND

A thumbnail sketch of the history and early cases on racial discrimination may be useful in placing the problem of school segregation in perspective.

The Civil War Amendments and Reconstruction Legislation

The tumultuous decade of Radical Reconstruction, 1865–75, was remarkable for its legislation: three constitutional amendments and a plethora of federal supporting legislation, all aimed at providing freedmen with liberty, equality, and suffrage.

In 1865, Congress passed and the states shortly thereafter ratified the Thirteenth Amendment prohibiting "slavery" and "involuntary servitude" in the United States. It nationalized the right to freedom, and Congress made itself the instrument to enforce this right "by appropriate legislation." Three-quarters of a century after the drafting of the Constitution, the Negro was recognized by law as five-fifths of a human being.

Under the lenient Reconstruction policies of Presidents Lincoln and Johnson, the former Confederate states retained substantial political autonomy. Although the South abolished slavery, it began to impose restrictive laws (the so-called Black Codes) on the movement and actions of the freedmen. It erected a new structure for perpetuating the old philosophy of keeping blacks in an inferior position, although now it was based on a caste system rather than on slavery.

The findings of the Joint Committee of Reconstruction, established by Congress in 1865, led most congressmen to believe that strong federal intervention was needed if the gains of the war were not to be nullified. Consequently, one of the first acts of Congress to enforce the Thirteenth Amendment was passage of the Civil Rights Act of 1866, aimed at overturning the Black Codes. It defined citizenship to include blacks and made the federal courts the protectors of their rights. The underlying premise of the legislation was that the liberty secured by emancipation is really inseparable from the equality due under the law.

Fears that in the future a different majority in Congress might repeal the civil rights statutes, or that the federal courts might invalidate them as an impermissible extension of federal power into the legislative jurisdiction of the states, led to the passage and eventual ratification in 1868 of the Fourteenth Amendment. It was the centerpiece of congressional Reconstruction.

The first section of the Fourteenth Amendment is expressly targeted at the states: "*No State* shall" "deprive" or "deny" certain basic rights. The reason for this focus is that the rights enumerated in the first eight Amendments were originally secured against the federal government only. It has been ruled by Chief Justice Marshall back in 1833 (*Barron* v. *Baltimore*) that, in a federal system, the Bill of Rights does not protect individuals from actions by state governments. The passage of the fourteenth Amendment filled the gap. State officials—not federal authorities or private persons—are now restrained by the United States Constitution from intruding upon rights of due process and of equality.

The language of the first section is also general and sweeping: states are forbidden to "deprive *any* person" or "deny to *any* person" the protected rights. Unlike the two companion Amendments of that era, there is no specific reference to slavery or to race. Although the original purpose of the Fourteenth Amendment was to ensure the constitutionality of federal civil rights legislation and to restore the former Confederate states to their place in the Union, the breadth of the language has made it possible for courts of ensuing generations to apply its provisions to a multitude of issues that were never anticipated by the framers. The Due Process Clause, in particular, has become today the most important and prolific source of constitutional limitations on "state action" (that is, legislation, policies, decisions, or any other kind of actions by legislators, police, school board members, or any other officials of the state).

It was unquestionably a revolutionary Amendment. It altered the balance of power in the federal compact. The fifth section empowered Congress to enforce these newly created constitutional rights by "appropriate legislation." Of course, what exactly is "appropriate" is a source of never-ending debate. At the time, however, Congress promoted itself as the buffer between the reconstructed states of the South and its people by passing legislation that placed the rights of freedom beyond the pale of discriminatory local statutes.

The Fifteenth Amendment guarantee of suffrage in 1869 and the accompanying legislation to implement it capped the efforts to establish full citizenship rights for blacks. The last major plank of Radical Reconstruction legislation came with the Civil Rights Act of 1875, enacted under the enforcement provision of the Fourteenth Amendment. It was the most sweeping statute of its kind to date. It guaranteed to all persons, regardless of race or color, the "equal enjoyment of the accommodations . . . of inns, public conveyances on land or water, theaters" and of other public facilities. Unsegregated schools were not included in the lengthy list, probably because it was not a critical issue at the time and public education was still in a rudimentary state (Franklin 1956).

Dismantling the Federal Protection

By the late 1870s Reconstruction passion had run its course. There was widespread sentiment in Congress and throughout the North that as much as could be accomplished for the political and civil rights of freedmen had been accomplished.

Now they were on their own. Outside the South, the nation was poised on the threshold of unprecedented industrial growth and its attention, therefore, turned mainly to economic matters. Moreover, after a costly war, Congress was not about to do more for the economic opportunities of the four million blacks it had emancipated. Without land, education, money, or the means of livelihood, most freedmen were reduced to peonage as sharecroppers.

On the political and legal front, there was growing sentiment in the post-Reconstruction years that the Civil War Amendments and the federal enforcement legislation may have upset the federal compact. With the war crisis over, there was thought to be less justification for overcentralization of federal power, and the pendulum began to swing back to the components of the Union. The Supreme Court, which had laid low and deferred to Congress during Reconstruction, began to reassert itself by defining a new federal-state equilibrium (*Slaughter-House Cases*, 1873). Meanwhile, many southern states enacted measures that had the potential effect of disenfranchising blacks, such as gerrymandering election districts and requiring a literacy test and a poll tax, although technically these measures comported with the Thirteenth Amendment. The Supreme Court upheld these statutes because they did not, on their face, discriminate between the races (*Williams* v. *Mississippi*, 1898).

Many southern whites had viewed the Civil Rights Act of 1875 with contempt and often violated it with impunity. The federal government brought a continuing stream of lawsuits on behalf of blacks whose rights under the Act allegedly were violated. In the *Civil Rights Cases* (1883), the Supreme Court struck down the public accommodations section of the Act. It held that Congress had exceeded its authority because the Fourteenth Amendment outlaws discriminatory action only when undertaken by state officials and not by private persons—even though the private businesses in question, such as restaurants, inns, theaters, and stores, were open to the public at large. Moreover, the excluded blacks had suffered wrongs merely to their "social rights," and not to their protected political or civil rights. The Court concluded that "there must be some stage in the progress of his elevation [from slavery] when he takes the rank of a mere citizen, and ceases to be the special favorite of the laws" (p. 25).

The Rise of Jim Crow Legislation

The *Civil Rights Cases* sent a clear signal that the safeguarding of rights of blacks no longer rested with the federal courts, but was left to the tender mercies of the states. It was an "important stimulus to the enactment of segregation statutes" (Franklin 1956, p. 6). Heretofore, racial discrimination in public accommodations had not been universal. The owners decided for themselves whom they would accommodate. By the 1890s, segregation laws were in force. Racial discrimination was now legalized; there was a state-mandated caste system. Only two decades after the victory at Appomattox, the Jim Crow era had begun.

The Fourteenth Amendment lay nearly unrecognizable as a result of Supreme Court interpretations. Black hopes for equality under this crowning achievement of Reconstruction received their *coup de grâce* in *Plessy* v. *Ferguson* (1896). The Louisiana legislature, in "an act to promote the comfort of passengers," decreed that railway companies "shall provide equal but separate accommodations for the white and color races" under penalty of fine or imprisonment. The Supreme Court sustained the statute: racially separate facilities, so long as they are equal, do not offend the Fourteenth Amendment. In other words, segregation was not the kind of racial discrimination prohibited by the Constitution.

Three years later, the Court decided for the first time a case involving racial separation in the schools (*Cumming* v. *County Board of Education*, 1899). A Georgia county provided a public high school for whites but none for blacks. The black plaintiffs did not seek to enforce *Plessy* (that is, the creation of a separate but equal black school) but demanded, instead, punitive relief: the shutdown of the white school until it was either desegregated or a black school established. The Court unanimously refused to grant relief.

Segregation laws, which began with passenger trains, spread to encompass virtually every aspect of life: restaurants, bus depots, water fountains, public restrooms, parks, barbershops—even separate Bibles for black witnesses to swear by on the witness stand. In 1908, the Court went even further than *Plessy* to uphold legislation outlawing voluntary contact in a biracial private college (*Berea College* v. *Kentucky*). By 1920, school segregation was nearly universal in the South, and residential segregation was authorized in many cities. These laws were designed to inoculate against the supposedly contaminating effects of interracial social contact in public places. They symbolized the social inferiority of blacks, a symbol that was unneeded and largely nonexistent during antebellum days because of the manifest inequality inherent in slavery.

Challenging School Segregation

The systematic challenge to school segregation began in the New Deal years, spearheaded by black lawyers from the national office of the National Association for the Advancement of Colored People (NAACP). The initial strategy was to seek enforcement of the separate-but-equal principle of *Plessy*. In the fullness of time, a frontal assault would be launched against the essential legitimacy of enforced separation. Until then, the demand was for actual equality, not just theoretical equality. The target of the early test cases were graduate and professional schools. It was less threatening to the white citizenry to challenge segregation there than in the local public schools. The numbers of those seeking admission to post-collegiate education were fewer than to primary and secondary schools. There is also no tradition of community involvement in institutions of higher learning. Against the national tapestry of a conservative Supreme Court, an impoverished economy, and a public not yet ready to recognize full equality for its fellow black citizens, the litigation strategy of the NAACP was not imprudent.

The first case came up in 1938: *Missouri ex rel. Gaines* v. *Canada*. The University of Missouri Law School refused to consider the application of a black candidate. The Court held that under *Plessy* a person was entitled to equal access to legal education within the state. Hence, Missouri had to admit the student or build a separate but equal law school for blacks. It was a milestone decision. The implications of putting a state to the choice of desegregating or establishing a whole new institution were monumental.

No major legal offensives were undertaken in the ensuing years while the nation was at war. The postwar years saw colleges swamped with veterans, supported by GI benefits and anxious to make up for lost time. The few black institutions simply were incapable of accommodating the number of qualified candidates. Wholesale litigation at the graduate school level was resumed.

Two principal cases appeared before the Supreme Court at the same time. In *Sweatt* v. *Painter* (1950), the University of Texas Law School denied admission to a black student on racial grounds. The legislature then provided a makeshift law school consisting of three basement rooms in the State Capitol and staffed by three part-time faculty members. The Court, for the first time, ordered an all-white school to admit a black student on the rationale that the separate colored school was unequal. Pointedly, however, the Court added that "[we need not] reach petitioner's contention that *Plessy* v. *Ferguson* should be re-examined in light of contemporary knowledge respecting the purposes of the Fourteenth Amendment and the effects of racial segregation" (p. 636).

In *McLaurin* v. *Oklahoma State Regents* (1950), a black teacher applied for admission to the only graduate school of education in the state in order to study for the Ph.D. Justice Thurgood Marshall, then chief counsel of the NAACP, recounts that McLaurin was deliberately selected over eight other eligible plantiffs. The reason was to deflect anticipated insinuations that the real motive for these desegregation lawsuits was to achieve intermarriage. McLaurin was 68 years old (Kluger 1977, p. 266).

McLaurin was admitted on a segregated basis. He was required "to sit apart at a designated desk in an anteroom adjoining the classroom; to sit at a designated desk on the mezzanine floor of the library, but not to use the desks of the regular reading room; and to sit at a designated table and to eat at a different time from the other students in the school cafeteria" (*McLaurin,* p. 640). It was apartheid within an all-white school. The case posed in sharp relief the validity of the separate-but-equal principle. McLaurin, unlike Sweatt, was not denied unequal educational facilities with respect to curriculum, faculty, library, and so forth. At stake was the concept of segregation itself—the humiliation of being set apart, by law, solely on account of race.

The Supreme Court ruled that "state imposed restrictions which produce such inequalities cannot be sustained." The "restrictions placed on him . . . handicapped [him] in his pursuit of effective graduate education" (p. 641). Nimbly, the Court sidestepped the *Plessy* issue by deliberately avoiding the use of the word "segregation." Left unanswered was whether segregation is itself an impermissible "restriction."

The walls did not crumble with these victories. *Sweatt* and *McLaurin* made it clear that there had to be equality or the separation would be invalid. Of course, there was room for argument over how equal was the equality. Diehard opponents of desegregation tried to resist with court fights each time. Throughout the South, the right to equal educational facilities from kindergarten to graduate school had to be litigated over and over again. It was like trying to cut one hair at a time.

Two years earlier, the NAACP had scored a major victory in the area of housing segregation. In *Shelley* v. *Kraemer* (1948), the Supreme Court ruled that racially restrictive covenants—then a principal private means of discrimination in housing—were unenforceable by resort to the courts. In light of this decision and the graduate school cases, the time seemed ripe for a frontal attack on *Plessy* and for shifting the battleground to one of the most sensitive areas of all, the public schools.

School desegregation lawsuits were begun almost simultaneously throughout the South, with the purpose of amassing a record of the pervasiveness of educational inequality for presentation before the Supreme Court. The outcome of several cases—arising in Delaware, South Carolina, Virginia, and Kansas—were eventually joined for consideration together by the highest tribunal in the land under the collective title of *Brown* v. *Board of Education.*

3.3. DOCTRINES OF EQUALITY AND THE SOCIAL SCIENCE CONTEXT

The "Separate-But-Equal" Doctrine

PLESSY v. FERGUSON

163 U.S. 537 (1896)

Mr. Justice BROWN, after stating the case, delivered the opinion of the court.

This case turned upon the constitutionality of an act of the General Assembly of the State of Louisiana, passed in 1890, providing for separate railway carriages for the white and colored races. Acts 1890, No. 111, p. 152.

The first section of the statute enacts "that all railway companies carrying passengers in their coaches in the State, shall provide equal but separate accommodations for the white and colored races, by providing two or more passenger coaches for each passenger train, or by dividing the passenger coaches by a partition so as to secure separate accommodations: *Provided,* That this section shall not be construed to apply to street railroads. No person or persons, shall be admitted to occupy seats in coaches, other than the ones assigned to them on account of the race they belong to."

By the second section it was enacted "that the officers of such passenger trains shall have power and are hereby required to assign each passenger to the coach or compartment used for the race to which such passenger belongs; any passenger insisting on going into a coach or compartment to which by race he does not belong, shall be liable to a fine of twenty-five dollars, or in lieu thereof to imprisonment for a period of not more than twenty days in the parish prison. . . .

The third section provides penalties for the refusal or neglect of the officers, directors, conductors and employees of railway companies to comply with the act, with a proviso that "nothing in this act shall be construed as applying to nurses attending children of the other race." The fourth section is immaterial.

The information filed in the criminal District Court* charged in substance that Plessy, being a passenger between two stations within the State of Louisiana, was assigned by officers of the company to the coach used for the race to which he belonged, but he insisted upon going into a coach used by the race to which he did not belong. Neither in the information nor plea was his particular race or color averred.

The petition for the writ of prohibition averred that petitioner was seven eighths Caucasian and one eighth African blood; that the mixture of colored blood was not discernible in him, and that he was

---

*Presided by Judge J. Ferguson, the named defendant.

entitled to every right, privilege and immunity secured to citizens of the United States of the white race; and that, upon such theory, he took possession of a vacant seat in a coach where passengers of the white race were accommodated, and was ordered by the conductor to vacate said coach and take a seat in another assigned to persons of the colored race, and having refused to comply with such demand he was forcibly ejected with the aid of a police officer, and imprisoned in the parish jail to answer a charge of having violated the above act.

The constitutionality of this act is attacked upon the ground that it conflicts both with the Thirteenth Amendment of the Constitution, abolishing slavery, and the Fourteenth Amendment, which prohibits certain restrictive legislation on the part of the States. . . .

2. By the Fourteenth Amendment, all persons born or naturalized in the United States, and subject to the jurisdiction thereof, are made citizens of the United States and of the State wherein they reside; and the States are forbidden from making or enforcing any law which shall abridge the privileges or immunities of citizens of the United States, or shall deprive any person of life, liberty or property without due process of law, or deny to any person within their jurisdiction the equal protections of the laws. . . .

The object of the amendment was undoubtedly to enforce the absolute equality of the two races before the law, but in the nature of things it could not have been intended to abolish distinctions based upon color, or to enforce social, as distinguished from political equality, or a commingling of the two races upon terms unsatisfactory to either. Laws permitting, and even requiring, their separation in places where they are liable to be brought into contact do not necessarily imply the inferiority of either race to the other, and have been generally, if not universally, rec-

ognized as within the competency of the state legislature in the exercise of their police power. The most common instance of this is connected with the establishment of separate schools for white and colored children, which has been held to be a valid exercise of the legislative power even by courts of States where the political rights of the colored race have been longest and most earnestly enforced.

One of the earliest of these cases is that of *Roberts* v. *City of Boston,* 5 Cush. 198, in which the Supreme Judicial Court of Massachusetts held that the general school committee of Boston had power to make provision for the instruction of colored children in separate schools established exclusively for them, and to prohibit their attendance upon the other schools.

In the *Civil Rights Cases,* 109 U.S. 3, it was held that an act of Congress, entitling all persons within the jurisdiction of the United States to the full and equal enjoyment of the accommodations, advantages, facilities and privileges of inns, public conveyances, on land or water, theatres and other places of public amusement, and made applicable to citizens of every race and color, regardless of any previous condition of servitude, was unconstitutional and void, upon the ground that the Fourteenth Amendment was prohibitory upon the States only. . . . In delivering the opinion of the court Mr. Justice Bradley observed that the Fourteenth Amendment "does not invest Congress with power to legislate upon subjects that are within the domain of state legislation; but to provide modes of relief against state legislation, or state action, of the kind referred to. It does not authorize Congress to create a code of municipal law for the regulation of private rights; but to provide modes of redress against the operation of state laws, and the action of state officers, executive or judicial, when these are subversive of the fundamental rights specified in the amendment. . . ."

[I]t is also suggested by the learned counsel for the plaintiff in error that the same argument that will justify the state legislature in requiring railways to provide separate accommodations for the two races will also authorize them to require separate cars to be provided for people whose hair is of a certain color, or who are aliens, or who belong to certain nationalities, or to enact laws requiring colored people to walk upon one side of the street, and white people upon the other, or requiring white men's houses to be painted white, and colored men's black, or their vehicles or business signs to be of different colors, upon the theory that one side of the street is as good as the other, or that a house or vehicle of one color is as good as one of another color. The reply to all this is that every exercise of the police power must be reasonable, and extend only to such laws as are enacted in good faith for the promotion for the public good, and not for the annoyance or oppression of a particular class. . . .

So far, then, as a conflict with the Fourteenth Amendment is concerned, the case reduces itself to the question whether the statute of Louisiana is a reasonable regulation, and with respect to this there must necessarily be a large discretion on the part of the legislature. In determining the question of reasonableness it is at liberty to act with reference to the established usages, customs and traditions of the people, and with a view to the promotion of their comfort, and the preservation of the public peace and good order. Gauged by this standard, we cannot say that a law which authorizes or even requires the separation of the two races in public conveyances is unreasonable, or more obnoxious to the Fourteenth Amendment than the acts of Congress requiring separate schools for colored children in the District of Columbia, the constitutionality of which does not seem to have been questioned, or the corresponding acts of state legislatures.

We consider the underlying fallacy of the plaintiff's argument to consist in the assumption that the enforced separation of the two races stamps the colored race with a badge of inferiority. If this be so, it is not by reason of anything found in the act, but solely because the colored race chooses to put that construction upon it. The argument necessarily assumes that if, as has been more than once the case, and is not unlikely to be so again, the colored race should become the dominant power in the state legislature, and should enact a law in precisely similar terms, it would thereby relegate the white race to an inferior position. We imagine that the white race, at least, would not acquiesce in this assumption. The argument also assumes that social prejudices may be overcome by legislation, and that equal rights cannot be secured to the negro except by an enforced commingling of the two races. We cannot accept this proposition. If the two races are to meet upon terms of social equality, it must be the result of natural affinities, a mutual appreciation of each other's merits and a voluntary consent of individuals. As was said by the Court of Appeals of New York in *People v. Gallagher*, 93 N.Y. 438, 448, "this end can neither be accomplished nor promoted by laws which conflict with the general sentiment of the community upon whom they are designed to operate. When the government, therefore, has secured to each of its citizens equal rights before the law and equal opportunities for improvement and progress, it has accomplished the end for which it was organized and performed all of the functions respecting social advantages with which it is endowed." Legislation is powerless to eradicate racial instincts or to abolish distinctions based upon physical differences, and the attempt to do so can only result in accentuating the difficulties of the present situation. If the civil and political rights of both races be equal one cannot be inferior to the other civilly or politically. If one race be inferior to the other socially, the Constitution of the United States cannot put them upon the same plane. . . .

The judgment of the court below is, therefore,

Affirmed.

Mr. Justice HARLAN dissenting.

By the Louisiana statute, the validity of which is here involved, all railway companies (other than street railroad companies) carrying passengers in that State are required to have separate but equal accommodations for white and colored persons. . . .

Thus the State regulates the use of a public highway by citizens of the United States solely upon the basis of race.

However apparent the injustice of such legislation may be, we have only to consider whether it is consistent with the Constitution of the United States.

That a railroad is a public highway, and that the corporation which owns or operates it is in the exercise of public functions, is not, at this day, to be disputed. . . .

It was said in argument that the statute of Louisiana does not discriminate against either race, but prescribes a rule applicable alike to white and colored citizens. But this argument does not meet the difficulty. Every one knows that the statute in question had its origin in the purpose, not so much to exclude white persons from the railroad cars occupied by blacks, as to exclude colored people from coaches occupied by or assigned to white persons. . . . No one would be so wanting in candor as to assert the contrary. The fundamental objection, therefore, to the statute is that it interferes with the personal freedom of citizens. "Personal liberty," it has been well said, "consists in the power of locomotion, of changing situation, or removing one's person to whatsoever places one's own inclination may direct, without imprisonment or restraint, unless by due course of

law." 1 Bl. Com. *134. If a white man and a black man choose to occupy the same public conveyance on a public highway, it is their right to do so, and no government, proceeding alone on ground of race, can prevent it without infringing the personal liberty of each. . . .

The present decision, it may well be apprehended, will not only stimulate aggressions, more or less brutal and irritating, upon the admitted rights of colored citizens, but will encourage the belief that it is possible, by means of state enactments, to defeat the beneficent purposes which the people of the United States had in view when they adopted the recent amendments of the Constitution, by one of which the blacks of this country were made citizens of the United States and of the States in which they respectively reside, and whose privileges and immunities, as citizens, the States are forbidden to abridge. Sixty millions of whites are in no danger from the presence here of eight millions of blacks. The destinies of the two races, in this country, are indissolubly linked together, and the interests of both require that the common government of all shall not permit the seeds of race hate to be planted under the sanction of law. What can more certainly arouse race hate, what more certainly create and perpetuate a feeling of distrust between these races than state enactments, which, in fact, proceed on the ground that colored citizens are so inferior and degraded that they cannot be allowed to sit in public coaches occupied by white citizens? That, as all will admit, is the real meaning of such legislation as was enacted in Louisiana.

The arbitrary separation of citizens, on the basis of race, while they are on a public highway, is a badge of servitude wholly inconsistent with the civil freedom and the equality before the law established by the Constitution. It cannot be justified upon any legal grounds.

If evils will result from the commingling of the two races upon public highways established for the benefit of all, they will be infinitely less than those that will surely come from state legislation regulating the enjoyment of civil rights upon the basis of race. We boast of the freedom enjoyed by our people above all other peoples. But it is difficult to reconcile that boast with a state of the law which, practically, puts the brand of servitude and degradation upon a large class of our fellow-citizens, our equals before the law. The thin disguise of "equal" accommodations for passengers in railroad coaches will not mislead anyone, nor atone for the wrong this day done. . . .

N O T E S   A N D   Q U E S T I O N S

1.　*Plessy* was the first case to come before the Supreme Court that squarely placed in issue the validity of segregation laws under the Fourteenth Amendment. Justice Brown's opinion was the most detailed and authoritative judicial analysis of their validity, since no subsequent case undertook to re-examine this analysis until *Brown* some half a century later.

　　When Justice Brown says that the Louisiana statute does not violate the Fourteenth Amendment, does he mean it does not violate the Due Process Clause, or the Equal Protection Clause, or both? According to the dissent of Justice Harlan, which provision is being violated?

　　What practical difference does it make for social policy and for the adjudication of future cases whether the instant case is decided on one or the other provision of the Fourteenth Amendment?

2.　A word on the standards of judicial review may be appropriate here. A somewhat more detailed treatment will be provided in section 3.6.

　　In reviewing the constitutionality of legislation or any official action, a court does not pass on the wisdom or substantive merits of the legislation or action, but only on its validity under the Constitution. A court reviews, not makes, legislation. Given this judicial function, nobody would disagree with Justice Harlan's opening statement: "However apparent the injustice of such legislation may be, we have only to consider whether it is consistent with the Constitution of the United States."

　　Perhaps two of the provisions that are most frequently claimed to be violated by state legislation are the Due Process and Equal Protection clauses. The judicial test or standard for review to determine if due process is violated is the "rule of reason," or simply "reasonableness." Not all state restrictions on an individual's life, liberty, or property are prohibited by the Fourteenth Amendment. Only those restrictions that are imposed without "due process," that is, imposed in some basically unfair way, are prohibited. Specifically, the test is whether the challenged statute bears some reasonable relation to permissible legislative ends. If the statute is reasonable—if it can be justified in terms of legitimate governmental objectives so that it can be said to be a fair statute—then it passes muster under the Due Process Clause, regardless of what a court might think of its inherent merits.

　　One of the standards for review under the Equal Protection Clause is also reasonableness. (Other standards will be mentioned in section 3.6.) The inquiry is whether there exists a rational basis for the classifications or distinctions set forth in the legislation. Not all unequal treatment of individuals by the state is prohibited. Only those inequalities that are unjustifiable—that are unrelated to a valid governmental purpose—offend the Equal Protection Clause.

　　The reasonableness standard under both clauses is essentially the same. To determine if the state restriction violates due process or if the state classification violates equal protection, each must bear a rational relationship to some valid state goal(s). Courts determine whether the legislation is reasonable or arbitrary (hence unconstitutional) by scrutinizing the factual circumstances of the case, the nature of the individual interests involved, and the purported governmental interests at stake.

3.　Black (1960, p. 422) writes that "the fault of *Plessy* is in the psychology and sociology of its minor premise."

Major (legal) premise　The Fourteenth Amendment requires that legislation be reasonable;

Minor (factual) premise   the Louisiana statute requiring separate but equal railway accommodations is reasonable;

Conclusion   therefore, the Louisiana statute does not violate the Fourteenth Amendment.

This is not to say, of course, that when judges are deciding a case, they actually think in syllogistic terms or that their conclusions are always rigorously deduced from general premises. However, it is to say that when the judicial mind reaches the ultimate outcome, the written opinion that seeks to explicate the rationale for that outcome can be reformulated in syllogistic form as an aid to analyzing its internal logic.

What were the factual assumptions or empirical bases for Justice Brown's middle premise that the statute in question was reasonable? Was he wrong—Black claims he was—in light of the psychology and sociology of his day? For an evaluation of the social science bases of *Plessy*, see Bernstein (1963).

4.   The Court said that segregation laws do not impose or imply black inferiority except as such inequality is in the eye of the beholder. Of course, if the Court determined that the state-mandated separation was based on racial attitudes pertaining to the status of blacks, then the legislation would have to be declared unreasonable and invalid since no legitimate governmental purpose would be served. Nonetheless, to deny the degrading impact of segregation borders on the disingenuous (Woodward 1966).

One basis for the Court's assertion that segregation legislation does not imply black inferiority is that it is a long established custom in the South. Franklin (1956) writes:

> The enactment of state segregation statutes is a relatively recent phenomenon in the history of race relations in the United States. Of course, there had been numerous segregative practices and some segregation statutes for many years, even before the nineteenth century. But it was not until the final quarter of the nineteenth century that states began to evolve a systematic program of legally separating whites and Negroes in every possible area of activity. And it was not until the twentieth century that these laws became a major apparatus for keeping the Negro "in his place." They were generally comprehensive and acceptable, because they received their inspiration from a persistent and tenacious assumption of the innate inferiority of the Negro and because they had their roots deep in the antebellum period. . . . [p. 1]

The demand for Jim Crow laws was initially strongest from lower class whites, especially when freedmen came into economic competition for subsistence wages. "For the poor white, caste would protect class" (Bernstein 1963, p. 202).

5.   Looking at the language of the Fourteenth Amendment, and considering the Reconstruction milieu in which it was passed, do you agree with Justice Brown's interpretation that this Amendment was intended to secure equality of political and civil rights but not of social relationships—that is, that it addresses only the problem of racial discrimination but not of racial segregation? On the tangled history of the Fourteenth Amendment and the intent of its framers, see Graham (1950), Kelley (1956), and Bickel (1955).

6.   The *Roberts* case of 1850 mentioned by Justice Brown has been a frequently cited legal precedent for school segregation. Notwithstanding the fact that the Massachusetts legislature abolished segregation in the Boston public schools a mere five years later (see *Brown* v. *Board of Education*, 1954, fn. 6), was it appropriate authority for the court to rely on in deciding this Fourteenth Amendment case?

7.   What are the implications of the Court's pointed mention of the fact the Homer Plessy was "seven eighths" Caucasian and one eighth African blood"?

8.   Three years after *Plessy*, the Court decided for the first time a case involving separate schools for white and black children. In denying a plea that the local white school be closed until a school for blacks were established, the Court said in an unanimous opinion:

> [T]he education of people in schools maintained by state taxation is a matter belonging to the respective states, and any interference on the part of Federal authority with the management

of such schools cannot be justified except in the case of a clear and unmistakable disregard of rights secured by the supreme law of the land. We have here no such case to be determined. . . . [*Cumming* v. *County Board of Education* (1899, p. 545)]

The opinion was written by Justice Harlan.

The Social Science Context

The studied ambiguity in the language of the Constitution gives judges considerable latitude for creative lawmaking. To say that the protection of the laws must be "equal," or that deprivation of rights must not be "without due process," is but to license judges to engage in policy-making, to define what is equal or due. All words are "symbols of meaning." If "individual words are inexact symbols, with shifting variables, their configuration can hardly achieve invariant meaning or assure definiteness" (Frankfurter 1961, p. 75). The Constitution, after all, is a broad declaration of national policy, and the Supreme Court can—and has—acted as a super-legislature. In the process of "interpreting" the Constitution in judicial review, it can formulate policy.

The meaning given to the words of the Constitution does not spring Minerva-like from within the four corners of the document. One source of meaning are extralegal facts—that is, facts derived from outside the law itself—that are pertinent to the adjudication of the case. "[E]very constitutional issue contains important factual elements which control the decision, whether they are expressly considered or remain buried in the mental equipment which the judge brings to the decisional process" (Karst 1960, p. 84). Since constitutional cases usually involve wide-ranging issues of social policy, and these issues often implicate broad social, economic, and behavioral facts, the social sciences have a role in the adjudication by laying bare the relevant factual elements. There is a dialectical relationship between these facts and the law. "[N]o law, written or unwritten, can be understood without a full knowledge of the facts out of which it arises and to which it is to be applied" (Brandeis 1916, p. 467). Law defines what are the relevant facts to be considered in a given case, but new facts, in turn, can also help beget new law.

We turn now to a brief sketch of the social science background in which the *Plessy* and *Brown* decisions were decided in order to set the stage for a more in-depth inquiry into the role of extralegal data in shaping constitutional lawmaking.

BIOLOGICAL PERSPECTIVES ON SOCIAL BEHAVIOR

In the post–Civil War era, Herbert Spencer's Social Darwinism—the transliteration of Darwin's evolutionary theory to a social milieu—was one of the most influential ideologies in America. Indeed, it became nearly synonymous with social science and had a profound influence on the founders of modern sociology and social psychology (Hofstadter 1966). It set the framework for the study of human behavior.

Its basic thesis, simply put, was that unbridled social competition for the survival of the fittest in society was in accord with the laws of nature. Hence, any artificially induced changes in behavior, such as by legislation, were deleterious to the human species and to society at large. Any social dislocations and disadvantages arising from unregulated economic competition would, in the long run, take care of themselves. The less the state intervenes in regulating human affairs, the greater is the opportunity for individual liberty and initiative. People will adapt to the environment on their own if they want to survive.

In the arena of race relations, notions of survival of the fittest, universal competition, and adaptability of the human species conditioned almost all scientific and common thinking. The leading sociologist of the day, William Graham Sumner (1906) of Yale, and formerly a theologian, published a monumental work on folkways which provided a Social Darwinist justification for racial segregation. This book recapitulated his lectures and articles over the past fifteen years. Sumner proposed that in the struggle for existence leading to the establishment of social organization, there developed "folkways" or ingrained habits that are prime movers of human behavior. Like instincts, they are uniform, universal, imperative, and invariable. They are ineradicable by laws and unchangeable by the schemes of social reformers. Racial attitudes are instinctual and racial separation is a deeply embedded habit of the human race. The implication was that it would have been futile for the Supreme Court to even attempt to invalidate segregation practices because they are inherent in the nature of things. "Law-ways cannot change folkways," was Sumner's well-known dictum. Thus, Justice Brown's factual assumptions were not only grounded in popular thought but were, in his time, credible or at least plausible in the context of the prevailing social "science." As Justice Holmes said of Spencer in a letter, "I doubt if any writer of English except Darwin has done so much to affect our whole way of thinking about the universe" (in Howe 1961, p. 58). In dissenting opinions, too, he protested that "the Fourteenth Amendment does not enact Mr. Herbert Spencer's Social Statics" (*Lochner* v. *New York*, 1905, p. 75). "Undoubtedly the greatest practical triumph of Social Darwinism . . . was achieved in the courts." They were the "approving sponsor[s] of these ideas" and "translated them into what was, for all practical purposes, the policy of the national government" (Rosen 1972, p. 26).

The influence of Social Darwinism lingered until about 1920. Anti-black sentiment, shared by some noted social scientists, reached its zenith around that period. The introduction and widespread use of intelligence testing served to reinforce the belief in the innate inferiority of blacks when the results showed their generally lower scores. Moreover, the dominant scientific view was that intelligence was wholly or mainly a function of heredity. This, coupled with the biological imperative of racial "instincts," was said to justify existing social institutions designed to perpetuate black subordination. Such was the view of William McDougall of Harvard who, in 1909, published the first *Introduction to Social Psychology* text. It underwent some two dozen editions and was widely used in the formation of a whole generation of social psychologists.

ENVIRONMENTAL PERSPECTIVES ON SOCIAL BEHAVIOR

By the 1930s, the amount of biological and social science literature purporting to prove the inferiority of blacks declined markedly (Newby 1965). Gradually, the scientific community began to conceptualize the individual as a product and a producer of his environment, and to discard models of behavior rooted in inevitable biological forces. This new way of looking at the springs of human conduct and relationships carries a political message, namely, that law-ways can change folkways.

Social psychologists were among those who inspired the reaction against Social Darwinism. Only some of the highlights of their writings will be mentioned. George Cooley (1902) developed the concept of the "looking glass self" to account for how a person's self-definition consists of the reflected estimation of others. It challenged the notion that the lower status of blacks is merely a self-imposed badge of inferiority. George H. Mead (1934) shed further insights into the socialization processes by which self-concepts are formed. He, too, concluded that a person's identity arises out of the internalization of attitudes and influences of others in society. The so-called Chicago school of sociology of the 1920s carried out a number of studies of urban blacks relying on an environmental perspective (Faris 1967). In anthropology, major new studies were proposing that culture, not racial inheritance, was the main shaping force in the development of mental and social characteristics (Boas 1911).

By the late 1920s, the counterattack on racism was in full swing among social scientists. Otto Klineberg (1934), a Columbia social psychologist, conducted some classic studies on intelligence that debunked the "selective migration" theory prevalent a few years earlier. To sustain the belief in black intellectual retardation, this theory explained the higher IQ scores of northern blacks over southern blacks in terms of selective migration: the smartest ones moved north. Klineberg's research revealed what was then not common knowledge: Improvement in social and educational opportunities enhances IQ and school achievement scores. He found, for example, a high positive association between length of residence in the north and IQ test performance.

John Dollard, a Yale social psychologist, published another seminal contribution in 1937: *Caste and Class in a Southern Town*. He dismissed the contention that segregation attitudes were based on the natural inequality of the races. He located them, instead, partly on the psychological need of whites to avenge the loss of the Civil War and partly on the social and economic advantages that accrued to whites by the perpetuation of these attitudes.

Probably the most comprehensive work of all that served as the main frame of reference for nearly all the scientific literature on race relations was *An American Dilemma* (1944), by the Swedish social economist Gunnar Myrdal and a team of social science contributors. It sought to explain the economic roots and consequences of segregation. When slavery ended, the social caste system began, and underlying both practices was economic exploitation of blacks. A vicious circle, then, developed throughout the generations: The deprivation of economic opportunities provided the pretext for social discrimination which, in turn, fueled further economic discrimination.

In short, the common theme echoed in the scholarly literature on the eve of the *School Segregation Cases* was that if black Americans appeared inferior in jobs, schools, IQ tests, and other aspects of social life, it was in large measure because the larger white society had deliberately kept them in the lower rungs. Social science research and opinion by midcentury had come a long way from Social Darwinist ideology. And just as the quasi–social science of racial instincts and folkways was the factual bedrock of Justice Brown's interpretation of equality in 1895, so, too, would the modern social science on the environmental malleability of human behavior appear as a central theme in Chief Justice Warren's definition of equality in 1954. And so when the NAACP lawyers prepared for the long-awaited assault on public school segregation, it was to the social scientists that they turned for assistance in persuading the Supreme Court that separate-but-equal facilities do not result in equality.

THE EFFECTS OF SEGREGATION AND THE CONSEQUENCES OF DESEGREGATION: A SOCIAL SCIENCE STATEMENT*

FOREWORD

The editors of the Minnesota Law Review greatly value the opportunity to make this brief available to the profession. It is the Appendix to Appellants' Briefs filed in the *School Segregation Cases,* in the Supreme Court of the United States, October Term, 1952: *Brown v. Board of Educa-*

*This statement was drafted and signed by the following sociologists, anthropologists, psychologists and psychiatrists, who have worked in the area of American race relations:
Floyd H. Allport, Syracuse, New York; Gordon W. Allport, Cambridge, Massachusetts; Charlotte Babcock, M.D., Chicago, Illinois; Viola W. Bernard, M.D., New York, New York; Jerome S. Bruner, Cambridge, Massachusetts; Hadley Cantril, Princeton, New Jersey; Isidor Chein, New York, New York; Kenneth B. Clark, New York, New York; Mamie P. Clark, New York, New York; Stuart W. Cook, New York, New York; Bingham Dai, Durham, North Carolina; Allison Davis, Chicago, Illinois; Else Frenkel-Brunswik, Berkeley, California; Noel P. Gist, Columbia, Missouri; Daniel Katz, Ann Arbor, Michigan; Otto Klineberg, New York, New York; David Krech, Berkeley, California; Alfred McClung Lee, Brooklyn, New York; R. M. MacIver, New York, New York; Robert K. Merton, New York, New York; Gardner Murphy, Topeka, Kansas; Theodore M. Newcomb, Ann Arbor, Michigan; Robert Redfield, Chicago, Illinois; Ira DeA. Reid, Haverford, Pennsylvania; Arnold M. Rose, Minneapolis, Minnesota; Gerhart Saenger, New York, New York; R. Nevitt Sanford, Poughkeepsie, New York; S. Stanfield Sargent, New York, New York; M. Brewster Smith, New York, New York; Samuel A. Stouffer, Cambridge, Massachusetts; Wellman Warner, New York, New York; Robin M. Williams, Ithaca, New York.

tion, Topeka, Kansas, No. 8; *Briggs v. Elliott,* No. 101; *Davis v. School Board of Prince Edward County,* No. 191.

Only the formal portions of the brief are omitted.

I.

The problem of the segregation of racial and ethnic groups constitutes one of the major problems facing the American people today. It seems desirable, therefore, to summarize the contributions which contemporary social science can make toward its resolutions. There are, of course, moral and legal issues involved with respect to which the signers of the present statement cannot speak with any special authority and which must be taken into account in the solution of the problem. There are, however, also factual issues involved with respect to which certain conclusions seem to be justified on the basis of the available scientific evidence. It is with these issues only that this paper is concerned. Some of the issues have to do with the consequences of segregation, some with problems of changing from segregated to unsegregated practices. These two groups of issues will be dealt with in separate sections below. It is necessary, first, however, to define and delimit the problem to be discussed. . . .

II.

At the recent Mid-century White House Conference on Children and Youth, a fact-finding report on the effects of prejudice, discrimination and segregation on the personality development of children was prepared as a basis for some of the deliberations.[2] This report brought together the available social science and psychological studies which were related to the problem of how racial and religious prejudices influenced the development of a healthy personality. It highlighted the fact that segregation, prejudices and discriminations, and their social concomitants potentially damage the personality of all children—the children of the majority group in a somewhat different way than the more obviously damaged children of the minority group.

The report indicates that as minority group children learn the inferior status to which they are assigned—as they observe the fact that they are almost always segregated and kept apart from others who are treated with more respect by the society as a whole—they often react with feelings of inferiority and a sense of personal humiliation. Many of them become confused about their own personal worth. On the one hand, like all other human beings they require a sense of personal dignity; on the other hand, almost nowhere in the larger society do they find their own dignity as human beings respected by others. Under these conditions, the minority group child is thrown into a conflict with regard to his feelings about himself and his group. He wonders whether his group and he himself are worthy of no more respect than they receive. This conflict and confusion leads to self-hatred and rejection of his own group.

The group goes on to point out that these children must find ways with which to cope with this conflict. Not every child, of course, reacts with the same patterns of behavior. . . .

Some children, usually of the lower socio-economic classes, may react by overt aggressions and hostility directed toward their own group or members of the dominant groups. Anti-social and delinquent behavior may often be interpreted as reactions to these racial frustrations. . . .

Middle class and upper class minority group children are likely to react to their racial frustrations and conflicts by withdrawal and submissive behavior. Or, they may react with compensatory and rigid conformity to the prevailing middle class values and standards and an aggressive determination to succeed in these terms in spite of the handicap of their minority status.

The report indicates that minority group children of all social and economic classes often react with a generally defeatist attitude and a lowering of personal ambitions. This, for example, is reflected in a lowering of pupil morale and a depression of the educational aspiration level among minority group children in segregated schools. In producing such effects, segregated schools impair the ability of the child to profit from the educational opportunities provided him. . . .

With reference to the impact of segregation and its concomitants on children of the majority group, the report indicates that the effects are somewhat more obscure. . . .

We return now to the question, deferred earlier, of what it is about the total society complex of which segregation is one feature that produces the effects described above—or, more precisely, to the question of whether we can justifiably conclude that, as only one feature of a complex social setting, segregation is in fact a significantly contributing factor to these effects.

To answer this question, it is necessary to bring to bear the general fund of psychological and sociological knowledge concerning the role of various environmental influences in producing feelings of inferiority, confusions in personal roles, various types of basic personality struc-

---

[2]Clark, K. B., *Effect of Prejudice and Discrimination on Personality Development*, Fact Finding Report Mid-century White House Conference on Children and Youth, Children's Bureau, Federal Security Agency, 1950 (mimeographed). [Subsequently published as *Prejudice and Your Child*, Clark (1966). Ed.'s note.]

tures and the various forms of personal and social disorganization.

On the basis of this general fund of knowledge, it seems likely that feelings of inferiority and doubts about personal worth are attributable to living in an underprivileged environment only insofar as the latter is itself perceived as an indicator of low social status and as a symbol of inferiority. In other words, one of the important determinants in producing such feelings is the awareness of social status difference. While there are many other factors that serve as reminders of the differences in social status, there can be little doubt that the fact of enforced segregation is a major factor. . . .

The preceding view is consistent with the opinion stated by a large majority (90%) of social scientists who replied to a questionnaire concerning the probable effects of enforced segregation under conditions of equal facilities. This opinion was that, regardless of the facilities which are provided, enforced segregation is psychologically detrimental to the members of the segregated group[12]. . . .

With reference to the probable effects of segregation under conditions of equal facilities on majority group members, many of the social scientists who responded to the poll in the survey cited above felt that the evidence is less convincing than with regard to the probable effects of such segregation on minority group members, and the effects are possibly less widespread. Nonetheless, more than 80% stated it as their opinion that the effects of such segregation are psychologically detrimental to the majority group members. . . .

III.

Segregation is at present a social reality. Questions may be raised, therefore,

as to what are the likely consequences of desegregation.

One such question asks whether the inclusion of an intellectually inferior group may jeopardize the education of the more intelligent group by lowering educational standards or damage the less intelligent group by placing it in a situation where it is at a marked competitive disadvantage. Behind this question is the assumption, which is examined below, that the presently segregated groups actually are inferior intellectually.

The available scientific evidence indicates that much, perhaps all, of the observable differences among various racial and national groups may be adequately explained in terms of environmental differences. It has been found, for instance, that the differences between the average intelligence test scores of Negro and white children decrease, and the overlap of the distribution increases, proportionately to the number of years that the Negro children have lived in the North. Related studies have shown that this change cannot be explained by the hypothesis of selective migration. It seems clear, therefore, that fears based on the assumption of innate racial differences in intelligence are not well founded. . . .

A second problem that comes up in an evaluation of the possible consequences of desegregation involves the question of whether segregation prevents or stimulates interracial tension and conflict and the corollary question of whether desegregation has one or the other effect. . . .

Under certain circumstances desegregation not only proceeds without major difficulties, but has been observed to lead to the emergence of more favorable attitudes and friendlier relations between races. Relevant studies may be cited with respect to housing, employment, the armed services and merchant marine, recreation agency, and general community life.

Much depends, however, on the cir-

[12]Deutscher, M. and Chein, I., The Psychological Effects of Enforced Segregation: A Survey of Social Science Opinion, *J. Psychol.*, 1948, 26, 259–287.

cumstances under which members of previously segregated groups first come in contact with others in unsegregated situations. Available evidence suggests, first, that there is less likelihood of unfriendly relations when the change is simultaneously introduced into all units of a social institution to which it is applicable, *e.g.*, all of the schools in a school system or all of the shops in a given factory. When factories introduced Negroes in only some shops but not in others the prejudiced workers tended to classify the desegregated shops as inferior, "Negro work." Such objections were not raised when complete integration was introduced.

The available evidence also suggests the importance of consistent and firm enforcement of the new policy by those in authority. It indicates also the importance of such factors as: the absence of competition for a limited number of facilities or benefits, the possibility of contacts which permit individuals to learn about one another as individuals, and the possibility of equivalence of positions and functions among all of the participants within the unsegregated situation. These conditions can generally be satisfied in a number of situations, as in the armed services, public housing developments, and public schools.

IV.

The problem with which we have here attempted to deal is admittedly on the frontiers of scientific knowledge. Inevitably, there must be some differences of opinion among us concerning the conclusiveness of certain items of evidence, and concerning the particular choice of words and placement of emphasis in the preceding statement. We are nonetheless in agreement that this statement is substantially correct and justified by the evidence, and the differences among us, if any, are of a relatively minor order and would not materially influence the preceding conclusions.

The "Separate-Is-Inherently-Unequal" Doctrine

BROWN v. BOARD OF EDUCATION OF TOPEKA

347 U.S. 483 (1954)

Mr. Chief Justice WARREN delivered the opinion of the Court.

These cases come to us from the States of Kansas, South Carolina, Virginia, and Delaware. They are premised on different facts and different local conditions, but a common legal question justified their consideration together in this consolidated opinion.[1]

In each of the cases, minors of the Negro race, through their legal representatives, seek the aid of the courts in obtain-

facilities for Negro and white students. Pursuant to that authority, the Topeka Board of Education elected to establish segregated elementary schools. Other public schools in the community, however, are operated on a nonsegregated basis. The three-judge District Court found that segregation in public education has a detrimental effect upon Negro children, but denied relief on the ground that the Negro and white schools were substantially equal with respect to building, transportation, curricula, and educational qualifications of teachers. 98 F. Supp. 797 . . .
[The other cases were: South Carolina, *Briggs v. Elliott*, 98 F. Supp. 529 (1951); Virginia, *Davis v. County School Board*, 103 F. Supp. 337 (1952); Delaware, *Gebhart v. Belton*, 91 A.2nd 137 (1952). A fifth case, *Bolling v. Sharpe*, 347 U.S. 497 (1954), was argued together with the preceding state cases but disposed of in a separate opinion because it involved public school segregation in the District of Columbia, and therefore decided under Fifth Amendment due process. Ed.'s note.]

[1]In the Kansas case, *Brown v. Board of Education*, the plaintiffs are Negro children of elementary school age residing in Topeka. They brought this action in the United States District Court for the District of Kansas to enjoin enforcement of a Kansas statute which permits, but does not require, cities of more than 15,000 population to maintain separate school

ing admission to the public schools of their community on a nonsegregated basis. In each instance, they had been denied admission to schools attended by white children under laws requiring or permitting segregation according to race. This segregation was alleged to deprive the plaintiffs of the equal protection of the laws under the Fourteenth Amendment. In each of the cases other than the Delaware case, a three-judge federal district court denied relief to the plaintiffs on the so-called "separate but equal" doctrine announced by this Court in *Plessy v. Ferguson*, 163 U.S. 537. Under that doctrine, equality of treatment is accorded when the races are provided substantially equal facilities, even though these facilities be separate. In the Delaware case, the Supreme Court of Delaware adhered to that doctrine, but ordered that the plaintiffs be admitted to the white schools because of their superiority to the Negro school.

The plaintiffs contend that segregated public schools are not "equal" and cannot be made "equal," and that hence they are deprived of the equal protection of the laws. Because of the obvious importance of the question presented, the Court took jurisdiction. Argument was heard in the 1952 Term, and reargument was heard this Term on certain questions propounded by the Court.

Reargument was largely devoted to the circumstances surrounding the adoption of the Fourteenth Amendment in 1868. It covered exhaustively consideration of the Amendment in Congress, ratification by the states, then existing practices in racial segregation, and the views of proponents and opponents of the Amendment. This discussion and our own investigation convince us that, although these sources cast some light, it is not enough to resolve the problem with which we are faced. At best, they are inconclusive. The most avid proponents of the post-War Amendments undoubtedly in-

tended them to remove all legal distinctions among "all persons born or naturalized in the United States." Their opponents, just as certainly, were antagonistic to both the letter and the spirit of the Amendments and wished them to have the most limited effect. What others in Congress and the state legislature had in mind cannot be determined with any degree of certainty.

An additional reason for the inconclusive nature of the Amendment's history, with respect to segregated schools, is the status of public education at that time. In the South, the movement toward free common schools, supported by general taxation, had not yet taken hold. Education of white children was largely in the hands of private groups. Education of Negroes was almost nonexistent, and practically all of the race were illiterate. In fact, any education of Negroes was forbidden by law in some states. Today, in contrast, many Negroes have achieved outstanding success in the arts and sciences as well as in the business and professional world. It is true that public school education at the time of the Amendment had advanced further in the North, but the effect of the amendment on Northern States was generally ignored in the congressional debates. Even in the North, the conditions of public education did not approximate those existing today. The curriculum was usually rudimentary; ungraded schools were common in rural areas; the school term was but three months a year in many states; and compulsory school attendance was virtually unknown. As a consequence, it is not surprising that there should be so little in the history of the Fourteenth Amendment relating to its intended effect on public education.

In the first cases in this Court construing the Fourteenth Amendment, decided shortly after its adoption, the Court interpreted it as proscribing all state-imposed discriminations against the Negro race.[5] The doctrine of "separate but equal" did not make its appearance in this Court until 1896 in the case of *Plessy v. Ferguson, supra,* involving not education but transportation.[6] American courts have since labored with the doctrine for over half a century. In this Court, there have been six cases involving the "separate but equal" doctrine in the field of public education. In *Cumming v. County Board of Education,* 175 U.S. 528, and *Gong Lum v. Rice,* 275 U.S. 78, the validity of the doctrine itself was not challenged. In more recent cases, all on the graduate school level, inequality was found in that specific benefits enjoyed by white students were denied to Negro students of the same educational qualifications. *Missouri ex rel. Gaines v. Canada,* 305 U.S. 337; *Sipuel v. Oklahoma,* 332 U.S. 631; *Sweatt v. Painter,* 339 U.S. 629; *McLaurin v. Oklahoma State Regents,* 339 U.S. 637. In none of these cases was it necessary to re-

examine the doctrine to grant relief to the Negro plaintiff. And in *Sweatt v. Painter, supra,* the Court expressly reserved decision on the question whether *Plessy v. Ferguson* should be held inapplicable to public education.

In the instant cases, that question is directly presented. Here, unlike *Sweatt v. Painter,* there are findings below that the Negro and white schools involved have been equalized, or are being equalized, with respect to buildings, curricula, qualifications and salaries of teachers, and other "tangible" factors. Our decision, therefore, cannot turn on merely a comparison of these tangible factors in the Negro and white schools involved in each of the cases. We must look instead to the effect of segregation itself on public education.

In approaching this problem, we cannot turn the clock back to 1868 when the Amendment was adopted, or even to 1896 when *Plessy v. Ferguson* was written. We must consider public education in the light of its full development and its present place in American life throughout the Nation. Only in this way can it be determined if segregation in public schools deprives these plaintiffs of the equal protection of the laws.

Today, education is perhaps the most important function of state and local governments. Compulsory school attendance laws and the great expenditures for education both demonstrate our recognition of the importance of education to our democratic society. It is required in the performance of our most basic public responsibilities, even service in the armed forces. It is the very foundation of good citizenship. Today it is a principal instrument in awakening the child to cultural values, in preparing him for later professional training, and in helping him to adjust normally to his environment. In these days, it is doubtful that any child may reasonably be expected to succeed in life if he

---

[5]Slaughter-House Cases, 16 Wall. 36, 67–72 (1873); Strauder v. West Virginia, 100 U.S. 303, 307–308 (1880): "It ordains that no State shall deprive any person of life, liberty, or property, without due process of law, or deny any person within its jurisdiction the equal protection of the laws. What is this but declaring that the law of the States shall be the same for the black as for the white; that all persons, whether colored or white, shall stand equal before the laws of the States, and, in regard to the colored race, for whose protection the amendment was primarily designed, that no discrimination shall be made against them by law because of their color? The words of the amendment, it is true, are prohibitory, but they contain a necessary implication of a positive immunity, or right, most valuable to the colored race,—the right to exemption from legal discriminations, implying inferiority in civil society, lessening the security of their enjoyment of the rights which others enjoy, and discriminations which are steps towards reducing them to the condition of a subject race. . . ."

[6]The doctrine apparently originated in Roberts v. City of Boston, 59 Mass. 198, 206 (1850), upholding school segregation against attack as being violative of a state constitutional guarantee of equality. Segregation in Boston public schools was eliminated in 1855. But elsewhere in the North segregation in public education has persisted in some communities until recent years. It is apparent that such segregation has long been a nationwide problem, not merely one of sectional concern.

is denied the opportunity of an education. Such an opportunity, where the state has undertaken to provide it, is a right which must be made available to all on equal terms.

We come then to the question presented: Does segregation of children in public schools solely on the basis of race, even though the physical facilities and other "tangible" factors may be equal, deprive the children of the minority group of equal educational opportunities? We believe that it does.

In *Sweatt v. Painter, supra,* in finding that a segregated law school for Negroes could not provide them equal educational opportunities, this Court relied in large part on "those qualities which are incapable of objective measurement but which make for greatness in a law school." In *McLaurin v. Oklahoma State Regents, supra,* the Court, in requiring that a Negro admitted to a white graduate school be treated like all other students, again resorted to intangible considerations: ". . . his ability to study, to engage in discussions and exchange views with other students, and, in general, to learn his profession." Such considerations apply with added force to children in grade and high schools. To separate them from others of similar age and qualifications solely because of their race generates a feeling of inferiority as to their status in the community that may affect their hearts and minds in a way unlikely ever to be undone. The effect of this separation on their educational opportunities was well stated by a finding in the Kansas case by a court which nevertheless felt compelled to rule against the Negro plaintiffs:

"Segregation of white and colored children in public schools has a detrimental effect upon the colored children. The impact is greater when it has the sanction of the law; for the policy of separating the races is usually interpreted as de-

noting the inferiority of the negro group. A sense of inferiority affects the motivation of a child to learn. Segregation with the sanction of law, therefore, has a tendency to [retard] the educational and mental development of negro children and to deprive them of some of the benefits they would receive in a racial[ly] integrated school system."

Whatever may have been the extent of psychological knowledge at the time of *Plessy v. Ferguson,* this finding is amply supported by modern authority.[11] Any language in *Plessy v. Ferguson* contrary to this finding is rejected.

We conclude that in the field of public education the doctrine of "separate but equal" has no place. Separate educational facilities are inherently unequal. Therefore, we hold that the plaintiffs and others similarly situated for whom the actions have been brought are, by reason of the segregation complained of, deprived of the equal protection of the laws guaranteed by the Fourteenth Amendment. This disposition makes unnecessary any discussion whether such segregation also violates the Due Process Clause of the Fourteenth Amendment.

Because these are class actions, because of the wide applicability of this decision, and because of the great variety of local conditions, the formulation of decrees in these cases presents problems of considerable complexity. On reargument,

---

[11]K. B. Clark, Effect of Prejudice and Discrimination on Personality Development (Midcentury White House Conference on Children and Youth, 1950); Witmer and Kotinsky, Personality in the Making (1952), c. VI; Deutscher and Chein, The Psychological Effects of Enforced Segregation: A Survey of Social Science Opinion, 26 J. Psychol. 259 (1948); Chein, What are the Psychological Effects of Segregation Under Conditions of Equal Facilities?, 3 Int. J. Opinion and Attitude Res. 229 (1949); Brameld, Educational Costs, in Discrimination and National Welfare (MacIver, ed., 1949), 44–48; Frazier, The Negro in the United States (1949), 674–681. And see generally Myrdal, An American Dilemma (1944).

the consideration of appropriate relief was necessarily subordinated to the primary question—the constitutionality of segregation in public education. We have now announced that such segregation is a denial of the equal protection of the laws. In order that we may have the full assistance of the parties in formulating decrees, the cases will be restored to the docket, and the parties are requested to present further argument on Questions 4 and 5 previously propounded by the Court for the reargument this Term.[13] The Attorney General of the United States is again invited to participate. The Attorneys General of the states requiring or permitting segregation in public education will also be permitted to appear as *amici curiae* upon request to do so by September 15, 1954, and submission of briefs by October 1, 1954.

It is so ordered.

[13][Questions 4 and 5 are reproduced in Chapter 4, section 4.2. Ed.'s note.]

NOTES AND QUESTIONS

1.   The decision-making process of the Supreme Court and its actual deliberations on specific cases are—and quite properly should be—known only to the Justices themselves. They are not matters of public record or disclosure, although they have been the subject of journalistic investigation (for example, Woodward and Armstrong 1979). The general procedures, however, are not veiled (see generally Wilkinson 1974; Morris 1974, pp. 67–75).

The yearly term of the Court begins in October and ends in June. During the weeks that are set aside for oral arguments, the Court is open from Monday to Thursday with Friday set aside for the Justices' private conference. Normally, thirty minutes is allocated to each side for argument, or one hour per case, and about four cases are heard each day. On Fridays, the Justices discuss among themselves the cases that have been argued and vote on them. A majority vote (5 of 9) is needed to dispose a case on its merits. There is considerable give-and-take in these sessions. Votes are changed on the basis of "bargaining" and assertions of "leadership" (Murphy 1962). A Justice's leverage in the discussions is his vote in the case; the sanction he can use is the threat of a dissent. The case is then assigned by the Chief Justice to a member of the Court to write an opinion. If the Chief Justice does not vote with the majority, then the task of assigning the writing falls on the senior Justice voting with the majority.

The weeks or oral argument are interspersed with recesses of two or three weeks during which time the Justices write opinions, read the briefs of the upcoming round of cases for hearing, and dispose of other Court business. The draft of an opinion is usually circulated by the author to the other Justices for comment. "Majority opinions have been rewritten as many as ten to twenty times before final agreement was reached" (Morris 1974, p. 75). Justices may decide then, on their own, to append dissenting or concurring opinions.

2.   The first oral argument on *Brown* was held in December 1952, and the Justices appeared to be of several minds. Outside observers conjectured that if they were going to strike down school segregation, the vote would have been a close one (Kluger 1977, p. 613). There was no question that such a vote would not have boded well for the Court or the nation. "Nothing could be worse from my point of view," said Justice Frankfurter, "than for this Court to make an abstract declaration that segregation is bad and then have it evaded by tricks" (in Friedman 1969, p. 48).

The reasons for the nonunanimity are not difficult to discern. The history of the Fourteenth Amendment and the intent of the framers on the issue of school segregation were unclear, and the Court needed some legal or historical footing for its decision, whichever way it came out. There were also social and political considerations. It was an explosive issue and surely any wariness the Court may have felt about brushing aside a deeply entrenched custom in the South was not misplaced. Nobody could foresee whether protracted domestic strife might ensue from a sudden desegregation order. Such an order would not only terminate separate schools but would also symbolize the beginning of the end of the whole social fabric of the South. In the national elections that year, Eisenhower had been voted

President by a landslide, and for the first time in some twenty years the Republicans controlled the White House and both houses of Congress. The posture of the new administration toward civil rights was not yet manifest.

The decision of the Court was to postpone a decision. This it did by the stop-gap measure of restoring the cases to the docket for reargument the next term, in October 1953. The Court specifically asked the parties to direct their second round of arguments to the history and intent of the Fourteenth Amendment. The Court also "invited" (read commanded) the Attorney General to take part in the oral argument (from which he had been absent the first time), presumably to learn the position of the Eisenhower Administration.

Chief Justice Vinson, a native son of the South, died in September 1953, and President Eisenhower nominated Governor Earl Warren of California as the successor. He came to the Court with no judicial experience and his first case was *Brown*. It is a reflection of his skill and interpersonal abilities that he was able to secure a unanimous decision when, just a few months earlier, the Justices were split. The significance of a unanimous opinion, especially in as sensitive a case as this one, cannot be over-stated. The legitimacy of the Court as the ultimate arbiter of disputes rests in large measure on the persuasiveness of the opinion justifying its decision. It has no means of its own to compel public compliance. The Court can only inspire it by the logic, authority, and moral force of its reasoning. When the Justices, sitting in the temple of American justice, speak with one voice, it is as if they—in their priestly raiment and putatively higher wisdom—have apprehended the truth and are now bringing it to the people. A single dissent can shatter this image. It suggests that there is no single truth, that the Justices are not above the rest of us with their partial and conflicting views.

3.   In the holding, did the Court squarely repudiate the separate-but-equal principle of *Plessy*? (See *Gayle* v. *Browder*, 1956.)

Indeed, did the Court ever suggest that the initial *Plessy* decision was wrong? Why did the Court take pains to establish the longevity of the separate-but-equal doctrine in education by tracing it back to *Roberts* v. *City of Boston* (1850), which antedated both *Plessy* (1896) and *Strauder* (1880, quoted in footnote 5)?

4.   A historical exegesis on the Fourteenth Amendment with respect to public school segregation is almost futile, since no readily available information about the framers' intent on that issue exists. Nonetheless, given the Court's order to address this matter on reargument, both sides enlisted distinguished historians to prepare history briefs. It would have been overreaching for the Court to impose a new meaning on the Fourteenth Amendment without at least considering its history and legislative purposes. The briefs could provide a historical peg on which to hang a new interpretation.

The historians participated not in the role of disinterested scholars but within the framework of advocacy. They sought to place the most favorable gloss on history without, of course, exceeding the limits of truthfulness. Those working on the NAACP side selectively manipulated history, "carefully marshalling every scrap of evidence in favor of the desired interpretation and just as carefully doctoring all the evidence to the contrary. . . ." The other side, likewise, engaged in "law office history," choosing some facts and interpreting other facts in order to make the most persuasive argument (Kelly 1965, p. 144). An unperceptive reader, examining the two history briefs, might well have concluded that each side had examined totally different evidence.

In the end, the Court in its opinion abruptly swept them all aside as "inconclusive." "The Court," said Kelly (1965), "rejected history in favor of sociology" (p. 144). In light of the Court's own struggle for a unanimous front, it is perhaps not surprising that it passed over the divided historians for the nearly unanimous social scientists.

Does it follow that when social science evidence is less than unanimous, as is often the case in many other social issues, it will be of little or no use in judicial decision-making?

5.   Even if the historical evidence on whether the Fourteenth Amendment was intended to prohibit segregated schools was inconclusive, that is not necessarily the end of any further historical analysis. The Constitution, after all, is a dynamic instrument and not a static body of rules. The Court has always recognized the adaptive genius of the Constitution by bringing within the ambit of the Fourteenth Amendment many different issues and litigants who were never contemplated initially by those who framed and ratified it. How might you argue that the Civil War Amendment was intended to forbid state-imposed restrictions on educational opportunity based on race?

6.   A handful of school desegregation precedents were cited in the opinion, but all were distinguished from the case at bar. More interesting are the cases that the Court could have, but did not, rely on. Like the watchdog in the Sherlock Holmes mystery ("The Silver Blaze") that did not bark, thereby providing a clue in something that did not exist, the Court purposely omitted any mention of all the post-*Plessy* decisions that had struck down racial classification laws in other areas, such as in housing (*Shelley* v. *Kraemer*, 1948) and in voting (*Guinn* v. *United States*, 1915; *Smith* v. *Allwright*, 1944). If no rational purpose sustained state-enforced segregated housing, for example, could a justifiable reason be found to sustain state-mandated segregated schooling? Could the Court have reached its decision in *Brown* relying on these cases? What would be the implications of a decision that did rely on them as legal authority? Would such a decision have disposed of the need to turn to social science authority?

7.   After touching upon history, the role of public education in contemporary society, and the legal precedents, the opinion turned to the psychological and educational consequences of segregation. The citation to the "modern authority" of social science in footnote 11 is probably one of the most famous and debated footnotes in the history of Supreme Court opinions.

The opinion is rather obscure on the most critical point: what exactly is the inequality that is being complained about? If the inequality refers not only to differences in tangible resources for black and white schools, but also to the wounding of the mind and spirit of black children by depriving them of equal educational opportunity, then why was this finding of psychological harm that is so crucial to the decision buried in a footnote?

Is the question of inequality solely an issue of fact? If so, why did the Court not scrutinize carefully the sufficiency of the social science evidence purporting to show the detrimental consequences of inequality? Indeed, if it is a factual issue and proof of harm is essential, does it mean that in subsequent challenges to segregated public beaches, golf courses, buses, and parks it would also be necessary to append "A Social Science Statement" on the psychological harm caused in each of these settings? (See the per curiam decisions in apparent reliance on *Brown:* respectively, *Baltimore* v. *Dawson*, 1955; *Holmes* v. *Atlanta*, 1955; *Gayle* v. *Browder*, 1956; and *New Orleans Park Association* v. *Detiege*, 1958.) In a challenge to a state medical school's policy that gives preferential admission to minority applicants, would a rejected white (but otherwise qualified) applicant have to prove that the racially-based policy "stamp[ed him] as inferior" and that it will "affect him throughout his life in the same way as the segregation of the Negro school children in *Brown I* would have affected them"? See *University of California Regents* v. *Bakke* (1977, p. 375).

Is the question of inequality solely an issue of law? That is, is the invalidity of state-imposed racial lines in public schools a matter resting only on authoritative judgment? What specific language in the opinion striking down separate schools bespeaks a normative judgment not grounded on empirical evidence? But if it is a purely legal decision, why was there no mention of the other racial classification cases?

8.   Wechsler (1959) has proposed that "neutral principles" govern constitutional decision-making. By that he meant that decisions should rest on "reasoning and analysis quite transcending the immediate result that is achieved" (p. 15). Decision-making, in other words, ought not be ad hoc and result-oriented. Neutral adjudication consists of dispassionate judging and generality in the reasons given for the conclusion. If the same and plainly articulated principles for the decision are applied to the full range of like issues, a losing party might take comfort in the knowledge that these principles could apply to its advantage in some future case.

Did the Court rely on neutral principles in deciding *Brown*?

Nobody can resist Wechsler's thesis that decision-making should be disinterested. Judges should not merely implement their private values. However, when a disputed policy matter involves the clash of two different values, a judge cannot escape the task of choosing between them. Are there objective and universal criteria for the exercise of value choices? Is reliance on social science evidence on the impact of the disputed policy (for example, the psychological harm of segregated schools) a neutral ground for choosing?

9.   Wechsler (1959) also argued that if separate schools are truly equal, the problem then "is not one of discrimination at all." Rather, it lies in "the denial by the state of the freedom to associate." He went on to say:

But if the freedom of association is denied by segregation, integration forces an association upon those for whom it is unpleasant or repugnant. . . . Given a situation where the state must practically choose between denying the association to those individuals who wish it, or imposing it on those who would avoid it, is there a basis in neutral principles for holding that the Constitution demands that the claims for association should prevail? [p. 34]

Do you agree that what the black plaintiffs were complaining about was the denial of the right to associate with whites? Assuming that it was, does social science provide a neutral basis for choosing between the conflicting claims for association or nonassociation? For response to Wechsler, see Pollak (1959), Black (1960), and Heyman (1961).

10.   Examine the form and style of the opinion. Is there any significance in titling these segregation cases after *Brown* v. *Board of Education* rather than any of the other three state cases decided together with it?

The opinion has been hailed as "a pronouncement second in importance only to President Lincoln's Emancipation Proclamation" (Muse 1964, p. 1). It certainly symbolized the reconsecration of the national aspiration for equality. One would have thought, therefore, that a landmark opinion such as this would contain a ringing declaration of human rights. However, except for that one soaring sentence prior to footnote 11 on how segregation "may affect [children's] hearts and minds in a way unlikely ever to be undone," the language in the rest of the opinion seems deliberately bland and dispassionate. There are no stirring words upon the deliverance of the oppressed, as in Lincoln's Proclamation; the incandescent rhetoric of a Frederick Douglass is absent. The *Plessy* principle merely has "no place" in contemporary public education. Justice Brown's underlying Social Darwinist premises were disposed of economically and matter-of-factly. What purposes are being served by an opinion that is restrained in style and thin in legal materials?

11.   Examine the language and substance of the final paragraph regarding the formulation of decrees. Were the political instincts of the Court sound? Did the Court handle adroitly the delicate issue of remedy and implementation? The social science brief had devoted nearly as much attention to the method and timing of desegregation as to the psychological effects of segregation. The Court cited only the latter evidence in support of the finding of a violation, but ignored the former evidence regarding the formulation of a remedy. Why?

3.4.   SOCIAL SCIENCE AT TRIAL: EXPERT TESTIMONY

Social science evidence and opinions were used by the NAACP in litigation prior to the School Segregation Cases, but not systematically or comprehensively. In challenging racially restrictive covenants in housing (*Shelley* v. *Kraemer*, 1948), an element of the proof was the impact of ghettoes on those confined therein and on the larger city as a whole. Data were introduced on the rates of immigration by race, the availability of housing in the postwar years, and the consequences of overcrowding for urban health, crime, and family life (Vose 1959; Kohn 1960). However, nothing in the Court's opinion striking down the enforceability of these restrictive covenants suggests the visible influence of the extralegal data. In the professional school cases (for example, *Sweatt* v. *Painter*, 1950), some social scientists were called upon to testify about the desirability of integrated graduate programs for educational purposes, and the absence of any inherent intellectual differences based solely on race. Again, the Court made no reference to social science in its decision.

When the drive against segregation in the public schools was launched, the NAACP legal staff decided to rely on social science as an integral part of their overall litigation strategy. The aim was to create in the trial courts a massive record of empirical evidence on the impact of segregation in order to lay a foundation for review by the Supreme Court. Thurgood Marshall (1952) wrote then that the *Plessy* "doctrine had become so ingrained that overwhelming proof was sorely needed to demonstrate that equal educational opportunity for Negroes would not be provided in a segregated system" (p. 322). When he learned of the social psychological studies of Kenneth Clark, he decided that "it was a promising way of showing injury to these segregated youngsters." Moreover, "we needed exactly that kind of evidence in the school case" (in Kluger 1977, p. 316).[*]

Clark, who later became a distinguished scholar in race relations and president of the City University of New York, served as general social science consultant to the NAACP. He assembled more than twenty leading social scientists to serve as expert witnesses in the four state school cases. The thrust of their testimony—based on specific studies, extrapolations from the general fund of social science knowledge, and an opinion survey of the social science community—was to show that segregation results in psychological and educational harm. Selections from the expert testimony in these trials are reproduced below.

Expert Testimony in South Carolina

Clark had designed a "dolls test" that purportedly illustrated the psychic damage to children resulting from segregation (Clark and Clark 1947). The results were also described in the White House Conference Report of 1950, later cited by the Supreme Court in footnote 11. He used the dolls with some children in Clarendon County and the findings were introduced at the trial through his expert testimony. The following is from the direct examination of Clark by Robert Carter, one of the NAACP attorneys:

A.   I made these tests on Thursday and Friday of this past week at your request, and I presented it to children in the Scott's Branch Elementary school, concentrating particularly on the elementary group. I used these methods which I told you about—the Negro and White dolls—which were identical in every respect save skin color. And, I presented them with a sheet of paper on which there were these drawings of dolls, and I asked them to show me the doll—May I read from these notes?

JUDGE WARING: You may refresh your recollection.

THE WITNESS: Thank you. I presented these dolls to them and I asked them the following questions in the following order: "Show me the doll that you like best or that you'd like to play with," "Show me the doll that is the 'nice' doll," "Show me the doll that looks 'bad,' " and then the following questions also: "Give me the doll that looks like a white child," "Give me the doll that looks like a colored child," "Give me the doll that looks like a Negro child," and "Give me the doll that looks like you."

By Mr. Carter:

Q.   "Like you?"

A.   "Like you." That was the final question, and you can see why. I wanted to get the child's free expression of his opinions and feelings before I had him identified with one of these two dolls. I found that of the children between the ages of six and nine whom I tested, which were a total of sixteen in number, that ten of those children chose the white doll as the preference; the doll which they liked best. Ten of them also considered the white doll a "Nice" doll. And, I think you have to keep in mind that these two dolls are absolutely identical in every respect except skin color. Eleven of these sixteen children chose the brown doll as the doll which looked "bad." This is consistent with previous results which we have obtained testing over three hundred children, and we interpret it to mean that the Negro child accepts as early as six, seven or eight the negative stereotypes about his own group. And, this result was confirmed in Clarendon County where we found eleven out of sixteen children picking the brown doll as looking "bad," when we also must take into account that over half of these children, in spite of their own feelings—negative feelings—about the brown doll, were eventually required on the last question to identify themselves with this doll which they considered as being undesirable or negative. It may also interest you to know that only one of these children, between six and nine, dared to choose the white doll as looking bad. The difference between eleven and sixteen was in terms of children who refused to make any choice at all and the children were always free not to make a choice. They were not forced to make a choice. These choices represent the children's spontaneous and free reactions to this experimental situation. Nine of these sixteen children considered the white doll as having the qualities of a nice doll. To show you that that was not due to some artificial or accidental set of circumstances, the following results are important. Every single child, when asked to pick the doll that looked like the white child, made the correct choice. All sixteen of the sixteen picked that doll. Every single child, when asked to pick the doll that was like the colored child, every one of them picked the brown doll. My opinion is that a fundamental effect of segregation is basic confusion in the individuals and their concepts about themselves conflicting in their self images. That seemed to be supported by the results of these sixteen children, all of them knowing which of those dolls was white and which one was brown. Seven of them, when asked to pick the doll that was like themselves; seven of them picked the white doll. This must be seen as a concrete illustration of the degree to which the pressures which these children sensed against being brown forced them to evade reality—to escape the reality which seems too overburdening or too threatening to them. This is clearly illustrated by a number of these youngsters who, when asked to color themselves—For example, I had a young girl, a dark brown child of seven, who was so dark brown that she was almost black. When she was asked to color herself, she was one of the few children who picked a flesh color, pink, to color herself. When asked to color a little boy, the color she liked little boys to be, she looked all around the twenty-four crayons and picked up a white crayon and looked up at me with a shy smile and began to color. She said, "Well, this doesn't show." So, she pressed a little harder and began to color in order to get the white crayon to show. These are the kinds of results which I obtained in Clarendon County.

Q.   Well, as a result of your tests, what conclusions have you reached, Mr. Clark, with respect to the infant plaintiffs involved in this case?

A.   The conclusion which I was forced to reach was that these children in Clarendon County, like other human beings who are subjected to an obviously inferior status in the society in which they live, have been definitely harmed in the development of their personalities; that the signs of instability in their personalities are clear, and I think that every psychologist would accept and interpret these signs as such.

Q.   Is that the type of injury which in your opinion would be enduring or lasting?

A.   I think it is the kind of injury which would be as enduring or lasting as the situation endured, changing only in its form and in the way it manifests itself.

MR. CARTER: Thank you. Your witness.*

---

*From Transcript of Record, *Briggs* v. *Elliott;* reproduced in Cahn 1955, pp. 161–63. Reprinted by permission of the publisher and Fred B. Rothman and Company. Copyright © 1955 by the *New York University Law Review.*

In addition to this specific study, Clark also testified on the basis of the general literature in the field:

> I have reached the conclusion from the examination of my own results and from an examination of the literature in the entire field that discrimination, prejudice, and segregation have definitely detrimental effects on the personality development of the Negro child. . . . The essence of this detrimental effect is a confusion in the child's concept of his own self-esteem—basic feelings of inferiority, conflict, confusion in his self-image, resentment, hostility towards himself, hostility towards whites. . . .

This was the essence of his findings presented in the preceding year in the White House Conference Report, which eventually was cited by the Supreme Court.

Several other social scientists also testified at the trial. The defense, however, did not cross-examine vigorously any of the experts and did not bother to introduce any social scientists to testify on its behalf. Apparently, on the defense team "nobody took [the social science evidence] seriously" (in Kluger 1977, p. 355).*

Expert Testimony in Virginia

Clark did not repeat the dolls test with the Prince Edward County, Virginia, students because of their high school age. Instead, he interviewed about a dozen adolescent students and then testified about their attitudes toward segregated schools. He reported that they all expressed negative reactions.

The cross-examination was jagged. After Clark said he was born in the Panama Canal Zone, the questioning went as follows:

> Q.   In view of your reference to Panama, I must inquire if you know—you appear to be of rather light color—what percentage, as near as you can tell us, are you white and what percentage some other?
> A.   I haven't the slightest idea. What do you mean by "percentage"?
> Q.   I mean are you half-white, or half-colored, and half Panamanian, or what?
> A.   I still can't understand you.
> Q.   You don't understand that question?
> A.   No. My parents were not born in Panama. My mother and father are from the West Indies. My father was born in Jamaica and so was my mother. They met in Panama, and I was the result.
> Q.   So you are, really, a West Indian?
> A.   I was not born in the West Indies; I was born in the Panama Canal Zone.

Defense counsel then lured Clark into conducting a sample interview with the attorney posing as one of the black students. According to an observer, the attorney "put on a moronic face and the accent of a little darkey," and left the inference that the students might have been coached in advance. "It brought the house down.

Everyone there enjoyed it—except maybe the [plaintiffs]" (in Kluger 1977, pp. 496–97).*

Among the other plaintiffs' experts was Isidor Chein of City College of New York and research director of the American Jewish Congress. He had co-authored "The Psychological Effects of Enforced Segregation: A Survey of Social Science Opinion" (Deutscher and Chein 1948) which was later cited in footnote 11. At the trial, he testified about the results of this survey. A questionnaire had been sent to members of the American Ethnological Society, the American Psychological Association, and the American Sociological Association, known to be concentrating on the area of race relations. Of the 849 questionnaires sent out, 61% were returned of which 6% came from the South. The survey contained three principal questions:

First, "Does enforced segregation have detrimental psychological effects on members of racial and religious groups which are segregated, even if equal facilities are provided?" Yes: 90%. No: 2%. No response or no opinion: 8%. Of the southern respondents, 91% said yes, and 6% said no.

Second, "Does enforced segregation have a detrimental effect on the group that enforces the segregation, even if that group provides equal facilities to the groups that are segregated?" Yes: 83%. No: 4%. No answer or no opinion: 13%. Of the southern respondents, 84% said yes, and 6% said no.

Third, "What is the basis for your opinions?" Based on multiple responses, 29% said their own research; 61% the research of others; 66% their own professional experience; and 48% the professional experience of others.

Cross-examination proceeded in part as follows:

Q.   Dr. Chein, just how do you spell your last name?

A.   C-H-E-I-N.

Q.   What kind of name is that? What sort of racial background does that indicate?

A.   The name is a poor English version of Hebrew which designates "charm."

Q.   What is your racial background?

A.   As Dr. Smith has testified, I could not give an honest answer to that because of the complexity of the concept. I think what you want to know is am I Jewish. [Reference is to M. Brewster Smith, a social psychologist then at Vassar College. Ed.'s note.]

Q.   Are you 100 percent Jewish?

A.   How do I answer that?

Q.   I don't know—you know.

A.   In all honesty, the framework of the question is not one which can be, as far as I know, intelligently answered. All of my—both of my parents and all of my ancestors, as far back as I know, were Jewish.

Q.   That answers my question. I simply wanted to find out what was the story about that. Where were you born?

A.   In the United States, in New York City.

Q.   Were your parents native born in the United States?

A.   No.

Q.   Where were they born?

A.   In Poland.

Q.   How long had they lived in this country when you were born?

A.   I am not sure—for some 20 years, I think. I was the youngest child.

. . .

Q.   Now take the Jews, they were discriminated against, were they not?

A.   Yes.

Q.   Is it your view that that has resulted in the Jew feeling inferiority as to status?

A.   Yes, sir.

Q.   You really believe that?

A.   I not only believe it, I have evidence to that effect. But this is to a much less marked degree than in the case of the Negro. As a matter of fact, in the social science literature the notion of self-hate first appeared in connection with a study of Jews. Jews are also people just like Negroes and other white people, people of other religious groups. They react to the same kind of social and psychological forces. If the weight of society bears against them, then they tend to share in the viewpoint of society. . . .

Q.   You agree that the Japanese and Chinese have great pride of race?

A.   There are Japanese and Chinese who do.

Q.   Do you not agree that the average Japanese or Chinese has pride of race?

A.   I am not too familiar with the Chinese and Japanese groups.

Q.   Do you know of any reason why the Negro in America should not be just as proud of his race as the Japanese or Chinese?

A.   I certainly do know a reason.

Q.   What?

A.   Because the state is saying to the Negro that he should have no pride in his race.*

The defense called three experts of its own: a psychiatrist, a clinical psychologist, and—the star witness—a noted experimental psychologist, Henry Garrett, chairman of the psychology department of Columbia University and a former president of the American Psychological Association. He was also Clark's former graduate adviser.

All three experts attacked the methodology and conclusions of the Deutscher and Chein survey and of Clark's earlier doll studies. They pointed out that psychology had not yet devised the means to measure precisely the personality effects of segregation. Their common theme was that so long as school facilities are equal, segregation is in the best interests of both races (Kohn 1960, p. 149). However, on cross-examination, each also made a surprising and possibly critical concession:

Q.   [I]n your opinion as a clinical psychologist, do you feel that racial segregation has an adverse effect on a healthy personality development?

A.   As an abstract statement—as a generality, let us put it that way—I should say yes. I think that anything that sets up artificial barriers, restricting communication between indi-

---

*From Transcript of Record, *Davis* v. *County School Board of Prince Edward County;* reproduced in Kluger 1977, pp. 493–94. Reprinted by permission of the publisher. Copyright ©1977 by Alfred A. Knopf, Inc.

viduals in a given community is, perhaps, at least theoretically, bad. But . . . I don't think a generality can actually be given.

· · ·

Q.   As a psychiatrist, do you feel that racial segregation is a social situation that has some effect upon personality development of the individual?

A.   Yes, I do.

Q.   As a psychiatrist, do you think that social situation is adverse or beneficial to the personality?

A.   I will have to say it is adverse to the personality.

· · ·

Q.   Do you consider, Dr. Garrett, that racial segregation, as presently practiced in the United States, and in Virginia, is a social situation which is adverse to the individual?

A.   It is a large question. In general, wherever a person is cut off from the main body of society or a group, if he is put in a position that stigmatizes him and makes him feel inferior, I would say yes, it is detrimental and deleterious to him.

Q.   . . . [D]o you know of any situation involving racial segregation of Negroes . . . where this stigmatism has not been put on the separation?

A.   I think, in the high schools of Virginia, if the Negro child had equal facilities, his own teachers, his own friends, and a good feeling, he would be more likely to develop pride in himself as a Negro, which I think we would all like to see him do—to develop his own potentialities, his sense of duty, his sense of art, his sense of histrionics. . . . [T]he Negroes might develop their schools up to the level where they would not [want to] mix themselves; and I would like to see it happen. I think it would be poetic justice. They would develop their sense of dramatic art, and music, which they seem to have a talent for—[and] athletics, and they would say, "We prefer to remain as a Negro group." . . .*

They also added, however, that the people of Virginia were not ready for desegregation, and hence any harm to black children was outweighed by the distress and disruption to their education that such an action would bring.

Cahn (1955) observed:

As any healthy-minded person reads the Virginia trial record, it is impossible not to contrast the altruism and sober dignity of the scientists with the behavior of defendants' counsel, who, by his manner of espousing the old order, exposed its cruelty and bigotry. Here was a living spectacle of what racial segregation can do to the human spirit. The segregated society, as defendants' own expert had said, was "sick"; and the tactics of cross-examination used by defendants' lawyer showed how very sick it was. I suggest that these pages of the record did not fail of notice in the deliberations of the United States Supreme Court. [pp. 165–66]†

Expert Testimony in Kansas

The principal expert of the NAACP in the *Brown* trial was Louisa Holt, a sociologist at the Menninger Clinic who also had psychoanalytic training. Of the many

---

*From Transcript of Record, *Davis;* reproduced in Kluger 1977, pp. 501–4. Reprinted by permission of the publisher. Copyright ©1977 by Alfred A. Knopf, Inc.

†Reprinted by permission of the publisher and Fred B. Rothman and Company. Copyright © 1955 by the *New York University Law Review.*

social scientists who testified in the various trial proceedings, none had a more discernible impact upon the language of the final Supreme Court decision than Holt.

Q.   . . . [D]oes enforced legal separation have any adverse effect upon the personality
development of the Negro child?

A.   The fact that it is enforced, that it is legal, I think has more importance than the mere
fact of segregation by itself does because this gives legal and official sanction to a policy which
is inevitably interpreted both by white people and by Negroes as denoting the inferiority of
the Negro group. Were it not for the sense that one group is inferior to the other, there
would be no basis—and I am not granting that this is a rational basis—for such segregation.

Q.   Well, does this interference have any effect, in your opinion, on the learning process?

A.   A sense of inferiority must always affect one's motivation for learning since it affects
the feeling one has of one's self as a person. . . . That sense of ego-identity is built up on the
basis of attitudes that are expressed toward a person by others who are important—first the
parents and then teachers and other people in the community, whether they are older or
one's peers. It is other people's reactions to one's self that basically affects the conception of
one's self. . . . If these attitudes that are reflected back and then internalized or projected, are
unfavorable ones, then one develops a sense of one's self as an inferior being . . . and
apathetic acceptance, fatalistic submission to the feeling others have expressed that one is
inferior, and therefore any efforts to prove otherwise would be doomed to failure.

Q.   Now . . . would you say that the difficulties which segregation causes in the public
school system interfere with a well—development of a well-rounded personality?

A.   I think the maximum or maximal development of any personality can only be based
on the potentialities which that individual himself possesses. Of course they are affected for
good or ill by the attitudes, opinions, feelings which are expressed by others and which may
be fossilized into laws. . . . I feel, if I may add another word, I feel that when segregation
exists, it's not something . . . directed against people for what they are. It is directed against
them on the basis of who their parents are. . . . [M]y understanding . . . of the American
tradition, religious tradition as well as set of values and ethos, determining much of our most
valued and significant behavior, hinges upon a belief of treating people upon their own
merits, and we are inclined to oppose a view which states that we should respect people or
reject them on the basis of who their parents were.

Q.   Now, Mrs. Holt . . . is the integration of the child at the junior high school level, does
that correct these difficulties which you have just spoken of, in your opinion?

A.   I think it's a theory that would be accepted by virtually all students of personality
development that the earlier a significant event occurs in the life of an individual the more
lasting, the more far-reaching and deeper the effects of that incident, that trauma, will be.
The more—the earlier an event occurs, the more difficult it is later on to eradicate those
effects.*

Impact of the Social Science Testimony on the Trial Courts

The impact was inconclusive. In South Carolina, the trial court viewed the
social science evidence as unproved and irrelevant in any event (*Briggs* v. *Elliott*, 1951,

---

*From Transcript of Record, *Brown* v. *Board of Education;* reproduced in Kluger, 1977, pp. 421–22. Reprinted by
permission of the publisher. Copyright © 1977 by Alfred A. Knopf, Inc.

pp. 535–37). The court in Virginia stated that segregation was a venerable custom of the people of the state. "We have found no hurt or harm to either race. This ends our inquiry" (*Davis* v. *County School Board*, 1952, p. 340). It did add that segregation had "begotten greater opportunities for the Negro" (p. 340), though greater than what the court did not say.

Segregated schools were also upheld by the trial court in *Brown*. However, as sort of a consolation prize to the NAACP, the court appended to its opinion a list of "Findings of Fact." One of the findings restated Louisa Holt's testimony, and this was the paragraph that eventually found its way into the Supreme Court's opinion.

In the Delaware case, the court, paraphrasing the social science testimony, determined that "the Negro's mental health and therefore his educational opportunities are adversely affected by state-imposed segregation in education" (*Gebhart* v. *Belton*, 1952, p. 865). It ordered the immediate admission of black students to all-white public schools, the first time in history that a court had ordered racial desegregation. The court expressly declined, however, to overrule the *Plessy* principle.

Thus, when these cases came up before the Supreme Court, it was not at all clear what impact the social science record would have upon the Justices, and whether they would even consider it in their decision-making.

NOTES AND QUESTIONS

---

1.   If the finding of constitutional violation rests upon the factual claim of psychological harm, then careful scrutiny of the studies that lead to the claim must be undertaken. The defense's cross-examination of the NAACP's experts, as the trial transcripts show, was particularly inept. What criticisms of methodology and research design might you raise about the dolls study?

For critiques of the social science evidence, see generally Cahn (1955), Gregor (1963), and van den Haag (1960). For a more elaborate and rigorous replication of the dolls study, see Radke and Trager (1950).

2.   The original dolls study was conducted by Clark and his wife before the school litigation (Clark and Clark 1947). They compared black children in a segregated Arkansas school (N = 134) with those in an integrated Massachusetts school (N = 119). When asked to choose the "doll that looks like you," 29% of the Arkansas sample chose the white doll compared with 39% of the Massachusetts group. The Clarks concluded: "The southern children . . . in spite of their equal favorableness toward the white doll, are significantly less likely to reject the brown doll (evaluate it negatively) as compared to the strong tendency for the majority of the northern children to do so" (p. 611). Compare this statement with the testimony given in the South Carolina trial. Later, Clark (1966) wrote: "The apparent emotional stability of the southern Negro child may be indicative only of the fact that through rigid racial segregation and isolation he has accepted as normal the fact of his inferior social status. Such acceptance is not symptomatic of a healthy personality" (p. 45).

3.   Questions of research methodology go to the *weight* or *sufficiency* of the evidence. They attempt to challenge the probative force of the expert's testimony. Another major issue regarding evidence introduced in court pertains to *materiality*—are the facts *relevant* to the legal matter under controversy? Questions about the validity of the conclusions and inferences that the expert draws from the data go to the issue of legal relevance.

What grounds exist for impeaching the materiality of the social science evidence, whether it be the expert testimony at trial or the brief on appeal?

3.5.   EVALUATING THE ROLE OF SOCIAL SCIENCE IN LAW CREATION

Up to the time of the appeal, the NAACP attorneys themselves had mixed reactions to the social science evidence. Some considered it "at best, a luxury and irrelevant" (in Kluger 1977, p. 321);* others felt that it was the "heart of our case" (in Friedman 1969, p. 3). Clark was always of the view that "the role of social science . . . was crucial . . . in supplying pervasive evidence that segregation itself means inequality" (in Friedman 1969, p. xxxvi). In the end, the decision was made to have Clark, together with two of his colleagues, prepare a statement summarizing the social science knowledge on the effects of segregation and desegregation. No specific mention was made of the dolls studies. The other side remained unimpressed. South Carolina's counsel, John Davis (the unsuccessful Presidential candidate in 1924), brushed it aside: "[N]othing in [the social science statement] requires special comment. I can only say that if that sort of 'guff' can move any court, 'God save the State!' " (in Kluger 1977, p. 577).*

As it turned out, the Court was moved enough to insert footnote 11. Its implications became the subject of intense public debate. James Reston of the *New York Times,* in a column headlined "A Sociological Decision," declared that "the Court's opinion read more like an expert paper on sociology than a Supreme Court opinion" (May 18, 1954, p. 14). The reliance on social science was thought to diminish the legitimacy of the decision. Several southern legislatures passed resolutions condemning the decision and specifically the footnote. The Florida legislature protested that the Court "predicated its determination of the rights of the people upon the psychological conclusions . . . rather than the legal conclusions" (in Rosen 1972, p. 177).

Reactions to the footnote among legal and social science scholars were also mixed, even among those in agreement with the decision (for example, Rosen 1972, p. 172; Swisher 1954, p. 158). The following comments by Cahn, a noted legal scholar, and the subsequent rebuttal by Clark, cast in sharp relief some of the questions concerning the role of social science in law creation.

---

*Reprinted by permission of the publisher. Copyright ©1977 by Alfred A. Knopf, Inc.

JURISPRUDENCE

Edmond Cahn

. . .

SCIENCE OR COMMON SENSE?

A DANGEROUS MYTH. In the Virginia case and to a lesser extent in the other litigations, various psychiatrists, psychologists,

Reprinted by permission of the publisher and Fred B. Rothman and Company. Copyright ©1955 by the *New York University Law Review* [30 (1955): 150–69].

and social scientists gave expert testimony concerning the harmful effects of segregation on Negro school children. In addition, some of appellants' witnesses prepared an elaborate statement on the subject, which, signed by a total of thirty-two experts, was submitted to the Supreme Court as an appendix to appellants' brief. In the months since the utterance of the *Brown* and *Bolling* opinions, the impression has grown that the outcome, either entirely or in major part, was caused by the testimony and opinions of the scientists, and a genuine danger has arisen that even lawyers and judges may begin to entertain this belief. The word "danger" is used advisedly, because I would not have the constitutional rights of Negroes—or of other Americans—rest on any such flimsy foundation as some of the scientific demonstrations in these records.

The moral factors involved in racial segregation are not new—like the science of social psychology—but exceedingly ancient. What, after all, is the most elementary and conspicuous fact about a primitive community if not the physical proximity of human beings mingling together? . . .

So one speaks in terms of the most familiar and universally accepted standards of right and wrong when one remarks (1) that racial segregation under government auspices inevitably inflicts humiliation, and (2) that official humiliation of innocent, law-abiding citizens is psychologically injurious and morally evil. Mr. Justice Harlan and many other Americans with responsive consciences recognized these simple, elementary propositions before, during, and after the rise of "separate but equal." For at least twenty years, hardly any cultivated person has questioned that segregation is cruel to Negro school children. The cruelty is obvious and evident. Fortunately, it is so very obvious that the Justices of the Supreme Court could see it and act on it even after reading the labored attempts by plaintiffs' experts to demonstrate it "scientifically." . . .

Professor Kenneth B. Clark of the psychology department of City College acted as general social science consultant to the NAACP legal staff and served as liaison between the lawyers and the scientists. His endeavors having been long and arduous, perhaps it was natural that he should exaggerate whatever the experts contributed to the case. In an article written while the country was waiting for the Supreme Court's decisions, he asserted, "*Proof* of the arguments that segregation itself is inequality and that state imposed racial segregation inflicts injuries upon the Negro *had to come from the social psychologists and other social scientists.*" (Emphasis supplied.)

When Professor Clark wrote this, he could not have known that Chief Justice Warren's opinions would not mention either the testimony of the expert witnesses or the submitted statement of the thirty-two scientists. The Chief Justice cushioned the blow to some extent by citing certain professional publications of the psychological experts in a footnote, alluding to them graciously as "modern authority." In view of their devoted efforts to defeat segregation, this was the kind of gesture a magnanimous judge would feel impelled to make, and we are bound to take satisfaction in the accolade. Yet, once the courtesy had been paid, the Court was not disposed in the least to go farther or base its determination on the expert testimony. . . .

When we come to explain why the statement signed by the thirty-two social scientists went without mention by Chief Justice Warren, I find myself at a disadvantage. Only the reader's assistance can rescue me. I have examined the text of this statement, which has become easy of access by being reprinted in a law review. My personal, subjective reaction is that the text conveys little or no information beyond what is already known in "literary psychology" (by which I mean such psychological observations and insights as one finds continually in the works of poets, novelists, essayists, journalists, and religious prophets). The statement's vocabulary and style would not be called "literary;" I refer only to its substance. . . .

WITHOUT SALT, NO SCIENCE. . . . As the courts' exclusionary rules of evidence tend to relax more and more, the scientists will appear more frequently to testify as expert witnesses. How much respect should the judges extend to their testimony?

The answer depends in large measure on the scientists. If I have been right in suggesting that their evidence in the desegregation cases seemed persuasive because it happened to coincide with facts of common knowledge, they surely cannot rely on having the same advantage in every future litigation. It is predictable that lawyers and scientists retained by adversary parties will endeavor more aggressively to puncture any vulnerable or extravagant claims. Judges may learn to notice where objective science ends and advocacy begins. At present, it is still possible for the social psychologist to "hoodwink a judge who is not over wise" without intending to do so; but successes of this kind are too costly for science to desire them.

For one thing: Merely translating a proposition of "literary" psychology into the terms of technical jargon can scarcely make it a scientific finding. For another: Just because social psychology is in a youthful and somewhat uncertain stage, the utmost rigor should be imposed on its *intermediate* processes.

The point is vital, involving as it does not only social psychology's prestige in the courts but—what is ultimately more valuable—its capacity to evolve and progress as a cumulative body of tested knowledge and approved method. Among the major impediments continually confronting this science are (1) the recurrent lack of agreement on substantive premises, and (2) the recurrent lack of extrinsic, empirical means for checking and verifying inferred results. As long as these disadvantages remain, and they are likely to remain in some measure for a very long time, social psychology will need, above all things, the use of scrupulous logic in its internal, intermediate processes. If the *premises* must be loose, the *reasoning* from them should be so much tighter; and if the final *results* cannot be validated precisely by ex-

ternal tests, then the *methods* of inference should be examined and re-examined all the more critically. It is meticulous standards that bring respect and credence to scientific testimony. When a social psychologist is called to serve as a "friend of the court," he should be able to assume our belief that his best friend, his premier loyalty, is always the objective truth.

SOME OF THE CONSEQUENCES. Obviously, the *Brown* and *Bolling* opinions are susceptible of more than one interpretation. My views do not agree with those of some very able commentators, who consider that the opinions show important marks of the psychologists' influence. Granting this variety of interpretations, does it really matter whether the Supreme Court relies or does not rely on the psychologists' findings? Does it make any practical difference?

I submit it does. In the first place, since the behavioral sciences are so very young, imprecise, and changeful, their findings have an uncertain expectancy of life. Today's sanguine asseveration may be cancelled by tomorrow's new revelation— or new technical fad. It is one thing to use the current scientific findings, however ephemeral they may be, in order to ascertain whether the legislature has acted reasonably in adopting some scheme of social or economic regulation; deference here is shown not so much to the findings as to the legislature. It would be quite another thing to have our fundamental rights rise, fall, or change along with latest fashions of psychological literature. Today the social psychologists—at least the leaders of the discipline—are liberal and egalitarian in basic approach. Suppose, a generation hence, some of their successors were to revert to the ethnic mysticism of the very recent past; suppose they were to present us with a collection of racist notions and label them "science." What then would be the state of our constitutional rights? Recognizing as we do how sagacious Mr. Justice Holmes was to insist that the Constitution be not tied to the wheels of any economic system whatsoever, we ought to keep it similarly uncommitted in relation to the other social sciences.

There is another potential danger here. It concerns the guarantee of "equal protection of the laws." Heretofore, no government official has contended that he could deny equal protection with impunity unless the complaining parties offered competent proof that they would sustain or had sustained some permanent (psychological or other kind of) damage. The right to equal protection has not been subjected to any such proviso. Under my reading of the *Brown* and *Bolling* opinions, this would remain the law. But if, in future "equal protection" cases, the Court were to hold that it was the expert testimony that determined the outcome of *Brown* and *Bolling,* the scope of the constitutional safeguard might be seriously restricted. Without cataloguing the various possibilities, one can discern at least that some of them would be ominous. It is not too soon to say so, for basic rights need early alarms. . . .

THE DESEGREGATION CASES: CRITICISM OF THE SOCIAL SCIENTIST'S ROLE

Kenneth B. Clark

Basic to the direct and indirect criticisms which have been raised concerning the role of social scientists in the school desegregation cases is the generally unstated question of the propriety of social scientists playing any role in this type of legal controversy. . . . Serious discussion of whether social scientists should play a role in the legal processes related to the desegregation of the public schools would

seem no more or less justified than discussions of the following questions:

Should social scientists play a role in helping industry function more efficiently—make larger profits—develop better labor management relations—increase the sense of satisfaction among the workers? . . .

The psychological significance of the fundamental problem posed by questioning the relationship between social scientists and the desegregation cases may be even more clearly illustrated by asking the analogous question:

Should biological scientists play a role in guiding medical research and practices?

The answers to the above questions would seem so obviously positive that one is forced to question the validity of the question which is implicit in the criticisms which have been raised concerning the role of the social scientists in the desegregation cases. . . .

The criticisms of Professor Cahn take many forms. Essentially, however, he states that it is incorrect to believe the *Brown* decision was "caused by the testimony and opinions of the scientists" and that the constitutional rights of Negroes or any other Americans should not "rest on any such flimsy foundation as some of the scientific demonstrations in these records." He contends that the cruelty inherent in racial segregation "is obvious and evident." . . .

Professor Cahn implies that the primary motive of the social psychologists who participated in these cases was not "strict fidelity to objective truth." This is a serious, grave, and shocking charge.

Professor Cahn did not present evidence to support his implication that the social scientists who participated in these cases, and particularly this writer, betrayed their trusts as scientists. He merely makes

Reprinted with permission from *Villanova Law Review* Volume 5 No. 2, pp. 224–235. Copyright © 1959 by Villanova University.

the assertion that some day judges will be wise and will be able to notice "where objective science ends and advocacy begins." . . .

When the lawyers of the NAACP, in their understandable zeal to develop the strongest possible case, asked the social scientists whether it was possible to present evidence showing that *public school segregation*, in itself, damaged the personalities of Negro children, it was pointed out to them that the available studies had so far not isolated this single variable from the total social complexity of racial prejudice, discrimination, and segregation. It was therefore not possible to testify on the psychologically damaging effects of segregated schools alone. Such specific evidence, if available at all, would have to come from educators and educational philosophers. Some of the more insistent lawyers felt that only this type of specific testimony would be of value to them in these cases. It was pointed out to these lawyers that if this were so then the social psychologists and other social scientists could not be of any significant, direct help to them. A careful examination of the testimony of the social scientists, found in the record of these cases and the Social Science appendix submitted to the United States Supreme Court, will show that the social scientists presented testimony, opinion, and information consistent with the available empirical studies, conclusions, and observations. They presented this information with caution and restraint befitting their roles as trained and disciplined scientists. As expert witnesses, they made not a single concession to expediency, to the practical and legal demands of these cases, or even to the moral and humane issues involved as they adhered to their concept of "strict fidelity to objective truth." Certainly Professor Cahn cannot be the judge of whether his concept of "strict fidelity to objective truth" in the field of social science is more acceptable or valid than theirs. . . .

It is difficult to determine precisely what Professor Cahn means by "objective truth." According to his article "most of mankind already acknowledged . . . that segregation is cruel to Negro children, involves stigma and loss of status. . . ." Professor Cahn contends, however, that when scientists attempt to demonstrate these same "well-known facts" through their use of the methods and approaches of science, they "provide a rather bizarre spectacle." What is more, he maintains they exaggerate their role, their methods are questionable, their logic and interpretation weak and fallacious, and they distort their findings as they become advocates who seek to "hoodwink" judges. A serious question would be: How could the social scientists be so unreliable yet nonetheless come out with a picture of social reality which Professor Cahn and everyone else "already knew"?

Professor Cahn presents a novel concept of the relationship between common knowledge and scientific knowledge. The logic of his position rests upon the premise that science concerns itself with one order of reality which is distinct from other forms of reality or truth—that a scientific "fact" has different attributes or characteristics than a "fact" of common knowledge. Another related theme which runs through his comments is that a "legal fact" is distinct from both a "scientific fact" and a "fact of common knowledge." . . .

The development of science as an approach to the determination of truth involved the development of methods for the control of errors in human observation, judgment, biases, and vested interests. These were the factors which seemed to have distorted man's concept of, or blocked his contact with, the "truth" or "facts" of experience. When they are operative, man's "common knowledge" becomes inconsistent with "scientific knowledge." When they are controlled or for some other reason non-operative, "common knowledge" and "scientific knowledge" are coincident—both reflecting the nature of reality, truth, or facts, as these are knowable to the human senses and intelligence.

Science is essentially a method of controlled observation and verification for the purpose of reducing human errors of observation, judgment, or logic. Science begins with observation and ends by testing its assumptions against experience. It is not a creation of another order of reality. In a very basic sense there cannot be a "legal fact" or a "fact of common knowledge" which is not at the same time a "scientific fact." Whenever this appears to be true, one or the other type of "fact" is not a fact.

THE BASIC ISSUE

After one has cut through the emotional irrelevancies of Professor Cahn's article, one is confronted with the basic circuitous plea that the law and the courts of the land should be isolated in Olympian grandeur from the other intellectual and scientific activities of man. Specifically, Cahn seems primarily—even if unconsciously—disturbed by the fact that the upstarts of the new social sciences should have been involved at all in these important cases which belonged exclusively to lawyers and students of jurisprudence. It is to be hoped that a decreasing number of lawyers believe that laws and courts are sacred and should be kept antiseptically isolated from the main stream of human progress. . . .

As Brandeis once said: "A judge is presumed to know the elements of law, but there is no presumption that he knows the facts." With the vast range and types of cases which come before the courts, it is unlikely that even the wisest judges and lawyers could be competent in all fields of human knowledge. One may presume that it was a recognition of these facts among others that influenced the decision of the lawyers of the NAACP to seek the help of social scientists in their attempt to overrule the *Plessy v. Ferguson* "separate but equal" doctrine which had dominated civil rights litigation since 1896. . . .

It may merely be coincidental that the lawyers of the NAACP succeeded in overruling the *Plessy* doctrine only after they enlisted an impressive array of social science testimony and talent and attacked this problem with this approach. . . .

NOTES AND QUESTIONS

1. Cahn's thesis is that the evidence of psychological harm was self-evident and, therefore, unneeded. Other legal scholars have also raised the same criticism, that the social science was "merely corroboratory of common sense" (Black 1960, p. 430). Do you find Clark's response persuasive?

2. If certain claims are self-evident, does it follow that they are necessarily true so as not to require proof? If psychological inequality is obvious, is the Fourteenth Amendment concept of equality also so plain in meaning as to dispense with any need of interpretation and proof?

3. Perhaps the issue is not whether the harm was universally obvious (including to southern whites in 1950), but that there were many who favored segregation despite knowledge of the harm it caused.

The governor of South Carolina wrote: "One cannot discuss this problem [of school desegregation] without admitting that, in the South, there is a fundamental objection to integration. White Southerners fear that the purpose . . . is to break down social barriers in the period of adolescence and ultimately bring about intermarrige of the races. . . . This is not petty prejudice. This is a serious problem in race relations" (Byrnes 1956, p. 104). At the time of the graduate school desegregation cases, a Texas poll showed that 80% of the white adult population wanted segregated universities (Kohn 1960, p. 141).

Interpretation of the meaning of constitutional provisions occurs in relation to the factual circumstances of the case. Do public attitudes toward segregation provide a factual basis for the Court to rule on the reasonableness of segregation legislation?

4.   Is the argument of self-evident harm applicable to racially separate schools that are not the result of state-mandated segregation?

5.   Do you agree with Clark that the role of social scientists in the school cases is "no more or less justified" than their role as consultants in industry? Is it valid to equate the role of social scientists to lawyers with the role of biologists to physicians?

3.6. SOCIAL SCIENCE ON APPEAL: THE BRANDEIS BRIEF

In the creation of law via the art of judicial interpretation, many different factors enter into the decision-making process: case precedents, legislative intent, the nature and limits of the judicial function, the social-political context, extralegal information from the social sciences and other disciplines, and not least, of course, the private values and philosophy of the judge. In examining the role and impact of social science in the adjudication of education equality, two opposing views have been considered: that the evidence "was not only crucial but . . . may well have been compelling" for the outcome (Rosen 1972, p. 172) and that the evidence was self-evident and unnecessary. We now turn to consider other possible roles of social science in lawmaking. We begin with an example drawn from the area of social welfare programs and then come back to *Brown*.

Due Process and the Brandeis Brief

Ironically, on Labor Day, 1905, an Oregon woman named Emma Gotcher worked longer than the statutory maximum of ten hours a day in a laundry. As a result, the owner, Curt Muller, was cited and fined $10. In those days, working women routinely put in thirteen hours or more per day at wages of $3 to $5 per week. The employer appealed his conviction all the way to the Supreme Court, arguing in his brief that Oregon's 10-hour law "destroy[s] the freedom of individual contract and the right of individual action." Thereupon, the National Consumers' League—a citizens' lobby for progressive causes such as the abolition of sweat shops—intervened in the case. It joined Oregon's Attorney General in inviting a leading New York lawyer to defend the statute. The lawyer, a one-time American Bar Association president and former ambassador to the Court of St. James, "could see no reason" why "a great husky Irish woman should not work in a laundry more than ten hours in one day, if her employer wished her to do so." One of the League's representatives at this meeting, a fiery woman labor activist who was known once to have slammed a door in Theodore Roosevelt's face, responded simply, in her most charming manner, "Why not, indeed?" (in Collins and Friesen 1983, p. 296). The League then turned to a Boston attorney, Louis D. Brandeis, a noted progressive advocate. He agreed to the defense of the legislation on the condition that the League gather (within a fortnight) extensive social, economic, and public health information on the effect of long working hours on women. He included this information in his brief on the grounds that "[legal] propositions are not considered abstractly, but always with reference to facts" (in Collins and Friesen 1983, p. 295). Thus, the stage was set for the contest between the laundress and the laundry owner, a contest that pitted progressive ideas against unfettered, free enterprise policies.

MULLER v. OREGON

208 U.S. 412 (1908)

Mr. Justice BREWER delivered the opinion of the court.

On February 19, 1903, the legislature of the State of Oregon passed an act (Session Laws, 1903, p. 148), the first section of which is in these words:

"SEC. 1. That no female (shall) be employed in any mechanical establishment, or factory, or laundry in this State more than ten hours during any one day. The hours of work may be so arranged as to permit the employment of females at any time so that they shall not work more than ten hours during the twenty-four hours of any one day." . . .

A trial resulted in a verdict against the defendant, who was sentenced to pay a fine of $10. The Supreme Court of the State affirmed the conviction, *State v. Muller*, 48 Oregon 252, whereupon the case was brought here on writ of error.

The single question is the constitutionality of the statute under which the defendant was convicted so far as it affects the work of a female in a laundry. That it does not conflict with any provisions of the state constitution is settled by the decision of the Supreme Court of the State. The contentions of the defendant, now plaintiff in error, are thus stated in his brief:

"(1) Because the statute attempts to prevent persons, *sui juris,* from making their own contracts, and thus violates the provisions of the Fourteenth Amendment, as follows:

" 'No State shall make or enforce any law which shall abridge the privileges or immunities of citizens of the United States; nor shall any State deprive any person of life, liberty, or property, without due process of law; nor deny to any person within its jurisdiction the equal protection of the laws.'

"(2) Because the statute does not apply equally to all persons similarly situated, and is class legislation.

"(3) The statute is not a valid exercise of the police power. The kinds of work proscribed are not unlawful, nor are they declared to be immoral or dangerous to the public health; nor can such a law be sustained on the ground that it is designed to protect women on account of their sex. There is no necessary or reasonable connection between the limitation prescribed by the act and the public health, safety or welfare." . . .

It is the law of Oregon that women, whether married or single, have equal contractual and personal rights with men. . . . Their rights in these respects can no more be infringed than the equal rights of their brothers. We held in *Lochner v. New York*, 198 U.S. 45, that a law providing that no laborer shall be required or permitted to work in a bakery more than sixty hours in a week or ten hours in a day was not as to men a legitimate exercise of the police power of the State, but an unreasonable, unnecessary and arbitrary interference with the right and liberty of the individual to contract in relation to his labor, and as such as in conflict with, and void under, the Federal Constitution. That decision is invoked by plaintiff in error as decisive of the question before. But this assumes that the difference between the sexes does not justify a different rule respecting a restriction of the hours of labor.

In patent cases counsel are apt to open the argument with a discussion of the state of the art. It may not be amiss, in the present case, before examining the constitutional question, to notice the course of legislation as well as expressions of opinion from other than judicial sources. In the brief filed by Mr. Louis D. Brandeis, for the defendant in error, is a very copious collection of all these matters, an epitome of which is found in the margin.[1] . . .

The legislation and opinions referred to in the margin may not be, technically speaking, authorities, and in them is little or no discussion of the constitutional question presented to us for determination, yet they are significant of a widespread belief that woman's physical structure, and the functions she performs in consequence thereof, justify special legislation restricting or qualifying the conditions under which she should be permitted to

toil. Constitutional questions, it is true, are not settled by even a consensus of present public opinion, for it is the peculiar value of a written constitution that it places in unchanging form limitations upon legislative action, and thus gives a permanence and stability to popular government which otherwise would be lacking. At the same time, when a question of fact is debated and debatable, and the extent to which a special constitutional limitation goes is affected by the truth in respect to that fact, a widespread and long continued belief concerning it is worthy of consideration. We take judicial cognizance of all matters of general knowledge.

It is undoubtedly true, as more than once declared by this court, that the general right to contract in relation to one's business is part of the liberty of the individual, protected by the Fourteenth Amendment to the Federal Constitution; yet it is equally well settled that this liberty is not absolute and extending to all contracts, and that a State may, without conflicting with the provisions of the Fourteenth Amendment, restrict in many respects the individual's power of contract. Without stopping to discuss at length the extent to which a State may act in this respect, we refer to the following cases in which the question has been considered: *Allgeyer v. Louisiana,* 165 U.S. 578; *Holden v. Hardy,* 169 U.S. 366; *Lochner v. New York,* 198 U.S. 45.

That woman's physical structure and the performance of maternal functions place her at a disadvantage in the struggle for subsistence is obvious. This is especially true when the burdens of motherhood are upon her. Even when they are not, by abundant testimony of the medical fraternity continuance for a long time on her feet at work, repeating this from day to day, tends to injurious effects upon the body, and as healthy mothers are essential to vigorous offspring, the physi-

---

[1] The following legislation of the States impose restrictions in some form or another upon the hours of labor that may be required of women. . . .
Then follow extracts from over ninety reports of committees, bureaus of statistics, commissioners of hygiene, inspectors of factories, both in this country and in Europe, to the effect that long hours of labor are dangerous for women, primarily because of their special physical organization. The matter is discussed in these reports in different aspects, but all agree as to the danger. It would of course take too much space to give these reports in detail. Following them are extracts from similar reports discussing the general benefits of short hours from an economic aspect of the question. In many of these reports individual instances are given tending to support the general conclusion. Perhaps the general scope and character of all these reports may be summed up in what an inspector for Hanover says: "The reasons for the reduction of the working day to ten hours—(a) the physical organization of women, (b) her maternal functions, (c) the rearing and education of the children, (d) the maintenance of the home—are all so important and so far reaching that the need for such reduction need hardly be discussed."

cal well-being of women becomes an object of public interest and care in order to preserve the strength and vigor of the race. . . .

Still again, history discloses the fact that woman has always been dependent upon man. . . . As minors, though not to the same extent, she has been looked upon in the courts as needing especial care that her rights may be preserved. . . . Even though . . . she stood, so far as statutes are concerned, upon an absolutely equal plane with him, it would still . . . justify legislation to protect her from the greed as well as the passion of man. The limitations which this statute places upon her contractual powers, upon her right to agree with her employer as to the time she shall labor, are not imposed solely for her benefit, but also largely for the benefit of all. Many words cannot make this plainer. The two sexes differ in structure of body, in the functions to be performed by each, in the amount of physical strength, in the capacity for long-continued labor, particularly when done standing, the influence of vigorous health upon the future well-being of the race, the self-reliance which enables one to assert full rights, and in the capacity to maintain the struggle for subsistence. This difference justifies a difference in legislation and upholds that which is designed to compensate for some of the burdens which rest upon her. . . .

The reason . . . rests in the inherent difference between the two sexes, and in the different functions in life which they perform.

For these reasons, and without questioning in any respect the decision in *Lochner v. New York*, we are of the opinion that it cannot be adjudged that the act in question is in conflict with the Federal Constitution, so far as it respects the work of a female in a laundry, and the judgment of the Supreme Court of Oregon is

Affirmed.

THE BRANDEIS BRIEF
Marion E. Doro

. . .

THE PHILOSOPHY OF THE BRANDEIS BRIEF

It is important to inquire about the nature of the social and economic views of Louis D. Brandeis as a means of understanding his "brief" and his consequent influence in American life. . . .

Brandeis sought social justice within the context of an "industrial democracy," which could be obtained only if laws were judged on the basis of the conditions which fostered them. Law should not exist for itself or be judged simply as an exercise of logic; to measure the law to fit a static structure of society was ill use of law in a dynamic society. Brandeis believed that law is properly used for the purpose of regulating relationships of men within society; he was fully aware that the relationships of men were in constant flux. . . . As society changes, these relationships change, and the law must be flexible enough to make these relationships productive. . . .

The broad basis from which he worked can be described as "institutionalism" or "contextualism." What was the economic and social context in which the problem had arisen? What factors contributed to its growth? How did existing legislation remedy the evil? What had been the experience of other states or countries with the same or similar problems? These factors he measured against his concept of the good society, where men were politically and economically free, where neither business nor labor were so powerful that they could dictate terms to one another.

Reprinted by permission of the publisher and William S. Hein and Company, Inc. Copyright © 1958 by the *Vanderbilt Law Review* [11 (1958): 784–899].

Business must prosper, but it could not sacrifice labor to do so; decent wages and working conditions, leisure time for thought and rest were labor's due. It was not enough that the laboring man be prosperous in material goods; he should have opportunities for growth and development. . . .

THE BRANDEIS BRIEF

TRADITIONAL ROLE OF LAW. At the turn of the century the function of interpreting the law was largely regarded as a matter of logic. The Court had accepted the theories of *laissez faire* economics, and the doctrine of evolution expounded by Herbert Spencer, to such an extent that any kind of regulation of private business was considered a violation of "liberty." Only exceptional circumstances which forced the attention of the members of the Court on matters other than the logic of the law would suffice to cause them to alter this view.

When it was recognized that political, economic and social considerations ought to be included in the process of determining the law, the legal tradition offered little means of placing such factual data before the judges. Thus decisions regarding matters of contract, in regard to labor or business regulation, were shaped by the personal philosophies of the Court members and the rigid pattern of law unleavened by knowledge of its relationship to society. Consequently the use of logic alone "resulted in proscribing any realistic test of legislative-judicial conclusions." The questions which needed to be asked, and answered, dealt with the social consequences of the law at issue and the consequences which could be expected to follow the judicial decision.

In reference to the first question regarding social consequences of the law, by what means were the judges to obtain the background of facts which led to its enactment? Many Justices felt this was the responsibility of the legislature, that law should be passed after legislative inquiry as to its needs had been made. Suppose, however, the Court would not accept the legislative decisions that the law was needed, how could the Court obtain sufficient data to discuss the law? In a sense this was the dilemma in *Lochner v. New York,* for the use of logic produced the rule that the restriction of employer-employee rights to contract over hours of labor violated due process. Justice Peckman refused to acknowledge that the health and welfare of employees provided any basis whatever for restricting business. It was clear that the Court would not uphold such legislation, *unless* it could be convinced that there was a reasonable relationship between such regulation and the public welfare.

It is at this crucial point in the history of constitutional development that Brandeis introduced his brief as "authoritative extra-legal data" to provide the Court with information as to the reasonable relation of the law to the object to be regulated. He differed from the other liberals of the day in the method he used. Rather than deal in invective and generalities, he examined the social ills in detail and offered concrete plans for social legislation. In effect, Brandeis was doing no more than taking cognizance of the facts of modern industrial life.

THE TECHNIQUE OF THE BRIEF: MULLER V. OREGON, 1908. As has been stated previously, the key to the Brandeis Brief was the *factual data* he submitted to show the *reasonableness* of the specific law at issue and the *relationship* of the regulation to the *needs* of society. In the briefs he presented, as a lawyer defending social legislation in four states, there is a definite pattern which he followed to prove his point. An analysis of these briefs and that data they include can be compiled into a single "brief" outline to illustrate Brandeis' methodology. The following construct represents the general pattern, omitting details and using the hours of labor for women as the subject.

Part First
  I. Legal Argument
    (Varying from two to forty pages, citing rules from supporting cases.)
Part Second
  II. Legislation Restricting Hours of Work for Women
    A. American Legislation
      1. List of States having such legislation
    B. Foreign Legislation
      1. List of countries having such legislation
    C. Summary of Combined Experience of Above Legislation
  III. The World's Experience upon which the Legislation Limiting the Hours of Work for Women is Based
    A. The Dangers of Long Hours
      1. Causes
        a. physical difference between men and women
        b. nature of industrial work
    B. Bad Effect of Long Hours on Health
      1. General injuries
      2. Problem of fatigue
      3. Specific evil effects on childbirth
    C. Bad Effect of Long Hours on Safety
    D. Bad Effect of Long Hours on Morals
    E. Bad Effect of Long Hours on General Welfare
  IV. Shorter Hours the Only Possible Protection
  V. Benefits of Shorter Hours
    A. Good Effect on Individual
      1. Health
      2. Morals
      3. Home Life
    B. Good Effect on General Welfare
  VI. Economic Aspects of Short Hours
    A. Effect on Output
      1. Increases efficiency
      2. Improves product
    B. Aids Regularity of Employment
    C. Widens Job Opportunities for Women
  VII. Uniformity of Restriction Necessary
    A. Overtime Dangerous to Health
    B. Essential to Enforcement
    C. Necessary for Just Application
  VIII. Reasonableness of Short Hours
    A. Opinions of Physicians
    B. Opinions of Employers
    C. Opinions of Employees
  IX. Conclusion

The outline of the brief indicates the wealth of the material Brandeis presented to the court to support his very brief legal argument. The evidence he produced relied, as Jerome Frank described it, on facts that "do not involve witnesses' credibility." It reveals a concern for why legislation was passed, what it is intended to do, and the benefits, including a dollars and cents consideration, which will accrue to business and labor alike. Thus it was an intellectual inquiry whose ends were social justice. It is so persuasive in content that the burden of proof placed on the opposing party in the suit is almost impossible to overcome. The simplicity and clarity of the organized evidence is an invitation to apply a pragmatic test to the reasonableness of the law, and in the final analysis it becomes an irresistible force. . . .

The first successful use of the brief before the Supreme Court of the United States came in 1908, when Brandeis argued in *Muller v. Oregon* to sustain an Oregon law establishing a ten hour day for women employed in "any mechanical establishment, or factory or laundry." The argument consisted of two pages of the legal rules applicable to the case, and was followed by 102 pages of evidence. . . .

The most interesting aspect of the case is that Brandeis relied on the rule of *Lochner v. New York* to prove his point. He began by agreeing that "the right to purchase or sell labor is a part of the 'liberty' protected by the fourteenth amendment" *but,* he pointed out, "such 'liberty' is subject to *reasonable restraint* by the police power of the state *if* there is a relationship to public 'health, safety or welfare.' " Brandeis concluded that the statute was "obviously

enacted for the purpose of protecting the public health, safety and welfare" and submitted "the facts of common knowledge of which the Court may take judicial notice" as proof of his argument.

The supporting evidence which followed the argument deeply impressed the Court, and Justice Brewer, who delivered the opinion, quoted extensively from it. . . . Thus, for the first time in the history of the Court, due process was determined, not just by consideration of abstract legal concepts, but also on the basis of the social and economic implications of the law at issue. . . .

A Note on Due Process and Judicial Review

Two concepts—due process and standards for judicial review—are basic in reading constitutional law cases.

MEANINGS OF DUE PROCESS

State "Police Power"

At the turn of the century, a wide range of social welfare and economic legislation was enacted (such as that in *Muller*) to ameliorate some of the ills and injustices occasioned by the development of industrial capitalism. The legislation was passed pursuant to the states' so-called police or regulatory power to direct activities of persons within their jurisdictions. The term "police" derives from the Greek "polis" which refers to the city-state or polity. Police power is another name for the inherent power of the state to further the public welfare (which is the end of all government), even at the expense of private rights. It is the power "to prescribe regulations to promote the health, peace, morals, education, and good order of the people, and to legislate so as to increase the industries of the state, develop its resources, and add to its wealth and prosperity" (*Barbier* v. *Connolly*, 1885, p. 31). Statutes were enacted to set maximum hours and minimum wages, improve factory working conditions, curb monopolistic practices, and so on.

Procedural and Substantive Due Process

The meaning of "due process" has never received comprehensive and detailed explication. The original idea antedates the Fourteenth Amendment, going back as far as the Magna Carta (Chapter 39): "No free man shall be seized or imprisoned or stripped of his rights . . . except by . . . the law of the land." In early common law, due process referred to fair process. The state could not infringe upon individual rights and liberties except by fair legal procedures. Due process meant procedural due process, although the exact procedure due by the government to an individual was not defined in advance, only on a case-by-case basis. When the Fourteenth Amendment was adopted in 1868, the Due Process Clause was designed to secure the political and civil liberties of emancipated blacks against state action.

By the 1900s, a new meaning was grafted on to the Due Process Clause. To counter the negative effects of industrialization, states began promulgating regulatory legislation under their police power. But the definition of police power contains within itself its own limitation, namely, that the regulations serve to promote the public welfare. Business interests affected by these statutes began challenging their constitutionality as an overreaching of the police power. From the 1890s to 1937, the courts often sided with business in striking down such federal and state legislation as a deprivation of "liberty" or "property" without the "due process of law" guaranteed by the Fourteenth Amendment. This was done by broadening the scope of the Due Process Clause to protect private property and economic (that is, substantive) rights from state interference. Thus, a business corporation was held to be a "person" entitled to Fourteenth Amendment protection (*Santa Clara County* v. *Southern Pacific Railroad Co.*, 1880). The notion of "substantive due process" was solely a judicial creation of that era.

For example, in the *Lochner*-type situation, when statutes set maximum work hours, they were invalidated as an unreasonable (that is, unfair) restriction upon an individual's economic "liberty" under the Due Process Clause. The "liberty" mentioned in that clause "means not only the right of the citizen to be free from the mere physical restraint of his person, as by incarceration [procedural due process], but the term is deemed to embrace the right of the citizen to be free . . . to enter into all contracts which may be proper, necessary, and essential to carrying out [his livelihood]" (*Allgeyer* v. *Louisiana*, 1897, p. 589). The reasoning was that an employee has the liberty or right to freely contract for his labor. A statute that forbade employers from requiring employees to work more than a maximum number of hours was said to restrict that liberty. Of course, since the terms of work (especially in industrial settings) were dictated by employers, often on a take-it-or-leave-it basis, the substantive due process interpretation favored employers, not workers.

Reasonableness in Due Process Adjudication

The test or standard for deciding whether the challenged legislation comports with due process (either substantive or procedural) is by application of the rule of reason. A statute is invalid if it is unreasonable or arbitrary. To determine reasonableness, a court examines whether the legislation serves some legitimate public end or purpose; whether the means contained in the statute are reasonably adapted toward that end; and whether the means are unduly oppressive or unfair on the persons being regulated (*Lawton* v. *Steele*, 1894, p. 137). These questions are easily stated but defy further analysis in the abstract. They are answered only in the context of the specific facts of each case under review. As applied to the maximum hours problem, the standard for review was articulated as follows: "Is this a fair, reasonable, and appropriate exercise of the police power of the state, or is it an unreasonable, unnecessary, and arbitrary interference with the right of the individual to . . . enter into those contracts in relation to labor which may seem to him appropriate or necessary for the support of himself and his family?" (*Lochner* v. *New York*, 1905, p. 56).

The rule of reason in due process adjudication, or in any other legal context, is essentially a flexible standard that involves subjective evaluations of mixed questions of law (that is, of legal precedents and value judgments) and of fact. In theory, a court does not review the substantive merits or desirability of the legislation; it is not a matter "of substituting the judgment of the Court for that of the legislature" (*Lochner*, p. 56). A court considers only the reasonableness of the challenged statute. In reality, in substantive due process cases, a court often sat as a super-legislature to evaluate the wisdom of legislation, and to strike down state laws because they did not "embody a particular economic theory . . . [such as] laissez faire" (Justice Holmes dissenting in *Lochner*, p. 75).

Substantive Due Process and *Laissez Faire*

What Social Darwinism was to social relations in the late nineteenth century, the *laissez-faire* philosophy was to economic affairs. After the Civil War, when the nation began industrializing on a continental scale, the economic watchword was noninterference. There was a general belief in the wisdom of not tampering with the "natural laws" of the marketplace. Government regulation of business or social affairs was thought to be unwise and, in any event, ineffective. Courts tended to decide cases in ways that facilitated economic growth. They began with the premise of the absolute right and inviolability of private property, and defended that right over the need to remedy the social dislocations resulting from industrialization. The primary judicial tool for blocking social and economic regulations was substantive due process. It provided the legal justification and framework for laissez-faire economics. These were the days when "economic regulation was fighting for its life" (Jaffe 1967, p. 991). "Liberal" state legislatures pressed for improved labor conditions while the "conservative" Supreme Court resisted the changes. It justified its intervention as a mere restoration of the "natural" economic order which had been disrupted by reform legislation. The result in *Muller* was a departure from the prevailing practice of invalidating such state actions. Oddly, although Justice Brewer was no friend of labor, he apparently felt sympathetic to "the work of a female in a laundry," as he noted at the end of his opinion.

Due Process and the Brandeis Brief

Into this climate came Brandeis with his innovative brief in *Muller*. Until then, "social legislation was supported before the courts largely *in vacuo*—as an abstract dialectic between 'liberty' and 'police power,' unrelated to the world of trusts and unions, of large scale industry and all its implications" (Frankfurter 1932, p. 52). Its introduction for the first time of extralegal data was widely acclaimed as "one of the few inventions in legal technique that can be identified in a profession that is not notable for wandering off the beaten path" (Freund 1963, p. 151).

Brandeis has been described as "the social scientist with a conscience" (Konefsky 1961, p. 152). He was an advocate of social reform and he introduced this brief to support progressive social welfare legislation. So long as the courts themselves did not profess any interest in the wisdom or merits of legislation, he could argue that the presence of the massive social and economic information contained in the brief constituted grounds for finding the legislation a reasonable exercise of the police power. The mere existence of these facts—not necessarily their validity—was prima facie proof that the state had not acted arbitrarily in enacting the legislation.

The initial success of government lawyers using the Brandeis brief to sustain legislative exercises of the police power was facilitated by the failure of opposing counsel to file briefs with contradictory data. It should be added that this type of brief was not always decisive. "It is clear that when the Court wished to uphold social welfare measures, it generally accepted the validity of facts contained in Brandeis briefs. But whenever it chose to reject such legislation, the Court found extra-legal data spurious and unconvincing" (Rosen 1972, p. 90).

Demise of Substantive Due Process

The era of judicial nullification of regulatory legislation came to an end in 1937 when the Supreme Court, under the threat of a New Deal judicial reorganization bill (the so-called Court-packing plan), recognized the demands for relief in a post-Depression society. In an about-face, the Court began upholding fair labor statutes and legislation against sweat shops and child labor, all as reasonable and justifiable actions under the police power. The official internment occurred in 1963 when a unanimous Court declared that it refused to return to the time when laws were voided because they were thought by judges to be "incompatible with some particular economic or social philosophy" (*Ferguson* v. *Skrupa*, 1963, p. 729).

Once the Court abandoned substantive due process, the original reason for a Brandeis brief also was removed. The brief was resurrected about a dozen years later by NAACP lawyers for use in a different setting and for a different purpose: to challenge racial discrimination under the Equal Protection Clause.

STANDARDS FOR JUDICIAL REVIEW

The Concept of Judicial Review

American courts perform several functions. They settle disputes between private parties (for example, a personal injury case), as well as between society and an individual (for example, a criminal prosecution). Another function, exemplified by the cases in this chapter, is to ascertain whether state officials have acted beyond the bounds of their constitutional powers. This function is judicial review. It is the foundation of our legal system and a major focus of our study. The courts have the power to review activities by another branch of government when a challenge to their constitutionality is raised in a particular case (Article 3, Section 2 of the Constitution; *Marbury* v. *Madison*, 1803). The final arbiter of constitutionality is, of course, the United States Supreme Court. "Judicial review," says Morris (1974), "is one of the outstanding contributions of the United States to the science and art of government" (p. 60).

In passing on the constitutionality of legislation or any other state action, courts rely on two principal standards for their review: the rule of reason and strict scrutiny. Whether a court assumes an "activist" or "restrained" posture in reviewing the actions of the coordinate branches of government is partly determined by the standard used.

Reasonableness Standard

Certain powers are delegated by the Constitution to the government. A legislature, for example, could enact a statute setting maximum work hours or restrict the sale of liquor to persons under the age of 21. An employer might then challenge the validity of the regulatory legislation under the Due Process Clause; a 20-year-old might attack the validity of the liquor law under the Equal Protection Clause as an invidious discrimination based on age. In either instance, the standard or test in reviewing the validity of the legislation is reasonableness, or the rule of reason. In the first instance, as already discussed, the statute would be sustained if it reasonably seeks to fulfill the legitimate purpose for which maximum hours were imposed. In the latter, it would be upheld if the classification bore some rational relation to a valid state objective (*McGowan* v. *Maryland,* 1961, p. 425). Moreover, courts will even hypothesize what their purposes are if they are not explicitly stated in the legislation itself. Regardless of the merits of the statute, if there is any rational basis or justifiable purpose for it, courts will not strike it down.

This is a relaxed standard of review because, in practice, it means considerable deference to the legislative prerogative. Wide latitude is allowed the other branches of government when the standard is reasonableness. The premise is that there are issues that are best left to the wisdom of officials who are kept in check by the electoral process. A court would intervene only when the challenged action is clearly arbitrary.

Consequently, a presumption of constitutionality is said to attach to legislation. It is assumed valid until proven otherwise. The burden of proof is placed on the plaintiff to prove its invalidity; it is not placed on the state to prove its validity. The plaintiff, as the challenger who seeks to disturb the status quo, has the burden of coming forward with evidence (legal and/or extralegal) to show that the legislation is open to rational question. Moreover, if a court is unpersuaded after hearing all the evidence—that is, the court is in equipoise—the plaintiff loses because the burden was not met. The plaintiff is the party that suffers the risk of nonpersuasion.

Strict Scrutiny or Compelling Interest Standard

The compelling interest standard, which is much higher than reasonableness, is triggered in either of two situations. One is when governmental action impairs the exercise of a fundamental right specifically guaranteed in the first eight Amendments (speech, press, religion, jury trial, and so forth), or one not expressly stated in the Bill of Rights but deemed important to preserve basic civil and political rights (such as interstate travel and voting). Under our constitutional system of government, the majority cannot via the political process take away any of these fundamental rights. They are placed above the rough-and-tumble of everyday politics and secured by the courts. Courts are more activist in the sense of being more likely to invalidate official actions that infringe upon these rights. There is a presumption of invalidity against such actions: "There may be a narrower scope for the operation of the presumption of constitutionality when legislation appears on its face to be within the specific prohibition of the Constitution, such as those of the first ten Amendments, which are deemed equally specific when held to be embraced within the Fourteenth" (*United States* v. *Carolene Products Co.*, 1938, p. 152, n. 4).

The standard is also applied when the state classifies people according to "suspect" criteria, specifically race and national ancestry. They are suspect because they are the grounds for governmental action targeted at those categories of people who are "saddled with such disabilities, or subjected to such a history of purposeful unequal treatment, or relegated to such a position of political powerlessness as to command extraordinary protection from the majoritarian political process" (*San Antonio Independent School District* v. *Rodriguez*, 1973, p. 28). The use of this standard when race is involved was first announced in connection with the Japanese-American relocation cases: "[A]ll legal restrictions which curtail the civil rights of a single racial group are immediately suspect. . . . This is not to say that all such restrictions are unconstitutional. It is to say that courts must subject them to the most rigid scrutiny" (*Korematsu* v. *United States*, 1944, p. 216).

When a court determines that the challenged state action encroaches upon a fundamental right, or that it classifies people on a suspect basis, it abandons the traditional principle of presumptive constitutionality. The burden no longer rests on the plaintiff to show the invalidity of the state action. Plaintiff need only make a prima facie (on its face) showing of invalidity, aided as it is by the presumption of invalidity. The burden is now up to the state to show a compelling or overriding justification for its action. This means that the courts will strictly scrutinize the legislation to see that it is precisely tailored to accomplish its purpose, and that there is no less drastic means of fulfilling it (*Dunn* v. *Blumstein*, 1972). As a practical matter, once this standard is used, the state action is very likely to be found unconstitutional. The Supreme Court, in consequence, has been reluctant to expand the range of fundamental interests and suspect classifications.

NOTES AND QUESTIONS

---

1.   At the time of the litigation, Muller would seem to have had an almost airtight Fourteenth Amendment challenge to the Oregon statute by reason of the *Lochner* precedent. How did the Court rule against Muller "without questioning in any respect the decision in *Lochner* v. *New York*"?

2.   Compare footnote 11 in *Brown* with footnote 1 in *Muller*, and their respective accompanying texts. What are some of their similarities and differences?
Note, too, the choice of words in both opinions. If segregated schools are "inherently unequal," and there is an "inherent difference" between the two sexes, are the extralegal authorities cited in the two footnotes really necessary to the disposition of both of these cases?

3.   What are the similarities and differences between the brief in *Muller* and the "social science statement" in *Brown*?

4.   We have already considered different views on the relevancy and necessity of the social science evidence in *Brown*. What other interpretations of the role of social science in the school desegregation problem are suggested by the following statement in *Bolling* v. *Sharpe* (1954), a companion case of *Brown*: "[C]lassifications based solely on race must be scrutinized with particular care" (p. 499).

5.   The extralegal information in *Muller* was presented by the proponent of the public welfare regulation; in *Brown*, by the opponent of school segregation. What is the legal significance of using that information for one or the other purpose? See generally Freund (1963, p. 152) and Pollak (1959).

6.   Doro, in his article, says that the Brandeis brief is "so persuasive in content" that it "becomes an irresistible force." But in arguing a minimum wage case, Brandeis conceded: "Each one of these statements contained in the brief in support of the contention that this is wise legislation might upon further investigation be found to be erroneous, each conclusion of fact may be found afterwards to be unsound—and yet the constitutionality of the act would not be affected thereby. This court is not burdened with the duty of passing upon the disputed [facts] . . ." (Argument in *Stettler* v. *O'Hara,* 1917; in Fraenkel 1934, p. 65).

     He never claimed that the facts were incontestable. Indeed, the "facts" in *Muller* were more in the nature of plausible hypotheses about the impact of long hours on the health and welfare of women than empirical findings of established reliability and validity. At best, the "facts" in a Brandeis brief were "nascent social science" evidence (Rosen 1972, p. 84).

     Granted the *relevance* of the extralegal data, why is a court "not burdened with the duty of passing upon" their adequacy or *weight*? For what legal purposes were the "data" offered if not for the truth of the fact asserted?

7.   The social science evidence in *Brown* can also be characterized as "nascent." The dolls studies and the opinion survey certainly were not beyond methodological impeachment. Yet, the Supreme Court opinion recognized the relevance of the evidence and seemed not to worry about the question of sufficiency or weight. Was the Court justified in not demanding a higher order of empirical proof? When would the use of "nascent" social research clearly be insufficient?

8.   Broadly speaking, courts consider two kinds of facts according to the function they are engaged in.

     The usual fare of judicial business is adjudicating disputes. This consists, in oversimplified form, in applying a governing rule of law to the facts of the dispute in order to reach a decision. The rule is a normative kind of major premise (*X*), and the conclusion (*Y*) follows if the facts (*A, B, C*) constituting the minor premise are proven. These facts are typically of a historical nature and concern the immediate party litigants; they are facts about who did what to whom, where, when, and how. "Were the brakes of the car functioning properly at the time of the accident?" "Has pretrial publicity prejudiced community attitudes toward the defendant?" These are examples of "adjudicative fact" that the trier of fact must decide (Davis 1958, section 15.03).

     Courts are reluctant to admit their other function, that of creating law, and when they do engage in judicial legislation, it is often said to be interstitial and elaborative. But as Justice Holmes (1881) early indicated with respect to the common law, "in substance the growth of the law is legislative. · . . . The very considerations which judges most rarely mention, and always with an apology, are the secret root from which the law draws all the juices of life. I mean, of course, considerations of what is expedient for the community concerned" (p. 35). This is all the more so in constitutional adjudication, which is judge-made law *par excellence*. In reviewing legislation and interpreting the Constitution, courts perform as a third legislative chamber (Hand 1958, Chapter 2).

     When a court is acting legislatively, it is deciding not just the immediate case before it, but also similar "cases" that may arise in the future. The decision is of interest not only to the adversaries but also to all others similarly situated. In judicial legislation, a court needs to be informed about facts beyond the current adjudicative issues. It needs to look at general social, economic, and behavioral facts that are in the realm of prediction and probability. "What are the psychological effects of segregated education?" "Do long working hours have a detrimental effect on the health and welfare of women?" These are questions of "legislative fact" (Davis 1958, §15.03). They look into the future; they are of concern to society as a whole, in addition to the particular litigants, because the possible legal consequences that might ensue therefrom would apply to all.

     There are, also, facts of a mixed nature: adjudicative facts with legislative fact implications. The results of the dolls test with the sixteen plaintiff children of Clarendon County, South Carolina, are an example. For purposes of the general classification scheme, these may be treated as mainly legislative facts. These are facts built upon a complex pattern of data and inference. The further removed they are from the immediate parties—that is, the more they deal with broad phenomena and trends—the more assistance a court will need (Note, *Harvard Law Review*, 1948). Our main concern is with the use of social science evidence to establish legislative facts in constitutional adjudication.

We can now carry a step further the basic syllogistic model of judicial decision-making (rule X, applied to facts A, B, C, results in decision Y). In a given case, the facts (minor premise), whether adjudicative or legislative, could be in dispute (for example, is the true state of affairs A, B, C or A, B, E?). Or the proper rule (major premise) to apply to the facts, once they are determined, could also be in question (for example, does rule X or rule Z govern?) The choice of rule (or choice of values, if you will, since legal rules embody normative considerations) will obviously affect the outcome of the case (decision Y or not-Y). Or both the facts and the governing rule could be in dispute.

There are four possible combinations of facts and rules, depending on whether they are disputed or not. They represent four principal ideal types—in the Weberian sense of theoretical constructs about reality—of judicial decision-making:

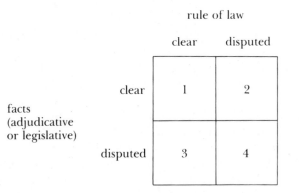

Query: In which cell(s) can social science evidence be used in judicial decision-making and for what purpose(s)?

3.7.   READING JUDICIAL OPINIONS

Reading judicial opinions is, obviously, unlike reading the social science literature. A charcoal outline of the structure of an opinion may provide some guidance in learning to read cases.

There are four main elements to any opinion: (1) the facts of the case (a statement of the circumstances underlying the controversy, usually found toward the beginning of the opinion); (2) the legal issue(s) or question(s) (the substance of the dispute, constituting the subject matter of the appeal); (3) the holding or decision (the resolution of the controversy, containing the rule or principle of law for which the case stands and which would govern like cases in the future); (4) the reasoning (an explication or justification of the decision, based on legal precedents, social policy considerations, extralegal facts, and/or other grounds).

Critical reading of opinions is an acquired skill. The aim is to learn to cut through the prose to get to the crux of the opinion and extract the proposition of law for which the case stands. In addition, given our particular interests and purposes, we also want to learn how empirical research is used (or not used) by a court in reaching its decision.

A useful tool in learning to read cases is "briefing." This refers to the preparation of a summary of the essential points of a case, resulting in a "case-brief." (It is not to be confused with an appellate brief, which consists of the written arguments of counsel submitted to an appellate tribunal.) The brief—or précis—of a case would consist of the aforementioned four headings, each followed by one or two short paragraphs. For our purposes, a fifth heading should be added: the role of social science in the case. The entire brief need not exceed one-half page, typed single-spaced.

Structure and Analysis of a Case

STATEMENT OF FACTS

The facts of a case are determined at trial. In a nonjury case, the trial judge is the fact-finder. He usually prepares a written and signed "Findings of Fact" that summarize his factual conclusions. They become the basis for the statement of facts presented by the appellate court in its opinion, unless during the appellate proceedings the findings are challenged by a litigant as being unsupported by the available evidence.

In a jury case, rarely are there separate findings of fact. The jury typically enters only a conclusion: guilty or not guilty, liable or not liable. On review, the appellate court summarizes the facts based on the evidence in the trial transcript (aided by the fact-summaries contained in the appellate briefs of both sides) and assumes that conflicting evidence was resolved by the jury in favor of the winning party.

It is important to stress that "the facts" recited in the appellate opinion do not represent a complete, coherent story of the dispute. They are, rather, a highly abstracted, distilled version of the raw events that occurred. From the time the dispute first arises to its description in an appellate opinion, the circumstances of the case are subjected to continued sieving and screening at each successive step in the proceedings. Initially, the attorneys select only certain facts from the totality of events as being relevant to legal adjudication. At trial, the evidence introduced to establish these facts is filtered through layers of exclusionary rules of evidence designed to safeguard procedural objectives such as relevancy and reliability. The trial judge further sifts through the admissible evidence to arrive at findings of fact. The appellate court then canvasses the trial record and selects certain facts for inclusion in the opinion as the "statement of facts." Since the decision has to subsume the particulars (the facts) of the case under general propositions (the rules or principles), the facts are described in abstract form. A specific fact is significant not in itself but only as a representative of a general category—Linda Brown, the plaintiff, is but a representative of black school children attending segregated schools. By now, of course, the statement may be a faint image of what happened in real life. Moreover, not all the facts in the opinion are necessarily relevant to the eventual decision. It falls to the reader to filter "the facts" to determine those that have legal bearing on the case.

"The facts" of the opinion, even if they bear little resemblance to the raw facts of life, are nonetheless critical for adjudication purposes. These are the facts that the court is adopting as the basis for decision, and we must treat them as if they constituted the complete and true record of the controversy.

To determine which are the legally relevant or significant facts—that is, those that affect the outcome of the case—one needs to read the entire opinion to have an idea of the legal issue before the court. There is a reciprocal relationship between facts and law. "The issues of fact arise out of the law," said Hart and McNaughton (1959, p. 61). The tangible equality of public schools, for example, is a relevant fact in *Brown* because of the *Plessy* doctrine that is at issue. On the other hand, "at the point of application of law, the issues of law also arise out of the facts" (p. 61). The psychological harm of segregation is also a relevant fact (leaving aside its weight or importance to the outcome) because it provides the basis for the new legal argument of intangible or psychological inequality under the Fourteenth Amendment. Thus, in trying to ascertain the legally relevant facts of a case, one has to engage in circular reasoning: One has to determine the legal rule or principle applicable to the facts and, simultaneously, one has to determine the (relevant) facts that make the rule or principle applicable in the first instance. This is one of the unique characteristics of case analysis and of legal reasoning generally.

Legal relevance is not an absolute quality; it is a matter of degree. Some facts may be undisputably relevant because the court expressly says so, or because it relies on them in the reasoning of the case. Others may be clearly irrelevant, even though they may be interesting and material by other (nonlegal) criteria. For example, in the South Carolina school case that led to *Brown*, the original plaintiff—a teacher and pastor—was fired from his job, shot at, sued on trumped-up criminal charges, and his house burned because he sought educational equality for his children. It was also the first time in the memory of the local inhabitants that a black person had ever filed suit against a white official, the school board chairman (Kluger 1977). These facts are not directly relevant to the legal issue and therefore do not appear in the statement of facts in *Brown* or in the lower court opinion. Finally, there are facts that fall in the middle of the relevance continuum. The impact of these facts on the decision is usually subject to dispute. The facts of footnote 11 in *Brown* are a classic example. It follows, then, that often there is no single, "correct" version of the significant facts of a case. What is significant can be subject to different interpretations.

After a summary of the relevant facts, the case-brief might include a short description of the procedural history of the case up to the time of the appeal; that is, which side won at the earlier stages of litigation and what relief was granted by the lower courts. For the purposes that we are reading opinions, a summary of the procedural posture of the case will be usually unnecessary.

THE LEGAL ISSUE(S) OR QUESTION(S)

Case analysis requires identification of the substantive legal issue(s) or question(s) presented for appellate review. Each issue in the case-brief should be stated in question form for which a yes or no answer can be given. For example, in *Brown* the Chief Justice stated as follows the question presented: "Does segregation of children in public schools solely on the basis of race, even though the physical facilities and other 'tangible' factors may be equal, deprive the children of the minority group of equal educational opportunities?" Notice that this statement incorporates the key relevant facts and the legal principle that is called into play by these facts.

Not all judges are so helpful as to clearly state the question before proceeding to answer it. It is then up to the reader to extract and frame the question from the body of the opinion. If the relevant facts are subject to dispute, then so can the formulation of the legal question since it, in turn, rests upon the facts. Indeed, the statement of the question is quite significant because the manner in which it is phrased may well predetermine the answer. It is not uncommon to find opposing counsel in their respective briefs defining somewhat differently the legal issue in the case. Even the court's own statement of the legal question, if expressly given, needs to be read critically. A court may not have stated the question adequately, or it may have failed to identify or even acknowledge other legal issues posed by the facts of the case, either by oversight or deliberately. In briefing a case, you should state what you think is the court's formulation of the issue. Then, if you find the court's formulation unsatisfactory, you can write down your understanding of the issue separately and at the end of the case-brief (for example, under a sixth heading consisting of your own notes and questions about the case).

THE DECISION OR HOLDING

The decision or holding is the court's answer to the legal question and can be stated in your case-brief in a single word: yes or no. The combination of the legal issue and the holding, stated in terms of the legally relevant facts, gives the proposition of law for which the case stands. For example, the principle of *Brown* is that racial segregation of children in public schools, even though the physical facilities and other tangible factors may be equal, deprives the children of the minority group of equal educational opportunities under the Fourteenth Amendment. This underlying principle of the decision is called the *ratio decidendi*.

There is no such thing in our judicial system as a single decision applicable to only a particular case. The reason no decision ever stands on its own is because, under our case law system, every decision subsumes the particular facts of a dispute under general propositions of law. These propositions may be established ones, as in the instance of legal precedents, or they may be newly created in the course of deciding the immediate case. In either event, the proposition of law would cover a whole class of similar disputes; otherwise, the decision rendered in the case would be deemed unprincipled—that is, arbitrary and without legal basis.

The underlying principle or rule of a case—a principle is simply a super-rule, one that embraces more specific rules; racial equality is a principle, whereas non-segregation in schools is a rule—may be broadly or narrowly read. A basic tenet in reading opinions is that the principle or rule should always be read narrowly, with reference to the specific facts of the controversy. Justice Roberts once likened the holding to a restricted train ticket that is good for only one train on a given day and at a specified hour. Llewellyn (1930) cautions, "What is not in the facts cannot be present for decision. Rules which proceed an inch beyond the facts must be suspect" (p. 47). Any language in the opinion that is broader than needed to state what the case stands for is not controlling law; it is not part of the holding. It is known as judicial "dicta"—wayside remarks, illuminating perhaps, but not binding on future cases.

For example, the holding of *Brown* concerns only the applicability of the *Plessy* doctrine to the public schools. It says nothing about its continued applicability in railway accommodations, public parks, or other segregated institutions. There is language that permits an expansive reading of the holding. Toward the end of the opinion, the Court talks about "the wide applicability of this decision." This is merely dictum, though it can be seized upon at a later date as a persuasive (but not binding) basis for contending that *Brown*'s principle should be expanded to other areas of society.

THE REASONING

An opinion consists of more than just the facts and the principled decision. The bulk of the opinion consists of the court's detailed explanation or reasoning for its decision. There are a number of grounds, or combinations thereof, that a court might rely upon in seeking to justify the case outcome. A principal basis is legal precedent. If there are cases with identical or similar facts to the present case, the propositions of law of those prior cases would be applied—the past speaks to the present, providing for stability and consistency in judicial decision-making. Of course, there could be a range of conflicting precedents (Llewellyn 1960, pp. 77–91) or a court might refuse to follow established authority in deciding the case before it. In such instances, other grounds must be given for the decision. These may include reference to historical practices, considerations of social utility, a balancing of normative values, reliance on social science information—in short, a whole range of rational (nonarbitrary) grounds other than legal authorities as such.

In briefing a case, you should summarize in a few sentences the court's rationale for its holding. In a separate section at the end of the brief, you may want to jot down your own evaluation and criticisms of the stated reasoning.

ROLE OF SOCIAL SCIENCE

"The great tides and currents which engulf the rest of men," Judge Cardozo (1921) once said, "do not turn aside in their course and pass the judges by" (p. 168). At least they should not. One criterion in selecting the cases reproduced in this book is that the legal issues implicated social "tides and currents" and that the opinions used or could have used pertinent social research evidence in addressing them. To the preceding four parts of the traditional case-brief, we would advise the student to include a fifth section that expressly focuses on the role of social science in the case. The purpose of briefing is not only to summarize a case but also to encourage active and critical reading of opinions. You may want to record your questions of the empirical assumptions made by the court, or sketch your ideas for empirical research based upon assertions made in the opinion.

Synthesis of Cases: Building the Apperceptive Mass

Cases are the building blocks of judge-made law. The first step in reading cases is to analyze and dissect them into their component parts: facts, issue, holding, reasoning, and role of social science. Case briefing, we have indicated, is a useful means for developing this analytical capacity so essential to legal thinking, as well as for providing summaries for review at the end of the course. The next step, after cases have been analyzed and briefed, is to pull them together into some kind of cohesive whole. The notes and questions in this book following the opinions are intended to guide in the analysis. The synthesis, however, is largely left to you.

A keynote of the case system is that no case occurs in a legal vacuum. A case becomes meaningful only when it is read in relation to the backdrop of other cases. As Judge Cardozo (1921) noted: "The implications of a decision may in the beginning be equivocal. New cases by commentary and exposition extract the essence. At last there emerges a rule or principle which becomes a datum, a point of departure, from which new lines will be run" (p. 48). Thus, doctrinal developments may not be obvious except over the long haul, after a series of cases have been adjudicated. Judges write opinions with the assumption that they will be read by those with the requisite background of information. This assumption obviously does not hold for students or for lawyers who are unfamiliar with the area covered by the cases. This is why after one has read a number of cases and developed a conceptual frame of reference, new cases will appear to blossom and old ones will acquire new significance. The same can be said, of course, about the reading of social research studies. The meaning and full import of a study is usually not apparent except in relation to other studies in that area and to the underlying theory or hypothesis that is being tested.

Case synthesis is the process of comparing and interrelating the holdings of different cases. Given cases of similar facts, do they result in similar outcomes? If not, can the different results be reconciled or harmonized in some principled way? Llewellyn (1930) has called case synthesis "the game of matching the cases" (p. 49). It is from the pulling together of diverse cases, rather than from a specific rule as found in a particular case, that one gains a perspective on how courts deal with a problem area. It is from this synthesis that one has a basis for anticipating how courts will dispose of future similar cases. For example, the principle that the state cannot separate or discriminate persons on account of race initially emerged not from any single case, but from a systematic collating of various desegregation cases (*Brown* and subsequent desegregation decisions in other areas).

Analysis involves examining cases one by one, and synthesis requires integrating them into an ordered pattern. Each case-brief should be prepared in terms of what the instant case contributes to what one already knows about the subject. Llewellyn (1930) describes case synthesis as enlarging one's apperceptive mass. This quaint concept, from the days when psychology was not yet divorced from metaphysics, refers to the totality of perceptions and impressions that constitute and control the mind. Each new input is not sorted into a separate mental compartment, but is assimilated into old ones to create this aggregate that is more than the sum of its parts. He exhorts: "[Y]ou require, each day, each week, to build your new material together with your old. You require to enlarge, above all you require to consolidate, your apperceptive mass in law. You require to bring to each new case and each new briefing the *whole* of the body of the knowledge you have that far met" (p. 56).

With experience, you will be able more readily to identify the relevant facts, pinpoint the legal issues, critique the reasoning of opinions, and sense when and how social science is used in law. You will be able to locate a case as one piece of a larger jigsaw puzzle. The fit might not be perfect, but there will be an existing background for the figure. Likewise, you may discover that even after reading a case many times, you are still finding a new meaning or point of view to it.

Thus, in addition to briefing individual cases, it is advisable from time to time—at the end of each two or three chapters—to integrate them in a separate outline. Because this book contains relatively few cases, the background needed for the synthesis is provided by the overview essays at the beginning of each chapter. Your responsibility is to trace the interconnections between the cases and the empirical readings within each chapter and between the chapters. In this chapter, for instance, there are common themes—in terms of both legal principles and social science applications to them—between school segregation and social welfare legislation. Later, as you progress through the book, you should compare these materials with, say, those on racial discrimination in jury selection (Chapter 7).

Learning through cases is a slow-moving process. Its momentum comes not from quickly canvassing a broad swath of readings, but from thoughtful analysis and synthesis of the few, purposefully selected cases and the associated social science literature. Our aim is to build and cultivate your apperceptive mass in law *and* social science.

REFERENCES

Allegeyer v. Louisiana, 165 U.S. 578 (1897).

Anastasi, A. *Fields of Applied Psychology.* New York: McGraw-Hill, 1957.

Baltimore v. Dawson, 350 U.S. 877 (1955).

Barbier v. Connolly, 113 U.S. 27 (1885).

Barron v. Baltimore, 33 U.S. (7 Pet.) 243 (1833).

Berea College v. Kentucky, 211 U.S. 45 (1908).

Bernstein, B. J. "Plessy v. Ferguson: Conservative Sociological Jurisprudence." *Journal of Negro History* 48 (1963): 196–205.

Bickel, A. "The Original Understanding and the Segregation Decision." *Harvard Law Review* 69 (1955): 1–65.

Black, C. L., Jr. "The Lawfulness of the Segregation Decisions." *Yale Law Journal* 69 (1960): 421–30.

Boas, F. *The Mind of Primitive Man.* New York: Macmillan, 1911.

Bolling v. Sharpe, 347 U.S. 497 (1954).

Brandeis, L. D. "The Living Law." *Illinois Law Review* 10 (1916): 461–71.

Briggs v. Elliott, 98 F. Supp. 529 (E.D. S.C. 1951).

Brown v. Board of Education of Topeka, 347 U.S. 483 (1954).

Byrnes, J. F. "Guns and Bayonets Cannot Promote Education." *U.S. News and World Report* 41 (1956): 100.

Cahn, E. "Jurisprudence." *New York University Law Review* 30 (1955): 150–69.

Cardozo, B. N. *The Nature of the Judicial Process.* New Haven: Yale University Press, 1921.

Civil Rights Cases, 109 U.S. 3 (1883).

Clark, K. B. "Desegregation: An Appraisal of the Evidence." *Journal of Social Issues* 9 (1953): 1–76.

———. "The Desegregation Cases: Criticism of the Social Scientist's Role." *Villanova Law Review* 5 (1959–60): 224–54.

———. *Prejudice and Your Child,* 2nd ed. Boston: Beacon Press, 1966.

———, and Clark, M. P. "Emotional Factors in Racial Identification and Preference in Negro Children." In *Readings in Social Psychology,* edited by T. M. Newcomb and E. Hartley. New York: Henry Holt, 1947.

Collins, R. K. L., and Friesen, J. "Looking Back on Muller v. Oregon." *American Bar Association Journal* 69 (1983): 294–8.

Cooley, C. H. *Human Nature and the Social Order.* New York: Charles Scribner's Sons, 1902.

Cumming v. County Board of Education, 175 U.S. 528 (1899).

Davis v. County School Board, 103 F. Supp. 337 (E.D. Va. 1952).

Davis, K. C. *Administrative Law Treatise.* St. Paul, Minn.: West, 1958.

Deutscher, M., and Chein, I. "The Psychological Effects of Enforced Segregation." *Journal of Psychology* 26 (1948): 259–87.

Dollard, J. *Caste and Class in a Southern Town.* New Haven: Oxford University Press, 1937.

Doro, M. E. "The Brandeis Brief." *Vanderbilt Law Review* 11 (1958): 784–899.

Dunn v. Blumstein, 405 U.S. 330 (1972).

Faris, R. E. *Chicago Sociology: 1920–1932.* San Francisco: Chandler, 1967.

Ferguson v. Skrupa, 372 U.S. 726 (1963).

Fraenkel, O. K., ed. *The Curse of Bigness: Miscellaneous Papers of Justice Brandeis.* New York: Viking Press, 1934.

Frankfurter, F. *Cases and Other Materials on Administrative Law.* New York: Corporation Trust, 1932.

———. "Reflections on Reading Statutes." In *The Supreme Court: Views from Inside,* edited by A. F. Westin. New York: W. W. Norton, 1961.

Franklin, J. H. "History of Racial Segregation in the United States." *Annals* 304 (1956): 1–9.

Freund, P. A. *The Supreme Court of the United States.* Cleveland: World, 1963.

Friedman, L., ed. *Argument: The Oral Argument Before the Supreme Court in Brown v. Board of Education of Topeka, 1952–55.* New York: Chelsea House, 1969.

Gayle v. Browder, 352 U.S. 903 (1956).

Gebhart v. Belton, 87 A.2d 862 (Del. Ch. 1952).

Graham, H. "The Anti-Slavery Backgrounds of the Fourteenth Amendment." *Wisconsin Law Review* 1950 (1950): 479–507.

Greenberg, J. "Social Scientists Take the Stand: A Review and Appraisal of Their Testimony in Litigation." *Michigan Law Review* 54 (1956): 953–70.

Gregor, A. J. "The Law, Social Science, and School Segregation: An Assessment." *Case Western Reserve Law Review* 14 (1963): 621–36.

Guinn v. United States, 238 U.S. 347 (1915).

Hamilton, A.; Jay, J.; and Madison, J. *The Federalist.* Washington, D.C.: National Home Library Foundation, 1938.

Hand, L. *The Bill of Rights.* Cambridge, Mass.: Harvard University Press, 1958.

Hart, H. M., and McNaughton, J. T. "Evidence and Inference in the Law." In *Evidence and Inference,* edited by D. Lerner. Glencoe, Ill.: Free Press, 1959.

Hazard, G. C. "Limitations on the Uses of Behavioral Science in the Law." *Case Western Reserve Law Review* 19 (1967): 71–76.

Heyman, I. "The Chief Justice, Racial Segregation, and the Friendly Critics." *California Law Review* 49 (1961): 104–25.

Hofstadter, R. *Social Darwinism in American Thought,* rev. ed. Boston: Beacon Press, 1966.

Holmes v. Atlanta, 350 U.S. 879 (1955).

Holmes, O. W. *The Common Law.* Boston: Little, Brown, 1881.

Howe, M. DeW., ed. *Holmes-Pollock Letters.* Cambridge, Mass.: Belknap Press, 1961.

Jaffe, L. L. "Was Brandeis an Activist? The Search for Intermediate Premises." *Harvard Law Review* 80 (1967): 986–1003.

Kalven, H., Jr. "The Quest for the Middle Range: Empirical Inquiry and Legal Policy." In *Law in a Changing America,* edited by G. C. Hazard. Englewood Cliffs, N.J.: Prentice-Hall, 1968.

Karst, K. L. "Legislative Facts in Constitutional Litigation." *Supreme Court Review* 1960 (1960): 75–112.

Kelly, A. "The Fourteenth Amendment Reconsidered." *Michigan Law Review* 54 (1956): 1049–86.

Kelly, A. H. "Clio and the Court: An Illicit Love Affair." *Supreme Court Review* 1965 (1965): 119–45.

Klineberg, O. "Cultural Factors in Intelligence Test Performance." *Journal of Negro Education* 3 (1934): 478–83.

Kluger, R. *Simple Justice.* New York: Alfred A. Knopf, 1977.

Kohn, J. "Social Psychological Data, Legislative Fact, and Constitutional Law." *George Washington Law Review* 29 (1960): 136–65.

Konefsky, S. J. *The Legacy of Holmes and Brandeis.* New York: Collier Books, 1961.

Korematsu v. United States, 323 U.S. 214 (1944).

Lawton v. Steele, 152 U.S. 133 (1894).

Llewellyn, K. N. *The Bramble Bush: On Our Law and Its Study.* Dobbs Ferry, N.Y.: Oceana, 1930.

———. *The Common Law Tradition: Deciding Appeals.* Boston: Little, Brown, 1960.

Lochner v. New York, 198 U.S. 45 (1905).

Marbury v. Madison, 5 U.S. (1 Cranch) 137 (1803).

Marshall, T. "An Evaluation of Recent Efforts to Achieve Racial Integration in Education Through Resort to the Courts." *Journal of Negro Education* 21 (1952): 316–26.

McDougall, W. *Introduction to Social Psychology.* Boston: J. W. Luce, 1909.

McGowan v. Maryland, 366 U.S. 420 (1961).

McLaurin v. Oklahoma State Regents for Higher Education, 339 U.S. 637 (1950).

Mead, G. H. *Mind, Self, and Society.* Chicago: University of Chicago Press, 1934.

Missouri ex rel. Gaines v. Canada, 305 U.S. 337 (1938).

Morris, A. A. *The Constitution and American Education.* St. Paul, Minn.: West, 1974.

Muller v. Oregon, 208 U.S. 412 (1908).

Münsterberg, H. *On the Witness Stand.* New York: McClure, 1908.

Murphy, W. F. "Marshaling the Court: Leadership, Bargaining, and the Judicial Process." *University of Chicago Law Review* 29 (1962): 640–72.

Muse, B. *Ten Years of Prelude: The Story of Integration Since the Supreme Court's 1954 Decision.* New York: Viking Press, 1964.

Myrdal, G. *An American Dilemma.* New York: Harper, 1944.

Newby, I. A. *Jim Crow's Defense: Anti-Negro Thought in America, 1900–1930.* Baton Rouge: Louisiana State University Press, 1965.

New Orleans Parks Association v. Detiege, 358 U.S. 54 (1958).

Note. "Social and Economic Facts—Appraisal of Suggested Techniques for Presenting Them to the Courts." *Harvard Law Review* 61 (1948): 692–702.

Plessy v. Ferguson, 163 U.S. 537 (1896).

Pollak, L. H. "Racial Discrimination and Judicial Integrity: A Reply to Professor Wechsler." *University of Pennsylvania Law Review* 108 (1959): 1–34.

Radke, M. T., and Trager, H. G. "Children's Perceptions of the Social Roles of Negroes and Whites." *Journal of Psychology* 29 (1950): 3–33.

Roberts v. City of Boston, 59 Mass. 198 (1850).

Rosen, P. L. *The Supreme Court and Social Science.* Urbana: University of Illinois Press, 1972.

San Antonio Independent School District v. Rodriguez, 411 U.S. 1 (1973).

Santa Clara County v. Southern Pacific Railroad Co., 118 U.S. 394 (1880).

Shelley v. Kraemer, 334 U.S. 1 (1948).

Slaughter-House Cases, 83 U.S. (16 Wallace) 36 (1873).

Smith v. Allwright, 321 U.S. 649 (1944).

Stettler v. O'Hara, 243 U.S. 629 (1917).

Strauder v. West Virginia, 100 U.S. 303 (1880).

Sumner, W. G. *Folkways.* Boston: Ginn, 1906.

Sweatt v. Painter, 339 U.S. 629 (1950).

Swisher, C. B. *The Supreme Court in Modern Role.* New York: New York University Press, 1954.

Tocqueville, A. de *Democracy in America.* Garden City, N.Y.: Doubleday, 1969.

United States v. Carolene Products Co., 304 U.S. 144 (1938).

University of California Regents v. Bakke, 438 U.S. 265 (1977).

van den Haag, E. "Social Science Testimony in the Desegregation Cases: A Reply to Professor Kenneth Clark." *Villanova Law Review* 6 (1960): 69–79.

Vose, C. E. *Caucasians Only: The Supreme Court, the NAACP, and the Restrictive Covenant Cases.* Berkeley: University of California Press, 1959.

Wechsler, H. "Toward Neutral Principles of Constitutional Law." *Harvard Law Review* 73 (1959): 1–35.

Wilkinson, J. H., III. *Serving Justice: A Supreme Court Clerk's View.* New York: Charterhouse Books, 1974.

Williams v. Mississippi, 170 U.S. 213 (1898).

Woodward, B., and Armstrong, S. *The Brethren: Inside the Supreme Court.* New York: Simon & Schuster, 1979.

Woodward, C. V. *The Strange Career of Jim Crow,* 2d ed. New York: Oxford University Press, 1966.

CHAPTER 4

Implementation and Expansion of Law: Case Study of Southern and Northern School Desegregation

4.1. INTRODUCTION AND OVERVIEW

The *Brown* decision led Thurgood Marshall, then chief counsel to the NAACP, to exult that school segregation in America would be eliminated within five years and that in another decade or so all forms of segregation would be stamped out (Kluger 1977, p. 714). To die-hard segregationists, however, May 17, 1954, was "Black Monday." The decision unleashed widespread resentment and bitterness in parts of the South. Ninety-six southern congressmen issued the "Southern Manifesto" vowing use of "all lawful means" to resist integration (Sarratt 1966, p. 41). Boards of supervisors in over half the counties of Virginia passed resolutions affirming their unalterable opposition to desegregated schools in the Commonwealth (Brief for Appellees, *Davies* v. *County School Board*, 1954). The Eisenhower Administration neither endorsed nor repudiated *Brown*. In Congress, powerful southern committee chairpersons filibustered civil rights bills. The implementation of *Brown,* therefore, had to come from the federal courts. After a fifty-week cooling-off period, the Supreme Court issued a decree calling for the admission to public schools on a "racially nondiscriminatory basis with all deliberate speed" (*Brown* v. *Board of Education*, 1955, or *Brown II,* to distinguish it from the earlier decision on the merits, or *Brown I*).

Throughout the latter half of the 1950s, the lower federal courts began to strike down segregation in nearly every other area of public life—public parks, beaches, golf courses, municipal housing developments, athletic events, and so forth—and the Supreme Court sustained them in per curiam decisions based on *Brown I*. The application of that decision to these other areas was problematic, because the opinion had focused narrowly on the role of public education in society and had avoided a more general racial classification analysis. The logic of invoking the detrimental psychological effects of segregated schools for the purpose of ending, say, segregated beaches, was not self-evident. The Court, however, was not troubled

107

by these flaws in reasoning. Over the next dozen years, the activist Warren Court in case after case struck down racial inequality in virtually every realm of American society.

Brown was the catalyst for the civil rights movement of the fifties and sixties. A few months after the implementation decree, the Montgomery, Alabama, boycott to protest Jim Crow in public transportation was begun by the Reverend Martin Luther King, Jr. One year later, the Supreme Court struck down segregation in buses (*Gayle* v. *Browder,* 1956), interring *Plessy* v. *Ferguson* (1896) at long last. In 1960, when four black college students were refused service at a lunch counter, the sit-ins began. Nonviolent marches and demonstrations swept across the South. "The Movement" reached its zenith in August 1963 when 200,000 citizens converged on the Washington Monument "to bear peaceful witness to the black American's petition for something called Freedom-Now. It may have been the most romantic single event of twentieth-century America" (*Newsweek,* September 10, 1963, p. 24).

The legislative and executive branches of the federal government joined in the drive for racial equality that the judiciary had initiated a decade earlier. In 1964, Congress passed the landmark Civil Rights Act and the Twenty-fourth Amendment banning the poll tax; the following year the Voting Rights Act was enacted. There is one ironic note to this chapter of American history. After *Brown,* desegregation proceeded relatively quickly and peaceably on all fronts except one: the public schools. The movement began with the schools, and when it was over the one institution that remained the most segregated was still the local schoolhouse. This chapter focuses on the on-going process of school desegregation and on the role of social science in that process.

We begin in section 4.2 with *Brown II* and the "Brandeis Brief" submitted by state officials. In a reversal of pre-1954 roles, segregationists relied heavily on social science evidence to perpetuate dual schools or delay desegregation, while integrationists now rested their case primarily on the newly established precedent. The post-*Brown* years in the South, described in section 4.3, unfolded in two stages: initially, token desegregation until the late sixties while the Supreme Court kept itself on the sidelines; then massive desegregation in the early seventies when the Court, its patience exhausted by the dilatory tactics and subterfuges to circumvent integration, strode back to center field. The culmination came with the announcement of desegregation guidelines in *Swann* v. *Charlotte-Mecklenburg Board of Education* (1971).

By the mid-seventies, more desegregation had been achieved in the South than in the ghettoes of the North and the barrios of the West. At the time of *Brown,* schools outside the South were not segregated by law; they were segregated in fact, supposedly as a result of "natural" demographic and social-economic changes. This distinction between de jure and de facto segregation provided the justification for the courts to refuse to apply *Brown* and its progeny to northern (including western) schools.

Faced with the prospect of regional discrimination, with one Constitution for the North and another for the South, the Supreme Court broadened the meaning of de jure segregation to encompass the particular circumstances of northern schools (section 4.4). By 1974, court-ordered desegregation was underway, although the line was drawn at merging inner city schools with outlying suburban districts (*Milliken* v. *Bradley*). Extensive and highly sophisticated social research was presented by expert witnesses on both sides in the northern litigation. Sections 4.5 and 4.6 deal with the effects of desegregation on academic achievement, self-esteem, racial attitudes, residential segregation, and the so-called white flight phenomenon.

The mixing of low income minority students with middle class white students led to second-generation problems: resegregation within the classrooms of desegregated schools (section 4.7). A disproportionate number of minority students scored lower on standardized achievement and intelligence tests and were relegated to inferior ability groups or tracks. Legal challenges to these ostensibly legitimate education placements served, in effect, to put the intelligence tests themselves on trial (*Larry P.* v. *Riles,* 1979). Section 4.8 examines the legal standards for evaluating these tests, which were derived from litigation on the racially discriminatory impact of personnel tests designed by industrial psychologists.

Today, school desegregation has come a long ways since *Brown.* Issues that were once clear are now almost hopelessly confused; the integration goals that seemed reasonable are now unreachable or have been transformed. In law and in social research, there is dissensus rather than consensus, complexity and variability rather than simplicity and certainty. It is against this changing background that we will examine in section 4.9 the role of social science in implementing and expanding the law.

4.2.   IMPLEMENTATION OF BROWN

After the first round of argument in *Brown I,* the Court requested further reargument on several issues, including on the following two questions:

4. Assuming it is decided that segregation in public schools violates the Fourteenth Amendment.

(a) would a decree necessarily follow providing that, within the limits set by normal geographic school districting, Negro children should forthwith be admitted to schools of their choice, or

(b) may this Court, in the exercise of its equity powers, permit an effective gradual adjustment to be brought about from existing segregated systems to a system not based on color distinctions?

5. On the assumption on which questions 4 (a) and (b) are based, and assuming further that this Court will exercise its equity powers to the end described in question 4 (b),

(a) should this Court formulate detailed decrees in these cases;

(b) if so, what specific issues should the decrees reach;

(c) should this Court appoint a special master to hear evidence with a view to recommending specific terms for such decrees;

(d) should this Court remand to the courts of first instance with directions to frame decrees in these cases, and if so what general directions should the decrees of this Court include and what procedures should the courts of first instance follow in arriving at the specific terms of more detailed decrees? [*Brown I,* 1954, pp. 495–96, fn. 13]

It is one thing to announce a constitutional entitlement; it is quite another to formulate and implement the mechanics of desegregation. The former is principally a matter of legal judgment informed, as appropriate, by social science analysis; the latter is mainly one of social engineering and political wisdom. More is at stake than simply the dismantling of dual school systems that have lasted for over half a century. Public schools are intertwined with other social institutions, and people otherwise indifferent to community affairs tend to take a proprietary interest in the neighborhood schools that their children attend. School desegregation affects the entire social fabric of the community.

Over one dozen briefs were filed for *Brown II* by appellants, appellees, and parties appearing as *amicus curiae* (the federal government, state governments, and private organizations). The South, in general, was unapologetic in its opposition to prompt desegregation. The briefs and oral arguments warned the Supreme Court not to press the wreath of thorns on the South's head. The Commonwealth of Virginia argued "the necessity for gradual adjustment" in light of intense public opposition. In *Brown I*, it had scoffed at the social science evidence presented by the plaintiffs; now, it resisted a desegregation decree on the grounds of insufficient social science information:

> [T]he facts of record relate only to the effect of *segregation*; what any detailed decree entered must be based on is evidence as to the effect of *integration*. They are very different facts; they require very different expert testimony to determine. But none of this evidence is now of record. [Brief for Appellees, *Davis* v. *County School Board*, 1954]

The distinction made in this argument would reappear some twenty years later in the northern school desegregation litigation. The State of Florida presented its own "social science appendix" to its brief (reproduced below) in support of gradual desegregation. There were hints of defiance in the oral arguments. An attorney for Clarendon County, South Carolina, responded as follows to a question by Chief Justice Warren regarding future compliance: "[I] would have to tell you that right now we would not conform [to any Supreme Court decree]—we would not send our white children to the Negro schools" (in Kluger 1977, p. 732).* Others sounded a more subdued note. The Attorney General of Texas said, "Texas loves its Negro people, and Texas will solve their problems in its own way" (in Kluger 1977, p. 734).

The NAACP again placed Kenneth Clark in charge of marshaling the social science evidence. The compilation took up an entire issue of the *Journal of Social Issues* (Clark 1953), and its principal findings were incorporated into the text of the NAACP brief:

> The underlying assumption [of state officials]—that change in attitude must precede change in action—is itself at best a highly questionable one. There is a considerable body of [social psychological] evidence to indicate that attitude may itself be influenced by situation and that, where the situation demands that an individual act as if he were not prejudiced, he will so act, despite the continuance, at least temporarily, of the prejudice. [Brief for Appellants, *Brown* v. *Board of Education*, 1954]

Clark also distilled from the research literature five conditions for peaceful and effective desegregation. Curiously, they were cited (without attribution) in the "Brandeis Brief" of Florida in support of gradual desegregation! The NAACP concluded by urging the Court to mandate desegregation within one year. The battlelines for

---

*Reprinted by permission of the publisher. Copyright ©1977 by Alfred A. Knopf, Inc.

Brown II were thus clearly drawn: a forthwith, iron-fisted decree or a leisurely, sweet-reasonableness approach.

AMICUS CURIAE BRIEF OF THE ATTORNEY GENERAL OF FLORIDA IN THE SUPREME COURT OF THE UNITED STATES, OCTOBER TERM 1954, IN BROWN v. BOARD OF EDUCATION OF TOPEKA

Appendix A: Results of a Survey of Florida Leadership Opinion on the Effects of the U. S. Supreme Court Decision of May 17, 1954 Relating to Segregation in Florida Schools

INTRODUCTION

. . .

In anticipation of the preparation of a brief for submission in response to this invitation, the Attorney General of the State of Florida requested the assistance of social scientists and other educators in compiling facts concerning the problems which the State of Florida would encounter in complying with the decision of the Court.

This is their report. . . .

THE REPORT AND THE CONCLUSIONS*

Just as the effects of segregation, held by the Court to be discriminatory, are essentially psychological, the problems of desegregation are also social and psychological as much as they are legal. . . .

[The purpose of the report was to predict "the problems which might arise if desegregation of public schools were undertaken." The data consisted of "expressed attitudes of various groups of leaders, both white and Negro, toward the court's decision and toward the possible implementation of it in Florida." Opinion

questionnaires were mailed to nine groups of white leaders and two groups of black leaders throughout the state. The white groups were Florida peace officers, school principals, PTA presidents, school board members, local judges and prosecutors, newspaper editors, radio station managers, state legislators, and ministers. The black groups were school principals and PTA presidents. A total of 7749 questionnaires were mailed; 51 percent were returned in usable form. The sample of black respondents was 266 (pp. 116, 135). Ed.'s note.]

GENERAL CONCLUSIONS

1. On the basis of data from all relevant sources included in this study, it is evident that in Florida white leadership opinion with reference to the Supreme Court's decision is far from being homogeneous. Approximately three-fourths of the white leaders polled disagree, in principle, with the decision. There are approximately 30 percent who violently disagree with the decision to the extent that they would refuse to cooperate with any move to end segregation or would actively oppose it. While the majority of white persons answering opposed the decision, it is also true that a large majority indicated they were willing to do what the courts and school officials decided.*

2. A large majority of the Negro leaders acclaim the decision as being right.

---

*Prepared by Dr. Lewis Killian, Department of Sociology, Florida State University. [See also Killian (1956). Ed's note.]

---

*[For example, percentage agreeing/disagreeing with *Brown* among white groups: principals, 52.9/40.4; PTA presidents, 29.6/66.1; editors, 50.0/42.4; legislators, 31.6/64.6. From Table 3, p. 138.

Percentage willing/unwilling to comply with Court order among white groups: principals, 84.5/13.6; PTA presidents, 51.2/46.1; editors, 70.3/26.3; legislators, 50.6/48.1. From Table 4, p. 139. The figures do not total 100 percent for each group because of "neutral" opinion or missing responses. Ed.'s note.]

3. Only a small minority of leaders of both races advocate immediate, complete desegregation. White leaders, if they accept the idea that segregation should be ended eventually, tend to advocate a very gradual, indefinite transition period, with a preparatory period of education. Negroes tend to advocate a gradual transition, but one beginning soon and lasting over a much shorter period of time*. . . .

4. [R]egional, county and community variations in responses to questionnaires and interviews are sufficiently marked to suggest that in some communities desegregation could be undertaken now if local leaders so decided, but that in others widespread social disorder would result from immediate steps to end segregation. There would be problems, of course, in any area of the state, but these would be vastly greater in some areas than in others.

5. While a minority of both white and Negro leaders expect serious violence to occur if desegregation is attempted, there is a widespread lack of confidence in the ability of peace officers to maintain law and order if serious violence does start. This is especially true of the peace officers themselves, except in Dade County. This has important implications. While it is true that expressed attitudes are not necessarily predictive of actual behavior, there seems little doubt that there is a minority of whites who would actively and violently resist desegregation, especially immediate desegregation. It has been concluded from the analysis of experience with desegregation in other areas, "A small minority may precipitate overt resistance or violent opposition to desegregation in spite of gen-eral acceptance or accommodation by the majority."[2]

6. Opposition of peace officers to desegregation, lack of confidence in their ability to maintain law and order in the face of violent resistance, and the existence of a positive relationship between these two opinions indicates that less than firm, positive action to prevent public disorder might be expected from many of the police, especially in some communities. Elected officials, county and school, also show a high degree of opposition. Yet it has been pointed out, again on the basis of experience in other states, that the accomplishment of efficient desegregation with a minimum of social disturbance depends upon:

A. A clear and unequivocal statement of policy by leaders with prestige and other authorities;

B. Firm enforcement of the changed policy by authorities and persistence in the execution of this policy in the face of initial resistance;

C. A willingness to deal with violations, attempted violations, and incitement to violations by a resort to the law and strong enforcement action;

D. A refusal of the authorities to resort to, engage in or tolerate subterfuges, gerrymandering or other devices for evading the principles and the fact of desegregation;

E. An appeal to the individuals concerned in terms of their religious principles of brotherhood and their acceptance of the American traditions of fair play and equal justice. [These five points are quoted from Clark, *supra* note 2, p. 54. Ed.'s note.]

It may be concluded that the absence of a firm, enthusiastic public policy of making desegregation effective would create the type of situation in which at-

---

*[For example, percentage favoring immediate/very gradual/somewhat gradual desegregation among white groups: principals, 3.1/71.7/19.5; PTA presidents, 4.3/65.1/13.7; editors, 5.1/60.2/19.5; legislators, 11.4/49.4/17.7. Among black groups: principals, 9.8/31.6/55.7; PTA presidents, 13.9/26.7/46.5. From Table 9, p. 144. Ed.'s note.]

2. Kenneth B. Clark, "Findings," *Journal of Social Issues,* IX, No. 4 (1953), 50.

titudes would be most likely to be translated into action.

7. In view of white feelings that immediate desegregation would not work and that to require it would constitute a negation of local autonomy, it may be postulated that the chances of developing firm official and, perhaps, public support for any program of desegregation would be increased by a decree which would create the feeling that the Court recognizes local problems and will allow a gradual transition with some degree of local determination.

8. There is a strong likelihood that many white children would be withdrawn from public schools by their parents and sent to private schools. It seems logical, however, that this practice would be confined primarily to families in the higher income brackets. As a result, a form of socio-economic class segregation might be substituted for racial segregation in education. . . .

BROWN v. BOARD OF EDUCATION OF TOPEKA [BROWN II]

349 U.S. 294 (1955)

Mr. Chief Justice WARREN delivered the opinion of the Court.

These cases were decided on May 17, 1954. The opinions of that date, declaring the fundamental principle that racial discrimination in public education is unconstitutional, are incorporated herein by reference. All provisions of federal, state, or local law requiring or permitting such discrimination must yield to this principle. There remains for consideration the manner in which relief is to be accorded.

Because these cases arose under different local conditions and their disposition will involve a variety of local problems, we requested further argument on the question of relief. In view of the nationwide importance of the decision, we invited the Attorney General of the United States and the Attorneys General of all states requiring or permitting racial discrimination in public education to present their views on that question. The parties, the United States, and the States of Florida, North Carolina, Arkansas, Oklahoma, Maryland, and Texas filed briefs and participated in the oral argument.

These presentations were informative and helpful to the Court in its consideration of the complexities arising from the transition to a system of public education freed of racial discrimination. The presentations also demonstrated that substantial steps to eliminate racial discrimination in public schools have already been taken, not only in some of the communities in which these cases arose, but in some of the states appearing as *amici curiae,* and in other states as well. Substantial progress has been made in the District of Columbia and in the communities in Kansas and Delaware involved in this litigation. The defendants in the cases coming to us from South Carolina and Virginia are awaiting the decision of this Court concerning relief.

Full implementation of these constitutional principles may require solution of varied local school problems. School authorities have the primary responsibility for elucidating, assessing, and solving these problems; courts will have to consider whether the action of school authorities constitutes good faith implementation of the governing constitutional principles. Because of their proximity to local conditions and the possible need for further hearings, the courts which originally heard these cases can best perform this judicial appraisal. Accordingly, we believe it appropriate to remand the cases to those courts.

In fashioning and effectuating the decrees, the courts will be guided by equitable principles. Traditionally, equity has been characterized by a practical flexibility in shaping its remedies and by a facility for adjusting and reconciling public and private needs. These cases call for the exercise of these traditional attributes of equity power. At stake is the personal interest of the plaintiffs in admission to public schools as soon as practicable on a nondiscriminatory basis. To effectuate this interest may call for elimination of a variety of obstacles in making the transition to school systems operated in accordance with the constitutional principles set forth in our May 17, 1954, decision. Courts of equity may properly take into account the public interest in the elimination of such obstacles in a systematic and effective manner. But it should go without saying that the vitality of these constitutional principles cannot be allowed to yield simply because of disagreement with them.

While giving weight to these public and private considerations, the courts will require that the defendants make a prompt and reasonable start toward full compliance with our May 17, 1954, ruling. Once such a start has been made, the courts may find that additional time is necessary to carry out the ruling in an effective manner. The burden rests upon the defendants to establish that such time is necessary in the public interest and is consistent with good faith compliance at the earliest practicable date. To that end, the courts may consider problems related to administration, arising from the physical condition of the school plant, the school transportation system, personnel, revision of school districts and attendance areas into compact units to achieve a system of determining admission to the public schools on a nonracial basis, and revision of local laws and regulations which may be necessary in solving the foregoing problems. They will also consider the adequacy of any plans the defendants may propose to meet these problems and to effectuate a transition to a racially nondiscriminatory school system. During this period of transition, the courts will retain jurisdiction of these cases.

The judgments below, except that in the Delaware case, are accordingly reversed and the cases are remanded to the District Courts to take such proceedings and enter such orders and decrees consistent with this opinion as are necessary and proper to admit to public schools on a racially nondiscriminatory basis with all deliberate speed the parties to these cases. . . .

It is so ordered.

NOTES AND QUESTIONS

---

1. *Brown II* begins by restating "the fundamental principle" of *Brown I*. Is it, in fact, an accurate restatement of the 1954 holding?

2. In *Brown I*, the Chief Justic had exhibited judicial statesmanship. In *Brown II*, faced with a politically explosive issue and lacking any precedents for guidance, he strove to reach a Solomonic solution. He treaded a thin line between resoluteness and accommodation on the question of timing. On the one hand, he ordered a "prompt and reasonable start" to desegregation and refused to let the Constitution yield to public opposition; on the other, he proposed no fixed date for completion, repeatedly deferred to "local conditions" and "local problems," and agreed to grant "additional time" as necessary. The formula used for this compromise was "all deliberate speed"—a phrase that combines opposite ideas for epigrammatic effect. On balance, was the baby split exactly down the middle?

3. The Supreme Court avoided stepping into the role of a super–school board. It gave the primary responsibility for desegregation to the local school authorities, supervised by the local federal judges. It urged the South to submit its own desegregation plans. Control, then, was placed in the hands of southerners themselves. The Court sought to induce compliance by persuasion and mutal participation rather than by judicial fiat. Perhaps the Court sensed that, in the long run, only the white South could truly deliver its fellow black citizens from inequality. Maybe the Court felt that the best it could do at that time was to declare the wrongfulness of a state-imposed caste system and then let the people who supported it figure out a way to dismantle it.

4.   Guidelines were given to the school boards but none to the reviewing federal courts. The latter were told only to be "guided by equitable principles." Consequently, desegregation was to proceed on a case-by-case basis by striking a balance between individual and community interests.

Now, with the benefit of some thirty years of hindsight, would you say that the Court decided the issues of the mechanics of desegregation—when, who, how—wisely in *Brown II*?

5.   Despite the extensive reliance on social science evidence by both sides in there respective briefs, there was no mention of it at all in the *Brown II* opinion. Why?

4.3.   POST-BROWN SOUTHERN SCHOOL DESEGREGATION

For a quarter of a century after *Brown I*, nearly every school desegregation lawsuit arose in the South. The existence of a constitutional violation was not at issue at this time. It had been disposed of by the 1954 decision. The litigated question pertained to the remedy for that violation—what was the nature and extent of corrective action that could be ordered by the courts? *Brown II* had been purposely vague on this matter. The history of southern school desegregation unfolded in two stages: from token desegregation (1955–67) to massive desegregation (1968–72) (Read 1975; Wilkinson 1978).

Token Desegregation

The federal district courts, set adrift without any clear mandate other than to exercise their equity power, were beset by demands from both sides: black plaintiffs sought desegregation with "speed," while school officials urged that desegregation be "deliberate." The Supreme Court stayed above the fray, content to observe from the sidelines. It would be over a decade before the Court intervened to amplify the mandate.

The most important lower court interpretation of *Brown II* occurred in the Clarendon County, South Carolina, case that was remanded for implementation. In *Briggs* v. *Elliott* (1955), Judge Parker wrote:

> [I]t is important that we point out exactly what the Supreme Court has decided and what it has not decided in this case. It has not decided that the federal courts are to take over or regulate the public schools of the states. It has not decided that the states must mix persons of different races in the schools or must require them to attend schools or must deprive them of the right of choosing the schools they attend. What it has decided, and all that it has decided, is that a state may not deny to any person on account of race the right to attend any school that it maintains. . . . Nothing in the Constitution or in the decision takes away from the people freedom to choose the schools they attend. The Constitution, in other words, does not require integration. It merely forbids discrimination. [p. 777]

The "Parker Doctrine" became the major stumbling block to desegregation. Its thesis—that integration and desegregation are descriptive of two different concepts—served to deflect the impact of *Brown* without outright defiance. It provided a legal underpinning for tokenism until it was finally repudiated by the Fifth Circuit in 1967 (*U.S.* v. *Jefferson County Board of Education*).

Throughout the remainder of the fifties and into the sixties, "all deliberate speed" came to mean "all conceivable delay." Desegregation litigation was a disheartening process, mired in delays and obstructions that were countenanced by some federal district court judges. The example of examples was the New Orleans school case. Over a ten-year period, there were forty-one separate judicial decisions reviewing the validity of forty-two statutes (Inger 1969). Even the token desegregation of the Little Rock, Arkansas, high school in 1957 required the help of federal troops. It was one of the most serious federal-state confrontations in history. The Supreme Court, in what is perhaps the only opinion personally signed by all nine justices, declared that no opposition, however intense, would be allowed to block the implementation of *Brown*. It again stopped short, however, of issuing concrete guidelines (*Cooper* v. *Aaron,* 1958).

In addition to proceeding "deliberately," state officials devised two principal means for resisting integration. One was the promulgation of pupil placement laws. Students were initially assigned to segregated schools, and then requests for transfers were considered on an individual basis according to nonracial criteria such as aptitude test scores, the "psychological effect upon the [transferring] pupil," "the possibility or threat of friction or disorder among pupils," "the possibility of breaches of the peace or ill-will . . . within the community," and so on (Alabama Code, Titles 52–56, §61(4), 1960). These laws were initially sustained as constitutional on their face because of state discretion in matters of educational policy. When it became clear, however, that they were used to obstruct desegregation, the courts struck them down on the ground that the initial assignment was based on race.

These laws were succeeded by freedom-of-choice plans. Each student could exercise a choice of school subject to space availability. For many blacks, there was no real choice as revealed in the following court description:

> There followed . . . numerous acts of violence and threats directed against Negro members of the community, particularly those requesting transfers of their children into formerly all-white schools. Shots were fired into houses, oil was poured into wells. . . . [A]n implicit threat was carried home to everyone by publication of the names of Negro applicants for transfer. [*Coppedge* v. *Franklin County Board of Education,* 1968, p. 411]

By 1965, about 57% of voluntary desegregation plans in the South were based on freedom-of-choice (U.S. Commission on Civil Rights 1966, p. 29).

Massive Desegregation

The Supreme Court finally intervened in 1968 in *Green* v. *County School Board* to declare at an end the days of token desegregation. For over a dozen years, desegregation was borne by the few black children "courageous enough to break with tradition" (p. 436). Hereafter, the school boards have "the affirmative duty to take whatever steps to convert to a unitary system in which racial discrimination would be eliminated root and branch" (pp. 437–38). They must come forward "with a plan that promises realistically to work, and promises realistically to work now" (p. 439). Freedom-of-choice plans, as they were then operated, were invalidated. For the first time, the Court pointed to an immediate integration remedy rather than to merely non-segregation. A year later, it ruled that "[c]ontinued operation of segregated schools under a standard of allowing 'all deliberate speed' for desegregation is no longer constitutionally permissible" (*Alexander* v. *Holmes County Board of Education*, 1969, p. 20).

The result was a new wave of litigation to test the viability of new freedom-or-choice plans and to clarify the meaning of a "unitary system" and of plans that "work." Attention increasingly fastened on the racial proportions in the student bodies. The Court was pressed to amplify its guidelines and it eventually attempted to do so in *Swann* v. *Charlotte-Mecklenburg Board of Education* (1971).

SWANN v. CHARLOTTE-MECKLENBURG BOARD OF EDUCATION

402 U.S. 1 (1971)

Mr. Chief Justice BURGER delivered the opinion of the Court. . . .

This case and those argued with it arose in States having a long history of maintaining two sets of schools in a single school system deliberately operated to carry out a governmental policy to separate pupils in schools solely on the basis of race. That was what Brown v. Board of Education was all about. These cases present us with the problem of defining in more precise terms than heretofore the scope of the duty of school authorities and district courts in implementing *Brown I* and the mandate to eliminate dual systems and establish unitary systems at once. . . .

I.

[The Charlotte-Mecklenburg school system encompasses Charlotte, North Carolina, and its environs. During 1968–69, about 71 percent of the students were white and 29 percent black. Two-thirds of the black students in Charlotte attended schools "which were totally Negro or more than 99% Negro." The federal district court rejected as unsatisfactory three desegregation plans proposed by the school board. It then accepted a plan, prepared at the court's request by an educational expert, which would have involved extensive busing and promised to produce student bodies that were 9 percent to 38 percent black. The Fourth Circuit Court of Appeals rejected this plan as an unreasonable burden on the schools and its pupils. Ed.'s note.]

II.

[W]e should now try to amplify guidelines, however incomplete and imperfect, for the assistance of school authorities and courts. The failure of local authorities to meet their constitutional obligations aggravated the massive problem of converting from the state-enforced discrimination of racially separate school systems. This process has been rendered more difficult by changes since 1954 in the structure and patterns of communities, the growth of student population, movement of families, and other changes, some of which had marked impact on school planning, sometimes neutralizing or negating remedial action before it was fully implemented. . . .

III.

The objective today remains to eliminate from the public schools all vestiges of state-imposed segregation. . . .

If school authorities fail in their

affirmative obligations . . . judicial authority may be invoked. Once a right and a violation have been shown, the scope of a district court's equitable powers to remedy past wrongs is broad, for breadth and flexibility are inherent in equitable remedies. . . .

In seeking to define even in broad and general terms how far this remedial power extends it is important to remember that judicial powers may be exercised only on the basis of a constitutional violation. Remedial judicial authority does not put judges automatically in the shoes of school authorities whose powers are plenary. Judicial authority enters only when local authority defaults. . . .

IV.

We turn now to the problem of defining with more particularity the responsibilities of school authorities in desegregating a state-enforced dual school system in light of the Equal Protection Clause. . . .

In *Green*, we pointed out that existing policy and practice with regard to faculty, staff, transportation, extracurricular activities, and facilities were among the most important indicia of a segregated system. . . . Independent of student assignment, where it is possible to identify a "white school" or a "Negro school" simply by reference to the racial composition of teachers and staff, the quality of school buildings and equipment, or the organization of sports activities, a *prima facie* case of violation of substantive constitutional rights under the Equal Protection Clause is shown.

When a system has been dual in these respects, the first remedial responsibility of school authorities is to eliminate invidious racial distinctions. . . .

The construction of new schools and the closing of old ones are two of the most important functions of local school authorities and also two of the most complex. . . . Over the long run, the conse-

quences of the choices will be far reaching. People gravitate toward school facilities, just as schools are located in response to the needs of people. The location of schools may thus influence the patterns of residential development of a metropolitan area and have important impact on composition of inner-city neighborhoods.

In the past, choices in this respect have been used as a potent weapon for creating or maintaining a state-segregated school system. In addition to the classic pattern of building schools specifically intended for Negro or white students, school authorities have sometimes, since *Brown*, closed schools which appeared likely to become racially mixed through changes in neighborhood residential patterns. . . .

In devising remedies where legally imposed segregation has been established, it is the responsibility of local authorities and district courts to see to it that future school construction and abandonment are not used and do not serve to perpetuate or re-establish the dual system. . . .

V.

The central issue in this case is that of student assignment, and there are essentially four problem areas: . . .

(1) RACIAL BALANCES OR RACIAL QUOTAS. . . . It would not serve the important objection of *Brown I* to seek to use school desegregation cases for purposes beyond their scope, although desegregation of schools ultimately will have impact on other forms of discrimination. We do not reach in this case the question whether a showing that school segregation is a consequence of other types of state action, without any discriminatory action by the school authorities, is a constitutional violation requiring remedial action by a school desegregation decree. This case does not present that question and we therefore do not decide it.

Our objective in dealing with the issues presented by these cases is to see that school authorities exclude no pupil of a racial minority from any school, directly or indirectly, on account of race; it does not and cannot embrace all the problems of racial prejudice, even when those problems contribute to disproportionate racial concentrations in some schools.

In this case it is urged that the District Court has imposed racial balance requirements of 71%–29% on individual schools. . . .

If we were to read the holding of the District Court to require, as a matter of substantive constitutional right, any particular degree of racial balance or mixing, that approach would be disapproved and we would be obliged to reverse. The constitutional command to desegregate schools does not mean that every school in every community must always reflect the racial composition of the school system as a whole. . . .

[T]he use made of mathematical ratios was no more than a starting point in the process of shaping a remedy, rather than an inflexible requirement. . . . In sum, the very limited use made of mathematical ratios was within the equitable remedial discretion of the District Court.

(2) ONE-RACE SCHOOLS. The record in this case reveals the familiar phenomenon that in metropolitan areas minority groups are often found concentrated in one part of the city. In some circumstances certain schools may remain all or largely of one race until new schools can be provided or neighborhood patterns change. . . .

In light of the above, it should be clear that the existence of some small number of one-race, or virtually one-race, schools within a district is not in and of itself the mark of a system which still practices segregation by law. The district judge or school authorities should . . . be concerned with the elimination of one-race schools. No per se rule can adequately embrace all the difficulties of reconciling the competing interests involved; but in a

system with a history of segregation the need for remedial criteria of sufficient specificity to assure a school authority's compliance with its constitutional duty warrants a presumption against schools that are substantially disproportionate in their racial composition. . . .

(3) REMEDIAL ALTERING OF ATTENDANCE ZONES. The maps submitted in these cases graphically demonstrate that one of the principal tools employed by school planners and by courts to break up the dual school system has been frank—and sometimes drastic—gerrymandering of school districts and attendance zones. An additional step was pairing, "clustering," or "grouping" of schools with attendance assignments made deliberately to accomplish the transfer of Negro students out of formerly segregated Negro schools and transfer of white students to formerly all-Negro schools. More often than not, these zones are neither compact nor contiguous; indeed they may be on opposite ends of the city. As an interim corrective measure, this cannot be said to be beyond the broad remedial powers of a court. . . .

No fixed or even substantially fixed guidelines can be established as to how far a court can go, but it must be recognized that there are limits. The objective is to dismantle the dual school system. . . .

(4) TRANSPORTATION OF STUDENTS. . . . No rigid guidelines as to student transportation can be given for application to the infinite variety of problems presented in thousands of situations. Bus transportation has been an integral part of the public education system for years, and was perhaps the single most important factor in the transition from the one-room schoolhouse to the consolidated school.

Absent a constitutional violation there would be no basis for judicially ordering assignment of students on a racial basis. All things being equal, with no history of discrimination, it might well be desirable to assign pupils to schools nearest their homes. But all things are not equal in a system that has been deliberately constructed and maintained to enforce racial segregation. . . .

An objection to transportation of students may have validity when the time or distance to travel is so great as to either risk the health of the children or significantly impinge on the educational process. District courts must weigh the soundness of any transportation plan in light of what is said in subdivisions (1), (2), and (3) above. It hardly needs stating that the limits on time of travel will vary with many factors, but probably with none more than the age of the students. . . .

VI.

. . .

At some point, these school authorities and others like them should have achieved full compliance with the Court's decision in *Brown I*. The systems would then be "unitary" in the sense required by our decisions in *Green* and *Alexander*.

It does not follow that the communities served by such system will remain demographically stable, for in a growing, mobile society few will do so. Neither school authorities nor district courts are constitutionally required to make year-by-year adjustments of the racial composition of student bodies once the affirmative duty to desegregate has been accomplished and racial discrimination through official action is eliminated from the system. This does not mean that federal courts are without power to deal with future problems; but in the absence of a showing that either the school authorities or some other agency of the State has deliberately attempted to fix or alter demographic patterns to affect the racial composition of the schools, further intervention by a district court should not be necessary. . . .

It is so ordered.

NOTES AND QUESTIONS

1.   *Swann* is an enigmatic opinion with language citable for almost any proposition. To a field already saturated with lawsuits, it simply fueled more litigation. What are some of the principal unanswered questions regarding the authority for desegregation, the indicia of desegregated schools, and the remedies for desegregating student populations?

2.   The opinion concludes with a cryptic note: Once schools are unitary, there is no longer any need for yearly adjustments. The Court seems to tantalize the lower courts and school officials with the prospect of ending the endless cycles of litigation. What new issues are created by this dictum?

3.   *Swann* focuses on "vestiges of state-imposed segregation." *Brown I* involved state-mandated or de jure segregation. *Swann*, however involved segregation-in-fact. At the time of the lawsuit, there was no racial assignment law. Pupils were assigned to neighborhood schools with the freedom to transfer if they so wished. The segregation was of the de facto variety. Nonetheless, the Court found a constitutional violation because of the "vestiges" of past racial laws—that is, because of what might be termed "past de jure" segregation. Thus, the combination of vestigial segregation with current de facto segregation triggers the application of desegregation remedies.

Since there was no finding of current de jure segregation, is the desegregation remedy benefiting the present students actually based on the injury inflicted upon past generations of students by the old racial laws?

Is the Court justified in assuming that a causal link exists between the pre-1954 racial laws and the contemporary segregation in neighborhood residences and schools? What kinds of evidence would be needed to establish the chain of causation? Who should bear the burden of proving it? What are the implications of allocating this burden?

4. Fiss (1971) argues that "the primary concern of the Court [was] the segregated patterns themselves rather than the causal relation of past discrimination to them. The attention paid to past discrimination can be viewed as an attempt by the Court to preserve the continuity with *Brown*" (pp. 204–5).

Swann, on its facts, applies only to schools with a history of de jure segregation at the time of *Brown I*; it applies, that is, to southern and border states. With respect to the most emotionally laden issue, that of busing, the Court says: "All things being equal, with no history of discrimination, it might well be desirable to assign pupils to schools nearest their homes." What are the implications for northern school desegregation?

5. Reconsider the role of social science in *Brown I* in the retrospective light cast by *Swann*. Cahn and other legal scholars had proposed that footnote 11 was inessential to the holding (Chapter 3, section 3.5). *Swann* declares an affirmative obligation to end continuing racial imbalance in schools formerly segregated by law. Does the justification for imposing this burden rest on the assumption that the detrimental psychological and learning effects of de jure segregation (as found in *Brown I*) carry-over to the present de facto situation? If, as Cahn said, the wrong was inherent in the state-mandated apartheid, and these racial laws have since been removed, what other basis is there for ordering desegregation?

6. A major test of footnote 11 occurred almost a decade later in Georgia (*Stell* v. *Savannah-Chatham County Board of Education*, 1963). The NAACP sued to enjoin the continuation of biracial schools. Some white students intervened on the side of the school board. They called several noted social scientists to the stand, including Henry E. Garrett, emeritus professor of psychology at Columbia University, Ernest van den Haag, lecturer in sociology at the New School for Social Research, and R. Travis Osborne, professor of psychology at the University of Georgia. They testified that "differences in specific capabilities, learning progress rates, mental maturity" and "differences in physical, psychical, and behavioral traits" made it "impossible for Negro and white children of the same chronological age to be effectively educated in the same classrooms," causing children of both races "grave psychological harm" (p. 668).

The NAACP conceded the authority of these witnesses, called no experts of its own, and simply argued that the social science evidence was irrelevant because *Brown I* had held that "segregation itself injures Negro children in the school system" (p. 676).

The federal district court ruled that "the existence or non-existence of injury to white or Black children from integrated or segregated schooling is a matter of fact for judicial inquiry and was so treated in *Brown*" (p. 678). It recognized the conflicting evidence in *Brown* and the present case. However, because "plaintiffs could have shown supporting authority . . . had they wished" but they failed to do so, the "court must assume that the truth lies on the side of the evidence of injury given in this case rather than that given in *Brown*" (p. 680). Since the white interveners had successfully disproved the factual basis of *Brown*, the decision was held to be inapplicable to the instant case and the lawsuit was dismissed.

What result on appeal, and why? (For the decision of the Fifth Circuit, see *Stell*, 1964. An overview of the role of social scientists in the defense of segregation from 1954 to 1966 is found in Newby 1967.)

4.4. EXPANSION OF SCHOOL DESEGREGATION TO THE NORTH

By the start of the seventies, school desegregation efforts in the South were largely completed. In 1971, 43.9% of black children in the South attended predominantly white schools, compared with only 27.8% in the North and West (*Keyes* v. *School District No. 1*, 1973, p. 218, n. 3). No sector of the nation had achieved anything near the extent of desegregation of the South.

Throughout the fifties and sixties, racial imbalance in barrio and ghetto schools was mostly ignored. Desegregation was thought to be a "southern problem." Early lawsuits against the school systems of cities such as Gary, Indiana (*Bell* v. *School City*, 1963), Kansas City, Missouri (*Downs* v. *Board of Education*, 1964), and Cincinnati, Ohio (*Deal* v. *Cincinnati Board of Education*, 1966), were unsuccessful. Federal appellate courts denied that there was a constitutional duty to abolish de facto segregation, and the Supreme Court refused to grant certiorari.

Meanwhile, two demographic shifts were taking place that made more acute the racial imbalance in northern schools. One was the northward migration of southern blacks. In 1954, 70% of the country's blacks resided in southern and border states; in 1970, the figure had dropped to 55% (U.S. Commission on Civil Rights, 1966). The other shift was the exodus of the white middle class to suburbia. Rising incomes, improved transportation, government support of middle class housing, fear of city crime, and search for different lifestyles were all factors associated with suburbanization. The trend has steadily accelerated since the early fifties. As whites moved out, southern blacks, seeking better job opportunities, moved in. The result has been that the inner core of the major northern cities has become occupied mainly by blacks and blue collar whites too poor to move.

Two years after *Swann*, the Supreme Court finally put the North on notice that it also had to comply with the mandate of *Brown*. The first northern school case decided by the Court arose in Denver (*Keyes* v. *School District No. 1*, 1973). The Court found that the school board had engaged in intentional (de jure) segregative acts in a mostly black neighborhood of Denver by manipulating attendance zones, selecting school sites "with conscious knowledge that it would be a segregated school" (p. 201), and deliberately assigning pupils to one-race schools. The de jure violation was found even though the board had never operated under legislation that permitted or required racial separation as in *Brown* and *Swann*.

In *Keyes*, then, the Court introduced a new definition of de jure violation applicable to northern circumstances: intentional segregation actions by school officials that result in racial imbalance. "We emphasize that the differentiating factor between de jure segregation and so-called de facto segregation to which we referred in *Swann* is purpose or intent to segregate" (p. 208). Racial imbalance that is not the product of official action and does not have a history of segregation by law is not subject to Equal Protection attack. The Court again drew the line between de jure and de facto segregation but side-stepped the issue of the validity of this distinction.

In a 7 to 1 vote—its first nonunanimous decision in a school desegregation case—the Court held that "a finding of intentionally segregative school board actions in a meaningful portion of a school system, as in this case [that is, the black neighborhood], creates a presumption that other segregated schooling within the system [that is, the rest of Denver] is not adventitious" (p. 208). City-wide desegregation was ordered when the school board was unable to overcome the presumption that the wrong done in one part of the system had infected the whole.

To win a desegregation remedy, there must be a finding of purposeful or intentional segregation. This requirement is easier met in the southern than in the northern case. When there is current or past segregation by law, there is a presumption of unconstitutionality and the burden rests at the outset upon the state to refute the prima facie case of segregation established by the racially identifiable schools. In the North, without prior racial legislation, the schools are presumed to be constitutional. *Keyes* establishes the allocation of burden of proof in de facto cases. The challenger initially has the burden of making a prima facie case of segregation by proving intentional segregative acts by school officials in at least a "meaningful" portion of the school system. The law then presumes that the segregation has reciprocal effects on the rest of the system. At this point, the burden shifts to school officials to disprove any segregative intent. Proving the negative, obviously, is not easy. If they fail to meet the burden, the court may decree district-wide remedies.

Denver is not representative of the northern urban metropolis. In part this is because blacks constitute a minority of the city's population. More typical is Detroit. It has a bull's-eye population pattern: a predominantly black inner core surrounded by rings of white suburbs. A steady migration of middle class whites to the suburbs has left a city that is mainly poor (black and white) and aged. In 1946, the Detroit school population was 46% black; in 1974, 72%; and it is forecast that in 1990 it will be virtually 100% black (*Bradley* v. *Milliken*, 1971, p. 586). Thus, in Detroit and other large northern cities, it is not only a problem of racially separate schools; it is also racially separate communities within a single metropolitan area. Against the background of the "growing separation between the poor and the affluent . . . between Negroes and whites" in the nation's urban centers (U.S. Commission on Civil Rights, 1966, p. 17), the Supreme Court handed down its decision on the Detroit school case in 1974.

MILLIKEN v. BRADLEY

418 U.S. 717 (1974)

Mr. Chief Justice BURGER delivered the opinion of the Court.

We granted certiorari in these consolidated cases to determine whether a federal court may impose a multi-district, areawide remedy to a single-district *de jure* segregation problem absent any finding that the other included school districts have failed to operate unitary school systems within their districts, absent any claim or finding that the boundary lines of any affected school district were established with the purpose of fostering racial segregation in public schools, absent any finding that the included districts committed acts which effected segregation within the other districts, and absent a meaningful opportunity for the included neighboring school Districts to present evidence or be heard on the propriety of a multi-district remedy or on the question of constitu-

tional violations by those neighboring districts.

I.

. . .

[Plaintiffs (appellees here) are the NAACP and individual parents and students. Defendants (appellants) include Governor Milliken of Michigan, the State Board of Education, and the Detroit Board of Education. Ed.'s note.]

The District Court found that the Detroit Board of Education created and maintained optional attendance zones within Detroit neighborhoods undergoing racial transition and between high school attendance areas of opposite predominant racial compositions. These zones, the court found, had the "natural, probable, foreseeable and actual effect" of allowing white pupils to escape identifiable Negro schools. . . .

The District Court found that in the operation of its school transportation program, which was designed to relieve over-crowding, the Detroit Board had admittedly bused Negro Detroit pupils to predominantly Negro schools which were beyond or away from closer white schools with available space.

With respect to the Detroit Board of Education's practices in school construction, the District Court found that Detroit school construction generally tended to have a segregative effect with the great majority of schools being built in either overwhelmingly all-Negro or all-white neighborhoods so that the new schools opened as predominantly one-race schools. . . .

The District Court also held that the acts of the Detroit Board of Education, as a subordinate entity of the State, were attributable to the State of Michigan, thus creating a vicarious liability on the part of the State. . . .[7]

Turning to the question of an appropriate remedy for these several constitutional violations, the District Court . . . [ordered state defendants] to submit desegregation plans encompassing the three-county metropolitan area despite the fact that the 85 outlying school districts of these three counties were not parties to the action and despite the fact the there had been no claim that these outlying districts had committed constitutional violations. . . .

[A divided Court of Appeals affirmed the District Court's findings of de jure segregation in the Detroit school system and agreed that "the only feasible desegregation plan" involves crossing boundary lines between Detroit and the surrounding suburbs. Ed.'s note.]

II.

Viewing the record as a whole, it seems clear that the District Court and the Court of Appeals shifted the primary focus from a Detroit remedy to the metropolitan area only because of their conclusion that total desegregation of Detroit would not produce the racial balance which they perceived as desirable. . . .

Here the District Court's approach to what constituted "actual desegregation" raises the fundamental question, not presented in *Swann*, as to the circumstances in which a federal court may order desegregation relief that embraces more than a single school district. The court's analytical starting point was its conclusion that school district lines are no more than arbitrary lines on a map drawn "for political convenience." Boundary lines may be bridged where there has been a constitutional violation calling for interdistrict relief, but the notion that school district lines may be casually ignored or treated as a mere administrative convenience is contrary to the history of public education in our country. No single tradition in public education is more deeply rooted than local control over the operation of schools; local autonomy has long been thought essential both to the maintenance of community concern and support for public schools and to quality of the educational process. . . .

The metropolitan remedy would require, in effect, consolidation of 54 independent school districts historically administered as separate units into a vast new super school district. Entirely apart from the logistical and other serious problems attending large-scale transportation of students, the consolidation would give rise to an array of other problems in financing and operating this new school system.

---

[7] The District Court briefly alluded to the possibility that the State, along with private persons, had caused, in part, the housing patterns of the Detroit metropolitan area which, in turn, produced the predominantly white and predominantly Negro neighborhoods that characterize Detroit. . . .

The Court of Appeals, however, expressly noted that . . . "[it] has not relied at all upon testimony pertaining to segregated housing. . . ."

Accordingly, in its present posture, the case does not present any question concerning possible state housing violations.

Some of the more obvious questions would be: What would be the status and authority of the present popularly elected school boards? Would the children of Detroit be within the jurisdiction and operating control of a school board elected by the parents and residents of other districts? What board or boards would levy taxes for school operations in these 54 districts constituting the consolidated metropolitan area? . . .

The controlling principle consistently expounded in our holdings is that the scope of the remedy is determined by the nature and extent of the constitutional violation. Before the boundaries of separate and autonomous school districts may be set aside by consolidating the separate units for remedial purposes or by imposing a cross-district remedy, it must first be shown that there has been a constitutional violation within one district that produces a significant segregative effect in another district. Specifically, it must be shown that racially discriminatory acts of the state or local school districts, or of a single school district have been a substantial cause of interdistrict segregation. . . . Conversely, without an interdistrict violation and interdistrict effect, there is no constitutional wrong calling for an interdistrict remedy. . . .

The record before us, voluminous as it is, contains evidence of *de jure* segregated conditions only in the Detroit schools; . . . to approve the remedy ordered by the court would impose on the outlying districts, not shown to have committed any constitutional violation, a wholly impermissible remedy based on a standard not hinted at in *Brown I* and *II* or any holding of this Court. . . .

IV.

. . .

[T]he judgment of the Court of Appeals is reversed and the case is remanded

for further proceedings consistent with this opinion leading to prompt formulation of a decree directed to eliminating the segregation found to exist in Detroit city schools, a remedy which has been delayed since 1970.

Reversed and remanded.

Mr. Justice STEWART, concurring.

. . .

This is not to say . . . that an interdistrict remedy of the sort approved by the Court of Appeals would not be proper, or even necessary, in other factual situations. Were it to be shown, for example, that state officials had contributed to the separation of the races by drawing or redrawing school district lines . . . or by purposeful, racially discriminatory use of state housing or zoning laws, then a decree calling for transfer of pupils across district lines or for restructuring of district lines might well be appropriate. . . .

Since the mere fact of different racial compositions in contiguous districts does not itself imply or constitute a violation of the Equal Protection Clause in the absence of a showing that such disparity was imposed, fostered, or encouraged by the State or its political subdivisions, it follows that no interdistrict violation was shown in this case.[2] . . .

Mr. Justice DOUGLAS, dissenting.

_____

[2]My Brother MARSHALL seems to ignore this fundamental fact when he states that "the most essential finding [made by the District Court] was that Negro children in Detroit had been confined by intentional acts of segregation to a growing core of Negro schools surrounded by a receding ring of white schools." This conclusion is simply not substantiated by the record presented in this case. The record here does support the claim made by the respondents that white and Negro students within Detroit who otherwise would have attended school together were separated by acts of the State or its subdivision. However, segregative acts within the city alone cannot be presumed to have produced—and no factual showing was made that they did produce—an increase in the number of Negro students in the city as a whole. It is this essential fact of a predominantly Negro school population in

. . .

Metropolitan treatment of metropolitan problems is commonplace. If this were a sewage problem or a water problem, or an energy problem, there can be no doubt that Michigan would stay well within federal constitutional bounds if it sought a metropolitan remedy. . . . Here the Michigan educational system is unitary, maintained and supported by the legislature, and under the general supervision of the State Board of Education. The State controls the boundaries of school districts. . . . Education in Michigan is a state project with very little completely local control, except that the schools are financed locally, not on a statewide basis. . . .

As I indicated in *Keyes*, there is so far as the school cases go no constitutional difference between *de facto* and *de jure* segregation. Each school board performs state action for Fourteenth Amendment purposes when it draws the lines that confine it to a given area, when it builds schools at particular sites, or when it allocates students. The creation of the school districts in Metropolitan Detroit either maintained existing segregation or caused additional segregation. Restrictive covenants maintained by state action or inaction build black ghettos. It is state action when public funds are dispensed by housing agencies to build racial ghettos. Where a community is racially mixed and school

authorities segregate schools, or assign black teachers to black schools or close schools in fringe areas and build new schools in black areas and in more distant white areas, the State creates and nurtures a segregated school system, just as surely as did those States involved in Brown v. Board of Education, when they maintained dual school systems. . . .

[S]ince Michigan by one device or another has over the years created black school districts and white school districts, the task of equity is to provide a unitary system for the affected area where, as here, the State washes its hands of its own creations.

Mr. Justice WHITE, with whom Mr. Justice DOUGLAS, Mr. Justice BRENNAN, and Mr. Justice MARSHALL join, dissenting.

The Detroit school district is both large and heavily populated. . . . If "racial balance" were achieved in every school in the district, each school would be approximately 64% Negro. A remedy confined to the district could achieve no more desegregation. . . .

SOCIAL SCIENCE AND THE COURTS: THE DETROIT SCHOOLS CASE

Eleanor P. Wolf

[INTRODUCTION]

. . .

I undertook a study of all the testimony presented in the course of the landmark Detroit case in order to discover what kinds of social-science materials were

Detroit—caused by unknown and perhaps unknowable factors such as in-migration, birth rates, economic changes, or cumulative acts of private racial fears—that accounts for the "growing core of Negro schools," a "core" that has grown to include virtually the entire city. The Constitution simply does not allow federal courts to attempt to change that situation unless and until it is shown that the State, or its political subdivisions, have contributed to cause the situation to exist. No record has been made in this case showing that the racial composition of the Detroit school population or that residential patterns within Detroit and in the surrounding areas were in any significant measure caused by governmental activity. . . .

Reprinted with permission of the author and the publisher from: *The Public Interest*, No. 42 (Winter, 1976), pp. 102–120. ©1976 by National Affairs, Inc. [Bracketed headings were not in the original article. Ed.'s note.]

introduced, and to evaluate their quality and comprehensiveness. . . .

The basic material for analysis was the verbatim transcript of the 41-day trial, held in 1971, as well as many of the exhibits offered in evidence, plus the transcript of the court hearings conducted the following year on alternative plans for desegregation. The chief areas of social-science concern, broadly classified, were 1) the extent, nature, and causes of racial separation in urban neighborhoods; 2) the economic, social, and psychological factors—both in and out of school—believed to be associated with various aspects of learning; and 3) the allegations and refutations of segregative practices within the school system. I had not foreseen the extent to which social-science materials would be involved in this last category, but there proved to be many references to demographic, sociological, and psychological factors in the course of disputed testimony concerning the reasons for the consequences of various school system policies and practices. A completely unexpected category was the rather considerable amount of testimony (and controversy) about methodology, some of it in response to challenges to the validity of evidence that had been introduced.

[TESTIMONY ON SEGREGATED HOUSING]

The decision of the Federal District Court on September 27, 1971, declaring Detroit schools to be segregated *de jure* was marked by the unusual prominence given to consideration of demographic trends and to an extended discussion of the nature and causes of racially segregated housing. . . . [The] findings were a largely accurate reflection of the testimony that had been presented on a wide range of specific topics in this general subject area: the measurement of segregation in housing; comparisons between the housing patterns of blacks and white ethnics; practices and policies, past and present, of the real estate industry; economic factors in residential choices of blacks; the impact upon housing patterns of government policy in urban renewal, public housing, FHA, and other federal programs; and the earlier judicial enforcement of restrictive covenants. Both the trial and the remedy hearings were marked by frequent references to "white flight" and its alleged causes; and school policy decisions, past and projected, were frequently rationalized by references to "white flight" and to the operation of the "tipping point" in schools and in housing.

Judge Roth's decision drew the following conclusions about the causes of residential segregation:

While the racially unrestricted choice of black persons and economic factors may have played some part in the development of this pattern of residential segregation it is, in the main, the result of past and present practices and customs of racial discrimination both public and private, which have and do restrict the housing opportunities of black people. On the record, there can be no other finding.

The record, however, was entirely the presentation of the plaintiffs. Because the defendants took the legal position that testimony about housing was irrelevant to the charge that Detroit's schools were segregated *de jure,* they offered no evidence on this subject. Regardless of the legal aspects, the fact that all of the housing witnesses were selected by one side tended to restrict the range of issues and narrow the perspective offered in this testimony. . . .

[CRITIQUE OF THE TESTIMONY]

Since legal advantage, rather than sociological relevance, governed the choice of materials to be presented, there was no testimony that reflected the studies of scholars who attribute greater importance to the economic ability of blacks or who stress the significance of the social class distribution of blacks in accounting for the residential preferences of *whites*. There was no testimony that emphasized the similarities, rather than the differences, between the residential behavior of blacks and that of other ethnic groups. . . . There was no reference to research revealing the continuing strength of social relationships among ethnic groups (including blacks) despite cultural assimilation.[9] The testimony on the causes of racial transition in urban neighborhoods was very sparse, consisting of references to solicitation by real-estate agents and the racial prejudice of whites. No testimony challenged the assertion that there is a "corresponding effect" between the racial composition of a school and that of a neighborhood—the phrase suggests a force of comparable magnitude in either direction. . . .

[I]t is surprising to discover that the 6th Circuit Court of Appeals, while upholding the finding that Detroit schools were segregated *de jure*, . . . removed all the references to housing that had been so prominent in Judge Roth's decision. . . .

Perhaps the Appeals Court recognized that, given the continued legality of geographical assignment, the emphasis Judge Roth had placed on residential segregation and demographic changes greatly weakened the charges against the school system. But the housing evidence, although ignored by the 6th Circuit Court of Appeals, played a very important role in

---

[9]Henry Aaron has pointed out in *Shelter and Subsidies* (Washington, Brookings Institution, 1972) that if all non-blacks exercise their preferences for "own-group majority" living situations, segregation occurs without discrimination (p. 17). Many studies show the persistence of social relationships and "clustering" among a variety of white ethnics. . . . The durability of black social ties and the tendency to "cluster," even in the absence of exclusion, has been noted by Philip Hauser, "Demographic Factors in the Integration of the Negro," in Talcott Parsons and Kenneth Clark, eds., *The Negro American* (Boston: Beacon Press, 1966), p. 96. . . .

the Detroit case. In addition to the expert witnesses on housing, there was testimony by several black real-estate brokers. Their plain-spoken narrative accounts of rebuff, subterfuge, and humiliation in their attempts to secure listings in white areas are very moving. Comments (in the transcript) from the defendants' counsel and the reports of observers at the trial suggests that this material also made a deep impression upon the listeners, and especially upon Judge Roth. . . .

[TESTIMONY ON PSYCHOLOGICAL AND LEARNING ASPECTS OF BIRACIAL SCHOOLING]

A considerable amount of expert testimony on education was offered during both the trial in 1971 and the hearing on desegregation plans conducted by Judge Roth in 1972. A wide range of issues was covered, some at great length, some briefly: the relationship between a child's background and academic achievement; the definition and measurement of socioeconomic status; the class-linked differences in attitudes, values, and overt behavior; and various problems in the definition and measurement of intelligence. There was a great deal of testimony on the effects of varying degrees of race and social-class mixture upon academic achievement, and upon other outcomes such as self-concept, motivation, aspirations, racial attitudes, and race relations. There was testimony on the effects of "tracking," ability-grouping, and the validity of tests used for such placement. There were presentations on the allocation of a variety of educational resources, with much emphasis on teachers' training, experience, skills, attitudes, and expectations. . . .

[CRITIQUE OF THE TESTIMONY]

Taken as a whole, the expert testimony about education was characterized by a number of serious omissions. There were no references to the differences in educational achievement between ethnic groups at similar income levels, although such differences are widely known and reasonably well documented. . . . [I]t was never revealed that the capacity of schools to eradicate [entry-level differences between black and white pupils] has not thus far been demonstrated. . . . No expert questioned the many exaggerated assertions made by both sides concerning research findings on the effects of teacher attitudes (the so-called "expectancy hypothesis") on student achievement, despite a considerable array of critical material on this work.

Perhaps most crucial of all, there was no serious challenge to the exaggerated claims, made by expert witnesses on both sides, of the power of racial and social-class mixture of classmates to improve the educational performance of low-achieving students. . . . The general import of the testimony on education was such as to persuade a reasonable man without research training or academic background that the proper kind of race-class mix in the classroom would heighten aspirations, improve motivation, raise self-esteem, and improve the academic performance of low-achieving black children. Simultaneously, contact with these children would reduce the prejudices and correct the stereotypes of whites, thus improving race relations. But there is little support in the professional literature for this dubious set of propositions. . . .

The expert testimony, then, on both housing and education was marked by a high degree of consensus. . . . We have already noted that there appeared to be genuine agreement between the adversaries on the benefits of integration, the harm of racial isolation in schools, and the moral and ideological imperatives of the goal of integration.

If the contrast in statements made by Judge Roth before and after the trial is

an indication of his beliefs, this high degree of consensus by experts was not without effect. The judge was a conservative among Democrats and had not been associated with civil-rights efforts. His pre-trial ruling in favor of a voluntary integration plan . . . indicates his original intention. . . .

The instrument eventually chosen to attain [desegregation] was a metropolitan plan of unprecedented dimensions. . . . The legal basis cited for this remedy, however, was not the social-science testimony, but the evidence of constitutional violations within the school system. . . .

[TESTIMONY ON DE JURE SCHOOL VIOLATIONS]

It is hard to escape the conclusion that Judge Roth's use of school violations was a reluctant concession to the requirements of legal precedent. "It is unfortunate," he declared "that we cannot deal with public school segregation on a no-fault basis, for if racial segregation . . . is an evil . . . it should make no difference whether we classify it *de jure* or *de facto*. . . . Our objective . . . should be to remedy a condition which we believe needs correction.". . .

The school-violations testimony is voluminous—and formidable. . . .

One category of school violations concerned site-selection. The facts here were not in doubt: The newly built Joffe Elementary School, for example, was small and the only children who lived nearby (and not so nearby) were black; it was thus predictable that it would be a "one-race school." Does this constitute segregation *de jure*? The District Court so ruled; the Appeals Court concurred; and the Supreme Court let the decision stand. . . .

Most scholars minimize the power of site-selection to alter the pattern of racial imbalance in large cities with substantial black populations. But the assertion that site-selection was a powerful influence was scarcely challenged directly. . . . Nobody was willing to say publicly what most said privately: that the policy was virtually meaningless and, for the City of Detroit, incapable of contributing to the aim of promoting integration from the time it was adopted. . . .

[Other kinds of unconstitutional conduct by school officials consisted of busing black students but not white students, using optional attendance zones in changing neighborhoods to enable whites to avoid going to mostly black schools, and manipulating boundary lines to perpetuate racial separation. Wolf systematically disputes each of these conclusions on the grounds that "incomplete and inaccurate factual material was accepted as evidence." Ed.'s note.]

[TESTIMONY ON RESEARCH METHODOLOGY]

In the course of these several thousand pages there were many disputes and explanations (some brief, some lengthy) concerning various techniques and methods of research: the validity and adequacy of sampling procedures and questionnaire results; the use of census data to make inference about school populations; the meaning of sampling error; the difference between cross-sectional and longitudinal analysis; the statistical significance of difference in samples and difference in total-enumeration procedures; the identification of variables as dependent or independent; the problems of regression-analysis; the ascertainment of item-reliability in an index; the appropriate indices for the measurement of socio-economic status; . . . and, finally, the meaning and use of the chi-square test.

Some of these controversies and explanations illustrate the problems faced by courts in cases where scientific materials are offered. There were some explanations which required a fair amount of

knowledge of quantitative techniques—which, as it appears from the record, some of those present, including the judge, did not have. . . .

[CONCLUSION]

What is the appropriate role for social science in the courtroom? The growing reluctance to use research findings and scholarly opinion as grounds for desegregation orders seems a proper recognition of the "revisionist" character of scientific knowledge. . . . In the future new knowledge may support, question, or reverse earlier findings. . . .

Regardless of the extent to which the social-science evidence offered in a desegregation case is used as legal underpinning for the court's decision, such material appears to have an important influence upon the general perspective of judges. Many pages of the transcript in the Detroit case read like a one-student seminar session. The expert-witness/teacher instructs and explains; the judge/student asks a question. . . . But there are many aspects of courtroom procedural tradition which are educationally disadvantageous: the long time lapse between opposing witnesses testifying on the same topic; the absence of direct confrontation between experts who offer contradictory evidence, especially concerning the nature of factual material; the extreme deference shown to the court's remarks, which allows half-truths to stand uncorrected. . . . The court is a poor classroom. . . . The source of some of these problems is in the very nature of the adversary system, and this raises the question whether matters of educational policy are appropriately handled by judicial proceedings. . . .

The law literature contains many procedural suggestions aimed at modifying some of those aspects of adversary proceedings that most academic witnesses find so distasteful. Among these suggestions are proposals for court-appointed masters to evaluate evidence, panels of consultants, joint committees of legal and behavioral-science scholars to prepare written submissions and other materials, and "devil's advocates" (a title peculiarly appropriate for these school-segregation cases) to argue unpopular positions. . . .

Social-science testimony *is* being used in these school cases, and it should be of better quality than much that was offered during the Detroit case. . . .

NOTES AND QUESTIONS

1.   *Milliken* marks the first major retreat by the Supreme Court in the area of school desegregation. It was decided in the post–civil rights era: Congress was busily attaching anti-busing riders to educational funding bills and the Nixon Administration talked about a period of "benign neglect" of black grievances. As Justice Marshall stated in his dissent, "Today's holding, I fear, is more a reflection of a perceived public mood that we have gone far enough in enforcing the Constitution's guarantee of equal justice than it is the product of neutral principles of law" (pp. 814–15). He predicted that the Detroit-only desegregation would lead to even more rapid white flight (p. 801).

2.   The events that preceded the lawsuit help place the case in perspective (Grant 1971, 1975).

In 1965, Detroit had one of the largest public school systems in the country. It was also one of the most progressive with respect to integration. The school board, dominated by a liberal-labor-black coalition, hired and promoted black teachers, criticized textbook publishers for not including materials on the black experience, and was unswervingly committed to integration. The school board president and the school superintendent were winners of NAACP awards.

Then came the Detroit riots during the summer of 1967 and the rise of new ideologies—community control and black power—that challenged the integration ideal. Black advocates of community control pushed through the state legislature a bill requiring the decentralization of Detroit schools in 1969. At that time, the city's electorate was 44% black, but black students composed 64% of the school population. The idea of community control was to carve the city's school system into racially homogeneous regional districts in order to achieve black control of black schools. These advocates were no longer committed to integration. In any event, they did not believe integration was possible so long as there was a majority of white voters.

The school board remained solidly pro-integration. Under the new decentralization law, it redrew the boundaries of regional districts so as to include both black and white schools. In addition, it adopted an integration plan that involved two-way busing for the first time: sending white students to predominantly black schools.

With visions of mass busing into and out of Detroit's violence-ridden ghettos, white voters rallied swiftly to block the integration plan. The school board members who had voted for the plan were removed in a recall election. The Michigan legislature passed a bill prohibiting the implementation of the integration plan without disturbing the decentralizing scheme. Proponents of integration were shocked by these political developments and in August 1970 began a full scale court challenge to the anti-integration provision of the state law. The case was assigned by the luck of the draw to Judge Roth. After the trial, he ordered the most sweeping interdistrict desegregation plan in the history of the Republic: the busing of 40% of the 780,000 students in all grade levels in 53 school districts, in order to produce a ratio of 20–30% black to 80–70%white in each school.

3.   The last sentence of the majority's opinion is not without irony: It orders intradistrict desegregation in a district that is 64% black and growing.

4.   *Milliken* does not mean the end of the line from *Brown*. Desegregation continues unabated on an intradistrict basis. The Denver and Detroit cases have focused attention on the large cities. But, as Pettigrew (1975) notes, there is a lot of "mopping up" to be done elsewhere in the North in small and medium-sized communities. Cumulatively, they are responsible for a significant proportion of northern school segregation. Because of the smaller black population in these communities, desegregation is possible without a metropolitan remedy.

Milliken also does not speak to voluntary interdistrict integration. When cities and suburbs are consolidated into a single school system, thereby sacrificing the neighborhood school concept (as in Miami–Dade County and Nashville–Davidson County), the integration has not led to mostly one-race schools (Farley 1975, p. 192).

5.   Did the Court say that there can never be an interdistrict remedy absent an interdistrict violation? Can the holding be limited narrowly to the facts of the case so as to prevent a permanent bar to desegregating inner city schools?

6.   Because of the difficulties of proof, the allocation of the burden of proof may determine which side will prevail. Who has the burden with respect to showing an interdistrict effect? Must plaintiffs prove that de jure segregation in Detroit has a segregative effect on the suburban schools? Or do school officials have the obligation of showing no causal link between suburban and inner city schools? Do the presumptions and allocations of burdens announced in the Denver case apply to the Detroit case?

7.   Is the result in Detroit reconcilable with the logic and language of the Charlotte case?

8.   For more on intradistrict de jure segregation, see *Dayton Board of Education* v. *Brinkman* (1979) and *Columbus Board of Education* v. *Penick* (1979).

9.   Consider the alternative remedies upon a finding of a constitutional violation if intradistrict desegregation is largely futile and metropolitan busing is precluded.

Upon remand, the new trial judge in the Detroit case ordered very limited reassignment of only 10% of the students within the city. The judge also required the State of Michigan (a reluctant defendant) and the Detroit school board (an enthusiastic and willing defendant) to share equally in the multi-million-dollar financing of extensive educational programs in the city schools, including the establishment of (a) reading and communication skills training to remedy the effects of past discrimination, (b) in-service training for faculty and staff to ease the desegregation process, (c) an educational and psychological testing program free from racial or cultural bias, and (d) counseling and career guidance programs. The Supreme Court unanimously sustained these orders (*Milliken* v. *Bradley*, 1977, or *Milliken II*). The NAACP described the new plan as "racist" and "a return to *Dred Scott*," and continued to insist on expanded busing with Detroit (Wolf 1981, pp. 237–38).

What is the relationship between these remedies and the wrong found in *Milliken I*? If the State of Michigan was not vicariously liable for the acts of the Detroit school board according to *Milliken I*, what is the basis for imposing upon the State the cost of implementing the decrees of *Milliken II*?

Is the Court implicitly saying that the psychological stigma described in *Brown* can now be removed without an integration remedy? Are the courts recognizing that there might be more public acceptance of expending tax dollars for compensatory education in ghetto schools than for busing? Does *Milliken II* mark the start of a modern, northern version of the *Plessy* doctrine: "mostly separate but equal in tangible resources"?

On the other hand, "*Milliken II* may well stand for the time-honored proposition that exigency creates its own rules of constitutional decisionmaking" (Yudof 1978, p. 105). The school board willingly relinquished its autonomy in exchange for the opportunity to dip into the state treasury under the authority and supervision of the federal courts. The state may have had no choice but to acquiesce in the plan because the Detroit school system was "chaotic and incapable of effective administration": The superintendent had "little direct authority" and board members were "busily engaged in politics" rather than in educational matters (*Milliken II*, p. 296). Consequently, Justice Powell complained in a concurring opinion that "the District Court virtually assumed the role of school superintendent and school board" (p. 297).

10.   Evaluation of compensatory education programs under Title I of the Elementary and Secondary Education Act of 1965 has shown no significant relationship between increased resources and improved test achievement scores. Most large surveys of the large national compensatory education programs have shown no beneficial results on the average (Weinberg 1977, p. 228). However, the evaluation studies also caution that these findings are not conclusive because of the weak sampling procedures and suspect research designs.

11.   The community control movement originated in Harlem and Bedford-Stuyvesant (New York City) in the late sixties. Its thrust was to break up large urban school districts and give black parents a greater voice in making educational policy and selecting teachers and administrators in mostly black schools (Comment, *California Law Review*, 1973). Its rationale, as stated by one proponent, is that "Opposition to segregation need not imply opposition to majority black schools" (in Bell 1975a, p. 595). "Judicial hostility to majority black schools reinforces the national belief that majority black schools are bad schools. Such belief insures that integration in education must continue to reflect the preference for middle class white behavior and precludes the possibility of identifying or developing appropriate black educational behavior in a majority black setting" (p. 594).

This alternative was tried out in Atlanta. The school system there is mostly black. In 1952, blacks composed 32% of the student population; in 1974, 82%. The local NAACP, defying the national office, agreed to forego busing in exchange for faculty desegregation and the appointment of black administrators. The compromise was judicially sanctioned (*Calhoun* v. *Cook*, 1973), but the Atlanta chapter was suspended for its apostasy by the NAACP (Wilkinson 1979, p. 233).

The efficacy of this remedy is subject to dispute. The early evaluations revealed "serious community conflict with no demonstrable educational gains" (Orfield 1978, p. 168). Black school officials confronted—unsuccessfully—the same problems as their white predecessors. The critical evidence itself has been roundly criticized by community control advocates (Yudof 1975, p. 429). Bell (1979) has described some all-black inner city schools that have gained reputations for academic excellence, in part because the parents have assumed an active role in their children's learning. He has also pointed out "how little serious research into effective black schools have been undertaken" (p. 1841, n. 45)—experts and the media tend to treat them as isolated, nonreplicable curiosities.

12.   In 1954, compelled racial separation in schools was said to be harmful. By the late sixties, with the quickening of black cultural consciousness and the rise of black power, voluntary racial separation was thought to be beneficial. As a result, the basic objective of *Brown* was called into question. Was the intent of *Brown* to impose integration upon the races? Or was it to declare equal educational opportunity in which judicially ordered integration, including the use of busing, was only one of the means—but surely not the only one—for attaining this goal? That is, is integration to be equated with equality?

There are an increasing number of members of the black community who are also questioning the effectiveness of school integration via compulsory busing. For example, in Dallas's school desegregation case, a "Black Coalition to Maximize Education," composed of "a substantial body of blacks who are opposed to any escalation in the use of racial balance remedies to cure the effects of school segregation," sought instead alternative remedies "to improve educational quality and eliminate the disparity in academic achievement . . ." (*Tasby* v. *Wright*, 1981, p. 690). In the Nashville school case, a "dramatic role reversal" was observed by the court, whereby "a white majority in the school board, acting on the advice of a white desegregation expert, recommended to the court *more* busing to achieve *more* racial balance," whereas black plaintiffs urged "*less* busing, more neighborhood characteristics to the assignment plan, and the possibility of majority black schools" (*Kelley* v. *Metropolitan County Board of Education*, 1980, p. 184).

Suppose that minority students in a community have a genuine choice between attending an integrated school or an all-minority school. Is the self-imposed segregation in the public schools constitutional? Would your answer depend upon the educational effectiveness of the all-minority school? (See *Hart* v. *Community School Board*, 1974.)

13.   A voluntary approach to desegregation is the magnet school. By offering unique educational programs, it attracts a broad cross-section of students (Orfield 1978). However, the result is often a handful of elite schools (with the top students and the most funds) which are partially integrated (because whites do not flock to inner city magnets) within the larger, segregated school district (*Wall Street Journal*, May 3, 1984, p. 1).

4.5.   SOCIAL SCIENCE IN POST-BROWN SCHOOL DESEGREGATION

Wolf's article, which has since been expanded to book length (Wolf 1981), can be appreciated at several levels. It is a detective story that seeks to unravel a couple of mysteries: How could one of the most pro-integration school boards in the nation be found culpable of racial discrimination? And what prompted the extraordinary conversion of the judge from pretrial skeptic to posttrial champion of massive busing? It is also a methodical summary and unrelenting critique of the social science evidence that was introduced to support an integration remedy. The appellate opinions in *Milliken* made no reference at all to empirical data. Unless one sat through the trial or, as Wolf did, painstakingly combed through tens of thousands of pages of court transcript, one would not have realized that voluminous expert testimony had been presented at both the trial and remedy proceedings. Finally, perhaps the most controversial level at which the article can be read is the ideological. Wolf is one of the chief sociological rhetoricians of the national mood of the late seventies and the eighties that is popularly described as the "new conservatism." Neoconservatives challenged the traditional liberal ideal of racial integration, no matter what the means or cost. Wolf places in juxtaposition the opposing claims based on social science and legal doctrines and by deft argument and counterargument attempts to justify a commitment to the status quo.

The kinds of evidence adduced at trial in the Detroit case are generally representative of that used in other northern school cases. They include the causes and extent of neighborhood and school segregation; white flight and resegregation; the effects of desegregated schooling on academic achievement, self-concept, and interracial attitudes of students; and the purportedly unconstitutional practices of school officials. We shall examine some of the social research in each of the foregoing categories. As you read this material, consider the legal purposes for which the research data are being introduced. Consider, too, the influence that the empirical evidence can have upon judicial decision-making.

Residential Segregation and School Segregation

For nearly six weeks during the Detroit trial, plaintiffs' expert witnesses set forth "the most extensive testimony ever presented on the interrelationship between segregation in the schools and in housing" (Grant 1975, p. 862). The theory was that government agencies and policies contributed to residential segregation which, coupled with the seemingly neutral policy of assignment to neighborhood schools, resulted in racially imbalanced schools—that de facto segregation was really de jure segregation once removed. As Wolf noted, it was a wholly one-sided presentation—defendants introduced no rebuttal evidence.

A noted demographer, Taeuber (1975), testified that black poverty was not a cause of residential segregation. According to census figures, there was no difference in the average rent paid by blacks and whites in Detroit. Housing of poor whites was not interspersed with that of poor blacks. He also eliminated personal choice as a cause. Polls showed that less than 20% of blacks prefer to live in all-black neighborhoods. According to census data, European ethnic groups were far less segregated from native whites than were blacks.

Moreover, Taeuber pointed out—based on a "complex interplay of hypotheses and evidence" (p. 847)—that reciprocal causal effects appear between residential and school segregation. A neighborhood social policy, superimposed upon a racially homogeneous neighborhood, results in a mostly one-race school. Conversely, perceptions of the racial composition of a school affect decisions on residential choice. Both patterns developed together and reinforced each other in Detroit. Consequently, he predicted that "desegregation of schools would have a cumulatively increasing effect on residential desegregation" (p. 844).

Taeuber concluded that "the prime cause of residential segregation by race has been discrimination, both public and private" (p. 840). There was substantial evidence in the record of governmental involvement in housing segregation (Taylor 1975). In the 1930s and 1940s, federal agencies actively fostered segregation by encouraging homeowners to use racially restrictive covenants in deeds. An FHA Underwriting Manual at that time proposed, for the ostensible purpose of neighborhood stability, that "properties shall be occupied by the same social and racial classes" (in Goodman 1972, p. 332, n. 192). Until the mid-fifties, state agencies assigned public housing on a racial basis. The subsequent promulgation of fair housing legislation was insufficient to eradicate past discrimination. Residential mobility occurs mostly in the early family stage of the life cycle, and housing policies of thirty years ago continue to affect where people presently live. Despite the economic gains of blacks in the past two decades, levels of residential segregation in the nation's urban areas has not declined (Farley 1975).

At the trial, Judge Roth found as follows (*Bradley* v. *Milliken*, 1971):

> Governmental actions and inactions at all levels, federal, state, and local, have combined with those of private organizations such as loaning institutions and real estate associations and brokerage firms, to establish and to maintain the pattern of residential segregation throughout the Detroit metropolitan area. . . .
>
> When we speak of governmental action we should not view the different agencies as a collection of unrelated units. . . . [A]ll of them, including the school authorities, are, in part, responsible for the segregated condition which exists. And we note that just as there is an interaction between residential patterns and the racial composition of the schools, so there is a corresponding effect on the residential pattern by the racial composition of the schools. [p. 587]

NOTES AND QUESTIONS

---

1. According to Wolf (1981), the plaintiffs' expert testimony on housing segregation was of "poor quality" (p. 70), "misleading" (p. 77), and "not the result of a review of research on the matter" but "a lawyer's argument" to justify a finding of de jure segregation (p. 33). She chided Taeuber for his "advocacy role," saying that if he had been giving a "scientific paper" rather than testifying in court, he would have made reference to "contrary evidence" (p. 34). Consider and evaluate two of the counterarguments made by Wolf (1981):

Black residential segregation in the north is merely a "conjunctural phenomenon involving the acts of millions of households over the years," such acts consisting in "large part" of "white avoidance" (read: white prejudice). Since racial concentrations in housing are of long-standing, antedating New Deal policies, they cannot be traced unequivocally to "discriminatory acts of government" (p. 33). In effect, Wolf says, what the government has not done, it should not intervene to undo.

Taeuber testified that residential choice for blacks was negligible. He referred to a national poll showing that 66% of blacks want to live in integrated neighborhoods, 20% prefer all-black areas, and 14% are undecided. Wolf combined the 20% with one-half of the undecided group to conclude that 27% of blacks favor all-black neighborhoods. This new figure was sufficiently large to support the inference that own-group preference—not discrimination—"might be an important influence" of residential segregation (p. 34). Wolf also cited other national surveys that indicate that blacks are concerned not so much with actually living next to whites as with the right to do so. If there were truly open occupancy, she suggests, there would still be voluntary enclaves of mostly black areas as there are of predominantly Jewish and other ethnic areas. Ties of kinship and friendship channel residential behavior. Wolf concludes that the "prospects for stable residential mixtures seem dim" (pp. 41–42).

2.   Despite the abundance of testimony on racial containment in housing, the Supreme Court deliberately avoided any mention of it. How and why did the majority sidestep the issue?

Justice Stewart in a concurring opinion seems to leave the door open for a metropolitan remedy in the future. Yet, he says in footnote 2, "No record has been made in this case" to show that governmental activity is related to school segregation and housing segregation. Taeuber (1975) noted wryly, "I don't know whether to feel insulted or challenged" (p. 833). Is his open door illusory? What is the implication of Justice Stewart's characterization of the causes of racial containment as not merely "unknown" but also "perhaps unknowable"?

3.   In the Detroit case, much of the social science evidence introduced at the trial (for example, the residential segregation data) was irrelevant and unnecessary under the existing law (because school officials are not responsible for racial imbalances arising solely from demographic changes); hence, it went unmentioned in the appellate opinions. Despite the absence of any legal need for such proof, it can be argued that there is an underlying pressure to offer some factual evidence to justify desegregation beyond reliance on case precedents. Social science can have an indirect impact on decision-making by changing the social outlook of judges.

There is a story inside the story of the Detroit school case: the evolution in attitudes of Judge Roth and one of the attorneys during the trial as a result of their exposure to the expert testimony (Grant 1975). In 1970, the judge was unfavorably disposed toward integration. He criticized it as "forced feeding" and suggested that "outsiders" leave the city alone. Eighteen months later, he developed a deep commitment to integration and ordered the most massive metropolitan desegregation plan in the country. "[W]ithout his conversion, it is unlikely that the Detroit school case would have become very significant in the history of school desegregation litigation" (p. 851).

Equally remarkable was the midtrial conversion of counsel for intervening defendants (the white parents resisting the school board's integration plan). The attorney was no champion of integration. Yet, later in the trial, he conceded that Detroit was segregated with respect to housing and schools and went on to endorse a metropolitan remedy! His change moved the judge. "We all got an education during the course of the trial," Judge Roth commented afterward (p. 865).

The change of heart of Judge Roth came about after weeks of hearing social science testimony. Based on her analysis of the trial transcripts, Wolf (1981) concluded: "I am convinced, although I cannot prove the point, that in Detroit as in some other cases," the testimony on residential segregation and the reciprocal effects on school segregation aroused the judge's sense of wrong and provided him with the justification for finding de jure violations by school officials. The testimony on social-educational benefits "misled" the judge to the view that racially mixed classrooms were the necessary, the desirable remedy (pp. 81, 101). In fact, Judge Roth confided that these data were "the keys to understanding the case" (Grant 1975, p. 863). In essence, social science "was an important aspect of Judge Roth's indoctrination" (Wolf 1981, p. 119). "Liberal" social scientists, too, argue that "the relevance of 'irrelevant' [expert] testimony" in school desegregation litigation lies precisely in the experts' function to "sensitize" or "educate" judges, who typically come from "conservative backgrounds," about racial discrimination in society at large (Sanders *et al.* 1981–82, pp. 403, 422).

Are you persuaded by this "brainwashing" hypothesis? See Ravitch (1982) and Book Review (1982, p. 956). Consider Cahn's description (1961) of the art of advocacy:

> [I]f you wish a judge to overturn a settled and established rule of law, you must convince both his mind and his emotions, which together in indissociable blend constitute his sense of injustice. . . . His mind must see not only that the law has erred but also that the law itself proffers a remedy. Then he can feel free to correct the error without betraying the consistency and continuity of the legal order because he will only be replacing mistaken law with correct law. . . . All this he may determine to do—if you are able to arouse the propulsive force in his sense of injustice, i.e., the excitement of glands and emotions that any man may experience when he witnesses the inflicting of injustice. [p. 129]

Does the suggestion that decisions are conditioned on emotive experiences triggered by expert testimony represent a substitution of the rule of the judge—or the vicarious rule of the social scientist—for the rule of law? How is society safeguarded against idiosyncratic judicial decision-making?

White Flight

White flight refers to the transfer of white students out of schools that are about to be or are in the process of being desegregated and into private schools or other public (typically suburban) schools. The transfer may or may not be accompanied by residential relocation. Although not expressly stated, the prospect of white flight was an underlying factor in Judge Roth's decision to order interdistrict desegregation. Experts had testified at trial that a 55% black student body was the minimum tipping point above which resegregation would quickly accelerate (Levin 1978, p. 21). We will first consider briefly the empirical literature on white flight that is said to result from judicially mandated desegregation. Then we will turn to the question of whether a court may take into account the possibility of white flight as a justification for fashioning a less than comprehensive remedy.

THE SOCIAL SCIENCE DEBATE ON WHITE FLIGHT

Subsequent research undermined the apparent expert consensus on the white flight issue in the Detroit case. In the widely publicized Boston school desegregation case, "voluminous affidavits and other materials by social scientists on the subject of white flight" were introduced (this time by both parties) and extensively summarized in the opinion of the First Circuit Court of Appeals (*Morgan* v. *Kerrigan*, 1976, p. 420, n. 29). The evidence, characterized as " 'legislative facts' relevant to a determination of the law," illustrate the complexity and dissensus of expert opinion on this matter.

The Boston school board initially submitted an affidavit and a report by James S. Coleman, professor of sociology at the University of Chicago (Coleman, Kelly, and Moore 1975). This report concerned trends in school segregation from 1968 to 1973. The main conclusion was that "massive white flight will occur when there is a significant decrease in segregation in a city where there is a high proportion of blacks in the central city and suburbs of a significantly different racial composition" (*Morgan*, p. 420). No substantial white flight was found in middle-sized cities. The implication of the results was that extensive and rapid school desegregation ordered by the courts defeated the purpose of increasing interracial contact. Unless the white flight was arrested, busing to achieve racial balancing in urban schools would likely produce resegregation between urban and suburban school districts.

This report had an enormous impact on the national debate on compulsory busing (Orfield 1978, p. 147). It also elicited attacks of unusual ferocity in academic circles. Since Coleman had co-authored earlier the *Equality of Educational Opportunity* (1966) survey that became the chief empirical authority for the academic benefits of integration, "his 'defection' seemed especially traitorous" to civil rights groups and to integration-minded social scientists (Ravitch 1978, p. 135).

Rebuttals were promptly published and some were introduced in evidence by plaintiffs in the Boston case. Pettigrew and Green (1976) criticized Coleman's methodology, "claiming that the source of his raw data is unknown; that failure to evaluate large cities which have been subject to massive desegregation orders separately from large cities which have not been subject to court orders undermines the study's relevancy; and that failure to control for other variables, which may be correlated with white flight, jeopardizes the validity of his conclusions" (*Morgan,* p. 420). Others testified that "white exit to private schools is a short term phenomenon and that declines in white population in the cities are part of a long term demographic trend independent of desegregation" (*Morgan,* p. 420).

The principal counter study was conducted by Rossell (1975) and also filed in evidence by plaintiffs. Relying on data from eighty-six northern school districts subject to court-mandated desegregation, the study concluded that "white flight is minimal and a temporary reaction to school desegregation" (p. 421). Whites tended to jump ship before the start of desegregation or during the first year of its implementation; thereafter, white enrollment stabilized.

Coleman, in turn, submitted further affidavits defending his study and criticizing the reports of his critics. Faced with the rounds of evidence and counter-evidence produced by "forensic social science," the First Circuit said with a touch of exasperation:

> Throughout this series of submissions this court has been burdened with reports written for sociologists by sociologists utilizing sophisticated statistical and mathematical techniques. We lack the expertise to evaluate these studies on their merits. We do come to one conclusion, however. The relationship between white flight and court ordered desegregation is a matter of heated debate among experts in sociology, and a firm professional consensus has not yet emerged. . . . [p. 421]

The court then proceeded to "reject all these materials as irrelevant to the issues before us" (p. 420).

Since the Boston case, the debate has cooled but the issue has not been fully resolved (Clotfelter 1978). The range of disagreements, however, has narrowed. For example, it is now recognized that the mixed results may be due in part to the fact that different studies do not always distinguish between different forms of white flight. School desegregation can be brought about by "natural" processes of residential succession: blacks move in as whites move out, and the racial composition of both the neighborhood and the school changes concomitantly. In this situation, the determination of causal relationships between school desegregation and white flight becomes problematic. Any number of factors may be associated with the trend toward white suburbanization, including urban pollution, crime, living costs, and taxes in addition to school desegregation itself. On the other hand, when school desegregation is induced by court decree, it may not necessarily lead to neighborhood desegregation and, eventually, to resegregation. The link between the decline in white enrollment and the decree is less tenuous when massive out-migration to the suburbs is not simultaneously occurring. It is difficult to partial-out long-term ecological changes from court-ordered desegregation.

Differences over the measurement of white flight are another reason for the conflicting claims. Ravitch (1978) pointed out that Coleman measured white flight in a way that magnifies the phenomenon whereas Rossell's method minimized it. For example, suppose there are 200,000 white students in a school district and they comprise 80% of the entire student population. Upon desegregation, 40,000 transfer out, so that the proportion of whites drops to 76.2%. A 3.8% decrease may be deemed "minimal," especially if the white enrollment stabilizes thereafter. On the other hand, 40,000 represents 20% of all of the white students. It can also be said that the departure of one out of every five white students is "massive."

Whatever the cause of white flight and however the figures are characterized, there is virtually no dispute on one point: at least some decline in white enrollment goes hand in hand with court-ordered desegregation. In 1979, less than half as many white students were in the Boston public schools as when busing began in 1974 (Comment, *Virginia Law Review*, 1980, p. 966). When mandatory busing went into effect in Los Angeles in 1978, 30% to 50% of white students scheduled to be bused left the school system (U.S. Commission on Civil Rights 1979, pp. 50–51; Bell 1979, p. 1837). Surveys have shown that racist attitudes are correlated more "strongly and consistently" with anti-busing positions than self-interest, including educational or other nonracial grounds for opposing busing: "[I]t is not the buses but the blacks who arouse the ire of so many whites . . . across the nation" (McConahay 1982, pp. 714– 15).

Rossell (1978) has since conceded the validity of Coleman's basic conclusion, despite differences over methodology and practical implications:

> On the average, a city school system less than 25 percent black can expect to lose 5 percent of its white enrollment with an average two-way desegregation plan (30 percent blacks, 5 percent whites reassigned, and a reduction in segregation of − 30) and 9 percent of its white enrollment with the most extensive plan (60 percent blacks, 25 percent whites reassigned, and a reduction in segregation of −67). City school systems with 35 percent or more black students can expect to lose 8 percent of their white enrollment with the average desegregation plan and 14 percent with the most extensive plan. [pp. 181–82]

Rossell concludes that despite the white flight, school desegregation is "quite successful" because it achieves racial mixing. There is a net gain (17% to 25%) in the number of white students enrolled in the mostly black schools.

JUDICIAL RESPONSES TO WHITE FLIGHT

The lower federal courts are divided on whether white flight can be taken into account in formulating desegregation plans. Most deny that it is a legitimate consideration.

In *Brunson* v. *Board of Trustees* (1970), the Fourth Circuit upheld a desegregation plan that would disperse white students throughout the school system, resulting in a 5% to 17% white enrollment in black majority schools. The issue of white flight was hotly debated. A dissenting opinion urged the court not to "ignore reality" and to observe "some degree of moderation in selecting a remedy" to avoid resegregation (p. 822). It cited extensive earlier testimony by Thomas F. Pettigrew, professor of social psychology at Harvard and a leading expert on integration and race relations. Pettigrew had distinguished between "desegregation," or "the mere mix of bodies, black and white, in the same school," from "integration," or "quality of the mix . . . [with] special emphasis on cross-racial acceptance." He further testified that the academic achievement benefits of integration for black students drop when their numbers exceed 35% or 40% of the student population. Hence, he advocated "the establishment of an optimum 30% black to 70% white ratio in as many schools as possible through the use of educational parks and through disregard of traditional school district lines" (p. 823, n. 1).

A concurring opinion lambasted "the invidious nature of the Pettigrew thesis":

> Its central proposition is that the value of a school depends on the characteristics of a majority of its students and superiority is related to whiteness, inferiority to blackness. Although the theory is couched in terms of "socio-economic class" and the necessity for the creation of a "middle-class milieu," nevertheless, at bottom, it rests on the generalization that, educationally speaking, white pupils are somehow better or more desirable than black pupils. This premise leads to the next proposition, that association with white pupils helps the blacks and so long as whites predominate does not harm the white children. But once the number of whites approaches minority, then association with the inferior black children hurts the whites and, because there are not enough of the superior whites to go around, does not appreciably help the blacks. . . .
>
> I too am dismayed that the remaining white pupils in the Clarendon County [South Carolina] schools may well now leave. But the road to integration is served neither by covert capitulation nor by overt compromise, such as adoption of a schedule of "optimal mixing." [pp. 826, 827]

Four years after this decision, only one white student was enrolled in the Clarendon County school system (Craven 1975, p. 155).

The Supreme Court, in ruling on de jure segregation, forbade lower courts to consider the prospect of white flight or community resistance when such arguments were clearly a "sham" or "mask" to resist integration (*U.S.* v. *Scotland Neck Board of Education,* 1972, (p. 491). The applicability of this decision to de facto segregation cases that are untainted by discriminatory motives is unclear.

In the Boston school case, the First Circuit opined that "What the layman calls 'resegregation' is not constitutionally recognized segregation." "This racial isolation becomes constitutionally significant only when the district boundaries are drawn with segregative intent. . ." (*Morgan,* p. 422). The Seventh Circuit also ruled that white flight is "not an acceptable reason for failing to dismantle a dual school system" in Indianapolis, despite undisputed evidence that it would accelerate when the proportion of black students approached 40% (*U.S.* v. *Board of School Commissioners,* 1971, p. 676; and 1974, p. 80).

More recently, however, some courts have begun to allow the consideration of white flight under certain circumstances. The Second Circuit, for example, upheld a New York school board policy limiting the enrollment of minority students to not exceed 50% in any desegregated school. The board had undertaken voluntary desegregation and engaged in good faith efforts to preserve integration in the face of steadily declining numbers of white students (*Parent Association* v. *Ambach,* 1979; see also *Crawford* v. *Board of Education,* 1976).

The problem of white flight raises a basic policy issue: What is the understanding of the mandate of *Brown?* Do school officials have an affirmative duty to achieve integration of the races in the schools? Or is the mandate merely that actions and policies of school officials be race-neutral, that is, free of any discriminatory motive or intent (the old Parker doctrine)? Query: What are the implications of each of these interpretations of *Brown* for the validity of white flight as a factor in limiting desegregation remedies?

Academic Achievement, Self-Concept, and Race Relations

A BRIEF SUMMARY OF THE COLEMAN REPORT

James S. Coleman

The *Equality of Educational Opportunity* Report contains seven sections dealing with different aspects of educational opportunity. . . .

[S]ections 2 and 3 have been seen as the most relevant to questions of school policy, and it is almost exclusively the conclusions represented in these sections that have been the subject of the discussion and controversy surrounding the Report. These sections describe the results of a national survey which covered approximately 4000 elementary and secondary schools. This large survey study was designed to identify the extent and sources of inequality of educational opportunity among six racial and ethnic groups (Negroes, Puerto Ricans, American Indians, Mexican Americans, Oriental Americans, and whites). . . .

The aim of section 2 is to give some indicators of inequality of opportunity by measuring qualities of inputs to schools, the most traditional conception of what constitutes school quality. It used the characteristics of schools that principals, superintendents, and school boards traditionally employ in comparing the "quality of education" their schools provide. These are items such as teachers' salary, the number of books in the library (and books per student), the age of buildings and of textbooks, the degree of teachers and principals, specialized facilities and curricula, free kindergarten, and nearly all the objective measures of schools that exist in principals' records or that can be obtained

from averaging responses of teachers to questionnaires. . . . Finally, the chapter contains measures of another input to schools that obviously affects the opportunity of each student in the school: the characteristics of other students in the school. Their socioeconomic background and characteristics of their home environment, their race, their attitudes, and their aspirations were included in these tabulations.

The results of all these statistical comparisons can be summarized in only the most superficial way. They show differences between schools attended by each of the minorities and whites, and in particular between schools attended by Negroes and whites in the same geographic region. In general, the differences show whites attending school with greater resources, although this is not uniformly true, and perhaps the most striking point is the small size of the differences. The differences between locales (in particular, North-South differences, and to a lesser extent, metropolitan-nonmetropolitan differences) are for most resources strikingly greater than within-locale or national differences between schools attended by minority students and those attended by white.

This finding has been one of the conclusions in the Report most subject to attacks by its critics, who argue that differences in the resources of schools attended by Negroes and whites are masked in one way or another. It is true that the reported differences do not show everything—for example, the fact that it probably costs more to run a school at the same level in the ghetto than in a suburb. To compete successfully for the same teachers, urban systems must pay higher salaries; among other things, depreciation on textbooks and buildings is greater, and the tabulation of numbers of books in the library does not show the quality of the books. Nevertheless, the criticism probably stems largely from the preconceptions that influence perception: many persons, white and Negro, when they see a school attended largely by black students, unconsciously depreciate it, seeing it as inferior, and then search for physical reasons to justify this perception.

The differences that do show up strongly in the mass of statistics in section 2 are largely differences in the student bodies. . . .

[O]ne might summarize these differences in school characteristics by saying that the major differences stem from the racial segregation of student bodies, and the racial matching of teachers and students. There are some differences in other inputs to schools, but these are not as large as had been generally believed.

Section 3 focuses on the outputs of schools, using achievement of various sorts as measures of output. The aim of the report was to use achievement output as the criterion by which various input differences might be evaluated: by assessing what inputs to the schools were most important for achievement, the relative importance of the input differences found in section 2 could be determined. . . .

In the measurement of achievement itself, a number of results were evident. In all areas of achievement tested (verbal skills, mathematical skills, and in higher grades, tests in practical knowledge, natural sciences, social sciences, and humanities), results were similar. The whites and Oriental Americans achieved at comparable levels in all grades tested (1, 3, 8, 9, and 12), and the other minorities achieved at a level sharply lower, with Negroes and Puerto Ricans achieving lowest of all. . . .

When the relative importance of school factors for achievement was assessed, achievement for each racial group separately was regressed upon various school factors, after family background characteristics were controlled. This con-

trol was carried out so that those school factors most highly correlated with family background would not spuriously show a high relation to achievement. In carrying out this control, however, the analysis showed what had already been well-known: the powerful relation of the child's own family background characteristics to his achievement, a relation stronger than that of any school factors. . . .

The general result was that the factors that, under all conditions, accounted for more variance than any other were the characteristics of the student's peers: those that accounted for the next highest amount of variance were teacher's characteristics; and finally, other school characteristics, including per pupil expenditure on instruction in the system, accounted for very little variance at all. The total variance accounted for by these three sets of school factors was not large—in fact, an analysis of variance showed that only 10 percent of the variance in achievement lay between schools (for each racial group separately), most of it residing within schools. . . .

These results of the analysis of the relation of school characteristics to achievement have produced the largest portion of controversy surrounding the Report—a result which is to be expected, since they constituted the major causal inferences in the Report, and causal inferences from statistical analysis are always subject to debate, whether the issue be smoking and lung cancer or school factors and achievement.

The results clearly suggest that school integration across socioeconomic lines (and hence across racial lines) will increase Negro achievement, and they throw serious doubt upon the effectiveness of policies designed to increase non-personal resources in the school. A simple general statement of the major result is that the closest portions of the child's social environment—his family and his fellow students—affect his achievement most, the more distant portion of his social environment—his teachers—affect it next most, and the non-social aspects of his school environment affect it very little. This of course is an oversimplification because of the interactions of some of these factors; but the results remain, with clear implications for school policies designed to increase the achievement of minority groups and lower-class white students.

THE EVIDENCE ON BUSING

David J. Armor

. . .

Few persons, perhaps, know of the role played by the social sciences in helping to sustain the forces behind desegregation. It would be an exaggeration to say they are responsible for the busing dilemmas facing so many communities today, yet without the legitimacy provided by the hundreds of sociological and psychological studies it would be hard to imagine how the changes we are witnessing could have happened so quickly. At every step—from the 1954 Supreme Court ruling, to the Civil Rights Act of 1964, to the federal busing orders of 1970—social sciences research findings have been inextricably interwoven with policy decisions. . . .

THE INTEGRATION POLICY MODEL . . .

The integration model which is behind current public policy is rooted in social science results dating back to before World War II. The connections between segregation and inequality were portrayed by John Dollard and Gunnar Myrdal in the first prestigious social science studies to show how prejudice, discrimination, segre-

Reprinted with permission of the author and the publisher from: *The Public Interest*, No. 28 (Spring, 1972), pp. 90–126. ©1972 by National Affairs, Inc.

gation, and inequality operated to keep the black man in a subordinate status.

Along with these broad sociological studies there also appeared a number of psychological experiments which were to play a crucial role in the policy decisions. The most notable were the doll studies of Kenneth and Mamie Clark. They found that preschool black children were much less likely than white children to prefer dolls of their own race. . . . In other words, segregation leads to serious psychological damage to the black child; that damage is sufficient to inhibit the kind of adult behavior which might enable the black man to break the circle.

How could the circle be broken? This question plagued a generation of social scientists in quest of a solution to America's race problems. Of a number of studies appearing after the war, two which focused upon the effects of segregation and integration upon white racial attitudes had especial impact. The first was a section of Samuel Stouffer's massive research on the American soldier during World War II. Stouffer found that white soldiers in combat companies with a black platoon were far more likely to accept the idea of fighting side by side with black soldiers than were white soldiers in non-integrated companies. The second was the study by Morton Deutsch and Mary Evans Collins of interracial housing. Comparing residents of similar backgrounds in segregated and integrated public housing projects, they found that whites in integrated housing were more likely to be friendly with blacks, to endorse interracial living, and to have positive attitudes towards blacks in general than were whites living in the segregated projects. . . .

The culmination of this research was Gordon Allport's influential work, *The Nature of Prejudice*. Using the work of Stouffer, Deutsch and Collins, and others, he formulated what has come to be known as the "contact theory":

Contacts that bring knowledge and acquaintance are likely to engender sounder beliefs about minority groups. . . . Prejudice . . . may be reduced by equal status contact between majority and minority groups in the pursuit of common goals. The effect is greatly enhanced if this contact is sanctioned by institutional supports (i.e., by law, custom, or local atmosphere), and it is of a sort that leads to the perception of common interests and common humanity between members of the two groups.

The clear key to breaking the vicious circle, then, was contact. By establishing integrated environments for black and white, white prejudice would be reduced, discrimination would decline, and damaging effects upon the black child's feelings and behavior would be reduced. . . .

With the 1954 decision [of *Brown* v. *Board of Education*], . . . contact theory became an officially sanctioned policy model, and the Southern public school systems became prime targets for its implementation. . . .

[The] policy model may be summarized as follows: . . . [T]he elimination of segregation in schooling should act as a countervailing force for black students by increasing achievement, raising aspirations, enhancing self-esteem, reducing black/white prejudices and hostility, and enabling black students to find better educational and occupational opportunities. It then follows that social and economic inequalities would be lessened and the vicious circle would be bent if not broken. . . .

[T]he school integration programs we review here have two important characteristics in common that may limit generalizability. First, they are examples of "induced" integration as opposed to "natural" integration. Induced integration is brought about by the decision of a state or local agency to initiate a school integration program (sometimes voluntary, sometimes mandatory), rather than by the "natural" process whereby a black family makes an individual decision to relocate in a pre-dominantly white community. Second, all of these programs have had to use varying amounts of busing to accomplish integration. This makes it difficult to separate out the potential effects of busing, if any, from the integration experience *per se*. In other words, *we will be assessing the effects of induced school integration via busing,* and not necessarily the effects of integration brought about by the voluntary actions of individual families that move to integrated neighborhoods. This is a more limited focus, yet induced integration, usually necessitating some amount of busing, is precisely the policy model that has been followed (or is being considered) in many communities throughout the country.

THE DATA

Many of the cities which desegregated their schools to achieve a racial balance have conducted research programs to evaluate the outcomes of desegregation. It is from these studies that we can derive data to test the school and busing hypotheses stemming from the integration policy model. . . .

The data we will use can be classified into two parts. The first part consists of findings from a study of Boston's METCO program, for whose research design, execution, and analysis we are partly responsible. The data are more complete and offer a more thoroughgoing test of the policy model than many other studies we have seen. The METCO program buses black students of all age levels from Boston to predominantly white middle-class schools in the suburbs. Approximately 1500 black students and 28 suburban communities have participated since the program began in 1966; the study from which our data will be taken covers the period from October 1968 to May 1970. The study used a longitudinal design that called for achievement testing for all students and a questionnaire for the junior and senior high students in three waves: the first at the beginning of the school year in October 1968; a second in May 1969; and a third in May 1970. (For a variety of reasons, the achievement testing was not done for the third wave.) The questionnaire covered several areas, including academic performance, aspirations and self-concept, relations with and attitudes toward white students, and attitudes toward the program.

The METCO study also included a small control group consisting of siblings of the bused students matched by sex and grade levels. The fact that the siblings were from the same families as the bused students means that there is an automatic control for social class and other tangible and intangible family factors. Since the high application rate usually prevented the busing program from taking more than one applicant per family, we had reason to believe that the control students would not differ substantially from the bused students along the important dimensions of ability, aspirations, and so forth. . . .

The second part of the data comes largely from reports on integration programs in four other Northern cities throughtout the country. . . . [The four reports are from White Plains, New York; Ann Arbor, Michigan; Riverside, California; and Hartford, Connecticut. Ed.'s note.]

THE FINDINGS: ACHIEVEMENT

None of the studies were able to demonstrate conclusively that integration has had an effect on academic achievement as measured by standardized tests. Given the results of the Coleman study and other evaluations of remedial programs (e.g., Head Start), many experts may not be surprised at this finding. To date there is no published report of *any* strictly educational reform which has been proven substantially to affect academic achievement; school integration programs are no exception. . . .

While none of these studies are flawless, their consistency is striking. Moreover, their results are not so different from the results of the massive cross-sectional studies. An extensive reanalysis of the Coleman data showed that even without controlling for social class factors, "naturally" integrated (i.e., non-bused) black sixth-grade groups were still one and one-half standard deviations behind white groups in the same schools, compared to a national gap of two standard deviations. This means that, assuming the Coleman data to be correct, the *best* that integration could do would be to move the average black group from the second percentile to the seventh percentile (on the *white* scale, where the average white group is at the fiftieth percentile). But the social class differences of integrated black students in the Coleman study could easily explain a good deal of even this small gain. . . .

ASPIRATION

In the METCO study we found that there were no increases in educational or occupational aspiration levels for bused students. . . ; on the contrary, there was a significant decline for the bused students, from 74 percent wanting a college degree in 1968 to 60 percent by May 1970. . . .

At the very least, we can conclude that the bused students do not improve their aspirations for college. The same is true for occupational aspirations, and in this case both the bused students and the controls show a similar pattern. We should point out, however, that the initial aspiration levels are already very high; Coleman found that only 54 percent of white twelfth graders in the urban North aspired to college, and 53 percent expected a professional or technical occupation. Therefore, even the slight decline we have found still leaves the bused students with relatively high aspirations compared to a regional norm. Moreover, when achievement is taken into account, black students actually have higher aspirations than white students at similar levels of achievement. In this respect, some educators have hypothesized that integration has a *positive* effect in lowering aspirations to more realistic levels; of course, others would argue that any lowering of aspirations is undesirable. . . .

RACE RELATIONS

One of the central sociological hypotheses in the integration policy model is that integration should reduce racial stereotypes, increase tolerance, and generally improve race relations. Needless to say, we were quite surprised when our data failed to verify this axiom. Our surprise was increased substantially when we discovered that, in fact, the converse appears to be true. . . .

[T]hese changes reflect ideological shifts. . . . The bused students are much more likely to support the idea of black power than the control students. . . . This is the clearest indication in our data that integration heightens black racial consciousness and solidarity.

The changes do not appear to be in ideology alone. From 1969 to 1970 the bused students reported less friendliness from whites, more free time spent with members of their own race, more incidents of prejudice, and less frequent dating with white students. . . . In other words, the longer the contact with whites, the fewer the kinds of interracial experiences that might lead to a general improvement in racial tolerance. . . .

SOCIAL CLASS

It is difficult to separate race and social class, since black families as a group tend to be lower than white families on most socio-economic measures. To the extent that the distinction can be made, however, no uniquely social class factors have

been reported that would contradict the findings presented so far. . . .

[DISCUSSION OF RESULTS]

Why has the integration policy model failed to be supported by the evidence on four out of five counts? How can a set of almost axiomatic relationships, supported by years of social science research, be so far off the mark? Part of the reason may be that the policy model has failed to take into account some of the conditions that must be placed upon contact theory; but we believe that there may be other reasons as well having to do with (1) inadequate research designs, (2) induced versus "natural" factors, and (3) changing conditions in the black cultural climate.

Most of the methodological procedures which have been used to develop various components of the integration policy model are not adequate. The single most important limitation is that they have been cross-sectional designs. That is, the studies have measured aspects of achievement or race relations at a single point in time, with causal inferences being drawn from comparisons of integrated groups with segregated groups. Such inferences are risky at best, since the cross-sectional design cannot control for self-selection factors. . . .

The second reason for our findings in the race-relations realm may have to do with the relatively contrived nature of current school integration programs. In all of the programs reviewed, the integration has been induced by the actions of state or local agencies; it has not occurred in a more natural way through individual voluntary actions. . . .

The final major reason why the integration policy model may fail is that the racial climate has changed drastically in the years since the Allport work and the Supreme Court decision. The most noteworthy change, of course, has been in the attitudes of black people. Although the majority of blacks may still endorse the concept of integration, many younger black leaders deemphasize integration as a major goal. Black identity, black control, and black equality are seen as the real issues, and integration is regarded as important only insofar as it advances these primary goals. . . .

POLICY IMPLICATIONS

. . .

The available evidence on busing, then, seems to lead to two clear policy conclusions. One is that massive mandatory busing for purposes of improving student achievement and interracial harmony is not effective and should not be adopted at this time. The other is that *voluntary* integration programs such as METCO . . . should be continued and positively encouraged by substantial federal and state grants. Such voluntary programs should be encouraged so that those parents and communities who believe in the symbolic and potential (but so far unconfirmed) long-run benefits of induced integration will have ample opportunity to send their children to integrated schools. . . .

BUSING: A REVIEW OF "THE EVIDENCE"

Thomas F. Pettigrew, Elizabeth L. Useem, Clarence Normand, and Marshall S. Smith

David Armor's "The Evidence on Busing" presented a distorted and incomplete review of this politically charged topic. We respect Armor's right to publish

Reprinted with permission of the principal author and the publisher from: *The Public Interest*, No. 30 (Winter, 1972), pp. 88–118. ©1972 by National Affairs, Inc.

his views against "mandatory busing." But we challenge his claim that these views are supported by scientific evidence. A full discussion of our reading of the relevant research would be too lengthy and technical for the non-specialist. We must limit ourselves here to outlining and discussing briefly our principal disagreements with Armor, which center on four major points.

First, his article begins by establishing unrealistically high standards by which to judge the success of school desegregation. "Busing," he claims, works only if it leads—in *one* school year—to increased achievement, aspirations, self-esteem, interracial tolerance, and life opportunities for black children. And "busing" must meet these standards in *all* types of interracial schools; no distinction is made between *merely desegregated* and *genuinely integrated* schools.

This "integration policy model," as it is labeled, is *not* what social scientists who specialize in race relations have been writing about over the past generation.* Indeed, Armor's criteria must surely be among the most rigid ever employed for

---

*[The authors later elaborate the first point as follows:

"At the heart of [Armor's] misconception is a persistent misreading of Gordon Allport's theory of intergroup contact. Armor cites a quotation from Allport delineating the crucial conditions that he held to be essential before positive effects could be expected from intergroup contact. . . . Yet Armor summarizes this quotation by stating: 'The clear key to breaking the vicious circle, then, was contact.' This is *not* what Allport wrote; the key, Allport argued, is contact *under particular conditions*. . . .

"The basic weakness, then, in this description of an 'integration policy model' is that it assumes positive results for *all* interracial schools rather than for just those meeting the conditions for optimal contact. . . . [I]t is important to distinguish between desegregation and integration. Desegregation is achieved by simply ending segregation and bringing blacks and whites together; it implies nothing about the quality of the interracial interaction. Integration involves Allport's four conditions for positive intergroup contact, cross-racial acceptance, and equal dignity and access to resources for both racial groups. . . ." Ed.'s note.]

the evaluation of a change program in the history of public education in the United States.

Second, the article presents selected findings from selected studies as "*the* evidence on busing." The bias here is twofold. On the one hand, the few studies mentioned constitute an incomplete list and are selectively negative in results. Unmentioned are at least seven investigations—from busing programs throughout the nation—that meet the methodological criteria for inclusion and report *positive* achievement results for black students. These seven studies are widely known. . . .

Positive findings are also obscured by the utilization of an unduly severe standard. The achievement gains of black students in desegregated schools are often compared with white gains, rather than with the achievement of black students in black schools. But such a standard ignores the possibility that *both* racial groups can make more meaningful educational advances in interracial schools. Indeed, this possibility actually occurs in three of the cities mentioned by Armor. Yet he does not inform us of this apparent dual success of desegregation; instead, "busing" is simply rated a failure because the black children did not far outgain the improving white children.

Third, the paper's anti-busing conclusions rest primarily on the findings from one short-term study conducted by Armor himself. This investigation focused on a voluntary busing program in metropolitan Boston called METCO. Yet this study is probably the weakest reported in the paper. Our reexamination of its data finds that it has extremely serious methodological problems.

Two major problems concern deficiencies of the control group. To test the effects of "busing" and school desegregation, a control group should obviously consist exclusively of children who neither are "bused" nor attend desegregated

schools. But our check of this critical point reveals that this is not the case. Among the 82 control students used to test the achievement effects of METCO at all 10 grade levels, we obtained records on 55. Only 21 of these 55 actually attended segregated schools in the tested year of 1968–69. Many of the 34 (62 percent) desegregated children by necessity utilized buses and other forms of transportation to get to school.

Incredible as it sounds, then, Armor compared a group of children who were bused to desegregated schools with another group of children which included many who *also* were bused to desegregated schools. Not surprisingly, then, he found few differences between them. . . .

Serious, too, is an enormous nonresponse rate in the second test administration. . . . For the elementary students, only 51 percent of the eligible METCO students and 28 percent of the eligible "control" students took part in both of the achievement test sessions. The achievement results for junior and senior high students are also rendered virtually meaningless by the participation of only 44 percent of the eligible METCO students and 20 percent of the eligible "control" students. Compare these percentages to the survey standard of 70 to 80 percent, and one can appreciate the magnitude of the possible selection bias introduced into the METCO results by the widespread lack of student participation. Efforts to compensate for these high non-response rates through the use of cross-sectional samples that also suffer from extensive non-response are insufficient. . . .

Consequently, Armor's sweeping policy conclusion against "mandatory busing" is neither substantiated nor warranted. Not only does it rely upon impaired and incomplete "evidence," but in a real sense his paper is not about "busing" at all, much less "mandatory busing." Three of the cities discussed—among them Boston, the subject of Armor's own research—had *voluntary*, not "mandatory busing.". . .

Fourth, objections must be raised to the basic assumptions about racial change that undergird the entire article. Public school desegregation is regarded as largely a technical matter, a matter for social sci-entists more than for the courts. Emphasis is placed solely on the adaptive abilities of black children rather than on their constitutional rights. Moreover, the whole national context of individual and institutional racism is conveniently ignored, and interracial contact under any condition is assumed to be "integration.". . .

N O T E S   A N D   Q U E S T I O N S

The Civil Rights Act of 1964, prohibiting discrimination in education, employment, housing, and voting, also directed the U.S. Office of Education to conduct a survey on educational opportunity in the nation. James Coleman, then professor of social relations at the Johns Hopkins University, was selected to head the research team. The so-called Coleman Report of 1966, involving a sample of 645,000 pupils, has been described as "an enterprise of near Promethean daring . . . perhaps the second largest in the history of social science" (Moynihan 1967, p. 3). It was the first national survey of the effects of biracial schooling. Its impact upon judicial, legislative, and administrative officials has been immense.

Armor's article appeared in the midst of an election year debate on anti-busing legislation. Expectedly, it received extensive media coverage; *The Public Interest* even held a prepublication press conference in anticipation of its impact. It was often cited in Congress as scientific evidence in support of the emerging white consensus against busing. Scholarly rebuttals such as those by Pettigrew et al. received far less public attention.

Effects on Academic Achievement

1.   The optimal research design to study the effects of biracial schooling is, of course, the controlled experiment. Students are randomly assigned to schools identical except for their different racial compositions and their achievement levels are measured at intervals over time. Whatever differences emerge can then be attributed with confidence to the manipulated feature. For obvious reasons, genuine experiments are unfeasible in this area.

"Indirect" experiments are the closest approximation. In one study, for example, black pupils from inner city schools who volunteered to be bused to suburban white schools were randomly assigned to either busing or no busing groups. This differential treatment was justified because there were more volunteers than could be accommodated in the desegregation plan (Mahon and Mahon 1971). The limited opportunities for carrying out indirect experiments restrict the usefulness of this research design for wide scale evaluations.

2.   Coleman relied on a nonexperimental survey using a cross-section design to assess the consequences of "natural" desegregation. Using data drawn from different sections of the country at one common point in time, he examined the relationships between a number of variables with no control over the conditions in which these variables operated or the circumstances that accounted for the presence of the pupils in integrated or segregated schools.

The principal drawback of any correlational study is the difficulty, if not impossibility, of specifying causal relationships with any reasonable certainty. The finding that the achievement of black children rises with the social class level of their school peers may be a spurious rather than a true relationship, given the possibility of confounding effects of uncontrolled (third) variables. Black children who voluntarily attend majority white schools are usually not there by accident. If they outperform their counterparts in segregated schools, it may not be because their middle class schoolmates are more stimulating but because they themselves possess characteristics that influence achievement.

Coleman was certainly cognizant of these difficulties and he statistically controlled for such background factors as parental education, family size and father absence, and reading materials in the home. What other factors should have been held constant?

For methodological criticisms of the Coleman Report—for example, third variable controls were inadequate to their purpose; measurement of social class based on parental education alone was insufficient—see Mosteller and Moynihan (1972) and Bowles and Levin (1968).

3.   Armor purported to study the effects of mandatory desegregation using a longitudinal design with before/after measures and a control group. What bias is present in sibling matching for control?

4.   Pettigrew's criticism of Armor's criterion of desegregation success illustrates how the fact of measurement can subtly redefine the basic policy question. Since 1954, the Supreme Court has never again relied on social science evidence on academic or psychological harm to black children in finding constitutional violations or fashioning remedies in school desegregation cases. The post-*Brown* social research, however, has made harm or benefit the key justification for court imposed desegregation. It has solidified the role of achievement scores as a critical test of whether induced desegregation is worth the candle.

Since the Coleman Report, the attainment of equal educational opportunity has been operationalized in terms of raising the test scores of disadvantaged black pupils. But does the issue of whether and how much to desegregate turn on the gain or nongain of a few points in standardized tests? Suppose it is shown that similar gains can be accomplished by curricular reform and better teaching—is induced desegregation less urgent if it is sufficient but not necessary for improving academic performance? At the bottom of the Pettigrew-Armor dispute there is disagreement not only on methodology and results, but also on the basic policy and research questions to be raised: what is meant by "equal educational opportunity" and how should it be measured?

5.   To the question "What is the effect of school desegregation on the academic achievement of black students?" the best that can be said at this time is, "Sometimes it works, and sometimes it doesn't" (Crain and Mahard 1978, p. 47). Whether or not it works depends on a host of circumstances related to when and how the desegregation process is carried out. The research design and measurements used to evaluate the results also influence the conclusions. Consequently, there can be no single, definitive study of the question. One has to review the empirical literature as a whole to see if any general pattern of results emerges.

Since the publication of the Armor article, several comprehensive literature reviews have appeared and all reach a more optimistic conclusion about the academic benefits of desegregation than did Armor. "The consistent finding," says Crain and Mahard (1978), "is that black achievement is higher in predominantly white schools" (p. 21). Examining fifty-two studies of court-imposed desegregation, they found that "positive findings outnumber negative findings [including Armor's Boston study] by a ratio of three to one" (p. 24). The average gain in achievement was one-half of a grade equivalent during the first one or two years of desegregation, or approximately .2 standard deviations (p. 49).

A survey of forty-four published and unpublished studies of both mandated and "natural" desegregation showed black achievement gains in ten studies, no changes or mixed results in twenty-three studies, and impaired performance in only one study (Stephan 1978, p. 232). Another reviewer concluded that "the greatest number of studies report positive gains as a result of desegregation, although it is clear that much additional research is needed before the findings can be fully understood and translated into effective policy" (Weinberg 1975, p. 242).

The consensus on the absence of any detrimental effects of desegregation on achievement is even stronger. It is the rare study that shows test performance of either white or black students to be adversely affected by desegregation (Weinberg 1975, p. 243; Crain and Mahard 1978, p. 18; St. John 1975), notwithstanding Wolf's claim (1981) to the contrary (p. 230).

6.   Subsequent studies to the Coleman Report suggest that the characteristics of fellow students are effective mainly at the classroom level rather than at the school level. The racial or social class balance of the individual classroom, rather than of the school, was found to exert the stronger influence upon student achievement (U.S. Commission on Civil Rights 1966, vol. 2, pp. 41–42; McPartland 1969; Cohen, Pettigrew, and Riley 1972).

7.   The fact that desegregation appears to be associated with some minority achievement gains is not to say that the reasons for this result are understood. The processes of classroom learning are not well known, regardless of race. What explanatory hypotheses, drawn from the social psychological literature (for example from basic research on social comparison processes, role theory, achievement motivation, teacher expectancies), could be put forth to provide a conceptual foundation for the desegregation-achievement relationship?

8.   The impact of mandatory versus voluntary desegregation is still uncertain. These two forms of desegregation may well be two different phenomena. Mandatory plans often involve institutional changes in the receiving school to serve better any special needs of minority students, including in-service training of teachers, curricular changes, faculty desegregation, and the like. Voluntary plans could entail nothing more than racial balancing of students. Moreover, these volunteer students are self-selected. What reasons are there to expect greater or more consistent academic improvement under mandatory or voluntary plans, either on a short-term or long-term basis?

9.   Pettigrew's social psychological differentiation between "integration" and "desegregation" (whether voluntary or induced) is a useful one. An instance of induced desegregation without integration was the experience of Riverside, California. Gerard and Miller (1975) found no evidence that it led to black achievement gains; in fact, there were some negative effects when classrooms were composed of more than 80 percent white students. They emphasized, however, that even four years later, the bused minority students were still treated as outsiders. White teachers and students were generally patronizing and deprecating toward them. The results indicated that social climate of the classroom is a key ingredient in academic success.

Results such as these have led Gerard (1983), a noted and "liberal" social psychologist, to concede, clad in sack cloth, that "social scientists were wrong in the belief that change would come easily. . . . [M]any of us were blinded by our ideology. . . . A good deal of damage has been done by recommendations [made in the "Social Science Statement" of 1954] that were based not on hard data but mostly on well-meaning rhetoric" (p. 875).

10.   Rist's account (1978) of voluntary desegregation of an upper income, all-white elementary school in Portland, Oregon, is another painful example of how desegregation ought not to be conducted. As with most voluntary plans, dispersal of minority students throughout the system was the norm. This particular school received about thirty black students. With the best of intentions, school officials sought to treat black students just like white students. They equated integration with racial assimilation: "socializing nonwhite students to act, speak, and believe very much like white students" (p. 15). The all-white faculty and administration had never taught a black child, and no special training was given them to welcome the new arrivals.

From the start, the low income blacks had trouble keeping up with the high achieving whites. Some teachers physically separated the one or two black students in each classroom for special instruction, but no other help was provided. Soon, teachers were exchanging "horror stories" about their black pupils, and some older white students cursed and taunted the black youngsters on the playground and in the bus. By the end of the year, some of the black students had adjusted and performed satisfactorily and others had dropped out. One fourth-grader, on the day before he left to transfer back to his former black school, "went around telling everyone how he hated them and hoped they would all die" (p. 165). Bell (1979) notes that the "systematic, mostly unthinking devastation" wreaked upon some of these children "probably has been replicated in many school integration efforts across the country" (pp. 1829, 1831). It is this kind of desegregation experience that has led critics to argue that "in order for schools to successfully teach black children, they will have to incorporate the cultural wisdom and experience of black families and meaningfully collaborate with parents and community" (Lightfoot 1978, p. 129). Whether and how this can be accomplished outside the context of all-black schools remains to be seen.

To assess, then, the impact of school desegregation on minority achievement as if everything else is equal is a spurious inquiry. Everything else is never equal; there are many other factors at play besides the racial or social class mixture.

Effects on Self-Concept

11.   The initial and most frequently cited justification for ending biracial schools was the one stated in *Brown I*: segregating black students "generates a feeling of inferiority" which, in turn, "affects [their] motivation . . . to learn" and retards their "educational and mental development" (p. 494). While the

Court dealt specifically with de jure segregation, some social scientists have stated that these detrimental personality effects flow from the very fact of racial separation, whether caused by state edicts or ecological changes (for example, Fisher 1967). This notion of a negative self-image among segregated black children had wide currency until the late sixties. With the start of northern school desegregation, social scientists began re-examining this notion and finding little or mixed empirical support for it. The recent literature distinguishes different dimensions of the global and shadowy construct of self-concept: racial identification or preference, self-esteem, and academic self-evaluation.

12.   The racial identification research is beset by conceptual and methodological problems (Weinberg 1977; Epps 1978). Clark had asserted that segregated black children have a negative self-image because they tended to prefer white dolls. One reviewer now describes it as "a paradigm in search of a phenomenon" (Banks 1976, p. 1179).

The evidence is equivocal. White preference results may or may not be obtained depending upon the experimental procedures used (Banks 1976). Racial attitudes are acquired by children in distinct stages, and studies of racial identification need to take into account this developmental pattern. Preferences expressed at an early age do not necessarily last into adolescence and adulthood (Katz 1976).

The most extensive study was done in the evaluation of the school desegregation in Riverside, California (Gerard and Miller 1975). No correlation was found between the self-esteem of minority children (measured by age-graded mental health tests) and their racial preferences (using photographs instead of dolls). The two are separate concepts, and a one-to-one relationship between them cannot be facilely assumed.

13.   Despite the proliferation of research on self-esteem, self-concept, and related constructs pertaining to one's sense of personal worth, there is "little agreement among researchers on the meaning of the terms" (Epps 1978, p. 65) or on the impact produced by school desegregation (St. John 1975; Weinberg 1977; Epps 1978). The results are mixed: Some studies find that minority children have higher self-concepts in desegregated schools, others find lower, and still others find no relationship at all. "At best, all that can be said is that there is little evidence that desegregation impairs black self-esteem; nor can it be said that desegregation, in itself, enhances self-esteem." In any event, contrary to Armor's results, recent reviews of the literature indicate that "there is no reason to believe that blacks suffer from low self-esteem" (Epps 1975, p. 312).

14.   Academic self-evaluation was examined in the Coleman Report. Students were asked to evaluate their ability to learn and to estimate their own intelligence relative to that of their peers. There was little difference between black and white students (1966, pp. 323–24). The new surge of black pride and self-imposed separation has also given a new dimension to the question of segregation and self-image. At least, there is now "serious doubt on the notion that segregated education generates feelings of inferiority" (Goodman 1972, p. 409).

Effects on Interracial Attitudes

15.   Another proposition put forth by social scientists at the time of *Brown I,* independent of the hypothesis about the effects on achievement and self-concept, was that desegregation would reduce prejudice and hostility between blacks and whites. A function of public education is to prepare children for membership in the multiracial and multicultural society that is America. The assumption is that one-race schools nurture intolerance in children, and in the long run it has a fallout effect on the level of prejudice in society as a whole. Integrated schools, on the other hand, provide an opportunity for children of diverse heritages to learn together and thereby develop mutual respect and acceptance. They are incubators of racial harmony. The conceptual and empirical basis for this view was provided by Allport's "equal status contact" hypothesis (1954, p. 261; Amir 1976; McConahay 1981, p. 35). It turned on its head the Social Darwinist premise of Sumner that law-ways cannot change folkways.

Is Allport's hypothesis applicable to the classroom setting? What is meant by "equal status" between middle income whites and low income blacks who are competing for grades and social leadership? For opposing views, compare Cook (1979), one of the signers of the "Social Science Statement" of 1954 (contemporary social scientists have "misdirected their efforts," focusing on conditions known to minimize rather than enhance the effectiveness of desegregation; p. 434) with Gerard (1983), who "probably would have signed [the "Statement"] . . . if [he] had been asked to do so" (it is "extraordinarily quixotic" to assume that the four conditions for positive intergroup contact "would or could be met in the typical school system . . ."; p. 870).

16.   Reviews of the literature on school desegregation and interracial attitudes show inconclusive results: "For every study showing certain effects, another study reaching opposite results can be cited. . . . [T]he findings are of such a mixed character that any attempt to use this evidence on the psychosocial effects of desegregation in a court could easily be contradicted by citing another study with opposite results" (Cohen 1975, p. 297; St. John 1975; Stephan 1978).

One reason for this uncertainty is the low methodological quality of most studies. "[T]here are apparently no experimental or quasi-experimental studies with sufficient methodological rigor to shed any light on the effects of school desegregation on either student racial attitudes or behavior" (McConahay 1978, p. 84). "[R]ecent reviews . . . agree unanimously that the literature is a methodological cesspool" (McConahay 1982, p. 36). Correlational surveys have shown that white students in naturally desegregated schools have friendlier, more respectful attitudes toward blacks (U.S. Commission on Civil Rights 1966, vol. 2, pp. 47, 139). However, the results are subject to chicken-and-egg problems of interpretation: biracial schools may make children more tolerant, but parents who send their children there are likely to be tolerant in the first place and to have inculcated such values at home.

Another reason for the mixed results is the absence of any theory that explains why and how school desegregation affects racial attitudes. Does school segregation enhance prejudice or does school desegregation decrease prejudice? Legally, this is not a fastidious distinction. The text of the Fourteenth Amendment is in the negative: It restrains the state from acting discriminatorily, but it does not demand that the state act affirmatively in the first instance. The role of the state is to be neutral. Therefore, there is no obligation on the schools to intervene to decrease pre-existing private prejudice; there is an obligation to prevent the increase of prejudice.

Such a theory would have to take into account the intervening factors that operate in desegregated schools and classrooms; that is, it would have to focus on higher-order relationships. For example, the Riverside study found that white students made fewer friends with black students when there were racially biased teachers (Gerard and Miller 1975, p. 94). The racial composition of the student body is another factor. The tolerance of white students in naturally desegregated schools diminishes when black enrollment exceeds 50% (U.S. Commission on Civil Rights 1966, vol. 2, p. 139).

"Does desegregation foster more tolerant racial attitudes?" is basically an unanswerable question. There are countless factors inside and outside the school setting that could influence the relationship. Prejudice in American society has a long history. It seems unrealistic to expect school desegregation to usher in the New Jerusalem and that, overnight, the lion will lay down with the lamb. Schools mirror the social stratification and racial discrimination of the larger society.

What other questions, more limited in scope and empirically answerable, could be framed for future investigation in this area?

Implications for Law

17.   The de jure/de facto distinction has implications for the use of social science evidence in challenging school segregation. When segregation is tolerated or required by law, the presumption of constitutionality is reversed (see Chapter 3, section 3.6). The challenger, entitled to factual doubt, need only show the possibility of harm. A court is justified in accepting "sloppy" social science for this purpose.

Strict scrutiny is also triggered when the state action infringes upon a fundamental right with explicit or implicit constitutional protection (for example, suffrage, interstate travel). A neighborhood school policy, when superimposed upon existing residential segregation, results in de facto school segregation. If equal educational opportunity—defined to include the right to attend integrated schools—is a fundamental right, then even a rational justification for this attendance policy would not shelter it from equal protection attack. The burden is on school officials to come forward with a compelling reason for that policy; failing that, it would be struck down as an invidious classification.

The Supreme Court has yet to articulate what makes certain rights, not found in the letter of the Constitution, fundamental. *Brown I* contains language that could be relied upon to argue that public education is a fundamental interest: It is the "very foundation of sound citizenship"; the state has "a principal interest in awakening the child to cultural values." Education not only increases social-economic opportunities later in life. The opinion of Chief Justice Warren also suggests that it is a precondition to free speech and representative self-government. It is necessary for the enlightened exercise of First Amendment rights.

In 1973, in a decision upholding the validity of state educational finance procedures that rely on local property wealth as a determinant of local school expenditures, the Supreme Court refused to recognize the fundamental nature of education (*San Antonio Independent School District* v. *Rodriguez*). The Court noted the division of opinion among social scientists on "the extent to which there is a demonstrable correlation between educational expenditures and the quality of education" and therefore refrained from passing on this issue. Query whether the result would have been different if there had been near unanimity in the expert testimony as in *Brown I.*

18.   With strict scrutiny foreclosed, the validity of "pure" de facto segregation rests on challenging the reasonableness of the neighborhood school policy. Because the alleged harm of this policy is not self-evident and a presumption of validity attaches thereto, "the de facto racial imbalance would have to be shown to be educationally or psychologically harmful." The challenger has the affirmative duty of proving—using reliable and valid data rather than merely plausible hypotheses—that "de facto segregation inflicted the same . . . harm as the statutorily-imposed segregation outlawed in *Brown*" (Levin and Moise 1975, p. 71).

This legal argument is no stronger than its empirical premises. Can a case against de facto segregation be built on the extant evidence on achievement, self-concept, and interracial attitudes? On the evidence on residential segregation? Is more needed than a showing of differential racial impact to find an Equal Protection violation?

19.   There are three interrelated elements in any school desegregation case: determining the violation, framing the remedy, and evaluating the effects of the remedy. For which of these purposes has social science evidence been most effectively used in the southern and northern school cases?

Unconstitutional Practices of School Authorities

A basic teaching of the post-*Brown* cases is that there is no judicial remedy for segregated schools without first establishing a constitutional violation. Evidence of purposeful discrimination is the "trigger" that fires the "cannon" of mandatory desegregation (Fiss 1971, p. 705). A court must find the smoking gun before it can order that the smoke be cleared. Judge Roth's findings of several kinds of unconstitutional conduct by Detroit school officials, though sustained by the appellate courts, were dismissed by Wolf (1981) as "absurd" and "inadequate" (pp. 201, 202).

Judge Roth's opinion, paradoxically, devoted more space to praising the pro-integration efforts of the Detroit School Board than to discussing its purported violations. Since no-fault liability is inexistent under present law, Wolf (1981) argues that the conclusions on school violations are merely legal fictions in order to hold school authorities culpable—the violations are the smoking gun. She derides the linkage between the violations and segregated schools as an "unsubstantiated causal theory" (p. 243), "a kind of legal hocus-pocus" (p. 292) that is "deceptive and harmful to judicial credibility" (p. 243). Others, too, have acknowledged that the causal link is a makeshift concept (Fiss 1971; Justices Powell and Rehnquist dissenting in *Dayton Board of Education* v. *Brinkman,* 1979). "It is astonishing," she writes, "that sociologists and demographers have not challenged this [causal] analysis" (p. 335, fn. 36). She does not deny that *some* violations have occurred in the past, but insists that "racial predominance violates the Constitution only if it can be shown that acts of school authorities played a *substantial* causal role" (p. 345, emphasis added).

NOTES AND QUESTIONS

1.   Wolf is right in asserting that if official misconduct contributed to only a small proportion of the variance, such actions are not *the* cause of segregation. But is the issue one of measuring the marginal increment in school segregation due to these violations? Or is it one of deciding whether to attribute responsibility to school and state officials even if their roles in causing segregation in the past and/or legitimating racial imbalances in the present are small or unmeasurable? That is, is the task one of "sociological-demographic analysis" (Wolf 1981, p. 257) or of normative judgment?

2.   Does *Swann* require a showing of "substantial" unconstitutional behavior for a finding of wrong? Is Wolf's criticism of the attenuated causal nexus a quarrel with the social research presented at the trial or with the substantive law?

3.   Wolf's observation that social science experts were used primarily by the plaintiffs rather than the defendants in the Detroit litigation is also true in other school desegregation cases. Sanders *et al.* (1981–82) interviewed the attorneys and experts in seventeen different lawsuits, involving small and large school districts, both in the north and in the south, in 1979 and 1980. In eleven of the seventeen cases, plaintiffs presented expert witnesses to prove a constitutional violation; defendants did so in only three of the cases. Several interrelated reasons accounted for this imbalance. Defense attorneys said they had difficulty recruiting scholars to testify on behalf of school authorities. As one put it:

> It's not fashionable to be defending these lawsuits. . . . We would find people who because of peer pressure did not want to testify for the defendant, regardless of what the facts were. . . . We were told, off the record, that if they did work for our side, . . . [t]heir access to grants, to promotions, to new relationships in their professions would be greatly jeopardized. [p. 415]

The paucity of experts for the defense stems not only from their ideological tilt and their fears of adverse career consequences, but also from the tactical decision of defense attorneys not to use counter experts. The bottom line in the defense of school officials is absence of intentional wrongdoing. With this narrow (and technically correct) definition of the legal issue, empirical evidence on residential segregation and on academic performance is arguably irrelevant. The defense focus is on the specific actions and motives of school officials—facts of an adjudicative nature. The social science focus is on the broader societal pattern of racism—facts of a legislative nature. In the view of one defense lawyer, the experts are "full of bull" and their testimony is "a waste of time." "[W]e would [be] better off if we could agree that they would have no sociologists and we would have no sociologists and we would just present our facts to the court . . ." (p. 419). For the same reason, defense lawyers often make little effort to cross-examine rigorously plaintiffs' experts. The study also suggests another explanation for the nonuse of social scientists by the defense. Only 20% of the defense attorneys in these seventeen cases had previously participated in a school desegregation lawsuit, compared to 75% of the plaintiff attorneys (p. 416). The latter were usually associated with a national organization (for example, the NAACP, the ACLU, or the Department of Justice) which had extensive experience in this area of law and had a ready network of seasoned expert witnesses it could call upon. Defense counsel typically consisted of a local law firm that had represented the school system in the past on labor relations or other routine business, but not on civil rights matters.

   Are there no tactical advantages for the defense in calling its own social science experts? Should the defense introduce evidence showing that most scholars are reluctant to testify on behalf of school boards because they believe their careers may be jeopardized?

4.   Figure 4.1 sketches in oversimplified form the legal issues and the accompanying social research from *Brown I* to *Milliken*. Obviously, both the law and the empirical research have grown more complex and uncertain since 1954. It is no longer simple to find the smoking gun. There may be no single gun or there may be many guns. In any event, there is smoke everywhere—and deciding how to clear the smoke is not any easier.

FIGURE 4.1

Summary of the Kinds of Social Science Evidence Presented and Their Legal Uses in Southern and Northern Cases

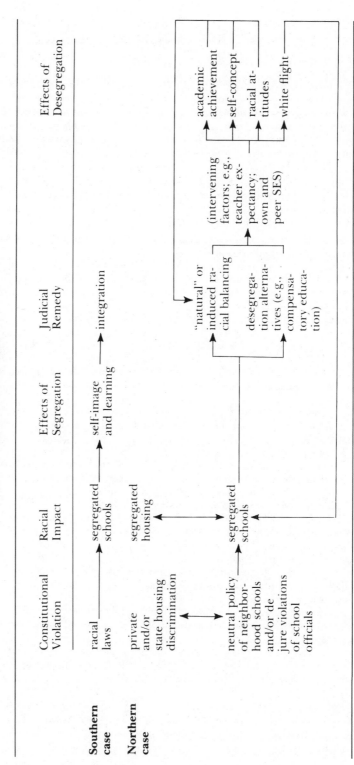

4.6.   REINTERPRETATION OF BROWN*

Evolving Interpretations of Brown:
Input and Output Perspectives

Depending on one's view of what *Brown* promised, it stands as a monument to unfulfilled hopes (racially segregated schools remain the norm in most large cities today) or to judicial power to effect social change (it did, quite simply, bury Jim Crow). There is a fundamental ambiguity in *Brown* regarding the constitutional entitlement it created and the remedy it implied upon its violation. This ambiguity has colored the subsequent development of all racial discrimination law.

On the one hand, *Brown* can be interpreted as proscribing color-conscious policies and actions that result in racial exclusion. Official apartheid is inherently wrong because it rests upon assumptions of racial superiority and inferiority that are repugnant to American aspirations of equality. The remedy for its violation is color-blind decision-making: "equal educational opportunit[y]." The emphasis is on equality of access to schools rather than on the quality of the schooling. This is an "input perspective" on the system of segregation. It seeks to identify and neutralize the specific "villains" who are the "cause" of the wrong.

On the other hand, *Brown* can be seen as safeguarding minority children against the social, psychological, and educational harms said to result from racial segregation. The constitutional right is defined in terms of the consequential injury. The remedy for its breach is color-conscious decision-making: racial integration. This relief promises more than just open access and an end to racial exclusion. It mandates deliberate racial mixture in order to bestow upon the underclass the purported advantages of exposure to the upperclass. This is an "output perspective" on segregation. It looks to the results of segregation, irrespective of their cause, with the purpose of improving the lot of the constitutionally protected group.

Through the years, liberals have clung steadfastly to the original understanding of *Brown* that racial integration and equal educational opportunity are inextricably related—the former guarantees the latter. When schools were, in fact, separate and unequal, pragmatic and moral considerations supported the integrationist strategy. Because white-dominated school boards favored white schools, black children had to go to the same schools attended by white children in order to receive the same educational package. "To get what the white kids have, you must go to where the white kids are."

Today, developments on several fronts—intradistrict equalization of educational funding; widespread white and emerging black opposition to involuntary busing; changing demographic patterns that frustrate intradistrict desegregation; doubts about the claimed benefits of racial integration in the classroom—render school desegregation an increasingly elusive remedy in the nation's metropolitan areas. The revisionist view does not equate the right to equal educational opportunity with the right to an integrated education. Instead, it reinterprets *Brown* as promising only

*This section is a revised version of part of an article by W. Loh: "In Quest of *Brown*'s Promise: Social Research and Social Values in School Desegregation," *Washington Law Review* 58 (1982): 129–74. Reprinted by permission of the publisher. Copyright ©1982 by the Washington Law Review Association.

nondiscriminatory access, a modern version of the old Parker Doctrine that desegregation-does-not-mean-integration.

The Detroit Case: Throughput Perspective

Pressed by competing demands for busing and for neighborhood schools, the *Milliken* Court strove for a balance between activism and restraint. Consistent with its other post-*Brown* decisions, it avoided any finding on the harm of segregation. If the wrong is defined in terms of its effects rather than its cause, then racial imbalances in every sphere of life, whether de jure or de facto, must be eradicated "root and branch"—a true *Green*-ing of America. The output perspective implicates system-wide relief. The Court, wisely, has abstained from a sweeping, panoramic analysis of segregation. It has not stigmatized all fruits of past segregation as original sin. An equality-cum-integration remedy on any large scale could have a dislocative impact on the white majority. The new conservatism fears that massive racial balancing would undermine the social-political consensus of our multi-ethnic society. What the Court has done, instead, in this case and in others, is to attribute the "cause" of segregation to specific "villains"—including integration-minded school boards—and find them culpable of de jure violations. Although Wolf reviles this causal analysis as unscientific and "legal hocus-pocus," it is a pragmatic means of distinguishing between permissible and impermissible forms of racial imbalance depending upon the equities of a particular case. The requirement of proximate causation implicit in the intentional discrimination serves to limit the widespread allocation of blame. If everyone is responsible, nobody is.

In the Detroit case, the Court adopted an input perspective on the violation, but did not confine the remedy to guaranteeing equal opportunity—"the proper objective of public policy," according to the new conservative view. It recognized that a colorblind remedy can be and is "an obstacle to school integration; facially neutral decisions can result in disproportional racial impact. The Court steered a middle-of-the-road course between color-conscious and colorblind remedial strategies. *Milliken II* affirmed the trial court's decree that the State of Michigan and the Detroit School Board expend $5.8 million in compensatory education, training, and counseling programs for students, faculty, and staff of the city schools, in addition to any intradistrict busing and in lieu of any interdistrict busing. It signaled the end of the integration line of *Brown* and the start of the neo-*Plessy* doctrine of mostly-separate-but-equal, at least when demographic conditions such as those of Detroit prevail.

This outcome suggests a third way of analyzing the promise of *Brown*: a "throughput perspective." The preceding two perspectives tend to slight the education component in *Brown* v. *Board of Education*. They focus on the inputs of discriminatory actions that produce racial imbalances, or on the outputs of new racial balances and social-educational improvements upon desegregation. The throughput perspective attends more to the quality of the schooling than to racial considerations. *Milliken II* should be seen against the background of a growing "effective education movement" in the black community that rejects racial integration as necessary to black educational achievement. It believes that predominantly black schools that "incorporate the cultural wisdom and experience of black families and meaningfully collaborate with parents and community" can foster academic excellence.

Table 4.1 summarizes the three perspectives on the constitutional entitlement and remedy promised by *Brown*. The doctrinal difficulty with the throughput per-

TABLE 4.1

Perspectives on *Brown's* Promise

	Brown's Promise	
	Entitlement	**Remedy**
Input perspectives	de jure segregation (color-conscious decisions) are inherently unequal	right to *equal* (colorblind) educational opportunity
Output perspectives	freedom from social-educational harms of segregation	right to *integrated* (color-conscious) education
Throughput perspectives	(undefined)	right to *effective* education

spective is that it offers a new remedy without a corresponding redefinition of the underlying right that triggers it. Educational effectiveness is nonactionable because the Court has ruled that the Fourteenth Amendment does not embrace a fundamental guarantee of quality education, (*San Antonio Independent School District* v. *Rodriguez*, 1973), and no right in *Brown* supports educational remedies to equalize racially separate schools. *Milliken II* and subsequent lower court decisions have nimbly sidestepped this issue by finding de jure violations and using this fiction as the constitutional peg upon which to hang the effective education remedy.

In summary, the Court in the Detroit case takes on the role of a virtuoso playing two keyboards. On the left keyboard, he plays the traditional liberal music; on the right, the new conservative sound. To the first audience, the notes of racial equality give courage to carry on with reform; to the second audience, the score of equal opportunity gives assurance that the existing class structure will not be fundamentally altered. The playing of both keyboards indicates the dilemma of resolving conflicting claims of high dimension. The Court opted, as it sometimes does when faced with a lack of consensual values, for a kind of rough justice or Solomonic compomise rather than a clear choice between the competing interests. It gave dignity and credibility to both claims and attempted to frame a middle course remedy. By recognizing and articulating the felt needs of the age, the Court assisted in the ongoing creation of national values in the context of which the political processes of government can act to resolve the conflict.

Implications for Social Research

The perspectives on *Brown's* meaning bear implications for empirical inquiry on school desegregation. So long as the remedial objective was integration, social science also adopted an output perspective on research. In the mid-fifties psychologists conducted small-scale experimental studies on the social and personality effects of segregation. In the mid-sixties, sociologists gathered extensive cross-sectional data and applied sophisticated multivariate analyses to examine the social and educational effects of "natural" desegregation. In the mid-seventies, revisionist sociologists conducted similar large-scale surveys on the effects of "induced" desegregation via mandatory busing. In all these instances, the basic research question was, "What is the effect of school segregation or desegregation on certain outcomes?" The question presumed a global impact of racial and/or social class composition on the dependent measures. Researchers were interested in establishing first-order relationships. There is a certain allure to the idea that heterogeneity in the schools based on race and/or social class can bring about the educational and social millennium.

After the mid-seventies, coincident with the emergence of the effective education movement, social scientists began to pay more attention to conditions inside the schools. They noted that factors such as the nature of intergroup contact and the social climate of the classroom can be as important, if not more so, as simple racial balancing. Social psychologists differentiated between "merely desegregated" and "genuinely integrated" schools (Pettigrew *et al.*, 1972). The former refers to a mere racial bouillabaisse and implies nothing about the quality of racial interaction that is a precondition to effective learning. The latter involves the presence of those conditions, identified by Gordon Allport, as necessary for favorable intergroup relations: equal status, common goals, noncompetitive atmosphere, and institutional resources. Researchers began to examine higher-order relationships. The question they asked was, "Under what circumstances can schools maximize the desired outcomes?"

The throughput perspective directs researchers to think about the remedy in terms of an ongoing process rather than as a final product. It focuses attention not only on what goes into and what comes out of the school system, but also on the myriad of events that transpire in between. School desegregation, in short, cannot be thought of as a kind of experimental treatment in education. The analogy fails because desegregation programs are not all alike. The quality of education may be entirely different in schools with the same racial balance because the conditions of learning and interracial contact are different. It is unrealistic to expect desegregation to have any across-the-board impact on educational performance or any other outcome. The emphasis in the eighties is on the situational factors that influence the result (for example, the conditions of "cooperative learning" in racially-mixed groups; Slavin 1980), and researchers are undertaking in-depth, longitudinal studies of a given school or school district in order to supplement the cross-section surveys of the past two decades (see Gerard 1983).

4.7.   SECOND-GENERATION PROBLEMS IN SCHOOLS: INTELLIGENCE TESTING

With the onset of massive desegregation, teachers began reporting behavior problems and academic deficiencies among the newly transferred black students—the "casualties of de jure segregation," as one court described them (*Hobson* v. *Hansen*, 1967, p. 443). The behavior problems were met with discipline. By the late sixties, it was apparent that in desegregated schools in both the North and the South, a disproportionate number of black students were suspended, subjected to corporal punishment, and expelled more often than white students (Hearings on Equal Educational Opportunity, 1970; the last has been termed the academic equivalent of "capital punishment"; Yudof 1974). The academic deficiencies resulted in the disproportionate placement of black pupils in educationally inferior ability tracks or in programs for the educable mentally retarded (E.M.R.).

The courts initially were reluctant to intrude into what was seen as intra-school matters that were best left to the discretion and competence of the schoolmaster. However, as school desegregation was followed increasingly by racially discriminatory actions within the classrooms of unitary schools, they moved in. Thus, during the first generation of judicial intervention, the unit of attention was the "macro" level of the school district; in the next generation, the focus shifted to the "micro" level of the classroom. Large-scale issues of inequality between schools were succeeded by minute details of inequality within schools. In this section, we will concentrate on one type of generation problem: the use of intelligence tests in E.M.R. placements.

Although standardized intelligence testing became widespread during the First World War, it did not come under judicial scrutiny until the late sixties. The legal challenge arose in two areas in which testing was extensively used: public employment and education. The discriminatory racial effects that resulted from the use of these seemingly neutral tests prompted the scrutiny.

In the schools, there were three principal uses of intelligence tests (which are individually administered) and aptitude tests (which are group-administered intelligence tests) that came under legal challenge. One was as a screening procedure for admission of black students to white schools. In the post-*Brown* token desegregation period, the pupil placement laws relied on both types of testing as a covert means of blocking black transfers. "It may not be coincidence," Bersoff (1979) noted, "that from 1957 until 1966, the use of standardized tests doubled" (p. 39, n. 53). At the time, the validity of the tests themselves was never called into question. When pupil placement laws were struck down, the tests were not enjoined from use so long as they were administered to all transferring students, white and black, and were not otherwise applied to perpetuate dual school systems.

A second use was to group students of homogeneous abilities into separate educational tracks within a school. Such groupings serve valid educational functions such as tailoring academic programs to individual ability. However, the track method can become suspect when it first begins to flourish during the school desegregation process and a disproportionate number of minority children are placed in the inferior tracks, resulting in resegregation within the classrooms.

In the landmark case of *Hobson* v. *Hansen* (1967), Judge Skelly Wright abolished tracking as it was then practiced in the Washington, D.C. public schools. He did not treat the overrepresentation of poor and black students in the lower tracks as racially motivated, though this pattern was a "precipitating cause" of the inquiry (p. 513). Instead, in some ninety pages of fact-finding, he dwelt on the lack of a rational connection between tracking and the aptitude tests used for the groupings. "[B]y definition the basis of the track system is to classify students according to their ability to learn" (p. 513). However, he found that the aptitude tests did not measure "ability to learn," which he defined as "innate capacity to learn" (p. 514). The "students are in reality being classified . . . [on] factors which have nothing to do with innate ability" (p.

514). Since the tests were invalid for ability grouping, the tracking system was over-turned as a violation of the Equal Protection Clause.

Despite Judge Wright's analytical misstep of equating ability with innate en-dowment, the Court of Appeals affirmed his decision but interpreted his decree as abolishing the tracking program then in existence rather than ending all forms of ability grouping in the future (*Smuck* v. *Hobson*, 1969). Judge Wright's opinion, ac-cording to one commentator, has had "no impact" on the full panoply of school classifications and sortings based on aptitude tests (Kirp 1973, p. 753).

A third group for legal challenge was the use of intelligence tests for E.M.R. placement. This type of sorting is more onerous than tracking. Some minority educa-tors describe E.M.R. programs as the educational equivalent of "genocide" (Kirp 1973, p. 720). The student is set apart from the mainstream of the school, the label is stigmatizing, and future college and job opportunities are curtailed. About a decade after the challenge to tracking and aptitude tests, E.M.R. programs and the associated use of intelligence tests were put on trial in *Larry P.* v. *Riles*.

LARRY P. v. RILES

495 F. Supp. 926 (N.D. Ca. 1979)

PECKHAM, Chief Judge.

Plaintiffs, representing the class of black children in California who have been or in the future will be wrongly placed and maintained in special classes for the "ed-ucable mentally retarded" ("E.M.R.")[1] challenge the placement process for those classes and particularly certain uses of standardized individual intelligence ("I.Q.") tests in California. They contend that the I.Q. tests in their present form are biased and that defendants have dis-criminated against black children by using those tests. The tests allegedly result in the misplacement of black children in special classes that doom them to stigma, inade-quate education, and failure to develop the skills necessary to productive success in our society. Black children represent only 10 percent of the present general student

[1]Educable mentally retarded (E.M.R.) children are defined as incapable, "because of retarded intellectual development," of mastering the skills necessary to ad-vance beyond a minimal educational level. *See* Cal. Educ. Code § 56500.

population in California, but provide some 25 percent of the population enrolled in E.M.R. classes. . . .

A principal focus of this litigation is on testing—on the use of individual I.Q. tests—to classify black children and assign them to E.M.R. classes. Much of the more than 10,000-page transcript of the trial represents detailed expert testimony about these tests. The court has necessarily been drawn into the emotionally charged debate about the nature of "intelligence" and its basis in "genes" or the "environment." . . .

III.   HISTORY OF THE I.Q. TEST . . .

A.   THE EARLY HISTORY. We must recog-nize at the outset that the history of the I.Q. test, and of special education classes built on I.Q. testing, is not the history of neutral scientific discoveries translated into educational reform. It is, at least in the early years, a history of racial prejudice, of Social Darwinism, and of the use of the scientific "mystique" to legitimate such prejudices.

The first usable I.Q. tests were de-veloped in France in 1905 by Alfred Binet, who sought to distinguish between "backward" and "normal" children in Paris. He had no illusions that his test could measure innate traits. . . .

The early leaders of the I.Q. testing movement in the United States were quick to assume that the Binet tests measured an innate capacity fixed in the genes. Typical and of particular interest for the California story were the views of Professor Lewis Terman of Stanford, the well-known developer of the Stanford-Binet I.Q. test in 1916. According to Terman, his test could be employed as an objective tool to learn the identity of the "feeble-minded" and "borderline feeble-minded" and hopefully to discourage them from breeding. . . .

E.   THE USE OF I.Q. TESTS IN E.M.R. PLACE-MENT. There is no factual dispute about the matters just discussed. E.M.R. classes are "dead-end" classes for children thought to be incapable of learning the material taught in regular classes, and black children can be found in the classes in numbers grossly out of proportion to their representation in the student population. We turn now to the process by which the children are assigned to the E.M.R. classes, and particularly to the role of the I.Q. tests in that process. . . .

The available data suggest very strongly that, even if in some districts the I.Q. scores were not always determinative, they were pervasive in the placement process. . . .

Since January of 1975, I.Q. examinations no longer have been part of the E.M.R. placement process in California. The state testing moratorium has forced school districts to rely primarily on other factors for placement decisions. This reliance on alternatives sets up a kind of test of the I.Q.'s role in the overrepresentation of black children in E.M.R. classes. Unfortunately, the data do not clearly prove or disprove the hypothesis. It appears that the percentage of black children in E.M.R.

classes has not changed substantially. . . . Uncontradicted expert testimony based on [20 school districts with 80 percent black student population] indicates that [a] four percent drop in the placement of black children in E.M.R. classes—50 percent to 46 percent—is statistically significant. . . .

IV.   INTELLIGENCE TESTS

A.   INTRODUCTION: THE IMPOSSIBILITY OF MEASURING INTELLIGENCE. A large proportion of the 10,000 pages of transcript in this case concerns the I.Q. tests themselves, how they operate, and what they can and cannot measure and predict. While many think of the I.Q. as an objective measure of innate, fixed intelligence, the testimony of the experts overwhelmingly demonstrated that this conception of I.Q. is erroneous. Defendants' expert witnesses, even those closely affiliated with the companies that devise and distribute the standardized intelligence tests, agreed, with one exception, that we cannot truly define, much less measure, intelligence. We can measure certain skills but not native intelligence. Professor Robert Thorndike of Columbia, defendants' first expert witness, confirmed that the modern consensus represents a change from that held in the early years of the testing movement: "Everybody would acknowledge we would have no conceivable way of directly measuring native ability." . . .

I.Q. tests, like other ability tests, essentially measure achievement in the skills covered by the examinations. As stated by Professor Leon Kamin, Professor of Psychology from Princeton University,

I.Q. tests measure the degree to which a particular individual who takes the test has experience with a particular piece of information, the particular bits of knowledge, the particular habit and approaches that are tested in these tests. . . .

C. REASONS FOR THE DISPARITY IN I.Q. SCORES. Disparities in I.Q. test scores* between black and white children can be caused by various factors. . . .

2. THE SOCIO-ECONOMIC ARGUMENT. Dr. Riles [Superintendent of Public Instruction at the time of the trial] preferred to admit that the I.Q. tests were biased against the poor—black and white alike—not because of inferior genes or divergent cultures but because of their inferior homes and neighborhood environments. Again, according to Dr. Riles,

[T]he point I'm trying to make is that if they are poor and disadvantaged, it doesn't matter whether they are minority or majority. If they are poor and disadvantaged, yes, they are going to do less well on the test.

Poverty is clearly a handicap for children taking I.Q. tests. But the question before the court is whether such disadvantages leads not only to poorer test and school performance, but also to the condition of mental retardation thought to justify placement in E.M.R. classes. . . .

[I]t is clear that socio-economic status by itself cannot explain fully the undisputed disparities in I.Q. test scores and in E.M.R. placements. As one of defendants' experts, Professor Lloyd Humphreys of the University of Illinois, testified, "there are a very great many studies in which . . . the objective socio-economic status indices have been held constant. The almost uniform finding is that blacks still score lower than the whites." . . .

3. THE CULTURAL BIAS OF STANDARDIZED I.Q. TESTS. The insufficiency of the above explanation leads us to question the cultural bias of I.Q. tests. The first important inferential evidence is that the tests were never designed to eliminate cultural biases against black children; it was assumed in effect that black children were less "intelligent" than whites. Those who did not make that assumption recognized the problem of cultural bias, even if they did not try to investigate it systematically. Dr. David Wechsler in 1944, stated this problem quite strongly in his introduction to the WISC [Wechsler Intelligence Scale for Children], which he developed:

[W]e have eliminated the colored vs. white factor by admitting at the outset that our norms cannot be used for the colored population of the United States. Though we have tested a large number of colored persons, our standardization is based upon white subjects only. We omitted the colored population from our first standardization because we did not feel that norms derived by mixing the population could be interpreted without special provisos and reservations.

Wechsler's observations apply with equal force to the other standardized tests. The tests were standardized and developed on an all-white population, and naturally their scientific validity is questionable for culturally different groups. Black children's intelligence may be manifested in ways that the tests do not show, so that the existing tests developed on the white population obviously would be inadequate.

Another type of indirect or inferential evidence of cultural bias is the manner in which I.Q. scores of black children may be improved. For example, there was testimony that black children raised in a cultural environment closer to the white middle class mainstream tend to perform better on the tests, that black children raised by white parents tend to do better, and that early intervention programs can dramatically improve testing results. . . .

Cultural differences can also be

---

*[The court found on "the undisputed testimony of experts from both sides" that "black children score, on the average, one standard deviation below white children," or about fifteen points below (mean scores of 88 and 103, respectively—100 is the average score). Ed.'s note.]

found in specific test items. Some of these items have in fact become rather notorious, such as the "fight item" on WISC tests. This question asked children what they would do if struck by a smaller child of the same sex. The "correct" answer is that it is wrong to strike the child back. Young black children aged six and seven "missed" this item more than twice as often as their white counterparts. The difference can only be attributed to a cultural variation at that age. Similarly, it may be that such questions as who wrote Romeo and Juliet, who discovered America, and who invented the light bulb, are culturally biased. . . .

[T]here was general agreement by all sides on the inevitable effect of cultural differences on I.Q. scores. Put succinctly by Professor Hilliard, black people have "a cultural heritage that represents an experience pool which is never used" or tested by the standardized I.Q. tests. . . .

With the factual issues thus framed, we turn to the law.

V. LEGAL ANALYSIS

A. INTRODUCTION. Plaintiffs and the U.S. Department of Justice, as *amicus curiae*, have mounted a massive attack on E.M.R. classes built on I.Q. testing. . . .

There are a number of sources for plaintiffs' contentions. Plaintiffs and the Department of Justice invoke the Equal Protection Clauses of the United States and California Constitutions; Title VI of the Civil Rights Act of 1964, 42 U.S.C. § 2000d et seq. (hereinafter "Title VI") and [other federal legislation]. . . .

2. TITLE VI OF THE CIVIL RIGHTS ACT OF 1964: ONE APPLICATION OF AN "EFFECTS TEST." . . . Title VI provides that

No person in the United States shall, on the ground of race, color, or national origin, be excluded from participation in, be denied the benefits of, or be subjected to discrimination

under any program of activity receiving Federal financial assistance.

There is no question that defendants receive substantial federal assistance. . . .

The Supreme Court's signal Title VI case is *Lau* v. *Nichols,* 414 U.S. 563 (1974), holding specifically that "[d]iscrimination is barred *which has that effect even though no purposeful design is present.*" (Emphasis added.) In *Lau,* the Court found that Title VI and implementing regulations were violated by San Francisco's failure to provide English language courses for students of Chinese ancestry. That failure, according to the Court, violated Title VI, since it had an adverse impact on Chinese-Americans and "students who do not understand English are effectively foreclosed from any meaningful education."

The same kind of analysis is applicable to students placed in E.M.R. classes on the basis of criteria that result in a grossly disproportionate overenrollment of black children. . . . Placement mechanisms for E.M.R. classes operate with a discriminatory effect that, to paraphrase *Lau,* effectively forecloses a disproportionate number of black children from any meaningful education. On the basis of their different cultural background, which results particularly in lower scores on I.Q. tests, black children are subjected to discrimination analogous to that borne by many San Francisco Chinese, who, because of their cultural background, could not communicate effectively in English. . . .

If defendants could have shown here that disproportionate enrollment in E.M.R. classes actually reflected and tapped a greater incidence of mild mental retardation in the black children population, and not "cultural bias," then defendants' E.M.R. placement process could have survived. Further, if defendants could somehow have demonstrated that the intelligence tests had been "validated" for the purpose of E.M.R. placement of black children, those tests could have been utilized despite their disproportionate impact. As discussed elsewhere in this opinion, however, defendants did not make these showings. . . .

4. THE QUESTION OF VALIDATION DESPITE DISCRIMINATORY EFFECTS. "Validation" is the determination of whether the placement tests or other evaluation materials are suited for the purposes for which they are used. It is a concept familiar in the testing literature and has frequently been used to evaluate tests used for employment qualifications. To date, however, there are no cases applying validation criteria to tests used to E.M.R. placement. . . .

The important threshold question is whether "validation" of I.Q. tests and E.M.R. placement mechanisms requires the same showing that is required of employment tests in employment discrimination cases. . . .

As stated in the leading case of *Griggs* v. *Duke Power Co.,* 401 U.S. 424 (1971), tests shown to have a discriminatory impact cannot be utilized unless the employer meets "the burden of showing that any given requirement has a manifest relationship to the employment in question." If the employer meets the burden, the plaintiffs may then show that alternative selection devices exist that would serve the employer's legitimate interests without discriminatory effects. This three-part test frequently has been cited with approval in recent cases under Title VII of the Civil Rights Act of 1964. . . .

[There is] a fundamental difference between the use of tests in employment and education, at least in the early years of schooling. If tests can predict that a person is going to be a poor employee, the employer can legitimately deny that person a job, but if tests suggest that a young child is probably going to be a poor student, the school cannot on that basis alone deny that child the opportunity to improve and de-

velop the academic skills necessary to success in our society. Assignment to E.M.R. classes denies that opportunity through relegation to a markedly inferior, essentially dead-end, track.

Furthermore, in the employment sphere, predictions of performance must be made before entrusting a person with a particular job. In the educational setting as it relates to E.M.R. classes, the child is already in school and already doing poorly, so it can be predicted without tests that the poor performance will continue in the absence of remedial attention. Indeed, past performance in school is a better predictor than tests of future school performance.

Finally, it is only to be expected that children placed in E.M.R. classes will fall increasingly behind in their performance in academic skills, which the E.M.R. curriculum deemphasizes. Placing children with lower I.Q. scores in these classes thus necessarily is a self-fulfilling prophecy. The results of such placements cannot be the basis for test validation in an educational setting.

Nevertheless, a more useful analysis of validation in the educational setting can begin with the burden of proof allocation development in the employment discrimination area. We must inquire whether the tests have been validated for the black children who are members of the plaintiff class, given the disproportionately low test scores of those children and the critical effect of those scores in keeping black children from full participation in regular classes. . . .[84]

---

[84] While the terminology is not particularly helpful in this case, it may be noted that the validation inquiry generally is based on assessments of "content validity," "construct validity," or "predictive validity." *See generally* American Psychological Association, *Standards for Educational and Psychological Tests* (1974). The only predictive validity asserted by defendants is that borrowed from the employment testing area, and we have already denied the relevance of predictions of academic performance to validation for E.M.R. placement. Content validity, according to the expert tes-

The experts testifying in this case agree that I.Q. tests cannot measure innate intelligence, but they disagreed on whether the tests can measure the "mental ability" of children. . . . We will assume that the tests can accurately measure the mental ability of white children placed in E.M.R. classes, and ask if the tests as utilized for E.M.R. placement have been validated for black children.

The answer, as should be clear from the earlier discussion of the history and biases of I.Q. tests, is that validation has been assumed, not established, for blacks. . . .

Under these circumstances, defendants have failed to take the steps necessary to assure the tests' validity. They have committed a serious error that Title VII regulations warn against in the employment situation: . . . Whether or not the tests do what they are supposed to do, the law is that defendants must come forward and show that they have been validated for each minority group with which they are used. . . .

It turns out that very few studies have correlated scores on the standardized intelligence tests mandated in California until the testing moratorium with subsequent grades for black and white children. At least one of the major studies casts some doubt on the ability of the tests to predict grades of black as opposed to white children. This Goldman and Hartog study, based on a sample of 201 blacks and 430

whites, investigated correlations between the WISC and grade point average, and found the correlation to be .14 for blacks and .25 for whites. It concluded that the WISC "appeared to be differentially valid for white vs. minority children," and that, "The WISC has little or no validity for predicting the scholastic performance of black or brown children." . . .

The key finding of these studies of grade predictions is not the extent of the correlations between I.Q. test scores and school performance (although the correlations are not great), but rather that the I.Q. tests are differentially valid for black and white children. As noted before and consistent with the standards in the employment testing area, tests cannot be validated on black persons if they are differentially valid. Differential validity means that more errors will be made for black children than whites, and that is unacceptable. . . .

This conclusion, consistent with what one would expect given the historical development of the tests, compels a finding for plaintiffs on the issue of predictive validity. Even if predictive validity could form the basis of validation for E.M.R. diagnosis and placement, defendants would still be unable to prevail.

5. ALTERNATIVES TO I.Q. TESTING FOR E.M.R. PLACEMENT. Even if defendants had discharged their burden of showing a sufficient relationship of the test-centered placement process to E.M.R. status, plaintiffs would still be entitled to prevail if they could show that alternative devices for placement exist and would serve defendants' legitimate interests without the same discriminatory effect. Plaintiffs have met this burden. . . .

[T]he evidence showed that many schools are taking more time and care with their assessments for E.M.R. classification, relying more on observational data gathered both in and out of the classroom. School psychologists, teachers, and others

timony, determines whether all aspects of a given subject are measured. The practical utility of content validity assessments is generally limited to achievement tests. One of the essential aspects of E.M.R. status is that it presupposes mental retardation, not merely a limited academic achievement. . . . We are thus apparently left with construct validity—whether the tests measure the domain of skills that comprise mental ability. The definitions are sometimes confused, however, and the important concern is the practical one of establishing the relationship between I.Q. test scores of black children and the characteristics justifying their placement into special E.M.R. classes.

involved in the process are now making decisions based on a wide number of factors, and the evidence suggests that the results are less discriminatory than they were under the I.Q.-centered standard. Evaluations can and are taking place through, *inter alia*, more thorough assessments of the child's personal history and development, adaptive behavior both inside and outside of the school environment, and classroom performance and academic achievement. . . .

C. **THE EQUAL PROTECTION CLAUSES OF THE FOURTEENTH AMENDMENT.** This decision could rest on the federal statutory claims alone, but in this case it would be inappropriate to conclude our analysis there. . . . [In part, this is because the lawsuit was commenced under the Fourteenth Amendment and the preliminary injunction was issued on that constitutional ground. Ed.'s note.]

1. INTENTIONAL DISCRIMINATION. a. *Determining the standard.* It is now established that disproportionate impact, the central fact of the I.Q. tests and the E.M.R. placement process generally,

is not the sole touchstone of an invidious racial discrimination forbidden by the Constitution. Standing alone, it does not trigger the rule . . . that racial classifications are to be subjected to the strictest scrutiny and are justifiable only by the weightiest of considerations.

Washington v. *Davis,* 426 U.S. 229 (1976). Since the late 1960's, beginning especially with the Supreme Court's first case involving "de facto" segregation in a northern school district, *Keyes* v. *School District No. 1,* 413 U.S. 189 (1973), the Court has increasingly emphasized that the strict scrutiny applied to racial classifications is triggered only by actions that can "ultimately be traced to a racially discriminatory purpose." . . .

Under the present state of the law, therefore, a factual showing of discriminatory impact provides no simple shortcut to the ultimate fact—discriminatory intent. As Justice Powell indicated in his majority opinion in *Village of Arlington Heights,* the situation "demands a sensitive inquiry into such circumstantial and direct evidence of intent as may be available." 429 U.S. at 266 (1976). . . .

b. *Applying the law.* Discriminatory intent does not necessarily mean an intent to harm black children. Since *Brown* v. *Board of Education,* an intent to segregate minority children in separate schools has sufficed to prove a prima facie violation of the Fourteenth Amendment. An intent to segregate into special, all day classes is functionally indistinguishable. . . . Once such a purpose is shown, even if it was not the sole or predominant purpose behind the actions in question, then defendants must show that the actions would have resulted anyway in the absence of the prohibited motive. If such a showing is not made, then "judicial deference is no longer justified."

That deference cannot be justified in this case. . . .

First, it is obvious that the decision to require the administration of one of the approved I.Q. tests prior to E.M.R. placement had profound discriminatory effects. It doomed large numbers of black children to E.M.R. status. . . .

The historical background of the I.Q. decision provides a second essential source of evidence. As noted before in some detail, the history of I.Q. testing and special classes for E.M.R. of California is a tainted one. Notions of racial inferiority permeated the classes established after World War I, and I.Q. scores were used generally to justify the isolation of so-called inferior ethnic or racial groups thought to contain large numbers of "feebleminded." . . . [T]here has been a constitutionally prohibited "failure to fulfill the duty to eradicate the consequences of prior purposefully discriminatory conduct." . . .

[The opinion then describes at length the alleged "procedural and substantive irregularities" associated with the adoption of IQ testing for E.M.R. placement which, according to the court, constitute indicia of discriminatory purpose. For example, despite a legislative resolution indicating concern over the disproportionate minority placement, the State Department of Education (SDE) approved the use of IQ tests without explanation, without hearings, and without inquiry into their possible bias—a "very suspicious and inadequate" procedure. SDE officials, moreover, "testified that they believed the overenrollment of black and Chicano children in the E.M.R. classes accurately reflected the incidence of mental retardation among these children." Defendants also did "essentially nothing" to monitor and remedy the problem of disproportionate enrollments. In short, "the SDE's actions revealed a complacent acceptance of those disproportions," and "that complacent acceptance must be seen as a desire to perpetuate the segregation of minorities in inferior, dead end, and stigmatizing classes for the retarded." Ed.'s note.]

Plaintiffs have met their burden of proving discriminatory intent. Since there is no evidence that the state would have acted the same "had the impermissible purpose not been considered," we must now apply the "strict scrutiny test."

Under the strict scrutiny or compelling interest test, defendants cannot prevail unless they are able to justify the racial classification by showing that it was necessary to the accomplishment of a compelling state interest. Defendants can establish no compelling state interest in the use of the I.Q. tests nor in the maintenance of E.M.R. classes with overwhelming disproportions of black enrollment. With respect to the tests, defendants assert the need to avoid misclassification, their interest in fiscal control, and the lack of alternatives for E.M.R. placement. These post hoc justifications merit little analysis in light of earlier discussions. . . . Plaintiffs have proven their case under the Fourteenth Amendment. . . .

VI. REMEDY

. . .

B. PERMANENT INJUNCTIVE RELIEF
1. INTELLIGENCE TESTS. Defendants are enjoined from utilizing, permitting the use of, or approving the use of any standardized intelligence tests, including those now approved pursuant to Cal. Admin. Code §3401, for the identification of black E.M.R. children or their placement into E.M.R. classes, without securing prior approval by this court. . . .

2. DISPROPORTIONATE PLACEMENT. Defendants are hereby ordered to monitor and eliminate disproportionate placement of black children in California's E.M.R. classes. . . .

3. REEVALUATION AND OTHER CLASS RELIEF. To remedy the harm to black children who have been misidentified as E.M.R. pupils and to prevent these discriminatory practices from recurring in California with respect to a similarly situated class of youngsters in the future, the defendants shall direct each school district to reevaluate every black child currently identified as an E.M.R. pupil, without including in the psychological evaluation a standardized intelligence or ability test that has not been approved by the court. . . .

Following the reevaluation, an "individual educational plan" that specifies the type of supplemental assistance needed to allow the child to return to a regular classroom shall be prepared for each child reevaluated and found to have been misdiagnosed. Such assistance shall then be provided.

C. THE NECESSITY OF LIMITING THE SCOPE OF THE REMEDY

. . .

[P]laintiffs sought a court order mandating supplemental assistance to black disadvantaged children who are not in regular classes. While we recognize that California's educational system is failing to educate adequately a vast number of minority and disadvantaged students, that matter is not before the court. It is not the role of the court to reach out to order what would amount to a massive expenditure of funds for supplemental assistance. . . .

VII.   CONCLUSION

. . .

It may be that E.M.R. classes and the philosophy underlying them are educational anachronisms. They focus on a label—retardation—derived for the most part from arbitrary cut-off scores on standardized I.Q. tests, and that label is used to justify academic isolation in special dead-end classes.

A contrary educational philosophy has been gaining adherents. . . . This philosophy aims not at labeling a child and confining the "retarded" in special classes. Rather, it aims to diagnose learning problems, to take the child as he or she is, and to encourage remedial action through an individualized educational program. The ideal is also to keep children whenever possible in regular classes with nonhandicapped children. . . .

Educators have too often been able to rationalize inaction by blaming educational failure on an assumed inferiority of disproportionate numbers of black children. That assumption without validation is unacceptable and is made all the more invidious when "legitimated" by ostensibly neutral, scientific I.Q. scores. We [hope] . . . this will clear the way for more constructive educational reform.

NOTES AND QUESTIONS

Definitions of Test Bias

Much of the five months of trial and 10,000 pages of expert testimony dealt with test bias. It had been a concern of psychometricians long before the court challenges. Some eight different criteria or definitions of test bias have been formulated (Flaugher 1978), and Judge Peckham relied on three of them: mean differences, item bias, and predictive validity.

1.   If different groups (for example, blacks and whites) obtain significantly different average scores on a test when there is no reason to expect these differences, the test is considered to be biased. The key issue, of course, is whether there is some systematic explanation for the different scores.

2.   Judge Peckham quickly rejected the socioeconomic explanation. However, the available evidence indicates that it is a factor. Although the overwhelming majority of the poor are not mildly retarded, there is undisputable evidence that among the mildly retarded, the economically disadvantaged are overrepresented (Reschly 1980, p. 131). Inadequate nutrition, poor medical care, exposure to toxic substances in living quarters, and "psychosocial disadvantages" (Robinson and Robinson 1976) are associated with poverty and may interfere with normal neurological development in early childhood.

What are the legal consequences of a finding that there is bias in IQ tests?

3.   The most common criticism of standardized tests pertain to cultural bias in the items or questions. It is usually based on subjective opinions of minority group members. These opinions, in turn, inevitably are also culturally rooted. Thus, if the "correct" answer to the "fight item" on the WISC test reflects white cultural bias, as Judge Peckham claims, is the implication that black culture approves of youngsters striking back at smaller children?

Item bias should be assessed empirically rather than impressionistically by comparing the responses of subjects of different backgrounds. An empirical analysis of the WISC-R concluded that "the notion that there may be a number of items with radically different difficulties for children from different ethnic groups [white, black, Chicano] has not been supported" (Sandoval 1979, p. 925). Moreover, responses to selected items cannot be generalized to the entire test. Elimination of thirteen items perceived to be biased from a widely used eighty-two-item reading ability test "did not improve the performance of schools with high minority populations relative to their performance on the original 'biased' version" (Flaugher 1978, p. 675). Also, most studies of group intelligence tests show that item bias, if present, accounts for very little of the group differences observed (Reschly 1980, p. 127).

4.   Judge Peckham's finding of item bias has not been uniformly accepted by other federal judges. In an almost identical suit against the Chicago Board of Education, in which many of the same expert witnesses who testified in the San Francisco trial also appeared, Judge Grady of the Northern District of Illinois concluded that "the witnesses and the arguments which persuaded Judge Peckham have not persuaded me" (*Parents in Action on Special Education* v. *Hannon*, 1980, p. 882). He then reviewed every single item on the challenged tests (Stanford-Binet, WISC, and WISC-R) and found, based on his own intuitive judgment, that only one item on the first test and eight items on the other two tests were culturally biased or suspect. The biased questions asked, for example, what C.O.D. means and what a stomach does. The court concluded that these few biased items would not significantly taint the tests as a whole as culturally unfair and that when the test scores are used with other educational criteria for placement in E.M.R. classes, they do not result in discriminatory placement of black children. If Judge Peckham's conclusions were not well founded on psychometric evidence, Judge Grady's analysis "can best be described as naive, . . . unintelligent and completely empty of empirical substance" (Bersoff 1981, p. 1049).

5.   To speak of culture-free items may be meaningless because all aptitude and IQ tests, by definition, are culture-bound—they measure ability acquired in a given social setting: "All behavior is affected by the cultural milieu in which the individual is reared, and since psychological tests are but samples of behavior, cultural influence will and should be reflected in test performance. It is therefore futile to try to devise a test that is free from cultural influences" (Anastasi 1976, p. 345).

There have been several attempts to construct group (not individual) intelligence tests for college admissions that eliminate socioeconomic and cultural differences, but they all failed. Average test scores between these different groups continued to differ, and the tests predicted school achievement less well than conventional, non–culture-free tests (Flaugher 1978).

6.   The cultural orientation of test items is a matter of degree that varies with the characteristics of the examinee, rather than an absolute quality inherent in the items themselves. It may be more useful to think of culture-fair rather than culture-free tests. The former would be one that did not require such highly specific information that only few persons with particular backgrounds would possess. The "Black Intelligence Test for Cultural Homogeneity" or BITCH, for example, is so culture-specific that the average white person would score poorly (MacMillan and Meyers 1980, p. 140). The evidence that a conventional IQ test as a whole, not just selected items, is not culture-fair in the foregoing sense is, at best, "equivocal" (Reschly 1980, p. 127).

7.   Judge Peckham dealt with cultural bias solely as a technical problem of test construction. However, if this bias represents an inherent cultural influence, reflecting experiences and opportunities in white, middle class America, what basic questions of values and social policy lie behind this technical issue that should be addressed before attempting to revise the tests—assuming such revision were feasible?

8.   The court considered two criteria for the predictive validity of IQ tests: the prediction of school grades and the placement of black children in E.M.R. programs. Because both are different from selection for employment, the court also decided that predictive validation was not legally relevant to the disposition of the case. Why, then, did the opinion devote such extensive attention to the question of validation?

9.   With respect to predicting academic grades, the evidence is not as unequivocal as Judge Peckham makes it out to be. The Goldman and Hartig (1976) study cited in the opinion has been strongly criticized for correlating test scores with an overall grade point average that included nonacademic subjects. Nobody has ever proposed that the WISC predicts performance in art, music, and physical education classes. Other studies that correlate WISC-R scores with solely academic performance have shown no differential validity for white, black, Chicano, and Native American students. "Contrary to the Larry P. opinion, evidence for confirming the allegation of differential validity is quite limited. . . . Definitive conclusions regarding individual intelligence tests and [grades of] school age children cannot be made at this time" (Reschly 1980, p. 129).

10.   Judge Peckham noted that the correlations between the WISC and grade average were "not great" (.14 and .25 for blacks and whites, respectively). Psychometricians consider as acceptable validity correlations in the .30 to .40 range. Should a court adopt this magnitude of correlation as the legal standard of validity when tests are challenged as culturally biased? Should the legal standard be different for tests used in education and in employment? Do you agree that given Judge Peckham's discussion of validation, "it is unlikely that any of the currently used intelligence tests are valid, which casts doubt on the continued utility of traditional evaluations using psychology's storehouse of standardized ability tests" (Bersoff 1981, p. 1048)?

11.   The validity of the E.M.R. classification of black children was the central factual issue. Judge Peckham concluded that the "plaintiffs were not retarded according to the relevant evidence" and therefore wrongly classified. To reach that conclusion, the criteria for determining mental retardation (which supposedly is predicted by the IQ tests) need to be specified, and this Judge Peckham did not do.
    The American Association on Mental Deficiency recognizes four degrees of mental retardation: mild (or educable), moderate, severe, and profound (Grossman 1977). The first level, usually defined by an upper IQ limit of 70, represents normal though slow mental functioning. Mild retardation is not regarded as permanent or incurable, is not traceable to any biological causes, and is not pervasive in the sense of impairing every aspect of behavior. In contrast, the other three levels constitute "genuine" mental retardation: They are biologically based, permanent, and comprehensive in behavioral impact. The public does not distinguish between mild retardation, which is characteristic of most of the mentally retarded, and the more severe conditions.
    If by "not retarded" Judge Peckham meant that plaintiffs were not moderately to profoundly retarded, he is correct. However, this is not to say that they were not seriously deficient academically, or "mildly" retarded. Essentially, then, the issue is a semantic one, as Judge Peckham acknowledges at the conclusion of his opinion. Because of the social stigma and the life consequences that attach to being branded as "retarded," Judge Peckham's decision can be seen as a de-labeling solution. No longer will there be "focus on a label—retardation." Whether the affected students are hereafter identified as "potentially needy learners" (MacMillan and Meyers 1980, p. 136), academically handicapped students, or by some other nomenclature, there still remains the question of what to do.

Remedy and Violations

12.   At the "macro" level of school segregation, analysis of the problem of disproportionate racial impact normally defines its own remedy. Overrepresentation of students by race in the schools is cured by transferring the students around. At the "micro" level of within-school segregation, there is no obvious relationship between problem and remedy.

13.   Judge Peckham's remedy consists of five interrelated components. In the first three, he (a) bans the use of IQ tests for E.M.R. placement of black (but not of white) pupils, (b) requires the reevaluation by means other than these tainted tests of the current generation of black E.M.R. pupils and "similarly situated class of youngsters in the future," and (c) orders the elimination of black overrepresentation in E.M.R. classes.
    If, as he found, IQ tests were a key factor in E.M.R. placement decisions, why did he not limit the injunction to simply banning the use of the tests? Contrary to his finding, the available evidence shows that "the IQ test is *not* the primary basis for placement" (Lambert 1981, p. 946). "In California and

elsewhere, the child must first fail in a regular school program and be referred for evaluation before a test is administered" (p. 940). What was the effect on E.M.R. placements of the four-year testing moratorium?

The ceiling on black E.M.R. enrollment applies without regard to how the enrollees are identified, whether by IQ tests or other means. The irony is that standardized testing was originally introduced to prevent inaccurate teacher decisions about assignment to special educational classes. They were hailed as fairer than the alternative, subjective evaluations that the court now endorses (Ashurst and Meyers 1973; Cronbach 1975).

The order forbids the disproportional enrollment in E.M.R. classes. Should it have enjoined the disproportional identification of students with E.M.R. attributes?

14.   The last two components consist of (d) "supplemental assistance" in order to allow (e) "return to a regular classroom."

With respect to the fourth component, Judge Peckham quickly adds that it is not within his role to "order what would amount to a massive expenditure of funds for supplemental assistance." What distinguishes this case from the Detroit school case, where the judge ordered a massive expenditure of funds by Michigan for compensatory education of inner city school children (*Milliken II*)?

The last component is known in the trade as "mainstreaming." The effects of placing slow learners in regular classrooms need to be considered.

Studies of E.M.R. programs in this country and in Europe show "either no effect or marginal adverse effects on achievement" (Kirp 1973, p. 718). However, few conclusions of a definitive nature can be drawn. The typical evaluation compares E.M.R. children with those in regular classes who have similar IQ scores. The obvious sampling bias inherent in such a research design renders uncertain the interpretation of any differences in academic gains that might be found between the two groups. If there is no evidence that E.M.R. classes are more academically beneficial, then the empirical justification for mainstreaming turns on social psychological consequences.

E.M.R. classes are stigmatizing. Children can be cruel in teasing "dummies." Placement in classes separate from "normal" students officially brands the E.M.R. children as "different" and reduces their self-esteem. However, reviews of the literature indicate that transfer to regular classes is not necessarily the solution. Slow learners are not "very well accepted socially regardless of . . . the label being appended to them and regardless of the educational placement into which they are programmed" (MacMillan and Meyers 1980, p. 141; Semmel, Gottlieb, and Robinson 1979). In other words, the source of the stigma is not the E.M.R. enrollment as such, but the deficient academic performance that prompted the E.M.R. placement in the first instance.

15.   Mainstreaming within a school is the remedial equivalent of integration between schools. Both result in greater interracial mixture. *Riles* brings the integration goal of *Brown* from the school district level to the classroom level. School integration was empirically justified initially by its claimed favorable effects on minority achievement. Implicit in Judge Peckham's opinion is the assumption that lifting black children out of "dead-end," "markedly inferior" E.M.R. classes would also enhance educational opportunity. Is this a valid parallel? Are the reasons given to support and require school desegregation applicable to mainstreaming?

16.   Of the five interrelated parts of the remedy, which is the most important, and why?

17.   Analysis of the remedy suggests different ways of seeing what the case is all about. According to Judge Peckham, the problem was the use of culturally biased and invalid IQ tests as a principal basis for E.M.R. placement of black children, resulting in their overrepresentation in inferior classes. This is what triggered the remedial action. Testing was protrayed as the villain. As one of the plaintiffs' attorneys put it, the "intelligence test [was] on trial" (Madden 1980, p. 149).

Do you agree that misuse of testing was the underlying problem that the court was trying to rectify? A report of the Panel on Selection and Placement of Students in Programs for the Mentally Retarded of the National Research Council takes the position that "[D]isproportionality per se is not the problem; unequal numbers do not by themselves constitute an inequality" (Heller, Holtzman, and Messick 1982, p. x). Are there other smoking guns? The action of banning the IQ test recalls the ancient Greek custom of killing the courier who bore bad news.

18.   One commentator described *Riles* as a case of "wrong problem–right solution" (Reschly 1980, p. 123). Or is this a case of "right problem–wrong solution"? Another commentator, who served as an expert defense witness, reviewed the trial transcript and charged that "the court selectively reported on the evidence presented. . . ." One "should not conclude that the data the court refers to are representative of the total body of evidence in the trial record" (Lambert 1981, p. 950).

Legal Theories

The principle in school discrimination cases is that there is no judicial remedy unless there is a violation. To rectify a social problem, a court must first translate it into the language of a legal wrong. It has to be dressed in constitutional attire before a court will intervene.

19.   Under the rule of reason standard of review, the state classification must bear some reasonable connection to a legitimate state purpose, and the burden falls on the challenger to prove its arbitrariness. Under the facts of *Riles,* would the plaintiffs have prevailed if this standard had been applied?

20.   Under the strict scrutiny standard, invoked when the classification is deemed suspect or a fundamental right is infringed, the burden is on the state to show a compelling justification for the classification. If the IQ tests are facially neutral and there is no evidence that the schools purposely sought to place more blacks in E.M.R. classes based on the test scores, then the only basis for triggering this higher standard of review is if intelligence itself (without regard to race) is deemed a suspect classification.

For Fourteenth Amendment purposes, is intelligence analogous to race or national ancestry? Is dullness a stigmatized attribute like the other, more immutable suspect characteristics?

Or is intelligence more like economic advantage, a nonsuspect characteristic? Intelligence classifications, whether based on standardized tests, grades, or other evaluations, serve as meritocratic sieves, giving the most able members of society access to benefits (schooling, jobs, power, and so forth) denied to duller ones. Is unequal treatment of individuals by the state based on ability more justifiable than unequal treatment based on, say, national ancestry?

The traditional, two-tier model of Equal Protection presents a dichotomous approach to the review of state classifications: they are either suspect or not suspect. Alternately, one can think of a continuum of suspectness between the extreme standards of mere rationality and compelling interest. Some characteristics are more suspect than others; there are "hardcore" and "softcore" unequal treatments (see generally Gunther 1972).

Is intelligence a "semi-suspect" characteristic—less suspect than race, more suspect than wealth? What legal and practical implications flow from this view?

21.   The Fourteenth Amendment has been interpreted to require invidious purpose or intent in order to find a violation. Hence, it applies only to instances of de jure discrimination. Federal legislation employs a lower standard of proof. Titles VI and VII of the Civil Rights Act of 1964 do not require a showing of discriminatory purpose. This makes it easier to establish a statutory wrong than a constitutional wrong. It enables action against de facto discrimination.

22.   *Riles* applies *Griggs* and Title VII to the area of educational classifications. Is the tripartite test of *Griggs* more like the rational relation standard or more like the strict scrutiny standard?

23.   Is Judge Peckham's definition of discriminatory purpose the same as that used in the preceding cases on school segregation?

In the Detroit case, Wolf said that "Judge Roth's use of school violations was a reluctant concession to the requirements of legal precedent." Does the evidence in this case show improper motive or was Judge Peckham's long discussion of it simply judicial legerdemain whereby colorblind actions are transformed into color-based culpability?

24.   Does the discussion on intentional discrimination suggest other grounds for constitutional challenge?

25.   If E.M.R. classes are as stigmatizing and inferior as described in the opinion, white children—who compose the majority—would also seem to be deprived of equal educational opportunity. Does Judge Peckham's analysis imply a constitutional remedy for them? The overrepresentation of boys (by 36 percent, irrespective of race) in E.M.R. classes is more dramatic than the overrepresentation of girls. "In the current vernacular, special education is more sexist than racist" (Lambert 1981, p. 941). Does the logic of *Riles* compel schools to eliminate this gender disparity?

4.8.   SECOND-GENERATION PROBLEMS IN THE MARKETPLACE: EMPLOYMENT TESTING

Riles relied on *Griggs* because legal standards for evaluating the claimed discriminatory effect of psychological tests were developed principally in connection with employment tests. The various kinds of standardized psychological tests—employment tests, personality tests, intelligence tests, academic achievement tests—are distinguished from each other mainly by their use rather than by any psychometric features of the instruments themselves. In this action, we shall discuss briefly the leading trilogy of cases on testing validation. They involve employment tests but, as *Riles* noted, the same legal principles provide a "useful analysis of validation in the educational setting."

Testing in industry, as in the schools, is a big business. By one estimate, there are some 500 testing organizations in the country, and one report claimed that virtually every major employer makes some use of psychological tests (Haney 1982, p. 2, n. 4). From the beginning, the objectivity and accuracy of employment tests, as of intellectual aptitude tests, were articles of faith among the makers and administrators of these measures. By the mid-sixties, the validity and legitimacy of different psychological tests were called into question. The intrusiveness of personality tests prompted congressional concern over possible infringement of individual privacy. Subsequently, the spotlight turned to measures of intellectual abilities and work skills. The concern centered on the role of testing in impeding equal educational and employment opportunities. In the area of education, the debate over racial disparities in test scores and the reasons for these disparities was fueled by the disproportionate placement of minorities in separate classes within recently integrated schools. In the area of employment, Title VII of the Civil Rights Act of 1964 was a catalyst for increased scrutiny of possible discrimination in hiring and promotions by means of seemingly neutral tests. Thus, for the first time since the development of large scale testing in World War II, there was enhanced public awareness that maybe these tests helped to perpetuate if not create the differences that they appeared to measure.

Title VII

Title VII prohibits discrimination in employment. Section 703(a) states: "It shall be an unlawful employment practice for an employer . . . to . . . classify his employees in any way which would deprive or tend to deprive any individual of employment opportunities . . . because of such individual's race, color, religion, sex, or national origin." Section 703(h) addresses the issue of testing: "[I]t shall not be an unlawful employment practice for an employer . . . to give and act upon the results of any professionally developed ability test provided that such test, its administration or action upon the results is not designed, intended or used to discriminate because of race, color, religion, sex, or national origin. . . ." (42 U.S.C. § 2000e-2(a), 2(h), 1976).

The intent and language of section 703(h) were ambiguous, and it was left to the courts and the Equal Employment Opportunity Commission (EEOC, the enforcement agency for Title VII) to interpret the legislation. With the assistance of psychologists, EEOC promulgated "Guidelines on Employment Testing Procedures" (29 CFR §1607). Particular attention was given to standards of test validation—that is, the extent to which a test measures what it is said to measure. Test validity is central to the interpretation of whether a test is "used to discriminate." Rarely will a test maker be so unsubtle as to market a test that is "designed" or "intended" to discriminate. Most of the litigation under Title VII revolves around the discriminatory "use" of a facially neutral instrument. As a result of conflicting lower court holdings on discriminatory use, the Supreme Court granted certiorari in *Griggs*.

Griggs v. Duke Power Co. (1971)

Thirteen of the fourteen black employees of the Duke Power Company in North Carolina (which had a total of ninety-five employees) brought suit under Title VII on the grounds that two standardized personnel tests, which the company required for promotion, resulted in freezing them out of better positions. To be eligible for advancement, incumbent employees had to possess a high school education or take the "Wonderlic Personnel Test" (which purports to measure general intelligence) and the "Bennett Mechanical Comprehension Test" and achieve scores equivalent to the national median for high school graduates. The majority of the white employees who took these tests scored above the cut-off level, compared with 6% of the blacks. The high school completion or testing requirements were instituted, according to the company, to improve the overall quality of the work force. However, the company did not examine their relationship to job performance. No validation studies were conducted to determine if the tests bore a demonstrable relationship to successful performance of the jobs in question. Moreover, prior to the enactment of the Civil Rights Act, the company had a policy of overt racial discrimination in promotions. This conduct ceased in 1964, but the high school diploma and testing requirements were then instituted.

The Court held that these promotion requirements which were unproven to be job related, even if adopted without invidious racial purpose, were unlawful because they had a disproportionate impact upon blacks and operated to maintain the status quo of prior discriminatory practices. Specifically, with respect to discriminatory use of tests, the Court accorded "great deference" to the EEOC's interpretation of section 703(h). The administrative guidelines required that employers have available "data demonstrating that the test is predictive of or significantly correlated with important elements of work behavior . . . relevant to the job or jobs for which the candidates are being evaluated" (p. 435). These guidelines, then, construed section 703(h) to demand that employment tests be job related. The command of Title VII, said the Court, "is that any tests used must measure the person for the job and not the person in the abstract" (p. 437). In other words, "The touchstone is business necessity.

If an employment practice which operates to exclude Negroes cannot be shown to be related to job performance, the practice is prohibited" (p. 432). The Court then articulated the tripartite procedure, described in the *Riles* opinion, for proving the disparate impact of employment tests.

Albemarle Paper Co. v. Moody (1975)

Grigg's requirement of job relatedness was initially viewed by some commentators as "the death of employee testing" because of the heavy burden it imposed on employers (Johnson 1976, p. 1239). Actually, *Griggs* left unspecified the meaning of job relatedness. Four years later, the Court in *Albemarle* sought to define the standards of a job related test.

In this case, a group of black employees at a paper mill in North Carolina sued the owner alleging *inter alia* that the employment tests for promotions were racially discriminatory in violation of Title VII. The plant had several lines of progression, and as workers gained experience, they advanced to more skilled and better paid lines. In the 1950s, the company began using two tests ("Beta Examination" to measure nonverbal intelligence and "Wonderlic Test" Forms A and B to measure general verbal facility) to screen applicants for entry into the skilled lines. Until 1964, the skilled lines were expressly reserved for white employees. After 1964, when the segregation policy was abolished, the company allowed black employees to transfer to the skilled lines if they scored at or above the national norm for these two tests. Few blacks succeeded in doing so. The company never validated the tests for job relatedness. Some white incumbents in the skilled lines, who were hired before the adoption of the tests, were unable to achieve the cut-off score when they took the tests for the first time in 1971 (as part of a validation study described below), but they still retained their high-ranking jobs.

Four months before the trial, Albemarle engaged an industrial psychologist to validate the tests. He designed a concurrent validation study. The study dealt with ten job classifications (for example, stock room operator, power plant operator), selected from near the top of the progression lines (rather than from the bottom or entry level). Within each job classification, the psychologist compared the test scores of each employee with the independent rankings of the employee (relative to the employee's co-workers) made by two supervisors. The supervisors, of course, did not know the test scores. The expert computed the "phi coefficient" of correlation between the test scores and the average of the two supervisory rankings. The study showed statistically significant correlations between the Beta Examination and the subjective rankings for only three of the eight job classifications. Form A or Form B (which in theory are interchangeable measures) of the Wonderlic Test correlated significantly with the rankings in eight of the ten jobs. The study concluded that the tests were job related.

The Court disagreed. In ruling this validation study defective, the Court elaborated on how to demonstrate job relatedness. The main principle of test validation, which the Court adopted from the EEOC Guidelines (and which, in turn, were based upon the American Psychological Association's "Standards for Educational and Psychological Tests and Manuals"), is that the test must be shown, "by professionally accepted methods," to be "predictive of or significantly correlated with important elements of work behavior which comprise or are relevant to the job or jobs for which candidates are being evaluated" (p. 432). Judged by this principle, Albemarle's validation study was flawed in four respects.

First, even if the validation study was adequate, the two tests were not shown to be related to the particular jobs in the Albemarle plant. The psychologist failed to analyze the specific skills needed in the ten job categories, so there was no way of knowing if the tests measured those job skills. In general, "a test may be used in jobs other than those for which it has been professionally validated only if there are 'no significant differences' between the studied and unstudied jobs" (p. 433).

Second, the supervisors were not given specific information on the criteria for ranking employees. Different supervisors could have used different criteria, some of which may not have been job related. Thus, the validation criterion cannot be vague and subjective.

Third, the validation study was done only with workers at or near the top of the progression lines, not with workers at the bottom or entry levels of those lines. This is permissible only if job progression is "nearly automatic" for the "great majority" of new employees (p. 435). Otherwise, the test(s) must also be correlated with job performance at the lower levels. In this case, there was no finding of automatic or quick job progression.

Finally, the validation study was conducted with experienced, white workers in skilled lines, yet the tests were given to new job applicants and workers in unskilled lines, many of whom were black. Under the EEOC Guidelines, "[d]ata must be generated and results separately reported for minority and nonminority groups wherever technically feasible." Differential validation as to racial groups is "essential" (p. 436).

In summary, the procedural burdens articulated in *Griggs* and the standards of job relatedness established in *Albemarle* represent a rigorous approach to test validation under Title VII. The Court, in these cases, appeared "to hold the practitioners of psychological testing to the highest standards of their profession" (Haney 1982, p. 19). However, a report by the Committee on Ability Testing of the National Research Council has argued that the American Psychological Association's standards are too rarefied for the everyday world of employment testing. They are state-of-the-art judgments that were not intended to be ground rules for evaluating an employer's compliance with the Civil Rights Act. Even the best constructed tests cannot withstand legal challenge as to their validity if these standards are rigorously applied. Average test scores of minorities are and will be lower than average test scores of whites, so long as minorities are educationally and economically disadvantaged (Widgdor and Garner 1982).

Washington v. Davis (1976)

A year later, the Court appeared to lighten greatly the burden that the two preceding cases placed on employers to prove the job relatedness of their personnel tests and, at the same time, to abandon its deference to the rigorous validation guidelines of EEOC. In *Davis,* two black applicants to the District of Columbia police department were denied employment by reason of low scores on "Test 21," a federal civil service examination designed to measure general verbal ability. Since black applicants failed Test 21 disproportionately more frequently than white applicants, these two applicants challenged the use of the test on constitutional and statutory grounds. They claimed that the test was not job related and that it had a discriminatory racial impact. At the time of the litigation, blacks represented 44% of the police force; about the same proportion of new recruits were also black. It was undisputed that the police department was systematically and affirmatively recruiting black officers.

The Court began by declaring, "We have never held that the constitutional standard for adjudicating claims of invidious racial discrimination is identical to the standards applicable under Title VII . . ." (p. 240). Prima facie proof of an Equal Protection violation requires a showing of racially discriminatory purpose, as in the cases on de jure school segregation. On the other hand, prima facie proof of a Title VII violation requires only a showing of disproportionate impact—it is more akin to de facto school segregation, which is nonactionable. By placing the burden of proving discriminatory intent on the challengers to facially neutral tests, *Davis* severely limited constitutional attacks on employment testing.

The Court also ruled that Test 21 complied with statutory requirements, including the standards of Title VII. The trial judge had ruled and now the Court affirmed that this test "was directly related to the requirements of the police training program" (because some minimum verbal skills were essential to completion of the training curriculum), and that "a positive relationship between the test and training-course performance was sufficient to validate the former, wholly aside from its possible relationship to actual performance as a police officer" (p. 251). This lenient standard of validation, the Court claimed, is not "foreclosed by either *Griggs* or *Albemarle*" and, indeed, is a "much more sensible construction of the job-relatedness requirement" (p. 252).

The impact of *Davis* on Title VII validation standards is uncertain. Many lower courts have not diluted the rigorous standards of *Griggs* and *Albemarle*. As one court pointed out, "If employers were permitted to validate selection devices without reference to job performance, then non-job-related selection devices could always be validated through the simple expedient of employing them at both the pre-training and training stage" (*Craig* v. *County of Los Angeles*, 1980, p. 663).

NOTES AND QUESTIONS

---

1. After an employer establishes the job relatedness of an employment test according to the *Albemarle* standards, does that end a Title VII inquiry under *Griggs*?

2. Many employers routinely examine a job applicant's school transcript as a criterion in the screening process. The assumption is that a person who performed well in school is likely to perform well on the job. Was the *Davis* Court's correlation between test score and training course performance a "sensible construction of the job relatedness requirement," if training course performance is expected to be correlated with job performance?

3. Are the *Albemarle* standards so stringent that they exceed the present state-of-the-art capabilities of test developers and, therefore, if fully implemented, would force employers to end testing altogether? For example, the job relatedness of a test depends logically upon an analysis of the nature and functions of the job itself. How would one define—and who would define—the central features of, say, a police officer's job, the success of which a test is expected to measure? Different persons may have different and competing conceptions of the police role. If the legitimacy of a test is founded on its power to predict some job performance criteria, a test is only as good as the criteria themselves—and there may be no consensus on what constitutes good police performance. Is test validity ultimately a problem of test-job relationship or of definition (conceptual and empirical) of the nature of the job itself? How is the validity of the validation criteria determined?

4.   Personnel selection tests which are marketed have predictive validity coefficients of about .30 to .35, which means that only 9% to 12% (the square of the correlation coefficient, or "coefficient of determination") of the variance in job performance is accounted for by the test score—certainly nothing to write home about. (Tests of intellectual ability and achievement tend to have higher validity coefficients because they are usually correlated with scholastic criteria—namely, grades—which are based on similar paper-and-pencil tests; they are weak predictors, however, of nonacademic accomplishments.) If it is shown that the proportion of successful employees selected on the basis of test scores is significantly greater than the proportion of successful employees selected by chance, can it be said that the test is job related despite a coefficient of determination of 10%? The testing standards of the American Psychological Association (1974), relied upon in *Albemarle*, expressly refuse "to call for a particular level of validity or reliability" (p. 5). The "standards" of the guild are merely "statements of ideals or goals" (p. 8). Is the definition of the minimum acceptable criteria for tests an expert issue beyond the competence of the courts or a policy judgment about which psychologists have no special expert claim?

5.   The *Davis* court opined that "[b]eyond doubt . . . there is no single method for appropriately validating employment tests for their relationship to job performance." It observed that the standards of the American Psychological Association "accept three basic methods of validation": predictive validity, construct validity, and content validity (p. 248, n. 13). The implication is that these are alternative and equally satisfactory methods of validation. Which is the most stringent type of validation? Are the three types of validation appropriate for different purposes?

6.   In *United States* v. *South Carolina* (1977), plaintiffs challenged the use of scores on the National Teachers Examination (NTE) by South Carolina in decisions on teacher certification and salary increases. A disproportionately larger number of minorities failed the NTE. The state commissioned the Educational Testing Service (ETS), the NTE publisher, to perform a validation study. ETS sought to demonstrate content validity by determining the degree to which the content of the test matched the curriculum content of teacher training programs in the state. A large sample of professors from all of South Carolina's teachers colleges reviewed each examination question (organized by specialization areas) and decided whether that question "involved subject matter that was a part of the curriculum" at the reviewer's college. By this procedure, the study concluded that 63% to 98% of the questions had content validity. A three-judge panel ruled that the design of this study, though "novel," was "consistent with the basic requirements enunciated by the Supreme Court [in *Davis*]," and hence "was adequate for Title VII purposes" (pp. 1112, 1113). Do you agree that this was an "adequate" validation of a test which results in certifying disproportionately fewer black teachers and paying them less than their white counterparts?

7.   In *Guardians Association of New York City* v. *Civil Service Commission* (1980), black applicants for police officer positions argued that a test purporting to measure attributes such as personality, leadership, and aptitude should have been subject to construct validation rather than content validation. The Second Circuit perceptively observed that because it is easier to conduct content-oriented studies than empirically oriented studies, the distinction between different types of validation "has a significance beyond just selecting the proper technique for validating the exam; it frequently determines who wins the lawsuit" (p. 92). The court refused to be rigidly bound by a particular validation method in analyzing the job-relatedness requirement of Title VII. It ruled that if a test measures abstract qualities (constructs) relevant to many jobs, construct validation would be required. Thus, intelligence and aptitude tests would be subject to empirical validation. "But, as long as the abilities that the test attempts to measure are no more abstract than necessary, that is, as long as they are the most observable abilities of significance to the particular job in question, content validation should be available" (p. 93). As a result, the continued legality of content-oriented methods of employment selection has not been threatened.

8.   Advocates of standardized tests like to analogize the measures to a thermometer. If the thermometer shows that the patient has a temperature, the proper action is to treat the illness rather than to reject the thermometer. Tests reveal discomforting truths regarding the inadequate work skills of substantial numbers of minorities, the result of poor or limited educational opportunities. Hence, the solution to the disparate impact of personnel tests lies in the schools rather than in the workplace. Is this a persuasive argument?

9.   On the one hand, to the extent that tests yield some useful information (not otherwise readily available) about the likelihood that an applicant will perform successfully on the job, personnel selection based on test results promotes the efficiency of the work force and, ultimately, the national interest in greater productivity. On the other hand, there is also a national commitment to racial representativeness in the marketplace by ensuring equal economic opportunity. Can these competing interests be accommodated short of imposing test validation requirements that employers and test makers, even with the best of will, cannot meet?

4.9.   SOCIAL SCIENCE IN LAW CREATION AND EXPANSION: PERSPECTIVES AND OVERVIEW

From Consensus to Dissensus

A theme that emerges from the long history of school desegregation from *Brown* to the present is that things are no longer as simple as they appeared to be in 1954. With respect to both the legal doctrines and the associated empirical research, there is now more dissensus than consensus, more complexity than simplicity, more indeterminacy than certainty. "School desegregation," says Bell (1979), "is our twentieth century equivalent of the Christian Crusades. Once-clear issues are now hopelessly confused. Goals that seemed reasonable are now unattainable" (p. 1826).

In the area of legal policy, the choice used to be framed unambiguously: racial hegemony or racial equality. After state-mandated segregation was declared to be wrong, the remedy was also straightforward: racial integration.

Today, rarely does the wrong appear as overt and easily detectable as the segregation statutes of yesteryear. De facto segregation is part of the more general problem that Wilkinson (1974) has termed "invisible race discrimination" (p. 134). If a public employer hires only on the basis of job qualifications, but most of the successful applicants turn out to be whites; if a police officer stops and questions only those suspected of crime, but the majority of suspects happen to be blacks; if a school district seeks by its attendance policy only to preserve the advantages of neighborhood schools, but the result is mostly one-race schools—if, in short, facially neutral policies or actions result in disproportional racial impact, is there "invisible" discriminatory purpose with the neutral justifications serving as racial surrogates, or is the outcome the product of genuinely unbiased decision-making? A violation, once found, no longer implies a predictable remedy. Questions are now raised as to whether *Brown* stands for steadfast integration, no matter what the social costs, or merely for nondiscrimination on account of race. Liberal values which held sway during the fifties and sixties are increasingly forced into accommodation with neoconservative values of the seventies and eighties.

The related social research has also evolved along a similar path. As Judge

Wisdom (1975) describes its present status, "There is a vast amount of solid research on school desegregation . . . [but] there is little agreement on methodology or conclusions, even when the data relied on are the same" (p. 136, n. 18). The more sophisticated the studies become and the greater the knowledge gained, the greater, too, is our sense of the complexity of the issues, the more apparent our ignorance, and the more conflicting our explanations. When one thinks back about the assertions that were so confidently proclaimed—that segregation has negative psychological effects, period—based mainly on a doll study and on an opinion survey of social scientists, they cannot but evoke a sense of nostalgia for the simplicity of the past.

Law is an instrument of social policy. The dissensus over school desegregation reflects a disagreement over basic social values. Judge Roth observed that "the task we are called upon to perform is a social one which society has been unable to accomplish. In reality our courts are called upon in these school cases to attain a goal through the educational system by using the law as a lever" (in Wolf 1981, p. 283). There are two basic normative questions that underlie school desegregation. First, do we as a nation want to have an integrated society, relying on integrated public schools as a stepping-stone toward the ultimate goal? Second, if yes, is compulsory busing the desired means for achieving integrated schools? Traditional liberal ideology answers both questions affirmatively. The societal ideal is "one [racially integrated] nation, indivisible, with liberty and justice for all." Public education, *Brown* declared, "is the very foundation of good citizenship." Historically, it has been the main avenue for the assimilation of different ethnic groups into mainstream America. It is an article of faith that "Negro and white children playing innocently together in the schoolyard are the primary liberating promise in a society imprisoned by racial consciousness" (*Hobson* v. *Hansen*, 1967, p. 419).

The 1970s and 1980s have seen an increasing number of apostates in the civil rights temple. Legal scholars (for example, Bell 1980) and social scientists (for example, Armor 1972; Coleman, Kelly, and Moore 1975; Glazer 1978; Wolf 1976, 1981) who profess opposition to racial discrimination but nonetheless are profoundly skeptical of the validity and effectiveness of school integration via mandatory busing have been bitterly derided by Kenneth Clark as "neo-liberal revisionists." They are the intellectual vanguard of the "new conservatism" movement, an ideology that finds favor not only about the political elite (for example, the Reagan Administration's position is that "if there are students out there who do not want an integrated education, we should not be compelling them to get on a bus to have one" (*New York Times*, February 14, 1982, p. 14)) but increasingly also among the black community (see *Tasby* v. *Wright*, 1981, p. 690, where black parents urged alternatives to racial balancing to improve educational quality).

The new conservative vision of the preferred society comes at the end of the thirty-year journey of school desegregation from the south to the north. Not all social scientists in the revisionist camp bear the same ideological colors. Some, like Wolf (1981), denounce compulsory busing on the grounds, that it "does not appeal to [the] self-interest of blacks" (because there is no proof of its beneficial consequences) and it "lack[s] moral authority" (because of the contrived fiction of de jure violations) (p. 293). She challenges not only the means but also the ends of integrated schools in an integrated society: "[I]t is hard to see why such heterogeneous association between ethnic groups should be considered a goal which is either attainable or urgently required" (p. 300). Other critics of busing do not go that far (Glazer 1978; Ravitch

1980). They say they are in favor of neighborhood schools, not against racial integration. However, a clean separation between means and ends is difficult to maintain. Multiple roads to Rome is a poor model for the pursuit of values: basic values do not exist independently of the instrumentalities but are defined by them. Racial integration is an abstraction and ultimate ends are appraised in terms of the means they call for. Ends determine the means and vice versa. Wolf's position has the virtue of consistency. Rejection of busing in the face of massive residential segregation implies, in large measure, rejection of integrated schools and an integrated society.

Confronted with these revisionist arguments, integration advocates have become increasingly estranged from social scientists and have denounced their erstwhile allies. One of the sharpest critics was none other than Kenneth Clark. At the time of *Brown,* he declared that the "proof [of the wrongfulness of segregation] had to come from the social psychologists" (1953, p. 3). Twenty years later, he made a remarkable about-face. He complained that "social scientists are indistinguishable from politicians" and "no more dependable in the quest for social justice than other citizens" (1973, p. 120). He warned that "the business of social justice is too important to be left in the hands of . . . social scientists who are primarily responsive to majority fashion, prejudices, and power"; instead, he urged that citizens "put their faith and trust in our federal courts" (Clark 1977, p. 9). His criticisms of social science's role in constitutional adjudication were widely quoted in the press (*New York Times,* June 25, 1975, p. 49). The irony, of course, is that Clark's fear that a change in social science conclusions will force a change in constitutional policy was precisely the alarm that his legal critics, especially Edmond Cahn, sounded in the mid-fifties and which Clark then brushed aside (Chapter 3, section 3.5).

Lawmaking and Fact Determination

The essence of legal reasoning is the establishment of a logical connection between the supporting facts and the conclusions of law of a case. An appreciation for the relationship between law and facts in legal reasoning helps in analyzing the role of empirical inquiry in legal decision-making.

Edward H. Levi (1948) describes the nature of legal reasoning as follows:

> The basic pattern of legal reasoning is reasoning by example. It is reasoning from case to case. It is a three-step process described by the doctrine of precedent in which a proposition descriptive of the first case is made into a rule of law and then applied to a next similar situation. The steps are these: similarity is seen between cases; next the rule of law inherent in the first case is announced; then the rule of law is made applicable to the second case. [pp. 1–2]

The accompanying diagram illustrates the three steps of the process. At time 1, a case involving a social dispute is presented to a court for resolution. The litigants submit evidence for their respective sides on the issue in question. Some of the evidence is admitted and other evidence is excluded after being filtered through layers of evidentiary and procedural rules in order to ensure their reliability, materiality, and probative value. The judge determines the facts of the case based on the evidence admitted. Assume, for purposes of a simple example, that there are no existing rules of law which are directly applicable to the facts of this case. The judge must then formulate a

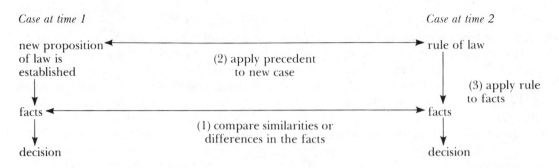

Case at time 1   *Case at time 2*

new proposition of law which, when applied to the facts found, results in a decision resolving the dispute.

At a later time 2, another dispute arises between some other parties, The judge compares the facts between these two cases. Again, for purposes of this illustration, assume that there are only these two cases for comparison and no others. If the critical facts are highly similar, then the proposition descriptive of the earlier case is made into a legal rule. Under the doctrine of precedent, this rule is applied by the judge to the facts of the new case in order to reach a decision. Counsel for the parties also engage in this reasoning process in trying to persuade the court. One side argues that the facts are similar and the precedent should apply to the present case; the other side argues that the facts are dissimilar and the prior rule is inapplicable. The position taken depends upon whether it is to one's advantage that the prior rule be applicable. The written opinion of the judge explaining his decision may or may not incorporate the arguments of the winning party.

An oversimplified overview of the law of school desegregation may make the process more concrete. At time 1, there arises a challenge to the validity of segregated railway cars. Based on the evidence presented by both sides, the court determines the facts of the case: racial segregation is a tradition in that part of the country, and statutes which follow social tradition are reasonable; there is a natural inequality between the races which law cannot restructure; and no annoyance or oppression is visited upon either race so long as the physical facilities in the cars are equal for both. The court then rules that segregated cars are not invalid.

At time 2, a court is faced with a controversy involving schools segregated by law. The judge determines on the evidence that the facts are similar to those of the railway cars case: The physical facilities of the schools are the same for both races. By the doctrine of precedent, the proposition descriptive of the earlier case—separate but equal treatment is valid—is made into a rule of law and applied to the present situation. The decision upholds the state policy of segregated school.

Another attack on segregated schools is mounted at a later time 3. The challengers present arguments and evidence to the effect that the facts of this case are different from the preceding ones. Included in the evidence are research findings showing the detrimental consequences of segregated (though equal) schools on the personality and educational performance of minority children. Suppose the court is persuaded that the prior rule should not apply. It has several options. It can expressly overturn the governing rule. It can distinguish the cases, so that a new rule applies to the present case but the prior rule remains intact. For example, by differentiating schools from railway cars, the court can limit the separate but equal principle to railway cars only. Or, it can ignore the prior rule and decide the present case on other grounds—in effect, it silently overrules the earlier case. Courts are reluctant to expressly overrule cases because it undermines the notion of precedent, designed to ensure stability and continuity in case law.

Suppose in this instance that the court overrules the prior cases. It decides that separate but equal schools are, in fact, unequal, and orders the desegregation of public schools. Where case law is concerned, despite the doctrine of precedent, a judge is not inextricably bound to statements made by prior judges, unless of course they are higher court judges. They become mere dictum and the judge makes his own decision. Determination of the facts is crucial. The judge can emphasize facts unavailable to or ignored by prior judges, such as the results of psychological research on the personality effects of segregation. Or, he may find irrelevant or erroneous facts which were deemed important in the past, such as the societal traditions approving of segregation.

To conclude the example, another case arises at time 4. Again a lawsuit against segregated schools is filed. Comparison of the facts of the case in time 3 and the present case reveals both similarities and differences. The key difference is that the segregated schools now are the result of residential housing patterns and not, as in the past, of deliberate governmental action. In addition, there is not total segregation, only disproportionate representation of races in a given school. However, there are some similarities in the effects on educational achievement. In this situation, there are arguably sufficient differences in the facts so that the rule of the case in time 3 does not apply, at least not in wholesale fashion. Yet the differences are not so great as to make the prior rule inapplicable. If a judge accepts this line of reasoning, he is in the position of having to apply the rule—but in some modified form—to the facts of the instant case.

This example illustrates the lawmaking process. At time 2, a court *applied* an existing rule, via the doctrine of precedent, to similar facts in the case in question. At time 3, a court *created* a new rule of law and overturned the past law, given the dissimilarity between the facts of the cases. And at time 4, a court *modified* or *expanded* the governing rule. Thus, the legal process is at once static and dynamic. The law is fixed and certain, expressed in a body of rules, which can be applied to diverse facts. And the law is also variable and changing, an analytical technique for reaching decisions in social disputes, in which the legal decision rules emerge in the process of analyzing facts. As Levi (1948) put it, "the rules change as the rules are applied" (pp. 3–4). The essence of legal reasoning is this determination of the facts. The findings of similarities or differences then trigger the application or nonapplication of a rule of law. It is reasoning by analogy and example based on facts (Murray 1982).

The analysis of facts and of rules of law are closely intertwined. On the one hand, similarity of facts calls into play a given legal rule: *ex facto jus oritur* (out of facts springs the law); on the other hand, it is this legal rule that made those facts legally significant in the first place (Hart and McNaugton 1959, p. 60). In legal reasoning, the mind constantly travels from facts to law and back to facts again, in a simulacrum of a feedback loop: "You cannot decide which facts matter unless you have already selected, at least tentatively, applicable decisional standards. But most of the time you cannot properly understand these legal standards without relating them to the factual situation of the case" (Damaška 1975, p. 1087, n. 8). Thus, the social psychological consequences of school segregation are facts which bring into operation the governing rule forbidding such segregation. But it is because of the existence of the rule that evidence has to be presented in support of these facts. This circular relationship between rule and facts is a central aspect of the way law works and evolves.

Legal reasoning is not, strictly speaking, perfectly logical reasoning. The determination of fact similarity is the crucial step in the process, yet there is no standard for ascertaining the necessary extent of similarity to invoke a given rule. Absent such an a priori standard, a judge—for reasons of justice and fairness—could classify facts as similar when they are somewhat different. The decision in the case would then be controlled by the governing precedent. Alternately, a judge could classify facts differently when they are somewhat similar. Precedent would then be inapplicable to the case. In both instances, a judge would justify the finding of similarity or difference based on the rule which arose from—and now is applied back to—the initial facts.

Legal reasoning is primarily a social process of problem-solving. The standard for determining similarity or difference is left ambiguous in order to allow law to change and grow. An open-textured, flexible approach (within procedural limits) to the determination of facts provides room for the infusion of new ideas into the lawmaking process. As society evolves, community values change, and knowledge is advanced by science, the courts can take into account these new developments by its fact determinations. Thus, because law is not a logical exercise carried out in a social vacuum, but a process which shapes and is shaped by social influences, its method of reasoning has to contain ambiguous categories (Levi 1948, pp. 3–4).

This basic account of the nature of legal reasoning places in perspective the role of empirical inquiry in the judicial process. It is this method of analogical reasoning that makes possible the introduction of research data—as well as of common ideas from society—into the lawmaking process. These nonlegal inputs of scientific and societal ideas enter into the law through the first step in legal reasoning, the comparison of facts. The analogies advocated by the litigants enable these ideas to have their day in court. The litigants themselves participate in the creation and expansion of laws. The ideas they bring help shape substantive justice, because the rule which emerges from the facts of the case will be the law for all.

REFERENCES

Albemarle Paper Co. v. Moody, 422 U.S. 405 (1975).

Alexander v. Holmes County Board of Education, 396 U.S. 19 (1969).

Allport, G. *The Nature of Prejudice.* New York: Addison-Wesley, 1954.

American Psychological Association. "Standards for Educational and Psychological Tests." *Manual of the American Psychological Association.* Washingon, D.C.: American Psychological Association, 1974.

Amir, Y. "The Role of Intergroup Contact in Change of Prejudice and Ethnic Relations." *Towards the Elimination of Racism,* edited by P. Katz. New York: Pergamon Press, 1976.

Anastasi, A. *Psychological Testing,* 4th ed. New York: Macmillan, 1976.

Armor, D. J. "School and Family Effects on Black and White Achievement." In *On Equality of Educational Opportunity,* edited by F. Mosteller and D. Moynihan. New York: Random House, 1972.

Armor, D. J. "The Evidence on Busing." *Public Interest* 28 (1972): 90–126.

Ashurst, D. E., and Meyers, C. E. "Social System and Clinical Model in the School Identification of the Educable Retarded." *Monographs of the American Association on Mental Deficiency* 1 (1973): 150–63.

Banks, W. C. "White Preference in Blacks: A

Paradigm in Search of a Phenomenon."
Psychological Bulletin 83 (1976): 1179–86.

Bell v. School City, 324 F.2d 209 (7th Cir.
1963); cert. denied, 377 U.S. 924 (1963).

Bell, D. A., Jr. *Race, Racism, and American Law.*
Boston: Little, Brown, 1975a.

———. "Waiting on the Promise of Brown."
Law and Contemporary Problems 39
(1975b): 341–73.

———. "Book Review." *Harvard Law Review* 92
(1979): 1826–44.

———. *Shades of Brown: New Perspectives on
School Desegregation.* New York: Teachers
College Press, 1980.

Bersoff, D. N. "Regarding Psychologists Tes-
tily: Legal Regulation of Psychological
Assessment in the Public Schools." *Maryland Law Review* 39 (1979): 27–120.

———. "Testing and the Law." *American Psychologist* 36 (1981): 1047–56.

Book Review. [E. Wolf's *Trial and Error.*] *Michigan Law Review* 80 (1982): 955–57.

Bowles, S., and Levin, H. M. "The Determinants of Scholastic Achievement: An
Appraisal of Recent Evidence." *Journal
of Human Resources* 3 (1968): 3–24.

Bradley v. Milliken, 338 F. Supp. 582 (E.D.
Mich. 1971).

Bradley v. Milliken, 402 F. Supp. 1096 (E.D.
Mich. 1975).

Brewer v. School Board, 434 F.2d 408 (4th Cir.
1969).

Brief for Appellants on Further Reargument in
the Supreme Court of the United States,
October Term 1954, in Brown v. Board
of Education, 1954.

Brief for Appellees on Further Reargument in
the Supreme Court of the United States,
October Term 1954, in Davis v. County
School Board of Prince Edward County,
1954.

Briggs v. Elliott, 132 F. Supp. 776 (E.D. S.C.
1955).

Brown v. Board of Education [Brown I], 347
U.S. 483 (1954).

Brown v. Board of Education [Brown II], 349
U.S. 294 (1955).

Brunson v. Board of Trustees, 429 F.2d 820
(4th Cir. 1970).

Cahn, E. *The Predicament of Modern Man.* New
York: Dell, 1961.

Calhoun v. Cook, 487 F.2d 860 (5th Cir. 1973).

Clark, K. B. "Desegregation: An Appraisal of
the Evidence." *Journal of Social Issues* 4
(1953): 1–77.

———. "Social Policy, Power, and Social Science Research." *Harvard Educational Review* 43 (1973): 113–21.

———. "Social Science, Constitutional Rights,
and the Courts." *Education, Social Science,
and the Courts,* edited by R. Rist and R.
Anson. New York: Teachers College
Press, 1977.

Clotfelter, C. J. "The Implications of Resegre-
gation for Judicially Imposed School
Segregation Remedies." *Vanderbilt Law
Review* 31 (1978): 829–54.

Cohen, D. K.; Pettigrew, T. F.; and Riley, R. T.
"Race and the Outcome of Schooling."
In *On Equality of Educational Opportunity,*
edited by F. Mosteller and D. Moynihan.
New York: Random House, 1972.

Cohen, D. K., and Weiss, J. A. "Social Science
and Social Policy: Schools and Race." In
*Education, Social Science, and the Judicial
Process,* edited by R. Rist and R. Anson.
New York: Teachers College Press,
1977.

Cohen, E. G. "The Effects of Desegregation on
Race Relations." *Law and Contemporary
Problems* 39 (1975): 271–99.

Coleman, J. S. "A Brief Summary of the Coleman Report." Harvard Educational Review, *Equal Educational Opportunity.* Cambridge, Mass.: Harvard University Press,
1969.

———; Kelly, S.; and Moore, J. "Trends in
School Segregation, 1968–73." Paper
presented at the American Educational
Research Association annual meeting,
April 2, 1975.

Coleman, J. S.; Campbell, E. Q.; Hobson, C. J.;
McPartland, J.; Mood, A. M.; Winfield,
F. D.; and York, R. L. *Equality of Educa-
tional Opportunity.* Washington, D.C.:
U.S. Government Printing Office, 1966.

Columbus Board of Education v. Penick, 443
U.S. 449 (1979).

Comment. "Alternative Schools for Minority
Students: The Constitution, the Civil
Rights Act and the Berkeley Experiment." *California Law Review* 61 (1973):
858–918.

Comment. "White Flight as a Factor in Desegregation Remedies: A Judicial Recognition
of Reality." *Virginia Law Review* 66
(1980): 961–81.

Cook, S. "Social Science and School Desegrega-
tion: 'Did We Mislead the Supreme
Court?'" *Personality and Social Psychology
Bulletin* 5 (1979): 420–437.

Cooper v. Aaron, 358 U.S. 1 (1958).

Coppedge v. Franklin County Board of Education, 394 F.2d 410 (4th Cir. 1968).

Craig v. County of Los Angeles, 626 F.2d 659
(9th Cir. 1980).

Crain, R. L., and Mahard, R. E. "Desegregation and Black Achievement: A Review of the Research." *Law and Contemporary Problems* 42 (1978): 17–56.

Craven, J. B. "The Impact of Social Science Evidence on the Judge: A Personal Comment." *Law and Contemporary Problems* 39 (1975): 150–56.

Crawford v. Board of Education, 17 Cal.3d 280 (1976).

Cronbach, L. "Five Decades of Public Controversy Over Mental Testing." *American Psychologist* 30 (1975): 1–14.

Damaška, M. "Presentation of Evidence and Factfinding Precision." *University of Pennsylvania Law Review* 123 (1975): 1083–1106.

Dayton Board of Education v. Brinkman, 443 U.S. 526 (1979).

Deal v. Cincinnati Board of Education, 369 F.2d 55 (6th Cir. 1966); cert. denied, 389 U.S. 847 (1967).

Dollard, J. *Caste and Class in a Southern Town.* New York: Doubleday, 1937.

Downs v. Board of Education, 336 F.2d 988 (10th Cir. 1964); cert. denied, 380 U.S. 914 (1965).

Epps, E. G. "The Impact of School Desegregation on Aspirations, Self-concepts, and Other Aspects of Personality." *Law and Contemporary Problems* 39 (1975): 300–13.

Epps, E. G. "The Impact of School Desegregation on the Self-evaluation and Achievement Orientation of Minority Children." *Law and Contemporary Problems* 42 (1978): 57–76.

Farley, R. "Residential Segregation and Its Implications for School Integration." *Law and Contemporary Problems* 39 (1975): 164–93.

Fisher, J. "Race and Reconciliation: The Role of the School." In *The Negro American*, edited by T. Parsons and K. Clark. Boston: Houghton-Mifflin, 1967.

Fiss, O. "The Charlotte-Mecklenburg Case—Its Significance for Northern School Desegregation." *University of Chicago Law Review* 38 (1971): 697–709.

Flaugher, R. "The Many Definitions of Test Bias." *American Psychologist* 33 (1978): 671–79.

Gayle v. Browder, 352 U.S. 903 (1956).

Gerard, H. B. "School Desegregation: The Social Science Role." *American Psychologist* 38 (1983): 869–877.

——— and Miller, N., eds. *School Desegregation: A Long-term Study.* New York: Plenum Press, 1975.

Glazer, N. *Affirmative Discrimination: Ethnic Inequality and Public Policy.* New York: Basic Books, 1978.

Goldman, R., and Hartig, L. "The WISC May Not Be a Valid Predicter of School Performance for Primary-Grade Minority Children." *American Journal of Mental Deficiency* 80 (1976): 585–87.

Goodman, F. I. "De Facto School Segregation: A Constitutional and Empirical Analysis." *California Law Review* 60 (1972): 275–437.

Grant, W. R. "Community Control Vs. Integration: The Case of Detroit." *Public Interest* 24 (1971): 62–79.

———. "The Detroit School Case: A Historical Overview." *Wayne Law Review* 21 (1975): 851–66.

Green v. County School Board, 391 U.S. 430 (1968).

Griggs v. Duke Power Co., 401 U.S. 424 (1971).

Grossman, H., ed. *Manual on Terminology and Classification in Mental Retardation.* Washington, D.C.: American Association on Mental Deficiency, 1977.

Guardians Association of New York City v. Civil Service Commission, 630 F.2d 79 (2d Cir. 1980).

Gunther, G. "The Supreme Court 1971 Term—Foreward: In Search of Evolving Doctrine in a Changing Court: A Model for a Newer Equal Protection." *Harvard Law Review* 86 (1972): 1–48.

Haney, C. "Employment Tests and Employment Discrimination: A Dissenting Psychological Opinion." *Industrial Relations Law Journal* 5 (1982): 1–86.

Hart, H. M., and McNaughton, J. T. "Evidence and Inference in Law." In *Evidence and Inference*, edited by D. Lerner. Glencoe, Ill.: Free Press, 1959.

Hart v. Community School Board, 383 F. Supp. 699 (E.D. N.Y. 1974).

Hearings on Equal Educational Opportunity Before the Select Senate Committee on Equal Educational Opportunity, 91st Congr., 2d Session, pt. 3-B, 1311 (1970).

Heller, K. A.; Holtzman, W. H.; and Mussick, S. (Eds.). *Placing Children in Special Education: A Strategy for Equality.* Wash. D.C.: National Academy Press, 1982.

Hobson v. Hansen, 269 F. Supp. 401 (D. D.C. 1967).

Inger, M. *Politics and Reality in an American city: The New Orleans School Crisis of 1960.* New York: Center for Urban Education, 1969.

Jensen, A. R. "How Much Can We Boost I.Q.

and Scholastic Achievement?" *Harvard Educational Review* 39 (1969): 1–123.

Johnson, J. G. "*Albemarle Paper Company v. Moody:* The Aftermath of *Griggs* and the Death of Employee Testing." *Hastings Law Journal* 27 (1976): 1239–62.

Katz, P. "The Acquisition of Racial Attitudes in Children." In *Towards the Elimination of Racism,* edited by P. Katz. New York: Pergamon Press, 1976.

Kelley v. Metropolitan County Board of Education, 492 F. Supp. 167 (M.D. Tenn. 1980).

Keyes v. School District No. 1, 313 F. Supp. 61 (D. Colo. 1970).

Keyes v. School District No. 1, 413 U.S. 189 (1973).

Killian, L. M. "The Social Scientist's Role in the Preparation of the Florida Desegregation Brief." *Social Problems* 3 (1956): 211–14.

Kirp, D. L. "Schools as Sorters: The Constitutional and Policy Implications of Student Classifications." *University of Pennsylvania Law Review* 121 (1973): 705–97.

Kluger, R. *Simple Justice.* New York: Alfred A. Knopf, 1977.

Lambert, N. "Psychological Evidence in *Larry P. v. Wilson Riles:* An Evaluation by a Witness for the Defense." *American Psychologist* 36 (1981): 937–52.

Larry P. v. Riles, 495 F. Supp. 926 (N.D. Ca. 1979).

Lau v. Nichols, 414 U.S. 563 (1974).

Levi, E. H. *An Introduction to Legal Reasoning.* Chicago: University of Chicago Press, 1948.

Levin, B. "School Desegregation Remedies and the Role of Social Science Research." *Law and Contemporary Problems* 42 (1978): 1–36.

———, and Moise, P. "School Desegregation Litigation in the Seventies and the Use of Social Science Evidence: An Annotated Guide." *Law and Contemporary Problems* 39 (1975): 50–133.

Levin, H. M. "Education, Life Chances, and the Courts: The Role of Social Science Evidence." *Law and Contemporary Problems* 39 (1975): 217–40.

Lightfoot, S. L. *Worlds Apart: Relationships Between Families and Schools.* New York: Basic Books, 1978.

Loh, W. D. "In Quest of *Brown*'s Promise: Social Research and Social Values in School Desegregation." *Washington Law Review* 58 (1982): 129–74.

MacMillan, D. C., and Meyers, C. E. "*Larry P:*

An Educational Interpretation." *School Review Psychology* 9 (1980): 136–48.

Madden, P. B. "Intelligence Test on Trial." *School Psychology Review* 9 (1980): 149–53.

Mahon, T., and Mahon A. "The Impact of Schools on Learning: Inner-City Children in Suburban Schools." *Journal of School Psychology* 9 (1971): 1–11.

McConahay, J. B. "The Effects of School Desegregation upon Students' Racial Attitudes and Behavior: A Critical Review of the Literature and a Prolegomenon to Future Research." *Law and Contemporary Problems* 42 (1978): 77–107.

———. "Reducing Racial Prejudice in Desegregated Schools." In *Effective School Desegregation: Equity, Quality, and Feasibility,* edited by W. D. Howley. Beverly Hills, Calif.: Sage, 1981.

———. "Self-interest Versus Racial Attitudes as Correlates of Anti-busing Attitudes in Louisville." *Journal of Politics* 44 (1982): 692–720.

McPartland, J. "The Relative Influence of School and Classroom Desegregation on the Academic Achievement of Ninth Grade Negro Students." *Journal of Social Issues* 25 (1969): 93–102.

Milliken v. Bradley, 484 F.2d 215 (6th Cir. 1973).

Milliken v. Bradley, 418 U.S. 717 (1974).

Milliken v. Bradley, 443 U.S. 267 (1977).

Morgan v. Kerrigan, 530 F.2d 401 (1976).

Mosteller, F., and Moynihan, D. *On Equality of Educational Opportunity.* New York: Random House, 1972.

Moynihan, J. "Education of the Urban Poor." *Harvard Graduate School Educational Association Bulletin* 12 (1967): 3.

Murray, J. R. "The Role of Analogy in Legal Reasoning." *UCLA Law Review* 29 (1982): 833–71.

Myrdal, G. *An American Dilemma.* New York: Harper, 1944.

Newby, I. A. *Challenge to the Courts: Social Scientists and the Defense of Segregation, 1954–1966.* Baton Rouge: Louisiana State University Press, 1967.

Orfield, G. "Research, Politics, and the Anti-busing Debate." *Law and Contemporary Problems* 42 (1978): 141–73.

Parent Association of Andrew Jackson High School v. Ambach, 598 F.2d 705 (2d Cir. 1979).

Parents in Action on Special Education v. Hannon, 506 F. Supp. 831 (N.D. Ill. 1980).

Pettigrew, T. F. "The Negro and Education."

Race and Social Sciences, edited by I. Katz and P. Gurin. New York: Basic Books, 1969.

———. "A Sociological View of the Post-Bradley Era." *Wayne Law Review* 21 (1975): 813–32.

———, and Green, R. "School Desegregation in Large Cities: A Critique of the Coleman "White Flight" Thesis." *Harvard Educational Review* 46 (1976): 1–23.

Pettigrew, T. F.; Useem, E. L.; Normand, C.; and Smith, M. S. "Busing: A Review of the Evidence." *Public Interest* 30 (1972): 88–118.

Plessy v. Ferguson, 163 U.S. 142 (1896).

Ravitch, D. "The "White Flight" Controversy." *Public Interest* 51 (1978): 135–49.

———. "Desegregation: Varieties of Meaning." *Shades of Brown: New Perspectives on School Desegregation,* edited by D. Bell. New York: Teachers College Press, 1980.

———. "Social Scientists on the Stand." *New Leader,* February 8, 1982, pp. 19–21.

Read, F. T. "Judicial Evolution of the Law of School Integration Since Brown v. Board of Education." *Law and Contemporary Problems* 39 (1975): 7–49.

Reschly, D. J. "Psychological Evidence in the Larry P. Opinion: A Case of Right Problem–Wrong Solution?" *School Psychology Review* 9 (1980): 123–35.

Rist, R. C. *The Invisible Children: School Integration in American Society.* Cambridge, Mass.: Harvard University Press, 1978.

Robinson, N., and Robinson, H. *The Mentally Retarded Child,* 2nd ed. New York: McGraw-Hill, 1976.

———. "School Desegregation and White Flight." *Political Science Quarterly* 90 (1975–76): 675–93.

Rossell, C. H. "School Desegregation and Community Social Change." *Law and Contemporary Problems* 42 (1978): 133–83.

San Antonio Independent School District v. Rodriguez, 411 U.S. 1 (1973).

Sanders, J.; Rankin-Widgeon, B.; Kalmuss, D.; and Chesler, M. "The Relevance of 'Irrelevant' Testimony: Why Lawyers Use Social Science Experts in School Desegregation Cases." *Law and Society Review* 16 (1981–82): 403–28.

Sandoval, J. "The WISC-R and Internal Evidence of Test Bias with Minority Groups." *Journal of Consulting and Criminal Psychology* 47 (1979): 919–27.

Sarratt, R. *The Ordeal of Desegregation.* New York: Harper & Row, 1966.

Semmel, M. I.; Gottlieb, J.; and Robinson, N. M. "Mainstreaming: Perspectives on Educating Handicapped Children in the Public Schools." In *Review of Research in Education,* vol. 7, edited by D. C. Berliner. Washington, D.C.: American Educational Research Association, 1979.

Slavin, R. E. "Cooperative Learning in Teams: State of the Art." *Educational Psychologist* 15 (1980): 93–111.

Smuck v. Hobson, 408 F.2d 175 (D.C. Cir. 1969).

St. John, N. "Desegregation and Minority Group Preference." *Review of Educational Research* 40 (1970):111–33.

———. *School Desegregation: Outcomes for Children.* New York: John Wiley, 1975.

Stell v. Savannah-Chatham County Board of Education, 220 F. Supp. 667 (S.D. Ga. 1963).

Stell v. Savannah-Chatham County Board of Education, 333 F.2d 55 (5th Cir. 1964).

Stephan, W. G. "School Desegregation: An Evaluation of Predictions Made in Brown v. Board of Education." *Psychological Bulletin* 85 (1978): 217–38.

Swann v. Charlotte-Mecklenburg Board of Education, 402 U.S. 1 (1971).

Taeuber, K. E. "Demographic Perspectives in Housing and School Segregation." *Wayne Law Review* 21 (1975): 833–50.

Tasby v. Wright, 520 F. Supp. 683 (N.D. Tex. 1981).

Taylor, W. L. "The Supreme Court and Urban Reality: A Tactical Analysis of Milliken v. Bradley." *Wayne Law Review* 21 (1975): 752–78.

United States Commission on Civil Rights. *Survey of School Desegregation in the Southern and Border States 1965–66.* Washington D.C.: U.S. Government Printing Office, 1966.

———. *Desegregation of the National Public Schools: A Status Report.* Washington, D.C.: U.S. Government Printing Office, 1979.

United States v. Board of School Commissioners, 332 F. Supp. 655 (S.D. Ind. 1971).

United States v. Board of School Commissioners, 503 F.2d 68 (7th Cir. 1974).

United States v. Jefferson County Board of Education, 372 F.2d 836 (5th Cir. 1966).

United States v. Jefferson County Board of Education, 380 F.2d 385 (5th Cir. 1967).

United States v. Scotland Neck Board of Education, 407 U.S. 484 (1972).

United States v. South Carolina, 445 F. Supp. 1094 (D.S.C. 1977).

Village of Arlington Heights v. Metropolitan

Housing Development Corp., 429 U.S. 252 (1976).

Washington v. Davis, 426 U.S. 229 (1976).

Weinberg, M. "The Relationship Between School Desegregation and Academic Achievement: A Review of the Research." *Law and Contemporary Problems* 39 (1975): 240–70.

———. *Minority Students: A Research Appraisal.* Washington, D.C.: National Institute of Education, 1977.

Wigdor, A. K., and Garner, W. R. (Eds.), *Ability Testing: Uses, Consequences, and Controversies.* Wash. D.C.: National Academy Press, 1982.

Wilkinson, J. H., III. *Serving Justice: A Supreme Court Clerk's View.* New York: Charterhouse Books, 1974.

———. "The Supreme Court and Southern School Desegregation, 1955–1970: A History and Analysis." *Virginia Law Review* 64 (1978): 485–559.

———. *From Brown to Bakke: The Supreme Court and School Integration, 1954–1968.* New York: Oxford University Press, 1979.

Wilson, J. Q. "On Pettigrew and Armor: An Afterword." *Public Interest* 30 (1973): 132–34.

Wisdom, J. M. "Random Remarks on the Role of the Social Sciences in the Judicial Decision-making Process in School Desegregation Cases." *Law and Contemporary Problems* 39 (1975): 134–49.

Wolf, E. "Social Science and the Courts: The Detroit School Case." *Public Interest* 42 (1976): 102–20.

———. "Northern School Desegregation and Residential Choice." *Supreme Court Review* 1977 (1977): 63–85.

———. *Trial and Error: The Detroit School Desegregation Case.* Detroit: Wayne University Press, 1981.

Yudof, M. G. "Suspension and Expulsion of Black Students from the Public Schools: Academic Capital Punishment and the Constitution." *Law and Contemporary Problems* 39 (1975): 375–411.

———. "School Desegregation: Legal Realism, Reasoned Elaboration, and Social Science Research in the Supreme Court." *Law and Contemporary Problems* 42 (1978): 57–110.

CHAPTER 5

Contraction and Abolition of Law: Case Study of the Death Penalty

5.1. INTRODUCTION

At periodic intervals since the founding of the Republic, the moral rightness and penological effectiveness of capital punishment have been the subject of intense public discourse and legislative action. Americans have always been aware of and held opinions about death and power; surely no adult is without some views on what it means for the state, with premeditation, to extinguish life. However, the legality of capital punishment was not seriously challenged until well into the second half of the twentieth century. On June 29, 1972, a fissured Supreme Court, consisting of five Justices each speaking only for himself, ruled that the death penalty as it was then imposed by the states was arbitrary and unevenhanded, and therefore in violation of the Eighth Amendment prohibition of "cruel and unusual punishment" (*Furman* v. *Georgia*). Immediately, some 600 theretofore condemned persons were spared from hanging, gassing, shooting, or electrocution. For opponents of capital punishment, it augured the beginning of the end of what Barzun (1964) has called "judicial homicide." It exalted the value of reverence for life over the primordial urge to avenge; life, no matter how distorted, violent, and criminal, is too precious to be taken away capriciously. But the Court's decision contained an implicit invitation to the states to recraft their death penalty statutes, and many states promptly enacted new legislation designed to repair the defects of the old. Then, four years later, a plurality of three Justices declared that capital punishment was not in and of itself cruel and unusual, so long as it was meted in a principled and fair manner. It is "an expression of society's moral outrage" at criminal conduct and, as such, retribution is "essential in an ordered society" (*Gregg* v. *Georgia*, 1976, p. 186). The machinery of death was once again set in motion. For proponents of capital punishment, the decision signaled the end of the beginning.

NOTE: This chapter was prepared with Barbara Critchlow, of the University of Washington, and Neil Vidmar, of the University of Western Ontario.

Today, capital punishment poses not only a pressing moral question but an arresting social problem as well. The number of death row inmates has swelled to over 1,200 (double that of a decade ago), spread out over 34 states, and it is presently increasing at a rate of 15 to 20 a month. Almost all of them are mired in elaborate and seemingly endless judicial procedures seeking to avoid or postpone the day of reckoning. But inevitably the day will come when all legal remedies are exhausted, and given the accumulated death row backlog, the nation may have to face the prospect of a blood bath—a prospect made all the more disturbing by the disproportionate number of racial minorities and the poor among the condemned.

This chapter traces the gradual contraction and attempted abolition of the law of capital punishment and the uses of social science in that process. To appreciate how and why the law evolved to its present form, it will be helpful to begin with a quick glance backward.

The Historical Scope of Capital Offenses

American criminal law is rooted in the English experience. In England, at the end of the fifteenth century, only eight capital offenses were recognized: murder, high treason, petty treason, larceny, robbery, burglary, rape, and arson. During the agricultural and industrial revolutions, a wide range of new capital crimes was created, so that by the late eighteenth century, the list had expanded to over two hundred. Property offenses rather than violent crimes accounted for the majority of capital convictions and executions. The expansion of death penalty legislation was associated with the growth of urbanization and wealth. Capital statutes "served the interests of private property and commerce" against those who might seek to undermine them (Bowers 1974, p. 170; Pritchard 1971). The usual mode of execution was by hanging, though beheading, disemboweling, and quartering were not unheard of. By the mid-nineteenth century, in the wake of social and economic reforms designed to ameliorate the dislocations caused by industrialization, most of the capital offenses were repealed. Thereafter, the death sentence was imposed and carried out principally for murder.

The American colonies inherited the large number of capital offenses and proceeded to add some of their own. Perhaps the most notorious were the theocratic crimes—blasphemy, idolatry, and witchcraft—of the Massachusetts Bay Colony in the mid-seventeenth century, which served to justify the witch hunts in Salem (Erikson 1966). Death for heretics became a means of enforcing compliance with the established religious orthodoxy. In the New World as in the Old, some of the more gruesome methods of execution, such as burning at the stake or impaling in the grave, were invented and used by religious authorities in times when the church was the dominant political authority and the basis for social organization (Bowers 1974, p. 166). Later, as the colony flourished as a center of trade, death for religious offenses was abolished.

The most significant expansion of capital statutes occurred with the growth of slavery and the plantation economy of the South. In the pre–Civil War years, several slavery-related capital offenses were created, including concealing a slave with intent to free him, inciting slaves to insurrection, circulating seditious literature among slaves, theft, and arson. "Next to theft, arson was the most common 'slave' crime, one which slaveowners dreaded almost constantly. Fire was a favorite means for aggrieved slaves to even the score with their masters" (Stampp 1956, p. 127). The reach of capital legislation was different for whites and for slaves. Virginia, for example, in the antebellum era defined five capital crimes for whites and up to seventy for slaves (Note, *Virginia Law Review,* 1972). Moreover, in some jurisdictions, slaves were sometimes subjected to more torturous methods of execution. Burning at the stake was authorized and performed as late as 1825 in South Carolina (Teeters and Hedblom 1967, p. 109). Slave owners were compensated, of course, by the state for executed slaves.

This quick overview of the expansion and contraction of the scope of capital statutes indicates that whatever legitimate, penological purposes the death penalty serves, it can also be used—even in societies with a democratic heritage—for extralegal purposes, be they religious, economic, political, or racial. Capital punishment can be an instrument by which the "top dog" can keep the "underdog" in check.

Statutory Reform and Repeal

The history of capital punishment in America until the 1960s is the history of periodic movements for its statutory repeal or, failing to attain that objective, for its reform by narrowing the scope of capital crimes and by civilizing the procedures by which death sentences are imposed and carried out. It is a checkered history of abolition, restoration, and reabolition that reflects the deep and continuing tension in the American psyche between the instincts of charity and retribution. The legislative pendulum seems to swing back and forth in roughly fifty-year cycles.

Modern abolitionist ideas find their source in the Enlightenment. An Italian jurist, Cesare Beccaria, is credited with publishing the first influential critique of the death penalty in his treatise *On Crime and Punishment* in 1764 (excerpted in Sellin 1967, p. 39). He proclaimed the inherent right to life and argued that nothing in the social contract certified the state to impose the sanction of death, which he termed "a war of the nation against the citizen." He urged reliance on utilitarian calculation (for example, the uselessness of executions as a deterrent to crime, the possibilities of rehabilitation of offenders) rather than reflex obedience to the early books of Scripture (for example, the Noahic commandment that "whoso sheddeth man's blood, by man shall his blood be shed," Genesis 9:6; and the *lex talionis:* "eye for eye, tooth for tooth, . . . life for life," Exodus 21:23–24). Beccaria's ideas dominated abolitionist thinking for the next 100 years and beyond.

Legislative reform in the United States began shortly after independence. It was brought about chiefly by the efforts of Benjamin Rush, a Philadelphia physician and signer of the Declaration of Independence, who was greatly influenced by Beccaria's treatise. Acknowledged as "the father of the [abolition movement] in the United States," Rush elicited the support of Benjamin Franklin and other prominent citizens to accomplish the first statutory reform in the nation (Bedau 1964, p. 8). The Pennsylvania legislature in 1794, as a compromise between total abolition and retention, adopted "degrees" of murder and limited the application of the death penalty to first degree homicide. This reform, however, had no immediate impact on the other states.

Abolitionist sentiment flowed again a generation later (1830s to 1850s). In New England and the Midwest, anti-gallows societies were organized and there was extensive lobbying for repeal and reform. In 1847, the Territory of Michigan eliminated all capital punishment except for treason (which it had never imposed), thereby becoming the first English-speaking jurisdiction in the world to achieve (de facto) abolition. Only two other states, Rhode Island and Wisconsin, followed suit in the pre–Civil War years (Filler 1952).

In this period, reform—a sort of guerrilla warfare against capital punishment—proved more successful than outright repeal. The list of capital crimes was shortened significantly, especially for property offenses. Several states also did away with the carnival-like atmosphere of public executions by performing them in the privacy of the prison yard scaffold. This reform "humanized" the execution process but also served to erode the state's interest in deterrence: the adage "out of sight, out of mind" could apply to capital punishment as well.

With the advent of the Civil War, the movement languished. Many of the death penalty abolitionists were also slavery abolitionists, and their energies were consumed by the more pressing issues of the day. The next major wave of abolitionist activity did not arise until after the turn of the century and the years before the First World War. The climate of the Progressive era gave death penalty reformers the opportunity to move in concert with other social reformers, including feminists, prohibitionists, and penal reformers. Nine states abolished capital punishment, but with American entry into the war, several of them restored it.

Again, where repeal failed, reform succeeded. Many states substituted discretionary sentencing for mandatory capital punishment. The purpose was to avoid putting the jury to the choice of either convicting a guilty person (and automatically sentencing him to death), or acquitting him (because he was not guilty enough to merit death). Mandatory punishment was thought to make convictions more difficult to secure. It was a reform favored by both sides. Abolitionists supported it because they viewed it as a first step toward their ultimate goal. Retentionists also favored it but for the opposite reason: if fewer persons are actually sentenced and executed, the drive for total abolition might be blunted.

The means of execution were made swift and painless. New York introduced the first electric chair late in the nineteenth century. There were some doubts as to its superiority over the gallows when the initial attempts, with clumsy and makeshift equipment, bungled. The condemned had to undergo re-electrocution. The development of execution by asphyxiation and by lethal gas then followed.

There also began a shift in the authority under which executions were carried out. With the growth of state penitentiaries and the centralization of penal authority, there was a corresponding movement toward the centralization of executions under state (rather than local) authority. With the adoption of more "humane" methods of execution, it became uneconomical to maintain an electric chair or a gas chamber in every town or county in a state (Bowers 1974, p. 11).

The mass slaughters of the Second World War spurred the postwar socialist and labor governments in Europe to abolish the death penalty. In England, a Royal Commission on Capital Punishment was formed in 1949 to gather research and hold hearings on the subject. It laid the foundation for parliamentary repeal some fifteen years later. In the United States, however, only six of the fifty states had abolished it by midcentury. In all the years of the abolitionist movement, there has never been anywhere near a majority of the states voting to repeal capital legislation. On the other hand, reforms in the scope and application of the death penalty have fared much better. Bedau (1964) observes that, paradoxically, these very reforms have "become the major obstacles to further statutory repeal. They have mitigated the rigidity and brutality of this form of punishment to a point where the average citizen no longer regards it as an affront to his moral sensibilities. As a consequence, he has no strong motive to press for further reduction, much less complete abolition, of the death penalty" (p. 14).

An associated reason for the failure of statutory abolition was the steady decline in the number of executions, from a high point of 191 in 1935 to 76 in 1955 and 7 in 1965. The rate of death sentences also declined regularly but less dramatically (Bedau 1964, p. 23). Thus, despite increases in the population and the crime rate, judges and juries seemed more and more reluctant to impose the death penalty, and state authorities seemed equally sparing in scheduling and performing executions. Even retentionists did not advocate with ardor or persistence the execution of every death-sentenced defendant. Under these circumstances, capital punishment in the 1950s and early 1960s was not perceived as a pressing social or moral issue. Except for the occasional *cause célèbre*, such as the execution of the Rosenbergs by the federal government or of Carryl Chessman by California, it did not evoke the same public concern and official response as did the other issues of the day, such as civil rights and the military excursions abroad.

The decline in executions resulted in an increase in the death row population which, in turn, led to more judicial appeals. From the 1930s to the 1960s, the number of appeals to the federal courts of all state-imposed death sentences rose from 3% to 32%, or a tenfold increase. As federal judges became increasingly willing to review capital cases and reverse state court decisions on constitutional grounds, state officials became more reluctant to schedule executions. By the 1960s, times were a-changing, and the nearly two-hundred-year-old movement begun by Benjamin Rush for statutory abolition and reform in state legislative chambers began to shift to constitutional abolition and reform in the federal courts. These early judicial challenges paved the way for the Supreme Court's direct ruling on the constitutionality of the death penalty in 1976.

The Start of Judicial Challenges

De Tocqueville observed with remarkable prescience over one hundred years ago that there is hardly a major social or political question in the United States that does not eventually turn into a judicial one. The federal judiciary, and especially the Supreme Court, typically has been more receptive than the other branches of government to the grievances of minority groups, whether "minority" is defined by race, political ideology, or criminal status. It has extended constitutional protection from the vicissitudes of the majoritarian political process to those who historically have been saddled with disabilities or have lacked political clout to exercise those rights guaranteed to all. Reforms are also wrought through the legislative, executive, and administrative processes, but to be successful they require widespread public support. Examples in point are the current movement in consumerism, environmentalism, and women's rights. Activists in these areas have pursued their causes mainly in the political and administrative forums, not in the courts. However, abolitionists have not succeeded in most legislatures because there has never been overwhelming popular consensus regarding their goal. The majority has been unresponsive to or skeptical of the claims advanced by capital defendants. Their advocates, and those of other minority viewpoints, have had to turn to the courts for redress. Life-tenured federal judges are somewhat more removed from the ebb and flow of electoral partisanship. They are in a better position to hear and maybe recognize unpopular causes, thereby give dignity to those espousing them and, eventually, facilitate their entry into the broader political arena. New ideas, not just political influence, can prompt change by the judiciary. When minority ideas are clothed in constitutional attire, linked to the lofty ideals and values embodied in the Bill of Rights, and marketed as reasonably deducible from precedents, the basis for court-sponsored reform is laid.

The issue of capital punishment was "judicialized" in the mid-sixties by a "rare conjunction of vigorous men and ripe ideas" (Meltsner 1973, p. 4). Three main ideas came to the fore in this period and were seized upon by lawyers and social scientists urging judicial reform and abolition.

One idea was equality. *Brown I* in 1954 heralded a new era of racial equality, and in the next decade or so, the principle of nonsegregation in public schools was successfully extended to strike down all forms of state required or supported racial discrimination in virtually every facet of public life: courtrooms, public facilities, employment, transportation, recreation, and so forth.

Another idea was procedural fairness. The 1960s saw a "due process revolution" in the rights of the criminally accused. The activist Warren Court, in addition to securing equal treatment for racial minorities, sought to safeguard the procedural rights of another politically powerless group in society, criminal defendants. It required the appointment of counsel for indigent defendants at trial, on the first appeal, and at certain pretrial stages of the criminal process such as preliminary hearing and stationhouse lineups; it obligated the police to warn suspects of their right to silence prior to custodial interrogations; it excluded from use in state trials any evidence procured by improper police searches and seizures; it circumscribed the scope of certain police field practices, such as stop-and-frisk; and so on. Whatever the practical effects of these pronouncements as they trickled down to the local level, to be interpreted and implemented by lower court judges and police who are not known to be generally sympathetic to the rights of criminal defendants, they at least served an important symbolic purpose. The decisions represented a reconsecration of the American democratic ideal that the state cannot intrude upon an individual's life, liberty, and security except by observing fair procedures. The history of American liberty, as Justice Frankfurter once remarked, is the history of legal procedure.

The third idea was the legality of capital punishment. Up to then, as already indicated, the periodic public and legislative debates centered on the morality and utility of the death penalty, not on its legality. By 1960, a number of legal scholars began to question seriously for the first time the constitutionality of this punishment (Gottlieb 1961; Oberer 1961; Morris 1960; Reichert 1959). At the same time, social scientists started to examine systematically its claimed deterrent effect on crime rates (for example, Sellin 1959). There was no unanimity of opinion, however, among the experts. The American Law Institute, an organization of prominent lawyers and judges, drafted in 1959 model legislation designed to stimulate reform in state penal codes. It proposed changes in capital trial procedures but took no official position on the death penalty itself. As late as 1967, the President's Commission on Law Enforcement and the Administration of Justice, which recommended changes in virtually every aspect of the criminal justice system, remained divided on the death penalty issue: "Some members of the Commission favor abolition of capital punishment, while others favor its retention," said the final report (p. 143).

These three ideas—racial equality, fairness in criminal procedure, and legality of capital punishment—converged in a single, specific topic: the legality of racial inequality in capital punishment for the offense of rape. Ideas require people and organizations to translate them into judicial action. As in the Civil War era when the abolitionists were drawn primarily from the ranks of anti-slavery activists, so too in the mid-twentieth century the proponents of judicial abolition came mostly from the civil rights movement. The principal organization spearheading the challenge was the same one that successfully ended segregated schools: the Legal Defense Fund of the NAACP (Meltsner 1973). By the mid- and late sixties, as "the Movement" began to wane and the federal government assumed the brunt of desegregation litigation under newly enacted civil rights legislation, the Legal Defense Fund turned to examine other areas of society that evidenced racial discrimination. One such area was criminal justice; and the particular issue it raised, involving a volatile mixture of race, death, and sexual crime, started the chain of judicial challenges to capital punishment. It is at this point, then, that the materials of this chapter begin.

Overview

The preceding two chapters looked at the creation and expansion of law. Now we turn to the contraction or restriction of the law with the purpose of its eventual abolition.

The first systematic attempt at restricting or abolishing capital punishment via the courts was prompted by the claim of racial discrimination in the execution of black rape defendants in the South (section 5.2). Elaborate statistical analyses were introduced in evidence in support of an equal protection challenge to the application of the death penalty, but a federal appellate court rejected the claim, declaring that it was "not certain" that "statistics will ever be [the defendant's] redemption" (*Maxwell* v. *Bishop*, 1968). The Supreme Court declined to pass on the racial inequality question.

Abolitionists then shifted to a different mode of attack. They challenged various aspects of the procedures by which capital trials are held and death sentences are imposed as violative of the due process guarantee of the Fourteenth Amendment. These challenges are described in section 5.3. One such procedural attack dealt with the death-qualification of prospective capital jurors: Does the exclusion for cause of venirepersons who are generally opposed to or have conscientious scruples against the death penalty result in a jury that is predisposed toward conviction? In *Witherspoon* v. *Illinois* (1968), the Supreme Court, presented with only a couple of weak empirical studies on this issue, nimbly sidestepped it. In 1980, the same question was raised before the California Supreme Court in *Hovey* v. *The Superior Court of Alameda County*. This time, an extensive body of research data on the conviction-proneness of death-qualified jurors, accumulated over the past dozen years, was made available to the court. The *Hovey* decision also avoided a direct answer, ostensibly because of methodological flaws in the studies.

When challenges to standardless capital sentencing and to single-verdict trials likewise proved unavailing, abolitionists finally had little choice but to raise the ultimate—and substantive—issue before the Supreme Court: Is the death penalty a "cruel and unusual punishment" proscribed by the Eighth Amendment? In *Furman* v. *Georgia* (1972), presented in section 5.4, the Court parried the question and ruled only that an arbitrary and capricious procedure for imposing the death sentence was cruel and unusual. Some Justices, however, in separate opinions examined public opinion on capital punishment. They considered it an indicator of society's "evolving standards of decency" and relevant in adjudicating the contemporary meaning of the Eighth Amendment. *Furman*, naturally, was a catalyst for research on death penalty attitudes, and the materials of this section include some of the surveys and field experiments conducted by social psychologists.

The second round of Eighth Amendment decisions took place four years later (section 5.5). In 1976, in *Gregg* v. *Georgia*, the Court upheld the constitutionality of the death penalty provided that it was imposed according to procedures that minimized arbitrariness and unevenhandedness. Statistical studies seem to cast doubt on whether post-*Furman* statutes that comply with *Gregg* standards do, in fact, result in nondiscriminatory sentencing.

At present, the Court has begun to show impatience with the tortuousness of the capital appeals process—the endlessly drawn out proceedings and repetitive demands for eleventh-hour stays of execution—which opponents of the death penalty are using to wage a guerrilla war on capital punishment itself. The final section (5.6) will attempt to pull together the cases and the social research and take into account the political context of constitutional adjudication.

5.2. EQUAL PROTECTION CHALLENGES

Racial differentiation in capital statutes of earlier years provides an instructive backdrop for understanding the equal protection challenges of the 1960s to racial inequality in rape executions.

In the pre–Civil War years, more striking than the proliferation of capital statutes to protect the institution of slavery was the statutory differentiation by race with respect to the crime of rape. The death penalty for rape has always been concentrated in southern and border states. The penal code of antebellum Georgia, for example, required mandatory death—though subject to the pardoning power of the governor—for slaves and "free persons of color" who were convicted of "committing a rape or attempting it on a free white female" (Cobb 1851, p. 987). A white man convicted of raping a slave woman or a free woman of color was fined and/or imprisoned at the court's discretion. Virginia's rape legislation at that time did not expressly identify the race of the offender and the victim, but it attained the same result by rendering blacks statutorily incompetent to testify against white defendants (Note, *Virginia Law Review*, 1972). Thus, the "death penalty served not only to protect and control the institution of slavery in the South, but also to articulate white supremacy in the social order" (Bowers 1974, p. 173). It buttressed the racial caste system.

Reconstruction legislation prohibited racial discrimination in punishments. Crimes for which previously only blacks could be executed were expanded to encompass all persons without regard to color. The subsequent enactment of Jim Crow legislation did not mark a return to explicit, racially based differences in punishments. However, so long as jury service was restricted to white males and the death penalty for rape was discretionary rather than mandatory, the practical effect was the same as before: blacks convicted of raping whites were executed with disproportionate frequency.

Reliable figures are not available until 1930. Between 1930 and 1976, 3,859 persons were executed for all crimes in the entire country (most of them in the South). For the offense of murder, 48% of those executed (1,630 out of 3,344) were black; for rape, 89% (405 out of 455) were black. The eleven former Confederate states accounted for 87% of all rape executions in the nation, and 91% of them were of blacks (U.S. Department of Justice 1971, p. 11; Murchison 1978, pp. 519–20).

The foregoing figures do not take into account executions outside the legal process. During the last two decades of the nineteenth century, lynchings outnumbered executions imposed under state and local authority (1,540 to 1,214), and most of them were against blacks in the South. In the first two decades of this century, lynchings still composed more than one-third of all (legal and extralegal) executions (Bowers 1974, p. 40).

These raw figures prompted more detailed analysis of the possibility that racial discrimination, rather than some other neutral factor, was responsible for the disproportionate number of blacks executed for rape. A study in Virginia found that every single rape execution in the state between 1908 and 1963 was of a black. It concluded that "there is more than a scintilla of evidence that there has been discrimination in the application of the death penalty," but nonetheless proposed that there is "no legal basis presently available which, absent any showing of actual prejudice, would persuade a court to reverse a conviction in a particular case" (Partington 1965, p. 63). A study in Texas of about the same time span discovered that the "dominant pattern is for the Negro male to get the death penalty for raping a white female" and that no Texas court has ever sentenced anyone to death for raping a black woman (Koeninger 1969, p. 138).

The most systematic study of the relationship between race, rape, and death was undertaken by Professor Marvin Wolfgang, and his research provided the empirical support for the Legal Defense Fund's opening assault on the legality of capital punishment in *Maxwell* v. *Bishop*.

STATEMENT OF PROFESSOR MARVIN E. WOLFGANG OF THE UNIVERSITY OF PENNSYLVANIA CENTER FOR STUDIES IN CRIMINOLOGY AND CRIMINAL LAW

Hearings before Subcommittee No. 3 of the Committee of the Judiciary, House of Representatives, 92nd Congress, 2d Session, on H.R. 8414, H.R. 12217, [et al. to suspend or to abolish the death penalty], March 16, 1972, Serial No. 29. Washington, D.C.: U.S. Government Printing Office, 1972.

. . .

II. RACIAL DISCRIMINATION IN THE IMPOSITION OF THE DEATH PENALTY FOR RAPE IN THE SOUTH, 1945–1965

In the summer of 1965 a unique survey was initiated to examine in refined detail the relationship between race and sentencing for rape in 11 southern and border states, in which rape is a capital crime. The study was suggested by the NAACP Legal Defense and Educational Fund Incorporated, and Professor Anthony Amsterdam and I worked together in the planning and preparation for the data collection in the field. At the Center for Studies in Criminology and Criminal Law at the University of Pennsylvania, I, with the help of the staff, conducted the statistical analyses of six states for inclusion as testimony in federal district court where the analyses were presented as evidence to support the contention of racial discrimination in the imposition of the death penalty.

For approximately ten weeks between June and August, 1965, about 30 law students, carefully selected from around the country, collected data on over 3,000 cases of convictions for rape in 250 counties in the 11 southern states. The

202 CONTRACTION AND ABOLITION OF LAW

counties were selected by careful statistical procedures to represent the urban-rural and black-white demographic distributions of all the 11 states. A 28-page schedule of information was used for data collection, on which information was recorded from court transcripts, prison records, and other data sources available. Objective, nonjudgmental standardized recording characterized the data collection process. For purpose of this testimony, I can only report briefly on the major purpose, methods and findings of this study.

The main purpose of the study was to determine whether race was associated with the imposition of the death penalty for persons convicted of rape. But more than this, we were interested in determining whether non-racial factors could account for the expectedly higher proportion of blacks sentenced to death. Variables that were examined, other than race of defendant, race of victim, and sentence, included those concerning the circumstances of the offense (for example, what degree of force was used and what amount of injury done the victim by the defendant; whether the offense was committed in the course of a burglary or unlawful entry in a building and whether the rape was accompanied by some other contemporaneous offense, such as robbery), the character of the defendant (age, marital status, occupation, prior criminal record, etc.), the character of the victim (age, marital status, dependent children, reputation for chastity, etc.), the nature of the relations between the defendant and victim (prior acquaintance, prior sexual relations, etc.) and the circumstances of the trial leading to a defendant's conviction (length of trial, plea, consent defense, etc.). . . .

Standard statistical procedures for determining the meaning of "statistical significance" were employed throughout the analyses that were made in Alabama, Arkansas, Florida, Georgia, Louisiana,

South Carolina and Tennessee. . . . For purposes of testifying before this Subcommittee, I have drawn together into a composite analysis some of the findings based on the data available in the states that have previously been individually analyzed. . . . I am submitting as appendix material to this testimony several illustrative tables which indicate the character of the research that has been done. . . .

In summary to this section of my testimony, we have found that during the twenty year period from 1945 to 1965 in seven southern states, Negro defendants convicted of rape were disproportionately frequently sentenced to death. Negro defendants convicted of rape of white victims were also disproportionately frequently sentenced to death, compared with all other defendants. In less than one time in 1000 could these associations have occurred by the operations of chance factors alone. We examined many non-racial variables connected with the offense, the defendant, the victim and the trial for the purpose of determining whether any of these variables, rather than the race of the defendant or race of the victim alone, could be responsible for the recorded fact that Negro defendants in significantly higher proportion than white defendants have customarily been sentenced to death. After careful statistical examination of all of the variables for which analysis could be made, I find that none of the non-racial variables—contemporaneous offense, prior criminal record of the defendants, a stranger relationship with the victim, display of a weapon, the use of force or the infliction of serious injury, et cetera—explains this sentencing differential. I therefore conclude that over at least a twenty year period there has been a systematic, differential sentencing practice of imposing the death penalty on Negroes and, most specifically, when the defendants are Negro and their victims are white. . . .

TABLE I

Race of Defendant by Type of Sentence

	Death		Other		Total	
	N	(%)*	N	(%)	N	(%)
Negro	110	(13)	713	(87)	823	(100)
White	9	(2)	433	(98)	442	(100)
Total	119		1,146		1,265	

Note: States included Florida, Georgia, Louisiana, South Carolina, Tennessee.
$X^2 = 41.9924$; $P < .001$.
*[Percentages were not in the original tables and are inserted here to facilitate reading. Ed.'s note.]

TABLE II

Racial Combinations of Defendant and Victim by Type of Sentence

	Death		Other		Total	
	N	(%)	N	(%)	N	(%)
Negro defendant and white victim	113	(36)	204	(64)	317	(100)
All other racial combinations of defendant and victim	19	(2)	902	(98)	921	(100)
Total	132		1,106		1,238	

Note: States include: Arkansas, Florida, Georgia, Louisiana, South Carolina, Tennessee.
$X^2 = 275.7192$; $P < .001$.

TABLE III

Contemporaneous Offense by Type of Sentence*

	Death		Other		Total	
	N	(%)	N	(%)	N	(%)
Contemporaneous offense	53	(28)	133	(72)	186	(100)
No contemporaneous offense	92	(10)	840	(90)	932	(100)
Total	145		973		1,118	

Note: States include: Arkansas, Florida, Georgia, Louisiana, South Carolina, Tennessee.
$X^2 = 47.65$; $P < .001$.
*[The marginals and X^2 value of Table III in the original were incorrect and have been recalculated. Ed.'s note.]

TABLE V

Contemporaneous Offense by Racial Combinations of Defendant and Victim

	Negro defendant and white victim		All other racial combinations of defendant/ victim		Total	
	N	(%)	N	(%)	N	(%)
Contemporaneous offense	58	(42)	81	(58)	139	(100)
No contemporaneous offense	88	(15)	480	(85)	568	(100)
Total	148		561		707	

Note: States include: Florida, Georgia, Tennessee.
$X^2 = 45.3139$; $P < .001$.

TABLE VI

Racial Combinations of Defendant/Victim by Type of Sentence Among All Cases in Which Defendant Committed a Contemporaneous Offense

	Death		Other		Total	
	N	(%)	N	(%)	N	(%)
Negro defendant and white victim	22	(39)	36	(61)	58	(100)
All other racial combinations of defendant/victim	2	(3)	79	(97)	81	(100)
Total	24		115		139	

Note: States included: Florida, Georgia, Tennessee.
$X^2 = 27.3231$; $P < .001$.

. . .

MAXWELL v. BISHOP

398 F.2d 138 (8th Cir. 1968)

BLACKMUN, Circuit Judge.

William L. Maxwell, a Negro and an Arkansas prisoner under sentence of execution on his 1962 conviction for the state crime of rape . . . petitions a second time for a federal writ of habeas corpus and, with its denial, a second time appeals. The points now urged to us are (1) that a prima facie case of racially discriminatory imposition of the death penalty for rape in Arkansas has now been established and remains unrebutted by the State; (2) that Arkansas' single verdict procedure is without appropriate standards, allows the jury to exercise its discretion irrationally, and is impermissible; and (3) that the decisions of the United States Supreme Court since Maxwell's first federal appeal demonstrate the error of our prior holding, adverse to the petitioner, on the jury selection issue.

We again review the background:

1. The offense for which Maxwell was charged was committed in the early morning of November 3, 1961, and in the City of Hot Springs, Garland County, Arkansas. Maxwell, who was 21 at the time, was arrested within two hours after the offense was committed. His convicting jury . . . imposed the death penalty.

2. Maxwell appealed. On this state appeal he challenged the sufficiency of the evidence; . . . [and] the constitutionality in application of the penalty statute. . . . All these points were decided adversely to the defense and the judgment of conviction was affirmed by a unanimous Supreme Court of Arkansas. . . .

[The details of the crime are described in the opinion of the Arkansas Supreme Court (Maxwell v. State, 1963): The victim, a 35-year-old white woman, lived with her helpless, 90-year-old father. The assailant entered their house at 3 A.M. by breaking the window screen. In the struggle, the victim bit her assailant's finger and caused bleeding. She was assaulted and her father was struck; the attacker kept threatening to kill them both. She was dragged to a remote spot two blocks from the house where, bruised and bleeding, she was raped. The identity of the attacker as the defendant was clearly established by blood and seminal stains, matching of hairs and clothing fibers, fresh injury to his finger, and the identification by the victim in the lighted living room. Confessions were not introduced at the trial, and defense presented no evidence. The state supreme court found the sufficiency of the evidence was "overwhelming" to sustain the rape conviction (p. 116). Ed.'s note.]

3. Maxwell, with new counsel, then filed a petition for a writ of habeas corpus in the United States District Court for the Eastern District of Arkansas. In that petition, as twice amended, he alleged [inter alia] unconstitutional application of [the death penalty statute]. Judge Young . . . denied the petition. . . . Maxwell v. Stephens, 229 F. Supp. 205 (E.D. Ark. 1964).

4. Judge Young, however, granted the certificate of probable cause . . . and stayed execution. With additional counsel from New York, an appeal was taken to this court. . . . [W]e reached the conclusion that Judge Young's decision was correct. Maxwell v. Stephens, 348 F.2d 325 (8th Cir. 1965). . . .

5. With still another name added to the list of Maxwell's counsel, a petition for certiorari was filed. This was denied, . . . 382 U.S. 944 (1965).

6. Execution was rescheduled but was stayed administratively until September 2, 1966.

7. Maxwell's second and present petition for a federal writ of habeas corpus was filed July 21, 1966, in the United States District Court for the Eastern District of Arkansas and came before Chief Judge Henley. The court denied the peti-

tion. Maxwell v. Bishop, 257 F. Supp. 710 (E.D. Ark. 1966).

8. The district court and a judge of this court successively declined to grant a stay of the execution or to issue a certificate of probable cause. But the Supreme Court granted leave to file a petition for a writ of certiorari, issued the writ, reversed the denial of the application for the certificate, and remanded the case with directions to issue it. Maxwell v. Bishop, 385 U.S. 650 (1967). Accordingly, the certificate was issued and the execution stayed, and the case is here on appeal. . . .

THE STATISTICAL ARGUMENT

Maxwell's present argument that Arkansas discriminates against Negroes in the application of the death penalty for rape, and thus violates the Equal Protection Clause . . . , rests on what is described as newly discovered evidence which became available since this court's disposition of Maxwell's first habeas appeal. It is said, in the words of the petition:

"This evidence consists of the results of a survey of rape convictions during the period 1945–1965 in a representative sample of nineteen counties comprising more than 47% of the population of the State of Arkansas. The survey was conducted in the summer of 1965, as part of a study of the application of the death penalty for rape in eleven southern states. This comprehensive study required the work of 28 law students throughout the summer, the expenditure of more than $35,000 and numerous hours of consultative time by expert[s]. . . ."

THE RECORD AND THE EVIDENCE. At a pretrial conference the district court was advised that the evidence to be presented on behalf of Maxwell was that which resulted from the survey and study so described, and that it would be presented through the testimony of Marvin Wolfgang, a criminologist-statistician on the faculty of the University of Pennsylvania. . . .

The study was carried out in twelve states. One of these was Arkansas. For the State of Arkansas the period investigated was that from January 1, 1945, to the summer of 1965. Not every Arkansas rape case during that period was included but every case which occurred in the sample counties was included. . . .

The approach was to develop a "null hypothesis" that there is no difference in the distribution of the sentence of death or life imprisonment imposed on negro and white defendants; the calculation of a theoretical frequency which represents the number of defendants expected to be sentenced to death if the null hypothesis is valid; the comparison of this theoretical frequency with the actual frequency in the collected data for each defendant-victim racial combination; and the determination whether the discrepancy between the expected and observed frequencies is great enough so that, under accepted statistical standards, that discrepancy can be said to be a product of the real phenomena tested rather than of the operation of chance within the testing process. . . .

The study disclosed that, in the 55 Arkansas cases, 34 defendants were Negroes and 21 were whites. . . .

From this Arkansas data and his study Dr. Wolfgang concluded . . . [1] that the critical variables were race of the offender, race of his victim, and sentence; (2) compared to other rape defendants, Negroes convicted of raping white victims were disproportionately sentenced to death; and (3) "no variable of which analysis was possible could account for the observed disproportionate frequency". . . .

[The Arkansas results were essentially the same as the composite results for the several southern states presented in the preceding excerpt of Wolfgang's congressional testimony, and therefore are not reproduced again. Ed.'s note.]

The State offered no evidence.

Such is the record. It is apparent from a reading of the record that the trial court was generous in its rulings on admissibility. Everything which the petitioner presented came in.

THE TRIAL COURT'S CONCLUSIONS ON THE STATISTICAL ARGUMENT. Chief Judge Henley, in his opinion, described the statistical argument as the "contention which has been urged most seriously here." . . . He noted that Dr. Wolfgang "concluded and the Court agrees, that the differential [in executions by race] could not be due to the operation of the laws of chance." . . . He acknowledged that "the statistical evidence produced in this case is more extensive and sophisticated than has been produced heretofore." Yet he was not convinced that "it is sufficiently broad, accurate, or precise as to establish satisfactorily that Arkansas juries in general practice unconstitutional racial discrimination in rape cases involving Negro men and white women. . . . The study does not indicate that Negro men convicted of raping white women invariably or even in a majority of cases receive the death penalty. . . . Only 7 Negro men were sentenced to die for raping white women. The case studies, and the number of death sentences imposed are simply too few in number to afford convincing proof of the proposition urged by petitioner." . . .

THE PETITIONER'S ARGUMENT. . . . The heart of the petitioner's statistical argument is . . . that on this record the petitioner has made a prima facie case of racial discrimination in sentencing and that he is entitled to prevail when, as here, the State presents no evidence or presents evidence of insufficient moment to overcome the prima facie case so established.

It is said that the Supreme Court of necessity has developed the doctrine that a prima facie showing of unequal racial treatment, calling state procedures in question, compels the inference that the

State is drawing the racial line unless it offers justification in non-racial factors for the disproportion. . . . It is argued that there is no reason why the prima facie approach should not be applied to the present case. If there are factors which offset Dr. Wolfgang's expert conclusion, they were in the power of the State to unearth and prove. "Every justification for shifting the burden of persuasion to the State . . . applies with evident force here." . . .

It is perhaps well to emphasize initially what the study and Dr. Wolfgang's testimony do not purport to do:

1. They do not relate specifically to Garland County where this particular offense was committed and where Maxwell was tried and convicted. They are concerned with 19 other Arkansas counties and with counties in 11 other states.

2. They admittedly do not take every variable into account.

3. They do not show that the petit jury which tried and convicted Maxwell acted in his case with racial discrimination.

4. They do not deny that generally the burden of demonstrating discrimination in penalty imposition is on the one who asserts it. . . .

Further, while it is true that it is in a sense the state which prosecutes, nevertheless the county has a character and a posture, too. Inasmuch as Garland County, as it was conceded, is in the predominantly white area of Arkansas, one might expect from the petitioner an argument that alleged southern injustice in interracial rape cases would be more apparent in such a county than in those areas where the Negro population is predominant. Yet the Garland County statistics . . . afford no local support to the petitioner's statistical argument. The evidence produced at the prior hearing and at this one discloses only Maxwell as a recipient of the death penalty in Garland County for rape. We are not yet ready to condemn

and upset the result reached in every case of a negro rape defendant in the State of Arkansas on the basis of broad theories of social and statistical injustice. This is particularly so on a record so specific as this one. And we are not ready to nullify this petitioner's Garland County trial on the basis of results generally, but elsewhere, throughout the South.

We therefore reject the statistical argument in its attempted application to Maxwell's case. Whatever value that argument may have as an instrument of social concern, whatever suspicion it may arouse with respect to southern interracial rape trials as a group over a long period of time, and whatever it may disclose with respect to other localities, we feel that the statistical argument does nothing to destroy the integrity of Maxwell's trial. Although the investigation and study made by Professor Wolfgang in the summer of 1965 is interesting and provocative, we do not, on the basis of that study, upset Maxwell's conviction and, as a necessary consequence, cast serious doubt on every other rape conviction in the state courts of Arkansas. . . .

We are not certain that, for Maxwell, statistics will ever be his redemption. The facts as to rape charges in Garland County are known and have been recited. Standing by themselves, they disclose nothing from which conclusions of unconstitutionality in application may appropriately be drawn. This situation—the aridity of the Garland County facts on which to claim unequal protection of the laws— forces Maxwell and his counsel to present his case on a state-wide and long-term historical approach, and even on a South-wide one, and to claim that conclusions which, at best, are necessarily general have valid application to Maxwell.

We do not say that there is no ground for suspicion that the death penalty for rape may have been discriminatorily applied over the decades in that large area of states whose statutes provide for it. There are recognizable indicators of this. But, as we have noted before, with respect to the issue of jury selection, improper state practice of the past does not automatically invalidate a procedure of the present. We do say that nothing has been presented in Maxwell's case which convinces us, or causes us seriously to wonder, that, with the imposition of the death penalty, he was the victim of discrimination based on race. . . .

NOTES AND QUESTIONS

---

1.   The roller-coaster ride of Maxwell through the federal courts is not atypical of the drawn-out, costly, complex, and dilatory proceedings that a death row inmate undergoes after his conviction is affirmed in the state appellate courts. After losing the appeal to the state supreme court, the convict can begin postconviction proceedings by petitioning a federal district court for habeas corpus relief. The "great" writ of federal habeas corpus, recognized in the Constitution (Article I, Section 9), is the principal means used today by state prisoners to obtain review of their convictions in the federal courts (*Brown* v. *Allen*, 1953). It requires a government official (for example, the prison warden) to bring the prisoner before a judge to review his claim that his federal constitutional rights were violated in the state proceedings so that, in consequence, he is being unlawfully detained. It developed out of the belief of federal judges that criminal defendants may not always get a fair shake in the state courts. The habeas corpus petition is a collateral attack that challenges the legality of the confinement; it is not an appeal on the merits of the conviction. The appellate courts are restricted in their capacity to review the facts that go to guilt or to the sentence imposed. They review only claimed infringements of guaranteed rights—they look at the rules of the game, not at the results—and especially in capital cases, as is apparent in Maxwell's case, they are often concerned with the substantive issues of guilt and appropriateness of the sentence.

A state prisoner, then, has two avenues of review: state appellate review and, if unsuccessful, federal habeas corpus review. If a habeas corpus petition is denied, it can be appealed to the federal appellate courts and, ultimately, to the Supreme Court. If the denial is affirmed at each successive level, the prisoner could initiate the process all over again by submitting a new petition (raising a different claim) to the federal district court, as did Maxwell. In noncapital cases, the prospect of a successful petition is minuscule; many are submitted, but few are heard.

Critics say that 98% of habeas corpus petitions are "frivolous" (Justice Clark dissenting in *Fay* v. *Noia*, 1963, p. 445) and can lead to a "procedural nightmare" (Burger 1970, p. 148). They can also be a source of unending mischief. Not only do the filings burden the appellate docket but, according to the U.S. Attorney General, they also make prisoners into "writ writers who never confront the fact of their guilt and get on with the process of rehabilitation" (*Wall Street Journal*, February 5, 1982). On the other hand, the availability of the remedy, notwithstanding its infrequent exercise, indicates a capacity for self-correction in the judicial process. For the condemned, the seemingly interminable rounds of proceedings at least give him a chance to postpone, maybe permanently, his date with the electrician.

2.   The state, rather cavalierly, did not dispute the soundness of the data or the analysis, and questioned only the conclusion that the petitioner sought to draw from the results. What criticisms might you raise about the research?

For a multivariate analysis of Wolfgang's data, see Wolfgang and Reidel (1976).

3.   Gibson (1978) has criticized the literature on racial discrimination in sentencing in terms of the unit of analysis employed. He noted that most studies have treated the cases as the unit of measurement rather than the decisions of individual judges within the court. The former approach is not sensitive to the possibility that within a jurisdiction there may be some judges who are prejudiced and some who are not. If their numbers are evenly balanced, or if the proportion of cases sentenced by prejudiced judges is small, racial differences would not be detected. Gibson analyzed criminal cases in a single trial court jurisdiction in Georgia and found no racial differentiation at the aggregate level. However, when the sentencing behavior of individual judges was examined, clear racial patterns could be seen for some of the judges.

Wolfgang's analysis was based on cases from randomly selected counties in the southern states. If his analysis had been based on individual judges or on purposely selected counties, it is possible that the magnitude of the racial differences he found would have been even greater.

4.   Judge Henley accepted Wolfgang's conclusion that sentencing patterns in Arkansas "could not be due to the operation of the laws of chance," but was unconvinced that "Arkansas juries in general practice unconstitutional racial discrimination in rape cases." Judge Blackmun also rejected the equal protection claim and expressed doubt that for Maxwell "statistics will ever be his redemption." When the Supreme Court granted certiorari, it, too, was unwilling to review whether Wolfgang's data proved racial discrimination. Why did all three federal courts resist the statistical evidence that brands hundreds of rape juries in the South as prejudiced? In *Brown I*, the Court was not reluctant to rely on the "modern authority" of social science studies showing the detrimental educational and personality consequences of school segregation on children, even though many of the studies (for example, Clark's doll experiment) were much weaker in design and methodology than Wolfgang's research. Why was social research successful in supporting the equal protection challenge to racial inequality in the public schools but not in rape executions?

5.   What would be the remedy if an equal protection violation had been found in this case? Would only black convicts be spared execution?

6.   In 1968, the Supreme Court agreed to review Judge Blackmun's decision, but limited it to certain procedural issues (whether there should be standards for capital sentencing and whether there should be bifurcated capital trials). The oral argument was held in March 1969. Two months later, the Court issued a brief order requesting reargument the following October, thereby postponing the decision. In May 1969, Justice Abe Fortas resigned. With only eight Justices on the bench, a split vote would have affirmed the Eighth Circuit's decision and removed the last judicial bar to Maxwell's execution. The case meant life or death for other southern black rape convicts, too. Given the wider consequences of the decision, Meltsner (1973, p. 187) has suggested that perhaps the reason for the Court's deferral of it was to await a replacement Justice.

By October 1969, there still was no new appointee and reargument was again postponed, this time indefinitely. Finally, Judge Blackmun of the Eighth Circuit was appointed and he promptly disqualified himself from sitting in review of his own decision. The reargument was held before eight Justices in May 1970. It was the first Supreme Court case on capital punishment in recent years, and it was expected to be significant enough so that other appeals and executions were placed on hold pending its announcement. The social temper then was tense: campus disorders, urban riots, high street crime, and an administration committed to the ideology of law and order. In this atmosphere, the Court rendered its opinion (*Maxwell* v. *Bishop*, 1970). It avoided resolution of the procedural issues, ignored the racial question, and disposed of the case on the narrowest possible ground: it remanded the case to the federal district court to determine if prospective jurors with scruples against the death penalty were wrongfully excluded at the trial eight years earlier in violation of *Witherspoon* v. *Illinois* (1968, discussed in the next section). The Court avoided adding grease to the fire, and Maxwell's long odyssey through the federal courts ended with a whimper.

7.   Almost a decade later, the Solicitor General of the United States, in an amicus brief supporting capital punishment, made a remarkable concession: "[Wolfgang's study was] a careful and comprehensive study, and we do not question its conclusion that during the twenty years in question, in southern states, there was discrimination in rape cases." He hastened to add that current "research does not provide support for a conclusion that racial discrimination continues . . ." (in Zeisel 1981, p. 458). Thus, the federal government belatedly admitted to what state officials have always denied, but also argued that racial discrimination in capital sentencing was all in the past and there was no evidence to support the claim that it is still prevalent today. Wolfgang's study may not have redeemed Maxwell, but if the Solicitor General is correct, it may have saved subsequent black rape convicts from being disproportionately sentenced to death. What broader implications can be drawn from this experience about the role of social research in changing legal doctrine and the administration of law?

5.3. DUE PROCESS CHALLENGES

Special measures of fairness are observed in capital trials. Because "death is different," the Supreme Court has recognized that "there is a corresponding difference in the need for reliability in the determination that death is the appropriate punishment in a specific case" (*Gardner* v. *Florida*, 1977, p. 363).

One such procedure is "death-qualification" of prospective jurors at voir dire: the exclusion for cause of venirepersons who express scruples against the death penalty. A death-qualified jury consists of jurors who survive elimination based on their attitudes toward the punishment. This procedure, unique to capital trials, was established in the mid-nineteenth century and remained unchallenged for 100 years. In those days, the death penalty was mandatory upon conviction of a capital offense. Consequently, venirepersons opposed to the sanction tended to vote "not guilty" rather than impose it on an otherwise guilty defendant: "If placed on the jury, [a scrupled juror] is compelled either to violate his oath or his conscience, and a man who would do either is unfit to serve as a juror" (*Williams* v. *State*, 1856, p. 392).

By the turn of the century, state penal codes had been reformed to make capital punishment discretionary. This enabled jurors opposed to the death penalty to vote for conviction and impose the sentence of life imprisonment. However, the death-qualification procedure for excluding scrupled venirepersons from deciding guilt and penalty continued in effect. It was not until 1961 that the question of whether this procedure results in a conviction-prone jury was squarely faced:

> [A] jury qualified on the death penalty will necessarily have been culled of the most humane of its prospective members. . . . Jurors hesitant to levy the death penalty would also seem more prone to resolve the many doubts as to guilt or innocence in the defendant's favor than would jurors qualified on the "pound of flesh" approach. . . . On what basis is it presumed that a death-qualified jury is as impartial on the guilt issue as one not so qualified? [Oberer 1961, pp. 549, 552]

In 1968, the Supreme Court agreed to review the conviction of an Illinois death row inmate, William Witherspoon, who eight years earlier had been convicted of murdering a Chicago policeman and had managed to postpone fifteen dates with the executioner. This case provided the Court with its first opportunity to address the constitutionality of death-qualification.

WITHERSPOON v. ILLINOIS

391 U.S. 510 (1968)

Mr. Justice STEWART delivered the opinion of the Court.

The petitioner was brought to trial in 1960 in Cook County, Illinois, upon a charge of murder. The jury found him guilty and fixed his penalty at death. At the time of his trial an Illinois statute provided:

"In trials for murder it shall be a cause for challenge of any juror who shall, on being examined, state that he has conscientious scruples against capital punishment, or that he is opposed to the same."

Through this provision the State of Illinois armed the prosecution with unlimited challenges for cause in order to exclude those jurors who, in the words of the State's highest court, "might hesitate to return a verdict inflicting [death]." . . .

I.

The issue before us is a narrow one. It does not involve the right of the prosecution to challenge for cause those prospective jurors who state that their reservations about capital punishment would prevent them from making an impartial decision as to the defendant's guilt. Nor does it involve the State's assertion of a right to exclude from the jury in a capital case those who say that they could never vote to impose the death penalty or that they would refuse even to consider its imposition in the case before them. For the State of Illinois did not stop there, but authorized the prosecution to exclude as well all who said that they were opposed to capital punishment and all who indicated that they had conscientious scruples against inflicting it.

In the present case the tone was set when the trial judge said early in the *voir dire,* "Let's get these conscientious objectors out of the way, without wasting any time on them." In rapid succession, 47 veniremen were successfully challenged for cause on the basis of their attitudes toward the death penalty. Only five of the 47 explicitly stated that under no circumstances would they vote to impose capital punishment. Six said that they did not "believe in the death penalty" and were excused without any attempt to determine whether they could nonetheless return a verdict of death. Thirty-nine veniremen, including four of the six who indicated that they did not believe in capital punishment, acknowledged having "conscientious or religious scruples against the infliction of the death penalty" or against its infliction "in a proper case" and were excluded without any effort to find out whether their scruples would invariably compel them to vote against capital punishment. . . .

II.

The petitioner contends that a State cannot confer upon a jury selected in this manner the power to determine guilt. He maintains that such a jury, unlike one chosen at random from a cross-section of the community, must necessarily be biased in favor of conviction, for the kind of juror who would be unperturbed by the prospect of sending a man to his death, he contends, is the kind of juror who would too readily ignore the presumption of the defendant's innocence, accept the prosecution's version of the facts, and return a verdict of guilt. To support this view, the petitioner refers to what he describes as "competent scientific evidence that death-qualified jurors are partial to the prosecution on the issue of guilt or innocence."[10]

The data adduced by the petitioner, however, are too tentative and fragmentary to establish that jurors not opposed to the death penalty tend to favor the prosecution in the determination of guilt.[11] We simply cannot conclude, either on the basis of the record now before us or as a matter of judicial notice, that the exclusion of

---

[10]In his brief, the petitioner cites two surveys, one involving 187 college students, W. C. Wilson, Belief in Capital Punishment and Jury Performance (Unpublished Manuscript, University of Texas, 1964), and the other involving 200 college students, F. J. Goldberg, Attitude Toward Capital Punishment and Behavior as a Juror in Simulated Capital Cases (Unpublished Manuscript, Morehouse College, undated). . . .

[11]During the post-conviction proceedings here under review, the petitioner's counsel argued that the prosecution-prone character of "death-qualified" juries presented "purely a legal question," the resolution of which required "no additional proof" beyond "the facts . . . disclosed by the transcript of the voir dire examination. . . ." Counsel sought an "opportunity to submit evidence" in support of several contentions unrelated to the issue involved here. On this issue, however, no similar request was made, and the studies relied upon by the petitioner in this Court were not mentioned. We can only speculate, therefore, as to the precise meaning of the terms used in those studies, the accuracy of the techniques employed, and the validity of the generalizations made. Under these circumstances, it is not surprising that the *amicus curiae* brief filed by the NAACP Legal Defense and Educational Fund finds it necessary to observe that, with respect to bias in favor of the prosecution on the issue of guilt, the record in this case is "almost totally lacking in the sort of factual information that would assist the Court."

jurors opposed to capital punishment results in an unrepresentative jury on the issue of guilt or substantially increases the risk of conviction. In light of the presently available information, we are not prepared to announce a *per se* constitutional rule requiring the reversal of every conviction returned by a jury selected as this one was.

III.

It does not follow, however, that the petitioner is entitled to no relief. For in this case the jury was entrusted with two distinct responsibilities: first, to determine whether the petitioner was innocent or guilty; and second, if guilty, to determine whether his sentence should be imprisonment or death. It has not been shown that this jury was biased with respect to the petitioner's guilt. But it is self-evident that, in its role as arbiter of the punishment to be imposed, this jury fell woefully short of that impartiality to which the petitioner was entitled under the Sixth and Fourteenth Amendments.

The only justification the State has offered for the jury-selection technique it employed here is that individuals who express serious reservations about capital punishment cannot be relied upon to vote for it even when the laws of the State and the instructions of the trial judge would make death the proper penalty. But in Illinois, as in other States, the jury is given broad discretion to decide whether or not death *is* "the proper penalty" in a given case, and a juror's general views about capital punishment play an inevitable role in any such decision.

A man who opposes the death penalty, no less than one who favors it, can make the discretionary judgment entrusted to him by the State and can thus obey the oath he takes as a juror. But a jury from which all such men have been excluded cannot perform the task demanded of it. Guided by neither rule nor standard, "free to select or reject as it [sees] it," a jury that must choose between life imprisonment and capital punishment can do little more—and must do nothing less—than express the conscience of the community on the ultimate question of life or death. Yet, in a nation less than half of whose people believe in the death penalty, a jury composed exclusively of such people cannot speak for the community. Culled of all who harbor doubts about the wisdom of capital punishment—of all who would be reluctant to pronounce the extreme penalty—such a jury can speak only for a distinct and dwindling minority. . . .

It is, of course, settled that a State may not entrust the determination of whether a man is innocent or guilty to a tribunal "organized to convict." It requires but a short step from that principle to hold, as we do today, that a State may not entrust the determination of whether a man should live or die to a tribunal organized to return a verdict of death. Specifically, we hold that a sentence of death cannot be carried out if the jury that imposed or recommended it was chosen by excluding veniremen for cause simply because they voiced general objections to the death penalty or expressed conscientious or religious scruples against its infliction.[21] No defendant can constitutionally be put to death at the hands of a tribunal so selected. . . .

To execute this death sentence would deprive him of his life without due process of law.

Reversed.

---

[21] . . . We repeat, however, that nothing we say today bears upon the power of a State to execute a defendant sentenced to death by a jury from which the only veniremen who were in fact excluded for cause were those who made unmistakably clear (1) that they would *automatically* vote against the imposition of capital punishment without regard to any evidence that might be developed at the trial of the case before them, or (2) that their attitude toward the death penalty would prevent them from making an impartial decision as to the defendant's *guilt*. Nor does the decision in this case affect the validity of any sentence *other* than one of death. Nor, finally, does today's holding render invalid the *conviction*, as opposed to the *sentence*, in this or any other case.

NOTES AND QUESTIONS

1. Trial by jury is "fundamental to the American scheme of justice" (*Duncan* v. *Louisiana*, 1968, p. 149), and the Sixth Amendment guarantees the right to an "impartial" jury. In a democratic society, the jury serves as a buffer between the accused, on the one hand, and an overzealous prosecutor or biased judge, on the other. An impartial jury consists of persons who are unbiased (who have not "formed such an opinion that [they] could not in law be deemed impartial," [*Reynolds* v. *United States*, 1878, p. 156]), and who constitute "a representative cross-section of the community" (*Williams* v. *Florida*, 1970, p. 100). Does the Witherspoon decision rest principally on the Sixth Amendment, the Due Process Clause, or both? What difference does it make on which ground(s) it rests?

In a random distribution of prospective jurors, one can expect to find a range of attitudes toward the death penalty as depicted in Figure 5.1. At the one end of the five-point scale are the "very anti" death penalty persons, those who the Court said would "automatically vote against the imposition of capital punishment" regardless of the evidence presented (group 1). They would always vote for life imprisonment (if the option were available) upon a finding of guilt. This category was divided by the Court into two subgroups, those who despite their "very anti" position could render "an impartial decision as to the defendant's *guilt*" and those who could not (groups 1a and 1b, respectively). Next are the "anti" death penalty persons, those who express "general objections to the death penalty or . . . conscientious or religious scruples against its infliction" (group 2). In the middle are those who are indifferent, neither for or against the death penalty (group 3). On the other side of the spectrum are the "pro" and "very pro" venirepersons (groups 4 and 5).

FIGURE 5.1

Spectrum of Death Penalty Attitudes

1 Very Anti		2 Anti	3 Indifferent	4 Pro	5 Very Pro
"automatically vote against capital punishment"		"general objections" or "conscientious or religious scruples"			
1a capable of "impartial decision" as to guilt	1b not capable of "impartial decision" as to guilt				

In terms of Figure 5.1, which groups (and subgroups) of prospective jurors can and cannot be excluded for cause by the prosecution according to *Witherspoon*?

2. Petitioner's argument, in essence, was as follows: The Sixth Amendment right to an impartial jury means an unbiased jury; a death-qualified jury is biased because it is more likely to convict; therefore, death-qualification violates the Sixth Amendment right. The correlation between "very anti" death penalty attitudes and reluctance to impose that penalty upon conviction is obvious enough. The intermediate premise of Witherspoon's argument is not intuitively apparent. What basis is there in the social psychological literature on attitudes and personality that could account for the hypothesized relationship between capital punishment views and propensity to convict or acquit?

3. Footnote 11 of the case provides a glimpse of the tactical uses of social research in constitutional adjudication. Petitioner, of course, had the burden of establishing the unconstitutionality of the Illinois procedure. In lower court proceedings, petitioner's counsel sought to sustain that burden solely with legal arguments, saying that "no additional proof" was necessary beyond the facts disclosed by the voir dire. In his brief before the Supreme Court, however, petitioner's counsel apparently changed his mind and cited, almost as an afterthought, two unpublished studies (footnote 10). As the Court observed, the results were "tentative and fragmentary" and, in any event, there was no opportunity to evaluate the methodology of these studies.

At the time of Witherspoon's appeal, there were some 500 death row inmates, most of whom had also been convicted by death-qualified juries. An adverse decision would have sealed the fate not only of Witherspoon but of several hundred other capital prisoners as well. Many of them were represented by the Legal Defense Fund. Consequently, upon seeing Witherspoon's brief and the two studies cited therein, the Fund rushed in with a lengthy *amicus* brief. The Fund argued that "with respect to bias in favor of the prosecution on the issue of guilt, the record in this case is 'almost totally lacking in the sort of factual information that would assist the Court' " (footnote 11). It urged that the bias issue not be decided until more rigorous empirical research was done. Instead, it proposed that "the jury which convicted and sentenced after exclusion of scrupled jurors did not reflect a cross-section of the community," because national polls had shown that about one-half of the adult population entertained doubts about the death penalty (Meltsner 1973, pp. 120–21). The Fund's alternative legal theory, restated in syllogistic form, was as follows: The Sixth Amendment right to an impartial jury requires that jurors represent a cross-section of the population with respect to death penalty attitudes; a death-qualified jury does not constitute a representative cross-section because of the exclusion of those opposed to the death penalty; therefore, the death-qualified jury violates the Sixth Amendment.

What tactical considerations are implicated in the Fund's request that the Court ignore the social science evidence presented by Witherspoon's counsel and that the Court decide the case on the cross-sectional representation theory? The Fund was unperturbed by its own use of "tentative and fragmentary" research in the *Brown* litigation (for example, Clark's dolls study). What differences, if any, exist between the issues of *Brown I* and *Witherspoon* that would justify the use of weak empirical evidence in one case but not in the other?

Suppose that the research presented by the petitioner to support the conviction-proneness theory had been conclusive and comprehensive. Would it have been dispositive of the issue or, as in Maxwell's case, would statistics also never be Witherspoon's redemption?

4. Petitioner argued *against* the exclusion of jurors opposed to the death penalty. Is there any basis in social science to support an argument *for* the exclusion of jurors favorable to the death penalty? Is the exclusion of jurors of both ends of the attitude spectrum the equivalent of the inclusion of the entire distribution of jurors?

5. W. White (1973) writes: "A defendant convicted by a death-qualified jury may argue that his rights under the equal protection clause are violated, because whereas defendants in noncapital cases are subject to one process of jury selection, the state, without any justifiable basis, has subjected the class of defendants to which he belongs to a different and prejudicial process of jury selection." He adds that "the interest of the state in seeking the death penalty is the only possible justification" for death-qualification, and "this interest is illusory" (pp. 1201, 1205). Do you agree?

6. *Witherspoon* was given retroactive effect by the Supreme Court. In news reports, "almost everyone questioned believed the decision meant the end of capital punishment in the United States" (Meltsner 1973, p. 124). It was assumed that the hundreds of death row inmates convicted by death-qualified juries would be entitled to resentencing before new juries who might decline to reimpose the death penalty, in part because of the changed climate of public opinion. As it turned out, *Witherspoon* did not result in de facto abolition; on the contrary, means were devised to circumvent its intent. Some states, for example, enacted legislation requiring any resentencing—resulting from the reversal of the death penalty by reason of *Witherspoon*—to be conducted by a judge rather than by a jury.

In subsequent capital cases, some state and federal courts also were not wholly faithful to *Witherspoon*. As in other areas of constitutional law (for example, the Parker Doctrine of *Brown I*), the Supreme Court decision underwent a transformation from its initial pronouncement to its eventual interpretation and application by the lower courts. In T. S. Eliot's words, in "The Hollow Men," "Between the idea and the reality . . . falls the Shadow."

Thus, in *People* v. *Speck* (1968), the first Illinois capital case after *Witherspoon*, some fifty jurors were excused because they had conscientious scruples, but none said he or she would never impose the death penalty. This death-qualified jury convicted the defendant of the murder of seven student nurses. The Illinois Supreme Court summarized the *Witherspoon* holding, noted its applicability to the instant case, and then affirmed the death sentence because the "atmosphere" of the voir dire was not prejudicial: "[T]he tone of the proceedings here indicates a sincere desire on the part of the prosecutor and the court (although perhaps not shared by the defense) to determine the jurors' qualifications according to the standard later held acceptable in *Witherspoon*" (p. 209). Clearly, this opinion disregards the language and intent of *Witherspoon*, even though the procedures of both Illinois cases were nearly identical.

Some courts have simply equated pre-*Witherspoon* state law with *Witherspoon* standards. A Texas court determined that a jury "selected in the traditional Texas manner" (that is, excluding scrupled venirepersons without any inquiry as to whether "they would vote against capital punishment regardless of the facts or circumstances of any case") "squares with the requirements of *Witherspoon*" (*Pittman* v. *State*, 1968, pp. 356–57). If anything, this procedure flies in the face of *Witherspoon* (Comment, *University of Chicago Law Review*, 1970, p. 770).

The Supreme Court did not state unequivocally whether improper exclusion of any venirepersons constitutes a violation, or whether only the general procedure of death-qualification must comport with *Witherspoon*. Some federal courts have held that the wrongful removal of a few prospective jurors is harmless error, because they have interpreted *Witherspoon* to apply only to "systematic exclusion of any significant element of the community" (*Bell* v. *Patterson*, 1968, p. 399). An approach that reviews the selection process as a whole rather than the challenge of individual venirepersons seems inconsistent with the spirit of *Witherspoon*.

This gap—between principle and practice, between the law-in-the-books and the law-in-action, between grandiloquent statements of lofty principles and their implementation in specific cases—is not unique or novel. The issue that needs to be considered is not just the fact of duality, but the *reasons* for its existence and the *method* by which it is perpetuated.

Why is *Witherspoon*—and other Supreme Court decisions for that matter—often honored in the breach? The *Speck* and *Pittman* (mis)interpretations of *Witherspoon* are quite out of proportion to the narrowness and clarity of the Court's holding. Amsterdam (1970) reminds us that "the significance of the Court's pronouncements . . . does not depend upon their correspondence with reality. Once uttered, these pronouncements will be interpreted by arrays of lower appellate courts, trial judges, magistrates, commissioners, and police officials. Their interpretation of the [pronouncement], for all practical purposes, will become the [law]" (p. 786). This lack of fit between the Court's pronouncements and their application by lower courts is similar to Friedman and Percival's notion (1981) of two-tiered justice in the criminal courts. One tier articulates and preserves the appearance of due process principles, and the other, less visible tier attempts to implement these principles amid immediately felt pressures for crime control. "Rights, due process, fairness can be important, not only in themselves, but also in propaganda. They seem timeless and classless, socially neutral in a word. The idea that this kind of justice exists may be a kind of soothing syrup for the masses." On the other hand, the "real day-by-day work" of the criminal courts goes on "unobserved, underneath" (p. 316).

Does the case-by-case method of decision-making—an incrementalist method characterized by the art of making hairline distinctions, minute qualifications, implied conditions, endless exceptions, and additional exceptions to the exceptions based upon the specific facts and equities at hand—facilitate the maintenance of the duality between the theory and practice of due process ideals? The very mode of adjudication appears to enable courts to give lip service to exalted principles and at the same time justify a deviation from them in particular instances (Davies 1982). "The intrinsic specificity of the case law method allied to the common law habit of declaration of broad principles rather than tight rulings, leads to grand civil rights rhetoric but plenty of scope for discretionary judicial practice" (McBarnet 1981, p. 46).

7.   Capital trials use single or split verdict procedures. In the single verdict trial, a single (death-qualified) jury decides guilt and penalty in the same trial. In the split or bifurcated trial, one (non–death-qualified) jury decides guilt and, upon conviction, a different (death-qualified) jury decides the penalty. In a variation of the bifurcated procedure, a single (death-qualified) jury decides guilt and penalty but in two separate trials.

If Witherspoon's conviction-proneness argument had prevailed, what would have been the effect of the decision on capital verdict procedures?

8. In *Crampton* v. *Ohio* (1971), the Court upheld the constitutionality of single-verdict sentencing. Crampton, who had shot his wife in the face while she sat on the toilet, argued that this procedure violated the Fifth Amendment right against self-incrimination. It forced him to choose between taking the stand to introduce mitigating evidence in support of lenient sentencing (thereby exposing himself to cross-examination about his past conduct that could impeach his credibility), and not taking the stand (thereby possibly going to his death without an opportunity to plead his case on the penalty question). Ohio argued that it was not an unfair procedure because mitigation could always be introduced by other witnesses or by Crampton's own attorney. The Court held that the Fifth Amendment is not so broad as to include the right "to speak to the jury free from any adverse consequences on the issue of guilt" that might arise from choosing to take the witness stand. Pleading the penalty issue personally has only "symbolic value" (p. 220). The Court observed that it is not "impermissible for a state to consider that the compassionate purposes of jury sentencing in capital cases [that is, the jury's discretion to decide death or life imprisonment] are better served by having the issues of guilt and punishment determined in a single trial than by focusing the jury's attention solely on punishment after the issue of guilt has been determined" (p. 221).

Crampton was decided solely on legal grounds. No social science evidence was introduced on appeal or mentioned in the opinion. Nonetheless, what empirical research issues are implicit in the single verdict and bifurcated verdict procedures?

HOVEY v. THE SUPERIOR COURT OF ALAMEDA COUNTY

168 Cal. Rptr. 128 (1980)

[Petitioner, accused of murder and kidnapping, brought a pretrial motion (writ of mandamus) to require the trial court to limit the exclusion for cause of prospective jurors. Ed.'s note.]

BIRD, Chief Justice.

. . .

III. THE ISSUES PRESENTED

The instant writ petition presents fundamentally two challenges to the current system of jury selection in capital cases.* First, must the class of prospective jurors, who may now be excluded for cause under *Witherspoon* standards from both phases of the trial, be narrowed to permit a specific sub-category to serve at the guilt phase? *Witherspoon* authorized the

exclusion for cause of prospective jurors who make "unmistakably clear" either (1) that they would automatically vote against the death *penalty* if there were a penalty phase, regardless of the evidence adduced at trial,[34] or (2) that their doubts about or opposition to capital punishment would preclude them from fairly and impartially determining *guilt* at the guilt phase.[35] Petitioner does not suggest that either of these two groups be allowed to serve at the penalty phase of a capital trial. Nor does he contend that the second group—those who could not be fair and impartial at the guilt phase—may serve at the guilt phase. Rather, it is argued that prospective jurors, who would automatically vote against death at the *penalty* phase, cannot constitutionally be excused for cause from sitting at the guilt phase if they can be fair and impartial *at that phase*.[36]

_____

*[California Penal Code §190.4(c) provides for bifurcated death penalty trials, but also requires that "the same jury" which convicts "shall" determine the penalty, "unless for good cause shown" the court orders the drawing of a new (penalty) jury. Ed.'s note.]

_____

[34]As a shorthand reference to this group, this opinion uses the term "automatic life imprisonment" group. The members of this group would automatically vote to impose life imprisonment in every capital trial.

[35]This second group will be referred to as the "guilt phase nullifiers."

[36]This group, which petitioner seeks to have included in the jury pool for the guilt phase of a capital trial, is

Two separate constitutional theories are advanced to reach this conclusion. One is bottomed on *Witherspoon.* Under it, petitioner contends there is evidence which can "establish" that a jury from which all "guilt phase includables" have been removed for cause is "less than neutral with respect to guilt."[38] The other constitutional theory relies on the "purpose and functioning" analysis developed in *Ballew* v. *Georgia,* and the line of decisions it represents. This theory would require the court to determine—under a "substantial doubt" standard—whether the interests protected by the Sixth Amendment are significantly inhibited by the disqualification at the guilt phase of all the "guilt phase includable" jurors.*

The second basic challenge to the current system of selecting a jury for a capital case focuses on the voir dire *procedure* by which the jury is selected, rather than on the *composition or functioning* of the jury itself. The argument is advanced that whoever is chosen to serve on a jury in a capital case, he or she will be affected by the methods now employed to identify those persons whose views on capital punish-

ment render them ineligible. The result, it is contended, is a jury likely to be "less than neutral" with respect to guilt and penalty. Petitioner suggests that certain procedural refinements would minimize this possibility.

IV. THE CONCEPT OF A NEUTRAL JURY

Central to the resolution of the *Witherspoon* issue is the concept of a constitutionally "neutral" jury. . . .

A neutral jury is one drawn from a pool which reasonably mirrors the diversity of experiences and relevant viewpoints of those persons in the community who can fairly and impartially try the case.

The concept of neutrality through diversity is demonstrated by the holding in *Witherspoon.* Assume that a jury must be empanelled to determine the question of punishment in a capital case. In the group of persons from the community who are statutorily competent to act as trial jurors, it can be expected that an entire spectrum of beliefs concerned the infliction of capital punishment [as follows]:

—"AUTOMATIC DEATH PENALTY" GROUP: will automatically vote for the death penalty;

—"FAVOR DEATH PENALTY" GROUP: favors the death penalty but will not vote to impose it in every case;

—"INDIFFERENT" GROUP: neither favors nor opposes the death penalty;

—"OPPOSES DEATH PENALTY" GROUP: opposes the death penalty but will not automatically vote against it in every case;

—"AUTOMATIC LIFE IMPRISONMENT" GROUP: will automatically vote for life imprisonment.

---

a subgroup of the "automatic life imprisonment" class. Its members will be referred to as the "guilt phase includables."

[38]. . . While the *Witherspoon* analysis does involve significant cross section concerns (as does the *Ballew* approach), it would appear that the purely cross sectional cases such as *Taylor* [v. *Louisiana* (1975)] and *Duren* [v. *Missouri* (1979)] represent a third line of constitutional analysis that is analytically separate from those of *Witherspoon* and *Ballew.* Petitioner has specifically declined to invoke the *Taylor* approach in the present case. Consequently, today's decision does not reach the validity of any argument based on a pure cross section analysis.

*[*Ballew* v. *Georgia* (1978) is reprinted in Chapter 8, section 8.2. In holding that a five-person jury violated the Sixth and Fourteenth Amendments, the Court determined that the purpose and function of the jury is to serve as a buffer between the state and the accused, and that this role is impaired when the composition of a jury is such (for example, five-person size) so as to (1) not "promote group deliberation" and (2) reduce the possibility of attaining a "cross-sectional representation" of the community. Ed.'s note.]

Under the state procedure in effect at the time Witherspoon's penalty was determined, all persons in the "oppose death penalty" group and the "automatic life imprisonment" group were excluded for cause. Thus, Witherspoon's jury was drawn from a pool of persons which did not reflect the range of community viewpoints on a critical aspect of the case. . . .

Manifestly, fair and impartial jurors will bring to the determination of guilt a diversity of experience, knowledge, judgment, and viewpoints, as well as differences in their "thresholds of reasonable doubt." If some of those jurors are systematically removed from the guilt determination, this may result in a disproportionate elimination of persons with characteristics favorable to the accused. If so, the ensuing jury will be "less than neutral with respect to guilt," just as the jury at the penalty phase in *Witherspoon* was not neutral with respect to penalty.[55]

V. THE EVIDENCE RELATING TO THE WITHERSPOON AND BALLEW CONTENTIONS

Roughly two dozen studies, experiments, and surveys were introduced at or were the subject of expert testimony during the evidentiary hearing below. . . .

CONVICTION PRONENESS

THE ZEISEL STUDY.[59] In the fall and winter of 1954–1955, Professor Hans Zeisel and two associates interviewed a number of jurors who had actually deliberated on felony cases in the Criminal Court of Chicago, Illinois, or the County Court of Kings County (Brooklyn), New York.

Zeisel's purpose was to explore whether the jurors' attitudes toward capital punishment correlated with a tendency to vote for guilt or acquittal in criminal cases. He asked the jurors whether they had any conscientious scruples against the death penalty and how they had voted on the first ballot after the jury started to deliberate.

Asking only these two questions would have resulted in a wholly uncontrolled study, for in this posture, the factor of the strength of the evidence had not been taken into account. Zeisel devised a rather ingenious question to get at this factor. He concluded that the strength of the evidence in a given case could be roughly estimated and compared with other cases by determining how the jury as a whole voted on the first ballot after deliberations began. Thus, a first ballot vote of 11-to-1 in favor of acquittal suggested a weak case against the accused; a 10-to-2 vote for acquittal indicated a weak case but not quite so weak; a 9-to-3 vote for acquittal, an even less weak case, and so on, through all 11 possible jury splits, to 11-to-1 for conviction. By grouping each juror's vote into one of the eleven categories or "constellations" based on the strength of the evidence—from the weakest prosecution evidence to the strongest—Zeisel could roughly control for the weight of the evidence. . . .

Zeisel ended up with data on 464 first ballot votes. . . .

Zeisel found that in 10 of the 11 constellations of evidence strength, jurors with conscientious scruples against capital punishment voted to acquit more often than jurors without such scruples.

Zeisel determined that these differences between the first ballot guilty votes of the jurors without conscientious scruples against capital punishment and the first ballot guilty votes of jurors with such scruples were statistically significant at the .04 level. . . .

---

[55]Many of the reasons underlying the constitutional requirement of neutrality are also concerns in the "jury purpose and functioning" analysis of *Ballew* v. *Georgia*. To this extent, then, *Witherspoon* and *Ballew* overlap.

[59]Zeisel, Some Data on Juror Attitudes Toward Capital Punishment (1968) (hereinafter, *Zeisel*).

THE JUROW STUDY.[67] Professor Jurow undertook the first controlled experiment in the post-*Witherspoon* era. His subjects were 211 employees at a Sperry-Rand Corporation plant on Long Island, New York. Virtually all of these individuals were eligible for jury duty. One-third of the subjects had had prior jury service. The group was overwhelmingly white (98.6 percent), fairly well educated and had relatively high median family income. Women constituted 26 percent of the subjects; Catholics nearly 50 percent; engineers 39 percent; and clerical workers and laborers 29 percent.

Jurow prepared two audiotapes of simulated criminal trials. A script was prepared for each case, which "attempt[ed] to weigh the evidence as evenly as possible between acquittal and conviction." The script included opening statements by the attorneys, witnesses' testimony, direct and cross examination, arguments of counsel, and the judge's instructions to the jury. The audiotapes were pretested to insure that the evidence was appropriately balanced and that the recordings were realistic and did enhance listener involvement.

The first audiotape lasted 33 minutes (case I). It involved "the murder of a liquor store proprietor during a holdup and the apprehension and trial of an ex-convict seen running from the vicinity of the store who denied any knowledge of the robbery and murder." The second tape (case II) lasted 50 minutes. It portrayed "a narcotics addict charged with robbing, raping, and killing a college girl in her apartment." At the conclusion of each tape, the subject/jurors were given time to think about their verdict and mark a ballot. There were no deliberations by the subject/jurors as a group.

The attitudes of the subject/jurors toward capital punishment were determined on a five-part spectrum. . . .

[Jurow constructed a five-point scale called a "Capital Punishment Attitude Questionnaire" (CPAQ) with two parts, (A) and (B).

The CPAQ(A) scale asked the subject to "check the *one* statement that *best* summarizes your *general views* about capital punishment" (Jurow 1971, Appendix A, p. 599):*

(1) I am opposed to capital punishment under any circumstances.
(2) I am opposed to capital punishment except in a few cases where it may be appropriate.
(3) I am neither generally opposed nor generally in favor of capital punishment.
(4) I am in favor of capital punishment except in a few cases where it may not be appropriate.
(5) I am strongly in favor of capital punishment as an appropriate penalty.

The CPAQ(B) scale asked a subject to "assume *you are on a jury* to determine the sentence for a defendant who has already been convicted of a serious crime" and to choose *one* of the following sentencing options provided by the law (Jurow 1971, Appendix A, p. 599):

(1) I could not vote for the death penalty regardless of the facts and circumstances of the case.
(2) There are some kinds of cases in which I know I could not vote for the death penalty even if the

---

[67]Jurow, New Data on the Effect of a "Death-Qualified" Jury on the Guilt Determination Process (1971), 84 *Harv. L. Rev.* 567 (hereinafter *Jurow*).

---

*Reprinted by permission of the author and publisher from G. L. Jurow, New Data on the Effect of a "Death-Qualified" Jury on the Guilt-Determination Process, *Harvard Law Review*, 1971, 84, 567–611. Copyright ©1971 by The Harvard Law Review Association.

law allowed me to, but others in which I would be willing to consider voting for it.

(3) I would consider all of the penalties provided by the law and the facts and circumstances of the particular case.

(4) I would usually vote for the death penalty in a case where the law allows me to.

(5) I would always vote for the death penalty in a case where the law allows me to. Ed.'s note.]

In both cases, Jurow found some tendency for an attitude favorable to capital punishment to correlate with a tendency to vote for conviction. In case I (the liquor store robbery-murder), this tendency was highly significant (the "p" value was less than .01); in case II, the tendency was at best marginally significant (the "p" value is greater than .05).

[The percentage of subjects voting guilty in case I, for each of the five response categories of CPAQ(B), was as follows (reorganized from Jurow 1971, Table II, p. 583):*

(1) 33% (7/21: 7 out of 21 subjects voted guilty)
(2) 29% (12/42)
(3) 45% (59/132)
(4) 91% (10/11)
(5) 80% (4/5)

$X^2 = 17.58$, $df = 4$, $P < .01$. There were no significant differences among the five response categories of CPAQ(A) for case I.

The percentage of guilty votes in case II on CPAQ(B) was as follows (reorganized from Jurow 1971, Table II, p. 583):

(1) 43% (9/21)
(2) 60% (25/42)
(3) 57% (76/132)
(4) 82% (9/11)
(5) 80% (4/5)

$X^2 = 5.58$, $df = 4$, $P > .05$. No significant differences were found in CPAQ(A) for case II. Ed.'s note.]

Jurow is not a definitive controlled study, however. Its presentation of evidence involved only oral, not visual, stimuli. The subjects were drawn from a limited population. There were no group deliberations and there may have been little felt responsibility on the part of the subjects as compared to actual jurors sitting in a real trial.[73] . . .

THE ELLSWORTH CONVICTION-PRONENESS STUDY.[76] The most recent controlled study of conviction proneness was undertaken in 1979 by Drs. Phoebe Ellsworth, William Thompson, and Claudia Cowan. They recruited as subjects 288 adults eligible for jury service in California. . . .

The subject/jurors participated in the study in groups of 12 to 36. They were shown a two-and-one-half hour videotaped reenactment of an actual criminal trial. . . .

After this videotape had been played, each subject/juror was asked to indicate how he or she would vote, based upon his or her "own personal individual decision." There were four possible verdicts. . . .

---

[73]Heretofore, this court has been "not willing to accept [Jurow's conclusions] as decisive" of the *Witherspoon* issue. This position represents the sound view that one study by itself can rarely justify altering constitutional practice. . . .

[76]Ellsworth et al., Juror Attitudes and Conviction Proneness: The Relationship between Attitudes towards the Death Penalty and Predisposition to Convict (1979, prepub. draft) (hereinafter, the *Ellsworth Conviction-Proneness Study*). [This study has been published. See Cowan, Thompson, and Ellsworth (1984). Ed.'s note.]

The subjects' views on capital punishment had been previously determined. Of the 288 persons participating in the experiment, 30 were "guilt phase includables" and 258 were "*Witherspoon*-qualified" (i.e., persons who could impose the death penalty in at least some circumstances).

These results of the *Ellsworth Conviction-Proneness Study* are shown in the accompanying table.

newspaper advertisement or venire list)—correlated with voting behavior. . . .

OVERVIEW OF CONVICTION-PRONENESS STUDIES

The expert witnesses called on behalf of the defense testified that the studies convincingly established a strong correlation between the tendencies of jurors to vote for conviction and juror attitudes to-

Ellsworth Conviction-Proneness Study: Juror Voting Behavior, Comparison of "*Witherspoon*-Qualified" and "Guilt Phase Includable" Jurors

Verdict	"Guilt Phase Includable" Jurors	"*Witherspoon*-Qualified" Jurors
First degree murder	3.3% (1)	7.8% (20)
Second degree murder	23.3 (7)	21.3 (55)
Manslaughter	26.7 (8)	48.9 (126)
Acquittal	46.7 (14)	22.1 (57)
	100.0% (30)	100.0% (258)

The results, Ellsworth concluded, "provide strong support for the hypothesis that death-qualified jurors are more likely to convict than are jurors excludable under the *Witherspoon* criteria. . . . The differences were highly significant ('p' value of less than .01). . . ."

Using a statistical process known as multiple regression analysis, Ellsworth also analyzed the data to determine whether the differences in the juror's voting behavior could be attributable to factors other than differences in the jurors' attitudes toward capital punishment. She found that none of the other factors examined—prior jury service, age, sex, and source from which the subjects were recruited (i.e.,

ward capital punishment. Dr. Zeisel noted, "[S]ince all of the studies show the same result, no matter with whom, no matter with what stimulus, no matter with what closeness of simulation, there is really only one conclusion that we can come to. The relationship is so robust—and this is a term of art among scientists—that no matter how strongly or how weakly you try to discover it in terms of your experimental design, it will come through." . . .

THE ATTITUDE SURVEYS

The several attitude surveys introduced below are relevant on both the *Witherspoon* and *Ballew* issues insofar as those surveys may show that persons who differ in their attitudes toward capital punishment also differ in other attitudes related to the criminal justice system. Such a showing would reinforce our confidence in the conviction-proneness studies' findings of a relationship between attitudes toward the death penalty and conviction proneness, since it would reasonably be anticipated that persons who differ on both capital punishment attitudes and voting behavior would also differ with respect to a number of other, related attitudes. . . .

THE ELLSWORTH ATTITUDE SURVEY.[97] The final attitude survey was conducted in April 1979 in Alameda County. The subjects were 811 persons randomly selected from the adult population of the county. All participants were registered to vote in the county or had a California driver's license; all lived in a household with an operational telephone.

The survey questionnaire was prepared by Drs. Ellsworth and Fitzgerald. The questions were pretested to insure that "the questions were comprehensible and the responses were sufficiently variable so that meaningful between-group comparisons would be possible." The survey was administered by the Field Research Corporation (FRC). The subjects were selected by FRC using a process known as random digit dialing, and the interviews were conducted by experienced professional interviewers at FRC. The methodology of this survey was universally praised by the experts below. . . .

The subjects were asked 13 attitudinal questions. There were statistically significant differences between the "guilt phase includable" subjects and the "*Witherspoon*-qualified" subjects on 11 of them.* . . .

As in many of the previous surveys, there was a majority of both groups who viewed the insanity defense as "a loophole allowing too many guilty people to go free," but the majority was much larger for the "*Witherspoon*-qualified" jurors (78 percent) than for the "guilt phase includable" group (59.2 percent). . . .

Differences in attitudes toward the privileges against self-incrimination were measured. . . . About one-third of the "*Witherspoon*-qualified" subjects (32.3 percent) indicated agreement with the statement "A person on trial who doesn't take the witness stand and deny the crime is probably guilty." Only 23.5 percent of the "guilt phase includables" agreed. . . .†

DEMOGRAPHIC CHARACTERISTICS

There has long been survey research done which related attitudes toward capital punishment to such demographic characteristics as race and sex. This research is relevant to the *Ballew* issue in the present case insofar as it may show that excluding persons based upon their opposition to capital punishment "foretells problems for the representation [on juries] of minority groups in the community."

Surveys conducted over the past thirty years by Gallup, Harris, and the National Opinion Research Center (N.O.R.C.) have uniformly shown that women are opposed to capital punishment

---

[97]Ellsworth & Fitzgerald, Due Process vs. Crime Control: The Impact of Death Qualification on Jury Attitudes (1979, prepub. draft). [This study has since been published. See Fitzgerald and Ellsworth (1984). Ed.'s note.]

*[The sample for the data analysis consisted of 717 persons. Based on attitudes toward the death penalty, 17% were classified as "guilt phase includable" and 83% as "*Witherspoon*-qualified." *Ellsworth Attitude Survey*, p. 5. Ed.'s note.]
†[The Jurow study also found highly significant correlations between the CPAQ items (A and B) and various established attitude measures (for example, the F-scale). Jurow (1971) concluded: "The more a subject is in favor of capital punishment, the more likely he is to be politically conservative, authoritarian, and punitive in assigning penalties upon conviction" (p. 578). Ed.'s note.]

more frequently than are men. From 1953 through 1978, Gallup and N.O.R.C. conducted nationwide polls asking the survey respondents, "Are you in favor of the death penalty for persons convicted of murder?" [T]here have been consistent differences between the responses of men and those of women, with women expressing opposition to the death penalty more often (by an average of 11 percent).* . . .

These differences between the sexes do not disappear when the question posed is tailored to the *Witherspoon* criteria. . . .

RACE. The disparities between whites and blacks are even greater than between males and females. [G]allup and N.O.R.C. polls during 1953 through 1978 have shown that blacks are much more opposed to capital punishment than are whites. The average difference in opposition to capital punishment over the entire 25-year period is 23 percent, but the gap has been increasing (it averaged 28 percent in the 1970s).† . . .

As was true for the sexual differences, the significant disparities remain when a *Witherspoon* question is posed. . . .

[T]hose correlations between opposition to capital punishment and racial and sexual characteristics "have tended to appear with boring regularity ever since these topics have been researched. . . ." "No one who has ever done [such] a survey . . . has failed to find" these differences.

VI. CRITICISMS OF THE STUDIES RELATING TO THE WITHERSPOON AND BALLEW CONTENTIONS

The Attorney General raises several major methodological arguments to attack the conclusions which petitioner would draw from these studies. . . .

[T]here is a . . . telling criticism of the conclusions which petitioner seeks to draw from the evidence relating to the *Witherspoon* and *Ballew* issues. The pool of jurors eligible to serve in a capital trial in California consists of those persons eligible to serve in a noncapital case whose attitudes toward capital punishment would place them in either the "favor death penalty," "indifferent," or "oppose death penalty" group. Thus, in order to establish that a capital case jury in this state is drawn from a pool that is less than neutral with respect to guilt or is inadequate to effectuate the purposes and functions of a jury, petitioner must establish deficiencies in a pool consisting of those *three* groups, i.e., the "California death-qualified" groups.

None of petitioner's studies expressly focused on a pool comprised in this manner. They do focus on the deficiencies in a pool of "*Witherspoon*-qualified" jurors. However, at least in theory, a pool of "*Witherspoon*-qualified" jurors differs from a pool of "California death-qualified" jurors. The former contains a fourth group in addition to the three "California death-qualified" groups, i.e., a "*Witherspoon*-qualified" jury pool also contains the "automatic death penalty" group.[110] Thus, in order to draw conclusions about a pool of "California death-qualified" jurors on the basis of the evidence introduced below, petitioner must be able to account for the "automatic death penalty" jurors. It is asserted by the Attorney General that petitioner is unable to do this in a scientifically adequate fashion. In short, petitioner is said to have proved the wrong proposition.

Petitioner seeks to overcome the critique in several ways. First, he contends that the "automatic death penalty" group

---

*[For example, those favoring the death penalty: 77% males, 66% females in 1953; 76% males, 66% females in 1978. *Hovey*, p. 164. Ed.'s note.]

†[For example, those favoring the death penalty: 72% whites, 64% blacks in 1953; 73% whites, 46% blacks in 1978. *Hovey*, p. 165. Ed.'s note.]

---

110. . . .[T]he exclusion of this ["automatic death penalty"] group is required by statute in [California].

is a tiny group compared to the "*Witherspoon*-qualified" groups as a whole. If this were true, it is urged, then the results of petitioner's studies would not be appreciably altered by subtracting the few "automatic death penalty" jurors from the large class of "*Witherspoon*-qualified" jurors.

However, there is no reliable evidence in the record to support petitioner's assumption as to the minute size of the "automatic death penalty" group. The defense experts below repeatedly admitted that "nobody knows" the size of this group. . . .

Petitioner's assertion that the *Ellsworth Conviction-Proneness Study* demonstrates the nonneutrality of a "California death-qualified" jury presents another problem as well. Even if this study reliably showed that "California death-qualified" jurors tend to be more conviction-prone than "guilt phase includable" jurors, it does not necessarily follow that the former would also tend to be more conviction-prone than are jurors in a noncapital case. It is this latter showing which is the crux of the *Witherspoon* issue. However, the study's omission of the "automatic death penalty" group—which comprises an unknown proportion of the pool of jurors in noncapital cases—renders unsound petitioner's leap from the results of this study [that "California death-qualified" jurors are more conviction-prone than "guilt phase includable" jurors] to the conclusion that "California death-qualified" jurors are also more conviction-prone than a "neutral" jury. . . .

Therefore, until further research is done which makes it possible to draw reliable conclusions about the nonneutrality of "California death-qualified" juries in California, this court does not have a sufficient evidentiary basis on which to bottom a constitutional holding under *Witherspoon* and *Ballew*. It is, indeed, unfortunate that so much research, time, and

energy has been expended in this area with the result that no one stopped to consider the differences between a "*Witherspoon*-qualified" jury and a "California death-qualified" jury.

The trial court properly rejected petitioner's motion under *Witherspoon* and *Ballew* to limit the exclusion for cause of jurors unalterably opposed to capital punishment.

VII. THE USE OF SEQUESTRATION IN DEATH-QUALIFYING A JURY

Petitioner asks this court to consider whether the procedures currently used in this state to identify death-qualified jurors alter the jury to the detriment of an accused. . . .

Presently, the defense counsel and the prosecutor have the right to question potential jurors about their attitudes toward the death penalty in order to lay a foundation for possible challenges for cause. The voir dire is usually conducted in open court with the entire jury panel present. Although each juror is questioned personally, he or she has the opportunity to observe the examination of many other venirepersons. . . .

The process presently used focuses attention on penalty before the accused has been found guilty. As a result, some jurors may be more likely to believe the accused is guilty as charged. Modern psychological theory suggests several reasons to anticipate such a result. . . .

Few human impulses are more fundamental than the need to make sense of one's surroundings. . . . [V]enirepersons who are in the unfamiliar and imposing surroundings of a courtroom, undergoing the oftentimes elaborate and sometimes baffling ritual of voir dire, will typically seek cues about appropriate ways of thinking, feeling, and believing. Such venirepersons are likely to look to the behavior of the most knowledgeable and respected figures in the courtroom, i.e., the judge and counsel. . . .

Jurors undergoing death-qualification would have reason to infer that the judge and the attorneys personally believe the accused to be guilty or expect the jury to come to that conclusion. Only such an inference could serve to explain to the jurors why so much time and energy are devoted to an extensive discussion of penalty before trial. Provided with these cues from people who are not only experts in the courtroom but are also presumably acquainted with all the evidence in the case, the relevant law, and the "correct" application of the one to the other, death-qualified jurors may themselves become more inclined to believe that the accused is guilty as charged. . . .[121]

The fact that the court dismisses those venirepersons who express unequivocal opposition to the death penalty is likely to be interpreted by the remaining jurors as an indication that the judge in particular and the law in general disapprove of such attitudes. . . .

When people are continually exposed to a stimulus which is intimidating or frightening to them, they become desensitized to what they earlier found to be threatening. In a capital voir dire, prospective jurors are repeatedly prompted to think about the penalty decision they may later be called upon to make. What was

initially regarded as an onerous choice, inspiring caution and hesitation, may be more readily undertaken simply because of the repeated exposure to the idea of taking a life. . . .

In 1979, Dr. Craig Haney, an assistant professor of psychology at the University of California at Santa Cruz, devised a controlled study to determine whether the process of death-qualification actually alters jurors' states of mind so that it affects their evaluation of guilt or their choice of penalty. The subjects of the experiment were selected from adults eligible for jury duty in Santa Cruz County who had responded to a local newspaper advertisement. The researchers screened the respondents by telephone, and eliminated from the study those whose attitudes about capital punishment disqualified them under the *Witherspoon* criteria.

Haney had prepared a two-hour videotape of a simulated voir dire in a capital trial. . . . Two of the venirepersons who were questioned on the videotape were confederates placed by Haney. These two were instructed to respond to the voir dire questions concerning capital punishment as if they had views which would render them ineligible under *Witherspoon*.

The 67 subjects of Haney's study were randomly divided into two groups for purposes of viewing the videotaped voir dire. Both groups were asked to imagine themselves to be "prospective jurors in this very case." One group—the "experimental" group—was shown the full two-hour videotape which included half an hour of death-qualification. The "control" group saw the same videotape with the death-qualifying segment deleted. . . .

After viewing the videotapes, both groups completed a questionnaire. Their responses were consistent with the predictions that the present procedures for death-qualifying a jury alter the jurors' perspectives.

Haney found that the "death-

---

[121]Studies in an area of social psychology called attribution research have identified another mechanism which suggests why the death-qualification process might influence a jury's determination of guilt or innocence. This research has demonstrated that imagining the occurrence of a possible event increases a person's belief that the event will come to pass. An imagining process also occurs in the death-qualifying voir dire. People are asked to consider what they would do if the trial were to proceed to the penalty phase. These venirepersons would accordingly be more likely to expect that the penalty phase will occur. Since the occurrence of the penalty phase is contingent on conviction and the finding of special circumstances, these venirepersons might also expect these intermediate steps to occur.

qualified" subject/jurors in his experimental group were more likely than those in the control group to believe the accused was guilty of first degree murder, a finding that was statistically significant. Moreover, the experimental group was more likely to think that the prosecutor and the defense attorney personally believed the accused guilty as charged. The subject/jurors in the experimental group were also more inclined to think that the judge believed the accused to be guilty as charged. . . .

The two groups were asked to select what they thought would be an appropriate penalty, assuming that the accused had been convicted and a special circumstance allegation of a prior conviction of first degree murder had been found true. Fifty-seven percent of the experimental group indicated that they would vote to impose the death penalty, compared to only 21.9 percent of the control group.

Haney's study has served to alert this court to some of the pernicious consequences of our current voir dire procedures in capital cases. . . .

The most practical and effective procedure available to minimize the untoward effects of death-qualification is individualized sequestered voir dire. Because jurors would then witness only a single death-qualifying voir dire—their own—each individual juror would be exposed to considerably less discussion and questioning about the various aspects of the penalty phase before hearing any evidence of guilt. Such a reduction in the pretrial emphasis on penalty should minimize the tendency of a death-qualified jury to presume guilt and expect conviction. . . .

VIII.

Since petitioner has failed to establish his *Witherspoon* and *Ballew* contentions, the only relief to which he is entitled is to have that portion of the voir dire of each prospective juror, which deals with issues other than those traditionally inquired into at any criminal trial, conducted outside the presence of the other prospective jurors. . . .

NOTES AND QUESTIONS

---

1. The Jurow study included two different attitude scales called CPAQ(A) and CPAQ(B). Persons endorsing statement 1 in CPAQ(B) correspond to what *Hovey* calls the "automatic life imprisonment" group. Persons subscribing to statements 2 to 5 on that scale are *Witherspoon*-qualified. In light of the *Witherspoon* opinion, what is the legal significance of Jurow's finding (in Case I) that responses on CPAQ(B), but not on CPAQ(A), were associated with guilty votes?

2. Why, according to the prosecutor, was the social research relied upon by the petitioner said to have "proved the wrong proposition"? Petitioner sought to challenge the exclusion for cause of the "guilt phase includables" (group 1a in Figure 5.1). If the challenge had succeeded, should those members of the "automatic death penalty" group (group 5) who are capable of an impartial decision as to guilt also not be excluded?

3. The California death-qualification procedure seeks a neutral jury (for guilt and sentence determinations) by excluding the "very pro" (group 5) and allowing challenges for cause of the "very anti" (group 1). Is it valid to assume that this method of eliminating the extremes of the attitude spectrum will result in a neutral jury? How would the assumption be tested empirically?

4. A Texas statute disqualified a prospective juror from serving in a capital case "unless he states under oath that the mandatory penalty of death or imprisonment for life will not affect his deliberations on any issue of fact". Texas argued that the resulting injury was neutral because the statute treated evenhandedly both extremes of the attitude spectrum: it permitted the disqualification of "very pro" and "very anti" venirepersons. Would the Texas procedure produce the same jury composition as the California procedure that excludes the "very pro" and allows challenges for cause of the "very anti"? Is the Texas procedure consistent with *Witherspoon*? (See *Adams* v. *Texas,* 1980.)

5.   Though the proposition proved by petitioner (that a *Witherspoon*-qualified jury is conviction-prone) was "wrong" in this case, nonetheless it was concededly "proven." Irrelevant as petitioner's data might have been in the California courts, is it sufficient to dispose on the merits the *Witherspoon* issue in the federal courts? What would be the practical and political implications of the Supreme Court's acceptance of the conviction-proneness claim?

6.   Although the *Witherspoon* and *Ballew* issues "overlap" (footnote 55), they are analytically severable. The former focuses on the relationship between capital punishment attitudes of death-qualified jurors and their guilt or penalty decisions. The latter considers whether the challenged jury procedure (be it jury size or death qualification) adversely affects "group deliberation" and "cross-sectional representativeness" of the jury. In support of the *Ballew* theory, petitioner presented demographic and attitudinal survey evidence showing, for example, that whites and men are more favorably disposed toward capital punishment than blacks and women. What additional empirical evidence did petitioner need to plead successfully the *Ballew* argument?

7.   In ordering that prospective jurors be questioned individually, the court relied on "several theories" from social psychology that suggest that group voir dire produces a state of mind that is conviction-prone and death-penalty-prone. These theories were presented in the context of the one and only study available on the subject at the time (Haney 1980). If, according to the court, the "sound view" is that "one study by itself can rarely justify altering constitutional practice" (footnote 73, referring to Jurow's study), why was it not unsound for the court to rely on Haney's study to change the voir dire procedure?

8.   One "theory" is that venirepersons, as uninformed laypersons, look to the judge and counsel as "knowledgeable and respected figures in the courtroom" for cues about appropriate attitudes and conduct. If judge and counsel are seen dismissing "very anti" venirepersons, the remaining ones would be inclined to think that the law favored conviction and death. But under the California procedure, venirepersons would also observe these respected figures dismissing the "very pro" ones. A symmetrical disapproval on the part of the law could also be inferred, thereby offsetting the prejudicial effect of this psychological process. Haney's videotape showed the disqualification of two "very anti" (confederate) venirepersons, but failed to include a similar disqualification of the "very pro." What other methodological criticisms can be raised of the Haney study? Examine the application of the other theories—formulated in different settings with different subject populations and for different purposes—to the voir dire process. Are the untoward effects of death-qualification the only conclusion that can be drawn from these theories?

9.   Even if group voir dire produces the claimed biasing effects, it does not necessarily follow that individual voir dire is "the most practical and effective procedure." What are alternative procedures?

10.   The mere fact of sequestration might not inhibit the tendencies of prospective jurors to prejudge. Voir dire is not simply an opportunity for counsel to inquire about venirepersons' attitudes toward the death penalty. It is also used as an opportunity to influence them subtly and indirectly before the start of the trial. Questions about punishment before the adjudication of guilt could create an atmosphere impregnated with the suggestion of guilt, regardless of whether the questions are asked individually or in a group. Propose a research design to assess the extent of the reactive effects of voir dire. If found to be present, what remedial measures would you suggest short of abolition of death-qualification?

    For a description of the psychology of the death-qualification process, based on interviews with jurors and observations of capital voir dires, see Haney (1984).

11.   In a memorandum opinion that reviews extensively the same research evidence presented in *Witherspoon* and *Hovey*, plus three or four new studies, Chief Judge Eisele of the U. S. District Court,

Eastern District of Arkansas, reached the opposite conclusion of the *Hovey* court: *Witherspoon*-excludable venirepersons who are capable of deciding impartially the issue of guilt or nonguilt of a capital defendant cannot be excluded from the guilt-determination phase of the trial merely because of their adamant opposition to the penalty itself (*Grisby* v. *Mabry,* 1983). He overturned the murder conviction of one of the petitioners and ordered the state to set this petitioner free or retry him using a bifurcated procedure, whereby a non-death-qualified jury would determine criminal liability and (upon conviction) another death-qualified jury would determine punishment. When dealing with life or death, "the cost-savings arguments of the state [a single jury to determine guilt and penalty is more economical and efficient] simply lose all force" (p. 1321).

Petitioners presented "a plethora of well-documented scientific research" and three expert witnesses (Craig Haney, a social psychologist-lawyer from the University of California at Santa Cruz; Reid Hastie, a social psychologist from Northwestern University; and Edward Bronson, a political scientist-lawyer from California State University at Chico). The experts testified that *Witherspoon*-qualified juries are more likely to convict than juries selected without regard to their views on the death penalty. They based their opinion on the studies cited in *Hovey* and a few new studies. Judge Eisele professed to be "impressed with the professionalism of these experts" (p. 1291). The State of Arkansas objected to the research on the same grounds that the Attorney General of California did. In Arkansas, both the "very anti-death penalty" ("Automatic Life Imprisonment") and the "very pro-death penalty" ("Automatic Death Penalty") venirepersons were excludable for cause, and none of the studies presented dealt with conviction-proneness without the inclusion of the "very pro" group. The response of the petitioners was that the size of this group is exceedingly small. A poll in Arkansas showed that only one percent of the sample believed in automatically imposing the death penalty (upon conviction for a capital offense), regardless of the facts. A Harris Poll in 1981 of a representative, national sample of adults also found that only one percent of the respondents held that opinion (p. 1307; see also Kadane 1984, p. 116). Therefore, the petitioners argued—and the court agreed—that the presence of this group in the simulated jury studies would not alter the results.

The state's expert was "Dr. Shure, a professor of psychology and sociology at U.C.L.A." The court observed that his "credentials are excellent," but "his interest and experience in the behavior of juries has been relatively limited" (p. 1307). He conducted a telephone survey of a nonrepresentative sample of 400 subjects in Los Angeles, specifically in Beverly Hills and neighboring areas which he acknowledged were "wealthy and conservative." After removing the "guilt phase nullifiers," the sample was reduced to 369. Using questions from Ellsworth's study (described in *Hovey*), he classified the remaining sample into three groups: Automatic Life Imprisonment (84 subjects, or 22.8% of the sample), Automatic Death Penalty (123 or 33.3%), and California Death-Qualified (162 or 43.9%). No other study has shown such a high percentage (33.3) of "very pro" respondents. "While having the highest regard for Dr. Shure's sincerity," Judge Eisele wrote, "the court is convinced that he is 'completely off the map' in his estimate of ADPs" (p. 1308).

12.   The inflated figure in the Los Angeles survey could be due to the question posed as well as to the nonrepresentative character of the sample. The following hypothetical case was described to the interviewees: A drug addict breaks into an apartment where a student couple is studying together, shoots the man, rapes and shoots the woman, but the woman survives to remain paralyzed, mute, and partially blind. The interviewee was then asked if he or she would vote for the death penalty in this case if the defendant was found guilty. Those who answered affirmatively were classified in the Automatic Death Penalty group. How should this question be redrafted in order to satisfy the criteria laid down in *Witherspoon?*

13.   In addition to the *Witherspoon* and *Ballew* issues, there is the third issue of whether the death-qualification process results in a jury that is nonrepresentative and therefore violates the cross-sectional requirement established by *Taylor* v. *Louisiana* (1975) and *Duren* v. *Missouri* (1979). The *Hovey* court sidestepped this issue (see footnote 38). In *Taylor* and *Duren*, the Supreme Court held that systematic underrepresentation of women in jury venires violated the cross-sectional principle of the Sixth Amendment right to an impartial jury. To establish a prima facie violation, the challenger must show that (1) a distinctive or cognizable group is (2) excluded or underrepresented in relation to its number in the community, and that (3) the exclusion or underrepresentation is due to systematic procedures in the jury selection process. Once the prima facie case is established, the burden shifts to the state to justify or explain why the procedures produce the exclusion or underrepresentation. In this Sixth Amendment analysis, the impact of the diminished numbers alone is sufficient to show a prima facie violation; proof of purposeful intent by the state to exclude or underrepresent the distinctive group is not necessary, as it would be under the Equal Protection Clause.

Grisby v. *Mabry* also ruled that the death-qualification procedure denied the petitioner a trial by jury representative of a cross-section of the community. Judge Eisele found that the tripartite test of *Duren* was satisfied. *Witherspoon*-excludables (Automatic Life Imprisonment) constitute a cognizable group, the exclusion (zero representation) of which during the guilt-determination phase constitutes a violation of the Sixth Amendment cross-sectional principle. The court again relied heavily on the same research evidence presented in *Hovey* in order to determine distinctiveness or cognizibility. "The evidence shows that '*Witherspoon* excludables' generally share an amalgam of interrelated attitudes toward the criminal justice system which is distinct from that possessed by 'death qualified' jurors" (p. 1283). All three expert witnesses for the petitioners described this shared attitudinal perspective as consisting of hostility toward defendants, favoritism toward the prosecution, bias toward racial minorities, and tepid support for constitutional rights. Moreover, the poll of Arkansas residents showed that death-qualification "clearly impacts more heavily upon blacks and women." About 45% of blacks were "very anti" the death penalty compared to 10% of whites; the figures for women were 21% and 8%, respectively (p. 1283). Judge Eisele was unmoved by the state's argument that the cross-sectional requirement applies only to venires, not to petit juries. *Ballew,* he noted, invalidated five-person juries in part because they undermined the representativeness of the (petit) jury. To mandate representativeness only in jury venires "flies in the face of the policies underlying the cross-section requirement" (p. 1285). Since the state failed to carry the burden of justifying the use of nonrepresentative and partial juries in the guilt-determination phase, the death-qualification process in Arkansas was declared unconstitutional.

5.4.   EIGHTH AMENDMENT CHALLENGES: ROUND ONE
The Social-Political Climate and the Evolution of Death Penalty Litigation

The latter half of the 1960s were turbulent and often sanguinary years. As the civil rights movement waned, upstaged by urban riots, the action shifted from the courtroom to the streets. The nation was consumed by the politics of war and peace. College campuses were wracked by dissent and unrest. Political assassinations and terrorist activities, at home and abroad, became regular front page news. The crime rate reached an all-time high. There were more presidential commissions studying and making recommendations about the incidence of street crime in this decade than in all of the preceding years of the Republic. "Law and order" was the rhetoric of the day. It was not an auspicious environment in which to nurture the ideals of reverence for life.

National polls conducted during this period (cited in *Hovey*) showed that most of the population favored capital punishment. All but about a handful of states authorized its imposition. Nonetheless, the number of executions had been dwindling for some time: 199 in 1935, 76 in 1955, and 7 in 1965. It seemed as though the public was ambivalent about the penalty. On the one hand, it did not want to disavow it completely and therefore opposed legislative repeal; on the other hand, it did not want to apply it on a regular basis. On the whole, there was no great public outcry for or against the death penalty. Except for the occasional, highly publicized capital case, the issue of the death penalty was not a salient or fashionable one. It was just another ripple in the sea of social ferment.

Prior to the sixties, judicial challenges to the death penalty were haphazard. Typically, counsel searched the trial transcript for procedural errors pertaining to the determination of guilt. Appeals, if won, often were on grounds unrelated to the death penalty. For example, in landmark decisions of the early 1930s that for the first time applied the Due Process Clause to state criminal processes, the Supreme Court established the right to appointed counsel for indigent defendants and the right to exclude coerced confessions, both in the context of capital appeals (*Powell* v. *Alabama*, 1932; *Brown* v. *Mississippi*, 1936). Challenges to capital trial procedures or to the death penalty itself were usually last-ditch efforts, filed with the care of a roll of the dice.

The judicial assault began in earnest with *Maxwell*. The Legal Defense Fund avoided a head-on attack on the constitutionality of capital punishment. Starting cautiously, it used ideas that were reasonable extensions of recent decisions. It applied equal protection analysis buttressed by empirical evidence, which it had used successfully in the school desegregation litigation, to the subject of criminal punishment. When it became apparent that the federal courts were unreceptive to the racial discrimination claim, the Fund had to change strategy. It broadened the scope of its representation. It sought to defend not only southern blacks convicted of rape, which were cases that presented the argument for abolition in its most favorable light, but also other death row inmates irrespective of race, crime, and geographical location.

The strategy, described by Meltsner (1973, pp. 106–8), was to raise due process challenges to a host of procedural aspects of capital trials, such as the death-qualification of venirepersons, split verdicts, and discretionary sentencing. The objective was to intervene in as many cases as possible throughout the country in order to delay, if not stop, executions. As these cases slowly wound their way through the various layers of appeal, the postponement of executions would create a logjam in death rows. If all the procedural challenges proved unsuccessful, there remained ultimately the Eighth Amendment challenge to the penalty itself. If that, too, proved unsuccessful and executions were resumed, the effect of this "moratorium strategy" would be to set the stage for a "blood bath" that nobody wanted (p. 107). Few state officials, the Fund reasoned, would want to preside over mass executions, especially in light of the decreasing frequency with which death sentences had been carried out in recent years. On the other hand, if the procedural appeals were fruitful, the death sentences (and maybe even the convictions) would be reversed. This purchased time for capital convicts. Legislatures would have to enact new procedures that survive constitutional scrutiny, and abolitionist forces could further delay or block their passage. Once the procedures were implemented, there was always a chance that the death penalty might not be reimposed at the resentencing. In short, the strategy was designed to bring about de facto abolition, if only for an interim period.

By 1971, the series of procedural attacks had come to a dead end. The Supreme Court had sidestepped the death-qualification issue and refused to strike down single verdict trials. The Court also rejected the claim that standardless jury sentencing was so open to caprice and arbitrariness as to constitute a lawless deprivation of life (*McGautha* v. *California*, 1971). The choice of life or death can properly be left to the unfettered discretion of the judge or jury. In any event, drafting standards for sentencing posed nearly "intractable" problems: "To identify before the fact those characteristics of criminal homicides and their perpetrators which call for the death penalty, and to express those characteristics in language which can be fairly understood and applied by the sentencing authority, appear to be tasks which are beyond present human ability" (p. 204).

Finally, after all the procedural challenges were exhausted, the Court gave notice that it would squarely face the issue of the legality of capital punishment itself. In 1971, it granted review to several cases that were eventually decided under the collective title of *Furman* v. *Georgia*. One case involved a violent rape of a 20-year-old woman by a prison escapee; another dealt with an accidental killing of the victim by a mentally deficient burglar; and the third involved the nonaggravated rape of a 65-year-old woman by a mentally deficient 20-year-old. In all three southern cases, the defendants were black and the victims white. (The appeal of a fourth case from California, involving a brutal rape and stabbing death of an elderly woman, was rendered moot when the California Supreme Court in *People* v. *Anderson* (1972) abolished the death penalty on the eve of the Supreme Court's decision. The death penalty was subsequently reinstated in California by public referendum.) The review was limited to the following question: "Does the imposition and carrying out of the death penalty [in these cases] constitute cruel and unusual punishment in violation of the Eighth and Fourteenth Amendments?"

Early Adjudication on the Eighth Amendment

A major hurdle to the substantive challenge is the absence of any language in the text of the Constitution expressly forbidding capital punishment. Several provisions of the Bill of Rights seem to presume its existence. The Fifth Amendment requires indictment by a grand jury for "capital or other infamous crimes" and prohibits double jeopardy of "life or limb." The Fourteenth Amendment bans the deprivation of "life, liberty, or property" without due process, a right that is premised on the availability of the death penalty.

The operative terms of the Eighth Amendment prohibition are vague and elusive. "Cruel and unusual" is a clause with a Delphic quality. It is rooted in the English Bill of Rights of 1689 and the circumstances surrounding its inclusion in the American Bill of Rights in 1789 have been reported by Granucci (1969). The initial language referred to "illegal and cruel" punishments, but in later drafts "cruel and unusual" was used. Historically, it was designed to forbid the excesses of punishment of the Stuart reign. "[T]here is no doubt whatever that in borrowing the language and in including it in the Eighth Amendment, our Founding Fathers intended to outlaw torture and other cruel punishments" (Justice Marshall in *Furman*, p. 318). The framers are also said to have adopted it to ban penalties disproportionate to the offense and penalties not sanctioned by the legal system (Granucci 1969).

Supreme Court decisions on the Eighth Amendment are meager. The entire judicial history that explicates the meaning of "cruel and unusual" can be recounted in a handful of cases. Eighth Amendment claims lay dormant because the clause was not made applicable to the states until 1962 (*Robinson* v. *California*), and because the Court took for granted that it applied only to penalties deemed cruel in 1789. The death penalty was generally assumed to be constitutional, and these few cases implicitly reaffirm it. A brief sketch of the main cases may help to provide a backdrop for *Furman*.

In *Wilkerson* v. *Utah* (1879), the Court for the first time squarely faced the issue of interpreting the meaning of "cruel and unusual." It unanimously upheld the sentence of public execution by musketry imposed upon conviction for premeditated murder. The execution itself, as distinguished from the method of imposition, was not even challenged by the petitioner. About a decade later, in the second Eighth Amendment case, the Court unanimously upheld electrocution as an appropriate means because it is "the most humane and practical method known to modern science of carrying into effect the sentence of death" (*In re Kemmler*, 1890, p. 444). Punishments are not necessarily "cruel" if the legislature prescribed it with a humane purpose. However, "punishments are cruel when they involve torture or a lingering death; but the punishment of death is not cruel within the meaning of that word as used in the Constitution. It implies there is something inhuman and barbarous— something more than the mere extinguishment of life" (p. 447).

Fifty years later, the Court again reviewed not the death penalty itself but the mode of its imposition. In *Louisiana ex rel. Francis* v. *Resweber* (1947), the Court refused to block a second attempt at electrocution when the first attempt, due to an electrical malfunction, failed. Although the bungled execution caused suffering in this one case, the cruelty proscribed is the "cruelty inherent in the method of punishment, not the necessary suffering involved in any method" (p. 464).

In the landmark case of *Weems* v. *United States* (1910), the Court introduced the notion of proportionality into the Eighth Amendment. An American employee of the Philippine government was convicted of falsifying a public document and sentenced under the Philippine Penal Code to fifteen years incarceration at hard labor with chains on ankles and perpetual surveillance. The Court examined the penalty in relation to the crime and pronounced it excessive: "Punishment for crime should be graduated and proportional to [the] offense" (p. 367). For the first time, the Court invalidated a statutorily prescribed penalty, but the Court did not articulate the standards for assessing proportionality.

A final pre-*Furman* case that contributed importantly to the meaning of the Eighth Amendment was *Trop* v. *Dulles* (1958). The denationalization of a native-born American by reason of a conviction by court-martial for wartime desertion was held to be "outside the bounds of traditional penalties," "more primitive than torture," and therefore "constitutionally suspect" (pp. 100, 101). Why loss of citizenship is a fate worse than death, the Court did not say. The plurality opinion recognized that the meaning of the clause changes over time and is not limited to the proscription of the same penalties of some two centuries ago: "[T]he Amendment must draw its meaning from the evolving standards of decency that mark the progress of a maturing society" (p. 101).

In summary, although no decision in over one hundred years of Eighth Amendment adjudication expressly ruled that the death penalty is a constitutional mode of punishment, the Court has stated repeatedly in dicta or implicitly assumed that it is legal. No systematic theory of the meaning of "cruel and unusual" emerges from these cases. The absence of helpful precedents, the elusiveness of the Eighth Amendment language, the presumption of constitutionality that ordinarily attaches to legislation, and the limited role of judicial review all came together to pose a formidable problem for judicial abolition. It was a tenuous base from which to launch the assault of *Furman*.

Round One

FURMAN v. GEORGIA
408 U.S. 238 (1972)

PER CURIAM

... The Court holds that the imposition and carrying out of the death penalty in these cases constitute cruel and unusual punishment in violation of the Eighth and Fourteenth Amendments. The judgment in each case is therefore reversed insofar as it leaves undisturbed the death sentence imposed. . . .

Mr. Justice DOUGLAS, Mr. Justice BRENNAN, Mr. Justice STEWART, Mr. Justice WHITE, and Mr. Justice MARSHALL have filed separate opinions in support of the judgments.

THE CHIEF JUSTICE, Mr. Justice BLACKMUN, Mr. Justice POWELL, and Mr. Justice REHNQUIST have filed separate dissenting opinions.

Mr. Justice DOUGLAS, concurring.

. . . There is increasing recognition of the fact that the basic theme of equal protection is implicit in "cruel and unusual" punishments. "A penalty . . . should be considered 'unusually' imposed if it is administered arbitrarily or discriminatorily." . . . "[T]he extreme rarity with which applicable death penalty provisions are put to use raises a strong inference of arbitrariness." The President's Commission on Law Enforcement and Administration of Justice recently concluded: "Finally there is evidence that the imposition of the death sentence and the exercise of dispensing power by the courts and the executive follow discriminatory patterns. The death sentence is disproportionately imposed and carried out on the poor, the Negro, and the members of unpopular groups."
. . .

[T]hese discretionary statutes are unconstitutional in their operation. They are pregnant with discrimination. . . .

Whether a mandatory death penalty would otherwise be constitutional is a question I do not reach. . . .

Mr. Justice BRENNAN, concurring.

The question presented in these cases is whether death is today a punishment for crime that is "cruel and unusual." . . .

The right to be free of cruel and unusual punishments, like the other guarantees of the Bill of Rights, "may not be submitted to a vote; [it] depend[s] on the outcome of no elections." "The very purpose of a Bill of Rights was to withdraw certain subjects from the vicissitudes of political controversy, to place them beyond the reach of majorities and officials and to establish them as legal principles to be applied by the courts." West Virginia State Board of Education v. Barnette, 319 U.S. 624 (1943). . . .

We know "that the words of the [Clause] are not precise, and that their scope is not static." We know, therefore, that the Clause "must draw its meaning from the evolving standards of decency that mark the progress of a maturing society." [Trop v. Dulles] . . .

At bottom . . . the Cruel and Unusual Punishments Clause prohibits the infliction of uncivilized and inhuman punishments. The State, even as it punishes, must treat its members with respect for their intrinsic worth as human beings. A punishment is "cruel and unusual," therefore, if it does not comport with human dignity.

The primary principle is that a punishment must not be so severe as to be degrading to the dignity of human beings. ["The barbaric punishments condemned by history," for example, torture,] . . . treat members of the human race as nonhumans, as objects to be toyed with and discarded. They are thus inconsistent with the fundamental premise of the Clause that even the vilest criminal remains a human being possessed of common human dignity. . . .

[The second principle is] that the State must not arbitrarily inflict a severe punishment. This principle derives from the notion that the State does not respect human dignity when, without reason, it inflicts upon some people a severe punishment that it does not inflict upon others. . . .

A third principle inherent in the Clause is that a severe punishment must not be unacceptable to contemporary society. Rejection by society, of course, is a strong indication that a severe punishment does not comport with human dignity. . . .

The final principle inherent in the Clause is that a severe punishment must not be excessive. A punishment is excessive under this principle if it is unnecessary. . . . If there is a significantly less severe punishment for which the punishment is inflicted, the punishment inflicted is unnecessary and therefore excessive. . . .

[These principles] are . . . interrelated, and in most cases it will be their convergence that will justify the conclusion that a punishment is "cruel and unusual." The test, then, will ordinarily be a cumulative one. . . .

I will analyze the punishment of death in terms of the principles set out above. . . .

Death is today an unusually severe punishment, unusual in its pain, in its finality, and in its enormity. No other existing punishment is comparable to death in terms of physical and mental suffering. Although our information is not conclusive, it appears that there is no method available that guarantees an immediate and painless death. . . .

["I . . . turn to the second principle":] There has been a steady decline in the infliction of this punishment in every decade since the 1930's, the earliest period

for which accurate statistics are available. In the 1930's, executions averaged 167 per year; in the 1940's, the average was 128; in the 1950's, it was 72; and in the years 1960–1962, it was 48. There have been a total of 46 executions since then, 36 of them in 1963–1964. Yet our population and the number of capital crimes committed have increased greatly over the past four decades. The contemporary rarity of the infliction of this punishment is thus the end result of a long-continued decline. . . .

When a country of over 200 million people inflicts an unusually severe punishment no more than 50 times a year, the inference is strong that the punishment is not being regularly and fairly applied. . . .

[The third principle:] I cannot add to my Brother MARSHALL's comprehensive treatment of the English and American history of this punishment. I emphasize, however, one significant conclusion that emerges from that history. From the beginning of our Nation, the punishment of death has stirred acute controversy. . . . At bottom, the battle has been waged on moral grounds. The country has debated whether a society for which the dignity of the individual is the supreme value can, without a fundamental inconsistency, follow the practice of deliberately putting some of its members to death. . . .

The progressive decline in, and the current rarity of, the infliction of death demonstrate that our society seriously questions the appropriateness of this punishment today. The States point out that many legislatures authorize death as the punishment for certain crimes and that substantial segments of the public, as reflected in opinion polls and referendum votes, continue to support it. Yet the availability of this punishment through statutory authorization, as well as the polls and referenda, which amount simply to approval of that authorization, simply underscores the extent to which our society has in fact rejected this punishment. When an unusually severe punishment is authorized for wide-scale application but not, because of society's refusal, inflicted save in a few instances, the inference is compelling that there is a deep-seated reluctance to inflict it. Indeed, the likelihood is great that the punishment is tolerated only because of its disuse. The objective indicator of society's view of an unusually severe punishment is what society does with it, and today society will inflict death upon only a small sample of the eligible criminals. . . .

The final principle to be considered is that an unusually severe and degrading punishment may not be excessive in view of the purposes for which it is inflicted. . . .

The [State's] . . . argument is that the threat of death prevents the commission of capital crimes because it deters potential criminals who would not be deterred by the threat of imprisonment. . . .

Proponents of this argument necessarily admit that its validity depends upon the existence of a system in which the punishment of death is invariably and swiftly imposed. Our system, of course, satisfies neither condition. A rational person contemplating a murder or rape is confronted, not with the certainty of a speedy death, but with the slightest possibility that he will be executed in the distant future. The risk of death is remote and improbable; in contrast, the risk of long-term imprisonment is near and great. In short, whatever the speculative validity of the assumption that the threat of death is a superior deterrent, there is no reason to believe that as currently administered the punishment of death is necessary to deter the commission of capital crimes. Whatever might be the case were all or substantially all eligible criminals quickly put to death, unverifiable possibilities are an insufficient basis upon which to conclude that the threat of death today has any greater deterrent efficacy than the threat of imprisonment. . . .

In sum, the punishment of death is inconsistent with all four principles. . . .

Mr. Justice STEWART, concurring.

. . . [A]t least two of my Brothers have concluded that the infliction of the death penalty is constitutionally impermissible in all circumstances under the Eighth and Fourteenth Amendments. Their case is a strong one. But I find it unnecessary to reach the ultimate question they would decide. . . .

These death sentences are cruel and unusual in the same way that being struck by lightning is cruel and unusual. For, of all the people convicted of rapes and murders in 1967 and 1968, many just as reprehensible as these, the petitioners are among a capriciously selected random handful upon whom the sentence of death has in fact been imposed. My concurring Brothers have demonstrated that, if any basis can be discerned for the selection of these few to be sentenced to die, it is the constitutionally impermissible basis of race. But racial discrimination has not been proved, and I put it to one side. I simply conclude that the Eighth and Fourteenth Amendments cannot tolerate the infliction of a sentence of death under legal systems that permit this unique penalty to be so wantonly and so freakishly imposed. . . .

Mr. Justice WHITE, concurring.

. . . In joining the Court's judgments . . . I do not at all intimate that the death penalty is unconstitutional *per se* or that there is no system of capital punishment that would comport with the Eighth Amendment. That question, ably argued by several of my Brethren, is not presented by these cases and need not be decided. . . .

[A] major goal of the criminal law—to deter others by punishing the convicted criminal—would not be substantially served where the penalty is so seldom invoked that it ceases to be the credible threat essential to influence the conduct of others. For present purposes I accept the morality and utility of punishing one person to influence another. . . . But common sense and experience tell us that seldom-enforced laws become ineffective measures for controlling human conduct and that the death penalty, unless imposed with sufficient frequency, will make little contribution to deterring those crimes for which it may be exacted.

The imposition and execution of the death penalty are obviously cruel in the dictionary sense. But the penalty has not been considered cruel and unusual punishment in the constitutional sense because it was thought justified by the social ends it was deemed to serve. At the moment that it ceases realistically to further these purposes, however, . . . its imposition would then be the pointless and needless extinction of life with only marginal contributions to any discernible social or public purposes. A penalty with such negligible returns to the State would be patently excessive and cruel and unusual punishment violative of the Eighth Amendment. . . .

Mr. Justice MARSHALL, concurring.

These three cases present the question whether the death penalty is a cruel and unusual punishment. . . .

[Justice Marshall began by examining the historical origins of the Eighth Amendment and found its progenitor contained in the English Bill of Rights (1689). "[T]he history of the clause clearly establishes that it was intended to prohibit cruel punishments." However, the word "unusual" was "inadvertent" in the English law, and he found nothing in the history to give flesh to its intended meaning.

He then turned to the few American cases to consider the construction given to the meaning of "cruel" by the Supreme Court, including *Wilkerson*, *In re Kemmler*, *Weems*, and *Trop* (see the beginning of this section, 5.4). From these cases, Justice Marshall extracted some principles to "serve as a beacon to an enlightened decision." The general principle is that the meaning of the Eighth Amendment must derive from "evolving standards of de-

cency," citing *Trop*. Thus, "a penalty that was permissible at one time in our Nation's history is not necessarily permissible today." In addition, he proposed two specific principles. First, "a penalty may be cruel and unusual because it is excessive and serves no valid legislative purpose." Second, "where a punishment is not excessive and serves a valid legislative purpose, it may still be invalid if popular sentiment abhors it." He conceded that no prior cases supported this last principle, though "the very notion of changing values requires that we recognize its existence." Ed.'s note.]

In order to assess whether or not death is an excessive or unnecessary penalty, it is necessary to consider the reasons why a legislature might select it as punishment for one or more offenses, and examine whether less severe penalties would satisfy the legitimate legislative wants as well as capital punishment. . . .

There are [several] purposes conceivably served by capital punishment [including retribution and deterrence]. . . .

The concept of retribution is one of the most misunderstood in all of our criminal jurisprudence. . . .

The fact that the State may seek retribution against those who have broken its laws does not mean that retribution may then become the State's sole end in punishing. Our jurisprudence has always accepted deterrence in general, deterrence of individual recidivism, isolation of dangerous persons, and rehabilitation as proper goals of punishment. Retaliation, vengeance, and retribution have been roundly condemned as intolerable aspirations for a government in a free society. . . . [T]he Eighth Amendment is our insulation from our baser selves. The "cruel and unusual" language limits the avenues through which vengeance can be channeled. . . . [R]etribution for its own sake is improper.

The most hotly contested issue regarding capital punishment is whether it is better than life imprisonment as a deterrent to crime. . . .

Abolitionists attempt to disprove . . . [the deterrence rationale] by amassing statistical evidence to demonstrate that there is no correlation between criminal activity and the existence or nonexistence of a capital sanction. Almost all of the evidence involves the crime of murder, since murder is punishable by death in more jurisdictions than are other offenses, and almost 90% of all executions since 1930 have been pursuant to murder convictions.

Thorsten Sellin, one of the leading authorities on capital punishment, has urged that if the death penalty deters prospective murderers, the following hypotheses should be true:

"(a) Murders should be less frequent in states that have the death penalty than in those that have abolished it, other factors being equal. . . .

"(b) Murders should increase when the death penalty is abolished and should decline when it is restored.

"(c) The deterrent effect should be greatest and should therefore affect murder rates most powerfully in those communities where the crime occurred and its consequences are most strongly brought home to the population.

"(d) Law enforcement officers would be safer from murderous attacks in states that have the death penalty than in those without it."[99]

Sellin's evidence indicates that not one of these propositions is true. . . .

There is but one conclusion that can be drawn from all of this—*i.e.*, the death penalty is an excessive and unnecessary punishment that violates the Eighth Amendment. The statistical evidence is not convincing beyond all doubt, but it is persuasive. It is not improper at this point to take judicial notice of the fact that for more than 200 years men have labored to demonstrate that capital punishment serves no purpose that life imprisonment could not serve equally well. And they have done so with great success. Little, if any, evidence has been adduced to prove the contrary. The point has now been reached at which deference to the legislatures is tantamount to abdication of our judicial roles as factfinders, judges, and ultimate arbiters of the Constitution. We know that at some point the presumption of constitutionality accorded legislative acts gives way to a realistic assessment of those acts. This point comes when there is sufficient evidence available so that judges can determine, not whether the legislature acted wisely, but whether it had any rational basis whatsoever for acting. We have this evidence before us now. There is no rational basis for concluding that capital punishment is not excessive. It therefore violates the Eighth Amendment.

In addition, even if capital punishment is not excessive, it nonetheless violates the Eighth Amendment because it is morally unacceptable to the people of the United States at this time in their history.

While a public opinion poll obviously is of some assistance in indicating public acceptance or rejection of a specific penalty, its utility cannot be very great. This is because whether or not a punishment is cruel and unusual depends, not on whether its mere mention "shocks the conscience and sense of justice of the people," but on whether people who were fully informed as to the purposes of the penalty and its liabilities would find the penalty shocking, unjust, and unacceptable.[145]

---

[99]T. Sellin, The Death Penalty, A Report for the Model Penal Code Project of the American Law Institute (ALI) 21 (1959).

[145]. . . It is therefore imperative for constitutional purposes to attempt to discern the probable opinion of an informed electorate.

In other words, the question with which we must deal is not whether a substantial proportion of American citizens would today, if polled, opine that capital punishment is barbarously cruel, but whether they would find it to be so in the light of all information presently available. . . .

Thus, I believe that the great mass of citizens would conclude on the basis of the material already considered that the death penalty is immoral and therefore unconstitutional. . . .

Mr. Chief Justice BURGER, with whom Mr. Justice BLACKMUN, Mr. Justice POWELL, and Mr. Justice REHNQUIST, join, dissenting.

. . . In the 181 years since the enactment of the Eighth Amendment, not a single decision of this Court has cast the slightest shadow of a doubt on the constitutionality of capital punishment. . . . Nonetheless, the Court has now been asked to hold that a punishment clearly permissible under the Constitution at the time of its adoption and accepted as such by every member of the Court until today, is suddenly so cruel as to be incompatible with the Eighth Amendment. . . .

A punishment is inordinately cruel, in the sense we must deal with it in these cases, chiefly as perceived by the society so characterizing it. . . . "The Amendment must draw its meaning from the evolving standards of decency that mark the progress of a maturing society." . . . [I]n a democratic society legislatures, not courts, are constituted to respond to the will and consequently the moral values of the people. . . . The critical fact is that this Court has never had to hold that a mode of punishment authorized by a domestic legislature was so cruel as to be fundamentally at odds with our basic notions of decency. Judicial findings of impermissible cruelty have been limited, for the most part, to offensive punishments devised without specific authority by prison officials, not by legislatures. . . . Whether or not provable, and whether or not true at all times, in a democracy the legislative judgment is presumed to embody the basic standards of decency prevailing in the society. . . .

There are no obvious indications that capital punishment offends the conscience of society to such a degree that our traditional deference to the legislative judgment must be abandoned. It is not a punishment such as burning at the stake that everyone would ineffably find to be repugnant to all civilized standards. Nor is it a punishment so roundly condemned that only a few aberrant legislatures have retained it on the statute books. Capital punishment is authorized by statute in 40 States. . . .

[It is argued] that the number of cases in which the death penalty is imposed, as compared with the number of cases in which it is statutorily available, reflects a general revulsion toward the penalty. . . . The selectivity of juries in imposing the punishment of death is properly viewed as a refinement on, rather than a repudiation of, the statutory authorization for that penalty. . . . Given the general awareness that death is no longer a routine punishment for the crimes for which it is made available, it is hardly surprising that juries have been increasingly meticulous in their imposition of the penalty. But to assume from the mere fact of relative infrequency that only a random assortment of pariahs are sentenced to death, is to cast grave doubt on the basic integrity of our jury system. . . . [I]f selective imposition evidences a rejection of capital punishment in those cases where it is not imposed, it surely evidences a correlative affirmation of the penalty in those cases where it is imposed.

Capital punishment has also been attacked as violative of the Eighth Amendment on the ground that it is not needed to achieve legitimate penal aims and is thus "unnecessarily cruel." . . . Those favoring abolition find no evidence that [the death penalty is a superior deterrent]. Those favoring retention start from the intuitive notion that capital punishment should act as the most effective deterrent and note that there is no convincing evidence that it does not. Escape from this empirical stalemate is sought by placing the burden of proof on the States and concluding that they have failed to demonstrate that capital punishment is a more effective deterrent than life imprisonment. . . . [T]o shift the burden to the States is to provide an illusory solution to an enormously complex problem. If it were proper to put the States to the test of demonstrating the deterrent value of capital punishment, we could just as well ask them to prove the need for life imprisonment or any other punishment. Yet I know of no convincing evidence that life imprisonment is a more effective deterrent than 20 years' imprisonment, or even that a $10 parking ticket is a more effective deterrent than a $5 parking ticket. In fact, there are some who go so far as to challenge the notion that any punishments deter crime. If the States are unable to adduce convincing proof rebutting such assertions, does it then follow that all punishments are suspect as being "cruel and unusual" within the meaning of the Constitution? . . .

The critical factor in the concurring opinions of both Mr. Justice STEWART and Mr. Justice WHITE is the infrequency with which the penalty is imposed. [This factor shows that] . . . juries and judges have failed to exercise their sentencing discretion in acceptable fashion. . . .

This claim of arbitrariness is not only lacking in empirical support, but also it manifestly fails to establish that the death penalty is a "cruel and unusual" punishment. The Eighth Amendment was included in the Bill of Rights to assure that certain types of punishments would never be imposed, not to channelize the sentencing process. The approach of these concurring opinions has no antecedent in the Eighth Amendment cases. It is essentially and exclusively a procedural due process argument.

This ground of decision is plainly foreclosed as well as misplaced. Only one year ago, in McGautha v. California, the Court upheld the prevailing system of sentencing in capital cases. . . .

Although the Court's decision in *McGautha* was technically confined to the dictates of the Due Process Clause of the Fourteenth Amendment, rather than the Eighth Amendment as made applicable to the States through the Due Process Clause of the Fourteenth Amendment, it would be disingenuous to suggest that today's ruling has done anything less than overrule *McGautha* in the guise of an Eighth Amendment adjudication. . . .

[The dissenting opinion of Mr. Justice Blackmun is omitted.]

Mr. Justice POWELL, with whom THE CHIEF JUSTICE, Mr. Justice BLACKMUN and Mr. Justice REHNQUIST join, dissenting.

. . . [The Court's judgment has a "shattering effect"] on the root principles of *stare decisis*, federalism, judicial restraint and—most importantly—separation of powers.

The Court rejects as not decisive the clearest evidence that the Framers of the Constitution and the authors of the Fourteenth Amendment believed that those documents posed no barrier to the death penalty. The Court also brushes aside an unbroken line of precedent reaffirming the heretofore virtually unquestioned constitutionality of capital punishment. . . . The Court's judgment not only wipes out laws presently in existence, but denies to Congress and to the legislatures of the 50 States the power to adopt new policies contrary to the policy selected by the Court. . . .

Petitioners' contentions are premised . . . on the long-accepted view that concepts embodied in the Eighth and Fourteenth Amendments evolve. They [argue] . . . that prevailing standards of human decency have progressed to the final point of requiring the Court to hold, for all cases and for all time, that capital punishment is unconstitutional. . . .

Any attempt to discern contemporary standards of decency . . . must take into account several overriding considerations which petitioners choose to discount or ignore. In a democracy the first indicator of the public's attitude must always be found in the legislative judgments of the people's chosen representatives. Forty states . . . still authorize the death penalty.
. . .

Any attempt to discern . . . where the prevailing standards of decency lie must take careful account of the jury's response to the question of capital punishment. During the 1960's juries returned in excess of a thousand death sentences, a rate of approximately two per week. Whether it is true that death sentences were returned in less than 10% of the cases as petitioners estimate or whether some higher percentage is more accurate, these totals simply do not support petitioners' assertion at oral argument that "the death penalty is virtually unanimously repudiated and condemned by the conscience of contemporary society." . . .

Much also is made of the undeniable fact that the death penalty has a greater impact on the lower economic strata of society, which include a relatively higher percentage of persons of minority racial and ethnic group backgrounds. . . .

Certainly the claim is justified that this criminal sanction falls more heavily on the relatively impoverished and underprivileged elements of society. The "have-nots" in every society always have been subject to greater pressure to commit crimes and to fewer constraints than their more affluent fellow citizens. This is, indeed, a tragic byproduct of social and economic deprivation. . . . The root causes of the higher incidence of criminal penalties on "minorities and the poor" will not be cured by abolishing the system of penalties. Nor, indeed, could any society have a viable system of criminal justice if sanctions were abolished or ameliorated because most of those who commit crimes happen to be underprivileged. The basic problem results not from the penalties imposed for criminal conduct but from social and economic factors that have plagued humanity since the beginning of recorded history, frustrating all efforts to create in any country at any time the perfect society in which there are no "poor," no "minorities" and no "underprivileged." The causes underlying this problem are unrelated to the constitutional issue before the Court. . . .

It seems to me that the sweeping judicial action undertaken today reflects a basic lack of faith and confidence in the democratic process. Many may regret, as I do, the failure of some legislative bodies to address the capital punishment issue with greater frankness or effectiveness. Many might decry their failure either to abolish the penalty entirely or selectively, or to establish standards for its enforcement. But impatience with the slowness, and even the unresponsiveness of legislatures is no justification for judicial intrusion upon their historic powers. . . .

[The dissenting opinion of Mr. Justice Rehnquist, with whom the Chief Justice, Mr. Justice Blackmun, and Mr. Justice Powell joined, is omitted.]

NOTES AND QUESTIONS

1.   The decision, by the narrowest of margins, was against almost all expectation. Given the social-political cross-currents of the day and the legal hurdles faced by the abolitionists, "it [is] not overstating

the matter to say that [the] victory for abolition would rank among the greatest surprises in American legal history" (Meltsner 1973, p. 287).

The brief "per curiam" ("for the Court") opinion reversed the death penalty in the three cases (and similar orders were entered in more than one hundred death penalty appeals then pending before the Court), but gave no reasoning for the decision. Each of the five concurring Justices gave separate reasons. Each read the cloudy historical and empirical record in somewhat different but not inconsistent manner. Compared, for example, with the unanimous opinion in *Brown I*, the absence of a commonly agreed basis for abolition dilutes the moral force of the decision and renders dubious its precedential value.

How does each of the five majority Justices define the issue in the case? What is the broadest ground of decision that underlies the five opinions? What are the implications for the meaning of the Eighth Amendment of an opinion that analyzes the legality of the death penalty solely in terms of "cruel," or of "unusual," or of both "cruel *and* unusual"?

2.   From the fact that executions are infrequently carried out, some of the majority Justices infer that they are arbitrary and "unusual." There are different kinds of arbitrariness in punishment: random selection (Justice Stewart's ingenious metaphor of a strike of lightning), purposeful selection based upon an invidious characteristic such as race, and systematic selection based upon nonsuspect criteria such as geographic location of the capital trial. In which sense is the death penalty "unusual" according to the different Justices?

The deterrence rationale of capital punishment is essentially the utilitarian argument that executions are tolerated as a means to a greater social good, namely, the prevention of future crime. Each execution trades a guilty person's life for several innocent persons' lives. The executed are drawn disproportionately from the poor and minorities. However, crime victims, too, are drawn disproportionately from these social categories, so it is their lives that are expected to be saved by the death penalty. Thus, is rough justice done even if executions are unequally applied?

3.   The Chief Justice argues that the paucity of executions need not necessarily lead to the inference of arbitrariness. It is also possible that juries and state officials exercise selectivity of choice. They err on the side of caution and reserve the death penalty for the most egregious transgressions. Infrequency of the sanction could be the antithesis of arbitrariness. How would you empirically test this informed selectivity hypothesis? Even when those executed and those spared are of equal culpability, is there any reason why the sparing and not the execution is wrong?

4.   The Chief Justice describes the opinions of Justices Stewart and White (who cast the swing votes) as consisting of "procedural due process" arguments disguised in Eighth Amendment language. Are there any objections to treating the Eighth Amendment as a repository of other, established constitutional theories?

5.   Does Justice Brennan's four-part test consist merely of hortatory statements or does it include useful standards for defining the meaning of cruel and unusual punishment?

6.   "At bottom," says Justice Brennan, "the battle [over capital punishment] has been waged on moral grounds." What are the competing moral issues that have incited such intense political, judicial, and scholarly debate? Do moral choices implicate an empirical assessment of the deterrent effect of the sanction? Is the question of whether murderers deserve to die the gravamen of the moral decision? Why should executions of convicted criminals (which are relatively infrequent) provoke greater consternation than shootings by police of fleeing, suspected criminals (which are relatively more common)? The very choice of the death penalty as a subject for debate reflects normative judgments—otherwise, why not divert the enormous resources spent on abolition to the reform of other problems of the criminal justice system (for example, prisons, drug abuse) that annually claim more people than the gas chamber? See Berns (1980) and Lempert (1981) for opposing positions on the moral basis of capital punishment.

7.   How would you respond to the Chief Justice's trenchant assertion that if capital punishment is excessive vis-à-vis life imprisonment, then logically Justice Marshall would also have to show—which he fails to do—that a 10-year prison sentence is excessive vis-à-vis a 5-year sentence, or that a $10 fine is excessive vis-à-vis a $5 fine?

8.   Whereas none of the Justices in the majority joined another one in concurrence, the four dissenters—all Nixon appointees—were unanimous in their agreement with each other's position. They took some shots at the opinions of the majority and scored some hits, exposing holes in the reasoning of the concurrences. Even at their most scathing, however, the dissenters said little in favor of the death penalty.

A major complaint of the dissenters is that the majority trespassed upon the policy-making domain of those directly responsive to the electorate. Eighth Amendment adjudication places the Court in a difficult position. On the one hand, the role of judicial review is limited to determining whether the challenged statute is reasonably related to permissible legislative ends, or whether it infringes upon protected interests. On the other hand, to decide whether a punishment is cruel and unusual, the Court must look at "evolving standards of decency." The determination of whether a law is decent or otherwise comports with community values would seem to be a function of the legislature, not the judiciary, because of the former's representative character. In adjudicating the constitutionality of the death penalty, the Court is called upon to make the kind of judgment ordinarily reserved to another branch of government. An eloquent attempt at resolving these conflicting functions was made by Justice Frankfurter in a different context:

> While the language of the Constitution does not change, the changing circumstances of a progressive society for which it was designed yield new and fuller import to its meaning. . . . This is the inescapable judicial task in giving substantive content, legally enforced through the Due Process Clause, and it is a task ultimately committed to this Court. It must not be an exercise of whim or will. It must be an overriding judgment founded on something much deeper and more justifiable than personal preference. . . . It must rest on fundamental presuppositions rooted in history to which widespread acceptance may fairly be attributed. Such a judgment must be arrived at in a spirit of humility when it encounters the judgment of the state's highest court. But, in the end, the judgment cannot be escaped—the judgment of this Court. [Concurring in *Sweezy* v. *New Hampshire*, 1957, pp. 266–67]

How vulnerable are the various opinions of the majority Justices to the criticism that they fail to respect the political processes of the states while reviewing the validity of death penalty legislation?

9.   Are the standards of review invoked in substantive due process and equal protection cases—"mere rationality" and "strict scrutiny" under the traditional two-tiered analysis—applicable to Eighth Amendment analysis? Do the concurring opinions of the majority and the dissenting opinions state which party has the burden of proof and what the quantum of that proof is in the review of the constitutionality of the death penalty? See generally Radin (1978) and Bice (1977).

10.   The majority opinions, however problematic they were jurisprudentially, had a clear and immediate impact on the administration of capital punishment. Legislators had to rewrite capital statutes and over 600 death row inmates were spared of execution. The broader repercussions of *Furman* for the criminal justice system are more difficult to foresee. What effects would you anticipate that abolition would have on prosecutorial charging practices, plea bargaining, trial rates, sentencing practices, prison reform, and parole policies?

11.   Legislators had basically two options after *Furman*. One was to enact mandatory death penalty statutes, an approach that most American jurisdictions had abandoned in the last century. What legal, ethical, and political questions are raised by mandatory sentencing? The other was to purge the claimed arbitrariness in sentencing by either formulating standards for the jury or judge to follow (a task which the Court had described the preceding year in *McGautha* v. *California* as "beyond present human ability" (p. 204)), or by defining narrowly the types of crimes for which the death penalty is authorized (for example, for the murder of a police officer in the line of duty). Under what circumstances would a legislative scheme of precisely defined capital offenses and/or of sentencing standards still be felled by the *Furman* ax?

Social Research on "Evolving Standards of Decency"

PUBLIC OPINION ON THE DEATH PENALTY

Neil Vidmar and Phoebe Ellsworth

. . .

The purpose of this Article is to assess public attitudes towards capital punishment by examining public opinion polls and other social science studies bearing on this issue. One goal is to provide legislative and judicial decisionmakers with a sounder social science base for evaluating public opinion about the death penalty. Another goal is to note the gaps in our knowledge of this subject, and to frame the sort of questions that need to be asked in future research. . . .

Our literature review is divided into [several] substantive areas. . . .

GENERAL SUPPORT FOR CAPITAL PUNISHMENT

. . . The overwhelming majority of the polls [from 1936 to 1969] have asked only general questions about the death penalty for murder. . . . The most recent poll show[s] 59% of the people supporting capital punishment. . . .

SUPPORT FOR CAPITAL PUNISHMENT UNDER SPECIFIC CIRCUMSTANCES

[A nationwide Harris Survey of June 1973 is] the most comprehensive survey of public attitudes toward the death penalty that we found in our literature search. The survey found that in response to the question, "Do you believe in capital punishment (the death penalty) or are you opposed to it?" 59 percent of the respondents gave support to capital punishment.

However, in another series of questions, respondents were given a list of crimes and asked whether they felt that all persons convicted of the crime should get the death penalty, that no one should get the death penalty, or that it "should depend on the circumstances of the case and the character of the person." The crimes and percentages of respondents endorsing each alternative are described in Table 1. It is clear that no more than 41 percent of the respondents favored a mandatory death sentence for any single type of the listed crimes. The other respondents were either opposed to capital punishment or felt it should be used in a discretionary way. . . .

EXPRESSED REASONS FOR FAVORING THE DEATH PENALTY

The most detailed and comprehensive inquiry into various common justifications for support of the death penalty was made in the 1973 Harris Survey. One question in that survey asked respondents whether they felt the death penalty was more effective as a deterrent than was a sentence of life imprisonment. Fifty-six percent of those interviewed indicated they felt it was more effective, while 32 percent felt that it was not. Among the proponents of capital punishment, 76 percent felt that it was more effective than a life sentence, but only 29 percent of capital punishment opponents felt that it was more effective. While this finding suggests the possibility that belief in the deterrent efficacy of capital punishment may be at least partially responsible for public support, there is one caveat that must be considered; expressed belief in deterrent efficacy may be seen by proponents as the most socially acceptable justification for favoring the death penalty and thus may be used as a cover for other, less acceptable reasons.

TABLE 1

Responses to June 1973 Harris Survey: Question on Who Should Get the Death Penalty

Crime	Response			
	All	**No One**	**Depends**	**Not Sure**
Killing policeman or prison guard	41%	17%	38%	4%
First degree murder	28	16	53	3
Skyjacking	27	27	41	5
Rape	19	27	50	4
Mugging	9	41	43	7
Bank robbery	8	43	43	6

Source, Harris Survey.

Additional questions on the Harris survey lend strong support to the hypothesis that for many respondents a belief in deterrence is not the more fundamental reason for favoring capital punishment. In one question respondents were asked, "[s]uppose it could be proved to your satisfaction that the death penalty was not more effective than long prison sentences in keeping other people from committing crimes such as murder, would you be in favor of the death penalty or would you be opposed to it?" Fifty-four percent of those who favored capital punishment said they would favor capital punishment even if it had no deterrent effect. . . .

Thus, these different ways of assessing reasons why people favor the death penalty yielded data that suggest that retribution may be an important motive in capital punishment attitudes. Taken by themselves, the data do not allow us to compare precisely the relative importance of retributive versus deterrence reasons for favoring the death penalty. . . .

LEVELS OF DEATH PENALTY ATTITUDES

Responses to generally phrased questions asking about support for, or opposition to, the death penalty do not reveal whether the view is embraced solely in an abstract manner without regard to how the person would feel or behave in more concrete situations. A person who says he favors the death penalty may be unwilling to see it carried out when faced with an actual execution or threat of execution. . . .

The 1973 Harris survey also indicates that respondents' self-predicted behavior as jurors is different than what might be implied from their general levels of support or opposition. Respondents were asked to assume that they were being considered as possible jurors in a trial where the defendant, if found guilty, would automatically be sentenced to death. Although 59 percent of them had previously expressed approval of the death penalty for certain crimes (with 31 percent opposed and 10 percent not sure) only 39 percent felt they could always vote guilty if guilt were proven for a crime that mandated the death sentence, another 33 percent could not say whether they would vote guilty even if guilt were proven, 16 percent said they would never vote guilty, and 12 percent were not sure. Thus, the basic findings are similar to those of Jurow. . . .

We should also note that the rather sharp difference in support for capital punishment at the general level and support for it in more specific circumstances is consistent with a hypothesis that some people may favor the *idea* of capital punishment either without realizing or without accepting its implications. . . .

TENTATIVE CONCLUSIONS

Much of the research on public opinion and capital punishment is not useful in the post-*Furman* era. Most of the polls have been superficial rather than comprehensive; generally, the questions have been asked with no attempt to discover why a respondent took a given position, how strongly he felt about his opinion, what kind of information he might use to justify his response, or whether he was really trying to substitute socially desirable answers for his own beliefs. Nevertheless, examination of the existing body of research does suggest a few tentative [conclusions]. . . .

First, despite the increasing approval for the death penalty reflected in opinion polls during the last decade, there is evidence that many people supporting the general idea of capital punishment want its administration to depend on the circumstances of the case, the character of the defendant, or both, rather than on the kind of nondiscretionary death penalty permissible under *Furman*.

Second, there is evidence that at least some of the support for capital punishment may stem from motives that are inconsistent with contemporary legislative and judicial goals. Some people may support the death penalty primarily for motives of retribution. . . .

NOTES AND QUESTIONS

---

1. According to several Justices in *Furman*, one "objective indicator" of prevailing "standards of decency" is public opinion. National polls on capital punishment are not, of course, tantamount to a plebiscite on the issue, since the very purpose of the Bill of Rights, as Justice Brennan noted, is to place certain subjects "beyond the reach of majorities." Nonetheless, polls are "a source of evidence" of "current social values," according to the Chief Justice. Justice Marshall goes so far as to say it is "imperative for constitutional purposes" to ascertain the attitudes of an "informed electorate."

2. A quick overview of the concept of opinion or attitude may be helpful. This concept is "the keystone in the edifice of American social psychology"; indeed, many "define social psychology as the scientific study of attitudes" (Allport 1967, p. 3). The traditional view of attitude as a learned response to some stimulus is that it consists of three components: a cognitive or knowledge component (a set of beliefs or information about the stimulus); an affective or emotional component (an evaluation—positive-negative, like-dislike—of the stimulus); and a motivational component (a state of readiness that predisposes one to act with respect to the stimulus). The enduring organization of these cognitive, affective, and dispositional processes vis-à-vis a stimulus is called an attitude or opinion.

It is well established in the research literature that attitudes are not perfectly correlated with behavior. Although a predisposition to respond (also described as incipient action or behavioral intention) is part of what makes up an attitude, it does not always or consistently predict how a person, in fact, will respond. A classic study in 1934 by LaPierre illustrates this point. A large number of restaurant and hotel proprietors were asked by mail if they would serve a Chinese couple, and the majority said no. However, when the couple actually showed up in these establishments, they were served in almost every instance (in Collins 1970, pp. 80–83).

Attitudes sometimes predict conduct and sometimes not, depending on different factors. The environmental context in which the attitude and the behavior are elicited may influence the relationship. In the LaPierre study, for example, the dress and amicability of the Chinese couple and the type of luggage they carried had as much an effect on the proprietors' actions as did their own attitudes toward the Chinese. The intensity of an attitude is another factor. A fervent opponent of capital punishment is unlikely to ever vote to impose it; a devout Christian Scientist is unlikely to enroll in medical school. On the other hand, an individual who does not feel and believe strongly about these issues is more likely to act in a nonuniform manner depending on the circumstances at hand.

3.   The Vidmar and Ellsworth article notes that polls which inquire about general opinions on the death penalty are "not useful in the post-*Furman* era." The polls usually measure only one component of opinion, the evaluative one. It is simplistic to consider a generalized expression of support or opposition as an indicator of "evolving standards of decency." That evaluation can vary when elicited under particular circumstances, as in the LaPierre study.

The disagreement between the Justices on what are the community attitudes toward the death penalty arises in part from their focus on the different dimensions of the attitude structure. For example, Justice Marshall looked at the relationship between the cognitive and affective components: If persons are informed about the facts of capital punishment, he reasoned, they would certainly oppose it. The dissenting Justices considered only the global evaluations (poll results) and actual conduct (jury sentences). The *Witherspoon* Court focused on the relationship between evaluations of capital punishment and the predisposition to vote in the role of a juror.

Thus, when the Justices refer to "public opinion," they have in mind different meanings or aspects of the concept. Which component or combination of components of the "attitude" toward capital punishment should be the constitutionally relevant indicator of "evolving standards of decency"? Is the substance of these decency standards an empirical issue to be ascertained by examining sophisticated attitude research of the kind proposed by Vidmar and Ellsworth, or is it essentially a normative matter that is beyond factual discernment?

4.   Other studies have validated the distinction between generalized evaluations of the death penalty and one's own potential behavior in a specific instance. Davidow and Lowe (1979) administered Jurow's CPAQ(A) and CPAQ(B) questionnaires (described in the *Hovey* opinion) to over 1600 law students, lawyers, and judges. The (A) version assesses general support or opposition and the (B) version measures predisposition to impose the death sentence if seated on a jury. They found that the majority of respondents in all three groups are able to and do make the distinction. Over three-fourths of those "in favor" or "strongly in favor" of capital punishment said they would still consider all of the penalties provided by the law and the facts and circumstances of the particular case," rather than "usually" or "always" vote for the death penalty when the sanction is legally justified. What implications would you draw from these results and from the Harris survey (described in the Vidmar and Ellsworth article) for the formulation of post-*Furman* capital sentencing legislation?

PUBLIC OPINION, THE DEATH PENALTY, AND THE EIGHTH AMENDMENT: TESTING THE MARSHALL HYPOTHESIS

Austin Sarat and Neil Vidmar

. . .

Our research strategy for this test consisted of three parts. First, we surveyed opinions about the death penalty in a random sample of subjects; next, we introduced experimental manipulations designed to produce "informed" opinion about capital punishment; finally, we re-

Reprinted by permission of the principal author, the publisher, and Dennis and Company. Copyright ©1976 by the *Wisconsin Law Review* [1976 (1976): 171–206].

measured subjects' attitudes to determine whether informed opinions were different from uninformed opinions.

A.   DESIGN AND PROCEDURES

During the spring and summer of 1975 a randomly selected sample of 200 adult residents of Amherst, Massachusetts was interviewed by a trained research team. . . .

Each interview began by presenting subjects with a questionnaire containing 18 statements designed to measure attitudes toward criminal punishment in general and toward various justifications for the death penalty. Three of these items measured the degree to which subjects endorsed retribution as a justification for criminal punishment and formed our "Retribution Scale." A second questionnaire . . . measured knowledge about the death penalty. A third questionnaire assessed support for or opposition to the death penalty by means of a 7-alternative scale ranging from "very strongly favor" to "very strongly oppose" the death penalty. . . .

In the second part of the interview the experimental manipulation was introduced. The heart of Justice Marshall's argument, one recalls, is not simply that people are relatively uninformed about capital punishment but rather, if they were informed, they would be inclined to reject it. We therefore wrote two 1500-word essays describing the kinds of scientific and other information which Marshall considers to be factual and which he thinks is important in making informed judgments about capital punishment. The first essay was concerned with the "Utilitarian" aspects of capital punishment and consisted of summaries of statistical studies, reports of personal experience and arguments about the psychology of deterrence as well as data on the recidivism rate among released murderers. The second, or "Humanitarian," essay discussed, first, the way

capital punishment has typically been applied and administered and, second, the psychological and physical aspects of execution. These essays constituted the substantive core of four information conditions: (1) utilitarian information only, (2) humanitarian information only, (3) utilitarian and humanitarian information combined, and (4) a control condition consisting of an essay about law which was entirely unrelated to death penalty issues. The survey respondents were assigned randomly to one of the four conditions. After an introduction that emphasized the interviewer's desire to familiarize the subject with the various issues involved, each subject was asked to read the materials in the essays carefully and thoughtfully. After reading these materials subjects were again asked about their attitudes toward capital punishment and about their evaluation of its application and effects.

B.   RESULTS

[The authors found a "substantial resemblance" between the death penalty attitudes of their study sample (for example, 54% favored capital punishment to some degree) and those of a larger national sample as shown by a poll. They also found their sample informed about certain aspects of the death penalty (for example, most knew that it was imposed disproportionately on the poor) but not about others (for example, its deterrent effect). But in the "strict sense" that Justice Marshall used the term, "few persons in our sample would be labelled 'informed' about the death penalty." Ed.'s note.]

. . .

INFORMATION AND ATTITUDE CHANGE. The heart of the Marshall hypothesis in *Furman* is that if the public were to be informed about the death penalty, they would find it unjust and immoral and reject it. Therefore, we have tried to test the extent to which death penalty attitudes and beliefs

TABLE 5

Mean Changes in Death Penalty Attitudes in Each Information Condition

	Before	After	Change
Utilitarian	3.36	3.93	.57
Humanitarian	3.52	3.75	.23
Combined	3.40	4.00	.60
Control	3.80	3.82	.02

might be changed by the kind of information which Marshall considers essential. . . .

[In general, the results showed that the direction of attitude] change in each condition was almost always toward the "opposed" position. The magnitude of such change was, however, not great; when change occurred it generally involved movement to the next alternative attitude rather than to an alternative several steps away. Finally, subjects whose attitudes changed tended to be persons who were moderate in their initial attitudes; those who strongly supported capital punishment were, with a few exceptions, unswayed by the information presented in the interview. . . .

[In Table 5,] death penalty scale responses were assigned a score from 1 (very strongly favor the death penalty) to 7 (very strongly oppose). Then a mean of the scores both before and after exposure to the information was calculated.

In sum, our results confirm Justice Marshall's expectation that the opinions of an informed public would differ significantly from a public unaware of the consequences and effects of the death penalty. The experiment indicates, furthermore, that it is information about the utilitarian aspects of capital punishment which is primarily responsible for bringing about these differences. . . .

RETRIBUTION AND DEATH PENALTY ATTITUDES. . . . In this study, although exposure to information about capital punishment was associated with diminished support for it among approximately 40 percent of our subjects, the remaining 60 percent displayed no change in their death penalty attitudes. . . . [I]t may be that some, especially those who would justify support for the death penalty on retributive grounds, simply found the information irrelevant in judging the propriety of capital punishment. This last possibility was tested by examining the relationship of subjects' retribution scores, their death penalty attitudes, and the degree of attitude change associated with the information manipulations.

On the basis of their responses to the retribution items in the questionnaires, all subjects were classified as being high or low in terms of their endorsement of retribution. Next, the mean death penalty attitudes of persons high and low in retribution were compared both before and after exposure to information about the death penalty. These data are summarized in Table 6.

. . . Comparing the means reported in Table 5 with those reported in Table 6, it appears that retributiveness is more important in differentiating among supporters and opponents of capital punishment

TABLE 6

Mean Death Penalty Attitudes by Information Conditions and Retribution

Condition	High Retribution		Low Retribution	
	Before	After	Before	After
Utilitarian	1.8	2.1	4.5	5.2
Humanitarian	1.9	1.9	4.8	5.2
Combined	2.1	2.3	4.5	5.4
Control	2.3	2.3	5.6	5.6

than is any of the kinds of information contained in the three experimental conditions. Furthermore, as Table 6 indicates, retributive motives are highly correlated with the extent of change in death penalty support produced by those conditions. In each of the conditions, persons low in retribution, persons whose level of support for the death penalty was initially quite low, nevertheless showed a further alteration in their positions. The effect of information among respondents scoring high on the measure of retribution was, in contrast, uniformly quite minimal. In terms of Marshall's theory, this latter change was clearly not of the magnitude which would be required if information about the death penalty is to be regarded as significant in altering the attitudes of those whose commitment to capital punishment results from an equal commitment to retribution as justification for such punishment.

[In summary,] even a cautious reading of our results leads to the conclusions that an informed public opinion about the death penalty may differ substantially from one that is uninformed and that these differences in support may be almost totally accounted for by persons who do not consider retribution as a legitimate, or at least important, justification for capital punishment. . . .

NOTES AND QUESTIONS

1.   The study's finding that retributiveness has a greater effect on death penalty attitudes than exposure to utilitarian or humanitarian information supports Justice Brennan's observation that "at bottom, the battle has been waged on moral grounds." The bottom line issue is the inherent permissibility of capital punishment rather than its practical wisdom or the humaneness with which it is carried out. Support for the death penalty that rests not on mere preference but on deeply held moral beliefs such as retribution tends to be impervious to rational persuasion. Kohlberg and Elfenbein (1976) suggest that "the growth of factual knowledge, in and of itself, will not necessarily bring about a change in public opinion; the impact that new facts will have upon the evolution of attitudes toward capital punishment is contingent upon the moral principles which are invoked by persons making judgments on the basis of those facts" (p. 251).

The social psychological literature distinguishes between attitudes and (moral) values. Attitudes are directed toward a specific stimulus; they pertain to preferences and imply a sense of desirability. Values refer to a more general orientation that reflects a person's normative code; they have the quality of categorical imperatives and connote a sense of obligation. In traditional Freudian theory, the acquisition of moral values is the development of the conscience or super-ego, the internalized arbiter of conduct. The two concepts overlap at the extremes of the attitude spectrum. "Very pro" death penalty persons, for example, are likely to believe in the rightness of the sanction as a means of retribution. Those who are "very anti" are likely to hold equally intense, but opposite, beliefs. Neither group is readily susceptible to social influence.

Is it necessary to qualify the conclusion of Sarat and Vidmar—"Our results confirm Justice Marshall's expectation that the opinion of an informed public would differ significantly from a[n uninformed] public"—in view of their results and the foregoing distinction between opinions and values?

2.   Does the procedure of the study invite interpretation of the results as a response to "demand characteristics" (Orne 1962)? These are explicit or implicit cues that tell subjects in experiments what responses are expected or desired. Subjects tend to be compliant and are eager to figure out the purpose of the study in order to "help" the researcher to confirm his hypothesis.

3.   Vidmar and Dittenhoffer (1981) replicated the study with the following changes. The subjects were English-speaking Canadians. They read supplementary articles and books in addition to the experimental essay which combined utilitarian and humanitarian information. The posttest occurred two weeks after the pretest and, prior to the posttest measurements, the subjects participated in a group discussion.

The results showed (as in the initial study) that there was more opposition to capital punishment after exposure to the information. The data did not indicate which categories of persons along the attitude spectrum changed the most. Retribution was also associated with opinions in favor of the death penalty, although (unlike the first study) it was not related to the opinion change.

4.   A study by Lord, Ross, and Lepper (1979) shows that individuals react to information in different ways depending on whether it supports or contradicts their existing views. The researchers gave subjects who either supported or opposed capital punishment information that either confirmed or disconfirmed their beliefs regarding the deterrent efficacy of the death penalty. The results indicate that attitudes were polarized: The "pro" subjects became more favorable toward the death penalty after exposure to the information, and the "anti" subjects became more opposed. Do these findings suggest the need for refinements in the methodology of the Sarat and Vidmar study?

5.   For discussions on the social psychological processes underlying attitudes toward legal punishment, including research on retributive justice, see Vidmar and Miller (1980).

5.5. EIGHTH AMENDMENT CHALLENGES: ROUND TWO

GREGG v. GEORGIA

428 U.S. 153 (1976)

Judgment of the Court, and opinion of Mr. Justice STEWART, Mr. Justice POWELL, and Mr. Justice STEVENS, announced by Mr. Justice STEWART.

The issue in this case is whether the imposition of the sentence of death for the crime of murder under the law of Georgia

violates the Eighth and Fourteenth Amendments. . . .

[Petitioner, while hitchhiking, shot and robbed the two men who had offered him a ride in their car. Ed.'s note.]

II.

. . . The Georgia statute, as amended after our decision in *Furman* v. *Georgia,* retains the death penalty for six categories of crime: murder, kidnapping for ransom or where the victim is harmed, armed robbery, rape, treason, and aircraft hijacking. The capital defendant's guilt or innocence is determined in the traditional manner, either by a trial judge or a jury, in the first stage of a bifurcated trial.

. . . After a verdict, finding, or plea of guilty to a capital crime, a presentence hearing is conducted. . . .

[At the hearing, the judge or jury is required to consider] "any mitigating circumstances or aggravating circumstances otherwise authorized by law and any of [ten] statutory aggravating circumstances which may be supported by the evidence . . ." [Georgia Code]. The scope of the nonstatutory aggravating or mitigating circumstances is not delineated in the statute. Before a convicted defendant may be sentenced to death, however, . . . [the jury or judge] must find beyond a reasonable doubt one of the 10 aggravating circumstances specified in the statute.[9] . . .

In addition to the conventional appellate process available in all criminal cases, provision is made for special expedited direct review by the Supreme

---

[9][Examples of statutory aggravating factors:]

"(1) The offense of murder, rape, armed robbery, or kidnapping was committed by a person with a prior record of conviction for a capital felony, or the offense of murder was committed by a person who has a substantial history of serious assaultive criminal convictions. . . .

"(4) The offender committed the offense of murder for himself or another, for the purpose of receiving money or any other thing of monetary value. . . .

"(7) The offense of murder, rape, armed robbery, or kidnapping was outrageously or wantonly vile, horrible, or inhuman in that it involved torture, depravity of mind, or an aggravated battery to the victim. . . .

"(8) The offense of murder was committed against any peace officer. . . .

The Supreme Court of Georgia . . . recently held unconstitutional the portion of the first circumstance encompassing persons who have a "substantial history of serious assaultive criminal convictions" because it did not set "sufficiently 'clear and objective standards.' "

Court of Georgia of the appropriateness of imposing the sentence of death in the particular case. The court is directed . . . to determine "(1) Whether the sentence of death was imposed under the influence of passion, prejudice, or any other arbitrary factor, and . . . (3) Whether the sentence of death is excessive or disproportionate to the penalty imposed in similar cases, considering both the crime and the defendant." If the court affirms a death sentence, it is required to include in its decision reference to similar cases that it has taken into consideration. . . .

III.

We address initially the basic contention that the punishment of death for the crime of murder is, under all circumstances, "cruel and unusual." . . .

[T]he Eighth Amendment has not been regarded as a static concept. As Mr. Chief Justice Warren said, in an oft-quoted phrase, "[t]he Amendment must draw its meaning from the evolving standards of decency that mark the progress of a maturing society." *Trop* v. *Dulles*. Thus, an assessment of contemporary values concerning the infliction of a challenged sanction is relevant to the application of the Eighth Amendment. As we develop below more fully, this assessment does not call for a subjective judgment. It requires, rather, that we look to objective indicia that reflect the public attitude toward a given sanction.

But our cases also make clear that public perceptions of standards of decency with respect to criminal sanctions are not conclusive. A penalty also must accord with "the dignity of man," which is the "basic concept underlying the Eighth Amendment." *Trop* v. *Dulles*. This means, at least, that the punishment not be "excessive." . . .

The most marked indication of society's endorsement of the death penalty for murder is the legislative response to *Fur-*

man. The legislature of at least 35 States have enacted new statutes that provide for the death penalty for at least some crimes that result in the death of another person. . . . All of the post-*Furman* statutes make clear that capital punishment itself has not been rejected by the elected representatives of the people. . . .

As we have seen, however, the Eighth Amendment demands more than that a challenged punishment be acceptable to contemporary society. The Court also must ask whether it comports with a basic concept of human dignity at the core of the Amendment. . . . [T]he sanction imposed cannot be so totally without penological justification that it results in the gratuitous infliction of suffering.

The death penalty is said to serve two principal social purposes: retribution and deterrence of capital crimes by prospective offenders.

In part, capital punishment is an expression of society's moral outrage at particularly offensive conduct. This function may be unappealing to many, but it is essential in an ordered society that asks its citizens to rely on legal processes rather than self-help to vindicate their wrongs.

Statistical attempts to evaluate the worth of the death penalty as a deterrent to crimes by potential offenders have occasioned a great deal of debate.[31] The results simply have been inconclusive. As one opponent of capital punishment has

said: "[A]fter all possible inquiry, including the probing of all possible methods of inquiry, we do not know, and for systematic and easily visible reasons cannot know, what the truth about this 'deterrent' effect may be. . . . A 'scientific'—that is to say, a soundly based—conclusion is simply impossible, and no methodological path out of this tangle suggests itself." C. Black, Capital Punishment: The Inevitability of Caprice and Mistake 25–26 (1974).

Although some of the studies suggest that the death penalty may not function as a significantly greater deterrent than lesser penalties, there is no convincing empirical evidence either supporting or refuting this view. We may nevertheless assume safely that there are murderers, such as those who act in passion, for whom the threat of death has little or no deterrent effect. But for many others, the death penalty undoubtedly is a significant deterrent. There are carefully contemplated murders, such as murder for hire, where the possible penalty of death may well enter into the cold calculus that precedes the decision to act. And there are some categories of murder, such as murder by a life prisoner, where other sanctions may not be adequate.

The value of capital punishment as a deterrent of crime is a complex factual issue the resolution of which properly rests with the legislatures, which can evaluate the results of statistical studies in terms of their own local conditions and with a flexibility of approach that is not available to the courts. . . .

. . . [T]he concerns expressed in *Furman* that the penalty of death not be imposed in an arbitrary or capricious manner can be met by a carefully drafted statute that ensures that the sentencing authority is given adequate information and guidance. As a general proposition, these concerns are best met by a system that provides for a bifurcated proceeding at which the sentencing authority is apprised of the

---

[31]See, *e.g.*, Peck, The Deterrent Effect of Capital Punishment: Ehrlich and His Critics, 85 Yale L.J. 359 (1976); Baldus & Cole, A Comparison of the Work of Thorsten Sellin and Isaac Ehrlich on the Deterrent Effect of Capital Punishment, 85 Yale L.J. 170 (1975); Bowers & Pierce, The Illusion of Deterrence in Isaac Ehrlich's Research on Capital Punishment, 85 Yale L.J. 187 (1975); Ehrlich, The Deterrent Effect of Capital Punishment: A Question of Life and Death, 65 Am. Econ. Rev. 397 (June 1975); Hook, The Death Sentence, in The Death Penalty in America 146 (H. Bedau ed. 1967); T. Sellin, The Death Penalty, A Report for the Model Penal Code Project of the American Law Institute (1959).

information relevant to the imposition of sentence and provided with standards to guide its use of the information. . . . [However], each distinct system must be examined on an individual basis. . . .

IV.

We turn now to consideration of the constitutionality of Georgia's capital-sentencing procedures. In the wake of *Furman*, Georgia amended its capital punishment statute, but chose not to narrow the scope of its murder provisions. . . .

Georgia did act, however, to narrow the class of murderers subject to capital punishment by specifying 10 statutory aggravating circumstances, one of which must be found by the jury to exist beyond a reasonable doubt before a death sentence can ever be imposed. In addition, the jury is authorized to consider any other appropriate aggravating or mitigating circumstances. . . .

These procedures require the jury to consider the circumstances of the crime and the criminal before it recommends sentence. No longer can a Georgia jury do as *Furman*'s jury did: reach a finding of the defendant's guilt and then, without guidance or direction, decide whether he should live or die. . . . As a result, while some jury discretion still exists, "the discretion to be exercised is controlled by clear and objective standards so as to produce non-discriminatory application."

As an important additional safeguard against arbitrariness and caprice, the Georgia statutory scheme provides for automatic appeal of all death sentences to the State's Supreme Court. . . . [That court] compares each death sentence with the sentences imposed on similarly situated defendants to ensure that the sentence of death in a particular case is not disproportionate. On their face these procedures seem to satisfy the concerns of *Furman*. . . .

The petitioner contends, however, that the changes in the Georgia sentencing procedures are only cosmetic. . . .

First, the petitioner focuses on the opportunities for discretionary action that are inherent in the processing of any murder case under Georgia law. He notes that the state prosecutor has unfettered authority to select those persons whom he wishes to prosecute for a capital offense and to plea bargain with them. . . . And finally, a defendant who is convicted and sentenced to die may have his sentence commuted by the Governor. . . .

The existence of these discretionary stages is not determinative of the issues before us. At each of these stages, an actor in the criminal justice system makes a decision which may remove a defendant from consideration as a candidate for the death penalty. *Furman*, in contrast, dealt with the decision to impose the death sentence on a specific individual who had been convicted of a capital offense. Nothing in any of our cases suggests that the decision to afford an individual defendant mercy violates the Constitution. . . .

[W]e hold that the statutory system under which Gregg was sentenced to death does not violate the Constitution. . . .

[The concurring opinion of Justice White, with whom The Chief Justice and Justice Rehnquest joined, is omitted. Justice Blackmun concurred separately in the judgment. The dissenting opinions of Justices Brennan and Marshall are omitted.]

NOTES AND QUESTIONS

1.   Shortly after *Furman*, a majority of states adopted new capital punishment statutes intended to withstand the challenge of arbitrary and capricious sentencing. Most of the state courts that reviewed

their constitutionality upheld them, so abolitionists went back to the Supreme Court. In 1976, in a series of five cases led by *Gregg*, the Court split three ways. Justices Brennan and Marshall declared all five statutes under review unconstitutional. The Chief Justice and Justices White, Blackmun, and Rehnquist declared all of them constitutional. Justices Stewart, Powell, and Stevens, who constituted the plurality, concluded that guided discretionary statutes are constitutional (*Gregg; Jurek* v. *Texas; Proffitt* v. *Florida*) and mandatory statutes violate the Eighth Amendment (*Woodson* v. *North Carolina; Roberts* v. *Louisiana*). The effect of the split was to uphold the discretionary schemes by a 7 to 2 vote and overturn the mandatory ones by a 5 to 4 vote.

2.   The plurality opinion in *Gregg* first states that the death penalty is not per se unconstitutional under the Eighth Amendment (substantive analysis), and then affirms the validity of the Georgia statute because of conformity with *Furman* (procedural analysis). What is the relationship between the Eighth Amendment analysis and the subsequent review of the Georgia legislation?

3.   The main teaching of *Furman* is that the death penalty cannot be imposed in an arbitrary and unprincipled manner. Consequently, statutes enumerated certain aggravating factors to guide the discretion of the sentencer. What are the standards by which these aggravating factors are chosen by the legislature in the first place? If there are no articulated standards, is the risk of arbitrariness simply pushed back from the sentencing stage to the legislative stage? For example, murder committed "for the purpose of receiving money" is one of the ten statutory aggravating factors. Why is a person who slays his or her spouse to collect the insurance more deserving of capital punishment than one who kills in order to be free to remarry?

4.   Standards are intended to focus the sentencer's attention on legitimate considerations (for example, circumstances of the crime) and block out legally irrelevant factors (for example, race). Vague standards are susceptible to arbitrary application and fail to serve this channeling function. In *Godfrey* v. *Georgia* (1980), the death penalty was imposed upon a finding that the murder was "outrageously or wantonly vile, horrible or inhuman" (the seventh aggravating circumstance). The Supreme Court held that this broadly worded standard is unconstitutionally vague, if it does not result in consistently executing only those whose crimes are horrible enough to be clearly distinguished from "normal" first-degree murder. What other aggravating factors could be challenged as insufficiently "clear and objective" (footnote 9 of *Gregg*)?

5.   The Georgia statute enumerates the grounds for imposing the death penalty (aggravating factors), but does not specify the bases for not imposing it. It simply allows the sentencing authority to consider "any mitigating circumstances." If discretion regarding the imposition of the death penalty must be guided, why is discretion regarding its nonimposition left unfettered? What are the standards to be applied in defining the criteria for mercy?

6.   The jury is asked to "consider" or weigh aggravating and mitigating factors. This implies comparability among the factors that are considered. What are the standards to guide a jury in comparing, for example, the killing of a police officer (an aggravating factor) and the youthfulness of the defendant (a mitigating factor)?

7.   The ultimate horror case, that courts are most vigilant about, is the execution of a completely innocent defendant. However, the far more common risk, Kaplan (1983) observes, is "when we execute someone whose crime does not seem so aggravated when compared to those of many who escaped the death penalty" (p. 576). Hence, another procedural safeguard against arbitrary decision-making in Georgia's capital sentencing scheme is appellate review according to the standard of proportionality. The Georgia Supreme Court must consider whether the death sentence is "excessive" in relation to the penalty imposed in "similar cases."

The courts have addressed the excessiveness issue in an intuitive and unsystematic manner. The approach of the Georgia Supreme Court is not atypical. The comparison pool consists of all murder convictions appealed to the state's highest court since 1973, of which only about 20% resulted in death sentences. From this pool, 5 to 20 "similar cases" (that resulted in death sentences) are selected and compared with the case under review. Few death sentences have been found to be excessive (Baldus 1980). The court usually stated its conclusion without elaborating on the details of the comparison. In general, it looked at salient features of the offense and the offender (for example, premeditation, bloodiness of the crime, prior criminal record) and compared them with those of the selected cases.

Critique this Georgia procedure. How should the pool of similar cases be defined? Should it include capital cases that were disposed by plea or that were not appealed? How might you quantify and render less subjective the process of determining excessiveness? For a proposed statistical approach, see Baldus et al. (1980). Suppose that one-half of the similar, comparison cases (however constituted) received life imprisonment—is this prima facie evidence that the death sentence in the specific case under review is unconstitutional? Is it desirable to establish a quantitative threshold of excessiveness?

8.   What substantive issues of equal protection are likely to be implicated by the procedural safeguard of comparative proportionality review?

9.   What effect, if any, does *Gregg* have upon *Crampton?* Upon *Witherspoon?*

10.   Nationwide, there is a homicide about every twenty-six minutes, yet only one hundred or so convicts are picked to die (Black 1980, p. 442). This is because unreviewable discretion—hence the omnipresent risk of arbitrariness—permeates every step of the criminal justice trail that leads to the electric chair. The prosecutor has unreviewable discretion with respect to charging and plea bargaining. A jury instructed on "lesser included offenses" has unreviewable discretion in finding a capital defendant guilty of such offenses rather than of the capital offenses. Gubernatorial clemency is entirely discretionary. Thus, the availability of clear and rational standards at the sentencing stage is no saving grace if decision-making at every stage of the criminal process, before and after sentencing, is not likewise principled. For this reason, Black (1974) argues that "the penalty of death cannot be imposed, given the limitations of our minds and institutions, without considerable measures both of arbitrariness and of mistake" (p. 24). At the core of *Furman's* notion of arbitrariness is human fallibility, and Black suggests that these errors are so human and so pervasive that they are essentially uncorrectable.

Is the plurality opinion's justification for not imposing standards outside the sentencing stage a persuasive one? Justice White, in a concurring opinion (not reproduced here), said that "the standards by which prosecutors decide to charge a capital felony will be the same as those by which a jury will decide the questions of guilt and sentence." If so, sentencing standards should help counteract or neutralize the possibility of arbitrariness at other stages of the criminal process, because these standards will also guide the discretion of other decision-makers. Is this proposition amenable to empirical testing?

The Deterrent Effect of Capital Punishment

The plurality opinion in *Gregg* stated that the empirical evidence on "the worth of the death penalty as a deterrent to crimes by potential offenders" is "inconclusive." It cited with approval Professor Black's assertion that a scientific conclusion on this issue is "simply impossible." In rebuttal, Professor Zeisel (1976) wrote that "both the Court's and Professor Black's views are wrong" and that "the evidence we have is quite sufficient if we ask the right question" (p. 318).

The concept of deterrence consists of two ideas. General deterrence refers to the capacity of the criminal law, via the threat of sanctions, to make citizens law-abiding. Special deterrence refers to the threat of further punishment of an offender who has already been convicted and sanctioned in order to render him less likely to recidivate. In both, the essence of deterrence or prevention is threat (Zimring and Hawkins 1973, pp. 91–248). The debate on the preventive effects of capital punishment pertains, obviously, to general prevention.

The ideal (though impossible) test of the general deterrent effect, according to Zeisel, would be an experiment in which persons convicted of a capital offense and born on odd-numbered days would be sentenced to death, and those born on even-numbered days would be sent to prison for life. (The issue is not simply whether capital punishment deters, but whether it deters more than life imprisonment.) The day of birth is simply a means for random assignment of individuals to the two groups. There are numerous studies that employ alternative procedures that approximate, with varying degrees of faithfulness, the design of this experiment. These research procedures are described in some detail by Zeisel and briefly summarized here.

One approach is to compare the capital crime rate before and after a state abolishes the death penalty. Another approach is to compare the capital crime rates of two jurisdictions, one with and the other without capital punishment, provided that they are otherwise similar. Thorsten Sellin pioneered and carried out most of the studies using these approaches. His results (summarized by Justice Marshall in *Furman*) and those of others have shown no differences in capital crime rates. Of course, unequivocal conclusions cannot be drawn from these data. Any deterrent effect could be dwarfed by the effect of uncontrolled variables. It is also impossible to prove a negative.

Zeisel suggests a variation of the between-states approach by adding a temporal dimension. For example, he reports the homicides per 100,000 population for the years 1920 to 1955 in Kansas (an abolitionist state that restored the penalty in 1935) and in Missouri (which kept the penalty through this period). The homicide rate (summarized here in five-year blocks and in rounded figures) in Kansas was 5, 5, 6, 5, 2, 2, 3, 2. In Missouri, the rate was 8, 12, 11, 10, 5, 6, 6, 5. Thus, the re-enactment of the death penalty in Kansas in 1935 (when there were five homicides per 100,000) was followed by a drop in the homicide rate in subsequent years (two per 100,000 in 1940). However, a cause-and-effect relationship cannot be inferred since the rate also declined in neighboring Missouri (from ten to five per 100,000) for the same interval despite the absence of any changes in capital statutes.

Other studies have refined these approaches by improving the comparability of the areas examined (for example, comparing homogeneous subsections of states rather than comparing entire states) and sharpening the indicator of capital crime (for example, looking only at police killings rather than homicides in general, because conviction of the former crime is more likely to result in the death penalty and is therefore a more sensitive measure of deterrence). These methodological improvements have "failed to reveal any difference between the threat of the death penalty and that of life imprisonment" (p. 327). Thus, the absence of any observable deterrent effect in different studies carried out at different times using different research designs gives credence to the belief that maybe it does not exist. Until *Gregg*, "the conclusion that the death penalty does not deter was the general consensus of the scientific community . . ." (Lempert 1981, p. 1206).

The theory of deterrence rests on the condition that the penalty is administered with severity, promptness, and certainty. For the most part, studies of the preventive effect of capital punishment using the aforementioned methods have concentrated only on severity. If sanctions deter, then the most severe sanction (death) should deter more than lesser ones (imprisonment). However, according to general deterrence theory, "severity acting alone is not associated with lower rates of crime" (Antunes and Hunt 1973, p. 158). There is "anecedotal but persuasive" evidence that an increase in the certainty of detection and punishment has greater general preventive effect than an increase in the severity of the sanction itself (Kadish and Paulsen 1975, p. 30). Thus, it has been argued that the reality of the threat for would-be criminals is not the theoretical availability of the death penalty but the actual frequency of its imposition. "The lesson to be learned from capital punishment is not that capital punishment does not deter, but that the improper and sloppy use of punishment does not deter. . . ." (Jeffrey 1965, p. 299). The argument is that if executions were carried out surely and promptly, the capital crime rate would be depressed.

In 1975, in an article subtitled "A Question of Life and Death," an economist, Isaac Ehrlich, was the first to apply multiple regression analysis to examine the relationship between the actual frequency of executions and capital homicide rates (see *Gregg*, footnote 31). This statistical technique is another means of simulating the aforementioned ideal experimental design. It isolates the effect of any one predictor variable (for example, executions) upon the criterion variable (homicide rate) under conditions that control for the possibly contaminating influences of the other predictor variables. Ehrlich examined whether the frequency of executions had an effect on the capital crime rate after controlling for the interference of other simultaneous predictor variables such as homicide arrest rates, homicide conviction rates, the unemployment rate, per capita income, the percentage of the population in the 14–24 age bracket, and the labor force participation rate. He concluded that "on the average the tradeoff between the execution of an offender and the lives of potential victims it might have saved was of the order of magnitude of 1 for 8 for the period 1933–67 in the United States" (p. 398). As might be expected, this study captured extraordinary attention and was appended by the Solicitor General to his brief in the *Gregg* case.

Regression analysis is a sophisticated technique, but it is also a delicate one that is sensitive to the kinds of control variables that are included and to technical refinements in the data. Several studies, cited in *Gregg* (footnote 31) and reviewed by Lempert (1981, pp. 1206–24) and Zeisel, have failed to replicate Ehrlich's finding or have succeeded only under limiting conditions. For example, some have noted that the noncontrol of certain factors associated with crimes could have produced a spurious correlation between executions and homicides. The proliferation of handgun ownership, rising racial tensions, and the frequency of life sentences are all factors which may predict the homicide rate better than executions. Others found that the relationship held up only under restrictive mathematical specifications (namely, converting the data to logarithmic form). Still others concluded that the claimed deterrent effect, if it exists, is detectable only in the latter part of the 1960s (when de facto judicial abolition, because of the "moratorium strategy," and crime rates simultaneously hit their peak). That is, when data from 1965–69 are omitted, the relationship between executions and homicides is no longer statistically significant. Since nothing in deterrence theory explains this sensitivity to time, the result could be a statistical aberration. In fact, some time-series analyses show the opposite of deterrence or a "brutalization" effect: In the months following each execution in New York between 1906 and 1963, there were two or three more homicides that would not have occurred otherwise (Lempert 1981, p. 1216).

On balance, after reviewing all these studies, Zeisel states that "the proper summary of the evidence on the deterrent effect of the death penalty" is as follows: "If there is one, it can only be minute, since not one of the many research approaches—from the simplest to the most sophisticated—was able to find it" (p. 338). A blue-ribbon Panel on Research on Deterrent and Incapacitative Effects of the National Research Council reached the same finding: "[T]he results of the analyses on capital punishment provide no useful evidence on the deterrent effect. . . . Our conclusion should not be interpreted as meaning that capital punishment does not have a deterrent effect, but rather that there is currently no evidence for determining whether it does have a deterrent effect" (Blumstein, Cohen, and Nagin 1978, p. 62). These conclusions are subject, of course, to methodological caveats. So long as the measures of homicide rates and execution rates are imprecise and studies fall short of a true experimental design, there always remains the possibility that an observed relationship may be spurious or that it might be altered if additional factors were controlled. So long as the death penalty is infrequently imposed, there is not a large enough data base for reliable statistical analysis of the claimed deterrent effect. In terms of the quantum of evidence available, however imperfect this evidence may be because of its nonexperimental nature, the bulk of it—with the exception of that of Ehrlich—shows no difference between capital punishment and life imprisonment with respect to the capital homicide rate. Hence, "for purposes of moral argument one must proceed as if the death penalty does not deter" (Lempert 1981, p. 1223).

Gregg also narrowed the scope of the deterrent claim. Justice Stewart said he could "safely assume" that there are types of murder, such as "murder for hire" and "murder by a life prisoner," where the death penalty could enter into the cold calculus that precedes the decision to act. Intuitively, one would expect that killing by a "lifer" would be a prime case for the operation of the deterrent effect. The facts are otherwise. Jailhouse murders are infrequent: In the past few years, about eighty inmates have been killed annually. Murder rates in and out of prison are about the same. However, in the 1970s, 40% of the inmate murders were committed by prisoners already serving life sentences for homicide. Also, 90% of these prison killings were in states that retained the death penalty. "The obvious conclusion is that the threat of execution is not much of a deterrent to an inmate bent on killing" (Newsweek, May 3, 1982, p. 90).

The debate on the penological effectiveness of capital punishment has raged for at least a couple of hundred years since Cesare Beccaria's influential treatise. And it is likely to continue, notwithstanding the paucity of empirical evidence in support of its alleged deterrent effect. There seems to be a deeply rooted belief in the inherent preventive value of the ultimate sanction. In consequence, there is an abiding resistance to any evidence that indicates the contrary. The tenacity with which the idea of deterrence is clung to by proponents of capital punishment suggests that perhaps, at bottom, one is not dealing with an empirical question. Deterrence may be a socially respectable, utilitarian justification for the moral judgment that the taking of human life by the state is permissible. As Vidmar and Ellsworth indicated in their article, the majority of the public believes in the deterrent effect of the death penalty, but this belief may simply be "a cover for other, less acceptable reasons" for favoring the sanction. (See also Vidmar and Miller 1980.) Gregg legitimized retribution as a motive for imposing capital punishment. Even then, the Court clothed this normative justification in functional attire: Retributive justice is "essential in an ordered society if citizens [are] to rely on legal processes rather than self-help to vindicate their wrongs."

If the issue of deterrence and the broader issue of the legality of capital punishment are, ultimately, moral issues, then the role of social research in their adjudication is obviously a limited one. But once it is decided that capital punishment does not violate Eighth Amendment values of mercy and sanctity of life, there still remains the procedural issue of how to administer it consistent with other constitutional values. The implementation of capital sentencing schemes, illustrated in the companion cases to *Gregg,* raises a host of empirical research issues. By addressing these procedural matters, social research may shape indirectly the evolution of the substantive question.

The Companion Cases

The *Gregg* analysis was applied to the other four cases in the series.

Proffitt v. *Florida:* Under the Florida scheme, upon conviction for first degree murder, a separate presentencing hearing is held before the jury where arguments may be presented and any evidence related to sentencing may be admitted. The evidence must bear on eight aggravating circumstances (for example, "The capital felony was committed for pecuniary gain"; the murder was "especially heinous, atrocious, or cruel") and seven mitigating ones specified in the legislation (for example, "the defendant has no significant history of prior criminal activity"; "the age of the defendant"). The jury is directed to weigh those factors and return an advisory verdict based upon a majority vote. The actual sentence is imposed by the trial judge. To pronounce death, the trial judge must put in writing his findings that the presence of at least one statutory aggravating circumstance has been proved beyond a reasonable doubt and that aggravation exceeds mitigation. To ensure uniform results, the death sentence is then reviewed by the state supreme court.

The plurality opinion declared Florida's procedure to comport with *Furman* because it guides the sentencer's discretion. The procedure also properly allows attention to the specific facts of the crime and the character of the defendant. The trifurcated system, with the judge rather than the jury imposing the sentence, was found not to be such a deviation from the Georgia format as to invalidate it.

Jurek v. *Texas:* The Texas scheme differed from that of Georgia and Florida. Instead of authorizing the death penalty for a broad category of murders and then limiting its imposition by prescribing specific aggravating factors which must be found in each case, the Texas statute limited the scope of capital homicides to intentional murders committed in five specified circumstances: murder of a police officer or fireman; murder committed in the course of kidnapping, burglary, robbery, forcible rape, or arson; murder while escaping or attempting to escape from prison; murder for remuneration; and murder of a prison employee by a prison inmate. Upon conviction, a separate presentence hearing is held before a jury, where any relevant evidence can be introduced for or against the death penalty. At this hearing, the jury must answer two questions: "whether the conduct of the defendant that caused the death of the deceased was committed deliberately and with reasonable expectation" that death would result; and "whether there is a probability that the defendant would commit criminal acts of violence that would constitute a continuing threat to society" (p. 269). If both questions are answered affirmatively and beyond a reasonable doubt, the death sentence is mandatory. There is expedited review of the sentence on appeal to the state supreme court.

The plurality ruled that the Texas scheme is sufficiently like those of Georgia and Florida to survive *Furman.* The enumeration of five categories of capital homicide was said to be the functional equivalent of a requirement that at least one statutory aggravating circumstance be present. The second question (pertaining to future dangerousness) opens the door for consideration of mitigating factors, as provided in the Georgia and Florida procedures. Thus, the Texas approach guides "the jury's objective consideration of the particularized circumstances of the individual offense and the individual offender" before sentencing and therefore passed muster (p. 274).

Woodson v. *North Carolina* and *Roberts* v. *Louisiana:* In the last two decisions of the *Gregg* series, the Court struck down mandatory death penalty statutes for first degree murder.

In the North Carolina case, mandatory sentencing was said to violate contemporary standards of decency. Most jurisdictions have discretionary sentencing in response to the long history of unfavorable jury reaction to the harshness of compulsory death. Nondiscretionary sentencing also continues to vest unfettered discretion in juries. A jury that believes the death penalty is unwarranted in a given first degree murder case would simply refuse to convict if there was no choice as to the sanction. A mandatory procedure merely pushes jury discretion back to the conviction stage. Another flaw is the "failure to allow the particularized consideration of the relevant aspects of the character and record of each convicted defendant" before decreeing the penalty. The Eighth Amendment notion that the penalty must accord with human dignity means that individualized sentencing is not just an "enlightened policy" but a "constitutional imperative" (p. 303).

The mandatory sentencing of Louisiana was overturned because it was found indistinguishable from the statute struck down in *Woodson*. Although Louisiana defined the scope of capital homicides more narrowly than North Carolina, it was still too inflexible and harsh to survive *Gregg*.

NOTES AND QUESTIONS

---

1. *Gregg* said that "each distinct system must be examined on an individual basis." Nonetheless, what are the procedural features common to the Georgia, Florida, and Texas statutes that enabled them to withstand constitutional scrutiny?

2. In upholding these three statutes, the Court assumes that the differences between them in standards and procedures are of no consequence to the jury. So long as there is individualized treatment, the statutes would be equally effective in precluding jury arbitrariness. On their face, are all three schemes likely to have the same impact on the jury? For example, is a Florida jury that is asked to render an "advisory verdict" likely to function the same as a Georgia or Texas jury that decides the real thing? Some Florida trial judges repeatedly override a jury's advisory sentence of life imprisonment and impose the death penalty (*Barclay* v. *Florida*, 1983, p. B5187). Is the human tendency toward mercy evoked equally by the Florida procedure that calls to the attention of the jury seven specific mitigating factors as by the Georgia procedure that asks the jury only to consider "any mitigation"? What are other features of these statutes that a social scientist would hypothesize might have different effects on the jury, even though these features are constitutionally fungible according to *Gregg*?

3. The Georgia scheme could be described as "semi-guided discretionary sentencing" because it enumerates aggravating but not mitigating factors. The Florida scheme is "fully-guided discretionary sentencing" because it enumerates the grounds for expressing both vengeance and mercy. And the Texas statute could be said to provide for "conditional mandatory sentencing"—the death penalty turns on the answers to the two questions. Justice Stevens conceded that it is "not easy to predict future behavior," but added hopefully: "The fact that such a determination is difficult, however, does not mean that it cannot be made" (*Jurek*, p. 274). The prediction of violent criminal conduct—whether for the purpose of making decisions regarding bail, parole, or sentencing to probation, imprisonment, or death—is considered to be "the greatest unresolved problem the criminal justice system faces" (in Monahan 1978, p. 244). Should judgments of mental health professionals about propensity for future criminality be permitted at the sentencing hearing? See *Barefoot* v. *Estelle* (1983). The research and the arguments comparing the success of actuarial and clinical predictions of dangerousness are summarized in Monahan (1981).

4.   Ohio's post-*Furman* statute requires the death penalty upon conviction for aggravated murder with at least one of seven specified aggravating circumstances found present, unless considering "the nature of the offender," the sentencer at a separate sentencing hearing determines that at least one of the following mitigating circumstances is established by a preponderance of the evidence: "(1) The victim of the offense induced or facilitated it. (2) It is unlikely that the offense would have been committed but for the fact that the offender was under duress, coercion or strong provocation. (3) The offense was primarily the product of the offender's psychosis or mental deficiency, though such condition is insufficient to establish the defense of insanity."

The constitutionality of this statute was reviewed in the context of a rather unusual case. The defendant, Sandra Lockett, helped plan the robbery of a pawn shop. She remained in the getaway vehicle while her male accomplice robbed and accidentally killed the pawnbroker. The actual killer pleaded guilty to the noncapital offense of aggravated robbery and received a life sentence. Lockett refused to plead guilty to the noncapital offense and was prosecuted and convicted for the capital offense of aggravated murder. She was sentenced to death even though she did not kill or intend to kill anyone. One might say that Lockett was sentenced to die because she insisted on being tried.

Is the Ohio statue constitutional under *Gregg* and its related cases? See *Lockett* v. *Ohio* (1978).

5.   *Furman* proscribed arbitrary sentencing but did not differentiate between types of capital offenses. Only three states in the post-*Furman* era—Georgia, Louisiana, and North Carolina—retained the death penalty for forcible rape. After *Gregg* struck down the compulsory sentencing of the last two states, Georgia was left as the only jurisdiction with a valid capital punishment law for rape. The next year, in *Coker* v. *Georgia* (1977), the Court overturned it. Four Justices, joined in the judgment by two concurring Justices, expressed an "abiding conviction" that the death penalty for the rape of an adult woman without any other physical violence is disproportionate to the seriousness of the crime (p. 598). Since the start of the judicial attempt at abolition, this was the first time that a majority of the Court relied purely on a substantive Eighth Amendment analysis rather than on procedural fairness.

6.   Georgia's capital sentencing scheme requires comparative proportionality review, but Texas' scheme does not; nonetheless, both statutes were upheld. In the post-*Gregg* years, over thirty states required by legislation or judicial decision some form of such review. The Georgia Supreme Court, in fact, has vacated several death sentences over the course of a few years because of comparative disproportionality. For example, the death penalty for felony murder was found excessive when a co-defendant received a life sentence in a subsequent trial (*Hall* v. *State*, 1978). The Suprme Court eventually had to decide whether the absence of any comparative review rendered a capital sentencing scheme, such as that of Texas, constitutionally infirm.

The decision came in *Pulley* v. *Harris* (1984). A 29-year-old defendant forced two teen-aged boys, who were sitting in their car eating hamburgers, to drive to a wooded area. He shot them despite their pleas for mercy, finished their hamburgers, and used their car in a bank robbery. (The defendant had an abused and unwanted childhood with an alcoholic father and a battered mother. At age 15, he was sentenced to a federal youth prison for car theft and over the next four years there was often raped. Thereafter, he developed a history of suicide attempts, emotional instability, and viciousness toward animals. These background facts are relevant to the determination of punishment even though one need not agree with the French saying that "To understand all is to forgive all.") Upon conviction for kidnapping, robbery, and first degree murder, the defendant was sentenced to death. On appeal, he pressed the claim, among others, that the California capital punishment law was invalid because it failed to require the state supreme court to compare a capital convict's sentence with sentences imposed in similar cases in order to determine whether they were proportionate. The Supreme Court rejected the claim. It held that the Eighth Amendment does not require, as an invariable rule in every case, that a state appellate court undertake such comparative review before it affirms a death sentence. "[T]hat some schemes providing proportionality reviews are constitutional does not mean that such review is indispensable. We take statutes as we find them" (p. B974). Besides, "Any capital sentencing scheme may occasionally produce aberrational outcomes," but this is a "far cry from the major systemic defects identified in *Furman*" (p. B983).

In the absence of any direct evaluation of whether similarly situated capital convicts are similarly sentenced, what other procedures are available by which an appellate court could determine whether capital punishment is imposed in a nonarbitrary and evenhanded manner? Can a court decide whether an outcome is aberrational or commonplace without comparative data?

7.   Constitutional litigation on the death penalty began, as we saw in section 5.2, with equal protection challenges to alleged racial discrimination in the sentencing of black defendants for the crime of rape. *Maxwell* v. *Bishop* (1978), as it turned out, did not inter the racial issue. Nearly two decades later, the litigation came full circle when abolition advocates again raised the claim of disparate racial treatment, but this time alleging a more subtle form of discrimination in the context of the crime of murder. In the late 1970s, the defense team of a Florida capital convict discovered serendipitously a statistical pattern that had not been perceived in the past. There were 114 men on the state's death row at the time of the appeal. Most of them (94%) had killed only white victims. Further research showed that 47% of black defendants arrested for killing a white in Florida were condemned to death, compared to 24% of white defendants arrested for killing a black (Zeisel 1981, pp. 458, 460). These data, suggestive of capricious sentencing based on race, were presented in the lower courts. The Fifth Circuit was unimpressed: "The allegation that Florida's death penalty is being discriminatorily applied to defendants who murder whites is nothing more than an allegation . . ." (*Spinkellink* v. *Wainwright*, 1978, p. 613). The defendant, who was white, was electrocuted.

8.   In a study of "arbitrariness and discrimination under post-*Furman* capital statutes," Bowers and Pierce (1980) estimated the number of homicide offenders (based on FBI and state crime reporting agency figures) in Florida, Georgia, Texas, and Ohio from about 1973 to 1977. They then determined the actual number of persons sentenced to death and computed the probability of the death penalty given a homicide for each of four offender/victim racial combinations (Table 2, p. 594). The results are summarized in their table presented on the next page.

The authors indicate that "the likelihood of a death sentence given a criminal homicide spans the criminal justice process from the initial investigation of the crime by the police through the sentencing of a convicted offender. That is, unlike studies that begin with a sample of indictments, these data will reflect the effects of differential law enforcement as well as differential court processing of criminal homicide cases. They incorporate the effects of discretion at arrest, charging, indictment, conviction, and sentencing in the handling of potentially capital crimes" (p. 593).* These four states accounted for about 70% of all capital sentences pronounced in the first five years after *Furman*.

What can you conclude from these data?

9.   There are a growing number of studies examining the race of the victim and of the defendant in the imposition of the death penalty. An analysis of cases under South Carolina's post-*Gregg* statute found that "While prosecutors sought the death penalty four times as often for blacks accused of killing whites as they did when blacks were accused of killing other blacks (p < .0001), they were only twice as likely to seek the death sentence when white defendants had white rather than black victims (p < .05)" (Jacoby and Paternoster 1982, pp. 384–5).

A large scale study by Samuel Gross and Robert Mauro examined some 17,000 homicide cases (in which negligence was not a factor and there were known suspects at least 15 years old) in eight states from 1976 to 1980. In each of these states, the study showed that the death penalty was more likely to be imposed when the victim was white. For example, in Georgia during this four-year period, there were 773 slayings of whites and the death penalty was imposed in 67 of the cases, or 8.7%. However, in the 1,345 slayings of blacks, only 12 cases resulted in death sentences, or less than 1%. The results in the other states are nearly as striking. In Florida, 114 death sentences were passed in the cases of 1,803 white victims, or 6.3%. However, the death penalty was handed down in only 14 of 1,683 homicides of black

---

*Reprinted with permission of the National Council on Crime and Delinquency, from William J. Bowers and Glenn L. Pierce, "Arbitrariness and Discrimination Under Post-*Furman* Capital Statutes," *Crime and Delinquency*, October 1980, vol. 26, p. 593.

Probability of Receiving the Death Sentence in Florida, Georgia, Texas and Ohio for Criminal Homicide, by Race of Offender and Victim (from effective dates of respective post-*Furman* capital statutes through 1977)

Offender/Victim Racial Combinations	Estimated Number of Offenders	Persons Sentenced to Death	Overall Probability of Death Sentence
Florida			
Black kills white	240	53	.221
White kills white	1768	82	.046
Black kills black	1922	12	.006
White kills black	80	0	.000
Georgia			
Black kills white	258	43	.167
White kills white	1006	42	.052
Black kills black	2458	12	.005
White kills black	71	2	.028
Texas			
Black kills white	344	30	.087
White kills white	3616	56	.015
Black kills black	2597	2	.001
White kills black	143	1	.007
Ohio			
Black kills white	173	44	.254
White kills white	803	37	.046
Black kills black	1170	20	.017
White kills black	47	0	.000

Reprinted with permission of the National Council on Crime and Delinquency, from William J. Bowers and Glenn L. Pierce, "Arbitrariness and Discrimination Under Post-*Furman* Capital Statutes," *Crime and Delinquency*, October 1980, vol. 26, p. 594.

victims, or less than 1%. The authors did not explore the reasons for these discrepancies, but they speculated on two possibilities: unconscious prejudice on the part of prosecutors, judges, and jurors who value the life of a white more than the life of a black, and the propensity of mostly white juries to identify with white victims. In short, the implication is that society takes murder more seriously when the victim is white (*New York Times*, January 5, 1984, p. 8).

10.   Many of the new studies, as yet unpublished, have been appended to the briefs of capital convicts who are appealing their sentences or seeking stays of execution in the lower courts. The Supreme Court has not squarely faced the new racial discrimination claim, although as Justice Brennan noted, "the issue cannot be avoided much longer" (dissenting in *Pulley* v. *Harris*, 1984, p. B995–6). Do the results of these post-*Gregg* studies support a stronger equal protection claim than Wolfgang's data in *Maxwell* v. *Bishop* (1968)? Since there is differential sentencing according to the victim's race in Georgia, what are the implications for the procedure of comparative proportionality review used by the Georgia Supreme Court?

11.   Would you expect that the cycle of reform observed in the challenge to differential sentencing in rape cases based on the defendant's race—first, presentation of empirical evidence of the improbability of the disparities due to chance alone; second, vigorous denial by state officials of any racial bias and rejection by the courts of the challenge; and third, changes in sentencing in the ensuing years that result in the diminution or elimination of the disparities, changes which "tacitly admit" the very bias denied earlier (Zeisel 1981, p. 468)—would be repeated in the challenge to differential sentencing in murder cases based on the victim's race?

5.6.   THE JURISPRUDENCE OF DEATH IN PERSPECTIVE

The ideas discussed in *Furman* and *Gregg,* though garbed in modern constitutional attire, are long-standing. From the debate between Caesar and Cato in ancient Rome on the legitimacy and efficacy of capital punishment to the opinions of the Justices of the Supreme Court in our day, "the main arguments for or against the death penalty have remained remarkably unchanged in the course of the centuries" (Hornum 1967, p. 55). The recurrent issues in the debate include the following: Does society have a right to exact retribution? To what extent does the death penalty deter criminality? Are there less costly alternatives to the death penalty that accomplish the same penological ends? How can society safeguard against the fallibility and unevenhandedness of human judgment in imposing the penalty? What is the prevailing community sentiment on the subject and how much weight should be given to it? What has been the experience of other jurisdictions with the abolition or reimposition of the death penalty? And, the preliminary jurisdictional issue, who is the proper authority to try to answer these questions?

In this country for the past two decades, the Supreme Court has taken on the task of addressing these questions. As with other matters that implicate wide-ranging social and political considerations (such as, for example, school desegregation), the issues raised by capital punishment were translated into the language of law and submitted to the Court for authoritative resolution. On the first question, the Court ruled that the state can, as a matter of principle, deprive a criminal offender of his life. On the remaining questions, however, the opinions in the first two rounds of litigation yielded no definitive and consistent answers. The opinions have been characterized as "glossolalial" (Justice Rehnquist in *Woodson* v. *North Carolina,* 1976, p. 317) and a "jurisprudential debacle" (Radin 1978, p. 998). The Chief Justice has conceded that the Court's signals in the cases shortly after *Furman* have not "always been easy to decipher" (*Lockett* v. *Ohio,* 1978, p. 602). No coherent pattern of reasoning underlies the decisions, no "neutral principles" (Wechsler 1959) emerge that transcend the particulars and explain the results.

The Politics and Dialectics of Adjudication

Doctrinal harmony is not the only way of evaluating the jurisprudence of capital punishment. There are limits to constitutional adjudication that account in part for the lack of clear signals. "The meaning of the Supreme Court's death penalty cases," Murchison (1978) suggests, is found in "the interplay of the judicial and political forces in contemporary American society" (p. 546). Ours is a system consisting of separate but coordinate branches of government, held together by a network of procedural checks and balances. One such procedure is judicial review: the power of the judiciary to evaluate the activities of another branch when their constitutionality is called into question. There is a continuing dialectic between the judicial and political arms of government. Legislators enact statutes: the Court passes on their constitutionality, sustaining or overturning them; modified or new statutes are enacted in response to the judicial action; constitutional challenges are mounted anew; and so on. Court decisions must be seen against this backdrop of the dynamics of the governmental process; they cannot be read in a political vacuum. Present meaning is breathed into the living Constitution as a result of this interchange. Answers to some of the recurrent questions in the debate on capital punishment are not found in Court opinions alone, as if doctrinal reasoning is all that counted, but they arise from the interactions between the Court, the public, and the latter's elected representatives.

By the mid-sixties, attempts at legislative reform and abolition had run their course. Proponents for change then turned to the federal courts which, at the time, were receptive to the claims of "minorities" (defined by race or criminal status) that they deserved protection from the majoritarian political process. For the first few years, the Supreme Court reacted cautiously to the challenges to capital trial procedures. It sidestepped the claim of racial discrimination in capital sentencing and deferred a ruling on the issue of the guilt bias of death qualified juries. It refused to countermand the legislative will regarding standardless sentencing and single verdict trials. The Court assiduously respected the political processes of the states but, at the same time, strove to find other grounds for sparing the capital convict of execution. The result was a decade-long de facto moratorium on executions that was broken in 1977 when Gary Gilmore went voluntarily before a firing squad in Utah (*Newsweek*, January 24, 1977, p. 35). These initial cases did not reach the ultimate substantive question nor did they result in sweeping decisions on the procedural questions. What they did was to purchase time for the legislative process to wrestle with and arrive at new answers to the enduring issues. The Court temporarily stalled executions and awaited the political response to its initiative.

By 1972, it became apparent that state legislatures were not about to change the status quo. Public opinion, though generally supportive of capital punishment, was riveted on other, more pressing social issues of the day. The death penalty was not a subject of great political visibility and interest. There was little public awareness of the burgeoning death row population, made all the larger by the judicial moratorium. The Court finally stepped into the breach. "*Furman* forced the political system to act if it wished to maintain the death penalty" (Murchison 1978, p. 540). The Court trod a middle ground between striking down and upholding capital sentencing statutes. It did not rule that the statutes were per se invalid, because it would have exposed itself to the criticism that it was acting as a super-legislature and substituting its penal philosophy for that of representative bodies of the states. Nor did it rule that the statutes were per se valid, because it would have abdicated its obligation of judicial review. Instead, the Court handed down a fairly narrow, procedural decision that was intended to be a catalyst for legislative action.

New death penalty statutes were promptly enacted by Congress and the states. The Court, having announced that the arbitrary imposition of the death penalty was unconstitutional, then stepped to the sidelines for a few years to observe without comment this new flurry of political activity. It was reminiscent of its action in *Brown*. There, after declaring segregated schools unconstitutional and ordering remedial action with "all deliberate speed," the Court also removed itself from centerstage and for several years thereafter let state and local officials work out their own solutions. In 1976, the Court pronounced judgment on the new legislative handiwork. *Gregg* deferred to the nationwide political consensus and the perceived mood of the citizenry. Most states had passed guided capital statutes and polls showed that the public was generally opposed to obligatory death sentences. The Court respected these national trends and upheld the validity of the death penalty. At the same time, it made it difficult to impose by overturning mandatory sentencing and requiring certain procedures and standards. *Gregg* completed what *Furman* started. It prescribed a remedy (standardized sentencing) for the constitutional wrong identified earlier (arbitrary sentencing).

In *Coker*, the Court invalidated Georgia's capital punishment for rape in a case involving an adult woman and no extrinsic physical violence. At the time, only three states made forcible rape a capital crime. The Court evaluated the statute by the "evolving standards of decency" of the nation, not of Georgia alone, and found the sanction to be disproportional to the offense. When the overwhelming majority of the states had rejected the death penalty for rapists, the court was unwilling to defer to the legislative will of a handful of jurisdictions.

Thus, with hindsight, we can see in the line of cases a pattern of growth as the law of capital punishment evolved from the interaction between the judicial and political processes. The Court adjudicates by interpreting the ambiguous text of the Constitution. It does so not only by ascertaining and reflecting the consensual values of society, as indicated by legislative pronouncements and public opinion. It also seeks to aid in the creation of national values. These normative judgments are then given a reasoned justification (admittedly feeble in the death penalty cases) based upon legal rules, social science information, philosophical arguments, and/or other grounds. The rationalization serves to explain the results in terms of general principles rather than idiosyncratic factors. The decision is designed to influence the electorate and its representatives, thereby setting in motion what G. E. White (1973) calls the "dialectics of adjudication": the processes of action and reaction, influence and response, between the judicial and political sectors of government (p. 296).

In each case, the Court proceeded with measured caution. To avoid any big and lasting mistakes, the Court refrained from making any big policy jumps. It avoided sweeping judgments whenever there were narrower grounds for decision. Each judgment produced a marginal change in the existing situation. The case method of adjudication lends itself well to this kind of "incremental decision-making" (Lindblom 1959; Daniels 1979). The Justices, like other social policy-makers, cannot contemplate in advance all the possible courses of action and their respective consequences. They had to take one step at a time. Depending in part on the feedback they received, their next step was forward or backward or sideways. They groped through the political mist for actions that satisfied their standard of craft and their vision of the desired policy. Each decision was a successive approximation of their objective, even as the objective itself continued to change under reconsideration. The sum of these incremental changes and the political response that they evoked constitute the present and still evolving jurisprudence of death.

The Death Sentence: A Compromise Sanction?

The vexing problem that triggered the efforts at judicial abolition in the mid-sixties is still with us today: Many are sentenced, few are executed, and the death row population keeps mushrooming. Since *Gregg*, juries across the nation have been imposing death sentences at the rate of about fifteen to twenty per month. Capital punishment is no longer mainly a southern phenomenon; now it is also prevalent in the Sun Belt states. In 1982, a milestone in the death row population was reached. The census of the damned burgeoned past 1,000, nearly double the number at the start of the judicial challenges two decades ago. Interviews with jurors indicate that they do not believe in the reality of executions. They impose the death sentence because they believe the defendant deserves it, but they seriously doubt whether it will ever be carried out. The figures do not belie their skepticism. The numbers executed in each of the five decades from 1930–39 to 1970–79 are, respectively, as follows: 1667, 1284, 717, 191, and 2. Although the pace has quickened in the early eighties (five were executed in 1983), it is still easier for the proverbial rich man to enter the Kingdom of Heaven than for the condemned to go to the gas chamber.

Capital convicts are mired in extended postconviction proceedings. Their chief weapon is the very tortuousness of the appeals process. By artful petitions and repetitive demands for eleventh-hour stays of execution, they have often fought the executioner to a draw. For the foreseeable future, so long as popular support for retaining the death penalty on the law books continues, the guerrilla struggle to thwart its imposition will likely continue too. The Court's patience with this abolitionist strategy appears to be running out. Chief Justice Burger has rebuked defense lawyers for turning capital appeals into a "sporting contest," and Justice Powell has expressed concern that stays of execution undermine public confidence in the courts. The Court has begun to streamline the appeals process to allow at least some executions to proceed. It has upheld the death sentence imposed as a result of procedures that were flawed but constitutionally "harmless" (*Barclay* v. *Florida*, 1983), deferred to the findings of fact and interpretations of law made by state courts in sentencing hearings (*Wainwright* v. *Goode*, 1983), and refused to mandate comparative proportionality review in every case (*Pulley* v. *Harris*, 1984).

Eventually, many death row inmates will have exhausted their legal remedies. The backlog of death sentences looms as a major social issue. Even proponents of capital punishment do not envision a sanguinary solution. "There won't be a blood bath," the attorney general of Florida said. (Florida has over 200 persons on death row, more than any other state.) He expects only 4 to 6 executions in the state in a given year (*Seattle Times*, January 8, 1984, p. A4). The attorney general of Georgia denied that there will be "a rampage to implement the death penalty" (*Newsweek*, October 17, 1983, p. 45). If they are not executed, their death sentences presumably would be commuted to life terms. (A "life" sentence may not necessarily be so. For example, of 102 defendants who were sentenced to die in San Quentin and had their sentences changed to life imprisonment, 29 have been paroled and 25 have release dates; *Newsweek*, May 24, 1982, p. 82.) It is a course that would surely be unacceptable to retentionists, partly because of the possibility of parole and partly because of their belief in the retributive and deterrent significance of executions. The imposition of the death penalty in the United States, then, remains largely an unpredictable event.

At present, death row inmates are in a state of limbo. Society has adjudged them as deserving of death, not of life in prison and certainly not of eventual release. On the other hand, there is greater public awareness of the omnipresent risk of mistake and unevenhandedness in sentencing, and hence a concomitant reluctance to actually carry it out. Perhaps the unarticulated, political solution to the choice between life and death is the existing, rough justice kind of compromise: life imprisonment under the perpetual threat of execution, for most (but not all) capital convicts. Until "evolving standards of decency" dictate otherwise, a capital sentence for most (but not all) defendants often represents not a sentence to death or to life, but to purgatory.

REFERENCES

Adams v. Texas, 448 U.S. 38 (1980).

Allport, G. W. "Attitudes." In *Readings in Attitude Theory and Measurement,* edited by M. Fishbein. New York: 1967.

Amsterdam, A. "The Supreme Court and the Rights of Suspects in Criminal Cases." *New York University Law Review* 45 (1970): 785–815.

Antunes, G., and Hunt, A. L. "The Deterrent Impact of Criminal Sanctions: Some Implications for Criminal Justice Policy." *Journal of Urban Law* 51 (1973): 145–61.

Baldus, D. C. "Quantitative Methods for Judging the Comparative Excessiveness of Death Sentences." In *The Use/Nonuse/Misuse of Applied Social Research in the Courts,* edited by M. J. Saks and C. H. Baron. Cambridge, Mass.: Abt Books, 1980.

———; Pulaski, C. A., Jr.; Woodworth, G.; and Kyle, F. D. "Identifying Comparatively Excessive Sentences of Death: A Quantitative Approach." *Stanford Law Review* 33 (1980): 1–74.

Barclay v. Florida, 103 S. Ct. 3383 (1983).

Barefoot v. Estelle, 103 S. Ct. 3418 (1983).

Barzun, J. "In Favor of Capital Punishment." In *The Death Penalty in America,* edited by H. A. Bedau. Garden City, N.Y.: Doubleday, 1964.

Bedau, H. A. *The Death Penalty in America.* Garden City, N.Y.: Doubleday, 1964.

Bell v. Patterson, 402 F. 2d 394 (10th Cir. 1968).

Berns, W. "Defending the Death Penalty." *Crime and Delinquency* 26 (1980): 503–18.

Bice, S. H. "Standards of Judicial Review Under the Equal Protection and Due Process Clauses." *Southern California Law Review* 50 (1977): 689–718.

Black, C., Jr. *Capital Punishment: The Inevitability of Caprice and Mistake.* New York: W. W. Norton, 1974.

———. "Objections to S. 1382, a Bid to Establish Regional Criteria for the Imposition of Capital Punishment." *Crime and Delinquency* 26 (1980): 441–52.

Blumstein, A.; Cohen, J.; and Nagin, D. (Eds.). *Deterrence and Incapacitation: Estimating the Effects of Criminal Sanctions on Crime Rates.* Wash., D.C.: National Academy of Sciences, 1978.

Bowers, W. *Executions in America.* Lexington, Mass.: Heath, 1974.

———, and Pierce, G. L. "Arbitrariness and Discrimination Under Post-*Furman* Capital Statutes." *Crime and Delinquency* 26 (1980): 563–635.

Brown v. Allen, 344 U.S. 443 (1953).

Brown v. Mississippi, 297 U.S. 278 (1936).

Burger, W. "Post-Conviction Remedies: Eliminating Federal-State Friction." *Journal of Criminal Law, Criminology, and Police Science* 61 (1970): 148–51.

Cobb, T. *A Digest of the Statute Laws of the State of Georgia* (§24 of the Penal Laws), 1851.

Coker v. Georgia, 433 U.S. 584 (1977).

Collins, B. E. *Social Psychology.* Reading, Mass.: Addison-Wesley, 1970.

Comment. "Jury Selection and the Death Penalty: *Witherspoon* in the Lower Courts." *University of Chicago Law Review* 37 (1970): 759–77.

Cowan, C. L.; Thompson, W. C.; and Ellsworth, P. C. "The Effects of Death Qualification on Jurors' Predisposition to Convict and on the Quality of Deliberation." *Law and Human Behavior* 8 (1984): 53–80.

Crampton v. Ohio, 402 U.S. 183 (1971).

Daniels, S. "Social Science and Death Penalty Cases." *Law and Policy Quarterly* 1 (1979): 336–72.

Davidow, R. P., and Lowe, G. D. "Attitudes of Potential and Present Members of the Legal Profession Toward Capital Punishment—A Survey and Analysis." *Mercer Law Review* 30 (1979): 585–614.

Davies, T. Y. "Do Criminal Due Process Principles Make a Difference?" *American Bar Foundation Research Journal* 1982 (1982): 247–68.

Duncan v. Louisiana, 391 U.S. 145 (1968).

Duren v. Missouri, 439 U.S. 357 (1979).

Erikson, K. T. *The Wayward Puritans.* New York: John Wiley, 1966.

Fay v. Noia, 372 U.S. 391 (1963).

Filler, J. "Movements to Abolish the Death Penalty in the United States." *Annals* 284 (1952): 124–36.

Fitzgerald, R., and Ellsworth, P. C. "Due Process vs. Crime Control: Death Qualification and Jury Attitudes." *Law and Human Behavior* 8 (1984): 31–52.

Frank v. Mangum, 237 U.S. 309 (1915).

Friedman, L. F., and Percival, R. V. *The Roots of Justice: Crime and Punishment in Alameda County, California—1870–1910.* Chapel Hill: University of North Carolina Press, 1981.

Furman v. Georgia, 408 U.S. 238 (1972).

Gardner v. Florida, 430 U.S. 349 (1977).

Gibson, J. L. "Race as a Determinant of Criminal Sentences: A Methodological Critique and Case Study." *Law and Society Review* 12 (1978): 455–78.

Girsh, F. G. "The *Witherspoon* Question: The Social Science and the Evidence." *NLADA Briefcase* 35 (1978): 99–125.

Godfrey v. Georgia, 446 U.S. 420 (1980).

Gottlieb, G. H. "Testing the Death Penalty." *Southern California Law Review* 34 (1961) 268–81.

Granucci, A. F. " 'Nor Cruel and Unusual Punishments Inflicted': The Original Meaning." *California Law Review* 57 (1969): 839–65.

Green, W. "An Ancient Debate on Capital Punishment." In *Capital Punishment,* edited by T. Sellin. New York: Harper & Row, 1967.

Gregg v. Georgia, 428 U.S. 153 (1976).

Grisby v. Marby, 569 F. Supp. 1273 (E. D. Ark. 1983).

Hall v. State, 247 Ga. 289 (1981).

Haney, C. "Juries and the Death Penalty: Readdressing the Witherspoon Question." *Crime and Delinquency* 26 (1980): 512–27.

———. "Examining Death Qualification: Further Analysis of the Process Effect." *Law and Human Behavior* 8 (1984): 133–52.

Hornum, F. "Two Debates." *Capital Punishment,* edited by T. Sellin. New York: Harper & Row, 1967.

Hovey v. The Superior Court of Alameda County, 168 Cal. Rptr. 128 (1980).

In re Kemmler, 136 U.S. 436 (1890).

Ingraham v. Wright, 430 U.S. 651 (1977).

Jacoby, J. E., and Paternoster, R. "Sentencing Disparity and Jury Packing: Further Challenges to the Death Penalty." *Journal of Criminal Law, Criminology, and Police Science* 73 (1982): 379–87.

Jeffrey, C. R. "Criminal Behavior and Learning Theory." *Journal of Criminal Law, Criminology, and Police Science* 56 (1965): 294–305.

Jurek v. Texas, 428 U.S. 262 (1976).

Jurow, G. L. "New Data on the Effect of a 'Death-Qualified' Jury on the Guilt-Determination Process." *Harvard Law Review* 84 (1971): 567–611.

Kadane, J. B. "After *Hovey:* A Note on Taking Account of the Automatic Death Penalty Jurors." *Law and Human Behavior* 8 (1984): 115–20.

Kadish, S., and Paulsen, M. *Criminal Law and Its Processes,* 3rd ed. Boston: Little, Brown, 1975.

Kamisar, Y.; LaFave, W. R.; and Israel, J. H. *Modern Criminal Procedure,* 5th ed. St. Paul, Minn.: West, 1980.

Kaplan, J. "The Problem of Capital Punishment." *University of Illinois Law Review* 1983 (1983): 555–77.

Kluger, R. *Simple Justice.* New York: Alfred A. Knopf, 1977.

Koeninger, R. L. "Capital Punishment in Texas, 1924–1968." *Crime and Delinquency* 15 (1969): 132–41.

Kohlberg, L., and Elfenbein, D. "Moral Judgments about Capital Punishment: A Developmental-Psychological View." In *Capital Punishment in the United States,* edited by H. A. Bedau and C. M. Pierce. New York: AMS Press, 1976.

Lempert, R. O. "Desert and Deterrence: An Assessment of the Moral Bases of the Case for Capital Punishment." *Michigan Law Review* 79 (1981): 1177–1231.

Lindblom, C. "The Science of Muddling Through." *Public Administration Review* 19 (1959): 79–88.

Lockett v. Ohio, 438 U.S. 602 (1978).

Lord, C. G.; Rose, L.; and Lepper, M. R. "Biased Assimilation and Attitude Polarization: The Effects of Prior Theories on Subsequently Considered Evidence." *Journal of Personality and Social Psychology* 37 (1979): 2098–2109.

Louisiana ex rel. Francis v. Resweber, 329 U.S. 459 (1947).

Maxwell v. Bishop, 398 F.2d 138 (8th Cir. 1968)

Maxwell v. Bishop, 398 U.S. 262 (1970).

Maxwell v. State, 370 S.W.2d 113 (1963).

Maxwell v. Stephens, 229 F. Supp. 205 (E.D. Ark. 1964); 348 F.2d 325 (8th Cir. 1965).

McBarnet, D. *Conviction: Law, the State, and the Construction of Justice.* Atlantic Highlands, N.J.: Humanities Press, 1981.

McGautha v. California, 402 U.S. 183 (1971).

Meltsner, M. *Cruel and Unusual: The Supreme Court and Capital Punishment.* New York: Random House, 1973.

Monahan, J. "The Prediction of Violent Criminal Behavior: A Methodological Critique and Prospectus." In *Deterrence and Incapacitation: Estimating the Effects of Criminal Sanctions on Crime Rates*, edited by A. Blumstein and D. Nagin. Wash., D.C.: National Academy of Sciences, 1978.

———. *Predicting Violent Behavior: An Assessment of Clinical Techniques.* Beverly Hills, Calif.: Sage Publications, 1981.

Moore v. Illinois, 403 U.S. 933 (1971).

Morris, A. "Thoughts on Capital Punishment." *Washington Law Review* 35 (1960): 335–61.

Murchison, K. M. "Toward a Perspective on the Death Penalty Cases." *Emory Law Journal* 27 (1978): 469–556.

Note. "Capital Punishment in Virginia." *Virginia Law Review* 58 (1972): 97–142.

Note. "Discretion and the Constitutionality of the New Death Penalty Statutes." *Harvard Law Review* 87 (1974): 1690–1719.

Oberer, W. "Does Disqualification of Jurors for Scruples Against Capital Punishment Constitute Denial of Fair Trial on the Issue of Guilt?" *Texas Law Review* 39 (1961): 545–67.

Orne, M. T. "On the Social Psychology of the Psychological Experiment." *American Psychologist* 17 (1962): 776–83.

Partington, D. H. "The Incidence of the Death Penalty for Rape in Virginia." *Washington and Lee Law Review* 22 (1965): 43–75.

People v. Anderson, 6 Cal.3d 628 (1972).

People v. Speck, 242 N.E.2d 208 (1968).

Pittman v. State, 434 S.W.2d 352 (Tex. Crim. App. 1968).

Powell v. Alabama, 287 U.S. 45 (1932).

President's Commission on Law Enforcement and the Administration of Justice. *The Challenge of Crime in a Free Society.* Washington, D.C.: U.S. Government Printing Office, 1967.

Pritchard, J. L. *A History of Capital Punishment.* Port Washington, N.Y.: Kennikat Press, 1971.

Proffitt v. Florida, 428 U.S. 242 (1976).

Pulley v. Harris, 44 CCH S. Ct. Bull. B966 (1984).

Radin, M. J. "The Jurisprudence of Death: Evolving Standards for the Cruel and Unusual Punishments Clause." *University of Pennsylvania Law Review* 126 (1978): 989–1064.

Reichert, W. O. "Capital Punishment Reconsidered." *Kentucky Law Journal* 47 (1959): 397–417.

Reynolds v. United States, 98 U.S. 145 (1878).

Roberts v. Louisiana, 428 U.S. 325 (1976).

Robinson v. California, 370 U.S. 660 (1962).

Sarat, A. "Deterrence and the Constitution: On the Limits of Capital Punishment." *Journal of Behavioral Economics* 6 (1977): 311–59.

———, and Vidmar, N. "Public Opinion, the Death Penalty, and the Eighth Amendment: Testing the Marshall Hypothesis." *Wisconsin Law Review 1976* (1976): 171–206.

Sellin, T. *The Death Penalty: A Report for the Model Penal Code Project of the A.L.I.,* 1959.

———, ed. *Capital Punishment.* New York: Harper & Row, 1967.

Spinkellink v. Wainwright, 578 F.2d 582 (5th Cir. 1978).

Stampp, K. *The Peculiar Institution: Slavery in the Antebellum South.* New York: Alfred A. Knopf, 1956.

State v. Lockett, 358 N.E.2d 1062 (Ohio 1976).

State v. Williams, 77 Mo. 310 (1883).

Strauder v. West Virginia, 100 U.S. 303 (1879).

Sweezy v. New Hampshire, 354 U.S. 234 (1957).

Tapp, J. L., and Kohlberg, L. "Developing Senses of Law and Legal Justice." In *Law, Justice, and the Individual in Society.* edited by J. L. Tapop and F. J. Levine. New York: Holt, Rinehart & Winston, 1977.

Taylor v. Louisiana, 419 U.S. 522 (1975).

Teeters, N. K., and Hedblom, J. H. *Hung by the Neck.* Springfield, Ill: Charles C Thomas, 1967.

Thiel v. Southern Pacific Co., 328 U.S. 217 (1946).

Trop v. Dulles, 356 U.S. 86 (1958).

United States Department of Justice, Bureau of

Prisons. National Prisoner Statistics, Bulletin No. 46. *Capital Punishment 1930–1970*. August 1971.

Vidmar, N., and Dittenhoffer, T. "Informed Public Opinion and Death Penalty Attitudes." *Canadian Journal of Criminology* 23 (1981): 43–56.

———, and Ellsworth, P. "Public Opinion on the Death Penalty." *Stanford Law Review* 26 (1974):1245–70.

———, and Miller, D. T. "Social Psychological Processes Underlying Attitudes Toward Legal Punishment." *Law and Society Review* 14 (1980): 565–602.

Wainwright v. Goode, 44 CCH S. Ct. Bull. P. B269 (1983).

Wechsler, H. "Toward Neutral Principles of Constitutional Law." *Harvard Law Review* 73 (1959): 1–35.

Weems v. United States, 217 U.S. 349 (1910).

White, G. E. "The Evolution of Reasoned Elaboration." *Virginia Law Review* 59: (1973): 279–302.

White, W. "The Constitutional Invalidity of Convictions Imposed by Death Qualified Juries." *Cornell Law Review* 58 (1973): 1176–1220.

Wilkerson v. Utah, 99 U.S. 130 (1879).

Williams v. Florida, 399 U.S. 78 (1970).

Williams v. State, 32 Miss. 389 (1856).

Witherspoon v. Illinois, 391 U.S. 510 (1968).

Wolfgang, M. E. "The Social Scientist in Court." *Journal of Criminal Law and Criminology* 65 (1974): 239–47.

———, and Reidel, M. "Rape, Racial Discrimination, and the Death Penalty." In *Capital Punishment in the United States*, edited by H. A. Bedau and C. M. Pierce. New York: AMS Press, 1976.

Woodson v. North Carolina, 428 U.S. 280 (1976).

Zeisel, H. "The Deterrent Effect of the Death Penalty: Facts v. Faiths." *Supreme Court Review* (1976): 317–43.

———. "Race Bias in the Administration of the Death Penalty: The Florida Experience." *Harvard Law Review* 95 (1981): 456–68.

Zimring, F., and Hawkins, G. *Deterrence: The Legal Threat in Crime Control.* Chicago: University of Chicago Press, 1973.

CHAPTER 6

Impact of Law: Case Study of Regulating Police Conduct

6.1. INTRODUCTION

The Police Function in a Democratic Society

BALANCING LAW AND ORDER

At the interface of a community and crime stands the police. In this country there are over 400,000 individuals in some 40,000 separate police agencies—one-third of them concentrated in the 55 largest urban police departments—engaged in the enterprise of enforcing the law and maintaining public order (Task Force Report 1967, p. 91). Other officials such as judges, prosecutors, defense attorneys, and corrections personnel are also in daily contact with crime and the public, but the police are the most visible and distinctive of all because only the police are right in the midst of where the action takes place: on the streets. They are the frontline of a community's day-to-day efforts to safeguard its citizens from the injury, losses, and fear occasioned by crime and the threat of crime. It is to the police rather than to these other officials of the criminal justice system that citizens first turn for protection of their persons, homes, and community.

There are limitations, of course, to the effectiveness of the police in deterring crime. Criminal behavior has been associated with a constellation of social forces, including poverty, poor race relations, family breakdowns, and decay of the inner cities. The police cannot and do not attempt to resolve the social conditions that enable crime to flourish.

Another limitation are the legal restrictions on police powers. Most peace-keeping and law enforcement actions can impinge directly upon a citizen's freedom of action. For example, frisking rock concert goers at the entry to the premises; stopping and questioning persons on the streets; searching homes and cars—these actions, which the police consider necessary and justifiable for carrying out their

273

obligations, nonetheless represent personal intrusions into the lives of citizens. They may affect a person's dignity, integrity, sense of privacy, or constitutionally protected liberty. Consequently, as the President's Commission (1967) observed, most people "both welcome official protection and resent official interference." Depending on how the police act, they may be seen as "protectors or oppressors, as friends or enemies" (p. 92). The most intrusive police actions occur, as is commonly known, in urban areas where the crime rates are the highest and the conditions of life are the worst. It is here in the densely populated cores of our major cities that the demand for police protection is the greatest. It is also here that most allegations of police misconduct are heard, and where a routine street encounter between an officer and a citizen can trigger a widespread riot.

While engaged in the competitive and sometimes dangerous task of ferreting out crime, the police in moments of excess zeal may undertake actions that threaten or infringe upon individual rights and freedoms that are fundamental in a democratic society. Ours is a government of laws, not of individuals, whether these individuals are judges, Presidents, or police officers. The history of American liberty, Justice Frankfurter observed in *McNabb* v. *United States* (1943), is the history of legal procedure—the history of how actions of government officials are controlled by law to prevent abuses of power. Thus, during the past fifty years or so, and especially during the decade of the 1960s, the more intrusive police procedures have been circumscribed by appellate court decisions: Interrogations must be preceded by warnings of the right to silence and to counsel; searches of premises require judicial warrants unless excused by specified exigencies; stop-and-frisks are justifiable only upon articulable suspicion that crime may be afoot; and so on. Many police and citizens feel that these judicially imposed restrictions on the police have unduly inhibited law enforcement and thereby rendered more difficult the protection of the public from crime. However, if the highly valued freedoms guaranteed to all persons—including criminal suspects who are legally presumed innocent of any wrongdoing until proven otherwise in court—are to be safeguarded and to flourish, the public monopoly of force cannot go unregulated.

There always has been and probably always will be an underlying tension between the competing demands of maintaining public security and protecting individual freedom. Packer (1964) has identified these two value perspectives as the "crime control model" and the "due process model" of the criminal process. The former has as its main objective the efficient apprehension and disposition of offenders in order to deter crime. The latter subordinates the control of criminal conduct to the goal of safeguarding individual dignity and autonomy. "The Crime Control model is administrative and managerial; the Due Process model is adversary and judicial. The Crime Control model may be analogized to an assembly line, the Due Process model to an obstacle course" (Packer 1966, p. 239).

The police function approximates the crime control model. The police concentrate on factual guilt; their norms are those of a productive enterprise: clearances by arrest. However, the courts attend to legal guilt or clearances by conviction, and the norms they set forth for police conduct attach paramount value to the fairness of law enforcement procedures. How the police carry out searches or interrogations is as important, if not more important, as the fruits produced thereby. These models embody polar opposites in values, though in practice the values are subject to compromise and modulation. The extent to which one or the other will be predominant at any given time will affect the outlook and outcome of the police function.

THE EXCLUSIONARY RULE

One of the most poignant issues that arises out of the oscillating balance between these two value perspectives is the exclusion from trial of evidence obtained by police actions deemed unlawful by the courts. The exclusionary rule is at present the main device for judicial review of police conduct. It manifests the principle that state power must be exercised within the framework of the law. It teaches that law enforcement, unchecked by law, can become a means of official oppression.

The exclusionary rule consists, in fact, of several rules, each designed to enforce a different constitutional right. There is a Fourth Amendment exclusionary rule for unreasonable police searches and seizures that violate the right to privacy (*Mapp* v. *Ohio*, 1961); a Fifth Amendment exclusionary rule for coerced or otherwise improper police interrogations that violate the right to silence (*Miranda* v. *Arizona*, 1966); a Sixth Amendment exclusionary rule for pre-indictment lineup identifications that violate the right to the presence of the suspect's counsel (*United States* v. *Wade*, 1967; see Chapter 10, section 10.2); and a Fourteenth Amendment exclusionary rule for evidence obtained by methods that "shock the conscience" and violate the requirement of due process (*Rochin* v. *California*, 1952).

The most frequently invoked of these rules pertain to Fourth Amendment and Fifth Amendment violations. Advocates of crime control values raise the loudest public clamor when "the criminal [goes] free" merely because "the constable has blundered" (*People* v. *Defore*, 1926, p. 21). This is because physical evidence (for example, narcotics, weapons) seized as a result of an improper search (for example, without a warrant) is inherently no less reliable an indicator of a suspect's guilt than if that evidence had been obtained legally. The probative value of the evidentiary items is unchanged by the method used in their acquisition. In comparison, the exclusion of confessions extracted by application of the third degree evokes less spirited opposition from the crime control camp. It is recognized that incriminating statements obtained by coercion may be untrue, and their admission at trial would undermine the reliability of the guilt-determination process. However, the exclusion of confessions which are obtained in violation of the *Miranda* warnings (regarding the right to silence and the right to counsel), but are otherwise noncoerced, has prompted almost as much criticism as the exclusion of the fruits of unreasonable searches and seizures.

The basic theme, then, that underlies the inquiry into the police role in a democratic system and that is the focus of this chapter is how the courts have strived to reach a proper equilibrium between crime control and due process values in the course of controlling the police—that is, how they have sought to ensure individual freedom consistent with the need for an orderly society. Our attention will center on the Fourth Amendment and Fifth Amendment exclusionary rules, which are intended, at least partly, to regulate police investigative practices. We will examine the impact of these judicial efforts to increase police accountability of its law enforcement methods and consider the uses of social science research in this process. The subject of judicial review of police behavior provides a case study of the effectiveness and limits of judge-made law as an instrument of organizational and behavioral change. To set the stage for the materials that follow, we turn next to a quick overview of the development of police forces.

A Brief History of the Police

The origins of the American police are rooted in early English history. Alfred the Great in the ninth century developed the simple expedient of paying private citizens for arresting offenders. The populace was divided into groups of ten families called "tithings." Each person was responsible for watching over the actions of others in the tithing. This unit was subsequently expanded tenfold to the "hundred," with one person—called the constable, who is the lineal antecedent of the modern police officer—in charge of keeping the weapons and organizing the group. Still later, the hundred was increased to encompass the county-wide "shire," under the supervision of an appointed "shire-reeve," who eventually became known as the "sheriff" (Schwartz and Goldstein 1970, pp. 32–34). In the ensuing centuries, other informal groups were developed to patrol the streets of large towns at night, including the so-called watch and ward.

The industrialization and urbanization of England in the eighteenth and early nineteenth centuries spurred the search for different and more effective ways of controlling crime in the rapidly growing cities. One development was the establishment of "public offices," later called police offices, which were headed by justices of the peace who employed paid constables to patrol a given neighborhood. Several independent and noncoordinated public offices existed in a single metropolitan area. In 1829, Sir Robert Peel, the home secretary, created the first city-wide police force in London. The officers, popularly called "Bobbies" after their founder, were placed in uniform and organized along military lines. Supervision of this force rested—as it does and other metropolitan forces still do today (Devlin 1958, pp. 17–19)—with the Home Secretary who, in turn, was accountable to Parliament. It was a novel effort at reconciling the need for police action and the protection of individual liberty.

The American colonists adopted the English system of law enforcement consisting of constable, sheriff, and watch and ward. With the growth of American cities in the nineteenth century, unified and full-time metropolitan police forces were established, the first one in Philadelphia in 1833. For a long time, the quality of these forces was poor. Salaries were low, officers were poorly trained if at all, corruption was common, and the public generally held the police in low regard. Police departments were often identified with the scandals of local politics of the period. A major source of the problem was political control of the police. High level police positions were considered patronage jobs, resulting in rapid turnover of police administrators. The potential for abuse is evident when control over departmental personnel and law enforcement policy is at the hands of political machine bosses.

Police reform at the turn of the century meant ridding the departments of political influence. Various efforts to this end were instituted. Police administrative boards, composed of noted judges, lawyers, and businessmen, were created with the purpose of appointing the top police executives and overseeing departmental affairs. The inexperience in police matters of the typical board members limited their effectiveness. Another reform effort was state control of local law enforcement. However, political friction often resulted because of the disharmony of views of state legislators,

representing rural constituencies, and of city officials, representing a more sophisticated urban population. A more successful effort at gaining political independence
for the police was the introduction of civil service appointments. This was one of the
main recommendations of a blue ribbon group concerned with criminal justice reform, the Wickersham Commission of 1931. Attempts at formal police training were
still another means of elevating the standards of police conduct, though in many parts
of the country it was not until the 1950s that police academies were established
(President's Commission 1967b, pp. 6–7).

Many of the issues that confront law enforcement today have their roots in
earlier years. This cursory history serves to highlight a few contemporary concerns.

The broad and largely unchecked discretionary authority of the police has a
long history. It goes back to the days when public offices were developed. When the
English justices of the peace relinquished their law enforcement duties to constables
and confined themselves to questions of law, the wide scope of their investigative
responsibilities was transferred wholesale to the police. This discretion to invoke or
not invoke the criminal process is one that the modern police officer continues to
exercise.

From the colonial days to the present, the social, political, and economic life of
the nation has become increasingly interdependent and centralized. The system of
law enforcement, however, has not kept apace. "America," noted the President's
Commission (1967b), "is a nation of small, decentralized police forces" (p. 3). There
are still a multitude of independent and local police units, each with responsibilities
that overlap and efforts that duplicate those of others. Within a 50-mile radius of
Chicago, for example, there are some 350 separate municipal, county, and state
police forces (LaFave 1965b, p. 597). The absence of a central authority to which all
the police are responsible results not only in administrative inefficiencies but also in
the lack of a common law enforcement policy. This further encourages the unfettered and uneven exercise of police discretion.

Memories of political control of the police of yesteryear inhibit current attempts by elected officials to reform the police. Today, reform means controlling the
discretionary authority of the police. The proposition that some checks on the police
are necessary in a democratic system is hardly disputed. Nonetheless, few efforts to
regulate police conduct have come forth from the legislative and executive branches
of government, in part because such efforts raise again the specter of political influence. As a result, the appellate courts have had to step into the regulatory vacuum.
A federal judge noted that "the courts have been left to make rules and apply
constitutional standards with little, if any, real knowledge or guidance regarding the
difficulties which face the police. . . . Moreover, Congress and the legislatures have
failed to make appropriate inquiry and statutory provision to meet the situation" (C.
J. Lumbard, *United States* v. *Fay*, 1963, p. 70). The national debate today centers on
whether the judiciary is adequate to the task of supervising police conduct via the
application of the exclusionary rule and, if not, what alternative means exist for
increasing police accountability of its actions.

OVERVIEW

In this chapter we shall look at both the law and the social research on judicial
controls of police behavior, in particular the impact of the Fifth Amendment ex-

clusionary rule on police interrogations and the Fourth Amendment exclusionary rule on police searches and seizures.

In the landmark decision of *Miranda* v. *Arizona*, reproduced in section 6.2, the Supreme Court set forth a new set of constitutional norms to govern interrogations. For the first time, it applied the Fifth Amendment privilege to the stationhouse and required the issuance of warnings prior to any questioning of a suspect in custody. It was an attempt to update the law of confessions to take into account the advances in psychological means of influence employed by the police.

Section 6.3 presents a social psychological study of interrogations conducted in New Haven shortly after the decision was announced. It attempted to measure the degree of coerciveness of detective interrogations, the impact of *Miranda* on the rate of confessions, and the necessity of confessions for solving crimes. The results clarify some of the factual premises on which *Miranda* rests and suggest directions for new studies.

The impact of the Fourth Amendment exclusionary rule on police field practice is examined in section 6.4 with a debate between two noted experts on the criminal process—a federal judge and a law professor—who assess the competing claims regarding the purposes and assumed consequences of this rule. It exposes how complex issues of value, law, and fact are intermingled in this area. Section 6.5 reviews empirical studies that attempt to trace the effects of the rule by using various sources of information, including court statistics on suppression motions, police interview, and observations of police in action. These materials provide an occasion to discuss issues of methodology and research design in empirical studies of judicial impact.

The exploration of alternatives to the exclusionary rule requires some background on the police. Section 6.6 describes briefly the social organization of a department, the patterns of recruitment and professional socialization, and the attitudes and personality characteristics of patrol officers. The theme is that change in individual police conduct depends, ultimately, on change in the police organization itself.

Judicial regulation via the exclusionary rule is premised on deterring or changing the conduct of individual officers. This is inherent in the case-by-case approach of judicial review. An alternative approach, presented in section 6.7, is self-regulation of the police via their own rule-making. It is based on the common-sensical idea that a lower echelon, frontline police officer is more likely to comply with rules of conduct that emanate from within the policy hierarchy than from outside the department, such as from the appellate courts. An analysis of this administrative model, whether or not it proves to be a feasible alternative, may spur critical thought on the advantages and shortcomings of the judicial model. The materials also make clear that the enduring question of how best to regulate the police in a democracy raises as many issues of social, organizational, and behavioral change as it does of legal rules.

In the final section (6.8), we stand back and view the subject from the wide-angle lens of jurisprudence. The cases of this chapter exemplify one of the ways law is created. Judges fashion rules of conduct by engaging in impact-thinking, that is, by trying to anticipate the social consequences of their decisions. We contrast this teleological or result-oriented style of decision-making with other styles that were illustrated by cases presented in the previous chapters, in order to assess the role of social science in the judicial process.

6.2. JUDICIAL REGULATION OF POLICE INTERROGATION

The Role of Police Interrogation

There are different forms of police questioning, each serving different objectives. There is field interrogation, which consists of stopping and questioning citizens in the streets by uniformed officers for the purpose of making brief, investigative inquiries or gathering intelligence. There is informal questioning or screening of a suspect at the time of booking by the arresting officer or desk sergeant for the purpose of recording fairly routine, basic information regarding the suspect and the circumstances of the arrest. And, finally, there is formal, custodial interrogation by detectives who are skilled in questioning techniques and who are seeking to elicit a confession or some other kind of information which can help solve the case. It is this last type that poses the most serious threat to basic liberties and has prompted the most judicial scrutiny.

It is generally assumed by the courts, the police, and advocates of crime control values that custodial and incommunicado interrogation is a necessary (even if not sufficient) tool of effective law enforcement. Definitive empirical knowledge on this point is lacking. It has been said, though, that interrogations in at least certain instances are "a practical necessity." "Many criminal cases [especially rapes, assaults, homicides], even when investigated by the best qualified police departments, are capable of solution only by means of an admission or confession from the guilty individual, or upon the basis of information obtained from the questioning of other criminal suspects" (Inbau 1961, p. 16). The notion that if police will investigate thoroughly enough in these cases they will discover clues that would lead to the offender is "pure fiction." Moreover, interrogation usually is effective only if it is prolonged, occurs in secret, and employs "less refined methods" (that is, methods of psychological influence that in ordinary business or social interaction would be deemed "deceitful or unethical").

If one starts with the premise that all convictions resulting from the use of stationhouse confessions are improper—because the interrogation procedures are inconsistent with social values of respect for individual dignity and free will, and/or because convictions based on self-accusations threaten our adversarial system of justice wherein the state has the burden of proving guilt—then there ought to be a blanket prohibition of all interrogations. This is obviously an unrealistic position and no court has ever endorsed it. There is a lingering distrust of police interrogation that has historical roots in the inquisitorial practices of the Star Chamber and the ecclesiastical High Commission. On the whole, the present posture of Anglo-American law toward interrogations is one of grudging acceptance of a necessary evil.

The judicial function, therefore, consists of defining the boundaries of permissible and nonpermissible interrogation methods. At the one end there is the application of the third degree which clearly offends civilized sensibilities. At the other end there is wholly innocuous and uncoercive questioning that poses no risks to the values sought to be safeguarded. In between lies a wide range of police methods of borderline legality. The history of judicial efforts to regulate police interrogations is the history of trial-and-error efforts to chart a course between the Scylla of unfettered questioning and the Charybdis of no questioning at all.

A Historical Sketch of Judicial Regulation of Interrogations

In early English common law, all out-of-court confessions, even when extracted by torture, were admissible. Legal restrictions limiting their use in evidence were laid down by the mid-eighteenth century. The principal criterion was voluntariness or noncoercion of the confession, that is, statements obtained without "flattery of hope," "the torture of fear," or other tactics that overwhelmed the exercise of free will (*The King* v. *Warickshall,* 1783, p. 235). An involuntary confession was deemed untrustworthy evidence and excluded from trial.

Although the great bulk of criminal litigation in this country occurs at the state level, it was not until 1936 that the Supreme Court for the first time reviewed a conviction in state court based on a coerced confession. In *Brown* v. *Mississippi,* the Court held that the admission of a confession obtained by methods that were "revolting to the sense of justice" amounted to a denial of the Fourteenth Amendment guarantees of due process. The decision constitutionalized the common law voluntariness test in order to enable the Court to gain jurisdiction over state confession cases. In that instance, several "ignorant Negroes" were charged and convicted for murdering a white man solely on the basis of their confessions. The transcript read "more like pages torn from some medieval account." A white mob, with the participation of the police, accused one of the blacks of the crime and upon his denial of it, "hanged him by a rope to the limb of a tree, and having let him down, they hung him again, and when he still protested his innocence, he was tied to a tree and whipped, and still declin[ed] to accede to the demand that he confess . . ." (p. 281). A couple of days later, the police "again severely whipped the defendant, declaring that he would continue the whipping until he confessed, and the defendant then agreed to confess to such a statement as the deputy [sheriff] would dictate. . . ." The other suspects were likewise whipped and had "their backs . . . cut to pieces with a leather strap with buckles on it" (p. 282).

In the succeeding years, the next five Supreme Court decisions on state confessions also involved uneducated and uncounseled black defendants in southern states, where the uncontroverted records disclosed long, secret sessions of intensive questioning and physical abuse. The Wickersham Commission, a prestigious group concerned with criminal justice reform, reported in the 1930s that "the extraction of confessions through police brutality was a widespread, almost universal, police practice" (President's Commission 1967, p. 93). Under these aggravated circumstances, the Court had no difficulty in reversing unanimously the convictions under the basic idea of fairness implicit in the due process guarantee. As a result, "the third degree is almost non-existent" today (p. 93).

The virtual abolition of physical coercion was replaced by increasingly sophisticated techniques of psychological coercion (for example, thirty-six straight hours of relentless questioning but no physical contact: *Ashcraft* v. *Tennessee,* 1944). For a generation after *Brown,* the Supreme Court adhered to the due process/voluntariness standard for reviewing confessions introduced in state trials. Under this test, a court looks at the "totality of the circumstances" bearing on a suspect's decision to talk. No one single factor can be isolated as being too objectionable as to require exclusion of the confession. Voluntariness depends, instead, on an examination of all of the circumstances, including the characteristics of the suspect (age, intelligence, emotional stability, and so forth) and the details of the interrogation (nature and extent of police overbearing) (*Spano* v. *New York,* 1959).

Due process/voluntariness can be an elusive standard that varies according to how tender or tough each suspect is. It is difficult to re-create after the fact the atmosphere of the interrogation so as to ascertain whether the confession was freely proffered. When the police use psychological methods of influence, mental coercion is more difficult to establish than brute force. Consequently, a "swearing contest" usually develops in court between the defendant and the police as to what happened behind the closed doors of the interrogation room. State trial courts tend to resolve any doubts in favor of the police and state appellate courts tend to defer to trial courts.

Thus, voluntariness is an issue of fact, and so long as state courts found no undue psychological coercion in most cases of police interrogation, the due process/voluntariness test was in effect nullified in practice. The Supreme Court, however, has often overturned confessions in state cases, finding involuntariness where lower courts had concluded otherwise. In part, this is because it is more difficult for local and state judges, who are close to the crime scene and are exposed firsthand to its impact, to separate the substance of a confession from the procedure by which it was obtained. They tend to construe the applicable law in ways that respond to the equities of a case. The more opprobrious the crime, the more likely is the tendency to focus on the guilt of the defendant than on the abstract norm of legality. Supreme Court justices, by reason of their more removed and detached position, are better able to separate these issues. Moreover, Amsterdam (1970) points out:

> To a mind-staggering extent—to an extent that conservatives and liberals alike who are not criminal trial lawyers simply cannot conceive—the entire system of criminal justice below the level of the Supreme Court of the United States is solidly massed against the criminal suspect. Only a few appellate judges can throw off the fetters of their middle-class backgrounds . . . and identify with the criminal suspect instead of with the policeman. . . . Trial judges still more, and magistrates beyond belief, are functionally and psychologically allied with the police, their co-workers in the unending and scarifying work of bringing criminals to book. [p. 792]

Recourse to the Supreme Court was not, however, a satisfactory long-term solution, because of the thousands of state confession cases that are tried annually, only one or two could be reviewed by the highest tribunal. As a result of the difficulty in defining a clear and predictable standard of voluntariness and the "sabotage" by police and lower courts of the due process rule by approving doubtful or borderline confessions, it was perhaps inevitable that the Supreme Court had to change to a different rule for controlling interrogations—one that was more fixed, absolute, and less susceptible to discretionary application.

The Court in 1964 formulated a more objective standard to determine the admissibility of state confessions. In *Escobedo* v. *Illinois,* the Court held that the results of pre-indictment interrogations (that is, interrogations conducted prior to the filing of formal charges in court) that "focused" on "a" suspect in custody and had the "purpose" of eliciting a confession were inadmissible if the suspect had not been warned in advance by the police of his right to silence and his request for counsel had been denied by the police. The pre-indictment right to counsel was an unprecedented step toward "judicializing" the police function. *Escobedo* underscored an institutional reason for the stricture against using improperly obtained confessions: safeguarding the integrity of the adversary process. The reliability of fact-finding at trial can be predetermined or undermined by the police methods used at the pretrial (police) stage. However, this rule evoked widespread criticism and disagreement over its scope and meaning. Since the police at times interrogate a suspect while transporting him to the stationhouse for booking, some critics feared that *Escobedo* would require placing defense attorneys around the clock in police cars.

The difficulties in implementing *Escobedo* led the Court, two years later, in *Miranda* v. *Arizona* (1966) to turn to the Fifth Amendment privilege as a means of reviewing state confessions. In so doing, it initiated a judicial revolution in the law of confessions and brought new intensity to the continuing debate over the proper exercise of judicial authority in regulating police conduct.

MIRANDA v. ARIZONA

348 U.S. 486 (1966)

Mr. Chief Justice WARREN delivered the opinion of the Court.

The cases* before us raise questions which go to the roots of our concepts of American criminal jurisprudence: the restraints society must observe consistent with the Federal Constitution in prosecuting individuals for crime. More specifically, we deal with the admissibility of statements obtained from an individual who is subjected to custodial police interrogation and the necessity for procedures which assure that the individual is accorded his privilege under the Fifth Amendment to the Constitution not to be compelled to incriminate himself. . . .

We start here . . . with the premise that our holding is not an innovation in our jurisprudence, but is an application of

*[*Miranda* is the collective name for four substantially similar cases arising in Arizona, California, Kansas, and New York. Ed.'s note.]

principles long recognized and applied in other settings. . . .

Our holding will be spelled out with some specificity in the pages which follow but briefly stated it is this: the prosecution may not use statements, whether exculpatory or inculpatory, stemming from custodial interrogation of the defendant unless it demonstrates the use of procedural safeguards effective to secure the privilege against self-incrimination. By custodial interrogation, we mean questioning initiated by law enforcement officers after a person has been taken into custody or otherwise deprived of his freedom of action in any significant way. As for the procedural safeguards to be employed, unless other fully effective means are devised to inform accused persons of their right of silence and to assure a continuous opportunity to exercise it, the following measures are required. Prior to any questioning, the person must be warned that he has a right to remain silent, that any statement he does make may be used as evidence against him, and that he has a right to the presence of an attorney, either retained or appointed. The defendant may waive effectuation of these rights, provided the waiver is made voluntarily, knowingly and intelligently. If, however, he indicates in any manner and at any stage of the process that he wishes to consult with an attorney before speaking there can be no questioning. Likewise, if the individual is alone and indicates in any manner that he does not wish to be interrogated, the police may not question him. The mere fact that he may have answered some questions or volunteered some statements on his own does not deprive him of the right to refrain from answering any further inquiries until he has consulted with an attorney and thereafter consents to be questioned.

I.

The constitutional issue we decide in each of these cases is the admissibility of statements obtained from a defendant questioned while in custody and deprived of his freedom of action. . . . They all thus share salient features—incommunicado interrogation of individuals in a police-dominated atmosphere, resulting in self-incriminating statements without full warnings of constitutional rights. . . .

Interrogation still takes place in privacy. Privacy results in secrecy and this in turn results in a gap in our knowledge as to what in fact goes on in the interrogation rooms. A valuable source of information about present police practices, however, may be found in various police manuals and texts which document procedures employed with success in the past, and which recommend various other effective tactics.
. . .

To highlight the isolation and unfamiliar surroundings, the manuals instruct the police to display an air of confidence in the suspect's guilt and from outward appearance to maintain only an interest in confirming certain details. The guilt of the subject is to be posited as a fact.

The interrogator should direct his comments toward the reasons why the subject committed the act, rather than court failure by asking the subject whether he did it. . . . These tactics are designed to put the subject in a psychological state where his story is but an elaboration of what the police purport to know already—that he is guilty. Explanations to the contrary are dismissed and discouraged.

The texts thus stress that the major qualities an interrogator should possess are patience and perseverance. . . .

"[H]e must rely on an oppressive atmosphere of dogged persistence. He must interrogate steadily and without relent, leaving the subject no surcease. He must dominate his subject and overwhelm him with his inexorable will to obtain the truth. . . . In a serious case, the interrogation may continue for days. . . ."

It is obvious that such an interrogation environment is created for no purpose other than to subjugate the individual to the will of his examiner. This atmosphere carries its own badge of intimidation. To be sure, this is not physical intimidation, but it is equally destructive of human dignity. . . . Unless adequate protective devices are employed to dispel the compulsion inherent in custodial surroundings, no statement obtained from the defendant can truly be the product of his free choice.

From the foregoing, we can readily perceive an intimate connection between the privilege against self-incrimination and police custodial questioning. It is fitting to turn to history and precedent underlying the Self-Incrimination Clause to determine its applicability in this situation.

II.

[W]e may view the historical development of the privilege as one which groped for the proper score of governmental power over the citizen. . . . [T]he constitutional foundation underlying the privilege is the respect a government—state or federal—must accord to the dignity and integrity of its citizens. To maintain a "fair state-individual balance," to require the government "to shoulder the entire load," to respect the inviolability of the human personality, our accusatory system of criminal justice demands that the government seeking to punish an individual produce the evidence against him by its own independent labors, rather than by the cruel, simple expedient of compelling it from his own mouth. . . .

We are satisfied that all the principles embodied in the privilege apply to informal compulsion exerted by law-enforcement officers during in-custody questioning. An individual swept from familiar surroundings into police custody, surrounded by antagonistic forces, and subject to the techniques of persuasion described above cannot be otherwise than under compulsion to speak. As a practical matter, the compulsion to speak in the isolated setting of the police station may well be greater than in courts or other official investigations, where there are often impartial observers to guard against intimidation or trickery. . . .

III.

We have concluded that without proper safeguards the process of in-custody interrogation of persons suspected or accused of crime contains inherently compelling pressures which work to undermine the individual's will to resist and to compel him to speak where he would not otherwise do so freely. . . .

It is impossible for us to foresee the potential alternatives for protecting the privilege which might be devised by Congress or the States in the exercise of their creative rule-making capacities. Therefore

we cannot say that the Constitution necessarily requires adherence to any particular solution for the inherent compulsions of the interrogation process as it is presently conducted. Our decision in no way creates a constitutional straitjacket which will handicap sound efforts at reform, nor is it intended to have this effect. However, unless we are shown other procedures which are at least as effective in apprising accused persons of their right of silence and in assuring a continuous opportunity to exercise it, the following safeguards must be observed.

At the outset, if a person in custody is to be subjected to interrogation he must first be informed in clear and unequivocal terms that he has the right to remain silent. . . . [S]uch a warning is an absolute prerequisite in overcoming the inherent pressures of the interrogation atmosphere. . . .

The warning of the right to remain silent must be accompanied by the explanation that anything said can and will be used against the individual in court. This warning is needed in order to make him aware not only of the privilege, but also of the consequences of foregoing it. . . .

The circumstances surrounding in-custody interrogation can operate very quickly to overbear the will of one merely made aware of his privilege by his interrogators. . . . Thus, the need for counsel to protect the Fifth Amendment privilege comprehends not merely a right to consult with counsel prior to questioning, but also to have a counsel present during any questioning if the defendant so desires. . . .

In order fully to apprise a person interrogated of the extent of his right under this sytem then, it is necessary to warn him not only that he has the right to consult with attorney, but also that if he is indigent a lawyer will be appointed to represent him. Without this additional warning, the admonition of the right to consult with counsel would often be understood as meaning only that he can consult with a lawyer if he has one or has the funds to obtain one. . . .

Once warnings have been given, the subsequent procedure is clear. If the individual indicates in any manner, at any time prior to or during questioning, that he wishes to remain silent, the interrogation must cease. . . . If the individual states that he wants an attorney, the interrogation must cease until an attorney is present. . . .

If the interrogation continues without the presence of an attorney and a statement is taken, a heavy burden rests on the Government to demonstrate that the defendant knowingly and intelligently waived his privilege against self-incrimination and his right to retained or appointed counsel. This Court has always set high standards of proof for the waiver of constitutional rights, and we reassert these standards as applied to in-custody interrogation. . . .

An express statement that the individual is willing to make a statement and does not want an attorney followed closely by a statement could constitute a waiver. But a valid waiver will not be presumed simply from the silence of the accused after warnings are given or simply from the fact that a confession was in fact eventually obtained.

The warnings required and the waiver necessary in accordance with our opinion today are, in the absence of a fully effective equivalent, prerequisites to the admissibility of any statement made by a defendant. No distinction can be drawn between statements which are direct confessions and statements which amount to "admissions" of part or all of an offense. . . .

Our decision is not intended to hamper the traditional function of police officers in investigating crime. . . . Such investigation may include inquiry of persons not under restraint. General on-the-scene questioning as to facts surrounding a crime or other general questioning of citizens in the fact-finding process is not affected by our holding. It is an act of responsible citizenship for individuals to give whatever information they may have to aid in law enforcement. In such situations the compelling atmosphere inherent in the process of in-custody interrogation is not necessarily present. . . .

V.

[W]e have concluded that statements were obtained from the defendants under circumstances that did not meet constitutional standards for protection of the privilege. . . .

Therefore, [the conviction of Miranda for kidnapping and rape is reversed]. . . .

It is so ordered.

Mr. Justice HARLAN, whom Mr. Justice STEWART and Mr. Justice WHITE join, dissenting. . . .

The Court's opening contention, that the Fifth Amendment governs police station confessions, is perhaps not an impermissible extension of the law but it has little to commend itself in the present circumstances. Historically, the privilege against self-incrimination did not bear at all on the use of extra-legal confessions, for which distinct standards evolved; indeed, "the *history* of the two principles is wide apart, differing by one hundred years in origin, and derived through separate lines of precedents. . . ." 8 Wigmore, Evidence §2266, at 401 (McNaughton rev. 1961). Practice under the two doctrines has also differed in a number of important respects. Even those who would readily enlarge the privilege must concede some linguistic difficulties since the Fifth Amendment in terms proscribes only compelling any person "in any criminal case to be a witness against himself." . . .

Mr. Justice WHITE with whom Mr. Justice HARLAN and Mr. Justice STEWART join, dissenting. . . .

[T]he court has not discovered or found the law in making today's decision, nor has it derived it from some irrefutable sources; what it has done is to make new law and new public policy in much the same way that it has in the course of interpreting other great clauses of the Constitution. . . .

First, we may inquire what are the textual and factual bases of this new fundamental rule. . . . [T]he Court conceded that it cannot truly know what occurs during custodial questioning, because of the innate secrecy of such proceedings. . . . Judged by any of the standards for empirical investigation utilized in the social sciences the factual basis for the Court's premise is patently inadequate. . . .

[E]ven if one were to postulate that the Court's concern is not that all confessions induced by police interrogation are coerced but rather that some such confessions are coerced and present judicial procedures are believed to be inadequate to identify the confessions that are coerced and those that are not, it would still not be essential to impose the rule that the Court has now fashioned. Transcripts or observers could be required, specific time limits, tailored to fit the cause, could be imposed, or other devices could be utilized to reduce the chances that otherwise indiscernible coercion will produce an inadmissible confession. . . .

All of this makes very little sense in terms of the compulsion which the Fifth Amendment proscribes. The amendment deals with compelling the accused himself. It is his free will that is involved. Confessions and incriminating admissions, as such, are not forbidden evidence; only those which are compelled are banned. I doubt that the Court observes the distinctions today. . . . [I]nstead of confining itself to protection of the right against compelled self-incrimination the Court has created a limited Fifth Amendment right to counsel. . . .

The rule announced today will measurably weaken the ability of the criminal law to perform [its] tasks. It is a deliberate calculus to prevent interrogations, to reduce the incidence of confessions and pleas of guilty and to increase the number of trials. . . . There is, in my view, every reason to believe that a good many criminal defendants who otherwise would have been convicted on what this Court has previously thought to be the most satisfactory kind of evidence will now, under this new version of the Fifth Amendment, either not be tried at all or will be acquitted if the State's evidence, minus the confession, is put to the test of litigation.

I have no desire whatsoever to share the responsibility for any such impact on the present criminal process. . . .

NOTES AND QUESTIONS

1.   The Court applied the Fifth Amendment privilege to custodial interrogation and discussed their interrelationship without specific reference to the facts of the case. Instead, it relied on police manuals and texts that describe recommended stratagems for interrogation. Why was there no description of the particulars of Miranda's own interrogation?

2.   The opinion of the Court can be recast in syllogistic form:

Major premise   The Fifth Amendment prohibits compulsion;
Minor premise   police custodial interrogations are "inherently" compulsive;
Conclusion   therefore, police interrogations are prohibited by the Fifth Amendment, unless preceded by warnings.

In dissent, Justice White argued: "Judged by any of the standards for empirical investigation utilized in the social sciences, the factual basis for the Court's [intermediate] premise is patiently inadequate. . . ." Do you agree?

Several times in the opinion, Chief Justice Warren stressed that custodial interrogations are "inherently" coercive. Note that in *Brown I*, he wrote that separate but equal educational facilities are "inherently" unequal.

3.   Separate lines of precedent are associated with out-of-court confessions (governed in early common law by the voluntariness test) and in-court confessions (governed by the privilege against self-incrimination). The Fifth Amendment privilege had its common law origins in the trial of radical Puritans in the mid-seventeenth century. They defended themselves against the charge of heresy on the procedural ground that "no man is obliged to produce himself," an old canon law precept. The exact source of the phrase "no man shall be compelled to be a witness against himself" is unknown, but by the late seventeenth century it had become a self-evident truth to protect individuals against interrogations without charges or interrogations that went beyond the scope of the official charges. It became the main shield of those prosecuted for the religious crime of heresy and the political crime of seditious libel.

Thus, there were two separate but parallel developments in the protection against interrogations: the common law voluntariness rule, aimed at pre-judicial interrogations by constables and private citizens serving in police roles, which was the precursor of the due process/voluntariness rule; and the common law privilege, aimed at in-court interrogations by state and ecclesiastical officials for crimes of belief and conscience, which was the precursor of the Fifth Amendment privilege. In 1966, the Supreme Court for the first time extended the constitutional privilege to protect against out-of-court, police interrogations regarding any kind of crime, not just those related to political expressions and worship. Thus, in dissent, Justice Harlan reminded the Court that "the history of the two principles is wide apart" and that there are "some linguistic difficulties" to this novel application of the Fifth Amendment.

The linguistic difficulty arises because of the particular meaning associated with the Fifth Amendment compulsion. The privilege forbids compelling any person to be a witness against himself—that is, it forbids legal compulsion in court. Legal compulsion exists if, in the absence of the privilege, a defendant is faced with the following cruel trilemma: If he refuses to take the stand, he is subject to contempt of court; if he takes the stand and testifies falsely, he is subject to perjury; and if he takes the stand and incriminates himself, he is subject to conviction. There is legal compulsion when these sanctions attach to taking the witness stand.

Technically, then, compulsion within the foregoing meaning of the Fifth Amendment is absent at the stationhouse. A suspect, unlike a court defendant, suffers no sanctions for prevaricating or refusing to talk to the police. A suspect is not a "witness" and is not legally "compelled" by the police. How does the Chief Justice resolve this "linguistic difficulty" so as to make the Fifth Amendment prohibition of compulsion applicable to the stationhouse?

4.   By practical necessity, police interrogation is inquisitorial. Its main purpose is not to uphold an individual's moral claim to mental freedom or to preserve choices that enhance his subsequent prospects of acquittal, but to get him to divulge information. The protections of the accusatorial process operate in the courtroom to create a semblance of equal footing between the antagonists. At the stationhouse, however, the advantage lies—and is expected by society to lie—with the police. Surely the Court was not so disingenuous as to believe that the police can interrogate effectively under strict application of Fifth and Sixth Amendment safeguards. If the police were actually judicialized, law enforcement would be undermined. What are some means whereby the police could subvert the spirit, if not the letter, of *Miranda*, so that the warnings would not "markedly decrease the number of confessions," as Justice Harlan feared? Instances of "police trickery" are described by White (1979) and Lewis and Peoples (1978, pp. 443–47).

5.   After the warnings are given, the Court says that a suspect "may knowingly and intelligently waive these rights." If the setting of custodial interrogation is as "inherently coercive" as the Court makes it out to be, how can a suspect feel free to waive? What standard would a court use in determining whether a waiver was in fact "knowing and intelligent"? Psychological testing has been used to establish a suspect's capacity to waive intelligently (*United States* v. *Frazier*, 1973). A state may have to undertake such testing to shoulder its burden of proving the suspect's comprehension (*Tague* v. *Louisiana*, 1980).

6.   The Court refused to say that "the Constitution necessarily requires adhesion to any particular solution." In fact, it urged Congress and the states to consider "potential alternatives for protecting the privilege" by the exercise of their "creative rule-making capacities." Since the issue of regulating police conduct is as much a subject of social engineering and behavioral control as it is of law, what alternatives to or modifications of *Miranda*—so as to constitute, according to the Court, "a fully effective equivalent" of warnings—might social scientists propose? •

7.   Subsequent cases have attempted to articulate the boundaries and nuances of meaning of the "Fifth Amendment right to counsel," to use the words of Justice White's dissent. Some of the questions addressed by *Miranda*'s progeny include the following:

> • What are some common modes and circumstances of interrogation that lie outside the ambit of *Miranda*? For example, is there "custodial" questioning when a suspect "voluntarily" comes to the stationhouse in response to an "invitation" by a police officer? See *Oregon* v. *Mathiason* (1977).
> • What constitutes an assertion of *Miranda* rights? For example, is the request by a juvenile suspect to see his parole officer (or his parents, best friend, or other trusted adult) tantamount to a request to see an attorney? See *Fare* v. *Michael C.* (1979).
> • How far may the language of the standard warnings be qualified or varied by the police and still pass muster? For example, is this modification constitutionally deficient: "You have the right to consult your attorney before making any statement . . . and you can have your attorney present while we interrogate you"? Or, "You have the right to be represented by an attorney who will be appointed by the . . . court in the event of insolvency on your part"? See *United States* v. *Contreras* (1981). Are warnings inadequate if the sequence in which they are delivered has been changed? See *California* v. *Prysock* (1981).
> • What constitutes "interrogation" within the meaning of *Miranda*? For example, in an arrest for drunken driving, is the officer's inquiry to the driver as to whether he would take a blood alcohol test an "interrogation" that must be prefaced by warnings? See *South Dakota* v. *Neville* (1983). In *Rhode Island* v. *Innis* (1980), a murder suspect was arrested near a school, repeatedly given the *Miranda* warnings, and then transported to the stationhouse in a police car. While enroute, two patrolmen, sitting next to the suspect, expressed concern to each other that the murder weapon could be found by school children, who might then be accidentally injured by it. The suspect interrupted the officers and offered to show them where the weapon was hidden at the scene of the arrest. Is this "conversation" between officers, which had the effect of appealing to the suspect's conscience, a form of interrogation without questioning that is the "functional equivalent" of direct interrogation? Is a pretrial psychiatric examination to determine competency to stand trial an "interrogation" which triggers the right to warnings, if the psychiatrist later testifies for the prosecution at the sentencing hearing that the defendant, based upon the earlier examination, is likely to be dangerous and therefore satisfies one of the statutory conditions for the imposition of the death penalty? See *Estelle* v. *Smith* (1981).
> • Can interrogation be resumed after the exercise of *Miranda* rights? For example, is reinterrogation permitted if conducted by a different officer, at a different location, regarding a different crime, provided that the initial invocation of rights is "scrupulously honored"? See *Michigan* v. *Mosley* (1975). Is it permitted if the suspect himself initiates further dialogue with the police? See *Wyrick* v. *Fields* (1982) and *Oregon* v. *Bradshaw* (1983).

Which of the foregoing questions can be translated into empirically testable propositions?

6.3. IMPACT OF MIRANDA ON POLICE INTERROGATION

INTERROGATIONS IN NEW HAVEN: THE IMPACT OF *MIRANDA*

Comment*

I. INTRODUCTION

. . .

The project attempts, essentially, to evaluate the claims that interrogations are inherently coercive and that *Miranda* will substantially impede successful law enforcement. [Several] questions are explored: What is the interrogation process like? What has been the impact of *Miranda* on the suspect's willingness to cooperate? How important are interrogations for successful solution of crime? . . .

III. SOURCES OF DATA AND METHODOLOGY

. . .

The foundation for this study was our observers' reports of the interrogations witnessed last summer. To supplement this data and round out our knowledge of police practices in New Haven, we interviewed at various times the detectives [and the] defendants who had been interrogated. . . .

A. OBSERVATIONS

. . .

[T]he period for which we report data began one week after the *Miranda* decision.

*[The student authors of this "Comment" are Michael Wald, Richard Ayres, David W. Hess, Michael Schantz, and Charles H. Whitebread II. Ed.'s note.]

Reprinted by permission of The Yale Law Journal Company and Fred B. Rothman and Company from *The Yale Law Journal*, Vol. 76, pp. 1519–1648. Copyright ©1967 by the Yale Law Journal Company, Inc.

Two students were in the police station at all times. They spent most of their time in the detective division, waiting for suspects to be brought in for questioning. Whenever a suspect was brought in, our observer was present in the interrogation room. The suspects were not told that the observer was a student and, as far as we can tell, most thought we were detectives. After the questioning the observer completed a questionnaire recording the events of the interrogation. . . .

B. POLICE INTERVIEWS

. . .

[S]ix months after the observations ended we interviewed 25 of the detectives to probe their opinions about the effect of *Miranda*. By this time they had adjusted to the decision and their attitudes should have solidified. These latter interviews, which averaged approximately three hours each, were generally conducted in the detectives' homes, on their own time. . . .

F. CONTROLS AND LIMITATIONS. Any empirical study necessarily has methodological shortcomings. . . .

1. CHANGES IN POLICE BEHAVIOR. To test whether our presence substantially affected police behavior, we tried to find out how the police acted before and after our observations. We interviewed 40 persons who had been interrogated during the four months preceding and following our three-month study. We asked them to describe the same features of their interrogations that our observers recorded in the police station. Assuming that the process might be perceived differently from the suspect's perspective, we also interviewed 20 of the people whom we saw questioned last summer. By asking them questions to

which we already had answers, we could tell how much, and on what points, their reports differed from those of our observers. This factor could then be applied to the interviews with the other suspects to estimate how accurate their reports were likely to be.

Almost half of the interviewed suspects whom we had observed described their interrogations differently than our observer. The discrepancies followed no pattern; some even reported the process more favorably, saying, for example, they had received *Miranda* warnings when our observer had not recorded any such warnings. However, most respondents reported a more hostile interrogation than our observer recorded. . . .

Yet, even if we do not assume any exaggeration by the groups we did not observe, their description of the process was so similar to what we did observe that we feel justified in assuming our presence did not markedly affect the detective's behavior. . . .

2. SIZE OF SAMPLE. Because of the low crime rate in New Haven our sample includes only 127 interrogations. . . .

The 127 interrogations constitute approximately 20 per cent of all the interrogations conducted during a year. It is likely that practices observed over a three-month period accurately reflect the general practices of the police. . . .

IV.   INTERROGATIONS IN NEW HAVEN

A. PSYCHOLOGICAL COERCION

. . .

All but nine of the 119 suspects brought into the Detective Division were interrogated. . . .

Overall, the entire process *usually* appeared quite haphazard. Since most arrests were not for crimes the detectives considered very serious, and since they sel-

dom arrested anyone without considerable evidence, they rarely felt a compelling need to pry information from suspects. However, when the crime was particularly serious, when the detectives felt they needed information from the interrogation, or when for some reason the suspect antagonized them, the interrogation was markedly more like that described in *Miranda*. . . .*

The Court's description of interrogations in *Miranda* dwelled with mingled horror and fascination on the various psychological "tactics" the police are instructed to use in breaking down a suspect. New Haven detectives employed most of the tactics listed [in police manuals] on occasion, thus in a sense justifying the Court's fears. . . . However, tactics were ignored in the typical interrogation. Even when tactics were used, they were generally rudimentary and were woodenly applied. . . .

B. ADHERENCE TO LEGAL NORMS

. . .

Despite the presence of our observers in the police station, the detectives gave all the advice required by *Miranda* to only 25 of 118 suspects questioned. Nonetheless most suspects did receive some advice. . . .

The detectives clearly gave more adequate advice later in the summer, however, as they became more accustomed to the *Miranda* requirements; much of the non-compliance may therefore have been transitional.

Despite increasing adherence to the letter of *Miranda*, however, [the] detectives complied less readily with its spirit. . . .

_____

*[The description goes on to say that, in contrast to the *Miranda* portrayal, the interrogation room "did not seem 'inherently coercive' to the observers"; most detectives were friendly or businesslike, not hostile, to most suspects; most interrogations were short, averaging thirty minutes. Ed.'s note.]

[They] commonly de-fused the advice by implying that the suspect had better not exercise his rights, or by delivering [their] statement in a formalized, bureaucratic tone to indicate that [their] remarks were simply a routine, meaningless legalism. . . . After they had finished the advice they would solemnly intone, "Now you have been warned of your rights," then immediately shift to a conversational tone to ask, "Now, would you like to tell me what happened?" . . .

C. THE MOST COERCIVE INTERROGATIONS.

Throughout the preceding discussion we have dealt with each aspect of psychological interrogation and adherence to legal norms in isolation, stressing the low level of coerciveness in most questioning. Here, we shall examine the 17 interrogations where the police put most of the elements of psychological interrogation together, isolated the suspect from friends, and disregarded his right to end questioning.

Five indicators of a coercive interrogation were used: (1) whether the attitude of the police towards the suspect was "hostile" or "ambiguous"; (2) whether the detectives employed three or more tactics; (3) whether they questioned the suspect for more than one hour; (4) whether they refused to stop questioning after the suspect indicated that he wanted to terminate the interrogation; (5) whether they neglected to tell the suspect he could contact friends or family until after questioning was completed. None of the interrogations in our sample included all five of these indicators. . . . We decided to examine closely the 17 interrogations wherein we found three or more of the indicators. . . .

Having isolated these interrogations, we tried to determine why the detectives had been more coercive in them. We found here, as in previous sections, that the detectives interrogated aggressively in serious crimes when they needed evidence to insure the suspect's conviction, when they needed the name of an accomplice, or when they felt the suspect could help them clear other crimes. . . .

The police gave noticeably more adequate advice of rights to these 17 suspects than to the sample as a whole. . . .

Despite the more adequate advice of rights given these suspects, the police were disproportionately successful in interrogating them. Seven of the suspects confessed; two admitted to their crimes; and two made incriminating statements. Only six of the 17 interrogations were unproductive. By comparison, only 21 suspects in the entire sample of 127 confessed, and only 11 made admissions. . . .

Our analysis of these 17 coercive interrogations thus indicates that the Court's fears of coerced confessions in *Miranda* are not groundless in New Haven, despite the lack of coercion in the typical interrogation. Aggressive interrogation pays off in confessions. Moreover, these cases suggest that the *Miranda* advice of rights does not reduce the value of coercion in obtaining confessions.

V. THE EFFECTS OF WARNINGS

. . .

Quantification requires the operations definition of categories and concepts which in ordinary usage would have rather fluid, qualitative meanings. A key concept in this section and in discussions of *Miranda* generally is the notion of a "successful" interrogation. It is often assumed that a successful interrogation is one which produces a written confession and an unsuccessful interrogation is one in which the suspect flatly refuses to talk. These polar categories, however, described only about one-third of the interrogations we observed. Our experience suggested dividing "successful" into four categories: (1) a confession; (2) an oral admission of guilt without a signed statement; (3) a signed statement that was incriminating but less than a full admission of guilt; or (4) oral evidence constituting less than a full admission of guilt without a signed statement. . . .

Twenty-seven of the suspects questioned received none of the *Miranda* warnings; 87 suspects received at least one. Our test hypothesis was that, all other things being equal, the detectives should have been more successful with the group not warned.

Considering as successful the interrogations that produced some evidence, our data suggests paradoxically that the detectives were more successful when some warning was given. [With warnings, there were 50 successful and 37 unsuccessful interrogations; without warnings, the figures were 8 and 19, respectively. These results were significant by the Chi Square test at the .01 level. This main order relationship between warning and successful interrogation persisted even when the analysis controlled for third variables such as seriousness of the crime and clarity of the warnings. From Table 11. Ed.'s note.]

In sum, our data indicate that the *Miranda* warnings . . . will not silence suspects and therefore will not cripple law enforcement as critics have claimed. The opposite side of this coin, however, is that warnings do not seem significantly to help the suspect to make a "free and informed choice to speak or assert his right to stand silent."*

---

*[In an appendix, the study suggests "a general theory of interrogation success" that could serve as a "guide for future research." A number of explanatory factors thought to be related to interrogation success were cross-tabulated with it, such as prior record, amount of evidence available at time of arrest, seriousness of the crime, race, and age of suspect. "Holding for third variables revealed that [the first three factors] were genuinely and independently related to interrogation success."

Prior criminal record success (41 unsuccessful cases and 29 successful cases with prior record; 16/24 without prior record). The more serious the crime, the more successful was the interrogation (32 unsuccessful and 26 successful with less serious crimes; 23/34 with more serious crimes). Finally, the more evi-

VI. THE ROLE OF INTERROGATIONS AND CONFESSIONS IN CRIMINAL LAW ENFORCEMENT

. . .

[A] small but growing number of officials and commentators have come to the conclusion that "the value of confessions in law enforcement has been grossly exaggerated." They argue that most cases can be solved by other investigative techniques. . . .

We have tried to explore [this issue] in estimating the importance of interrogations in meeting several major goals of law enforcement. We also have tried to determine the impact of *Miranda* on the success of those interrogations we ultimately considered important. Our information was obtained from three sources: our observers, the detectives, and police records. . . .

A. SOLVING CRIMES THROUGH INTERROGATION. To avoid confusion, our discussion uses a special vocabulary to classify interrogations. Interrogation is considered "necessary" to crime solution when there is both (1) insufficient evidence at the time interrogation begins to solve the crime,

---

dence of guilt confronting a suspect, the more likely was a successful interrogation (21 unsuccessful and 8 successful with little or no evidence; 35/50 with considerable evidence).

"Psychologically, the analysis suggests that prior record is the most important factor in determining . . . the interaction of detective and suspect. With a record, a suspect is more likely to be in sufficient control to evaluate the evidence and decide whether cooperation is the rational course of action." Such would be the educative consequences of a previous trip through the interrogation mill. "Without a prior record, a suspect is more likely to be at a detective's mercy." Here, seriousness of the crime and amount of evidence are more significant. "This theory suggests that, in principle, warnings might provide the knowledge and psychological strength necessary to alter the existing balance of forces," especially for those with little prior criminal experience. This assumes, of course, that the warnings are "comprehensible" or are not "rendered nugatory by the tone and manner of the interrogators." Ed.'s note.]

and (2) no alternative investigative means available to obtain such information. An interrogation is considered "successful" if a confession, admission, or incriminating statement is obtained. The number of necessary and successful interrogations reflects the actual current importance of questioning.

Using these definitions, we analyze [a question] relevant to the claim that interrogations are essential to law enforcement: In how many cases is questioning necessary? . . .

From information gathered at the stationhouse by the observers and from police files, each member of the project independently rated the amount of evidence available in each case into one of four categories.

(1) None;

(2) Some;

(3) Enough to take the case to trial;

(4) Probably enough to obtain a conviction.

These categories correspond to evidentiary standards commonly used in criminal cases. A case was coded "None" when the evidence seemed insufficient to establish probable cause for making an arrest. "Some" evidence would justify arrest and perhaps an indictment or information, but would not preclude a directed verdict. Cases were placed in the third category when the evidence would get the case to the jury but a guilty verdict did not appear certain. For cases in the fourth category, conviction would almost certainly result absent a strong defense by the suspect.

An estimate of investigative alternatives was obtained from the interrogating detectives in the interviews and supplemented by a check of the police files six months later. . . . The investigative alternatives were coded in four categories:

(1) None;

(2) Available but probably inadequate for conviction;

(3) Available and probably adequate for conviction;

(4) Further investigation unnecessary. . . .

A cross-tabulation of the four "evidence available" and four "investigative alternatives" categories would produce a confusing maze of 16 categories to describe the need for interrogation. To simplify presentation we devised an Evidence-Investigation Scale which distributes these 16 categories into four categories: (1) interrogation essential; (2) interrogation important; (3) interrogation not important; (4) interrogation unnecessary. (See Table 19.) . . .

If all investigative alternatives deemed "probably inadequate" were in fact inadequate, our analysis indicates that interrogations were an "important" or "essential" method of investigation in 12 of the 90 cases observed [see Table 20].

. . . In [most cases] the police had adequate evidence to convict the suspect without any interrogation. Interrogation usually just cemented a cold case or served to identify accomplices.

This finding is probably explained by the fact that the police were rarely able to arrest even a single person for crimes where no witnesses were available. . . . [T]here is strong evidence that confessions are of small importance, since arrests can be made only where the crime is for the most part already solved because such substantial evidence is available before interrogation. . . .

B. DETECTIVES' EVALUATION OF THE NEED FOR INTERROGATION TO SOLVE CRIMES. Our analysis can be compared with the detectives' views on the importance of interrogations. We obtained the detectives' opinions in 70 of the 90 cases. . . .

[T]he detectives considered interrogation important in 13 cases and unnecessary in 57. Ten of these were also labelled "necessary" in our analysis. . . .

TABLE 19

Distribution of Categories for an E-I Scale Analysis of the Need for Interrogation to Obtain Conviction

	Amount of Evidence			
	None	Some	Trial	Conviction
Investigative Alternatives None	Essential			
Available but probably inadequate	Important			
Available and probably adequate	Not important			
Further investigation unnecessary	Unnecessary			

TABLE 20

Need for Interrogation: E-I Scale Analysis, All Cases

	Number	Percent
Essential	3	3
Important	9	10
Not important	8	9
Unnecessary	69	77
Other*	1	1
	90	100

*Interrogation revealed that the suspect was innocent.

[T]he overlap—10 of 13 cases—is substantial. . . . More important, our interviews revealed that not even the detectives considered more than a small minority of interrogations "important," however they defined the term. . . .

IX. CONCLUSION

Our data and our impressions in New Haven converge to a single conclusion: Not much has changed after *Miranda*. Despite the dark predictions by the critics of the decision, the impact on law enforcement has been small. This is true for two reasons. First, interrogations play but a secondary role in solving the crimes of this middle-sized city, both because serious offenses are relatively infrequent and because the police rarely arrest suspects without substantial evidence. . . .

[U]nless the criminal is caught red-handed or unless witnesses are available, the police with their limited resources for scientific investigation cannot amass even enough evidence to arrest a suspect. And since such evidence when available is all but conclusive, by the time the police have a suspect the crime is solved, conviction is assured and interrogation is unnecessary.

The second reason for the almost nugatory impact of *Miranda* in New Haven should also apply as well to other cities: the *Miranda* rules, when followed, seem to affect interrogations but slightly. The police continue to question suspects, and succeed despite the new constraints.

This is not surprising when the realities of the interrogation room are considered. Warnings are not useless, but neither can they eliminate whatever "inherently coercive atmosphere" the police station may have. The suspect arrested and brought downtown for questioning is in a crisis-laden situation. The stakes for

him are high—often his freedom for a few or many years—and his prospects hinge on decisions that must be quickly made: to cooperate and hope for leniency, to try and talk his way out, to stand adamantly on his rights. . . .

The conclusion, inescapable, [is] that mere warnings cannot provide concrete "assurance of real understanding and intelligent exercise of the privilege of silence." . . . If such is the goal, this can be done only by providing each accused with counsel before the police begin questioning—someone who knows the system, the institutions, the personalities involved. The lone suspect cannot make a "free and informed" choice to speak or remain silent.

We believe that such an informed decision is the proper goal. And, therefore, we recommend that counsel should be assured to each suspect before the police interrogate. . . .

NOTES AND QUESTIONS

Methodological Issues: Reliability and Validity

1. To check for any possible changes in police behavior as a result of the presence of the observers, the authors interviewed suspects who were interrogated four months before (call it Time 1) and four months after (Time 3) the three-month period of the study (Time 2). The authors compared their own observations (at Time 2) with the reports of the suspects in Time 2, as well as with those of the suspects in Times 1 and 3. What other comparisons might have been made to determine if the observers' presence had any effect on what they were observing?

2. How would you ascertain and minimize the extent of measurement unreliability arising from nonrecording errors of the observers (for example, omission in recording police use of tactics or hostile acts)?

3. We not only see events, we perceive them—our past experiences, attitudes, and social expectations condition what we see and fill in any missing gaps in the observed event. Perception is a creative as well as a recording process. Different people may underreport or overreport observations of police misconduct. How would you measure and control for this source of observer unreliability?

Changes in attitudes of observers are not uncommon. As they gain the confidence of and become more friendly with the police, observers may become more sympathetic toward the police viewpoint. This socialization or co-optation effect is likely to influence their observations. Are there means of measuring and minimizing it?

For more on the methodology of "systematic social observation," see Reiss (1971b).

4.   We have already discussed briefly the question of measurement reliability: How accurate or error-free were the observations of the interrogations? Now we turn to the second basic concept in measurement theory, that of validity: Did the observations measure what they were supposed to measure, namely, coerciveness? That is, how do we know that the five-item index in fact measures coercion and not some other theoretical construct? The question of validity does not arise in the measurement of tangible, physical attributes. In determining how tall a person is, for example, one need not be concerned whether the measuring tape provides a valid measure of height. The only issue is the reliability of the measure. The measurement of intangible, psychological attributes such as "intelligence" or "coerciveness" does raise the question of validity.

There are different ways of ascertaining the validity of a measure. One way is predictive validity. If a measure predicts (that is, is correlated with) another attribute as anticipated, then it is said to show evidence of validity. The predictive validity of IQ tests for placement in "educable mentally retarded" classes, for example, was discussed in Chapter 4, section 4.7. Another way is construct validity. If the measure of a construct is correlated with the measures of other constructs as expected according to a theory, then there is evidence of construct validity. Thus, to *define* operationally a theoretical construct or concept (for example, coercion) is to specify a set of operations to *measure* it (the five-item index) and to *validate* the measure (that is, to determine that the index measures coercion and not, say, "police authoritarianism" or some other psychological dimension) implies a *test of the underlying theory* of the phenomenon under study (interrogations). Construct validation involves what Kaplan (1964) terms the "paradox of conceptualization": Concepts are needed to formulate a theory, but a theory is needed to arrive at the concepts (p. 53).

To illustrate, suppose that a theory of interrogation success includes the following proposition: The more "coercive" the interrogation, the more likely will be the "overbearing of the will" of the suspect. This simple theory has two concepts, and we shall assume that prior research has established that the concept of "overbearing" is validly measured by the index of confession rates. (Theory-building and testing in science constitute a continuing and cumulative process.) The measure of "coercion" is the five-item index devised by the Yale authors. If this index indeed measures "coercion," then we would expect to find a correlation or association with confession rates as predicted by the theory. To validate the measure is, in effect, to test the theory.

The foregoing is our reconstruction of the theory implicit in the Yale study. As it turned out, the study found a positive relationship between the five-item index and confession rates. If this expected correlation had not been found, the validity of the five-item index as a measure of "coercion"—as well as the validity of the theory itself—would have been called into question.

The theory of interrogation relied upon in the study was, of course, somewhat more elaborate. It also proposed, for example, that greater "coercion" would be exerted in cases involving "serious crimes." Assuming that "seriousness" is validly operationalized by felony offenses, a positive correlation would be expected between the five-item idex and felony (but not misdemeanor) cases. The results confirmed this hypothesized relationship and, thereby, gave added evidence of the validity of the coercion measure.

The foregoing process of validation of the coercion measure, which is to say the process of testing the theory of interrogation success, may be diagrammed as follows:

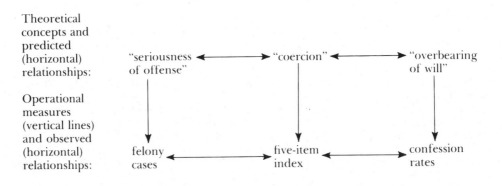

Theoretical concepts and predicted (horizontal) relationships: "seriousness of offense" ⟷ "coercion" ⟷ "overbearing of will"

Operational measures (vertical lines) and observed (horizontal) relationships: felony cases ⟷ five-item index ⟷ confession rates

As Kaplan (1964) notes, "The meaning of a theoretical term is fixed by horizontal as well as vertical members of the conceptual structure" (p. 57). The empirical meaning of a concept (coercion) depends on its relations to other concepts (overbearing; seriousness of offense) as fixed by their place in the theory. It is these other concepts, anchored in prior research or common experience, that allow for the meaning of the new concept (coercion). Construct validation, then, is not an either-or event. It is a continuing process of establishing correlations (horizontal relationships) with other operational indicators in order to strengthen the inferential (vertical) link between the measure at issue and the concept it purportedly measures.

5.   Another approach to the examination of the coerciveness of interrogations has been the extrapolation of findings from the social psychological literature to the stationhouse. Relying on tenuous analogies between certain social psychological studies (for example, on conformity and "experimenter effects") and questioning tactics described in police manuals, one writer concluded that "the Court's finding of inherent coercion even in ethical interrogations seems completely justified by the literature of social psychology" (Driver 1968, p. 44; see also Zimbardo 1967). What are the difficulties in using research conducted originally in other settings and for other purposes and transposing it to address questions of legal policy?

Impact of Warnings on Confessions

6.   Curiously, the study found more successful interrogations when warnings were delivered. This pattern persisted even after controlling for such "third variables" as seriousness of the crime and clarity of the warnings. How might you account for this result?

7.   Consider the implications of the authors' "general theory of interrogation success." The educated and well-to-do presumably would call their lawyer upon arrest and would know or be informed by their lawyer of the right to silence. Those who have been arrested and gone through the interrogation mill a number of times in the past presumably would have learned of their right not to talk. The authors' theory suggests that the warnings are most needed and helpful to those with limited past criminal experience and, of course, to those who do not have a retained lawyer. Does this theory support the argument that the underlying rationale of the *Miranda* warnings was to further equal treatment regardless of wealth and criminal experience rather than to preserve the privilege against self-incrimination?

8.   In studies of complex social problems, no single research method is sufficient to yield the needed information. A combination of approaches is desirable so that the deficiencies of one may be offset by the advantages of another. Studies of the impact of *Miranda* on confessions have relied on methods other than observation. Seeburger and Wettick (1967), for example, examined police records over a period of time. They analyzed every "cleared" case in the detective files of the Pittsburgh Police Department from about two years before *Miranda* to one year after. Their results showed that the percentage of suspects (based on several hundred cases) making incriminatory statements dropped from 48.5% to 27.1%, or a drop of about 21% (p. 13). They concluded that *Miranda* did have a detrimental effect on interrogation success.
        This study used a quasi-experimental research design, specifically, a "separate-sample pretest-posttest design" (Campbell and Stanley 1963, p. 53). A research design is the logical structure upon which the validity of the conclusions and inferences are grounded. The more rigorous the design, the greater is the internal validity of the study. Internal validity is the *sine qua non* of experimentation: Are the observed results attributable to the experimental treatment (or independent variable) rather than to some alternative uncontrolled factor(s)? The Seeburger and Wettick study did not employ a true experimental design because of the absence of randomization and of a control group (which, in their setting, was obviously impossible). As a result of these imperfections in design, there are plausible rival explanations for their result. There are several possible threats to the internal validity of any quasi-experimental design (Campbell 1970; Lempert 1966). Some of them, pertinent here, include the following:
        History: Events other than the *Miranda* decision may have occurred from the before period to the after period of the study, and they may account for the decline in confessions. For example, *Miranda* was only a part of the general due process revolution in criminal procedure of the 1960s that resulted in

greater judicial restrictions on police authority and, concomitantly, greater safeguards for the criminally accused.

Maturation: There may have been changes in the police themselves during the three-year period of the study that may have affected the interrogation results, independently of *Miranda.*

Selection: Another possible source of invalidity is the differential selection of cases for the before and after groups, thereby resulting in different levels of confession. The study did not indicate what types of crimes and suspects were involved in the two time periods. There could have been more serious offenses in the before period, and we know (from the Yale study) that the more serious the crime, the more coercive the interrogation, and the more likely a confession.

Regression: "Regression artifacts," notes Campbell (1970), "are probably the most recurrent form of self-deception in the experimental social reform literature" (p. 225). To determine regression effects, an extended time series is needed. This study used only two time periods. If there had been data showing instability in the rate of confessions at different time periods prior to 1964–66 (the before period in the study), and the rate in 1964–66 was exceptionally high, then the rate in the subsequent (or after) period would be, on the average, lower (that is, regress toward the general trend) purely as a function of the variability in the time series. The observed decline in confessions could have reflected a pseudo-shift due to the atypically high rate that prevailed at the before period.

What other plausible explanations based on history, maturation, and selection could account for the Seeburger and Wettick result?

9.   For an observational study of field (not custodial) interrogations by patrol officers (not detectives), see Reiss and Black (1967). Using the systematically recorded observations of students who rode police cars around the clock in several metropolitan areas, the authors found patterns similar to those of the custodial interrogation studies. Officers usually had evidence to arrest apart from the field interrogation results. Indeed, voluntary admissions of guilt were more frequent than admissions after questioning. Field interrogations, in short, were "unproductive" for the purpose of obtaining evidence for conviction. The study concluded that the "introduction of *Miranda*-type warnings into field settings would have little effect on the liability of suspects to criminal charges" (p. 56).

Practical and Symbolic Aspects of Warnings

10.   In the first round of impact studies after an important decision is handed down, the tendency of researchers is to examine main order effects: Do warnings affect confessions? Does school desegregation enhance minority student achievement and self-esteem? Does the death penalty decrease crime rates? And so on. The attention given to main effects eclipses the many other factors that intervene between the legal decision and the societal impact. When interaction effects are neglected, the results may appear contradictory. Sometimes a rule has an observable impact and sometimes not. The next and more important question, then, is under what circumstances will a rule have an effect?

One factor that mediates the impact of *Miranda* is the suspect's understanding of the warnings. A study by Medalie, Zeitz, and Alexander (1968) of Georgetown University examined the relationship between comprehension of the warnings and the subsequent exercise of the rights. They interviewed 85 post-*Miranda* defendants "supplied" by public defender agencies and the private bar in Washington, D.C. The researchers read the warnings one at a time to each defendant and then asked him what the warning meant. The responses were coded in terms of "understand" or "not understand." A fairly high rate of comprehension was found: 85% of the interviewees understood the right to silence and 82% the right to an attorney. Nonetheless, a sizable minority of those who understood the warnings chose not to exercise the rights. Of the 37 defendants who understood the right to silence, 15 (or 41%) gave a statement to the police. Of the 29 defendants who understood the right to an attorney, 10 (or 34%) opted not to have an attorney (p. 1377, Table 10).

These results have to be read with caution, given the small and selected sample and the fact that the interview did not duplicate the atmosphere of the interrogation room. The explanations given by the interviewees are still revealing. The reasons they gave for confessing included the belief that there was no harm in talking so long as there was no signed statement and the hope for more lenient treatment by adopting a cooperative posture. The reasons for not desiring an attorney were mixed: "The police have some lawyers of their own who [are] working with them" (p. 1375). "I wouldn't want one. That's the worst place to have a lawyer, because the police play it straight then. I wanted them to make a mistake" (p. 1378). For some, having a lawyer was a low priority concern: "[My] main concern was bond"; "I wasn't thinking about anything but calling my mother and wife" (p. 1378).

Thus, cognitive understanding of the warnings does not necessarily translate into the exercise of the rights warned. What other factors might influence the effect of *Miranda*?

For another interview study regarding the comprehension of warnings which reached similar results and was conducted in Denver, see Leiken (1970).

11.   One year after *Miranda*, the Supreme Court extended to juveniles the rights to counsel and to silence in juvenile court proceedings, but did not specifically deal with the application of these rights at the pretrial stage of police interrogation (*In re Gault*, 1967). The Court opined that "the greatest care must be taken to assure that [a minor's] admission [is] voluntary," without elaborating on the dimensions of that care (p. 55). The implication is that minors, because of their immaturity and vulnerability which place them at a disadvantage in the stationhouse, may require special protections not accorded to adults.

The overwhelming majority of juveniles (and adults) waive their *Miranda* rights. To determine the validity of a waiver by a juvenile, the Court requires only a consideration of the totality of circumstances (*Fare* v. *Michael C.*, 1979). That is, a reviewing court examines circumstances such as the age, intelligence, and prior experiences of the juvenile with the criminal justice system to assess whether the waiver was knowingly and voluntarily made. The specific factors to be considered and the weight to be attached to each are left to the discretion of the court. Some state courts have imposed a higher standard on the assumption that minors do not understand the warnings uttered by the police and therefore cannot make an informed choice to relinquish their rights. The Pennsylvania supreme court, for example, imposed a per se or nonwaivable right to have an "interested" adult (such as parent, guardian, or attorney) present to advise a juvenile prior to interrogation (*Commonwealth* v. *Roane*, 1974).

The issue of a juvenile's capacity to understand his rights was studied by Grisso (1980). He tested juveniles in a detention center regarding their comprehension of the words of *Miranda* (for example, by asking them to paraphrase the warnings and define key terms) and of the meaning of the rights communicated by the warnings (via standardized interview questions). The responses were compared to those of adult ex-offenders. He found that, as a class, "juveniles under the age of fifteen do not meet an adult level of understanding, while sixteen-year-olds generally do" (p. 1157). Intelligence was associated with increased comprehension. Prior court experience was related to increased understanding of the practical implications of the rights to silence and to counsel, but not to increased understanding of the words of the warnings. The "inescapable conclusion" is that suspects aged fifteen or younger should have an absolute right to the presence of counsel during interrogation (pp. 1161, 1166).

Does this recommendation necessarily follow from the findings? Why not draft simplified warnings for juveniles? Should one inquire whether judges are determining fairly the validity of waivers by juveniles under the totality test?

12.   The Court did not spell out what the "right to the presence of an attorney" means at the stationhouse. Justice Jackson suggested that "any lawyer worth his salt will tell the suspect in no uncertain terms to make no statement to the police under any circumstances" (*Watts* v. *Indiana*, 1949, p. 59). If all lawyers heeded his advice, there would be no confessions and interrogations would come to an end. Since statements are obtained by the police even at times when an attorney is available, there is need to find out the attorney's role at the stationhouse.

In the Georgetown study (Medalie, Zeitz, and Alexander 1968), volunteer lawyers from Washington, D.C., agreed to furnish indigent suspects with stationhouse counsel by being on call around the clock for a one-year period. Most of them had little or no experience in criminal law practice. An "astonishingly small number" of defendants (7% of 15,430 arrestees for the year) requested one of these volunteer attorneys. When counsel was requested, very little time was actually spent with the suspects: one-fourth of the attorneys (out of a total of 292) spent less than fifteen minutes; about one-half spent thirty minutes. The most common service rendered was the reiteration of legal rights. Non-*Miranda* services included assisting with bond, contacting friends and relatives, and aiding with various social problems. This volunteer project was discontinued partly because "very few interrogations [were] taking place" (over one-half of the defendants alleged that they had been questioned before the attorney arrived at the stationhouse) and partly because most of the attorneys felt they were performing no useful legal service (pp. 1389–90).

The Yale study (in a section of the article not reproduced here) also involved interviews with fifty-five of the most active members of the New Haven criminal bar. Normally, the attorneys said they advised their clients not to talk to the police. But forty of the attorneys also conceded that under certain circumstances they would urge cooperation. These included cases involving minors, morals offenses, and domestic disputes, and cases in which the police already had enough evidence of guilt without a confession. In these circumstances, the attorneys felt that detectives would reward cooperation by recommending leniency to the prosecutor in charging and/or in sentencing. Legal advice, in any event, is not necessarily the final word. Over two-thirds of the interviewed attorneys said that suspects do not invariably follow their advice (pp. 1600–05).

Systematic study of the role and impact of *Miranda* counsel is needed. The range of services that counsel can and should perform at the stationhouse remains to be mapped, and a starting point is to ascertain what counsel, in fact, does. There is a whole constellation of factors—the nature of the case, amount of evidence, competence of counsel, attorney-police relationship, defendant's trust in counsel—that can affect that role.

13.   Suppose that the requisite funds and authorization are secured to carry out a demonstration project of stationhouse counsel for arrestees. After the warnings are given to all arrestees brought to the stationhouse, one-half (based on random selection) are furnished immediately with an on-site attorney (which, of course, they are free to decline), and the other half are not automatically provided with counsel on the spot (unless they exercise their right and request counsel). What ethical, legal, and methodological issues does this experimental differentiation pose? What new information might this field experiment yield that interviews with attorneys would not provide?

14.   We know that the overwhelming majority of defendants plead guilty rather than go to trial. If a defendant heeds the warnings of the right to silence and later still pleads guilty, the effect of *Miranda* in such a case would be simply to defer the confession from the stage of police interrogation to the stage of prosecutor-defender plea bargaining. What are the tactical advantages, if any, for the defendant in postponing the moment of truth?

15.   Can *Miranda* be justified without reference to any impact upon confessions? Does its validity rest upon the outcome of interrogations?

By requiring only a *warning* of the right to the presence of counsel rather than the *actual presence* of counsel at each interrogation, or providing no safeguards at all, the Court appears to have undertaken the Solomonic judgment of "splitting the baby." Seen as a compromise decision, *Miranda*'s purpose seems to be to lessen the disadvantage a suspect has in dealing with the police but not to equalize the balance. The warnings make the interrogation process a bit less inquisitorial, but since most suspects may be expected to waive their right to presence of counsel, the police-suspect confrontation remains mostly a nonadversarial one. *Miranda* seeks the middle ground between the demands of crime control and due process.

Could or should the Court have been more forthright in explaining how it reached the particular equilibrium that it did in *Miranda*? What are other ways for arriving at the same result without relying on the device of warnings and the loophole of waiver?

16.   Although the outcome in terms of overall confessions may stay the same, the giving of the warnings serves in itself a symbolic function. The warnings may have a long-term educative effect on the police and the citizenry. Their utterances may sound like meaningless legalisms, but like all rituals, they also communicate an important message: that law enforcement in a democratic society is not above the law. The warnings represent a normative declaration of how the police ought to comport themselves and a reminder to the citizenry that their rights are not laid to rest at the stationhouse door. In the long run, *Miranda* could instill in both the police and the public a greater sensitivity to their respective responsibilities and rights.

The initial impact of *Brown I* was also mostly symbolic. It served as a catalyst for changes in social attitudes and values, but widespread school desegregation was not implemented in the South until more than a dozen years later and in the North it is still proceeding apace. *Brown II*'s rule of "all deliberate speed" was also a compromise decision. Does *Miranda* play the same role as *Brown* as a catalyst for attitude change in order to induce future behavioral change? Or are the two contexts—judicial regulation of school officials and of the police—too disparate to permit the drawing of parallels?

6.4. JUDICIAL REGULATION OF POLICE ENFORCEMENT PRACTICES

The Fourth Amendment Exclusionary Rule

HISTORICAL BACKGROUND

The decisional history, limited to headlines, unfolds in two major cases.

In *Weeks* v. *United States* (1914), the Supreme Court reversed a conviction based on contraband seized by federal officers after entering the premises without a warrant. It prohibited the use in the federal courts of evidence secured in violation of the Fourth Amendment. The establishment of this exclusionary rule gave expression to the principle that the power of the state must be exercised within the framework of the law.

The exclusion in state courts of illegally obtained evidence was not mandated until 1961 in *Mapp* v. *Ohio*. In that case, an anonymous caller informed the police that a bombing and arson suspect was hiding in Mrs. Mapp's home. The police arrived in force, forbade her lawyer from entering the house, and then broke down the door. They waived a piece of paper that they claimed was a search warrant. Mrs. Mapp grabbed the paper and placed it inside her blouse. The police forcibly retrieved it. Later, the state courts professed doubt that there ever was a search warrant. All that the police found in the search were some "lewd and lascivious" materials (p. 643). Mrs. Mapp was eventually convicted and sentenced to imprisonment for possession of pornography, then a crime under Ohio law. The Court reversed the conviction and acknowledged that "other remedies have been worthless and futile" in preventing police misconduct. It held that the exclusionary rule is a "constitutionally required—even if judicially implied—deterrent safeguard without insistence upon which the Fourth Amendment would have been reduced to 'a form of words' " (p. 652).

It was a landmark and controversial decision. According to one district attorney, "Police practices and prosecution practices were revolutionized" by *Mapp* (Specter 1962, p. 4). The New York City Police Commissioner said, "I can think of no decision in recent times in the field of law enforcement which had such a dramatic and traumatic effect as [*Mapp*]." It led to "modifying, amending, and creating new policies" and to holding retraining sessions "from the very top administrators down to each of the thousands of foot patrolmen" (Murphy 1966, pp. 940–41).

PROCEDURE OF EXCLUSION

The mechanics for invoking the exclusionary rule can be described briefly. At a pretrial hearing or a trial, defense counsel makes a motion to suppress evidence. Various technical and tactical reasons determine when a motion is raised. Generally, motions to exclude physical evidence obtained from allegedly unreasonable searches and seizures are made at the pretrial stage. Often it may be the only evidence available or its mere possession (for example, of narcotics) may be the crime. In such instances, if the evidence is suppressed, the prosecution is left with no case to take to court. Motions to exclude confessions resulting from allegedly improper interrogations are commonly made at trial, partly because there is usually enough other evidence for prosecution. For the most part, more suppression motions are made at the pretrial stage than at the trial stage, and typically these involve claims of Fourth Amendment violations.

Pretrial hearings to evaluate the legality of police conduct occupy a significant part of the business of the crowded lower courts of metropolitan areas. In Chicago, for example, about one-third of all court time in narcotics proceedings is spent on suppression hearings (Oaks 1970, p. 744). In its ideal form, defense counsel submits a memorandum or brief in support of the motion, describing the alleged police impropriety, giving reasons for the exclusion, and citing legal authorities. The prosecution files an opposing brief. At the hearing, the officer who conducted the search or seizure is sworn in and cross-examined for the purpose of establishing that his conduct leading to the evidence or the arrest was improper. The officer is also examined by the prosecution to disclose facts that would afford a basis in law for the search or seizure; the prosecution, in effect, attempts to rehabilitate the officer. This procedure is the source of the recurrent police complaint that it is the officer, and not the accused criminal, who is on trial. For the accused, especially in narcotics cases, this hearing may well be more important than the trial, because if the evidence is excluded, there likely will be no trial.

After the hearing, the trial judge gives his ruling. Either side may appeal from an unfavorable disposition. In practice, when a motion is granted, the prosecution usually dismisses the case because of the cost and time in pursuing an appeal—unless, or course, it is a particularly significant case.

The Purpose and Impact of the Exclusionary Rule

THE EXCLUSIONARY RULE: WHY SUPPRESS VALID EVIDENCE

Malcom R. Wilkey

America is now ready to confront frankly and to examine realistically both the achievements and social costs of the policies which have been so hopefully enacted in the past 40 years. . . .

We can see that huge social cost most clearly in the distressing rate of street crimes—assaults and robberies with deadly weapons, narcotics trafficking, gambling and prostitution—which flourish in no small degree simply because of the exclusionary rule of evidence. . . .

Though scholars have been shedding more and more light on [the exclusionary rule], few people have considered the enormous social cost of the exclusionary rule, and fewer still have thought about possible alternatives to the rule. I propose to do both those things in this article.

THE RULE'S MYSTIQUE

. . . The greatest obstacle to replacing the exclusionary rule with a rational process, which will both protect the citizenry by controlling the police and avoid rewarding the criminal, is the powerful, unthinking emotional attachment to the rule. . . . [Many citizens, lawyers, and judges] appear totally unaware that the rule was not employed in U.S. courts during the first 125 years of the Fourth

Amendment, that it was devised by the judiciary in the assumed absence of any other method of controlling the police, and that no other country in the civilized world has adopted such a rule. . . .

Realistically, the exclusionary rule can probably never be abolished until both the public and the Supreme Court are satisfied that there is available in our legal system a reasonably workable alternative. Unfortunately, the converse may also be true—we will never have any alternative in operation until the rule is abolished. So long as we keep the rule, the police are not going to investigate and discipline their own men, and thus sabotage prosecutions by invalidating the admissibility of vital evidence. . . .

THE COURT'S RATIONALE

Deterrence: During the rule's development, the Supreme Court has offered three main reasons for the rule. The principal and almost sole theory today is that excluding the evidence will punish the police officers who made the illegal search and seizure or otherwise violated the constitutional rights of the defendant, and thus deter policemen from committing the same violation again. The flaw in this theory is that there is absolutely no empirical data that excluding evidence against a defendant has anything to do with either punishing police officers or thereby deterring them from future violations. . . .

Privacy: From *Weeks* (1914) to *Mapp* (1961) the rule was also justified as protecting the privacy of the individual against illegal searches and seizures as guaranteed by the Fourth Amendment. The Supreme Court later downgraded the protection of privacy rationale, perhaps because of the obvious defect that the rule purports to do nothing to recompense innocent victims of Fourth Amendment violations, and the gnawing doubt as to just what right of privacy guilty individuals have in illegal firearms, contraband narcotics and policy betting slips—the frequent objects of search and seizure.

Judicial integrity: A third theme of the Supreme Court's justifying rationale, now somewhat muted, is that the use of illegally obtained evidence brings the court system into disrepute. In *Mapp* Justice Clark referred to "that judicial integrity so necessary in the true administration of justice." . . .

THE IMPACT OF THE RULE

It is undeniable that, as a result of the rule, the most valid, conclusive, and irrefutable factual evidence is excluded from the knowledge of the jury or consideration by the judge. As Justice Cardozo predicted in 1926, in describing the complete irrationality of the exclusionary rule:

The criminal is to go free because the constable has blundered. . . . A room is searched against the law, and the body of a murdered man is found. . . . The privacy of the home has been infringed, and the murderer goes free.

. . .

I submit that justice is, or should be, a truth-seeking process. The court has a duty to the accused to see that he receives a fair trial; the court also has a duty to society to see that all the truth is brought out; only if all the truth is brought out can there be a fair trial. The exclusionary rule results in a complete distortion of the truth. Undeniable facts, of the greatest importance, are forever barred. . . .

There have been several empirical studies on the effect of the exclusionary rule in five major American cities— Boston, Chicago, Cincinnati, New York and Washington, D.C.—during the period from 1950 to 1971. These have been recently collected and analyzed, along with other aspects of the exclusionary rule and its alternatives, by Professor Steven Schlesinger in his book, *Exclusionary In-*

justice: The Problem of Illegally Obtained Evidence.

Three of these studies concluded that the exclusionary rule was a total failure in its primary task of deterring illegal police activity and that it also produced other highly undesirable side effects. The fourth study, which said the first three were too harsh in concluding that the rule was totally ineffective, still said: "Nonetheless, the inconclusiveness of our findings is real enough; they do not nail down an argument that the exclusionary rule has accomplished its task." . . .

CRITICISMS OF THE RULE

By this point, we should be able to see that the exclusionary rule actually produces many effects opposite from those that the Court intended to produce. No matter what rationale we consider, the rule in its indiscriminate workings does far more harm than good and, in many respects, it actually prevents us from dealing with the real problems of Fourth Amendment violations in the course of criminal investigations.

In the eyes of the Supreme Court, the first and primary rationale of the exclusionary rule is deterrence. I submit that all available facts and logic show that excluding the most reliable evidence does absolutely nothing to punish and thus deter the official wrongdoer, but the inevitable and certain result is that the guilty criminal defendant goes free.

The second—now rather distant second—rationale in the eyes of the Court has been the protection of privacy. I submit a policy of excluding incriminating evidence can never protect an innocent victim of an illegal search against whom no incriminating evidence is discovered. The only persons protected by the rule are the guilty against whom the most serious reliable evidence should be offered. It cannot

be separately argued that the innocent person is protected *in the future* by excluding evidence against the criminal *now*, for this is only the deterrent argument all over again.

The third rationale found in the past opinions of the Court is that the use of illegally obtained evidence brings our court system into disrepute. I submit that the exclusion of valid, probative, undeniably truthful evidence undermines the reputation of and destroys the respect for the entire judicial system. . . .

OTHER DEFECTS OF THE RULE

The rule does not simply fail to meet its declared objectives; it suffers from five other defects, too. One of those defects is that it uses an undiscriminating, meat-ax approach in the most sensitive areas of the administration of justice. It totally fails to discriminate between the degrees of culpability of the officer or the degrees of harm to the victim of the illegal search and seizure.

It does not matter whether the action of the officer was grossly willful and flagrant or whether he was conscientiously using his very best judgment under difficult circumstances; the result is the same: the evidence is out. . . .

Another defect is that the rule makes no distinction between minor offenses and more serious crimes. The teenage runner caught with policy slips in his pocket and the syndicate hit man accused of first degree murder are each automatically set free by operation of the exclusionary rule, without any consideration of the impact on the community. . . .

A third problem is that, strangely, a rule which is supposed to discipline and improve police conduct actually results in encouraging highly pernicious police behavior. A policeman is supposed to tell the truth, but when he knows that describing the search truthfully will taint the evidence and free the suspect, the policeman is apt to feel that he has a "higher duty" than the truth. He may perjure himself to convict the defendant.

Similarly, knowing that evidence of gambling, narcotics or prostitution is hard to obtain under the present rules of search and seizure, the policeman may feel that he can best enforce the law by stepping up the incidence of searches and seizures, making them frequent enough to be harassing, with no idea of ultimate prosecution. . . .

Fourth, the rule discourages internal disciplinary action by the police themselves. Even if police officials know that an officer violated Fourth Amendment standards in a particular case, few of them will charge the erring officer with a Fourth Amendment violation: it would sabotage the case for the prosecution before it even begins. . . .

Finally, the existence of the federally imposed exclusionary rule makes it virtually impossible for any state, not only the federal government, to experiment with any other methods of controlling police. One unfortunate consequence of *Mapp* was that it removed from the state both the incentive and the opportunity to deal with illegal search and seizure by means other than suppression. . . .

ALTERNATIVES TO THE RULE

The excuse given for the persistence of the exclusionary rule in this country is that there is no effective alternative to make the police obey the law in regard to unreasonable searches and seizures. If this excuse did not come from such respected sources, one would be tempted to term it an expression of intellectual bankruptcy.

"No effective alternative"? How do all the other civilized countries control their police? By disciplinary measures against the erring policeman, by effective civil damage action against both the policeman and the government—not by freeing the criminal. Judging by police conduct in England, Canada and other nations, these measures work very well. Why does the United States alone rely upon the irrational exclusionary rule? . . .

[T]here seem to be two general approaches which might well be combined in one statute—internal discipline by the law enforcement authorities themselves, and external control by the courts or an independent review board.

INTERNAL DISCIPLINE

Disciplinary action against the offending law enforcement officer could be initiated by the law enforcement organization itself or by the person whose Fourth Amendment rights had been allegedly violated. The police could initiate action either within the regular command structure or by an overall disciplinary board outside the hierarchy of command. . . .

The person injured could also initiate action leading to internal discipline of the offending officer by complaint to the agency disciplinary board. Each enforcement agency or department could establish a process to hear and decide the complaint, providing both a penalty for the offending officer (if the violation were proved) and government compensation to the injured party.

This procedure would cover numerous cases in which citizens suffer violations of Fourth Amendment rights, but in which no court action results. . . .

The penalty against the officer would be tailored to fit his own culpability; it might be a reprimand, a fine, a delay in promotion, a suspension, or discharge. Factors bearing upon the extent of the penalty would include the extent to which the violation was willful, the manner in which it deviated from approved conduct, the degree to which it invaded the privacy of the injured party, and the extent to which human dignity and societal values were breached.

Providing compensation to the injured party from the government is necessary. . . . Policemen traditionally are not wealthy and the government has a deep purse. . . .

EXTERNAL CONTROL

When a prosecutor tries a defendant in the wake of a violation of Fourth Amendment rights, the court could conduct a "mini-trial" of the offending officer after the violation is alleged and proof outlined in the principal criminal case. This mini-trial would be similar to a hearing on a motion to suppress now, but it would be conducted after the main criminal case. The burden would be on the injured party to prove, by preponderance of the evidence, that the officer violated his Fourth Amendment rights. The policeman could submit his case to either the judge or the jury who heard the main criminal case. . . .

Such a mini-trial would provide an outside disciplinary force that the injured party could utilize in lieu of internal discipline by the agency. . . .

In those instances where police violate Fourth Amendment rights but the prosecutor does not bring charges against the suspect, the wronged party should be able to bring a statutory civil action against the government and the officer. . . .

CONCLUSION

. . . If we have a choice, let us calmly and carefully consider the available alternatives, draw upon the experience of other nations with systems of justice similar to our own, and by abolishing the rule permit in the laboratories of our 51 jurisdictions the experimentation with various possible alternatives promising far more than the now discredited exclusionary rule.

THE EXCLUSIONARY RULE IN HISTORICAL PERSPECTIVE: THE STRUGGLE TO MAKE THE FOURTH AMENDMENT MORE THAN "AN EMPTY BLESSING"

Yale Kamisar

In the 65 years since the Supreme Court adopted the exclusionary rule, few critics have attacked it with as much vigor and on as many fronts as did Judge Malcolm Wilkey. . . .

Because so many share Judge Wilkey's hostility to the exclusionary rule, it is important to examine and to evaluate Wilkey's arguments at some length. . . .

CRIME AND THE RULE

. . .

[J]udge Wilkey . . . claim[s] on his very first page that "[w]e can see [the] huge social cost [of *Weeks* and *Mapp*] most clearly in the distressing rate of street crimes . . . which flourish in no small degree simply because of the exclusionary rule." [I]t is disappointing to hear a critic repeat this charge, because after 65 years of debate, there was reason to hope that this criticism, at least, would no longer be made. As Professor James Vorenberg pointed out, shortly after he completed his two years of service as Executive Director of the President's Commission on Law Enforcement and Administration of Justice:

What the Supreme Court does has practically no effect on the amount of crime in this country, and what the police do has far less effect than is generally realized.

Even Professor Dallin Oaks (now a university president), upon whose work Judge Wilkey relies so heavily, advised a decade ago:

The whole argument about the exclusionary rule 'handcuffing' the police should be abandoned. If this is a negative effect, then it is an effect of the constitutional rules, not an effect on the exclusionary rule as the means chosen for their enforcement.

Police officials and prosecutors should stop claiming that the exclusionary rule prevents effective law enforcement. In doing so they attribute far greater effect to the exclusionary rule than the evidence warrants, and they are also in the untenable position of urging that the sanction be abolished so that they can continue to violate the [constitutional] rules with impunity.

. . .

A BASIC CONFUSION

. . . [P]olice and prosecutors have treated the exclusionary rule as if it were itself the guaranty against unreasonable search and seizure (which is one good reason for retaining the rule). At several places Judge Wilkey's article reflects the same confusion.

He complains, for example, that if a search or frisk turns up a deadly weapon, that weapon cannot be used in evidence if the officer lacked the constitutionally required cause for making the search or frisk in the first place. But this is really an attack on the constitutional guaranty itself, not the exclusionary rule. . . .

If we replace the exclusionary rule with "disciplinary punishment and civil penalties directly against the erring officer involved," as Judge Wilkey proposes, and if these alternatives "would certainly provide a far more effective deterrent than . . . the exclusionary rule," as the judge assures us, the weapon still would not be brought in as evidence in the case he poses because the officer would not *make* the search or frisk if he lacked the requisite cause to do so.

I venture to say that Judge Wilkey has confused the *content* of the law of search and seizure (which proponents of the exclusionary rule need not, and have not always, defended) with the *exclusionary rule*—which "merely states the consequences of a breach of whatever principles might be adopted to control law enforcement officers." The confusion was pointed out more than 50 years ago by [Connor Hall] . . . :

When it is proposed to secure the citizen his constitutional rights by the direct punishment of the violating officer, we must assume that the proposer is honest, and that he would have such consistent prosecution and such heavy punishment of the offending officer as would cause violations to cease and thus put a stop to the seizure of papers and other tangible evidence through unlawful search.

If this, then, is to be the result, no evidence in any appreciable number of cases would be obtained through unlawful searches, and the result would be the same, so far as the conviction of criminals goes, as if the constitutional right was enforced by a return of the evidence. . . .

If punishment of the officer is effective to prevent unlawful searches, then equally by this is justice rendered inefficient and criminals coddled. . . .

WAITING FOR ALTERNATIVES

Judge Wilkey makes plain his agreement with Chief Justice Burger that "the continued existence of [the exclusionary rule] . . . inhibits the development of rational alternatives." . . .

Thus, Judge Wilkey warns that "we will never have any alternative in operation until the rule is abolished. So long as we keep the rule, the police are not going to investigate and discipline their men, and thus sabotage prosecution by invalidating the admissibility of vital evidence. . . ."

In light of our history, these comments (both the Chief Justice's and Judge Wilkey's) are simply baffling. First, the fear of "sabotaging" prosecution has never inhibited law enforcement administrators from disciplining officers for committing the many unlawful searches of homes and automobiles of innocent people which turn up nothing incriminating, in which no arrest is made, about which courts do nothing, and about which we never hear.

Second, both defenders of the rule and its critics recognize that

there are large areas of police activity which do not result in criminal prosecutions [for example, arrest or confiscation as a punitive sanction, common in gambling and liquor law violations; illegal detentions which do not result in the acquisition of evidence; unnecessary destruction of property]—hence the rule has virtually no applicability and no effect in such situations.

Whatever the reason for the failure to discipline officers for "mistake" in these "large areas of police activities," it cannot be the existence of the exclusionary rule.

Finally, and most importantly, *for many decades* a majority of the states had no exclusionary rule but *none of them* developed any meaningful alternative. Thirty-five years passed between the time the federal courts adopted the exclusionary rule and the time *Wolf* [which made the Fourth Amendment applicable to the states] was decided in 1949, but none of the 31 states which still admitted illegally seized evidence had established an alternative method of controlling the police. Twelve more years passed before *Mapp* imposed the rule on the state courts, but none of the 24 states which still rejected the exclusionary rule had instituted an alternative remedy. This half-century of post-*Weeks* "freedom to experiment" did not produce any meaningful alternative to the exclusionary rule anywhere.

DISPARITY BETWEEN FACT AND THEORY

Of course, few critics of the exclusionary rule have failed to suggest alternative remedies that *might be devised* or that *warranted study*. None of them has become a reality. . . .

Judge Wilkey proposes that in lieu of the exclusion of illegally seized evidence there be a statutory remedy against the government itself to afford meaningful compensation and restitution for the victims of police illegality. . . . [L]eading commentators . . . made the same suggestion 20 years ago, but none of the many states that admitted illegally seized evidence at the time seemed interested in experimenting along these lines. . . . Abandoning the exclusionary rule without waiting for a meaningful alternative (as Judge Wilkey and Chief Justice Burger would have us do) will not furnish an incentive for devising an alternative, but *relieve* whatever pressure there now exists for doing so. . . .

[In a separate insert, the author writes:]

ARE COMPARISONS WITH OTHER COUNTRIES MEANINGFUL?

In his reliance on comparisons with other countries to attack the exclusionary rule, Judge Wilkey parts company with the two academicians he has chiefly leaned on, Steven Schlesinger and Dallin Oaks. Schlesinger saw little point in making comparisons between Canada and the United States. He recognized that there may be no comparable need for the exclusionary rule in Canada (and Western European Countries) for several reasons:

• Their police "are simply better disciplined than their American counterparts."
• Canada's crime rate, "especially that of violent crime, is substantially less than that of

the United States, thus putting less pressure on the police to deal with crimes by illegal methods."

• Canada's problem with crime is not exacerbated by the level of racial tension experienced in the United States.

Finally, Schlesinger noted, "it would seem that these factors which differentiate the Canadian law enforcement situation from the American are likewise present in the nations of Western Europe."

LEGISLATIVE OVERSIGHT

Some 20 years ago, Justice Jackson suggested another possible factor when he said:

I have been repeatedly impressed with the speed and certainty with which the slightest invasion of British individual freedom or minority rights by officials of the government is picked up in Parliament, not merely by the opposition, but by the party in power, and made the subject of persistent questioning, criticism, and sometimes rebuke. There is no waiting on the theory that the judges will take care of it. . . . [T]o transgress the rights of the individual or the minority is bad politics. In the United States, I cannot say that this is so.

More recently, an American political scientist furnished examples of "zealous legislative oversight" of the police of Scotland, Sweden, West Germany and France, indicating that it is still "good politics" in many European countries to observe civil liberties. It was noted, too, that "[c]ivilians do not just oversee but actually run most European police departments"; that several European countries reserve hundreds of positions for lawyers who are recruited directly into the upper ranks; that "European police departments place much more emphasis on education"; and that some European countries actually encourage complaints against police and, not infrequently, sustain them.

CANADA'S DIFFERENCES

How do other countries control their police without the exclusionary rule? At least with respect to Canada, Professor Oaks offers explicit answers, but his answers do not demonstrate the "irrationality" of the rule in the American setting. Rather, they indicate why Canada may not need an exclusionary rule, but why the United States still does.*

First, "police discipline is relatively common. . . . Second, police officers are occasionally prosecuted for criminal misconduct occurring in the course of their official duties." Oaks considers a third factor perhaps most important of all: ". . . an aggrieved person's tort cause of action against an offending police officer is a real rather than just a theoretical remedy. . . ."

But he suggests that the difference is more than simply the remedies. "[P]olice are greatly concerned about obeying the rules and very sensitive to and quick to be influenced by judicial criticism of their conduct," he writes. And Canadian prosecutors play a different role from that of American prosecutors. A prosecutor there "will sometimes exercise what he considers to be his teaching function with the police by refusing to introduce evidence that he considers to have been improperly obtained." Moreover, "Canadian prosecutors are part of the Ministry of Justice, which has . . . command authority over most of the police organizations . . ." and channels by which to correct offensive practices.

---

*[In 1982, Canada implemented a "Charter of Rights and Freedoms," which is equivalent to the Bill of Rights of the U.S. Constitution. The charter guarantees in section 8 the right to be "secure against unreasonable searches and seizures" and in section 24(2) allows the exclusion of illegally seized evidence if the court decides that its admission "would bring the administration of justice into disrepute." Prior to the implementation of this charter, Canadian courts (as Kamisar indicates) had generally admitted illegally seized evidence so long as it was relevant. The effect of this new exclusionary rule on the Canadian police remains to be seen. Ed.'s note.]

NOTES AND QUESTIONS

1.   As the Wilkey-Kamisar exchange illustrates, the focus of the debate on the Fourth Amendment exclusionary rule has shifted from its normative justification to its empirically based, deterrent justification. The argument of principle is that it is unseemly for judges to countenance police derelictions by admitting in evidence the tainted evidence. The "imperative of judicial integrity" (*Elkins* v. *United States*, 1960, p. 222) demands that courts not be partners to or profit from the wrongdoing of a coordinate branch of government. We must "preserve the judicial process from contamination," said Justice Brandeis. "If the Government becomes a law-breaker, it breeds contempt for the law" (dissenting in *Olmstead* v. *United States*, 1928, p. 485). This moralistic reasoning is weakened by exceptions to the exclusionary rule. For example, improperly seized evidence cannot be used to establish guilt but can be admitted to impeach the credibility and direct testimony of the accused if he opts to take the stand (*United States* v. *Havens*, 1980).

    Mapp's holding that the exclusionary rule is a "constitutionally required . . . deterrent safeguard" is somewhat ambiguous. It is unclear whether exclusion is constitutionally required as an integral part of the Fourth Amendment, or whether it is required only to the extent that it serves as a means of deterrence. The Court has since adopted an increasingly restrictive view. The "prime purpose" is to prevent "future unlawful police conduct" and not to secure a "personal constitutional right" of the defendant (*United States* v. *Calandra*, 1974, pp. 347–48). This instrumentalist rationale was a "late arrival" on the judicial scene (Kamisar 1983, p. 597). The amalgam of values on which the rule was premised during the first thirty-five years of its existence has receded into the background, if it is mentioned at all (*Michigan* v. *DeFillippo*, 1979, p. 38). Two consequences ensued from this shift.

    First, since the rule has been made to rest on an empirical foundation, the Court has waded into the ancillary debate on the efficacy of the deterrent effect. In 1960, it observed that "empirical statistics are not available" and expressed doubt whether they would ever be available: "Since as a practical matter it is never easy to prove a negative, it is hardly likely that conclusive data could ever be assembled" (*Elkins* v. *United States*, p. 218). A decade and a half later, it was still of the view that the burden of proving deterrence had not been met: "No empirical researcher, proponent or opponent of the rule, has yet been able to establish with any assurance whether the rule has a deterrent effect even in the situations in which it is now applied" (*United States* v. *Janis*, 1976, p. 450, n. 22). In the next section, we will examine the empirical literature.

    Second, the deterrence rationale has spawned cost-benefit evaluations of the rule. The Court has balanced the competing interests of individual liberty and police efficiency, often concluding that in collateral settings (that is, settings other than criminal trials, such as grand jury proceedings [*Calandra*] and civil tax actions [*Janis*]) and in criminal prosecutions of defendants who are the targets but not the victims of illegal searches (*United States* v. *Payner*, 1980), the "incremental" or "marginal" advantages of exclusion are outweighed by the "substantial" costs to society. Of course, if the Court begins its analysis skeptical that the deterrent effect can even be measured, it comes as no surprise that all recent cases involving exclusion in peripheral contexts come out in favor of the government. Ideology intrudes into the balancing process when incommensurables are compared. The values at stake, unlike consumer benefits, cannot be easily "priced" according to some standard scale. The cumulative effect of not applying the exclusionary rule to the many settings outside the criminal trial is bound to be felt eventually at the trial itself. In a system of law, changing some parts can have repercussions throughout the whole. Admitting illegally seized evidence outside a protected central area is like waging guerrilla warfare against the rule in the countryside. Thus, Justice Brennan expressed the "uneasy feeling" that "a majority of [his] colleagues [have] positioned themselves to abandon altogether the exclusionary rule" (dissenting in *Calandra*, p. 365) or, at least, to modify its thrust, as we shall see below.

2.   The causal model implicit in Wilkey's claim that evidentiary exclusion encourages street crime is that the rule (a) reduces convictions and (b) lets criminals go free, thereby (c) enabling them to prey upon society. Is this model intuitively sound?

3.   The rule comes into play at trial, but the majority of criminal cases are disposed without trial by plea bargain. The possibility of suppression may influence tactical decisions of the prosecution. For example, the anticipation of suppression might lead prosecutors to demand high bail as a means of punishing by pretrial detention those defendants who would escape conviction as a result of the successful exclusion of evidence (Geller 1981, p. 1645). What effect would you expect that exclusionary rule to have on plea rates, charging, and the severity of sentences?

4.   In support of his argument against the exclusionary rule, Wilkey points to the experience of Canada, England, and other Western Countries. There, he says, police misconduct is minimal and rights are safeguarded, all without reliance on the suppression of evidence. In point of fact, Bradley (1983) has observed that West Germany has a well-deveoped system of exclusionary rules founded on constitutional and statutory provisions. For example, under a constitutional doctrine of proportionality, judges balance on a case-by-case basis the methods used by the police and the seriousness of the charged offense. If the means of fighting crime are disproportional to the crime itself, the evidence is excluded despite its relevancy. However, unlike the American doctrine of exclusion, the purpose is not to deter police misconduct but, instead, to keep in balance the competing interests of effective law enforcement and protection of individual rights. To the extent that German law does not focus on whether the police broke the rules, it could be said that there is no exclusion of illegally obtained evidence. The reality is a bit more complex.

5.   Skolnick (1966) argues that the British police are not any more rule-respecting than the American police. They only appear to be more observant of legality:

> [T]he British policeman does not conform to rules so much as he knows how to present the appearance of conformity. By contrast, when the American policeman varies from canons of procedural regularity, his misbehaviors tend to be more visible. Reared in a society with finer social distinctions the British policeman is schooled in etiquette to a degree unknown to most Americans. [p. 66]*

The myth that English police do not use violence, perjury, and improper methods was shattered during the racial disturbances in English cities during the summer of 1981. "The most astonishing revelation of the riots," wrote a journalist, "was how the British police treated the people. But almost equally astonishing was how whites, blacks, and Asians were united in their hostility to the police" (Allman 1981, p. 16).

6.   Tort damages against errant officers and the government as an alternative to the exclusionary rule, advocated by Wilkey and other judges (Posner 1982) and proposed in several bills introduced in the 97th Congress (see Schlag 1982, pp. 907–13), are not common in practice. Most suspects are glad simply to be out of police clutches and they lack the knowledge and resources to sue. Juries are not sympathetic to suits against the police, especially if the plaintiff comes with unclean hands. Attorneys may be reluctant to take on such cases because of the need to maintain good relations with the police—for example, they may have to call on police testimony in another, future case. As a policy matter, making an officer personally liable may not be desirable. The public interest in law enforcement could be adversely affected if the policeman acts unusually cautiously to resolve any doubts in favor of his or her employer's pocketbook.

7.   Criminal prosecution of the police for illegal searches and seizures is also rare, notwithstanding the "mini-trial" proposed by Wilkey. Prosecutors are unwilling to file charges given their symbiotic relationship with the police and juries are unlikely to convict for what they perceive is only excess zeal in fighting crime (Chevigny 1969).

8.   Wilkey's criticism of the "meat-ax approach" of the rule—that it fails to discriminate between degrees of culpability of the officer—goes to the heart of the so-called good faith exception. In an *en banc* decision in *United States* v. *Williams* (1980), a thirteen-judge majority of the Fifth Circuit concluded that "evidence is not to be suppressed under the exclusionary rule where it is discovered by officers in the course of actions that are taken in good faith and in the reasonable, though mistaken, belief that they are authorized" (p. 840). This narrowing of the scope of the rule has been adopted by a few states. Colorado,

---

*Reprinted by permission of the publisher, from Jerome Skolnick, *Justice Without Trial: Law Enforcement in a Democratic Society.* Copyright ©1966 by John Wiley and Sons, Inc.

for example, provides that "otherwise admissible" evidence "shall not be suppressed by the trial court if the court determines that the evidence was seized . . . as a result of a good faith mistake or of a technical violation." Good faith errors include mistakes of fact ("reasonable judgmental error" concerning the facts of probable cause) and mistakes of law ("technical violations" in reliance on statutes or decisions that are later overruled or on a warrant that is later found invalid) (Colo. Rev. Stat. §16-3-308(1)(2)(1981)). The Attorney General's Task Force on Violent Crime (1981) has also criticized the exclusionary rule as a remedy that is often excessive in proportion to the violation and has recommended that "evidence should not be excluded from a criminal proceeding if it has been obtained by an officer acting in the reasonable, good faith belief that it was in conformity to the Fourth Amendment" (p. 55). Legislation to the same effect has been proposed at the federal level (The Exclusionary Rule Bills, 1982). This exception is said to flow from and to be consistent with the deterrence rationale. By definition, the rule does not serve its purpose when the police in good faith and reasonably do not know that they were acting unlawfully.

The broad language of the foregoing modifications of the rule leaves open many questions. How are suppression judges to determine what is and what is not good faith? Does the state have the burden of proving good faith or does the defendant have the burden of proving bad faith? In either case, does the proof entail a subjective inquiry into the state of mind of the officer and/or an objective assessment of the reasonableness of his conduct in light of his training and experience? If most police misconduct is not egregious and thus falls outside the scope of the good faith test, is the exclusionary rule rendered "an empty blessing"? Does the exception create an incentive for the police to remain in welcome ignorance of the law, since a claim of good faith is more credible if one has no reason to know whether certain conduct is unlawful?

The Supreme Court, "with apologies to all" (*Illinois* v. *Gates*, 1983, p. 2321), declined to rule on the good faith question, but agreed to address it in its subsequent term.

9.   The *Mapp* rule and the foregoing modifications and alternatives all fail to address a basic question: how to review the broad spectrum of police-citizen encounters that do not result in arrest or prosecution. When the police are seeking evidence to use at trial, a defendant's desire to avoid conviction is a powerful incentive to identify possible police misconduct. But if much of law enforcement has nonconviction objectives, many police derelictions may never come to light. Unless there is prosecution, most citizens—especially poor minority members—have an "almost total lack of effective channels for redress of complaints against police conduct" (National Advisory Commission on Civil Disorders 1968, p. 310).

6.5.   IMPACT OF THE EXCLUSIONARY RULE ON POLICE ENFORCEMENT PRACTICES

STUDYING THE EXCLUSIONARY RULE IN SEARCH AND SEIZURE

Dallin H. Oaks

. . .

ATTEMPTS TO MEASURE THE EFFECT ON THE EXCLUSIONARY RULE

This section examines both previously published and newly compiled evidence on the effect of the exclusionary rule pertaining to search and seizure on the criminal justice system, particularly on law enforcement personnel. Three research methods are represented in this data. The *before-after* method compares the conduct of law enforcement officers or the operation of the criminal justice system before and after adoption of the exclusionary rule. The *multiple-area* method compares the conduct of law enforcement officers or the operation of the criminal justice system in a jurisdiction that has the exclusionary rule with a jurisdiction that does not. These first two methods compare the ef-

Reprinted by permission of the publisher. Copyright ©1970 by the *University of Chicago Law Review* [37 (1970): 665–757].

fect of the rule at different times or in different jurisdictions. The third method, *field observation,* tries to determine the effect of the rule in a single area during a single period of time, such as by drawing inferences from the proportion of motions to suppress that are granted in a particular crime. The information has been obtained from a variety of sources including questionnaires, criminal justice system statistics and observation. The data is grouped according to those sources. . . .

MOTIONS TO SUPPRESS. Court statistics show the astonishing extent to which the exclusion of evidence—as measured by the incidence of motions to suppress—is concentrated in a few crimes. . . .

[O]ver 50 per cent of the motions to suppress in Chicago and the District [of Columbia] were filed in cases involving narcotics and weapons, even though these crimes accounted for a comparatively small proportion of the total number of persons held for prosecution. (The nationwide figures show that only 2 per cent of the total number of persons held for prosecution were charged with weapons or narcotics offenses.) In Chicago an additional 26 per cent of the motions to suppress were filed in gambling cases, which account for only 1 per cent of the national total of persons held for prosecution. . . . [T]he frequency of motions to suppress is a function of the relative importance, in the prosecution of a particular type of crime, of evidence that is obtained by means that can reasonably be challenged as improper. If so, then the law enforcement conduct that is supposed to be deterred by the exclusionary rule will probably be concentrated in the enforcement of those few crimes where motions to suppress are most numerous. Whether or not one accepts that hypothesis, the unequal distribution of motions to suppress among various crime categories should at least make one wary of attempts to use

overall crime statistics as an index of the effect of the exclusionary rule. . . .

The figures on motions to suppress in Chicago and the District of Columbia are in sharp contrast at every level. A few examples will suffice. The percent of gambling cases in which there is a motion to suppress is 81 per cent for Chicago but 12 per cent for the comparable felony in the District. . . . [A]djusted for differences in the number of reported arrests, Chicago has about two and one-half times more motions to suppress in felonies and misdemeanors than the District of Columbia.

Such contrasts are clearly attributable to important differences in the criminal justice systems of the two cities. These include differences in the receptivity of judges to claims of illegal search and seizure and differences in the structure of the system, as well as differences in police behavior. Comparative data cannot be evaluated accurately without taking account of these differences. The point is of enormous importance, especially where the researcher plans to use multiple area comparisons. . . .

[The author's figures on the frequency of motions to suppress as an indirect measure of the deterrent effect of the exclusionary rule as it operated in Chicago in 1950 and 1969 were later updated with 1971 data and combined for presentation purposes by James E. Spiotto, in "Search and Seizure: An Empirical Study of the Exclusionary Rule and its Alternatives."* Oaks was an adviser to Spiotto in his study, which was also conducted at the University of Chicago Law School. At this point, therefore, pertinent excerpts of the Spiotto article are reproduced and in-

*Reprinted by permission of the University of Chicago Press, from James E. Spiotto. "Search and Seizure: An Empirical Study of the Exclusionary Rule and Its Alternatives." *Journal of Legal Studies* 2 (1973): 243–78. Copyright © 1973 by the University of Chicago.

serted in lieu of Oak's original material with respect to motions to suppress.

Spiotto examined "the general increase of motions to suppress in the last 20 years" made at preliminary hearings in Chicago Felony Court, Narcotics Court, and Rackets Court (gambling and guns):

"A comparison of studies made between 1950 and 1971 indicates shifts in the number of motions to suppress—a marked decrease of such motions in gambling cases and a sharp increase in narcotics and gun cases (see Table 1). The decrease in motions to suppress made in gambling offenses is explainable in part by the fact that, during this period, federal authorities as a result of new legislation became involved in the prosecution of gambling offenses. This reduced the legal and social pressure on local Chicago police to search out and seize gambling paraphernalia and arrest violators, sometimes in questionable circumstances. The increase

in motions to suppress in narcotics and gun cases during the same period can be traced at least in part to increased social pressure for aggressive enforcement in these areas. Still, had the exclusionary rule deterred police from making illegal search and seizures, one might expect the number of motions to suppress to have declined in all offenses, not just in gambling. The data demonstrate otherwise. . . .

The most serious question, on which the present study casts some light, is whether the exclusionary rule is effective in deterring unlawful searches. . . .

As pointed out earlier in this study, during the period 1950–1970, in the course of which the exclusionary rule was introduced into Illinois, there was a proportional increase in motions to suppress for narcotics and guns. Yet it would seem that if the exclusionary rule had a strongly deterrent effect on the police, the proportional number of motions to suppress

TABLE 1

Motions to Suppress: 1950–1971

Gambling, Weapons, and Narcotics Cases in Branch 27 of the Municipal Court of Chicago, 1950

Offense	No. of Defs.	Defs. with Motion to Suppress (a)	Motions Granted (b)	Defs. with Motions Granted (a) × (b)
All gambling offenses	5,848	77%	99%	76%
Narcotics	288	19	100	19
Carrying concealed weapons	513	28	91	25
All above offenses	6,649	70	98	69

Source: Comment, Search and Seizure in Illinois: Enforcement of the Constitutional Right of Privacy, 47 Nw.U.L.Rev. 493, 498 (1952).

Gambling, Weapons, and Narcotics Cases in Branches 27 and 57 of the
Circuit Court in Chicago for 12 Sample Days in 1969

Offense	No. of Defs.	Defs. with Motion to Suppress (a)	Motions Granted (b)	Defs. with Motions Granted (a) × (b)
All gambling offenses	312	52%	86%	45%
Narcotics	457	34	97	33
Carrying concealed weapons	188	36	68	24
All above offenses	957	40	87	35

Source: Dallin H. Oaks, Studying the Exclusionary Rule in Search and Seizure, 37 U. Chi. L. Rev. 665, 685 (1970).

Gambling, Weapons, and Narcotics Cases in Branches 25, 27, and 57 of the
Circuit Court in Chicago for 3 Months (April, May, June) in 1971

Offense	No. of Defs.	Defs. with Motion to Suppress (a)	Motions Granted (b)	Defs. with Motions Granted (a) × (b)
All gambling offenses	824	32%	76%	24%
Narcotics	2,060	43	84	36
Carrying concealed weapons	929	36	62	22
All above offenses	3,813	39	77	30

Source: Compiled from examination of court records in Branches 25, 27, and 57 of the First District of the Municipal Department of the Circuit Court of Cook County for April, May, June of 1971.

Reprinted by permission of the University of Chicago Press, from James E. Spiotto, "Search and Seizure: An Empirical Study of the Exclusionary Rule and its Alternatives," *Journal of Legal Studies,* 2(1973): 243–78. Copyright ©1973 by the University of Chicago.

would have decreased over that period of time. . . ." (Spiotto 1973, pp. 246–48). Ed.'s note.]*

OBSERVATIONS OF POLICE BEHAVIOR. Detailed observation of police behavior has also yielded valuable insights into the effect of the exclusionary rule. Jerome S. Skolnick's notable book, *Justice Without Trial,* is the most fruitful source of information obtained by this technique. Over a period of fifteen months in 1962 and 1963, Skolnick carried out many weeks of intensive "participant observation" of the operations of the police of an unidentified city of 400,000. This included two weeks with police of the patrol division, six weeks direct observation of the vice control squad, four weeks with the burglary squad, and two weeks with the robbery and homicide detail. Skolnick's observations of the effect of the exclusionary rule on the police of this city may be summarized as follows:

(1) The exclusionary rule was "neutralized" in practice.
(2) The police viewed the rule not as guaranteeing greater protection of the freedom of decent citizens, but as unnecessarily complicating the task of detecting and apprehending criminals.
(3) Because the policeman's allegiance was to the police organization and to its network of professional responsibilities and evaluative standards, he did not respond to judicial interpretations of legality.
(4) The police organization interpreted its fundamental duty as the discovery of criminal activity. Remaining within the boundaries of the law was secondary. Consequently, when the police felt that the arrest and search and seizure rules constituted too great a hindrance to the apprehension and

conviction of criminals, they would "reconstruct a set of complex happenings in such a way that, subsequent to the arrest, probable cause can be found according to appellate court standards." In this way, "The policeman fabricates probable cause."
(5) "The policeman, as a tactical matter, recognizes an obligation to appear to be obeying the letter of procedural law, while often disregarding its spirit. Thus, the working philosophy of the police has the end justifying the means; according to this philosophy, the demands of apprehension require violation of procedural rules in the name of the higher justification of reducing criminality."
(6) "Since in the policeman's hierarchy of values, arrest and subsequent conviction are more important the 'bigger' the 'pinch,' compliance with the exclusionary rule seems contingent upon this factor."*

. . .

Writing just after the decision in *Mapp* v. *Ohio,* Francis A. Allen declared that up to that time, "no effective quantitative measure of the rule's deterrent efficiency has been devised or applied." That conclusion is not yet outdated. The foregoing findings . . . fall short of demonstrating a research method by which that important question could be determined. . . .

There is a more pervasive difficulty with all of the foregoing methods for measuring the deterrent effect of the exclusionary rule: they all tend to oversimplify an enormously complex inquiry. All suggest a simple answer to a simple question—whether or not the exclusionary rule deters police from illegal behavior. But the subject is not as simple as determining whether the suspect's fingerprint is on the gun, yes or no. Any attempt to determine whether or the extent to which the exclusionary rule affects the behavior of law enforcement personnel confronts an exceed-

*Reprinted by permission of the University of Chicago Press, from James E. Spiotto, "Search and Seizure: An Empirical Study of the Exclusionary Rule and Its Alternatives." *Journal of Legal Studies* 2 (1973): 243–78. Copyright © 1973 by the University of Chicago.

*Reprinted by permission of the publisher, from Jerome Skolnick, *Justice Without Trial: Law Enforcement in a Democratic Society.* Copyright ©1966 by John Wiley and Sons, Inc.

ingly complicated inquiry into human motivation within a complex social model, the criminal justice system.

We are just beginning to sense the complexities of the criminal justice system and its enormous variations from city to city and state to state. Variations in the organization and style of police departments, such as those discussed in James Q. Wilson's *Varieties of Police Behavior,* are bound to have an important effect on whether, when and how much a legal rule will affect police behavior. And it must be remembered that "the police" is not a monolithic entity. There are officers in positions of command, staff, specific assignment (like narcotics detail) and patrol, to name only a few. A policeman's perceptions of the search and seizure rules and of the exclusionary rule as an enforcement device are bound to be affected by his assignment and by the way he interacts with other police and with personnel in other parts of the criminal justice system. The role of the prosecutor is subject to great variation, as pointed out in the contrast between Chicago and the District of Columbia. And the manner in which courts perform their function is another variable of immense diversity.

In this incredibly diverse milieu of different police departments and criminal justice systems and different individual motivations and sensitivity to sanctions, the researcher must consider not one but a variety of possible effects, some long term and some short term, some subtle and some obvious. In addition to the direct deterrent effect of the exclusionary rule, he must try to measure its impact, such as its moral or educative effect.

In view of the complexity of the inquiry, it presently appears to be impossible to design any single test or group of tests that would give a reliable measure of the overall deterrent effect of the exclusionary rule on law enforcement behavior. But it is possible to nibble around the edges of the

problem by small inquiries that illuminate areas of special importance. . . .

LIMITATIONS UPON THE DETERRENT EFFECTIVENESS OF THE EXCLUSIONARY RULE

. . .

[T]he general deterrent effect of legal sanctions will be affected by the following conditions. . . .

1. RISK OF DETECTION, CONVICTION AND PUNISHMENT. A prime defect of the exclusionary rule is that police who have been guilty of improper behavior are not affected in their person or their pocketbook by the application of the rule. . . . So far as police command control is concerned, it is a notorious fact that police are rarely, if ever, disciplined by their superiors merely because they have been guilty of illegal behavior that caused evidence to be suppressed. . . .

2. SEVERITY OF PENALTY. The immediate impact of the exclusionary rule falls not upon the police but upon the prosecutor who is attempting to obtain a conviction. The impact is misplaced. The Presidential Commission's Report on the Police observed that the prosecutor "is not generally conceived of in this country as having overall responsibility for the supervision of the police." The relationship is generally that of independent and coordinate authorities, not always cooperating and sometimes even in conflict in the common task. The relationship can be explained in terms of the different motivations of prosecutor and police. The prosecutor's dominant career motivation is to prosecute and convict the guilty. The police, on the other hand, have a variety of motives other than to facilitate prosecutions. Consequently, the exclusionary rule is well tailored to deter the prosecutor from illegal conduct. But the prosecutor is not the guilty party in an illegal arrest or search and seizure. . . .

3.   COMPETING NORMS OF BEHAVIOR.
The exclusionary rule is unlikely to have a
controlling effect upon a wide range of
police behavior that is violative of the rules
of arrest and search and seizure because
any direct deterrent effect of the rule is
neutralized by the keenly felt needs of the
situation and by the competing norms of
police behavior. Skolnick found that
"norms located within police organization
are more powerful than court decisions in
shaping police behavior. . . ." Even if a
police officer's conduct was illegal and resulted in loss of a conviction, Skolnick observed that the officer was assured of the
sympathy of his superiors so long as he
acted "in conformity with administrative
norms of police organization. . . ."* A
police officer will be disciplined only if he
has failed to behave as a reasonable officer
should. . . .

7.   CLARITY OF THE RULE. The deterrent effectiveness of the exclusionary
rule is also dependent upon whether the
arrest and search and seizure rules that it is
supposed to enforce are stated with suffi-

cient clarity that they can be understood
and followed by common ordinary police
officers. This point applies not only to the
direct deterrent effect of the rule, but also
to its longer range moral and educative effect. If the rules are a clarion call for protecting the rights of the individual, then
the trumpet gives an uncertain sound.
Though undoubtedly clear in some areas
of police behavior, the rules are notoriously complex in others. As one critic observed with acid hyperbole, they "would
not deter or enlighten a policeman in Gary
with a Ph.D. who was going to law school at
night." . . .

The point of this section is not that
the exclusionary rule can have no direct
deterrent effect. There are probably situations where it deters. In crimes such as
homicide, where prosecution is almost a
certainty and where public interest and
awareness are high, the conditions for deterrence are optimal and the exclusionary
rule is likely to affect police behavior. The
point of this section is, rather, that there
are situations—and there are good reasons
to believe that these situations comprise a
majority of law enforcement activities involving arrest and search and seizure—
where conditions militate against the direct deterrent effect of the exclusionary
rule. . . .

*Reprinted by permission of the publisher, from
Jerome Skolnick, *Justice Without Trial: Law Enforce-
ment in a Democratic Society.* Copyright ©1966 by John
Wiley and Sons, Inc.

NOTES AND QUESTIONS

1.   The Spiotto study presents the percentage of defendants with motions to suppress and the percentage of motions granted for three different offenses over three time periods: twelve months in 1950,
twelve days in 1969, and three months in 1971. It is essentially an "interrupted time-series design"
(Campbell 1970, p. 222) with three uneven time intervals.

Mapp made the exclusionary rule obligatory in all states in 1961. However, many states on their
own initiative had already adopted an equivalent rule prior to the Supreme Court decision. Illinois
adopted its own exclusionary rule in 1923, or nearly half a century before *Mapp* (Comment, *Northwestern
University Law Review,* 1974, p. 755). Thus, the rule was continuously in effect in Chicago during the
three time periods of the Spiotto data. There is no "interruption" of the trend because of the introduction of an experimental treatment (the exclusionary rule). What problems of data interpretation does
this fact pose? Even if these figures tell how bad things are despite the existence of the rule, does it

necessarily follow that the rule has had no deterrent effect? Or, as one court put it, "if it snowed all summer, would it then be winter?" (*Matter of Storar*, 1981, p. 380).

2.   Elsewhere in his article Spiotto (1973) claimed that motions to suppress constitute "the only empirical mechanism available to measure illegal police practices and the workings of the exclusionary rule" (p. 246).* Do you agree? What problems of *validity* and *reliability* are posed by the use of the frequency of suppression motions as a measure of improper police enforcement, especially in before-after designs? Does the count of suppression motions (raised or granted) underestimate or overestimate the extent of illegal searches and seizures?

3.   Prosecutorial policies in a given jurisdiction may affect the frequency and success of suppression motions, apart from any deterrent effect of the exclusionary rule. In 65 other cities, less than 10% of motions are successful, compared with the 62% to 100% success rates in the Spiotto data for Chicago (Canon 1973, pp. 721–25). In Chicago, unlike the District of Columbia and other jurisdictions, there is no initial prosecutorial screening of cases prior to their going to court. Consequently, the suppression hearing in Chicago serves a filtering function that elsewhere is usually exercised by the prosecutor's office.

4.   Subsequent research confirms that suppression is invoked and granted relatively infrequently when there is advance screening of cases by the prosecutor. An analysis by the General Accounting Office of some 2,804 cases from 38 U.S. Attorneys' offices around the country showed that only 1 of every 10 defendants tried to suppress evidence. Federal judges granted the motion in about 1.3% of the cases altogether. More than half of the defendants who won their suppression motions were nonetheless convicted using other available evidence. Prosecutorial dismissals was another measure of the rule's impact. In this study, prosecutors dropped the charges because of anticipated exclusion in about .4% of all of the cases. The general conclusion was that the rule does not cripple federal law enforcement (Comptroller General of the United States 1979).

Similar analyses of state cases have yielded similar results. A study by the National Institute of Justice (1982) reported that only 4.8% of felony cases in California were dismissed by district attorneys because of illegal search and seizure problems. Although this was said to indicate "a major impact of the exclusionary rule on state proceedings" (p. 2), these cases amounted to less than 1% of the total number of felony complaints referred to district attorneys during the period of the study. Thus, "issues relating to the exclusionary rule 'may be substantial in terms of legal theory, [but] they appear to have little impact on the over-all flow of criminal cases after arrest'" (Geller 1981, p. 1644).

Appellate reversals of denials of suppression motions are uncommon. In a sample of 544 criminal appeals in one federal court, 151 raised Fourth Amendment issues, and only 8 of them were reversed. An analysis of 1,300 appellate rulings in state courts produced only 16 cases in which the evidence was suppressed (Davies 1982, pp. 265–66).

5.   Another confounding factor on suppression rates could be the increased availability of defense counsel. In the years following *Mapp*, the Court extended the right to counsel to all felony trials, to arraignments, to pretrial lineups, and to custodial interrogations. The increase in the number of defendants represented by attorneys enhances the likelihood that more suppression motions would be raised, independently of any impact of the exclusionary rule. The right to suppress evidence is part of the larger due process revolution in the criminal justice system brought about by the Warren Court decision of the 1960s. The effect of *Mapp* (or, for that matter, of *Miranda*) may be indistinguishable from the background of other cases, all of which were designed to elevate the standards of police behavior and safeguard individual liberties. Determining the impact of a particular decision may not be unlike determining the effect of a ripple started in a sea of social forces. These forces can send forth larger waves that drown out any effects of the decision itself.

6.   The frequency of suppression motions and of prosecutorial dismissals are indices of noncompliance with the Fourth Amendment. However, the deterrent value of the exclusionary rule lies in the

---

violations it prevents, not in the violations that occur despite it. As Morris (1982) observes, "police compliance with the exclusionary rule . . . consists of *not* conducting an illegal search" (p. 653). What would be valid indices of compliance? Do statistical studies focus on noncompliance because it is more easily measured? Do the results of such studies necessarily aid only one side of the debate?

The "totality of the evidence," writes Canon (1979), "does not support the . . . conclusion that the rule is inefficacious" as its opponents [for example, Spiotto 1973; Schlesinger 1979] claim, but "neither . . . does the evidence support the opposite conclusion" (p. 400). Given the difficulty and inconclusiveness of proof, does it follow that statistical studies are "irrelevant to the question of whether or not the rule should be modified or abolished" (Jensen and Hart 1982, p. 921)? Should the deterrence issue be resolved on the basis of burden of proof? Which side bears the burden, and why? Consider the following assertion by Kamisar (1983): "I do not think that the life of the exclusionary rule should depend on an empirical demonstration of its effects on police behavior any more than the continued validity of *Brown* v. *Board of Education* should depend on empirical data concerning the harmful effects of school segregation on black children" (p. 658).

7.   The processes by which the exclusionary rule "deters" the police need to be clarified. Is it valid to draw an analogy between the deterrent effect of the rule on the police and the deterrent effect of the criminal law on the citizenry? If the rule prevents police misconduct, does it do so in the same way that penal sanctions prevent criminal activity?

"Deterrence" is a concept that embraces different meanings. Oaks, in an unreproduced portion of his article, reviewed the social-legal literature on the deterrent effect of punishment. "Special deterrence" prevents wrongdoing by an individual through the direct imposition of sanctions. The exclusionary rule, obviously, does not even attempt this function, since evidentiary suppression does not punish the officer. As Wigmore (1923) complained, "Our way of upholding the Constitution is not to strike at the [officer] who broke it but to let off [the criminal] who broke something else," so that "both go free" (§2184). The penalty falls instead on the prosecutor. "General deterrence" refers to the preventive effect of sanctions on individuals who have not experienced them before. It discourages wrongdoing in two ways. "Direct deterrence" is the immediate compliance induced by the threatened sanction. It depends upon effective communication to the individual of the desired conduct and upon the individual's assessment of the costs and benefits of compliance. "Indirect and long-term deterrence" refers to the symbolic importance of sanctions in teaching what society deems appropriate conduct. Compliance can be effected quite apart from the sanctions themselves, as a result of an individual's internalization of the taught values. The deterrence language in Fourth Amendment discussions refers to general deterrence.

Oaks concludes that in most law enforcement actions, the prerequisites for direct and indirect preventive effects of the exclusionary rule are lacking. If so, is it "misleading" to talk about "deterring" the police? Would it aid thinking to excise that term from the search and seizure vocabulary and substitute, instead, the concept of "disincentive"? The rule may not deter police violations but it does reduce the incentives to violate (Kamisar 1983, p. 661). Another concept is "systemic deterrence." The rule is assumed to influence individual officers "through a police department's institutional compliance with judicially articulated Fourth Amendment standards" (Mertens and Wasserstrom 1981, p. 394). A particular officer may be indifferent or even hostile to certain procedural rights, but "police departments are not likely to share such a view, at least officially." The police are members of a hierarchical, bureaucratic organization, and top police executives "can be expected to encourage . . . compliance [by the rank-and-file] through training and [departmental] guidelines . . ." (p. 399). Is the notion of systemic deterrence any different from the professionalization of the police and enhanced internal discipline? Systemic or institutional compliance recognizes that the police organization must change if the individual officer is to change. It also "rests on the assumption that police officers follow departmental orders" (p. 395, n. 133). In the next two sections, we will examine more closely the processes of organizational and individual change in police departments.

8.   Arguments for and against the exclusionary rule turn as much on ideology and symbolism as on the facts of deterrence. Due process advocates claim that the rule "should be preserved for its symbolic value, not because of any impact it might be having on society." It reassures us that the "police do not behave lawlessly and that the courts do not condone such lawless behavior as occasionally occurs" (Canon 1982, p. 580). The police "are bound to view the elimination of the exclusionary rule as an indication that the Fourth Amendment is not a serious matter, if indeed it applies to them at all" (Loewenthal 1980, p. 30). In nondemocratic societies, there is not even the pretense of subordinating police power to the rule of law. Crime control advocates claim that abolition of the rule is symbolically important in controlling the fear of crime, even though the rule may have little effect on actual crime rates. "[W]e live by symbols," Geller (1981) argues. "If we fight the exclusionary rule, we may feel we're fighting crime. If we feel we're fighting crime, we may gain a sense of community pride that indirectly could actually help fight crime" (p. 1645).

6.6. SOCIAL PSYCHOLOGICAL AND LEGAL PERSPECTIVES ON THE POLICE

The basic issue is how to increase police accountability of their enforcement practices. The exclusionary rule is a means—at present, the principal means—for seeking to attain that end. But in assessing its effectiveness, we need to consider two further matters. First, what are the conditions of effectiveness? And second, are there other, nonjudicial means that might be as effective as, or more effective than, the rule in inducing police compliance? These questions lead us to inquire into the limits of judicial action in shaping social conduct, particularly of the police. In this section we shall address the first question, and in the next the second.

Levels of Analysis

The Oaks article points out that there is no simple "yes or no" answer to the question of the deterrent efficacy of the rule: "Any attempt to determine whether or not the extent to which the exclusionary rule affects the behavior of law enforcement personnel confronts an exceedingly complex inquiry into human motivation within a complex social model, the criminal justice system." In effect, Oaks proposes that it is not enough to look only at the input (rule) and the output (behavior), but that the throughput must also be taken into account. The kinds of mediating factors at work can be grouped as follows: the personality, motivation, and attitudes of police officers, or the individual level of analysis; the social norms and professional socialization of a police department, or the organizational level; and the communications between a police department and other units of the criminal justice system, or the system level.

From a social psychological viewpoint, search and seizure practices are part of the "role behavior" of the police—that is, they are standardized patterns of conduct that arise from the occupational tasks of law enforcement and are engaged in by any occupant of the police role regardless of personal predilections. In any attempt to change this role behavior, the individual psychology of the police officer, the social psychology of the police organization, and the sociology of the larger criminal justice system in which the police operate must be considered. As Katz and Kahn (1978) note, "The behavior of people in organizations is still the behavior of individuals, but it has a different set of determinants than behavior outside organizational roles" (p. 658). It is a "psychological fallacy" and a "gross oversimplification" to reason that because organizations are composed of individuals, one can change organizations by changing its members (p. 658). Most work-related behavior does not occur in a social and organization vacuum. It may be necessary to change the organization itself in order to induce any change in the role behavior of its members. The implication for inducing greater police compliance with the Fourth Amendment is that the method—whether it be the exclusionary rule or some other judicial or nonjudicial approach—has to have an impact not only on the individual errant officer but also on the organizational norms and processes of the police department itself.

Thus, to appreciate the conditions that limit the deterrent effect of the exclusionary rule and to consider alternative means of enhancing police accountability, some background knowledge on the police is helpful. We shall draw on the social science literature to sketch a basic profile of the police: the personal characteristics of officers, recruitment and socialization processes, organizational norms of police departments, and institutional relationships between the police and other agencies of the criminal justice system, particularly the courts.

Individual and Organizational Characteristics of the Police

The police are divided into specialized roles (traffic police, detectives, and so forth), but the "typical" role is that of the lower echelon, frontline, uniformed patrol officer or "cop" (constable on patrol). Because of the absence of lateral mobility into any police department, every officer has to begin by serving an apprenticeship as a patrolman. The constabulary role becomes the common role for all officers, regardless of rank in the organization. The following profile will be of the patrol officer.

SOCIAL-ECONOMIC BACKGROUND

Most persons entering the police ranks come from white, lower-middle class or working class backgrounds. They bring to the job certain values that are generally associated with these social classes: deference to authority, emphasis on self-respect, machismo, reliance on personal qualities rather than formal procedures, and the like (Hahn 1971; Brown 1981). Nationwide, less than one-third of the police have post-secondary education, but increasingly some college education is becoming the norm (President's Commission 1967b, p. 10). For many, becoming a police officer represents an advance over their father's occupational status. It is a chance for upward social mobility. Among some ethnic groups, there is a high proportion of family members in law enforcement. Two-thirds of Irish policemen in Chicago, for example, have relatives on the force, most of them from the immediate family (Hahn 1971). Police values and traditions may be transmitted at home as well as on the job. This familial influence reinforces the already tightly knit bonds characteristic of the police fraternity and renders more difficult outside efforts at reform.

SOCIALIZATION AND TRAINING

In the 1940s, training of new recruits in police academies began to be commonplace. The length of training varies greatly, from a couple of weeks to twenty-four weeks or more (Schwartz and Goldstein 1970, p. 41). Most of the time is devoted to such practical concerns as physical conditioning, firearms, patrol procedures, first aid, self-defense, and departmental rules and regulations. Relatively little attention is given to human relations and to the law of criminal procedure.

After graduation from the academy, the rookie officer is assigned to a precinct for patrol duty with a veteran officer as a partner. All new officers begin their police careers at the bottom as uniformed patrolmen. The unavailability of high or mid-level entry positions in the police organization tends to deter persons with skills and experience in other fields (for example, law, business) that are relevant to law enforcement. The rookie patrol officer serves for two or more years before becoming eligible for possible promotion.

The initial patrol experience serves as a rite of passage. Here is when the real occupational socialization begins. The newcomers are exposed to and "re-educated" in the norms and traditions of the existing police culture by their experienced partners. There is strong pressure to "belong" to the police brotherhood, to unlearn old values and conform to new ones (Niederhoffer 1967, pp. 211–13). This kind of on-the-job socialization helps to nurture the intense feelings of solidarity and camaraderie that color the police. "The most important question asked by patrolmen about a rookie is whether or not he displays the loyalty demanded by the police culture" (Brown 1981, p. 83). The peer influences among the lower echelon, frontline officers could also thwart the efforts of top police administrators and academy instructors to promote different law enforcement values and practices among the young, new recruits. This is one reason why police academy training is said to have little lasting effect on recruits after graduation (Harris 1973, p. 168).

ORGANIZATION AND FUNCTIONS

A police department is usually headed by a chief or commissioner who is responsible to the civilian executive of the local government, normally the mayor. The line divisions in the department are organized in a chain of command from the chief down to supervisory officers (captains, inspectors, and so forth) and to the backbone of the force, consisting of detectives (who investigate major crimes) and uniformed patrol officers (who do the bulk of peacekeeping, law enforcement, and social service duties).

Contrary to the cops-and-robbers image of police work conjured by television programs, most police—except detectives—spend only a minor portion of their time (estimated at about 20%) in criminal investigations (Broderick 1976, p. 75; Brown 1981, p. 322). Uniformed officers are busy mainly with routine patrol and maintaining order: assisting motorists, handling drunks, escorting dignitaries, intervening in domestic quarrels, processing juveniles, and the like. Much of the work is only peripherally related to law enforcement and can be better characterized as "general community service" (Schwartz and Goldstein 1970, p. 1). For example, in one 24-hour period, the police in one area of Chicago received 394 calls. Of these, 16% dealt with crimes, 44% with incidents that could involve crime but usually required only a warning, mediation, or assistance (such as public intoxication), and 40% with requests for service and information (Goldstein 1967).

Nonetheless, police work is viewed by the police themselves as involving primarily the investigation of crime and the identification and apprehension of criminals. Police agencies are geared toward a law enforcement rather than a community service model, and this is reflected in every aspect of the police function: in recruitment, training, organization, operations, and social values. The perpetuation of this one-dimensional conception of the nature of policing is a hurdle to improving the overall police function (Goldstein 1977, pp. 8–9).

PERSONAL CHARACTERISTICS

Obviously, not all officers are alike in personal characteristics and outlook. However, because of their self-selection, training, socialization, and work requirements, they—as an occupational group—share certain identifiable attributes and attitudes that are associated with the law enforcement role. These include suspiciousness, authoritarianism, and social distance.

Suspiciousness

"Suspicion," writes Hahn (1971), "probably has become the trademark of the police officer in his relations with other people" (p. 463; Wilson 1968, pp. 48–49). Although the sources of the "high level of suspiciousness" are said to be "a mystery" (Bartol 1983, pp. 58–59), it would seem that it is a disposition that is perhaps inherent in an occupation that demands continuous vigilance for potential crime situations. Other kinds of work may have higher injury and fatality rates, but law enforcement is the only nonmilitary activity where the risks of harm are mainly from personal violence. Thus, police experts exhort patrol officers to "be suspicious. This is a healthy police attitude" (Adams 1963, p. 28). They learn to be attentive to cues that past experience has taught them are a prelude to or are associated with possible criminal activity—for example, a dirty car with clean license plates and vice versa; uniformed deliverymen without a truck or merchandise; loiterers in public restrooms; exaggerated calm when stopped by an officer.

After years of street experience, the police tend to develop informal, behavioral profiles of potential criminals. Skolnick (1966) calls them "perceptual shorthands" to help identify "symbolic assailants" (p. 45). They introduce order and predictability into the policeman's world view. In a study of the Chicago Police Department, Davis (1975) reported that "according to a good many officers we have interviewed . . . all society is divided into two classes of people, the 'kinky' (criminal) class and the law-abiding class. The officers can tell which are which by physical characteristics and appearance—mostly hair and dress, but also the look in the eyes. The working principle is that searches of 'kinky' people for drugs and handguns are necessary and proper, whether or not the searches would be constitutional" (p. 18). These probabilistic judgments about criminality and the ensuing enforcement actions, unreasonable as they might appear to a neutral magistrate or lay observer, are explainable in part by the trained suspiciousness and cognitive outlook of the police.

Authoritarianism

Police incidents of heavy-handedness, unnecessary or excessive use of force, and demand for deference to authority are common knowledge. We need not wade into the debate on whether the police are basically authoritarian persons—whether they possess a "personality" that is different from those who are not policemen. Recent reviews of the literature conclude that evidence for a "global police personality"—including a pervasive authoritarian syndrome—is at best "equivocal and inconsistent" (Bartol 1983, p. 61). It is sufficient for our purposes to note that much of the outlook and conduct that has an authoritarian character can be accounted for solely in terms of the occupational demands of the police role and the organizational characteristics of police departments. Professional socialization may well override any personality styles. Veteran officers constantly remind rookies to take charge in confrontations and not back down: "'You've got to be tough, kid, or you'll never last' " (in Niederhoffer 1967, p. 53).

The heavy-handed manner in which the police sometimes patrol ghetto areas could reflect the bigotry and authoritarian traits of the individual officers. It could also be that they are simply actions needed to ensure their own safety and control a potentially dangerous situation. As James Baldwin (1962) wrote in *Nobody Knows My Name*, ghetto residents see the police as a symbol of oppression; they represent the white world's dominance. Even if an officer is personally "good-natured" and "insuperably innocent," the environment demands that he patrol Harlem "like an occupying soldier in a bitterly hostile country: which is precisely what, and where he is, and is the reason he walks in twos and threes" (p. 66). Simply put, "the only way to police a ghetto is to be oppressive" (p. 65).

Whether the springs of authoritarian conduct are thought to lie in the personality or in the organizational role of the police have implications for reform efforts. If it is a matter of fitting the right person to the job, reform would be geared mainly to recruitment and training. There have been proposals, for example, that the police recruit persons who are sensitive to others, who are more likely to use persuasion than force in influencing people, and who have the ability to make "delicate judgments concerning complex human behavior." Police training, moreover, ought to attend more to issues of psychology, minority relations, urban problems, and the like rather than to firearms, departmental regulations, and other conventional police academy subjects. Such changes, it is said, will "automatically" result in "improved police-community relations" (Terris 1967, pp. 67–69).

However, if social and organizational factors are important in molding the role behavior of the police, changes in recruitment are unlikely to have much of an effect. As Balch (1972) argues, "attracting more liberal, humane people to police work is not necessarily an answer," because it "may simply mean that college graduates will be 'busting heads' instead of high school drop-outs" (p. 143). From a social psychological perspective, role behavior is influenced by both individual and situational factors. A person's background and personality will interact with conditions in the work environment to affect job performance. Thus, if a police department is loosely organized, unprofessional, and lacks supervisory control, individual factors are likely to have a greater share in determining law enforcement practices. But if a department has rules of conduct, trains and motivates its force to comply with them, and monitors each officer's performance, the ground is less fertile for any authoritarian tendencies or racial prejudices to flower. In this view, to change individual police conduct toward greater compliance with constitutional norms requires change in the social organization of the police.

Social Distance

While police tend to be vigilant toward those whom they consider to be potential criminals, they also feel a sense of estrangement from the "conventional" citizenry with whom they identify. Their position of authority and their perception of danger around them make them feel isolated, and this isolation leads them to turn to one another for support. Prior friendships with civilians often weaken or end after one becomes an officer. To combat the social rejection, some conceal their police identity or fraternize mostly with other police (Stotland and Berberich 1979). In an interview, one officer said, "[I] try not to let people know I'm a policeman. Once you do, you can't have normal relations with them" (in Skolnick 1966, p. 51). This gap between the police and the wider community is not only an American phenomenon. In Britain, too, about two-thirds of the police sampled in surveys say they have difficulties making friends outside the force. As one constable put it, "[V]ery few [civilians] . . . accept us as just ordinary like them. . . . [A]t times that makes us lonely" (in Skolnick 1966, p. 49).*

The sense of separation is sometimes associated with a feeling of resentment toward a public that does not seem to appreciate the value of police work. Surveys indicate that only a small percentage of American officers believe that the public holds them in high esteem, even though polls show that they are not viewed as unfavorably as they think they are (Bartol 1983, pp. 70, 58). The attitude that "nobody likes us, so to hell with them" is not uncommon among some urban policemen (Hahn 1971, p. 454). In order to endure their work, they tend to espouse a cynical worldview: People would break the law with impunity if they knew they could get away with it (Niederhoffer 1967). The police also view themselves as a minority. The New York City Police Commissioner remarked: "The police officer, too, belongs to a minority group—a highly visible minority group, and is also subject to stereotyping and mass attack" (in Lipset 1969, p. 80). Thus, it is not surprising that police work ranks among the top of all occupations in psychological stress (Selye 1978).

The distance between the police and the community, especially the minority community, has obvious implications for the effectiveness of law enforcement. It also has an impact on police organization. The greater the sense of isolation, the greater is the internal social cohesion of the police and the resistance to outside efforts at police reform. The more the police are removed from the citizenry, the more it becomes an "introverted force" (Hahn 1971, p. 458). Some argue that by keeping the public at a distance, the police are able to create an aura of a semisecret society, and this "secrecy is one of the most effective sources of police power" (Manning 1977, p. 135).

SOCIAL AND ORGANIZATIONAL NORMS

Solidarity

The degree of internal cohesion or solidarity manifested by the police is virtually unmatched by other occupational groups. There is an extraordinarily strong sense of group identification, bordering on clannishness. The proportion of policemen participating in the activities of their professional associations is substantially higher than that of most other groups (Lundman 1980; Brown 1981).

Solidarity results in more than just social camaraderie. It can become an obsta-

---

*Reprinted by permission of the publisher, from Jerome Skolnick, *Justice Without Trial: Law Enforcement in a Democratic Society.* Copyright ©1966 by John Wiley and Sons, Inc.

cle to police reform. The common front of the police in the face of external or internal review can be accounted for by this social norm. The limited effectiveness of civilian review boards, which typically act in an advisory capacity only and have no supervisory influence (Hudson 1971; Schlesinger 1977), can be traced in part to the countervailing pressure of police culture for loyalty (Brown 1981, p. 84; Reiss 1971a, pp. 189–97). The most likely witnesses to a patrolman's actions are fellow officers, and they rarely incriminate each other. They usually support the challenged officer's version of the incident or deny knowledge of it. A study of one metropolitan police department concluded that it was nearly impossible for citizens to obtain redress of grievances because of the "blue curtain" and the use of trumped-up charges (for example, resisting arrest) in order to force complainants to drop their charges (Chevigny 1969, p. 27).

This code of silence is also found, of course, among members of other professions such as medicine and law when one of their own is called to task. However, it is perhaps more stringent among the police. Several factors encourage peer loyalty over integrity. Officers are dependent upon others for help in the field and they can ill risk a reputation for exposing their colleagues. The police see criticism of one of their members as criticism of the entire group. Moreover, they do not view routine deviations from legal norms as wrongdoing. They rationalize them as a practical need in the war against crime, so they perceive the challenges to their actions as unjustified (Goldstein 1977, pp. 165–66).

Police administrators, having risen from the constabulary ranks, also share (albeit perhaps less strongly) in this sense of fraternal bond. Hence, departmental sanctions for improper police actions tend to be mild or nonexistent. A study of 35 civil rights damage suits brought against the Chicago police in a seven-year period found that only 18 were successful. None of the 18 officers found in the wrong were disciplined by their supervisors, not even by reprimand (Oaks 1970, p. 717, n. 145). Similar observations of lenient departmental discipline, unless an officer acts in bad faith or outside the line of duty, have been reported in other locales (Hudson 1971, p. 518; Levine 1971, p. 205).

Interestingly, however, the tension that characterizes the relationship between the police and the public also spills over to the relationship between rank-and-file officers and police administrators. Patrolmen are often arrayed in opposition to their supervisors. They believe that only their peers are sympathetic to their needs and problems. They tend to resist any interference in their street authority by those in the upper echelons of the department (Banton 1964, pp. 115–19). This renders difficult hierarchical efforts at instilling discipline in the field. "Patrol solidarity thus thwarts the conscientious administrator, forcing him to regulate trifles [for example, tardiness], and this petty supervision increases the sense of patrol isolation, which heightens solidarity" (Batey 1976, p. 251).

The power of group norms and peer influences on individual attitudes and conduct is well documented (Katz and Kahn 1978, p. 390). It is not surprising, therefore, that police culture and on-the-job interactions with veteran patrolmen have a greater effect in shaping rookie officers than formal training in the police academy (Bittner 1970, p. 75). In any effort at changing the behavior of the police, whether it originates from inside or outside the department, one must come to grips with these social psychological processes.

Efficiency vs. Legality

In carrying out law enforcement tasks, the police are often caught between two competing expectations, efficiency and legality. On the one hand, police supervisors demand expeditious and reliable investigation and apprehension of criminal suspects. Productivity is indexed typically by "clearance by arrest," reflecting the ability to solve crimes, and not by convictions obtained in court. The police norm is that of a productive enterprise: efficiency in crime control. There can be considerable public pressure to compile impressive clearance rates. On the other hand, the appellate courts demand that the police function be subordinated to the rule of law. The manner in which the police obtain evidence about a suspect's possible guilt is as important as the fact of guilt itself. The police are expected to act in procedurally proper ways, even at the cost of inefficiency in crime control. They are expected to be rule-oriented as well as order-oriented—they have to honor and live by different and often contradictory organizational demands. If a department, for example, expects officers to carry out a minimum number of field investigations or issue a certain number of summonses, they would be less likely to observe those due process rules that might interfere with the attainment of their departmental quotas (Quick 1978, p. 31).

The need to compromise—to bend legal rules, administrative regulations, even personal standards—becomes an inarticulated part of policing. These accommodations are made at the street level, based upon the patrol officer's discretionary judgment, with few directions or little control from superior officers. Goldstein (1977) argues that if officers ignore their oath of office, neglect what they learned in the police academy, and bluff or lie about their encounters with citizens, they do so "not necessarily out of malevolence, but often out of desire to be helpful in the face of the irreconcilable demands upon them" (p. 10).

ATTITUDES TOWARD, AND COMPLIANCE WITH, LEGALITY

The overwhelming majority of the police view the norm of legality as a "judicializing" of the police role that only frustrates effective law enforcement (Lipset 1969; Wilson 1968). For them, criminals are the enemy. Criminals, by their definition, are outside the law, and they find it hard to understand the preoccupation of the appellate courts with the civil rights of such persons. Appellate judges are perceived as misguided in their efforts to give aid and comfort to the enemy. They resent the obstacles placed in law enforcement work and the undermining of their discretionary authority by the judiciary. They often interpret procedural rulings of the courts as a personal affront, aimed at hampering or even punishing the police (Quick 1978, p. 27). As one policeman complained, "These goddam search and seizures rules are our enemy. These sellers [of narcotics] get away with murder and we can't do a goddam thing about it. We know guys who are walking around Eastville with the stuff, but we can't bust 'em. . . . Sometimes, the only thing you can do is scare the hell out of the guy. . . . We tail them, harass them, give them a hard time" (in Skolnick 1966, p. 208).*

*Reprinted by permission of the publisher, from Jerome Skolnick, *Justice Without Trial: Law Enforcement in a Democratic Society.* Copyright ©1966 by John Wiley and Sons, Inc.

Although the police accept the judicial power to formulate rules of conduct, they do not necessarily see themselves as morally blameworthy when a court holds that their actions violate these rules and the evidentiary fruits thereof must be suppressed. Thus, the chief and the legal counsel of the Washington, D.C., Police Department "protest" strongly the view of the "police as the primary villains in a system where everyone else is carefully observing the rules." They argue that "the police are not the sole, nor even necessarily the principal, offenders" for the suppression of evidence. The responsibility for enforcement practices being illegal "ought to be viewed as resting . . . with other, presumably more sophisticated, elements of the criminal justice system" (meaning, presumably, the courts themselves for having formulated rules that handcuff the police in the first place) (Wilson and Alprin 1971, p. 488).

In the tug between the conflicting expectations of efficiency and legality in the law enforcement role, police culture may be more influential in determining an officer's conduct than appellate court pronouncements. The impact of legal rules is modified by the occupational culture and organizational structure of the police. Legality is seen through the spectacles of police values. The policeman on the street does not respond to this role tension by completely ignoring the legal constraints and letting the end of crime control justify the means. Nor does he always and fully comply with the spirit of legally approved procedures. Instead, the typical way of resolving this conflict is by engaging in what might be termed tactical compliance: observing the letter but not necessary the spirit of legal norms. As Skolnick (1966) puts it, "[T]he policeman respects the necessity for 'complying' with the [search and seizure] laws. His 'compliance,' however, may take the form of post-hoc manipulation of the facts rather than before-the-fact behavior" (p. 220).* That is, at the suppression hearing, the policeman gives an after-the-fact description of the action taken so as to make it appear to be in conformity with existing legal standards, regardless of whether he in fact acted that way. As Wilkey pointed out, in this respect the exclusionary rule may prompt an officer to "perjure himself [in order] to convict the defendant."

Observational and interview studies have shown that police compliance often means a subsequent dressing up of the initial conduct so as to take on the appearance, if not the reality, of legality. Judges and prosecutors in New York City report that they believe that the "police have been fabricating grounds of arrest in narcotics cases in order to circumvent the requirements of *Mapp*" (Comment, *Columbia Journal of Law and Social Problems*, 1968, p. 95). One reason for this post-hoc, technical compliance is the belief that obeying the spirit of procedural rules will seriously impair the investigation and apprehension of criminals. As one officer put it, "'Earl Warren might have been a great judge, but he couldn't have made your typical drug arrest without cutting a few corners'" (in Broderick 1976, p. 143). A study that observed the day-to-day routine of Philadelphia police concluded that Fourth Amendment violations are widespread. "There are no legal ways to enforce the drug laws on the streets, so any pressure on the police to make more drug arrests is an open encouragement to them to lie and violate their pledge to uphold the Constitution. . . . The same is true of gambling" (Rubinstein 1973, p. 376). Moreover, the study found that despite the legal

*Reprinted by permission of the publisher, from Jerome Skolnick, *Justice Without Trial: Law Enforcement in a Democratic Society.* Copyright ©1966 by John Wiley and Sons, Inc.

derelictions, a culpable patrolman was seldom disciplined by his superior since "he [was] honorably following the knowledge of his trade which is rooted in the realities of city life" (pp. 265–66).

This is not to say that the police are incapable of genuine compliance with legal norms or that tactical compliance is the dominant practice. When the police have a stake in securing a conviction, they take pains to conform to the form and substance of procedural law. The question is how to motivate the police to adopt that approach toward all law enforcement activities on a regular basis.

Institutional Relationships in the Criminal Justice System

In the report of the President's Commission on Law Enforcement and the Administration of Justice (1967a), the criminal justice system was conceived of as a social system, not as a balkanized aggregation of unrelated organizations. It recognized that disturbing the parameters of one part of the system had repercussions throughout the entire whole. The arrest rates of the police affect the work of prosecutors, judges, and correctional personnel, and their decisions, in turn, also have an impact on the police. Improvements in the police establishment must be accompanied by reforms in other parts of the system upon which the police so heavily depend. Conditions and procedures elsewhere can negate police efforts. The interdependence of the activities of these different organizations is what constitutes the connectedness of the system.

Thus, in considering the determinants of police conduct, we need to look not only at police personality and police organization, but also at the larger environment in which the police operate. In particular, we need to consider the communication between the police and other organizations in the criminal justice system, especially the courts. "Communication," Katz and Kahn (1978) state, "is the very essence of a social system" (p. 428). If the purpose of the exclusionary rule is to deter over the short haul and to educate over the long haul, then the reasons for the exclusion need to be conveyed to the police so that they can adjust their behavior accordingly in the future. A theory of legal compliance by the police requires three basic conditions: clear, understandable rules of conduct; communication of these rules to the police; and the motivation to comply with them. In the preceding pages, we mentioned some of the personal and organizational characteristics that militate against compliance with the spirit of legal rules. We now turn to the clarity and communication of these rules—system-level variables—that affect police conduct.

EDUCATIVE EFFECT OF THE SUPPRESSION HEARING

The procedure of the suppression as it occurs in its ideal form was described in section 6.4. In practice, "local judges are time and time again called upon to evaluate questioned police conduct without an adequate development of the facts, without a sufficient presentation of existing authority, and without the necessary understanding of the law enforcement context within which the practice in question occurs" (LaFave 1965a, p. 401).

In the crowded lower trial courts of larger cities, the evaluation of police behavior occupies a major portion of court docket. The only real issues in these suppression hearings is the propriety of the police intrusion. The majority of the run-of-the-mill cases are processed in assembly-line fashion. Defense counsel make motions orally without giving in advance the reason for suppression and without citing legal precedents. Prosecutors usually have no opportunity to prepare in advance their opposition to the motions. Questions asked of the officers on the stand tend to be more or less standard ones, raised in almost every search and seizure case, designed to elicit facts that would lead a judge to conclude that the conduct either does or does not pass muster.

Under these circumstances, the development of the factual circumstances of the police intrusion is typically incomplete and little additional guidance is afforded the judge for his decision. Judges seldom inquire if there is a departmental policy behind the specific policy conduct in question, in order to know if the officer conformed to or deviated from the policy in the particular case. Even if they ask, trial counsel would be hard-pressed to describe the policy (if one exists) and its rationale. Judges, then, do not have a broad frame of reference for their decision-making. "Most often, the process of judicial review is seen as a decision about the propriety of the actions of the individual officer rather than a review of department administrative policy. . . . As a result, police are not encouraged to articulate and defend their policy" (President's Commission 1967b, p. 41). Thus, "there is no assurance that the trial court's [suppression] decision will be sound" (LaFave 1965a, p. 400).

Moreover, when the motion is eventually decided, often the ruling is unaccompanied by any opinion or even an oral explanation. An officer, "upon hearing the judge declare 'motion granted,' usually departs with a bewildered expression on his face; seldom does he have any clearer understanding of the limitations on his authority than he had prior to the hearing. The assumption apparently is that police practice is positively influenced by exclusion of evidence even without police knowledge of why the decision was made" (LaFave 1965a, p. 403). The outcome is usually "not even communicated to the police administrator, and the prevailing police practice often continues unaffected by the decision of the trial judge" (President's Commission 1967b, p. 41; Goldstein 1977, p. 326). In short, the suppression hearing is not the most conducive setting for the police about lawful practices.

CLARITY AND COMMUNICATION OF LEGAL NORMS

Chief Justice Burger (1964) has observed that most policemen have neither "the time or inclination to read the opinions of appellate courts, and even if they did so it is hardly likely that they can grasp their full import without sustained expert guidance. . . . [Hence], we cannot blame him too much for not accepting what he does not understand" (p. 11). This guidance is unavailable to the police from other agencies in the criminal justice system. Unlike Canada, where prosecutors have authority over the police, in this country the police and the prosecution are independent and coordinate branches of government. Prosecutors have no overall responsibility for supervising or educating the police. They are usually detached from and uninformed about the day-to-day police enforcement practices and policies that precipitate the exclusionary rule. In many jurisdictions, communication between the two agencies is virtually nonexistent. "[T]he prosecutor assigned to [a] case rarely assumes it is his duty to inform the police department of the meaning of [a court] decision or of its intended impact upon current police practice (LaFave and Remington 1965, p. 1005). For this reason, some of the larger police departments have legal counsel to help make judicial standards intelligible.

Most trial judges, too, "indicate that they have no more responsibility for explaining decisions to police than they have with regard to private litigants" (President's Commission 1967b, p. 41). In an adversarial system of justice, it may be unethical or at least unseemly for judges to tutor the police. Such "teamwork" might raise public skepticism about judicial impartiality. Besides, some tension and antagonism between the regulator and the regulated are inevitable in an adversary setting. These institutional constraints of effective communication of legal norms tend to reinforce the police's guild-like commitment to its autonomy in law enforcement.

Time and the capacity to read or understand judicial opinions are not the only limits to the efficacy of court regulation of the police. The legal norms themselves may not be clear. Appellate decisions, especially those of the Supreme Court, filter down to frontline police only through the refracting prisms of lower court judges. It is these judges' interpretations and applications of higher court opinions that are "the law" in the local jurisdiction (Amsterdam 1970, p. 785). Different judges in the same court district may interpret and apply the broadly formulated norms differently. What may be reasonable police conduct to one judge may be unreasonable to another. The inconsistency in the suppression decisions of local judges leads to "judicial shopping." Experienced defense counsel try to maneuver cases before certain judges who are known to disapprove of particular law enforcement practices (LaFave 1965a, p. 405). Although much attention has been given to disparities in judicial sentencing, differences in suppression decisions have provoked less scrutiny. At the very least, the nonuniformity in the evaluation of police practices compounds the difficulty of communicating to the police the standards for future behavior.

6.7. SELF-REGULATION OF THE POLICE BY RULE-MAKING

LAW ENFORCEMENT POLICY: THE POLICE ROLE

President's Commission on Law Enforcement and the Administration of Justice

POLICE ATTITUDE TOWARD THEIR ROLE IN THE DEVELOPMENT OF LAW ENFORCEMENT POLICIES

The absence of carefully developed policies to guide police officers in handling the wide variety of situations which they confront is in sharp contrast to the efforts taken to provide detailed guidance for other aspects of police operations.

Like all military and semimilitary organizations, a police agency is governed in its internal management by a large number of standard operating procedures. Elaborate regulations exist dealing with such varied phases of an agency's internal operations as the receipt of complaints from citizens, the keeping of records, and the transportation of nonpolice personnel in police vehicles. Established procedures govern such matters as the replacement of vehicles, uniforms, and ammunition. . . .

In contrast, there have been only occasional efforts to make use of a deliberative planning process to develop policies to guide and control police officers in dealing with the variety of situations that require the exercise of some form of police authority. . . .

There are a number of factors which account for the general failure of police to develop policies for dealing with crime and potential crime situations, in contrast to their willingness to do so for issues of internal management of the department.

In the first place, devising procedures for handling routine matters of internal management can be done with relative certainty and assurance that the decision will not be a subject of major debate in the community. Few people are concerned about these issues. . . .

Many police administrators are caught in a conflict between their desire for effective, aggressive police action and the requirements of law and propriety. Direct confrontation of policy issues would inevitably require the policy administrators to face the fact that some police practices, although considered effective, do not conform to constitutional, legislative, or judicial standards. By adopting a "let sleeping dogs lie" approach, the administrator avoids a direct confrontation and thus is able to support "effective" practices without having to decide whether they meet the requirements of law.

The police administrator has greater control over management questions than he does over the criminal justice process, responsibility for which he shares with the legislature, the courts, the prosecutor, and other agencies. The fact that the courts in particular have assumed increasing responsibility for control in this area has resulted in a prevalent attitude by police administrators that criminal justice policy decisions are not their concern. . . .

THE NEED TO RECOGNIZE THE POLICE AS AN ADMINISTRATIVE AGENCY WITH IMPORTANT POLICYMAKING RESPONSIBILITY

There are two alternative ways in which police can respond to the difficult problems currently confronting them:

(1) The first is to continue, as has been true in the past, with police making important decisions, but doing so by a process which can fairly be described as "unar-ticulated improvisation." This is a comfortable approach, requiring neither the police nor the community to face squarely the difficult social issues which are involved. . . .

(2) The second alternative is to recognize the importance of the administrative policymaking function of police and to take appropriate steps to make this a process which is systematic, intelligent, articulate, and responsive to external controls appropriate in a democratic society; a process which anticipates social problems and adapts to meet them before a crisis situation arises.

Of the two, the latter is not only preferable; it is essential if major progress in policing is to be made, particularly in the large, congested urban areas.

To assert the importance of the police playing an important role in the development of law enforcement policies in no way detracts from the importance of the legislature, the appellate and trial judiciary. . . .

However great the legislative contribution may be, experience demonstrates the legislatures can never deal specifically with the wide variety of social and behavioral problems which confront police. Legislation was inadequate to deal in detail with regulation of the economy during the depression of the 1930's. As a consequence, there was a great increase in the number of economic regulatory agencies and in the importance of the administrative process. The administrative agency has survived as an essential vehicle for the introduction of needed flexibility and expertise in the economic regulatory process.

Certainly there is no reason to expect the legislatures can be more effective with respect to the work of police than they were with respect to the task of the economic regulatory agency. The "administrative process" and administrative flexibility, expertise, and, most important, administrative responsibility are as necessary and as appropriate with respect to the regulation of deviant social behavior as they are with respect to other governmental regulatory activity. . . .

The judiciary has played and will undoubtedly continue to play an important role in the determination of what are proper law enforcement practices. . . .

How specifically courts become involved with detailed law enforcement practices in the future may well depend upon how willing legislatures and police are themselves to assume the responsibility for defining appropriate practices and insuring conformity with them. However, no matter how specifically judicial review may deal with enforcement practices, it cannot be an adequate substitute for responsible police administrative policymaking. Judicial review is limited, for the most part, to cases which "go to court," and many important and sensitive police practices used in maintaining public order and settling minor disputes are seldom reflected in court proceedings. In addition, judicial review is most effective if it relates to carefully developed administrative policies rather than to the sporadic actions of individual police officers. . . .

THE POLICY FORMULATION PROCESS

IDENTIFICATION

. . .

One method of identifying important issues is by the analysis of routine complaints that are received. . . .

Another method of identifying important issues is by observation of field procedures. . . .

A third method of identifying important issues is by analysis of court decisions. . . .

STUDY AND RESEARCH. . . . Research methods must be devised to produce accurate understanding of current practices and, so far as it is measurable, their impact upon crime and the community. Adequate evaluation of existing practices may require the collection of a substantial amount of data not now gathered. Study of alternative practices may be aided by a willingness to engage in experimentation and demonstration projects. . . .

In the creation of a research staff an effort should be made both to utilize the rich and untapped knowledge of experienced police officers and also the knowledge and technique of behavioral scientists. . . .

CONSULTATION BOTH WITHIN AND OUTSIDE THE POLICE AGENCY. The final stages in the formulative steps of the policy-making process should consist of achieving agreement on the part of the command staff of the agency and those outside the agency whose approval may be necessary or desirable. . . .

TRAINING. However successful a draftsman may be in building clarity and preciseness into a policy statement, dependence cannot be placed upon the written word in order to achieve effective implementation. Opportunities must be afforded for officers at the lowest level in the organization to ask questions and, more importantly, to gain a full understanding of how the policy came about and why it is important that it be implemented. An officer who knows why a policy is adopted is more likely to comply with it and, to the extent that he identifies with the new policy, is more likely to work toward its successful implementation. . . .

REVIEW. Flexibility is one of the major objectives in the formulation of policy. . . . A decision as to what constitutes proper guidelines for the police must, therefore, be subject to frequent review to assure that adequate room is allowed for the exercise of an officer's judgment, but to assure as well that the guidelines are not so broad as to encourage or allow for the making of arbitrary decisions. . . .

PROPOSED IMPROVEMENTS IN METHODS OF INTERNAL CONTROL

. . .

[T]he mere adoption of administrative polices will not alone achieve compliance. This will require "good administration," that is, the use of the whole array of devices commonly employed in public administration to achieve conformity. These include, but are not limited to, the setting of individual responsibility, the establishment of systems of accountability, the designing of procedures for checking and reporting on performance, and the establishment of methods for taking corrective action. . . .

The success of internal controls as applied to such matters appears to be dependent upon two major factors: (1) the attitude and commitment of the head of the agency of the policies being enforced and (2) the degree to which individual officers and especially supervisory officers have a desire to conform. . . .

[EXTERNAL CONTROL: JUDICIAL REVIEW]

. . .

[T]he function of the trial judge in excluding evidence which he determines to have been illegally obtained places him very explicitly in the role of controlling police practices. However, trial judges have not viewed this role as making them responsible for developing appropriate police policies. . . .

It is possible and certainly desirable to modify the current system of judicial control and to make it consistent with and, in fact, supportive of the objective of proper police policymaking. To accomplish this would require some basic changes in judicial practice:

When a trial judge is confronted with a motion to suppress, he, and the appellate court which reviews the case, should request a showing of whether the conduct of the officer in the particular case did or did not conform to existing departmental policy. If not, the granting of such a motion would not require a reevaluation of department policy. . . .

If departmental policy were followed, the judge would be given an opportunity to consider the action of the individual officer in light of the overall departmental judgment as to what is proper policy. Hopefully, a judge would be reluctant to upset a departmental policy without giving the police administrator an opportunity to defend the reasons for the policy, including, where relevant, any police expertise which might bear upon the reasonableness of the policy. . . .

NOTES AND QUESTIONS

Policing the Police: Judicial, Legislative, and Administrative Regulation

1.   Judge McGowan (1972) observed that "everybody, it sometimes seems, makes rules for the police but the police themselves" (p. 667). Hyperbole aside, the principal source of rules for law enforcement practices has been and continues to be the appellate courts, especially the Supreme Court.

The foregoing excerpts from the President's Commission (1967b) stated that judicial review as a means of regulating the police was not entirely adequate, partly because it evaluated "sporadic actions of individual police officers" rather than "carefully developed administrative policies." This point is noteworthy. Appellate courts normally play a backstopping role: They review the legality of policies promulgated in the first instance by legislative, administrative, or executive branches of government.

However, in the area of law enforcement, they review individual behavior rather than institutional policy.

In appraising an articulated policy, whether it be a statute or an administrative regulation, a court has the background information to enable it to grasp the nature and purpose and intended consequences of the subject under review. The parameters of the policy are stated; the connections with other related policies are perceptible; the underlying social values are more or less apparent. However, in evaluating individual police conduct, a court operates in a conceptual void (Amsterdam 1970). For example, a court would review the propriety of a warrantless search carried out by a particular officer in a given situation. Such a review would rarely be in the context of the police department's overall search policy. The facts are frozen in the record below, and the legal issues framed by counsel focus mainly on the admissibility of the evidence rather than on the indirect shaping of future police conduct by suppression. The reviewing judge would not know whether the warrantless search was an isolated incident reflecting the discretion of the particular officer or a common practice stemming from an invisible department-wide policy. Thus, courts are called upon to rule on individual actions that are rule-less.

2.   Another limitation on judicial formulation of general rules or policies for the police inheres in the case-by-case method of adjudication. Courts, obviously, have no supervisory power over the police. Moreover, the rules that they do formulate are done so in a piecemeal and reactive fashion because of the nature of judicial review. Courts are powerless to initiate the review process. The cases presented for review do not arrive in a planned, coherent sequence, nor do they always fit neatly into some overall framework. It is a defendant's personal interests that determine whether a case is appealed, not some public interest in law enforcement policy. If there are few cases, a court has only bits and pieces of information, which may be too fragmentary to enable it to see the picture in the round. Judges might not grasp the wider implications and effects of the rules they fashion beyond the particular case at hand.

3.   An oft-heard police criticism is that appellate judges are inexpert in law enforcement matters, removed from the day-to-day operations of the police, and therefore not competent to instruct the police on how to do their business. Is appellate inexpertness necessarily a disadvantage? What are other limits to the capacity of the judiciary to serve as an architect of a comprehensive code of police conduct?

4.   There is a ubiquitous lack of statutory regulation of the police. Most state codes give minimal attention to the police stage of the criminal process. The "vast abnegation of responsibility [by Congress and the state legislatures] . . . for legal rule-making has forced the Court to construct all the law regulating the everyday functioning of the police" (Amsterdam 1970, p. 790).

Legislatures believe that because police-citizen relationships are of constitutional dimension, the responsibility rests with the judiciary. The police themselves, though vocal critics of the exclusionary rule, have not sought legislative clarification for their authority. They have preferred the ambiguity of seldom-litigated procedures.

5.   Despite the great flexibility and discretion that police have in law enforcement, they have generally not exercised that power to formulate their own enforcement policies. The idea of the police policing themselves, at least in part, is not quixotic. There are some police departments that have already put into effect self-regulation regarding selected aspects of law enforcement.

The legal unit of the Washington, D.C., Police Department, for example, has drafted guidelines that have been approved and implemented by the police chief on the use of deadly force, eyewitness identifications, and car searches (Wilson and Alprin 1971). In the eyewitness area, for example, the rules prescribe how long and under what circumstances the pretrial identifications can be held. The Supreme Court decisions on the subject have "raised more questions for police administrators than they answered." The decisions do not say when showups (one-on-one confrontations) may be employed. The department decided on a flat one-hour rule: If a suspect is arrested within one hour of the commission of the offense, he can be returned to the crime scene for a showup identification with the victim or witness; after one hour, this type of confrontation is prohibited (p. 496). All members of the department are instructed in these rules, and noncompliance leads to disciplinary action ranging from warnings, to fines, and ultimately to discharge. The rules are also the subject of departmental promotion examinations. The expectation of police administrators is that such self-imposed regulations might "prove to be a far more effective control of police 'misconduct' than any of the exclusionary rules have been" (p. 499).

In 1980, a "Police Intelligence Ordinance" was implemented in Seattle to govern all police intelligence investigations. Although promulgated by the city council, the administrators of the Seattle Police Department had a substantial say in its formulation. It is the first ordinance of its kind in the nation. It spells out in detail when and how and about whom the police may gather information, the kinds of intelligence that can and cannot be collected, the training programs and internal disciplinary procedures that must be developed to enforce the policy, the external (nonjudicial) means of auditing police compliance, and so on.

For examples of other police regulations that represent administrative responses to Supreme Court decisions, see the President's Commission (1967b, pp. 38–40); Batey (1976, pp. 261–62); and Mertens and Wasserstrom (1981, pp. 399–401).

6.   The formulation of norms of conduct for law enforcement is a complex and demanding task. It requires drafting and communication skills and knowledge about decisional law where principles are amorphous and changing. It also demands intimate familiarity with prevailing police practices and an understanding of the politics, personalities, and institutions of the local criminal justice system as a whole.

The starting point of the policy formulation process, according to the President's Commission (1967b), is an identification of important police practices that are in need of such administrative policy-making. It recommends the "observation of field procedures" and the use of "the knowledge and technique of behavioral scientists." If you were a social science consultant to a police department which was interested in promulgating norms of conduct, what kinds of studies would you propose?

7.   The President's Commission (1967b) recognizes that "consultation" outside the police agency "may be necessary or desirable" in the policy-making process, but avoids taking a position on the nature of such consultation and on whether it should be required.

Should there be broad public participation in police rule-making? One suggestion is that the Administrative Procedure Act—which outlines the rule-making procedure for federal administrative agencies and which has been lauded as "one of the greatest inventions of modern government" (Davis 1969, p. 67)—be used by the police as a model for their policy-making (Davis 1975, pp. 98–113). Essentially, the proposed rules would be published, interested parties would have an opportunity to submit written comments, and public hearings would be held to review the rules and consider the community reactions. The idea is that an open process of policy-making is as important as the final policy itself. The process can have an educative effect both on the public (raising community consciousness of the issues at stake) and on the police (writing down and justifying the guidelines of one's behavior summons greater rationality).

Or should the enunciation of policy be a task for the police only? As it is, without any rule-making to circumscribe their discretionary authority, the police already feel isolated from the public at large and resist any outside interference in law enforcement. The few police departments which have promulgated some rules have done so with little or no meaningful community participation (Wilson and Alprin 1971).

Is there a "consultation" procedure that might represent a middle-of-the-road position between the "open" and "closed" approaches to police rule-making?

8.   The President's Commission (1967b) proposes that the guidelines be such that there is "adequate room" for "the exercise of an officer's judgment," but at the same time "not so broad" as to permit "the making of arbitrary decisions."

The feasibility or desirability of having meticulously detailed canons of conduct is subject to dispute. Skeptics argue that police work is basically an "art," that it varies from case to case, and that "there are no set rules, nor even general principles" to guide it. "Each policeman must, in a sense, determine the standard to be set based upon his own experience." [H]e is a policyforming police administrator in miniature, who operates beyond the scope of the usual device for control" (Smith 1960, p. 19). Police work is also seen as a "craft," learned by apprenticeship rather than formal training, and built upon personal experience instead of codified norms (Wilson 1968, pp. 278–84).

On the other hand, if self-regulation means broad statements of principles that address the overall style or strategy of law enforcement but not specific individual conduct, the result could be the "semblance of rule governance without much actual governing" (Batey 1976, p. 259, fn. 65). There is the risk that very general rules may become just so much boilerplate and merely add the appearance of legitimacy to police discretion.

What can social science contribute to the search for the proper balance between particularized rules and broad norms? Are certain kinds of law enforcement conduct more amenable to rule governance than others?

Internal Control: Motivational Bases of Compliance

9.   The President's Commission (1967b) recognizes that the mere adoption of rules will not ensure compliance—in addition, officers must "have a desire to conform." Demanding as is the task of rule formulation, the task of inducing rule compliance is perhaps more challenging.

The objective is to change the role behavior of the policeman, and the determinants of such change are found mainly in organization structure rather than in individual personality. Katz and Kahn (1978) have identified three motivational bases of organizational functioning that appear applicable to the police setting: "legal compliance and punishment," "extrinsic rewards," and "internalized motivation" (p. 408). We shall consider each in turn.

10.   "Legal compliance and punishment" represents a simple machine theory of motivation. "Any rule or directive from the proper authority must be obeyed because it is the law" (p. 406). Compliance is enforced by the threat of punishment. The reason for obeying has no relation to the conduct itself. This "tends to produce performance at the minimum acceptable level" (p. 425). The application of the exclusionary rule or of other judicial remedies such as monetary damages and criminal prosecution is based essentially on a "compliance and punishment" motivation model—that is, on negative reinforcement.

11.   "Extrinsic rewards" refer to economic and social rewards that are not inherent in the work itself but nonetheless enhance performance. The basic principle derived from behavioral psychology is that positive reinforcement of desired actions is more effective than negative reinforcement of undesired actions. In this view, it is better to reward an officer for making a lawful search than to punish him for making an unlawful one.

Psychologists and lawyers have urged "implementing legal policies [for the police] through operant conditioning" (Levine 1971, p. 195). "The first requirement of an effective system for police discipline," writes Batey (1976), "is the formalized use of positive reinforcement" (p. 252). The advocates of the Skinnerian approach to police reform have yet to present detailed blueprints for behavioral modification. Their proposals have been made only in general terms: for example, payment of bonuses for "excellent conformity with departmental goals"; development of evaluation methods to assess "good performance" in both routine, daily activities and in highly visible criminal investigations (Batey 1976, pp. 253–54; Quick 1978; Hyman 1979); and use of intermittent rather than continuous reinforcement in order to elicit a high level of the desired responses (Levine 1971).

This approach is effective in motivating and changing individual behavior, but is it applicable to organizations? Can a system of individual reinforcement schedules be set up when police work is highly interdependent? "O.B.Mod." (organizational behavior modification) has been applied with some success when the rewarded behaviors are observable and countable, such as piece rates in factory assembly lines. Extraordinary police actions (heroism, a major arrest) are easy to recognize, but how is the bulk of routine patrol activity to be evaluated? Perceptions of inequity and problems with morale may arise from differential reinforcement. In industrial settings, "singling out of individuals for their extra contributions to the cause is not the most effective and reliable means of evoking high motivation for the accomplishment of organizational objectives" (Katz and Kahn 1978, p. 410). If individual performance is difficult to assess, should there be across-the-board reinforcement for all members of a group (a specialized unit or an entire precinct) based upon the overall performance? Would such an interdependent payoff system generate among the police a sense of shared responsibility and greater peer pressure to conform to the desired conduct?

12.   There is "internalized motivation" when conforming to the right conduct is intrinsically rewarding. Organizational goals are incorporated as part of one's personal value system, so that one wants to do what one is expected to do. "Internalization of organizational goals is at once the most effective of motive patterns and the most difficult to evoke" (Katz and Kahn 1978, p. 425). The long-term, educative purpose of the exclusionary rule is, in effect, to instill in the police an "inner voice" that directs their compliance with constitutional norms.

Internalized motivation is developed in part by increasing the sense of self-determination and responsibility over one's actions. "If people are involved in determining policies and share in the returns from collective effort, they regard the organization as of their own making" (Katz and Kahn 1978, p. 378). If organizational norms and procedures are designed so that members feel that they can personally identify with them, the performance of their obligations is likely to be more intrinsically self-rewarding.

In the police setting, what organizational changes need to be effected to harness this means of reforming police conduct? Given the dissensus on the values and priorities of law enforcement, is internalized motivation a viable basis for change?

13.   Another possible source of influence is the motivational power of the peer group. Manipulations of rewards and punishments represent a form of vertical control by superiors. Horizontal control by peer pressure can be just as effective. The principal contribution of group dynamics research to organizational behavior has been the demonstration of the impact of the primary group on shaping individual attitudes and conduct. The need for group affiliation opens a person to peer influence. The "Peer Review Panel" of the Kansas City Police Department is an attempt to use police solidarity in disciplinary reform. This panel of patrolmen investigates citizen complaints and makes recommendations to supervisors regarding any sanctions (Batey 1976, p. 255). If effective, a disciplinary procedure that relies on peer evaluation can lead to greater professionalization of the police.

External Control: Judicial Review

14.   To urge self-regulation of the police is not to say that there should be no external control of law enforcement, especially by the judiciary. This would be untenable in a constitutional scheme of government. It is to say that the focus and scope of judicial review should be changed without, however, abdicating ultimate control.

At present, judicial review in a suppression case focuses on the propriety of the individual officer's challenged conduct (for example, presenting a showup), rather than on the validity of the departmental policy, if available (for example, regulations on how, where, and when to conduct pretrial identifications). The President's Commission (1967b) recommends that trial and appellate judges raise two basic questions in suppression cases: First, did the officer in the particular case conform to existing departmental policy? Second, is the policy itself valid or constitutional? The implications of this proposal merit examination.

Obviously, if there is no existing policy, the present form of judicial review would continue. If a court decides that a showup in a given instance was proper, the identification evidence is admissible; if not, the exclusionary rule is applied.

If there is a departmental policy, four outcomes are possible:

First, the officer's actions are found to conform to the policy and the policy itself is held to be legitimate. In this case, the motion to suppress would be denied and the officer, presumably, would be rewarded by the department.

Second, the officer's conduct conforms to the policy, but the policy is ruled unconstitutional. Should the exclusionary rule be applied in this instance? What should be the consequence for the officer who obeyed rules later adjudged invalid? The department, of course, would be expected to redraft the policy.

Third, the officer's actions do not conform to the policy, but the policy passes muster. Should the evidence be excluded in this situation? What means of internal control need to be undertaken?

Finally, both the nonconforming conduct and the policy are invalid. The application of the exclusionary rule here should not be problematic.

Once a particular departmental policy has been reviewed by the courts and not found wanting, are there reasons why individual police actions in the future under this policy should still be reviewed by the courts rather than by the police themselves?

Police Rule-making and Community Attitudes

15.   A basic issue is how to induce police departments to assume the responsibility for self-regulation in the first place. After all, rule-making is a self-imposed cutback in their discretionary power.

The President's Commission (1967b) gives several reasons why police administrators have not assumed this responsibility with alacrity. There are also the problems of lack of resources and of cost. Only large departments have legal staff and police legal advisers serve mostly in action-oriented roles rather than in policy-making. Systematic research data on police practices, useful in formulating policy, is often lacking. The preparation of just one narrowly focused regulation may take months of work and undergo numerous drafts, so that even large departments are unable to produce more than a few regulations each year.

16.   The police have a monopoly over the use of legitimate force in society, and the self-regulation approach seeks to place that power under the aegis of articulated and uniform rules. If the police do not undertake rule-making on their own, should they be constitutionally compelled to do so by the courts? As an alternative approach, what rewards can be given to the police for promulgating rules?

17.   The fact that legislatures have not seen fit to impose upon the police the duty to make rules raises the question of whether the larger community really wants—via its elected representatives—to limit the police.

According to some police critics, responsibility for law enforcement rests ultimately upon the citizenry, and "there is something in most of us that does not want the police to change." On the one hand, the public and the media decry the rising tide of street crime and demand vigorous law enforcement. On the other, they also profess to want the police to behave according to due process of law. This, it is said, is "sheer hypocrisy." What most people really want is order (crime control) while preserving only the appearance, if not the reality, of law (due process). The police depend upon the community for their rewards, and seldom are they rewarded for conforming to legality. Public attention and monies go to the apprehension of criminals, the recovery of stolen goods via "sting" operations, and so on. If the community appears more concerned with curbing crime than with observing civil liberties, the police will respond to this conception of justice. Consequently, "the police continue to adhere to their old customs because they know that their superiors and much of the rest of society approve. They have no motive to change" (Chevigny 1969, p. 281).

Do you agree with the foregoing analysis? Does it follow that the prospect of infusing law enforcement with the rule of law is more illusory than real until there is a change in public attitudes? Does it support the argument that the judiciary should impose upon the police the constitutional obligation to formulate rules?

18.   The effect of social attitudes on law enforcement is also reflected in the substantive criminal law. We have seen that the exclusionary rule is invoked mostly in narcotics, gambling, and weapons offenses. The first two are "victimless crimes." They are said to be victimless because a "victim" in a gambling or narcotics case, unlike an assault victim, is typically a third party who is offended by the activity. The state then intervenes to prosecute a defendant who voluntarily participated in the forbidden conduct. They are "crimes" in the sense that they violate conventional morality. Morality, so goes a philosophical argument, gives cohesion to society, and hence must be enforced by criminal sanctions.

Morals legislation is usually broadly drafted and promulgated with the knowledge that it will be difficult to enforce fully, thereby opening the door to discretionary—and potentially inconsistent and unequal—police action. Some jurisdictions forbid all forms of gambling, but as a practical matter the police need to exercise discretion as to whom and when they will arrest for gambling. Thus, police conduct and the substantive criminal law are interdependent. It is not surprising that police searches of premises were much more frequent during the Prohibition era than before, since searches were the primary tool of enforcement (Arnold 1935, p. 164). A cost of that kind of moralistic criminal statute was an increase in the invasion of privacy of the home. When legislation is difficult to enforce, especially under restrictive procedures set forth by the courts, the police may ignore these restrictions or engage in tactical compliance. The frequency of police deviations from legality, and therefore the frequency with which the exclusionary rule is invoked, is associated with the content of the criminal code. To reform the police, whether by suppression of evidence or administration rule-making, may require also reform of the criminal law itself.

A Summing Up

The materials of this chapter dealt with the social impact of law, specifically, the impact of the Fifth and Fourth Amendment exclusionary rules upon police conduct. The question of the deterrent efficacy of these rules implicates a broader problem: how to enhance police accountability. One need not declare oneself uncompromisingly for or against these rules to justify inquiry into alternative ways of inducing police reform. The basic problem of how to control the discretion of lower echelon, frontline officers is one that raises issues of applied behavioral change as well as issues of law and social policy.

Theoretically, the police are expected to engage in full enforcement of the criminal law. In practice, of course, it is impossible not to make choices on when and whether to invoke the criminal process and how far to proceed in that process. Criminal statutes are often broadly drafted and public opinion may not tolerate full enforcement of all laws at all times. Discretion is needed for individualization of justice, in order to tailor the law enforcement response to the particular circumstances at hand. The policeman exercises greater discretion than a judge or a prosecutor or any other criminal justice official.

Inevitable and indispensable as it may be, discretion also carries risks. Discretion begins where law ends, and when discretion is abused, injustice occurs. "Perhaps nine-tenths of injustice in our legal system flows from discretion and perhaps only one-tenth from rules" (Davis 1969, p. 25). A patrolman's discretion is largely invisible, beyond the review of his supervisors and the courts. It is also exercised in an ad hoc manner—"unarticulated improvisation," the President's Commission (1967b) called it.

Thus, despite the pretense that a policeman is a ministerial officer who merely enforces rather than makes policy, in fact he does create policy via his discretionary actions. Selective enforcement and underenforcement are surreptitious forms of policy-making. In the absence of police self-regulation via rule-making, it is the officers on the streets who by their conduct establish de facto policy. In this respect, the police are different from other organizations. In most bureaucracies, policy is made by upper echelon executives. As one descends the organizational hierarchy, there is less and less discretion. Clerical and assembly line workers have little authority to make choices among different courses of action or inaction. In a police department, this pattern is reversed: There is more discretion at lower levels. As the President's Commission (1967a) noted, "law enforcement policy is made by the policeman"—not by the police chief (p. 10).

The task of regulating the police in a democratic society is the task of confining their discretion within the boundaries of law. Court-created norms of how to conduct interrogations or searches and seizures represent attempts to limit police discretion, and the suppression doctrine is the principal means for enforcing compliance with them. An analysis of the effectiveness of this "judicializing" of the police function provides a case study for a theory of legal impact.

In this chapter, we have touched upon three interrelated elements that are a part of any impact theory. First, the change agent or the source of the legal norms: *Who* should regulate the police? The proposed self-regulation model—with police administrators formulating the norms and the courts thereafter reviewing them—represents a compromise between the extremes of exclusive judicial governance and unfettered police self-governance. Rule-making does not bestow any new power for policy-making that the police did not previously have. It simply transfers the locus of that power from the patrolmen to the highest echelons of the department. The Supreme Court itself said in *Miranda* that the Constitution does not "necessarily require adherence to any particular solution" for controlling interrogations. Indeed, it urged Congress and the states to exercise "creative rulemaking capacities." "Even under the shadow of constitutional commands, there is room for experimentation in law enforcement methods" (McGowan 1972, p. 677).

Second, the content of the behavioral norms: *What* should be the rules for governing the various law enforcement practices? The suppression doctrine says nothing about how police should interrogate or conduct searches, but obviously the purpose of suppression cannot be realized unless there is content to the Fifth and Fourth Amendments, respectively. These norms cannot be drafted in the abstract. Empirical observation of field practices is needed in order to devise realistic rules of conduct.

And third, the motivational bases of compliance: *How* are the police to be induced to obey these norms? Rules are not self-applying. The task of shaping police conduct is, at bottom, one of social engineering. The conventional judicial methods of evidentiary exclusion, monetary damages, and criminal prosecution are all premised on a negative reinforcement approach to behavioral change. The administrative method of self-regulation, because it relies on internal control, makes available other means of change, including positive reinforcement and peer influence.

The problem of regulating the police, then, involves a complex inquiry at several different levels of analysis. To reform the police—regardless of who promulgates the norms, what their content consists of, and how compliance with them are effected—may entail changing not only the attitudes and behavior of individual officers, but also the organizational functioning of the police, the communications between the police and other criminal justice agencies, the substantive criminal law, and community attitudes. In short, a theory of legal impact needs to take into account analyses of individual change, organizational change, and social change, as well as legal change.

6.8.   A JURISPRUDENCE OF IMPACT

No single, common method of appellate decision-making underlies the functions of law creation and application. "[T]here exists no authoritative body of learning or generally agreed upon ideas on the subject of how legal decisions are actually arrived at, to say nothing of how they ought to be arrived at" (Cowan 1963, p. 508). Nonetheless it is possible to identify some distinct methods or styles of decision-making. A judge's express or implicit conception of the nature and purposes of law and his mode of thinking or of rationalizing the results of his thinking are bound to have an effect on the substantive outcome of a case. They will also influence his use of social science in reaching or in justifying his decision.

The cases in this chapter, and in the three preceding chapters, were selected in part to exemplify various methods of decision-making, each of which reflects different jurisprudential perspectives on the judicial process. We shall touch upon two of them here: deductive syllogism, associated with formalist jurisprudence, and impact analysis, associated with purposive jurisprudence.

At this time, we shall merely spotlight key features of these styles of appellate decision-making. The historical background of these jurisprudential traditions and the social-cultural context from which they emerged are covered more extensively in Chapter 12. A preview of this subject now serves several purposes. These processes of judicial reasoning provide a framework for pulling together the different substantive topics canvassed thus far. At this halfway mark, an introduction to some of the ways that judges think and justify their decisions may add a new dimension to the analysis of cases. It may be helpful to articulate that which may have been sensed only intuitively in the course of reading the opinions of the past chapters.

Deductive Syllogistic Method

A conception of law that flowered in the nineteenth century, when American society was relatively static and the model of the physical world was dominated by Newtonian mechanics, was that of a closed system of rules, logically and systematically ordered—"a seamless web of immutable truths" (Miller 1965, p. 370). It was a "mechanical jurisprudence" (Pound 1908), in which the task of a judge was to apply the proper legal rule (major premise), selected from the pantheon of existing rules, to the facts of a case (minor premise), in order to deduce the conclusion. The opinion in *Plessy* v. *Ferguson* (1896; Chapter 3, section 3.4) is a classic example.

This method of decision-making, though associated with the formalist school of jurisprudence which was dominant in the last century, still maintains a hold on current legal thinking. Although the social-economic values that were originally sustained with this method are now outmoded, the rule-deductive style of reasoning itself remains an integral part of the modern lawyer's intellectual equipment. The process of extracting principles from past cases and applying them to decide new ones is still the bedrock of legal analysis.

Impact Analysis Method

Since Holmes's well-known epigram (1881), "The life of the law has not been logic; it has been experience" (p. 1), American jurisprudential thought has looked increasingly forward to the consequences of decisions rather than backward to first principles. A judicial decision "must be judged by the results it achieves, not by the niceties of its internal structure," wrote an early critic of the formalist approach. "It must be valued by the extent to which it meets its end, not by the beauty of its logical processes or the strictness with which its rules proceed from the dogmas it takes for its foundation" (Pound 1908, p. 605). John Dewey (1938) argued that "the sanctification of ready-made antecedent, universal principles as a method of thinking is the chief obstacle" to social reforms and "to social advance by means of law" (p. 27).

The formalist method represents a jurisprudence of antecedents: Decisions are based on deductions from certainties. It is a kind of programmed or prefabricated decision-making, and some judges and scholars estimate that the "predestined outcome" of cases, based on the application of precedent, may run as high as 90 percent (Clark and Trubek 1961, p. 256, n. 7).

Impact analysis is a "jurisprudence of consequences": "Choices are made by [judges] from many competing principles (or inconsistent interests), not because of compelling law, but because of an evaluation of what the impact of given decisions is thought to be" (Miller 1965, p. 372). A basis for deciding between conflicting values is to anticipate the possible social and behavioral effects of the alternative courses of action. The choice of an applicable rule would depend, at least in part, on the extent to which that rule would help realize the desired end. For example, in weighing the different values at stake in the School Segregation Cases, one factor in the choice was the impact of segregation on minority children's learning and emotional development. In deciding whether to impose the exclusionary rule in *Mapp*, a factor in the balancing of crime control and due process value was the deterrent effect of the rule on future police behavior. The death penalty decisions also implicated prospective thinking about the impact of abolition on crime.

To decide, then, is to choose, and to choose is to predict. This teleological or result-oriented approach to decision-making emerged as a central feature of jurisprudential thought in the aftermath of the Second World War. In an era when the ideals of civilization and justice were put to the test, law was seen as an instrument for policy-making—for "the ever more complete achievement of the democratic values that constitute the professed ends of American polity" (Lasswell and McDougal 1943, p. 206). For this purpose, policy-oriented theorists of law urged the adoption of "goal-thinking," "trend-thinking," and "scientific thinking" to complement deductive thinking (p. 216). There were calls for an "experimental jurisprudence," that is, "a science of law based on a rigorous application of the scientific method" and "devoted to the study of the phenomena of lawmaking, the effect of law upon society, and the efficiency of laws in accomplishing the purposes for which they came into existence" (Beutel 1957, p. 18).

The key notion in impact analysis is that decisions are evaluated and criticized in terms of postulated goals and that continuing feedback of the effects of decisions is needed to improve decision-making. Justice Cardozo (1924) observed that "some of the errors of courts have their origin in imperfect knowledge of the economic and social consequences of a decision" (p. 116). And Justice Frankfurter (1954) once inquired "where we can go to find light on what the practical consequences of [our] decisions have been. . . . [T]o the extent that they may be relevant in deciding cases, they ought not to be left to the blind guessing of myself and others only a little less informed than I am" (p. 17).

The materials of this chapter exemplify the result-oriented method of decision-making, as applied to the problem of police regulation. Of course, it is not a method unique to law. There are analogues in other disciplines. It is no coincidence that the rise to prominence of this method corresponded with the blooming of the "policy sciences." In the areas of public administration and organizational behavior, impact analysis is known as "rational-comprehensive" or "scientific" decision-making (Lindblom 1959; March and Simon 1958). Concepts and skills from economics, psychology, statistical decision theory, operations research, and other disciplines were applied to aid in the rational treatment of policy matters. The method consists basically of the following sequence of steps (Mayo and Jones 1964, pp. 348–50):

- identification of the issue or problem that needs resolution (for example, determination of the kinds of police enforcement practices that are subject to abuse of discretion)
- clarification of the objectives and values sought to be achieved (for example, deterrence of police misconduct)
- mean-ends analysis: consideration of alternative courses of action for achieving the postulated objectives (for example, comparison of tort damages versus the exclusionary rule as different means for changing police conduct)
- projection of the possible social, economic, and behavioral outcomes of each of the possible courses of action (for example, costs and deterrent impact of the exclusionary rule)
- consideration of other factors in the setting that could affect the realization of the desired objectives (for example, police cultural norms that are barriers to external reform)
- choice of the course of action (for example, adoption of the exclusionary rule)
- evaluation of the actual consequences, intended and unintended, of the action taken (for example, empirical impact studies of *Mapp*)
- proposals for change, based at least partly on the impact data, in the means adopted earlier, in order to attain better the postulated objectives; and/or proposals for change in the objectives themselves, if their attainment is unfeasible (for example, recommendation of police self-regulation in lieu of, or in addition to, the exclusionary rule).

Impact analysis, then, consists of three interrelated components: (1) prediction (anticipation by judges of the effects of alternative rules as a basis for choice); (2) description (data collection and hypothesis testing by researchers regarding the social impact of the decision); (3) prescription (criticism and reformulation of the rule based in part on the empirical research—informed commentary on the decision products of a court becomes a part of the lawmaking process of the judiciary).

NOTES AND QUESTIONS

1.   Impact-analysis is a rational-comprehensive style of thinking because it attempts to consider all possible factors in reaching a decision. Is prediction of possible consequences a satisfactory basis for choosing between competing values and objectives, especially when there is no consensus on what are the desired ends in the first place?

In public administration, Lindblom (1959) proposes that there often is no clear-cut, agreed-upon objectives, and the decision-makers "are reduced to deciding policy without clarifying objectives first" (p. 82). Given dissensus on social ends, he argues "it is not irrational for a [decision-maker] to defend a policy as good without being able to specify what it is good for (p. 84). Public administration is "the science of muddling through" (p. 79). What are examples of cases that we have considered thus far in which judges made law without clarifying the underlying purposes? Since judges are expected to justify in their opinions the reasons for their decisions, how do they discharge that responsibility when the objectives and values are uncertain or in conflict?

2.   Does impact analysis assume a degree of rationality, intellectual capacity, and information availability that is too optimistic? If tracing all the important consequences of the different available alternatives prior to acting taxes the limits of decision-makers, how then do they anticipate the impact of their actions?

Simon (1957) suggests that decision-makers do not search among the range of possible actions and select the best one. Instead they seek a course of action that is satisfactory or merely good enough—they "satisfice" rather than "maximize" the desired objectives. What cases presented thus far illustrate judicial equivalents of "satisficing"?

3.   The two styles of decision-making—deductive syllogism and impact analysis—are not mutually exclusive. What features of these methods can be combined? What cases illustrate hybrid decision-making? What other methods of decision-making are demonstrated in the cases of the previous chapters?

REFERENCES

Adams, T. F. "Field Interrogations." *Police*, March–April 1963.

Allman, T. D. "Pomp and Desperation." *Harper's*, November 1981, pp. 14–18.

American Bar Association, Project on Standards for Criminal Justice. *Standards Relating to the Urban Police Function*. Chicago: American Bar Association, 1972.

American Law Institute. *A Model Code of Pre-arraignment Procedure*. Study draft no. 1. Philadelphia: American Law Institute, 1968.

———. *A Model Code of Pre-arraignment Procedure*. Proposed official draft. Philadelphia: American Law Institute, 1975.

Amsterdam, A. G. "The Supreme Court and the Rights of Suspects in Criminal Cases." *New York University Law Review* 45 (1970): 785–815.

———. "Perspectives on the Fourth Amendment." *Minnesota Law Review* 58 (1974): 349–477.

Arnold, T. W. *The Symbols of Government*. New Haven: Yale University Press, 1935.

Ashcraft v. Tennessee, 322 U.S. 143 (1944).

Attorney General's Task Force on Violent Crime. *Final Report*. Washington, D.C.: U.S. Government Printing Office, 1981.

Balch, R. "The Police Personality: Fact or Fiction?" *Journal of Criminal Law, Criminology, and Police Science* 63 (1972): 106–19.

Baldwin, J. *Nobody Knows My Name*. New York: Dell, 1962.

Banton, M. *The Policeman in the Community*. New York: Basic Books, 1964.

Bartol, C. R. *Psychology and American Law*. Belmon, Ca.: Wadsworth, 1983.

Batey, R. "Deterring Fourth Amendment Violations Through Police Disciplinary Reform." *American Criminal Law Review* 14 (1976): 245–72.

Beutel, F. *Experimental Jurisprudence.* Lincoln: University of Nebraska Press, 1957.

Bittner, E. *The Functions of the Police in Modern Society.* Chevy Chase, Md.: National Institute of Mental Health, Center for Studies of Crime and Delinquency, 1970.

Boyd v. United States, 116 U.S. 616 (1886).

Bradley, C. M. "The Exclusionary Rule in Germany." *Harvard Law Review* 96 (1983): 1032–66.

Broderick, J. J. *Police in a Time of Change.* Morristown, N.J.: General Learning Press, 1976.

Brown, M. K. *Working the Street: Police Direction and the Dilemmas of Reform.* New York: Russell Sage Foundation, 1981.

Brown v. Mississippi, 297 U.S. 278 (1936).

Burger, W. E. "Who Will Watch the Watchmen?" *American University Law Review* 14 (1964): 1–23.

California v. Prysock, 453 U.S. 355 (1981).

Campbell, D. T., and Stanley, J. C. *Experimental and Quasi-Experimental Designs for Research.* Chicago: Rand McNally, 1963.

———. "Legal Reforms as Experiments." *Journal of Legal Education* 23 (1970): 217–40.

Canon, B. C. "Is the Exclusionary Rule in Failing Health? Some New Data and a Plea Against a Precipitous Conclusion." *Kentucky Law Journal* 62 (1973): 681–730.

———. "Testing the Effectiveness of Civil Liberties Policies at the State and Federal Levels: The Case of the Exclusionary Rule." *American Politics Quarterly* 5 (1977): 57–82.

———. "The Exclusionary Rule: Have Critics Proven That It Doesn't Deter Police?" *Judicature* 62 (1979): 398–403.

———. "Ideology and Reality in the Debate over the Exclusionary Rule: A Conservative Argument for its Retention." *South Texas Law Journal* 23 (1982): 559–82.

Caplan, G. "The Case for Rulemaking by Law Enforcement Agencies." *Law and Contemporary Problems* 36 (1971): 500–514.

Cardozo, B. N. *The Growth of the Law.* New Haven: Yale University Press, 1924.

Chevigny, P. *Police Power: Police Abuses in New York City.* New York: Pantheon Books, 1969.

Clark, C., and Trubek, D. "The Creative Role of the Judge: Restraint and Freedom in the Common Law Tradition." *Yale Law Journal* 71 (1961): 255–76.

Comment. "Interrogations in New Haven: The Impact of *Miranda.*" *Yale Law Journal* 76 (1967): 1519–1648.

Comment. "Effect of Mapp v. Ohio on Police Search and Seizure Practices in Narcotics Cases." *Columbia Journal of Law and Social Problems* 4 (1968): 87–104.

Comment. "Critique: On the Limitations of Empirical Evaluations of the Exclusionary Rule. A Critique of the Spiotto Research and United States v. Calandra." *Northwestern University Law Review* 69 (1974): 740–98.

Commonwealth v. Roane, 459 Pa. 389 (1974).

Comptroller General of the United States. *Impact of the Exclusionary Rule on Federal Criminal Prosecutions.* Report No. G-B-D-79-45, April 19, 1979.

Cowan, T. A. "Decision Theory in Law, Science, and Technology." *Rutgers Law Review* 17 (1963): 499–530.

Davies, T. Y. "Do Criminal Due Process Principles Make a Difference? *American Bar Foundation Research Journal* 1982 (1982): 247–68.

Davis, K. C. *Discretionary Justice: A Preliminary Inquiry.* Baton Rouge: Louisiana State University Press, 1969.

———. *Police Discretion.* St. Paul, Minn.: West Publishing Co., 1975.

Devlin, P. *The Criminal Prosecution in England.* New Haven: Yale University Press, 1958.

Dewey, J. *Logic: The Theory of Inquiry.* New York: Henry Holt, 1938.

Driver, E. D. "Confessions and the Social Psychology of Coercion." *Harvard Law Review* 82 (1968): 42–61.

Elkins v. United States, 364 U.S. 206 (1960).

Escobedo v. Illinois, 378 U.S. 478 (1964).

Estelle v. Smith, 451 U.S. 454 (1981).

Fare v. Michael C., 442 U.S. 707 (1979).

Frankfurter, F. *Some Observations on Supreme Court Litigation and Legal Education.* Chicago: University of Chicago Law School, 1954.

Geller, W. A. "Is the Evidence in on the Exclusionary Rule?" *American Bar Association Journal* 67 (1981): 1642–45.

Gideon v. Wainwright, 372 U.S. 335 (1963).

Goldstein, H. "Police Policy Formulation: A Proposal for Improving Police Performance." *Michigan Law Review* 65 (1967): 1123–46.

———. *Policing a Free Society.* Cambridge, Mass.: Ballinger, 1977.

Grisso, T. "Juveniles' Capacities to Waive *Miranda* Rights: An Empirical Analysis." *California Law Review* 68 (1980): 1134–1166.

Hahn, H. "A Profile of Urban Police." *Law and Contemporary Problems* 36 (1971): 449–66.

Harris, R. N. *The Police Academy: An Inside View.* New York: Wiley, 1973.

Holmes, O. W. *The Common Law.* Boston: Little, Brown, 1881.

Hudson, J. R. "Police Review Boards and Police Accountability." *Law and Contemporary Problems* 36 (1971): 515–38.

Hyman, E. M. " In Pursuit of a More Workable Exclusionary Rule: A Police Officer's Perspective." *Pacific Law Journal* 10 (1979): 33–68.

Illinois v. Gates, 103 S. Ct. 2317 (1983).

Jensen, D. L., and Hart, R. "The Good Faith Restatement of the Exchange Rule." *Journal of Criminal Law and Criminology* 73 (1982): 916–38.

Inbau, F. "Police Interrogation—A Practical Necessity." *Journal of Criminal Law, Criminology, and Police Science* 52 (1961): 16–46.

Kamisar, Y. "The Exclusionary Rule in Historical Perspective: The Struggle to Make the Fourth Amendment More Than 'an Empty Blessing.' " *Judicature* 62 (1979): 337–50.

———. "Does (Did) (Should) the Exclusionary Rule Rest on a 'Principled Basis' Rather than an 'Empirical Proposition.'" *Creighton Law Review* 16 (1983): 565–667.

Kaplan, A. *The Conduct of Inquiry.* San Francisco, Ca.: Chandler, 1964.

Kaplan, J. "The Limits of the Exclusionary Rule." *Stanford Law Review* 26 (1974): 1027–55.

Katz, D., and Kahn, R. L. *The Social Psychology of Organizations,* 2nd ed. New York: John Wiley, 1978.

LaFave, W. R. "Improving Police Performance Through the Exclusionary Rule——Part I: Current Police and Local Court Practices." *Missouri Law Review* 30 (1965a): 391–458.

———. "Improving Police Performance Through the Exclusionary Rule——Part II: Defining the Norms and Training the Police." *Missouri Law Review* 30 (1965b): 567–610.

———, and Remington, F. "Controlling the Police: The Judge's Role in Making and Reviewing Law Enforcement Decisions." *Michigan Law Review* 63 (1965): 987–1012.

Lasswell, H., and McDougal, M. "Legal Education and Public Policy: Professional Training in the Public Interest." *Yale Law Journal* 52 (1943): 203–95.

Leiken, L. S. "Police Interrogation in Colorado: The Implementation of Miranda." *Denver Law Journal* 47 (1970): 1–53.

Lempert, R. "Strategies of Research Design in the Legal Impact Study." *Law and Society Review* 1 (1966): 111–32.

Levine, J. P. "Implementing Legal Policies Through Operant Conditioning: The Case of Police Practices." *Law and Society Review* 6 (1971): 195–222.

Lewis, P. W., and Peoples, K. D. *The Supreme Court and the Criminal Process.* Philadelphia: W. B. Saunders, 1978.

Lindblom, C. "The Science of 'Muddling Through'" *Public Administration Review* 19 (1959): 79–88.

Lipset, S. M. "Why Cops Hate Liberals and Vice Versa." *Atlantic Monthly,* March 1969, pp. 76–83.

Loewenthal, M. "Evaluating the Exclusionary Rule in Search and Seizure." *University of Missouri–Kansas City Law Review* 49 (1980): 24–40.

Lundman, R. J., ed. *Police Behavior: A Sociological Perspective.* New York: Oxford University Press, 1980.

Manning, P. K. *Police Work: The Social Organization of Policing.* Cambridge, Mass.: M.I.T. Press, 1977.

Mapp v. Ohio, 367 U.S. 643 (1961).

March, J. G., and Simon, H. A. *Organizations.* New York: John Wiley, 1958.

Matter of Storar, 52 N.Y. 363 (1981).

Mayo, L. H., and Jones, E. M. "Legal-Policy Decision Process: Alternative Thinking and the Predicative Function." *George Washington Law Review* 33 (1964): 318–456.

McGowan, C. "Rule-making and the Police." *Michigan Law Review* 70 (1972): 659–94.

McNabb v. United States, 318 U.S. 332 (1943).

Medalie, R. J.; Zeitz, J.; and Alexander, P. "Custodial Interrogation in Our Nation's Capital: The Attempt to Implement *Miranda.*" *Michigan Law Review* 66 (1968): 1363–1407.

Mertens, W. J., and Wasserstrom, S. "Foreword: The Good Faith Exception to the Exclusionary Rule: Deregulating the Police and Derailing the Law." *Georgetown Law Journal* 70 (1978): 365–463.

Michigan v. DeFillippo, 443 U.S. 31 (1979).

Michigan v. Mosley, 423 U.S. 96 (1975).

Miller, A. S. "On the Need for 'Impact Analysis' of Supreme Court Decisions." *Georgetown Law Journal* 53 (1965): 365–401.

Miranda v. Arizona, 384 U.S. 486 (1966).

Morris, A. M. "The Exclusionary Rule, Deterrence, and Posner's Economic Analysis of Law." *Washington Law Review* 57 (1982): 647–67.

Murphy, M. J. "The Problem of Compliance by Police Departments." *Texas Law Review* 44 (1966): 939–64.

National Advisory Commission on Civil Disorders (the "Kerner Commission"). *Report.* New York: Bantam Books, 1968.

National Advisory Commission on Criminal Justice Standards and Goals. *Police.* Washington, D.C.: U.S. Government Printing Office, 1973.

National Institute of Justice. *The Effects of the Exclusionary Rule: A Study in California.* Washington, D.C.: U.S. Government Printing Office, 1982.

Niederhoffer, A. *Behind the Shield: The Police in Urban Society.* Garden City, N.Y.: Doubleday, 1967.

Oaks, D. "Studying the Exclusionary Rule in Search and Seizure." *University of Chicago Law Review* 37 (1970): 665–757.

Olmstead v. United States, 277 U.S. 438 (1928).

Oregon v. Bradshaw, 103 S. Ct. 2830 (1983).

Oregon v. Mathiason, 429 U.S. 492 (1977).

Packer, H. L. "Two Models of the Criminal Process." *University of Pennsylvania Law Review* 113 (1964): 1–68.

———. "The Courts, the Police, and the Rest of Us." *Journal of Criminal Law, Criminology, and Police Science* 57 (1966): 238–43.

People v. Defore, 242 N.Y. 13 (1926).

Plessy v. Ferguson, 163 U.S. 537 (1896).

Posner, R. A. "Excessive Sanctions for Governmental Misconduct in Criminal Cases." *Washington Law Review* 57 (1982): 635–46.

Pound, R. "Mechanical Jurisprudence." *Columbia Law Review* 8 (1908): 605–23.

President's Commission on Law Enforcement and the Administration of Justice. *Crime in a Free Society.* Washington, D.C.: U.S. Government Printing Office, 1967a.

———. *Task Force Report: The Police.* Washington, D.C.: U.S. Government Printing Office, 1967b.

Quick, A. T. "Attitudinal Aspects of Police Compliance with Procedural Due Process." *American Journal of Criminal Law* 6 (1978): 25–56.

Quinn, J. "The Effect of Police Rulemaking on the Scope of Fourth Amendment Rights." *Journal of Urban Law* 52 (1974): 25–54.

Reiss, A. J., Jr. *The Police and the Public.* New Haven: Yale University Press, 1971a.

———. "Systematic Observation of Natural Social Phenomena." In *Sociological Methodology,* edited by H. L. Costner. San Francisco, Ca.: Jossey-Bass, 1971b.

———, and Black, D. J. "Interrogation and the Criminal Process." *Annals* 374 (1967): 47–57.

———, and Bordua, D. "Environment and Organization: A Perspective on Police." In *The Police: Six Sociological Essays,* edited by D. Bordua. New York: John Wiley, 1967.

Rhode Island v. Innis, 446 U.S. 291 (1980).

Robinson, C. D. "Police and Prosecutor Practices and Attitudes Relating to Interrogation As Revealed by Pre- and Post-Miranda Questionnaires: A Construct of Police Capacity to Comply." *Duke Law Journal* 1968 (1968): 425–524.

Rochin v. California, 342 U.S. 165 (1952).

Rubinstein, J. *City Police.* New York: Farrar Straus & Giroux, 1973.

Schlag, P. J. "Assaults on the Exclusionary Rule: Good Faith Limitations and Damage Remedies." *Journal of Criminal Law and Criminology* 73 (1982): 875–915.

Schlesinger, S. R. *Exclusionary Injustice: The Problem of Illegally Obtained Evidence.* New York: Marcel Dekker, 1977.

———. "The Exclusionary Rule: Have Proponents Proven That It Is a Deterrent to Police?" *Judicature* 62 (1979): 404–9.

Schwartz, L. B., and Goldstein, S. R. *Law Enforcement Handbook for Police.* St. Paul, Minn.: West, 1970.

Seeburger, R. H., and Wettick, R. S., Jr. "*Miranda* in Pittsburgh—A Statistical Study." *University of Pittsburgh Law Review* 29 (1967): 1–26.

Selye, H. "The Stress of Police Work." *Police Stress* 1 (1978): 7–8.

Simon, H. *Administrative Behavior,* 2nd ed. New York: Macmillan, 1957.

Skolnick, J. *Justice Without Trial: Law Enforcement in a Democratic Society.* New York: John Wiley, 1966.

Smith, B., Sr. *Police Systems in the United States,* 2nd rev. ed. New York: Harper, 1960.

South Dakota v. Neville, 103 S. Ct. 916 (1983).

Spano v. New York, 360 U.S. 315 (1959).

Specter, A. "Mapp v. Ohio: Pandora's Problems for the Prosecutor." *University of Pennsylvania Law Review* 111 (1962): 4–45.

Spiotto, J. E. "Search and Seizure: An Empirical Study of the Exclusionary Rule and Its Alternatives." *Journal of Legal Studies* 2 (1973): 243–78.

Stotland, E., and Berberich, J. "The Psychology of the Police." In *Psychology of Crime and Criminal Justice* edited by H. Toch. New York: Holt Rinehart & Winston, 1979.

Tague v. Louisiana, 444 U.S. 469 (1980).

Terris, B. J. "The Role of the Police." *Annals* 374 (1967): 58–69.

The Exclusionary Rule Bills: Hearings on S. 101, S. 751, and S. 1995 Before the Subcommittee on Criminal Law of the Senate Committe on the Judiciary, 97th Congress, 1st and 2d Sess. (1982).

The King v. Warickshall, 1 Leach 263, 168 Eng. Rep. 234 (K.B. 1783).

Tiffany, L. P. *Detection of Crime: Stopping and Questioning, Search and Seizure, Encouragement and Entrapment.* Boston: Little, Brown, 1967.

United States v. Calandra, 414 U.S. 338 (1974).

United States v. Contreras, 667 F.2d 976 (11th Cir. 1981).

United States v. Fay, 323 F.2d 65 (2d Cir. 1963).

United States v. Frazier, 476 F.2d 891 (1973).

United States v. Havens, 446 U.S. 620 (1980).

United States v. Janis, 428 U.S. 433 (1976).

United States v. Payner, 447 U.S. 727 (1980).

United States v. Wade, 388 U.S. 218 (1967).

United States v. Williams, 622 F.2d 830 (5th Cir. 1980).

Watts v. Indiana, 336 U.S. 917 (1949).

Weeks v. United States, 232 U.S. 383 (1914).

White, W. S. "Police Trickery in Inducing Confessions." *University of Pennsylvania Law Review* 127 (1979): 581–629.

Wigmore, J. *Wigmore on Evidence,* 2d ed. Boston: Little, Brown, 1923.

Wilkey, M. R. "The Exclusionary Rule: Why Suppress Valid Evidence." *Judicature* 62 (1978): 214–32.

Wilson, J. Q. *Varieties of Police Behavior.* Cambridge, Mass.: Harvard University Press, 1968.

Wilson, J. V., and Alprin, G. M. "Controlling Police Conduct: Alternatives to the Exclusionary Rule." *Law and Contemporary Problems* 36 (1971): 488–99.

Wilson, O. "How the Police Chief Sees It." *Harper's* April 1964, p. 140.

Witt, J. W. "Non-coercive Interrogation and the Administration of Criminal Justice: The Impact of *Miranda* on Police Effectuality." *Journal of Criminal Law and Criminology* 64 (1973): 320–32.

Wolf v. Colorado, 338 U.S. 25 (1949).

Wyrick v. Fields, 103 S. Ct. 394 (1982).

Zimbardo, P. "The Psychology of Police Confessions." *Psychology Today* 1 (1967): 17–27.

PART III

SOCIAL RESEARCH AND PROCEDURAL JUSTICE: FACT-FINDING IN THE TRIAL PROCESS

CHAPTER 7

Selection of the Jury:
Case Study of Jury Impartiality

7.1. INTRODUCTION

The gravamen of law is *how* a judgment is reached, more so than *what* that judgment is. Fact-finding procedures at trial are the institutional components of what we have called procedural justice. We begin the study of procedural justice by examining the jury because it is "the nerve center of the fact-finding process" (*Estes* v. *Texas*, 1965, p. 545). This centuries-old Anglo-American institution represents a remarkable political ideal of using lay members of a local community in the administration of justice. It emerged as the principal legal method of dispute resolution because it seemed more rational than alternative means. A group of twelve or fewer individuals, more or less randomly and involuntarily recruited by the state from the local population, is convened for the purpose of resolving controversies at a particular trial. The jurors hear the evidence, deliberate in secret, and report a final decision without giving any reasons or an accounting for the verdict to any authority. After this relatively short period of public service, they are dismissed and disappear to private life. Matters of life, liberty, and property are thus often entrusted by the state to a transient group of lay persons rather than to professional decision-makers such as judges.

Origins of the Jury

The name "jury" indicates the nature of its pedigree. It comes from the Latin "iurare," which means "to swear" to tell the truth. Although jury-like groups were known in the ancient Greco-Roman world, the modern jury has its roots in early Anglo-Saxon and Norman history (Devlin 1956, pp. 3–14; Thayer 1898, pp. 47–182). Before the twelfth century, civil and criminal disputes were settled by recourse to celestial intervention rather than to human reason. The most common method of proof in criminal cases was the ordeal. Under ecclesiastical superintendence the accused was dropped in a pit of water. If he sank, that meant he was "accepted" by

Providence via this element of nature and was adjudged innocent; if he floated, that meant he was "rejected" and therefore guilty. There were also ordeal by fire (carrying heated stones or iron—if the subsequent burn healed, he was declared innocent) and ordeal of the morsel (that did or did not stick in the throat). The Normans brought to England trial by battle between the disputants or their proxies, with right equated with victory. Civil disputes were resolved by the taking of oaths. A party who swore a false oath was believed to expose himself to the judgment of God, more fearful than the judgment of man. Disputants were sometimes supported by oath-helpers or com-purgators who swore to their faith in a party's veracity rather than to the facts of the dispute. The side with the most number of credible compurgators prevailed. Today, it may all be very reminiscent of fraternity hazing, but there was a wisdom of sorts in these modes of conflict resolution: They reflected well the deeply felt beliefs of the times. They may not have produced accurate findings, but the medieval populace thought that they did, and therefore the results were perceived as legitimate.

In time, the validity of these methods of proof was called into question. The use of juries to dispense justice in civil and criminal cases began or became common during the reign of Henry II (1154–1189). Early jury trials dealt with disputes relating to land. An agreed body of neighbors, knowledgeable about the facts, answered upon oath which of the two parties was entitled to the property. When a party received twelve oaths in his favor, he won. On the criminal side, the parent of jury trial was the royal inquest. Norman officials periodically visited the boroughs of the realm to inquire about local concerns. These inquiries or inquests (conducted by Frankish monarchs since the ninth century and brought to England in 1066) involved calling a group of twelve freemen, compelling them to take an oath, and asking them for information needed for public administration. These men were called jurors because they had sworn to tell the truth. At the Assize of Clarendon (1166), the jury underwent a metamorphosis from an administrative fact-finding body to a criminal justice institution. Thereafter, at royal inquests, jurors were required to report on criminal activity in their vicinage. Since they were usually witnesses to offenses or had information about offenders, they presented criminals for subsequent adjudication by ordeal. This jury of presentment or accusation was the forerunner of the modern grand jury.

In 1215, Pope Innocent III, by decree of the Fourth Lateran Council, forbade clerics from taking part in the ordeal, relying in part on Jesus' admonition: "Thou shalt not tempt the Lord thy God" (Matthew 4:7). Consequently, new methods of guilt-adjudication had to be devised. In England, both criminal and civil matters were eventually turned over to the jury for disposition. In 1219, King John ordered royal judges to urge criminal defendants to "put [themselves] upon God and the country" (Devlin 1956, p. 10), that is, to consent to trial by their countrymen. Defendants would plead "not guilty" and then be tried by jury. Those who refused to plea either got no trial at all and were condemned simply on the accusation or were coerced by the *peine forte et dure* (piling rocks on the defendant's chest until he pleaded or was crushed to death). As with any legal reform, trial by jury was not immediately accepted. Only gradually did it replace older methods of adjudication. Trial by compurgation, for example, co-existed with trial by jury for a generation or two before it lapsed into desuetude.

Trial, such as it then was, bore little resemblance to today's proceedings. No distinction was drawn initially between the trial jury and the presenting jury. The nascent trial jury acted on what it already knew or thought it knew about the case. A central feature of the medieval jury was its self-informing character. Its task was to deliver a verdict, not to listen to the evidence. The notion of having uninformed jurors receive evidence presented by the parties in court evolved very slowly. By the mid-fourteenth century, presenting jurors no longer sat at the trial itself, and by the time of Sir Edward Coke (1552–1634), the impartial jury trial as we now know it had come into being.

From its English home, the jury was exported abroad. During the French Revolution, it was viewed as a democratic institution for the administration of criminal justice. From France, the jury was carried eastward across Europe under the influence of the Napoleonic Wars. In the days of the British Empire the jury also migrated in the opposite direction. Today, the idea of lay participation, in some form or another, in criminal adjudication is fairly widespread, although there are many nations in which criminal trials are the exclusive domain of professional judges.

The Sixth Amendment Jury and the Seventh Amendment Jury

This system of administration of justice has sparked extensive commentary. In this country, by the middle of the century, Broeder (1955) estimated that some three hundred articles had already been written on the jury. They consist of historical and doctrinal scholarship on the constitutional right to a jury trial, normative arguments about the purposes of the jury and its role in a democratic society, and analyses of administrative and financial considerations (court delay, costs, and so forth) incident to the implementation of jury trials. No small part of the legal and policy discussion rests on factual predicates regarding how the jury actually operates. There is also a systematic body of empirical research on the social organization and functioning of the jury. To narrow the scope of our coverage, we shall focus only on selected aspects of this right where issues of law, policy, and fact intersect.

There is a Seventh Amendment right to a jury in civil cases ("In suits at common law, where the value in controversy shall exceed twenty dollars, the right of trial by jury shall be preserved . . .") and a Sixth Amendment right to a jury in criminal cases ("In all criminal prosecutions, the accused shall enjoy the right . . . to an impartial jury of the State and district wherein the crime shall have been committed . . ."). The argument for preserving the jury in the criminal context is more compelling because life and liberty, not just property, are at stake. The results of a criminal prosecution are generally more consequential for society. Criminal cases join issues of individual liberty and social order. The Supreme Court implicitly subscribes to the received view that the civil jury is less important than the criminal jury in terms of its social impact and symbolic significance (Lempert 1981, p. 81). It has not yet held that the Seventh Amendment right, unlike the Sixth Amendment right, is essential to the scheme of ordered liberty, and therefore has not made it binding on the states. Much of the literature on the fairness, reliability, and efficiency of the jury has revolved around the criminal jury. Social research has also largely neglected the civil counterpart. For these reasons, our coverage will concentrate primarily, but not exclusively, on the criminal jury of the Sixth Amendment.

We have divided the materials into two parts. This chapter deals with the processes of selecting a jury, and the next chapter looks at the social organization and functioning of the jury. The common theme to both chapters is the constitutional guarantee of an "impartial jury." We begin with jury selection because the claim of race and sex discrimination in choosing prospective jurors raises threshold questions of impartiality. Unless a jury consists of a fair cross section of the community, it cannot discharge the responsibilities for which it was called into existence. The issue of nondiscriminatory selection is also intertwined, as we shall see in the next chapter, with the issues of jury size and jury decision-making rules. The jury deliberation process and the eventual outcome depend, in part, on who serves on the jury. Together, then, Chapters 7 and 8 present a body of law and social science that elaborates on the meaning of "impartiality." The subject of the jury provides a case study on how legal policy and empirical analysis intermesh to shape procedural justice.

Overview

The attempt to secure race-neutrality in jury selection began with equal protection challenges to the systematic exclusion or underrepresentation of prospective black jurors in the trials of black defendants. A jury is only as good as its members. If a jury is to be an instrument of public justice, embodying community values, it should be representative of the range of people and views contained in that community. An unrepresentative jury has less claim to the legitimacy of its decisions. The selection of the venire from which a grand jury (that determines indictments) and a petit jury (that decides guilt) are empaneled goes to the core of the right to an impartial jury. We start in section 7.2 with the standards for prima facie proof of purposeful discrimination under the Fourteenth Amendment (*Swain* v. *Alabama*, 1965).

The legal issue of how large a disparity—between actual and expected numbers of minority members in a venire—must be in order to be adjudged invalid can be aided by the application of statistical decision theory. The Supreme Court has applied the binomial formula for the standard deviation and ruled that a disparity greater than two or three standard deviations raises a suspicion of discriminatory selection (*Castaneda* v. *Partida*, 1977). Other courts have used other statistical tests of significance, such as the Chi square test and the Z test of a normal probability distribution, to determine the chance occurrence of the observed disparity before rejecting the null hypothesis of race-neutral selection (*People* v. *Powell*, 1974). We will discuss in section 7.3 the methods of statistical proof of discrimination and the legal issues that arise when quantitative analysis is used in litigation.

The problem of underrepresentation (rather than total exclusion) arising from facially neutral procedures can be a subtle form of "invisible" discrimination. It is not unique to the jury but is found in various other contexts as well, such as employment, housing, voting, and schooling. Section 7.3 also touches upon Title VII and §1981 challenges to the underrepresentation of minorities in the labor market (*Hazelwood School District* v. *United States*, 1977; *Gay* v. *Waiters' and Dairy Lunchmen's Union, Local 30*, 1980). It provides an opportunity to compare the constitutional and statutory standards of proof and to consider whether the statistical methods of proof used in jury discrimination cases are applicable to employment discrimination.

In contrast to the imposing conglomeration of legal barriers against discrimination in the selection of the jury venire, the legal safeguards against discrimination in the impaneling of the petit jury itself are minimal. The Supreme Court has declined to invalidate the use (or misuse) of peremptory challenges in any particular voir dire for excluding minority members or other identifiable groups (*Swain* v. *Alabama*, 1965). Thus, if a representative venire contains, say, six minority members and each party is allowed six peremptory strikes, the party opposed to seating any minorities in the jury box could legitimately remove all six solely because of their group affiliation. Section 7.4 looks at the voir dire process and explores why the courts are more reluctant to intervene at the petit jury stage than at the venire stage.

In the absence of detailed procedural rules governing voir dire, lawyers have turned to social scientists for assistance in choosing "unbiased" jurors (unbiased against their own side). The conventional wisdom is that trials can be won or lost at voir dire. During the early 1970s, "scientific" jury selection was introduced by the defense in criminal trials with "political" overtones. Social scientists constructed demographic and attitudinal profiles of prospective jurors likely to be favorably disposed toward the defendant(s), which lawyers then used as guides in voir dire selection. A decade later, the techniques have been expanded and applied to large scale antitrust litigation and other civil cases. The materials in section 7.5 describe the use of scientific jury selection in a highly publicized murder trial and explore the methodological, ethical, and policy issues incident to its use.

In addition to personal characteristics that may predispose jurors toward acquittal or conviction, a second source of juror partiality is prejudicial pretrial publicity. The final section (7.6) examines judicial safeguards designed to remedy or prevent this bias, namely, change of the trial to a venue untouched by publicity or prior restraint of the media (*Nebraska Press Association* v. *Stuart*, 1976), respectively.

7.2. DISCRIMINATION IN JURY SELECTION

SWAIN v. ALABAMA

380 U.S. 202 (1965)

Mr. Justice WHITE delivered the opinion of the Court.

The petitioner, Robert Swain, a Negro, was indicted and convicted of rape in the Circuit Court of Talladega County, Alabama, and sentenced to death. His motions to quash the indictment, to strike down the trial jury venire and to declare void the petit jury chosen in the case, all based on alleged invidious discrimination in the selection of jurors, were denied. The Alabama Supreme Court affirmed the conviction . . . , and we granted certiorari.

In support of his claims, petitioner invokes the constitutional principle announced in 1880 in Strauder v. State of West Virginia, 100 U.S. 303 where the

Court struck down a state statute qualifying only white people for jury duty. . . . Although a Negro defendant is not entitled to a jury containing members of his race, a State's purposeful or deliberate denial to Negroes on account of race of participation as jurors in the administration of justice violates the Equal Protection Clause. . . .

But purposeful discrimination may not be assumed or merely asserted. . . . It must be proven. . . .

We consider first petitioner's claims concerning the selection of grand jurors and the petit jury venire. The evidence was that while Negro males over 21 constitute 26% of all males in the county in this age group, only 10 to 15% of the grand and petit jury panels drawn from the jury box since 1953 have been Negroes, there having been only one case in which the percentage was as high as 23%. In this period of time, Negroes served on 80% of the grand juries selected, the number ranging from one to three. There were four or five Negroes on the grand jury panel of about 33 in this case, out of which two served on the grand jury which indicted petitioner. Although there has been an average of six to seven Negroes on petit jury venires in criminal cases, no Negro has actually served on a petit jury since about 1950. In this case there were eight Negroes on the petit jury venire but none actually served, two being exempt and six being struck by the prosecutor in the process of selecting the jury.

It is wholly obvious that Alabama has not totally excluded a racial group from either grand or petit jury panels, as was the case in Norris v. Alabama, 294 U.S. 587. . . . Moreover, we do not consider an average of six to eight Negroes on these panels as constituting forbidden token inclusion within the meaning of the cases in this Court. . . . Nor do we consider the evidence in this case to make out a prima facie case of invidious discrimination under the Fourteenth Amendment.

Alabama law requires that the three jury commissioners in Talladega County place on the jury roll all male citizens in the community over 21 who are reputed to be honest, intelligent men and are esteemed for their integrity, good character and sound judgment. Ala. Code, Tit. 30, §§20, 21 (1958). In practice, however, the commissioners do not place on the roll all such citizens, either white or colored. A typical jury roll at best contains about 2,500 names, out of a total male population over 21, according to the latest census, of 16,406 persons. Each commissioner, with the clerk's assistance, produces for the jury list names of persons who in his judgment are qualified. The sources are city directories, registration lists, club and church lists, conversations with other persons in the community, both white and colored, and personal and business acquaintances.

Venires drawn from the jury box made up in this manner unquestionably contained a smaller proportion of the Negro community than of the white community. But a defendant in a criminal case is not constitutionally entitled to demand a proportionate number of his race on the jury which tries him nor on the venire or jury roll from which petit jurors are drawn. . . . Neither the jury roll nor the venire need be a perfect mirror of the community or accurately reflect the proportionate strength of every identifiable group. . . . We cannot say that purposeful discrimination based on race alone is satisfactorily proved by showing that an identifiable group in a community is underrepresented by as much as 10%. . . . Here the commissioners denied that racial considerations entered into their selections of either their contacts in the community or the names of prospective jurors. There is no evidence that the commissioners applied different standards of qualifications to the Negro community than they did to the white community. Nor was there any meaningful attempt to demonstrate that the same proportion of Negroes qualified under the standards being administered by the commissioners. It is not clear from the record that the commissioners even knew how many Negroes were in their respective areas, or on the jury roll or on the venires drawn from the jury box. The overall percentage disparity has been small, and reflects no studied attempt to include or exclude a specified number of Negroes. Undoubtedly the selection of prospective jurors was somewhat haphazard and little effort was made to ensure that all groups in the community were fully represented. But an imperfect system is not equivalent to purposeful discrimination based on race. We do not think that the burden of proof was carried by petitioner in this case. . . .

Affirmed.

Mechanics of Jury Selection

To place the *Swain* problem in legal context, the general procedure of jury selection needs to be outlined.

Selection procedures are prescribed by statute and they vary from state to state. In the federal courts, it is prescribed by the Jury Selection and Service Act of 1968. The main objective of these procedures is to ensure fairness in the selection process. It must not "systematically exclude distinctive groups in the community and thereby fail to be reasonably representative thereof" (*Taylor* v. *Louisiana*, 1975). In the state system, there are three main methods of jury selection, and some variations or combinations thereof: a random process often based on voter registration lists or tax rolls; a "key man" procedure whereby jury commissioners solicit and receive names of prospective jurors from "key men" (business leaders, political figures, and so forth) in the jurisdiction; and a mixed, somewhat arbitrary procedure such as was in effect in Alabama at the time of the *Swain* case. The Alabama Code defined the eligible jury population as consisting of male citizens in the community over 21 years, who are reputed to be honest, intelligent, and esteemed for integrity, good character, and sound judgment. The jury commissioners of Talladega County, at their discretion, collected names for the jury list from a variety of sources such as voter registration lists, church lists, and key men contacts. In short, the procedure was—in the Court's description—"somewhat haphazard" in ensuring that "all groups in the community were fully represented." But apparently it was not grossly haphazard or arbitrary in the Court's judgment so as to be constitutionally unfair.

The steps in the jury selection process, speaking generally, are as follows. First, the eligible population is defined by statute. Second, a jury list or master jury wheel is drawn up by jury commissioners or other local officials. In most states, the statutes defining the eligible population are "directory" only so that, in practice, officials seldom compile a complete list of eligible potential jurors. They have considerable discretion in controlling the composition of this pool if procedures other than purely random ones are used. Third, a qualified jury list or wheel is prepared after otherwise eligible potential jurors are excluded, excused, or exempted according to the statutory guidelines. For example, economic hardship is often a recognized reason for excuse from jury service. Certain professional groups such as attorneys are exempted from service. Fourth, from the qualified jury list, a smaller sample is drawn (by random or nonrandom procedures, depending on the jurisdiction) to form the jury panel or venire consisting of thirty to sixty persons. Venirepersons receive notices to appear for possible jury service. From this qualified jury list is also selected a grand jury. This body composed of sixteen to twenty-three persons meets behind closed doors to receive evidence presented by the prosecutor and to determine whether to issue an indictment, or formal written accusation, charging a defendant with the commission of a crime. Finally, by the voir dire process of in-court questioning of venirepersons, the petit jury (six to twelve persons) is selected to determine the verdict at trial. The specific selection procedure in a given state may vary somewhat from the foregoing general description but, on the whole, it is a fairly representative one.

Judicial review of the fairness of selection can be exercised with real efficiency only at the level of defining the eligible population. The statutory categories can be tested against constitutional standards with relative ease. Statutes which exclude non-whites from jury duty are clearly unconstitutional as found in *Strauder* v. *West Virginia* (1880), cited in the *Swain* case. Statutes which require jurors to be literate are reasonable on their face, although literacy tests can be susceptible to abuse, as has happened in voter registration.

The real sources of possible unfairness lie in the broad discretion of jury officials at the points of drawing up the master jury wheel, the qualified jury wheel, and the venire. Seldom are master jury wheels complete lists of the eligible population. Even when voter registration lists are used, which are more representative than such haphazard sources as key men contacts or business club lists, such lists may be incomplete and thus not reflective of the cross section of the community, particularly of the poor and of minorities (Kairys, Kadane, and Lehoczky 1977). Some states permit the expansion of voter lists to include such varied sources as welfare rolls and driver licenses. At the qualified jury wheel level, the vague statutory standards (for example, hardship excuse) are applied at the discretion of the jury officials. Indeed, they sometimes add inclusion or exclusion requirements of their own which are not described in the statute (Note, *Virginia Law Review*, 1966). They have discretion not only in composing the master and qualified jury wheels but also in the selection of the venire itself. Decisions by jury officials which stop short of total, blatant exclusion of distinctive groups are not easily challenged in court.

Grounds for Challenging Jury Selection

There are three major bases of litigation regarding discrimination in jury selection. The first basis of challenge is the statutory standards of eligibility or of exemptions and excuses. This does not pose difficult issues. Exclusion of women and racial minorities has been held illegal. Exemptions for certain professional groups have usually been ruled to constitute a reasonable and justifiable exercise of legislative policy. A second basis of challenge is the procedure by which the names of potential jurors are drawn at any given stage of the selection process, such that the objective of a representative cross section is undermined. The challenged procedure may be attacked on statutory grounds for deviation from the legislatively prescribed standards, and/or on constitutional grounds for violation of the Due Process Clause or Equal Protection Clause of the Fourteenth Amendment and the Sixth Amendment impartial jury right. The third basis of challenge is that the results of the selection procedure—regardless of the propriety of the procedure itself—are discriminatory in that distinctive groups are either totally excluded or substantially underrepresented in the jury panel. The principal source of jury litigation today consists of challenges to the procedure and/or results of the selection process.

A facially neutral procedure which results in total exclusion of minority members has been held to violate the Equal Protection Clause (*Norris* v. *Alabama*, 1937; cited in *Swain*). Thus, jury selection statutes which are facially discriminatory are unconstitutional, and those which are facially neutral are also unconstitutional if they nonetheless result in systematic and complete exclusion.

The more difficult problem today, which is posed in *Swain*, is this: Is there discrimination when a "somewhat haphazard" (but still constitutionally acceptable) procedure results in underrepresentation of minority members in the venire? Since not every discrepancy between the eligible population and the venire is constitutionally fatal, how does one draw the line between "large" and "small" underrepresentation for purposes of finding illegal discrimination?

Swain held that an 11% to 16% discrepancy between the number of eligible blacks in the local eligible population and in the venire panels (for the grand jury and petit jury), over a period of several years, does not constitute a prima facie case of invidious, systematic discrimination in violation of the Equal Protection Clause.

The elements of the test need to be examined carefully because they define the kinds of proof—including proof by empirical data—which are required. First, "prima facie" refers to the standard of proof needed to establish invidious or purposeful discrimination. The party challenging the selection procedure has the burden of proving it is discriminatory. That party, in this instance the defendant, need not prove it beyond a reasonable doubt, the standard used for criminal convictions. A much lower standard, lower than even the civil standard of preponderance of the evidence, is sufficient: prima facie. Once evidence is adduced to meet this standard, then "the burden shifts to the state to rebut the presumption of unconstitutional action by showing that permissible, facially neutral selection criteria and procedures have produced the monochromatic result" (*Alexander* v. *Louisiana,* 1972, p. 632). Initially, then, a presumption of constitutionality attaches to state procedures. Once the defendant succeeds in establishing a prima facie case, the presumption is rebutted, and the state must now come forth with evidence to show that the exclusion or underrepresentation was brought about by untainted procedures.

There are three basic elements to a prima facie case. First, the claimed discrimination must be directed toward a constitutionally protected or cognizable group, such as a racial minority. Second, the discrimination has to be invidious or purposeful on the part of jury officials. Absent intent to discriminate, even substantial underrepresentation could be found not violative of the Equal Protection Clause. For instance, if the reason for underrepresentation is that most of the minority venire persons voluntarily sought to be excused from jury service because of the economic hardship it would cause, arguably it cannot be said that the state engaged in "purposeful" discrimination. And third, the purposeful discrimination has to be systematic, that is, over a period of time, in order for it to be unlawful. Discrimination which occurs in just one instance is not sufficient. A continuous official pattern of bias needs to be established.

NOTES AND QUESTIONS

---

1.   According to the Court, how did Alabama rebut the presumption of unconstitutionality? What other kinds of evidence, derived from empirical research, could the state have used to show that it had no design to discriminate?

2.   Notice the role of procedural rules—the prima facie standard of proof and rebuttable presumptions—in defining the scope and use of empirical data in litigation. Compare the use of social science data in the school desegregation cases discussed in Chapter 3 with the use of statistical proof in the jury discrimination cases. What are the similarities and differences in the use of empirical information in these two instances? How essential is such information in the school and jury cases?

3.   Is this statement of the Court correct: "We cannot say that purposeful discrimination based on race alone is satisfactorily proved by showing that an identifiable group in a community is underrepresented by as much as 10%"? Suppose that 15% of the eligible jurors in a jurisdiction are black. The venire lists contain, on the average, 8% blacks. By what percentage are blacks underrepresented in the venire?

4.   Justice White compared the percentage difference between the number of eligible blacks in the population (26%) and in the jury panel (10% to 15% over the years). He concluded that there was no purposeful discrimination because "the overall percentage disparity [11% to 16%] has been small." A rule of law should articulate a reasoned connection between the facts and the conclusion. Does Justice White present any reason for drawing the line at 10% to 15% other than that these happen to be the figures in this case? Is there a general rule in the *Swain* opinion as to when discrepancies are large enough to be deemed evidence of discriminatory design?

5.   In the social sciences, the likelihood of the obtained results is tested against an external comparison standard, namely, the results expected by chance. If the results are unlikely to have occurred below a certain pre-established probability baseline—and the odds of five in one hundred is a commonly used cut-off level—then they are deemed to be due to other than mere happenstance. This notion of statistical decision theory has been applied by Finkelstein (1966) to the problem of jury discrimination. He suggests that the principle in *Swain* and related cases is the intuitive equivalent of ideas used in probability theory.

His thesis is that the likelihood of discrimination in jury selection can be inferred on the basis of a binomial probability distribution model, because the process of selecting venire persons is equivalent to a series of Bernoulli trials. In probability theory, the repeated tossing of a coin is an instance of a series of Bernoulli trials because there are only two possible outcomes for each toss or trial (heads or tails), the probabilities for each outcome are constant throughout all the tossings (always .5 for heads or tails), and the tosses are independent of each other in the sense that the outcome of one toss does not affect another one. Likewise, when venirepersons are selected, there are two possible racial results, the likelihood of a black or white person is constant, and each selection is independent of others.

A binomial distribution, then, is one in which the observed events can have only two outcomes or values, and it can be applied to compute the likelihood that certain observations would occur by chance. Given 25% (rounded off from 26%) adult male blacks in the population, and the drawing of thirty venires between 1955 and 1962 composed of five or fewer blacks (b) in each venire, the probability of obtaining by chance this result of five or fewer blacks is, according to Finkelstein's application of the binomial formula, as follows:

$$P\,(b \le 5) = \sum_{b=0}^{b=5} \binom{30}{b} (1/4)^b (3/4)^{30-b}$$
$$= .20260.$$

(One could also simply use a table of binomial probabilities, such as is found in the appendix of some statistics books, to establish the probability of the event's occurrence.) On the average, one venire in five would have five or fewer blacks solely by chance. In *Swain*, however, this result occurred not just once, but thirty consecutive times from 1955 to 1962. Applying the product rule of probability (the probability of the joint occurrence of independent events is equal to the product of their respective individual probabilities), the likelihood of this result is .20 to the thirtieth power. This means that "only one in more than one hundred million trillion groups each containing thirty venires would consist solely of venires which were not more than 15% Negro" (Finkelstein 1966, p. 357). Since this likelihood is less than the .05 criterion usually accepted in social research for statistical significance, the conclusion is that nonrandomness (that is, discriminatory purpose) operated in the selection process.

In sum, Justice White compared the eligible population with the observed venire. Finkelstein suggests that the observed results should be compared with the expected venire based on change. The two comparisons are diagrammed on page 363.

Does the application of statistical decision theory here imply that judicial decisions regarding discrimination can be the result of mathematical proof? Do you agree that a prima facie case of intentional discrimination can be equated with improbable selection outcomes? What more proof, other than probability figures, might a court require before finding there is purposeful discrimination, and why?

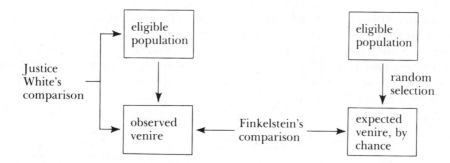

Post-Swain Underrepresentation Cases

Supreme Court cases after *Swain* have grappled with the problem of whether more than only statistical discrepancy is needed to establish purposeful discrimination.

In *Whitus* v. *Georgia* (1967), blacks constituted 27.1% of the taxpayers (statutory qualification for jury service) in the county but only 7.8% were represented in the petit jury venire. "While unnecessary to our disposition of the instant case, it is interesting to note the 'probability' involved in the situation before the Court. . . . Assuming that 27% of the list was made up of the names of qualified Negroes, the mathematical probability of having seven Negroes [that is, 7.8%] on a venire of 90 is .000006" (fn. 2, p. 552). The Court thus took notice of the large statistical disparity but yet found it "unnecessary" for striking down the selection process. This was because the Tax Digest from which the names were culled was itself a segregated system. An identification code was placed beside the names of taxpayers who were black so that the jury commissioners were aware of the race of those called for jury service.

In *Alexander* v. *Louisiana* (1972), the jury commissioners compiled a list from nonracial sources and sent out information questionnaires for grand jury service. The questionnaire included a space for racial designation. Blacks constituted 21% of the local population presumptively eligible for service. About 14% of the questionnaires returned were from blacks. By means of two culling-out procedures, when racial identifications were plainly visible, the pool was reduced to only 7% blacks. After another screening procedure, the grand jury venire was drawn and the percentage of blacks dropped to 5%. The commissioners testified that race was not a consideration. The Court found that "the progressive decimation of potential Negro grand jurors is indeed striking here, but we do not rest our conclusion that petitioner has demonstrated a prima facie case of invidious racial discrimination on statistical improbability alone, for the selection procedures themselves were not racially neutral" (p. 630).

Swain (which has not been overruled) and its progeny suggest two elements for a prima facie case of purposeful discrimination. One is the extent of statistical disparity between the proportion of eligible minority members in the population and in the venire. This disparity may be small (equal to or less than 11% to 16%, the cutoff point established in *Swain*), or large (greater than 11% to 16%), or such as to constitute total exclusion rather than just underrepresentation. The second element is procedural discrepancy. It may be small (for example, a subjective though facially neutral selection procedure such as the key man system) or large (for example, racially based selection procedures, as in *Whitus*, or neutral procedures which are clearly applied in a discriminatory fashion). These deviations, of course, are relative and the dichotomy serves only as a rough classification. The result is the accompanying table:

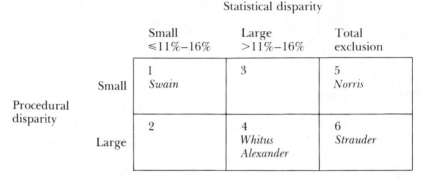

Statistical disparity

		Small ≤11%–16%	Large >11%–16%	Total exclusion
Procedural disparity	Small	1 *Swain*	3	5 *Norris*
	Large	2	4 *Whitus* *Alexander*	6 *Strauder*

Cells 5 and 6 represent obvious cases: If there is total exclusion, there is purposeful discrimination regardless of the propriety of the procedure itself. That is, when a facially neutral procedure results in no minorities at all in the venire, despite their eligible numbers in the population, there is almost an irrebuttable presumption of discriminatory design.

Cell 1 represents the facts of the *Swain* case. The statistical disparity was small and so was the procedural disparity ("somewhat haphazard" process); there was no prima facie case of discrimination.

Cell 4 includes the *Whitus* and *Alexander* cases. The selection methods were clearly opprobrious and the underrepresentation was larger than that tolerated by *Swain*.

Following the reasoning of *Whitus* and *Alexander*, what should be the result in cases which fall in cell 2?

What should be the result in cases which fall in cell 3?

7.3. LEGAL AND STATISTICAL PROOF OF DISCRIMINATION

Proof in Jury Cases

CASTANEDA v. PARTIDA

430 U.S. 482 (1977)

Mr. Justice BLACKMUN delivered the opinion of the Court.

The sole issue presented in this case is whether the State of Texas, in the person of petitioner, the Sheriff of Hidalgo County, successfully rebutted respondent prisoner's prima facie showing of discrimination against Mexican-Americans in the state grand jury selection process. . . .

II.

Respondent, Rodrigo Partida, was indicted in March 1972 by the grand jury of the 92d District Court of Hidalgo County for the crime of burglary of a private residence at night with intent to rape. Hidalgo is one of the border counties of southern Texas. After a trial before a petit jury, respondent was convicted and sentenced to eight years in the custody of the Texas Department of Corrections. He first raised his claim of discrimination in the grand jury selection process on a motion for new trial in the State District Court. In support of his motion, respondent testified about the general existence of discrimination against Mexican-Americans in that area of Texas and introduced statistics from the 1970 census and the Hidalgo County grand jury records. The census figures show that . . . 79.1% of the county's population was Mexican-American.

Respondent's data compiled from the Hidalgo County grand jury records from 1962 to 1972 showed that over that period, the average percentage of Spanish-surnamed grand jurors was 39%. . . . On the list from which the grand jury that indicted respondent was selected, 50% were Spanish-surnamed. The last set of data that respondent introduced, again from the 1970 census, illustrated a number of ways in which Mexican-Americans tend to be underprivileged, including poverty-level incomes, less desirable jobs, substandard housing, and lower levels of education.[8] The State offered no evidence at all

either attacking respondent's allegations of discrimination or demonstrating that his statistics were unreliable in any way.

III.

. . . Thus, in order to show that an equal protection violation has occurred in the context of grand jury selection, the defendant must show that the procedure employed resulted in substantial underrepresentation of his race or of the identifiable group to which he belongs. The first step is to establish that the group is one that is a recognizable, distinct class, singled out for different treatment under the laws, as written or as applied. Next, the degree of underrepresentation must be proved, by

---

[8]At oral argument, counsel for petitioner suggested that the data regarding educational background explained the discrepancy between the percentage of Mexican-Americans in the total population and the percentage on the grand jury lists. For a variety of reasons, we cannot accept that suggestion. . . .

[T]he data are incomplete in some places. . . . The census reports for educational background cover only those who are 25 years of age and above. Yet the only age limitation on eligibility for grand jury service

is qualification to vote. During the period to which the census figures apply, a person became qualified to vote at age 21. . . .

[E]ven assuming that the statistics for persons age 25 and over are sufficiently representative to be useful, a significant discrepancy still exists between the number of Spanish-surnamed people and the level of representation on grand jury lists. . . . [The Court noted that 22.9% of Spanish-surnamed persons aged 25 and over had *no* schooling, according to the 1970 census. Of all persons in this age group who *had* some schooling, the same census results showed that 65% were Spanish-surnamed and 35% were non-Spanish-surnamed. Ed.'s note.] The 65% figure still creates a significant disparity when compared to the 39% representation on grand juries shown over the 11-year period involved here.

The suggestion is made in the dissenting opinion of The Chief Justice that reliance on eligible population figures and allowance for literacy would defeat respondent's prima facie showing of discrimination. But the 65% to 39% disparity between Mexican-Americans *over* the age of 25 who have some schooling and Mexican-Americans represented on the grand jury venires takes both of The Chief Justice's concerns into account. Statistical analysis indicates that the discrepancy is significant. If one assumes that Mexican-Americans constitute only 65% of the jury pool, then a detailed calculation reveals that the likelihood that so substantial a discrepancy would occur by chance is less than 1 in 10^{50}.

We prefer not to rely on the 65% to 39% disparity, however, . . . [because] the record does not show any way by which the educational characteristics are taken into account in the compilation of the grand jury lists. . . .

comparing the proportion of the group in the total population to the proportion called to serve as grand jurors, over a significant period of time. This method of proof, sometimes called the "rule of exclusion," has been held to be available as a method of proving discrimination in jury selection against a delineated class. Finally, as noted above, a selection procedure that is susceptible of abuse or is not racially neutral supports the presumption of discrimination raised by the statistical showing. . . .

B. In this case, it is no longer open to dispute that Mexican-Americans are a clearly identifiable class. The statistics introduced by respondent from the 1970 census illustrate disadvantages to which the group has been subject. . . .

The disparity proved by the 1970 census statistics showed that the population of the county was 79.1% Mexican-American, but that, over an 11-year period, only 39% of the persons summoned for grand jury service were Mexican-American. This difference of 40% is greater than that found significant in *Turner v. Fouche*, 396 U.S. 346 (1970) (60% Negroes in the general population, 37% on the grand jury lists). Since the State presented no evidence showing why the 11-year period was not reliable, we take it as the relevant base for comparison. The mathematical disparities that have been accepted by this Court as adequate for a prima facie case have all been within the range presented here. . . . We agree with the District Court and the Court of Appeals that the proof in this case was enough to establish a prima facie case of discrimination against the Mexican-Americans in the Hidalgo County grand jury selection.[17]

Supporting this conclusion is the fact that the Texas system of selecting grand jurors is highly subjective. The facial constitutionality of the key-man system, of course, has been accepted by this Court. Nevertheless, the Court has noted that the system is susceptible of abuse as applied. Additionally, as noted, persons with Spanish surnames are readily identifiable.

The showing made by respondent therefore shifted the burden of proof to the State to dispel the inference of intentional discrimination. Inexplicably, the State introduced practically no evidence. . . . The commissioners themselves were not called to testify. . . . Without some testimony from the grand jury commissioners . . . it is impossible to draw any inference about literacy, sound mind and moral character, and criminal record from the statistics about the population as a whole. . . .

---

[17]If the jurors were drawn randomly from the general population, then the number of Mexican-Americans in the sample could be modeled by a binomial distribution. See Finkelstein, The Application of

Statistical Decision Theory to the Jury Discrimination Cases, 80 Harv. L. Rev. 338, 353-356 (1966). . . . Given that 79.1% of the population is Mexican-American, the expected number of Mexican-Americans among the 870 persons summoned to serve as grand jurors over the 11-year period is approximately 688. The observed number is 339. Of course, in any given drawing some fluctuation from the expected number is predicted. The important point, however, is that the statistical model shows that the results of a random drawing are likely to fall in the vicinity of the expected value. The measure of the predicted fluctuations from the expected value is the standard deviation, defined for the binomial distribution as the square root of the product of the total number in the sample (here 870) times the probability of selecting a Mexican-American (0.791) times the probability of selecting a non–Mexican-American (0.209). Thus, in this case the standard deviation is approximately 12. As a general rule for such large samples, if the difference between the expected value and the observed number is greater than two or three standard deviations, then the hypothesis that the jury drawing was random would be suspect to a social scientist. The 11-year data here reflect a difference between the expected and observed number of Mexican-Americans of approximately 29 standard deviations. A detailed calculation reveals that the likelihood that such a substantial departure from the expected value would occur by chance is less than 1 in 10^{140}

C. In light of our holding that respondent proved a prima facie case of discrimination that was not rebutted by any of the evidence presently in the record, we have only to consider whether the District Court's "governing majority" theory filled the evidentiary gap. In our view, it did not dispel the presumption of purposeful discrimination in the circumstances of this case. Because of the many facets of human motivation, it would be unwise to presume as a matter of law that human beings of one definable group will not discriminate against other members of their group. . . .

Furthermore, the relevance of a governing majority of elected officials to the grand jury selection process is questionable. The fact that certain elected officials are Mexican-American demonstrates nothing about the motivations and methods of the grand jury commissioners who select persons for grand jury lists. The only arguably relevant fact in this record on the issue is that three of the five jury commissioners in respondent's case were Mexican-American. Knowing only this, we would be forced to rely on the reasoning that we have rejected—that human beings would not discriminate against their own kind—in order to find that the presumption of purposeful discrimination was rebutted. Without the benefit of this simple behavioral presumption, discriminatory intent can be rebutted only with evidence in the record about the way in which the commissioners operated and their reasons for doing so. It was the State's burden to supply such evidence, once respondent established his prima facie case. The State's failure in this regard leaves unchallenged respondent's proof of purposeful discrimination. . . .

IV.

Rather than relying on an approach to the jury discrimination question that is as faintly defined as the "governing major-

ity" theory is on this record, we prefer to look at all the facts that bear on the issue, such as the statistical disparities, the method of selection, and any other relevant testimony as to the manner in which the selection process was implemented. Under this standard, the proof offered by respondent was sufficient to demonstrate a prima facie case of discrimination in grand jury selection. Since the State failed to rebut the presumption of purposeful discrimination by competent testimony, despite two opportunities to do so, we affirm the Court of Appeals' holding of a denial of equal protection of the law in the grand jury selection process in respondent's case.

It is so ordered.

. . .

Mr. Chief Justice BURGER, with whom Mr. Justice POWELL and Mr. Justice REHNQUIST join, dissenting.

. . . What the majority characterizes as a prima facie case of discrimination simply will not "wash." The decisions of this Court suggest, and common sense demands, that *eligible* population statistics, not gross population figures, provide the relevant starting point. . . .

The failure to produce evidence relating to the eligible population in Hidalgo County undermines respondent's claim that any statistical "disparity" existed in the first instance. . . . After all, the presumption of constitutionality attaching to all state procedures has even greater force under the circumstances presented here, where exactly one-half the members of the grand jury list now challenged by respondent were members of the allegedly excluded class of Mexican-Americans. . . .

The statistics relied on in the Court's opinion suggest that 22.9% of Spanish-surnamed persons over age 25 in Hidalgo County have had no schooling at all. Since one requirement of grand jurors in Texas is literacy in the English language, approximately 20% of adult-age

Mexican-Americans are very likely disqualified on that ground alone.

The Court's reliance on respondent's overbroad statistics is not the sole defect. As previously noted, one-half of the members of respondent's grand jury list bore Mexican-American surnames. . . . Since respondent was indicted in 1972, by what appears to have been a truly representative grand jury, the mechanical use of

Hidalgo County's practices some 10 years earlier seems to me entirely indefensible. We do not know, and on this record we cannot know, whether respondent's 1970 gross population figures, which served as the basis for establishing the "disparity" complained of in this case, had any applicability at all to the period prior to 1970. . . .

NOTES AND QUESTIONS

---

1.   In terms of the earlier matrix defining invidious discrimination founded on statistical and/or procedural disparity, in which cell would *Castaneda* be located?

2.   The Court noted, "Inexplicably, the state introduced practically no evidence." What demographic, statistical, and social science information would you recommend that the state present in order to rebut the presumption of unconstitutionality? The dissenting opinion by Justice Powell (not reproduced here), joined by the Chief Justice and Justice Rehnquist, indicated that "one may agree that the disproportion did not occur by chance without agreeing that it resulted from purposeful invidious discrimination" (p. 508). Thus, even if the state should concede that the underrepresentation of Mexican-Americans was highly improbable, it could still prevail by explaining the causes of the underrepresentation. What are some possible neutral causes?

Recall that in *Maxwell* v. *Bishop*, Judge Blackmun also noted that "The State offered no evidence" (Chapter 5, section 5.2). In both southern and northern school desegregation cases, the school boards seldom rest their defense on empirical research evidence. What factors are common to claimed racial discrimination in jury selection, capital sentencing, and school enrollments, so that plaintiffs are more likely to use social science evidence than defendants?

3.   The lower court and Justice Powell in his dissent filled the evidentiary gap with a so-called governing majority theory. They assumed that all Mexican-Americans—indeed, that members of all minority groups—have an "inclination to assure fairness" to other members of their group (p. 516). Justice Marshall felt compelled to write a concurring opinion in order to express his "profound disagreement" with the above view:

> In the first place, Mr. Justice POWELL's assumptions about human nature, plausible as they may sound, fly in the face of a great deal of social science theory and research. Social scientists agree that members of minority groups frequently respond to discrimination and prejudice by attempting to disassociate themselves from the group, even to the point of adopting the majority's negative attitudes towards the minority. Such behavior occurs with particular frequency among members of minority groups who have achieved some measure of economic or political success and thereby have gained some acceptability among the dominant group. [p. 503]

What available research and theory in the social psychology of intergroup relations supports Justice Marshall's position? And Justice Powell's position? In either event, should scientific generalizations about behavior be made the foundation for a constitutional ruling in this case? That is, how central to the legal issue of purposeful discrimination is the factual question of how "top dogs" treat "underdogs" of the same ethnic background within a given community?

4.   Footnote 17 appears steeped in statistical arcana. Actually, the statistical test that Justice Blackmun uses to determine whether the disproportionately small number of Chicanos in the venires was large enough to constitute prima facie evidence of invidious selection—namely, the standard deviation—is "probably the single most important statistical concept used in legal cases" (Barnes 1983, p. 75). It is a key element in quantitative proof in discrimination litigation. It provides a standardized criterion for judging the extent of variation (deviation) of observed outcomes from expected (chance) outcomes. Justice Blackmun applies the binomial distribution (a distribution of randomly drawn events that have only two possible outcomes, such as a white juror or nonwhite juror) as a means for computing the standard deviation. The formula for the standard deviation of events with a binomial distribution is the square root of the (a) size of the sample under consideration (870 persons summoned for grand jury duty), (b) multiplied by the expected value of one of the outcomes (the expected number of Chicanos in the venire, which mirrors their number in the population, or 79.1%), and (c) multiplied by the expected value of the second outcome (the expected number of non-Chicanos in the venire, which is also equal to their percentage in the population, or 20.9%).

Using these figures, the standard deviation is 12—that is, one standard deviation in *Castaneda* is equal to 12 jurors. The difference between the expected number of Chicano grand jurors (688, or 79.1%) and the observed outcome (339, or 39%) is 349—there are 349 fewer Chicanos on the venire than expected by chance. To judge how large this difference is, the underrepresentation of 349 persons is divided by the 12 people in one standard deviation, which equals 29. This means that the difference (349) is 29 standard deviations below what is expected by chance. In the social sciences, Justice Blackmun says, a difference between the observed and expected outcomes of "greater than two or three standard deviations . . . would be suspect." In this case, since 29 is so much greater than 2 or 3, he concludes that the underrepresentation of Chicanos is constitutionally impermissible.

The social science criterion he employed is defined by reference to the normal distribution curve (a symmetrical, bell-shaped graph where the variable of interest, for example, the number of Chicano jurors in the venire, is plotted on the abscissa, and the frequency of occurrence of this variable is plotted on the ordinate). The mean or average value on this curve is 688 Chicano jurors. That is, if one were to draw—randomly and repeatedly—samples of 870 venirepersons from a population containing 79.1% Chicanos, on the average each of these samples will have 688 Chicanos. Some samples may have more and some may have less (because of random fluctuations or sampling error in the drawing process), but most samples should have a number close to 688. When the disparity between the number actually selected and the number expected is measured in units of standard deviations, one can determine the probability of the observed disparity occurring by chance. Here, one standard deviation represents 12 jurors. One standard deviation above the expected value is $688 + 12 = 700$ jurors, and one standard deviation below is $688 - 12 = 676$ jurors; two standard deviations above or below the expected value equal 688 ± 24; and three standard deviations above or below the expected outcome equal 688 ± 36.

When a sample is thought to be normally distributed around the mean or expected value, 68.26% of the observed outcomes will be within one standard deviation above or below the expected outcome, 95.44% will be within two standard deviations of the expected value, and 99.74% will be within three standard deviations. Virtually all of the observed outcomes (99.99%) will be within four standard deviations. A criterion of "greater than two . . . standard deviations" signifies that only 5% (rounded off from .0456) of the randomly drawn venire samples of size 870 will be more than two standard deviations from the expected number—that is, only one out of twenty samples will have more than 712 Chicanos or fewer than 664. In this case, the underrepresentation of 349 Chicano jurors is a whopping 29 standard deviations from 688. The likelihood of such an extreme variation arising by reason of chance alone is 1 in 10^{140}.

When the observed difference is so large, the Court says, "then the hypothesis that the jury drawing was random would be suspect." This "hypothesis," known as the "null hypothesis," is the initial assumption that jury selection is race-neutral. The "alternative hypothesis" is that purposeful design rather than randomness lies behind the selection process. This assumption of randomness is akin to the presumption of innocence in criminal cases and the presumption of statutory validity in constitutional litigation. Statisticians, like fact-finders, are subject to two possible types of error in making decisions. "Type 1 error" is a decision that wrongly rejects the null hypothesis. It occurs when one concludes that the null hypothesis is false (for example, that the selection is not random or that the criminal defendant is not innocent) when, in fact, it is true. "Type 2 error" is the failure to reject the null hypothesis (for example, concluding that the selection is random or that the defendant is innocent) when it is false. The law has always worried more about fact-finders committing a Type 1 error than a Type 2 error. The standard of proof beyond a reasonable doubt, for example, implies that the law is more willing to risk setting free some guilty defendants than to risk convicting innocent ones. The same is true in scientific research. The greater error is to wrongfully add to the store of knowledge by claiming that there is an effect or relationship when none exists (the sin of commission) than to fail to discover this effect (the sin of omission).

The probability value of .05 adopted by Justice Blackmun (that is, the likelihood of "greater than two . . . standard deviations") is an arbitrary but generally accepted cutoff point in social research for deciding whether an observed result is due to something other than sampling error. It is known as the level of (statistical) significance. Researchers reject the null hypothesis when an observed outcome occurs less often than an agreed upon significance level, which is usually .05. It represents the level of confidence that must be met to reject the null hypothesis. It is the probability of making a Type 1 error. Statistical tests of significance, such as that used in *Castaneda*, calculate the probability that an observed result is due to chance occurrence and if that probability is equal to or less than .05, the null hypothesis is rejected.

Here, the probability of an underrepresentation of 349 Chicanos as a result of random selection is 1 in 10^{140}, quite a bit less than the .05 level. Thus, one can infer that something other than chance is going on in the summoning of venirepersons in Hidalgo County. For Justice Blackmun, the process appears "suspect"—there is, here, the smell of the rodent.

5.   Does the fact that an observed value will occur at random only once in twenty mean that there is a 95% chance that it was the product of deliberate action? The requirement of invidious purpose for an equal protection violation implies showing a causal connection between the observed results and the challenged procedure. Does statistical inference—the process of saying something about an entire population based upon limited information from a sample—supply the causal link?

6.   The decision of the Court appears to turn on the result of the statistical test. This result, of course, depends on the numbers that are plugged into the formula. Chief Justice Burger vigorously objected to the figures used by Justice Blackmun. Whose numbers are more convincing? Do you agree with the dissent that reliance on data of the previous ten years is "entirely indefensible"? Is there a single "correct" set of figures to use in the arithmetic? Compute the deviation of observed outcomes from expected outcomes using the figures of the dissent, or other (given or estimated) figures that are most favorable to the State of Texas—does it exceed the "two or three standard deviations" test of the Court? Clearly, quantification does not replace advocacy in proof of discrimination.

7.   The underrepresentation of women on jury panels has been decided on Sixth Amendment rather than equal protection grounds. In *Duren* v. *Missouri* (1979), a male defendant convicted of murder appealed on the basis that women, who composed 54% of the eligible population in the jurisdiction, were systematically excluded because of a state law that provided exemptions from jury duty upon request for women (but not for men), resulting in jury venires that averaged only 14.5% women. The Court held that such exemptions "result[ing] in jury venires averaging less than 15% female" violated the Sixth Amendment right to an impartial jury selected from a fair cross section of the population. Statistical disparity alone—without proof of purposeful discrimination, as is required under Fourteenth Amendment analysis—was ruled sufficient to establish a prima facie violation of the cross-section principle. Missouri failed to advance a "significant state interest" to justify the exemption of women, so the jury selection procedure was declared unconstitutional.

The Court examined the absolute disparity between the percentage of adult women in the country and their percentage in the venires. It did not define the minimum disparity needed for a prima facie violation, and it did not analyze the disparity in terms of standard deviations as in *Castaneda*. Large absolute disparities such as those present in *Castaneda* (40%) and *Duren* (39.5%) are unlikely to pass muster under the standard deviation analysis.

However, the *Duren* test and the *Castaneda* test may not necessarily yield the same result when the percentage-points difference is less striking. Lower courts, for example, have found no Sixth Amendment violation when the absolute disparity between the percentage of a distinctive group in the population and the percentage of that group in the venire is less than 10% (*United States* v. *Maskeny*, 1980). Barnes (1983) points out that "a disparity too small to be significant in absolute terms may rise to significance under the [*Castaneda* criterion]" (p. 128). To illustrate, given an absolute deviation of 10% (12% minorities in the eligible population and 2% in the venire) and a venire size of 30, the disparity is

1.69 standard deviations below chance expectation. However, given the same 10% disparity but a venire size of 300, the disparity is 5.33 standard deviations. Thus, the standard deviations increase as the venire increases even though the 10% difference is constant, because the standard deviation formula takes into account group size and the simple subtraction of percentages does not. In other words, as the venire size expands, there is a lower probability of finding no minorities in the venire. The courts have been unwilling to say that the *Castaneda* analysis is the only accepted approach or even the preferred one.

PEOPLE v. POWELL
40 Cal. App. 3d 107 (1974)

[Defendants Powell and Smith were convicted of first-degree murder in Los Angeles County Superior Court and their appeals were consolidated. One of the issues on appeal was whether minority and lower social-economic groups were improperly underrepresented in the jury venire. This portion of the opinion by J. Vogel, is reproduced. Ed.'s note.]

VALIDITY OF SELECTION
PROCEDURE

. . .

It is important to understand that appellants' primary assault was based upon an attempted showing that the actual number of persons selected for jury service from designated areas was so disproportionate to the expected probable draws that the burden of proving the legality of the venire shifted to the People. The demonstration was premised on the application of a statistical formula designated Chi square. This technique was employed to show whether or not a segment of the community had been chosen for jury service in numbers consistent with a random selection from the general population. In this case, appellants employed the Chi square formula in an effort to show that there was an improbable disparity between the number of certain minorities actually selected for jury service and their numbers in the general population for designated districts. Appellants contend that such disparity implies that a random selection of the jury venire was unlikely.

The evidence offered in support of the motion was profuse, redundant and frequently recondite. It required nearly six months for its production. No useful purpose would be served in making a detailed exposition of this evidence in this opinion. Therefore only pertinent parts will be set forth.

In response to the motion, the People produced evidence outlining the method by which the jury venires were and had been selected in Los Angeles County for the time periods in question. This evidence served as a useful backdrop to an understanding of the issue. . . .

[It is the Jury Commissioner's] responsibility to provide residents of the County to serve as jurors in cases conducted by the Superior Court. . . .

In making the selection from the Register of Voters the Jury Commissioner used a key number system, selecting prospective jurors from every sixth precinct and having the Registrar of Voters draw every fifth name from each of the designated precincts. . . .

This process results in two venires per calendar year. . . .

The Jury Commissioner called for a list of prospective jurors ten times greater than that needed. This was done in anticipation that for every registered voter that qualified, nine would either not respond, be excused or not qualify. For each of the 1968 venires the Jury Commissioner expected to need 8,000 qualified jurors. Therefore, he asked that the Registrar of Voters provide him with approximately 80,000 names. . . .

We emphasize that the first step in the selection process is the random withdrawal of names from the list of those who have registered to vote within the County. This approach is unassailable. . . .

The Register of Voters probably constitutes the most pervasive listing of qualified citizens from both sexes, all races and all walks of life that is readily available to the government for its jury selection. . . . Therefore, appellants are prima facie confronted with a jury venire for Los Angeles County, apparently selected at random and in accordance with judicially approved methods. The burden then fell on them to prove that the procedures followed operated systematically to exclude identifiable segments of the community resulting in a venire that did not fairly reflect a cross section of the community.

In this case appellants asked that certain comparisons be made of the results of this selection process in four areas selected by appellants. . . . The Watts and Avalon Districts were selected because they are predominantly populated by members of the black community; the Boyle Heights District was selected because of the fact that it is heavily populated by persons with Spanish surnames; and the Mulholland District was an arbitrary designation of an area that is purported to be populated predominantly by "Caucasians." . . .

In support of the motion appellants called Nancy Ward for the purpose of offering certain demographic information. She was the research director of the Los Angeles County Human Relations Commission. . . . Based on a variety of computations and formulations, Ward made certain estimates and projections as to the adult population for the designated areas within Los Angeles County and the County as a whole. These estimates and projections purported to produce population information covering the period for the jury selection. . . .

Ward used the confidential statistics of the County Mental Health Department to determine what percentage of the population within each district was adult. . . . The most basic deficiency in her computations and projections is her total disregard of whether the adults in the sample districts were registered voters. Because the Register of Voters was the exclusive source for the selection of jury venires—other than the rare nomination by a judge of the court—it was only the registered adult population to which she should have referred for comparison purposes. Thus, her estimates concerning the populations, prospective jury lists and approved jury lists were calculated with reference to a general adult population. . . .*

Ultimately, appellants demonstrated that the number of qualified jurors selected for the period in question was less than the number estimated by Ward with respect to Avalon, Boyle Heights and Watts. By this demonstration as will be more expansively discussed, appellants attempted to prove through statistical calculation that the probability of disparity was so great that it must be presumed to be the result of a systematic exclusion of members of the minority community. . . .

---

*[Ward estimated (1) the total adult population, (2) the black adult population, (3) the "prospective juror list" (minorities and nonminorities), (4) the "prospective juror list" (minorities only), (5) the "approved juror list" (minorities and nonminorities), and (6) the "approved juror list" (minorities only) for each of the four districts as follows (the figures pertain to the 1968 venire in question):

Avalon: (1) 25,200, (2) 24,100, (3) 493, (4) 468, (5) 37, (6) 35. Boyle Heights: (1) 46,000, (2) 29,900, (3) 901, (4) 568, (5) 68, (6) 44. Mulholland: (1) 29,900, (2) —, (3) 509, (4) —, (5) 40, (6) —. Watts: (1) 12,200, (2) 10,700, (3) 238, (4) 218, (5) 18, (6) 16.

The procedure by which these estimates were derived was not described in the opinion. Although these expected figures are divided by minority and nonminority categories, no similar racial breakdown was given for the data on the observed number of jurors (presented later in the text of the opinion). Ed.'s note.]

Appellants also called Dr. Wayne Zimmerman to apply the projections of Ward concerning jury selection and composition. He used Ward's estimated projections as a part of the statistical analysis about which he testified. Zimmerman holds a Ph.D. in psychology with a major in psychometrics. . . .

Zimmerman was cognizant of the actual number of prospective jurors that qualified for the [1968] jury venire. He used this as one factor in an equation for the purpose of attempting to demonstrate that the numbers of prospective jurors that qualified from Avalon, Boyle Heights and Watts were numerically deficient. The witness employed the Chi square formula. As mentioned, the formula required two factors for its computation: the observed number of jurors that qualified and the estimated number of jurors that would be expected to qualify as jurors within the designated districts. Zimmerman used the computed conclusions of Ward for the second factor, the expected number of qualified jurors.

In essence, the witness made these computations to produce a Chi square number which could then be referred to a standard table of Chi square values indicating a numerical probability for measuring the degree of expectancy for the actual number of approved jurors. . . . According to Zimmerman the probability of the observed number of prospective jurors that qualified and were selected from each of the designated districts is demonstrated as follows:

District	Observed Selected Jurors	Probability of Occurrence
Avalon	25	.05
Boyle Heights	37	.0003 or .0004
Mulholland	43	.6
Watts	11	.1

Quite obviously appellants are attempting to fashion their argument after the opinion of the United States Supreme Court in Whitus v. Georgia (1967), 385 U.S. 545. . . . The judicial system should pay attention to evidence that shows an apparent and meaningful disparity between the presence of identifiable segments of the community—racial, economic, ethnic— and their absence from the jury venires. From demonstrated improbabilities courts may infer that the selection system is purposefully or systematically excluding certain segments of the community. . . .

The problem is that appellants employed a spurious factor in arriving at this Chi square number. Specifically, Ward's estimates were "soft" since they were arrived at without reference to the registered voter population and were otherwise largely speculative. The trial court was not required to accept these statistical conclusions unless it was persuaded that they were founded on substantially reliable data. . . .

NOTES AND QUESTIONS

1.   There is a major difference in the procedure of jury selection in *Powell* and in the cases from *Swain* to *Castaneda*. In *Powell*, the venire was drawn from voter registration lists using a random process. In the preceding cases, all originating in southern states, the sources were other than voter lists (or voter lists in

combination with a variety of other sources) and the selection was by a nonrandom or discretionary process. A strong presumption of constitutionality attaches to random drawings from voter lists. In fact, in federal courts, "there is no case in which exclusive reliance on voter registration lists has been invalidated" (Gewin 1975, p. 817).

According to the court, the evidence was "profuse, redundant and frequently and recondite," and it required nearly six months to assemble. It is ironic, then, that the first expert witness for the defense should present a statistical analysis that was flawed in such an elementary fashion. Further, with respect to the second witness (the psychometrician), what evidence in addition to his Chi square analysis should have been presented?

2.   The Avalon and Watts districts are predominantly black. However, the same census map shows that there are several other districts in Los Angeles County which also have a large black population. The appellant never explained why these two mostly black districts were selected and not the others. What limitations are placed on the conclusions of the expert witnesses by selective sampling?

3.   The court, without much elaboration, relied on the Chi square formula to evaluate the null hypothesis that the selection process is race-neutral. The standard deviations approach compares the observed results (for example, number of minorities in venire) with the expected results (number based upon their proportion in the relevant population). The Chi square test is somewhat similar. It compares the observed number with the expected number, but it does so for both categories (minorities and whites). The formula for the Chi square value is:

$$X^2 = \frac{(Om - Em)^2}{Em} + \frac{(Ow - Ew)^2}{Ew}.$$

where Om is the observed number of minorities, Em is the expected number of minorities, Ow is the observed number of whites, and so on. This test determines whether proportionately fewer minorities than whites are selected. An advantage of the Chi square test over the binomial formula for the standard deviation (applied in *Castaneda*) is that the former is suitable for the analysis of more than two categories (for example, comparing numbers of blacks, whites, Asians, and Chicanos in a venire) whereas the latter is limited to a distribution of events with only two outcomes (for example, comparing whites and minorities).

To illustrate, here is an hypothetical example (with only two categories). Suppose that minorities compose 8% of the population eligible for jury duty. The size of each venire is 200, and over the years, each of the venires has included 7 minority members. Since the expected number of minorities in each venire is 16 (8% of 200), how likely is the observed result due to chance occurrence? We apply the Chi square formula:

$$X^2 = \frac{(7 - 16)^2}{16} + \frac{(193 - 184)^2}{184} = 5.50.$$

The Chi square of 5.50 can be translated into a probability value that indicates the likelihood that the null hypothesis is true. By consulting a table of Chi square values (found in statistics texts), we find that the Chi square must equal (or exceed) 5.41 to be significant at the .02 level, and 6.64 to be significant at the .01 level, given one degree of freedom. (Degrees of freedom refers to the number of categories that can be freely chosen mathematically. In general, it is equal to the number of categories minus one—in this example, $2 - 1 = 1$. That is, once the numbers in one category—for example, seven minorities—are determined, the numbers in the other category—$200 - 7 = 193$ whites—are fixed. Given two categories, we have freedom to choose the numbers in one category only—hence one degree of freedom.) In this case, the probability of a Type 1 error is between 2% and 1% if the null hypothesis is rejected. It is unlikely, therefore, that so few minorities were selected merely by coincidence.

4.   Apply the binomial formula for the standard deviation to the foregoing hypothetical. How many standard deviations is the selected number of minority venirepersons (7) from the expected number (16)? Is that disparity suspect under *Castaneda*?

5.   Re-examine and critique the application of the Chi square test in *Powell*.

6.   In the southern jury discrimination cases, the courts have adopted a case-by-case approach to evaluate the alleged discrimination in each instance. They examine the specific procedures and particular circumstances of each case. In contrast, when random methods and voter lists are used, typical of northern jurisdictions, the courts feel less need for a particularized assessment of each case. The jury discrimination problem could be addressed on a systemic or per se basis rather than case-by-case. The courts could require the use of voter lists and random selection on the grounds that due process prohibits haphazard selection procedures as unfair. In *Taylor* v. *Louisiana* (1975), the Supreme Court rejected this per se approach. The administration of criminal justice has traditionally been a matter of local control, and the Court declined to fashion detailed jury selection codes for state courts since "the fair cross-section principle must have much leeway in application" (p. 530). Political considerations of federalism are at odds with statistical criteria of fairness.

7.   In jurisdictions where particular groups fail to register to vote and therefore are underrepresented in voter registration lists, the master jury wheel can be supplemented with names from other sources in an effort to cure the nonrepresentativeness. Assume that minorities compose 12.5% of the voting age population and 11% of the registered voters in a given jurisdiction. There are a total of half a million names on the voter registration list. Does this list underrepresent minorities so as to taint a jury selected therefrom?

Proof in Other Contexts

In 1897, Holmes foresaw that "for the rational study of law, the black-letter man may be the man of the present, but the man of the future is the man of statistics . . ." (p. 409). Today, "at least a rudimentary knowledge of statistical reasoning is essential if attorneys and judges are to function effectively in . . . litigation" (Kaye 1982, p. 837). Before the 1970s, no federal opinions discussed the statistical significance of data. By the early 1980s, in contrast, 130 cases did so (American Statistical Association 1983, p. 3).

In discrimination litigation, especially, inferential statistics is an accepted—if not always sufficient—method of proof. It provides an objective basis for drawing inferences from incomplete information. A statistician can assist a lawyer in drawing a random sample from the population in question, specify how large that sample must be to permit conclusions at a given level of confidence, analyze the sample data, quantify the uncertainties or error risks in deriving population estimates from the sample, and assess the statistical significance of observed differences obtained by sampling (Barnes 1983, p. 32; Curtis and Wilson 1979).

Quantitative analysis contributes to but does not replace legal analysis. Calculation of the standard deviation, for example, indicates the likelihood of observing very few minority venirepersons (relative to the proportion of minorities in the relevant population) if the selection process is random. However, the law must still define how large a disparity is sufficient to establish a prima facie case of illegality. The specification of the relevant population, which determines the figures to be used in the statistical computations, is also a threshold legal question. Thus, law defines the probative relevance of the numbers. Conard (1967) likens the role of statisticians in litigation to that of laboratory technicians in a hospital. They are called upon to perform quantitative analyses of various body fluids, but they are not in charge of diagnosis and treatment of the patient. The job of the attending physician is to know what fluids to analyze and, after the results come back, to understand what the quantities signify. The physician need not become a chemist or serologist, and the latter does not take over the physician's role. Similarly, lawyers define the legal questions that could be illuminated by statistical analysis. Merely thinking about a problem in quantitative terms can yield new insights. Baldus and Cole (1980) suggest that "over the long run, the intelligent use of statistics promises to increase the consistency of the decided cases, thereby adding coherence to the law of discrimination" (p. 5).

The problem of underrepresentation of distinctive groups is not limited, of course, to the area of jury venires. "Invisible race discrimination" (Wilkinson 1974, p. 134) can be found elsewhere in modern society: in employment, housing, voting, and public education, to name the most common areas of alleged discrimination. When procedures or actions which are facially neutral and rationally related to some permissible purpose result, nonetheless, in disproportionate racial impact, is there "invisible" discrimination with the neutral justifications serving as racial surrogates, or is the outcome the product of genuinely unbiased decision-making? This section presents cases involving employment discrimination for the purpose of illustrating the application to this area of the statistical tests used in jury discrimination. The quantitative analysis of the likelihood of underrepresentation is the same whether it occurs in the judicial system or in the marketplace, although the legal standards for inferring discrimination may differ depending on the context.

HAZELWOOD SCHOOL DISTRICT v. UNITED STATES

433 U.S. 299 (1977)

Mr. Justice STEWART delivered the opinion of the Court.

The petitioner Hazelwood School District covers 78 square miles in the northern part of St. Louis County, Mo. In 1973 the Attorney General brought this lawsuit against Hazelwood and various of its officials, alleging that they were engaged in a "pattern or practice" of employment discrimination in violation of Title VII of the Civil Rights Act of 1964. . . .

Hazelwood hired its first Negro teacher in 1969. The number of Negro faculty members gradually increased . . . [to] 22 of 1,231 in the 1973 school year. By comparison, according to 1970 census figures, of more than 19,000 teachers employed in that year in the St. Louis area, 15.4% were Negro. . . . Apart from that school district, 5.7% of the teachers in the county were Negro in 1970. . . .

The District Court ruled that the Government had failed to establish a pattern or practice of discrimination. . . . The statistics showing that relatively small num-bers of Negroes were employed as teachers were found nonprobative, on the ground that the percentage of Negro pupils in Hazelwood was similarly small [about 2%]. . . .

The Court of Appeals for the Eighth Circuit reversed. . . . [It] rejected the trial court's analysis of the statistical data as resting on an irrelevant comparison of Negro teachers to Negro pupils in Hazelwood. The proper comparison, in the appellate court's view, was one between Negro teachers in Hazelwood and Negro teachers in the relevant labor market area. Selecting St. Louis County and St. Louis City as the relevant area, the Court of Appeals compared the 1970 census figures, showing that 15.4% of teachers in that area were Negro, to the racial composition of Hazelwood's teaching staff. In the 1972–1973 and 1973–1974 school years, only 1.4% and 1.8%, respectively, of Hazelwood's teachers were Negroes. This statistical disparity, particularly when viewed against the background of the teacher-hiring procedures that Hazelwood had followed, was held to constitute a prima facie case of a pattern or practice of racial discrimination. . . .

This Court's recent consideration in *Teamsters v. United States,* 431 U.S. 324, of the role of statistics in pattern-or-practice suits under Title VII provides substantial guidance in evaluating the arguments advanced by the petitioners. In that case we stated that it is the Government's burden to "establish by a preponderance of the evidence that racial discrimination was the [employer's] standard operating procedure—the regular rather than the unusual practice." We also noted that . . . where gross statistical disparities can be shown, they alone may in a proper case constitute prima facie proof of a pattern or practice of discrimination.

There can be no doubt, in light of the *Teamsters* case, that the District Court's comparison of Hazelwood's teacher work force to its student population fundamentally misconceived the role of statistics in employment discrimination cases. The Court of Appeals was correct in the view that a proper comparison was between the racial composition of Hazelwood's teaching staff and the racial composition of the qualified public school teacher population in the relevant labor market. . . .

What the hiring figures prove obviously depends upon the figures to which they are compared. The Court of Appeals accepted the Government's argument that the relevant comparison was to the labor market area of St. Louis County and the city of St. Louis, in which, according to the 1970 census, 15.4% of all teachers were Negro. The propriety of that comparison was vigorously disputed by the petitioners, who urged that because the city of St. Louis has made special attempts to maintain a 50% Negro teaching staff, inclusion of that school district in the relevant market area distorts the comparison. Were that argument accepted, the percentage of Negro teachers in the relevant labor market area (St. Louis County alone) as shown in the 1970 census would be 5.7% rather than 15.4%.

The difference between these figures may well be important; the disparity between 3.7% (the percentage of Negro teachers hired by Hazelwood in 1972–1973 and 1973–1974) and 5.7% may be sufficiently small to weaken the Government's other proof, while the disparity between 3.7% and 15.4% may be sufficiently large to reinforce it.[17]

[A] determination of the appropriate comparative figures in this case will depend upon further evaluation by the trial court. . . . And only after such a determination is made can a foundation be established for deciding whether or not Hazelwood engaged in a pattern or practice of

---

[17]Indeed, under the statistical methodology explained in *Castaneda v. Partida,* involving the calculation of the standard deviation as a measure of predicted fluctuations, the difference between using 15.4% and 5.7% as the areawide figure would be significant. If the 15.4% figure is taken as the basis for comparison, the expected number of Negro teachers hired by Hazelwood in 1972–1973 would be 43 (rather than the actual figure of 10) of a total of 282, a difference of more than five standard deviations; the expected number in 1973–1974 would be 19 (rather than the actual figure of 5) of a total of 123, a difference of more than three standard deviations. For the two years combined, the difference between the observed number of 15 Negro teachers hired (of a total of 405) would vary from the expected number of 62 by more than six standard deviations. Because a fluctuation of more than two or three standard deviations would undercut the hypothesis that decisions were being made randomly with respect to race, each of these statistical comparisons would reinforce rather than rebut the Government's other proof. If, however, the 5.7% areawide figure is used, the expected number of Negro teachers hired in 1972–1973 would be roughly 16, less than two standard deviations from the observed number of 10; for 1973–1974, the expected value would be roughly seven, less than one standard deviation from the observed value of 5; and for the two years combined, the expected value of 23 would be less than two standard deviations from the observed total of 15. A more precise method of analyzing these statistics confirms the results of the standard deviation analysis. See F. Mosteller, R. Rourke, & G. Thomas, Probability with Statistical Applications 494 (2d ed. 1970).

These observations are not intended to suggest that precise calculations of statistical significance are necessary in employing statistical proof, but merely to highlight the importance of the choice of the relevant labor market area.

racial discrimination in its employment practices in violation of the law.

We . . . [remand] the case to the Dis-trict Court for further findings as to the relevant labor market area. . . .

It is so ordered.

NOTES AND QUESTIONS

---

1.   The Court dismissed as "misconceived" the curious reasoning of the trial court that the small numbers of black teachers were "nonprobative" (read: justified) because of the small numbers of black pupils in Hazelwood. However, the Court disagreed with the court of appeals on whether the relevant market included the city of St. Louis. On remand, what considerations should the trial court evaluate in determining the proper comparison figures?

2.   Footnote 17 applies the "greater than two or three standard deviations" rule of *Castaneda*. It is not the only means of testing the statistical significance of disparities, but it is an intuitively understandable procedure and therefore has been applied frequently since it received the Court's imprimatur (Baldus and Cole 1980, p. 295). For purposes of review, redo the *Hazelwood* calculations using the formula presented in *Castaneda*.

3.   The comparison according to the Court is between the percentage of black teachers hired by Hazelwood and the percentage of black teachers in St. Louis county (either with or without the city of St. Louis). However, not all black teachers may be interested or available to work in Hazelwood. What other kinds of data should a court examine besides hiring figures?

4.   The Court says that if the percentage of black teachers hired by Hazelwood (3.7%; actually, the correct sum is 3.2% = 1.4% + 1.8%) is compared with 5.7%, the disparity "may be sufficiently small to weaken the Government's" proof of discrimination. Alternately, "the disparity between 3.7% and 15.4% may be sufficiently large to reinforce it." Does statistical inference justify these suggestions about a causal link between numerical disparities and prohibited employment practices? Is rejection of the null hypothesis as a result of finding a statistically significant disparity equivalent to accepting the alternative hypothesis?

5.   In footnote 17 the Court adopts the .05 level of significance used in *Castaneda*. If the 5.7% figure is used, the likelihood of hiring so few black teachers in Hazelwood (15 in 1972–74) is greater than .05 (less than two standard deviations)—hence, the charge of discrimination in recruitment is "weaken[ed]." It is conventional in social research to adopt this probability value as the level of confidence for rejecting the null hypothesis. Researchers are reluctant to claim that they have discovered an effect or established a scientific relationship unless that result occurs by coincidence less than 5% of the time. However, are there any a priori reasons why the conventions of social science should be used in legal proof? After all, the standard of proof in civil litigation—a "preponderance of the evidence," generally understood to mean somewhat more than .50—is much lower. Indeed, should varying levels of statistical significance be adopted for legal proceedings depending upon the nature of the case? For example, should a less demanding level (say .10) be used in proof of racial discrimination in death penalty sentences (see *Maxwell* v. *Bishop*, Chapter 5) than in employment discrimination? Should the same level be used in jury discrimination and employment discrimination? See Kaye (1982, p. 840).

If the courts are not to follow mechanically the conventions of social science, on what bases are they to choose the appropriate level of significance? Should they evaluate the social costs of a Type 1 error in different kinds of cases? It is possible that different statistical tests of significance may yield different results even when applied to the same data. How is a court to decide which is the appropriate test to apply? Given these difficulties, should a court simply forget about statistical significance and rely on its own intuition (as in *Swain*) on whether an observed disparity indicates something more than mere coincidence? The *Hazelwood* Court itself said, at the end of the learned statistical footnote, that it had "not intended to suggest that precise calculations of statistical significance are necessary. . . ." For arguments against the use of statistical inference in legal proof, see Cohn (1980).

6.   The Court concluded that the number of blacks hired (15) during the two-year period deviated from the expected number (23) by less than two standard deviations, and the probability of this occurrence by chance was greater than .05. However, in a dissenting opinion (not reproduced above), Justice Stevens compared this disparity between 15 and 23 and wrote: "[O]ne of my law clerks advised me that given the size of the two-year sample, there is only about a 5% likelihood that a disparity this large would be produced by a random selection from the labor pool. . . . [H]is calculation was made using the method described in H. Blalock, *Social Statistics* 151–173 (1973) . . ." (p. 318, n. 5).

These conclusions appear inconsistent because the majority used a two-tailed test of statistical significance and the dissent used a one-tailed test. The probability of two standard deviations is .05 when there is no a priori reason to expect that the observed number (of blacks hired) will be greater or fewer than the expected number (based upon the proportion of blacks in the relevant labor market). A two-tailed test evaluates a deviation that can occur in either direction. A one-tailed test evaluates the likelihood due to chance alone of a deviation in only one direction, the anticipated direction. A deviation need not be as large to achieve the .05 level of significance under a one-tailed test as under a two-tailed test. Thus, in *Hazelwood*, Kaye (1982, p. 841) noted that 15 is 1.73 standard deviations from 23 using a one-tailed test, which corresponds to a significance level of .04. In basic social research, the more common approach is to use a two-tailed test. Do you agree that "the Court was simply mistaken in concluding that the .05 [level] was not satisfied by the statistical evidence . . ." (p. 841)?

GAY v. WAITERS' AND DAIRY LUNCHMEN'S UNION, LOCAL 30

489 F. Supp. 282 (N.D. Ca. 1980)

SCHWARZER, District Judge

This is an action for alleged discrimination by defendants in hiring, promoting and transferring black males into waiter positions. Plaintiffs sue on behalf of themselves and a class consisting of black males who were denied employment as waiters. The only defendants remaining in the case are The St. Francis Hotel Corporation ("St. Francis") and Hilton Hotels Corporation ("Hilton"). . . .

THE STANDARD OF PROOF UNDER SECTION 1981

At the threshold lies the question of the quantum of proof required of plaintiffs. This case is brought under Section 1981, not Title VII of the Civil Rights of 1964 (42 U.S.C. §2000e et seq.). . . . [This Court concludes] that proof of discriminatory intent is required in actions brought under Section 1981. . . . [42 U.S.C. 1981 (1976) provides: "All persons within the jurisdiction of the United States shall have the same right . . . to the full and equal

benefit of all laws and proceedings for the security of persons and property as is enjoyed by white citizens. . . ." Ed.'s note.]

ELEMENTS OF THE PRIMA FACIE CASE

Plaintiffs contend that the defendant hotels engaged in a pattern or practice of purposeful discrimination against black male applicants for positions as waiters. The record is devoid of any direct evidence of intent to discriminate. . . .

Teamsters v. United States, 431 U.S. 324 (1977), established that purposeful employment discrimination may be proved by statistical evidence. The Court said:

Statistics showing racial or ethnic imbalance are probative in a case such as this one only because such imbalance is often a telltale sign of purposeful discrimination; absent explanation, it is ordinarily to be expected that nondiscriminatory hiring practices will in time result in a work force more or less representative of the racial and ethnic composition of the population in the community from which employees are hired. Evidence of longlasting and gross disparity between the composition of a work force and that of the general population thus may be significant. . . .

431 U.S. at 340 n. 20. The Court agreed that the government had made out a prima facie case under Title VII by proving, in addition to individual instances of discrimination, that in communities where 10 to 50 percent of the population was black, defendant employed not a single black line driver before the suit was commenced. . . .

Whether . . . an inference [of discriminatory intent] may be drawn from evidence of disparate impact turns on a sensitive and practical evaluation of the full factual context. In cases of employment discrimination, where proof of intent rests on statistical evidence of impact, that impact must be "longlasting and gross" to sustain the inference that the defendant acted for the purpose of creating or maintaining it.

Another feature of statistical evidence that must be borne in mind is that, contrary to the illusion of certainty which it may create, it does not afford a mathematically precise basis for decision. . . . As the Supreme Court noted in *Hazelwood*, quoting from *Teamsters*, "[S]tatistics . . . come in infinite variety . . . [T]heir usefulness depends on all of the surrounding facts and circumstances."

THE RELEVANT LABOR MARKET

The statistical analysis must begin with a determination of the pool of individuals available and qualified to become waiters for the defendant hotels and the percentage of black males in that pool. Whether or not an inference of discriminatory impact and purpose arises from the percentage of blacks hired or promoted by the defendants depends on the choice of the proper labor market for statistical comparison. The parties are in fundamental disagreement on this issue, and have presented largely contradictory expert opinions. . . .

[For example, with respect to the "relevant population," plaintiff's expert advocated using general population figures rather than civilian labor force data, since the former index yields a larger number of blacks than the latter. The defendant's expert, of course, favored using labor force statistics. The court sided with the defense because the general population includes groups (for example, the disabled, inmates, those not seeking work) which are not likely to supply applicants for waiter positions and therefore is a less accurate indicator of the available labor pool.

With respect to the "relevant employment qualifications," plaintiff contended that all persons of the relevant population with normal intelligence and physical capabilities should be counted, on the grounds that waitering does not require any special competencies. Defendant responded that only experienced waiters should be included, since prior work experience is a hiring criterion in luxury hotels. The Court decided that the skills in question are readily acquired and, therefore, prior experience is not a "manifestly job-related qualification for waiters."

The parties also differed on the "relevant geographic area," "relevant time," and "relevant earnings bracket" in determining the "relevant labor market" (of blacks available for the waiter jobs). Ed.'s note.]

[T]he Court finds the appropriate comparison is with a labor market consisting of all males, aged 21 to 64, in the civilian labor force in the weighted San Francisco/Oakland SMSA [Standard Metropolitan Statistical Area] as shown in the 1970 census.

The statistical data offered by plaintiffs produce a black availability figure of 11.1% in that market, or availability pool. The choice of a particular figure should, however, not be permitted to create the illusion of certainty or precision. . . . [N]o single figure provides a reliable estimate of availability. The entire process is perhaps more calculated to exclude gross error than to lead to precise answers. The Court concludes that the analysis producing an availability figure of 11.1% is the one which, in the circumstances of this case, appears to be the most rational and valid. . . .

[THE TIME PERIOD FOR THE STATISTICAL ANALYSIS]

Inasmuch as the question to be decided is whether defendants engaged in purposeful discrimination during the years at issue [1970–79], comparisons must be based on defendants' employment practices—hiring, transfer and promotion of black males into waiter positions—during that period. Because of the nature of the statistical tests applied, the question arises whether to use aggregate figures for the whole period or to divide it into parts. This choice necessarily has an effect on the outcome of the analysis. The same percentage of blacks actually hired could be statistically significant or not, depending on the number of hires; the more years grouped together, the larger the number, the more significant statistically is a given percentage variation from the number of black hires expected. . . .

Reliance on one test of a single time period would be especially inappropriate, moreover, where the issue is intent and the test is whether the disparities were so "longlasting and gross" that an inference of purposeful discrimination arises. A more satisfactory indication of intent is the pattern of cumulative results. The racial makeup of progressively increasing numbers of hires, year by year, is relevant to what the defendants might have known about the racial impact of their hiring practices over time. . . .

The data are as follows: [Only portions of the data for the St. Francis Hotel

are reproduced. They should suffice for illustrative purposes. Some calculation errors in the original table, pointed out by Barnes (1983, p. 228), have been corrected. The significance levels (last column), based on two-tailed tests, were presented elsewhere in the opinion and are added to the table on page 382. Ed.'s note.]

STATISTICAL ANALYSIS—PRIMA FACIE CASE

Having determined the pool of available workers, the percentage of blacks in that pool, and the rate at which blacks were hired by defendants, it is possible to draw certain statistical conclusions. The statistical test employed estimates the likelihood that the variation between the observed data (i.e., the actual number of blacks hired) and the expected (based on the percentage of blacks in the availability pool) is consistent with random selection, given the total number hired. . . .

Although, as the Supreme Court [in *Castaneda*] has observed, fluctuations of more than two or three standard deviations "would undercut the hypothesis that decisions were being made randomly," it does not follow that an inference of purposeful discrimination must arise. Whereas here, the plaintiffs' proof rests essentially on comparisons with an availability percentage constructed for trial purposes, the disparity must be so gross as not to be dependent on defendants' contemporary knowledge of that rate. . . .

To evaluate the statistical evidence in an intent case, one must also, insofar as possible, consider the data in the light in which they appeared to the defendant at the time. In the case of the St. Francis, after hiring no blacks in 1970 and only one in 1971, the rate of hiring increased to over five percent on a cumulative basis. Only for the entire 1970–75 period does

St. Francis Hotel: Hire, Promotion and Transfer Date[32]

Period	Positions Filled	Blacks	% Black	Expected No. of Blacks at 11.1%	Z Statistic	% Probability of Chance Occurrence
. . .						
1970–1971	35	1	2.9%	3.9	−1.55	12.12%
. . .						
1970–1975	256	13	5.1%	28.4	−3.07	.22%
. . .						
1970–1979	390	28	7.2%	43.3	−2.46	1.38%

the disparity exceed three standard deviations. . . .

Thus, even though a Z statistic of three indicates a probability of random occurrence of only .22%, viewing the data as a whole the Court cannot conclude that they raise an inference of purposeful discrimination. "The mathematical conclusion that the disparity between . . . two figures is 'statistically significant' does not, however, require an *a priori* finding that these deviations are 'legally significant.' "

---

[32] The Z statistic is computed as a part of a statistical test, the so-called Z test. It is based on an assumed normal distribution of observed values around any expected value. The variation between observed values and the expected value (here the percentage of blacks in the availability pool) is measured in terms of standard deviation (or standard error). The Z statistic reflects the number of standard deviations by which the observed value differs from the expected value. By reference to tables based on the normal distribution curve, the Z statistic can be used to determine the probability that the observed value is the product of random selection or occurrence.

The formula for calculating the standard deviation is derived from an equation which mathematically described the normal distribution. This formula was set out by the Supreme Court in *Hazelwood* and in another context in Castaneda v. Partida; other courts have applied the formula in employment discrimination cases. The standard deviation is equal, in this case, to the square root of the product of the probability of drawing a nonblack (.889) and the probability of drawing a black (.111), multiplied by the square root of the sample size. Given a sample size of 100, for example, the formula in this case would be:

$$\sqrt{.111 \times .889} \times \sqrt{100} = 3.14.$$

The standard deviation (or standard error) for this sample would therefore be approximately 3. Statistical theory tells us that if 100 samples were drawn independently and at random from the same population group, in 95 of the draws the observed number of blacks would be within two standard deviations of the expected number of blacks, i.e., approximately between 17 and 5. To put it differently, if there were fewer than 5 or more than 17 blacks in a sample of 100, the probability of obtaining that number as a result of random selection is less than five percent.

The Z statistic is equal to the difference between the expected number (11.1% of the sample) and the actual number of blacks hired divided by the standard deviation:

$$Z = \frac{(\text{Actual Number}) - (\text{Expected Number})}{(\text{Standard Deviation})}.$$

The Z statistic thus reflects the number of standard deviations between expected and actual hires. Under the formulae stated above, the standard deviation tends to decrease as the sample size increases; as a necessary corollary, the Z statistic tends to increase as the standard deviation decreases.

The probability that a particular observed value would occur by chance can be estimated by consulting a table that shows the probability, in a normal distribution, of a random variation equal to the Z statistic. A Z statistic of 2.00, for example, indicates a less than 5% likelihood that the observed value would occur by chance. Such a result is described as being significant at the .05 level. . . .

United States v. Test, 550 F.2d 577, 584 (10th Cir. 1976) (jury selection case). The Supreme Court, while noting that disparities "greater than two or three standard deviations" would be suspect to a social scientist, has never accepted that level as sufficient to raise an inference of intent. In the cases in which it has applied this analysis to determine the presence of purposeful discrimination, it has relied on disparities ranging from five to 29 standard deviations. See *Castaneda* and *Hazelwood*. Statistical disparities considerably more gross and long-lasting than those found here being required to support an inference of purposeful discrimination, the Court finds and concludes that plaintiffs have failed to establish a prima facie case as to their class claims under Section 1981. . . .

For the reasons stated, the complaint must be dismissed and judgment entered for defendants, the parties to bear their own costs.

It is so ordered.

NOTES AND QUESTIONS

1. The Z test is another measure of statistical significance. The Z score, obtained by using the formula given by the Court in footnote 32, indicates the number of standard deviations an observed value is from the expected value. By finding this Z score in a table of normal probabilities, usually printed in the back of any statistics text, we can determine the likelihood of chance deviation—where this disparity is measured in terms of standard deviations—of the observed value from the expected value.

Apply the Z test to the hypothetical example given earlier (7 minorities in a venire of 200, where minorities compose 8% of the eligible population). The calculations should yield a Z score of −2.34 (the negative sign indicates that the expected number exceeds the observed number). Consulting a table of normal probabilities, we find that the likelihood of a score of −2.34 if the null hypothesis is true is .019 (using a two-tailed test). This means there is a 1.9% chance of randomly selecting a number of minority jurors (7) that is that many standard deviations (3.83) above or below the expected number (16). Otherwise stated, there is a 1.9% chance of wrongly rejecting the null hypothesis of race-neutral selection. Notice that the Z test gives a more precise estimate of the risk of a Type 1 error than does the Chi square test (between 2% and 1%, as described earlier).

2. The court says that only in the 1970–75 period (of the St. Francis Hotel data) does the disparity "exceed three standard deviations" (exactly 3.07 standard deviations). The significance level of this disparity occurring by chance, using the Z test, is .0022. Since the disparities for all of the time periods are in the one anticipated direction (underrepresentation rather than overrepresentation), would it be proper to use a one-tailed test of significance? If so, would the deviations in the other time periods be statistically significant?

3. The choice of the "relevant" population for statistical comparison is critical to the determination of discriminatory impact and purpose. Hence, both sides presented voluminous descriptive statistical proof regarding the expected percentage of blacks in the pool of potential job candidates. Plaintiffs typically advocate for the highest possible expected number, thereby magnifying the disparity, and defendants naturally argue for the lowest possible figure. The more precise the estimate by the court, the narrower is the range of alternative, nonrandom explanations for any disparities. The *Gay* case shows that a major part of discrimination litigation is determining the numbers to be inserted in the statistical formulas.

4. The judicial analyses of statistical disparities in employment discrimination assume that race-neutral hiring will mirror the percentage of minorities in the labor force. However, "labor market economics recognizes that an employer does not engage in truly random hiring practices" (Smith and Abram 1981, p. 52). Selective—but not necessarily discriminatory—reasons enter into the process of hiring. Job recruitment is unlike the selection of outcomes by lottery; it does not follow the luck of the draw. Is the process of hiring employees sufficiently distinct from the process of selecting jurors so that the standards of statistical proof formulated in jury discrimination cases are inapposite to employment discrimination cases?

5.   The legal challenge to disproportionate impact or underrepresentation can be based on the Sixth Amendment, the Fourteenth Amendment, Title VI, Title VII, section 1981, or a combination of constitutional and statutory grounds. Is the legal standard of proof of discrimination the same under each of these approaches? Is the level of statistical certainty needed to establish a prima facie case the same under each of these approaches?

6.   Consider the following cases which raised equal protection challenges to racial underrepresentation in various contexts:

Northern school segregation: The problem of de facto school segregation in northern cities was examined in Chapter 4. It can be seen as an instance of "underrepresentation" of minority students in certain schools. Assuming that this disproportionate pattern is not the result of actions or policies of school officials, but can be accounted for by other nonschool related factors such as residential housing trends, the question is whether this underrepresentation (segregation) is a constitutional violation. "A law claimed to be discriminatory must be traced to discriminatory purpose. Black and white schools in a community are not alone violative of Equal Protection. The differentiating factor between de jure segregation and so called de facto segregation . . . is purpose or intent to segregate" (*Keyes* v. *School District No. 1*, 1973, p. 208).

Employment discrimination: *Washington* v. *Davis* (1976). Justice White held that a verbal aptitude test used in screening prospective recruits for a police department training program, which was nonracial on its face but which resulted in the exclusion of a disproportionate number of black candidates, did not violate the Equal Protection Clause or Title VII of the Civil Rights Act of 1964. Under Title VII, employees "need not concern themselves with the employer's possibly discriminatory purpose but instead may focus solely on the racially differential impact of the challenged hiring or promotional practices" (p. 238). On the other hand, "we have never held that the constitutional standard for invidious racial discrimination is identical to the standards applicable under Title VII" (p. 239). Under the equal protection test, "disproportionate impact is not irrelevant but it is not the sole touchstone of an invidious racial discrimination. . . . Standing alone, it does not trigger the rule . . . that racial classifications are to be subjected to the strictest of scrutiny and are justifiable only by the weightiest of considerations" (p. 242).

Exclusionary zoning: *Arlington Heights* v. *Metro Housing Corp.* (1977). Justice Powell, for the Court, held that a municipality's denial of an application for rezoning from single family to multiple family, thereby preventing construction of a housing project that would have benefited primarily low income blacks, was not a violation of equal protection despite the disproportionate impact upon blacks of such action unless discriminatory motive could be shown. "Determining whether invidious discriminatory purpose was a motivating factor demands a sensitive inquiry into such circumstantial and direct evidence of intent as may be available. The impact of official action . . . may provide an important starting point. . . . Absent a pattern as stark as that [of total exclusion of a racial category], impact alone is not determinative, and the Court must look to other evidence" (p. 266).

Municipal elections: *City of Mobile* v. *Bolden* (1980). In Mobile, Alabama, blacks constitute 45% of the local electorate. No black has ever been elected to the city council or the mayor's office, ostensibly because voting is city-wide rather than by wards (and most blacks are congregated within certain areas of the city). The Supreme Court rejected a challenge to require the city to switch to a ward-based election procedure. There was no violation of the Equal Protection Clause, the Court said, because there was no proof of purposeful discrimination, only of disproportional impact.

In these five different contexts—jury selection, school segregation, employment, housing, and voting—the underlying fact pattern is roughly the same: Actions or procedures designed to serve neutral (nonracial) ends nonetheless cause a disproportionate racial impact. The result is not as blatant as outright exclusion of minority members, but the discriminatory effect is still there (arguably in more subtle fashion).

In each of these situations, the constitutional test for determining discrimination appears to be the same. There must be discriminatory motive in addition to discriminatory impact. Yet, in the jury selection case (*Castaneda*), the challenger claiming discrimination won, whereas in the cases on employment (*Davis*), housing (*Arlington Heights*), voting (*Mobile*) and schools (de facto segregation), the challenger lost. Is *Castaneda* inconsistent with these other cases? The facts appear to be the same, and the legal rule is the same, yet the conclusions were different. Consistency and symmetry in the law seems more of an ideal than an ever-present reality. Or is *Castaneda* distinguishable from these other cases?

A more basic question needs to be raised that underlies all of these different discrimination situations. Why is motive or purpose a key element in the constitutional test of discrimination? It is a nebulous, slippery concept, difficult to establish empirically, and obviously the principal obstacle to successful anti-discrimination litigation. Can you suggest an alternative test? Should the stigmatizing psychological effects of discrimination be taken into account?

7.4. DISCRIMINATION IN PEREMPTORY CHALLENGES

SWAIN v. ALABAMA

380 U.S. 202 (1965)

[The first half of the opinion dealing with underrepresentation in the jury venire was reproduced earlier in this chapter. Here is the second half of Mr. Justice White's opinion. Ed.'s note.]

Petitioner makes a further claim relating to the exercise of peremptory challenges to exclude Negroes from serving on petit juries. . . .

In this case the six Negroes available for jury service were struck by the prosecutor in the process of selecting the jury which was to try petitioner. . . .

Alabama contends that its system of peremptory strikes—challenges without cause, without explanation and without judicial scrutiny—affords a suitable and necessary method of securing juries which in fact and in the opinion of the parties are fair and impartial. This system, it is said, in and of itself, provides justification for striking any group of otherwise qualified jurors in any given case, whether they be Negroes, Catholics, accountants or those with blue eyes. Based on the history of this system and its actual use and operation in this country, we think there is merit in this position. . . .

The persistence of peremptories and their extensive use demonstrate the long and widely held belief that peremptory challenge is a necessary part of trial by jury. Although "[t]here is nothing in the Constitution of the United States which requires the Congress [or the States] to grant peremptory challenges," nonetheless the challenge is "one of the most important of the rights secured to the accused." . . .

The function of the challenge is not only to eliminate extremes of partiality on both sides, but to assure the parties that the jurors before whom they try the case will decide on the basis of the evidence placed before them, and not otherwise. . . .

The essential nature of the peremptory challenge is that it is one exercised without a reason stated, without inquiry and without being subject to the court's control. While challenges for cause permit rejection of jurors on a narrowly specified, provable and legally cognizable basis of partiality, the peremptory permits rejection for a real or imagined partiality that is less easily designated or demonstrable. It is often exercised upon the "sudden impressions and unaccountable prejudices we are apt to conceive upon the bare looks and gestures of another," upon a juror's "habits and associations," or upon the feeling that "the bare questioning [a juror's] indifference may sometimes provoke a resentment." It is no less frequently exercised on grounds normally thought irrelevant to legal proceedings or official action, namely, the race, religion, nationality, occupation or affiliations of people summoned for jury duty. For the question a prosecutor or defense counsel must decide is not whether a juror of a particular race or nationality is in fact partial, but whether one from a different group is less likely to be. It is well known that these factors are widely explored during the voir dire, by both prosecutor and accused. This Court has held that the fairness of trial by jury requires no less. Hence veniremen are not always judged solely as individuals for the purpose of exercising peremptory challenges. Rather they are challenged in light of the limited knowledge counsel has of them, which may include their group affiliations, in the context of the case to be tried.

With these considerations in mind, we cannot hold that the striking of Negroes in a particular case is a denial of equal protection of the laws. In the quest for an impartial and qualified jury, Negro and white, Protestant and Catholic, are alike subject to being challenged without cause. To subject the prosecutor's challenge in any particular case to the demands and traditional standards of the Equal Protection Clause would entail a radical change in the nature and operation of the challenge. . . .

In the light of the purpose of the peremptory system and the function it serves in a pluralistic society in connection with the institution of jury trial, we cannot hold that the Constitution requires an examination of the prosecutor's reasons for the exercise of his challenges in any given case. The presumption in any particular case must be that the prosecutor is using the State's challenges to obtain a fair and impartial jury to try the case before the court. The presumption is not overcome and the prosecutor therefore subjected to examination by allegations that in the case at hand all Negroes were removed from the jury or that they were removed because they were Negroes. . . .

Affirmed.

Objectives of Voir Dire

The preceding sections dealt with challenges to the entire array of prospective jurors because of unrepresentativeness or underrepresentation of certain groups, purportedly due to discriminatory selection. We now focus on challenges to individual jurors within the array during the voir dire process. Voir dire (Old Norman French, loosely translated as "see them speak the truth") is an "examination" of a prospective juror "face to face, in the presence of the court," for the purpose of assessing his fitness to pass judgment in a particular case (*Pointer* v. *United States*, 1894, p. 408).

The present system of exclusions is rooted in the English common law. In the years after the Norman Conquest, the jury—consisting of witnesses to a crime—was used as an inquisitorial device for the discovery of criminals. From these origins the idea evolved that the Crown had the right to select the best informed witnesses. This notion, in turn, led to the development of unlimited peremptory challenges for the prosecution in criminal cases. In 1305, the unlimited right was abrogated by parliamentary decree (the "Ordinance for Inquests") and the Crown was obligated to show cause for every challenge. Since then, in England, the prosecution has not had right to peremptory challenges. By the fifteenth century, the right was firmly established as a right of the defendant—not of the state—in felony trials. The courts, however, construed the aforementioned ordinance so as to create a functional equivalent for the Crown's peremptory, called the right to "stand aside" for cause. In this country, most states were slow to accord the peremptory challenge to the prosecution because it was considered primarily a shield for the defense against jurors who were conviction-prone or too subservient to the state. It was not until 1870 that most state legislatures granted the right to the prosecution. Thus, the defendant's right and the state's right to exclude without cause stem from different historical traditions (Comment, *Virginia Law Review*, 1966, pp. 1170–72).

The questioning of venirepersons serves several functions. The most obvious and legally recognized purpose is to obtain information needed to ascertain an individual's partiality. The voir dire is essentially "a self-disclosure interview" (Suggs and Sales 1981, p. 247). Of course, neither party really wants an impartial juror; each wants jurors favorable to its side. The adversarial clash at voir dire should produce, in theory, surviving jurors who are, in Lord Coke's words, "indifferent as they stand unsworn" (in Babcock 1975, p. 551). An "indifferent" juror does not imply one who is wholly devoid of bias. The Supreme Court has recognized that such a requirement would set an "impossible standard" (*Irvin* v. *Dowd*, 1961, p. 723). People have opinions, values, knowledge, and experiences which color their judgment and which they cannot easily shed at the courthouse door. The expectation is that a juror's "qualifications as to impartiality" merely fall within "minimum standards" (*Beck* v. *Washington*, 1962, p. 557). At the venire level, as we have already seen, the courts have defined impartiality in terms of selecting a representative cross section of the community. The right to an impartial jury means, in effect, an equal opportunity for all biases to be represented in the venire. A range of viewpoints can thereby be brought to bear on the fact-finding process. At the individual level, the cross-sectional principle translates into the idea that " 'impartial' jurors are ones who would at least be willing to be persuaded and influenced by the life experiences of others" (Babcock 1975, p. 552). Thus, once an impartial selection procedure yields a venire composed of different biases, a purpose of voir dire challenges according to the *Swain* Court is "to eliminate extremes of partiality on both sides"—that is, to exclude those who are beyond rational persuasion. The opportunity to challenge particular individuals can complement nondiscriminatory selection of the venire by eliminating from the pool those with insuperable bias.

A second purpose of voir dire is a tactical one: to influence jurors before the start of the trial. Counsel may try to plant in the minds of potential jurors the seeds of a certain argument or line of proof. Counsel may also attempt to create a favorable personal impression or establish in advance a good rapport with the jury. Based on observations in a federal district court, one study estimated that 80% of voir dire time was used for covert persuasion (Broeder 1965). Other studies estimate a lower figure, 40% (Balch et al. 1976). Whatever the actual rate, this kind of advocacy is not uncommon, even though "the main and, in theory, . . . only legitimate function" of voir dire is to qualify unbiased jurors (Kaplan and Waltz 1965, p. 92).

A third and related purpose is educational. By answering questions about their own views and making a public commitment to impartiality, jurors may be educated into their proper role. The voir dire can serve as a socialization process, a "rite of passage" to juryhood (Balch et al. 1976). The right to challenge jurors also "teaches the litigant, and through him the community, that the jury is a good and proper mode for deciding matters . . . because in a real sense the jury belongs to the litigant: he chooses it" (Babcock 1975, p. 552). By exercising peremptory challenges, he can exclude those from "his" jury that he—for whatever reason—does not want on it. A symbolic-didactic value of the right to exclude potential jurors is that the jury is not only supposed to be impartial, but that it should also appear to be impartial to those whose life or liberty are at stake.

Procedure of Voir Dire

Challenges for cause are usually based on rather narrowly specified and demonstrable grounds of partiality, such as expressed bias or kinship or friendship with one of the litigants. Prospective jurors who admit having formed an opinion on the merits of the case but nonetheless declare themselves capable of impartial judgment cannot, usually, be struck for cause. Judges feel uncomfortable divining a person's "true" state of mind, and they are reluctant to impugn the credibility of an otherwise qualified juror who professes impartiality.

Unlike the narrowness of justified exclusions, peremptory challenges are issued without reason or judicial control. Their allocation and number varies with the severity of the crime and the jurisdiction. For example, in the federal courts, twenty peremptory challenges are allowed to each side in a capital trial. For noncapital felony cases, the defense is entitled to ten peremptory challenges and the prosecution to six (Federal Rules of Criminal Procedure, 24(a)).

The questioning of venirepersons may be conducted by the judge, by counsel, or by both, depending on the jurisdiction. Less than half of the states permit counsel to exercise primary control over voir dire in both criminal and civil cases. In the federal system, the conduct and scope of voir dire is left to the trial court's discretion, subject to "the essential demands of fairness" (*Aldridge* v. *United States*, 1931, p. 310). In practice, state and federal judges over the years have increasingly assumed a dominant role. A survey of the federal bench found that about 70% of the judges conduct the questioning themselves, although they accept supplementary questions from counsel which they ask in the form requested or in edited form (Bermant and Shapard 1981, pp. 80–82). Appellate courts tend to defer to the lower courts' discretion in voir dire, and they seldom reverse a trial judge's decision to disallow counsel's questions that might lead to exclusion without cause.

Federal judges try to accommodate their procedures to the norms and traditions of the state bench of the jurisdiction in which they are located. With respect to peremptory challenges, there are two common procedures. One is the struck jury method. Its distinctive feature is that all challenges for cause are ruled on by the judge (based upon questions posed by counsel and/or the judge) before any peremptory challenges are exercised by the parties. This results in a pool of prospective jurors, all of whom have survived justified exclusions, which counsel is then free to whittle down without giving any reasons. A second method consists of exercising sequentially the challenges for and without cause. After each juror is questioned, counsel must decide whether to accept or reject that juror. In this sequential method, since counsel does not have the chance to inspect in advance the entire pool, there is always the risk that a peremptorily excluded juror might be followed by someone even more unsatisfactory—and peremptories, unlike challenges for cause, are limited. This kind of uncertainty is absent, of course, in the struck jury method. The aforementioned survey found that 55% of federal judges use the struck jury procedure (Bermant and Shapard 1981, p. 94).

Although the *Swain* Court observed that the peremptory challenge is "one of the most important of the rights secured to the accused," its practice has been marked by increasing contention and criticism. A principal complaint by the courts is that "excess rococo examination" of prospective jurors by counsel has reached the point where "the trial structure is endangered" (*People* v. *Crowe*, 1973, p. 819).

The voir dire can be time-consuming. The selection of a jury in the criminal trial of a Black Panther activist took thirteen weeks and involved the examination of 1,550 venirepersons. The voir dire in the murder trial of Sirhan Sirhan lasted six weeks and 250 venirepersons were questioned. One noted defense lawyer likened the prolonged voir dire to the "[courtroom] counterpart of the legislative filibuster" (in Kamisar, LaFave, and Israel 1980, p. 1350). These instances, however, are exceptional. In most cases and in most places, it is not such a drawn-out affair. A study in Los Angeles Superior Court estimated that voir dires conducted by attorneys averaged 135 minutes, by attorneys and judge 111 minutes, and by judge alone 64 minutes (Babcock 1975, p. 563, n. 69). Judge-conducted examination is speedier because judges do not probe as deeply or as extensively as counsel. For example, if a prospective juror in a criminal trial responds affirmatively to the question of whether he has ever been a victim of crime, a judge would probably ask if that experience would preclude his ability to decide impartially in the present case. If the answer is negative, that will usually end the inquiry. A defense attorney, however, would want to know more about the nature of the crime, the legal outcome of that earlier event, and so on. Counsel has the incentive to examine more thoroughly and also the capability to do so because of his knowledge of the circumstances of the case at bar, both of which a judge may lack.

The scope of voir dire can be circumscribed by the judge's discretion to restrict the number and types of questions asked by counsel. Another judicially imposed limitation is en masse rather than individual questioning. It is easier for a juror to not respond if an inquiry is addressed to an entire group instead of to him personally. In observing some two dozen federal jury trials, Broeder (1965) recorded several instances of jurors who sat mute during block questioning and later turned out to be acquainted with or had ties to the litigants. It is not surprising, then, that attorneys advocate unfettered participation in voir dire. The ABA Commission on Standards for Judicial Administration (1976) has proposed that "counsel for each side should have the right, subject to reasonable time limits, to question jurors individually and as a panel," instead of leaving it to the court's discretion (p. 26). Some even argue that this right is of constitutional dimension (Gutman 1972). Judges, on the other hand, especially federal judges, strongly favor bench-conducted voir dires, ostensibly to expedite and improve the process. Judges also seem to assume that if the venire was fairly selected so as to compose a representative cross section, its members can be seated in the jury box without much ado.

NOTES AND QUESTIONS

1.   There is an elaborate body of doctrine designed to safeguard against abuses in the selection of the venire. Underrepresentation of distinct groups in the venire can be a prima facie violation of the Sixth and Fourteenth Amendments. This safeguard is a hollow one if there is unchecked use of peremptory challenges based on group affiliation during the voir dire. By the Court's own admission, peremptories are not constitutionally required, yet this device can be used to deny certain groups the right to participate in the administration of justice.

The *Swain* decision could be "a blank check for discrimination" (Comment, *Virginia Law Review*, 1966, p. 1175). The absence of minorities (or other distinct groups) from a jury, especially when they constitute a sizable proportion of the community, tends to undermine the perceived validity of the verdict. Thus, when an all-white, all-male jury acquitted four white police officers of the killing of a black insurance salesman in Miami, black neighborhoods erupted for several days in the worst riots in the history of the city (Gillespie 1980). The legitimacy of the jury and of the criminal courts generally is called into question when those members of the community who are most concerned with the issues at stake are not represented in the decision-making process.

2.   In this case, the striking of all black members in the jury was held not invalid. According to the Court, when would such use (or misuse) of the peremptory challenge be improper? Since not one single black had "actually served on the petit jury since 1950," what must the defense show to rebut "the presumption . . . that the prosecutor is using the State's challenges [properly] . . . ," and what are the logistical problems of proof?

3.   The Court considered the right of the prosecution to peremptory challenges to have the same weight as the right of the defense. Even if the scales of justice are to be evenly held between the two sides, and leaving aside the different historical origins of the right, does it follow—as a matter of social policy— that the peremptory challenge is entitled to the same protection in the hands of the prosecution and of the defense?

4.   The supreme courts of California (*People* v. *Wheeler*, 1978) and Massachusetts (*Commonwealth* v. *Soares*, 1978) have gone beyond *Swain* and held that under their respective state constitutional provisions for an impartial jury, the peremptory challenge cannot be used by any party to remove a potential juror solely because of his group affiliation. The courts also emphasized that proportional representation of groups in the petit jury is not required. How would one show "strong likelihood"—the standard set in these cases—that potential jurors were removed solely because of ethnicity or religion?

      In the preceding venire discrimination cases, the courts have compared the expected and observed numbers of minorities in the venire in order to establish a prima facie case of systematic underrepresentation. Can a similar analysis be used at the jury level to show that the frequency of a prosecutor's peremptory challenges of minorities exceeds chance expectations, thereby shifting the burden to the state to prove any nonracial grounds for exclusion? How would the expected rate of peremptory challenges be calculated, and what kinds of information would be needed for the calculation?

5.   Of the two procedures of peremptory challenges, the strike method and the sequential method, is one more susceptible to discriminatory application than the other? Does the presumptive inviolability of the peremptory challenge extend to the particular method of challenge?

6.   The *Swain* Court alluded to "the function [the peremptory system] serves in a pluralistic society." In England, challenges for cause are made on very circumscribed grounds and challenges without cause are rarely exercised by either side. Counsel, according to Lord Justice Devlin (1956), "should address the jury as an impersonal body of twelve and the less they know about them as men and women, the better" (p. 34). He recalled, however, a case in which the court discovered after the trial that two of the jurors did not understand English (p. 35). What is the relationship between social heterogeneity and the exercise of peremptories?

7.   The possibility of prosecutorial abuse in systematically excluding death-scrupled venirepersons from capital juries was investigated by Winick (1982). He analyzed the transcripts of the voir dire of all the venirepersons (629) in all of the death penalty trials (33) in one judicial district of Florida over a five-year period, starting shortly after the promulgation of a new capital punishment law in 1974. He found that 28.2% (15 of 52) of nonscrupled venirepersons were peremptorily challenged by the state, compared to 76.9% (40 of 52) of scrupled venirepersons (p. 28). This difference was highly significant (greater than 7.6 standard deviations) by application of the binomial distribution. The likelihood of obtaining this difference by chance is the equivalent of obtaining 33 heads in a row by flipping an unbiased coin (p. 35). The relationship remained unchanged after controlling for several third variables such as gender, employment status, and partiality. For example, among those prospective jurors whose impartiality was questioned, 76.9% of the scrupled were removed peremptorily, but only 26.7% of the nonscrupled were struck without cause (p. 34). The study concluded that there was systematic use of the peremptory challenge so as to cause substantial underrepresentation of scrupled jurors in capital trials. What prophylactic measures, if any, might prevent the nullification of the safeguards of *Witherspoon* v. *Illinois* (see Chapter 5, section 5.3) by the (mis)use of *Swain*?

8.   Trial lawyers like to claim that they sometimes win cases at the jury selection stage by astute exercise of peremptories. Some researchers have been skeptical of this claim: After observing many criminal trials in federal court, Broeder (1965) concluded that the "voir dire was grossly ineffective not only in weeding out 'unfavorable' jurors but even in eliciting data which would have shown particular jurors as very likely to prove 'unfavorable' " (p. 505). A systematic, experimental study of the impact of peremptories on trial outcomes was conducted by Zeisel and Diamond (1978). They concluded that "lawyers apparently do win some of their cases, as they occasionally boast, during or at least with the help of voir dire" (p. 519). Their original and elegant study merits description in more detail.

The authors secured the cooperation of several judges and attorneys in twelve criminal trials in the United States District Court for the Northern District of Illinois. In addition to the real jury (impaneled after "for cause" challenges by the judge, followed by peremptory challenges by counsel), the researchers selected two mock or shadow juries: One was the "English jury," obtained by random selection of unexamined venirepersons, and the other was composed only of jurors who had been peremptorily challenged in the selection of the real jury. The mock juries were treated the same as the real juries (for example, they were given copies of documents and received judicial instructions). After the trial, they cast a predeliberation individual ballot and then deliberated and rendered a group verdict.

At first glance, one might be inclined to compare the English jury (a "control" group selected without voir dire) and the real jury. As it turned out, the English jury was initially different from and therefore not comparable with the real jury—the former were more conviction-prone. The authors then reconstructed a hypothetical control group, called "jury without [peremptory] challenge" (JWC), for each of the twelve trials. The JWC consisted of jurors who would have decided the case had there been no peremptory challenges. It was reconstructed simply by reading (from the transcript of the voir dire) the names of the first twelve venirepersons who were not excused for cause. For example, suppose that of the first fifteen persons who are examined in one case, the first three are struck for cause, the next nine are seated, and the last three are excused peremptorily. The JWC consists of the seated nine and the last three—these twelve persons would have composed the actual jury if no peremptories had been allowed. However, since peremptories are allowed, the real jury in this case consisted of the nine who were seated and three others (say, venirepersons numbered sixteen to eighteen) who survived challenges for and without cause in the next round of voir dire. The experimental purpose was to compare the decisions of the JWCs and the real juries—any differences would then be attributed to the effect of the peremptory challenge.

The dependent variable was not the group verdict, since members of the JWC never met together to deliberate. Instead, the authors relied on the predeliberation, individual decisions. Earlier research (Kalven and Zeisel 1966) had shown a very high correlation between the predeliberation individual ballot and the postdeliberation group verdict. If most individual decisions are for acquittal, the final verdict is also likely to be for acquittal. If most individual votes are for conviction (say nine out of twelve, or 75%), the probability of a guilty conviction is high (.90).

To ascertain the first ballot vote of each JWC, the authors had to ascertain the individual votes of the two subgroups constituting the JWC: those peremptorily challenged (three persons in the above example) and those real jury members who also would have been on the JWC (the nine seated persons in the example). The authors knew the votes of the first subgroup because these persons were in the mock jury. (A few refused to participate in the mock jury, and the authors simply guessed their votes based upon the votes of the majority.) The votes of the second subgroup were estimated from the overall first ballot votes of the real juries. (With the real juries, because of reasons of privacy, the researchers knew only the overall pattern of the first vote, not the votes of each individual juror.) For example, if the real jury split 8 to 4 for conviction on the first ballot, the researchers assumed that the nine persons belonging to this jury would have split 6 to 3 for conviction.

Thus, from the estimated first ballot of each JWC, the study estimated the likely group verdict in each case and compared it with the verdict of the real jury. In seven of the twelve trials, the peremptory challenge had virtually no effect on the outcome—there was no significant difference in the probability of guilty verdicts between JWCs and real juries. In the remaining five cases, there was an impact: "[P]eremptory challenges had a substantial role in altering the likelihood of guilty verdicts" (p. 508). This effect was in the direction of acquittals. The reason why the exercise of peremptories favors the defense could not be isolated in this study. It could be due to the superior performance of defense counsel, or the greater number of peremptories granted to the defense, or a combination of these and other (unexamined) factors.

9. A number of methodological features limit the internal and external validity of the foregoing study. The twelve cases do not constitute a probability sample, so the figure of five-twelfths cannot be generalized. The calculations of the dependent variable were predicated on assumptions that have been sharply criticized (Bermant and Shapard 1981, pp. 102–5). For example, since the researchers never knew how the individuals on the real juries actually voted, their estimates may be unreliable. The estimate of the votes of peremptorily challenged members who refused to participate, based on the votes of those who participated, is also questionable. Accepting, however, for purposes of discussion, the facial validity of the results, what are the policy implications for the practice of peremptory challenges? Can one draw conclusions about the wisdom of allocating more peremptories to the defense than to the prosecution? In a follow-up experiment, how might you measure or control for the skills of opposing counsel? Voir dire serves qualifying as well as advocacy functions. How would you partial out the influence of one from the other in determining the impact of peremptories on verdicts?

10.   The voir dire paradigm lends itself to the testing of hypotheses extrapolated from studies on social influence. For example, is increased self-disclosure by prospective jurors more likely under judge-conducted or attorney-conducted questioning? In an interview, "too great a status differential between interactants may lead to an interviewing bias effect" (Suggs and Sales 1981, p. 253). The respondent feels pressure to tailor his answers to the interviewer's expectations. In the courtroom, a judge has higher standing and is more removed from jurors than are the attorneys. Can one then conclude that "attorneys are probably better suited to conduct the voir dire," because they are more similar to and at an intermediate social distance from jurors (p. 253)? Another example of an issue that is amenable to experimental study is the method of addressing questions to the prospective jurors. Which method—en masse questioning, individual questioning in the presence of other group members, or individual questioning in isolation—is most conducive to attaining the different objectives of voir dire? Does the method of questioning an individual in front of his peers resemble sufficiently the classic paradigm used by Asch (1958) so that substantial conformity to the majority's position can be expected? What other situational factors in voir dire might shape the responses of prospective jurors?

7.5.   JUROR PARTIALITY AND PERSONAL CHARACTERISTICS: METHODS OF SELECTION

THE USES OF SOCIAL SCIENCE IN TRIALS WITH POLITICAL AND RACIAL OVERTONES: THE TRIAL OF JOAN LITTLE

John B. McConahay, Courtney J. Mullin, and Jeffrey Frederick

INTRODUCTION

One unintended by-product of the zealous prosecution of political and racial militants in the recent past has been the increased participation by social scientists in the judicial arena. The presence of social psychologists and sociologists was obvious in the more publicized cases, e.g., the Harrisburg Eight, the Camden 28, and the Gainesville Eight. Applied social scientists

have also worked in trials involving persons from the right wing of the political spectrum, e.g., Mitchell-Stans, and in an increasing number of lesser known criminal cases. Now, at least two organized groups of social scientists, the National Jury Project and the Raleigh-based Psychology and Law Center, are permanently established for consultation in both criminal and civil litigation. In this article we will draw upon our experiences in another of the better-known trials, that of Ms. Joan Little, to illustrate some of the contributions of social scientists to the judicial process and to discuss some of the issues raised by the application of social science to the law.

The Joan Little case began in Washington, North Carolina. Early on the morning of August 27, 1974, Clarence Alligood, the night jailer for the Beaufort County jail, was found dead in a locked cell in the women's section of the jail. Alligood,

Reprinted by permission of the principal author and the publisher. Copyright ©1977, Duke University School of Law [*Law and Contemporary Problems* 41 (1977): 205–29].

a sixty-four-year-old white male, had ice pick punctures in his body and semen on his leg, and his pants and shoes were outside the cell. The person incarcerated in the cell during the preceding weeks was Joan Little, a twenty-year-old black female. Both Ms. Little and the keys to the cell and jail were missing. Over the next few days, there was an extensive search for Ms. Little in Beaufort and adjacent counties. She was on the verge of being declared an outlaw when, accompanied by her attorney, Jerry Paul, she turned herself in to the authorities in Raleigh. She was immediately charged with first degree murder. On April 28, 1975, her trial was moved from Beaufort to Wake County (Raleigh), North Carolina. And on August 15, after a trial of five weeks, she was acquitted of all charges. . . .

II.   CHANGE OF VENUE MOTION

When a case has received publicity which would make it extremely difficult to impanel a fair jury or when the issues surrounding the case arouse the racial, political, sexual, or other prejudices of a large segment of the population of the judicial district, a change of venue is one means of increasing the likelihood that the defendant will receive a fair trial. The usual grounds for a change of venue motion are prejudicial publicity or prejudicial attitudes towards the client in the district.

Social scientists who are authorities in communications research and public opinion have been called upon to testify that the evidence presented indicates that prejudice against the defendant is so high that a fair and impartial jury cannot be impaneled in that district.

The evidence presented may vary from copies of newspaper clippings and government press releases to affidavits from people in the community, but the best evidence from the standpoint of the social scientist is data from carefully conducted public opinion polls. To have scientific validity, these polls must have at least two features: 1) they must be based upon a random sample of persons in the judicial districts, and 2) at least two judicial districts must be polled. . . .

It is our opinion that the most important thing we did to insure a fair trial and an acquittal for Joan Little was to present evidence and testimony that secured a change of venue for her trial.

The North Carolina statutes regarding a change of venue permit the trial judge to move a trial from its original county to a contiguous county if, in the opinion of the trial judge, a fair and impartial jury cannot be impaneled in the original county. If he or she has doubts that a fair jury can be impaneled in a contiguous county, the judge may, at his or her discretion, remove the trial to another county in a contiguous judicial district. Thus, according to the statutes, it was theoretically possible for the trial judge to remove Joan Little's trial to any one of twenty-three counties within the area generally known as the eastern region of North Carolina. It was the defense's position, however, that the cultural and ethnic homogeneity of the whites in the region created a commonly held value structure that made it impossible for Ms. Little to receive a fair trial in any one of these eastern counties.

In all of these counties agriculture is the primary source of income, the population is spread relatively sparsely across the land, and there has been little in or out migration among whites during this century. Hence, we could expect a great deal of intergenerational continuity in political and value socialization to produce a high degree of conservatism in the white people of the region. We expected the conservatism of the whites (whom our surveys revealed to be overrepresented in all of the jury pools in the counties of the region) to be reflected in their commonly held, stereotypical attitudes towards race, towards women, towards those in authority, towards women who have been raped, and towards capital punishment. All of these attitudes could strongly influence the final decision of those who would judge Joan Little.

Though we were prepared to argue for a change of venue, county by county for each of the twenty-three eastern counties, Judge McKinnon ruled that he would allow a change of venue from Beaufort County, the indicting county, to Pitt County. He agreed with us that there would be little chance of securing a fair and impartial jury in Beaufort and he felt that Pitt had more adequate courtroom facilities as well as a larger police force to deal with the expected demonstrators. All other eastern counties were ruled out of consideration.

The defense then tried to convince Judge McKinnon that a move to Pitt would not improve Ms. Little's chances of getting a fair jury. In order to do that, it would be necessary to move to the more urban Piedmont area of the state. To substantiate our argument, we presented data from the random sample telephone surveys we had conducted in each of the twenty-three counties of the eastern region and in one Piedmont county, Orange. . . .

These data show that there were no differences among the counties in the respondents' perceived level of exposure to the case. Over 75 per cent of those surveyed in these (and the other twenty-two) counties said that they had heard "a lot" about the case. The data also show that though Pitt and Beaufort did not differ significantly from one another in preconceptions of guilt and racial attitudes, they did differ significantly from Orange County. Hence, we argued that, while a move to Pitt would gain nothing, a move to Orange would make it much more likely that a fair and impartial jury could be impaneled.

We further substantiated our case by introducing evidence developed by academic experts working independently of the defense team. We introduced a survey by the University of North Carolina showing results very similar to ours. Dr. Paul Brandis, also of the University of North Carolina and an authority on the effects of publicity upon attitudes, introduced a content analysis showing that newspaper coverage in the eastern region would induce prejudice. This was buttressed by introducing all newspaper clippings about the Little case from newspapers in the region.

Expert testimony was also given by Professor Robin Williams of Cornell University who indicated for the court the "resonating effects" which could be expected to occur in a community such as the eastern region of North Carolina. Williams explained that in such areas there exists a societal standard commonly held by the people of the region. Word-of-mouth information dispersal is the primary method by which people become aware of events occurring within their communities. In the case of unusual events that break with the general standards, this procedure serves as a tool to indicate to all inhabitants of the community how people "should" feel about this incident.

Finally, the defense introduced one hundred two affidavits or statements from persons in Pitt County which stated that most people in the county had already formed an opinion about the case.

We convinced Judge McKinnon. Although he did not move the trial to Orange County, where the University of North Carolina has its main campus, he did move it to Wake County, which is also in the Piedmont region and is the location of Raleigh, the state's capital and one of its largest cities. . . .

III. JURY SELECTION

. . .

In the trial of Joan Little, the judge asked potential jurors, in groups of twelve, general questions—largely regarding their ability to serve for the expected four- to six-week period. Then they were examined individually out of the sight and hearing of other jurors. The prosecution questioned them first and, if they were not excused for cause, made a decision to accept or peremptorily challenge the juror. Once it had passed a juror, the prosecution could not change its decision. At this point, the potential juror was examined by the defense and, if the person was not excused for cause, the defense had to decide to accept or use one of its peremptory challenges. If the defense accepted a juror, he or she was immediately sequestered in the jury room. This process continued until sixteen jurors (twelve regular jurors and four alternates) were seated. The process of jury selection took ten working days during which over two hundred potential jurors were interviewed.

Six streams of data were combined in the defense's decision to accept or reject a potential juror. First, on the basis of a random sample survey of Wake County, we had developed a mathematical model of the juror who would be ideal for the defense. Second, we observed the behavior of the potential juror during the voir dire and rated him or her on a psychological characteristic known as authoritarianism. Third, we observed the "body language" including both kinesic and paralinguistic behavior in order to determine the degree to which a potential juror was defense or prosecution oriented. Fourth, the attorneys drew upon their voir dire experience and common sense. Fifth, we had a psychic who observed the potential jurors and advised us of their aura, "karma," and psychic vibrations. Finally, Ms. Little was asked how she felt about any juror whom we were seriously considering accepting.

We shall go into more detail on the first three of these in the next few sections of this article. It is beyond the scope of our task here to make any comments upon the judgments of the attorneys, the psychic, or

Ms. Little except to note three observations. First, all streams of data pointed to the same decision in about 90 per cent of the cases. Second, when there was disagreement, a majority of the lawyers and Ms. Little usually went with the decision indicated by the scientific evidence. Finally, given the political nature of the trial, the publicity value of a psychic should not be underestimated. He helped to keep the eyes of the world upon the defense, the prosecution, the judge, and Raleigh, North Carolina.

A. THE SURVEY AND MATHEMATICAL MODEL. Although it was expensive to construct (about $35 thousand), the most important scientific tool we had was the mathematical model of the defense's ideal juror based upon a random sample survey of Wake County. Its effectiveness rested upon two assumptions which, fortunately, proved to be justified. First, we assumed that the jury pool would be close to a random sample of the citizens of Wake County eligible for jury service. Second, we assumed that those characteristics of the survey respondents which enabled us to predict opinions regarding Joan Little's guilt or innocence in the sample survey would also enable us to predict them in the jury pool.

In order to facilitate a general understanding of the mathematical model by readers unfamiliar with statistical methods, it will be described in a brief, nontechnical fashion. The basic idea behind this approach is that individuals who are predisposed to believe that the defendant in question is guilty will differ from other individuals with respect to a number of observable characteristics. Once these characteristics have been identified for the population as a whole, they can be used to predict the predispositions of each potential juror.

Before the model can be employed, a survey of attitudes in the particular geographical area of interest must be undertaken. This provides an assessment of the attitudinal composition of that area from which the mathematical model will then generate its predictions. The mathematical model itself is a predictive hybrid of several statistical techniques. First, we chose an appropriate measure of the attitudes or opinions we wished to predict, i.e., belief in the guilt or innocence of the accused. Next, a series of statistical techniques was employed to determine what demographic characteristics of the respondents in the sample would act as predictors of these important opinions. Demographic characteristics might include age, race, sex, political and religious affiliations.

In the first phase of the procedure, an attempt was made to divide the sample into groups possessing similar opinions. That is, if those of higher ages and lower ages differed in their opinions regarding the guilt or innocence of the accused, it would be helpful to divide the sample into younger and older age groups before an attempt was made to formulate predictions of their important opinions. This was accomplished by using a modified version of a statistical computer program known as AID (Automatic Interaction Detection).

The AID program searched the survey data until it had successfully divided the sample into as many groups as possible based upon the homogeneity of the sample members' opinions. Membership in any one homogeneous group was often defined by several demographic characteristics—for example, young democrats with at least a college education. As a result of this first phase, our ability to predict opinions was increased by decreasing the variability of our sample.

After the sample was divided into groups of individuals with fairly similar opinions, each group was examined to establish which of their social and psychological characteristics were important with respect to our ability to predict a potential juror's opinions. In more technical terms,

this phase was concerned with the formulation of predictive equations for jurors' opinions. In order to do this we used a technique known as multiple regression, which enabled us to develop a mathematical model of the opinions of potential jurors based upon a series of characteristics that differed from one demographic group to another. An example of this would be the case where one group produced by phase I consisted of young democrats with at least a college education. For members of this group we may need to know the sex, religious attitudes, and income characteristics of the individuals. In another group from phase I, e.g., democrats over forty-five years old with a high school education, the terms in the predictive equation might be the type of magazines read, sex, and preferred presidential candidate.

Though the social and psychological factors used to predict opinions varied from group to group, they combined to form the same thing: a prediction of the likelihood that a potential juror would be willing to vote Joan Little not guilty before hearing any of the evidence.

One of the advantages of this procedure is obvious. Regardless of what a juror might say during the voir dire, by observing or obtaining his or her demographic characteristics (age, education, etc.) and social-psychological characteristics (politics, reading habits, etc.), the mathematical model enabled us to predict how predisposed he or she was to side with the prosecution or defense. Potential jurors might lie about their preconceptions of guilt or innocence, but they were much less likely to lie about their age or education.

A second advantage is not so obvious. Because the judge permitted both prosecution and defense to send out with the jury summons a questionnaire concerning the jurors' demographic characteristics, we were able to get a preliminary estimate of what proportion of the jury pool would be predisposed to be "pro-defense" or "pro-defendant" before the voir dire began and before we had seen a single juror. The advantage here is that in the early part of the voir dire we could afford to let some promising jurors go because we knew that better potential jurors would appear later. Many of the news reporters failed to see how important this was. Informally, if not in print or on the air, they expressed the opinion that the mathematical model and the other scientific procedures were not necessary because anyone would have known we wanted health food waitresses (the final jury had two of them) and a former drama major turned record store manager. What they failed to notice was that we got these persons as jurors because we had not already filled the slots with secretaries and IBM engineers.

B. AUTHORITARIANISM. Although we expected the math model to be between 85 per cent and 95 per cent accurate, we supplemented it with courtroom observations of authoritarianism and body language. Our observations of authoritarianism were based upon the theory of the authoritarian personality developed in the 1950's by researchers at the University of California at Berkeley.

According to this theory, which is supported by mountains of empirical research, extreme authoritarians are rigid, racist, anti-semitic, sexually repressed, politically conservative, highly punitive individuals who will accept the word of an authority figure over that of a lesser person. The authoritarian is servile and obsequious in subordinate position, but takes out all of his or her pent-up hostility and frustration upon those perceived to be in violation of the conventional norms of society.

It is obvious that no defense attorney would want a jury loaded with extreme authoritarians. . . .

The procedure for observing pro-spective jurors and rating their level of authoritarianism was developed by Richard Christie for use in the Harrisburg Eight trial. Christie had refined the procedure in a number of subsequent criminal trials, and in fact he was present at the Little trial to observe the potential jurors and to train others in the use of his observation and rating technique.

The authoritarianism rating scale we used in the courtroom ranged from a low of zero which represented minimum authoritarianism to a high of thirty which represented maximum authoritarianism. The neutral point between high authoritarian and low authoritarian behavior was fifteen. Christie's experience in a number of trials suggested that the average American rated about twenty on this scale of authoritarianism. By observing the authoritarianism-related behavior of potential jurors—their rigidity, their sexual prudery, their introspectiveness, and so on—three social psychologists were able to rate reliably the person's level of authoritarianism. When a decision was made to accept or reject a potential juror, these independently made, written ratings were combined to feed an authoritarianism rating into the decision making process.

The average rating assigned by our observers to all persons who were interviewed for Ms. Little's jury was 21.02, which is not very different from the general American population. On the other hand, the average for the sixteen seated jurors was 14.03. For the twelve who made the final decision to acquit her, the average authoritarianism rating was 12.95. Thus, we were able to pick a jury which was significantly less authoritarian than the jury pool as a whole.

C. BODY LANGUAGE. In a highly publicized case such as Ms. Little's, there were some people who actively desired to be on the jury. These people might have said whatever was necessary to insure that they were picked for the jury. Some of them could be expected to be pro-defense, some to be pro-prosecution. It was crucial for the defense to determine in some way the truthfulness of the jurors being selected. To do this, we called upon the newly emerging science of kinesics and paralinguistics, i.e., body language.

Although people frequently communicate their true feelings in the words they speak, it is now clear that we can also communicate a great deal of information by means of our body movements, gestures, positions, vocal intonations, pauses and the like. In other words, it is not what we say but the way we say it. We are perfectly capable of expressing one type of attitude with our language and a diametrically opposed attitude with our body language, for example, by unduly long pauses when speaking or by loudness or softness of the voice.

Our approach was to measure the levels of anxiety expressed by the individuals being questioned. We employed five variables to determine the kinesic response (body movement, body orientation, body posture, eye contact, and hand movement). We also employed two paralinguistic measures (vocal intonation and vocal hesitancy).

No single kinesic or paralinguistic response determined the acceptance or rejection of any juror. We were looking for patterns of behavior. Human communication is extremely complex and one must look at the whole in order to make any determination as to the attitudes being expressed. Some popular writers on the subject would have one believe that a single gesture indicative of an overall attitude. In truth, the single gesture must be deeply incorporated into a pattern of response expressed throughout the body and by the voice.

David Suggs, of the University of Nebraska, was our expert on body lan-guage. He and one and sometimes two other observers trained by him noted each prospective juror's pattern of kinesic and paralinguistic behavior (described above) and rated the juror on a scale ranging from one point, least favorable to the defense, to five points, most favorable to the defense. These preliminary ratings were written down independently by each observer and then combined to form a final five point rating of the juror's attitude towards the defense (a high score indicating maximum favorableness).

To assess the relationship between the measures made on the basis of authoritarianism and body language, we correlated the two scales. The overall correlation was $-.79$. The correlation was high and indicated that authoritarianism was associated with being least favorable towards the defense. The correlation was not so high, however, as to indicate that the two scales were simply measuring the same phenomena. Each measure both reinforced and added to the other. The use of both approaches insured more complete knowledge of the attitudes of the potential jurors than the use of either alone.

D. THE FINAL DECISION. When, in the course of the voir dire, a member of the defense team thought that a decision should be made on the potential juror under consideration, a conference was called. At this point, the members of the team put their heads together in a fashion that resembled a football huddle. Each social scientist read to the team from a written estimate of the potential juror based upon the juror's demographic rating, authoritarianism, or body language. In this way we minimized the influence upon an estimate from one technique (e.g., body language) by another technique (e.g., authoritarianism). The attorneys, the psychic, and Ms. Little also indicated their opinions of the potential juror in this "huddle." One of three decisions was made: accept, reject, or obtain more information.

If the decision was to accept, we either indicated acceptance at the time or asked a few more "soft" questions in order to educate the juror and establish further rapport. If the decision was to reject, we began a line of questioning which attempted to get the potential juror excused for cause. The defense team was very successful at getting people whom we did not want excused by the judge for cause. By the time we were choosing the twelfth juror, we had thirteen of our original fourteen peremptory challenges left while the prosecution had expended eight of its original nine peremptories.

When there were disagreements among the members of the team about a given juror, we continued to obtain information by asking more informational questions until we could reach agreement to accept or reject. As indicated above, when we had sufficient information, the scientific evidence pointed toward the same decision in over 90 per cent of the cases. Furthermore, as our advantage over the prosecution in peremptory challenges increased, we became more and more cautious about whom we accepted so that if only one of the streams of scientific data suggested a rejection, we rejected. This meant that we were virtually unanimous about the sixteen jurors finally accepted.

At the close of the five week trial, the jury took seventy-eight minutes to find Ms. Little not guilty of all charges. . . .

NOTES AND QUESTIONS

Systematic Jury Selection

1.   A word, first, on nomenclature. We shall refer to the application of social psychological methods in the voir dire process as systematic jury selection. The term scientific jury selection, which is often used to describe it, is not entirely appropriate. These methods are applied in conjunction with and as a supplement to the informed judgment of the attorney conducting the voir dire. We will also leave out of our discussion the use by attorneys of psychological advice which is based mainly on ad hoc, clinical judgment rather than systematically collected data. For example, Bryan, Jr. (1971), has described "hypnoanalytic" methods for assessing unconscious motives of prospective jurors in the courtroom. He indicates that he has been successful in a number of celebrated trials but the scientific underpinnings of his methods remain unclear (Vidmar 1976).

2.   Systematic jury selection is a recent development, born in the context of the highly politicized criminal cases of the early 1970s. One of the first published reports concerned the jury selection in the conspiracy trial of the Berrigan brothers and other antiwar activists, held in Harrisburg, Pennsylvania, for allegedly plotting to blow up the heating pipes of the Pentagon and kidnapping the Secretary of State (Schulman et al. 1973). It has also been used in the Angela Davis trial (Moore 1974; Sage 1973); the Wounded Knee trial of Native American activists Russell Means and Dennis Banks (Time, January 28, 1974, p. 60); the conspiracy trial of John Mitchell and Maurice Stans for allegedly impeding a Securities and Exchange Commission investigation of a fugitive financier (Zeisel and Diamond 1976); the "Camden 28" trial (Christie 1977); a civil damage suit against the Chicago Police Department for killing of Black Panther Party members (Berk 1976); and in a score of other cases. "[A]n eminent criminal lawyer . . . was so impressed by how [this method] helped him size up jurors in a part of the country where values and customs were unknown to him that he now uses it in four out of his five cases" (Hunt 1982, p. 73). Systematic jury selection provoked little public attention in the early "Harrisburg Conspiracy" and Angela Davis cases. The same effort in the Mitchell-Stans trial aroused considerable critical comment and public concern about "jury stacking" and "jury manipulation" (for example, Etzioni 1974). Appar-

ently the use of survey techniques by a professional consultant, at a cost of thousands of dollars, in conjunction with the acquittal verdict in that case triggered the commotion. Thus, by the time of the Joan Little trial, social scientists already had a few years of experience with jury selection (Bonora and Krauss 1979).

3.   The logic of using survey research in jury selection is straightforward. It consists, in essence, of three steps. First, a random sample is drawn from the population and the demographic profile of this sample is compared with that of the venire panel. If the venire was randomly drawn, the profiles should match. If they do not because there is a substantial underrepresentation of a distinct, cognizable group, then a constitutional challenge to the composition of the venire can be mounted on the authority of *Casteneda* and the line of cases discussed earlier. Second, once it is assured that the survey sample and the venire are equivalent groups, a survey of the randomly drawn sample is conducted. The purpose is to determine the demographic, personal, and attitudinal characteristics associated with being a "favorable" juror—favorable, that is, to one's own side. It is basically a predictive validity study. Third, once these characteristics are identified, they become the basis for the social scientist's recommendation for selection of individual jurors in the courtroom. This method can be diagrammed as follows:

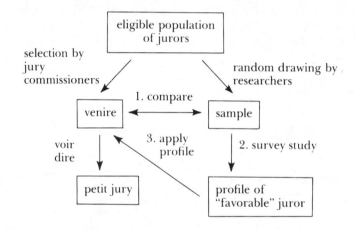

There are, of course, additions and variations to this basic procedure (Kairys, Shulman, and Harring 1975). For example, in the "Harrisburg Conspiracy" trial (Schulman et al. 1973), the use of the favorable juror profile in voir dire was supplemented by reports from "community scouts" regarding individual venirepersons. These scouts were persons of long standing in the community who knew or had access to local information about particular venirepersons. Their reports provided a check on the predictive validity of the survey results. In the Harrisburg case, the researchers also attempted to predict possible coalitions between prospective jurors. That is, from the probabilistic profile drawn from the survey group data, they sought to predict not only the behavior of an individual juror but also the social interactions between jurors during the deliberation phase. They wanted to ensure that jurors favorably disposed toward the defendant would have other jurors who would lend them support in the face of pressures from those jurors urging conviction. In another trial, for example, the researchers urged the rejection of several male venirepersons of high social status who were potentially favorable to the defense, on the grounds that they could be rivals of a woman venireperson whom the defense hoped would be the jury foreperson (Christie 1977).

4.   In the Little case, the various strands of information used in choosing prospective jurors—survey data, authoritarianism ratings, attorneys' judgments, body language, psychic's intuitions—were very highly correlated. But suppose they had not fit into a neat pattern—the demographic indices of a favorable juror did not coincide with the attitudinal predictors, or the latter were at variance with the attorney's judgment. If a large number of peremptory challenges were available, the defense could afford to make conservative decisions and reject any juror who was not rated favorably according to each and every one of the information sources. But if the number of peremptories were limited, how would you choose jurors with mixed ratings? How would you weight the different predictors?

5.   Perhaps the most interesting and the hardest question to answer is, "Does it work?" Is this elaborate and expensive method of jury selection successful? Indeed, what are the criteria which define success?

One way to assess the method is according to case outcome. It has resulted in acquittals or hung juries in about a score of cases. In only two or three instances did it result in convictions. Absent a control group, of course, it cannot be inferred that the high acquittal rate was the direct product of the use of social science at voir dire. A trial is a complex process and any number of factors or combinations of factors, in addition to the selection process at voir dire, could have been responsible for the favorable verdicts. In several of the well-publicized trials, including the Little trial, the amount and quality of the prosecution's evidence was unusually weak to begin with. Systematic jury selection has been applied mostly in conspiracy cases which are difficult for the prosecution to prove under most circumstances. Defense counsel retained in these cases were also of the highest caliber. The political dimension of these cases allows more room for the expression of the jury's sense of equity than in garden variety criminal cases. What the outcomes would have been in these cases if the government's evidence was stronger, or defense counsel less illustrious, or the ideological or racial element absent, is an open question (Saks 1976).

How would you design a field experiment to test the effect of systematic jury selection on verdicts? What possible alternative rival hypotheses would you seek to control for? What independent variables need to be studied? What methodological artifacts need to be controlled? Might the mere presence of social scientists and psychics in the courtroom, which in itself is uncommon, trigger any process that could affect the outcome? What are the "demand characteristics" of the situation and how might jurors be affected?

What does the following laboratory experiment (by Horowitz 1980) tell us about the comparative effectiveness of voir dire methods? Law students were trained in either conventional voir dire or social science selection (for example, using personality and demographic data based on a prior survey of prospective jurors) and assigned to observe the voir dire examination of mock jurors in one of four types of cases (illegal drug sale, court martial, murder, and drunk driving). The students predicted how the prospective jurors would vote. The jurors were then assigned to one of the four cases, listened to an audiotape of the trial, and rendered a verdict. The results showed that in the first two types of cases, the social science trained students predicted the jurors' verdicts more accurately than the conventionally-trained students. The earlier survey had shown that certain characteristics are associated with attitudes toward drug and court martial cases, so this finding was not surprising. The conventionally-trained students performed better in the murder case and there were no differences between the two groups in the drunk driving case.

6.   Schulman et al. (1973) conducted posttrial interviews with jurors to determine their votes and patterns of social interaction during the deliberation period. This information provided a check on the predictive power of their selection techniques. They claim an "accuracy" rate of 70% or better in predicting juror behavior (Vidmar 1976). What methodological problems do you see in this means of evaluating effectiveness?

7.   The article by McConahay et al. (1977) points out that the challenges to the composition of the venire panel and the venue were "perhaps more important than the jury selection in determining the outcome of the trial." The research for both of these challenges was preliminary to and necessary for the construction of the "favorable" juror profile. This suggests that indices other than, or additional to, case outcomes might be more appropriate for assessing impact of systematic jury selection. An important secondary consequence of this method is to educate prospective jurors about the pervasiveness and the ramifications of prejudice. One cannot discount the possibility that the mere use of behavioral scientists at trial has a talismanic effect on the attorneys themselves, giving a psychological edge to one side and dispiriting the other. How would you evaluate the selection method in light of these less tangible indices?

Predicting Verdicts from Jurors' Characteristics

The importance that attorneys attach to voir dire is predicated on the assumption that personal characteristics of jurors are an important determinant of the eventual verdict. A jury selection manual flatly asserts that "the people who constitute the jury can have as much or more to do with the outcome of a trial as the evidence and arguments" (Kairys, Schulman, and Harring 1975, p. 1). Attorneys have always relied on their intuition and experience in choosing the kinds of persons who might be sympathetic to their side. With the development of systematic jury selection, they have turned to social scientists for assistance in voir dire. Mathematical models for predicting "favorable" jurors also rest on the premise that decisions of potential jurors are influenced by their background (for example, race, social class, education, sex), social attitudes (for example, political preferences, racial attitudes), and/or personality characteristics (for example, authoritarianism, dogmatism). Even previous jury duty may affect how a juror evaluates the evidence (Kerr 1981). The assumption, in other words, is that human conduct is caused—or at least conditioned—by socialization experiences and personal makeup. Behavior is relatively consistent at different times and in different places. Consequently, if the demographic and individual characteristics of a prospective juror are known, his voting tendency can be predicted before the trial even begins.

However, there are empirical and theoretical grounds for questioning the validity of this heroic assumption and, thereby, the marginal effectiveness of systematic jury selection over conventional jury selection. Consider, for example, the assumed relationship between the attribute of authoritarianism and the propensity to convict. Some researchers claim that this personality dimension is "one of the best predictors of conviction proneness we have encountered" (Ellison and Buckhout 1981, p. 191). The jurors in the Little case were chosen partly because of their significantly lower authoritarianism ratings relative to the general population, and they acquitted. On this basis, some advocate "trial by a jury of attitudinally similar peers" (Mitchell and Byrne 1973, p. 128) and the psychological screening of prospective jurors as a precondition for qualification (Emerson 1968).

The available research belies the assumption of such a simple relationship. Since 1970, there have been a large number of jury simulations on the effects of various personality and demographic characteristics of mock jurors on their decision-making (see, for example, Gerbasi, Zuckerman, and Reis 1977; Nemeth 1981). In general, "although the literature indicates that authoritarians do indeed recommend more severe punishment . . . , only a single study has shown that they are more likely to vote for conviction (Bray and Noble, 1978)" (Greenberg and Ruback 1982, p. 143). Another review also concluded that "the claim that high authoritarian jurors have a proclivity for guilty verdicts is basically unwarranted" (Davis, Bray, and Holt 1977, p. 341). Despite the lack of convincing evidence, it is still an article of faith among some social scientists that "authoritarianism is an influential factor in the jury process" (Bartol 1983, p. 139).

With respect to individual differences other than authoritarianism, there also is no unequivocal proof of a direct, one-to-one relationship with conduct. One study presented a videotaped trial to 480 actual jurors and then correlated their decisions with their responses to 27 attitudinal and demographic questions. Only four of these "predictors" correlated with juror verdicts, and together they accounted for only 13% of the variance in decision-making (Saks and Hastie 1978, pp. 65–66). Such "weak relationships between the personal characteristics of jurors and the decisions they make are by far the rule, not the exception" (p. 66). Penrod (1979) presented four audiotaped trials (involving murder, rape, robbery, and a tort suit) to a sample of 367 actual jurors. Each trial, lasting about thirty minutes, adhered to the usual procedure of opening and closing statements, witnesses' testimony, and judicial instructions. The jurors then rendered individual (not group) verdict preferences. These responses were subjected to regression analysis to determine whether the verdicts could be predicted from personal information of the jurors. In the four cases, these predictors accounted for only 4% to 16% of the variance in jurors' judgments. Penrod concluded that it is "[not] possible to predict jurors' verdict preferences on the basis of juror characteristics or attitudes" (p. 174). In another simulated jury study, nine demographic variables accounted for only 8% of the variation in jurors' decisions in a felony-murder case, and certain social opinions (for example, toward punishment) accounted for only 10% (Hepburn 1980).

None of these studies, it should be pointed out, compared these predictions with judgments of attorneys. The issue of interest is not the absolute magnitude of the correlation coefficients, but the relative superiority of this method over conventional voir dire. It is possible that attorneys predict juror decisions no better, or even worse, than the mathematical models. These studies cast doubt on the basic predicate of systematic jury selection, but they do not directly show that it is less effective than attorney-conducted selection.

The notion that *who* a person is determines *how* that person acts, irrespective of the social context, is also at odds with recent thinking on the nature of personality. Traditionally, psychologists viewed behavior as the product of more or less stable personality characteristics. Since the late 1960s, a different conceptualization of social behavior has gained currency. The springs of conduct are now increasingly located in situational influences rather than in individual traits. If how people behave depends significantly on the circumstances in which they find themselves, "the assumption of massive behavioral similarity across diverse situations no longer is tenable" (Mischel 1968, p. 296). Social behavior is context-specific; its "causes" are said to lie outside rather than inside the person. It is a "fundamental attribution error" to "[account] for behavior in terms of the traits or dispositions of the people who perform it rather than the characteristics of the situation in which it occurs" (Haney 1982, p. 30). With respect to social attitudes, which are less enduring and more malleable than personality traits, social psychologists have also recognized that they are seldom reliable predictors of future conduct (Ajzen and Fishbein 1980).

In the trial setting, features of the proceeding itself are the decisive influences on the jury verdict. Those who are impaneled are solemnly instructed in the obligations of a juror, to lay aside personal biases and decide solely on the evidence presented in accordance with established rules of law. There is little reason to believe that the person's background and attitudes would override the effect of these situational forces. (There are, of course, hopelessly biased persons, but they would probably have been excluded for cause.) We know that most criminal cases that go to trial have fairly clear outcomes. Kalven and Zeisel (1966) found that judges agreed with the verdict returned by the jury in about 75% of the cases sampled (p. 56). Simulation "studies are unanimous in showing that evidence is a substantially more potent determinant of jurors' verdicts than the individual characteristics of jurors" (Saks and Hastie 1978, p. 68). Moreover, jurors deliberate together to reach a common verdict, and "small-group researchers have long recognized that individual difference variables account for little of the variation in group performance . . ." (p. 66).

This is not to say that jurors' characteristics have no impact on their decisions. Rather, their impact, if any, is likely to be mediated by situational factors of the trial. Work needs to be done on how individual and contextual factors combine or interact to influence jury decision-making. For example, women (mock) jurors have been found to be more conviction prone than their male counterparts in rape cases but not in other criminal prosecutions (Greenberg and Ruback 1982, pp. 143–44). A juror's racial biases could come into play in a housing discrimination case but not in a burglary trial. The amount of evidence available might also determine the extent to which extralegal influences intrude in the decisional process. If the evidence is clear and unambiguous, as it is in about 70% of criminal cases according to one estimate (Lempert 1975), there is less room for the expression of individual differences. In the other 30% of the cases, systematic jury selection could have an effect.

A model of the "favorable" juror, like any other statistical model, necessarily simplifies the reality it is intended to simulate. It cannot and need not incorporate all aspects of the reality in order to yield useful predictions. However, as Finkelstein (1978) cautioned in another context, there is a tendency in model building "to sweep away complexity to permit mathematical accessibility. This drive for quantification sometimes tempts the [researcher] to ignore or reject complicating factors that are nonetheless essential to the legal picture. The lawyer may be an unwitting accomplice in this process if he limits his role to a passive understanding of his expert's work, and fails to pursue a critical evaluation from a carefully focused legal point of view" (pp. 11–12). Complicating factors that are absent in juror selection models are the nature and strength of the evidence. Thus, instead of measuring global personality traits or general social attitudes, a more fruitful approach to jury selection might be to examine situationally specific attributes of jurors that might predispose them to decide one way or another. The prediction of the outcome would be based on matching characteristics of the jurors with characteristics of the case to be tried. For particular cases under specified conditions, "scientific" selection of jurors may yet prove to be superior to attorneys' judgments.

Expansion and Refinements of the Method

Some of the social scientists involved in the "Harrisburg Conspiracy" trial helped to establish the National Jury Project in 1975. Staffed by a handful of modestly paid employees and backed by part-time volunteers (liberal and leftist social scientists and lawyers), this nonprofit organization assisted in jury selection on behalf of dozens of activist and indigent defendants. By the end of the 1970s and in the 1980s, word of the techniques had gotten around and an increasing number of lawyers, generally representing major corporations embroiled in large-scale products liability and antitrust litigation, began to call on social scientists and market researchers. Today, social research is used more often in civil than in criminal trials, and the procedures have been extended to include jury persuasion as well as jury selection (Hunt 1982).

One expansion of the method is the use of a shadow jury. Lawyers for IBM hired social scientists to select a mock jury composed of individuals with demographic and personal characteristics similar to those of the real jury then sitting in an antitrust trial. The case involved a $300 million suit filed by California Computer Products, Inc., against IBM. The shadow jury sat in on the trial every day. In the evenings, the members reported their reactions to the arguments and evidence presented that day. The IBM attorneys received daily feedback on the effectiveness of their persuasion. They learned when they were proceeding too fast or too slow, how clearly they were addressing the jury, and so on (*Wall Street Journal*, April 3, 1981, p. 27). When the shadow jury was discovered by the press two months into the trial, it attracted so much controversy that it was disbanded. IBM eventually won the case.

The shadow jury technique was used in another major antitrust suit by MCI Communications Corp. against AT&T. The attorneys for MCI hired a large market research firm to construct a profile of the favorable juror: self-made, competitive, first- or second-generation American, intelligent, and susceptible to claims of unfair practices by mighty corporations against small competitors. In addition, a shadow jury was selected and the attorneys rehearsed their presentations in front of this mock jury before appearing in court. The deliberations of the mock jurors were observed through one-way mirrors and analyzed by the social scientists. The sessions yielded some valuable tips. For example, the MCI lawyers discovered that a point of law, favorable to their side, was difficult for the mock jurors to grasp, so they took pains to present it clearly to the real jury. Also, the shadow jury rendered a verdict for MCI but awarded damages of only $100 million, far short of the $900 million requested. The mock jurors reported that they arrived at the lower figure because it was MCI's lost profit by reason of AT&T's monopolistic practices. Subsequently, with new mock jurors, the attorneys avoided mentioning the $100 million figure in order not to give them a comparison standard. This time the mock jury awarded $900 million. At the conclusion of the trial, the real jury found for MCI and awarded it $600 million, the largest damage award in antitrust history (*Newsweek*, March 9, 1981, p. 84; Cahn 1983).

Needless to say, companies pay handsomely for such research services. The head of a consulting firm that specializes in jury research tells lawyers, "If it isn't worth spending $50,000 for jury research for your case, forget it. And a full-scale workup can run as much as $500,000" (Hunt 1982, p. 73). Other consultants say that "scaled-down simulations can be run and analyzed for as little as a few thousand dollars and are therefore practical in medium-sized cases as well" (Cahn 1983, p. 1074).

What new developments or refinements in the technology of systematic jury selection would you suggest? At present, as with any new technology, it is a costly and time-consuming process. With the ready availability of computers and data storage systems, how might one standardize the method so that it could be used as a routine tool in a given jurisdiction? See Comment, *University of Detroit Journal of Urban Law* (1978).

Policy and Legal Issues

8.   The use of systematic jury selection in voir dire raises a host of difficult ethical and policy issues. For purposes of this discussion, assume that the technology is, in fact, effective, however effectiveness is defined. Is it the systematic jury selection method itself or the inequitable use of this method that poses risks? To date, in criminal cases it has been used exclusively by defense counsel. Do you see possible inequities arising if and when the government avails itself of this method? Would these inequities be minimized if the state were to subsidize the use of social scientists by indigent defendants for jury selection purposes? Some jurisdictions now provide for state-paid expert witnesses—such as psychiatrists and ballistics experts—to indigent defendants. Alternatively, should the defense be allowed discovery of the results of the prosecution's selection study? If both sides construct and use their own predictive models for the same trial, would the effects of the method be counterbalanced or neutralized?

9.   Etzioni (1974) has sharply criticized the use of this technology as a form of jury stacking which threatens the institution of the jury trial. He makes four proposals to check possible abuses: (a) Decrease the number of excuses from jury duty in order to increase the venire array and thereby render it more representative of the population; (b) curb the number of peremptory challenges; (c) bar the out-of-courtroom investigation of prospective jurors; and (d) allow only judges to conduct the voir dire questioning. Evaluate each of these proposals. If implemented, what impact would each have on systematic jury selection and on the guarantee of an impartial jury trial? For additional criticisms and comments, see Herbsled, Sales, and Berman (1978) and Hunt (1982).

10.   Is the issue of an impartial jury a matter of having a bias-free jury or of having a jury with a representative cross section of the biases of the community? In this perspective, voir dire is a process to ensure that a wide range of biases are represented in the composition of the jury. If, for instance, most of the members of a community have values and attitudes which do not predispose them favorably to a defendant, is it "stacking" the jury to use social science methods to include prospective jurors with minority viewpoints? Would there be any need for using these methods if the community was already biased in favor of a defendant?

11.   Critics of systematic jury selection also say that it tends to undermine our adversarial system of justice. In principle, there is a balance between the prosecution and the defense. The government usually has greater resources than an individual defendant, but the balance is supposedly restored by procedural rules which place the burden on the government. Thus, an accused is presumed innocent until proven guilty by the state; self-accusation is not tolerated. The state also has to come forward with the evidence; the accused has only to rebut whatever is presented. These ground rules equalize the match and with competent counsel on both sides vigorously advocating the respective positions, justice is supposed to emerge. Systematic jury selection, it is argued, by stacking the jury with members who are sympathetic to the defendant, tips the carefully designed balance to the advantage of the accused.

In practice, however, the balance of justice is seldom in equipoise. The advantage is massively on the side of the state. Consider the following factors in evaluating the effect of systematic jury selection on the adversarial system. The federal government, in certain conspiracy trials, can choose the site of prosecution. In the trial of the Berrigan brothers, the government chose Harrisburg, Pennsylvania, a small, very conservative town known to be in favor of the Vietnam War. Since the defendants had raided draft boards in Philadelphia and New York, and the charge was conspiracy to destroy the heating pipes in the Pentagon, the government could have conducted the trial in these two cities or in Washington, D.C. Likewise, in the Pentagon Papers trial of Daniel Ellsberg in 1973, the government chose southern California as the trial site. The voir dire revealed that many of the prospective jurors had some ties to the defense industry which is predominant in that area. The government could have prosecuted Ellsberg in Washington, D.C.

The investigative resources of the state simply cannot be matched by individuals. The FBI has been used to investigate the backgrounds and views of prospective jurors (Van Dyke 1977, p. 616). In a prosecution for income tax evasion, the Justice Department obtained tax records of venirepersons from the IRS and used the Postal Service to check the backgrounds of prospective jurors (Okun 1968). Local prosecutors not infrequently maintain "black lists" of jurors who have voted for acquittal in any case. When these persons appear again for jury service, they are challenged on a peremptory basis. Up to now, systematic jury selection methods have scrupulously respected the privacy of prospective jurors. Unlike the government inquiries, the behavioral scientists address their questions to a random sample from the population and not to members of the venire panel itself.

The sequestration of the jury can also operate to the state's advantage. The purpose is to insulate the jury from trial publicity and any improper influences. But it could also have the unintended effect of biasing the jury toward the state. In some cases, the government has provided the jury with special dining and entertainment during the period of sequestration. In one instance, a juror was provided an escort of U.S. marshals to watch a ball game in which his son was playing (Van Dyke 1977). The effects of long periods of sequestration on jury deliberations and outcome have not been investigated. Undoubtedly such long periods generate internal pressures, but the impact of virtual isolation on jury behavior has been subject only of conjecture.

12.   The preceding discussion has already suggested a number of complex legal issues which are emerging as a result of this technology. If the method can be standardized and used on a relatively routine basis for certain types of cases in a given jurisdiction, what procedural safeguards will be needed to protect the privacy of prospective jurors? Is there a constitutional right under the Due Process Clause or the Sixth Amendment guarantee of *effective* counsel to state-appointed behavioral scientists for indigent defendants?

13.   The theme of this chapter is the right to an impartial jury trial. So far, we have seen three ways in which control over impartiality can be exerted: challenge to venire composition if cognizable groups are underrepresented; challenge to venue if the population is biased; and challenges (peremptory or for cause) at voir dire.

Notice that the means for ensuring impartiality in the first instance are different from those at voir dire. By looking at population bias and venire composition, the inquiry is a relatively objective one and rests on aggregate statistical data. A survey can indicate the extent of bias in the community. Statistical impact data and analysis of the selection procedures used can reveal whether there has been purposeful discrimination against cognizable groups such that they are underrepresented in the venire. There are also extensive legal rules, from *Swain* to *Castaneda,* which attempt to guarantee a representative cross section of the population in the venire. Thus, the control for impartiality is exercised at two threshold points: the community itself and the institutional procedures for selection into the venire.

On the other hand, the control for impartiality at the voir dire is primarily an inquiry into the state of mind of prospective jurors. Each individual is questioned regarding possible biases. In contrast to the well-developed body of law on venire composition, there is hardly any law regarding the voir dire. The selection of petit jurors is largely a matter of trial court discretion. What possible reasons might underlie the different judicial treatment of venire selection and petit jury selection?

14. In *Ristiano* v. *Ross* (1976), the Supreme Court set narrow constitutional limits to questioning about prejudice in state trials. A black defendant was prosecuted for assaulting a white guard. At voir dire, the judge refused to inquire if the venirepersons were biased against blacks. Only questions regarding possible "general bias" of prospective jurors, without any mention of race, were permitted. The Court upheld the conviction and ruled that questioning about specific (racial) prejudice at voir dire is permissible only if there is a nexus between the prejudice feared and the issues which are likely to arise at trial. In this instance, there was no connection between the mere fact of different racial identities of the parties and the crime of assault. Racial identity alone is not constitutionally determinative of the right to question venirepersons about racial prejudice. The decision reaffirms the traditional discretion of the trial judge in voir dire and shows a remarkable solicitude for biases in prospective jurors.

At bedrock rests a key assumption regarding the psychology of prejudice. The Court assumes that latent prejudices are triggered by issues at the trial which are related to those prejudices. Cases which do not expressly deal with prejudice (for example, an ordinary assault case in contrast to, say, a housing discrimination case) "are [less] likely to intensify any prejudice that individual members of the jury might harbor" (p. 597). This "intensification" notion suggests that latent prejudice interacts with the facts of a case, and this interaction brings the prejudice to the surface. If such facts are present in a case, the voir dire questioning can touch upon the specific issue of prejudice, and venirepersons found to be biased can be disqualified for cause.

Prior to *Ristiano,* questioning on racial bias was generally allowed as a matter of trial court discretion, and persons so found were disqualified. The psychological assumption is that biases are not issue-specific, that they manifest themselves across different issues and situations. Racial prejudice has, so to speak, a "main effect" on juror behavior. With *Ristiano,* the assumption is that racial prejudice and case issues have an "interaction effect" on behavior. Which assumption accords more with present psychological theory and evidence on human prejudice? Can you suggest a study or a series of interlocking studies designed to test these assumptions? What impact does *Ristiano* have for voir dire questioning using systematic jury selection methods? That is, how would you assess prejudice in prospective jurors if specific questions are disallowed for want of nexus?

If questioning is allowed, is disclosure of racial bias more likely to occur when the prospective juror responds in open court or in private? See Nietzel and Dillehay (1982).

15. The higher standard used in federal trials was announced by Justice White in a plurality opinion in *Rosales-Lopez* v. *United States* (1981): Failure to honor a defendant's request to inquire into bias "will only be reversible error where the circumstances of the case indicate that there is a reasonable possibility that racial or ethnic prejudice might have influenced the jury" (p. 1637). A situation in which the defendant is accused of a violent crime, and both the defendant and the victim are members of different racial backgrounds, would fall within the "reasonable possibility" standard. This test was not met in the case at bar, since the defendant was a Mexican-American charged with smuggling Mexicans into the United States. Surely the Court knows what everybody else knows, that there is the possibility of prejudice in less inflamed situations than interracial violence. Are there sound reasons of policy for thus restricting the scope of voir dire? Propose a less restrictive test that nonetheless meets the objections to unfettered questioning about racial bias.

7.6.   JUROR PARTIALITY AND PRETRIAL PUBLICITY: REMEDIAL AND PREVENTIVE SAFEGUARDS

There are two principal sources of juror partiality: (1) individual characteristics that predispose jurors toward acquittal or conviction (discussed in the preceding section)—the voir dire process, including the use of systematic selection techniques, is the principal means of screening for this type of bias; and (2) pretrial publicity. A representative jury may not necessarily ensure an impartial jury because it may be representative of a community inflamed by prejudicial publicity.

A study by Constantini and King (1980–81) indicates that the latter source has a greater effect on the propensity of prospective jurors to prejudge guilt. They conducted telephone surveys of large probability samples of prospective jurors in California in connection with three highly publicized criminal cases. Prejudgment (as indexed by belief in defendant's guilt or by self-evaluations of impartiality) was highly correlated with prior knowledge about the case gained from the media and with such personal characteristics as general attitudes toward crime, gender, and education. Multivariate analyses showed that prior knowledge was the most important variable in predicting potential bias in jurors. In one case, it was "ten times more important than any of the other three [individual characteristics] and four times as important as the other three combined" (p. 33).

This section deals with juror partiality arising from pretrial publicity. The courts have devised various corrective and preventive measures for this bias. Remedies during judicial proceedings include (a) changing the trial to a venue untouched by publicity, (b) postponement of the trial until public attention ebbs, (c) searching questioning at voir dire, (d) judicial admonitions to the jury to set aside pretrial media information, (e) sequestration of the jury, and (f) the ultimate palliative of reversal on appeal (*Sheppard* v. *Maxwell*, 1966, pp. 357–62). The preventive approach reaches back to the pre-judicial phase and nips the problem at the source by banning publication or broadcasting all or parts of the case, at least until the trial is concluded. Preventive measures include gagging the press and/or the police and the attorneys. We shall focus on the remedy of venue change and the use of opinion surveys for that purpose, and then turn to the safeguard of prior restraint of the media.

Remedying Pretrial Publicity: Change of Venue

When there is demonstrated a reasonable likelihood of substantial prejudice in the community, a trial court at its discretion may grant a change of venue. Traditionally, the evidence in support of the motion for change consists of affidavits of community leaders regarding their perceptions of public opinion and documentary proof of pretrial media publicity. In the early 1950s, opinion surveys were introduced in order to assess more directly and systematically the extent of community prejudice (Woodward 1952). The early attempts to use survey data ran afoul of the hearsay barrier. Typically, the survey researcher presents the procedures and results in court via testimony and/or written statements. Since the researcher is describing opinions of respondents which were recorded by interviewers and, in turn, processed and analyzed by others, the in-court testimony constitutes hearsay several times removed. The respondents themselves are not in court so they cannot be subjected to cross-examination, under oath, for evaluation of veracity. Consequently, survey data were ruled inadmissible (Barksdale 1957).

By the mid-sixties, as courts became educated in sampling statistics and opinion polls, they became more receptive to their use in a variety of noncriminal cases. The hearsay objection was sidestepped by admitting the data under one of the many exceptions to the rule. For example, an opinion poll can be admitted not for the truth asserted therein but to show the state of mind of the respondent. If a survey in support of a trademark infringement lawsuit showed that 90% of the sample think the two brands are the same, the result may be admissible solely to show the confusion of the respondents, not that they are in fact the same. The modern approach is to weigh the value of the survey evidence against the unreliability inherent in any hearsay. If other methods of obtaining the information are impractical and the risks of error have been minimized, survey data are usually admitted. The issue, then, becomes one of the methodological adequacy of the survey. It is no longer a threshold issue of admissibility of survey opinions as such (Zeisel 1968).

In this changed judicial climate, criminal defense attorneys once again began to support their motions for venue change with survey evidence. The American Bar Association's standards on "Fair Trial and Free Press" expressly endorsed the use of "qualified public opinion surveys or opinion testimony offered by individuals or . . . the court's own evaluation" to determine whether "there is a substantial likelihood that . . . a fair trial by an impartial jury cannot be had" as the result of "dissemination of potentially prejudicial material" (ABA Standing Committee on Association Standards for Criminal Justice 1982, Standard 8-3.3(c)). Imaginatively designed research even included a field experiment within a survey in order to pinpoint the sources of bias. In a Canadian case, a defendant was prosecuted for fraud. The prosecution came in the wake of a highly publicized, unrelated trial involving the defrauding of senior citizens. This defendant had also been a defendant (along with others) in the earlier, publicized trial and had been convicted. Vidmar and Judson (1981) conducted telephone surveys which showed that one-half of the respondents said they could not be impartial jurors in a fraud trial, even if they were judicially instructed to set aside their biases and decide solely on the evidence presented. The respondents were also asked to evaluate their ability to be impartial under one of four randomly assigned conditions: the defendant had no prior criminal record, a conviction for assault, a conviction for fraud, or a conviction for fraud in the earlier, publicized case. The last condition elicited the highest level of expressed bias. These results showed the prejudicial effect of defendant's prior conviction. The motion was granted largely on the expert testimony on the survey study.

However, the successful uses of survey research in this instance and in the Joan Little case represent the exception rather than the rule. Indeed, since the mid-sixties, for the most part "the reported cases in which public opinion sampling was introduced . . . have either denied the motion while attributing little or no weight to the poll, or if granting the motion, have still attributed little weight to the poll" (Pollock 1977, p. 280). The reasons for the relative lack of success of scientific surveys for this particular legal use are not always apparent, since some judges continue to rely on the hearsay objection as a handy rationale for denying the motion. Some researchers "speculate that the major cause lies with poorly conceived and conducted surveys" (Hans and Vidmar 1982, pp. 52–53). They point out surveys which used very small and unrepresentative samples. Other polls asked questions which were not relevant to the legal issues. For example, interviewers were asked if they recognized defendant's name and how much they liked the defendant. The inference was that negative attitudes toward a defendant can be equated with potential juror bias. However, judges have long sensed—and empirical studies have since confirmed—that general attitudes of prospective jurors (for example, against the death penalty) do not necessarily result in actions (for example, acquittal) consistent with those attitudes (this is the *Witherspoon* issue discussed in Chapter 5, section 5.3). Hans and Vidmar (1982) propose that "it may be preferable to first ask people open-ended questions regarding the case and then provide them with more specific questions about how they might behave as jurors in this case" (p. 52). Notwithstanding sound methodology, survey evidence does not always have a decisive impact because the requested remedy is one that courts grant only in extraordinary circumstances, such as when all other remedial measures are inappropriate.

N O T E S   A N D   Q U E S T I O N S

Survey Research to Establish Community Bias

1.   Suppose that at a pretrial hearing on a motion for change of venue, defense counsel introduces a social scientist who testifies about a survey he has conducted that purportedly shows community bias toward the defendant. If you are with the prosecution which is resisting the motion, what questions would you ask of the expert witness and what criticisms might you raise regarding the procedure, results and conclusions? The facts of the following case are adapted, in abbreviated and modified form, from an actual trial and survey study reported by Nietzel and Dillehay (1983; "Case II" of four reported cases).

The defendant, a 52-year-old black prison trusty, is charged with the rape and murder of a white woman in her apartment. Extensive pretrial publicity focused on the defendant's long criminal record and the security lapses in the trusty program. This program was terminated prior to the start of the trial because of this crime. The social scientist testifies that he conducted a telephone survey of the county in question and of a neighboring county (which was the desired venue by the defense). From a telephone directory, he randomly selected names. About 25% of those he called refused to participate in the survey. The final sample of respondents consisted of 33 adults and 30 adults in the two respective counties, all of whom were elegible for jury service. He says "There are no firm rules for sample size," but in his experience, "Judges are usually satisfied with samples of this size" (p. 317). The interviewers were college students who were trained in the use of a standardized questionnaire. They introduced themselves as researchers for the public defenders's office and said that they were calling to see how county voters "feel about our criminal justice system." Confidentiality of answers was promised. The results of the answers to several key questions asked of the samples in the original venue county and in the neighboring county were, respectively, as follows (pp. 322–27):

— Had read or heard anything about the case: 97% vs. 50%
— Were able to name defendant: 30% vs. 0%
— Believed in defendant's guilt: 41% vs. 10%
— Believed there is much evidence against defendant: 21% vs. 3%
— Favored death penalty for defendant if found guilty: 41% vs. 10%
— Thought fair trial was possible in locale: 71% vs. 57%
— Knew that defendant was a trusty at time of crime: 73% vs. 17%
— Acknowledged that trusty status affected opinion about guilt: 18% vs. 17%

Except for the last question, the differences between the responses of the two groups were statistically significant. He concludes that these figures show that there is a "reasonable likelihood" (which is the governing legal standard in the jurisdiction) of prejudice in the original venire and of not being able to impanel an impartial jury. (In the actual case based on the foregoing facts, the trial court granted the motion.)

2.   Is the following observation, made a generation ago by Justice Frankfurter, still valid? "Science with all of its advances has not given us instruments for determining when the impact of such newspaper exploitation has spent itself, or whether the powerful impression bound to be made by such inflaming articles as here preceded the trial can be dissipated in the mind of the average juror by the tame and often pedestrian proceedings in court" (*Stroble* v. *California*, 1952, p. 181).

3.   Survey research allows us to make estimates about the population based on information obtained from a randomly selected subset or sample thereof. The various techniques of drawing random samples is the specialized subject of sampling statistics. (For example, there is simple random sampling: every person in the population has an equal chance of being included in the sample, such as would occur if the names of all persons were placed in an urn and the names were then drawn by chance; stratified sampling: the population is divided into strata, such as occupational groups, and persons are randomly selected from each stratum; cluster sampling: the population is divided into clusters, such as census tracts, and persons are randomly selected from each of the randomly chosen clusters; and so forth.) The representativeness of the sample is determined by the method that is selected (namely, random or nonrandom), not by its size. However, sample size does have a bearing on the accuracy of the estimates of the population.

    A domestic example may help illustrate these points. Suppose that you wish to know if a cauldron of soup is sufficiently salted. You need not consume the whole cauldron to find out. Tasting a spoonful will do, provided you stir the soup thoroughly so that each drop has an equal chance of being included in the spoonful. Even after stirring, and assuming your gustatory sense is reliable, the spoonful will not reflect exactly the saltiness of the whole cauldron. In statistical terms, the inaccuracy of measures based on a sample is called "sampling error." The range of this error can be specified in terms of "levels of confidence" expressed in probability terms. (For example, suppose that in a randomly drawn sample, 41% of respondents say the accused is guilty. If the application of statistical formulas shows the sampling error is, say, ± 6% and the confidence level of the sample result [41%] is .05, this means that in 95 out of 100 times, the number of persons in the population who believe the accused is guilty will fall between 35% and 47%.) Moreover, the sampling error can be reduced by increasing the sample size, though beyond a certain point, the reduction is marginal. Tasting a cupful will yield a more accurate measure than tasting a spoonful, but consuming a quart of the soup is not likely to improve the estimate much more than sampling the cupful. The larger the sample, the smaller the sampling error. If the quantity of soup you sample is the entire cauldron, there is no sampling error because the sample equals the population. Statistical formulas show that the sampling error is inversely proportional to the square root of the sample size. By quadrupling the sample size, the sampling error is reduced by one half. Thus, to assess the probative value of a survey, one needs to know the sampling procedure, the sampling error, and the sample size.

    Should the courts specify the confidence levels for the accuracy of survey data, since sampling error can be reduced at will by increasing sample size?

Survey Research to Establish Trademark Infringement

4.   Survey research yields numbers. One must still draw conclusions from these numbers. What proportion of the population must express prejudice before a court should conclude that it is not likely that an impartial jury can be impaneled? An overwhelming majority? A substantial minority? Should the results of past surveys of community bias be used as "norms" to guide the decision (Nietzel and Dillehay 1983, p. 335)? Should the cut-off point vary according to the nature of the case, the amount of publicity, and the liberalism or conservatism of the community?

    Another area of law in which survey research is extensively used, and in which the same issue of line drawing arises, is trademark infringement. A trademark is any word or symbol used by a producer to identify his product (Lanham Act §45, 15 U.S.C. §1127, 1976). It is valuable intellectual property because not only does it distinguish the product from its competitors, but it can also generate consumer demand if it is widely recognized and respected. A new mark is not accorded protection by the Patent and Trademark Office if it is so similar to an already registered mark as to "likely . . . cause confusion or to cause mistake, or to deceive." Thus, the owner of a trademark can sue someone who designates his product by a similar name so as to cause consumer confusion. For example, the publisher of *Seventeen* magazine brought a trademark infringement action against the manufacturer of "Miss Seventeen" girdles (*Triangle Publications* v. *Rohrlick*, 1948). The trial judge and the majority of the Second Circuit simply assumed that the new mark created confusion. In dissent, Judge Frank acidly observed that "neither the trial judge nor any member of this court is (or resembles) a teen-age girl," so that empirical inquiry rather than judicial notice should be relied upon to determine whether "any [confusion] existed between plaintiff's magazine and defendant's girdles" (p. 976).

The trademark statute says nothing about the proportion of consumers who must likely be confused in order for liability to lie. "[T]he range of numbers adopted by the courts in different cases have varied widely" (*Processed Plastic Co.* v. *Warner Communications*, 1982, p. 857). Does the determination of the threshold for consumer confusion involve different considerations than the determination of the threshold for community bias in criminal proceedings?

5.   The questions that are (and are not) asked, and the manner in which they are phrased, affect the responses elicited. What additional questions should have been included in the above rape-murder survey, in order to determine whether venue change was warranted?

6.   The importance of scrutinizing survey questions for legal relevance can be illustrated with another example from trademark law. In 1935, Parker Brothers registered "Monopoly" as a trademark for a board game. In the early 1970s, an economics professor invented and tried unsuccessfully to market a new board game called "Bust the Trust." He then repackaged it in a way similar to "Monopoly" and called it "Anti-Monopoly." The result was commercial success. General Mills, the successor to Parker Brothers, protested the use of that name. Anti-Monopoly, Inc., the marketing organization, took the offensive and sued for declaratory judgment against the continued use of the "Monopoly" trademark. General Mills counterclaimed for trademark infringement. After several years of trials and appeals, Anti-Monopoly won. The Ninth Circuit ruled that "the word 'Monopoly' has become 'generic' and that the regulation of it as a trademark is no longer valid" (*Anti-Monopoly, Inc.* v. *General Mills Fun Group, Inc.*, 1982, p. 1326). The Supreme Court denied certiorari.

Under the Lanham Act, a trademark is cancelled if it becomes "the common descriptive name of an article" (15 U.S.C. §1064(2), 1976). Trademarks which were initially symbols to identify their producer can, over time, become symbols to identify the product categories. For example, "thermos," "yo-yo," "brassiere," "aspirin," and "cellophane" were all initially registered marks. When they became assimilated into ordinary speech and were used to describe the product rather than the brand, legal protection was forfeited. The trademarks became "generic" and, therefore, invalid. The reason is that trademark law safeguards only the source-denoting function. "One competitor will not be permitted to impoverish the language of commerce by preventing his fellows from fairly describing their own goods" (p. 1319). A novel feature of this case was that there was only one board game that fit the description of "Monopoly." In the aspirin and thermos bottle cases, for example, there were several competing brands within the product category.

"The principal evidence" on the issue of whether "Monopoly" had become generic since it was registered in 1935 consisted of several surveys of consumer opinion (p. 1323). We shall briefly describe some of the surveys.

"The Brand-name Survey." General Mills asked respondents whether "Monopoly" is a "brand-name" or "common name." The interviewer explained that "By *brand* name, I mean a name like *Chevrolet*, which is made by *one* company; by common name, I mean "automobile," which is made by a number of different companies" (p. 1323). The respondent was given a list of brand names (for example, Tide, Coke) and common names (for example, refrigerator, margarine), plus the word "Monopoly." Over two-thirds correctly identified brand names and almost 90% correctly identified common names. "Monopoly" was identified as a brand name by 63% of interviewees (in Zeisel 1983, p. 902). The court said that the results had "no relevance" to the legal issue, since "Under the survey definition, 'Monopoly' would have to be a 'brand name' because it is made by only one company" (p. 1323). How would you reformulate the question to make it legally relevant? Do you expect the reformulated question to produce different results?

"The Thermos Survey." Anti-Monopoly adopted a procedure used in an earlier survey of thermos bottles and asked respondents as follows: "Are you familiar with business board games of the kind in

which players buy, sell, mortgage and trade city streets, utilities and railroads, build homes, collect rents and win by bankrupting all other players, or not?" About 53% said they were. Those persons were then asked: "If you were going to buy this kind of game, what would you ask for, that is, what would you tell the sales clerk you wanted?" About 80% said: "Monopoly." This was "compelling evidence," the court said, that "Monopoly" has become generic (p. 1323). Do you agree? Does the "sneaked-in plural" of board "games," despite the qualifying phrase "of this kind," bias the question (Zeisel 1983, p. 901)?

"The Motivation Survey." Anti-Monopoly designed a telephone survey to ascertain the meaning of "Monopoly." In response to the first question, "Are you aware of 'Monopoly,' the business board game produced by Parker Brothers?", about 92% said yes. Of these, 62% had bought it or intended to buy it. The interviewer then inquired into their reasons for purchasing the game. These were open-ended questions and the interviewees often gave multiple answers, such as liking the game, believing it was an educational game, and so on. After these preliminary questions, the respondents who said they had purchased or would purchase it were given a choice of two statements and were asked which better reflected their reasons. Sixty-five percent chose: "I want a 'Monopoly' game primarily because I am interested in playing 'Monopoly.' I don't much care who makes it." Thirty-two percent chose: "I would like Parker Brothers' 'Monopoly' game primarily because I like Parker Brothers' products" (p. 1324). The court looked at the 65% figure and concluded that "Monopoly" meant primarily the game and not its producer. Are the wording and order of these series of questions, which were designed by Anti-Monopoly, biased in the direction of showing "genericness"?

"The Tide Survey." General Mills fought back with its own motivation survey. It replicated Anti-Monopoly's survey but substituted instead "Tide" (a well-established trademark in the detergent industry) for "Monopoly." Of those who said they had bought or would buy Tide, 68% said they would buy it "primarily because [they] like Tide detergent." (Note that the figure on the comparable question regarding the reason for buying "Monopoly" was 65%.) The remainder of the sample said they would buy Tide "primarily because [they] like Procter and Gamble's products," or gave other reasons, or no reasons. The court denied that these results show Tide's trademark would be forfeited, "a *reductio ad absurdum* of [Anti-Monopoly's] motivation survey" (p. 1326). What do you conclude from "The Tide Survey"?

7.   Should surveys designed for use in litigation—whether in a criminal proceeding or a trademark action—be carried out by independent third parties? Are such studies more likely to pose legally relevant questions and be more "objective" than litigant-sponsored surveys?

The Free Press/Fair Trial Controversy

The Sixth Amendment right to an impartial jury (and hence to a fair trial) is not absolute, but has to be accommodated to the First Amendment guarantee of the free flow of information. They are, as Justice Black said, "two of the most cherished policies of our civilization, and it would be a trying task to choose between them" (*Bridges* v. *California*, 1941, p. 260). This is the dilemma known as "fair trial and free press" among lawyers and "free press and fair trial" among journalists.

At the outset, we should clear the underbrush by making two points. First, there is no inherent incompatibility between the rights of free press and fair trial as such. The most salivating headlines, pandering to the basest of human prejudices, would raise only an issue of reportorial taste, not of threat to a fair trial, if the judicial proceeding was held before a judge and not a jury. The assumption is that a judge, unlike lay jurors, is capable of blocking out these outside influences in the course of deliberation. The issue, then, is a much narrower one: Does pretrial press coverage impregnate the jury with bias so as to deprive an individual of an impartial jury trial? Mere exposure to pretrial publicity should not be equated with prejudicial pretrial publicity. Ignorance of public affairs is not necessarily a desired attribute of the impartial juror (Hassett 1980). Second, the number of trials actually tainted by pretrial publicity are very few. Of the tens of thousands of criminal cases processed each year, possible prejudicial effect occurs in only a fraction of the less than 1% of the cases that even raise it (Wright 1966, p. 435). However, because of the symbolic importance of the cases in which the pretrial publicity is prejudicial, the significance of the issue is by no means a function of the proportionate number of instances in which it arises. Its rarity simply cautions us to seek curative or prophylactic measures that are no more drastic than what the illness requires.

THE FIRST AMENDMENT

The bedrock of the First Amendment is liberty of expression: "Congress shall make no law . . . abridging the freedom of speech, or of the press. . . ." This is what justifies its firstness. It is addressed to freedom of speech or of the press, and the courts have had a long-standing practice of making interchangeable use of speech cases in press cases, and vice versa. The two liberties go together; one cannot be said to be free to speak but not to publish. Despite the interrelatedness of the two clauses, there is a key distinction between them. The right to speak freely pertains to the individual, as do all of the other guarantees of the Bill of Rights. The only right that protects an institution rather than an individual is "of the press." In Justice Stewart's words (1975), it is a "structural" guarantee. "The publishing business is the only organized private business that is given explicit constitutional protection" (p. 633). This is because the press serves not only to inform the citizenry of what is going on in the world; it also is a watchdog of government. The First Amendment entrusts the reporting and commentary on the branches of government to a "fourth estate" and seeks to keep it free from state control. In this monitoring role, the press has an adversarial relationship with the government. A free and activist press can be a threat to a closed and entrenched authority. Thus, judicial attempts to restrict the media have society-wide repercussions. Many are the stories of official improprieties exposed and miscarriages of justice prevented because of alert and vigorous reporting.

THE SOCIAL-LEGAL BACKGROUND

Since the early days of the Republic, there has been an unbroken line of *causes célèbres* that have engaged public and media interest because of the people involved, the nature of the acts, or the implications that they hold for society at large. The Supreme Court's approach to the problem unfolds in three phases.

In the treason trial of Aaron Burr before the Supreme Court, Chief Justice Marshall cast what may have been the first stone in the free press/fair trial controversy (*United States* v. *Aaron Burr,* 1807). There was extensive newspaper commentary on Burr's guilt. The Chief Justice refused to disqualify prospective jurors solely because they were knowledgeable about the case and had formed opinions about it. To do so, he said, "would exclude intelligent and observing men, . . . and would perhaps be applying the letter of the rule requiring an impartial jury with a strictness which is not necessary for the preservation of the rule itself." Instead, he vigorously questioned the venirepersons to determine if they would "close [their] mind[s] against the testimony" (p. 51). His approach, then, was to assess the relative openmindedness of jurors at voir dire rather than the content of newspaper reports and its impact on the public.

This approach prevailed for some 150 years. Appellate courts did not find trials to be unfair despite widespread prejudicial publicity, so long as jurors declared themselves capable of deciding impartially. The 1960s saw a major departure from Chief Justice Marshall's assumption of no lack of harmony between pretrial knowledge and trial fairness. In *Irvin* v. *Dowd* (1961), the Court for the first time reversed a conviction because of prejudicial media coverage. News stories about "Mad Dog" Irvin blanketed the community. Of the 430 veniremen, 370 believed in the defendant's guilt; so did 8 of the 12 seated jurors, but they claimed they could weigh the evidence objectively. The Court, however, discounted the jurors' claim, given the tide of public passion incited by the media. The defendant was retried and, in a more subdued atmosphere, he was again convicted.

Two years later, the Court once more remanded a case for retrial because of massive pretrial television publicity (*Rideau* v. *Louisiana,* 1963). Under the guise of a television "interview," the sheriff elicited self-incriminating statements from the suspect. The "interview" was then telecast three times and was seen by several of the jurors. The Court did not even pause to review the voir dire. Instead, it ruled for the first time that presumed or potential bias, not actual prejudice, was sufficient for reversal. The Court departed from its long-standing and exclusive focus on the openmindedness of jurors.

After formally recognizing the potentially biasing influence of pretrial publicity, the Court affirmatively set forth for trial judges the means by which it could be resisted at the threshold. In *Sheppard* v. *Maxwell* (1966), the media saturated Cleveland with information about the defendant's guilt. In addition, "bedlam reigned at the courthouse during the trial and newsmen took over practically the entire courtroom, hounding most of the participants in the trial . . ." (p. 355). Twelve years after the verdict, the Court vacated the conviction because the trial court had failed even to attempt to insulate the proceedings from the Roman holiday atmosphere. The Court endorsed several procedural safeguards, enumerated earlier, for remedying the pretrial bias. The express approval of change of venue as a corrective measure paved the way for increased use of opinion surveys as evidence in support of requests for such change.

The preceding three cases were the first systematic judicial efforts to accommodate the right of the public to be informed and the right of a defendant to a fair trial. It was probably prompted by the publicity surrounding Lee Harvey Oswald, the suspected assassin of President Kennedy. Bar groups have concluded that had Oswald lived, he would not have had an opportunity for a fair trial because of the conduct of the Dallas police and of the media. Under the glare of floodlights and cameras in the stationhouse, the police disclosed evidence and repeatedly pronounced Oswald's guilt. The presidential commission which investigated the assassination—known as the Warren Commission (1964) after its chairman, the Chief Justice—reprimanded the media for trying and convicting Oswald on the basis of the police declarations. It is perhaps no coincidence that the Court addressed the free press/fair trial issue at this time, after decades of inattention.

In response to the Warren Commission's report (1964), the American Bar Association established an Advisory Committee on Fair Trial and Free Press. Its report (hereinafter called ABA Report 1968) proposed standards that became the model for voluntary "Bench-Bar-Press Guidelines" drafted by various states (see, for example, *Federated Publications v. Swedberg*, 1981). One standard of the ABA Report urged that qualified opinion surveys be declared admissible. Until then, this kind of empirical evidence was more often than not excluded on grounds of hearsay. The substantive reason probably was that such data shows only potential bias in a community, and the conventional rule is that actual bias of prospective jurors must be demonstrated. Consequently, the proposal was coupled with the recommendation that "a showing of actual prejudice shall not be required" (p. 8). The ABA Report and the express approval in *Sheppard* of venue change as a corrective measure resulted in decreased reluctance by the lower courts to accept opinion surveys in support of such change.

During the 1960s, the Court sought to neutralize but not eliminate pretrial media influence. It purposely refused to stamp it out at its source by applying any sanctions against the press. The approach seemed to be that the judiciary and the bar should put their own houses in order before telling the press what to do. In the second half of the 1970s, some lower courts began to censor or sanction the media. In the past, the Supreme Court had restricted the power of the courts to hold the press in contempt for publishing materials attacking judicial decisions (*Bridges* v. *California*, 1941). Actions against the press remained a dormant issue until the post-Watergate years, when reportorial probing of integrity in government extended beyond the executive branch. One might muse that some courts did not welcome the intensive scrutiny of their proceedings by investigative journalists. Injunctions against the media rose sharply. In this context, the Supreme Court decided *Nebraska Press Association* v. *Stuart* (1976), marking the third phase in the evolution of the controversy between the First and Sixth Amendments.

Preventing Pretrial Publicity: Prior Restraint

**NEBRASKA PRESS ASSOCIATION
v. STUART**

427 U.S. 539 (1976)

Mr. CHIEF JUSTICE BURGER delivered the opinion of the Court.

The respondent State District Judge entered an order restraining the petitioners from publishing or broadcasting accounts of confessions or admission made by the accused or facts "strongly implicative" of the accused in a widely reported murder of six persons. We granted certiorari to decide whether the entry of such an order on the showing made before the state court violated the constitutional guarantee of freedom of the press.

I.

On the evening of October 18, 1975, local police found the six members of the Henry Kellie family murdered in their home in Sutherland, Neb., a town of about 850 people. Police released the description of a suspect, Erwin Charles Simants, to the reporters who had hastened to the scene of the crime. Simants was arrested and arraigned in Lincoln County

Court the following morning, ending a tense night for this small rural community.

The crime immediately attracted wide-spread news coverage, by local, regional, and national newspapers, radio and television stations. Three days after the crime, the County Attorney and Simants' attorney joined in asking the County Court to enter a restrictive order relating to "matters that may or may not be publicly reported or disclosed to the public," because of the "mass coverage by news media" and the "reasonable likelihood of prejudicial news which would make difficult, if not impossible, the impaneling of an impartial jury and tend to prevent a fair trial. . . ."

[The County Court entered a very broad order, enjoining the dissemination in "any form" of "any testimony" or evidence. The Nebraska Supreme Court sustained it with modifications, and it is the terms of the final modified order that are at issue. Ed.'s note.]

V.

. . .

[P]rior restraints on speech and publication are the most serious and the least tolerable infringement on First Amendment rights. A criminal penalty or a judgment in a defamation case is subject to the whole panoply of protections afforded by deferring the impact of the judgment until all avenues of appellate review have been exhausted. Only after judgment has become final, correct or otherwise, does the law's sanction become fully operative.

A prior restraint, by contrast and by definition, has an immediate and irreversible sanction. If it can be said that a threat of criminal or civil sanctions after publication "chills" speech, prior restraint "freezes" it at least for the time.

The damage can be particularly great when the prior restraint falls upon the communication of news and commentary on current events. Truthful reports of public judicial proceedings have been afforded special protection against subsequent punishment. . . . For the same reasons the protection against prior restraint should have particular force as applied to reporting of criminal proceedings. . . .

The authors of the Bill of Rights did not undertake to assign priorities as between First Amendment and Sixth Amendment rights, ranking one as superior to the other. . . . It is unnecessary, after nearly two centuries, to establish a priority applicable in all circumstances. . . .

VI.

We turn now to the record in this case to determine whether, as Learned Hand put it, "the gravity of the 'evil,' discounted by its improbability, justifies such invasion of free speech as is necessary to avoid the danger." *United States* v. *Dennis*, 183 F.2d 201, 212 (1950). To do so, we must examine the evidence before the trial judge when the order was entered to determine (a) the nature and extent of pretrial news coverage; (b) whether other measures would be likely to mitigate the effects of unrestrained pretrial publicity; (c) how effectively a restraining order would operate to prevent the threatened danger. . . .

A. In assessing the probable extent of publicity, the trial judge had before him newspapers demonstrating that the crime had already drawn intensive news coverage. . . .

Our review of the pretrial record persuades us that the trial judge was justified in concluding that there would be intense and pervasive pretrial publicity concerning this case. He could also reasonably conclude, based on common human experience, that publicity might impair the defendant's right to a fair trial. He did not purport to say more, for he found only "a clear and present danger that pretrial publicity *could* impinge upon the defendant's right to a fair trial." (Emphasis added.) His conclusion as to the impact of such publicity on prospective jurors was of necessity speculative, dealing as he was with factors unknown and unknowable.

B.   We find little in the record that goes to another aspect of our task, determining whether measures short of an order restraining all publication would have insured the defendant a fair trial. . . .

Most of the alternatives to prior restraint of publication in these circumstances were discussed with obvious approval in *Sheppard* v. *Maxwell.* . . .

We have therefore examined this record to determine the probable efficacy of the measures short of prior restraint on the press and speech. There is no finding that alternative measures would not have protected Simants' rights. . . .

C.   We must also assess the probable efficacy of prior restraint on publication as a workable method of protecting Simants' right to a fair trial, and we cannot ignore the reality of the problems of managing and enforcing pretrial restraining orders. . . .

[W]e note that the event disclosed by the record took place in a community of 850 people. It is reasonable to assume that, without any news accounts being printed or broadcast, rumors would travel swiftly by word of mouth. . . . But plainly a whole community cannot be restrained from discussing a subject intimately affecting life within it.

Given these practical problems, it is far from clear that prior restraint on publication would have protected Simants' rights. . . .

E.   The record demonstrates, as the Nebraska courts held, that there was indeed a risk that pretrial news accounts, true or false, would have some adverse impact on the attitudes of those who might be called as jurors. But on the record now before us it is not clear that further publicity, unchecked, would so distort the views of potential jurors that 12 could not be found who would, under proper instructions, fulfill their sworn duty to render a just verdict exclusively on the evidence presented in open court. We cannot say on this record that alternatives to a prior restraint on petitioners would not have sufficiently mitigated the adverse effects of pretrial publicity so as to make prior restraint unnecessary. Nor can we conclude that the restraining order actually entered would serve its intended purpose. Reasonable minds can have few doubts about the gravity of the evil pretrial publicity can work, but the probability that it would do so here was not demonstrated with the degree of certainty our cases on prior restraint require.

Of necessity our holding is confined to the record before us. . . . However difficult it may be, we need not rule out the possibility of showing the kind of threat to fair trial rights that would possess the requisite degree of certainty to justify restraint. This Court has frequently denied that First Amendment rights are absolute and has consistently rejected the proposition that a prior restraint can never be employed.

[W]e reaffirm that the guarantees of freedom of expression are not an absolute prohibition under all circumstances, but the barriers to prior restraint remain high and the presumption against its use continues intact. We hold that, with respect to the order entered in this case prohibiting reporting or commentary on judicial proceedings held in public, the barriers have not been overcome; to the extent that this order restrained publication of such material, it is clearly invalid. . . . [T]he judgment of the Nebraska Supreme Court is therefore *Reversed.*

NOTES AND QUESTIONS

1.   The Court's opinion distinguishes between subsequent punishment and prior restraint of the press. The former is an a posteriori sanction of the speaker or publisher after the act of communication because of objection to the content. The latter is an a priori suppression of future speech or publication, with penalties attaching only if the order is violated and the communicator is subsequently found in contempt of court. It is a more direct method of restricting or censoring expression.

The Court says that subsequent punishment is the lesser evil because it only "chills" speech, and prior restraint is the greater evil because it "freezes" it. The rationale of the distinction is rooted in the Madisonian idea that a free press is essential to a free society. Consequently, abuse by the press is a price that a free society has to pay. Before this case, most of the prior restraints invalidated by the Court were in the fields of obscenity and libel. A libeler has a right to publish malicious gossip, though he may be subject to civil or criminal sanctions afterward. By not imposing a prior restraint, protection is given to expression in its emergent state.

Do you agree that this distinction as to which is the greater or the lesser evil is applicable in the area of free press/fair trial? Suppose the Nebraska legislature had enacted a statute forbidding the publication in the pretrial stage of any criminal case of information exactly the same as that contained in the prior restraint order of the present case. The press cannot report confessions or other "strongly implicative" facts. The penalty for violation is a stiff fine or jail term. Clearly, this statute is not a prior gag order; it is a subsequent punishment. Is it constitutional? Is its chill less than the freeze of a gag order?

2.   The balancing test used by Chief Justice Burger is Justice Holmes's "clear and present danger" principle as reformulated by Judge Learned Hand in terms of a tripartite test. Although the Chief Justice rejects an absolute bar on prior restraints and limits the holding to the facts of the case, could it be said that the tripartite test results, in practice, in an absolute bar? How feasible is it to meet each of the three conjunctive parts of this test?

3.   Applying the first prong of the tripartite test to the facts of this case, the Chief Justice says cryptically, "[The trial judge's] conclusion as to the impact of such publicity on prospective jurors was of necessity speculative, dealing as he was with factors unknown and unknowable." Compare this statement with footnote 2 of Justice Stewart's concurring opinion in the Detroit busing case (Chapter 4, section 4.4), in which he also pronounces—with a ring of finality—that predominantly black urban schools are "caused by unknown and perhaps unknowable factors. . . ." What is meant by "unknowable" in these two settings?

4.   A prior restraint order is unlikely to be issued after *Nebraska Press Association*. Subsequent punishment of the press, even if applied, would not prevent unwanted publicity. What other judicial orders might a defendant seek to forestall disclosure before and during trial? See *Gannett Co., Inc.* v. *DePasquale* (1979) and *Richmond Newspapers, Inc.* v. *Virginia* (1980).

Research on Pretrial Publicity

"[F]ew if any First Amendment problems have called forth such extensive efforts to investigate empirical issues" (Schmidt 1977, p. 454). Yet, the *Nebraska Press Association* opinion is virtually devoid of any reference to the social science literature. One reason may be the quality of the research.

THE ABA REPORT

The ABA Report (1968) contained an extensive review of the social psychological literature on persuasion as extrapolated and applied to the trial setting (pp. 60–

79; Appendix A, pp. 158–91). It has been described as "the most significant single source of factual information about the extent of pretrial publicity" (Schmidt 1977, p. 445). Although the subject of mass communications and opinion change is a traditional one for research, until this time there had been few empirical studies on the specific issue of jury bias as a result of pretrial publicity. Even Kalven and Zeisel's seminal study (1966) of the jury did not touch upon it. Here we will only summarize the Report's main conclusions drawn from this literature.

The first part dealt with the extent of pretrial publicity. Based on content analysis of newspapers, it found substantial dissemination of crime-related news, most of it originating from the police before a trial and from prosecutors during a trial. The most prejudicial information was a confession, followed by a defendant's prior record. In a questionnaire survey of attorneys and judges, the ABA Report found a widespread belief in the association between pretrial publicity and conviction rates (pp. 23–41). The second part concerned the effect of this publicity on the jury. The ABA Report relied on the general literature on opinion formation and change. It cited experiments showing that attitudes are formed with little or ambiguous information, and once established, they are highly resistant to change because of the internal pressures toward consistency with the initial impression (pp. 60–67).

There was little systematic analysis of the cause-effect relationship between news reports, judicial safeguards, and jury verdicts. On the one hand, it conceded that "[a]vailable data neither conclusively establish nor definitely refute . . . [the assumption] that presence of jurors who know of a case, or who have formed an opinion, poses a serious threat to the fairness of a trial" (p. 60). On the other hand, it went on to conclude, after filling the research gaps with anecdotal evidence drawn from various judicial cases, that "there is indeed a substantial danger of an unfair trial when potentially prejudicial information reaches the eyes or ears of the trier of fact" (p. 66).

The ABA Report's conclusion about the impact on the jury rested principally on intuition informed by suppositions drawn from the general scientific literature. It leaves the impression that all pretrial crime news is not only potentially prejudicial but also actually prejudicial. The inference is that the American jury is deficient in fortitude and fairmindedness when confronted with a barrage of pretrial publicity. Nonetheless, the ABA Report frequently hedged its statements with disclaimers such as, "There are no determinative empirical data that will supply ready answers to these questions" that lie at the foundation of the free press/fair trial issue. Perhaps it was the Advisory Committee's understandable eagerness to see its "liberal" recommendations implemented that led it to stretch what limited research data were available to fit its policy objectives.

EXPERIMENTAL STUDIES

Studies of the effects of pretrial publicity on mock juror verdicts have been reviewed by Simon (1977). There are serious methodological deficiencies in these studies so that they "[fail] to capture successfully the realism of a trial" (p. 520). To some extent these problems are familiar in all jury simulations, but in other areas there are usually some data and a body of theory that are not so infected, thereby permitting considered judgments about the implications of research that is of suspect external validity. This is not the case with research on free press/fair trial.

An experiment by Padawer-Singer and Barton (1975) is perhaps the best of the lot. Real jurors either were or were not exposed (just prior to the trial) to prejudicial newspaper clippings about the defendant. In addition, some of the jurors in both groups either were or were not subjected to voir dire examination. All the jurors then listened to a tape recording of the defendant's trial and deliberated until they reached a verdict or were deadlocked. The results showed that among exposed jurors, six convicted, one acquitted, and one hung; among nonexposed juries, two convicted, five acquitted, and six stalemated. The voir dire was inconclusive but it appeared to attenuate the effect of prejudicial reports.

Notwithstanding the weaknesses in its design, this research provides "the first and only hard empirical support of the conclusion that jurors allow pretrial publicity to influence their verdicts" (Simon 1977, p. 526). Hence, some media scholars are of the view that "scientific evidence proving that media publicity influences the parties to a trial is scant" (Graber 1980, p. 107).

The field of free press/fair trial is a fertile one for well-designed studies. What are some issues of legal policy that are amenable—but have not yet been subject—to empirical investigation?

REFERENCES

ABA Advisory Committee on Free Trial and Free Press. *Studies Relating to Fair Trial and Free Press.* Chicago: American Bar Association, 1968.

ABA Commission on Standards of Judicial Administration. *Standards Relating to Trial Courts.* Chicago: American Bar Association, 1976.

ABA Standing Committee on Association Standards for Criminal Justice. *Standards for Criminal Justice* (2d ed.). Boston: Little, Brown, 1982.

Ajzen, I., and Fishbein, M. *Understanding Attitudes and Predicting Social Behavior.* Englewood Cliffs, N.J.: Prentice-Hall, 1980.

Aldridge v. United States, 283 U.S. 308 (1931).

Alexander v. Louisiana, 405 U.S. 625 (1972).

American Statistical Association. *When Lawyers Count.* Mimeographed report, 1983.

Anti-Monopoly, Inc. v. General Mills Fun Group, Inc. 684 F.2d 1316 (9th Cir. 1982).

Arlington Heights v. Metro Housing Corp., 429 U.S. 252 (1977).

Asch, S. "Effects of Group Pressure upon the Modification and Distortion of Judgments." In *Readings in Social Psychology*, 3d ed., edited by E. Maccoby, T. Newcomb, and E. Hartley. New York: Holt, Rinehart & Winston, 1958.

Babcock, B. A. "Voir Dire: Preserving 'Its Wonderful Power.'" *Stanford Law Review* 27 (1975): 545–66.

Balch, R. W.; Giffiths, L. T.; Hall, E. O.; and Winfree, L. T. "The Socialization of Jurors: The Voir Dire as a Right of Passage." *Journal of Criminal Justice* 4 (1976): 271–83.

Baldus, D., and Cole, J. *Statistical Proof of Discrimination.* New York: McGraw-Hill, 1980.

Barksdale, H. *The Uses of Survey Research Findings as Legal Evidence.* New York: Printers' Ink Books, 1957.

Barnes, D. W. *Statistics as Proof.* Boston: Little, Brown, 1983.

Bartol, C. *Psychology and American Law.* Belmont, Ca.: Wadsworth, 1983.

Beck v. Washington, 369 U.S. 541 (1962).

Berk, R. "Social Science and Jury Selection: A Case Study of a Civil Suit." In *Psychology and Law*, edited by G. Bermant, C. Nemeth, and N. Vidmar. Lexington, Mass.: Heath, 1976.

Bermant, G., and Shapard, J. "The Voir Dire Examination, Juror Challenges, and Adversary Advocacy." In *The Trial Process*, edited by B. D. Sales. New York: Plenum Press, 1981.

Bonora, B., and Krauss, E., eds. *Jurywork:*

Systematic Techniques. Berkeley, Ca.: National Jury Project, 1979.

Bray, R. M., and Noble, A. M. "Authoritarianism and Decisions of Mock Juries: Evidence of Jury Bias and Group Polarization." *Journal of Personality and Social Psychology* 36 (1978): 1424–30.

Bridges v. California, 314 U.S. 252 (1941).

Broeder, D. W. "Memorandum on the Jury System." Hearings on Recordings of Jury Deliberations Before the Subcommittee to Investigate the Administration of the Internal Security Act of the Senate Committee on the Judiciary, 84th Congress, 1st Session, 64 (1955).

———. "The Voir Dire Examination—An Empirical Study." *Southern California Law Review* 38 (1965): 503–28.

Brooks v. Beto, 366 F.2d 1 (5th Cir. 1966).

Bryan, W., Jr. *The Chosen Ones: The Psychology of Jury Selection.* New York: Vantage Press, 1971.

Cahn, E. "Winning Big Cases with Trial Simulations." *American Bar Association Journal* 69 (1983): 1073–77.

Castaneda v. Partida, 430 U.S. 482 (1977).

Christie, R. "Probability vs. Precedence: The Social Psychology of Jury Selection." In *Psychology and the Law,* edited by G. Bermant, C. Nemeth, and N. Vidmar. Lexington, Mass.: Heath, 1977.

City of Mobile v. Bolden, 446 U.S. 55 (1980).

Cohn, R. M. "On the Use of Statistics in Employment Discrimination Cases." *Indiana Law Journal* 55 (1980): 493–513.

Comment. "*Swain v. Alabama:* A Constitutional Blueprint for the Perpetuation of the All-White Jury." *Virginia Law Review* 52 (1966): 1157–75.

Comment. "Computers and Scientific Jury Selection: A Calculated Risk." *University of Detroit Journal of Urban Law* 55 (1978): 345–70.

Commonwealth v. Soares, 387 N.E.2d 499 (1978).

Conrad, A. F. "The Quantitative Analysis of Justice." *Journal of Legal Education* 20 (1967): 1–20.

Constantini, E., and King, J. "The Partial Juror: Correlates and Causes of Prejudgment." *Law and Society Review* 15 (1980–81): 9–40.

Curtis, W., and Wilson, L. "The Use of Statistics and Statisticians in the Litigation Process." *Jurimetrics* 20 (1979): 109–20.

Davis, J.; Bray, R.; and Holt, R. "The Empirical Study of Decision Processes in Juries: A Critical Review." In *Law, Justice, and the Individual in Society,* edited by J. Tapp and F. Levine. New York: Holt, Rinehart & Winston, 1977.

Devlin, P. A. *Trial by Jury.* London: Stevens, 1956.

Duren v. Missouri, 439 U.S. 357 (1979).

Ellison, K., and Buckhout, R. *Psychology and Criminal Justice.* New York: Harper & Row, 1981.

Emerson, C. D. "Personality Tests for Prospective Jurors." *Kentucky Law Journal* 56 (1968): 832–54.

Estes v. Texas, 381 U.S. 532 (1965).

Etzioni, A. "Creating an Imbalance." *Trial* 10 (1974): 28, 30.

Federated Publications v. Swedberg, 96 Wn.2d 13 (1981).

Finkelstein, M. "The Application of Statistical Decision Theory to the Jury Discrimination Cases." *Harvard Law Review* 80 (1966): 338–76.

———. *Quantitative Methods in Law.* New York: Free Press, 1978.

Gannett Co., Inc. v. DePasquale, 443 U.S. 368 (1979).

Gay v. Waiters' and Dairy Lunchmen's Union, Local 30, 489 F. Supp. 282 (N.D. Ca. 1980).

Gerbasi, K. C.; Zuckerman, M.; and Reis, H. T. "Justice Needs a New Blindfold: A Review of Mock Jury Research." *Psychological Bulletin* 84 (1977): 323–45.

Gewin, W. "An Analysis of Jury Selection Decisions." Appendix to Foster v. Sparks, 506 F.2d 805 (5th Cir. 1975).

Gillespie, M. "What the Miami Race Riots Mean to All of Us." *Ms.,* April 1980, p. 87.

Graber, D. *Mass Media and American Politics.* Washington, D.C.: Congressional Quarterly Press, 1980.

Greenburg, M. S., and Ruback, R. B. *Social Psychology of the Criminal Justice System.* Monterey, Ca.: Brooks/Cole, 1982.

Gutman, S. M. "The Attorney-Conducted Voir Dire of Jurors: A Constitutional Right." *Brooklyn Law Review* 39 (1972): 290–329.

Haney, C. "Employment Tests and Employment Discrimination: A Dissenting Psychological Opinion." *Industrial Relations Law Journal* 15 (1982): 1–86.

Hans, V. P., and Vidmar, N. "Jury Selection." In *The Psychology of the Courtroom,* edited by N. L. Kerr and R. M. Bray. New York: Academic Press, 1982.

Hassett, J. M. "A Jury's Pre-trial Knowledge in Historical Perspective: The Distinction

Between Pre-trial Information and 'Prejudicial' Publicity." *Law and Contemporary Problems* 43 (1980): 155–68.

Hazelwood School District v. United States, 433 U.S. 299 (1977).

Hepburn, J. R. "The Objective Reality of Evidence and the Utility of Systematic Jury Selection." *Law and Human Behavior* 4 (1980): 89–102.

Herbsled, J. D.; Sales, B. D.; and Berman, J. J. "When Psychologists Aid Voir Dire: Legal and Ethical Considerations." In *Social Psychology and Discretionary Law*, edited by L. Abt and I. Stuart. New York: Van Nostrand Reinhold, 1978.

Holmes, O. W. "The Path of the Law." *Harvard Law Review* 10 (1897): 457–78.

Horowitz, I. A. "Juror Selection: A Comparison of Two Methods in Several Criminal Cases." *Journal of Applied Social Psychology* 10 (1980): 86–99.

Hunt, M. "Putting Juries on the Couch." *New York Times Magazine*, November 28, 1982, p. 70.

Irvin v. Dowd, 366 U.S. 717 (1961).

Kairys, O.; Kadane, J. S.; and Lehoczky, J. P. "Jury Representativeness: A Mandate for Multiple Source Lists." *California Law Review* 65 (1977): 776–827.

———; Schulman, J.; and Harring, S., eds. *The Jury System: New Methods for Reducing Prejudice*. Philadelphia: National Jury Project and National Lawyers Guild, 1975.

Kalven, H., and Zeisel, H. *The American Jury*. Boston: Little, Brown, 1966.

Kamisar, Y.; LaFave, W. R.; and Israel, J. H. *Modern Criminal Procedure* (5th ed.). St. Paul, Minn.: West, 1980.

Kaplan, J., and Waltz, J. *The Trial of Jack Ruby*. New York: Macmillan, 1965.

Kaye, D. H. "The Numbers Game: Statistical Inference in Discrimination Cases." *Michigan Law Review* 80 (1982): 833–56.

Kerr, N. L. "Effects of Prior Juror Experience on Juror Behavior." *Basic and Applied Social Psychology* 2 (1981): 175–193.

Keyes v. School District No. 1, 413 U.S. 189 (1973).

Lempert, R. "Uncovering 'Nondiscernible Differences': Empirical Research and the Jury Size Cases." *Michigan Law Review* 73 (1975): 644–708.

———. Civil Juries and Complex Cases: Let's Not Rush to Judgment." *Michigan Law Review* 80 (1981): 68–132.

Maxwell v. Bishop, 398 U.S. 262 (1970).

McConahay, J. B.; Mullin, C. J.; and Frederick, J. "The Uses of Social Science in Trials with Political and Racial Overtones: The Trial of Joan Little." *Law and Contemporary Problems* 41 (1977): 205–29.

Mischel, W. *Personality and Assessment*. New York: John Wiley, 1968.

Mitchell, H. E., and Byrne, D. "The Defendant's Dilemma: Effects of Jurors' Attitudes and Authoritarianism on Judicial Decisions." *Journal of Personality and Social Psychology* 25 (1973): 123–29.

Moore, H. "Redressing the Balance." *Trial* 35 (1974): 29, 31, 35.

Nebraska Press Association v. Stuart, 427 U.S. 539 (1976).

Nemeth, C. "Jury Trials: Psychology and Law." In *Advances in Experimental Social Psychology*, vol. 13, edited by L. Berkowitz. New York: Academic Press, 1981.

Nietzel, M. T., and Dillehay, R. C. "The Effects of Variations in Voir Dire Procedures in Capital Murder Trials." *Law and Human Behavior* 6 (1982): 1–13.

———. "Psychologists as Consultants for Changes of Venue: The Use of Public Opinion Surveys." *Law and Human Behavior* 7 (1983): 309–35.

Norris v. Alabama, 294 U.S. 587 (1937).

Note. "The Congress, the Courts and Jury Selection." *Virginia Law Review* 52 (1966): 1069–1160.

Okun, J. "Investigation of Jurors by Counsel: Its Impact on the Decisional Process." *Georgetown Law Journal* 56 (1968): 839–92.

Padawer-Singer, A., and Barton, A. "The Impact of Pretrial Publicity." In *The Jury System in America*, edited by R. J. Simon. Beverly Hills, Ca.: Sage, 1975.

Penrod, S. "A Study of Attorney and 'Scientific' Jury Selection Models." Unpublished doctoral dissertation, Harvard University, 1979.

People v. Crowe, 8 Cal.3d 815 (1973).

People v. Powell, 40 Cal. App. 3d 107 (1974).

People v. Wheeler, 583 P.2d 748 (1978).

Pointer v. United States, 151 U.S. 396 (1894).

Pollock, A. "The Use of Public Opinion Polls to Obtain Changes of Venue and Continuances in Criminal Trials." *Criminal Justice Journal* 1 (1977): 269–88.

Processed Plastic Co. v. Warner Communications, 675 F.2d 852 (7th Cir. 1982).

Richmond Newspapers, Inc. v. Virginia, 448 U.S. 555 (1980).

Rideau v. Louisiana, 373 U.S. 723 (1963).

Ristiano v. Ross, 424 U.S. 582 (1976).

Rosales-Lopez v. United States, 451 U.S. 182 (1981).

Sage, W. "Psychology and the Angela Davis Jury." *Human Behavior,* January 1973, pp. 56–61.

Saks, M. "The Limits of Scientific Jury Selection." *Jurimetrics Journal* 17 (1976): 3–22.

———, and Hastie, R. *Social Psychology in Court.* New York: Van Nostrand Reinhold, 1978.

Schmidt, B. C. *"Nebraska Press Association:* An Expansion of Freedom and Contraction of Theory." *Stanford Law Review* 29 (1977): 431–76.

Schulman, J.; Shaver, P.; Colman, R.; Emrich, B.; and Christie, R. "Recipe for a Jury." *Psychology Today* 6 (1973): 37–44, 77–84.

Sheppard v. Maxwell, 384 U.S. 333 (1966).

Simon, R. J. "Does the Court's Decision in *Nebraska Press Association* Fit the Research Evidence on the Impact on Jurors of News Coverage." *Stanford Law Review* 29 (1977): 515–28.

Smith, A. B., Jr., and Abram, T. G. "Quantitative Analysis and Proof of Employment Discrimination." *University of Illinois Law Review* 1981 (1981): 33–74.

Stewart, P. "Or of the Press." *Hastings Law Journal* 26 (1975): 631–37.

Strauder v. West Virginia, 100 U.S. 303 (1880).

Stroble v. California, 343 U.S. 181 (1952).

Suggs, D., and Sales, B. D. "Juror Self-Disclosure in the Voir Dire: A Social Science Analysis." *Indiana Law Journal* 56 (1981): 245–71.

Swain v. Alabama, 380 U.S. 202 (1965).

Taylor v. Louisiana, 419 U.S. 522 (1975).

Thayer, J. B. *A Preliminary Treatise on Evidence at Common Law.* Boston: Little, Brown, 1898.

Tivnan, E. "Jury by Trial." *New York Times Magazine,* November 10, 1975, p. 30.

Triangle Publications v. Rohrlick, 167 F.2d 969 (2nd Cir. 1948).

United States v. Aaron Burr, 25 Fed. Cas. 48 (No. 14692g) (1807).

United States v. Maskeny 609 F.2d 183 (5th Cir. 1980).

Van Dyke, J. "Jury Selection Procedures: Our Uncertain Commitment to Representative Panels." *Case Western Reserve Law Review* 27 (1977): 609–22.

Vidmar, N. "Social Science and Jury Selection." Mimeographed. In *Psychology and the Litigation Process,* Department of Continuing Education, University of Toronto, 1976.

———, and Judson, J. "The Use of Social Science in a Change of Venue Application." *Canadian Bar Review* 59 (1981): 76–102.

"Warren Commission." *The Report of the President's Commission on the Assassination of President John F. Kennedy.* Washington, D.C.: U.S. Government Printing Office, 1964.

Washington v. Davis, 426 U.S. 229 (1976).

Whitus v. Georgia, 385 U.S. 545 (1967).

Wilkinson, J. H., III. *Serving Justice: A Supreme Court Clerk's View.* New York: Charterhouse, 1974.

Winick, B. J. "Prosecutional Peremptory Challenge Practices in Capital Cases: An Empirical Study and a Constitutional Analysis." *Michigan Law Review* 81 (1982): 2–98.

Witherspoon v. Illinois, 391 U.S. 510 (1968).

Woodward, J. "A Scientific Attempt to Provide Evidence for a Decision on Change of Venue." *American Sociological Review* 17 (1952): 447–52.

Wright, S. "Fair Trial—Free Press." 38 F.R.D. 435 (1966).

Zeisel, H. "The Uniqueness of Survey Evidence." *Cornell Law Review* 45 (1968): 322–46.

———, and Diamond, S. "The Jury Selection in the Mitchell-Stans Conspiracy Trial." *American Bar Foundation Research Journal* 1 (1976): 151–74.

———. "The Effect of Peremptory Challenges on Jury and Verdict: An Experiment in a Federal District Court." *Stanford Law Review* 30 (1978): 491–530.

———. "The Surveys that Broke Monopoly." *University of Chicago Law Review* 50 (1983): 896–909.

CHAPTER 8

Functioning of the Jury: Case Study of Jury Size, Verdict, and Litigation Complexity

8.1. INTRODUCTION

The idea of lay participation in the administration of justice has sparked, not surprisingly, extensive debate over the merits of the jury. Unabashed praise and unremitting scorn have been lavished upon this mode of dispute resolution by commentators on both sides of the Atlantic. Lord Justice Devlin (1956) wrote: "Each jury is a little parliament. The jury sense is the parliamentary sense. I cannot see the one dying and the other surviving. . . . [T]rial by jury is more than an instrument of justice and more than one wheel of the constitution: it is the lamp that shows that freedom lives" (p. 164). In contrast, an American critic complained, rather hyperbolically, about the delays, costs, and irrationality of the jury process: "Too long has the effete and sterile jury system been permitted to tug at the throat of the nation's judiciary as it sinks under the smothering deluge of the obloquy of those it was designed to serve. Too long has ignorance been permitted to sit ensconced in the places of judicial administration where knowledge is so sorely needed. Too long has the lament of the Shakespearean character been echoed, 'Justice has fled to brutish beasts and men have lost their reason' " (Sebille 1924, p. 55).

The merits of lay decision-making are evaluated in terms of the purposes which the jury serves. The Supreme Court, in an opinion by Justice Brennan, declared that "the purpose of the jury trial . . . in criminal and civil cases [is] to assure a fair and equitable resolution of factual issues" and "in criminal cases to prevent government oppression" by interposing between the two sides a group of the defendant's peers (*Colgrove* v. *Battin*, 1973, p. 157). The jury, like most other legal institutions, has multiple and sometimes competing ends. Its performance or impact cannot be tidily measured against a single avowed purpose. The arguments on behalf of or against the jury are made on different or shifting grounds which can be the despair of social scientists who would like to pin down one legal criterion for evaluation. We shall elaborate briefly each of these purposes in order to set the stage for the ensuing materials on jury functioning.

JURY COMPETENCE

One role of the civil jury and the criminal jury is to find the facts based upon the evidence adduced at trial and to apply to those facts the law as instructed by the judge at the end of the presentation of the evidence. In the eighteenth and early nineteenth centuries, the jury was empowered to decide both the facts and the law in reaching its decision. Today, its task is limited to the determination of the facts alone. The fact-finding function of the jury represents its principal glory or shame, depending upon its proponents or opponents, respectively. The former claim that twelve persons of average ability are better than one person (the judge) of purportedly superior ability. The group's pool of experience, collective memory, and mix of biases help to compensate for the lack of training in decision-making. In fact, the jury's amateur capabilities are said to be an asset because the jury brings a fresh perspective to each trial. Critics point out that the enhanced fact-finding ability of a group, even if true, is not always realized because of the somewhat haphazard methods by which jurors are selected. In the emotionally charged setting of a trial, lay persons are said to be incapable of remaining immune to extraneous social influences and personal biases. The conflicting assertions on the fact-finding merits of the jury rested largely on folk wisdom, educated guesses, and anecdotal evidence of trial lawyers rather than on systematic research until the publication in 1966 of *The American Jury*. Co-authored by Harry Kalven, a lawyer, and Hans Zeisel, a sociologist-lawyer, it is the classic work on jury functioning.

The book was one of the many products of the University of Chicago Jury Project. The seven-year project began in the 1950s with a substantial grant from the Ford Foundation and its broad purpose was to further social-legal research by intensive study of the jury. The evolution of this project and the difficulties of interdisciplinary collaboration were chronicled by Broeder (1958). The research generated a public outcry and a congressional investigation when it was disclosed that jury deliberations in several civil trials in a federal court had been videotaped without the jurors' knowledge, but with the consent of the judge and of counsel. The widespread, unfavorable commentary on this intrusion into jury privacy, notwithstanding its scientific justifications, led to the enactment of legislation prohibiting any eavesdropping on jury deliberations. The project never used any of the videotaped data, and Kalven and Zeisel relied on questionnaires and interviews to collect the information contained in their pioneering work.

A principal objective of the authors was to ascertain the fact-finding capability of the criminal jury. In the absence of any objective criterion of the "correct" decision in a case, they compared the verdicts of juries and judges. They reasoned that if lay persons were competent fact-finders, their decisions should match those of professional decision-makers. Conversely, the absence of consensus would support the critics' charge of jury lawlessness. To this end, they sent questionnaires to federal judges who had presided over criminal jury trials. Each judge was asked how he would have decided the case if there had been no jury at the trial. There are, of course, some methodological problems with a retrospective study using hypothetical judicial verdicts, but it was the only practical way of obtaining information on a large sample of trials.

The results, based on over 3,500 criminal trials held between 1954 and 1958, showed substantial agreement in verdicts between judge and jury. A judge either acquits or convicts, and a jury can acquit, convict, or be deadlocked (hang). The six possible combinations of judge-jury decision-making were distributed as follows: judge acquits/jury acquits, 13.4%; judge acquits/jury convicts, 2.2%; judge acquits/ jury hangs, 1.1%; judge convicts/jury acquits, 16.9%; judge convicts/jury convicts, 62.0%; judge convicts/jury hangs, 4.4%. Thus, both judge and jury agreed to acquit or to convict in (13.4 + 62.0 =) 75.4% of the cases (Kalven and Zeisel, 1966, p. 56). In a parallel study of some 4,000 civil jury trials, similar consensus was found between judge and jury on the issue of liability: Both found for the plaintiff in 47% of the cases and for the defendant in 31%, producing an overall agreement of 78% (pp. 63– 64).

No prior expectations existed in the legal community regarding the extent of convergence of judge and jury decisions. The Chicago Jury Project discovered that in three-fourths of the cases, whether the business is criminal or civil, laypersons reach the same result as learned judges—a sign of the jury institution's competence and stability.

JURY SOVEREIGNTY

The criminal jury has long been regarded a bulwark of liberty. One of the principal objections to the draft of the Constitution was its failure to guarantee jury trials, a defect remedied in the Bill of Rights (*The Federalist* No. 83). By providing the accused with the right to be tried by a jury of his peers, a buffer is interposed between the accused and an overzealous prosecutor or a biased judge. This function of preventing government oppression is related to a constellation of other social values surrounding the jury. The jury operates as the conscience of the community. Laypersons inject notions of equity and the community's sense of justice into the decision-making process and thereby temper the rigors of the law. The jury also provides an experience in civic education for the citizenry. By enabling laypersons to adjudicate important matters involving the state and/or their fellow citizens by applying the law of the land, jury service plays a teaching role in the democratic process. If the jury is to be an instrument of public justice, expressing community values, it needs to be representative of the range of views and beliefs contained in the community. The fulfillment of the jury's purposes is dependent upon the composition of its members; the jury has to be a representative cross section of the community. A consequence of broadly based participation is that the jury helps legitimate official action. Disputants and the public at large may be more accepting of unfavorable decisions if they are rendered by a representative body of their peers. Given its transient nature, the jury diverts away from the judge any public dissatisfaction which might otherwise be aimed at the court itself.

The jury's capacity to serve as the repository of the people's sense of reason and fair play is central to its function of safeguarding against government overreaching. Jury equity gives rise in criminal trials to the jury's power of nullification, also called the jury's prerogative of lenity or jury sovereignty. This power implies the right to set aside the judge's instructions on the applicable law as well as the evidence presented in order to reach an acquittal verdict based upon the popular sense of fairness and the wisdom of the common man. It does not mean that the jury is like a mini-legislature empowered to make or rewrite the law. It means only that the jury can ameliorate the harshness of the criminal law by interjecting communal standards of blameworthiness—rather than or in addition to legal standards of culpability—into its secret deliberations. And the jury sometimes does suspend the strict application of the law when it believes that the results would otherwise be unjust. "The pages of history shine on instances of the jury's exercise of its prerogative [of lenity]. Most often commended are the 18th century acquittal[s] . . . of seditious libel . . . and the 19th century acquittals in prosecutions under the fugitive slave law" (*United States* v. *Dougherty*, 1972, p. 1130). In modern times, cases in which this power is likely to be exercised include euthanasia, criminal prosecutions with ideological overtones (for example, the trials of Angela Davis and Joan Little), and crimes of conscience. Of course, the dark side of this prerogative is that the jury can also act from prejudice. The pages of history also reveal the jury immunizing those charged with committing crimes against members of minority or unpopular groups.

Jury sovereignty is part of the broader and age-old issue of reconciling legal rules and equitable results within the administration of justice. Law, by definition, embodies formal, relatively stable, and universal rules applicable in an impartial and equal manner to all. At the same time, rules cannot always be applied rigidly if justice is to be done in a specific case. Whereas the judge provides uniformity in the administration of justice via adherence to precedents, the jury provides for individualization of justice. The power of nullification enables the jury to individualize the law without following or creating precedent—to render particularized justice without betraying the commitment to evenhanded application of law. The question, then, is the actual extent and the proper role of the jury in bending rules (and "finding" facts) in order to do equity.

In criminal cases, only a general verdict (guilty or not guilty) is required. The jury need not divulge the reasons for its decision and acquittals are not reversible by the trial judge. Because of the general verdict, a jury can reach a result without following the substantive rules of law and even without giving weight to the evidence presented. In this respect, the jury is an "aresponsible agency" (Calabresi and Bobbitt 1978, pp. 57–79). The medieval power of the courts to punish jurors for corrupt or incorrect verdicts was repudiated in 1670 in *Bushell's Case*. Members of the jury which had acquitted William Penn for unlawful assembly, in spite of the judge's attempt to starve them into a guilty decision, had been fined and imprisoned for delivering a verdict against the evidence. (In London's Old Bailey courthouse, the site of Penn's trial, hangs a tablet that "commemorates the courage and endurance of the Jury [mentioning juror Edward Bushell by name] . . . who refused to give a verdict against [Penn]. . . ." It is the only trial so memorialized.) This case established that the jury's verdict is final, so that, in effect, the jury has the power to find facts and apply the given law to those facts according to its own conscience and without fear of judicial reprisal. Juries which were trying defendants critical of the state had to be protected themselves from possible state intimidation.

However, in civil cases, the state has greater control over the jury. A court can order a new trial, or set aside the jury's verdict if contrary to the preponderance of the evidence, or instruct the jury to issue a directed verdict on behalf of one of the parties—after presentation of the evidence but before jury deliberation—because the evidence clearly supports (in the court's judgment) the position of that party. In addition, in civil but not in criminal cases, special verdicts can be requested. The jury can be instructed to decide a series of specific questions drafted by the attorneys and posed by the judge (for example, did the defendant exercise due care in driving the car? Did plaintiff contribute to the accident by driving too slowly?) which are prerequisite to reaching the general verdict of liability or no liability. These questions provide the outside world with a glimpse of the decision-making processes of the jury by requiring it to announce its intermediate decisions. The different values and the greater stakes present in criminal trials compared with civil trials make the jury in the first instance far less accountable in any way for its general verdict. Thus, in criminal cases, a jury can blunt the force of the general rule and take into account extralegal factors in reaching its decisions which it is precluded from doing in civil cases. In the protected privacy of its retirement, a jury in a criminal trial can supply the flexibility to legal rules which is essential to working justice in particular circumstances.

Critics (for example, Simson 1976) and proponents (for example, Scheflin and Van Dyke 1980) of jury sovereignty—of the jury's "power to bring in a verdict in the teeth of both law and facts," in the words of Justice Holmes (*Horning* v. *District of Columbia*, 1920)—are numerous and vocal. One of the sharpest critics was Judge Jerome Frank. In his opinions (for example, *Skidmore* v. *Baltimore and Ohio R.R.*, 1948) and scholarly writings (1930, pp. 173–78), he expressed the view that juries applied law they did not understand to facts they could not get straight—that juries were, in fact, the supreme example of irrationality in the law. Even if juries do understand, they do not feel bound by instructions, and such "jury law" or lawlessness undermines the certainty and predictability which characterize the rule of law. It is curious that Judge Frank, who was an enthusiastic advocate of rapprochement between law and the social sciences, in this instance engaged in cavalier fact-finding. He did not consider as problematic the factual premises of his conclusions.

Proponents respect the jury's discretion. As the conscience of the community, the jury's sovereignty rests on notions of right which it shares with the community. The power to render inconsistent verdicts, according to Judge Learned Hand, a noted contemporary of Judge Frank, is desirable because it introduces "a slack into the enforcement of law, tempering its rigor by the mollifying influence of current ethical conventions" (*U.S. ex rel. McCann* v. *Adams*, 1942). The Supreme Court has also recognized this feature of the jury. Justice White in *Duncan* v. *Louisiana* (1968) wrote that the "jury's power to displace law by appeal to conscience is fundamental to the American system of government" (p. 156).

Two traditions, then, coexist in the jury. One is the unreviewable and irreversible power of the jury in criminal cases to acquit in disregard of law and evidence. The other is the legal practice and precedent of instructing juries in both criminal and civil cases that they must follow and apply the law to the facts that they determine. The task is to strike a balance between discretion and legal certainty—in other words, to keep equity and rule in equilibrium.

The American Jury offers a lode of insights into jury sovereignty. Kalven and Zeisel examined not only the magnitude of consensus between judge and jury but also the reasons for dissensus. As described earlier, the verdicts were different in about one-fourth of the criminal cases. Moreover, the jury's disagreement with the judge was largely in the direction of favoring the defendant. The jury is more lenient than the judge (judge convicts/jury acquits) in 16.9% of the cases, and the jury is less lenient (judge acquits/jury convicts) in 2.2% of the cases. On balance, jury trials show a net leniency of (16.9 − 2.2 =) 14.7%. That is, a defendant would fare better 14.7% of the time in a jury trial than a bench trial. This result confirms the belief that a jury of one's peers is more likely than a judge to give the benefit of the doubt to the accused. The jury's role in safeguarding against state oppression is manifested in its prodefense orientation. (In contrast, although the level of judge-jury disagreement was almost the same in criminal and civil cases, the civil jury is about as likely to find for the plaintiff as for the defendant when it disagrees with the judge—Kalven and Zeisel 1966, p. 63.)

Moreover, the authors found that the reasons for the criminal jury's disagreements with the judge were highly consistent. These reasons, and the percentage of cases reflecting each reason, were as follows: sentiments about the law, 29%; sentiments about the defendant, 11%; evidentiary issues, 54%; facts known only to the judge, 2%; and disparity in competence of counsel, 4%. The authors state that "unless at least one of these factors is present in a case, judge and jury will not disagree" (p. 109).

The conclusion they draw from these results is that the jury does understand the evidence and is a generally competent fact-finder. In addition, the jury does not deviate substantially from legal instructions; when it does, the deviation is stable and consistent (for example, juries tend to apply the law of self-defense more liberally than judges). This consistency of deviation from law in several areas suggests the absence of jury capriciousness or abuse of discretion. In short, it can be inferred that jury equity and legal rule are in some kind of reasonable balance. The fears of Judge Frank and others that the criminal jury, because of the power of the general verdict, could turn into a runaway institution, spreading anarchy in the administration of justice, do not seem to be founded.

Empirical research such as that of Kalven and Zeisel does not, of course, settle value-ridden controversies regarding jury competence and jury sovereignty. Normative judgments are beyond the scope of factual analysis. However, research data can aid in narrowing a controversy, eliminating erroneous factual premises, and suggesting different ways of looking at the issues. The result is a clearer focus on the policy arguments and perhaps less fanciful, more modest claims by partisans and opponents of the jury.

CONSTITUTIONAL DIMENSIONS OF JURY FUNCTIONING

By jury functioning we mean the deliberation process and the ensuing verdict. Numerous factors influence jury functioning, including the composition of its members, the physical and social organization of the group, and the evidence presented at the trial.

Who decides a case has some effect on *how* the evidence is evaluated and *what* the outcome will be. The individual characteristics and demographic background of jurors are therefore taken into account in the voir dire process. However, as we indicated in the preceding chapter, there is no research evidence that these factors are major determinants of trial results in most cases.

Physical organization refers to the size of the group and the spatial arrangements of its members. Social structure pertains to the communications, social status, subgroup coalitions, the decision-making rules that prevail within the group. Both features are related. In the 1950s and early 1960s, during the heyday of group dynamics research, social psychologists examined the effects of group size on the participation and performance of its members in a variety of tasks. Nearly all of these studies involved small groups other than the jury (Thomas and Fink 1963). On the issue of voting protocol, whether by unanimous or majority decision, "hardly any empirical research existed" (Saks and Hastie 1978, p. 83). The few jury-specific studies were carried out principally by social psychologists associated with the Chicago Jury Project. They focused on the impact of group geography on jury behavior. They looked, for example, at the seating pattern of twelve-member juries. Jurors located at the ends of the jury table were more likely to be selected foreman. Those positioned at the ends and in the middle initiated and received more communication that those seated elsewhere. The geometry of the table shaped the flow of discussion and the definition of social status within the group (Strodtbeck, James, and Hawkins 1957; Strodtbeck and Hook 1961; Stasser, Kerr, and Bray 1982).

In the early 1970s, issues of physical and social organization of the jury were thrust into the constitutional limelight. The Supreme Court ruled that criminal and civil juries of six rather than twelve members did not violate, respectively, the Sixth and Seventh Amendment rights to trial by jury. It also held that verdicts by majority rather than unanimous votes (in twelve-member juries) did not infringe upon the Sixth Amendment guarantee of an impartial jury. These decisions rested on an analysis of the purposes of the jury, and social scientists were quick to generate data evaluating the factual predicates and social impact of the rulings.

Another influence on jury verdicts is the evidence: its weight, credibility, and direction. Kalven and Zeisel (1966) found not only that the jury is a competent trier (compared with the judge), but that "the evidence itself is a major determinant of the decision of both judge and jury" (p. 162). This is not surprising since the evidence in the majority of cases clearly points toward conviction (52%) or acquittal (5%) (p. 134). Laboratory studies too show that "evidence is a substantially more potent determinant of jurors' verdicts than the individual characteristics of jurors" (Saks and Hastie 1978, p. 68).

Kalven and Zeisel dealt with the criminal jury. In the early 1980s, the competency of the civil jury began to occupy the research agenda. The research interest was sparked by litigation on whether subject matter complexity creates an exception to the Seventh Amendment right to jury trial. The lower federal courts have been divided in their judgments of the ability of the jury to comprehend and rationally decide complex cases (for example, large-scale antitrust suits), involving voluminous evidence, esoteric theories, and technical issues (for example, economic models and statistical analyses of market share) (Lempert 1981). The Supreme Court has not ruled on the question, but the answer could turn on scientific evidence about the fact-finding capabilities of civil juries.

The coverage of the materials that follow is centered on the constitutional aspects of jury functioning as they intersect with social research. Our primary attention will be on the impact of jury size and verdict rules on the representativeness and decision-making of criminal juries. We will also touch upon the effect of litigation complexity on the decision-making of civil juries.

OVERVIEW

The selection and functioning of the jury are intertwined. The right to an impartial jury and the social values that undergird it provide the common framework for the materials of the preceding chapter and the present one.

We begin in section 8.2 with *Williams* v. *Florida* (1970). The Court declared that there is "no discernible difference" between juries of twelve and six members with respect to the purpose of preventing government oppression, and therefore upheld the smaller-sized jury. Three years later, the Court sanctioned the size reduction of the federal civil jury (*Colgrove* v. *Battin,* 1973), its faith in the functional equivalence of the different-sized juries unshaken. Eight years after *Williams,* every member of the Court concluded in *Ballew* v. *Georgia* (1978) that conviction by a five-member jury stretched the Sixth Amendment beyond the breaking point. In the intervening years, there developed a substantial body of empirical and statistical studies comparing the effects of different-sized juries. This literature was summarized by Justice Blackmun in *Ballew,* and we shall discuss some of the studies.

Section 8.3 examines *Apodaca* v. *Oregon* (1972), which sustained the constitutionality of majority verdicts, and evaluates its impact upon the representativeness and functioning of the jury. It also examines the issue of whether criminal juries should be expressly informed of their nullification power (*United States* v. *Dougherty,* 1972). These opinions on size and verdict rules are significant not only because they cite social science in fashioning procedural justice, but also because they implicate changing views on federal-state relations in the administration of criminal justice. The jury cases need to be located in this broader political context.

Problems of measurement and research design in the study of jury behavior are highlighted in section 8.4. We consider the trade-offs between internal and external validity inherent in different methodologies, such as archival research, field experiments, and laboratory simulations. Most of the research since *The American Jury* has consisted of laboratory studies with mock jurors. The relevance of these studies for theory-testing and policy-making is a subject of continuing debate.

The encroachment on the right to a criminal jury trial, started in the 1970s by legislative and judicial efforts to reduce jury size and allow nonunanimous verdicts, has continued into the 1980s with proposals to create a complexity exception to the Seventh Amendment civil jury. This exception rests on the factual predicate that juries, unlike judges, are incapable of deciding fairly and rationally in cases involving voluminous evidence and difficult issues. Section 8.5 examines the clash between the right to a fair trial and the right to a jury trial (*In re Japanese Electronic Products Antitrust Litigation,* 1980) and considers the social research needed to inform the debate.

8.2. EFFECTS OF SIZE ON JURY FUNCTIONING

WILLIAMS v. FLORIDA

399 U.S. 78 (1970)

Mr. Justice WHITE delivered the opinion of the Court. . . .

The question in this case then is whether the constitutional guarantee of a trial by "jury" necessarily requires trial by exactly 12 persons, rather than some lesser number—in this case six. We hold that the 12-man panel is not a necessary ingredient of "trial by jury," and that respondent's refusal to impanel more than the six members provided by Florida law did not violate petitioner's Sixth Amendment rights as applied to the States through the Fourteenth.

We had occasion in *Duncan v. Louisiana* to review briefly the oft-told history of the development of trial by jury in criminal cases. That history revealed a long tradition attaching great importance to the concept of relying on a body of one's peers to determine guilt or innocence as a safeguard against arbitrary law enforcement. That same history, however, affords little insight into the considerations that gradually led the size of that body to be generally fixed at 12. . . . In short, while sometime in the 14th century the size of the jury at common law came to be fixed generally at 12, that particular feature of the jury system appears to have been a historical accident, unrelated to the great purposes which gave rise to the jury in the first place. The question before us is whether this accidental feature of the jury has been immutably codified into our Constitution. . . .

We do not pretend to be able to divine precisely what the word "jury" imported to the Framers, the First Congress, or the States in 1789. It may well be that the usual expectation was that the jury would consist of 12, and that hence, the most likely conclusion to be drawn is simply that little thought was actually given to the specific question we face today. But there is absolutely no indication in "the intent of the Framers" of an explicit decision to equate the constitutional and common-law characteristics of the jury. Nothing in this history suggests, then, that we do violence to the letter of the Constitution by returning to other than purely historical considerations to determine which features of the jury system, as it existed at common law, were preserved in the Constitution. The relevant inquiry, as we see it, must be the function that the particular feature performs and its relation to the purpose of the jury trial. Measured by this standard, the 12-man requirement cannot be regarded as an indispensable component of the Sixth Amendment.

The purpose of the jury trial, as we noted in *Duncan*, is to prevent oppression by the Government. "Providing an accused with the right to be tried by a jury of his peers gave him an inestimable safeguard against the corrupt or overzealous prosecutor and against the compliant, biased, or eccentric judge." *Duncan v. Louisiana*, at 156. Given this purpose, the essential feature of a jury obviously lies in the interposition between the accused and his accuser of the commonsense judgment of a group of laymen, and in the community participation and shared responsibility that results from that group's determination of guilt or innocence. The performance of this role is not a function of the particular number of the body that makes up the jury. To be sure, the number should probably be large enough to promote group deliberation, free from outside attempts at intimidation, and to provide a fair possibility for obtaining a representative cross-section of the community. But we find little reason to think that these goals are in any meaningful sense less likely to be achieved when the jury numbers six, than when it numbers 12—particularly if the requirement of unanimity is retained. And, certainly the reliability of the jury as a factfinder hardly seems likely to be a function of its size.

It might be suggested that the 12-man jury gives a defendant a greater advantage since he has more "chances" of finding a juror who will insist on acquittal and thus prevent conviction. But the advantage might just as easily belong to the State, which also needs only one juror out of twelve insisting on guilt to prevent acquittal.[47] What few experiments have oc-

---

[47]It is true, of course, that the "hung jury" might be thought to result in a minimal advantage for the defendant, who remains unconvicted and who enjoys the prospect that the prosecution will eventually be dropped if subsequent juries also "hang." Thus a 100-man jury would undoubtedly be more favorable for defendants than a 12-man jury. But when the com-

curred—usually in the civil area—indicate that there is no discernible difference between the results reached by the two different-sized juries.[48] In short, neither currently available evidence nor theory[49]

suggests that the 12-man jury is necessarily more advantageous to the defendant than a jury composed of fewer members.

Similarly, while in theory the number of viewpoints represented on a randomly selected jury ought to increase as the size of the jury increases in practice the difference between the 12-man and the six-man jury in terms of the cross-section of the community represented seems likely to be negligible. Even the 12-man jury cannot insure representation of every distinct voice in the community, particularly given the use of the peremptory challenge. As long as arbitrary exclusions of a particular class from the jury rolls are forbidden . . . , the concern that the cross-section will be significantly diminished if the jury is decreased in size from 12 to six seems an unrealistic one. . . .

Affirmed.

---

parison is between 12 and six, the odds of continually "hanging" the jury seem slight, and the numerical difference in the number needed to convict seems unlikely to inure perceptibly to the advantage of either side.

[48]See Wiehl, *supra*, n. 25, at 40–41; Tamm, *supra*, n. 25, at 134–136; Cronin, Six-Member Juries in District Courts, 2 Boston B. J. No. 4, p. 27 (1958); Six-Member Juries Tried in Massachusetts District Court, 42 J. Am. Jud. Soc. 136 (1958). See also New Jersey Experiments with Six-Man Jury, 9 Bull. of the Section of Jud. Admin. of the ABA (May 1966); Phillips, A Jury of Six in All Cases, 30 Conn. B. J. 354 (1956).

[49]Studies of the operative factors contributing to small group deliberation and decisionmaking suggests that jurors in the minority on the first ballot are likely to be influenced by the proportional size of the majority aligned against them. See H. Kalven & H. Zeisel, The American Jury 462–463, 488–489 (1966) . . . ; cf. Asch, Effects of Group Pressure Upon the Modification and Distortion of Judgments, in Readings in Social Psychology 2 (G. Swanson, T. Newcomb & E. Hartley et al., eds., 1952). See generally Note, On Instructing Deadlocked Juries, 78 Yale L. J. 100, 108 and n. 30 (and authorities cited), 110–111 (1968). Thus if a defendant needs initially to persuade four jurors that the State has not met its burden of proof

in order to escape ultimate conviction by a 12-man jury, he arguably escapes by initially persuading half that number in a six-man jury; random reduction, within limits, of the absolute number of the jury would not affect the outcome. . . .

N O T E S   A N D   Q U E S T I O N S

1. The Court engaged in three lines of reasoning to reach its decision. The first was historical analysis. It looked at common law history and the intent of the framers of the Constitution to discern the proper jury size. This historical approach is not uncommon in due process analysis. To determine what is the process due to an individual accused of crime, the particular procedure that is being challenged is examined in light of past practices. If tradition and "immemorial usage" have not sanctioned the procedure, it may fail to pass constitutional muster. With respect to jury size, the practice has always been to have twelve members. If the legislative debates during the adoption of the Bill of Rights contain no mention of jury size, the reason may have been because a size of twelve was universally assumed. Blackstone's *Commentaries,* the most influential legal treatise in colonial America, stated that a jury trial meant trial by twelve persons (Vôl. 4, pp. 349, 352). (The provenance of the number twelve is a matter of historical speculation, but romantic explanations abound: the twelve tribes of Israel, the twelve officers of Solomon (I Kings 4:7), the twelve Apostles, the twelve astrological signs, not to mention "an early English abhorrence of the decimal system" (Devlin 1956, p. 8)—hence, twelve pennies to the shilling.) Yet, the Court brushed aside six centuries of common law history as mere "accident." It also glossed over the fact that four Supreme Court decisions, from 1898 to 1930, have held that in federal trials the Sixth Amendment right to jury trial means a jury of size twelve. ("[T]rial by jury as . . . recognised in this country and England when the Constitution was adopted . . . [means] that the jury should consist of twelve men, neither more nor less. . . ." *Patton* v. *United States,* 1930, p. 288.)

Two years earlier, in *Duncan* v. *Louisiana* (1968), the Court per Justice White held that the Sixth Amendment right to a jury trial was applicable to the states. One of the grounds for that decision was the historical tradition dismissed in *Williams*—since colonial times and the early days of the Republic, the right to jury trial has always been guaranteed. This is another instance of "law office history" (Kelly 1965) or forensic history.

After the heavy-handed treatment of history, Justice White turned to a functional, or policy, analysis. "The relevant inquiry, as we see it, must be the function that the particular feature performs and its relation to the purposes of the jury trial." The jury's purpose in a criminal case is to provide a buffer for the accused from the unfair exercise of state power via an overzealous prosecutor or a biased judge. The issue of jury size depends upon its impact on this purpose. If six members do not undermine the buffer function, it is constitutional. This impact is operationally indexed in terms of promoting "group deliberation" and securing a "representative cross-section of the community." The functional test can be summarized as follows:

Legal issue	Immediate goals: means to attain ultimate purpose	Ultimate purpose of jury
12 vs. 6 members	(1) group deliberation: quality and outcome	prevent oppression: jury as buffer
	(2) representative cross section	

Finally, the Court turned to empirical evidence and claimed that there is "no discernible difference" between the results reached by the two different-sized juries. The "few experiments" referred to in footnote 48 of the opinion were impressions of judges and court administrators, not controlled studies.

The Court's reasoning, then, can be cast in syllogistic form:

Major premise   Twelve is constitutional (based on history and precedents);
Minor premise   the effects of six are only "negligibly" different from the effects of twelve (in terms of the two intermediate goals);
Conclusion   therefore, six is constitutional.

2.   The reduction from twelve to six members will have virtually no effect on the cross-sectional representativeness of the jury, according to the Court. Arguably, this reduction might result in minority underrepresentation in the petit jury. Given the percentage of minority members in a community who are eligible to serve on a jury, we can apply the binomial distribution to compute the probability of obtaining by chance no minority members at all in six- and twelve-person juries. With 10% eligible minority members, the likelihood of an all-white jury is .282 with twelve-member juries and .531 with six-member juries (Lempert 1975, p. 669). (That is, the probability that twelve jurors in a row will be white is. $90^{12} = .282$ and that all six jurors in a group of six will be white is $.90^6 = .531$.) Thus, with this size reduction, out of every 100 juries there will be an increase of one-fourth (.531 − .282 = .249) in the number of monochromatic juries—hardly a "negligible" difference. However, with 50% of eligible minority members in the population, the odds of no minorities being chosen are .000 and .016 in the twelve- and six-member juries, respectively. The impact of size reduction on all-white juries becomes negligible as the proportion of minorities in the population increases.

What factors does this probabilistic analysis fail to take into account in determining underrepresentation of the jury? Do they invalidate the random process model of jury selection?

3.   What is the effect of *Williams* on the line of cases from *Swain* to *Partida* discussed in the previous chapter?

4.   The criterion of group deliberation would seem to encompass both the quality of the deliberation process and the outcome or verdict. Consider first the outcome. In addition to acquittal or conviction, the jury might not be able to reach a consensus—it is hung. A stalemated jury is valued in our criminal justice system because it symbolizes the societal commitment to minority viewpoints. A minority group (defined by race, opinions, or any other dimension) can thwart the majority will. Of course, if hung juries occurred all the time, the criminal process would be paralyzed. For the individual defendant, it is an important option. In some cases, the best that can be hoped for is a stalemated jury.

In footnotes 47 and 49 of the opinion, Justice White says that it is the "proportional size" of the majority aligned against the minority, rather than the absolute size of the jury, that affects stalemated outcomes. Thus, hung juries are equally likely to occur in a 10-to-2 vote in a twelve-member jury as in a 5-to-1 vote in a six-member jury. In support, he cited the classic study on majority influence by Solomon Asch. Does Asch's study support this proportional hypothesis?

The national rate of stalemates in twelve-person juries is 5.5%. A preliminary study indicates that the rate for six-person juries in Miami is 2.4%, or a drop of 50% (Zeisel 1971, p. 720). Absent controlled comparisons, what alternative factors could account for this drop?

5.   A field experiment by Roper (1980) examined the impact of jury size on hung juries. He presented in a courtroom a 90-minute videotape of a criminal trial (based on an actual case, where the evidence was evenly balanced and the jury deadlocked) to 110 mock juries of 5, 6, and 12 members, all of whom were volunteers selected from actual jury rolls in Kentucky. At the conclusion of the videotape but prior to the start of group deliberation, each juror cast a ballot in order to ascertain the extent of agreement within the group. If there was no unanimity on the first ballot, the group deliberated for as long as necessary to reach a verdict of guilty or not guilty. If the group was stalemated after several ballots, a hung jury was declared.

The results showed that when there were "viable minorities" on a jury (for example, 2 or more persons who disagreed with the rest of the group on the first ballot), 27% of these juries (10 out of 37) were hung. With "nonviable minorities" (only 1 juror dissenting from the group on the first ballot), 12% (2 out of 17 juries) were hung (p. 989). In addition, the larger the jury, the more likely it was that a viable minority would emerge: 80% of the 12-member juries had 2 or more dissenters, compared with 33% of the 6-member juries and 14% of the 5-member juries (p. 988). Therefore, as expected, larger juries hung more often: 24% (8 out of 33 juries) of the 12-member juries compared with 5% (1 out of 21) of the 6-member juries (p. 990).

Typically, in a deadlocked jury, the majority favors conviction and the minority favors acquittal (Flynn 1977). A hung jury means that a minority of the group has reasonable doubts about the defendant's guilt. Hence, Roper's results suggest that smaller juries could increase the likelihood of wrongful convictions (Type 1 error) and decrease the likelihood of wrongful acquittals (Type 2 error).

6.   What relationship, if any, would you expect between jury size and plea bargaining?

7.   What hypotheses does the literature on small groups research suggest about the relationship between group size and the quality (not just outcome) of group decision-making? See Rosenblatt and Rosenblatt (1973) and Lempert (1975) for opposite views on whether this research justifies any general conclusions as applied to the jury setting.

8.   To interpose a representative body of laypersons as a buffer between the individual and the state serves, in effect, the purpose of giving the benefit of the doubt to the individual. "If the defendant preferred the common-sense judgment of a jury to the more tutored but perhaps less sympathetic reaction of the single judge, he was to have it," wrote Justice White in *Duncan* v. *Louisiana* (1968). Kalven and Zeisel (1966) have confirmed the prodefendant tilt of the jury. In their survey, it will be recalled, they compared actual jury verdicts with the retrospective decisions of the judges who presided over those trials. They found that juries are more lenient than judges in about 15% of the cases (p. 56). Does the *Williams* decision alter the balance between judge trial and jury trial?

9.   The Court perceived "no discernible difference" in the functioning between the different-sized juries. If empirical research that was above methodological reproach showed a difference as discernible as between night and day, would the six-member jury automatically be deemed unconstitutional? If empirical studies showed that size reduction makes "some difference" which only "somewhat impairs" the values of a jury trial, would the six-member jury still be constitutional? How would the Court draw the line between "no" difference and "some" difference? Are there standards other than the purposes of the jury and the history of the jury for defining the extent to which a decision-making group can qualify as a "jury" within the meaning of the Sixth Amendment, despite a smaller number and some differences in functioning?

10.   In *Brown I*, social science was used by the Court to preserve constitutional rights; in *Williams*, it appears to have been used for the opposite effect. Was Edmond Cahn right when he warned that "we ought to keep [the Constitution] uncommitted in relation to the social sciences" because, otherwise "our fundamental rights rise, fold, or change along with the latest fashions of psychological literature" (see Chapter 3, section 3.5)? Or, do you agree with the view that "[t]he jury size cases are very different from the [school] segregation cases, and the influence of the results of empirical research should be quite different" (Lempert 1975, p. 706)?

11.   Three years after *Williams*, the Court upheld the size reduction of the federal civil jury: "[A] jury of six satisfies the Seventh Amendment's guarantee of trial by jury in civil cases" (*Colgrove* v. *Battin*, 1973, p. 160). The Court's belief in the functional equivalence of the twelve- and six-member juries remained unshaken: "[F]our very recent studies have provided convincing empirical proof of the correctness of the *Williams* conclusion that 'there is no discernible difference between the results reached by the two different-sized juries' " (p. 159, n. 15). (The validity of these studies were evaluated by Zeisel and Diamond in an article reproduced later in this chapter.) "[T]he purpose of the jury trial in . . . civil cases," the Court said, is "to assure a fair and equitable resolution of factual issues," and size reduction does not impair this purpose (p. 157).

   One meaning of a fair and equitable jury decision is a reliable or reproducible decision— different, randomly selected juries presented with the same evidence and following the same decision-making rules should arrive at the same result. In reality, of course, there is variability in jury decisions. Different persons and different groups of persons see and evaluate information differently. The jury institution exists precisely because of this heterogeneity. If everyone weighed evidence equally, a one-person jury would be as good as an *n*-person jury, and every jury would be as good as every other.

   Suppose, then, that a civil jury is deciding the issue of the amount of damages. Given the same case facts, different juries might arrive at somewhat different damage awards. The distribution of the size of these awards could be modeled by a normal, bell-shaped curve (Kaye 1980, p. 1022). The question of interest is whether a reduction in jury size will increase the variability—and, hence, the unfairness—of damage awards. Given an expected jury award (say, a mean of $3,500) and the variation around it (say, a standard deviation of $1,000), we can compute the standard error of the judgments of randomly drawn juries of different sizes. The standard error tells us how such a particular sample statistic (a particular jury award) is likely to vary from the population (or expected) value. It is equal to the square root of the variance of the sample divided by the sample size, or the standard deviation divided by the square root of the sample size. Thus, with twelve jurors, the damage awards have a standard error of $289 ($1000/\sqrt{12}$), and with six jurors, the standard error is $408 ($1000/\sqrt{6}$) (Kaye 1980, p. 1024, n. 77). In this example, the diminution of the jury by one-half results in an increase of 1.4 times the variability of awards. Experiments with mock jurors have also shown that "smaller [criminal] juries have a greater propensity to be inconsistent [in their decision]" (Roper 1980, p. 992). Why do smaller groups render less stable judgments than larger groups?

BALLEW v. GEORGIA

435 U.S. 223 (1978)

   Mr. Justice BLACKMUN announced the judgment of the Court and delivered an opinion in which Mr. Justice STEVENS joined.

   This case presented the issue whether a state criminal trial to a jury of only five persons deprives the accused of the right to trial by jury guaranteed to him by the Sixth and Fourteenth Amendments. Our resolution of the issue requires an application of principles enunciated in *Williams v. Florida*, 399 U.S. 78 (1970),

where the use of a six-person jury in a state criminal trial was upheld against similar constitutional attack. . . .

III.

   When the Court in *Williams* permitted the reduction in jury size—or, to put it another way, when it held that a jury of six was not unconstitutional—it expressly reserved ruling on the issue whether a number smaller than six passed constitutional scrutiny. . . . The Court refused to speculate when this so-called "slippery slope" would become too steep. We face now, however, the two-fold question whether a further reduction in the size of the state criminal trial jury does make the grade too dangerous, that is, whether it inhibits the functioning of the jury as an institution to a significant degree, and, if so, whether any state interest counterbalances and justifies the disruption so as to preserve its constitutionality.

Williams v. Florida and *Colgrove v. Battin* generated a quantity of scholarly work on jury size.[10] These writings do not draw or identify a bright line below which the number of jurors would not be able to function as required by the standards enunciated in *Williams*. On the other hand,

they raise significant questions about the wisdom and constitutionality of a reduction below six. We examine these concerns:

First, recent empirical data suggest that progressively smaller juries are less likely to foster effective group deliberation. At some point, this decline leads to inaccurate fact-finding and incorrect application of the common sense of the community to the facts. Generally, a positive correlation exists between group size and both the quality of group performance and group productivity. A variety of explanations has been offered for this conclusion. Several are particularly applicable in the jury setting. The smaller the group, the less likely are members to make critical contributions necessary for the solution of a given problem. Because most juries are not permitted to takes notes, . . . memory is important for accurate jury deliberations. As juries decrease in size, then, they are less likely to have members who remember each of the important pieces of evidence or argument. Furthermore, the smaller the group, the less likely it is to overcome the biases of its members to obtain an accurate result. When individual and group decisionmaking were compared, it was seen that groups performed better because prejudices of individuals were frequently counterbalanced, and objectivity resulted. . . .

Second, the data now raise doubts about the accuracy of the results achieved by smaller and smaller panels. Statistical studies suggest that the risk of convicting an innocent person (Type I error) rises as the size of the jury diminishes. Because the risk of not convicting a guilty person (Type II error) increases with the size of the panel, an optimal jury size can be selected as a function of the interaction between the two risks. Nagel & Neef concluded that the optimal size, for the purpose of minimizing errors, should vary with the importance attached to the two types of

---

[10]*E.g.*, M. Saks, Jury Verdicts (1977) (hereinafter cited as Saks); Bogue and Fritz, The Six-Man Jury, 17 S. Dak. L. Rev. 285 (1972); Davis, et al., The Decision Processes of 6- and 12-Person Mock Juries Assigned Unanimous and Two-Thirds Majority Rules, 32 J. Pers. and Soc. Psych. 1 (1975); Diamond, A Jury Experiment Reanalyzed, 7 U. Mich. J. L. Rev. 520 (1974); Friedman, Trial by Jury: Criteria for Convictions, Jury Size and Type I and Type II Errors, 26-2 Am. Stat. 21 (April 1972) (hereinafter cited as Friedman); Institute of Judicial Administration, A Comparison of Six- and Twelve-Member Civil Juries in New Jersey Superior and County Courts (1972); Lempert, Uncovering "Nondiscernible" Differences: Empirical Research and the Jury-Size Cases, 73 Mich. L. Rev. 643 (1975) (hereinafter cited as Lempert); Nagel & Neef, Deductive Modeling to Determine an Optimum Jury Size and Fraction Required to Convict, 1975 Wash. U. L. Q. 933 (hereinafter cited as Nagel & Neef); New Jersey Criminal Law Revision Commission, Six-Member Juries (1971); Pabst, Statistical Studies of the Costs of Six-Man versus Twelve-Man Juries, 14 Wm. & Mary L. Rev. 326 (1972) (hereinafter cited as Pabst); Saks, Ignorance of Science Is No Excuse, 10 Trial 18 (Nov.–Dec. 1974); Thompson, Six Will Do, 10 Trial 12 (Nov.–Dec. 1974); Zeisel, Twelve is Just, 10 Trial 13 (Nov.–Dec. 1974); Zeisel, . . . And Then There Were None: The Diminution of the Federal Jury, 38 U. Chi. L. Rev. 710 (1971) (hereinafter cited as Zeisel); Zeisel, The Waning of the American Jury, 58 A. B. A. J., 367 (1972); Zeisel & Diamond, "Convincing Empirical Evidence" on the Six Member Jury, 41 U. Chi. L. Rev. 281 (1974) (hereinafter cited as Zeisel & Diamond); Note, The Effect of Jury Size on the Probability of Conviction: An Evaluation of *Williams v. Florida*, 22 Case W. Res. L. Rev. 529 (1971) (hereinafter cited as Note, Case W. Res.); Note, Six-Member and Twelve-Member Juries: An Empirical Study of Trial Results, 6 U. Mich. J. L. Ref. 671 (1973); Note, An Empirical Study of Six- and Twelve-Member Jury Decision-Making Processes, 6 U. Mich. J. L. Ref. 712 (1973).

mistakes. After weighing Type I error as 10 times more significant than Type II, perhaps not an unreasonable assumption, they concluded that the optimal jury size was between six and eight. As the size diminished to five and below, the weighted sum of errors increased because of the enlarging risk of the conviction of innocent defendants.

Another doubt about progressively smaller juries arises from the increasing inconsistency that results from the decreases. Saks argued that the "more a jury type fosters consistency, the greater will be the proportion of juries which select the correct (*i.e.*, the same) verdict and the fewer 'errors' will be made." M. Saks, Jury Verdicts, 86–87 (1977). From his mock trials held before undergraduates and former jurors, he computed the percentage of "correct" decisions rendered by 12-person and six-person panels. In the student experiment, 12-person groups reached correct verdicts 83% of the time; six-person panels reached correct verdicts 69% of the time. The results for the former juror study were 71% for the 12-person groups and 57% for the six-person groups. . . .

Third, the data suggest that the verdicts of jury deliberation in criminal cases will vary as juries become smaller, and that the variance amounts to an imbalance to the detriment of one side, the defense. Both Lempert and Zeisel found that the number of hung juries would diminish as the panels decreased in size. Zeisel said that the number would be cut in half—from 5% to 2.4% with a decrease from 12 to six members. Both studies emphasized that juries in criminal cases generally hang with only one, or more likely two, jurors remaining unconvinced of guilt. Also, group theory suggests that a person in the minority will adhere to his position more frequently when he has at least one other person supporting his argument. In the jury setting the significance of this tendency is demonstrated by the following figures: If a minority viewpoint is shared by 10% of the community, 28.2% of 12-member juries may be expected to have no minority representation, but 53.1% of six-member juries would have none. Thirty-four percent of 12-person panels could be expected to have two minority members, while only 11% of six-member panels would have two. As the numbers diminish below six, even fewer panels would have one member with the minority viewpoint and still fewer would have two. The chance for hung juries would decline accordingly.

Fourth, what has just been said about the presence of minority viewpoint as juries decrease in size foretells problems not only for jury decisionmaking, but also for the representation of minority groups in the community. The Court repeatedly has held that meaningful community participation cannot be attained with the exclusion of minorities or other identifiable groups from jury service. . . . Although the Court in *Williams* concluded that the six-person jury did not fail to represent adequately a cross-section of the community, the opportunity for meaningful and appropriate representation does decrease with the size of the panels. Thus, if a minority group constitutes 10% of the community, 53.1% of randomly selected six-member juries could be expected to have no minority representative among their members, and 89% not to have two. Further reduction in size will erect additional barriers to representation.

Fifth, several authors have identified in jury research methodological problems tending to mask differences in the operation of smaller and larger juries. For example, because the judicial system handles so many clear cases, decisionmakers will reach similar results through similar analyses most of the time. One study concluded that smaller and larger juries could disagree in their verdicts in no more than 14% of the cases. Disparities, therefore, appear in only small percentages. Nationwide, however, these small percentages will represent a large number of cases. And it is with respect to those cases that the jury trial right has its greatest value. When the case is close, and the guilt or innocence of the defendant is not readily apparent, a properly functioning jury system will insure evaluation by the common sense of the community and will also tend to insure accurate factfinding. . . .

IV.

While we adhere to, and reaffirm our holding in *Williams v. Florida,* these studies, most of which have been made since *Williams* was decided in 1970, lead us to conclude that the purpose and functioning of the jury in a criminal trial is seriously impaired, and to a constitutional degree, by a reduction in size to below six members. We readily admit that we do not pretend to discern a clear line between six members and five. But the assembled data raise substantial doubt about the reliability and appropriate representation of panels smaller than six. Because of the fundamental importance of the jury trial to the American system of criminal justice, any further reduction that promotes inaccurate and possibly biased decisionmaking, that causes untoward differences in verdicts, and that prevents juries from truly representing their communities, attains constitutional significance. . . .

V.

With the reduction in the number of jurors below six creating a substantial threat to Sixth and Fourteenth Amendment guarantees, we must consider whether any interest of the State justifies the reduction. We find no significant state advantage in reducing the number of jurors from six to five.

The States utilize juries of less than 12 primarily for administrative reasons. Savings in court time and in financial costs are claimed to justify the reductions. The financial benefits of the reduction of 12 to six are substantial; this is mainly because fewer jurors draw daily allowances as they hear cases. On the other hand, the asserted saving in judicial time is not so clear. Pabst in his study found little reduction in the time for voir dire with the six-person jury because many questions were directed at the veniremen as a group. Total trial time did not diminish, and court delays and backlogs improved very little. The point that is to be made, of course, is that a reduction in size from six to five or four or even three would save the States little. They could reduce slightly the daily allowances, but with a reduction from six to five the saving would be minimal. If little time is gained by the reduction from 12 to six, less will be gained with a reduction from six to five. Perhaps this explains why only three States, Georgia, Louisiana, and Virginia, have reduced the size of juries in certain nonpetty criminal cases to five. Other States appear content with six member or more. In short the State has offered little or no justification for its reduction to five members.

Petitioner, therefore, has established that his trial on criminal charges before a five-member jury deprived him of the right to trial by jury guaranteed by the Sixth and Fourteenth Amendments. . . .

Mr. Justice POWELL, with whom THE CHIEF JUSTICE and Mr. Justice REHNQUIST join, concurring in the judgment.

I concur in the judgment, as I agree that use of a jury as small as five members, with authority to convict for serious offenses, involves grave questions of fairness. As the opinion of Mr. Justice Blackmun indicates, the line between five- and six-member juries is difficult to justify, but a line has to be drawn somewhere if the substance of jury trial is to be preserved.

I do not agree, however, that every feature of jury trial practice must be the same in both federal and state courts. Because the opinion of Mr. Justice Blackmun today assumes full incorporation of the Sixth Amendment by the Fourteenth Amendment contrary to my view in *Apodaca*, I do not join it. Also, I have reservations as to the wisdom—as well as the necessity—of Mr. Justice Blackmun's heavy reliance on numerology derived from statistical studies. Moreover, neither the validity nor the methodology employed by the studies cited was subjected to the traditional testing mechanisms of the adversary process. The studies relied on merely represent unexamined findings of persons interested in the jury system.

For these reasons I concur only in the judgment.

NOTES AND QUESTIONS

1.   A century and a half ago, Justice Story wrote that "the trial by jury is justly dear to the American people. . . . [E]very encroachment upon it has been watched with great jealousy" (*Parsons* v. *Bedford*, 1830, p. 445). While *Williams* occasioned no popular outcry, perhaps because the decision came in the guise of a procedural adjustment that did not purport to encroach upon the jury trial right itself, scholars were quick to react against the size reduction as a veiled curtailment of the constitutional guarantee. In the eight years after *Williams*, they published numerous empirical and statistical studies that generally questioned the representativeness and performance of smaller juries. The only member of the *Ballew* Court who saw fit to review this literature was Justice Blackmun, and from the studies cited he arrived at two conclusions.

First, he said, "[W]e adhere to and reaffirm our holding in *Williams*. . . ." His reasoning can be cast in the following syllogistic form:

Major premise   Twelve is constitutional (—this is axiomatic);
Minor premise   the effects of six are different from the effects of twelve (as shown by the research);
Conclusion   therefore, six is constitutional (—*Williams* is reaffirmed).

Is Justice Blackmun's stubborn clinging to precedent an instance of intentional disregard or distortion of social science evidence? See Sperlich (1978), Tanke and Tanke (1979), and Kaye (1980).

Second, relying on *Williams*'s functional analysis but without following the logic to its ultimate conclusion, he got off the slippery slope:

Major premise   Six is constitutional (as established by *Williams*);
Minor premise   the effects of five are not discernibly different from the effects of six (as extrapolated from the research);
Conclusion   therefore, five is unconstitutional.

Successive reductions in jury size will, of course, impair the purpose and functioning of the jury, such as by reducing the cross-sectional representation from the community. Earlier we indicated that the chances of all-white membership in a twelve-person jury (given 10% minorities in the population) is .28. In a six-person jury (given the same population parameters), the probability increases to .53. In a five-member jury, the likelihood rises to .59. A reduction from six to five members, then, increases the likelihood of all-white juries by only 6%. Thus, in extrapolating from the research, Justice Blackmun took into account the direction—but not the magnitude—of the effects of size reduction. If going from 12 to 6 impairs the jury, going from 6 to 5 impairs it further and to an unconstitutional degree.

2.   Of the score of studies cited by Justice Blackmun, only one—by Nagel and Neef—purported to address size issues within the range of interest in *Ballew*. Was his reliance on this study appropriate in light of the authors' conclusion? Moreover, is it desirable to give judicial approval to the assumption

underlying the conclusion, namely, "weighing Type I error as 10 times more significant than Type II" is "not . . . unreasonable"?

3.   Recognizing, perhaps, the shortcomings of his functional analysis, Justice Blackmun presented an alternative test for determining the permissible reduction in size, based upon a balancing of state and individual interests. What factors should be taken into account in this balancing process? Does balancing provide a reliable means for drawing the line between different-sized juries?

4.   Justice Powell conceded to some arbitrariness in striking down five-person juries, but he insisted that "a line has to be drawn somewhere." Line drawing is something that judges and lawyers do all the time, but as Justice Frankfurter noted in a different context, "the fact that a line has to be drawn somewhere does not justify it being drawn anywhere" (*Pearce* v. *Commissioner*, 1942, p. 558).

Do you agree with Justice Powell's view that Justice Blackmun's "heavy reliance on numerology" was neither "wise" nor "necessary"? Does the cited research merely ornament a result predetermined on other grounds? A year after *Ballew*, an opinion of the Court by Justice Rehnquist again reflected the constraints of precedent. He ignored the figures from the numerarium and once more reiterated, unapologetically, the *Williams* dogma: "[A] jury of 12 is neither more reliable as a factfinder, more advantageous to the defendant, nor more representative of the variety of viewpoints in the community than a jury of six" (*Burch* v. *Louisiana*, 1979, p. 135, n. 7).

8.3.   EFFECTS OF DECISION RULES ON JURY FUNCTIONING

APODACA v. OREGON

406 U.S. 404 (1972)

Mr. Justice WHITE announced the judgment of the Court and an opinion in which THE CHIEF JUSTICE, Mr. Justice BLACKMUN, and Mr. Justice REHNQUIST joined.

Robert Apodaca, Henry Morgan Cooper, Jr., and James Arnold Madden were convicted respectively of assault with a deadly weapon, burglary in a dwelling, and grand larceny before separate Oregon juries, all of which returned less than unanimous verdicts. The vote in the cases of Apodaca and Madden was 11-1, while the vote in the case of Cooper was 10-2, the minimum requisite vote under Oregon law for sustaining a conviction. . . . [A]ll three sought review in this Court upon a claim that conviction of crime by a less than unanimous jury violates the right to trial by jury in criminal cases specified by the Sixth Amendment and made applicable to the states by the Fourteenth. We granted

certiorari to consider this claim, which we now find to be without merit. . . .

I.

Like the requirement that juries consist of 12 men, the requirement of unanimity arose during the Middle Ages and had become an accepted feature of the common-law jury by the 18th century. But, as we observed in *Williams*, "the relevant constitutional history casts considerable doubt on the easy assumption . . . that if a given feature existed in a jury at common law in 1789, then it was necessarily preserved in the Constitution." . . . [A]s in *Williams*, . . . we must turn to other than purely historical considerations.

II.

Our inquiry must focus upon the function served by the jury in contemporary society. As we said in *Duncan*, the purpose of trial by jury is to prevent oppression by the Government by providing a "safeguard against the corrupt or overzealous prosecutor and against the compliant, biased, or eccentric judge." . . . A requirement of unanimity, however, does not materially contribute to the exercise of a commonsense judgment. . . . [A] jury will come to such a judgment as long as it consists of a group of laymen representative of a cross section of the community who have the duty and the opportunity to deliberate, free from outside attempts at intimidation, on the question of a defendant's guilt. In terms of this function we perceive no difference between juries required to act unanimously and those permitted to convict to acquit by votes of 10 to two or 11 to one. Requiring unanimity would obviously produce hung juries in some situations where nonunanimous juries will convict or acquit.[5] But in either case, the interest of the defendant in having the judgment of his peers interposed between himself and the officers of the State who prosecute and judge him is equally well served. . . .

IV.

Petitioners also cite quite accurately a long line of decisions of this Court upholding the principle that the Fourteenth Amendment requires jury panels to reflect a cross section of the community. They then contend that unanimity is a necessary precondition for effective application of the cross section requirement, because a rule permitting less than unanimous verdicts will make it possible for convictions to occur without the acquiescence of minority elements within the community. . . .

All that the Constitution forbids, however, is systematic exclusion of identifiable segments of the community from jury panels and from the juries ultimately drawn from those panels; a defendant may not, for example, challenge the makeup of a jury merely because no members of his race are on the jury, but must prove that his race has been systematically excluded. No group, in short, has the right to block convictions; it has only the right to participate in the overall legal processes by which criminal guilt and innocence are determined.

We also cannot accept petitioners' second assumption—that minority groups, even when they are represented on a jury, will not adequately represent the viewpoint of those groups simply because they may be outvoted in the final result. They will be present during all deliberations, and their views will be heard. We cannot assume that the majority of the jury will refuse to weigh the evidence and reach a decision upon rational grounds, just as it must now do in order to obtain unanimous verdicts, or that a majority will deprive a man of his liberty on the basis of prejudice when a minority is presenting a reasonable argument in favor of acquittal. . . .

We accordingly affirm the judgment of the Court of Appeals of Oregon.

Mr. Justice POWELL, concurring . . . in the judgment in [*Apodaca;* from the companion case of *Johnson* v. *Louisiana,* 406 U.S. 356, pp. 366–80].

. . .

I concur in the plurality opinion in this case insofar as it concludes that a defendant in a state court may constitutionally be convicted by less than a unanimous verdict, but I am not in accord with a major premise upon which that judgment is based. Its premise is that the concept of jury trial, as applicable to the States under the Fourteenth Amendment, must be identical in every detail to the concept required in federal courts by the Sixth Amendment. I do not think that all of the elements of jury trial within the meaning of the Sixth Amendment are necessarily

---

[5] . . . [W]hen juries are required to be unanimous, "the probability that an acquittal minority will hang the jury is about as great as that a guilty minority will hang it." H. Kalven & H. Zeisel, The American Jury 461 (1966).

embodied in or incorporated into the Due Process Clause of the Fourteenth Amendment. . . .

[In] holding that the Fourteenth Amendment has incorporated "jot-for-jot and case-for-case" every element of the Sixth Amendment, the Court derogates principles of federalism which are basic to our system. In the name of uniform application of high standards of due process, the Court has embarked upon a course of constitutional interpretation which deprives the States of freedom to experiment with adjudicatory processes different from the federal model. At the same time, the Court's understandable unwillingness to impose requirements which it finds unnecessarily rigid (e.g., *Williams* v. *Florida*) has culminated in the dilution of federal rights which were, until these decisions, never seriously questioned. . . .

Mr. Justice DOUGLAS, with whom Mr. Justice BRENNAN and Mr. Justice MARSHALL concur, dissenting [from *Johnson* v. *Louisiana*, 406 U.S. 356, pp. 380–94].

. . .

I could construe the Sixth amendment, when applicable to the States, precisely as I would when applied to the Federal Government.

The plurality approves a procedure which diminishes the reliability of jury. . . .

The diminution of verdict reliability flows from the fact that nonunanimous juries need not debate and deliberate as fully as must unanimous juries. . . .

Indeed, if a necessary majority is immediately obtained, then no deliberation at all is required in these States.

(There is a suggestion that this may have happened in the 10-2 verdict rendered in only 41 minutes in Apodaca's case.) To be sure, in jurisdictions other than these two States, initial majorities normally prevail in the end, but about a tenth of the time the rough and tumble of the juryroom operates to reverse completely their preliminary perception of guilt or innocence. . . .

Moreover, even where an initial majority wins the dissent over to its side, the ultimate result in unanimous jury States may nonetheless reflect the reservations of uncertain jurors. I refer to many compromise verdicts on lesser-included offenses and lesser sentences. Thus, even though a minority may not be forceful enough to carry the day, their doubts may nonetheless cause a majority to exercise caution. . . .

The new rule also has an impact on cases in which a unanimous jury would have neither voted to acquit nor to convict, but would have deadlocked. In unanimous jury States, this occurs about 5.6% of the time. Of these deadlocked juries, Kalven and Zeisel say that 56% contain either one, two, or three dissenters. In these latter cases, the majorities favor the prosecution 44% (of the 56%) but the defendant only 12% (of the 56%). . . . H. Kalven & H. Zeisel, The American Jury 461, 488 (Table 159) (1966). By eliminating the one and two dissenting juror cases, Oregon does even better, gaining 4.25 convictions for every acquittal. While the statutes on their face deceptively appear to be neutral, the use of the nonunaminous jury stacks the truth-determining process against the accused. Thus, we take one step more away from the accusatorial system that has been our proud boast. . . .

NOTES AND QUESTIONS

1.   The reasoning in this case is the same as in *Williams*. A shift from a unanimous to a majority decision rule is not impermissible if the ultimate function of the jury is not thereby impaired, as measured by the two-pronged test. This time, without citing "experimental" evidence as in *Williams*, the

Court simply concluded, "In terms of this function, we perceive no difference between juries required to act unanimously [or by majority vote]."

Consider the criterion of a representative cross section of the community. The Court recognizes the long line of cases from *Swain* onward designed to safeguard this objective. But then Justice White goes on to say, "No group, in short, has the right to block convictions; it has only the right to participate in the overall legal processes by which criminal guilt and innocence are determined." Thus, if a juror disagrees with the majority and insists on not finding the defendant guilty because, in this juror's judgment, the government has not met the high burden of proof, Justice White would characterize the behavior of this juror as blocking a conviction. The assumption seems to be that defendants are guilty and therefore deserving of conviction before the jury verdict is rendered.

2.   Zeisel (1971) has suggested that the majority verdict rule could reduce the chances of a representative cross section of the community in the jury box. Suppose there are 10% minority members in the eligible population. Applying the binomial distribution, the expected number of minority members in one hundred randomly selected juries of twelve persons each is as follows (p. 722):

Expected number of minority members	Number of juries
None	28
One	38
Two	23
Three or more	11

Under a unanimous rule, out of every one hundred juries, how many juries will have at least one minority member? Under a 10-to-2 majority rule, out of every one hundred juries, how many juries will there be in which the majority can disregard the views of the two-person minority? Comparing, then, the unanimous versus the majority juries, by how much is the effective representation of minorities in juries reduced under a 10-to-2 decision rule?

3.   What is the relationship between the issues of venire underrepresentation, jury size, and verdict rule? With respect to the ideal of a representative cross section, do the cases in these three areas produce the same or different effects? What are the consequences for the values of the jury, as identified by Justice White, of allowing both reduced jury size and a majority verdict? If a statute provides that noncapital defendants shall be tried before a jury of nine persons, seven of whom must concur to render a verdict, is it constitutional?

4.   A statute provides that in jury trials of noncapital criminal cases, the accused "shall be tried before a jury of six persons, five of whom must concur to render a verdict." Is it constitutional? See *Burch* v. *Louisiana* (1979).

5.   Consider the criterion of meaningful group deliberation. According to Justice White, under a majority decision rule, "[minority group members] will be present during all deliberations, and their views will be heard." Present they will be if there is no purposeful discrimination in the selection process or abuse of the peremptory challenge by excluding all minority members. The issue is whether their views will be heard. In the companion case of *Johnson* v. *Louisiana* (1972), Justice White for the majority upheld a 9-to-3 majority rule and stated: "A majority will cease discussion and outvote a minority only after reasoned discussion has ceased to have persuasive effect or to serve any other purpose. . . ." If a 9-to-3 decision is sufficient to convict and the distribution of votes on the first ballot is 9-to-3 for conviction, what is the incentive for the majority to continue "reasoned discussion" with the minority?

What kind of a research design would you propose to assess the effect of majority/unanimous decision rules on the quality or meaningfulness of group deliberation? Indeed, how would you operationalize this dependent variable?

6.   Unlike the issue of the effects of jury size, empirical research on the effects of verdict rules is "sparse" (Bartol 1983, p. 146). However, from studies involving unanimous verdicts, some extrapolations can be drawn about the possible effects of majority verdicts on promoting or dampening group deliberation.

Jury deliberation appears to proceed in two phases. Initially, there is a general exploration of the issues and of the evidence. A first ballot is taken either at the start or at the end of this first phase in order to ascertain the extent of consensus in the jury. After this vote, the second and principal phase begins. Attention focuses on specific points of disagreement and the interchange of views becomes more spirited. This latter phase consists essentially of efforts by jurors in the majority on the first ballot—and, in most instances, there is a simple majority for conviction or acquittal—to persuade those in the minority to conform to the majority's position (Hawkins 1962; Stasser and Davis 1981).

Kalven and Zeisel (1966) found a high correlation between the first phase (and often predelibera-tion) ballot of individual jurors and the final group verdict. Specifically, in a twelve-member jury, when there were no guilty votes on the first ballot, 100% of the cases (N = 26) resulted in not-guilty verdicts. When there were one to five guilty votes on the first ballot (that is, a majority for acquittal), 91% of the cases resulted in not-guilty verdicts, 2% in guilty verdicts, and 7% in stalemates (based on N = 41). When the votes on the first ballot were evenly split, six for conviction and six for acquittal, the final verdict was also split: 50% of the cases were decided guilty, and 50% not guilty (N = 10). When there were seven to eleven guilty votes on the first ballot (that is, a majority for conviction), only 5% of the cases resulted in not-guilty verdicts, 86% resulted in guilty verdicts, and 9% were hung (N = 105). Finally, when there was unanimity for conviction on the first ballot, 100% of the cases resulted in guilty verdicts (N = 43) (Table 139, p. 488).

They concluded that "with very few exceptions the first ballot decides the outcome of the verdict." If so, "the real decision is often made before the deliberation begins" (p. 488). Dramatic instances of the lone juror—as memorialized by Henry Fonda in the film "Twelve Angry Men"—who by sheer force of will and persuasive power succeeds in turning around the eleven other jurors happens only rarely in real life. Their study showed that an initial minority of three or four members is needed to hang a twelve-member jury. Thus, the only effect that Justice White was willing to concede in *Apodaca* was that unanimous verdicts "would obviously produce [more] hung juries" than majority verdicts. Kalven and Zeisel found that 5.6% of the trials in unanimous jurisdictions were deadlocked, compared with 3.1% in majority jurisdictions (p. 461). For Justice White, this difference apparently was not large enough.

Jury deliberation, then, is primarily a consensus-producing process rather than a group decision-making process. "The deliberation process might well be likened to what the developer does for an exposed film: it brings out the picture, but the outcome is pre-determined" (p. 489). Under a majority rule, it is possible that minority viewpoints could simply be ignored in the discussion. In some mock jury studies, "jurors even asked why time was spent debating with minority jurors when their votes were superfluous" (Saks and Hastie 1978, p. 86).

Racial minorities or women cannot be systematically underrepresented in the jury venire. However, once they are seated in the jury box, they potentially could be frozen out of meaningful delibera-tion by reason of a majority verdict rule. Is their role on juries, then, mainly cosmetic? Is it necessary to assume that racial minorities or women would always or often espouse a different position from that of majority members (white men) in order to challenge the integrity of the jury decision-making process?

7.   If a jury cannot reach agreement, some courts will give an *"Allen* instruction" that directs the dissenting jurors to consider whether they might not reasonably doubt the correctness of their position in light of the opposing view of the majority (*Allen* v. *United States*, 1896). Whether this is really a "dynamite charge," as some defense counsel claim, that blasts open deadlocked juries (and thereby blows away the defendant), remains to be investigated.

8.   The consensus-building process in jury deliberation has been observed in simulated studies and labeled the "group polarization phenomenon": "The average postgroup response will tend to be more extreme in the same direction as the average of the pregroup response" (Myers and Lamm 1976, p. 603). This means that group discussion tends to magnify (polarize) the individual preferences that existed before the discussion. If most members lean in one direction prior to their assembling as a group, the ensuing deliberation simply draws them further in the same direction and puts pressure on the dissent-ers to conform. This phenomenon has been found in groups involved in making ethical and business decisions as well as judgments of criminal liability.

What are the implications for jury research and for trial advocacy of the finding that verdicts are largely predictable from the judgments of individual jurors prior to deliberation? Recall, too, that social attitudes, personality traits, and demographic characteristics of jurors have not been proved to be strong predictors of individual judgments or of group verdicts (see Chapter 7, sections 7.4 and 7.5).

9.   For various cognitive, mathematical, and computer models of juror and jury decision-making, see Penrod and Hastie (1979), Pennington and Hastie (1981), and Kaplan (1982). They are "new and incomplete," and "considerable work remains to be done before they are ready to [be] appl[ied] to the judicial process" (Bartol 1983, p. 165).

UNITED STATES v. DOUGHERTY

473 F.2d 1113 (D.C. Cir. 1972)

LEVENTHAL, Circuit Judge:

Seven of the so-called "D.C. Nine" bring this joint appeal from convictions arising out of their unconsented entry into the Washington offices of the Dow Chemical Company, and their destruction of certain property therein. . . . [Appellants defaced the premises by spilling about a bloodlike substance, as a symbolic protest of Dow Chemical's manufacture of napalm, used by the American military in the then on-going Vietnam War. The trial judge ruled that "the War in Vietnam is not an issue in this case." Ed.'s note.]

Appellants urge [several] grounds for reversal, [including] as follows: . . . The judge erroneously refused to instruct the jury of its right to acquit appellants without regard to the law and the evidence, and refused to permit appellants to argue that issue to the jury. . . .

There has evolved in the Anglo-American system an undoubted jury prerogative-in-fact, derived from its power to bring in a general verdict of not guilty in a criminal case, that is not reversible by the court. . . .

Since the jury's prerogative of lenity, again in Learned Hand's words introduces a "slack into the enforcement of law, tempering its rigor by the mollifying influence of current ethical conventions," it is only just, say appellants, that the jurors be so told. It is unjust to withhold information on the jury power of "nullification," since conscientious jurors may come, ironically, to abide by their oath as jurors to render verdicts offensive to their individual conscience, to defer to an assumption of necessity that is contrary to reality.

This so-called right of jury nullification is put forward in the name of liberty and democracy, but its explicit avowal risks the ultimate logic of anarchy. This is the concern voiced by Judge Sobeloff . . .:

No legal system could long survive if it gave every individual the option of disregarding with impunity any law which by his personal standard was judged morally untenable. . . .

The statement that avowal of the jury's prerogative runs the risk of anarchy, represents, in all likelihood, the habit of thought of philosophy and logic, rather than the prediction of the social scientist. But if the statement contains an element of hyperbole, the existence of risk and danger, of significant magnitude, cannot be gainsaid. In contrast, the advocates of jury "nullification" apparently assume that the articulation of the jury's power will not extend its use or extent, or will not do so significantly or obnoxiously. Can this assumption fairly be made? We know that a posted limit of 60 m.p.h. produces factual speeds 10 or even 15 miles greater, with an understanding all around that some "tolerance" is acceptable to the authorities, assuming conditions warrant. But can it be supposed that the speeds would stay substantially the same if the speed limit were put: Drive as fast as you think appropriate, without the posted limit as an anchor, a point of departure?

Our jury system is a resultant of many vectors, some explicit, and some rooted in tradition, continuity and general understanding without express formulation. A constitution may be meaningful though it is unwritten, as the British have proved for 900 years.

The jury system has worked out reasonably well overall, providing "play in the joints" that imparts flexibility and avoids undue rigidity. An equilibrium has evolved—an often marvelous balance—with the jury acting as a "safety valve" for exceptional cases, without being a wildcat or runaway institution. There is reason to believe that the simultaneous achievement of modest jury equity and avoidance of intolerable caprice depends on formal instructions that do not expressly delineate a jury charter to carve out its own rules of law. . . .

The way the jury operates may be radically altered if there is alteration in the way it is told to operate. The jury knows well enough that its prerogative is not limited to the choices articulated in the formal instructions of the court. The jury gets its understanding as to the arrangements in the legal system from more than one voice. There is the formal communication from the judge. There is the informal communication from the total culture—literature (novel, drama, film, and television); current comment (newspapers, magazines and television); conversation; and, of course, history and tradition. The totality of input generally conveys adequately enough the idea of prerogative, of freedom in an occasional case to depart from what the judge says. Even indicators that would on their face seem too weak to notice—like the fact that the judge tells the jury it must acquit (in case of reasonable doubt) but never tells the jury in so many words that it must convict—are a meaningful part of the jury's total input. Law is a system, and it is also a language, with secondary meanings that may be unrecorded yet are part of its life.

When the legal system relegates the information of the jury's prerogative to an essentially informal input, it is not being duplicitous, chargeable with chicane and intent to deceive. The limitation to informal input is, rather a governor to avoid excess: the prerogative is reserved for the exceptional case, and the judge's instruction is retained as a generally effective constraint. . . .

Moreover, to compel a juror involuntarily assigned to jury duty to assume the burdens of mini-legislator or judge, as is implicit in the doctrine of nullification, is to put untoward strains on the jury system. It is one thing for a juror to know that the law condemns, but he has a factual power of lenity. To tell him expressly of a nullification prerogative, however, is to inform him, in effect, that it is he who fashions the rule that condemns. That is an overwhelming responsibility, an extreme burden for the jurors' psyche. And it is not inappropriate to add that a juror called upon for an involuntary public service is entitled to the protection, when he takes action that he knows is right, but also knows is unpopular, either in the community at large or in his own particular grouping, that he can fairly put it to friends and neighbors that he was merely following the instructions of the court.

In the last analysis, our rejection of the request for jury nullification doctrine is a recognition that there are times when logic is not the only or even best guide to sound conduct of government. . . .

What makes for health as an occasional medicine would be disastrous as a daily diet. The fact that there is widespread existence of the jury's prerogative, and approval of its existence as a "necessary counter to case-hardened judges and arbitrary prosecutors," does not establish as an imperative that the jury must be informed by the judge of that power. . . . An explicit instruction to a jury conveys an implied approval that runs the risk of degrading the legal structure requisite for true freedom, for an ordered liberty that protects against anarchy as well as tyranny. . . .

BAZELON, Chief Judge, concurring in part and dissenting in part. . . .

My disagreement with the Court concerns the issue of jury nullification. . . . I see no justification for, and considerable harm in, [the majority's] deliberate lack of candor. . . .

We are left with a doctrine that may "enhance the over-all normative effect of the rule of law," but, at the same time, one that must not only be concealed from the jury, but also effectively condemned in the jury's presence. Plainly, the justification for this sleight-of-hand lies in a fear that an occasionally noble doctrine will, if acknowledged, often be put to ignoble and abusive purposes—or, to borrow the Court's phrase, will "run the risk of anarchy." . . . No matter how horrible the effect feared by the Court, the validity of its reasoning depends on the existence of a demonstrable connection between the alleged cause (a jury nullification instruction or argument to the jury on that issue) and that effect. I am unable to see a connection.

To be sure, there are abusive purposes, discussed below, to which the doctrine might be put. The Court assumes that these abuses are most likely to occur if the doctrine is formally described to the jury by argument or instruction. That assumption, it should be clear, does not rest on any proposition of logic. It is nothing more or less than a prediction of how jurors will react to the judge's instruction or argument by counsel. And since we have no empirical data to measure the validity of the prediction, we must rely on our own rough judgments of its plausibility.

The Court reasons that . . . the spontaneous and unsolicited act of nullification is thought less likely, on the whole, to reflect bias and a perverse sense of values than the act of nullification carried out by a jury carefully instructed on its power and responsibility.

It seems substantially more plausible to me to assume that the very opposite is true. The juror motivated by prejudice seems to me more likely to make spontaneous use of the power to nullify, and more likely to disregard the judge's exposition of the normally controlling legal standards. The conscientious juror, who could make a careful effort to consider the blameworthiness of the defendant's action in light of prevailing community values, is the one most likely to obey the judge's admonition that the jury enforce strict principles of law. . . .

I do not seen any reason to assume that jurors will make rampantly abusive use of their power. Trust in the jury is, after all, one of the cornerstones of our entire criminal jurisprudence. . . . Nevertheless, some abuse can be anticipated. If a jury refuses to apply strictly the controlling principles of law, it may—in conflict with values shared by the larger community—convict a defendant because of prejudice against him, or acquit a defendant because of sympathy for him and prejudice against his victim. Our fear of unjust conviction is plainly understandable. But it is hard for me to see how a nullification instruction could enhance the likelihood of that result. The instruction would speak in terms of acquittal, not conviction, and it would provide no comfort to a juror determined to convict a defendant in defiance of the law or the facts of the case. . . .

As for the problem of unjust acquittal, it is important to recognize the strong internal check that constrains the jury's willingness to acquit. Where defendants seem dangerous, juries are unlikely to exercise their nullification power, whether or not an explicit instruction is offered. Of course, that check will not prevent the acquittal of a defendant who may be blameworthy and dangerous except in the jaundiced eyes of a jury motivated by a perverse and sectarian sense of values. But whether a nullification instruction would make such acquittals more common is problematical, if not entirely inconceivable. In any case, the real problem in this situation is not the nullification doctrine, but the values and prejudice that prompt the acquittal. And the solution is not to condemn the nullification power, but to spotlight the prejudice and parochial values that underlie the verdict. . . .

NOTES AND QUESTIONS

---

1.   To tell or not to tell the jury, that is the question. Should the answer rest primarily on normative grounds, as Judge Leventhal suggests, or on empirical grounds, as Judge Bazelon implies? What empirically testable propositions are set forth in each opinion? Is the recognition of the de facto power of lenity, coupled with the refusal to expressly avow that right by instruction, a judicial "sleight-of-hand," as Judge Bazelon puts it, or a form of Solomonic compromise to confine its exercise to occasional cases, as Judge Leventhal argues?

2.   Informing the jury of its nullification power, Judge Leventhal says, is akin to allowing the jury to determine what is the "appropriate" speed limit "without the posted limit as an anchor." Is the analogy valid?

3.   Horowitz (in Horowitz and Willging 1984) performed a laboratory experiment comparing the verdicts of mock juries who were informed of the nullification power with the verdicts of those who received standard instructions without any mention of nullification. He found that juries informed about nullification "were less likely to convict a defendant in an euthanasia case in which a suffering patient was disconnected from life-support systems by a sympathetically portrayed nurse, and more likely to convict in a drunk-driving case in which the defendant was clearly negligent" (p. 195). Moreover, these juries spent more time during the deliberation talking about their personal experiences as they pertained to the legal issues, and less time discussing the trial evidence. Assuming that these results are generalizable to real juries, do they support Judge Leventhal's position or Judge Bazelon's position?

4.   Two states permit jury nullification instructions, Indiana and Maryland (Scheflin and Van Dyke 1980, pp. 79–85). This opens up the possibility of field experiments that compare the impact of not only the presence or absence of nullification instructions, but also different wordings of these instructions. Some Maryland courts instruct as follows:

> Members of the Jury, this is a criminal case and under the Constitution and the laws of the State of Maryland in a criminal case, the jury are the judges of the law as well as of the facts in the case. So that whatever I tell you about the law, while it is intended to be helful to you in reaching a just and proper verdict in the case, it is not binding upon you as members of the jury and you may accept or reject it. And you may apply the law as you apprehend it to be in the case [*Wyley* v. *Warden*, 1967, p. 743, n. 1].

As a safeguard against jury lawlessness, either party may request the judge to give the jury an advisory instruction on the law, and the judge must do so under Maryland law. Would an instruction such as the following one neutralize the effect of the nullification instruction: "[You are not to] apply the law as you think it ought to be or what it should be, but what, in fact, it is in this case" (*Hamilton* v. *State*, 1971, p. 98)?

  Compare the Maryland nullification instruction with the ones below. On its face, which instruction is most likely to move a jury to exercise lenity?

Pattern Instruction for Kansas. "It is presumed that juries are the best judges of fact. . . . [J]udges are presumed to be the best judges of the law. Accordingly, you must accept my instructions as being correct statements of the generally accepted legal principles that apply in a case of the type you have heard. . . . Even so, it is difficult to draft legal statements that are so exact that they are right for all conceivable circumstances. Accordingly, you are entitled to act upon your conscientious feeling about what is a fair result in this case and acquit the defendant if you believe that justice requires such a result." (The Kansas Supreme Court subsequently overturned this instruction. Scheflin and Van Dyke 1980, p. 64.)

U. S. District Court Judge Fisher's instruction. "[I]f you find that the overreaching participation by Government agents . . . as you have heard them was so fundamentally unfair as to be offensive to the basic standards of decency, and shocking to the universal sense of justice, then you may acquit any defendant to whom this defense applies." (This instruction was given in the trial of antiwar activists who were charged with destroying records at a local selective service office. Scheflin and Van Dyke 1980, p. 53.)

5.   Since most jurisdictions do not allow nullification instructions, studies could focus on the efficacy of other indirect and subtle ways of "reminding" jurors of that power. In closing arguments, counsel could present the case as a call to conscience, without expressly inviting the jury to suspend the application of the judge's instructions of law. At voir dire, counsel could preemptorily challenge prospective jurors who answered "yes" to a question such as: "If Robin Hood was prosecuted for robbery, would you convict him of that charge even if he gave all the stolen money to the poor?"

Political Policy and the Jury Cases

The foregoing cases on jury size and decision-making rules cannot be read in a political vacuum. These decisions are noteworthy not only because they involve substantial use (by at least some members of the Court) of social science, but also because they reflect broader political and jurisprudential trends in the area of criminal justice. An underlying political consideration in *Ballew* as revealed by Justice Blackmun's application of the balancing approach is the issue of federalism—of striking a balance between the authority of the federal courts to review the constitutionality of legislation and the authority of state governments to regulate their own affairs, in this instance the size of state juries. His opinion emphasized that only three states have reduced jury size to five persons, implying that in this context the argument of federally compelled uniformity between the states has less force. This issue of preserving our federal system of government constitutes the political backdrop of the jury cases. In the broad sweep of constitutional history, the balance between state and federal control over the state criminal process has gone through three distinct stages. A quick overview of the evolution of these stages helps place in wider perspective the development of procedural justice in state criminal courts, including the right to an impartial jury.

The first stage was characterized by a policy strongly supportive of state autonomy over centralized power. From the founding of the Republic to the first third of the twentieth century, the criminal justice system of the different states was governed principally by state and local law. Federal constitutional law that applied to protect the procedural rights of individuals prosecuted in federal courts was irrelevant to state cases: The Bill of Rights initially bound only the actions of the national government, not of state governments. The American criminal process has always been highly decentralized and subject to local control. For example, there has always been a lingering fear of national police force, and the decentralization and fragmentation of the criminal process is perhaps most obvious with respect to the police.

In the 1930s, in cases involving procedural unfairness (for example, denial of appointed counsel) to indigent black defendants convicted of capital crimes in southern state courts, the Supreme Court for the first time made one of the guarantees of the Bill of Rights enforceable against the states (*Powell* v. *Alabama*, 1932). This marked the second stage in state-federal relations—the start of the "nationalization" of state criminal processes. The federal Constitution as well as state law (state constitution, legislation, decisions) now became sources of procedural justice for state defendants. However, it was not until the 1960s that the wholesale attempt to raise the quality of state criminal justice to the federal level was carried out by the "liberal" Warren Court. The result was a significant expansion of the power of the federal courts to oversee day-to-day matters of criminal justice administration—for example, police interrogations (*Miranda*), counsel at police lineups (*United States* v. *Wade;* see Chapter 10), right to a jury trial (*Duncan* v. *Louisiana*, 1968)—that historically had been within the almost exclusive control of state and local authorities. There was a centralization of state criminal procedures insofar as constitutionally based rights of the accused were concerned. The objective was to erase the dual standard of justice in the state and federal systems. The justice afforded a defendant ought not vary depending on the forum in which he is tried, since there is only one national Constitution for the land.

The *Williams, Apodaca,* and *Ballew* decisions in the 1970s intimate the beginning of a third stage in the evolution of federal-state relations. These decisions were made against the backdrop of a changing social-political climate—one that saw a nation increasingly worried about street crime, disenchanted with the centralization of power in the federal government, desirous of greater control over its local institutions, skeptical of national solutions to local problems, and drifting rightward at the polls. In this context of the "new conservatism," the theme of state sovereignty again strikes a responsive popular chord. By the mid-1970s and into the 1980s, as enthusiasm for federal intervention wanes, it is once more respectable to advocate for states' rights.

The jury cases reveal the Burger Court's solicitude for the states in the federal system. Once the basic right to a jury trial is assured in state courts, it is no longer up to the federal courts to dictate to their state counterparts how that right ought to be implemented. Different states have different needs and resources, and state officials are in a better position than federal judges to determine whether certain jury sizes or verdict rules are the more appropriate for their own jurisdictions. The movement of the 1960s toward federally compelled uniformity between the states in the administration of criminal justice has been blunted.

Thus, *Williams* reaffirms the right to a jury trial as announced in *Duncan*, but it narrows the scope of the right by allowing smaller juries. When the Sixth Amendment was stretched to its limit in *Ballew*, the Court drew the line. The scope was further narrowed in *Apodaca* by allowing nonunanimous verdicts. To the extent that these issues implicate jury representativeness and functioning, they go to the substance of the right itself.

Re-examine the *Apodaca* case in light of the foregoing overview. Note the alignment of votes of the justices: Four join the plurality opinion (Chief Justice Burger, Justices White, Blackmun, and Rehnquist); four dissent (Justices Brennan,

Douglas, Marshall, and Stewart); and one concurs (Justice Powell). This voting pattern presages the political policy issue raised again in *Ballew*. The plurality justices and Justice Powell concluded that unanimity is not required in state criminal trials, and the dissenting justices disagree. The dissenting justices and Justice Powell suggested that unanimity is required in federal criminal trials under the Sixth Amendment, and the plurality justices seemed to disagree. Thus, the position of the plurality could result in the lowering of the federal standards to the state level, and the position of the dissenters would raise state standards to the federal level. Justice Powell adopts a middle-of-the-road position: separate state and federal standards consistent with "principles of federalism."

    Evaluate the applicability of the foregoing three-stage cycle to the school desegregation decisions (Chapters 3 and 4) and to the death penalty cases (Chapter 5).

8.4.   METHODOLOGICAL ISSUES IN JURY RESEARCH

"CONVINCING EMPIRICAL EVIDENCE" ON THE SIX MEMBER JURY

Hans Zeisel and Shari Seidman Diamond

· · ·

    [T]he Court asserted [in *Colgrove* v. *Battin*] that "four very recent studies have provided *convincing empirical evidence* of the correctness of the *Williams* conclusion that 'there is no discernible difference between the results reached by the two different sized juries.' " . . . [T]he Court was misled; the four studies do not support this proposition. . . . [T]his article will analyze the four studies cited in *Colgrove* and suggest several study designs that would produce the needed evidence.

I.   THE FOUR STUDIES

    On the surface all four studies do what their summaries claim: they compare the performance of twelve-member and six-member juries. Two of the studies, in

Washington[10] and New Jersey,[11] compare jury trials within a system that allows litigants to choose between the two jury sizes. A third study, in Michigan,[12] also used actual trial results in what is called a before-and-after study. Until July, 1970, civil cases in Michigan were tried before juries of twelve; after that date jury size was reduced to six. The fourth study[13] was a laboratory study in which experimental juries viewed the same videotaped trial, and jury size was randomly varied by the experimenter. . . .

A.   THE WASHINGTON STUDY. Civil jury trials in the state of Washington are held before six-member juries, unless one of the litigating parties requests a twelve-member jury. The authors of this study

[10]Bermant & Coppock, *Outcomes of Six- and Twelve-Member Jury Trials: An Analysis of 128 Civil Cases in the State of Washington*, 48 Wash. L. Rev. 593 (1973) [hereinafter cited as *Washington Study*].
[11]Institute of Judicial Administration, A Comparison of Six- and Twelve-Member Juries in New Jersey Superior and County Courts (1972) [hereinafter cited as *New Jersey Study*].
[12]Note, *Six-Member and Twelve-Member Juries: An Empirical Study of Trial Results*, 6 U. Mich. J. L. Reform 671 (1973) [hereinafter cited as *Michigan Study*].
[13]Note, *An Empirical Study of Six- and Twelve-Member Jury Decision-Making Processes*, 6 U. Mich. J. L. Reform 712 (1973) [hereinafter cited as *Laboratory Study*].

tried to determine whether there is any difference between six- and twelve-member juries by comparing the results of 128 workmen's compensation trials.

Where an attorney is presented with the opportunity to demand a twelve-member jury, he or she is likely to do so only for a reason. The jury fee is usually twice that for a six-member jury, and the attorney knows that the court may view the larger jury as an added burden. Whenever the studied attribute is present for a reason, rather than after random distribution by chance, surface comparisons between results become meaningless. . . .

The Washington investigators recognized this problem, but thought it could be circumvented by words, stating "if we may properly assume that the assignment of jury size was essentially random . . . then we may conclude that the use of the smaller jury introduced no systematic bias into the trial outcomes."

The investigators have ignored the fact that "random assignment" does not describe a selection *result;* it is a characteristic of the selection *procedure,* namely one that leaves the selection to chance. Lawyer stipulations, however, are anything but random events; there is good evidence that lawyers are more likely to opt for the larger jury if the amount in controversy is larger. It is therefore irrelevant to report the Washington finding that, in these workmen's compensation trials, six- and twelve-member juries found in equal proportions for the plaintiff, because not only the jury size, but also probably the amount in controversy, was different.

B.   THE NEW JERSEY STUDY. The New Jersey study, also conducted in a system in which the litigants had a choice of jury size, recognized the possibility that different types of cases might be presented to the two types of juries and documented the impossibility of direct comparison. Yet the study failed to deal with this difficulty

and, in its summary conclusion, thereby misled the unwary reader.

The study leaves no doubt as to the major differences between the cases tried before the two types of juries. Both settlements and verdicts of twelve-member juries are, on the average, three times as great as for the six-member jury cases. Twelve-member jury cases also tended to be more complex. . . .

The study's finding on trial time was that "cases tried before twelve-member juries take approximately twice as much trial time as those tried before six (11 hours compared to 5.6). One important reason . . . is that the cases tend to be more complicated." There is nothing wrong with this statement; there is no hint that smaller jury size has anything to do with reducing trial time. Yet the summary begins with the statement that "[u]se of six-member juries in civil cases can result in substantial savings in trial time. . . ." There is not a shred of evidence to support this claim. Indeed, a reasonable conclusion would be that the trial time difference was caused by the decreased complexity of the cases, and not by a decrease in jury size. . . .

C.   THE MICHIGAN LABORATORY EXPERIMENT. The Michigan laboratory study avoided the difficulties of comparability of cases by showing just one videotaped case to a series of six- and twelve-member juries. . . .

The experiment . . . had a . . . serious drawback. The use of only one trial had the disadvantage of narrowing the experimental experience and increasing the difficulties of drawing general conclusions. This drawback was aggravated by the fact that this trial was very special. The evidence in the case overwhelmingly favored the defendant; of sixteen juries, not one found for the plaintiff. This overpowering bias makes the experiment irrelevant. On the facts of this case, any jury under any rules would probably have arrived at the same verdict. Hence, to conclude from this experiment that jury size generally has no effect on the verdict is impermissible. . . .

D. THE MICHIGAN BEFORE-AND-AFTER STUDY. The twelve-member jury was replaced in Michigan on July 23, 1970 by the six-member jury. If nothing but jury size had changed at that time, it would be sensible to compare trial results before the change with results after it. The trouble is that unknown simultaneous changes may have also affected the trial results, and it is difficult to exclude such a possibility. In this study the situation is worse, because two important changes are known to have occurred at the crucial point in time. A mediation board was instituted, and procedural rules were modified to allow discovery of insurance policy limits. Under these circumstances it is difficult, if not impossible, to say whether any observed change or part of a change is due to the reduction in jury size or the other changes. If the various causes operate in opposite directions, a finding of no difference might be equally spurious.

To illustrate this point, consider the study's data that the average award in automobile negligence cases in which the jury found for the plaintiff was $11,147 with twelve-member juries and $23,768 with six-member juries. The probability of settling a particular case without trial is related to the size of that case; the largest cases are least likely to be settled. If the creation of the mediation board and better discovery procedures increased the proportion of settled cases, the average size of cases reaching trial would be increased. The data therefore could not be used to support a conclusion that six-member juries give higher damage awards. . . .

II.   SATISFACTORY EXPERIMENTS

Although no study has produced satisfactory evidence regarding the impact of six-member juries, there are strategies for studying this question that would produce the needed information.

The ideal research design would test the effects of jury size in a jurisdiction in which six-member juries are optional. A series of cases could be tried simultaneously before two juries, one composed of six members and the other of twelve. The parties' counsel would select eighteen jurors to form the two juries; before the trial, without the knowledge of either jury, the attorneys and the court would decide which jury would decide the case. The jurors would not learn whether their jury made the real decision until deliberations were completed. This design would permit a comparison of jury reactions to the same trial and would allow a direct assessment of the effect of jury size. While this design would not violate the essential rights of the litigants or the integrity of the trial, it would require the consent of the trial court and the litigants.

In the next best design, comparable sets of cases would be tried before six- and twelve-member juries. Again, one would choose a jurisdiction in which jury size is optional. The study would exclude all cases in which a party insisted on a twelve-member jury or chose a six-member jury for reasons other than the lower fee. In the remaining cases, the parties would be indifferent about jury size, and the attorneys would be asked to agree to a lottery to determine whether their case would be tried before a six-member or twelve-member jury. In these cases, all litigants would pay only the six-member jury fee. This random assignment of cases would provide a properly controlled experiment in which comparable sets of cases are tried by six- and twelve-member juries. . . .

CONCLUSION

The flaws in these studies are, as we have shown, not complex and surely not beyond the reach of modest expertise. It would be unfair, however, to place the blame for accepting unsatisfactory evidence entirely on the Supreme Court. If lawyers and social scientists write poor studies, and if legal journals publish them, the courts should be entitled to cite them. . . .

Perhaps the ultimate solution lies in eliminating a misleading label. "Empirical evidence" is a pleonasm; all evidence is, or ought to be, empirical. The term has come to distinguish systematically gathered facts from the facts in the individual case as they are traditionally defined. Perhaps the time has come when "empirical" legal studies should simply be called legal studies. Such wording would reflect a desire for critical and intelligent use of these studies as an integral part of legal analysis. . . .

UNCOVERING "NONDISCERNIBLE" DIFFERENCES: EMPIRICAL RESEARCH AND THE JURY SIZE CASES

Richard O. Lempert

. . .

PROBLEMS OF JURY-SIZE RESEARCH

My point is . . . that typical strategies of legal-impact research, such as those utilized in the *Colgrove* real-world studies, are unlikely to uncover differences associated with jury size however well they control for those plausible rival hypotheses that form the usual threats to the validity of impact research. The reason lies in the unamenability of the jury-size problem to the usual techniques of aggregate data analysis.

The difficulties of the real-world approach are best illustrated if we look at the careful research designs that Zeisel and Diamond present in the latter part of their *Colgrove* article. Their "ideal" design would require a jurisdiction in which six-member juries were optional. During the experimental period, cases in that jurisdiction would be tried simultaneously before two juries, one of six and one of twelve members. . . .

In the abstract, this design and analytical framework might seem ideal. It has the particular virtue of revealing verdict differences on a case-by-case basis. However, it holds a major trap for the unwary researcher: In any actual study, data analysis is likely to proceed on the implicit assumption that each trial provides an occasion on which any existing jury-size effects can, with a certain *constant* probability, be expected to appear. If, for example, in thirty out of one hundred trials the simultaneous verdicts were different, the researcher probably would conclude that there were substantial jury-size effects. If, on the other hand, differences arose in only five out of one hundred pairs of verdicts, the conclusion probably would be that jury-size effects were minimal. But the probability of divergent verdicts in any particular case may be close to zero. A five per cent disagreement rate may reflect disagreement in all or a substantial percentage of those cases where jury size *reasonably* could be expected to influence jury verdicts.

MOST CASES ARE CLEAR

One may test this last point by attempting to estimate the fraction of cases in which jury size can be expected to have a reasonable probability of affecting the verdict. The best empirical starting point for making such an estimation is Kalven and Zeisel's *The American Jury*. In this book the authors perform a radical version of the experiment that Zeisel and Diamond propose. Instead of comparing the verdicts reached by juries of twelve with those reached by juries of six, they compare the verdicts of juries of twelve with those of "juries" of one, the judge. The difference between judges and twelve-member juries in socioeconomic status, legal sophistication, role conceptions, and cognitive processes of evidence evaluation are likely to exceed substantially the differences between six- and twelve-member juries with respect to these factors. Thus, one may take the percentage of verdict agreement between judges and twelve-member juries as a minimum estimate of the percentage of cases in which jury-size effects could be expected to have virtually no influence on the ultimate verdict. . . . [The author goes on to propose that the maximum possible difference between six- and twelve-person juries is 30%. In *The American Jury*, a 30% disagreement was found between the verdicts of twelve-person juries and the trial judge (or one-person "jury"). The author then refines this estimate by eliminating those cases of disagreement in which size effects are very unlikely because the differences are attributable to factors other than size. For instance, a certain number of the disagreements between the one-person "jury" and the twelve-person jury result from differences over evidentiary factors or sentiments about the defendant. The author arrives at a final estimate of 14.1% as the proportion of cases in which jury size has a reasonable likelihood of influencing verdicts. Ed.'s note.]

This final estimate explains why real-world research, even research as carefully designed as Zeisel and Diamond's "ideal" experiment, is likely to lend apparent support to the Supreme Court's conclusion that there is no discernible difference in the verdicts rendered by different-sized juries. There are simply too few cases in which it is reasonable to suppose that size effects will be manifested in divergent verdicts. If, for example, size affects verdicts in one third of the cases where such effects appear possible, the aggregate data collected in a Zeisel and Diamond ideal experiment would reveal fewer than five divergencies in every hundred trials. Since some divergent verdicts might be expected to occur by chance, such a low figure would lead most to conclude too hastily that the *Williams* decision was right and that jury size has little or no impact on jury verdicts.

SELECTION EFFECTS AND MISLEADING AGGREGATES

An an alternative to their ideal design, Zeisel and Diamond describe a "next best" design that in their view approximates a controlled experiment by randomly assigning cases to six- and twelve-member juries. . . . Although this type of design might be appropriate for some legal-impact research, it has flaws not shared by the ideal design that further increase the likelihood that experimentation will reveal no association between jury size and jury verdicts.

The first flaw is that only cases in which both attorneys are indifferent to jury size will be examined. If attorneys generally have any intuitive appreciation of situations in which jury size might affect verdicts, the proportion of experimental trials with a reasonable probability of size effects will be even smaller than was the case with the ideal experiment. Indeed, the experiment might prove impossible in some circumstances. If in criminal cases defendant's attorneys regard hung juries as victories, one might expect them always to insist on twelve-member juries.

The second and more basic flaw of this next best design turns on the fact that the data will have to be aggregated for analytical purposes. If, for example, the six-member jury trials result in forty per cent defendants' verdicts while the twelve-member trials result in sixty per cent defendants' verdicts, the experimenter presumably would conclude that a size effect exists. If, on the other hand, both sets of trials resulted in forty-five per cent defendants' verdicts, the likely conclusion would be that there was no size effect. Yet the latter finding would disguise a twenty per cent disagreement rate between the two types of juries if the twelve-member panels decide ten percent of the cases for the defendant when the six-member panels would have found for the plaintiff and vice versa. In other words, to the extent that size effects are not directional, differences between the verdicts of six- and twelve-member juries will, in the aggregate, cancel out. Such nondirectionality appears particularly likely in civil litigation. Kalven and Zeisel point out that in the civil cases they have studied, the judge finds for the plaintiff fifty-seven percent of the time, hardly a great difference. But an examination of case-by-case statistics reveals a twenty-two per cent rate of judge-jury disagreement. Zeisel and Diamond's next best design would show only the two per cent disagreement rate; their ideal design would report twenty-two per cent disagreement. The flaws inherent in the next best design appear so severe that the results of such research can never substantially support the proposition that jury size has no effect on jury verdicts.

TESTING STATISTICAL SIGNIFICANCE

Totally apart from the design used, one characteristic of most empirical analysis enhances the probability that research will fail to discern actual differences in verdicts rendered by different-sized juries. This feature is the routine reliance on significance tests with conventional levels of statistical significance to determine whether differences deserve to be treated as discernible. . . .

In a typical jury-size experiment the researcher tests the "null hypothesis" that jury size as an independent variable has no effect on jury verdicts as a dependent variable. A type I error would be to conclude that jury size affects jury verdicts when in fact it does not; a type II error would be to conclude that jury size does not affect jury verdicts when in fact it does. . . .

The difficulty with accepting conventional significance levels as a guide in jury-size research stems from the fact that these levels are selected to be very conservative with respect to type I error. This conservatism reflects the values of social science. Data-based theory must rest on relatively firm foundations. Multiple replications of research to ensure the reliability of findings are often expensive, difficult to accomplish, and rarely accompanied by the prestige accorded original studies. Hence original research must carry facial guarantees that the results reported are not artifacts of chance. Relatively stringent significance levels are therefore required before a relationship may be assumed to exist and a theory's support acknowledged.

The values of social science, however, are not the values of the law. When the Supreme Court rejects a constitutional attack on six-member juries partly on the ground that such a shift will not change trial results, surely the Court ought to be more concerned with type II error, the possibility that available research has failed to reveal true differences between the verdicts rendered by different size juries, than with type I error, the possibility that reported size effects do not in fact exist. Legally, the argument is that the framers of the Bill of Rights contemplated a body of twelve when they used the term "jury." Despite the Supreme Court's equivocation on this point in *Williams*, the history seems clear. Therefore, those who argue that jury size is not defined constitutionally, because size does not affect verdicts and hence has no relationship to sixth and seventh amendment values, should have the burden of empirically proving the lack of relationship. Instead, the uncritical use of significance tests in jury-size research puts a heavy burden of proof on partisans of the status quo. . . .

MEASURING VERDICT DIFFERENCES

Thus, I join Zeisel and Diamond in their call for further research, but I favor different strategies than the carefully controlled "real world" experimental approach they emphasize. . . .

Mock juries also provide the preferred strategy for examining other probable differences between juries of twelve and six. This "laboratory strategy" allows selection of cases that are sufficiently similar to reveal systematic but unanticipated size effects. In addition, members of visible minorities, such as blacks, could be placed on juries to determine the effects of their presence. Even if the presence of visible minorities had the same influence on juries of twelve as on those of six, the bare finding of influence would indicate likely size effects because the presence of one or more minority group members is more likely on larger juries.

The most important advantage of mock-jury experimentation is that it allows the researcher to monitor the deliberation process. In a close case it may be impossible to know or to prove that one outcome is better than another, yet it may be possible to conclude that a particular decision-making process is preferable. Thus, if research reveals that six-member juries tend to reach their verdicts by deliberations in which all jurors make rational contributions while twelve-member juries are dominated by one or two members or draw lots in frustration, one might well conclude that the quality of justice rendered by six is likely to be superior to that rendered by

twelve, even though nothing in observed verdict differences makes this conclusion obvious.

If mock juries are used, the researcher must be careful to avoid certain problems. The most obvious pitfall inheres in the choice of jurors. While college sophomores may be good subjects in experiments designed to explore basic social-psychological processes, a group composed of college students generally will be unsuited for jury-size research. There is simply too much evidence that juror interaction is strongly influenced by factors such as age and occupational status. The homogeneity of college students on these and other dimensions not only indicates that their deliberations are unlikely to represent actual jury deliberations, but also diminishes any advantage that juries of twelve enjoy over juries of six. . . .

Although access to real jurors is ideal, jury-size research probably should vary from the Chicago model in certain respects. Jurors in the Chicago project were neither examined on voir dire nor subjected to challenge. Yet voir dire questioning with a right to challenge adds an important element of realism to jury-size experimentation. Effective use of voir dire might minimize some of the differences between juries of six and twelve. The Chicago researchers' use of pre-deliberation votes also should be avoided. While such information is important to measure the effects of the deliberation process on individuals' attitudes, the work of Gerard and his associates indicates that prior written commitment will affect the extent to which individuals are influenced by groups. . . .

The selection and presentation of experimental cases also poses important problems. The facts of the cases used for a study of size effects must support at least two possible verdicts; otherwise there is little reason to expect that different-sized juries will decide differently. Civil cases have a particular advantage in that they generate information on two very different decision-making processes: the decision on liability and the decision as to damages. . . .

An additional advantage of using mock rather than real juries is that presentation of cases on audio or videotape ensures that the members of each experimental jury see essentially the same case. However, the use of such devices decreases the realism of the mock trial. This, plus the fact that mock jurors know that they are not actually determining an individual's fate, are probably the two most important weaknesses of this experimental approach. Both suggest that experimental juries will be less motivated to reach subjectively correct decisions and less willing to extend their deliberations than they would be if the cases were real. . . .

NOTES AND QUESTIONS

1.   Internal validity and external validity are two important methodological yardsticks. Internal validity is the *sine qua non* of any research design. It refers to the confidence with which a result is attributable to the independent variable or experimental treatment rather than to some alternative, uncontrolled factor(s). The more rigorous the research design in controlling for plausible rival hypotheses that explain the results, the greater will be the internal validity. External validity refers to the confidence with which a result is generalizable beyond the particular conditions of a study. When the same result is obtained in different studies carried out in different settings and using different methods, the confidence in its generality is enhanced. Internal validity is a necessary but not sufficient condition for external validity. If there are several competing explanations for a result, such that it is impossible to draw any firm causal inferences, the issue of generalizability does not even arise.

The two preceding articles assess several methodological approaches to studying jury functioning: archival research, field experiments with real juries, field experiments with mock juries, and laboratory simulations of juror or jury decision-making. What are the trade-offs between internal and external validity for each of these approaches?

2.   Lempert favors the laboratory approach, provided that the simulation is realistic and representative mock jurors are used. Laboratory simulations in this area are largely a post-1970 phenomenon. From 1964 to 1969, there were 21 such studies, but from 1970 to 1975, the number soared to 87 (Weiten and Diamond 1979, p. 73). An annotated bibliography of 160 simulated studies showed that about 90 percent were conducted within the past decade (Penrod 1979). Of the three major areas of psycholegal research (jury decision-making, eyewitness identification, and evidence rules), studies of mock jurors have been "by far the most voluminous and visible" (Ebbesen and Konečni 1982, p. 28). This interest was sparked by the participation of social psychologists in "scientific" jury selection on behalf of antiwar activists in the early 1970s. Subsequently, research attention expanded to encompass other features of the jury because it was a topic that had, in the parlance of the day, "social relevance." For reviews of this literature, see Erlanger (1970); Gerbasi, Zuckerman, and Reis (1977); Davis, Bray, and Holt (1977); Saks and Hastie (1978, pp. 47–99); Penrod and Hastie (1979); Weiten and Diamond (1979); Elwork, Sales, and Suggs (1981, pp. 8–34); Bray and Kerr (1982); Dane and Wrightsman (1982).

On the whole, the existing literature falls short of Lempert's ideal of jury simulation. A survey of 72 laboratory studies found that "nearly one-half . . . have been highly unrealistic" (Bray and Kerr 1982, p. 294). The paradigmatic procedure of these simulations is as follows. College students, playing the role of jurors, are randomly assigned—without voir dire or oath-taking—to experimental and control groups. Because of the contrived nature of experimental procedures, the independent (or manipulated) variable is given a prominence disproportionate to its actual effect in the real world. The "trial" consists of a couple of written pages that summarize the facts of the case. Then, without any judicial instructions, the jurors render individual decisions after little or no group deliberation. The responses are recorded on a continuous scale of guilt. (Simulation studies representative of this genre, which examine the effects of variables other than size and verdict rules, are reproduced in Chapter 9.)

The artificiality of such simulations may well bias the results. For example, Bermant et al. (1974)

examined the mode of presentation in simulation research. They exposed mock jurors to one of four treatments: a four-page summary of the evidence; a thirty-page transcript of the trial; an audiotape based on the transcript; or the audiotape and a slide show that depicted the courtroom and the various actors at the trial. The facts and evidence presented by each of these modalities were, of course, identical. The results showed a direct relationship between the proportion of individual, not-guilty decisions (without group deliberation) and the degree of realism of the simulation. The number of subjects voting not guilty in the four conditions were, respectively, 30%, 43%, 67% and 78%.

Other procedural features also limit external validity. The content of the trial materials is typically highly abbreviated and not very complex. What impact would you expect this to have on the responses of mock jurors? In over two-thirds of the laboratory studies, the dependent variable has been juror decision rather than jury verdict (Bray and Kerr 1982, p. 294). Kalven and Zeisel's survey (1966), it will be recalled, found a high correlation between the (predeliberation) first ballot and the final verdict (p. 488). Does this finding justify equating individual decisions with group decisions in laboratory settings?

3.   More realistic scenarios and more representative jurors do not necessarily lay to rest the issue of generalizability. Simulation is a form of role-playing, and mock jurors—even when highly involved in their roles—may comport differently than their real counterparts. Zeisel and Diamond (1978) compared shadow juries (randomly selected from the venire) and actual juries (selected by voir dire) who sat through the same trials in a U.S. District Court. They found that the former rendered more guilty verdicts than the latter. This difference could be due to the knowledge of shadow jurors that their decisions had no real-life consequences but, of course, it could also be attributed to the different selection procedures.

At issue is the validity of role-playing as a method for studying complex social processes. Some researchers argue that "the only way" to gain "a true understanding of the [legal] system's operation . . . is to study the system *in vivo*." Simulation studies are validated ultimately by testing their conclusions against data obtained in the real world. Therefore, "it would seem more reasonable to *begin* by studying the real-world system and then go back to the laboratory to study the specifics . . . rather than *vice versa*" (Konečni, Mulcahy, and Ebbesen 1980, p. 91). The rationale for this approach derives from studies that show that different research methods can produce different results. For example, in ascertaining the factors that determine judicial sentencing decisions, Konečni and Ebbesen (1982b) analyzed court files, interviewed judges, and conducted laboratory simulations with judges. Each method yielded a different pattern of sentencing determinants, but the archival research proved to be the best in predicting the decisions. Hence, they urged that "preference should be given to real-world studies over simulations" (p. 323). In the jury field, other researchers likewise believe that simulation "generally appears inadequate to the task of understanding real juries" (Dillehay and Nietzel 1980, p. 250).

Do you believe in the blanket superiority of field methods over laboratory methods for studying legal processes? Does the adequacy of a particular method depend upon the nature of the problem to be investigated? In the absence of prior studies, how would one determine the preferred method for a particular problem?

4.   Social psychologists have conducted most of the laboratory studies and some of them have been their own sharpest critics. Vidmar (1979) charges that "much jury simulation research . . . can be fairly characterized as marked by (a) legal naiveté, (b) sloppy scholarship, and (c) overgeneralization combined with inappropriate value judgments" (p. 96). (With respect to value judgments, even the titles of articles—for example, "Justice Needs a New Blindfold"; Gerbasi, Zuckerman, and Reis, 1977—belie professions of scholarly detachment.) These failings, Vidmar says, render the studies "questionable" or "useless" in applied research (p. 97). These criticisms should be seen in longitudinal perspective. The charges are true with respect to most of the laboratory studies done before, say, the late 1970s, when the field was still relatively young. By the 1980s, however, the simulations have steadily become more sophisticated (for example, Severance and Loftus 1982, reproduced in Chapter 9, section 9.6). There is reason to hope that the criticisms will lose some of their force in the coming years.

A counterargument is that legal relevance need not be the criterion for appraising jury research. The simulated jury can be simply a setting for conducting basic research on, say, group dynamics or interpersonal relations. One commentator suggests that "psychological research should not be dictated by what law wants but by what psychologists find interest in studying," even if "the impact . . . on the judicial system . . . is minimal." The "worth" of jury research lies "predominantly in its attempts at theory building" (Bartol 1983, p. 167).

Is a clear separation between applied and basic research in this field possible or desirable? Should the "worth" of jury research be measured instead by the extent to which it illuminates or improves the jury institution, thereby helping to effectuate the values which underlie the right to jury trial?

5.   Critics of these laboratory simulations argue that if the research cannot be done properly, then it should not be undertaken: "[E]rroneous information obtained by scientific methods (and therefore carrying the aura of truth) is more harmful than no information at all, . . . especially when issues as sensitive as legal ones are being dealt with . . ." (Konečni and Ebbesen 1982a, p. 32). The alternative view is that "in new efforts it must be better to learn something, however imperfectly, than to withdraw from inquiry altogether when preferred methods are as a practical matter not available" (Kalven and Zeisel 1966, p. 39).

Which is the sounder position? Should the answer depend upon the purposes—theory-building or policy-making—for which the imperfect information is gathered?

8.5.   EFFECTS OF CASE COMPLEXITY ON JURY FUNCTIONING

Complexity and the Seventh Amendment

Thus far, we have looked at the effects of two independent variables of constitutional dimension (jury size and decision-making rules) on the dependent variables of the deliberation and verdicts of criminal juries. Now we turn to another variable, arguably also of constitutional status—namely, that of case complexity—and examine its impact on the functioning of the civil jury. The question is whether the right to a civil jury can be denied on the grounds that the parties are so numerous, the evidence so massive, the issues so complicated, and the duration of the trial so protracted that jurors would be unable to understand the case and decide it rationally. Whereas the issues of size reduction and nonunanimous verdicts purportedly modified only the scope but not the substance of the Sixth Amendment right, the issue of complexity threatens to curtail the Seventh Amendment right itself.

The complexity exception has not arisen in the criminal context. The criminal jury trial is inextricably associated with political freedom in the Anglo-American experience so that to abrogate the one is to undermine the other. Preservation of the criminal jury is more compelling because it is the only citizen institution that stands between an individual and the forces of the state. The civil jury is deemed less consequential because it adjudicates property or economic rights, not matters of life and death. "Indeed, the [Supreme] Court has paid the civil jury its 'ultimate' insult, for it has never held that the seventh amendment is, as part of the Bill of Rights, incorporated into the fourteenth amendment and thus binding on the states" (Lempert 1981, p. 81). Consequently, the scope and meaning of the Seventh Amendment are determined without reference to state law. If the civil jury is not essential to the scheme of ordered liberty, its curtailment is not constitutionally impermissible.

Despite its second class status, lay decision-making in civil matters advances significant social values. In addition to providing peaceful resolution of disputes, it serves to mitigate the literal demands of the law by interjecting the community's sense of justice. For example, juries often refuse to leave unremedied a partly negligent plaintiff in a contributory negligence jurisdiction. Popular wisdom, reflected in these verdicts, antedated and inspired the development of comparative negligence law. Jury equity allows the legal system to reach results which a judge is unable or unwilling to reach. Even Alexander Hamilton, who opposed the civil jury, conceded that it provided a check on the morality of governing elites (*Federalist*, No. 83). The possibility of nullification (or subterranean legislation) by the civil jury helps to safeguard economic liberties which, the framers of the Seventh Amendment realized, are related to political liberties (Wolfram 1973). Hence, the preservation of the civil jury merits respect. Even though a denial of the Seventh Amendment right might not precipitate the public clamor that a denial of its Sixth Amendment counterpart would arouse, it should prompt careful inquiry into the actual competence of the jury before a constitutional judgment is reached.

We know from the Kalven and Zeisel report that the level of jury-judge agreement on civil liability is quite high (78% of the time), about the same as the consensus on criminal guilt. If laypersons reach the same results as professional decision-makers, the inference is that the jury can decide by rational deduction from the facts in evidence and by application of the relevant law. Given the general capability of the jury in run-of-the-mill cases, the narrower issue is its competence in cases of extraordinary complexity. The measure of a lawsuit's complexity is not easily defined with any degree of precision. Courts have tended to rely on the "I know it when I see it" test. They have had no difficulty in recognizing complexity in the cases where the issue has been raised. For example, in *In re U.S. Financial Securities Litigation* (1979), a variety of plaintiffs filed some twenty suits (consolidated for trial) against a real estate development company and assorted individual and corporate defendants, alleging violations of securities law, fraud, and negligence. Pretrial discovery produced about five million documents. The federal district court judge estimated that the trial to determine the extent and amount of liability, if any, of each defendant to each plaintiff, as well as of defendants to each other, would take two years. During this time, the fact-finder would be presented with documents involving esoteric subject matter in economics, accounting, and securities. If stacked together, these papers would be as high as a three-story building or as long as the first ninety volumes of the *Federal Reporter, Second Series* (including headnotes). The judge also worried that there was no courtroom in the country large enough to seat all of the attorneys, not to mention the principal parties. While proclaiming faith in the jury system, the judge concluded that this case was beyond the ability of the jury. The Ninth Circuit reversed. It expressed great confidence in the capability of the jury to decide any case and held that there exists no complexity exception to the Seventh Amendment.

Analytically, there are three approaches to whether the Seventh Amendment applies to complex litigation. The first is historical. It rests on the legal-equitable distinction, with complex commercial cases analogized to equitable actions which are not triable by jury. The second is functional. It is based on a footnote in *Ross v. Bernhard* (1970), in which the Supreme Court appeared to ask trial judges to inquire into "the practical abilities and limitations of juries" in deciding the Seventh Amendment issue (p. 538, n. 10). The third involves the Fifth Amendment Due Process Clause. Under this approach, fairness requires a bench trial when a jury cannot comprehend the issues and the evidence in the case. The next section briefly describes the historical and functional approaches, and the following section focuses on the Fifth Amendment analysis.

Historical and Functional Approaches

The Seventh Amendment provides that "in suits at common law, . . . the right of trial by jury shall be preserved. . . ." Its surface simplicity is beguiling because the exact scope of its application is unclear. It "preserves" (not creates) the right only in suits denominated "at common law" as they existed in the English tradition in 1791, the year the Amendment was adopted. Jury trial is a demandable right only in "suits in which *legal* rights [are] to be ascertained and determined, in contradistinction to those where *equitable* rights alone [are] recognized, and equitable remedies [are] administered" (*Parsons* v. *Bedford*, 1830, p. 446).

In early English practice, there were separate courts, each having different jurisdiction over different kinds of claims. The two principal ones were common law courts (which tried legal issues before a jury) and equity courts or chancery courts (which heard equitable claims before a judge called the chancellor). (Other forums included admiralty courts which disposed of maritime cases.) In this context, "equity" does not refer to general principles of fairness, but to a distinct body of rules that supplemented and superseded the common law when legal remedies were inadequate or nonexistent. For example, the remedy of monetary damages for breach of contract was a "legal" issue which presumptively carried the right to jury trial. However, if a plaintiff requested the remedy of specific performance (a court order to the defaulting party to perform the contract), it was unavailable in the common law courts. It was an "equitable" issue within the jurisdiction of the chancellor.

The apparent exceptions to this practice were "actions for an account." These were cases involving financial transactions or business dealings in which the plaintiff alleged a balance ("account") was owed to him. When the accounting was deemed too complicated for a jury to unravel, the suit was tried in chancery court despite its legal nature.

The grounds for categorizing an action as legal or equitable—and, if legal, whether it is nonetheless triable in chancery—are found in long-ago practices of the English courts. Traditionally, then, resolution of the Seventh Amendment issue involved recourse to historical inquiry: Does the present action, for which jury trial is demanded, have any exact or analogical counterpart to "suits at common law" in 1791? If yes, and these suits were not exceptions to the practice, the right is preserved. Thus, courts have held that treble damage suits under modern antitrust laws are entitled to jury trials. Even though antitrust claims were unheard of in the eighteenth century, they are analogous to common law suits for monetary damages. However, when the antitrust or other commercial litigation is highly complicated, opponents of jury trial in such cases analogize them to equitable accountings in order to place them out of the reach of the Seventh Amendment (Devlin 1980). Proponents of jury trial, on the other hand, view these precedents as aberrational. They argue that equity assumed jurisdiction not because of the complexity of the accountings but because of chancery procedures unrelated to jury competence (Arnold 1980; Sperlich 1982).

This debate illustrates the basic difficulty with the historical approach. When modern suits such as complex antitrust litigation have no clear historical counterpart, and early chancery practices are murky to begin with, how is the Seventh Amendment issue decided? In response to this difficulty, the Supreme Court gradually moved away from an exclusively historical approach and embraced a policy in favor of jury trials. The catalyst for changes was the adoption in 1938 of the Federal Rules of Civil Procedure (FRCP), which merged courts of law and of equity into a consolidated jurisdiction. Merger enabled the simultaneous assertion of legal and equitable claims in a single action in the same court. Litigants no longer had to institute separate proceedings to seek relief by way of damages and injunction. After 1938, the only significance left to the legal-equitable distinction was that legal claims were still entitled to jury trial.

In a set of three cases, the Court expounded on the implications of merger for the Seventh Amendment. All the cases involved legal matters that were intermixed with equitable claims. In *Beacon Theatres, Inc.* v. *Westover* (1959), an antitrust case, the Court ruled that legal issues should be tried before equitable issues in order to preserve jury trial. (The right could be lost if equitable adjudication by the judge estopped the parties from relitigating the same fact issues before a jury.) Since 1791, equitable issues had been tried first. In reversing the sequence of litigation, the Court implicitly regarded jury trial as the preferred mode of adjudication. *Dairy Queen, Inc.* v. *Wood* (1962) involved an accounting for money owed and an injunction in a trademark dispute. The Court rejected the notion that labeling the suit as one for an "accounting" would determine the mode of trial. Given the availability of "masters" to assist juries, the Court suggested that accountings too complicated for the jury would be rare indeed.

Finally, in *Ross* v. *Bernhard* (1970), the Court again demonstrated its partiality for jury trial of legal issues in suits primarily intended to secure equitable relief. It extended the Seventh Amendment to legal claims in a stockholder's derivative suit (that is, a suit against the managers or directors of a corporation alleging harm to the corporation, and only indirect or derivative harm to the stockholder initiating the suit). Such an action in premerger days was cognizable only in equity, because courts of law refused to recognize a shareholder's standing to sue on behalf of his corporation. In a short and cryptic footnote, the Court set forth a tripartite test for determining whether any particular issue (rather than the overall action) is legal or equitable, and therefore triable by jury or judge:

> As our cases indicate, the "legal" nature of an issue is determined by considering, first, the pre-merger custom with reference to such questions; second, the remedy sought; and, third, the practical abilities and limitations of juries. Of these factors, the first, requiring extensive and possibly abstruse historical inquiry, is obviously the most difficult to apply. [p. 538, n. 10]

The first prong simply reaffirms the historical analogue approach. The second prong states the effect of the FRCP on remedies at law. Equity acts only when post-merger legal remedies are inadequate. The third prong represents a functional approach to the Seventh Amendment. It appears to raise to constitutional status the decision-making capability of the jury. The Court in *Ross* did not rely on the third prong nor did it indicate its weight in relation to the other prongs.

With rapid technological development, business expansion, and increased government regulation, commercial litigation has steadily become more numerous and more complex. Ironically, the foregoing Supreme Court cases, which offered an expansive view of the Seventh Amendment, came at a time when backlog, delay, and congestion in the civil courts were mushrooming. In the latter half of the 1970s and the early 1980s, faced with a growing number of mammoth suits, some federal district courts seized upon the functional analysis in the *Ross* footnote to sanction a complexity exception in actions which otherwise warranted jury trial. In a securities fraud suit, a court said that the third prong "must be seen as a limitation to or interpretation of the Seventh Amendment," even though a jury trial was supported by the first two prongs (*In re Boise Cascade Securities Litigation*, 1976, p. 105). Other district courts and some commentators have not read the footnote to mean that jury competence is the constitutional weathervane for the right to jury trial (*ILC Peripherals Leasing Corp. (Memorex)* v. *International Business Machines Corp.*, 1978; Sperlich 1982, pp. 407–10). Appellate court rulings are also in conflict and the Supreme Court has not yet addressed the issue.

The unresolved disputes over the history of chancery practices and the interpretation of footnote 10 have prompted some courts to consider a Fifth Amendment-based exception to the Seventh Amendment right. The case reproduced in the next section presents a balancing analysis based upon due process.

Fifth Amendment Due Process Approach

IN RE JAPANESE ELECTRONIC PRODUCTS ANTITRUST LITIGATION

631 F.2d 1069 (3d Cir. 1980)

SEITZ, Chief Judge.

. . . In an action for treble damages under the antitrust and antidumping laws, do the parties have a right to trial by jury without regard to the practical ability of a jury to decide the case properly?

[Two major domestic manufacturers of televisions sued seven of its Japanese competitors and nine of their subsidiaries, alleging that the defendants sought to drive American manufacturers out of the American market by selling televisions at artificially depressed prices. Plaintiffs further claimed that these dumping practices were part of a massive conspiracy in which defendants agreed amongst themselves and in concert with over ninety coconspirators around the world to maintain artificially low prices for Japanese televisions sold in the United States. Plaintiffs sought treble damages for the injuries sustained and also asked for injunctive relief. Several of the Japanese defendants, in turn, filed antitrust counterclaims.

Plaintiffs demanded trial by jury but fourteen of the defendants opposed it, arguing that the case was "too large and complex for a jury." Nine years of pretrial discovery had produced "millions of documents," and the district court predicted that the trial would last a full year. The sources of complexity included an enormous mass of financial and business documentation (involving, for example, matters of accounting, marketing practices in Japan and the United States, and pricing policies adjusted for currency fluctuation), highly technical data on "thousands of different [television] models," and "conceptually difficult legal and factual issues" on market shares and relevant product markets. The district court granted trial by jury and defendants brought this interlocutory appeal. Ed.'s note.]

IV.

. . .

[A]ppellants concede that a right to jury trial normally exists in suits for treble damages under the antitrust and antidumping laws. They argue that the seventh amendment does not guarantee a right to jury trial when any particular lawsuit, because of its extraordinary complexity, is beyond the ability of a jury to decide.

For the sake of clarity, we should state our understanding of complexity in this context. A suit is too complex for a jury when circumstances render the jury unable to decide in a proper manner. The law presumes that a jury will find facts and reach a verdict by rational means. It does not contemplate scientific precision but does contemplate a resolution of each issue on the basis of a fair and reasonable assessment of the evidence and a fair and reasonable application of the relevant legal rules. A suit might be excessively complex as a result of any set of circumstances which singly or in combination render a jury unable to decide in the foregoing rational manner. Examples of such circumstances are an exceptionally long trial period and conceptually difficult factual issues. . . .

The Supreme Court has supplied direct support for appellants' position only in a footnote to its opinion in *Ross v. Bernhard*. . . . The third prong of the test plainly recognizes the significance, for purposes of the seventh amendment, of the possibility that a suit may be too complex for a jury. Its inclusion in the three prong test strongly suggests that jury trial might not be guaranteed in extraordinarily complex cases, even though . . . Supreme Court cases, reflected in the first two prongs, would read the seventh amendment as applying to the suit. . . .

VI.

Both appellants . . . contend that the due process clause of the fifth amendment prohibits trial by jury of a suit that is too complex for a jury. They further contend that this due process limitation prevails over the seventh amendment's preservation of the right to jury trial. . . .

The primary value promoted by due process in factfinding procedures is "to minimize the risk of erroneous decisions." A jury that cannot understand the evidence and the legal rules to be applied provides no reliable safeguard against erroneous decisions. . . . [D]ue process precludes trial by jury when a jury is unable to perform [its] task with a reasonable understanding of the evidence and the legal rules. . . .

In the context of a lawsuit of the complexity that we have posited, . . . [the social functions of a jury] do not produce real benefits of substantial value. The function of "jury equity" may be legitimate when the jury actually modifies the law to conform to community values. However, when the jury is unable to determine the normal application of the law to the facts of a case and reaches a verdict on the basis of nothing more than its own determination of community wisdom and values, its operation is indistinguishable from arbitrary and unprincipled decisionmaking. . . .

The district court also noted that preservation of the right to jury trial is important because the jury "provides a needed check on judicial power." A jury unable to understand the evidence and legal rules is hardly a reliable and effective check on judicial power. . . .

Therefore, we find the most reasonable accommodation between the requirements of the fifth and seventh amendments to be a denial of jury trial when a jury will not be able to perform its task of rational decisionmaking with a reasonable understanding of the evidence and the relevant legal standards. . . .

VII.

The district court devoted most of its discussions . . . to a number of practical objections to the argument. We shall consider those objections in this section.

First, the district court challenged

the premise that a case could exceed a jury's ability to decide rationally and asserted that a jury was at least as able as a judge, the only alternative factfinder, to decide complex cases. The court noted that a jury possesses the wisdom, experience, and common sense of twelve persons. It has a greater effect than a judge in disciplining attorneys to present their cases clearly and concisely. . . .

Any assessment of a jury's ability to decide complex cases should include consideration not only of a jury's particular strengths and the possible enhancement of its capabilities but also of the particular constraints that operate on a jury in complex cases. The long time periods required for most complex cases are especially disabling for a jury. A long trial can interrupt the career and personal life of a jury member and thereby strain his commitment to the jury's task. The prospect of a long trial can also weed out many veniremen whose professional backgrounds qualify them for deciding a complex case but also prohibits them from lengthy jury service. Furthermore, a jury is likely to be unfamiliar with both the technical subject matter of a complex case and the process of civil litigation. The probability is not remote that a jury will become overwhelmed and confused by a mass of evidence and issues and will reach erroneous decisions. . . .

Given that a jury has both particular strengths and weaknesses in deciding complex cases, we cannot conclude *a priori* that a jury is capable of deciding a suit of any degree of complexity. . . .

A general presumption that a judge is capable of deciding an extraordinarily complex case, by contrast, is reasonable. A long trial would not greatly disrupt the professional and personal life of a judge and should not be significantly disabling. . . . [A judge's] experience can enable him to digest a large amount of evidence and legal argument, segregate distinct issues and the portions of evidence relevant to each issue, assess the opinions of expert witnesses, and apply highly complex legal standards to the facts of the case. . . .

The district court's second objection to appellants' due process argument was that the court can prevent an "irrational" verdict with its power to direct a verdict or to grant judgment n.o.v. [At the conclusion of the presentation of the evidence but before jury deliberation, the court can order (direct) the jury to return a verdict for one of the parties. Or, after the verdict, the court upon motion can set it aside as unreasonable and enter judgment *non obstante veredicto* (notwithstanding the verdict). Ed.'s note.] These devices enable the court to enter judgment against any party that has not submitted at least the minimal quantity of evidence necessary for a jury to decide reasonably in its favor. . . .

Denial of a jury trial may be necessary to minimize the risk of erroneous decisions. The district court's review of evidence on motions for directed verdict and judgment n.o.v. will not serve this purpose adequately. The court may not grant one of these motions if the evidence might reasonably support a verdict for either side. Thus, the court can only ensure that the jury will return one of a range of possible verdicts that the court finds reasonably but minimally supported by the evidence. Given that substantial property rights often are at stake in actions at law, we believe that due process requires a greater measure of reliability in the decisionmaking process. . . .

Finally, the district court feared that the authority to strike jury trial demands on case-by-case determinations of complexity would lead to the long-run dilution of the right to jury trial. . . .

We do not believe that a due process limitation allows the district courts a substantial amount of discretion to deny jury trials. . . . The complexity of a suit must be so great that it renders the suit beyond the ability of a jury to decide by rational means with a reasonable understanding of the evidence and applicable legal rules. Moreover, the district court should not deny a jury trial if by severance of multiple claims . . . or other methods the court can enhance a jury's capabilities or can reduce the complexity of a suit sufficiently to bring it within the ability of a jury to decide. Due process should allow denials of jury trials only in exceptional cases. . . .

IX.

. . . [Defendants] also argue that a propensity of two of [plaintiffs'] attorneys to make remarks prejudicial to Japanese makes a jury trial unsuitable for all of the Japanese defendants. . . . Should this case be tried to a jury, we are confident that the able district judge will ensure that appeals to racial bias and wartime prejudices do not influence the jury. . . .

[Reversed.]

NOTES AND QUESTIONS

1. The Third Circuit's decision clashed squarely with the earlier holding of the Ninth Circuit (*In re U.S. Financial Securities Litigation*, 1979, the facts of which were described above) that there is no complexity exception to the Seventh Amendment. The Ninth Circuit observed that the historical approach had been used for almost two hundred years and therefore refused to read the *Ross* footnote as establishing a functional approach. In any event, the court said, "there has been little substantive research" on "the practical abilities of jurors." To assume, without more, that jurors are incapable in complex cases "unnecessarily and improperly demeans the intelligence of the citizens of this Nation" (p. 430). Moreover, "no one has yet demonstrated how [a] judge can be a superior fact-finder" since he "generally does not have any more training or understanding of computer technology or economics than the average juror" (p. 431).

In light of the values served by the jury institution, do you agree with the Ninth Circuit's view that considerations of history (the first prong of footnote 10) should outweigh considerations of jury competence (the third prong) in determining the application of the Seventh Amendment to complex cases? This view, of course, renders nondispositive if not irrelevant any empirical jury research. In *Williams* v. *Florida* (1970), the Supreme Court brushed aside several centuries of experience with the twelve-member jury as a mere "historical accident" and adopted instead a functional analysis of the issue of jury size. Should the approach to the Seventh Amendment jury parallel that to the Sixth Amendment jury?

2. Underlying the arguments cloaked in constitutional and historical language are two basic empirical questions: Is the jury as competent as the judge? Does the choice make a difference on the trial outcome?

On the first question, as the Ninth Circuit noted, there has been little empirical research. In the absence of systematic information, Judge Seitz was careful in his choice of words: "The probability is not remote" that the jury is incompetent whereas "a general presumption" that the judge is competent is "reasonable." In their study of the criminal jury, Kalven and Zeisel also treated bench decisions as the "correct" result against which jury decisions are evaluated. The inquiry always focuses on the capability of the jury, not of the judge. Can the competence of either fact-finder be assessed independently of each other? Surely one could imagine a lawsuit that exceeds the ability of a judge to decide rationally. If both professional and lay fact-finders are equally befuddled by complexity, is there a right to a confused judge rather than a confused jury, or vice versa? Would any court trial at all under these circumstances be permitted by the Fifth Amendment?

The problem of complexity forces us to change our institutions of justice or accept their limits. Should adjudicatory responsibility for such disputes rest with other branches of government? See *Atlas Roofing Co.* v. *Occupational Safety and Health Review Commission* (1977).

3.   Litigants seek or oppose trial by jury because they believe that the outcome may turn on who is the fact-finder. The reasons that some defendants—such as Japanese manufacturers accused of predatory practices in the American market or big financial firms accused of defrauding investors—would not welcome trial by jury are obvious. Although the cases involve sophisticated issues, they are also like those criminal prosecutions with political overtones (for example, Joan Little's trial) in that they have ideological features which arouse the community's sense of justice. It is not surprising that "scientific" jury selection, which is predicated on the assumption that knowing the values of jurors can help predict the verdict, has been used mainly in criminal conspiracy and large scale antitrust litigation (Chapter 7, section 7.5). Kalven and Zeisel discovered that popular values intruded in jury decision-making only in close cases. Extralegal influences colored jurors' evaluation of facts and law when the evidence was not clearly tilted in one direction or another. A tide of complex information that overwhelms the comprehension capabilities of jurors could have the same effect as evenly matched evidence—it invites jury sovereignty to come into play. Is the possibility of nullification in these types of suits an argument for or against jury trial?

4.   Lempert (1981) suggests another reason why litigants favor or oppose jury trial: "[S]ince the parties will know which judge has been assigned the case before they must make a demand for jury trial or a motion to strike that demand, arguments over jury trial may be motivated more by the perceived sympathies of a known judge than by the predicted biases and competence of a still to be selected jury" (p. 85). As a practical matter, the choice of jury trial or bench trial may rest on tactical rather than constitutional considerations. What systematic differences, if any, would you expect between judicial and lay bias, and how might they affect the outcome of complex civil litigation?

5.   What are the benefits and drawbacks of each of the following research methods when applied to the study of jury competence in complex cases: courtroom observation; interviews with judges, jurors, and attorneys; laboratory simulation; documentary research (reading trial transcripts, and so forth); analysis of completed cases and comparison of judge-jury agreements in the mode of Kalven and Zeisel; and real world simulation with shadow juries in court (Zeisel and Diamond 1978)? These methodological issues are canvassed by Lempert (1981).

The relatively small number of complex cases tried to date precludes statistical analysis. Lempert (1981) proposes comparing cases of increasing degrees of complexity. If complexity impairs jury functioning, jury disagreement with judges should increase as complexity increases (p. 102). What are other research designs for handling the problem of small sample size?

6.   The Fifth Amendment overrides the Seventh Amendment when it is assumed that the jury cannot reach a rational verdict. This conflict between the two guarantees is not necessarily inevitable. Judge Seitz sought to harmonize them when he disallowed denial of jury trial if there were "other methods [whereby] the court can enhance a jury's capabilities or can reduce the complexity of a suit. . . ." Thus, he appears to redefine the focus of inquiry in two significant ways.

First, he calls for the development of ways to better jury functioning. Much of the simulation research conducted to date, as discussed in the preceding section of this chapter, highlights the susceptibility of jurors to extraneous influences. Studies are designed to show juror bias rather than to discover the conditions that promote juror rationality. Since there is a long-standing and undisputed judicial policy of preserving jury trials (within the limits of due process), "the most important question in jury research today is not, 'Do juries perform well or poorly?' It is, 'How may the jury system be improved?' " (Lempert 1981, p. 132).

Second, Judge Seitz suggests that the solutions to the problems posed by complex litigation might be found in reducing the complexity itself rather than in worrying about the competence of the jury. Traditionally, since the days of equitable accounting actions, courts have focused on the abilities of the decision-maker. Given the preservative mandate of the Seventh Amendment, courts also need to focus on the nature of the decisional task. There may be little one can do about the human limits of jurors or judges, but changes in trial procedures could simplify a lawsuit sufficiently to bring it within their decisional capabilities.

The problem of the impact of complexity on jury functioning is perhaps too broadly framed to be readily amenable to empirical research. Judge Seitz's proposals help to break it down into more manageable parts. By evaluating specific procedural renovations designed to reduce complexity and promote informed jury judgments, social scientists can contribute to small solutions for each small bite of the big problem.

7.   In modern times, efficient case management procedures have been introduced in the pretrial process to improve expedition and economy. However, after the jury is impaneled, the trial itself proceeds essentially as it would have a century or more ago. Gradually, some trial courts are instituting changes in the trial in an effort to render complex litigation more accessible to jurors (Strawn and Munsterman 1982). These reforms include:

- allowing the jury to retire with exhibits and transcripts, and to play back videotaped testimony in the jury room
- redrafting jury instructions so as to make them more comprehensible
- delivering instructions on law at the start of the trial or throughout the trial, rather than at the conclusion of the presentation of the evidence
- teaching jurors the relevant law via a series of judicial lectures before the trial begins
- permitting jurors to take notes during the trial
- incorporating the inquisitorial practice of allowing jurors to submit written questions to witnesses and to counsel during the trial

The effectiveness of some of these changes, in the absence of controlled studies, remains "uncertain" (Note, *Harvard Law Review*, 1979, p. 915).

8.   Jury functioning is intertwined with and partly dependent upon jury selection and composition. One court noted the difficulty of impaneling a representative jury in protracted suits. Because of the large number of exemptions and excuses that would have to be granted, the litigants may be left with housewives whose children had grown, retired persons, the unemployed, and those not needing gainful employment (*Bernstein* v. *Universal Pictures, Inc.*, 1978, p. 70). What changes might make feasible the representation of employed persons in numbers that more closely approximate their population proportion?

Early English law recognized "common" juries and "special" juries. The former included persons— as one court official in the 1850s tactfully put it—" 'unaccustomed to severe intellectual exercise or to protracted thought' " (in Devlin 1956, p. 4). The latter were composed of "persons of a somewhat higher station in society" who were specially qualified to evaluate the evidence (*R.* v. *Edmonds*, 1821, p. 1015). Today, qualifications for federal jury service require only a very basic level of literacy (28 U.S.C. §1861, 1976). A special or "blue ribbon" jury, which requires certain educational or experiential qualifications for service, could be an alternative to the traditional jury (Nordenberg and Luneborg 1982). Can the exclusion of less-educated persons from such petit juries in complex litigation be reconciled with the ideals of a democratic society and representative government?

Jury size and verdict rules influence decision-making. Do arguments for twelve-member juries and unanimous verdicts carry more force in complex cases?

9.   The Federal Rules of Civil Procedure (FRCP) make available a number of devices intended to streamline trial adjudication. Controlled studies could determine if these procedures are effective in reducing complexity and improving fact-finding.

Usually, a jury delivers a "general verdict" of liable or not liable and the damages, if any. Under FRCP 49, the court may require a jury to return a "special verdict" consisting of written findings on each factual issue. In that event, the court may submit to the jury written questions to be answered. Alternately, the court may require a general verdict accompanied by written interrogatories on factual issues. These alternatives to the general verdict do not simplify the trial but do allow a judge to channel jury deliberation and, thereby, perhaps render fact-finding more rational.

A trial need not take place all at once. Under FRCP 42, the court can sever the issues in a suit and order a separate trial of each issue. The result could be shorter and more clearly defined trials. Whether the outcomes under consolidated and separate trials are the same remains to be investigated. In a related vein, some courts have permitted seriatim litigation of issues. A jury renders a series of separate judgments on an issue-by-issue basis as the trial unfolds (Strawn and Munsterman 1982, p. 445).

FRCP 53b permits the court to appoint a "master" or expert to assist the jury with complicated

FIGURE 8.1

Stages of the Jury Process and Corresponding Research Issues

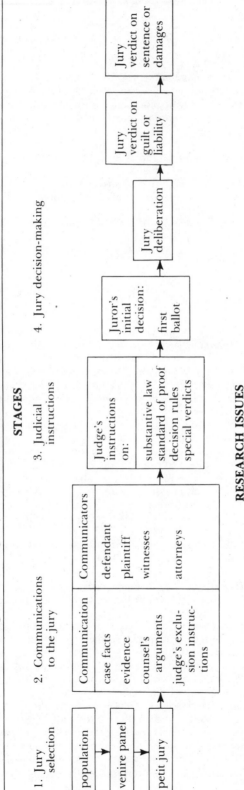

STAGES

1. Jury selection

2. Communications to the jury

3. Judicial instructions

4. Jury decision-making

RESEARCH ISSUES

1. Community bias
2. Representativeness of venire
3. "Scientific" jury selection
4. Peremptory challenges

1. Demographic, personality, and attitudinal characteristics of communicators and audience (jurors)
2. Content of communication
3. Order of communication
4. Complexity of communication

1. Mode of communicating instructions
2. Effect of judicial instructions
3. Quantification of standards of proof

1. Group dynamics of deliberation process
2. Fact-finding competence and equity of jury verdicts
3. Comparison of judge/jury verdicts
4. Effects of size and decision rules on deliberations and verdicts

issues. The master ostensibly does not supersede the jury because the jury is free to accept, reject, or give whatever weight it wishes to the expert's findings. However, "neutral" experts (especially from certain "schools" of economics and the social sciences) do not or may not be able to shed their theoretical and professional biases merely because their fees are paid by the court rather than by the litigants. (Chapter 13, section 3.2, examines this issue.) Whether juries defer unduly to the master's report and whether this added information simplifies or complicates the jury's task are empirical questions.

Other proposals abound for restructuring case complexity. Judge Higginbotham (1977) believes that effective presentation of the evidence is the key to jury competence. The issue is primarily one of counsel's ability to communicate rather than the jury's ability to comprehend (pp. 54–55). One means of disciplining attorneys so that they organize a complex mass of information into a form understandable to laypersons is by excluding cumulative or confusing evidence (under Federal Rules of Evidence 403). Another is by limiting in advance the number of hours or days allocated to counsel for the presentation of his case (*SCM Corp.* v. *Xerox Corp.*, 1978). For further discussions of strategies for coping with litigation complexity and their research implications, see Strawn and Munsterman (1982) and Lempert (1981).

Schematic Overview of the Jury Process and Jury Research

In the preceding chapter and in the present one, we focused on jury selection and jury functioning, respectively. There are, of course, other issues related to the jury which we have not covered. Figure 8.1 presents a schematic overview of the research literature, and it may help the student to locate the material of these chapters in the larger scheme of things. We organized the literature in terms of sequential stages in the jury process: (1) selection of the jury; (2) communications to the jury, that is, presentations of evidence by attorneys, witnesses, and litigants themselves; (3) judicial instructions to the jury; and (4) deliberation and decision-making by the jury. Corresponding to each of these stages, we have listed some of the areas for empirical research. In Chapter 9, we shall consider some of the legal and empirical issues that arise in the second and third stages.

REFERENCES

Allen v. United States, 164 U.S. 492 (1896).

Apodaca v. Oregon, 406 U.S. 404 (1972).

Arnold, M. S. "A Historical Inquiry into the Right to Trial by Jury in Complex Civil Litigation." *University of Pennsylvania Law Review* 128 (1980): 829–48.

Atlas Roofing Co. v. Occupational Safety and Health Review Commission, 430 U.S. 442 (1977).

Ballew v. Georgia, 435 U.S. 223 (1978).

Bartol, C. R. *Psychology and American Law*. Belmont, Ca.: Wadsworth, 1983.

Beacon Theatres, Inc. v. Westover, 359 U.S. 500 (1959).

Bermant, G.; McGuire, M.; McKinley, W.; and Salo, C. "The Logic of Simulation in Jury Research." *Criminal Justice and Behavior* 1 (1974): 224–33.

Bernstein v. Universal Pictures, Inc., 79 F.R.D. 59 (S.D. N.Y. 1978).

Bray, R. M., and Kerr, N. L. "Methodological Considerations in the Study of the Psychology of the Courtroom." In *The Psychology of the Courtroom*, edited by N. L. Kerr and R. M. Bray. New York: Academic Press, 1982.

Broeder, D. W. "The University of Chicago Jury Project." *Nebraska Law Review* 38 (1958): 744–61.

Burch v. Louisiana, 441 U.S. 130 (1979).

Bushell's Case, 124 Eng. Rep. 1006 (1670).

Cahn, E. "Jurisprudence." *New York University Law Review* 30 (1955): 150–69.

Calabresi, G., and Bobbitt, P. *Tragic Choices*. New York: W. W. Norton, 1978.

Colgrove v. Battin, 413 U.S. 149 (1973).

Dairy Queen, Inc. v. Wood, 369 U.S. 469 (1962).

Dane, F. C., and Wrightsman, L. S. "Effects of Defendants' and Victims' Characteristics on Jurors' Verdicts." In *The Psychology of the Courtroom,* edited by N. L. Kerr and R. M. Bray. New York: Academic Press, 1982.

Davis, J.; Bray, R.; and Holt, R. "The Empirical Study of Decision Processes in Juries: A Critical Review." In *Law, Justice, and the Individual in Society,* edited by J. Tapp and F. Levine. New York: Holt, Rinehart & Winston, 1977.

Devlin, P. A. *Trial by Jury.* London: Stevens, 1956.

———. "Jury Trial of Complex Cases: English Practice at the Time of the Seventh Amendment." *Columbia Law Review* 80 (1980): 43–107.

Dillehay, R. D., and Nietzel, M. T. "Conceptualizing Mock Jury-Juror Research: Critique and Illustrations." In *Review of Personality and Social Psychology,* edited by L. Wheeler. Beverly Hills, Ca.: Sage, 1980.

Duncan v. Louisiana, 391 U.S. 145 (1968).

Ebbesen, E. B., and Konečni, V. J. "Social Psychology and the Law: The Choice of Research Problems, Settings, and Methodology." In *The Criminal Justice System: A Social-Psychological Analysis,* edited by V. J. Konečni and E. B. Ebbesen. San Francisco: W. H. Freeman, 1982.

Elwork, A.; Sales, B. D.; and Suggs, D. "The Trial: A Research Review." In *The Trial Process,* edited by B. D. Sales. New York: Plenum Press, 1981.

Erlanger, H. A. "Jury Research in America: Its Past and Future." *Law and Society Review* 4 (1970): 345–70.

Flynn, L. J. "Does Justice Fail When the Jury is Deadlocked?" *Judicature* 61 (1977): 129–34

Frank, J. *Law and the Modern Mind.* New York: Tudor, 1930.

Gerbasi, K. C.; Zuckerman, M.; and Reis, H. T. "Justice Needs a New Blindfold: A Review of Mock Jury Research." *Psychological Bulletin* 84 (1977): 323–45.

Hamilton v. State, 12 Md. App. 91 (1971).

Hawkins, C. H. "Interaction Rates of Jurors Aligned in Factions." *American Sociological Review* 27 (1962): 689–91.

Higginbotham, P. E. "Continuing the Dialogue: Civil Juries and the Allocation of Judicial Power." *Texas Law Review* 56 (1977): 47–60.

Horning v. District of Columbia, 254 U.S. 135 (1920).

Horowitz, I. A., and Willgang, T. E. *The Psychology of Law: Integrations and Applications.* Boston: Little, Brown, 1984.

ILC Peripherals Leasing Corp. (Memorex) v. International Business Machines Corp., 458 F. Supp. 423 (N.D. Cal. 1978).

In re Boise Cascade Securities Litigation, 420 F. Supp. 99 (W.D. Wash. 1976).

In re Japanese Electronic Products Antitrust Litigation, 631 F.2d 1069 (3d Cir. 1980).

In re U.S. Financial Securities Litigation, 75 F.R.D. 702 (S.D. Cal. 1979).

Johnson v. Louisiana, 406 U.S. 356 (1972).

Kalven, H., and Zeisel, H. *The American Jury.* Boston: Little, Brown, 1966.

Kaplan, M. F. "Cognitive Processes in the Individual Juror." In *The Psychology of the Courtroom,* edited by N. L. Kerr and R. M. Bray. New York: Academic Press, 1982.

Kaye, D. "And Then There Were Twelve: Statistical Reasoning, the Supreme Court, and the Size of the Jury." *California Law Review* 68 (1980): 1004–43.

Kelly, A. H. "Clio and the Court: An Illicit Love Affair." *Supreme Court Review* 1965 (1965): 119–45.

Konečni, V. J., and Ebbesen, E. B. "Social Psychology and the Law: The Choice of Research Problems, Settings, and Methodology." In *The Criminal Justice System: A Social Psychological Analysis,* edited by V. J. Konečni and E. B. Ebbesen. San Francisco: W. H. Freeman, 1982a.

———. "An Analysis of the Sentencing System." In *The Criminal Justice System: A Social Psychological Analysis,* edited by V. J. Konečni and E. B. Ebbesen. San Francisco: W. H. Freeman, 1982b.

———; Mulcahy, E. M.; and Ebbesen, E. B. "Prison or Mental Hospital: Factors Affecting the Processing of Persons Suspected of Being 'Mentally Disordered Sex Offenders.' " In *New Directions in Psycholegal Research,* edited by P. D. Lipsitt and B. D. Sales. New York: Van Nostrand Reinhold, 1980.

Lempert, R. "Uncovering 'Nondiscernible' Differences: Empirical Research and the Jury Size Cases." *Michigan Law Review* 73 (1975): 644–708.

———. "Civil Juries and Complex Cases: Let's Not Rush to Judgment." *Michigan Law Review* 80 (1981): 68–132.

Miranda v. Arizona, 384 U.S. 486 (1966).

Myers D. G., and Lamm, H. "The Group Polarization Phenomenon." *Psychological Bulletin* 83 (1976): 602–27.

Nordenberg, M. A., and Luneborg, W. V. "Decisionmaking in Complex Federal Civil Cases: Two Alternatives to the Traditional Jury." *Judicature* 65 (1982): 420–31.

Note. "The Right to a Jury Trial in Complex Civil Litigation." *Harvard Law Review* 92 (1979): 898–918.

Parsons v. Bedford, 28 U.S. (3 Pet.) 433 (1830).

Patton v. United States, 281 U.S. 276 (1930).

Pearce v. Commissioner, 315 U.S. 543 (1942).

Pennington, N., and Hastie, R. "Juror Decisionmaking Models: The Generalization Gap." *Psychological Bulletin* 89 (1981): 246–87.

Penrod, S. "A Study of Attorney and 'Scientific' Jury Selection Models." Unpublished doctoral dissertation, Harvard University, 1979.

———, and Hastie, R. "Models of Jury Decision-making: A Critical Review." *Psychological Bulletin* 86 (1979): 462–92.

Powell v. Alabama, 287 U.S. 45 (1932).

R. v. Edmonds, 106 Eng. Rep. 1009 (K. B. 1821).

Roper, R. "Jury Size and Verdict Consistency: 'A Line Has to Be Drawn Somewhere'?" *Law and Society Review* 14 (1980): 977–95.

Rosenblatt, A. M., and Rosenblatt, J. C. "Six-Member Juries in Criminal Cases: Legal and Psychological Considerations." *St. John's Law Review* 47 (1973): 615–33.

Ross v. Bernhard, 396 U.S. 531 (1970).

Saks, M., and Hastie, R. *Social Psychology in Court.* New York: Van Nostrand Reinhold, 1978.

Scheflin, A., and Van Dyke, J. "Jury Nullification: The Contours of a Controversy." *Law and Contemporary Problems* 43 (1980): 51–115.

SCM Corp. v. Xerox Corp., 463 F. Supp. 943 (D. Conn. 1978).

Sebille, C. "Trial by Jury: An Ineffective Survival." *American Bar Association Journal* 10 (1924): 53–55.

Simson, G. "Jury Nullification in the American System: A Skeptical View." *Texas Law Review* 54 (1976): 488–506.

Skidmore v. Baltimore and Ohio R.R., 167 F.2d 54 (2d Cir. 1948).

Sperlich, P. W. "Trial by Jury: It May Have a Future." *Supreme Court Review* 1978 (1978): 191–224.

———. "The Case for Preserving Trial by Jury in Complex Civil Litigation." *Judicature* 65 (1982): 394–415.

Stasser, G., and Davis, J. H. "Group Decision Making and Social Influence: A Social Interaction Model." *Psychological Review* 88 (1981): 523–51.

———; Kerr, N. L.; Bray, R. M. "The Social Psychology of Jury Deliberations: Structure, Process, and Product." In *The Psychology of the Courtroom*, edited by N. L. Kerr and R. M. Bray. New York: Academic Press, 1982.

Strawn, D. U., and Munsterman, G. T. "Helping Juries Handle Complex Cases." *Judicature* 65 (1982): 444–47.

Strodtbeck, F. L., and Hook, L. H. "The Social Dimensions of a Twelve-Man Jury Table." *Sociometry* 24 (1961): 397–415.

———; James, R. M.; and Hawkins, C. "Social Status in Jury Deliberations." *American Sociological Review* 22 (1957): 713–19.

Tanke, E. D., and Tanke, T. J. "Getting Off a Slippery Slope: Social Science in the Judicial Process." *American Psychologist* 34 (1979): 1130–38.

Thomas, E. J., and Fink, C. J. "Effects of Group Size." *Psychological Bulletin* 60 (1963): 371–84.

United States ex rel. McCann v. Adams, 126 F.2d 974 (2d Cir. 1942).

United States v. Dougherty, 473 F.2d 1113 (D.C. Cir. 1972).

United States v. Wade, 338 U.S. 218 (1967).

Vidmar, N. "The Other Issues in Jury Simulation Research: A Commentary with Particular Reference to Defendant Character Studies." *Law and Human Behavior* 3 (1979): 95–106.

Weiten, W., and Diamond, S. S. "A Critical Review of the Jury Simulation Paradigm: The Case of Defendant Characteristics." *Law and Human Behavior* 3 (1979): 71–94.

Williams v. Florida, 399 U.S. 78 (1970).

Wolfram, C. W. "The Constitutional History of the Seventh Amendment." *Minnesota Law Review* 57 (1973): 639–747.

Wylie v. Warden, 372 F.2d 742 (4th Cir. 1967).

Zeisel, H. ". . . And Then There Were None: The Diminution of the Federal Jury." *University of Chicago Law Review* 38 (1971): 710–24.

———, and Diamond, S. S. " 'Convincing Empirical Evidence' on the Six-Member Jury." *University of Chicago Law Review* 41 (1974): 281–95.

———. "The Effect of Peremptory Challenges on Jury and Verdict: An Experiment in a Federal District Court." *Stanford Law Review* 30 (1978): 491–530.

CHAPTER 9

Presentations to the Jury:
Case Study of Evidence Rules

9.1. INTRODUCTION

"[T]hat which you hear me tell," said the "Third Gentleman" in Shakespeare's *The Winter's Tale,* "you'll swear you see, there is such unity in the proofs" (act 5, scene 2). The gentleman then described "many evidences" from which he inferred the proposition desired to be proved, namely, that the lost child was the King's daughter. In all of the Bard's plays, the words "proof" or "prove" recur some 350 times. Proof—the ratiocinative process of arriving at conclusions from available evidence—is a common aspect of human experience. People usually decide or act based upon inferences they draw from the information before them. Proof in a court of law is simply a more formalized application of a universal mode of thinking. "Legal proof," according to Wigmore (1937), is a "process of contentious persuasion" (p. 3). It seeks to move the mind of the trier to accept the conclusion derived from the facts offered to prove it. The procedural rules which govern proof at trial constitute the law of evidence, the subject of this chapter.

The Structure of Evidence Law

The rules of evidence "represent the most careful attempt to control the processes of communication to be found outside a laboratory" (Cleary 1952, p. 282). Thus, the presentation of evidence in court for the purpose of legal proof can be examined in terms of a persuasive communications paradigm: *Who* says *what, how,* and with what *effect.* The plethora of rules prescribed, in essence, who can present the evidence, what evidence can be admitted, and how the evidence should be introduced. The target of the persuasion is the trier, either jury or judge. This communications analogy obviously oversimplifies the law of evidence, but it serves to highlight its basic structure.

First, there is a set of rules which pertains to communicators, that is, to witnesses. They set forth the qualifications for competency and capacity of ordinary and expert witnesses and establish the limits for their support or impeachment upon questioning by counsel. There are also rules that prescribe the circumstances under which personal attributes of witnesses (for example, community reputation, bad character, prior convictions) can be brought out at trial.

A second category of rules has to do with the nature and presentation of the communication. The introduction at trial of different types of evidence (for example, documentary information, scientific evidence) is governed by different procedures. There are rules that prescribe the form and scope of questions (for example, direct versus leading inquiries) used to elicit evidence of a testimonial kind. Other rules structure the sequence or order of presentation of evidence by each side, or dispense with the need of proof altogether via the procedural device of legal presumptions.

A third set of rules controls the admission or exclusion of evidence at trial. It constitutes the most substantial and important component of the body of evidence law. Evidence that is otherwise relevant to what is sought to be proved may nonetheless be excluded on the basis of one of four rules: the hearsay rule (secondhand evidence is excluded because it might be improperly overvalued by the jury); the relevance rule (nonrelevant evidence, in the sense that its probative value is outweighed by the risks of prejudicial impact on the jury, is inadmissible); the opinion rule (statements of opinion rather than fact from ordinary witnesses are excluded because such judgments belong to the province of the jury); and the privilege rule (evidence that is privileged—for example, communications between attorney and client, doctor and patient, clergy and penitent, husband and wife—because it protects socially valued relationships is inadmissible). Each of these general rules has been spun into a multiplicity of refined discriminations and exceptions that specify the conditions under which normally inadmissible evidence becomes admissible. The hearsay rule, for example, has some two dozen exceptions, more or less. It is these exceptions that make for the complexity of evidence law.

Finally, there are rules that guide the deliberations of the jury at the end of the trial, after all the evidence has been presented. These concern the burden of proof. The sufficiency of the evidence to prove the disputed matter is evaluated by the trier according to standards that are stated in probabilistic terms, such as "by a preponderance of the evidence" in civil cases and "beyond a reasonable doubt" in criminal prosecutions.

The importance of evidence law in the trial process is substantial. No matter how strong a litigant's case, he is unlikely to prevail unless the supporting evidence can be made available to the trier. Evidence rules play a gatekeeping role in the courtroom—they condition if not control decision-making by determining the evidence that will be admitted or excluded.

The Rationale of Evidence Law

"It is important to remember that all of the fundamental rules have some *reason* underneath," Wigmore (1935) taught. The reasons may not be sound in point of practical policy and they may be buried from sight, but they are there. "Therefore, to understand the reason of the rules is to be half way towards mastery of the rules deduced from these reasons" (p. 5). The need for any rules to regulate the flow of communication in civil and criminal trials is said to rest on three rationales: practical necessity, the promotion of certain social values, and distrust of the jury (Aronson 1978, pp. 33–36).

There have to be some practical limits to the admissibility of evidence. Anything and everything cannot be considered if trials are not to be excruciatingly long and costly. Rules regarding relevancy, for example, seek to prevent needless repetition of cumulative evidence and obfuscation of the issues.

At trial, more is at stake than the truth of the matter in contest. Minimization of fact-finding errors is not necessarily the *summum bonum* of litigation. Evidence law also serves to effectuate goals extrinsic to truth determination. Rules that exclude hearsay not only ensure that admitted evidence is reliable but also make trials appear fairer. If litigants and the public perceive the dispute resolution process as impartial, they are more likely to accept the legitimacy of the outcome. The protection of certain confidential relationships or deterrence of police misconduct are examples of other values which are promoted by the exclusion of otherwise relevant and probative evidence.

The chief influence in the shaping of evidence law was the development of jury trial. The English law of evidence, according to Sir Henry Maine, "was in its origin a pure system of exclusion . . . which prevented large classes of testimony from being submitted to the jury" (in Wigmore 1940, vol. 1, p. 30). Rules of exclusion are not an inherent feature of a rational method of proof. Under inquisitorial procedures such as prevail on the Continent, there is no separate and systematic branch of law on evidence. The reason is that the judge dominates the trial, investigating, hearing, and weighing evidence virtually uninhibited by any procedural limitations. By training and experience, the inquisitorial judge is deemed an expert arbiter of facts.

The emergence of the modern jury trial in England around the sixteenth century caused judges to fear that their untrained, lay counterparts would be misled by false testimony and succumb to improper appeals to their emotions and sympathies. In its infancy, during the twelfth and thirteenth centuries, the jury was a self-informing group. Verdicts were based on information obtained in the vicinage rather than on what transpired in court. Over the course of the next two or three centuries, the process of trial was transformed, resulting in a corresponding change in the jury's role. The sworn testimony of witnesses gradually became the principal source of information and prospective jurors with pre-existing knowledge of the dispute were excluded from passing judgment.

Initially, judges punished jurors for returning "erroneous" verdicts (especially in political cases of seditious libel). Jurors could be subject to "attaint," a review of their verdict by a second jury. If the verdict was found demonstrably false, the original jurors were imprisoned or stripped of their personal property. The threat of attaint served to control verdicts. Once it became settled doctrine that the jury is the sole judge of the facts and its verdict is final and sacrosanct (*Bushell's Case,* 1670), judges began to fashion other means to control and diminish jury discretion. Otherwise, armed with the power of the general verdict, the jury could surreptitiously decide issues of law. Judges granted new trials or set aside the verdict instead of sanctioning jurors directly. They devised procedural means of control such as the directed verdict, the special verdict, and the judgment notwithstanding the verdict. Another method was to regulate the flow of information. By crystallizing the wisdom of generations of professional decision-makers in ready-to-hand rules, untrained citizens could be sheltered from the temptation of accepting uncritically any proffered evidence. It was only after the modern trial by jury was well established that the first treatise on evidence law was published (in 1726; Wigmore 1940, vol. 1, p. 11). Such was the origin, and such the spirit, of evidence rules. "[J]udicial oversight and control of the process of introducing evidence to the jury [was what] gave our system birth; and he who would understand it must keep this fact constantly in mind" (Thayer 1898, p. 181). The law of evidence is indelibly stamped as "the child of the jury system" (p. 266). In contrast, in nonjury proceedings, judges have been and still are exempt from scrupulous subservience to jury trial evidence rules. The application of evidentiary rules of exclusion is relaxed when the capability of the trier is presumed.

A unity of theme underlies the corpus of evidence law. The rules are intended to increase the likelihood that the trial outcome comports with the procedural values of administrative efficiency, fairness, and reliable fact-finding by the jury. These values are sometimes arrayed against each other and evidence rules may represent accommodations or compromises between them. On the whole, evidence law—like other procedural law—is not merely a set of technical rules for managing the traffic of communication in court. It is more than a manual of trial etiquette. By controlling the process of proof, it provides the context for the application of the substantive law. As Llewellyn (1962) noted, substantive law cannot be read except through the "spectacles of . . . procedure" at trial (p. 18).

Overview

The common law of evidence has been subject periodically to codification (Lempert and Saltzburg 1982, pp. 1189–96). The most recent and successful effort is found in the Federal Rules of Evidence (FRE), which became effective for all of the federal courts in 1975. Since then, the FRE have been adopted with some or no modifications by many states. In this chapter, the references to evidence law will be to the FRE. We have chosen several specific issues of evidence law for discussion here. They deal with *how* the evidence is proffered (issues of order and mode of presentation), *what* the evidence is (issues of admissibility and sufficiency), and what the *effect* is of the evidence on the jury after it has been filtered through the procedural rules (issues of the effectiveness and clarity of judicial instructions).

In section 9.2, we begin at the start of the trial and examine the (gross) order in which each side presents its main case and the (internal) order in which evidence is presented by each side. *Brooks* v. *Tennessee* (1972) reviews the constitutionality of a statute that requires the defense to structure the presentation of witnesses in a certain sequence. The legal issues are discussed in light of data from laboratory experiments on the impact of such order on the jury's decision. The sequence of proof-taking is related to the method of proof itself. We turn, next, to a brief comparison of the inquisitorial and adversarial styles of fact-finding and describe empirical research that purportedly shows the superiority of the latter in neutralizing judicial bias.

The mode of presentation of evidence—live or by videotape—is the subject of section 9.3. Recent technological advances have enabled the prerecording of witness testimony by videotape for subsequent use as evidence at trial. The basic issue is whether a videotaped trial is simply a substitute form of communication or whether the use of the electronic medium influences the evidence itself and the decision-making of jurors. If, indeed, "the medium is the message," behavioral and policy issues are implicated, as well as technical aspects of videotaping.

Evidence law consists primarily of rules that govern admissibility, and a basic principle of admissibility is evidentiary relevance. Section 9.4 focuses on two rules pertaining to limited relevance. One is the "other crimes evidence" rule: Prior convictions of a defendant are admissible to impeach his credibility if he takes the stand, but not to establish his propensity to commit the crime charged. The other rule concerns the admissibility of a codefendant's out-of-court confession (hearsay) for use against a nonconfessing defendant in a joint trial (*Bruton* v. *United States,* 1968). The effectiveness of judicial instructions limiting the relevance of the evidence to a specific purpose or party is evaluated in light of empirical studies and normative considerations.

The rationale for the prescribed (gross) order of presentation of evidence is based in part on the allocation and quantum of the burden of proof. The procedural rules that regulate the beginning and concluding phases of a trial are in symmetry. In section 9.5, we turn to the standards of proof used to assess the sufficiency of the evidence at the end of the trial. Lawyers and statisticians have sought to apply classical probability theory and Bayesian statistics to the measure of persuasion (*People* v. *Collins,* 1968). These efforts cast in sharp relief the purposes of trial and some of the differences between dialectical and scientific methods of fact-finding.

The effectiveness of instructions on limited admissibility and standard of proof depends, in part, on their comprehensibility by jurors. Pattern or standard instructions typically sacrifice clarity for legal accuracy. The final section (9.6) presents research on revising pattern instructions according to psycholinguistic principles and evaluating their effect on comprehension and verdicts.

9.2. ORDER OF PRESENTATION OF EVIDENCE

Stages in the Presentation of Evidence

The principal stages in the presentation of evidence and the steps within each stage—applicable generally to a civil or criminal trial—are summarized in Figure 9.1.

The first stage is the opening statement of the case. The party that bears the burden of proof—the side that has the responsibility of persuading the jury that the evidentiary proof proffered during the trial reaches the required level of probability: the plaintiff in a civil case, the prosecution in a criminal case—has the first opportunity to outline its case to the trier of fact. (For the purposes of this description, we will assume that it is a criminal jury trial.) The prosecution begins with a general description of the facts of the case and a preview of the evidence that it will present later. The purpose is to let the jury know in advance what the prosecution is all about. There can be no argument on the merits of the case at this point. A judge will usually limit the content of the opening statement to the alleged factual circumstances. An attorney cannot attempt to persuade the jury to accept his version of the facts via the device of the opening statement.

After the prosecution completes its opening statement, the defense may make a similar statement subject to the same constraints just noted or defer it until after the prosecution has terminated the presentation of all of its evidence. In a criminal trial, the defense does not have the responsibility of proving innocence—that is presumed by law. Instead, the state has the burden of proving guilt. For this reason, the defense may opt to waive making an opening statement until after the prosecution is finished

FIGURE 9.1

Steps in the Course of a Criminal Trial

1. Opening statement	1a	prosecution's opening statement
	1b	defense's opening statement

2. Presentation of evidence	2a	prosecution's case-in-chief
		    direct examination
		    cross-examination
		    re-direct
		    re-cross
		    prosecution rests

	2b	defense's case-in-chief
		    direct examination
		    cross-examination
		    re-direct
		    re-cross
		    defense rests

	2a′	prosecution's case-in-rebuttal repeat 2a, above
	2b′	defense's case-in-rejoinder repeat 2b, above

3. Closing argument or summation	3a	prosecution opens closing argument
	3b	defense's closing argument
	3c	prosecution's closing argument

4. Judge's instructions to the jury

5. Jury's deliberation and verdict

presenting its case. Such a deferral, however, occurs only seldom in practice, because it is deemed a risky tactic. By remaining silent at the outset of the trial, the defense allows the state to monopolize the opportunity to establish an initial rapport with the jury as well as its version of the facts of the case.

The second stage is the presentation of the cases-in-chief, first by the prosecution and then by the defense. The prosecution puts its case-in-chief (also called evidence-in-chief) by calling witnesses to testify and by introducing real evidence (physical objects) and documentary evidence. (In this chapter, we will attend only to testimonial evidence.) The testimony is elicited by the prosecutor's questions on direct examination. Leading questions—that is, ones that suggest their own answer, such as "You were driving on Main Street, weren't you?"—are not permitted on direct examination of one's own witnesses. This is to prevent influencing the witness's recollection of the facts. Leading questions are allowed on direct examination of an adverse or hostile witness (for example, a friend of the defendant who is called to the stand by the prosecutor to give testimony that might be used against the defendant could be expected to be hostile to the prosecution).

Any advantage the prosecution may have by presenting its evidence first is offset at least partially by the defense's right to cross-examine immediately after the direct examination of each witness is concluded. This right is part of the right to confront one's accusers that is guaranteed by the Sixth and Fourteenth Amendments. The defense could elect not to cross-examine the state's witnesses and later call them for examination during its case-in-chief. The more common practice is for prompt cross-examination to mitigate the impact of the direct testimony.

The scope of the content of the cross-examination is governed by the local law of the jurisdiction. Most states limit the cross-examination to what was testified on direct examination; that is also the rule in the federal courts (FRE 611b). Some states allow wide-open cross-examination so long as the evidence is relevant. In either instance, prompt cross-examination enables the defense to present its version of the facts before the prosecution completes its case-in-chief. It also permits the impeachment of the witness's credibility, by exposing the lack of ability or opportunity to observe the critical event, or raising questions about the witness's character and motivation, or revealing any prior convictions. So long as the direct examination and cross-examination of each witness is alternated, "it is doubtful that either party has a substantial advantage of position" in the presentation of the cases-in-chief (Lawson 1968, p. 544).

After the defense's cross-examination of each witness, the prosecution can have another turn at bat if it wishes. It can conduct a re-direct for the purpose of bolstering or rehabilitating the witness before the jury; the defense, in turn, has the option of a re-cross. The contents of all direct examinations and cross-examinations are confined to the elicitation of factual testimony. Neither side can engage in persuasive appeals to the jury at this stage.

The prosecution rests after presenting all of its evidence. By resting, the state says, in effect, that it has proved enough so that if the jury believes the evidence, it will render a guilty verdict. Now it is the defense's turn to present its case-in-chief, also denominated as evidence-in-defense or case-in-reply. It begins with an opening statement, unless it was delivered at the first stage, and continues with direct examination on a witness-by-witness basis. These defense witnesses are then subjected to cross-examination by the prosecution and, again, there is the opportunity for re-direct and re-cross. After putting in its case, the defense rests.

Sometimes there is a second round of presentations of evidence, consisting of the prosecution's case-in-rebuttal and the defense's case-in-rejoinder. The order and the constraints governing the direct examinations and cross-examinations during the first round again apply. Both sides may recall witnesses who appeared during the case-in-chief or call new witnesses. Finally, both parties announce they have closed, indicating that the hearing on the facts has come to an end. The trial proceeds to the stage of argument of counsel.

The third stage consists of the closing argument or summation. Up to this stage, the communications to the jury have been mainly via witness testimony regarding evidence about the facts. Now, for the first time, the attorneys can address the jury directly for the purpose of persuasion. Commentary on the evidence rather than presentation of evidence characterizes the summation.

Each side seeks to cast its case in the most favorable light possible. The presentation of evidence during the second stage is seldom done in a neat, orderly fashion: Different witnesses testify at different times; the testimony is interrupted by objections, court rulings, recesses; the jury may forget evidence introduced at the beginning of a long trial. The summation enables the attorneys to organize and clarify the evidence for the jury and to suggest reasonable inferences that could be drawn from it. They try to influence the jury to accept their respective version of the facts. They may point out extralegal factors to win the jury's sympathy (for example, the defendant leaves behind a destitute family). Since the defense goes first, it might try to anticipate some of the prosecution's summation arguments and rebut them in advance. The defense might also seek to remind the jury of its duties and the procedures of trial (for example, that it is up to the state to prove guilt, rather than to the defendant to prove innocence). Some of the flavor of a summation is captured by the advice supposedly given by a wizened counsel to a young, new assistant: "When the law is on your side but the facts are against you, hammer away at the judge; when the facts are on your side but the law is against you, hammer away at the jury; when both the law and the facts are against you, hammer away at the counsel table" (Cohn and Udolf 1979, p. 198).

In a civil case, the defendant goes first and the plaintiff has the last word. A typical statutory procedure is the following: "In the [closing] argument, the party having the burden of proof shall have the conclusion, and the adverse party [defendant] the opening" (Kentucky Rules of Civil Procedure, 43.02(5)). The plaintiff, then, has the right to have the first and the last word at a trial, a presumed advantage which is granted in order to compensate for shouldering the burden of proof.

In a criminal case, the order of summation is prosecution-defense-prosecution. Thus, "unless both parties shall waive argument and agree that the cause be submitted to the jury without argument, the prosecuting attorney shall make the opening argument and the counsel for defendant shall follow, and the prosecuting attorney shall conclude the argument" (Missouri Rules of Criminal Procedure, 20.02(7)). In other jurisdictions, the prosecution gives only one closing argument, after the defense completes its summation: "In the [concluding] argument, the attorney for the Commonwealth shall have the conclusion and the defendant or his attorney the opening" (Kentucky Rules of Criminal Procedure, 9.42(6)).

Following the summation, the judge informs the jury as to the applicable law to the case at bar. (In some states, the court's instructions precede the attorneys' summation.) The instructions state the elements of the crime charged against the defendant, and the jury must find that the prosecution has presented evidence as to each of these elements in order to return a conviction. The instructions also include general principles of the criminal law, such as the presumption of innocence, the standard of proof of beyond a reasonable doubt, and the importance of deciding solely on the basis of the evidence presented. In addition, the attorneys may submit to the judge proposed instructions on specific matters (for example, cautionary instructions on the risks of eyewitness testimony). Finally, the jury retires to deliberate and render its verdict.

Gross Order and Internal Order of Presentation

Gross order refers to the overall order in which each side presents its respective case-in-chief. In contrast, internal order refers to the sequence in which evidence is presented by each side within its case-in-chief (Thibaut and Walker 1975, p. 54).

In a criminal trial, the prosecution traditionally proceeds first and the defense follows. The rationale for the gross order is possibly related to the burden and its allocation. The responsibilities of pleading, producing, and persuading are usually allocated to the same party. A plaintiff has to plead, produce evidence, and persuade the jury that more likely than not the defendant was negligent. If after examining the evidence the jury is in equipoise with respect to the ultimate issue of negligence (that is, it finds the evidence of each side equally persuasive), the plaintiff loses. The prosecution has to accuse, produce evidence, and persuade the jury beyond a reasonable doubt that the defendant is guilty. Again, failure to persuade at the requisite level results in loss of the prosecution. The party that shoulders the burden of proof bears the risk of nonpersuasion. This risk is always allocated to the plaintiff or the prosecution, and the jury is so informed before it retires to deliberate.

Arguably, then, a reason for the traditional gross order of presentation is the allocation of the burden of proof. (It is arguable because this oft-stated justification has not been historically proven; R. Lempert, 1982, personal communication.) Since the plaintiff or the prosecution suffers the disadvantage of the risk of a directed verdict or dismissal, respectively, by the judge, and the risk of nonpersuasion of the jury, the policy has been to compensate the party with the burden of proof by granting it the right to open and to close the trial—that is, to have the first and the last word. The disadvantages of bearing the burden are offset by the presumed advantages of the order of proof. These two procedural features of trial are interrelated, and any inquiry into the effects of order of proof needs to take into account the allocation of the burden.

With respect to the sequence in which the evidence of each side is presented, the strongest or most important information may be presented last (climactic order) or at the outset (anticlimactic order). In a criminal case, the testimony of the defendant is usually considered to be one of the most important aspects of the defense, at least from the standpoint of the jury. This is all the more so since a defendant has a constitutional right not to take the stand. The legal and empirical questions raised by the internal order of presentation are addressed in *Brooks* v. *Tennessee* (1972).

BROOKS v. TENNESSEE

406 U.S. 605 (1972)

Mr. Justice BRENNAN delivered the opinion of the Court.

Petitioner was tried and convicted in the Circuit Court of Hamilton County, Tennessee, on charges of armed robbery and unlawful possession of a pistol. During the trial, at the close of the State's case, defense counsel moved to delay petitioner's testimony until after other defense witnesses had testified. The trial court denied this motion on the basis of Tenn. Code Ann. §40-2403 (1955), which requires that a criminal defendant "desiring to testify shall do so before any other testimony for the defense is heard by the court trying the case." . . . The defense called two witnesses, but petitioner himself did not take the stand. . . .

The rule that a defendant must testify first is related to the ancient practice of sequestering prospective witnesses in order to prevent their being influenced by other testimony in the case. Because the criminal defendant is entitled to be present during trial, and thus cannot be sequestered, the requirement that he precede other defense witnesses was developed by court decision and statute as an alternative means of minimizing this influence as to him. . . .

Despite this traditional justification, the validity of the requirement has been questioned in a number of jurisdictions as a limitation upon the defendant's freedom to decide whether to take the stand. . . . [W]e are persuaded that the rule embodied in §40-2403 is an impermissible restriction on the defendant's right against self-incrimination. . . .

Although a defendant will usually have some idea of the strength of his evidence, he cannot be absolutely certain that his witnesses will testify as expected or that they will be effective on the stand. They may collapse under skillful and persistent cross-examination, and through no fault of their own they may fail to impress the jury as honest and reliable witnesses. . . .

Because of these uncertainties, a defendant may not know at the close of the State's case whether his own testimony will be necessary or even helpful to his cause. Rather than risk the dangers of taking the stand, he might prefer to remain silent at that point, putting off his testimony until its value can be realistically assessed. Yet, under the Tennessee rule, he cannot make that choice "in the unfettered exercise of his own will." Section 40-2403 exacts a price for his silence by keeping him off the stand entirely unless he chooses to testify first. This, we think, casts a heavy burden on a defendant's otherwise unconditional right not to take the stand. . . .

Although the Tennessee statute does reflect a state interest in preventing testimonial influence, we do not regard that interest as sufficient to override the defendant's right to remain silent at trial. This is not to imply that there may be no risk of a defendant's coloring his testimony to conform to what has gone before. But our adversary system reposes judgment of the credibility of all witnesses in the jury. Pressuring the defendant to take the stand, by foreclosing later testimony if he refuses, is not a constitutionally permissible means of ensuring his honesty. It fails to take into account the very real and legitimate concerns that might motivate a defendant to exercise his right of silence. And it may compel even a wholly truthful defendant, who might otherwise decline to testify for legitimate reasons, to subject himself to impeachment and cross-examination at a time when the strength of his other evidence is not yet clear. For these reasons we hold that §40-2403 violates an accused's constitutional right to remain silent insofar as it requires him to testify first for the defense or not at all. . . .

[The Court also ruled that the Tennessee statute infringed the defendant's right to counsel because it restricted the defense in deciding whether and when the accused should take the stand. This Sixth Amendment portion of *Brooks* was later repudiated in *Lakeside* v. *Oregon* (1978) and therefore is not reproduced here. Ed.'s note.]

The judgment is reversed. . . .

It is so ordered.

Mr. Justice REHNQUIST, with whom THE CHIEF JUSTICE and Mr. Justice BLACKMUN join, dissenting.

While it is possible that this statute regulating the order of proof in criminal trials might in another case raise issues bearing on the privilege against self-incrimination, its application in this case certainly has not done so. Petitioner Brooks never took the stand, and it is therefore difficult to see how his right to remain silent was in any way infringed by the State. Whatever may be the operation of the statute of other situations, petitioner cannot assert that it infringed *his* privilege against self-incrimination—a privilege which he retained inviolate throughout the trial. . . .

I could understand, though I would not agree with, a holding that under these circumstances the Fourteenth Amendment conferred a right upon the defendant . . . to decide at what point during the presentation of his case to take the stand. . . .

In view of the strong sanction in history and precedent for control of the order of proof by the trial court, I think that

Tennessee's effort here to restrict the choice of the defendant as to when he shall testify, in the interest of minimizing the temptation of perjury, does not violate the Fourteenth Amendment. I would therefore affirm the judgment below.

NOTES AND QUESTIONS

1.   The statute represents a compromise between the need to sequester prospective witnesses before they testify (so that they do not influence each other), and the right of a defendant to be present at all times at his own trial (even though he may also be a prospective witness). The compromise is to give the defendant a choice to speak first, if he opts to speak at all, or else be forbidden from speaking later at any time.

This statute has no effect on a defendant who opts not to testify. It also has no effect on a defendant who opts to testify but does not care when he does it. It has an effect only on a defendant such as Brooks who, at the beginning of the trial, is undecided whether he wishes to testify and prefers to reserve the decision until he sees how the evidence unfolds.

2.   The majority held that this statute violated the Fifth Amendment because it pressured the defendant to take the stand at the start of his case-in-chief. The pressure is created by the penalty of precluding the opportunity to testify at a later time. The dissent said that no Fifth Amendment injury was suffered by the defendant because he never took the stand. The Fifth Amendment protects an individual from being compelled to speak over his objection, but if any compulsion was exerted upon Brooks, it was for him not to speak. Pressure to remain silent is not prohibited by the Fifth Amendment. Which reasoning do you find more persuasive, and why?

3.   One of the principal values served by the Fifth Amendment is a defendant's right to silence. In early common law, a defendant was forbidden to take the stand, in order to force the state to prove its accusation. The Tennessee statute also forbids the defendant to take the stand, unless he testifies first. Can it be said that this sanction reinforces the value of silence?

4.   In a separate dissenting opinion not reproduced here, Chief Justice Burger argued that the statutory sanction of precluding the defendant from testifying later was not invalid, because it simply forced the defendant to accelerate a decision that he would have had to make anyway: "[T]he only 'burden' cast on the defendant's choice to take the stand . . . is the burden to make the choice at a given point in time. That the choice might in some cases be easier if made later is hardly a matter of constitutional dimension" (*Brooks* v. *Tennessee,* p. 615). Is the question in this case merely one of *when* to testify (timing) or of *whether* to testify at all (right to silence)?

5.   Consider the control of the timing and sequence of the internal order of the defense's case-in-chief. "[*Brooks*] is difficult to defend on any grounds other than a defendant's right to take maximum tactical advantage of his own testimony" (Dix 1977, p. 240). *Brooks* constitutionalizes defendant's right to this control—it guarantees him the freedom to organize his evidence in any order that he thinks would be most persuasive to the jury. An underlying assumption of the Court, shared by authors of trial advocacy manuals, is that a climactic sequence has greater impact on the jury (Keeton 1954, p. 24).

If the defendant's (new) right to control the internal order of proof is the underlying rationale of this decision, why did it remain unarticulated in the majority's opinion? Why did it locate the textual basis for this right in the Fifth Amendment? The dissent suggests that the Due Process Clause of the Fourteenth Amendment would have been a more understandable premise for the Court's decision— that it is fundamentally unfair to deny a defendant the opportunity to present his case in the most persuasive light possible. Was the majority justified in ignoring this ground for its decision?

6.   The Sixth Amendment guarantees that "in all criminal prosecutions, the accused shall enjoy the right . . . to be confronted with the witnesses against him." This means that a defendant can demand that the state bring to court those witnesses who are accusing him of the crime charged, in order to subject them to cross-examination. The right of confrontation is implemented by the device of cross-examination.

Gross order of presentation is sometimes thought to be an "estimator-variable" rather than a "system-variable," to use Wells's terminology (1978). That is, it is assumed that gross order cannot be controlled by the party litigants because it is fixed by tradition and policy. A researcher can only estimate the effect of that variable upon the jury. If the first presentation has a greater impact, it is known in the social psychological literature as a primacy effect. If the second presentation is more persuasive, it is termed a recency effect.

But gross order can be a system-variable in that it can be altered to some extent by other parties. When the defense cross-examines a state witness immediately after completion of the direct examination, it is manipulating the gross order of proof. The prompt exercise of the confrontation right could nullify any primacy advantage of the prosecution. On the other hand, if the defense chooses to defer cross-examination until after the prosecution rests, any primacy effect from gross order remains intact.

Thus, *Brooks* closes the circle on order of proof: "Just as the confrontation clause constitutionalizes the defendant's right to control certain aspects of the 'gross' order of proof at trial, *Brooks* constitutionalizes the defendant's right to control the 'internal' order of proof within his own case-in-chief" (Westen 1978, p. 984).

7.   The flipside of *Brooks* would be a statute that sought to restrict the defendant's control of the gross order. Suppose that a statute provided that a defendant may cross-examine only after the prosecution closes its case-in-chief. The statute does not preclude a defendant from the right of confrontation; it only attempts to structure the timing of the cross-examination. Is the statute constitutional?

8.   Granting that the state has a legitimate interest in preventing defendants from bearing false testimony by tailoring their statements to fit the prior testimony of other defense witnesses, formulate an alternative to the Tennessee statutory scheme that would enable the state to achieve its objective and also survive constitutional attack.

Social Research on Order of Communications

There is extensive research literature on the effects of order of communications on opinion change. We will provide only a thumbnail sketch as background for the study of Walker, Thibaut, and Andreoli (1972) that follows.

The first study on gross order of presentation was conducted by Lund (1925). Two written communications of equal length and persuasive quality were prepared, adopting an affirmative or negative position on each of three controversial subjects (equal political rights, protective tariffs, and monogamous marriage). Half of the subjects received the affirmative communications first and the negative communications second. The order was reversed for the other half. Opinion measures were taken before any communications were given, and again after the first and after the second communications. The opinion change created by the first communication was greater than that induced by the second communication, regardless of the stance of the message. Lund described this result as the "Law of Primacy in persuasion" (p. 189).

A subsequent study by Cromwell (1950) found antipodal results: Speeches delivered second had a greater influence on the opinions of listeners than those presented first. A possible explanation for these conflicting findings could be the different measurement procedures used. Cromwell assessed the effects of the communications after both sides had been presented. Lund measured the subjects' opinions after each side had been presented. This may have forced the subjects to review the arguments, formulate their own conclusions, and commit themselves to a position on paper after being exposed to only one side. The tendency to remain internally consistent, especially after a public commitment of one's attitude is made, is well known. Consequently, Lund's subjects may have been less willing to change their opinions when the second communication was presented. The primacy effect could have been due to the repeated measurement rather than to the order of presentation.

In the mid-1950s, social psychologists at Yale under Carl Hovland conducted a systematic program of research on communication and persuasion, giving special attention to order effects. Hovland and Mandell (1957) replicated Lund's study using topics of greater current interest. No primacy effects were found. They again repeated Lund's study but added an extra group in which the subjects' opinions were measured only after both sides had been presented. They essentially combined the research designs of Lund and Cromwell. No effects of gross order were obtained. They concluded that primacy was not a principle of general application but that it occurred only under certain conditions.

The Yale group and subsequent researchers turned their attention to ascertaining the conditions under which communications are primacy-bound. We will briefly review some of these circumstances.

PRIOR FAMILIARITY WITH THE COMMUNICATION

Hovland (1957) conjectured that "it may be when no prior knowledge of the topic is involved, a law of primacy does operate" (p. 139). Based on this factor, Lawson (1968) distinguished between "experimentally-induced primacy" and "true primacy" experiments.

The former kind typically involved topics that were controversial or otherwise well known to the subjects, such as federally sponsored medical care (Cromwell 1950) or the sale of antihistamines without prescription (Hovland and Mandell 1957). One explanation for the primacy effect is that the audience receives a first or new communication with which it is unfamiliar. If, as was likely, subjects had already been exposed to and had formed an opinion on these highly publicized issues, the communication could not have created a primacy effect. The prior familiarity would have pre-empted its impact.

True primacy experiments present to the audience new information for the first time. The classic studies on impression formation are of this kind (Luchins 1957). Subjects were presented with a series of adjectives that described fictitious persons, such as intelligent-good-hardworking-passive. The only difference between two sets of descriptions was the order in which these adjectives were listed. The results showed that impressions about the personality of fictitious persons were influenced by the order of presentation of the traits. The first impressions created a set or expectancy that shaped subsequently received information. In other words, there was a primacy effect.

In 1961, Lana conducted a true primacy study of communications. He controlled for prior familiarity by selecting an obscure subject, the vivisection of animals. An informational lecture on this topic, without any attempt at persuasion, was first given to the subjects. The two opposing communications in favor of and against vivisection were presented in counterbalanced order. Opinion measures were taken at the conclusion of both messages. A primacy effect was found. "A communication presented first, whether pro or con, is more effective the more familiar the subject is [as a result of the experimental procedure] with the topic" (p. 575).

There are parallels between Lana's study and the trial process that suggest hypotheses about the order of communications in the courtroom. Jurors are like the subjects in true primacy research in that both have no prior familiarity with the subject or are uncommitted to any given side. The voir dire process serves to weed out prospective jurors who have formed an opinion about the case and are unable to set it aside. The cases-in-chief presented by the litigants are akin to Lana's informational lecture. The testimony by witnesses is mostly factual information, and any advantage of order is offset by the other side's right to immediate cross-examination. Finally, the summations by the attorneys resemble the persuasive communications of Lana's experiment. By the time counsel's argumentation begins, the jury has acquired a substantial amount of evidentiary information.

If one accepts these parallels, two hypotheses can be derived applicable to the trial context. First, it is only at the closing argument stage that order of communication is of relevance (Lawson 1968, p. 544). Second, at this summation stage, the party that goes first has an advantage.

DELAY BETWEEN OPPOSING COMMUNICATIONS

Another factor that seems to influence the outcome of primacy is the amount of time that elapses between opposing communications. In a jury simulation study, Miller and Campbell (1959) presented a tape of a product liability trial. Each side heard the same number of statements. Half of the subjects received first the plaintiff's side, followed by the defense; the other half heard the communications in reverse order. In addition, the experimenters varied the time interval between the two communications (immediate or one week) and between the end of the second communication and the dependent measure. This measure asked each subject to check "the degree to which he thought either the plaintiff or the defendant was responsible for the accident."

The unrepresentativeness of certain features of this procedure limits the generalizability of the results to the courtroom. Rarely, for example, does the defense proceed before the plaintiff; never is a jury asked to decide the liability of the plaintiff as the ultimate issue. Bearing these limitations in mind, the results showed a primacy effect when the two communications were presented contiguously and measurement of the dependent variable was delayed a week. When the messages were separated by a one-week interval and measurement was taken immediately after the second message, a recency effect was found.

According to Miller and Campbell, the primacy effect occurs because a communication that is presented first has "a greater probability that it will be believed." However, when a long period of time separates the two communications, details of the first are likely to be forgotten and, therefore, the second or more recent communication has the greater influence.

ANTICIPATION OF OPPOSING COMMUNICATIONS

The effect of primacy appears to be blunted by the anticipation of communications advocating the opposite viewpoint. Hovland, Janis, and Kelley (1953) noted that "even when a highly impressive communication is presented, members of an audience would be more cautious and less likely to adopt the new conclusion if they had previously learned that there are grounds for maintaining a different position" (pp. 294–95).

Luchins (1957) varied the order of presentation of information and the forewarning of subjects in the context of an impression formation experiment. When subjects were not forewarned of subsequent contradictory information, the usual, strong primacy effect was found. When they were cautioned before any information was given, a primacy effect was still found, though much weaker. Warnings introduced between the first and the second information produced a recency effect—subjects tended to discount the first and overemphasize the second. This study suggests that gross order effects can be controlled, although this conclusion could be limited to communications about personality characteristics.

However, if the influence of audience anticipation on order effects applies also to other kinds of communications, "one wonders what would happen to the totality of primacy and recency effects if subjects were warned . . . against both primacy and recency" (p. 71). In the trial setting, this warning is a built-in feature of the adversary process. Jurors know to withhold judgment because they expect that the information presented by one party will be disputed by the other. At the evidence presentation stage, with its alternating cycles of direct examination and cross-examination, one might expect order to have an effect. At the summation stage, defense attorneys often begin their closing argument by reminding the jury that this is their last statement and they will not have an opportunity to speak after the prosecution closes. It remains to be seen whether such reminders, like the forewarnings in the experiments, nullify any order effects.

A SUMMING UP

As Saks and Hastie (1978) point out, these experimental studies yield "no simple answer" to the question of the effects of gross order. "Sometimes primacy is found to operate, sometimes recency" (p. 106). Reviews of the literature on the effects of internal order show similar results—under some conditions a climactic sequence is more effective, and under others an anticlimactic sequence (Hovland, Janis, and Kelley 1953; Lawson 1970). Since the heyday of Hovland's program, as "inconsistent data accumulated and . . . each new study revealed unanticipated complexity," both "theoretical and empirical interest [in the area of communications research] has waned" (Bartol 1983, p. 232). The interest was revived in the 1970s and 1980s, as we shall see below, by psychologists and lawyers examining the effects of order in the courtroom.

The foregoing overview of the research leads us to a concluding observation. The results from these laboratory experiments cannot be extrapolated directly to the trial setting. One reason is that the data and the theoretical interpretations are vulnerable to scientific impeachment. More importantly, a trial consists of many unique procedural and evidentiary features that are not duplicated in the typical persuasive communication study. These features—stages of the trial, cross-examination, burden of proof, and so forth—are fundamental to fact-finding by an adversary process. They may influence the effects of order in ways that communication experiments do not even consider. Consequently, de novo research is needed on the impact of order at trial. Research must be done afresh that simulates as closely as possible the conditions of a trial, if the findings are to have some external validity. The study that is reproduced next is a first attempt in this direction.

ORDER OF PRESENTATION AT TRIAL

Laurens Walker, John Thibaut, and Virginia Andreoli

The order of evidence in an adversary proceeding has an important effect upon the final determination of guilt or innocence. This effect is complicated by the fact that the adversary process is ordered in two distinct ways: a "gross order" of presentation by each party; and, within this gross order, an "internal order" for the presentation of each party's case.

Gross order is determined by statute and judicial decision. . . .

There is, however, no established internal order for adversary proceedings; such ordering is typically left entirely to the participants. Nevertheless, most practitioners normally save their strongest, most convincing evidence for last. . . .

[T]he choice of both gross and internal order rests upon assumptions which are as yet unsubstantiated. While the effect of order on decision making has attracted the attention of psychological researchers, their work has little direct application to an adversary legal process: they have focused on either external *or* internal order; in the adversary model, the two factors always exist in combination. Moreover, few of these studies have dealt with legal material and none has been designed to include the essential characteristics of the legal fact-finding process. . . .

I.   METHOD

The experiment used a hypothetical case which could arise in either a civil or criminal context.[4] The case as explained was comprised of fifty brief factual statements, divided equally into "lawful" and "unlawful" bits of evidence. Through the prior use of scaling procedures, the impact of each "lawful" bit on a subject (acting as typical juror) was matched by an "unlawful" bit tending in the opposite direction.[*] Subjects were instructed to listen to the evidence and then decide whether the defendant's acts were lawful or unlawful.[6]

Into this setting the two variables of gross and internal order were introduced: In the gross order variable, either the unlawful facts were presented first, followed by the lawful facts, or vice versa; in the internal order variable all possible combinations of climactic and anticlimactic orderings within the two opposing pre-

The Yale Law Journal, Vol. 82, pp. 216–26. Copyright ©1972 by The Yale Law Journal Company, Inc.

[4]The case was explained by a brief summary: Adams (the defendant) and Zemp have been close friends for years. Recently they began to gamble heavily together and, as matters became involved, they met at a tavern to discuss their relationship. After a period of conversation Zemp knocked Adams to the floor and threw an object in his direction. Adams responded by stabbing Zemp in the stomach with a piece of glass. The law provides that it is unlawful to use more force in repelling an attack than a reasonable person would believe necessary in the same or similar circumstances.

[*][Examples of scaled unlawful facts: "The Defendant had been in a fight the night before the stabbing and lost." "Zemp is happily married and the father of four children." Examples of scaled lawful facts: "The Defendant was never known to have carried a gun or knife in his life." "Zemp had been lightweight boxing champion of the First Marine Division." From Thibaut, Walker, and Lind (1972, p. 392). Ed.'s note.]

[6]Each experimental session began when a group of undergraduate students reported to a large conference room at a specific time. A long table was situated at the front of the room, and two third-year law students sat at opposite ends of the table facing each other. The experimenter, a graduate student in psychology, sat at the center of the table facing the participating undergraduate students. Each subject was given an envelope containing the case summary and a series of questionnaires for use in the test session.

Reprinted by permission of The Yale Law Journal Company and Fred B. Rothman and Company from

sentations were compared.[7] Variations attributable to the individuals presenting the evidence were controlled for by alternating roles.

The effects of gross and internal ordering were measured by the judgments of the subjects as to whether the defendant's action was lawful or unlawful, and their certainty about those judgments. Each side presented its twenty-five bits of evidence five at a time. After each set of five bits had been presented, the subjects were asked to indicate the extent to which they *currently* considered the defendant's actions to be lawful or unlawful by checking a nine-point scale (one being unlawful, nine being lawful). After the last set of facts, the subjects were asked to indicate their final opinions on the case and their degree of certainty.

II. RESULTS

The subjects' final judgments are expressed in means in Table 1. Larger means indicate results more favorable to the defense; smaller means, more favorable to the prosecution.

Table 1 suggests that gross order does make a difference and that the second presenter is in the more advantageous position. In three of the four cases, the

party going second obtained more favorable results. Analysis of these data demonstrates that these column differences are highly significant (p < .001).

Table 1 also suggests important differences resulting from internal ordering. Comparison of the appropriately paired rows reveals that a climactic order in the *first* presentation produced substantially lower final means when the prosecution went first (column two). When the defense went first (column one), however, there was no corresponding favorable effect to the defense; indeed, there was a mildly unfavorable trend: Both climactic ordered means are slightly lower than their paired means. Statistical analysis indicates that this differential effect of internal order favorable to the climactic order (only when the prosecution went first) is highly significant (p < .001). As to *second* presentations the data appear to indicate that a climactic order is effective for both prosecution and defense. Statistical analysis demonstrates the internal order difference (generally favorable to the climactic order) to be only marginally significant (p < .052) and not significantly different for defense and prosecution presentations. . . .

III. DISCUSSION

The results of this experiment suggest that in a legal setting the impact of the final bits of evidence, in both gross order and internal order, is pervasive: In gross order, the side going second is strongly advantaged; internal order favor strong evidence occurring toward the end of the presentation except when the defense presents first.

In seeking to account for the gross order results, it is important to examine why facts presented *first* have less impact in a legal setting than elsewhere. First impressions normally have strong impact. . . . Once an early impression is formed, later inconsistent information is often "discounted" because the recipient of the in-

---

[7]The gross order comparison was created after the completion of the standard preliminaries. The two law students were introduced to the subjects as the attorneys for the defense and prosecution. These terms were adopted to differentiate the roles for the subjects but not to suggest a criminal as opposed to a civil trial. In one-half of the sessions, the subjects were told by the experimenter that the defense attorney would present his evidence first and that the prosecution attorney would follow; this procedure was then carried out. In the other sessions, the reverse order was announced and followed throughout the session. In all sessions the appropriate attorney stood and read aloud the lawful or unlawful facts, and then the second attorney presented his case in the same manner.

The internal ordering variable was introduced by having one or both of the two attorneys present their evidence in either the climactic (weak to strong) or anticlimactic (strong to weak) order.

TABLE 1

Mean terminal judgments: The higher the score the more lawful the case was judged.

| | Gross Order | |
Internal Order	Defense First, Prosecution Second	Prosecution First, Defense Second
First presentation weak to strong Second presentation strong to weak	3.94 (18)[a]	3.73 (15)
First presentation weak to strong Second presentation weak to strong	2.84 (19)	4.38 (16)
First presentation strong to weak Second presentation strong to weak	4.20 (15)	5.85 (19)
First presentation strong to weak Second presentation weak to strong	3.50 (20)	6.77 (17)

[a] Number of subjects in parentheses.

formation has relied on the first impression. However, the recipient of the information presented by each party in an adversary process knows that such information has been screened by the advocate and is thus plainly incomplete. Luchins has shown that by forewarning subjects of the imminence of additional information, the impact of early information is suppressed. Thus, when fact-finders know that early information is imperfect and that contrary information will follow, first impressions are not so strong that later information will be discounted. . . .

It is this posture of legal fact-finders, with their suspension of commitment and heightened receptivity to the subsequent presentation, that may favor the party going second. Such effects are further promoted, of course, by a sharpened recall of the more recently presented evidence.

As to internal order, strong evidence presented late in the argument (as in the climactic order) carries greater weight than that which is presented early (as in the anticlimactic order), particularly within the second presentations. It is only when the defense presents first that the climactic order carries no discernible advantage. This may be because in legal fact-finding greater *weight* is given to discernible differences in the strength of evidence presented by the advocate of guilt than to equally discernible differences in the strength of evidence presented by the advocate of innocence. Because "prizes" are not awarded for increasing evidence of innocence but, rather, graduated penalties are routinely calibrated to increasing evidence of guilt, fact-finders in a legal setting may naturally be expected to place most weight on differences in the strength of evidence of malfeasance. . . .

IV. CONCLUSION

The results of this experiment suggest: (1) It makes a difference whether one goes first or second in the adversary presentation of legal materials, and the second position is the more advantageous; (2) the ordering of weak and strong elements within presentation also produces a difference in results, and the weak to strong (climactic) order is the more effective. But this second finding is true regardless of gross order only for the plaintiff or prosecution; the climactic order is advantageous for the defense only within second presentations and there only to a relatively minor degree.

Assuming that the ideal order for adversary fact-finding is a sequence of evidence which eliminates any advantage gained solely because of order, these two findings suggest an optimal sequence for an adversary system: The advocate asserting guilt or fault should go first and present his case in a climactic order; the advocate defending should follow and also present his case in a climactic order. Both advocates are thus given effective resources: This sequence gives a gross order advantage to the defense, offset by the climactic order advantage given to the preceding prosecution or plaintiff presentation. . . .

The system, with its traditional gross order for opening statements and the presentation of evidence (prosecution or plaintiff first) provides the ideal order as long as both advocates follow their self-interest and present their evidence in a climactic order. The traditional adversary trial thus appears remarkably well arranged to neutralize the effects of order and thus maintain the fact-finding process relatively free of this powerful yet legally irrelevant influence.

NOTES AND QUESTIONS

---

1.   The authors begin by noting quite rightly that social psychological research on the effects of order of communications "has little direct application to an adversary legal process" because they do not "[incorporate] the essential characteristics of legal fact-finding." They seek to remedy this flaw by designing their experiment to simulate the trial process more faithfully. They titled their study the "order of presentation at trial." Is this description valid? Did their experimental procedure for communicating facts to the student fact-finders simulate the presentation of evidence stage, the opening statement stage, or the summation stage?

2.   Consider their procedure as a simulation of the presentation of evidence stage. The role of the jury, by definition, is to find the facts on the basis of the evidence presented. In what respects was the task assigned to the student "jurors" without any parallel in a real jury trial?

The experiment revealed a pervasive gross order effect—the party that goes second has a greater impact. Before making the generalization that there is a recency effect in trials, what other fundamental variable should have been included in this or any other study that purports to investigate gross order, if the procedure is to have verisimilitude to actual trials?

3.   Does their procedure simulate the closing argument stage? In a trial, the jurors do not come to the summation without prior information about the case. They have already been exposed to the cases-in-chief of the prosecution and of the defense. In this experiment, the student fact-finders hear the facts for the first time when the attorneys speak. How do you think this difference might alter the effects of order?

Since the students had no prior information, is the study's procedure more like the opening statement stage? If so, is it valid to claim that this is a study of presentation order "at trial" when the "trial" concludes with the opening statements?

4.   Assume, for discussion purposes, that the procedure simulates the summation stage. The authors found a recency effect that favors the defense. In actual criminal trials, the prosecution has the last word—not the defense, as in the experiment. In fact, the typical summation order is prosecution-defense-prosecution. The prosecution has both the first and the last word, not only in the summation stage but in the entire trial. What do the authors mean by a recency effect for the defense when, in actual practice, the defense is sandwiched in between the prosecution?

5.   It would appear that the prosecution always has the advantage since it has the right to open and to close. If there is a recency effect, the prosecution would benefit because it has the last word. If there is a primacy effect, it would also benefit because it has the first word. Either way, the prosecution is favored—unless the burden of proof reposed on the prosecution serves to neutralize the advantage of order.

The experiment simply asked the students to make judgments of lawfulness with respect to the facts presented. How would you modify this dependent measure in order to incorporate the burden of persuasion and thereby make the study more representative of trial adjudication?

6.   The experiment's results on internal order supported—but not strongly—the factual premise in *Brooks* that a climactic sequence for the defense could have greater persuasive impact upon the jury. Suppose that well-designed studies had shown the opposite result: a strong anticlimactic effect. Would the validity of the Tennessee statute be decided any differently? Or, perhaps more likely, suppose that these studies did not yield any unequivocal main effects of internal order. Instead, as with most social psychological processes, interaction effects were found: Under some conditions there was a climactic effect; under others there was an anticlimactic effect. What would be the role of these research findings in determining the legal issue?

7.   The literature on impression formation reviewed earlier suggests that if there is a primacy effect, it could be due to the fact that the first impression creates a mental set or expectancy that conditions the evaluation of subsequent information, at least with respect to the evaluation of personality attributes. The opening statement could provide an opportunity for counsel to establish in jurors a like mental set or "thematic framework" for organizing and interpreting the evidence to be presented later (Pyszczynski and Wrightsman 1981, p. 302). Experienced counsel know that the informational function of opening statements, limited to a preview of the evidence, can be transformed into a subtle attempt at persuasion or at facilitating the persuasive impact of the subsequent advocacy. What factors would you hypothesize might bear upon the efficiency of this covert purpose of opening statements and how would you design a study or studies to test them?

8.   Pennington (1982) conducted an experiment "designed to overcome [the methodological] short-comings [of Walker, Thibaut, and Andreoli] and hence determine whether order effects occur when a more realistic simulation of courtroom proceedings is achieved" (p. 320). He followed the English trial procedure of opening statements by the prosecution and the defense, the cases in chief by the prosecution and the defense, and the summation by the judge. College students read the transcript of a rape trial, approximately 3,000 words in length. Then, without any judicial instructions, they answered a questionnaire, including giving their individual judgments of guilt or nonguilt. Within the established gross order of the first two phases of the trial, the internal order was varied to produce a primacy effect (evidence implicating guilt was presented first) or a recency effect (evidence implicating guilt was presented last). The results showed that the greatest number of guilty judgments occurred when the inculpatory evidence was presented first. "The major question," according to the author, "is why we should find primacy effects when most other researchers find recency effects" (p. 330). He speculated that the longer the trial, the more likely a primacy effect because attention diminishes over time. He also suggested that rape trials are more emotionally involving than assault cases, and the testimony of the rape victim early in the trial is more likely to be imprinted in the jurors' memory. Thus, the amount of evidence presented and the nature of the charge may determine whether there are primacy or recency effects. What other conditions might account for finding one or the other effect?

Methods of Proof

The law of evidence cannot be discussed *in vacuo*. An analysis of the rules which govern proof-taking at trial needs to take into account their original rationale, namely, to shelter the jury from misleading evidence, and also the nature of the method of proof itself, namely, an adversarial style of developing the evidence in court. If the origins of the Anglo-American law of evidence are found in the jury trial, its contours are shaped by the contested trial. In Western civilization, the quest for rational methods of adjudication has taken two forms: an inquisitorial approach in which the evidence is developed principally by the judge uninhibited by rules of evidence and an adversarial approach in which the parties control the production of evidence and the judge is a neutral umpire who determines the admissibility of the evidence and instructs the jury in the applicable law. A key feature that distinguishes the two methods of fact-finding are the evidentiary rules of exclusion. The choice of fact-finder and assumptions about the fact-finder's competence give rise to the need for these rules.

Debate over the relative merits of the continental and the Anglo-American styles of proof-taking has raged for over a century. The arguments have been mostly speculative, resting on informed impressions and intuitive insights. In the 1970s, a social psychologist and a lawyer began an interdisciplinary research program designed "to define and clarify the nature of procedural justice through the application of social-psychological methods . . ." (Thibaut and Walker 1975, p. vii). Theirs was "the first systematic attempt" to apply laboratory experimentation to the study of legal proof (p. vii). The preceding article, "Order of Presentation at Trial," was a product of this program. Their research has centered on the effectiveness of inquisitorial and adversarial processes for the divination of truth. In the epistemology of legal procedure, they have provided an empirical *pied-à-terre*. In this section, we will sketch the key characteristics of these two processes and summarize one of their many experiments that purport to show that the adversary process is "clearly superior" (p. 118). In so doing, the interrelatedness of the law of evidence and the law of procedure should become manifest.

INQUISITORIAL AND ADVERSARIAL METHODS

The inquisitorial method of fact-finding grew out of the ecclesiastical courts. In the canon system of justice, judges directed the gathering of evidence and were the sole arbiters. In modern continental procedure, the French criminal process is an archetype of the inquisitorial model (Goldstein 1974). The central figures are the investigating magistrate (*juge d'instruction*) and the presiding judge at trial. The magistrate takes over the investigation of the case from the moment the arrest is made or the charge(s) filed. He gathers—unbounded by evidentiary restrictions—all probative evidence in a dossier which is sent to trial.

The trial itself is essentially a public recapitulation of the dossier. The judge, like the magistrate in the investigation phase, dominates the proceedings. Informed by the dossier, he interrogates the defendant and any other witnesses. There are no separate witnesses for the prosecution or the defense. In fact, the parties cannot prepare witnesses for trial. The "coaching" of witnesses common in the Anglo-American tradition comes perilously close to a criminal offense in the continental setting. Judicial interrogation is usually more like an informal conversation than a relentless cross-examination. Witnesses are asked to give a narrative account uninterrupted by questions or the invocation of exclusionary rules. The goal is to reconstruct the event in question. Afterward, the parties are allowed to question the witnesses in order to fill in the gaps or emphasize certain features of the testimony. Upon completion of the proof-taking, the parties offer summations of the facts and legal arguments.

In contrast to the active role of the continental judge in amassing and adjudicating the facts, the common law judge lets the parties control the investigation and development of the evidence. The paradigm of the adversary method is the keenly contested trial in which each party calls its own witnesses and seeks to present information favorable to its side. Fact-finding unfolds by the rival use of witnesses. It is an article of faith among Anglo-American lawyers that "cross-examination is the greatest legal engine ever invented for the discovery of truth" (Wigmore 1940, vol. 5, p. 29). The judge, not having been exposed to a dossier, lacks the background information needed to participate directly in the adjudication. His role is limited to refereeing the contest by deciding what evidence should or should not be admissible. The trier, then, hears two alternating, one-sided presentations filtered through the sieve of evidentiary rules.

The foregoing are idealized portrayals of the two approaches. There are no purely inquisitorial or purely adversarial systems. It would blink reality to ignore the inquisitorial elements in the American criminal process. For example, the grand jury serves investigative functions. American judges sometimes assume a proactive stance that belies the reactive umpire image (Frankel 1975). By the application of exclusionary rules and instructions on the law, they can influence the proceedings and restrain the jury. In some jurisdictions, they can also appoint experts, comment on the evidence, and even summon witnesses. Conversely, continental processes do not faithfully conform to the inquisitorial model. In practice, a magistrate could leave much of the pretrial investigation to the police, as is the American custom. At trial, attorneys sometimes play a more substantial role in the production of evidence than inquisitorial norms suggest. Despite the overlap between these two methods of proof in their day-to-day operations, epistemologically there are still clear differences in their central tendencies.

One implication of these procedural differences is the effect on the impartiality of the judge. The continental judge learns about the case from the dossier, which could lead him to form tentative preconceptions before the trial. Instead of discovering or reconstructing what happened, he may set out to confirm his a priori hypotheses. The Anglo-American judge would be disqualified if he had comparable prior knowledge. By leaving the production of evidence to the dialectics of partisan inquiry, he avoids the pitfalls of premature judgment. As one advocate of the sporting model put it, "An adversary presentation seems the only effective means for combating [the] natural human tendency to judge too swiftly in terms of the familiar which is not yet fully known" (Fuller 1961, p. 44). This specific issue—the claimed superiority of the adversary method over the inquisitorial method in counteracting judicial bias—was the subject of an experiment by Thibaut, Walker, and Lind (1972), described below.

STUDY OF JUDICIAL BIAS IN INQUISITORIAL AND ADVERSARIAL METHODS

The hypothetical case for this experiment was the same stabbing incident employed in the study on order of presentation (see footnote 4 of the article by Walker, Thibaut, and Andreoli reproduced in the preceding section). The issue presented by the case was the limits of lawful self-defense. The decision-makers or "judges" were college students tested in groups of seven to twelve. The details of the case were presented to them in fifty brief factual statements, half of which had been scaled to suggest that the stabbing in self-defense was lawful, and the other half to suggest that it was unlawful. Thus, the basic procedure of the study was identical to the one on order of presentation.

Into this setting, three independent variables were introduced, of which only two are of interest here. The first was method of proof. To simulate the adversary mode, the factual statements were read to the subjects by two law students who were seated at separate tables bearing the signs "prosecution" and "defense." The "prosecutor" read the twenty-five unlawful statements and the defense read the twenty-five lawful ones. To mimic the inquisitorial style, all fifty statements were read by one person, whose role was "intended to resemble that of a *juge d'instruction*" (p. 393). Subjects were randomly assigned to one or the other condition.

The second variable was decision-maker bias. The continental judge is thought to be biased by reason of exposure to the dossier prior to trial. "Bias" as operationalized by the authors meant an a priori "expectation that the test case will yield a given outcome," namely, the unlawfulness of the self-defense (p. 394). To this end, half of the subjects were made to believe that the defendant's act was unlawful, while the other half remained "unbiased." To create the biased condition, the experimenter read six cases to the subjects. The facts of these cases were very similar to the facts of the test case. The experimenter told the subjects that the "correct result," in five of the six cases, was unlawful conduct by the defendant. This biasing procedure created the expectation or mental set that the defendant, in the test case, acted in unlawful self-defense.

The defendant measure consisted of ratings on a nine-point scale of the lawfulness of the stabbing (one = unlawful, nine = lawful). Nine ratings were taken during the course of the presentation of the fifty factual statements, but the principal measure employed in the analysis of the results was the tenth and last rating. Except for rendering these judgments, the subjects at all times and in all conditions sat passively, simply listening to the information presented.

The results showed that the biasing procedure was effective. The average unlawful rating (on the tenth judgment) was 2.94 for the biased group and 4.01 for the unbiased group. The former group, then, had "an expectation of an unlawful outcome" before the start of the "trial" (p. 396).

The results also provided "empirical support for the general claim . . . that an adversary presentation apparently counteracts decisionmaker bias" (p. 397). Among biased subjects, the average unlawful ratings obtained with the inquisitorial and adversarial methods were, respectively, 2.17 and 3.62. This difference was statistically significant. Among unbiased subjects, the respective ratings were 4.27 and 3.76, a difference which was not beyond chance occurrence. In effect, the authors say that the inquisitorial approach does not neutralize pre-existing judicial bias and, therefore, is more prone to err in the direction of convicting the defendant. The adversary approach, on the other hand, errs in the opposite direction of giving the benefit of the doubt to the defendant.

In subsequent experiments, Thibaut and Walker and their associates have explored other dimensions of these two methods of proof (Lind and Walker 1979). They found no differences in the quantum of facts generated by these methods, although "client centered" attorneys presented the facts in a more one-sided manner than "court centered" attorneys of the continental system. They have also examined the subjective reactions of the subjects to different methods of adjudication. In general, there was greater satisfaction with and perceived fairness of the adversary method compared with the inquisitorial one, regardless of the trial outcome. Their basic conclusion is that the Anglo-American procedure "is superior to other classes of procedures . . . both [in] subjective and normative appraisals of its performance" (Thibaut and Walker 1975, p. 118). These findings have been used to develop a general theory of legal procedure for "analyzing and classifying all conflict resolution procedures" (Thibaut and Walker 1978, p. 541). They identify three types of disputes: "truth conflicts" (disputes about empirical facts), best resolved by nonadversary procedures because they introduce less bias at the information gathering stage; "interest conflicts" (disputes about the distribution of matters of economic value), best settled by adversary means because they result in greater equity and fairness by allowing the litigants to control the gathering and presentation of evidence; and "mixed conflicts," best addressed by a bifurcated procedure that uses inquisitorial methods for determining truth and adversarial methods for adjudicating conflicts of interest.

Though path-breaking and imaginative, their research on procedural justice has not been immune to sharp criticism for its methodological and conceptual flaws (Damaška 1975; Hayden and Anderson 1979). Our discussion will focus on the experiment just described.

NOTES AND QUESTIONS

1.   Is the reading of the factual statements a valid (though stylized) representation of the Anglo-American and continental methods of developing evidence? Design an alternative research procedure that better captures the quintessence of the two methods.

2.   Critique the authors' operational definition of "bias." Did their biasing manipulation create "bias" in its commonly understood meaning of partiality? Notice that there was no objective or independent criterion for determining the "correct" result, that is, whether the defendant's act was lawful or not.

3.   On what other dimensions, besides the neutralizing of judicial bias and number of facts elicited, can these two methods be compared empirically?

4.   Consider the following experiment designed to compare the efficacy of inquisitorial and adversarial procedures (and other procedures, such as plea bargaining, which need not concern us here) and to "correct . . . [the] methodological shortcomings in previous studies [by Thibaut and Walker]" (Austin et al. 1981, p. 286). Women college students were shown a videotaped re-enactment of a criminal proceeding in which the defendant was charged with leaving the scene of a car accident. The subjects saw either an adversary proceeding with direct and cross examination by counsel or an inquisitorial proceeding with the judge calling all the witnesses and conducting the questioning. The testimony given in both proceedings was identical. The outcome of the two types of proceedings was systematically varied. In one half of the cases, the outcome was "favorable" (the judge reduced the felony charge to a misdemeanor conviction), and in the other half the outcome was "unfavorable" (the judge certified the case to a court of general jurisdiction for possible felony prosecution). After viewing the videotape, the subjects completed twenty-seven rating scales that assessed a variety of opinions, including the perceived fairness of the proceeding and the perceived satisfaction of the defendant with the outcome. The results showed that both proceedings were perceived as uniformly and moderately fair. However, the perceived satisfaction of the defendant depended upon the type of proceeding. The defendant was thought to be most satisfied when the adversary proceeding led to a favorable outcome, and least satisfied when the adversary proceeding led to an unfavorable outcome. The authors concluded that these results "[c]ontradict previous studies [by Thibaut and Walker] which report adversarial to be the most preferred dispute resolution procedure within all outcome conditions" (p. 281). They also suggested that the fairness with which a proceeding is conducted may be more important than the nature of the proceeding itself. What conclusions, if any, would you draw from this experiment?

5.   A trial is not purely an exercise in cognition. Social values other than impartial fact-finding are also served by adjudication. Thus, even if there are differences in the fact-finding effectiveness of the two methods, it cannot be said necessarily that one is "superior" to the other. Each method is embedded in a unique institutional context. The adversary approach is part of the larger common law tradition of individualized justice, case-by-case adjudication, and malleable decisional precedents. The inquisitorial mode is indistinguishable from the civil law tradition of standardized justice, uniform adjudication, and decisional standards based on precise, codified rules. It would seem only natural that these different systems of law should give rise to different methods of proof. Perhaps the more important issue for social research is not the comparative merits of the two methods, but how each method can be improved in order to serve the interests of justice of their respective legal systems.

9.3.   MODE OF PRESENTATION OF EVIDENCE

By the 1970s, the state of the art of videotape technology had become rather sophisticated. Its applications in television news and entertainment programs and in classrooms grew rapidly. In this context, it did not take unusual prescience to declare that "one day very soon now, a courtroom somewhere in this illustrious land will introduce a sweeping change in the present system of trial by jury. . . . A jury will have decided the issues of a lawsuit by merely viewing and hearing the entire proceedings of a trial on a television screen . . . ." (Morrill 1970, p. 237). In 1971, in the Court of Common Pleas in Sandusky, Ohio, the first videotaped trial was held (McCrystal and Maschari 1980). Since then, a number of state and federal courts have allowed the videotaping of at least certain limited types of testimony for use at trial. The advent of the videotaped trial is seen as a "historic breakthrough" in the administration of justice, involving a "marriage between technologists, behavioral scientists, and the legal profession" (Clark 1975, p. 327).

The basic issue is whether the presentation of evidence by this electronic recording medium is the same as live communication. On the one hand, it is said that videotaped material is merely a new method of presenting evidence (Kornblum 1972). It is simply a substitute form of conveying information; the evidence is unaffected by the channel in which it is transmitted. On the other hand, "Will attending a (televised) movie instead of a trial affect the verdict?" (Johnson 1974, p. 27). The television screen that is interposed between the jurors and the trial participants creates a certain psychological distance because of the loss of the living presence. The transmission via this screen may also have an impact on the communication itself in terms of how it is processed and how jurors respond to it. In McLuhan's (1964) celebrated phrase, "The Medium is the Message" (p. 7). The transfer of a trial from its original live context to the electronic medium could alter a whole complex of relationships in unanticipated ways.

Applications to the Judicial Process

There are several major uses of videotape technology in the judicial process.

Extrajudicial activities of governmental agencies, particularly the police, are sometimes recorded on videotape when these activities are expected to be scrutinized subsequently by the courts. For example, videotapes of police lineups, interrogations and confessions, sobriety tests for drivers, and investigations of crime scenes have been accepted in evidence by many courts.

Pretrial depositions and trial proceedings are usually recorded stenographically by court reporters. Some states have authorized the videotaping of depositions and of complete trials as a substitute for stenographic reporting. In addition to cost savings, the videotape can provide a record of contextual factors such as voice intonation, inflection, and nonverbal cues, which are absent in a written record.

The application that has stirred the most interest and controversy in the legal profession, and that is our main focus, is the prerecording of testimony by videotape for subsequent use as evidence at trial, in lieu of the live presence of the witness. The general procedure is as follows. A witness testifies under oath under questioning by lawyers of both sides. Any objections by counsel are noted, but the questioning is not curtailed, since the judge is usually absent at the testimony-taking. After all the witnesses have been videotaped, the master tape is reviewed by the attorneys and the judge in chambers. The judge rules on objections and both the formal objections and the objectionable statements are deleted from the tape. The parties also agree on the order of presenting the testimony of the various witnesses, by juxtaposing different parts of the tape. Not only testimonial evidence but demonstrative evidence as well (for example, the scene of the accident) can be videotaped for use as evidence. At the trial itself, the attorneys impanel the jurors and deliver live opening statements. Then the prerecorded videotaped testimony of the witnesses is presented on television monitors. If necessary, live exhibits may be introduced by counsel at appropriate intervals. Throughout the videotape presentation, the judge is not in the courtroom, though the attorneys are present. Finally, live closing arguments are made and prerecorded judicial instructions to the jury are delivered on the television monitors (Comment, *Columbia Journal of Law and Social Problems*, 1973, pp. 365–66).

The extensiveness of the use of prerecorded videotaped evidence in any given trial will vary. It can range from a completely prerecorded trial, including the opening and closing statements, to the prerecording of testimony of only one or two witnesses. At present, most videotaped trials fall somewhere between the two extremes, depending on the nature and complexity of the case.

There are four sets of issues in any videotaped trial: technical issues regarding equipment and operational procedures; administrative considerations regarding time savings and cost effectiveness of this medium; the behavioral impact of videotaped trials on the courtroom participants; and constitutional and policy issues. We will attend primarily to the behavioral and legal policy issues; but because all of the issues are interrelated, we will begin with a quick overview of the technical and administrative aspects.

Technical Aspects

The hardware and operating procedures of videotape technology affect production quality which, in turn, may have behavioral effects on actors and viewers. We leave aside matters of equipment and their different technical capacities and limit our focus to production techniques.

When communication is filtered through the medium of a videotape camera, there is some inherent transformation of the message. There is no electronic fidelity to live communication. The location of cameras and microphones involves not only a technical decision but represents an editorial judgment as well. Television production manuals note that "everything the camera sees, it necessarily interprets. It is innately selective" (in Doret 1974, p. 245). The camera becomes the juror's eye. It locks his view, narrows his focus, and restricts his autonomy of observation. The blocking out of background cues may eliminate distraction but at the same time may require intense concentration. The potential for editorializing by the cameraman is substantial.

Picture composition is also subject to technically induced bias in the viewer. The zoom technique, for example, which allows close-up shots without moving the position of a camera, forces the viewer to pay attention to certain aspects of physiognomy. Continual zooming on the disfiguring scars of a plaintiff in an automobile accident suit may well create a more forceful impression of injury than wide-angle shots. The discretion in the editing of the master tape is another potential source of bias. The splicing and combination of separately taped testimonies may result in a whole that is more than the sum of its parts. Thus, studies on the effects of videotaped trials on the jury have to take into account differences within the videotape medium itself.

Economies and Efficiencies

The reduction of court congestion is an oft-stated rationale. By videotaping and previewing the evidence, attorneys for both sides can work out evidentiary disputes about admissibility out of court and therefore expedite the flow of the trial. Improved justice is also thought to result from this efficiency. Judges would have more time to reflect and even do research on evidentiary challenges before ruling on them, and jurors would not be biased by hearing evidence that is subsequently ruled inadmissible because it would be deleted from the tape. Substantial saving in judicial time is expected. Judges need not be in attendance during the taping of the testimony. Later in chambers, they can turn directly to those portions of the tape that raise evidentiary questions. They also need not be present during the presentation of the videotape to the jury at trial. With all this free time, judges presumably could turn to the trying of other cases and thereby reduce the court docket.

Prerecorded videotaping also saves time and reduces costs to witnesses. In a live trial, all the witnesses need to be present at one place and at one time. By taping testimony of witnesses in segments, at different times and places at their convenience, the spatial and temporal restrictions of a trial are obviated. This procedure might also increase the number of witnesses who would otherwise be unwilling or unable to take time off to testify at a trial. A particular advantage would be the increase in the availability of eminent expert witnesses located far from the place of trial. They would presumably be more willing to be videotaped in their own offices at their own convenience than to travel across the country for a personal appearance. The first videotaped trial took one day, including the live voir dire and closing arguments. In a live trial, the presiding judge estimated it would have taken two or three days (Mc-Crystal and Young 1973).

Behavioral Impact on the Jury

An overriding question in videotaped trials is the impact on the ultimate jury verdict. Granting that the electronic medium inherently distorts the communication, does this nonetheless influence the final decision? And granting that the claimed efficiencies and economies are established, do they justify the use of videotaped trials if it is shown that jury judgments are thereby altered? The research that follows attempts to answer some of these questions.

THE EFFECTS OF VIDEOTAPE TESTIMONY IN JURY TRIALS: STUDIES ON JUROR DECISION MAKING, INFORMATION RETENTION, AND EMOTIONAL AROUSAL

Gerald R. Miller, David C. Bender, Frank Boster, B. Thomas Florence, Norman Fontes, John Hocking, and Henry Nicholson

. . .

The initial research was designed to answer [the following] questions: (1) Do the responses of jurors exposed to a live trial differ from those exposed to a videotaped trial? (2) Do the responses of jurors exposed to inadmissible testimony differ from those not exposed to such testimony?

SELECTING THE STIMULUS TRIAL. Since videotape has thus far been accepted more widely in the civil than in the criminal arena, a civil case [*Nugent* v. *Clark*] was selected. . . . [This was] an automobile injury case involving the question of contributory negligence on the part of the plaintiff.

EDITING THE TRANSCRIPT. For the most part, the content and structure of the trial transcript were left unchanged. . . .

PREPARING THE TRIAL.

CASTING. . . . Except for the judge and the bailiff . . . all participants in the trial were professional actors and actresses.

EQUIPMENT. . . . The trial was recorded by using a split-screen technique that partitioned the television screen so as to show the three perspectives simultaneously. The full courtroom shot appeared on the lower half of the screen; the close-up of the witness and the witness stand was located in the upper left quarter; and the upper right quarter of the screen contained a view of the bench and the questioning attorney. This system, besides being technically feasible, would hold the attention of the jurors while allowing them to see, hear, and identify all relevant participants in the courtroom. . . .

NUGENT v. CLARK STUDY 1: LIVE v. VIDEOTAPE TRIALS

PROCEDURES.

THE LIVE PRESENTATION. Fifty-two jurors from the Genessee County Circuit Court (Flint, Michigan) jury panel served as subjects on their final day of jury service. . . .

On the day of the trial, the jurors were brought into the courtroom and seated in the spectator section facing the hearing area. The judge then explained that the videotape recording cameras in the courtroom were for the purpose of making a record of the trial for possible later appeal or review. The judge further explained that the abnormally large size of the jury was to allow a group of researchers from Michigan State University, who were interested in jury size, to analyze the results of the trial. The jurors were assured that they were the actual determiners of the verdict in the case, and that their decision would be binding on the litigants. Because of the large jury size, the judge explained, voir dire would be accomplished by means of a written questionnaire.

After the voir dire questionnaires had been completed by the jurors and the attorneys had examined them, four jurors were peremptorily dismissed, a move made to heighten realism. After these preliminaries, the judge started the trial and the taping began. As mentioned earlier, all technical personnel and control equipment were located in the judge's chambers outside the view of the jurors.

The trial proceeded in 50-minute segments through the judge's final instructions to the jury. Recesses were taken after each 50-minute segment. In all, the trial was conducted in a manner as closely conforming to normal trial procedure as possible. Visual exhibits were distributed at the appropriate times. When the trial ended, the jurors went to the jury assembly room, where an experimenter administered the "jury size" questionnaire.

After completing the questionnaire, all jurors were completely debriefed. Very little suspicion about the reality of the trial was expressed either orally during the debriefing session or on the questionnaires. Jurors did not deliberate, since, for purposes of this study, we were interested only in what jurors take to the jury room with them.

THE VIDEOTAPE PRESENTATION. Subjects were 45 jurors from Genessee County who viewed the videotape trial on the last day of their jury service 1 month later. The same research personnel were used, and the two attorneys were again present to conduct an ostensible written voir dire and to observe the trial. The single variation in procedure was that the trial was viewed by jurors on six television monitors placed in the spectator section of the courtroom, rather than being seen live. The judge's preliminary instructions to the jury addressed this difference, explaining the split-screen system and admonishing the jurors that, although the trial would be viewed on television, it was fully as important as any trial they had sat on during their term of jury service. Visual exhibits were distributed at the appropriate times. At the conclusion of closing arguments, the judge entered the courtroom and read instructions to the jury. . . .

THE QUESTIONNAIRE. . . . Specifically, the questionnaire posed two questions directly: (1) Was the defendant in fact negligent, and if so, was the plaintiff contributorily negligent? (2) If the verdict necessitated monetary awards to the plaintiffs, what was the juror's judgment as to the magnitudes of those awards? Further, the questionnaire was designed to measure juror perception of attorney credibility, juror retention of substantive information, and juror motivation and interest. . . . [Credibility and motivation were measured by several seven-point semantic differential scales. Retention was measured by a forty-item examination of true-false and multiple-choice questions. Ed.'s note.]

RESULTS AND DISCUSSION. . . . Analysis of [the] data revealed no evidence that the mode of presentation significantly influenced jurors' attributions of negligence. Although jurors found for the plaintiff somewhat more frequently in the videotape trial (that is, they found the defendant, Frank Clark, solely negligent with greater frequency), these differences do not reach statistical significance. [In the live trial, 13 out of 44 jurors (about 30%) found for the plaintiff; in the videotape trial, the figure was 20 out of 41 (about 48%). Ed.'s note.]

[T]he mode of presentation [also did not] significantly affect the amount of award given by jurors who found for the plaintiffs. . . . [Mean award for Mrs. Nugent: live trial, $20,538; videotape trial, $17,975.]

Jurors' perceptions of credibility were uniformly high for both attorneys and did not differ significantly between the two trials. . . .

The jurors' retention of trial-related information was not significantly influenced by the medium of presentation. Of a possible score of 40, the mean retention score for jurors in the live trial was 31.1, while the score for jurors in the videotape trial was 29.8. The difference is not statistically significant. . . .

Juror interest and motivation did not vary significantly as a result of watching a live or videotape trial, suggesting that there is nothing inherently less interesting or motivating about watching a videotape trial rather than the live counterpart. . . .

On the basis of the results of this study and the impressions gleaned while conducting the research, we find that the videotape trial format does not produce detrimental effects on juror responses. . . .

[STUDY] 3: THE EFFECTS OF THE DELETION OF INADMISSIBLE TESTIMONY

Proponents of the use of videotape in jury trials have argued . . . that, because of this ability to edit, . . . inadmissible evidence can be suppressed so as not to taint a jury's verdict. The present study tested the validity of [this claim]. . . .

PROCEDURE. One hundred and twenty jurors serving on the Wayne County Circuit Court (Detroit, Michigan) panel, who voluntarily returned for "further jury service" during the week following the end of their term of regular jury service, were instructed that they would serve as jurors in change-of-venue trials. They were further told that a representative from Michigan State University would be administering a questionnaire on jury size to them subsequent to the trial and prior to their deliberation. The jurors were then randomly assigned to one of seven experimental trials, each trial using a split-screen tape of *Nugent* v. *Clark* containing from zero to six instances of inadmissible testimony. At the conclusion of the videotape presentation, each group completed the "jury size" questionnaire. . . .

CONCLUSIONS. The study uncovered none of the effects of inadmissible testimony predicted. No statistically significant differences in attribution of negligence resulted from experimentally varying the amounts of inadmissible material in the trial. Similarly, no statistically significant differences were found in the amount of money awarded to the plaintiff or in the jurors' perception of attorney credibility. However, these results are preliminary only, for the findings of no differences may be attributable to one or more of three factors. First, the inadmissible testimony may have had too small an effect in relation to the length of the trial. . . . Second, the inadmissible testimony may have been neither supportive enough of plaintiff's case nor damning enough for defendant's case to have had an appreciable effect on verdict, award, or attorney credibility. Third, the large amount of money asked for by the plaintiff very likely suppressed any differences in juror response caused by the varying amount of inadmissible testimony in the seven versions of the trial. When a large amount of money is asked for, there is a tendency for jurors to choose a round number near one of the extremes of allowable awards. . . .

[In other studies, not reproduced here, the authors found no differences between split-screen and full-screen video-tape presentations. They did find better information retention with black-and-white videotape than with color videotape. Ed.'s note.]

NOTES AND QUESTIONS

---

1.   The simulated trial (except for the absence of group deliberation and verdict) was admirable for its verisimilitude to actual trials. Miller and his colleagues have set a high standard for simulated jury research. Ironically, however, it is precisely the verisimilitude of the videotaped trial to an actual live trial that reduces the generalizability of the results. The videotaped trial in the experiment should have simulated an actual videotaped trial rather than an actual live trial. Their videotaped presentation was perhaps too smooth and cohesive. Actual videotaped trials tend to be segmented and discontinuous, because the testimony of witnesses is prerecorded at different times and different places and then juxtaposed. Also, the judge is normally not shown in the videotape, since he is typically absent at the taping. Miller et al.'s videotape procedure, then, minimizes the differences between live trials and actual videotape trials as they are presently conducted. This point is made not so much to criticize what was not done, as to indicate again the importance of variations in the technical aspects in affecting the behavioral impact.

2.   In research, one normally seeks to reject the null hypothesis that the independent variable makes no difference or has no impact. Miller et al., however, are not out to reject the null hypothesis. To the contrary, because of the policy implications of videotaped trials, their interest is in not rejecting the null hypothesis. What are the implications of using inferential statistics to "prove" there are no differences?

3.   The findings may not be as unequivocal as they were reported to be. Other researchers have reanalyzed Miller et al.'s data and reached the opposite conclusion: There is "a significantly different pattern for jurors' verdicts [on liability] in the video trials" (Williams et al. 1975, p. 383, n. 31). In Miller et al.'s Study 1, about 30% of the live trial jurors had found the defendant negligent, compared with 48% of the video trial jurors, but this difference was not statistically significant. Since Miller et al. used the same research paradigm for their several studies, Williams et al. combined the responses of all the video trial jurors in these different studies and compared them with the original group of live trial jurors. This comparison showed that significantly greater attributions of negligence were rendered by video trial jurors (48% to 62%). They acknowledged, however, that "technically, a combining of the results of separate studies conducted under varying stimulus conditions can be only suggestive. . . ." Nonetheless, they emphasized that the frequency of liability judgments, which is consistently higher in video trials, "brings into question [Miller et al.'s] finding of 'no difference' . . ." (n. 31).

4.   To assess the impact on the jury of deleting inadmissible evidence, Miller and his associates compared seven conditions differing in the frequency of items of tainted information, from zero (or control group) to six. Does this design adequately test the question of interest?

5.   An unexplored area of research is the effect of cultural conditioning by television on jurors' perceptions of videotaped trials. Informal interviews with lawyers and judges suggest that television shows such as "Perry Mason" "influence jurors' expectations and decisions." One survey indicated that jurors who are regular television watchers expect real trials to be as fast-paced and dramatic as television criminology, and they become dissatisfied and restless when they are not. A Los Angeles prosecutor opined that "TV has changed the shape of the criminal justice system more than anything I know of" (Siegel 1980, p. A3).

6.   Except for a handful of instances to date, videotaped trials have been used principally in civil cases. Are there any justifications for why videotape technology should or should not be applied to criminal proceedings?

7. During the taping of the witnesses' testimony and during presentation of the videotape to the jury, the judge is normally absent. This judicial time-saving feature of the medium is one of its principal attractions. Should there be a constitutional right to the presence of the judge at these two times?

8. At present, there is no single, legally permissible production procedure for videotaped trials. As the use of videotape increases, undoubtedly there will be considerable variability in local practices, thereby raising the possibility of greater medium distortion of the communication. Assuming that it would be desirable to have uniform standards in videotaping for court purposes, what should these standards include?

9. A trial carries social-pedagogic metamessages in addition to serving a fact-finding purpose. It reminds the community of the principles that it holds important. It can be a forum for the expression of ideological views. In criminal cases, it is an outlet for community reprobation of the convicted defendant. The objections to and the striking of inadmissible evidence at trial engender in the jury and the public an appreciation of the rules of fair play in legal fact-finding (Bermant and Jacoubovitch 1975, p. 1008). The ceremony and ritual of the trial lend legitimacy to the judicial process. Do videotaped presentations, which efficiently fragment the trial proceedings and sever testimony-taking from the courtroom, jeopardize the symbolic aspects of the trial?

10. The Sixth Amendment guarantees the right to a public trial. This guarantee is rooted in a historical distrust of secret judicial proceedings. Without public access, the courts could become instruments of governmental abuse, and freedom would be compromised. The assembly of persons in the courtroom also impresses upon trial participants the seriousness of the event and announces to society the operation of the deterrent effect of the criminal law.

    If the public can attend a live trial, obviously it can also attend a videotaped trial. However, does "public trial" include the right to attend the videotaping of the testimony, which usually is not held in the courtroom? Is the loss of the symbolic power of public attendance on a witness who is testifying in private before a camera sufficient so as to raise a constitutional objection?

Television Cameras in the Courtroom

    In an electronic age, "public trial" comes to mean television broadcast of a trial. Media videotaping *of* trials and the use of videotaped testimony *in* trials implicate different issues, but both subjects share a common focus: Does communications technology alter the conduct and outcome of trials?

    In *Estes* v. *Texas* (1965), salad oil magnate Billie Sol Estes, a prominent citizen of the Lone Star State, was convicted in a trial which was televised over his objection. The Supreme Court reversed on the grounds that obtrusive television equipment prejudiced the defendant's right to a fair trial under the Due Process Clause. The Court worried that telecasting would have adverse effects on the jury's attentiveness, the witnesses' testimony, the judge's objectivity, the attorneys' effectiveness, and the defendant's dignity and ability to concentrate on the proceedings. The decision left unsettled whether all televised trials are inherently unfair.

    The answer came sixteen years later. In *Chandler* v. *Florida* (1981), two police officers appealed their convictions for burglary on the basis that the presence of television cameras at trial hampered their defense and denied them an impartial jury. After noting the sophistication of modern videotape technology (no cumbersome wires, artificial lights, or whirring noises that accompanied the television crews of the previous decade), the Court unanimously ruled that the defendants had not shown with sufficient "specificity that the presence of cameras impaired the ability of jurors to decide the case on only the evidence or that . . . any of the participants [had been adversely affected]" (p. 581). The Court acknowledged that "the general issue of the psychological impact of broadcast coverage upon the participants in a trial . . . is still subject to sharp debate . . ." (p. 578). The "experiments and surveys" are "limited" and "non-scientific." Nonetheless, "it is still noteworthy that the data now available do not support . . . the thesis that the presence of the electronic media, *ipso facto*, interferes with trial proceedings." However, the Court warned, "further research may change the picture" (p. 576, no. 11). Systematic studies on the effects of cameras on trial participants remain to be done (Cohen 1982, p. 290).

In the aftermath of *Chandler*, state courts struggled to define the threshold of interference caused by cameras beyond which there is an "adverse psychological impact" that is inherently lacking in due process (*Chandler*, p. 575). The Florida Supreme Court formulated a "qualitative difference test": "The presiding judge may exclude electronic media coverage of a particular participant only upon a finding that such coverage will have a substantial effect upon the particular individual which would be qualitatively different from the effect on members of the public in general and such effect will be qualitatively different from coverage by other types of media" (*State* v. *Palm Beach Newspapers, Inc.*, 1981, pp. 546–47). What might constitute a provable qualitative difference? Is the test amenable to operational definition and measurement? Should there be psychological evaluation of particular individuals to determine if they would be substantially affected by the telecasting? What other standards would you suggest that a court use to determine whether the presence of cameras infringes upon a fair trial?

9.4.   ADMISSIBILITY OF EVIDENCE

The Basic Policy and Principle of Evidence Law

The basic policy of evidence law is to admit all evidence that would aid the truth-seeking function of trial, unless there are valid reasons to exclude it. Thayer (1898) stated the policy as follows: "(1) That nothing is to be received which is not logically probative of some matter requiring to be proved; and (2) that everything which is thus probative should come in, unless a clear ground of policy or law excludes it" (p. 530). This is also the prevailing view today. "The distinct tendency of the Federal Rules of Evidence is to admit rather than exclude" (Weinstein and Berger 1976, pp. 105–10). The rationale is that anything which throws light on a controversy should be considered by the jury, subject to the judge's discretion to set reasonable bounds. The policy manifests a trust in the intelligence of the jury to reach a correct decision when all the facts are presented.

However, not all evidence can or should be admitted. The law of evidence consists primarily of exclusionary rules that determine admissibility. These rules, as we have indicated earlier, can be categorized into four sets: hearsay, relevancy, privilege, and opinion evidence rules. The principle that underlies this complex mosaic of exclusionary rules is evidentiary relevance. Only relevant evidence is admissible (FRE 402). Relevance refers to the probative value of evidence—whether there is a logical relationship between the evidence presented and the facts sought to be proven at the trial" (FRE 401).

The trial judge determines relevance according to a balancing test: "Although relevant, evidence may be excluded if its probative value is substantially outweighed by the danger of unfair prejudice, confusion of the issues, or misleading the jury, or by considerations of undue delay, waste of time, or needless presentation of cumulative evidence" (FRE 403). At his discretion, the judge weighs the probative value or relevance of the evidence against the probative dangers.

The notion of relevance needs to be distinguished from that of sufficiency. The two concepts reflect the division of labor between jury and judge. The jury decides the ultimate issue of the sufficiency or weight of the evidence—was enough evidence presented to satisfy the burden of persuasion? The judge decides the initial issue of relevance—does the particular evidence tend to establish or disprove the disputed factual matter for which it was offered? If it does not, the jury is not allowed to consider this evidence. If its relevance is disputable, judges usually let it in "for what it's worth" and let the jury decide.

The usual procedure at trial is for evidence offered by a party to be received unless it is objected to by the opponent. If the objection is grounded on nonrelevance, the judge applies the balancing test. If the objection is overruled and the evidence admitted, the opponent can make an exception to the judge's ruling and later use it—if he should lose at trial—as a basis for claiming error of law on appeal.

As a result of dealing with countless factual circumstances involving relevancy, the courts over the years have formulated rules that standardize and thereby dispense with ad hoc balancing of probative value against prejudice. When similar situations arise repeatedly and the same decision is rendered in each case, the decisions eventually become hardened into rules to guide future instances.

The "Other Crimes Evidence" Rule

A large group of exclusionary rules fall under the rubric of rules of relevancy. One such rule is the "other crimes evidence" rule: "Evidence of other crimes, wrongs, or acts is not admissible to prove the character of a person in order to show that he acted in conformity therewith" (FRE 404(b)). Thus, a defendant's past criminal record cannot be introduced in the prosecution's case-in-chief to show his likelihood of committing the crime charged. A number of policy reasons underlie this rule.

One reason is the fear that a jury might overestimate the predictive relationship between past criminality and present conduct. As a general proposition, there might be a relationship between these two factors, but it is hazardous to forecast propensity to crime in any particular instance. A second reason is the risk that a jury might be tempted to convict a defendant because he is an incorrigible offender, deserving of punishment. If a jury knows he is a "bad" person, it might not sympathize as much with him as with one without a record of past misdeeds, and therefore adjudge him by a lower standard of proof. Finally, there is the normative consideration, related to the presumption of innocence, that a defendant should be protected from inculpation by proof of former wrongdoings. It seems unfair to saddle a person forever with the record of the past, especially if one subsequently leads a blameless life.

As with nearly all legal rules, there are exceptions. One exception is to admit other crimes evidence for the limited purpose of impeaching defendant's credibility, if he chooses to take the stand (FRE 404(a)(3)). A defendant with a criminal record faces the dilemma of whether or not to testify. If he exercises his Fifth Amendment privilege, the jury will probably take into account his silence and draw adverse infer-ences from it, despite the fact that the prosecution and the judge are forbidden to comment on his silence and despite cautionary instructions by the judge to avoid drawing such inferences. Consequently, about 90% of defendants testify at trial (Note, *Columbia Journal of Law and Social Problems*, 1968, p. 222). However, if he waives his constitutional privilege, the prosecution is allowed to cross-examine the defendant and expose his prior record in order to impeach his trustworthiness. The risk to the defendant is that the jury, upon hearing the other crimes evidence, may use it for the unauthorized purpose of guilt determination. The judicial safeguard is the limiting instruction (FRE 105). If the defendant takes the stand, the court protects his interest not by excluding altogether the other crimes evidence, but by instructing the jury—upon request of the defendant—to consider it only for the authorized purpose. The instruction restricting the evidence to its proper scope represents a compromise between total exclusion of the evidence and its unfettered admission.

The other crimes evidence rule illustrates the accommodation of competing values in the trial process. As Louisell and Williams (1960) state, "Accurate fact-finding is an important, but not the only, ideal of the adjudicatory system in a liberty-loving society. . . . The persistence of the privilege against self-incrimination is a testimonial that, with us, there are values more pervading and controlling than efficiency in finding out the truth in litigation" (p. 413).

Effectiveness of Limiting Instructions

A fundamental premise of the limiting instruction would appear to be that jurors are able and willing to compartmentalize the evidence as directed. Common experience, however, suggests that this kind of mental process is less easily achieved than assumed. One of the paradoxes of evidence law is that instructions are given despite the recognition by the legal community itself of their possible futility.

Justice Jackson noted that "the naive assumption that prejudicial effects can be overcome by instructions to the jury . . . all practicing lawyers know to be unmitigated fiction" (*Krulewitch* v. *United States*, 1949, p. 453). Judge Learned Hand described it as a "mental gymnastic which is beyond not only their [the jury's] powers, but anybody's [sic] else" (*Nash* v. *United States*, 1932, p. 1007). Perhaps one of the strongest critics of limiting instructions was Judge Frank (1930):*

> These instructions are like exorcising phrases intended to drive out evil spirits; phrases once earnestly thought to be efficacious, now no longer believed in, yet an inextricable part of the conventionalized system of observances. Perhaps, too, the more unintelligible and technical instructions on the law may be considered as part of this mechanism of exorcism, resembling the 'tremendous words' from Hebrew and Greek, such as Schemhamphora or Tetragram-maton which the medieval exorcists employed to scare away the minions of Satan. [p. 184]

Social scientists have evaluated empirically the effectiveness of limiting instruc-tions. The following experiment puts to the test the validity of the foregoing criti-cisms.

---

*Reprinted by permission of the publisher. Copyright ©1930 by the Tudor Publishing Company.

SECTION 12 OF THE CANADA EVIDENCE ACT AND THE DELIBERATIONS OF SIMULATED JURIES

Valerie P. Hans and Anthony N. Doob

. . .

METHOD

EXPERIMENTAL DESIGN. The experiment was designed to assess the effects of a defendant's criminal record on both individual and group verdicts of his guilt. Presence or absence of the defendant's record and whether verdicts were made individually or in groups were varied orthogonally. There were 20 persons in each of the individual verdict conditions, and 15 groups comprised of four persons in each of the group verdict conditions.

SUBJECTS. Subjects were 160 men and women living in or visiting the Toronto area. Forty of these were undergraduate students at the University of Toronto who were paid for their participation in the experiment. The remaining 120 were visitors to the Ontario Science Centre in Toronto who volunteered for participation in the experiment. . . .

PROCEDURE. Subjects were randomly assigned to and participated in one of the four conditions of the experiment.

Subjects were told to imagine that they were jurors, sitting in court on jury duty. They were told that their task was to reach a verdict in the case before them. Each person then read a description of a hypothetical case about a man accused of burglary.

It described the court proceedings in the burglary case. A woman testified

that while she was at a party, her unoccupied home had been broken into. Approximately $200 had been stolen. As she arrived home, she caught a glimpse of the burglar fleeing through the back yard. She immediately reported the incident to the police. The police picked up a man in the vicinity who fitted her description and who had $200 in the glove compartment of his car. In a police line-up, this man was positively identified by the woman as the burglar. The girlfriend of the accused testified, however, that the accused was with her at the movies at the time of the break-in. The defendant took the stand and stated that the events of the evening in question were just as his girlfriend had testified.

At this point in the experiment, half of the subjects received an additional piece of information—that the accused had been previously convicted of burglary (Record condition). These subjects were also given the "judge's instructions" which are given whenever a defendant's record is made known to the jury. These instructions were as follows:

In the judge's instructions to the jury, the judge noted that, according to law, the accused person's prior criminal record should not be used to determine whether or not the defendant is guilty. Prior record should be used only to determine the credibility of the defendant, that is, whether he is to be believed as a witness.

After reading the case, either with or without the record information and judge's instructions, subjects either (a) made an individual decision about the defendant's guilt, or (b) engaged with three others in a simulated jury deliberation and reached a group verdict. The experimenter was not present during the group discussions and the case description was not available to subjects during the verdict-making process.

DATA ANALYSIS FOR THE JURY DELIBER-ATIONS. In order to determine the manner in which the defendant's record may have influenced discussions in the group deliberation of the case, tape recordings of the group discussions were made. The group deliberations were analyzed by first breaking down each discussion into codes representing different types of statement. Approximately 45 different classes of statements were coded in this manner. For example, statements about the strength of the evidence, probable guilt, the line-up, the alibi, the defendant's credibility and mention of other specific pieces of evidence were all assigned different codes. . . .

[As a check on the success of the record manipulation, the authors found that Record groups deliberated 1.4 times longer than No Record groups. Ed.'s note.]

RESULTS AND DISCUSSION

EFFECT OF RECORD ON VERDICTS. We predicted that there would be differences between the number of subjects deciding guilty verdict in the Record and No Record conditions. We thought that more persons reading a case who had information about the defendant's prior conviction would choose to convict the defendant than persons who did not have the record information. We also predicted that the presence of record would increase the percentage of guilty verdicts whether verdicts were made individually or in groups. The results . . . partially supported our predictions. The juries who had the record information were significantly more likely to convict the defendant than the juries without the record information ($p < .01$, Fischer exact test).* However, the presence of record did not seem to make much of a difference in the percentage of guilty verdicts when the verdicts were made individually. . . .†

CONTENT OF THE JURY DELIBERATIONS. Examination of the content of the deliberations for the Record and No Record groups indicated numerous ways in which the presence of record appeared to alter the deliberation process.

INITIAL STATEMENTS. Comparison of the initial statements (the first ten codes of each group discussion) made by members of Record and No Record groups revealed that members of Record groups were significantly more likely to make initially negative or damaging statements about the defendant's case, while members of No Record groups were more likely to make initially positive or favorable statements about the defendant's case. . . .

EVIDENCE. Differences between Record and No Record group discussions of the evidence in the case were striking. Although the identical case was given to Record and No Record groups, Record groups considered the evidence against the defendant to be stronger than did No Record groups. This trend manifested itself in two ways: First of all, Record groups were significantly more likely than No Record groups to state that the evidence against the defendant was strong. Furthermore, Record groups tended to bring up more frequently than No Record groups the facts in the case that were most damaging to the defendant. . . .

REASONABLE DOUBT. . . . Record groups discussed more often the standard by which they should decide the defendant's

---

*[Percentage of group guilty verdicts: 40% in Record condition, 0% in No Record condition; N = 15 groups/condition. From Table 1 of article. Ed.'s note.]

†[Percentage of individual guilty verdicts: 45% in Record condition, 40% in No Record condition; N = 20/ condition. From Table 1. Ed.'s note.]

guilt, although exactly how the issue was considered by Record and No Record groups cannot be determined from the frequency comparison data. . . .

SUMMARY AND CONCLUSIONS

The present research leaves little doubt that knowledge of a previous conviction biases a case against the defendant. The likelihood that a jury will convict the defendant is significantly higher if the defendant's record is made known to the jury. The fact that the defendant has a record permeates the entire discussion of the case, and appears to affect the juror's perception and interpretation of the evidence in the case. . . .

The data indicate that the case is biased against the Record defendant in ways which are contrary to the specifications of s. 12 of the Canada Evidence Act. This evident failure to follow instructions suggests that similar instructions of judges in actual court cases might well be futile.

NOTES AND QUESTIONS

1.   The authors found 40% guilty verdicts in the Record group that was given the limiting instruction, and no guilty verdicts at all in the No Record group. They concluded that the instruction was "futile." Is this conclusion wholly justified? Is Record vs. No Record the only comparison of interest? Furthermore, should one ignore the fact that the *majority* of the jury groups—60%, or eight out of fifteen groups—found the defendant *not* guilty?

2.   If prior record is introduced, defense counsel is not limited to requesting a limiting instruction or remaining silent and hoping that the jury will not notice it. He can discuss the prior record openly before the jury and seek to explain it or mitigate its impact. He can also describe to the jury the reasons for the instruction. Whether these actions have a greater cleansing effect than the mere presence or absence of judicial admonitions remains to be investigated.

3.   Sometimes the instructions are given at the time of the introduction of the evidence (as in the Hans and Doob study), sometimes at the end of the trial together with the final charge, and sometimes on both occasions. What effect would you expect the timing of the instructions to have on the jury's ability to limit the evidence to its rightful purpose?

4.   Another experiment on the effectiveness of limiting instructions was done by the British team of Cornish and Sealy (1973). The two studies merit comparison because they seem to arrive at opposite results. Cornish and Sealy claim that their mock juries "do take account of a judicial instruction to disregard similar convictions" (p. 222).
     Their procedure was as follows: Jurors listened to a lengthy tape recording of either a theft trial or a rape trial, both re-enacted from transcripts of actual proceedings. In the theft case, the defendant put his own good character in evidence, and this allowed the prosecution to impeach on cross-examination by introducing his previous convictions. In the rape case, the information about the prior record was slipped in accidentally by a codefendant. In both sets of cases, the variable of prior record was further manipulated by making it either similar or dissimilar to the present charge.
     At the end of the taped trial, the jurors were instructed as to the other crimes evidence and the burden of persuasion. Some subjects were instructed to disregard the prior conviction for the purpose of determining guilt; others received no instruction on this issue. After the instructions, individual juror verdicts were recorded. The percentages of individual guilty verdicts in the two trials for the four main groups (labeled X, Y, Z, and Co by the authors) are reproduced below.

	Cornish and Sealy individual verdicts for		**Hans and Doob** individual/group verdicts for
	rape	theft	robbery
(X) Similar prior record; no instruction	36%	57%	
(Y) Dissimilar prior record; no instruction	9%	33%	
(Z) Similar prior record; disregard instruction	29%	35%	45%/40%
(Co) Control: no prior record	29%	27%	40%/0%

(The rape trial involved two codefendants. The reproduced data are for verdicts on the codefendant named "Bryce.")

To facilitate comparison, the results of Hans and Doob are presented again adjacent to Cornish and Sealy's data. The "Record" treatment in the former study is equivalent to the Z group; the "No Record" treatment is like the Co group.

Cornish and Sealy compared groups X and Z and concluded that judicial instructions are effective—there are fewer convictions when jurors are told to disregard the evidence of prior convictions for the same charge. Hans and Doob, on the other hand, compared the equivalent of groups Z and Co and concluded that instructions are "futile." Can the interpretation of these two sets of data be reconciled?

5.   Limiting instructions come into play because legal relevance does not have an absolute quality. Evidence may be relevant for one purpose but not another, as exemplified by other crimes evidence. Evidence may also be relevant against one party but not another in a multiparty trial. This type of limited relevance was addressed by the Supreme Court in *Bruton* v. *United States* (1968).

In this case, two defendants (Evans and Bruton) were accused of the same crime of robbery. They were jointly tried for reasons of administrative efficiency. At the close of the prosecution's direct case, the trial judge cautioned the jury as follows: "A confession made outside of court by one defendant may not be considered as evidence against the other defendant, who was not present and in no way a party to the confession. Therefore, if you find that a confession was in fact voluntarily and intentionally made by the defendant Evans, you should consider it as evidence in the case against Evans, but you must not consider it, and should disregard it, in considering the evidence in the case against the defendant Bruton" (p. 125).

In an opinion by Justice Brennan, the Court reversed Bruton's conviction and held that "because of the substantial risk that the jury, despite instructions to the contrary, looked to the incriminating extrajudicial statements in determining petitioner's guilt, admission of Evans' confession in this joint trial violated petitioner's right of cross-examination secured by the Confrontation Clause of the Sixth Amendment" (p. 126). The Court "acknowledge[d] the impossibility of determining whether in fact the jury did or did not ignore Evans' statement . . . in determining petitioner's guilt." But "despite the concededly clear instructions to the jury," the introduction of Evans' confession posed such a "substantial threat" to Bruton that "The effect is the same as if there had been no instruction at all" (p. 137).

Evans' statement, insofar as Bruton was concerned, was hearsay. Hearsay evidence is secondhand evidence, "a story out of another man's mouth" (McCormick 1972, section 245). The admission of hearsay, subject to numerous exceptions, is generally prohibited for two interrelated reasons: a tale of a tale is deemed to be untrustworthy, unless there are special circumstances to indicate otherwise; and, the source of the tale is not on the witness stand and not under oath so that he cannot be confronted by the accused and his demeanor cannot be evaluated by the jury. Thus, the Court could have decided the case without reaching the constitutional question. The unsworn, out-of-court confession of Evans, who was unavailable for cross-examination because of his exercise of the Fifth Amendment privilege, was clearly inadmissible as hearsay. Instead, the Court invoked the Sixth Amendment and refused to accept the limiting instruction as an "adequate substitute" for Bruton's right of cross-examination (p. 137). The broader issue of whether the admission of other kinds of hearsay evidence violates the Confrontation Clause was left unanswered.

In reaching its decision, the Court relied on *Jackson* v. *Denno* (1964). Under the challenged New York procedure in that case, a jury first hears a confession to determine whether it is voluntary. If the jury decides it was freely given, it then evaluates the weight of the confession; if the jury decides it was coerced, the judge then instructs the jury to disregard it in determining guilt. The Supreme Court held that this procedure violated the Due Process Clause in presuming the jury's ability to disregard—as judicially instructed—a defendant's involuntary confession.

Justice Brennan in *Bruton* reasoned that a codefendant's confession that inculpates a nonconfessing defendant is more prejudicial in the eyes of the jury than a defendant's own confession. The former is harder to compartmentalize into permissible and impermissible purposes. Under the New York procedure, the jury is told to disregard the defendant's confession entirely if it is found to have been given involuntarily. In joint trials, the confession of the codefendant is never deleted from the case. The jury is told to consider it in determining the guilt of the codefendant and to ignore it in determining the guilt of the defendant. Justice White, dissenting in *Bruton*, argued the opposite: "There are good reasons . . . for distinguishing the codefendant's confession from that of the defendant himself and for trusting in the jury's ability to disregard the former when instructed to do so" (p. 139). A defendant's own admission of guilt "possesses greater reliability and evidentiary value than ordinary hearsay." Also, unsworn statements of a partner in crime have "traditionally been viewed with special suspicion" because of the partner's interest in exonerating himself (p. 141). Which view do you find more persuasive, and how would you design a study to test these rival assumptions?

6. There are alternatives to the limiting instruction in the *Bruton* situation. One is total exclusion of the codefendant's confession. This obviously disadvantages the prosecution, because it would not be able to use the confession even against the confessing codefendant. The state would agree to this option only if it felt it had enough other evidence to secure a conviction, aside from the confession.

A second option is severance of the defendants at trial. Separate trials are not favored by the prosecution and the courts because of the cost, delay, and inconvenience involved.

A third option that seems to be the most popular in the lower courts is the "edited confession," a compromise between the first two options. A codefendant's confession that implicates another nonconfessing defendant is admissible when references to the latter defendant are omitted or substituted by an "X" or "another person" in lieu of his name. This process is known as redaction. In the absence of empirical information on the efficacy of redaction, one can only surmise that when two defendants are on trial at the same time charged with the same offense, and there is other evidence in the case linking the codefendants in the commission of the offense, the jury is capable of guessing the identity of the anonymous nobody referred to in the confession. In light of *Bruton*, is redaction constitutional?

7. There is an apparent paradox in the law's attitude toward the impact of instructions. In some circumstances it presumes their futility; in others it assumes their effectiveness. The limiting instruction has been likened to a "judicial placebo" (*United States* v. *Grunewald*, 1956, p. 574). The analogy is apt because it implies that sometimes the pretended cure works and sometimes it does not. The question is whether there is a consistent pattern or principle underlying the seemingly conflicting judicial views on the jury's ability to heed instructions.

Why is a limiting instruction on other crimes evidence deemed effective, but a similar instruction limiting a codefendant's statement only to himself deemed per se ineffective?

Self-incriminating statements obtained in violation of *Miranda* warnings are inadmissible for proving guilt but are admissible for impeaching the defendant if he opts to testify (*Harris* v. *New York*, 1971). Why is a *Harris* jury deemed capable of confining the defendant's inculpatory statements to impeachment purposes, but a *Bruton* jury is deemed incapable of confining the codefendant's inculpatory statement to the codefendant and a *Jackson* jury is similarly incapable of disregarding the defendant's involuntary confession?

Some states have habitual criminal statutes which provide for stiffer penalties upon repeated convictions. In order to prove that a defendant is a habitual offender, the prosecution introduces at the start of the trial the record of his past convictions. The jury is instructed, of course, as to its limited relevance. The Supreme Court has sustained such statutes from due process attack. "To say that the United States Constitution is infringed simply because this type of evidence may be prejudicial and limiting instructions inadequate to vitiate prejudicial effects would make inroads into the entire complex code of state and evidentiary law, and would threaten other large areas of trial jurisprudence" (*Spencer* v. *Texas*, 1967, p. 562). Again, are there circumstances here that justify the assumption that the effect of instructions is or should be different from that in *Bruton* and *Jackson*?

8.   Do the results of the following study by Kassin and Wrightsman (1981) lend support to the *Jackson* Court's assumption about the effect of instructions? College students read a 22-page transcript of a prosecution for auto theft. The testimony indicated that the police stopped and arrested the defendant for speeding. (*Miranda* warnings were not included in this hypothetical case.) The confession was made at the scene to the officer (who later so testified at trial) under one of three circumstances: spontaneous confession of the theft; confession after promises of leniency; or confession after threats of punitive consequences. (Under the due process test, the communication to a suspect of possible leniency or harm could render a confession involuntary.) At the end of the transcript, the subjects read the standard instructions about burden of proof. In addition, some subjects were told to disregard the confession only if they believed it was involuntary, and other subjects were given no instructions about the confession. (The study included other experimental conditions which are not relevant here.) Individual (not collective) judgments of guilt were rendered. One half of the subjects found the defendant guilty. However, there was no difference in guilty decisions between those who were instructed and those who were not instructed, regardless of the circumstances (that is, the voluntariness) of the confession.

9.   In addition to joinder of defendants (as in *Bruton*), there can be joinder of charges against one defendant in a single trial (for example, a defendant is prosecuted for three bank robberies which occurred at different times and different places). Under Rule 8(a) of the Federal Rules of Criminal Procedure (FRCrP), the government may join several charges if they are of "the same or similar character or are based on the same act or . . . [constitute] parts of a common scheme or plan." There are obvious economies to joinder. But there is also the risk of compromising the right to a fair trial if joinder of defendants conveys the impression to the jury that "birds of a feather flock together," and if joinder of offenses tends to establish that "where there's smoke, there is fire." Therefore, the FRCrP, Rule 14, provides that "If it appears that a defendant or the government is prejudiced by a joinder of offenses or of defendants . . . , the court may order . . . separate trials . . . ." In ruling on a motion to sever, a trial court at its discretion weighs the possible prejudice to the defendant against the public interest in avoiding duplicating trials in which the same issues are relitigated. Reversal of convictions for failure to grant a severance motion is rare. In one such rare case, the defendant was charged with sixty-four counts of "homosexual sodomitic acts" in one indictment and with promoting prostitution and other sexual offenses in two other indictments. The appellate court held that joining the first indictment with the other two raised the possibility of improper conviction on the latter two indictments based upon assumptions of criminal propensity (*People* v. *Shapiro*, 1980).

Of the three grounds for joinder under Rule 8(a), is there any one ground which poses the greatest potential for prejudice with the least promise of judicial economy? Of the following sources of potential prejudice, described in *Drew* v. *United States* (1964), which ones are most likely to be found in each of the three grounds for joinder: (1) confusion in the presentation of separate defenses; (2) "the jury may use the evidence of one of the crimes charged to infer a criminal disposition . . . from which to find [defendant's] guilt of the other crime or crimes charged"; (3) "the jury may cumulate the evidence of the various crimes charged and find guilt when, if considered separately, it would not so find" (p. 88)?

10.   In lieu of severance, a trial court may seek to neutralize any potential bias by instructions. Evidence relevant to one charge may not be relevant to another charge, so the court can instruct the jury to consider the evidence for each charge separately. Several experimental studies have concluded that joinder of charges enhances the conviction rate and that judicial instructions are not significantly effective.

The experiment by Tanford and Penrod (1982) is representative of the genre. College undergraduates read summaries of a case in which the defendant was prosecuted on two charges of rape, one charge of sexual assault, and one charge of criminal trespass. Each offense occurred at different times and places and involved different victims. The evidence on any one charge was not directly related to the evidence on the other charges. Subjects assigned to the "joined trial condition" read summaries of two, three, or four offenses merged in a single trial. For example, in the joined trial of three offenses, the written summary presented all three indictments at the outset (as occurs in actual practice), followed by opening statements, direct and cross examinations, closing statements, and judicial instructions. At the end, the subjects rendered individual (not group) judgments of guilt on each of the charged offenses, all at the same time. Subjects assigned to the "sequential trials condition" read summaries of two, three, or four trials presented in sequence, each trial involving only one charge. For each trial, the procedure was the same as in the joined trial (that is, the summary began with the indictment and opening statements, and concluded with the instructions). However, these subjects rendered individual judgments of guilt at the end of each successive trial. As part of the general instructions, some of the subjects in the joined trial condition and in the sequential trials condition were also given the following judicial instruction: "Be sure to judge each case individually in making your decision—treat each offense as a separate crime" (p. 459). The total time for the experiment ranged from 30 minutes to one hour.

The results showed that in the joined trial, the proportion of guilty verdicts was consistently high regardless of the number of charges (two, three, or four) that were merged. In the sequential trials, the proportion of guilty verdicts increased as the number of trials (two, three, or four) increased. In practice, the comparison of interest is not between a joined trial and sequential trials, since the purpose of severance is to have separate trials by different juries. Therefore, in a second study, the authors replicated the initial study with some modifications, the principal one being the addition of a condition in which there is only one trial on one offense. (The nature of the offense—rape, sexual assault, trespass—was varied.) The results again showed the prejudicial effect of joinder: for each of the three categories of offenses, a joined trial produced a higher proportion of guilty verdicts than a single offense trial.

The judicial instructions did not significantly reduce the proportion of guilty verdicts, a finding confirmed in other studies (for example, Greene and Loftus 1981). The results also showed that in a joined trial, in contrast to a single offense trial, the subjects evaluated the defendant more negatively and these evaluations correlated positively with judgments of guilt. This finding suggests that joining offenses leads subjects to perceive the defendant as having a criminal predisposition. Moreover, in a joined trial, the subjects rated the evidence as more incriminating than that presented at a single offense trial. This result supports the notion that jurors might aggregate the evidence of the various crimes charged.

Do data from research such as the foregoing one justify the blanket indictment of joined trials as "institutionalized prejudice" (Greene and Loftus 1981)? In *Ashe* v. *Swenson* (1970), four masked men were charged with robbing six men who were playing poker. One defendant, Ashe, was charged with six separate robberies. Would it be in Ashe's interest to have six separate trials? Suppose that in the prosecution of a defendant on four separate charges, the government's evidence is strong on one of the charges but weak on the other three. Would the defendant want to insist on joinder in the hope that reasonable doubt on the weak charges will carry over to the strong charge? What are other possible conditions in which joinder may not be prejudicial to the defendant and may, indeed, even be advantageous? Re-examine the procedure of Tanford and Penrod's experiment. Are there features in the study that maximize the finding of a prejudicial effect? Can social research provide a calculus for determining whether or not the potential prejudice to a defendant is offset by the benefits of judicial economy?

Empirical and Normative Justifications of Instructions

The evaluation of judicial instructions cannot be made solely on empirical grounds—on whether or not they have an impact on the jury. Apart from the issue of effectiveness, there are policy considerations that argue for the use or nonuse of these instructions.

Instructions provide a basis for appeal and a means for doing substantive justice on review. The determination that an instruction was ineffective, or that one should have been given when it was not, provides a procedural peg on which an appellate court can hang a reversal. In theory, appellate tribunals do not reconsider the facts but only review issues of law. In actuality, cases are mostly won or lost at trial rather than on appeal. "The reason for this is that appellate judges in reviewing cases seek generally to ensure that justice was done below; they are less concerned with upholding the letter of the law. Consequently, except to some extent when constitutional values are implicated, appellate courts will rarely reverse trial courts for mistaken rulings of evidence law unless they have some reason to suspect the substantive justice of the trial result" (Lempert and Saltzburg 1982, p. 2). Appellate judges bend the procedural law in order to reach a fair result.

Thus, even if an appellate judge personally believes in the futility of instructions, he might still rule that the absence of an instruction at trial was reversible error so that the defendant can have another day in court. If on retrial the defendant is reconvicted despite instructions properly issued, then it could be said that a "correct" result has been reached.

Justice Jackson observed that evidence law appears "paradoxical and full of compromises" because it seeks to maintain a "balance between adverse interests" (*Michelson* v. *United States,* 1948, p. 486). Instructions can be seen as an attempt to balance competing interests in reliable fact-finding and social values extrinsic to the truth function of trial. Consider, for example, the instruction that limits the use of prior record. If the prosecution is allowed to introduce the prior record as part of its case-in-chief, there is the possibility of prejudicial impact on the jury. In addition, to hold a person accountable on the basis of his past misdeeds is inconsistent with our notions of fairness. However, we know that many offenders are recidivists and that, as an actuarial matter, there is a high correlation between past and present conduct. To the extent that accurate fact-finding is an important objective, evidence of prior crimes should be allowed as one of the pieces of information for the fact-finder to consider. In European civil law countries, other crimes evidence is admissible to show a defendant's bad character or propensity to commit the crime charged. Weinstein and Berger (1976) believe that the wholesale exclusion of prior record "would probably have as its principal consequence a lessening of the reliability of jury verdicts" (pp. 105–36).

What the law of evidence does, then, is to compromise between the extremes of unlimited admission and blanket exclusion. It strikes the balance between probative value and prejudice or unfairness by allowing the evidence for an intermediate purpose (to impeach credibility) but not the ultimate purpose (to establish guilt). The limiting instruction is a device by which the law lets the jury make the judgment. It can interject its notions of popular justice in the decision-making process. Under its power of nullification, it can bend the facts and thwart the law's commands in order to reach what it considers a right result.

As it turns out, the available data support the view that the limiting instructions helps to preserve the procedural equilibrium. The studies by Hans and Doob and by Cornish and Sealy, when put together, show that admitting evidence of prior record is indeed a *via media* between unlimited admission and blanket exclusion. Convictions are highest under unlimited admission, lowest under complete exclusion, and in between under limited admission. The question of the effectiveness of these instructions, then, depends on the comparisons that are made. Limiting instructions are effective (in the sense of reducing guilty verdicts) when compared with the admission of the evidence without any instructions. They are obviously not effective or less effective when compared with the exclusion of the evidence. And this, we suggest, is precisely the Solomonic compromise that the instructions were intended to effectuate.

Thus, there are two distinct yet related questions in the evaluation of judicial instructions. One is a factual question that is responsive to empirical research: Are the instructions effective? This has been the focus of our discussion so far. But it is apparent from the cases cited that the appellate courts have been raising another, normatively oriented question: Should the evidence have been excluded? The answer to this issue may furnish the response to the empirical question. If a court decides that the evidence should have been excluded, it would say that the instructions were ineffective. If it decides that no harm ensued from its admission, it would conclude that there is no basis for claiming that the instructions were not effective. Efficacy of instructions, then, is principally a judicial conclusion to rationalize the admission or exclusion of evidence made on normative grounds. This interpretation may explain the seemingly paradoxical attitude of the law toward these instructions, sometimes saying they are futile, sometimes saying they work, but never abandoning them altogether.

The decision as to whether the evidence should have been excluded or not at trial would seem to depend on the nature and extent of the harm caused by its admission. One could imagine a continuum of harm. At the one end, the admission of evidence would be deemed to constitute an irrebuttable presumption of harm because, despite its probative value, it would clearly prejudice the jury or would infringe upon a constitutionally protected right. Here, social values other than accurate fact-finding take precedence, and courts are likely to claim that instructions are in themselves ineffective.

At the opposite end, the harm is deemed to be *de minimis* and consequently the courts are unwilling to conclude that the instructions, under these conditions, are ineffective. If the admitted evidence implicates no constitutional values and it does not appear that a defendant has otherwise been harmed by it (for example, because there is overwhelming other evidence to support the conviction apart from the prejudicial evidence), appellate judges are likely to let the jury verdict stand.

Finally, there is the large, nebulous, middle zone of the continuum, and here is where the difficult decisions lie. Again, the challenged evidence implicates no specific constitutional provision but a general issue of fairness is raised. In reviewing whether the admission was proper, courts balance the probative value of the evidence and the state's interests in its admission, on the one hand, against the harm to the defendant from its prejudicial impact, on the other. Unless the balance tilts decisively one way or the other, courts are unlikely to disturb the jury's decision.

In this middle range the possibilities for empirical research are the greatest. The factual issue of efficacy of instructions comes to the fore when the answer is not foreclosed or determined a priori by legal policy considerations. If the critical evidence is not inherently inadmissible or irreparably prejudicial, the jury can consider it for what it is worth. The task is not simply to determine whether the instructions are effective but also the conditions which affect efficacy. The study of the determinants of the effectiveness of instructions is essentially an inquiry into the parameters of jury equity.

9.5. SUFFICIENCY OF EVIDENCE

The procedural and evidentiary rules that govern the trial process are intertwined. *How* proof is introduced at trial, namely, the gross order of presentation of evidence, is related to *how much* proof is needed to prevail. This section examines the sufficiency of the proffered evidence: Does it reach the threshold of proof required by law? The materials that follow discuss the standards of legal proof, focusing on the sufficiency of objective and subjective probabilistic evidence in criminal and civil adjudication. An analysis of efforts to rigorously quantify legal proof should lead to an appreciation of the costs and benefits of "trial by mathematics" and, more importantly, to insights into what the trial process is and ought to be.

Burden of Production and Burden of Persuasion

The burden of proof, though stated in the singular, entails two distinct and interrelated obligations: the burden of production and the burden of persuasion (Thayer 1898, chapter 9).

The first, known also as the burden of going forward with the evidence, is the responsibility of a party to produce enough evidence to satisfy a judge that the case is worthy of consideration by the jury. The judge scrutinizes first the proffered evidence to determine whether it provides at least minimal support for the allegations of the case, before it goes to the jury for its decision.

The burden is allocated initially to the party who pleads the existence of the disputed fact, normally the plaintiff or the prosecution. Its purpose is to ensure that juries are precluded from rendering verdicts in cases not grounded in evidence. It allows the judge rather than the jury to decide the case if the plaintiff or the prosecution fails to come forward with enough evidence to have a trial. When this responsibility is not successfully discharged, a judge can order a directed verdict in favor of the defense in a civil case, or achieve the same result in a criminal case by a dismissal of the charges against the defendant. When the responsibility is met, the burden of production shifts to the adversary to come forward with rebuttal evidence. During the course of the trial, this burden may shift back and forth between the parties.

Once enough evidence is produced, the second burden comes into operation. The party that shoulders the burden of persuasion must persuade the fact-finder that the evidence tendered reaches the required level of sufficiency.

In a civil case, the burden is allocated to the plaintiff, since it is the "accusing" party and the one who seeks to change the status quo. The main purpose of the burden is to prevent jury indecision or a "tie" verdict. If after evaluating all of the evidence the jury is in equipose, finding the evidence of both sides equally persuasive, there needs to be a rule that announces which side wins. "There are no ties or sudden death overtimes in litigation" (Winter 1971, p. 337). By allocating the burden of persuasion to the plaintiff, it is the plaintiff who loses if the jury finds the evidence split evenly in sufficiency. In this sense, the plaintiff bears the risk of nonpersuasion.

In a criminal case, the burden is placed on the prosecution. Whereas this burden disadvantages somewhat the plaintiff in a civil lawsuit, it disadvantages greatly the state in a criminal trial. The standard for the burden of persuasion in a criminal case ("beyond a reasonable doubt") is much higher than that in a civil case ("preponderance of the evidence"). By setting a high quantum of persuasion, the law deliberately ensures that any error in the verdict is unidirectional, against the state. The premise is that Type 1 errors (false positives) are less tolerable than Type 2 errors (false negatives). The policy of the law is that it is better to risk letting the guilty go free than to risk convicting the innocent.

However, the law does not go so far as to require absolute certainty in the correctness of the verdict. The threshold of proof required for conviction or liability falls short of unequivocal persuasion. In a criminal prosecution, the proof need not be beyond all doubt in order to secure a guilty verdict—only beyond a reasonable doubt. One reason for setting a less than perfect measure of persuasion is that, in a trial, a decision must be rendered within the limits of the evidence adduced and within some reasonable time frame. In scientific fact-finding, a researcher can defer reaching conclusions while he gathers more and more information that reaches the level of reliability generally accepted in the scientific community. In adjudication, however, to postpone a verdict until the evidentiary gaps are filled and all doubt is erased in the mind of the fact-finder is both impractical and undesirable. A final, authoritative judgment has to be rendered to settle the dispute, even if there is some uncertainty. The question is how much uncertainty or imperfection in proof is allowed at the time of the decision.

In other words, the law compromises the truth-finding function of trial. Reliability is one of the main values of procedural justice, but in practice something less than perfect reliability in fact-finding is tolerated. Otherwise, social disputes might never get settled by the adjudicative process. This compromise is articulated in the formulas for the standard of proof.

STANDARD OF PROOF IN CRIMINAL CASES

The highest standard of proof in law—"beyond a reasonable doubt"—is constitutionally required for criminal conviction (*In re Winship*, 1970). The explication of this standard to the jury has been a perennial concern. It is an old maxim that all definitions are dangerous, and definitions often need more explanation than the term explained. There have been literally hundreds of definitional attempts by the courts over the years. Some paint the lily in defining it: "It is that state of the case which, after the entire comparison and consideration of all the evidence, leaves the minds of jurors in that condition that they cannot say they feel an abiding conviction, to a moral certainty, of the truth of the charge" (*Commonwealth* v. *Webster*, 1850, p. 320). The Supreme Court described it as "utmost certainty" of guilt (*In re Winship*, 1970, p. 364). Since it is usually at the discretion of the trial judge whether to explain it to the jury, unless the jury expressly requests it, some state courts simply declare it "needs no definition" (*People* v. *Cagle*, 1969, p. 204) or that it "is almost incapable of any definition which will add much to what the words themselves imply" (*State* v. *Sauer*, 1888, p. 438).

What is clear is that this standard does not require absolute certitude for conviction. If it did, quite possibly there might be very few convictions, an endless round of hung juries, and hence a paralysis of the criminal justice process. It might also diminish the deterrent effect of the criminal law. The standard of reasonable doubt, then, can be seen as an attempt to balance the practical requirements of criminal justice administration, on the one hand, and the normative concern with minimizing the risks of wrongful convictions, on the other.

STANDARD OF PROOF IN CIVIL CASES

The deprivation of property by civil liability infringes upon a less protected interest than the loss of life or liberty by criminal sanction. Consequently, a lower question of proof is expected in civil cases: Proof "by a preponderance of the evidence," sometimes phrased in terms of "more likely than not"—proof that leads a fact-finder to find that the existence of the disputed fact is more likely than its nonexistence. Whereas the criminal standard is stated according to the amount of doubt in the mind of the fact-finder, the civil standard focuses on the likelihood of the evidence. This likelihood is said to correspond to a subjective certainty of more than .50. This decision rule, according to the Supreme Court, means that both sides "share the risk of error in roughly equal fashion" (*Addington* v. *Texas*, 1979, p. 423). In practice, jurors and judges appear to translate the standard into a higher probability estimate. Surveys by Simon and Mahan (1971) show that jurors interpret it as .75, and judges as .55.

The metaphysics of "preponderance" has been a subject of extensive judicial pondering. Some courts define it objectively as a determination of the balance of probabilities. The Washington Pattern Jury Instructions (Civil) states that "it means you must be persuaded, considering all the evidence in the case, that the proposition on which [the party] has the burden of proof is more probably true than not true" (21.01). This interpretation asks the jury to decide which side has the more probable evidence, and that is the side that will win. Other courts seem to define "preponderance" in terms of a higher threshold of proof by requiring the fact-finder to have an actual belief in or be convinced of the truth of the fact established by the preponderance of evidence. Thus, a verdict must be based on what the jury finds "to be facts rather than what they find to be 'more probable' " (*Lampe* v. *Franklin American*, 1936, p. 723). Finally, there are courts that deem the preponderance standard to be one of "common knowledge" and therefore in no need of explication (McCormick 1972, section 339).

QUANTIFICATION OF EVIDENCE AND OF STANDARDS OF PROOF

Proof involves drawing inferences from the evidence. Since no conclusion can be drawn from facts without some step of inductive inference, all factual evidence is ultimately statistical and all proof is ultimately probabilistic. Lawyers have long been inclined to quantify the probability notions that lie inchoate behind legal evidence and the formulas of proof. The lure of making fact-finding more objective and precise by attaching numerical values to qualitative information is hard to resist.

Quantification has typically consisted of informal, homespun statistics, presented at the summation stage of the trial. Courts give wide berth to hypothetical assumptions and rhetorical flourishes in the argumentation of counsel that would have been inadmissible had they been made during the case-in-chief. In one celebrated closing statement, a lawyer urged the jury to "take up your table of logarithms and figure away until you are blind, and such an accident could not happen in as many thousand, billion, trillion, quintillion years as you can express by figures" (McCormick 1972, section 204).

With the development of the calculus of probability and its widespread use, there began more formal efforts to quantify the probative force of particular evidence and the measure of persuasion itself. At trial, the probability evidence is introduced by an expert witness, either as part of his testimony explaining how he arrived at his conclusions or as a lecture to the jury so that they may apply it in their deliberation. Both raise questions of relevance and admissibility. The following case is one of the first to deal explicitly with the application of probability theory to criminal proof.

Using Objective Probability Estimates at Trial

PEOPLE v. COLLINS

66 Cal. Rptr. 497 (1968)

SULLIVAN, Justice.

We deal here with the novel question whether evidence of mathematical probability has been properly introduced and used by the prosecution in a criminal case. While we discern no inherent incompatibility between the disciplines of law and mathematics and intend no general disapproval or disparagement of the latter as an auxiliary in the fact-finding processes of the former, we cannot uphold the technique employed in the instant case. . . .

A jury found defendant Malcolm Ricardo Collins and his wife defendant Janet Louise Collins guilty of second degree robbery. Malcolm appeals from the judgment of conviction. Janet has not appealed.

On June 18, 1964, about 11:30 A.M. Mrs. Juanita Brooks, who had been shopping, was walking home along an alley in the San Pedro area of the City of Los Angeles. She was pulling behind her a wicker basket carryall containing groceries and had her purse on top of the packages. She was using a cane. As she stooped down to pick up an empty carton, she was suddenly pushed to the ground by a person whom she neither saw nor heard approach. She was stunned by the fall and felt some pain. She managed to look up and saw a young woman running from the scene. According to Mrs. Brooks the latter appeared to weigh about 145 pounds, was wearing "something dark," and had hair "between a dark blond and a light blond," but lighter than the color of defendant Janet Collins' hair as it appeared at trial. Immediately after the incident, Mrs. Brooks discovered that her purse, containing between $35 and $40, was missing.

About the same time as the robbery,

John Bass, who lived on the street at the end of the alley, was in front of his house watering his lawn. His attention was attracted by "a lot of crying and screaming" coming from the alley. As he looked in that direction, he saw a woman run out of the alley and enter a yellow automobile parked across the street from him. He was unable to give the make of the car. The car started off immediately and pulled wide around another parked vehicle so that in the narrow street it passed within six feet of Bass. The latter then saw that it was being driven by a male Negro, wearing a mustache and beard. At the trial Bass identified defendant [Malcolm] as the driver of the yellow automobile. . . .

On the day of the robbery, Janet was employed as a housemaid in San Pedro. Her employer testified that she had arrived for work at 8:50 A.M. and that defendant had picked her up in a light yellow car about 11:30 A.M. On that day, according to the witness, Janet was wearing her hair in a blond ponytail but lighter in color than it appeared at trial.

There was evidence from which it could be inferred that defendants had ample time to drive from Janet's place of employment and participate in the robbery. Defendants testified, however, that they went directly from her employer's house to the home of friends, where they remained for several hours. . . .

At the seven-day trial the prosecution experienced some difficulty in establishing the identities of the perpetrators of the crime. The victim could not identify Janet and had never seen defendant. The identification by the witness Bass . . . was incomplete as to Janet. . . .

In an apparent attempt to bolster the identifications, the prosecutor called an instructor of mathematics at a state college. Through this witness he sought to establish that, assuming the robbery was committed by a Caucasian woman with a blond ponytail who left the scene accompanied by a Negro with a beard and mustache, there was an overwhelming probability that the crime was committed by any couple answering such distinctive characteristics. The witness testified, in substance, to the "product rule," which states that the probability of the joint occurrence of a number of *mutually independent* events is equal to the product of the individual probabilities that each of the events will occur. *Without presenting any statistical evidence whatsoever in support of the probabilities for the factors selected,* the prosecutor then proceeded to have the witness *assume* probability factors for the various characteristics which he deemed to be shared by the guilty couple and all other couples answering to such distinctive characteristics.[10]

Applying the product rule to his own factors the prosecutor arrived at a probability that there was but one chance in 12 million that any couple possessed the distinctive characteristics of the defendants. Accordingly, under this theory, it was to be inferred that there could be but one chance in 12 million that defendants were innocent and that another equally distinctive couple actually committed the robbery. . . .

[T]he specific technique presented through the mathematician's testimony and advanced by the prosecutor to measure the probabilities in question suffered from two basic and pervasive defects—an inadequate evidentiary foundation and an inadequate proof of statistical independence. First, as to the foundation requirement, . . . the prosecution produced no evidence whatsoever showing, or from which it could be in any way inferred, that only one out of every ten cars which might have been at the scene of the robbery was partly yellow, that only one out of every four men who might have been there wore a mustache, that only one out of every ten girls who might have been there wore a ponytail, or that any of the other individual probability factors listed were even roughly accurate. . . .

But, as we have indicated, here was another glaring defect in the prosecution's technique, namely an inadequate proof of the statistical independence of the six factors. . . . To the extent that the traits or characteristics were not mutually independent (e.g., Negroes with beards and men with mustaches obviously represent overlapping categories), the "product rule" would inevitably yield a wholly erroneous and exaggerated result even if all of the individual components had been determined with precision.

In the instant case, therefore, because of the aforementioned two defects—the inadequate evidentiary foundation and the inadequate proof of statistical independence—the technique employed by the prosecutor could only lead to wild conjecture without demonstrated relevancy to the issues presented. It acquired no redeeming quality from the prosecutor's statement that it was being used only "for illustrative purposes" since, as we shall point out, the prosecutor's subsequent utilization of the mathematical testimony was not confined within such limits.

We now turn to the second fundamental error caused by the probability testimony. . . .

The prosecution's approach . . . could furnish the jury with absolutely no guidance on the crucial issue: *Of the admittedly few such couples, which one, if any, was*

---

[10] . . . The prosecutor . . . proposed the individual probabilities set out in the table below. . . .

Characteristic	Individual Probability
A. Partly yellow automobile	1/10
B. Man with mustache	1/4
C. Girl with ponytail	1/10
D. Girl with blond hair	1/3
E. Negro man with beard	1/10
F. Interracial couple in car	1/1000

guilty of committing this robbery? Probability theory necessarily remains silent on that question, since no mathematical equation can prove beyond a reasonable doubt (1) that the guilty couple *in fact* possessed the characteristics described by the People's witnesses, or even (2) that only *one* couple possessing those distinctive characteristics could be found in the entire Los Angeles area.

As to the first inherent failing we observe that the prosecution's theory of probability rested on the assumption that the witnesses called by the People had conclusively established that the guilty couple possessed the precise characteristics relied upon by the prosecution. But no mathematical formula could ever establish beyond a reasonable doubt that the prosecution's witnesses correctly observed and accurately described the distinctive features which were employed to link defendants to the crime. Conceivably, for example, the guilty couple might have included a light-skinned Negress with bleached hair rather than a Caucasian blond. . . .

Confronted with an equation which purports to yield a numerical index of probable guilt, few juries could resist the temptation to accord disproportionate weight to that index; only an exceptional juror, and indeed only a defense attorney schooled in mathematics, could successfully keep in mind the fact that the probability computed by the prosecution can represent, *at best,* the likelihood that a random couple would share the characteristics testified to by the People's witnesses—*not necessarily the characteristics of the actually guilty couple.*

As to the second inherent failing in the prosecution's approach, even assuming that the first failing could be discounted, the most a mathematical computation could *ever* yield would be a measure of the probability that a random couple would possess the distinctive features in ques-

tion. . . . Even accepting this conclusion [of one in 12 million] as arithmetically accurate, however, one still could not conclude that the Collinses were probably *the* guilty couple. On the contrary, as we explain in the Appendix, the prosecution's figures actually imply a likelihood of over 40 percent that the Collinses could be "duplicated" by at least *one other couple who might equally have committed the San Pedro robbery.* . . .*

[T]he prosecutor told the jurors that the traditional idea of proof beyond a reasonable doubt represented "the most hackneyed, stereotyped, trite, misunderstood concept in criminal law." He sought to reconcile the jury to the risk that, under his "new math" approach to criminal jurisprudence, "on some rare occasion . . . an innocent person may be convicted." "Without taking that risk," the prosecution continued, "life would be intolerable . . . because . . . there would be immunity for the Collinses, for people who chose not to be employed to go and push old ladies down and take their money and be immune because how could we ever be sure they are the ones who did it?"

In essence this argument of the prosecutor was calculated to persuade the jury to convict defendants whether or not they were convinced of their guilt to a moral certainty and beyond a reasonable doubt. Undoubtedly the jurors were unduly impressed by the mystique of the

---

*[Using the prosecution's figures, the court's analysis in a lengthy Appendix showed that as the total number of all couples who conceivably might have been in the area of the robbery approaches 12 million (concededly a "not determinable" figure), the probability of another couple as distinctive as the Collinses rises to 41%. "Thus the prosecution's computations, far from establishing beyond a reasonable doubt that the Collinses were the couple described by the prosecution's witnesses, imply a very substantial likelihood that the area contained *more than one* such couple. . . ." In other words, the statistics showed—at best—that the Collinses belonged to a category of couples with the inculpating characteristics, not that they were, in fact, the guilty couple. Ed.'s note.]

mathematical demonstration but were unable to assess its relevancy or value. Although we make no appraisal of the proper applications of mathematical techniques in the proof of facts . . . , we have strong feelings that such applications, particularly in a criminal case, must be critically examined in view of the substantial unfairness to a defendant which may result from ill conceived techniques with which the trier of fact is not technically equipped to cope. . . . We feel that the technique employed in the case before us falls into the latter category.

We conclude that the court erred in admitting over defendant's objection the evidence pertaining to the mathematical theory of probability and in denying defendant's motion to strike such evidence. . . . [W]e think that under the circumstances the "trial by mathematics" so distorted the role of the jury and so disadvantaged counsel for the defense, as to constitute in itself a miscarriage of justice. . . . The judgment against defendant must therefore be reversed. . . .

NOTES AND QUESTIONS

---

1.   The *Collins* case: The court said that there was no proof of the independence of the characteristics assumed in the product rule. However, Fairley and Mosteller (1974) have suggested an interpretation that presents a more favorable argument for the prosecution. An assumption of dependent characteristics is more reasonable than one of independence. Hence, the prosecutor could have employed a product rule for dependent events: If $P(F)$ is the probability of characteristic F occurring, and $P(E|F)$ is the probability that characteristic E occurs given that F occurs, then the probability of both E and F occurring is given by the product: $P(F \text{ and } E) = P(F)[P(E|F)]$.

Working backward from the table in footnote 10 of the opinion, the frequency of interracial couples who drive cars is 1 in 1,000; among interracial couples who drive, 1 in 10 include a black with a beard; and so on. Each individual probability is interpreted as a conditional probability, given the preceding characteristics. The product of these conditional probabilities gives the probability of the joint occurrence of these characteristics.

A second ground for exclusion was the absence of evidentiary foundation to support the probability estimates. The prosecution could have conducted a survey of the relevant population to determine the proportion of women with blond ponytails, the proportion of yellow cars, and so on. Fairley and Mosteller (1974) point out that the dependence problem could have been handled by examining pairs and triples of characteristics in the sample. For example, out of a sample of 1,000 cars at a given time, one could compute how many have three of the critical characteristics (blond ponytail, yellow, black with mustache). One can then define a range of possible probabilities for the occurrence of these three characteristics in that sample.

2.   For discussion purposes here, assume that the court's objections had been overcome at trial—that there was an evidentiary foundation, that the product rule was properly applied, and that there was only one couple in the jurisdiction that had these magical characteristics. The question, then, is whether probabilistic proof of the kind introduced would be admissible to establish the identity of the perpetrator. Other courts have consistently skirted this issue and have relied on evidentiary grounds to reject the probabilistic proof. The New Mexico Supreme Court, for instance, held that "mathematical odds are not admissible as evidence to identify a defendant in a criminal proceeding so long as the odds are based on estimates, the validity of which have not been demonstrated" (*State* v. *Sneed*, 1966, p. 802).

Put another way, should probabilistic proof of the identity of the criminal defendant be admitted since it is simply another form of expert proof, subject to the usual safeguards of cross-examination and opportunity to rebut with the defense's own (or state-appointed) statistical expert? Should it be admissible if, in addition, the safeguard of cautionary jury instructions regarding statistics was included?

3. The courts have sometimes upheld probabilistic proof of individual events, but more frequently they have ruled it improper (Tribe 1971; Kaye 1982, p. 488). What is needed is a delineation of when and why statistical proof is admissible or not for a given evidentiary purpose. For a broader analysis of the proper role of statistics as an auxiliary to legal fact-finding, we will examine three other cases and then compare them with *Collins*.

4. The heroin case: *Turner v. United States* (1970). A federal statute prohibited the knowing possession of illegally imported heroin. The defendant was arrested for possessing heroin, but to secure a conviction under this statute, the prosecution also had to prove that defendant knew it was illegally imported. To facilitate the obviously difficult task of proving a person's state of mind, Congress created a statutory presumption that permitted, but did not require, a jury to find from the proven fact of heroin possession the presumed fact of knowledge of illegal importation.

The Supreme Court affirmed the conviction and ruled the presumption to be constitutional. The Court reviewed legislative records establishing the presumption that showed overwhelming evidence that 98% of all the heroin in this country was illegally imported. "To possess heroin is to possess imported heroin," since "little if any heroin is made in the United States"; thus, "Turner doubtless knew that the heroin he had [275 bags] came from abroad" (p. 410). This presumption comported with due process because there was a rational connection—established beyond a reasonable doubt by the 98% figure—between the proven fact and the presumed fact.

A word, here, on the concept of presumption. A presumption is an evidentiary rule established by statute or case law to aid the party with the burden of proof by permitting a jury to infer the existence of an ultimate or presumed fact Y from proof of some other fact X. Presumptions give the effect of law to normal inferences that people would draw from a given fact (for example, heroin possession; ten-year disappearance of a person), in the absence of direct proof of the ultimate fact (for example, knowledge of illegal importation; the person is dead). The effect of a presumption in a criminal case is to create a permissible inference for the jury. It enables the prosecution to take an otherwise weak case to the jury. The jury, of course, is not required to accept the inference of Y, and the defendant is not obligated to rebut it.

There are numerous presumptions in criminal and civil law. They serve to rectify an imbalance resulting from one side's superior access to proof. They also represent estimates of probability, based on experience, that proof of X renders inference of the existence of Y sufficiently probable that the sensible and time-saving thing to do is to assume the truth of Y, unless the jury decides otherwise.

5. The bus case: *Smith v. Rapid Transit, Inc.* (1945). Plaintiff was driving on Main Street of a small city at 1 A.M. when she observed a blue bus—later described only as a "great big, long, wide affair"—coming toward her. She had to swerve to the right and collided with a parked car. In a suit against the defendant bus company for personal injuries sustained by the allegedly negligent operation of the blue bus, the plaintiff's only proof that this bus belonged to the defendant was that four-fifths of all blue buses in the city were owned and operated by Rapid Transit, Inc. The defendant had the sole franchise for operating a bus line on Main Street. In affirming a directed verdict for the defendant, the Supreme Judicial Court of Massachusetts said: "The most that can be said of the evidence in the instant case is that perhaps the mathematical chances somewhat favor the proposition that a bus of the defendant caused the accident. This was not enough" (p. 470).

The court did not say *how* much more or *what* more is "enough" to establish liability for damages. Does the quoted statement mean that a higher margin of probabilistic proof is needed? Or does it mean that additional, nonprobabilistic, particularized proof is required to show that the negligent bus belonged to the defendant? This is the problem of "naked statistical evidence" (Kaye 1980, p. 601): Is statistical proof alone sufficient to warrant a finding for its proponent or, at least, to shift the burden of production to the opponent? In the absence of individualized proof of identity, the presentation of generalized proof based upon statistical odds serves, in effect, to articulate the preponderance standard in starkly numerical terms.

6. The falling barrel case: *Byrne v. Boadle* (1863). A barrel of flour fell out of a window of a warehouse onto the head of a passing pedestrian. The hapless plaintiff, to recover, had to prove that some negligent act of omission by the defendant warehouse caused the fall. Chief Baron Pollock wrote: "There are certain cases of which it may be said *res ipsa loquitur*. . . . (T)he mere fact of an accident's having occurred is evidence of negligence . . ." (p. 300). This Latinism ("the thing speaks for itself") expresses a rule of circumstantial evidence in tort law that enables a plaintiff to satisfy the burden of production by proving that he has been injured by an event of a sort that normally would not have occurred but for negligence. It permits but does not compel a jury inference of defendant's fault from the circumstances of an unusual accident. This doctrine is not a true presumption because it does not result in a directed verdict for the plaintiff if the defendant fails to rebut the inference. As a practical matter, it may produce the same result as a presumption in that it allows the plaintiff to take the case to the jury, which may then find for the plaintiff.

If warehouse barrels are within the control of the defendant, and it is within common knowledge and experience that such barrel fallings do not occur unless there is fault, the case can go to the jury. Suppose, however, that it cannot be said that it is within common knowledge that such unexplained accidents are due to negligence. Should plaintiff be allowed to introduce statistical evidence showing that four-fifths of all falling barrels from warehouse windows are the result of negligent acts?

In the bus case, the fact that 80% of blue buses belonged to the defendant was not sufficient to impose liability. In this instance, is reliable proof that 80% of barrel fallings result from negligence also not enough to impose liability?

7.   The foregoing cases capture some of the issues in probabilistic proof of individual instances. In the two criminal cases, the courts ruled the attempts at quantification to be improper in *Collins* and proper in the heroin case. In the two civil cases, the proof was excluded in the bus case and admissible in the falling barrel case. Instead of focusing on a case-by-case analysis of details to determine admissibility, we need to seek the general principles that courts appear to be using implicitly in passing on such proof. Four overlapping questions can help guide the inquiry (Loh 1979, pp. 25–28). They do not identify the only ways of mapping the field, but they provide a starting point for sketching a broader analysis of the proper role of statistics in legal fact-finding.

The first question is the general purpose for which statistical proof is introduced: Is it used as an aid to rule-making to design procedural or evidentiary rules of law by which lawsuits are generally conducted, or is it used as an aid to fact-finding to resolve conflicting claims of a particular adjudication? For which of these two general purposes was probabilistic proof used in each of the four cases?

The second question concerns the particular purpose for which the proof is introduced: Is it used to determine the occurrence of an event or a party's state of knowledge, on the one hand, or to establish the identity of a party, on the other? Why are courts more reluctant to use probability evidence for proof of who did it (whose bus ran over defendant's car?) than for showing what happened (did the barrel fall because of negligence?)? Why is the use of the 98% probability estimate for raising an inference about defendant's knowledge of illegal importation less objectionable than the probability estimate of one in twelve million figure to identify the magical couple? Are the courts justified in accepting the application of probability theory to prove discriminatory intent and/or impact in the selection of jury venires and in the hiring of employees (see Chapter 7, section 7.3), but not in the *Collins* case and in the bus case?

The third question concerns the source that evaluates the statistical proof: Is it presented to aid the jury or a rule-making body such as a legislature or an appellate court? The concern that lay fact-finders might be swayed by the overbearing impressiveness of figures such as one in twelve million, thereby eclipsing the weight of seemingly less dramatic, conventional evidence, is understandable. But legislators and appellate judges, untutored in probability theory, are not necessarily immune to influence by numbers.

Quantification of the probative value of evidence invites, directly or indirectly, quantification of the standard of proof. The final question is: Do the social costs of articulating in numerical form the risk of an erroneous verdict (Type 1 error) outweigh the benefits?

Legal scholars (Tribe 1971; Brilmayer and Kornhauser 1978; Nesson 1979) and philosophers of science (Cohen 1977) have objected "to constru[ing] Anglo-American standards of judicial proof in terms of mathematical probabilities" (Cohen 1977, p. 116). They say there is something special about adjudicatory proof that makes probability theory inapposite. Tribe argues that the appearance of precision which numbers import may undermine the expressive purposes of trial. The Supreme Court said, "It is critical that the moral force of the criminal law not be diluted by a standard of proof that leaves people in doubt whether innocent men are being condemned" (*In re Winship*, 1970, p. 364). Beyond a reasonable doubt implies a subjective state of certitude. To permit the state to adjudge guilt without that requisite certainty would undercut public confidence in the criminal law. Declaring in advance the acceptable rate of false positives dehumanizes justice and diminishes respect for the individual. "[T]here is something intrinsically immoral," says Tribe, in telling oneself " 'I believe there is a chance of one in twenty that this defendant is innocent, but a 1/20 risk of sacrificing him erroneously is one I am willing to run in the interest of the public's—and my own—safety' " (p. 1372). There is an ethical difference between unintended and officially tolerated wrongful convictions. In short, it may be the better part of wisdom to leave some matters unspoken.

Nesson (1979) has pointed out another value in obscurity. The perceived legitimacy of adjudication depends in part on its authoritative finality. There needs to be closure in the settlement of disputes. Trial by ordeal may not have produced accurate results, but because of its Judgment Day quality, the outcome was respected by the medieval populace. Authoritative resolution, Nesson argues, may be more important than the ascertainment of truth, especially when the facts are uncertain (p. 1194). So long as the standard of proof is left ambiguous, the public can assume that it shares with the jury—which is supposedly representative of the community—common conceptions of the quantum of evidence needed to impose blame and punishment. The secrecy that surrounds jury deliberations fosters this assumption. Once the standard is quantified, others can question the verdict if they have a higher or lower subjective threshold of proof, and the finality of adjudication is gone. Thus, "any conceptualization of reasonable doubt in probabilistic form is inconsistent with the functional role that the concept is designed to play" (p. 1225).

8.   Some mathematically sophisticated legal scholars (Finkelstein 1978; Kaye 1979) and social scientists (Saks and Kidd 1980–81) disagree that the laws of probability should be suspended in the courtroom. While acknowledging that a trial serves the aforementioned symbolic purposes, they suggest that statistical decision theory has a rightful role in aiding the jury's evaluation of probabilistic identification evidence. Their proposal to use Bayesian-computed probabilities to decide the relevance of evidence proffered at trial is described in the next section. The opposing contentions in this debate engage thought on the nature and purposes of trial.

Using Subjective Probability Estimates at Trial

OBJECTIVE AND SUBJECTIVE PROBABILITY

There are two main schools of thought on the meaning of "probability." The classical school, originating with R. A. Fisher, E. Pearson, and others, operationalizes the concept in terms of the relative frequency of an event. If one tosses a fair coin N times and X heads occur, the relative frequency of heads is X/N. Over repeated tosses, the relative frequency is expressed as the probability of obtaining heads, or .50. Classical statistical theory is useful for estimating the likelihood of repeatable, random events based upon sample data. This objective or relative frequency approach coincides with the lay conception of probability.

The subjectivist or personalist school views probability as a measure of personal uncertainty regarding the likelihood of a unique event. It seeks to quantify the degree of belief a person holds about the occurrence of an event. Subjective or intuitive probability is defined in terms of the odds a person would accept on a bet as to the truth of a proposition. For example, a trial is a unique event. The results of a trial, unlike the outcomes of a coin toss, are not equally likely, mutually exclusive, and endlessly repetitive events. It is meaningless to speak of the probability of a defendant's guilt or liability in the sense of relative frequency. To say that the odds are .75 that a defendant is culpable is to imply that he was tried N times and that in three-fourths of the trials the verdict went against him. Thus, a concept of probability that reveals something about the observer rather than the observed event is more suitable for modeling the decision-making of jurors.

This subjectivist approach is associated with Bayesian statistics, named after the eighteenth-century English clergyman Thomas Bayes, who derived its basic theorem. Bayes' Theorem is an accepted mathematical technique for calculating the impact of (objective) probabilistic information on initial (subjective) probability estimates. Based upon the computation of conditional probabilities (that is, the probability of one event given the probability of another event), it describes how subsequent statistical evidence alters existing degrees of belief. It is used to aid decision-making in economics, business, medicine, and psychology, and, according to its advocates, it should also be used in trial adjudication.

BAYES' THEOREM

In its simplest form, Bayes' Theorem states the following relationship between two events, A and B:

$$P(A/B) = \frac{P(A)P(B/A)}{P(A)P(B/A) + P(\text{not-}A)P(B/\text{not-}A)}.$$

$P(A)$ is the probability of occurrence of A and $P(\text{not-}A)$ is the probability of nonoccurrence of A. $P(A/B)$ is the probability of occurrence of A given the probability of occurrence of B. $P(B/A)$ is the conditional probability of B given A, and $P(B/\text{not-}A)$ is the conditional probability of B given the probability of nonoccurrence of A. The derivation of this formula from axioms of probability theory is available in any standard statistics text. We shall limit our exposition to two illustrations of the practical applications of the formula, one pertaining to school admissions and the other to trial evidence.

APPLICATION OF THE THEOREM TO SCHOOL ADMISSIONS

Since Bayes' Theorem calculates conditional probabilities, it is used in prediction and selection tasks where initial probabilities are known and new statistical information is taken into account. Suppose that records at a college show that 70% of its students graduate. Among those who graduated, 80% scored above 650 on the college boards; among those who failed or dropped out, only 30% scored above 650. The college decides to raise the minimum test score for admission to 650. What is the probability that an applicant with a score of 650 or higher will graduate? We want to calculate the impact of new information on test scores on the existing information on graduation rates.

Let A = graduation and B = score of 650 or higher. We know from experience that $P(A) = .70$, so $P(\text{not-}A) = .30$. $P(B/A)$ is the probability of a score above the cut-off, given that the student graduated, or .80. $P(B/\text{not-}A)$ is the probability of a score above the cut-off, given that the student did not graduate, or .30. Inserting these values into the formula shows that

$$P(A/B) = \frac{(.70)(.80)}{(.70)(.80) + (.30)(.30)} = \frac{.56}{.56 + .09} = .86.$$

The probability of graduating given a test score at or above 650 (.86) is greater than the probability in general of graduating (.70). The formula reveals how much the odds of graduation are increased when the admission standard is raised to 650, given the prior graduation rate.

APPLICATION OF THE THEOREM TO IDENTIFICATION EVIDENCE

Bayesian statistics can describe how probabilistic evidence would influence a rational juror's evaluation of the odds of a defendant's culpability, provided there is other evidence linking the defendant to the case. Finkelstein and Fairley (1970) demonstrated its application with the following example:

> [A] woman's body is found in a ditch in an urban area. There is evidence that the deceased had a violent quarrel with her boyfriend the night before. He is known to have struck her on other occasions. Investigators find the murder weapon, a knife which has on the handle a latent palm print similar to defendant's print. The information in the print is limited so that an expert can say only that such prints appear in no more than one case in a thousand. [p. 496]

Under the relative frequency approach to probability, the 1/1000 statistic is not very meaningful. Following the reasoning of the *Collins* court, it does not measure the likelihood of defendant's guilt. The expert's quantification of the print's rarity may tempt jurors to give it disproportionate weight. Opponents of "trial by mathematics" would urge exclusion of the statistical evidence because "the seeming inexorability of numbers" would dwarf the soft, nonquantified evidence and mislead the jury (Tribe 1971, p. 356). If admitted, they would insist that the judge caution the jury that there might be other persons with similar prints, in order to avoid "find[ing] guilt by categories" (Nesson 1979, p. 1225). The question is how to inform the jury of the probative value of the unusual print without conveying a deceptive precision.

Finkelstein and Fairley's answer (1970) is to educate jurors in Bayesian calculations. The total probative value of the evidence is assessed in two steps. First, the trier evaluates the qualitative evidence (violent quarrel, prior assaults) and arrives, introspectively, at an initial probability of defendant's guilt, or $P(A)$. Assume that the trier is unconvinced up to this point that defendant is the murderer. If he were asked to quantify his subjective estimate of guilt, he might say, for example, .10. This figure can be interpreted, according to Finkelstein and Fairley, as a relative frequency of guilt over many similar cases. It can be characterized as an estimate of the proportion of cases in which a defendant, given the foregoing pattern of qualitative evidence, was, in fact, guilty. In a large number of trials with the same facts, $P(A) = .10$ means that an acquittal verdict would be correct 9 times out of 10. This is only an approximation of the true probability of guilt, since there is no independent measure of relative frequency. Therefore, some argue that "subjective probabilities cannot be given a standard frequency interpretation" (Brilmayer and Kornhauser 1978, p. 140). Others defend Finkelstein and Fairley's approach (Kaye 1979, p. 52). For present purposes, in order to present the mathematical approach to adjudication in its strongest light, we shall assume that a trier's intuitive estimates conform to the axioms of classical probability theory.

In the second step, the trier combines the (objective) probability of the palm print ($P(B) = .001$) with the prior (subjective) probability of guilt ($P(A) = .10$) according to Bayes' formula. The initial probability of not guilty is $P(\text{not-}A) = 1$-

$P(A) = .90$. The probability that the print belongs to defendant given that he is guilty is $P(B/A) = 1$. That is, if defendant is the murderer, the prints will match. The probability that the print belongs to defendant given that he is not guilty is $P(B/\text{not-}A) = .001$. There is a 1/1000 chance that a randomly chosen person from the population will have prints that match those of the murderer. Hence, the subsequent probability of guilt given the print information is

$$P(A/B) = \frac{(.10)(1)}{(.10)(1) + (.90)(.001)} = .991.$$

The equation shows how a juror's initial low estimate of defendant's guilt is dramatically altered by the introduction of the quantified print evidence.

Finkelstein and Fairley propose showing the jury a chart of $P(A/B)$ values for various prior probabilities and probabilistic evidence. The following is a condensed version of their chart (p. 500):

		$P(A)$		
		.10	.50	.75
	.50	.181	.666	.857
$P(B/\text{not-}A)$	.10	.526	.909	.967
	.001	.991	.9990	.9996

A juror can look at this chart and see how his initial subjective estimate (if he had one) would be modified by the objective probabilistic evidence. If his initial judgment of guilt is .50 and he is then told that the odds of having the particular print are 1/1000, he can see that the subsequent probability of guilt rises to .999. The expert does not, of course, channel the jurors' attention to any particular $P(A)$ value. He testifies only as to the likelihood of the print and describes in general terms how the chart is to be read. The chart is a pedagogical tool that describes the probative force of probabilistic evidence.

Bayesian calculations show how a rational decision-maker evaluates statistical evidence if he were behaving according to the Bayesian model. There is a normative quality to the model. It does not describe how real jurors decide; it prescribes how they should decide. If some jurors do not conform to the model, its assumptions about rational decision-making are not necessarily disproved. The model of the rational man of economic theory is not undercut by the existence of persons (for example, Buddhist monks) who do not act to maximize utility (Kaye 1979, p. 54). The question, then, is not whether Bayesian inference faithfully models actual decisional processes, but whether it generates more reliable judgments than intuitive assessments of probabilistic evidence. In fields as diverse as physics, genetics, insurance, economics, and gambling, it is well known that formal probability calculations provide more accurate predictions of outcomes than intuitive reasoning about probabilistic information. Since all evidence is ultimately probabilistic, jurors, too, make probabilistic judgments, though not in numerical terms. Whether the laws of probability are superior to unguided intuition in the courtroom setting is an empirical issue. Some social scientists, relying on human information processing studies, claim that it is

(Saks and Kidd 1980–81). We turn next to the empirical defense of trial by mathematics.

SYSTEMATIC BIASES IN DECISION-MAKING

Opponents of trial by mathematics argue that technically unimpeachable uses of probability theory are still open to normative objections. Saks and Kidd challenge the factual premises of the normative arguments "from an empirical point of view." The claims that people discount qualitative variables for quantitative variables, or that symbolic functions of trial are more important than reliable fact-finding, either "stand without supporting evidence" or are contradicted by the evidence (p. 125). They concede that there may be some social costs in the use of probability theory in litigation, but they declare that "even more harm may be inherent in not using [it]" (p. 125). The reason is that "abundant evidence from psychological research . . . suggests that in many contexts decisionmakers' intuitive common-sense judgments depart markedly and lawfully . . . from actual probabilities" (p. 127). To prefer intuitive decisions rather than explicit calculations of probability is "much like a patient who would rather have a human physician make a wrong diagnosis than allow a computer to make a correct one" (p. 146).

They cite studies by mathematical psychologists showing systematic errors in decision-making. For illustrative purposes, two of the studies will be described. In one experiment, subjects were given the description of a man: John is 39 years old, married, with two children, active in local politics, collects rare books, and is competitive, argumentative, and articulate. They were then asked to estimate the probability that John is a lawyer. One group of subjects was told that the foregoing description was a summary profile drawn from a population consisting of 70 lawyers and 30 engineers. The median probability estimate was .95. Another group was told that the population from which John's profile was drawn consisted of 30 lawyers and 70 engineers. The median estimate of these subjects was also .95. The Bayesian model would lead us to expect that the population base rates would influence the judgment. As it turned out, subjects ignored the quantitative information and relied on the case-specific information because it fit their existing stereotype of lawyers (political, argumentative, and so forth). The numbers did not dwarf the qualitative variables. In a third group of subjects, no individualized information about John was presented. In this situation, subjects relied on the given base rates in estimating the probability that John was a lawyer.

In another experiment, subjects read a brief description of a hit-and-run case. Two cab companies (blue and green) operate in the area. Since the accident occurred at night, the identity of the culpable cab company was at issue. A witness reported that the hit-and-run cab was blue. Vision tests showed that the witness's identifications, under conditions similar to the accident, were correct 80% of the time. There was also evidence that 85% of all cabs in the area are green, and 15% are blue. The task of the subjects was to estimate the probability that the cab was blue. The typical estimate was .80. This study, like the previous one, shows that people are insensitive to base rate information. They ignore the statistical evidence and focus on particularized information (in this instance, the reliability of the witness, which was defined numerically). If they had been instructed in Bayesian analysis, they would have discovered that the probability that the cab was blue, given the truth of the witness's testimony, is .41 (p. 130, n. 9).

According to Saks and Kidd, studies such as these show that people have difficulty combining base rate data (what lawyers would call "legislative facts") with case-specific information ("adjudicative facts") and thereby make consistently inaccurate judgments. People judge the likelihood of an event by evaluating the case facts in terms of their own cognitive maps (for example, stereotypes of lawyers, prior experience with observational reliability) rather than against the background information of generalized odds. Other reviews of the psychological literature also conclude that decisions (typically involving simple tasks performed in a laboratory) are less accurate than the predictions generated by probabilistic models (Hogarth 1981). People stubbornly resist changing their judgments even when given new information. They are confident of their decisions and ignore base-rate information. Saks and Kidd propose a "modest suggestion" which they think lawyers should find "comfortingly traditional": Use experts to "offer their data, their algorithms, and their Bayesian Theorems" and subject them to cross-examination to correct for technical errors. The choice, they claim, is not between "humans and mathematics," but between "explicitly presented computing and subjective computing" (pp. 147, 148).

NOTES AND QUESTIONS

1.   According to Bayes' formula, a prior belief in the truth of the proposition to be proved is necessary in order to calculate the subsequent probability, once the new statistical evidence is acquired. So long as a party successfully discharges the burden of production, jurors should have some evidentiary basis for the initial probability estimates. However, to the extent that the prior probability is unreliable, so will the subsequent probability that the formula generates. A threshold issue is whether jurors are capable of converting, meaningfully and reliably, their initial assessments into numerical terms.

This technique forces a juror to reach a quantitative estimate in his mind early in the trial. Normally, the trier is asked to suspend judgment until the end of trial, after all the evidence has been presented. Tribe (1971) argues that to invite jurors to make interim estimates of guilt during the course of the trial is to replace the presumption of innocence with the presumption of guilt. He fears that explicit reliance on Bayesian calculations may change the character of the trial itself (pp. 1368–69).

There is no empirical research that bears directly upon whether and how jurors' verdicts are influenced by their interim judgments as each item of evidence is sequentially presented. In a classical study of the impact of evidence on jurors, Weld and Danzig (1940) recorded eighteen judgments of mock jurors during the course of the trial, prior to the final verdict. These judgments showed the seesaw effects of the adversary process. Alternating presentations by the two sides pushed the judgments back and forth. It is possible, then, that the order of presentation may mitigate any effects of interim decisions.

However, research by Schum and Martin (1982) on "cascaded inference" suggests that there is a difference between making a single judgment after all the evidence is presented and making a series of conditional judgments (using Bayesian calculations) during the presentation of the evidence. Complex inferential reasoning is cascaded or hierarchical in nature: A number of intermediate mental steps are needed before a judgment or conclusion can be drawn from the available evidence. Given a mass of evidence, a decision-maker decomposes it into smaller parts and evaluates the probative weight of each part or combinations of parts to reach the final judgment. Wigmore (1937) called this task of inductive inference "catenated" reasoning (p. 13). Bayes' Theorem provides a mathematical tool for partitioning and combining the links in the chain of inferential reasoning.

In one study, Schum and Martin presented brief descriptions of twelve felony cases to subjects. Each case described the crime, the defendant, and various items of evidence. One group of subjects estimated the likelihood of each defendant's guilt after assessing all the evidence of each case. They aggregated the evidence in some intuitive fashion and gave a single judgment in each case. Another group received extensive instructions on Bayesian calculations and estimated several conditional probabilities of guilt for each case. These subjects had to decompose the mass of evidence and render fine-grained judgments. The results showed that the judgments of the second group were superior in the sense that they were significantly more consistent. There was substantial agreement between the subjects in assessing the probative value of the evidence. In contrast, the holistic judgments of the first group of subjects were highly variable. The deliberately contrived nature of the experiment precludes generalizations to actual trials, but the results should at least caution against assuming that Bayesian instructions merely aid intuitive fact-finding.

2. Predictive judgments are probabilistic in nature. There is an extensive literature showing that statistical judgments (that is, evaluations made according to a predetermined rule for counting and weighing information) are more reliable than subjective or clinical judgments. In such diverse fields as psychiatric diagnosis, academic performance, criminal sentencing, and parole release, quantitative methods have usually produced more accurate predictions than qualitative assessments (Underwood 1979, pp. 1420–32). This difference between standardized judgments based on statistics and individualized judgments based on intuition mirrors the familiar tension in law between rule and discretion. The issue of interest here is whether statistical approaches are also superior in trial adjudication. Indeed, one should inquire whether they can even be properly applied in this field.

Subjective probability treats the decision-maker as a bookmaker. The Bayesian approach forces us to conceptualize a juror's decision as a wager on contested issues of fact. He makes book on defendant's culpability. However, betting—or predicting—deals with uncertain events that have not yet occurred. Probability theory is usually applied to estimate the likelihood of future outcomes: Will the high school applicant for admission successfully graduate from college? Which horse is most likely to win the race? What are the odds that the patient has a particular ailment? Legal fact-finding, however, deals with postdiction rather than prediction. It seeks to find out what has already happened. Is the difference between future and past occurrences relevant to the application of probability theory?

Implicit in the idea of bookmaking is that bets must be able to be settled. "The outcome must be knowable otherwise than from the data on which the odds themselves are based" (Cohen 1977, p. 90). Thus, college graduation—predicted from a student's prior academic record and test scores—can be independently determined. In a horse race, the camera at the finish line tells whether the favored horse won. However, bets about disputed facts at trial are not settled afterward. Unless "the truth" can be extracted from the defendant after trial (perhaps by some Orwellian machine that is undisputedly reliable), truth is what the trier decides. Is the application of probability calculus to juror decisions, then, fundamentally misconceived? Or is it meaningful to use the bookmaker model even when there is no way of ascertaining independently the outcome of the wager?

3. Saks and Kidd (1980–81) conclude that human decision-making "tend[s] predictably to be incorrect" (p. 130). "People systematically violated the principles of rational decisionmaking when judging probabilities . . ." (p. 131). The studies show a discrepancy between how subjects decide and how the statistical model says they ought to decide. Do you agree that the former is "incorrect" and the latter "correct"? If people deviate from the ideal specified by the model, should people be made to conform to the model? Schum and Martin (1982) note: "[W]e can never ask how correct or accurate is a person's assessment of the probative weight . . . of evidence given at trial. Such evidence involves unique or one-of-a-kind events and each fact finder evaluates the evidence according to personal strategies . . ." (p. 124). Would Kalven and Zeisel's approach (1966) of obtaining the decisions of judges provide a suitable yardstick for evaluating the correctness of the decisions of jurors? How should juror decision-making be evaluated if not in terms of accuracy?

4. Saks and Kidd treat the introduction of statistical models at trial as simply a matter of improving "decisionmaking technology." After all, they say, if "people trust their pocket calculators . . . whose workings they do not begin to comprehend," by parity of reasoning they should have faith in mathematical tools that decide "more accurately than people do" (p. 148). However, does the adoption of this "technology" take on the characteristics of a value choice? In the pursuit of precision, what other (undisclosed or unintended) purposes are sought by quantification? What effect would you expect the use of Bayesian statistics by jurors to have upon the rate of convictions and of liability verdicts? Does an increase in fact-finding "accuracy" mean a decrease in Type 1 errors or Type 2 errors? What values are sacrificed when society permits legal sanctions to be imposed based upon statistical predictions, even when the figures are exceedingly accurate?

5. A few courts have admitted Bayesian calculations in paternity trials (Ellman and Kaye 1979). Typically, a plaintiff offers the results of serological tests to establish that the defendant and the child both have a set of genes found in only, say, 1 out of 100 men in the population. Does this number imply that the odds are .99 that the defendant is the father?

9.6.   COMPREHENSIBILITY OF INSTRUCTIONS ON EVALUATING EVIDENCE

Back in 1930, Judge Frank (1930)* wrote: "Time and money and lives are consumed in debating the precise words which the judge may address to the jury, although everyone . . . knows that those words might as well be spoken in a foreign language. . . . Yet, every day, cases . . . are reversed by upper courts because a phrase or sentence, meaningless to the jury, has been included in or omitted from the judge's charge" (p. 181). One generation later, the same lament was voiced by Judge Schwarzer (1981): "Prevailing practices of instructing juries are often so archaic and unrealistic that even in relatively simple cases what the jurors hear is little more than legal mumbo jumbo to them" (p. 732). If the profession seems resigned to the existence of purportedly "meaningless" judicial instructions, one reason may be that its members have not been socialized to view this state of affairs as problematic. For example, a casebook on civil procedure tells law students that "instructions tend to be prolix and incomprehensible, but the judge will do the best he can and the jury will do the best they can" (Louisell and Hazard 1968, p. 12). Instructions are essential to ensuring that juries return verdicts consistent with law and the evidence adduced at trial. Laypersons cannot be expected to properly consider evidence for one purpose but not another or to find liability by a preponderance of the evidence, if these concepts are not understandable to them. The evolution of jury instructions in this country sheds some light on why their lexical obscurity has long been regarded by their drafters with equanimity.

Historical Background

Instructions were developed by English judges after *Bushell's Case* (1670) as one of several means of controlling the jury. The American colonists, however, viewed judges and juries as more or less equals in the judicial process. Devoted to liberty and distrustful of judges appointed by the King, they jealously watched over the independence of the jury. In the early years of the Republic, judges often did not charge the jury, and when they did, the instructions were delivered in the vernacular and jurors were not obligated to abide by them (Nelson 1975, pp. 18–20). Moreover, as Chief Justice Jay explained in 1794, jurors had the "right . . . to determine the law as well as the fact in controversy. . . . [B]oth objects [were] lawfully within [their] power of decision" (*Georgia* v. *Brailsford*, p. 4).

By the end of the nineteenth century, the tide of opinion changed: Distrust of judges gave way to apprehension about unbridled jury discretion. The industrial and commercial developments of the period demanded certainty in the administration of law. There were fears that popular prejudices might find their way into jury verdicts. There were also doubts that in a rapidly changing society, jurors from different backgrounds would decide according to consensual norms (Nelson 1975, pp. 165–

*Reprinted by permission of the publisher. Copyright ©1930 by the Tudor Publishing Company.

69). Consequently, by legislation or judicial regulation, trial judges began to instruct juries on the applicable law. American courts increasingly relied on postverdict remedies and retrials to restrict jury decision-making, much like their English counterparts had started doing earlier. And in 1895, the Supreme Court annulled the right of federal juries to decide legal issues in criminal cases, though it recognized that their power to do so surreptitiously continued by reason of the general verdict (*Sparf and Hansen* v. *United States*).

Even the appellate courts sought to superintend indirectly the course of jury trials. On appeal, they considered not only whether the evidence supported the jury verdict, but they also scrutinized any claims of error in the accuracy of the instructions in stating the law. Normally, each side submits to the trial judge the instructions it wishes delivered to the jury. The judge may opt to use the instructions of one party, or a combination of both parties' instructions, or draft his own in addition to or in lieu of the proffered ones. Attorneys seeking the benefit of repetition of points of law favorable to their side will request redundant instructions. Trial courts often oblige because rejected instructions can be grounds for appeal. The more rigorous the appellate review, the more complex and periphrastic will be the instructions delivered by judges in the hope of avoiding reversals.

By the 1930s, it was clear that reform was needed. Committees of judges began to draft pattern or standard instructions. Based on appellate court decisions, these model instructions were written so as to be widely applicable regardless of the facts of any particular case. Today, nearly all the states have adopted pattern instructions and some make their use compulsory. They are intended to save time, improve legal accuracy, replace partisan instructions of counsel, reduce appeals (and thereby reduce appellate court caseloads), and improve jury comprehension. The results have been mixed. In Illinois, for example, where pattern instructions are mandatory, a before-after comparison of over 2,000 state supreme court cases found no differences in the frequency of appeals and of reversals. Other states have experienced a marginal reduction of reversals (Nieland 1979). The instructions do not necessarily lend themselves to ease of comprehension. They tend to be abstract in order to encompass as many factual circumstances as possible, and attorneys tend to tailor them to the particularities of their own case. Indeed, some drafters say that the most important aim is "to correctly state the law. This is true regardless of who is capable of understanding it" (in Schwarzer 1981, p. 739). On the whole, pattern and unstandardized instructions are still viewed through the knothole of a distant appellate fence.

RESEARCH ON COMPREHENSIBILITY

In 1977, New York enacted the first "plain English" law in the nation. It required certain consumer contracts to be "written in non-technical language and in a clear and coherent manner . . ." (N.Y. Gen. Oblig. Law, §5-701(b)(c) (1978)). The "Plain English Movement"—aimed at improving lay readability of common legal documents such as insurance policies and warranties—then spread to other states, the federal government, and the private sector. Although some believe it is "naive" to think that "linguistic reform can change sociolegal realities" (Danet 1980, p. 490), the movement had a fallout effect on judicial instructions. Social scientists began to assess the comprehensibility of pattern instructions and to rewrite them according to psycholinguistic principles.

In general, the research shows relatively low levels of juror comprehension. For example, jurors in one study were exposed to a videotaped presentation of the Florida pattern jury instructions and then tested for comprehension with multiple-choice questions. Although they performed better than a control group that did not hear the instructions, they still had 27% errors on the test. Other studies found that large samples of jurors in the Midwest understood only one half of civil and criminal pattern instructions (Elwork, Sales, and Alfini 1982). Some researchers concluded that linguistic construction, rather than substantive law, was responsible for the comprehension difficulties (Charrow and Charrow 1979). They rewrote some of the California civil pattern instructions, eliminating legal jargon, multiple negatives, the passive voice in subordinate clauses, and the like. They found improved comprehension with the revised version.

These initial studies have some methodological flaws. There is no evidence that the results have external validity. Comprehension needs to be measured not in the abstract but in the context of applying the instructions to the facts of a case. The findings obtained in a classroom-like setting cannot be generalized directly to the courtroom. If the comprehension of jurors in actual trials is as poor as these studies imply, one would not expect that their verdicts would match judges' verdicts as closely as Kalven and Zeisel (1966) have shown they do. In addition, the legal adequacy of psycholinguistic improvements needs to be validated. An understandable instruction may not necessarily state the law accurately. The research of Severance and Loftus, reproduced below, attempts to overcome these difficulties and represents the state of the art in improving the comprehensibility of instructions.

IMPROVING THE ABILITY OF JURORS TO COMPREHEND AND APPLY CRIMINAL JURY INSTRUCTIONS

**Laurence J. Severance and
Elizabeth F. Loftus**

. . .

ENHANCING THE MEANING OF CRIMINAL JURY INSTRUCTIONS (STUDY 3)*

The purpose of Study 3 was to develop and empirically test revisions in the

*[This article reported three studies, of which only the third is reproduced here. Study 1 sought to identify the difficulties that actual juries have in understanding criminal jury instructions. The authors analyzed all the written questions submitted by deliberating juries to judges in a sample of 405 trials in

target instructions to enhance subjects' comprehension and ability to apply the instructions. . . .

The task of revising jury instructions must . . . be not only to enhance meaning but also to retain legal sufficiency. This requires input from both psy-

King County, Washington. "[A] significant number" of the questions requested clarification regarding pattern instructions, such as the definition of "reasonable doubt" (p. 172). This study served to identify some of the unclear instructions, which the authors then rewrote and tested in their subsequent experiments.

Study 2 examined the ability of mock jurors to comprehend and apply several instructions. Subjects watched a videotaped burglary trial and afterward received either (a) no instructions, (b) pattern instructions concerning the jury's general responsibilities, or (c) the foregoing general instructions and specific pattern instructions (for example, regarding "reasonable doubt" and limited admissibility of evidence). There were no differences in verdicts among the three conditions. The rate of errors in comprehension was only slightly less for those given pattern instructions (groups b and c) than for those without any instructions. "Overall, these data suggest that the standard pattern instructions do not convey the full meaning they were intended to convey" (p. 183). Ed.'s note.]

chological and legal perspectives. We . . . examined the standard pattern instructions in light of psycholinguistic principles and proposed changes in the language to improve meaning. . . .

These proposed changes were then submitted for comment and criticism to two legal scholars familiar with the issues relevant to criminal jury instructions in order to seek validation from a legal perspective as to the probable adequacy of the revised instructions. Further revisions were made as necessary to satisfy their concerns. . . . The results of these procedures appear in Table 4 [on next page], where standard pattern instructions and our revisions are listed. . . .

OVERVIEW. Study 3 employed a 3 x 2 between-subjects factorial design with three levels of Instructions (No Instructions, Pattern Instructions, Revised Instructions) and two levels of Opportunity to Deliberate (Deliberation, No Deliberation). . . .

METHOD. Subjects were 216 college students who were also registered voters, recruited from psychology courses at the University of Washington. The same videotaped trial and procedures employed in the previous experiment were used in this experiment. . . . [The description of the method that follows was taken from Study 2. Ed.'s note.]

Subjects participated in groups of three or more. In all cases, there were six persons in each deliberating jury. A total of 36 persons participated in each of the six experimental groups.

The videotaped trial was a burglary trial in which the accused allegedly took tools from a construction site. The trial was an enactment, occurring in an actual court with an actual judge and credible actors as witnesses. The facts were intentionally balanced so that the defendant was not clearly innocent or guilty. The defendant in the trial had one prior conviction, which he

admitted to while being questioned as a witness. The trial lasted one hour.

All instructions used in the study were pattern instructions developed for juries in criminal trials in the state of Washington. The No Instructions groups received no instructions. . . . [Subjects in the Revised Instructions group and in the Pattern Instructions group heard a tape recording of the respective instructions at the close of the videotaped trial. These included general instructions on the duties of jurors and specific instructions on legal concepts such as reasonable doubt and limited admissibility. Ed.'s note.]

Half of the participants were randomly assigned to deliberate and the other half were not. Those in the deliberating groups were given a written set of the judge's instructions, asked to choose a foreperson, placed in a room to deliberate, and asked to notify the experimenter when a verdict had been reached. They were then left to deliberate for up to thirty minutes. All deliberations were tape recorded. Upon reaching a verdict, or after 30 minutes, each subject was given a questionnaire to complete. Subjects in the No Deliberation condition were each given a questionnaire immediately after the trial (and instructions) had been presented.

All subjects responded to identical questionnaire items. The questionnaires first elicited a verdict of "guilty" or "not guilty." . . .

The comprehension measures were presented in a multiple choice format. . . .

The application measures consisted of ten single-paragraph descriptions of factual situations, each of which asked for a judgment that tested subjects' abilities to use concepts embodied in the pattern instructions in order to reach a legally correct decision. . . .

RESULTS.

VERDICTS. Overall, 77 subjects (35.6 percent) found the defendant guilty, and

TABLE 4

Examples of Pattern Instructions and Their Revised Counterparts

Use of Prior Conviction to Impeach a Defendant

Pattern instruction: Evidence that the defendant has previously been convicted of crime is not evidence of the defendant's guilt. Such evidence may be considered by you in deciding what weight of credibility should be given to the testimony of the defendant and for no other purpose.

Revised instruction: Evidence that the defendant has previously been convicted of a crime is not evidence of the defendant's guilt in this case. You may not use this evidence in deciding whether he or she is guilty or innocent. You may use evidence of prior convictions only to decide whether to believe the defendant's testimony and how much weight to give it.

Reasonable Doubt

Pattern instruction: A reasonable doubt is one for which a reason exists. A reasonable doubt is such a doubt as would exist in the mind of a reasonable person after fully, fairly and carefully considering all of the evidence or lack of evidence. If after such consideration, you have an abiding belief in the truth of the charge, you are satisfied beyond a reasonable doubt.

Revised instruction: A reasonable doubt about guilt is not a vague or speculative doubt but is a doubt for which a reason exists. A reasonable doubt is a doubt that would exist in the mind of a reasonable person after that person has fully, fairly and carefully considered all of the evidence or lack of evidence. If, after such thorough consideration, you believe in the truth of the charge, you are satisfied beyond a reasonable doubt.

If you are satisfied beyond a reasonable doubt that all elements of the charge have been proved, then you must find the defendant guilty. However, if you are left with a reasonable doubt about the proof of any element, then you must find the defendant not guilty.

General Introductory Instruction

Pattern instruction: It is your duty to determine the facts in this case from the evidence produced in court. It is also your duty to accept the law from the court, regardless of what you personally believe the law is or ought to be. You are to apply the law to the facts and in this way decide the case. . . .

Revised instruction: As jurors in this case, you have several duties: First, it is your duty to determine the facts in this case from the evidence produced in court; Second, it is your duty to accept the law as I will instruct you, regardless of what you personally believe the law is or ought to be; Third, to reach a verdict, you are to apply the law to the facts and in this way decide the case. . . .

To reach a verdict, your decision must be unanimous. [This last sentence was not contained in the pattern instruction. Ed.'s note.]

---

139 subjects (64.4 percent) found the defendant not guilty. . . . [T]he independent variables did significantly affect verdicts in this study. There are fewer guilty verdicts among deliberating jurors than nondeliberating jurors. . . . The instructions jurors received affected verdicts. . . . [Among deliberating jurors, the number of guilty verdicts for No Instructions, Pattern Instructions, and Revised Instructions was, respectively, 14, 6, and 1. Among nondeliberating jurors, the number of

guilty verdicts for these three conditions was, respectively, 20, 19, and 17. From p. 189. Ed.'s note.]

COMPREHENSION. . . . The overall comprehension error rate was 29.3 percent with No Instructions compared to an error rate of 24.3 percent when . . . Pattern Instructions were available, and a 20.3 percent error rate when the Revised Instructions were available. Post hoc tests revealed that in these overall results, the No Instructions condition differed significantly from the other two instruction conditions, . . . but the difference between the latter two conditions, though in the predicted direction, was not significant.

[There was] a consistent pattern of results across each of the target instructions included in the study. Errors in comprehension were consistently lower when pattern instructions were presented and were lower still when Revised rather than Pattern instructions were provided. . . . [For example, the percentage of errors in No Instructions, Pattern Instructions, and Revised Instructions regarding "limited admissibility" was, respectively, 47.3% (a), 34.0% (b), and 31.5% (c). (Percentages with different subscripts differed at the .05 level of significance.) The percentage of errors regarding "reasonable doubt" for each of the three conditions was, respectively, 24.1% (a), 22.3% (a), 20.2% (a). From p. 190. Ed.'s note.]

ABILITY TO APPLY INSTRUCTIONS. . . . [P]attern Instructions produced a significant increase in the percentage of correct applications of the law over the No Instructions condition, and the Revised Instructions led to a further increase in accuracy. . . . [The overall mean percentage of correct applications for No Instructions, Pattern Instructions, and Revised Instructions was, respectively, 56% (a), 61% (b), 68% (c). Percentages with different subscripts were significantly different at the .05 level. From p. 191. Ed.'s note.]

The opportunity to deliberate af-fected subjects such that those who deliberated comprehended the general instructions better than those who did not deliberate. . . .

QUALITY OF DELIBERATIONS. [T]he quality of deliberations was evaluated by having independent judges code the content of the deliberations into a series of categories which were then submitted to analysis. . . . [T]he groups that received instructions discussed less irrelevant information, i.e. information not brought up in the trial. Post hoc analysis of this effect showed significant differences between No Instructions ($\bar{X}$ = 15.5), and Pattern Instructions ($\bar{X}$ = 5.75), and also between No Instructions and Revised Instructions ($\bar{X}$ = 3.38). . . .

[J]urors' statements asking for or offering clarification of facts were marginally affected by the Instruction manipulations, with those who received No Instructions tending to request most clarification, those who received Pattern Instructions requesting less, and those who received Revised Instructions requesting least clarification. . . . [These differences were not statistically significant. Ed.'s note.]

DISCUSSION AND CONCLUSIONS

Study 3 provides concrete evidence that psycholinguistic changes in pattern instructions can improve jurors' abilities to both comprehend and apply jury instructions. The most powerful indication of these effects is the overall improvement in subjects' abilities to apply the instructions after receiving Revised Instructions as compared to Pattern or No Instructions. . . . In addition, the pattern of comprehension results is consistent, with lowest error rates among subjects who received Revised Instructions. . . .

If jurors' understanding of the instructions is improved by psycholinguistic revisions, what are the implications for their behavior in deliberations? The results of this study suggest two answers. First, the data on verdicts indicate fewer guilty verdicts among deliberating jurors who receive instructions than among deliberating jurors who receive no instructions. . . . This relationship between Instruction condition and verdicts may be due to an increased understanding of the law fostered by the instructions. . . .

Given the ambiguous facts in the videotaped trial used in our research, the jury instructions tended to reduce guilty verdicts to the extent that they were understood and properly applied, particularly among deliberating jurors. By comparison, if the facts had clearly indicated guilt, clear instructions might have enhanced the number of guilty verdicts. In general, we would predict that clearly understood instructions on the law will enhance a just determination of guilty or not guilty by sharpening the relevant decision criteria that jurors are supposed to apply to the facts.

The content analysis of the deliberations suggests a second way in which instructions helped to focus jurors on the relevant issues. Subjects who received instructions talked less about irrelevant facts and appeared to need less clarification of the evidence than subjects who did not receive instructions. These results tended to be most pronounced among the subjects receiving the Revised Instructions. The data thus suggest that the quality of deliberations as well as the verdicts may be affected by the degree to which jurors understand their duties. . . .

NOTES AND QUESTIONS

1.   Is there any inherent reason why psycholinguistic improvements in pattern instructions should produce fewer convictions? Compare the standard and revised versions—does the latter have a pro-defense bias? The two legal scholars evaluated only the substantive accuracy of the revision. There was no independent assessment of the ideological tilt, if any, of the instructions. How would you determine whether decreased or increased guilty verdicts, incident to the rewriting of instructions, is the more accurate or reliable outcome? A replication of Study 3 with real jurors again showed a lower percentage of guilty judgments with revised instructions (8%) than with pattern instructions (22%), but only after group deliberation. There was no difference if judgments were recorded without prior deliberation (Severance, Greene, and Loftus 1984, Table 3).

2.   Despite the improved comprehension with the revised instructions, the subjects still had an overall error rate of 20.3%. A similar experiment by Elwork, Alfini and Sales (1982) found that rewritten instructions still produced 22% errors in a comprehension test administered to real jurors, after they had watched the videotape of an actual trial and had engaged in deliberation (p. 442). (In contrast, jurors who received the nonrevised instructions had 60% errors on the same test.) How should one determine the minimum acceptable level of comprehensibility? Should this level vary according to the importance of the instruction in question (for example, a higher level for instruction on the standard of proof)? Should comprehensibility, as well as accuracy, be made a basis for appeal?

3.   Is the rewriting of instructions, like the quantification of probabilistic evidence at trial, more than a technical task in that it implicates unarticulated normative choices? Whose interests are being served by being more precise? Do the advantages of linguistic clarity always outweigh the value of intended ambiguity? If jurors are to be fully informed on the applicable law, they could be taught by means of judicial lectures (before or after the trial) rather than by brief instructions. The present system of instructions can be seen as a middle-of-the-road position between comprehensive instruction (which would make jurors more like judges) and no instruction at all (which would leave unchecked the jury's popular sense of rightness). Is the equilibrium disturbed when the instructions are rendered more understandable?

4. Clearer language is only one facet of the instruction process. Timing may also influence comprehension. Rule 30 of the Federal Rules of Criminal Procedure states that "the court shall instruct the jury after the arguments are completed." A similar provision is found in the Federal Rules of Civil Procedure (R. 51). Thus, jurors could listen to days or weeks of evidence without knowing the standards by which they are to evaluate it. Some state court judges have tried giving preliminary instructions at the beginning of the trial and additional instructions during the course of the trial (Avakian 1979). The efficacy of such segmented instructions remains to be investigated fully (Kassin and Wrightsman 1979). The relative desirability of oral or written presentation of instructions, which is usually left to the trial court's discretion, is also in need of empirical inquiry. Experimentation could show whether the availability of written instructions in the jury room would sidetrack jurors into legal arguments or make their deliberations more informed and efficient.

REFERENCES

Addington v. Texas, 441 U.S. 418 (1979).

Aronson, R. H. "The Federal Rules of Evidence: A Model for Improved Evidentiary Decisionmaking in Washington." *Washington Law Review* 54 (1978): 31–64.

Ashe v. Swenson, 397 U.S. 436 (1970).

Austin, W.; Williams, T. A.; Worchel, S.; Wentzel, A. A.; and Siegel, D. "Effect of Mode of Adjudication, Presence of Defense Counsel, and Favorability of Verdict on Observers' Evaluation of a Criminal Trial." *Journal of Applied Social Psychology* 11 (1981): 281–300.

Avakian, S. "Let's Learn to Instruct the Jury. . . ." *Judges' Journal* 18 (1979): 41.

Bartol, C. R. *Psychology and American Law.* Belmont, Ca.: Wadsworth, 1983.

Bermant, G., and Jacoubovitch, M. D. "Fish Out of Water: A Brief Overview of Social and Psychological Concerns About Videotaped Trials." *Hastings Law Journal* 26 (1975): 998–1011.

Brilmayer, L., and Kornhauser, L. "Review: Quantitative Methods and Legal Decisions." *University of Chicago Law Review* 46 (1978): 116–53.

Brooks v. Tennessee, 406 U.S. 605 (1972).

Bruton v. United States, 391 U.S. 123 (1968).

Bushell's Case, 124 Eng. Rep. 1006 (1670).

Byrne v. Boadle, 159 Eng. Rep. 299 (1863).

Chandler v. Florida, 449 U.S. 560 (1981).

Charrow, R. P., and Charrow, V. "Making Legal Language Understandable: A Psycholinguistic Study of Jury Instructions." *Columbia Law Review* 79 (1979): 1306–74.

Clark, T. C. "Introduction to Symposium."

Brigham Young University Law Review 1975 (1975): 327–30.

Cleary, E. W. "Evidence as a Problem in Communicating." *Vanderbilt Law Review* 5 (1952): 277–95.

Cohen, J. "Cameras in the Courtroom and Due Process." *Washington Law Review* 57 (1982): 277–92.

Cohen, L. *The Probable and the Provable.* London: Oxford University Press, 1977.

Cohn, A., and Udolf, R. *The Criminal Justice System and Its Psychology.* New York: Van Nostrand Reinhold, 1979.

Comment. "Videotape Trials: Legal and Practical Implications." *Columbia Journal of Law and Social Problems* 9 (1973): 363–93.

Commonwealth v. Webster, 59 Mass. (5 Cush.) 295 (1850).

Cornish, W. R., and Sealy, A. P. "Juries and Rules of Evidence." *Criminal Law Review* 17 (1973): 208–28.

Cromwell, H. "The Relative Effect on Audience Attitude of the First Versus the Second Argumentative Speech of a Series." *Speech Monograph* 17 (1950): 105–27.

Damaška, M. "Presentation of Evidence and Factfinding Precision." *University of Pennsylvania Law Review* 123 (1975): 1083–1106.

Danet, B. "Language in the Legal Process." *Law and Society Review* 14 (1980): 445–564.

Dix, G. E. "Administration of Texas Death Penalty Statutes: Constitutional Infirmities Related to the Prediction of Dangerousness." *Texas Law Review* 55 (1977): 1343–1414.

Doret, D. M. "Trial by Videotape—Can Justice

Be Seen to Be Done?" *Temple Law Quarterly* 47 (1974): 228–68.

Drew v. United States, 331 F.2d 85 (D.C. Cir. 1964).

Ellman, I. M., and Kaye, D. "Probabilities and Proof: Can HLA and Blood Group Testing Prove Paternity?" *New York University Law Review* 54 (1979): 1131–62.

Elwork, A.; Alfini, J. J.; and Sales, B. D. "Toward Understandable Jury Instructions." *Judicature* 65 (1982): 433–43.

———; Sales, B. D.; and Alfini, J. J. *Making Jury Instructions Understandable.* Charlottesville, Va.: Michie/Bobbs-Merrill, 1982.

Estes v. Texas, 381 U.S. 532 (1965).

Fairley, W. B., and Mosteller, F. "A Conversation about *Collins.*" *University of Chicago Law Review* 41 (1974): 242–53.

Finkelstein, M. O. *Quantitative Methods in Law: Studies in the Application of Mathematical Probability and Statistics to Legal Problems.* New York: Free Press, 1978.

———, and Fairley, W. B. "A Baysian Approach to Identification Evidence." *Harvard Law Review* 83 (1970): 489–517.

Frank, J. *Law and the Modern Mind.* New York: Tudor, 1930.

Frankel, M. E. "The Search for Truth: An Umpireal View." *University of Pennsylvania Law Review* 123 (1975): 1031–59.

Fuller, L. "The Adversary System." In *Talks on American Law,* edited by H. Berman. New York: Vintage Books, 1961.

Georgia v. Brailsford, 3 U.S. (3 Dall.) 1 (1794).

Goldstein, A. "Reflections on Two Models: Inquisitorial Themes in American Criminal Procedure." *Stanford Law Review* 26 (1974): 1009–25.

Greene, E., and Loftus, E. F. "When Crimes Are Joined at Trial: Institutionalized Prejudice?" Paper presented at the meeting of the American Psychology-Law Society, Boston, 1981.

Hans, V. P., and Doob, A. N. "Section 12 of the Canada Evidence Act and the Deliberations of Simulated Jurors." *Criminal Law Quarterly* 18 (1976): 235–53.

Harris v. New York, 401 U.S. 222 (1971).

Hayden, R. M., and Anderson, J. K. "On the Evaluation of Procedural Systems in Laboratory Experiments." *Law and Human Behavior* 3 (1979): 21–38.

Hogarth, R. M. "Beyond Discrete Biases: Functional and Dysfunctional Aspects of Judgmental Heuristics." *Psychological Bulletin* 90 (1981): 197–217.

Hovland, C. I. "Summary and Implications." In *The Order of Presentation in Persuasion,* edited by C. I. Hovland. New Haven: Yale University Press, 1957.

———; Janis, I. L.; and Kelley, H. H. *Communication and Persuasion.* New Haven: Yale University Press, 1953.

———, and Mandell, W. "Is There a Law of Primacy in Persuasion?" In *The Order of Presentation in Persuasion,* edited by C. I. Hovland. New Haven: Yale University Press, 1957.

In re Winship, 397 U.S. 358, (1970).

Jackson v. Denno, 378 U.S. 368 (1964).

Johnson, R. "Just Because You Can't Televise Trials Doesn't Mean You Can't Bring a Television to Court." *Juris Doctor* 4 (1974): 25–27.

Kalven, H., Jr., and Zeisel H. *The American Jury.* Boston: Little, Brown, 1966.

Kassin, S. M., and Wrightsman, L. "On the Requirements of Proof: The Timing of Judicial Instruction and Mock Juror Verdicts." *Journal of Personality and Social Psychology* 37 (1979): 1877–87.

———, and ———. "Coerced Confessions, Judicial Instructions and Mock Juror Verdicts." *Journal of Applied Social Psychology* 11 (1981): 489–506.

Kaye, D. "The Laws of Probability and the Law of the Land." *University of Chicago Law Review* 47 (1979): 34–56.

———. "Naked Statistical Evidence." *Yale Law Journal* 89 (1980): 601–11.

———. "The Limits of the Preponderance of the Evidence Standard: Justifiably Naked Statistical Evidence and Multiple Causation." *American Bar Foundation Research Journal* 1982 (1982): 487–516.

Keeton, R. *Trial Tactics and Methods.* New York: Prentice-Hall, 1954.

Kornblum, G. "Videotape in Civil Cases." *Hastings Law Journal* 24 (1972): 9–36.

Krulewitch v. United States, 336 U.S. 440 (1949).

Lakeside v. Oregon, 435 U.S. 333 (1978).

Lampe v. Franklin American, 96 S.W.2d 710 (1936).

Lana, R. E. "Familiarity and Order of Presentation in Persuasion." *Journal of Abnormal and Social Psychology* 62 (1961): 573–77.

Lawson, R. G. "Order of Presentation as a Factor in Jury Persuasion." *Kentucky Law Review* 56 (1968): 523–55.

———. "Experimental Research on the Organization of Persuasive Arguments: An Application to Courtroom Communications." *Law and Social Order* 4 (1970): 579–608.

Lempert, R., and Saltzburg, S. *A Modern Ap-*

proach to Evidence, 2d ed. St. Paul: West, 1982.

Lind, E. A. "The Psychology of Courtroom Procedure." In *The Psychology of the Courtroom,* edited by N. L. Kerr and R. M. Bray. New York: Academic Press, 1982.

———, and Walker, L. "Theory Testing, Theory Development, and Laboratory Research on Legal Issues." *Law and Human Behavior* 3 (1979): 5–19.

Llewellyn, K. N. *Jurisprudence: Realism in Theory and Practice.* Chicago: University of Chicago Press, 1962.

Loh, W. D. "Some Uses and Limits of Statistics and Social Science in the Judicial Process." In *Social Psychology and Discretionary Law,* edited by L. E. Abt and I. R. Stuart. New York: Van Nostrand Reinhold, 1979.

Louisell, D. W., and Hazard, G. C., Jr. *Cases and Materials on Pleading and Procedure,* 2nd ed. Mineola, N.Y.: Foundation Press, 1968.

———, and Williams, H. *The Parenchyma of Law.* Rochester, N.Y.: Professional Medical Publications, 1960.

Luchins, A. S. "Primacy-Recency in Impression Formation." In *The Order of Presentation in Persuasion,* edited by C. I. Hovland. New Haven: Yale University Press, 1957.

Lund, F. H. "The Psychology of Belief." *Journal of Abnormal and Social Psychology* 20 (1925): 174–96.

McCormick, C. T. *McCormick on Evidence,* 2nd ed. St. Paul, Minn.: West, 1972.

McCrystal, J. L., and Maschari, A. B. "Will Electronic Technology Take the Witness Stand?" *University of Toledo Law Review* 11 (1980): 239–54.

McLuhan, M. *Understanding Media: The Extensions of Man.* New York: McGraw-Hill, 1964.

Michelson v. United States, 335 U.S. 469 (1948).

Miller, G. R.; Bender, D. C.; Boster, F.; Florence, B. T.; Fontes, N.; Hocking, J.; and Nicholson, H. "The Effects of Videotape Testimony in Jury Trials: Studies on Juror Decision Making, Information Retention, and Emotional Arousal." *Brigham Young University Law Review* 1975 (1975): 331–73.

Miller, N., and Campbell, D. "Recency and Primacy in Persuasion as a Function of the Timing of Speeches and Measurements." *Journal of Abnormal and Social Psychology* 59 (1959): 1–9.

Miranda v. Arizona, 384 U.S. 486 (1966).

Morrill, A. E. "Enter—The Videotape Trial." *John Marshall Journal of Practice and Procedure* 3 (1970): 237–59.

Nash v. United States, 54 F.2d 1006 (2d Cir. 1932).

Nelson, W. *Americanization of the Common Law.* Cambridge, Mass.: Harvard University Press, 1975.

Nesson, C. R. "Reasonable Doubt and Permissive Inferences: The Value of Complexity." *Harvard Law Review* 92 (1979): 1187–1225.

Nieland, R. *Pattern Jury Instructions: A Critical Look at a Modern Movement to Improve the Jury System.* Chicago: American Judicature Society, 1979.

Note. "To Take the Stand or Not to Take the Stand: The Dilemma of the Defendant with a Criminal Record." *Columbia Journal of Law and Social Problems* 4 (1968): 215–29.

Pennington, D. C. "Witnesses and Their Testimony: Effects of Ordering on Juror Verdicts." *Journal of Applied Social Psychology* 12 (1982): 318–33.

People v. Cagle, 244 N.E.2d 200 (1969).

People v. Collins, 66 Cal. Rptr. 497 (1968).

People v. Shapiro, 50 N.Y. 2d 747 (1980).

Pyszczynski, T. A., and Wrightsman, L. S. "The Effects of Opening Statements on Mock Jurors' Verdicts in a Simulated Criminal Trial." *Journal of Applied Social Psychology* 11 (1981): 301–13.

Saks, M. J., and Hastie, R. *Social Psychology in Court.* New York: Van Nostrand Reinhold, 1978.

Saks, M. J., and Kidd, R. F. "Human Information Processing and Adjudication: Trial by Heuristics." *Law and Society Review* 15 (1980–81): 123–60.

Schum, D. A., and Martin, A. W. "Formal and Empirical Research on Cascaded Inference in Jurisprudence." *Law and Society* 17 (1982): 105–52.

Schwarzer, W. W. "Communicating with Juries: Problems and Remedies." *California Law Review* 69 (1981): 731–69.

Severance, L.; Greene, E.; and Loftus, E. "Towards Criminal Jury Instructions That Jurors Can Understand." *Journal of Criminal Law and Criminology* (1984): in press.

Severance, L. J., and Loftus, E. F. "Improving the Ability of Jurors to Comprehend and Apply Criminal Jury Instructions." *Law and Society Review* 17 (1982): 153–97.

Siegel, B. "Has Television Tipped the Scales of

Justice?" *Seattle Times,* July 6, 1980, p. A3.

Simon, R., and Mahan, L. "Quantifying Burdens of Proof." *Law and Society Review* 5 (1971): 319–30.

Smith v. Rapid Transit, Inc., 317 Mass. 469 (1945).

Sparf and Hansen v. United States, 156 U.S. 51 (1895).

Spencer v. Texas, 385 U.S. 551 (1967).

State v. Palm Beach Newspapers, Inc., 395 So.2d 544 (Fla. 1981).

State v. Sauer, 38 Minn. 438 (1888).

State v. Sneed, 414 P.2d 858 (1966).

Tanford, S., and Penrod, S. "Biases in Trials Involving Dependants Charged with Multiple Offenses." *Journal of Applied Social Psychology* 12 (1982): 453–80.

Thayer, J. *A Preliminary Treatise on Evidence at the Common Law.* Boston: Little, Brown, 1898.

Thibaut, J. "A Theory of Procedure." *California Law Review* 66 (1978): 541–60.

———, and Walker, L. *Procedural Justice: A Psychological Analysis.* Hillsdale, N.J.: Lawrence Erlbaum, 1975.

———; Walker, L.; and Lind, E. "Adversary Presentation and Bias in Legal Decisionmaking." *Harvard Law Review* 86 (1972): 386–401.

Tribe, L. H. "Trial by Mathematics: Precision and Ritual in the Legal Process." *Harvard Law Review* 84 (1971): 1329–93.

Turner v. United States, 396 U.S. 398 (1970).

Underwood, B. "Law and the Crystal Ball: Predicting Behavior with Statistical Inference and Individualized Judgment." *Yale Law Journal* 88 (1979): 1408–48.

United States v. Grunewald, 233 F.2d 556 (2d Cir. 1956).

Walker, L.; Thibaut, J.; and Andreoli, V. "Order of Presentation at Trial." *Yale Law Journal* 82 (1972): 216–26.

Weinstein, J. B., and Berger, M. A. *Weinstein's Evidence.* New York: Matthew Bender, 1976.

Weld, H. P., and Danzig, E. R. "A Study of the Way in Which a Verdict Is Reached by a Jury." *American Journal of Psychology* 53 (1940): 518–36.

Wells, G. "Applied Eyewitness-Testimony Research: System Variables and Estimator Variables." *Journal of Personality and Social Psychology* 36 (1978): 1546–57.

Westen, P. "Order of Proof: An Accused's Right to Control the Timing and Sequence of Evidence in His Defense." *California Law Review* 66 (1978): 935–85.

Wigmore, J. H. *A Students' Textbook on the Law of Evidence.* Brooklyn, N.Y.: Foundation Press, 1935.

———. *The Science of Judicial Proof,* 3d ed. Boston: Little, Brown, 1937.

———. *Wigmore on Evidence,* 3d ed., vol. 1. Boston: Little, Brown, 1940.

———. *Wigmore on Evidence,* 3d ed., vol. 5. Boston: Little, Brown, 1940.

Williams, G. R.; Farmer, L. C.; Lee, R. E.; Cundrick, B. P.; Howell, R. J.; and Rooker, C. K. "Juror Perception of Trial Testimony as a Function of the Method of Presentation: A Comparison of Live, Color Video, Black-and-White Video, Audio, and Transcript Presentations." *Brigham Young Law Review* 1975 (1975): 375–422.

Winter, R. K. "The Jury and the Role of Nonpersuasion." *Law and Society Review* 5 (1971): 335–44.

CHAPTER 10

Extrajudicial Influences on the Jury Before Trial: Case Study of Eyewitness Identification

10.1. INTRODUCTION

An objective of trial is to ascertain the "truth," that is, to reach a reliable determination of the facts of a disputed matter. In a criminal trial, to ascertain the truth means to determine the guilt or nonguilt of the accused. During the 1960s, the Supreme Court initiated sweeping changes in the administration of criminal justice by establishing constitutionally based procedural safeguards for the accused both before and at trial. Thus, as discussed in Chapter 6, the Court excluded from use in state criminal trials any evidence directly obtained by law enforcement officials in violation of Fourth Amendment strictures against unreasonable searches and seizures (*Mapp* v. *Ohio*, 1961) and draped the Fifth Amendment immunity mantle over the accused at the moment of custodial interrogation (*Miranda* v. *Arizona*, 1966).

These constitutional safeguards, however, do not have as their only or primary function the ascertainment of truth. They also serve to deter official wrongdoing and to protect the integrity of the judicial process. Thus, the exclusion of evidence obtained by an improper search may result in the acquittal of those who, in fact, perpetrated a crime as well as those who are wholly innocent. There are policy reasons relating to how evidence is procured, which are apart from the trial issue of whether the defendant committed the alleged offense, that justify the procedural rule of exclusion. Many of the decisions of the Supreme Court in the area of the criminal process do not deal directly with the basic trial issue of safeguarding against wrongful convictions.

A major exception is the landmark trilogy of *Wade-Gilbert-Stovall* (*United States* v. *Wade; Gilbert* v. *California; Stovall* v. *Denno*) decided on June 12, 1967. For the first time, the Court established constitutionally derived procedural safeguards to govern

---

Note: This chapter was prepared with the collaboration of Edith Greene of the University of Washington.

eyewitness identification evidence in federal and state criminal trials. Since unreliable pretrial identifications are said to be a major source of erroneous convictions at trial, these cases expressly address the truth-ascertainment function of the fact-finding process.

The Relationship Between Pretrial and In-Court Identification

The Sixth Amendment guarantees that "in all criminal prosecutions, the accused shall enjoy the right . . . to be confronted with the witnesses against him . . . and to have the Assistance of Counsel for his defense." An in-court personal identification of a defendant by an eyewitness is highly damaging to the accused. A confession is perhaps the only other type of evidence that is more persuasive to a jury. The right of confrontation consists of the opportunity to cross-examine in an attempt to impeach the testimony or discredit the credibility of the witness. This right may be compromised in an eyewitness case because the in-court identification may represent the witness's recall of a pretrial, stationhouse identification rather than of the original observation at the crime scene. The following example illustrates this source of bias.

A prosecutor is conducting a direct examination of the complaining witness in a rape case. After eliciting the facts of the crime, he asks: "And is the person who raped you in this courtroom?" "Yes," says the witness. "Will you please point out this person?" The witness, then, dramatically points to the defendant sitting at defense counsel's table. "Let the record show that the witness has identified the defendant as the person who committed the crime," concludes the prosecutor.

This kind of in-court identification is usually extremely damaging to the defense. Juries attach substantial weight to it. However, there are two possible sources of error, which defense counsel will attempt to expose on cross-examination. One is the inherent unreliability of eyewitness testimony due to the vagaries of human perception and memory. In this example, the defense attorney might begin by probing the accuracy of the identification by this witness at the crime scene. He cross-examines her as to the amount of lighting at the place of rape that night, the stressfulness of the situation, and so on, all designed to create reasonable doubt in the minds of the jurors as to the reliability of the initial observation.

Then he asks: "Prior to the identification you've just made, have you identified the accused at any other time since the alleged rape?" "Yes I have." "When and where was that?" "About a week or so after the rape," answers the witness. "The police called me to the stationhouse to see a lineup of suspects. They had five men in the lineup, including the defendant. They asked me if the rapist was there. I identified him."

Thus, in addition to any unreliability resulting from frailties in human information processing, there is possibly a second, situationally induced source of bias in the stationhouse identification. The in-court identification is subject to two different interpretations. One is that the accused is the person who committed the crime, based on the witness's recollection of the on-scene encounter. The other is that the accused is not the rapist but simply a person (perhaps similar in features to the actual rapist) seen for the first time at the lineup, when the witness was susceptible to police persuasion to make a positive identification. Once the lineup identification is made, the witness is unlikely to alter a publicly made judgment. If the latter interpretation is the case and defense counsel is unsuccessful in impeaching the witness's testimony at trial by showing the prejudicial police influence, the fate of the defendant is, in effect, determined in advance at the pretrial stage, not at trial.

In the criminal process, the pretrial stage is essentially the police stage—the police conduct investigations, arrests, searches, and seizures to gather evidence for use by the prosecutor later at trial. As the above example illustrates, the manner in which the police obtain information can subsequently taint the fairness of the trial itself. To a far greater extent than the public realizes, the American criminal process is the pretrial process. Most suspects never journey past the stationhouse. Kamisar (1965) has described the criminal process as consisting of two simultaneous shows, one in the "mansion," or courtroom, and the other in the "gatehouse," or police station. The show in the mansion is stirring and dignified, the public is invited, individual liberties are celebrated, and the supposed enemy of the state is accorded every respect and protection. This is the show that the public knows and approves of. But in the gatehouse of the criminal process, constitutional rights are checked at the door, the suspect is depersonalized, and the harsh realities of law enforcement are faced. The elaborate legal rules required in the mansion mean little in the stationhouse; here, a de facto inquisitorial system operates. "Society does not know or care" about this second, far bigger but less visible, show (p. 19). The public wants criminals tried and put away but is not curious as to how the police do it provided it gets done. Yet, there is no escaping the fact that the inquisitorial processes before trial shape or even determine adversarial fact-finding at trial. In the context of eyewitness identifications, "the trial which might determine the accused's fate may well not be that in the courtroom but that at the pretrial confrontation, with . . . the witness as the sole jury . . ." (*United States* v. *Wade*, 1967, p. 235).

Parameters of the Problem

The *Wade* Court devoted ten full pages to the dangers inherent in eyewitness identification, pointing out that "the annals of criminal law are rife with instances of misidentification" (p. 229). Others, too, have claimed a high rate of erroneous convictions (for example, Levine and Tapp 1973, p. 1081; Sobel 1982, p. 1.2; Comment, *Dickinson Law Review*, 1978, p. 467). In a study of 65 innocent men who were convicted, it was found that 29 were adjudicated guilty on the basis of eyewitness testimony. These 29 were identified by a total of 140 witnesses, or an average of 5 witnesses per defendant (Borchard 1932).

It is impossible to estimate reliably the number of erroneous convictions, but anecdotal reports of their occurrence need to be placed in perspective. It is highly unlikely that this kind of injustice is a common outcome in criminal prosecutions. Only 10% of cases nationwide go to trial. Of these cases, the identity of the perpetrator is not an issue because the accused is arrested in the act of commission, or there is a confession, or identity is admitted but guilt is contested, or some other reason. Most crimes are property crimes (burglaries, auto thefts, and so forth) in which proof of identity is seldom by eyewitness. Personal crimes (assaults, statutory rapes) typically involve parties who are acquainted with each other. It is in robberies that the use of eyewitness identification is most prevalent (*United States* v. *Wade*, 1967, p. 230). The identity of the perpetrator is usually at issue, and because the opportunity for observation is often fleeting and under stressful circumstances, the capacity of the eyewitness for reliable observation and remembering is called into question. Sobel (1972) estimates that eyewitness evidence is used in about 5% of criminal trials.

Even when identity is contested, it should be pointed out that most are not "pure identification" cases where there is nothing but eyewitness testimony to establish guilt. Most are "identification plus" cases where circumstantial evidence or other kinds of evidence are also available. Obviously, the former is more fraught with risk of a wrongful conviction, but fortunately its incidence is "rare" (Sobel 1972, p. 11). A blue-ribbon commission on eyewitness identifications chaired by Lord Chief Justice Devlin (1976) examined every criminal case involving a lineup in England and Wales during 1973. Of the 2,116 cases, in 45% of them the suspects were identified at the lineup. Of these, only 357 (or about 16% of the total number) were "pure identification" cases, and nearly three-fourths resulted in convictions. In nearly all of the identification cases decided by the Supreme Court, there has been ample evidence to connect the defendant with the crime, apart from the identification testimony.

Miscarriage of justice because of mistaken identification or prejudicial pretrial publicity tends to garner headline attention perhaps out of the proportion to its actual incidence. This, of course, in no way diminishes the seriousness of these problems because they undermine the truth-finding ideal of trial. It does suggest that preventive or remedial measures need not be more drastic than what the ills require (such as outright exclusion of all eyewitness identification testimony).

It is important to distinguish at the outset two distinct sources of erroneous pretrial identification. One is the normal and universal fallibility of the human mind to observe, retain, and recall accurately. The senses are not like a camera that records and plays back faithfully. One not only sees but perceives, and the constructive—rather than reduplicative—processes of the mind add to and alter the representation of the event as it is stored in memory. The second source is the susceptibility of the mind to suggestive influences, especially at the stage of retrieval from memory. It is here that the most distortion occurs because of situational factors and persuasion. Of concern to the law are suggestions arising from police identification practices that aggravate or even create the fallible eyewitness identification.

There are four types of police identification practices that could have a suggestive effect. A showup is a confrontation between the suspect alone and the witness. It may occur at the crime scene (typically when the police happen by when a crime is underway and they arrest a suspect on the spot) or later at the stationhouse. A stationhouse lineup is essentially a "multiple choice recognition test" (Woocher 1977, p. 986), in which the witness is presented with a parade of suspects. A photographic identification can be conducted in either showup or lineup form. And finally, there is informal identification in the field. For example, the police may arrange for a witness to ride in an unmarked patrol car and observe a suspect standing on a street corner, or "coincidentally" encounter the suspect in a courthouse corridor at the time of a bail hearing. The manner in which these identification procedures are carried out by the police could bias an eyewitness who was unsure to begin with. Wittingly or not, an officer who was absent at the crime scene can become in practical effect the main identifying witness.

Our concern is not with deliberate prevarication. As Williams (1963) notes, "[I]t is comparatively rare in a civilized society for an innocent person to be put in peril of conviction by the lying testimony of the prosecution; the real danger is of mistaken evidence" (p. 89). Nor is our concern here with intentional police misconduct. Instead, our attention centers on involuntary errors made by witnesses while identifying in good faith and on unintentional police influence at the stationhouse (for example, subtle suggestions which even the officer might not be conscious of, such as the hint of recognition when the witness's gaze turns to the suspect in the lineup).

Figure 10.1 summarizes the three principal stages at which identifications occur and the two sources of bias. The central question is whether the in-court identification at Time 3 represents a recall of the original observation at Time 1 (with the fallibility inherent to all such observations), and/or a recall of the stationhouse identification at Time 2 (with the possibility of police suggestion before or during the viewing). Our emphasis will not be on documenting these sources of bias. We will attend, instead, to the procedural safeguards the law has erected at trial to neutralize these pretrial biases and to research on their purported effectiveness.

FIGURE 10.1

Stages of Identification and Sources of Bias

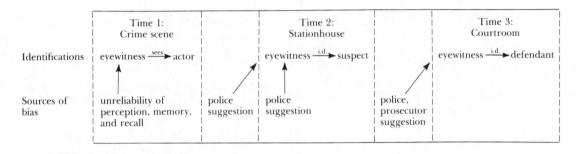

Overview

We begin in section 10.2 with the right to counsel as the safeguard against suggestive police identification procedures at lineups (*United States* v. *Wade*, 1967). Subsequent Supreme Court decisions all but dismantle this means of protection by triggering the right only after formal charges are filed. Where the right to counsel is unavailable, the reliability of pretrial identification evidence is evaluated by a due process balancing test (*Manson* v. *Brathwaite*, 1977). These cases provide the legal backdrop for social research designed to evaluate and improve the accuracy of lineup identifications.

Section 10.3 reviews the psychological research bearing on the reliability of eyewitness identifications. The established view is that human perception, memory, and recall are inherently fallible and therefore eyewitness testimony should be presumed suspect. The revisionist view challenges the assertion that eyewitnesses are generally untrustworthy and raises questions about the methodological, conceptual, and ideological underpinnings of the available research.

The next two sections examine the legal safeguards against the fallibility of eyewitness identifications. Section 10.4 describes the use of expert witnesses by presenting excerpts from a trial transcript of a psychologist's testimony. It also discusses the admissibility of expert testimony on eyewitness identifications (*United States* v. *Amaral*, 1973). Section 10.5 examines the use of cautionary instructions as a safeguard (*United States* v. *Telfaire*, 1972) and reviews research designed to improve jury comprehension of such instructions.

10.2. SAFEGUARDS AGAINST SUGGESTIVE POLICE IDENTIFICATION PROCEDURES

Presence of Counsel

UNITED STATES v. WADE

388 U.S. 218 (1967)

Mr. Justice BRENNAN delivered the opinion of the Court.

The question here is whether courtroom identifications of an accused at trial are to be excluded from evidence because the accused was exhibited to the witnesses before trial at a postindictment lineup conducted for identification purposes without notice to and in the absence of the accused's appointed counsel.

The federally insured bank in Eustace, Texas, was robbed on September 21, 1964. A man with a small strip of tape on each side of his face entered the bank, pointed a pistol at the female cashier and the vice president, the only persons in the bank at the time, and forced them to fill a pillow case with the bank's money. The man then drove away with an accomplice waiting in a stolen car outside the bank. On March 23, 1965, an indictment was returned against respondent Wade and two others for conspiring to rob the bank and against Wade and the accomplice for the robbery itself. Wade was arrested on April 2, and counsel was appointed to represent him on April 26. Fifteen days later an FBI agent, without notice to Wade's lawyer, arranged to have the two bank employees observe a lineup made up of Wade and five or six other prisoners and conducted

in a courtroom of the local county courthouse. Each person in the line wore strips of tape such as allegedly worn by the robber and upon direction each said something like "put the money in the bag," the words allegedly uttered by the robber. Both bank employees identified Wade in the lineup as the bank robber.

At trial, the two employees, when asked on direct examination if the robber was in the courtroom, pointed to Wade. The prior lineup identification was then elicited from both employees on cross-examination. At the close of testimony, Wade's counsel moved for a judgment of acquittal or, alternatively, to strike the bank official's courtroom identifications on the ground that conduct of the lineup, without notice to and in the absence of his appointed counsel, violated . . . his Sixth Amendment right to the assistance of counsel. The motion was denied, and Wade was convicted. . . .

II.

[I]n this case it is urged that the assistance of counsel at the lineup was indispensable to protect Wade's most basic right as a criminal defendant—his right to a fair trial at which the witnesses against him might be meaningfully cross-examined. . . .

[O]ur cases have construed the Sixth Amendment guarantee to apply to "critical" stages of the proceedings. . . .

[T]he principle of Powell v. Alabama and succeeding cases [pertaining to right to counsel] require that we scrutinize *any* pretrial confrontation of the accused to determine whether the presence of his counsel is necessary to preserve the defendant's basic right to a fair trial as affected by his right meaningfully to cross-examine the witnesses against him and to have effective assistance of counsel at the trial itself. It calls upon us to analyze whether potential substantial prejudice to defendant's rights inheres in the particular confrontation and the ability of counsel to help avoid that prejudice.

III.

The Government characterizes the lineup as a mere preparatory step in the gathering of the prosecution's evidence, not different—for Sixth Amendment purposes—from various other preparatory steps, such as systematized or scientific analyzing of the accused's fingerprints, blood sample, clothing, hair, and the like. We think there are differences which preclude such stages being characterized as critical stages at which the accused has the right to the presence of his counsel. Knowledge of the techniques of science and technology is sufficiently available, and the variables in techniques few enough, that the accused has the opportunity for a meaningful confrontation of the Government's case at trial through the ordinary processes of cross-examination of the Government's expert witnesses and the presentation of the evidence of his own experts. . . .

IV.

But the confrontation compelled by the State between the accused and the victim or witnesses to a crime to elicit identification evidence is peculiarly riddled with innumerable dangers and variable factors which might seriously, even crucially, derogate from a fair trial.

The vagaries of eyewitness identification are well-known; the annals of criminal law are rife with instances of mistaken identification. . . . A commentator has observed that "[t]he influence of improper suggestion upon identifying witnesses probably accounts for more miscarriages of justice than any other single factor—perhaps it is responsible for more such errors than all other factors combined." Wall, *Eye-Witness Identification in Criminal Cases* 26. Suggestion can be created intentionally or unintentionally in many subtle ways. And the dangers for the suspect are particularly grave when the witness' opportunity for observation was insubstantial, and thus his susceptibility to suggestion the greatest.

Moreover, "[i]t is a matter of common experience that, once a witness had picked out the accused at the line-up, he is not likely to go back on his word later on, so that in practice the issue of identity may (in the absence of other relevant evidence) for all practical purposes be determined there and then, before the trial. . . ."

But as is the case with secret interrogations, there is serious difficulty in depicting what transpires at lineups and other forms of identification confrontations. "Privacy results in secrecy and this in turn results in a gap in our knowledge as to what in fact goes on. . . ." Miranda v. State of Arizona. For the same reasons, the defense can seldom reconstruct the manner and mode of lineup identification for judge or jury at trial. Those participating in a lineup with the accused may often be police officers; in any event, the participants' names are rarely recorded or divulged at trial. The impediments to an objective observation are increased when the victim is the witness. Lineups are prevalent in rape and robbery prosecutions and present a particular hazard that a victim's understandable outrage may excite vengeful or spiteful motives. In any event, neither witnesses nor lineup participants are apt to be alert for conditions prejudicial to the suspect. . . . Moreover any protestations by the suspect of the fairness of the lineup made at trial are likely to be in vain; the jury's choice is between the accused's unsupported version and that of the police officers present. In short, the accused's inability effectively to reconstruct at trial any unfairness that occurred at the lineup may deprive him of his only opportunity meaningfully to attack the credibility of the witness' courtroom identification. . . .

Since it appears that there is grave potential for prejudice, intentional or not, in the pretrial lineup, which may not be capable of reconstruction at trial, and since presence of counsel itself can often avert prejudice and assure a meaningful confrontation at trial, there can be little doubt that for Wade the post-indictment lineup was a critical stage of the prosecution at which he was "as much entitled to such aid [of counsel] . . . as at the trial itself." Powell v. State of Alabama. Thus both Wade and his counsel should have been notified of the impending lineup, and counsel's presence should have been a requisite to conduct of the lineup, absent an "intelligent waiver. . . ."

Legislative or other regulations, such as those of local police departments, which eliminate the risks of abuse and unintentional suggestion at lineup proceedings and the impediments to meaningful confrontation at trial may also remove the basis for regarding the stage as "critical."[30]

But neither Congress nor the federal authorities has seen fit to provide a solution. What we hold today "in no way creates a constitutional straitjacket which will handicap sound efforts at reform, or is it intended to have this effect." Miranda v. State of Arizona.

V.

We come now to the question whether the denial of Wade's motion to strike the courtroom identification by the bank witnesses at trial because of the absence of his counsel at the lineup required, as the Court of Appeals held, the grant of a new trial at which such evidence is to be excluded. We do not think this disposition can be justified without first giving the Government the opportunity to establish by clear and convincing evidence that the in-court identifications were based upon observations of the suspect other than the lineup identification. . . . Where, as here, the admissibility of evidence of the lineup identification itself is not involved, a per se rule of exclusion of courtroom identification would be unjustified. A rule limited solely to the exclusion of testimony concerning identification at the lineup itself, without regard to admissibility of the courtroom identification, would render the right to counsel an empty one. The lineup is most often used, as in the present case, to crystallize the witnesses' identification of the defendant for future reference. We have already noted that the lineup identification will have that effect. The

---

[30]Thirty years ago Wigmore suggested a "scientific method" of pretrial identification "to reduce the risk of error hitherto inherent in such proceedings." Wigmore, *The Science of Judicial Proof* 541 (3d ed. 1937). Under this approach, at least 100 talking films would be prepared of men from various occupations, race, etc. Each would be photographed in a number of stock movements, with and without hat and coat, and would read aloud a standard passage. The suspect would be filmed in the same manner. Some 25 of the films would be shown in succession in a special projec-

tion room in which each witness would be provided an electric button which would activate a board backstage when pressed to indicate that the witness had identified a given person. Provision would be made for the degree of hesitancy in the identification to be indicated by the number of presses. Of course, the more systematic and scientific a process or proceeding, including one for purposes of identification, the less the impediment to reconstruction of the conditions bearing upon the reliability of that process or proceeding at trial. . . .

State may then rest upon the witnesses' unequivocal courtroom identification, and not mention the pretrial identification as part of the State's case at trial. . . .

We think it follows that the proper test to be applied in these situations is that quoted in Wong Sun v. United States, "Whether, granting establishment of the primary illegality, the evidence to which instant objection is made has been come at by exploitation of that illegality or instead by means sufficiently distinguishable to be purged of the primary taint." . . . Application of this test in the present context requires consideration of various factors; for example, the prior opportunity to observe the alleged criminal act, the existence of any discrepancy between any pre-lineup description and the defendant's actual description, any identification prior to lineup of another person, the identification by picture of the defendant prior to the lineup, failure to identify the defendant on a prior occasion, and the lapse of time between the alleged act and the lineup identification. It is also relevant to consider those facts which, despite the absence of counsel, are disclosed concerning the conduct of the lineup. . . .

We . . . think the appropriate proce-dure to be followed is to vacate the conviction pending a hearing to determine whether the in-court identifications had an independent source, or whether, in any event, the introduction of the evidence was harmless error. . . .

[Reversed and remanded.]

Mr. Justice WHITE . . . dissenting in part and concurring in part.

. . . The premise for the Court's rule is not the general unreliability of eyewitness identifications nor the difficulties inherent in observation, recall, and recognition. The Court assumes a narrower evil as the basis for its rule—improper police suggestion which contributes to erroneous identifications. The Court apparently believes that improper police procedures are so widespread that a broad prophylactic rule must be laid down, requiring the presence of counsel at all pretrial identifications, in order to detect recurring instances of police misconduct. I do not share this pervasive distrust of all official investigations. . . .

I would not extend [the adversary] system, at least as it presently operates, to police investigations and would not require counsel's presence at pretrial identification procedures. . . .

NOTES AND QUESTIONS

---

1. There is a syllogistic simplicity to the Court's analysis:

Major premise The right to counsel attaches at every critical stage of a criminal proceeding;
Minor premise a (postindictment) lineup is a critical stage (because suggestive influences at the lineup may undermine the right to confrontation at the trial);
Conclusion therefore, the right to counsel attaches at a (postindictment) lineup.

2. There are two aspects to the scope of the right to counsel. There is a right to appointed in-court assistance of counsel and to pretrial assistance of counsel.

The Sixth Amendment is generally construed to make counsel available at the trial itself. Therefore, to make the assistance of appointed counsel for indigent defendants applicable at a pretrial phase, the Court shifts to a "critical stage" analysis. A critical stage is one at which the defendant has to assert certain rights or raise certain defenses which may be lost if not invoked. Critical stages include arraignment (during which a defendant enters a plea before a judge), preliminary hearing (a mini-trial in which the state must show that the defendant probably committed the charged offense and therefore should be made to stand trial), and postindictment police interrogations. In what respects is a (postindictment) lineup different from these other critical stages so that, arguably, the right to counsel is less compelling at an identification session?

3.   In *Miranda* v. *Arizona* (Chapter 6, section 6.2), the Court required the police to warn suspects of their right to counsel. Why were no warnings required by *Wade* prior to lineups? Using the *Miranda* warnings as a model, what warnings would you draft for use by the police in lineups?

4.   Is waiver of the right to counsel at interrogations equivalent to waiver of the right to counsel at lineups? In terms of the functions that counsel serves in these two police situations, can it be argued that allowing waivers is less justifiable at lineups than at interrogations, or vice versa?

5.   The broad purpose for requiring presence of counsel at lineups is clear. It is a means of safe-guarding the right to confrontation at trial because the attorney can reconstruct what happened at the lineup and thereby have the needed information to attempt to impeach the in-court identification.
     But what is the specific role of counsel at the lineup itself? Should he be there just as a passive observer? The California Supreme Court has interpreted *Wade* to mean that "counsel plays only a limited role at the lineup itself" (*People* v. *Bustamante*, 1981, p. 583). If so, why is an attorney needed? Why not simply require a videotape of any lineups and later make it available to the defense, since there are not enough court-appointed lawyers and public defenders to serve indigent suspects around the clock? And since many suspects waive their right to counsel, a videotape would seem to be a more effective way of preserving a record of the pretrial confrontation.
     Can the attorney engage in a participatory, adversarial role? Can he object to the composition of the lineup, make suggestions to the police (and need the police comply?), and cross-examine the eyewit-ness? The flipside of the coin of suggestive influence by the police is coaching of the suspect by counsel. If the suspect had an Afro haircut and a dashiki at the crime scene, can the attorney advise that he cut his hair and wear a coat and tie at the lineup? Should a prosecutor then be present at the lineup, too? Would the next logical step be to bring a magistrate to the stationhouse to mediate disputes between both sides?
     Ours is an adversarial system of justice, but traditionally the adversarial procedure has been limited to the judicial component of the system. The police component, by the nature of its investigative function, is an *ex parte*, inquisitorial process. By requiring counsel at lineups or the giving of warnings of the right to counsel and to silence at custodial interrogations, the Court has transposed the adversarial model of trial onto the pre-judicial police stage.

6.   Despite the Court's dictum that "we scrutinize *any* pretrial confrontation . . . to determine whether the presence of his counsel is necessary," the facts of the case would limit the holding to post-indictment lineups. In terms of the dangers of police suggestion and the general unreliability of eyewitnesses, is the distinction between a preindictment and postindictment lineup meaningful? What reasons might the police have for conducting a lineup either before or after the formal accusation?

7.   The viability of a right is directly proportional to the enforcement remedy. Based on the "fruit of the poisonous tree" doctrine (*Wong Sun* v. *United States*, 1963), the Court said that the in-court identification ("fruit") can be excluded if it is derived from a stationhouse lineup conducted without the presence of counsel ("poisoned tree"). The fruit is automatically excluded if it results from "exploitation" of the primary illegality (for example, if the prosecution had elicited the tainted lineup identification from the witness on direct examination). However, if the prosecution does not exploit the poisoned tree by bringing out the lineup identification in its case-in-chief, the in-court identification could escape exclusion. The fruit can be unpoisoned if the witness had an independent source for the in-court identification—independent, that is, from the tainted lineup.
     In *Wade*, there was no exploitation because the lineup identification was elicited by the defense on cross-examination; therefore, the prosecution was allowed to show an independent source. Of the six possible independent sources enumerated in the opinion, does each one offer a wholly separate basis for the in-court identification? That is, are any of the sources themselves subject to police suggestion?

8.   Suppose an eyewitness identifies the defendant in court as the person who robbed her. The witness further testifies that the robber put a gun to her face so that she got a good look at him, and she would never forget that face for the rest of her life. On cross-examination, it is brought out that she identified the defendant at the lineup at which counsel was absent. The defense moves to strike the in-court identification as poisoned fruit. The prosecution then conducts a redirect examination. Q: "How do you know that this defendant is the man who robbed you?" A: "Because I remember him. The face of that robber is indelibly etched in my mind, and the defendant matches my mental picture of the robber." Is the in-court identification admissible? See *United States* v. *Crews* (1980).

9.   The first major retreat of the Burger Court from the vigorous safeguarding of the rights of the accused that characterized the Warren Court was in the area of pretrial identification. In *Kirby* v. *Illinois* (1972), the Court upheld the validity of a preindictment showup at the stationhouse conducted without an attorney present. The plurality opinion, announced by Justice Stewart, paid lip service to *Wade* but limited its scope. The right to counsel is "historically and rationally applicable only after the onset of formal prosecutorial proceedings" (p. 690). The police can now simply delay formal charges until after the lineup.

10.   The Court continued its retreat in *United States* v. *Ash* (1973). It held that there is no right to counsel in a postindictment photo identification because the Sixth Amendment guarantee applies only to trial-like confrontations. The use of photos is not trial-like because of the physical absence of the suspect.
     Suppose that a suspect invokes his right to counsel at a lineup. The police arrange for an attorney to be there, but the witness is not present. Instead, the police take a picture of the lineup and, after the attorney has departed, show the picture to the witness for identification. Is this procedure constitutional? See *People* v. *Lawrence* (1971) and *State* v. *Gaitor* (1980).

11.   A showup identification made at a preliminary hearing is subject to the *Wade* right to counsel (*Moore* v. *Illinois*, 1977). Even when a formal indictment has not been issued, the adversary process begins with this hearing.

Reliability of Identifications

MANSON v. BRATHWAITE

432 U.S. 98 (1977)

Mr. Justice BLACKMUN delivered the opinion of the Court.
     [Glover, a black undercover state police officer, stood for two or three minutes at an apartment door and made a purchase of heroin. The lighting was good and he had an opportunity to see the seller. Glover then left the building and reported to Detective D'Onofrio, who was waiting outside, giving him a description of the seller: "a colored man, approximately five feet eleven inches tall, dark complexion, black hair, short Afro style, and having high cheekbones, and of heavy build. . . ." Based on this description, D'Onofrio obtained a single photograph from police files and left it in Glover's office. Two days later, while alone, Glover

viewed the photograph and identified it as that of the seller. Three months later, the seller was arrested. At trial, Glover testified to the photographic identification in his office and also made an in-court identification of the seller (defendant Brathwaite). Ed.'s note.]
     This case presents the issue as to whether the Due Process Clause of the Fourteenth Amendment compels the exclusion, in a state criminal trial, apart from any consideration of reliability, of pretrial identification evidence obtained by a police procedure that was both suggestive and unnecessary. . . .

IV.

     [T]he courts of appeals appear to have developed at least two approaches to [this issue]. . . . The first, or *per se* approach, employed by the Second Circuit in the present case, focuses on the procedures employed and requires exclusion of the out-of-court identification evidence, without regard to reliability whenever it has been obtained through unnecessarily suggestive confrontation procedures. The justifications advanced are the elimination of evidence of uncertain reliability, deterrence of the police and prosecutors, and the stated "fair assurance against the awful risks of misidentification."

The second, or more lenient, approach is one that continues to rely on the totality of the circumstances. It permits the admission of the confrontation evidence if, despite the suggestive aspect, the out-of-court identification possesses certain features of reliability. Its adherents feel that the *per se* approach is not mandated by the Due Process Clause of the Fourteenth Amendment. This second approach, in contrast to the other, is *ad hoc* and serves to limit the societal costs imposed by a sanction that excludes relevant evidence from consideration and evaluation by the trier of fact. . . .

There are, of course, several interests to be considered and taken into account. . . . *Wade* and its companion cases reflect the concern that the jury not hear eyewitness testimony unless that evidence has aspects of reliability. It must be observed that both approaches before us are responsive to this concern. The *per se* rule, however, goes too far since its application automatically and peremptorily, and without consideration of alleviating factors, keeps evidence from the jury that is reliable and relevant.

The second factor is deterrence. Although the *per se* approach has the more significant deterrent effect, the totality approach also has an influence on police behavior. The police will guard against unnecessarily suggestive procedures under the totality rule, as well as the *per se* one, for fear that their actions will lead to the exclusion of identifications as unreliable.

The third factor is the effect on the administration of justice. Here the *per se* approach suffers serious drawbacks. Since it denies the trier reliable evidence, it may result, on occasion, in the guilty going free. . . .

We therefore conclude that reliability is the linchpin in determining the admissibility of identification testimony. . . . The factors to be considered . . . include the opportunity of the witness to view the criminal at the time of the crime, the witness' degree of attention, the accuracy of his prior description of the criminal, the level of certainty demonstrated at the confrontation, and the time between the crime and the confrontation. Against these factors is to be weighed the corrupting effect of the suggestive identification itself.

V.

We turn, then, to the facts of this case and apply the analysis:

1. The opportunity to view. Glover testified that for two to three minutes he stood at the apartment door, within two feet of the respondent. . . . Glover looked directly at his vendor. . . . Natural light from outside entered the hallway through a window. There was natural light, as well, from inside the apartment.

2. The degree of attention. Glover was not a casual or passing observer, as is so often the case with eyewitness identification. Trooper Glover was a trained police officer on duty—and specialized and dangerous duty. . . . Glover himself was a Negro and unlikely to perceive only general features of "hundreds of Hartford black males," as the Court of Appeals stated. . . .

3. The accuracy of the description. Glover's description was given to D'Onofrio within minutes after the transaction. It included the vendor's race, his height, his build, the color and style of his

hair, and the high cheekbone facial feature. . . . No claim has been made that respondent did not possess the physical characteristics so described. . . .

4. The witness' level of certainty. There is no dispute that the photograph in question was that of respondent. Glover, in response to a question whether the photograph was that of the person from whom he made the purchase, testified: "There is no question whatsoever." This positive assurance was repeated.

5. The time between the crime and the confrontation. Glover's description of his vendor was given to D'Onofrio within minutes of the crime. The photographic identification took place only two days later. . . . Although identifications arising from single-photograph displays may be viewed in general with suspicion, we find in the instant case little pressure on the witness to acquiesce in the suggestion that such a display entails. . . .

Although it plays no part in our analysis, all this assurance as to the reliability of the identification is hardly undermined by the facts that respondent was arrested in the very apartment where the sale had taken place, and that he acknowledged his frequent visits to that apartment. . . .

The judgment of the Court of Appeals is reversed.

It is so ordered.

NOTES AND QUESTIONS

1. Photo identification (a "rogues' gallery") is employed at different stages of the criminal process. During investigation, when the perpetrator is still at large, the police might show mug shots to eyewitnesses in an effort to identify a suspect. Not only is this a useful police tool but it also spares the innocent the ignominy of arrest. Mug shots might also be used when the police already have a suspect in custody. This practice is criticized but generally condoned by the lower courts (Sobel 1982, p. 5.4). Finally, just before trial, the prosecution might show photos to witnesses in preparation for the in-court identification. Of course, the line between "preparing" and "prompting" a witness is not always clear.

2. The use of mug shots during investigation to find suspects is common practice and certainly not in itself objectionable. But suppose an eyewitness identifies a suspect from the mug shots, and the police arrest the suspect and then present the suspect in a lineup (with presence of counsel) for identification by the eyewitness. In light of the preceding cases, does this procedure pass constitutional muster?

3. A variant of this procedure is the use of composite drawings prior to a lineup. The eyewitness describes to a police artist the features of the suspect and, together, they create a composite sketch of the suspect. The police arrest a person who looks like the drawing of the suspect, and this person is subsequently identified in a proper lineup by the eyewitness. Again, is this lineup identification admissible?

Design a study to examine the influence, if any, of the identification by mug shot or composite drawing upon the subsequent lineup identification.

4. Under the "balancing" or "totality of the circumstances" test, the fact that an identification procedure is unnecessarily suggestive (that is, unfair or potentially prejudicial) is not sufficient; it must also be inaccurate (that is, unreliable or actually prejudicial). Reliability is determined by looking at the factual circumstances of each case, and in this instance, Justice Blackmun mentions five specific factors. Notice that several of these factors are taken from the independent source test of *Wade*. *Wade* looked at these factors only to determine the admissibility of an in-court identification; *Brathwaite* extends them to evaluate the admissibility of a pretrial identification. Because of their similarity, courts have tended to use them interchangeably (*Kusley* v. *State*, 1982, p. 1338). What are the policy and practical implications of using the same criteria for determining the admissibility of these two different kinds of identifications?

5.   Under this totality test, if a suspect is correctly identified as guilty, the identification evidence can be used at trial even though identification procedure might be suggestive or unfair. Most state courts, in the wake of *Brathwaite,* allow suggestive evidence so long as it is reliable. Admissibility hinges on the witness's ability to identify the suspect, not on the conduct of the police (Jonakait 1981, p. 515). Do you agree that the issues of guilt of the suspect and procedural fairness by the police can be or should be separated?

The due process test is also used to determine the validity of confessions (*Spano* v. *New York,* 1959). Suppose that the police apply undue coercion and extract a confession, but there is independent basis for determining that the suspect is guilty and therefore the confession is reliable. Should the confession be admissible despite the coercive interrogation procedure? If not, how would you distinguish an unfair interrogation from an unfair identification?

6.   What are the advantages and disadvantages of the ad hoc, balancing approach of *Brathwaite* under the Due Process Clause compared with the per se, categorical approach of *Wade* under the Sixth Amendment?

7.   Prior to *Wade,* there had been virtually no legislative controls over lineups and no administrative regulations promulgated by the police themselves to minimize suggestiveness. In *Miranda* v. *Arizona* (1966), the Court urged Congress and the states to devise ways of safeguarding the right to silence during interrogations, because "the Constitution [does not] necessarily require adherence to any particular solution for the inherent compulsion" in questioning. Until alternative procedures are formulated, the Court requires warnings. In *Wade,* likewise, the Court emphasized that legislation or police department regulations that eliminate the risks of suggestion at lineup "may also remove the basis for regarding the stage as 'critical.' "

Subsequently, with the shift in emphasis in decisional law from right to counsel (*Wade*) to the reliability of identification (*Brathwaite*), many police departments began to heed the Court's call to promulgate regulations to ensure the fairness of lineups. Such regulations also help solidify the state's case and render less likely protracted litigation on the reliability issue. Some state supreme courts endorsed the idea of prescribing lineup standards by administrative rule-making in lieu of case-by-case adjudication (*State* v. *Greene,* 1979, p. 1371; *People* v. *Bustamante,* 1981, p. 583). For model lineup standards drafted by commentators, see American Law Institute (1975, pp. 662–67) and Sobel (1982, pp. 10.6–10.10).

The following lineup procedure was jointly developed by the prosecutor and public defender of Clark County (Las Vegas), Nevada. Does this procedure adequately safeguard against suggestive influence? Are there any additions or modifications that you would propose? Compare this procedure with Wigmore's "scientific method" described in footnote 30 of the *Wade* opinion—which one is more likely to produce more reliable identifications?

CHECKLIST FOR LINE-UP IDENTIFICATION*

1.   No line-up identification should be held without discussing the legal advisability of such line-up with the office of the District Attorney.

2.   No line-up should be held without a member of the District Attorney's office being present.

3.   No line-up should be held without a member of the Public Defender's office [or privately retained attorney] being present.

---

*Reprinted by permission of the publisher from F. T. Read, Lawyers at line-ups: constitutional necessity or avoidable extravagance? *UCLA Law Review* 17 (1969): 339–407, Appendix D, pp. 397–98. Copyright © 1969 by the Regents of the University of California.

4.   Insofar as possible, all persons in line-up should be of the same general age, racial and physical characteristics (including dress).

5.   Should any body movement, gesture, or verbal statement be necessary, this should also be done uniformly and any such movement, gesture, statement be done one time only by each person participating in the line-up and repeated only at the express request of the person attempting to make identification.

6.   The customary line-up photograph should be taken, developed as soon as possible and a copy of such photograph made available immediately to the Public Defender's office.

7.   If more than one person is called to view a line-up, the persons should not be allowed, before the completion of all witness[es]' attempted identification, to discuss among themselves any facet of their view of the line-up or the result of their conclusions regarding the same.

8.   All witnesses who are to view the line-up should be prevented from seeing the suspect in custody and in particular in handcuffs, or in any manner that would indicate to the witness the identity of the suspect in question.

9.   All efforts should be made to prevent a witness from viewing any photographs of the suspect prior to giving the line-up.

10.   All conversation between the police officer and prospective witnesses should be restricted to only indispensable direction. In all cases nothing should be said to the witness to suggest suspect is standing in the particular line-up.

11.   Should there be any more than one witness, only one witness at a time should be present in the room where the line-up is conducted.

. . .

14.   Each witness, as he appears in the room where the line-up is conducted, should be handed a form for use in the identification. [The form asks the witness to "place an 'X' in the appropriate square corresponding to the number of the person in the line-up" and to sign it.]

Research on Lineup Identifications

In the wake of the promulgation of lineup regulations by police departments, social psychologists began to undertake simulation studies of lineups in an effort to identify the variables that influence identification accuracy. These studies could provide an empirical basis for drafting or revising the regulations and for judicial determinations of fairness. So long as the effect of these variables can be controlled (for example, the effect of lineup size, which is a "system variable" to employ Wells's language [1978]) and not merely estimated (for example, the effect of race of suspect, which is an "estimator variable"), there is a potential opportunity for researchers to help improve this aspect of police investigation. Some representative examples of research on these two kinds of variables are described below.

LINEUP INSTRUCTIONS

It is not uncommon for the police to instruct a witness, prior to viewing a lineup, that they "have the man" and that he is among those taking part in the lineup.

Most courts have not found such an instruction so unduly suggestive as to constitute reversible error, since "it is generally assumed if one is called to examine a photographic or physical lineup, . . . there is a suspect in the crowd" (*State* v. *Wright*, 1982, p. 1097).

To determine the effect of this instruction on the rate and accuracy of identifications, Malpass and Devine (1980) presented to 350 students "a realistically staged vandalism of moderate seriousness" (p. 350). A vandal interrupted a lecture, ransacked some equipment, and ran out of the classroom. The students were then told that the event was staged and were asked to attend a lineup on a subsequent day. One hundred students showed up and each individually observed a five-person corporeal lineup. Half of the witnesses received the "biased instruction" that the vandal was in the lineup, and the others were given the "unbiased instruction" that the vandal "may or may not be present." In addition, for every other witness, the vandal was absent from the lineup and replaced by a look-alike alternate (that is, a "blank" lineup). The frequency of choosing and of errors (incorrect identifications), respectively, for the four conditions were as follows: (1) biased instruction/vandal present: 100% choosing rate, 25% error rate; (2) unbiased/present: 83%, 17%; (3) biased/absent: 78%, 78%; (4) unbiased/absent: 33%, 33%. The study concluded that unbiased instructions result "in fewer choices and fewer false identifications without a decrease in correct identifications" (p. 351).

Can these results be generalized to actual police lineups? Do they challenge judicial rulings that such biasing instructions, though suggestive, do not result in unreliable identifications? The authors replicated the study and, to lend greater realism, did not inform the students that the vandalism was staged. The lineups were conducted by uniformed police officers at a student center. This time, the instructions appeared to have no impact on the rate or accuracy of identifications (p. 353).

LINEUP SIZE

The typical regulation, such as that of Clark County, consists of a check list of factors that intuition and experience suggest are potential sources of unreliability. A drawback of this approach is that the relative weights of these different factors are unknown. There is no basis for assuming that biased instructions produce more unreliable identifications than, say, the composition of the lineup. Consequently, there are no general standards for determining which and how many of these factors need to be complied with by the police in order for the lineup to pass muster.

Some researchers have devised a different approach for assessing the fairness of a lineup. They have used the identifications of mock witnesses to construct a single, summary index of overall fairness. Doob and Kirshenbaum (1973) defined a biased lineup as "one where a person who was not a witness to the crime is more likely to pick the suspect of the lineup than we would expect by chance (where chance is defined as $1/n$, n being the number of people in the lineup" (p. 290). Thus, a six-person lineup would be deemed biased by this criterion if the proportion of mock witnesses choosing the suspect exceeds one-sixth, the value specified by the null hypothesis.

Others, however, suggest that "nominal size" (the total number of persons) is less important for determining fairness than "functional size" (the number of lineup members resembling the suspect) (Wells, Leippe, and Ostrom 1979, p. 285). Functional size can be less than nominal size if some of the lineup members are easily perceived by witnesses as nonsuspects. For example, if the suspect is known to be a man, and the six-man lineup is expanded to include five additional "fillers" or "foils" who are women, this lineup would be biased according to the Doob-Kirshenbaum test because the proportion of mock witnesses choosing the suspect would remain at 1/6 while the chance baseline is 1/11. Obviously, if none of the mock witnesses choose any of the women, these added fillers are functionally irrelevant to the identification—it is as if the women were not present in the lineup. Consequently, Wells et al. propose another index, D/n (where D is the number of mock witnesses choosing the suspect and n is the total number of mock witnesses who view the lineup), or its reciprocal, n/D, which measures "functional size." The two indices yield the same information, except that the former is expressed in terms of a fraction and the latter in terms of an integer.

Wells et al. give an example based upon an actual case (p. 290). Eyewitnesses to a bank robbery provided a physical description of the alleged culprit and then correctly identified him in a six-person corporeal lineup. To support the defense argument that the lineup was unfair, the researchers calculated post hoc the functional size of the lineup. They gave sixty mock witnesses (students) the eyewitnesses' description of the suspect and a photograph of the lineup that had been presented to the eyewitnesses. The students were tested individually and asked to identify the suspect. Forty-one of the students made a choice, and of this number, twenty-five (or 60%) chose the correct suspect. The functional size of the lineup was only 1.6 members (41/25). (The number of mock witnesses needed to determine functional size was based upon the number needed to produce a 95% confidence interval of $\pm.5$. It is a parameter estimation procedure.)

Is the viewing of a corporeal lineup the equivalent of viewing a photographic lineup? What should be the acceptable functional size? How would the police determine in advance the functional size of a lineup? Is functional size an adequate operational measure of the due process test of fairness prescribed by *Brathwaite*? Does this index of departure from nominal size merit more weight in determining reliability than, say, biased instructions or any other potential source of bias enumerated in the Clark County check list? For further mathematical elaboration of this concept, see Malpass (1981).

LINEUP SIMILARITY

Defense claims of an unfair lineup due to its composition have generally been rejected except for the most blatant instances of dissimilarity (for example, a black suspect in an all-white lineup). Due process challenges on the grounds that the defendant was much older, or shorter, or had longer hair, or was distinctively attired have not prevailed because, as one court put it, "there is no requirement that a defendant in a lineup must be surrounded by people nearly identical in appearance" (*Wright* v. *Smith*, 1977, p. 342). Researchers have oppugned this judicial attitude because, they claim, it rests on erroneous behavioral assumptions.

One study examined the effect of lineup similarity on identification accuracy (Lindsay and Wells 1980). As lineup members look more alike, making the witness's task of recognition more difficult, there could be a decrease in wrong identifications (thereby safeguarding the rights of suspects) or there could be a decrease in both wrong and correct identifications (an equal reduction of both would be a tradeoff between promoting the interests of suspects and of law enforcement).

The study involved a staged theft. Each student was seated alone in a room and was completing a questionnaire when a man entered, engaged in brief conversation, picked up a calculator lying on a table, and quickly departed. The entire incident took twelve seconds. The experimenter then returned and asked the student "to assume that a theft had occurred" (p. 306) and to identify the thief from a six-man photographic lineup, with the option of choosing "none of the above." There were two independent variables: (1) "criminal present lineup" or "criminal absent lineup" (identical lineup except that the picture of the thief was replaced by a picture of a look-alike, a Caucasian with light brown hair and moustache), and (2) "high lineup similarity" (all the foils resembled the thief) or "low lineup similarity" (the foils were Asians and Caucasians with black hair and beard).

The results (based on ninety-four subjects) are summarized in the accompanying table. The authors conclude that "high-similarity lineups reduce the rate of false identifications of innocent suspects more rapidly than the rate of correct identifications of guilty suspects" (p. 313). It is important to note how they define a false identification. "[T]he identification of any lineup member other than the original criminal . . . is not necessarily a false identification" because foils are known (to the police) to be innocent (p. 305). The researchers assume that the police place only one suspect per lineup. "It is only the identification of an innocent suspect that deserves the label 'false identification.' Choices of foils might be more appropriately labeled 'failure to identify the suspect'" (p. 306).

What other conclusions can be drawn from this table? Do these results impeach

Proportions of Witnesses Choosing the Guilty or Innocent Suspect from the Photo Array as Functions of the Presence or Absence of the Criminal and the Similarity Manipulation

	Choice of Guilty Suspect	Choice of Innocent Suspect	Choice of Foil	No Choice
Low lineup similarity				
Criminal present	.71	—[b]	.12	.18
Criminal absent	—[b]	.70	.04	.26
High lineup similarity				
Criminal present	.58	—[b]	.29	.13
Criminal absent	—[b]	.31	.41	.28

[b] cannot occur.

the courts' intuition that some dissimilarity does not necessarily obviate the fairness of a lineup? (Note that "low similarity" in this study involved gross dissimilarity.)

WITNESS CONFIDENCE

One of the variables to be considered in reviewing the fairness of an identification under *Brathwaite's* due process test is "the witness' level of certainty." The common-sense assumption is that a witness's confidence in his or her own identification is correlated with the accuracy of that identification. Confidence is an "estimator variable" which cannot be directly controlled by criminal justice officials, but which is nonetheless relied upon by judges and juries as an indicator of reliability. Research attempting to test the validity of this assumption has yielded mixed results. A review of twenty-five studies found about an equal number of studies showing a positive relationship and no relationship (or even negative relationship) between confidence and accuracy (Deffenbacher 1980). The review sought to reconcile these conflicting findings by suggesting that when the original observation and the subsequent identification are carried out under "optimal" conditions (that is, conditions that facilitate accurate identifications, such as ample opportunity to observe, prior familiarity with the suspect, unbiased lineup instructions), a positive correlation will obtain. This optimality hypothesis, which includes the reliability factors enumerated in *Brathwaite,* accounted for many but not all of the inconsistent results. Nonetheless, the review concluded that "the judicial system should cease and desist from a reliance on eyewitness confidence as an index of eyewitness accuracy" (p. 258).

In the Lindsay and Wells study of lineup similarity, the confidence of the subjects in their identifications was also recorded on seven-point scales. They found no correlation between confidence and accuracy, even when the identification setting was "optimal" (low similarity, criminal present). Other researchers propose that the "reality" of these simulation studies may be a mediating factor. The witnesses know it is "only" an experiment with no real-life consequences for the victim or suspect. Brigham (1980) undertook a study of "high mundane realism" (p. 318). "Customers" visited convenience stores, and two hours later, "law interns" came and showed the store clerks six-person photographic lineups. The customer was present in the lineup and the foils were similar to him. About 80% of the clerks made a choice and indicated the degree of their confidence on a four-point scale. A substantial correlation (.50) was found: Among those who were most certain, 85% were accurate, while among those who were least certain, only 17% (or one-sixth, the chance level) were accurate. The study concluded that this is "an area in need of further clarification" (pp. 317, 318; see also Brigham et al. 1982).

FURTHER RESEARCH

What other system-level variables might influence identification accuracy and merit empirical study?

Do the foregoing studies support the proposal that the police present at least two lineups to each witness, one of which is a "blank" lineup?

Police regulations of photographic lineups have been less common than those of corporeal lineups. In the absence of standards, for example, police sometimes insert more than one photograph of a suspect in the same display, and courts have not struck down this practice (*People* v. *Guillebeau,* 1980). Draft a set of model regulations governing the composition of photo spreads.

10.3.   PSYCHOLOGY OF EYEWITNESS IDENTIFICATION

The current research on the psychology of eyewitness identification represents the outgrowth of four distinct yet interrelated strands of inquiry.

Witness reliability. One of the earliest uses of psychology in action was to determine the testimonial certitude of courtroom witnesses. At the turn of the century, German psychologists (Stern 1910) developed the *Aussage* or remembrance experiments. Laboratory subjects were presented with pictures and later asked to recall the details under questioning or free narration. Typically, the results showed considerable error, and these were generalized to show the unreliability of witnesses. The procedure was later refined to simulate the observation and reporting of a real event. This became known as the "reality experiment." The first one was conducted in 1901 by a law professor at Stern's suggestion. An unexpected staged altercation erupts in the middle of a lecture and students are subsequently asked to report the incident in detail. Again, incompleteness and inaccuracy characterize the reports. The first book in English on legal psychology contained descriptions of a number of such experiments (Münsterberg 1908). Revised and made more sophisticated over the years, the reality experiment became the prototype of current psychological research in this area.

Evidence. The psychology of evidence flourished in the late 1920s and 1930s, pioneered by the collaborative efforts of Hutchins, a lawyer, and Slesinger, a psychologist. They set out to reconstruct the body of evidence law by re-examining its premises in light of the available understanding of perception, memory, learning, and emotion. Their essays were informed analyses of law with proposals for reform of evidence rules (for example, Hutchins and Slesinger 1929). They relied as often on untested generalizations and conjecture as on research data to critique the law. In the tradition of advocacy, they selected the most persuasive evidence available and, in this instance, it came from the developing field of experimental psychology.

Perception, memory, and recall. Basic experimental research on perception, memory, and recall during the past fifty years or so undergirds current work. Bartlett's (1932) classic study of remembering showed that it is a constructive rather than reproductive process. Instead of simply storing and retrieving information, it is "an effort after meaning" (p. 44). Memory, like perception, is a dynamic process, selecting and organizing inputs in psychologically meaningful ways. Subsequent research elaborated on the theme that the mind is not a mirror that merely reflects the external world, but is affected by needs, expectancies, and other factors so that it creates its own vision of reality. This research provided the theoretical framework and methodology for much of the applied research on eyewitness testimony (Clifford and Bull 1978; Loftus 1979; Yarmey 1979).

Social psychology. Experimental psychology tends to study cognitive processes of individuals in isolated, controlled settings. It does not take into account the social context of perception and memory. But the general unreliability of eyewitness identification involves a combination of fallible cognitive processes and social suggestion. Thus, the classic studies of social perception and social psychology of the past quarter of a century provide another basis for contemporary work on eyewitness research. These studies describe the motivational bases of perception (the "New Look" school of the 1950s; Bruner 1958), the interaction of sensory and social inputs in perception (Allport 1955), the conformity to majority pressure and other social influence (Asch 1958; Sherif 1958), and the workings of small groups (Collins and Raven 1968).

In the past decade there has been an increasing body of new research expressly concerned with applications to the area of criminal identifications, and it has been referred to as "applied eyewitness testimony research" (Wells 1978). It represents the convergence of the early reality experiments, the reform-inspired attention to the psychology of evidence, and the basic advances in experimental and social psychology. It is against this brief historical backdrop that the following overview of the psychological research should be seen.

DID YOUR EYES DECEIVE YOU? EXPERT PSYCHOLOGICAL TESTIMONY ON THE UNRELIABILITY OF EYEWITNESS IDENTIFICATION

Frederic D. Woocher

. . .

PSYCHOLOGICAL RESEARCH FINDINGS

Research on the psychological dimensions of eyewitness identification has emerged from a combination of somewhat distinct fields of specialization within experimental psychology, including perception, memory and social psychology. Although experimental psychologists traditionally have concentrated their efforts on pure research and only occasionally have alluded to the practical effects of their findings, some of their earlier works in applied psychology, dating back to the 19th century, explored relevant areas of "legal psychology." In particular, having observed that major discrepancies often existed between different eyewitness ac-

counts of the same event, many psychologists began to study the psychology of testimony and later to examine experimentally the fallibility of perception, the unreliability of memory and the inaccuracy of eyewitness identifications.[13]

The need for scientific study in this area was occasioned by the earlier "sensationalist" thinking in the field, which assumed that the human brain operates more or less as a mechanical recording device: A person sees everything and records this information on a memory "tape." When necessary to describe a past event, the person simply selects the appropriate memory tape and plays it back, producing

[13]One of the most common techniques used to demonstrate the fallibility of personal identification is to stage a "mock crime" before a group of observers. Dr. Hugo Münsterberg probably first used this method of study, H. Münsterberg, [*On the Witness Stand* (1908)], at 49–54, although it has been repeated so often in law and introductory psychology classes that the results are no longer reported. The scenario runs generally as follows: At some point in the middle of the professor's lecture, a stranger enters the room, confronts the professor or a student, feigns an assault on that person, and quickly runs off. Members of the audience are then asked to give descriptions of the attacker and the event.

Such experiments yield almost uniform results: Most observers make significant errors on almost every facet of the description, from the duration of the event, the physical description of the attacker and the clothing worn, to the words spoken, the weapon used and even the sequence of events. . . .

a faithful recounting of the original perception.

Over the past half-century, however, psychological research emphatically has demonstrated the invalidity of this conception and has revealed that the "videotape recorder" analogy is misleading in three respects discussed briefly here and analyzed more fully in the remainder of this section. First, perception is not a mere passive recording of an event but instead is a constructive process by which people consciously and unconsciously use decisional strategies to attend selectively to only a minimal number of environmental stimuli. Second, over time, the representation of an event stored in memory undergoes constant change; some details are added or altered unconsciously to conform the original memory representation to new information about the event, while others simply are forgotten. Finally, the manner in which information is retrieved from memory almost always distorts the remembered image; most often, very powerful —yet imperceptibly subtle—suggestions shape the resulting recollection.

1. PERCEPTION OF THE ORIGINAL EVENT.

PERCEPTUAL SELECTIVITY. The inherent limitations of the human brain are the major source of inaccuracy in perception. People can perceive only a limited number of the simultaneous stimuli in the environment at any time; the number of these that can be encoded in memory is even smaller. In order to cope with these innate limitations, an observer develops unconscious strategies to aid in the selectivity of perceptual processes and ultimately to concentrate attention on the most necessary and useful details. In short, a human must "learn" how to perceive efficiently. . . .

[N]umerous studies have confirmed that even trained observers find it difficult to describe such obvious physical charac-

teristics as height, weight and age. Lay witnesses surely must recognize and relate specific details of physiognomy much more inaccurately than these trained, objective observers. . . .

TIME PERCEPTION. Humans also find it especially difficult to perceive time accurately, that is, to estimate either the duration of an event or the interval between successive events. Studies have shown that people tend to judge time by the amount of activity occurring; during sudden, action-packed events such as crimes, people almost always overestimate the length of time involved because the flurry of activity leads them to conclude that a significant amount of time has passed. . . .

POOR OBSERVATION CONDITIONS. In addition to perceptual inaccuracies caused by the brain's inherent limitations, many identification errors are due to the circumstances of the observation. A major variable influencing perception is the duration of the observation period. Crimes in which the primary evidence is an eyewitness identification characteristically are brief, fast-moving events; the victim and witnesses consequently will have difficulty getting a sufficiently good "look" to allow them to process enough visual features of the event and the offender to make a reliable subsequent recognition. . . .

STRESSFUL SITUATION. Another important environmental factor limiting the accuracy of perception is the stressful situation facing the victim. Although judges and juries often may be convinced by the victim's assertion that "I was so frightened that his face is etched in my memory forever," psychological research demonstrates that perceptual abilities actually *decrease* significantly when the observer is in a fearful or anxiety-provoking situation.

Studies have shown that an increase in anxiety generally produces a cluster of certain physiological responses. The frightened victim or eyewitness may report increases in heart rate, rapid breathing and excessive perspiration, but usually does not notice that the anxiety also has caused fixation of the eyes. Yet, because visual information is processed by contrasting successive retinal images, this fixation reduces visual acuity, particularly for details on the periphery of the environment.

Excessive anxiety also produces involuntary cognitive reactions in the observer, who often will attempt to cope with a frightening situation simply by rejecting it. This phenomenon of "perceptual defense" may cause a frightened victim . . . to "close" her mind—and eyes—in order to block out and avoid recognition of stimuli that might produce anxiety. . . .

EXPECTANCY. Although many of the organic and environmental limitations on perceptual abilities come quickly to mind, other social psychological factors operate more subtly, if quite powerfully, to distort perception. In order to compensate for the perceptual selectivity made necessary by the brain's limitation, observers make extensive use of expectancy, not only in developing strategies for determining what to look at, but also in interpreting what they see. Because the human mind can process only a small portion of what is visible at any given time, it develops the ability to form conclusions about what has been perceived based on limited amounts of sensory information. It accomplishes this task by integrating fragmentary visual information into existing conceptual schemata based upon a fund of general knowledge acquired over time. In essence, witnesses unconsciously reconstruct what *has* occurred from what they assume *must have* occurred. Consequently, they exhibit a pronounced tendency to perceive the expected. . . .

PERSONAL NEEDS AND BIASES. In addition to expectancies caused by prior experience and information about the world,

the personal needs and motives of the observer also distort perception.[39] In short, witnesses tend to see when they *want* to see. Thus, the need and desire to produce a complete description of an assailant may foster perception that is more the product of an unconscious imagination than a keen eye.

Personal biases and latent prejudices also shape expectancies, often distorting perceptions to fit the various stereotypes that all humans possess.[40] Social psychology experiments indicate that people tend to correlate physical characteristics with personality traits, and that perceptual distortion increases when the viewer regards objects unfavorably. These findings imply that a victim may unwittingly distort her perception of an assailant to include physical features that the victim associates with the personality traits typified by the criminal's behavior.

CROSS-RACIAL IDENTIFICATIONS. Finally, considerable evidence indicates that people are poorer at identifying members of another race than of their own. Some studies have found that, in the United States at least, whites have greater difficulty recognizing black faces than vice

---

[39] . . . In some famous experiments, psychologists showed meaningless inkblot pictures to a group of subjects who had undergone varying degrees of food deprivation. When they asked the subjects for descriptions, the researcher found that the hungrier the subjects the more likely they were to report having seen some type of food. The "need" to see food had increased the likelihood that the subject would see food. Levine, Chein & Murphy, The Relation of the Intensity of a Need to the Amount of Perceptual Distortion: A Preliminary Report, 13 *J. Psych.* 283 (1942). . . .

[40] In a classic experiment on the effects of social prejudice on perceptions, psychologists showed subjects a picture of several people on a subway train, including a white man holding an open razor and apparently arguing with a black man standing next to him. When asked to describe what they had seen, over half the subjects reported that the black man was brandishing the razor. G. Allport & L. Postman, *The Psychology of Rumor* 75 (1965). . . .

versa. Moreover, counterintuitively, the ability to perceive the physical characteristics of a person from another racial group apparently does not improve significantly upon increased contact with other members of that race. Because many crimes are cross-racial, these factors may play an important part in reducing the accuracy of eyewitness perception.

2.   ENCODING AND STORAGE IN MEMORY.

MEMORY DECAY OVER TIME. Even if someone accurately perceived an event, its representation in the observer's memory would not remain entirely intact for very long. People forget both quickly and easily. The phenomenon of forgetting what once has been perceived and encoded in memory, known as "retroactive inhibition," is one of the earliest and most consistent findings of cognitive psychology. Simply put, the more time that has elapsed since the perception of some event—and, therefore, the more intervening occurrences that must be stored in memory—the poorer a person's memory is of that event. Particularly with visual images, memory begins to decay within minutes of the event, so that considerable memory loss probably occurs during the many days— and often months—that typically elapse between the offense and an eyewitness identification of the suspect in a criminal case.

FILLING GAPS IN MEMORY. Many psychologists once thought that automatic decay of the memory trace caused all distortions of memory. More recently, however, they have discovered that memory, like perception, is an active, constructive process that often introduces inaccuracies by adding details not present in the initial representation or in the event itself. The mind combines all the information acquired about a particular event into a single storage "bin," making it difficult to distinguish what the witness saw originally from what she learned later. Because all of the research on human memory indicates that the actual memorial representation must decay in accuracy over time, any reported increases in the completeness of a description come only at the risk of a reduction in the description's correctness. If a witness' description of a suspect becomes more detailed as the investigation proceeds from the police report through the preliminary hearing to trial, the witness in this situation probably unconsciously has changed the image in memory to include details subsequently acquired from, for example, newspaper reports of the event or a mug shot of the defendant.

Moreover, because of a psychological need to reduce uncertainty and eliminate inconsistencies, witnesses have a tendency not only to fill any gaps in memory by adding extraneous details but also to change mental representations unconsciously so that they "all make sense.". . . In the context of an eyewitness identification of a criminal defendant, such unconscious modifications of memory can have tragic consequences.[53]

---

[53]Psychological research has shown that people often have difficulty remembering the context in which they originally learned an item of information. . . .

A recent experiment using a "blank" lineup that did not contain the actual criminal but did include one or two people whose pictures previously were included in a photo array demonstrated that lineup witnesses possibly will misidentify an individual whose mug shot they had seen, even if they earlier had failed to select him in the photo array. K. Deffenbacher, E. Brown & W. Sturgill, Memory for Facts and the Circumstances of their Encounter (1975) (unpublished study conducted at the University of Nebraska) (copy on file with Stanford Law Review). [Published in *Journal of Applied Psychology* 62 (1977): 311. Ed.'s note.]

The dangers resulting from the difficulties people have in remembering the circumstances under which they saw an individual are not limited to photo arrays and subsequent corporeal lineups. The possibility always exists that the witness is quite accurate in recalling an individual but completely wrong in remembering the circumstances under which he encountered that person. Glanville Williams describes several mistaken identifications resulting from "unconscious transference," in which, for example, a

Although a careful defense attorney and a scrupulous prosecutor might take measures to shield a witness from exposure to certain types of information obtained after the event itself, such as viewing the defendant in custody prior to identification, recent experiments have demonstrated that some suggestions work so subtly as virtually to make it impossible to prevent their incorporation into the witness' memory. The leading series of experiments in this area suggests that the mere wording of a question put to an eyewitness during a deposition, an interview or at the trial itself may affect not only the immediate answer but also the witness' memory of the original event as well as any answers to subsequent questions about that event.[55] By implication, therefore, even routine police interrogation of the witness immediately after the crime may plant subtle suggestions that unconsciously become incorporated into the witness' memory of the event.[56] . . .

---

waitress identifies the defendant as having been in her cafe with the murder victim when, in fact, the defendant had been in that cafe on a few earlier occasions but was out of town at the time of the crime. G. Williams, [*The Proof of Guilt*, 3rd ed. (1963) at 91–92.
. . .
[55]In one study, after seeing a movie of a traffic accident, researchers asked the subjects a series of questions about the accident, including some that contained presuppositional information about nonexistent events. For example, some were asked, "How fast was the car going when it passed the barn while travelling down the country road?"—even though there had been no barn. When asked a week later whether they remembered seeing a barn in the movie, these subjects answered affirmatively 10 times more often than subjects who had not received the presuppositional information. Loftus, Leading Questions and the Eyewitness Report, 7 *Cognitive Psych.* 560 (1975). . . .
[56]In phrasing the questions asked of the eyewitness, the police investigator unconsciously may induce the eyewitness subsequently to include information in his memorial representation of the events. For example, the police may ask the victim of a robbery to describe the gun that the assailant used and even might show the victim several types of firearms. Although the victim originally may have been unsure whether the assailant actually had a gun, these questions may incor-

3. RETRIEVAL OF INFORMATION FROM MEMORY.

INADEQUACY OF VERBAL DESCRIPTIONS. The final source of errors in identification, and the one discussed most thoroughly in the legal literature, is the process by which information is retrieved from memory for purposes of making an identification. Because few eyewitnesses have the artistic ability to draw an accurate representation of the criminal—the closest analogy to free recall—the criminal justice system must rely upon the eyewitness' vocabulary. Initially, therefore, the recall process suffers from the inadequacy of the verbal form to convey fully the physiognomical details of the witness' memory of the offender. Moreover, numerous studies have shown that even the most free and accurate form of verbal recall—a narrative description unprompted by questions—results in exceedingly incomplete information retrieval. On the other hand, as the questions become more structured in order to achieve completeness, the resulting responses become more inaccurate, because witnesses may feel compelled to answer questions completely in spite of incomplete knowledge. Faced with this inverse relationship between accuracy and completeness of a description, law enforcement officials generally opt for the latter at the expense of the former.

SUGGESTION IN THE COMPOSITION OF AN IDENTIFICATION TEST. In order to obtain identifications, police must rely on structured "recognition" tests, such as lineups and photo arrays, even though these procedures are notoriously unreliable because of their potential for exposing the witness to suggestive influences. Much already has been written on the dangers involved in the use of such techniques for identification purposes. . . .

---

porate their suggestions into the witness' memory, causing him to believe that he really had seen a gun. . . .

Note: Did Your Psychologist Deceive You?

The principal message that emerges from the research—to be read with trumpets blaring—is that OBSERVATIONS ARE UNTRUSTWORTHY! Eyewitness testimony, quite simply, is "notoriously unreliable," Woocher asserts, more so than the courts are willing to acknowledge. "In report after report, we have been informed of the inability of witnesses to accurately select from lineups or photo spreads or of the variability among eyewitnesses in their descriptions of a common event, or of the malleability of the memory of a witness" (Yuille 1980, p. 338). "[L]egal testimony is replete with potential inaccuracies and misconceptions, regardless of the avowed certainty of the witness" (Bartol 1983, p. 190). "[E]yewitness testimony . . . is not any kind of magic pipeline to the truth"; it is "overvalued as a sacred element of evidence" and "*any* eyewitness report" (emphasis added) should be evaluated "skeptically." Decisions such as *Brathwaite* are derided as "a step backward into the nineteenth-century view" of human perception (Ellison and Buckhout 1982, pp. 128, 80–81). The reluctance of the courts to embrace wholeheartedly these claims is railed as "reactionary and closed minded" (Buckhout; quoted in Wells 1978, p. 1547). Psychologists, it sometimes seems, sound like the Howard Cosell of academia. There is no way of determining directly the proportion of eyewitnesses in actual cases who are untrustworthy. But those in a position to make informed guesses, namely trial attorneys, suggest a less alarming scenario. In a statewide survey of prosecuting attorneys in Florida, the majority indicated that 90-95% of eyewitness identifications they encountered were probably correct. Defense attorneys as a group have a stake in impeaching the credibility of eyewitnesses. But even among this group, the same survey showed that the majority said that about 75% of identifications they encountered were probably correct (Brigham et al. 1982, p. 679). A "revisionist" view, therefore, may be in order. The methodological, conceptual, and ideological underpinnings of the research need to be scrutinized if a balanced perspective is to be restored.

In addition to the basic premise that eyewitnesses are inherently unreliable, researchers in this area assert a second proposition: there is unwarranted and excessive trust in eyewitness evidence. "[J]urors," Loftus (1979) says, "rarely regard eyewitness testimony with any skepticism" (p. 197). If eyewitnesses are generally inaccurate but jurors nonetheless overbelieve them, then the inference is that the admission of eyewitness testimony at trial will likely increase wrongful convictions. The foundation for the basic premise is studies that show that people are inaccurate in the laboratory. We shall begin by examining some of these studies to see if certain features of the experimental procedures might inflate or enhance inaccuracy. Even if the procedures are not biased, we need to inquire if the inaccuracy of subjects in the laboratory can be generalized to eyewitnesses in the real world, given the contrived nature of the typical experiment in this field. And finally, even if the results are generalizable, we should consider whether the claim that many innocent defendants are being convicted on the basis of false eyewitness reports is a conclusion that necessarily follows.

1.   *Self-selection of subjects.* The inference drawn from simulation studies is that actual eyewitnesses in real life settings are probably as inaccurate as the experimental subjects. It is possible, however, that the reported inaccuracies are magnified because of the procedures used.

Consider the method of selecting witnesses. In the real world, witnesses who agree to attend a police identification session are self-selected. One likely basis for the self-selection is claimed accuracy of observation. For example, if twenty persons are at a bank when a robbery occurs, maybe only five or six will agree to identify the suspect at a subsequent lineup. It is possible that only those who really got a good look at the robber would come forward. Those who did not notice all the details of the crime would decline to participate. In contrast, in a staged crime in a classroom, all of the students in attendance would be asked to describe the incident and the suspect. The accuracy scores in reality experiments consist of averages of the reports of the entire sample of subjects, irrespective of whether they paid attention to the staged event or not. If the studies included only those students who said they watched the entire event carefully, the reported accuracy rate could rise substantially.

Thus, because "we do not know the role of 'volunteerism' in eyewitness research . . . [i]naccurate eyewitnesses" may be "overrepresented" (Yuille 1980, p. 338).

2. *Unreality of simulation.* The fact that classroom students or laboratory subjects know that it is a staged crime may also produce inflated fallibility figures. They may be less reticent to hazard a guess when no actual consequences attach to their decisions. In the studies, seldom are the witnesses also the victims of the crime. These methodological drawbacks limit the external validity or generalizability of the research.

One study examined the effect of deliberately enhancing the penal consequences of simulated crimes (Malpass and Devine 1980). Students viewed a classroom incident of vandalism but were not told that it was staged. At the subsequent lineup procedure, the students overheard a conversation on the possible consequences to the vandal if he were identified: either "trivial" (reprimand by college officials) or "severe" (criminal prosecution and jail term). Subjects in the "severe" group made fewer identification errors (25%) than those in the "trivial" group (70%) when the vandal was present in the lineup (p. 353). These findings are consistent with what we know about the performance of simulated jurors. Real juries are less likely to convict than mock juries (Zeisel and Diamond 1974, p. 281), and the greater the verisimilitude in jury simulations, the lower is the rate of guilty verdicts (Bermant et al. 1974, pp. 230–31). "Perhaps . . . simulations have inherently trivial consequences . . . and this difference is responsible for the contrasting results" (Malpass and Devine 1980, p. 357), whether these results are of eyewitness identifications or jury decisions.

Some researchers claim that knowledge of the staged character of a crime does not affect eyewitness performance (Murray and Wells 1982). The basis of their claim is a study in which college students witnessed a staged theft while participating as subjects in a psychology experiment. One group was then informed that it was staged but was asked to pretend that the theft was real. The other group was not informed. (However, several subjects in the latter group told the experimenter that they disbelieved the incident and were dropped from the analysis of the results. How many other subjects were skeptical about the reality of the theft but remained silent is unknown.) A campus policeman arrived and asked the subjects (in both groups) to identify the suspect in a photographic lineup of six persons. Whether subjects were informed or not informed had no effect on their choices of the lineup suspect or on their willingness to make an identification. This experiment tells us something about the effect of the disclosure on identifications made in the contrived setting of the laboratory. But to suggest that the uninformed subjects somehow resemble witnesses to an actual crime is surely stretching the simulation to its breaking point.

Because the data on eyewitness fallibility have been gathered mostly in (unrealistic) laboratory settings, some researchers acknowledge that "whether subject witnesses in research projects behave similarly to real eyewitnesses is not clear" (Yuille 1980, p. 343). Until researchers can show that their conclusions can survive the transportation from the laboratory to the real world, they will continue to be greeted with some skepticism by the legal community.

3. *Deceiving the memory of observers.* Elizabeth Loftus has conducted imaginative experiments designed to show the malleability and fallibility of memory—that is, memory is reconstructive in nature, so that past experiences are changed or reconstructed rather than simply and faithfully recalled. This demonstration is done by incorporating postobservation misinformation in a person's memory of the observed event.

For example, subjects were shown slides of a car accident (Loftus, Miller, and Burns 1978). Later they were given multiple choice questions, some of which contained misinformation. One question asked if the car had stopped at the stop sign when, in fact, the slide had shown a yield sign. In a subsequent recall test, only 41% of the misinformed subjects correctly remembered the nature of the traffic sign compared to 75% of the control (nondeceived) subjects. Similarly, in "reality" experiments, student observers included a moustache in their description of a thief because, after the fact, the professor conducting the staged theft planted that misinformation.

Yuille (1980) has provided an alternative explanation for these results. Since perception is said to be selective, it is entirely possible that the observers never paid any attention to the traffic sign. It was only one small item in the totality of events. Consequently, when a reputable source such as a university professor supplies information about the sign, those who did not initially see it will accept it. Postevent information adds to rather than reconstructs the memory of those who were not observant.

Yuille repeated the study but made changes to make the procedure "more typical of real-life situations" (p. 339). First, each subject gave a written description of the accident after seeing the slides but before being given the misleading information. The police often obtain witness statements at the crime scene. Second, the period of time between the viewing of the accident and the presentation of the misinformation was shorter than in the Loftus research. This study found that 80% of the misinformed subjects were accurate under these circumstances. Moreover, none of the subjects who mentioned the stop sign in their initial descriptions were led astray by the deception.

Based upon this study and subsequent ones, Yuille concludes that "witnesses to real events may not be as malleable as Dr. Loftus' and other eyewitness data suggest . . . [there is] hope that memory distortions may be less easily obtained in the normal course of a police investigation" (p. 339). Research on postevent misinformation "may be less a comment on the fallibility of human memory and more of a statement of the credibility of professors and researchers as sources of [trustworthy information]" (p. 338).

4. *Inconsistent results.* The research literature on eyewitness identification is an example of "forensic social science" (Rivlin 1973), or law office psychology, whereby investigators selectively emphasize some results and elide others in order to marshal the most persuasive argument possible for their point of view. We have already noted, for example, that about the same number of studies confirm or disconfirm a relationship between witness confidence and identification accuracy (Deffenbacher

1980). While acknowledging that the relationship is "far more complicated" than supposed, unqualified assertions such as the following are still made: "[T]he judiciary's belief that accuracy can be assumed merely on the basis of the confidence expressed by eyewitnesses is untenable" (Bartol 1983, p. 180).

Other examples abound. Woocher suggests that "lay witnesses surely must recognize . . . details of physiognomy much more inaccurately than . . . trained, objective observers." However, assuming that police are trained observers, some reviews of the literature on "police effectiveness as witnesses" show "mixed results" (Yuille 1980, p. 339; Clifford and Bull 1978) and others conclude that "police officers are no more accurate than ordinary citizens," perhaps even "more likely to misinterpret events" (Bartol 1983, p. 190). Woocher also asserts, based on "considerable evidence," that "people are poorer at identifying members of another race than of their own." A concurring opinion by Judge Leventhal (in *United States* v. *Telfaire*, 1972, reprinted in section 10.6 below) pointedly observed that the evidence is not uniform and that one published study showed that black subjects recognized white faces more accurately than black faces. Other researchers have also cast doubt on the claim that cross-racial identifications are per se unreliable. In a field study by Brigham et al. (1982), law interns asked clerks working alone in convenience stores to identify from photographic lineups two male customers, one black and one white, who had been in the store two hours earlier. The study found that "White clerks were equally likely to be accurate in identifications of the white customer (31.3%) and of the black customer (32.3%), whereas black clerks were correct 44.4% of the time for the white customer and 55.6% of the time for the black customer" (p. 678). Moreover, the more frequent the number of interracial experiences in the past, the more accurate the cross-racial identifications of the white clerks.

The party line is that stress impairs rather than enhances an eyewitness's reliability. For example, Woocher says that "psychological research demonstrates that perceptual abilities actually *decrease* significantly when the observer is in a fearful or anxiety-provoking situation." Others point out that "Unfortunately, there is little basis for this claim" (McCloskey and Egeth 1983, p. 557). In a review of 19 studies on the effect of stress on accuracy of eyewitnesses, 10 of the studies showed an impairment and 9 of the studies showed either an improvement or no effect. The reviewer explained these inconsistent findings by proposing that they fit the inverted U-shape curve between stress and performance (known as the Yerkes-Dodson law): performance is best at intermediate levels of stress or arousal and is worst at very high or very low levels (Deffenbacher 1983). It may well be true that eyewitnesses are most accurate when they are only moderately anxious or fearful, but this is only a hypothesis. There is no metric for calibrating and comparing the levels of stress in the different studies. To reconcile the conflicting results by suggesting that the studies showing improved accuracy may have involved moderate stress is an after-the-fact account that may or may not be empirically warranted.

5. *Wrongful convictions.* If jurors are said to be unduly trusting of eyewitness testimony and if such testimony is unreliable, then the use of such testimony at trial may increase the frequency of wrongful convictions. Critics of eyewitness testimony concede that "No one really knows" what this frequency is, and that "Our evidence . . . is purely anecdotal" (Loftus 1983, p. 564). There are many widely publicized cases of persons wrongly charged or convicted of crimes, and the injustice is not recognized until later when a look-alike confesses to have perpetrated those crimes. However,

unsubstantiated assertions of "hundreds" of such cases strain credulity, if only because relatively few criminal cases go to trial and fewer still rest solely on eyewitness evidence (see section 10.1 above).

The problem with the claim of increased wrongful convictions is that, in the real world, this claim is difficult to prove or disprove. In an imperfect world, there will always be some nonguilty persons who are convicted. But there is no way of directly ascertaining the proportion of verdicts which are wrong or, more specifically, the proportion of verdicts which are wrong as a result of erroneous identifications. In the absence of baseline figures, it is difficult to evaluate the claim that unjust outcomes are somehow unacceptably high, either in absolute terms or relative to wrongful convictions in nonidentification cases.

An indirect test is to compare the conviction rates in cases with and without eyewitness testimony. If the cases are otherwise similar and jurors are overcredulous of eyewitnesses, there should be more convictions when eyewitnesses are introduced. McCloskey and Egeth (1983) have summarized the results of two field studies by other researchers that bear upon this issue. One study in Los Angeles looked at the results of all criminal cases over a fifteen-month period. It found that the ratio of convictions in cases with at least one eyewitness identification to convictions without such evidence was 1.1 to 1.0. Another study in Indiana analyzed some 200 criminal cases over a three-year period. The results showed that convictions were no more likely when there were eyewitness identifications than when there were no eyewitnesses. Of course, as with all correlational studies, there can be other uncontrolled factors that account for the findings (for example, the prosecution's case may have been weaker when eyewitnesses were available). It could still be that eyewitnesses have a prejudicial effect on a trial, but that effect, if it exists, is not a dramatic and easily detectable one.

There have also been experimental studies on the effect of eyewitness testimony on convictions. For example, Loftus (1979, p. 117) asked college students to read a brief summary of a felony-murder trial and then make individual (not group) judgments of guilt (without any judicial instructions of any kind). One group of subjects read only about the physical evidence linking the defendant to the crime; 18% of them gave guilty ratings. A second group read about the physical evidence plus the identification of an eyewitness; 72% of this group judged the defendant guilty. A third group was exposed to the same evidence as the second group. In addition, this group also read a cross-examination which discredited the eyewitness. (The eyewitness had poor eyesight and was not wearing corrective lenses at the time of the identification.) In this third group, 68% gave guilty ratings. This experiment was said to show that jurors are overtrusting of eyewitnesses even when they are discredited, thereby producing a high rate of convictions. However, other studies using similar procedures have not replicated the results. After reviewing these studies, McCloskey and Egeth (1983) concluded: "In our research, we have frequently seen subjects, who read trial summaries and arrived at verdicts, vote not guilty in spite of a stated belief that an eyewitness who identified the defendant was probably correct" (p. 554). The higher acquittal rates in subsequent experiments could have been due to the insertion of judicial instructions regarding proof beyond a reasonable doubt, instructions which were not given in the Loftus study. Other discrepancies between the studies (for example, the high conviction rate even with discredited eyewitnesses in the Loftus study, but not in subsequent studies) remain unexplained.

"[W]e really do not know the reasons for the low acquittal rates in some studies," Loftus (1983) acknowledges (p. 568). It may well be that "there are conditions under which simulated jurors are highly believing of eyewitness testimony and other conditions under which they are not" (p. 568), but what these conditions are remain to be clarified. It can be said that the claim that eyewitness testimony leads to more convictions, whether these convictions are accurate or not, has not been definitively established in the laboratory.

6. *Conditions of accuracy.* Experience and common sense indicate that eyewitness reports are sometimes inaccurate and sometimes accurate. Unsubstantiated assertions of "hundreds of cases [of] innocent men and women" being "convicted, imprisoned, and even executed on the strength of . . . unchecked but false eyewitness reports" (Ellison and Buckhout 1981 p. 80) strain credulity, if only because relatively few criminal cases go to trial and fewer still rest solely on eyewitness evidence (see section 1 above). The more meaningful and difficult question is *when* eyewitness reports are reliable or not. Findings of highly inaccurate identifications could be an artifact of unrepresentative subjects and procedures, as discussed before. They could also reflect simply a spurious relationship. Behavior is typically the product of the combined, interactive effect of different factors impinging upon it. There may well be no single, direct relationship between identification reliability and any of the system-level variables that have been manipulated experimentally. The influence of any given variable may depend upon levels of other, mediating variables present in the simulated setting. In real life, everything is related to everything else. If these other variables are taken into account in the research, eyewitness identification may well turn out to be more accurate than is supposed. Realism of simulation is an example of one such mediating or third variable. The more realistic the procedures, the greater will be the accuracy.

It is necessary to examine the interaction effects between the different factors that affect the identification process. For experimental psychologists to declare, without more, that eyewitness testimony is usually fallible is as sweeping and oversimplified an assertion as that made by social psychologists at the time of *Brown,* namely, that school desegregation is directly related to the educational performance of black children. Just as subsequent desegregation research focused on the *conditions* under which racial intermixture enhanced or impeded academic achievement, so, too, future eyewitness research needs to focus on higher-order relationships. It needs to identify the circumstances in which cognitive processes are more likely or less likely to be accurate. At present, "researchers of eyewitness behavior are certainly nowhere near being able even to catalog such interactive effects" (Deffenbacher 1980, p. 258).

7. *Standard of accuracy.* The claim that identifications are often mistaken presumes a standard or baseline of accuracy. The law has not articulated the degree of reliability necessary for an identification to satisfy due process. Researchers, however, appear to be using an implicit standard of reliability that is higher than that evidenced by the courts. Thus, in the vandal study, when the vandal was present in the lineup, the rate of correct identifications was 75% and 83% for the conditions of biased and unbiased instructions, respectively (Malpass and Devine 1980). In the lineup similarity study, when the criminal was present, the rate of correct identifications was 71% and 58% for the conditions of low similarity and high similarity, respectively. To suggest that "mistaken identity from lineups is often the rule and not the exception" (Yarmey 1979, p. 159)—when in some simulation studies (and relatively unrealistic

ones, at that) more than one-half of the witnesses are accurate—is either to ignore contradictory data or to imply reliance on a very high standard of proof. Perhaps researchers assume that lineup identifications must be accurate "beyond a reasonable doubt" before they deem them reliable. The courts, on the other hand, are undoubtedly applying a lower standard, such as "more likely than not" accurate or maybe even "probably" accurate.

8. *Ideological premise of the research.* A pervasively negative evaluation of eyewitnesses colors the entire psychological research in this field. Even when psychologists recognize that "eyewitness testimony may be highly reliable under some conditions and extremely unreliable in other settings," they are almost exclusively and obsessively preoccupied with the conditions of unreliability (Bartol 1983, p. 169).

One can only speculate on the reasons for this negative emphasis. Espousal of a particular theory of perception and memory is one factor. The psychology of eyewitness testimony is rooted in the reconstructive view of the mind: Perception is selective and the processes of remembering are malleable. This view challenged the earlier "sensationalist" or "trace" theory, which conceived of the mind as a videotape recorder: Perception passively records events and memory consists of relatively accurate traces of these events; if the traces decay or cannot be retrieved, recall becomes inaccurate. Evidence on the fallibility of eyewitnesses vividly demonstrates the reconstructive theory.

Another reason could be the "striking, attention-getting nature of the findings" on fallibility (Yuille 1980, p. 344). One psychologist muses that "low accuracy rates may be preferred among researchers . . . as infinitely more interesting, more publishable, and more socially important" (Wells 1978, p. 1551). The courts have been relying on eyewitness testimony since time immemorial, and scientific endorsement of this practice by confirming the reliability of such evidence is hardly likely to prickle the ears of the legal profession. Thus, psychologists tend "to oversell the legal implications of their work and . . . expect their findings to be regarded as virtual saviors of the integrity of the legal system" (Greer 1971, p. 142).

More generally, the psychology of eyewitness behavior is consistent with the long-standing association between social science and liberal social and political values. This is a fact that social researchers have readily acknowledged and subjected to self-examination. The profession tends to attract those who are more interested in shaping the future than in preserving the past. Teaching and research focus on, say, the "psychology of social change," not on the "psychology of the status quo." As we have seen in the school desegregation and death penalty cases, social scientists have offered expert testimony far more frequently on behalf of those challenging existing practices than on behalf of state officials defending them. It is not surprising, therefore, that psychologists are not perceived as neutral scientists when they testify as expert witnesses for the defense. Their ostensible purpose is merely to "inform" the jury about scientific knowledge regarding the unreliability of eyewitnesses in general, and thereby reduce the risks of wrongful conviction. But the scientific presentation is only a guise for casting doubt on the testimony of the prosecution witness. Thus, a survey of lawyers in Florida indicates that they view expert testimony on eyewitness research as "solely aimed at the acquittal of suspects" (Brigham 1980, p. 318).

Even if we assume that expert psychological testimony is successful in neutralizing the purported faith that jurors have in eyewitness testimony, and that this newly found skepticism indeed reduces the rate of wrongful convictions, this result is not achieved without cost. Tradeoffs between wrongful convictions and wrongful acquittals are inevitable; one cannot reduce the first type of error without also increasing the second type. "In signal detection terms, it is unfortunate but true that except in situations involving very high signal-to-noise ratios, one cannot eliminate false alarms [incorrect convictions] without also eliminating hits [correct convictions] merely by shifting one's decision criterion [that is, by making jurors more skeptical and therefore less likely to convict]" (McCloskey and Egeth 1983, p. 552). Psychologists appearing as experts seem to operate on the premise that it is better that many guilty defendants be set free in order to minimize the chances of convicting an innocent party. This is certainly a defensible normative stance, regardless of how frequently wrongful convictions actually occur. The objection is only to the nondisclosure of this advocacy purpose. Even as ardent an advocate of the use of social research in the courts as Judge Bazelon (1982) has complained, though not in the specific context of eyewitness testimony, that "Behavioral scientists who appear in the public arena . . . often do not expose the values underlying their choice of facts" and that "[they] often operate with hidden agendas" (pp. 115-6).

Eyewitness research is a good example of how values intrude in scientific inquiry, from the selection of the problem for study, to the formulation of hypotheses, to the handling and interpretation of data. Research, like perception, is selective; some facts are attended to and others are neglected. Empirical knowledge is not found in facts themselves but in the way they are organized in relation to some interpretive scheme. This scheme (for example, the reconstructive model) shapes the researchers' perceptions of social reality and explains why things are the way they seem to be.

If memory is as malleable as it is now claimed to be, why do researchers create laboratory conditions to demonstrate that memory can be made less accurate rather than more reliable? Some studies have shown that identification reliability can be enhanced without biasing or deceiving witnesses. Subjects given a "guided recollection" of the staged crime seen several months earlier were more accurate in lineup identifications. Other studies have identified circumstances in which "eyewitness reports are generally accurate" (Yuille 1980, p. 339). If cognitive processes seem inordinately fallible, it may well be because the experiments that yield those results involve situations that are unrepresentative of the kind in which people normally function. Consciously or not, prodefense values are molding the conduct and the conclusions of scientific investigation of eyewitness testimony. Unless, as a first step, there is increased self-awareness and disclosure of these values, researchers risk setting out to confirm what they already believe.

10.4. SAFEGUARDS AGAINST FALLIBLE EYEWITNESS IDENTIFICATION: EXPERT TESTIMONY

We have examined two safeguards against the situationally derived bias of police suggestion: the constitutional right to counsel and the nonconstitutional alternative (endorsed by the Supreme Court) of articulated standards for lineups. Neither safeguard effectively controls the bias that arises from the general fallibility of perception, memory, and recall. We turn now to other nonconstitutional, procedural safeguards against this second source of bias.

The first safeguard is simply a blanket exclusion of eyewitness testimony because of its inherent unreliability. This option has never been embraced by the courts. The remedy is too drastic, especially since most cases are not instances of "pure identification." Nonetheless, in a particular case, despite absence of official wrongdoing at the pretrial identification, if the circumstances show it was so inherently unreliable as to poison the in-court identification, the fruit would be excluded under *Brathwaite*. These exclusionary determinations are made on a case-by-case basis. Of course, if it appears that a given eyewitness is so unreliable, the testimony will probably be discounted by the jury anyway. The exclusion, then, is largely an added precaution.

Whereas the exclusionary remedy goes to the issues of admissibility, the other safeguards pertain to the weight of the identification. A second safeguard is the use of psychologists as expert witnesses testifying about the general fallibility of eyewitnesses. It is often used in conjunction with a third safeguard, that of cross-examination of the eyewitness by defense counsel. A fourth means of protection is for the judge to issue cautionary instructions to the jury at the end of the trial, warning about the potential unreliability of such identifications. This section will concentrate on expert testimony and the following section on cautionary instructions.

Example of Expert Testimony

THE PHYSIOLOGY OF EYEWITNESS TESTIMONY: EYEWITNESS IDENTIFICATION

Marshall Houts

[In the felony-murder trial of *People v. Garcia*, expert psychological testimony on eyewitness identifications was introduced. The transcript of this testimony was published in *Trauma* and excerpts are reproduced below.

The facts were as follows. On the evening of October 12, 1977, two gunmen robbed a liquor store in Watsonville, California. One stood in front of a young male clerk with a drawn gun and demanded the money. The other stood five feet away with a gun pointed at a second, older male clerk. The young clerk (J. Melville) turned, heard a shot, and dove to the floor. When he looked up, the first robber was almost out of the door and the second

was in the doorway. The older clerk was dead. Melville sounded an alarm and a security guard arrived in five minutes.

Melville was then interviewed at the stationhouse. He described the first gunman as a 32- to 37-year-old Mexican, about 5'7" to 5'8", with stocky build, around 175 to 180 pounds, with a round face, collar-length black hair, mustache, and wearing a short-sleeve shirt. He described the revolver as a .38 or .357, of blue steel with about a four-inch barrel. Melville and a police artist constructed a composite drawing of the gunman.

On subsequent days, Melville viewed two lineups and did not identify anyone. On October 26, he looked at a large set of black-and-white mug shots and picked the photograph of J. Garcia. (In fact, there were two photos of Garcia and he identified only the second one.) On October 31, Melville picked Garcia's picture from an array of six color photographs, saying, "This is the guy. I wouldn't forget the face." Four days later, he wrongly selected an officer from another lineup based upon the similarity of the officer's voice to that of the gunman. Melville again looked at the color photographs and decided that the selection of Garcia because of his looks was correct, rather than his selection of the officer because of his voice.

Garcia was arrested for robbery and murder. He was 29 years old, 5'10", 242 lbs., had a heavy accent, and was a member of Nuestra Familia, a Mexican-American prison gang. He also had tattoos all over both arms and a deformed left hand. At a subsequent preliminary hearing, Melville testified that he did not notice the robber's left hand.

The only other witness was the security guard (R. Campbell). He had driven by the store at 10 to 20 m.p.h. and had seen two Mexicans inside. On December 5, he picked Garcia out of the six color photographs, but admitted seeing the composite drawing in the newspaper before the identification.

The state's sole evidence in this capital case was the eyewitness testimony of Melville and the guard. The trial ended with a hung jury and on retrial the jury again was stalemated. Expert testimony given during the first trial, and excerpted below, dealt with psychological processes relevant to the facts of the case. Ed.'s note.]

. . .

The Court: Mr. Christensen, do you intend to call any witnesses?

Mr. Christensen (defense counsel): Yes, I do, your Honor.

The Court: Okay.

Mr. Christensen: Call Dr. Elizabeth Loftus.

The Clerk: You do solemnly swear that the testimony you are about to give shall be the truth, the whole truth, and nothing but the truth, so help you God?

The Witness: I do.

The Clerk: Be seated up there.

By Mr. Christensen:

Q. Would you state your name and occupation please?

A. My name is Elizabeth Loftus, and I'm [a professor] at the University of Washington in Seattle. . . .

[VOIR DIRE BY DEFENSE]

[Dr. Loftus first described her qualifications in response to counsel's questions: degrees, teaching experience, publications, awards and honors, professional lectures to legal organizations, government grants for her laboratory, and prior expert testimony in eight states. Ed.'s note.]

. . .

Q. Doctor, is there a generally accepted theory on how memory works?

A. Yes, there is. It's generally accepted among the experimental psychologists in my field that memory does not work like a videotape recorder. . . .

In a sense, we construct what we routinely call "a memory."

Now, we make a distinction between three major phases in this process of this memory, or information processing system. . . . [The acquisition, retention, and retrieval phases were described briefly. Ed.'s note.]

Mr. Christensen: Thank you, Doctor. Mr. Harry has a few questions.

The Court: Go ahead.

[VOIR DIRE BY PROSECUTION]

By Mr. Harry [prosecutor]:

. . .

Q. And in your [studies], you have reenactments of crimes; is that correct?

A. Well, it's true; they aren't real crimes.

Q. They are reenactments, and they are filmed. Is that proper?

A. That's true. . . .

Q. Where do you get the subjects to be tested?

A.   Most of the subjects come from psychology classes. . . .

Q.   And the students are university students at the Washington University?

A.   It's the University of Washington. . . .

Q.   And who designs the experiments?

A.   I'm principally responsible for designing the experiments. . . .

Q.   Well, did all the experiments work out the way you thought they would before you started the experiment?

A.   No.

Q.   And if it works out, you publish it; and if it doesn't work out, you sort of go back to "go," and start again; is that right?

A.   That's usually what happens.
. . .

Q.   And so when the experiment produces the result which you like, you publish a paper on that; and when it produces a result that wasn't what your hypothesis started out to be, you don't publish that?

A.   No, that's not quite accurate.

Q.   You are saying that if the result comes out different than what you thought it would be, you recalculate the material, and then draft a new hypothesis to match that material?

A.   Well, oftentimes that's what happens. . . .

Q.   Now, do you conduct the testing yourself?

A.   I might supervise the first few sessions of an experiment; but I don't actually sit in on the data collection phase, no.
. . .

Q.   [D]o you compile the data based upon the answers received from the booklet? [The "booklet" is simply the response sheet used by subjects in recording their answers. Ed.'s note.]

A.   We get much of our information from the booklets, yes.

Q.   Well, do you reach some kind of an average of what the six subjects saw or reported to have been able to see in the film? . . . [Earlier, Dr. Loftus said that subjects were tested in groups of about six persons. Ed.'s note.]

A.   Yes, the final data . . . [are percentage averages].

Mr. Harry (approaching blackboard): Your Honor, may I use this just for a second for a rough diagram?

The Court: Yes.

By Mr. Harry:

Q.   Let's say that this is subject one and you have your test results up here, the items they should have seen. Do you then score them, subject one saw this item, but missed this one, but saw that one and missed this one and saw those two?

A.   We might do that.

Q.   And do you do something similar to that with number two and all the way down to six?

A.   It's possible that we would do that.

Q.   So that one may totally disagree with six. It's possible, is it not?

A.   It's possible that one might see completely different items than six, yes.

Q.   And they may have been asked different questions dealing with the same item; is that right?

A.   Well, the problem we are having here is that there are certain things I can say about my typical experiment, and you are now attempting to add too much to what is typical, and losing the thread of what I actually do in my experiments. We'd probably be better off if I gave you an example of an experiment. . . .

The Court: Is that what you want, Mr. Harry?

Mr. Harry: No, your Honor. I would like her just to tell us how she arrives at her averages. The method of testing, not the results.

Mr. Popin (defense counsel): Your

Honor, I object to that question. That question is so broad it is meaningless and incomprehensible to anyone.

The Court: You do it in the way you would like to do it, Dr. Loftus.

The Witness: All right. Let me show you one of my recent experiments. . . . [She then described the study summarized in footnote 55 of Woocher's article. Ed.'s note.]

Q. [I]n order to find [out about your experiments, I] would have to go to the University of Washington, [I] would have to take the test booklets, [I] would have to determine from that to check on what you did to determine whether you were accurate; isn't that right?

A. Well I'm not sure what you mean. In my scientific articles, the experiments are described in quite a bit of detail.

Q. The methods of conducting the experiments were described?

A. That's right. . . .

Mr. Harry: Nothing further, your Honor.

The Court: Mr. Christensen?

Mr. Christensen: Thank you, your Honor.

[DIRECT EXAMINATION]

By Mr. Christensen:

Q. Dr. Loftus, are you familiar with the cases of People versus Garcia and People versus Lawrence?

A. Yes, I am.

Q. And how did you attain that familiarity?

A. I read all of the police reports. I read an initial statement given by a person involved in the case, Melville; I read another statement given by another person named Campbell. I read testimony from the preliminary hearings; and I had a number of conversations with different people about the case. . . .

Mr. Harry: . . . I intend to interpose an objection. I don't object to her looking at the reports, but I'm going to object to his question that follows.

The Court: I'm going to ask you to step out for about five minutes, ladies and gentlemen, very quickly.

(The jury leaves the courtroom.)

[ARGUMENT ON ADMISSIBILITY OF EXPERT TESTIMONY]

The Court: Yes, Mr. Harry?

Mr. Harry: Your Honor, my objection is based upon the proffered testimony of Dr. Loftus that, first of all, she is an expert in conducting experiments and giving addresses and writing of articles regarding the results of those tests; but she is not an expert in determining the ability to perceive, recollect and identify based upon Mr. Melville and Mr. Campbell.

She can only talk about her general testing that she has conducted; and I think that from the questions on voir dire, it's very clear that they have not been conducted on actual eyewitness victims of robberies and murder; and that she has really no expertise that she can bring to this Court except for one purpose; and this is the purpose which I feel the defense is offering the evidence.

And that is to somehow collaterally impeach Mr. Melville and Mr. Campbell as to their ability to perceive, recollect and to describe what happened.

The Court: This testimony is not being offered for that purpose, Mr. Harry. It's been specifically rejected for that purpose. . . .

Mr. Harry: All right. I will withdraw the point, then.

The Court: All right. Go ahead.

Mr. Harry: . . . She said she read Mr. Melville's report and she read Mr. Campbell's report and she read over the police report. . . .

[T]he only reason she could be reading those [reports] and the only reason she would be offering any evidence regarding those is to impeach those witnesses.

The Court: I disagree with you. I want you to hear this, too, Dr. Loftus, so you understand what the ground rules are.

I have previously indicated that, as far as I'm concerned, relevant evidence for the jury to consider, if it comes from somebody who has expertise in knowing what the factors are, are the factors that go into identification.

Now, you mentioned acquisition, retention, retrieval. Previously, you testified at the hearing we had regarding what the important factors are, and the way in which there are certain misconceptions about how important these factors are. Do you follow me?

The Witness: Yes.

The Court: Now, those things, as far as I'm concerned, are relevant for the jury to consider here.

The only purpose in terms of what we are talking about here, of Dr. Loftus having read the reports, the preliminary hearing transcript and so on, is to allow her to know what the facts are in this case.

I am not going to allow Mr. Christensen to ask her questions that would indicate in any way an opinion on her part about whether this is a good identification or a bad identification by either Mr. Melville or Mr. Campbell.

But she is entitled to talk about the factors that would be involved if somebody was robbed at gunpoint in a store of the kind that we are dealing with, under the circumstances that we are dealing with. . . .

Mr. Harry: Your Honor, for clarification, the factors involved are factors that would come into play from her experiments and not from the facts as existing in this—

The Court: Let me deal with that for a moment. Now, Dr. Loftus, . . . with regard to the experiments that you have been involved with, have you specifically worked on experiments which were intended to attain the kind of information we are talking about here? What are the important factors—

The Witness: Yes.

The Court: —when somebody is robbed and they are later asked to recall what happened?

The Witness: Yes.

The Court: That is, some studies have been specifically directed toward that?

The Witness: Yes, they have. . . .

The Court: Okay. Mr. Harry, as far as I'm concerned, Dr. Loftus is qualified to testify. . . .

Mr. Christensen: Your Honor, purposefully, I did not use the hypothetical— I did not set the stage to duplicate this case. And I purposefully asked her whether or not she had reviewed these materials.

I thought that was the most fair way of getting into the factors that may be involved in this particular case, without having her express an opinion [regarding the accuracy of the eyewitnesses' identifications]. . . .

The Court: Bring the jury in, would you please?

The Bailiff: Yes, your Honor.

(The jury enters the courtroom.)

[DIRECT EXAMINATION, RESUMED]

By Mr. Christensen:

. . .

Q. And I would like to ask you whether or not there are certain factors that may affect eyewitness identification in the case of People versus Garcia and Lawrence? Do you understand what I'm saying?

A. Yes. . . .

Q. Okay. . . . What about the factors of stress. . . . Does [stress] have a

meaning in relation to eyewitness identification?

A.   Yes, it does, because there is a
relationship between stress and memory or
eyewitness ability.

Q.   Can you describe what that relationship is?

A.   Yes. I will use the diagram. . . .

The relationship is an inverted U-
shape function, and this is called the
Yerkes-Dodson Law, named after the two
psychologists that discovered it in 1908.

What this is saying is that under
very high stress or fear or arousal, and also
under very, very low stress, such as when
you are just waking up in the morning, we
are less good rememberers and perceivers
than we are under ordinary, optimal, moderate levels of stress.

So we are actually performing best
at an optimal or moderate level of stress.
. . .

Q.   And with high stress or very
low stress, memory is going to be at the
lower level or not as good; is that what you
are saying?

A.   That's correct.

Q.   Okay. Is the presence of a
weapon a factor that is involved in how
good or bad an eyewitness identification is?

A.   Yes. It's a factor. In fact, the
factor has been called "weapon focus." . . .

Q.   Have there been studies on this
to know why that is the case that people
can identify the weapon?

A.   There is one study that was
performed at Oklahoma State University
within the last couple of years, showing
that weapon focus did occur; that in a condition where there is a weapon present,
people are good at remembering the
weapon. They are less good at remembering the person who was holding the
weapon than in the corresponding controlled condition.

However, we don't have a very detailed understanding of why this occurs.
Just that it does occur. . . .

Q.   Thank you. Are you familiar
with the concept called "cross-racial
identification"?

A.   Yes, I am.

Q.   And what is meant by that?

A.   A cross-racial identification is one
in which a member of one race attempts
to identify a member of a different race.

Q.   Has that concept been studied
by psychologists?

A.   Yes, it has. . . . The repeated
finding in studies of cross-racial identification [between whites and blacks] is
that we are less good, less accurate at identifying a member of another race than we
are at identifying members of our own
race. . . .

Q.   Based upon your background,
experience, education, do you have an
opinion as to whether or not the concepts
would apply to a Caucasian and Mexican-
American?

A.   In my opinion, the cross-racial
problem that exists with these other
groups would extend into a cross-racial
identification with whites and Mexican-
Americans, yes.

Q.   Thank you. Has there been any
determination of why it's more difficult to
identify a person of a different race?

A.   Well, there have been many hypotheses . . . [but] really there exists no
good explanation for this finding, although the finding holds up repeatedly.
. . .

[CROSS-EXAMINATION]

By Mr. Harry:

. . .

Q.   [L]et's use your "weapon focus"
example. If someone is using a weapon
and the person observing the weapon has a
rather high stress from that, it may not
bother some people and it may cause a
very high stress factor for some other people; is that correct?

A.   Well—

Q. According to your tests.

A. I think it's possible that someone could feel very comfortable around weapons and not become stressed by them and such a person might even, in the presence of a weapon, still be at a moderate stress level. . . .

Q. . . . So if the event is significant and the person has the capacity or ability to observe, then according to your analogy here with the Yerkes-Dodson Law, if it produces high stress, how would the significance of that be affected, if it's a very significant event to the perceiver or an insignificant event?

A. If an overall event is significant to someone, the person's probably going to be able to remember that that event happened; but if the person was extremely stressed, he would not be able to remember the details of that event particularly well. . . .

Q. So the significance depends upon the person perceiving it; isn't that right?

A. Well, the significance would depend on the witness, yes. . . .

Q. Would it be fair to say that high stress interferes with the ability to remember the details?

A. Yes.

Q. But it would also be fair to say that if it is an important event, then the focus is on a particular significant event and that the memory is improved?

A. Something that is particularly significant or important, which causes one to focus on it, would tend to improve or enhance the memory for that aspect, yes. . . .

Q. And it is fair to say that even though you have tested and experimented with the "weapon focus" aspect of your work, that there are people who, even though the weapon is there and the stress situation is high, they do remember things; is that right?

A. Well, that would certainly be true, yes. . . .

Mr. Harry: Nothing further. Thank you, Dr. Loftus.

The Court: Mr. Christensen?

Mr. Christenen: I have no further questions.

NOTES AND QUESTIONS

1.   In addition to the factors of stress, "weapon focus," and cross-racial identification, the direct examination also brought out other factors that were not reproduced here: "retention interval" between the crime and the identification (the longer the interval—two weeks for Melville and seven weeks for Campbell—the less accurate will be the memory, according to the "Ebbinghaus forgetting curve"); "postevent information" (the newspaper photograph of Garcia that Campbell saw prior to the stationhouse identification could have reconstructed his memory of the original crime scene observation, thereby biasing the stationhouse identification); and "unconscious transference" (when Melville saw a second photograph of Garcia, he would have been identifying—unconsciously—the image of the first photograph rather than the face seen at the crime scene).

The cross-examination was relatively short. In addition to the excerpted sections, it also covered "retention interval." It did not touch upon the other factors at all.

2.   The prosecutor's voir dire attempted to cast doubt on the data sources, procedures, and analyses of the studies upon which the expert witness's opinions are based. Did it seem effective?

3.   Houts (1981) evaluated the effectiveness of the cross-examination as follows: "The cross-examination takes about the only line open to the prosecutor: he cannot effectively challenge the accuracy or scientific basis of what the witness has said; rather, he must show that even though the jury accepts her opinions, they do not necessarily apply to this case" (p. 439). The prosecutor indeed can and should try to show that the testimony on the unreliability of eyewitnesses in general does not necessarily apply to the perception, memory, and recall of the particular eyewitnesses in this case. Although the trial court "specifically rejected" the admission of this testimony to collaterally impeach the reliability of Melville and Campbell, the actual impact (if not ostensible purpose) of the expert's testimony was to create doubt in the minds of the jurors. It would be disingenuous to believe that a courtroom is a classroom for a dispassionate lecture on the factors that bias eyewitness identifications.

However, surely that is not "the only line open." Given your knowledge of social research, if you were the prosecutor in this case, how would you "effectively challenge the accuracy or scientific basis" of each of the points made by the expert? Consider, for example, the testimony on "weapon focus." Dr. Loftus acknowledged that her claims were based upon only one (unpublished) study. (In her book, she further describes this single study which purportedly demonstrates the phenomenon of "weapon focus" as "suggestive . . . but far from conclusive" [Loftus 1979, p. 36].) Suppose that she goes on to say: "I believe that a weapon captures the attention of a witness because of . . . a traditional literature that suggests that people will fixate on unusual or highly informative objects" (Loftus 1983, p. 569). What questions would you ask on cross-examination?

4.   Of course, there is no direct way of ascertaining how instrumental the expert testimony was in producing the nonconviction outcome. What other facts in this particular case might have influenced the jury to not convict?

Admissibility of Expert Testimony on Eyewitness Identifications

UNITED STATES v. AMARAL

488 F.2d 1148 (9th Cir. 1973)

TURRENTINE, District Judge:
[Defendant was indicted and convicted of bank robbery. One of the grounds of appeal was that "the trial court abused its discretion in refusing to allow the defense to present testimony by an alleged expert witness regarding the reliability of eye-witness testimony." Ed.'s note.]

We find that these contentions are without merit, and we accordingly affirm the conviction. . . .

The general test regarding the admissibility of expert testimony is whether the jury can receive "appreciable help" from such testimony. 7 Wigmore, Evidence §1923 (3d ed., 1940). The balancing of the probative value of the tendered expert testimony evidence against its prejudicial effect is committed to the "broad discretion" of the trial judge and his action will not be disturbed unless manifestly erroneous.

The countervailing considerations most often noted to exclude what is relevant and material evidence are the risk that admission will 1) require undue consumption of time, 2) create a substantial danger of undue prejudice or of confusing the issues or of misleading the jury, 3) or unfairly and harmfully surprise a party who has not had a reasonable opportunity to anticipate the evidence submitted. Scientific or expert testimony particularly courts the second danger because of its aura of special reliability and trustworthiness. . . .

Whether the court below erred in excluding the alleged expert testimony regarding the credibility of eye-witness identification, therefore, must be decided in reference to the four outlined criteria: 1) qualified expert; 2) proper subject; 3) conformity to a generally accepted explanatory theory; and 4) probative value compared to prejudicial effect.

At the trial, defense counsel moved to introduce the alleged expert testimony of Dr. Bertram Raven, a holder of a doctoral degree in psychology. Dr. Raven's testimony, as was made clear by the defense's offer of proof, was to be in regards to the effect of stress on perception and, more generally, regarding the unreliability of eye-witness identification. The trial court below considered this a novel question and, in view of the Government's opposition, requested both sides to submit authorities supporting their respective contentions. No appellate to trial court decision was cited by either counsel resolving the issue facing us on appeal.

The trial court excluded the proffered testimony of Dr. Raven on the ground that "it would not be appropriate to take from the jury their own determination as to what weight or effect to give to the evidence of the eye-witness and identifying witnesses and to have that determination put before them on the basis of the expert witness testimony as proffered."

Our legal system places primary reliance for the ascertainment of truth on the "test of cross-examination. . . ."

Certainly effective cross-examination is adequate to reveal any inconsistencies or deficiencies in the eye-witness testimony. Here defense counsel uncovered no confusion or uncertainty as to identity in any of the various witnesses. . . .

Accordingly, we hold that the court below did not err in excluding the testimony of Dr. Raven.

We need not reach the question, even assuming our competency to pass on it, whether the proffered testimony was in accordance with a generally accepted theory explaining the mechanisms of perception. Furthermore, while we see the dangers of admitting such testimony in terms of confusing the jurors and undue delays, we believe that our holding makes it unnecessary to analyze those dangers in detail.

NOTES AND QUESTIONS

Procedure for Using Expert Witnesses

1.   *Amaral* is the leading opinion on using expert psychological testimony on eyewitness fallibility. It is the first attempt to outline the conditions for admissibility of expert testimony in this subject matter, and its principles have been reaffirmed repeatedly by the Supreme Court (*United States* v. *Nobles*, 1975, p. 241, n. 16), other federal courts of appeal (for example, *United States* v. *Thevis*, 1982), and by state appellate courts (for example, *Arizona* v. *Chapple*, 1983). An ordinary witness is qualified to testify if he has firsthand knowledge of the event testified to (that is, it is not based on hearsay). An expert witness must have the capacity to draw inferences from facts that a jury would not be competent to do, because the subject of the inference is beyond the ken of laypersons (McCormick 1972, p. 29).

2.   Expert testimony may be presented before a judge or a jury. In the former instance, defense counsel makes a motion for exclusion of the eyewitness identification either at a pretrial hearing or during the trial itself. In arguments before the judge alone, defense counsel introduces an expert to inform the court about the risks of eyewitness identifications. Trial judges are generally cognizant of the fallibility of the human mind and senses, but they may not be familiar with the relevant research.

In the latter instance, defense counsel usually calls the expert witness to the stand in conjunction with cross-examination of the eyewitness and the officer who conducted the pretrial identification. The role of the expert is to inform the jury about the research on the fallibility of eyewitnesses. The testimony normally is of a general kind, enumerating specific factors that are known to result often in unreliability. Rarely do experts venture an opinion as to the reliability of the particular eyewitness in the case. Indirectly, of course, the purpose is to cast doubt on the accuracy of the eyewitness identification.

3.   With respect to the admissibility of confessions, due process requires that a trial court conduct a separate hearing—outside the presence of the jury—as to the voluntariness of the confession (*Jackson* v. *Denno*, 1964). If the judge determines that it was voluntarily given, the prosecution can introduce it into evidence so that the jury can hear it. If the judge determines that it was obtained by coercion, the confession is excluded and the jury never hears about it. Prior to *Jackson* v. *Denno*, the jury determined both the voluntariness of the confession and the weight or probative value of the confession. The reason for splitting the two functions was the fear that lay jurors would be unduly influenced by the substance of the confession and therefore be more likely to convict regardless of how the confession came about.

Suppose that a defendant contends that a preindictment lineup was highly suggestive, thereby biasing the subsequent in-court identification by the eyewitness. An eyewitness identification is believed to have a powerful impact on the jury. Arguably, lay jurors are incapable of separating the identification, made self-confidently by the eyewitness, from the suggestive conditions of the lineup, just as they are incapable of separating the truthfulness of a confession from the improper coercion exercised in the interrogation room.

Should due process require that a trial court conduct a separate hearing—outside the presence of the jury—regarding the suggestiveness of police identification procedures before the jury hears about the eyewitness identification? What kinds of research evidence would be relevant to the analysis? See *Watkins* v. *Sowders* (1981).

4.   Failure to appoint a psychologist to assist the defense by testifying on the unreliability of eyewitness identifications (pursuant to a statute providing for the appointment of "investigative, expert" services for indigents when "necessary for an adequate defense") was held not to be reversible error, absent a showing of prejudice caused by the failure to appoint (*United States* v. *Sims*, 1980). What empirical evidence might be marshaled in support of an appeal of this decision?

Admissibility of Expert Testimony—General Principles

5.   The fundamental proposition of case law and evidence rules is that the propriety of receiving expert testimony in general rests with the sound discretion of the trial court; reversals for abuse of that discretion are rare (McCormick 1972, p. 30). The reported appellate cases show that expert testimony on the reliability of eyewitness identifications has been excluded more often than it has been admitted. "The admissibility of this type of expert testimony is strongly disfavored by most courts" (*United States* v. *Sims*, 1980, p. 1375). "[R]esearch has not produced a single appellate decision in which such expert testimony was held admissible or its exclusion held to be an abuse of discretion. Cases to the contrary are legion" (*State* v. *Galloway*, 1979, p. 741, C. J. Reynoldson concurring and citing twenty cases; see also *Hampton* v. *State*, 1979, citing other cases to the same effect. The disfavor of the courts has been conceded by Elizabeth Loftus 1979, pp. 198–99). On successive occasions, Washington appellate courts have upheld the exclusion of Loftus's testimony (for example, *State* v. *Cook*, 1982). No court has yet said that such testimony must be admitted as a matter of law. However, since the *Galloway* decision by the Iowa Supreme Court, the Arizona Supreme Court in *State* v. *Chapple* (1983) has ruled that the exclusion of Loftus's testimony in that particular case was reversible error. Both cases are discussed below.

Of course, not all cases involving expert psychological testimony reach appellate review. It is only after a defendant is convicted and if the proffered testimony was ruled inadmissible that a foundation is laid for appellate consideration. Those cases in which the testimony was admitted or the defendant was acquitted would not raise this issue or would not be appealed at all. Appellate decisions, therefore, are not necessarily a reliable indicator of the frequency of admission in the trial courts. A Kansas court noted that two psychologists (Elizabeth Loftus and Robert Buckhout) had been allowed to testify as eyewitness identification experts in some fifty-four trials altogether (*State* v. *Warren*, 1981, p. 1243).

6.   Some trial courts which have allowed experts to testify as to the general factors that affect the reliability of identifications have also set some limiting conditions. For example, an expert was not permitted to respond to hypothetical questions that called for comment on the specific factors that affect the accuracy of eyewitness identifications. These specific factors were similar to the particular circumstances of the case. The reason was that the responses would usurp the jury's fact-finding role. The defendant argued that the denial of hypothetical questions prevented the jury from understanding the scientific evidence, but the appellate court held that it was not an abuse of the lower court's discretion (*State* v. *Cook*, 1982).

In other jurisdictions, "the use of hypothetical questions in the examination of expert witnesses is a well established practice" (*Barefoot* v. *State*, 1980). In that case, two psychiatrists responded to a hypothetical fact situation (based on the evidence) that asked whether the individual would likely commit future acts of violence. Their affirmative responses were not excluded even though they had not personally examined the defendant. The issue, the court ruled, was one of weight rather than admissibility of the testimony.

Other courts have received the expert's general opinion (that there was a "real possibility" of misidentification of a suspect who is identified by an examination of photographs three years after the crime) but refused the expert's explanation that the opinion was based on experiments performed by other researchers. The trial court's exclusion was held not to be an abuse of discretion even though under the law of evidence on expert testimony the offered explanation could have been received (*State* v. *Galloway*, 1979, p. 739).

7.   The courts have given various justifications for not receiving expert testimony on eyewitness reports, and these can be organized into five major categories.

(a) Perhaps the most commonly given justification for exclusion is that the expert usurps the jury's traditional function of determining the ultimate facts (in this instance, the fact of the reliability or unreliabity of the eyewitnesses). (Rule 704 of the Federal Rules of Evidence [FRE] has repudiated the "ultimate issue" rule, consistent with its basic approach of admitting all expert testimony when it may be helpful to the trier of fact; FRE 702.)

(b) Expert testimony has also been excluded because the fallibility of eyewitnesses is not deemed to be beyond common knowledge and expertise of the jury (*United States* v. *Thevis*, 1982, p. 641). This is the second criterion of *Amaral*. So long as cross-examination is available, it is assumed that "the jury [is] fully capable of assessing the eyewitness' ability to perceive and remember . . . without the aid of expert testimony" (*United States* v. *Fisher*, 1979, p. 383). (Modern evidence rules do not require that the subject matter of the expert testimony be beyond the ken of the lay fact-finder; FRE 702.)

(c) Another basis for exclusion is that the expert testimony is not probative or relevant—there is no logical relationship between the scientific testimony presented and the facts sought to be proven at trial. Thus, according to the Iowa Supreme Court, "explanation of the scientifically identified mechanisms which bring about memory decay may be of academic interest, but it is of little aid to the jury in judging reliability of the particular eyewitness identification before them" (*State* v. *Galloway*, 1979, p. 741). However, according to the Arizona Supreme Court, it is precisely "the 'generality' of the testimony . . . which favors admission." Experts may give an exposition of scientific principles and leave it to the trier to apply them to the facts of the case (*State* v. *Chapple*, 1983, p. 1219).

(d) Doubts about the reliability of the scientific claims underlie some of the decisions to exclude expert testimony. This, too, goes to the issue of probative values, which is an element of *Amaral*'s fourth criterion. For example, when an expert conceded that prior research on cross-racial identifications was "inadequate," a court sustained the exclusion on the grounds that "work in [this area] remains inadequate to justify its admission into evidence" (*United States* v. *Watson*, 1978, p. 369). Another court has observed that the catch-all rationale of invading the province of the jury may well mask other, unstated justifications such as the possible unreliability of the scientific evidence (*United States* v. *Fisher*, 1979, p. 383). An English report on eyewitness identifications recognized their potential fallibility but found the available research wanting: "[T]he stage seems not yet to have been reached at which the conclusions of psychological research are sufficiently widely accepted or tailored to the needs of the judicial process to become the basis for procedural change"(Devlin 1976, p. 73).

(e) The prejudicial effect of expert testimony is another consideration in the decision whether to exclude. In applying a balancing test, trial judges have often found the probative value offset by its prejudice.

A source of prejudice is confusion of issues at trial. Normally, expert testimony is used to supply knowledge that is not known to or that is helpful to the trier. Expert eyewitness testimony, however, is also used to impeach—by implication, if not directly—the credibility of a prosecution witness. "To admit such testimony in effect would permit the proponent's witness to comment on the weight and credibility of opponents' witnesses and open the door to a barrage of marginally relevant psychological evidence" (*United States* v. *Thevis*, 1982, p. 641). There is the fear that the expert testimony might "cause the trial to become not only a trial of the defendant but also a trial of the witness" (*Hopkins* v. *State*, 1972, p. 220).

Another source of prejudice is rooted in the infrequently stated but constant preoccupation of the courts that a well-credentialed, university professor might be perceived by the jury as possessing an "aura of special reliability and trustworthiness," despite the uncertainties in the research evidence (*United States* v. *Fosher*, 1979, p. 383). The concern is that a lay trier might attach more weight to this kind of expert evidence than is warranted.

What are other possible prejudicial consequences that outweigh the benefits of admitting the expert testimony? Are there circumstances in which the benefits would exceed the costs?

8.   Evaluate the foregoing five rationales. Do they provide a principled basis for exclusion? Formulate other arguments, based on reasons of policy and/or scientific evidence, for and against admissibility.

Admissibility of Expert Testimony—Specific Examples

9.   Consider the facts of the following three illustrative cases. In the first two cases, the exclusion of expert testimony at trial was upheld on appeal, and in the third case it was overturned.

United States v. *Thevis* (1982). Thevis (and several co-defendants) were convicted by a jury of several acts under the Racketeer Influenced and Corrupt Organizations Act (RICO) in the course of conducting an interstate pornography business. These acts included the murders of two competitors in the business, arson against competitors, and the murder of a government witness (a former employee of Thevis who had helped dispose of the body of one of Thevis' victims and of other incriminating evidence) in order to prevent his testimony at trial. The trial lasted eight weeks and the government presented a massive case consisting of physical and circumstantial evidence, tape recordings, and eyewitness testimony. The trial record totalled 118 volumes or about 16,000 pages. One basis of the appeal was the exclusion of expert testimony by Dr. Robert Buckhout, a psychologist at Brooklyn College. Two eyewitnesses, both experienced airline pilots, placed Thevis at the scene of the murder of the government witness. Dr. Buckhout offered to testify that "the ability of airplane pilots to make eyewitness identifications is not greater than that of other persons." The trial court excluded the proffered testimony, saying that the subject of cognitive processes was within the expertise of the jury and "therefore the probative value of the evidence was substantially outweighed by the possibility of prejudice emanating from this 'expert' testimony." The Fifth Circuit upheld the exclusion, noting that its decision is "supported by other circuits' uniform approval of excluding testimony exactly like Buckhout's" (p. 641).

State v. *Galloway* (1979). The defendant was convicted of first degree murder of a grocery store clerk, a crime that occurred in the course of a robbery carried out by the defendant and two other men. More than three years after the shooting, two witnesses selected a photograph of the defendant and identified him as the robber who fired the shot. Both witnesses subsequently also selected the defendant in a lineup. Their testimony was the principal evidence in the state's case. The trial court excluded the defense's offer of proof in which Dr. Elizabeth Loftus testified that there was "a real possibility of misidentification" as a result of examining photographs three years after the event. Dr. Loftus based her opinion in part on an experiment conducted by Robert Buckhout. Dr. Buckhout staged an assault (that lasted forty-two seconds) on a college campus and it was witnessed by 141 persons. Seven weeks later, all the witnesses were presented with six photographs and were asked to identify the assailant. Only 40% could do so. In upholding the exclusion, the majority opinion of the Iowa Supreme Court simply said that "admissibility of such evidence rests within the sound discretion of the trial court. We cannot say that discretion was abused in this case" (p. 739). However, the court nonetheless overturned the conviction because the prosecutor, whether intentionally or not, failed to disclose exculpatory evidence to the defense. Before the trial, the defendant moved for disclosure of police reports describing the witnesses' photographic identifications. The prosecutor denied that such information was available. After trial, it turned out that such reports existed, and they revealed that one eyewitness had identified, with varying degrees of certainty, other individuals and stated that they resembled the murderer. A new trial was ordered.

State v. *Chapple* (1983). Chapple was convicted of three counts of first degree murder and two counts of illegally transporting drugs. The facts, as the court noted, are "complicated" and "bizarre.' Coley, a drug dealer in Washington, D.C., arranged with Scott, a middleman in Phoenix, for the purchase of a large quantity of marihuana. Scott and his sister, Buck, found a supplier named Varnes. Some years earlier, Coley, Varnes and a third person named Logan had been arrested together in connection with a heroin transaction. Scott picked up Coley at the Phoenix airport and found him accompanied by two strangers, identified only as "Dee" and "Eric." Scott drove all three to the rendezvous place where they met Buck and waited for the arrival of Varnes. The conversation between Coley, Dee, and Eric, as well as their actions (cleaning their guns), led Scott to believe that they probably did not intend to pay Varnes for the goods, and he so informed his sister. Varnes arrived with two men. When the three men were alone in a room with Dee and Eric, several shots were heard. Varnes and his aides were found dead. Scott helped Dee and Eric load the bodies into Varnes' car, which was then doused with gasoline and set afire. The parties then left the scene of the crime and returned to Scott's house. Coley paid Scott and Buck $500 each and flew back to Washington, D.C. under the name of "Logan." Eric and Dee drove off with the marihuana. Fear or remorse, or both, drove Scott to see a lawyer, who negotiated an immunity deal for him and persuaded him to surrender to the police.

Scott and Buck promptly identified Coley in photographic lineups prepared by the police. Scott also pointed to a photograph of a person and said that it resembled Dee, but that he was not sure. The photograph was actually of a person named Logan, but no follow-up was made of this identification. About four months later, Scott identified Eric in another photographic lineup, but he failed to identify a photograph of Chapple. (Buck was not shown the set of pictures that included Chapple.) More than one year later, both Scott and Buck were shown a lineup with nine photographs. The sixth picture was of Chapple and the seventh was of Eric. Again, both witnesses identified Eric and this time they also identified Chapple as "Dee." When asked by the police why he had not identified Chapple earlier, Scott explained that he did not recall seeing a photograph of Chapple among the multitude of pictures he had examined.

Eric was never found, but Chapple was apprehended and convicted solely on the identifications of the photograph, and of the defendant himself at trial, made by Scott and Buck. At trial, the defendant did not contest any of the foregoing facts. His only defense was that he was not "Dee." Three defense witnesses testified that Chapple was in Cairo, Illinois, on the day of the crime. To rebut the testimony of Scott and Buck, the defense called Dr. Elizabeth Loftus and offered her expert testimony. Outside the presence of the jury, Loftus offered to testify on the following points: the identifications were probably unreliable because of the one year interval between the crime and the presentation of the defendant's photograph; the identifications were probably unreliable because the witnesses were under tension and stress (with the two killers at large); Scott's identification of Chapple could have been the product of unconscious transference (that is, the identification was based on the remembered picture of the earlier lineup when Scott failed to identify Chapple); Eric's picture next to Chapple's may have "heightened the memory transfer" and thus contributed to an unreliable identification; the confidence with which Scott and Buck identified the defendant in court is unrelated to the accuracy of the identification; and the conversations that Scott and Buck must have had between them regarding the identity of Dee were likely to reinforce their (probably mistaken) individual identifications. The trial judge precluded this expert testimony, saying "I don't find anything that's been presented . . . that isn't within the common experience of the people of the jury" (p. 1220).

The Arizona Supreme Court found the preclusion to be error and reversed the conviction. The court conceded that prior cases "have uniformly affirmed trial court rulings denying admissibility" (p. 1218). Its ruling, therefore, was quite narrow: "We reach the conclusion that Dr. Loftus should have been permitted to testify on the peculiar facts of this case and have no quarrel with the result achieved in the vast majority of cases . . ." (p. 1224). The "key issue" in determining admissibility is whether the eyewitness research is a "proper subject" for expert testimony under *Amaral*. The test of proper subject, according to the court, is "whether the subject of inquiry is one of such common knowledge that people of ordinary education could reach a conclusion as intelligently as the [expert] witness" (p. 1219). Although lay persons on the jury might not need to be enlightened about the risks of eyewitness fallibility in general, the court concluded that they might not be cognizant of the specific variables that shape the accuracy or inaccuracy of eyewitness identifications. Exposition of the scientific research that bears on these variables cannot be precluded, because the expert testimony could be "of considerable assistance in resolving some of the factual contentions raised" (p. 1222).

10.   Do you agree that the "key issue" is proper subject matter rather than any of the other three criteria of *Amaral*? On this key issue, how would you reconcile the conflictory rulings of *Thevis* (eyewitness reliability is within the common knowledge of the jury) and *Chapple* (jury needs expert assistance)? The Arizona court repeatedly emphasized the "peculiar facts" of the case, but a dissenting judge asserted "I am unable to distinguish the case at bench from the wealth of cases where identification is in issue [and exclusion of expert testimony is upheld]" (p. 1227). What are the special facts, if any, that distinguish *Chapple* from *Thevis* and *Galloway*?

11.   A survey in Florida found that all the prosecutors said that expert eyewitness testimony should "never" or "rarely" be admitted, whereas three-fourths of the public defenders believed that it should be admitted "fairly often" or "routinely" (Brigham 1980, p. 319). Thus, prosecutors see the issue as one of admissibility, and defense counsel see it in terms of weight (of the expert testimony). Which is the sounder position?

12. An argument for admitting expert testimony is that by informing jurors about the scientific knowledge on eyewitness identifications, they will be helped in making more accurate evaluations of the reliability of eyewitnesses. In an experiment by Wells, Lindsay, and Tousignant (1980), subjects viewed a staged crime and then a photographic lineup. Some made a correct lineup identification and others an incorrect one. All subjects were questioned about the crime setting, the appearance of the suspect, and the like. These questions were intended to simulate a direct examination. The responses were videotaped and shown to other subjects (mock jurors) who then judged whether the eyewitnesses had made correct or incorrect identifications. Before making these judgments, some of the "jurors" were given expert psychological advice. They were told that eyewitnesses are generally unreliable and that there is no correlation between the accuracy of an identification and the confidence of the eyewitness in his own identification. The results showed that the expert advice reduced the credibility of the eyewitnesses—the "jurors" given the advice found the eyewitnesses less believable than the "jurors" who were not so advised. However, the expert advice had no effect on their ability to discern between accurate and inaccurate eyewitnesses.

For an overview of other studies, see Hosch (1980) and Egeth and McCloskey (1983).

13. There are many other issues for research. Is the expert's impact mediated by the presence and quantum of corroborating evidence? Is expert testimony more effective than traditional safeguards such as skillful cross-examination of the eyewitness (as assumed by *Amaral*) or cautionary instructions to the jury (discussed in the next section)? Is the use of an expert by the prosecution (thereby initiating a battle of experts) likely to be as effective as skillful cross-examination of the defense expert by a prosecutor who is well-versed in social research?

14. McCloskey and Egeth (1983) are of the view that a battle of experts "would almost certainly work to the detriment of the psychological profession, creating (or sustaining) the impression of psychology as a subjective, unscientific discipline . . . ." Although engineers and physicians are also found on opposite sides in a trial, they do not suffer a significant loss of public credibility because of the long record of achievements of their respective disciplines. Psychology, however, "does not have the sort of strong public reputation needed to endure battles of experts without significant damage" (p. 559). What arguments would you make in rebuttal?

Research Pertinent to Expert Testimony

15. To determine whether psychological knowledge is within the realm of popular understanding, researchers have administered multiple choice tests to college students and nonstudent adults. The test questions asked, for example, about the effect of stress upon memory and the accuracy of cross-racial identifications—items on which "research can give reasonably unequivocal answers" (Deffenbacher and Loftus 1982, p. 16). Respondents answered correctly roughly one-half of the questions (that is, the answers coincided with the conclusions of researchers). This performance, though significantly better than the level expected by guessing (25%: four reply options per question), was "not terribly impressive in absolute terms. It is reasonable to assume that laypersons and the legal profession would not be impressed with anything less than 85% . . . [accuracy on various items]" (p. 20). Hence, the researchers concluded that scientific knowledge is not within common knowledge. Assuming the validity of these results, do they undermine this rationale for exclusion?

16. There have been simulation studies of the impact of expert testimony on the trial. For example, Loftus (1980) asked students to read a 250-word essay that described the evidence against a defendant. It was essentially a "pure identification" case. The victim had several drinks, went to sleep at 3:30 A.M., and woke up at 5:00 A.M., when he was hit in the head by an assailant with a pistol. The victim said that he had never seen the assailant before and described him in some detail. A week later, he identified a suspect in a lineup. The next day, he had a car accident and claimed that the other driver (who was not the same man identified in the lineup) was the actual assailant. The trial of the driver (defendant) was held three months later.

One-half of the subjects read, in addition, a 200-word essay that described a defense expert's testimony about the unreliability of eyewitnesses. The expert said that stress, alcohol, and cross-racial identifications (white victim, black defendant) can reduce perceptual and memorial abilities. The other subjects were not exposed to the expert testimony.

Subjects deliberated in groups of six for a maximum of thirty minutes. Without the expert testimony, seven juries convicted, two acquitted, and one stalemated. On the average, each jury spent 6.8 minutes discussing the eyewitness identification. With the expert testimony, three juries convicted, four acquitted, and three reached no decision because of lack of time. The average discussion time on the eyewitness identification was 10.6 minutes. Loftus concluded that expert testimony reduces convictions and increases the amount of attention jurors give to eyewitness reports.

What features of the experiment reduce the external validity of the results? Why is increased deliberation time on the identification evidence necessarily a salubrious effect? Does this study tell us whether the courts are justified in their worry that jurors may give undue weight to scientific testimony?

10.5. SAFEGUARDS AGAINST FALLIBLE EYEWITNESS IDENTIFICATION: CAUTIONARY INSTRUCTIONS

UNITED STATES v. TELFAIRE

469 F.2d 552 (D.C. Cir. 1972)

PER CURIAM:

[A black defendant was convicted of robbery based upon the identification of a white victim. The court ruled that the trial judge's failure to initiate a cautionary instruction on eyewitness identifications even in the absence of a request by defense counsel was not prejudicial error. However, "to further the administration of justice," the court appended a "model instruction," reproduced below. The court added, elliptically, "It is not being set forth in terms of compulsion, but a failure to use this model, with appropriate adaptations, would constitute a risk in future cases that should not be ignored unless there is strong reason in the particular case. . . ." Ed.'s note.]

APPENDIX: MODEL SPECIAL INSTRUCTIONS ON IDENTIFICATION

One of the most important issues in this case is the identification of the defendant as the perpetrator of the crime. The Government has the burden of proving identity, beyond a reasonable doubt. It is not essential that the witness himself be free from doubt as to the correctness of his statement. However, you, the jury, must be satisfied beyond a reasonable doubt of the accuracy of the identification of the defendant before you may convict him. If you are not convinced beyond a reasonable doubt that the defendant was the person who committed the crime, you must find the defendant not guilty.

Identification testimony is an expression of belief of impression by the witness. Its value depends on the opportunity the witness had to observe the offender at the time of the offense and to make a reliable identification later.

In appraising the identification testimony of a witness, you should consider the following:

(1) Are you convinced that the witness had the capacity and an adequate opportunity to observe the offender?

Whether the witness had an adequate opportunity to observe the offender at the time of the offense will be affected by such matters as how long or short a time was available, how far or close the witness was, how good were lighting conditions, whether the witness had had occasion to see or know the person in the past. . . .

(2) Are you satisfied that the identification made by the witness subse-

quent to the offense was the product of his own recollection? You may take into account both the strength of the identification, and the circumstances under which the identification was made.

If the identification by the witness may have been influenced by the circumstances under which the defendant was presented to him for identification, you should scrutinize the identification with great care. You may also consider the length of time that lapsed between the occurrence of the crime and the next opportunity of the witness to see defendant, as a factor bearing on the reliability of the identification. . . .

(3) You may take into account any occasions in which the witness failed to make an identification of defendant, or made an identification that was inconsistent with his identification at trial.

(4) Finally, you must consider the credibility of each identification witness in the same way as any other witness, consider whether he is truthful, and consider whether he had the capacity and opportunity to make a reliable observation on the matter covered in his testimony.

I again emphasize that the burden of proof on the prosecutor extends to every element of the crime charged, and this specifically includes the burden of proving beyond a reasonable doubt the identity of the defendant as the perpetrator of the crime with which he stands charged. If after examining the testimony, you have a reasonable doubt as to the accuracy of the identification, you must find the defendant not guilty.

BAZELON, Chief Judge, concurring:

. . . [I] wholeheartedly concur in the promulgation of a model identification instruction which deals realistically with the shortcomings and trouble spots of the identification process. . . . But . . . [it does not go] far enough.

The available data, while not ex-haustive, unanimously supports the widely held commonsense view that members of one race have greater difficulty in accurately identifying members of a different race. The problem is by no means insubstantial; a significant percentage of the identifications in this jurisdiction are interracial. Yet, we have developed a reluctance—almost a taboo—to even admit the existence of the problem, let alone provide the jury with the information necessary to evaluate its impact.

This reluctance apparently grows out of a well-intentioned effort to insulate criminal trials from base appeals to racial prejudice. But I cannot agree that because any discussion of this identification problem necessarily refers to racial differences, such discussion is, as one New York appellate court has held, "prejudicial" and "divisive." . . .

It follows that counsel should be allowed to urge the jury to consider whether the inter-racial character of an identification affects its reliability. I also believe that when the issue is raised, the jury should be *instructed* to consider the matter. The jury's knowledge of the relevant factors should not turn on the inadvertence or inexperience of trial counsel, and this is particularly so where the issue of identity *is* the question of guilt or innocence. Moreover, by offering something like the following instruction, the court sets the narrow context in which racial differences are relevant, and further ensures that jury consideration of these differences stays within such properly delineated bounds.

In this case the identifying witness is of a different race than the defendant. In the experience of many it is more difficult to identify members of a different race than members of one's own. If this is also your own experience, you may consider it in evaluating the witness's testimony. You must also consider, of course, whether there are other factors present in this case which overcome any such difficulty of identification. For example, you may conclude that the witness has had sufficient contacts with members of the defendant's race that he would not have great difficulty in making a reliable identification.

LEVENTHAL, Circuit Judge, concurring:

This is to add a thought as to useful procedure for consideration of the possibility of separate instruction on inter-racial identifications, discussed in Chief Bazelon's separate opinion.

In my judgment, this subject is not appropriate for inclusion in the model instruction provided with the opinion. Whether this case may involve a problem of inter-racial identification is not knowable from the record, and the point was not argued by counsel. The issue arose only because the court became concerned with the responsibility of trial judges to focus on the general issue of identification, concluding the time is ripe to fashion a model instruction that will help make this "a matter of routine" for trial judges.

A model instruction serves a useful function of survey and synthesis, to distill outstanding judgments on matters that have been pondered by this and other courts. The issue of inter-racial identifications is not ripe for this kind of distillation of wisdom involving as it does a matter on which there is only "meager data" and an assertion of "common sense" views that merit further consideration. What seems obvious to one judge, based on his experience, may be questioned by another. . . . When we are dealing with an instruction to the jury on "the law," we are or should be dealing with propositions that reflect the wisdom of the community.

My own reflections on the subject have been enhanced by some surprises encountered in a little reading undertaken after this subject arose in conference. Although some writers say it is "a well established socio-psychological phenomenon"

that members of one race recognize each other more readily than members of another race, it develops that in at least one study—which apparently sought to confirm another point, that Negroes are more likely to recognize whites than vice versa—the data seemed to show that Negroes recognize white faces with greater accuracy than black faces.[4] If this is true, it would be necessary to investigate the possible explanations, and to provide the explanations and qualifications needed if a model instruction is to avoid distortion, and possibly outright error.

If the instruction refers to the ultimate ingredients of the problems of identification, it might well have to note that identifiability depends on the ability (and opportunity) of the individual as perhaps influenced by such matters as his attitude toward the other race, the extent to which his ability to distinguish may have been enhanced by need or reward for such ability in past situations, and the factor whether in the individual instance the subject being identified had homogeneous characteristics. . . .

The wisdom of making haste slowly in discerning the generalization ready for inclusion in model instructions is underscored when what is involved is as sensitive as race relations in our society. If the subject of inter-racial identification is to be covered in instructions that are informative and objective, we may be opening the door to questioning and proffers of proof so that every time a witness makes an identification of an offender of another race, he is subject to cross-examination on the nature and extent of his contacts with and attitudes (favorable or not) toward the other race. The more I ponder the problems, the better I understand the kernel of

[4] . . . See R. M. Malpass (of U. of Illinois) and J. Kravitz (of Howard University), Recognition for Faces of Own and Other Races, 13 J. of Personality and Social Psychology (1969) 330, 332.

wisdom in the decisions that shy away from instructions on inter-racial identifications as divisive. . . .

What strikes me is that this is the kind of issue which appellate judges should explore with trial judges, and with lawyers, in a manner more like that of a legislative committee, than a decision in an adversarial proceeding. . . . At least where problems require careful further exploration . . . a more felicitous means of conducting such exploration [would involve]

common meetings on common problems between members of bench (trial as well as appellate judges), bar, and social scientists; providing time for further explorations after initial discussion; enhancing collaborative conference as distinguished from competitive or adversarial skirmish.

Mulling and interchange always take time. Yet if the problem of inter-racial identification is to be considered with discernment as well as authority, that time would be well spent.

NOTES AND QUESTIONS

---

1.   The model instructions of *Telfaire* alert jurors to various objective factors (for example, opportunity to observe) that might result in unreliable identifications. Most of them, it should be noted, come from *Wade*'s independent source test. There is no mention of the psychological factors that contribute to eyewitness fallibility. This source of bias was also not confronted in *Wade*. Yet, the Court of Appeals was certainly cognizant of the psychological research literature, as the exchange between Judge Bazelon and Judge Leventhal on cross-racial identification demonstrates. Why, then, do the instructions omit reference to the psychology of eyewitness identification, if this is the central issue?

2.   Compare this exchange between Judges Bazelon and Leventhal on eyewitness instructions with their exchange in *United States* v. *Dougherty* (Chapter 8, section 8.3) on jury nullification instructions. What are the different philosophical views regarding the nature of the law and the role of judicial policy-making that inform Judge Bazelon's embrace and Judge Leventhal's wariness of social research?

3.   Today, most federal courts of appeal approve the use of the *Telfaire* instructions or similar ones, though they seldom reverse convictions when trial courts refuse to issue them (Holtshouser 1983). The practice in state appellate courts varies greatly. Some jurisdictions, such as Washington, disallow cautionary instructions on eyewitness identifications because they are construed as an improper judicial commentary on the evidence (*State* v. *Jordan*, 1977). Discussion of the conditions of accurate identification is left to counsel's argument. Others require them under certain circumstances. The Kansas Supreme Court ruled that when "there is a serious question about the reliability of the identification, a cautionary instruction should be given advising the jury on the factors to be considered in weighing the credibility of the eyewitness . . ." (*State* v. *Warren*, 1981, p. 1244). Most states, however, allow but do not mandate them (for example, *State* v. *Guster*, 1981).

4.   Research by Greene (1983) attempted "to simplify the language [of the *Telfaire* instruction] . . . in order to make it clear and logical to jurors" and "to include more data from psychological research that jurors may use to appraise a witness' testimony" (pages unnumbered). A one-and-a-half-hour-long videotaped trial involving an assault prosecution was shown to 139 actual jurors. There were two independent variables. One was strength of the identification, either "strong" or "weak" (that is, observation of the suspect under bright lights, at close proximity, and so on, or under poor visual conditions, respectively). The other was type of instructions: *Telfaire* instructions, revised instructions, or no cautions at all. All jurors received the usual instructions on the elements of the crime and the standard of proof. They deliberated in groups of five to seven persons, for a maximum of thirty minutes. Then they recorded their individual judgments of guilt and answered a multiple choice test on the findings of eyewitness research.

The relevant portions of the revised instructions, dealing with the factors affecting the accuracy of identifications, were as follows:

> . . . In evaluating the testimony of any eyewitnesses, you should consider two sets of factors: first, factors present when the incident occurred; second, factors affecting the later identification.
>
> Factors present when the incident occurred are: (a) how much time was available for observation; (b) how well the scene was lit; (c) how far the eyewitness was from the incident.
>
> You should also consider how well the eyewitness could see and hear at the time. For example, if a witness is afraid or distracted, his or her capacity to perceive and remember is reduced.
>
> A second set of factors affect later identification. You should consider how much time passed between the incident and the identification. For example, identification errors increase as time passes. You should also consider the circumstances surrounding the identification. For example, an identification made from a fair lineup of similar individuals is more reliable than other forms of identification such as viewing a suspect alone. You should also consider how certain the eyewitness was in making the identification. Certainty may or may not mean that the identification is accurate.
>
> If, after considering all of these factors, you have a reasonable doubt about the accuracy of the eyewitness' identification of the defendant as the person who may have committed a crime, then you must find the defendant not guilty.

Both sets of instructions were given to some ninety judges for evaluation. About 62% of the judges rated the revised instructions as "very effective" or "extremely effective" in "conveying legal concepts to the jury," but only 23% so rated the *Telfaire* instructions.

The results of the experiment showed that jurors who received the revised instructions had the most number of correct answers on the multiple choice test. Moreover, when the identification was strong, none of them found the defendant guilty. In contrast, 35% of those who received no instructions rendered guilty decisions. When the identification was weak, there were no guilty judgments at all by any of the jurors.

The author concluded that the simplified instructions were "better" and "more effective" than the *Telfaire* instructions in "educating jurors about the vagaries of eyewitness [identification]" and urged the use of the former by the courts. Evaluate the methodology and normative premises of this research. In revising instructions, where does a social scientist draw the thin line between an instruction that "cautions" and one that "educates" (read: persuades)?

5.   A distinguished commission on eyewitness identification appointed by the British Home Secretary proposed that "pure identification" cases should not be sufficient for conviction absent exceptional circumstances. Specifically, it recommended that trial judges be required "to direct the jury that it is not safe to convict upon eyewitness evidence unless the circumstances of the identification are exceptional or the eyewitness evidence is supported by substantial evidence of another sort, and to indicate to the jury the circumstances, if any, which they might regard as exceptional . . . ." If there are no such circumstances or supporting evidence, the jury must be instructed to return a verdict of not guilty (Devlin 1976, pp. 149–50). Does the psychological literature provide a foundation for such a drastic instruction? Does the same literature inform us on the exceptional circumstances when eyewitness testimony is reliable?

REFERENCES

Adams v. United States, 392 F.2d 574 (D.C. Cir. 1968).

Allport, F. H. *Theories of Perception and the Concept of Structure.* New York: John Wiley, 1955.

American Law Institute. *A Model Code of Pre-arraignment Procedure.* Philadelphia: American Law Institute, 1975.

Asch, S. "Effect of Group Pressure upon the Modification and Distortion of Judgments." In *Readings in Social Psychology,* 3rd ed., edited by E. Maccoby, T. Newcomb, and E. Hartley. New York: Holt, Rinehart & Winston, 1958.

Barefoot v. State, 596 S.W. 2d 875 (Tex. Crim. App. 1980).

Bartlett, F. C. *Remembering: A Study in Experimental and Social Psychology.* London: Cambridge University Press, 1932.

Bartol, C. *Psychology and American Law.* Belmont, Ca.: Wadsworth, 1983.

Bazelon, D. L. "Veils, Values, and Social Responsibility." *American Psychologist* 37 (1982): 115–21.

Bermant, G.; McGuire, M.; McKinley, W.; and Salo, C. "The Logic of Simulation in Jury Research." *Criminal Justice and Behavior* 1 (1974): 224–33.

Borchard, E. *Convicting the Innocent.* New Haven: Yale University Press, 1932.

Brigham, J. C. "Perspectives on the Impact of Lineup Composition, Race, and Witness Confidence on Identification Accuracy." *Law and Human Behavior* 4 (1980): 315–22.

———, and Barkowitz, P. "Do They All Look Alike?" The Effect of Race, Sex, Experience and Attitudes on the Ability to Recognize Faces." *Journal of Applied Social Psychology* 8 (1978): 306–18.

———; Maass, A.; Snyder, L. D.; and Spaulding, K. "Accuracy of Eyewitness Identifications in a Field Setting." *Journal of Personality and Social Psychology* 42 (1982): 673–81.

Brown, E.; Deffenbacher, K.; and Sturgill, W. "Memory for Faces and the Circumstances of Encounter." *Journal of Applied Psychology* 62 (1977): 311–18.

Bruner, J. S. "Social Psychology and Perception." In *Readings in Social Psychology*, 3rd ed., edited by E. Maccoby, T. Newcomb, and E. Hartley. New York: Holt, Rinehart & Winston, 1958.

Buckhout, R. "Eyewitness Testimony." *Scientific American* 231 (1974): 23–31.

Clifford, B. R., and Bull, R. *The Psychology of Person Identification.* London: Routledge & Kegan Paul, 1978.

Collins, B., and Raven, B. "Group Structure: Attraction, Coalitions, Communication, and Power." In *Handbook of Social Psychology*, vol. 4, 2nd ed., edited by G. Lindzey and E. Aronson. Cambridge, Mass: Addison-Wesley, 1968.

Comment. "Expert Testimony on Eyewitness Perceptions." *Dickinson Law Review* 82 (1978): 465–87.

Deffenbacher, K. A. "Eyewitness Accuracy and Confidence: Can We Infer Anything About Their Relationship?" *Law and Human Behavior* 4 (1980): 243–60.

———. "The Influence of Arousal on Reliability of Testimony." In *Evaluating Witness Evidence: Recent Psychological Research and New Perspectives*, edited by B. R. Clifford and S. Lloyd-Bostock. Chichester, England: John Wiley, 1983.

———, and Loftus, E. F. "Do Jurors Share a Common Understanding Concerning Eyewitness Behavior?" *Law and Human Behavior* 6 (1982): 15–30.

Devlin, P. *Report to the Secretary of State for the Home Department of the Departmental Committee on Evidence of Identification in Criminal Cases.* London: Her Majesty's Stationery Office, 1976.

Doob, A. N., and Kirshenbaum, H. M. "Bias in Police Lineups: Partial Remembering." *Journal of Police Science and Administration* 1 (1973): 287–93.

Egeth, H. E., and McCloskey, M. "Expert Testimony about Eyewitness Behavior: Is it Safe and Effective?" In *Eyewitness Testimony: Psychological Perspectives*, edited by G. Wells and E. F. Loftus. London: Cambridge University Press, 1983.

Ellison, K., and Buckhout, R. *Psychology and Criminal Justice.* New York: Harper & Row, 1981.

Erdelyi, M. H., and Kleinbard, J. "Has Ebbinghaus Decayed with Time: The Growth of Recall (Hypermnesia) over Days." *Journal of Experimental Psychology: Human Learning and Memory* 4 (1978): 275–87.

Gideon v. Wainwright, 372 U.S. 335 (1963).

Gilbert v. California, 388 U.S. 263, (1967).

Greene, E. L. "Judges' Instruction on Eyewitness Testimony: Evaluation and Revision." Unpublished draft of doctoral dissertation, University of Washington, 1983.

Greer, D. S. "Anything But the Truth? The Reliability of Testimony in Criminal Trials." *British Journal of Criminology* 11 (1971): 131–64.

Hampton v. State, 285 N.W. 868 (Wisc. 1979).

Holtshouser, S. E. "Eyewitness Identification Testimony and the Need for Cautionary Jury Instructions." *Washington University Law Quarterly* 60 (1983): 1387–1433.

Hopkins v. State, 480 S.W.2d 212 (Tex. Crim. App. 1972).

Hosch, H. M. "Commentary: A Comparison of Three Studies of the Influence of Expert Testimony on Jurors." *Law and Human Behavior* 4 (1980): 287–96.

Houts, M. "The Physiology of Eyewitness Testimony: Eyewitness Testimony." *Trauma* 23 (1981): 4.7–4.46.

Hutchins, R. M., and Slesinger, D. "Legal Psychology." *Psychological Review* 36 (1929): 13–26.

Jackson v. Denno, 378 U.S. 368 (1964).

Jonakait, R. N. "Reliable Identification: Could the Supreme Court Tell in *Manson v. Brathwaite?*" *University of Colorado Law Review* 52 (1981): 511–28.

Kalven, H., and Zeisel, H. *The American Jury.* Boston: Little, Brown, 1966.

Kamisar, Y. "Equal Justice in the Gatehouses and Mansions of American Criminal Procedure." In *Criminal Justice in Our Time*, edited by Y. Kamisar, F. Inbau, and T. Arnold. Charlottesville: University of Virginia Press, 1965.

Kamisar, Y.; Lafave, W; and Israel, J. *Modern Criminal Procedure*, 5th ed. St. Paul, Minn: West, 1980.

Kirby v. Illinois, 406 U.S. 682 (1972).

Kusley v. State, 432 N.E.2d 1337 (Ind. 1982).

Levine, F. J., and Tapp, J. L. "The Psychology of Criminal Identification: The Gap from *Wade* to *Kirby.*" *University of Pennsylvania Law Review* 121 (1973): 1079–1131.

Lindsay, R. C. L., and Wells, G. "What Price Justice? Exploring the Relationship of Lineup Fairness to Identification Accuracy." *Law and Human Behavior* 4 (1980): 303–14.

Loftus, E. F. *Eyewitness Testimony.* Cambridge, Mass.: Harvard University Press, 1979.

———. "The Impact of Expert Psychological Testimony on the Unreliability of Eyewitness Identification." *Journal of Applied Psychology* 65 (1980): 9–15.

———. "Silence Is Not Golden." *American Psychologist* 38 (1983): 564–72.

———. Miller, D. G., and Burns, H. J. "Semantic Integration of Verbal Information into a Visual Memory." *Journal of Experimental Psychology* 4 (1978): 19–31.

Malpass, R. S. "Effective Size and Defendant Bias in Eyewitness Identification Lineups." *Law and Human Behavior* 5 S(1981): 299–310.

Malpass, R. S., and Devine, P. G. "Realism and Eyewitness Identification Research." *Law and Human Behavior* 4 (1980): 347–58.

Manson v. Brathwaite, 432 U.S. 98 (1977).

Mapp v. Ohio, 81 U.S. 1684 (1961).

McCloskey, M., and Egeth, H. E. "Eyewitness Identification: What Can a Psychologist Tell a Jury?" *American Psychologist* 38 (1983): 550–63.

McCormick, C. *The Law of Evidence*, 2nd ed. St. Paul, Minn.: West, 1972.

Miranda v. Arizona, 384 U.S. 486 (1966).

Moore v. Illinois, 434 U.S. 220 (1977).

Münsterberg, H. *On the Witness Stand.* New York: Doubleday Page, 1908.

Murray, D. M., and Wells, G. L. "Does Knowledge that a Crime Was Staged Affect Eyewitness Performance?" *Journal of Applied Social Psychology* 12 (1982): 42–53.

People v. Bustamante, 177 Cal. Reptr. 576 (1981).

People v. Gillebeau, 107 Cal. App. 3d 531 (1980).

People v. Lawrence, 4 Cal.3rd 273 (1971).

Powell v. Alabama, 287 U.S. 45, (1932).

President's Commission on Law Enforcement and the Administration of Justice. *Task Force Report: The Courts.* Washington D.C.: U.S. Government Printing Office, 1967.

Quinn, J. R. "In the Wake of *Wade*: The Dimensions of Eyewitness Identification Cases." *University of Colorado Law Review* 42 (1970): 135–58.

Read, F. T. "Lawyers at Line-ups: Constitutional Necessity an Avoidable Extravagance?" *UCLA Law Review* 17 (1969): 339–407.

Reiss, A., and Black, D. "Interrogation and the Criminal Process." *Annals* 374 (1967): 47–57.

Rivlin, A. M. "Forensic Social Science." *Harvard Educational Review* 43 (1973): 61–75.

Sherif, M. "Group Influences upon the Formation of Norms and Attitudes." In *Readings in Social Psychology*, 3rd ed., edited by E. Maccoby, T. Newcomb, and E. Hartley. New York: Holt, Rinehart & Winston, 1958.

Simon, R. "Does the Court's Decision in Nebraska Press Association Fit the Research Evidence on the Impact on Jurors of News Coverage?" *Stanford Law Review* 29 (1977): 515–28.

Sobel, N. R. *Eyewitness Identification: Legal and Practical Problems.* New York: Clark Boardman, 1972.

———. *Eyewitness Identification: Legal and Practical Problems*, 2nd ed. New York: Clark Boardman, 1982.

Spano v. New York, 360 U.S. 315 (1959).

State v. Chapple, 660 P. 2d 1208 (Ariz. 1983).

State v. Cook, 639 P.2d 863 (Wash. App. 1982).

State v. Gaitor, 388 So.2d 570 (Fla. App. 1980).

State v. Galloway, 275 N.W.2d 736 (Iowa 1979).

State v. Greene, 591 P.2d 1362 (Or. 1979).

State v. Guster, 421 N.E.2d 157 (Ohio 1981).

State v. Jordan, 17 Wash. App. 542 (1977).

State v. Warren, 635 P.2d 1236 (Kan. 1981).

State v. Wright, 410 So.2d 1092 (La. 1982).

Stern, W. "Psychology of Testimony." *American Journal of Psychology* 21 (1910): 270–75.

Stovall v. Denno, 388 U.S. 293 (1967).

Swain v. Alabama, 380 U.S. 202 (1965).

United States v. Amaral, 488 F.2d 1148 (9th Cir. 1973).

United States v. Ash, 413 U.S. 300 (1973).

United States v. Brown, 501 F.2d 146 (9th Cir. 1974).

United States v. Collins, 395 F. Supp. 629 (M.D. Pa. 1975).

United States v. Crews, 445 U.S. 463 (1980).

United States v. Fosher, 590 F.2d 381 (1st Cir. 1979).

United States v. Hearst, 412 F. Supp. 883 (N.D. Cal. 1976).

United States v. Hodges, 515 F.2d 680 (7th Cir. 1975).

United States v. Nobles, 422 U.S. 225 (1975).

United States v. Sims, 617 F.2d 1371 (9th Cir. 1980).

United States v. Telfaire, 469 F.2d 552 (D.C. Cir. 1972).

United States v. Thevis, 665 F.2d 616 (5th Cir. 1982).

United States v. Wade, 388 U.S. 218 (1967).

United States v. Watson, 587 F.2d 365 (7th Cir. 1978).

Wall, P. *Eyewitness Identification in Criminal Cases.* Springfield, Ill.: Charles C. Thomas, 1965.

Watkins v. Sowders, 449 U.S. 341 (1981).

Wells, G. L. "Applied Eyewitness-Testimony Research: System Variables and Estimator Variables." *Journal of Personality and Social Psychology* 12 (1978): 1546–57.

———; Leippe, M. R.; and Ostrom, T. M. "Guidelines for Empirically Assessing the Fairness of a Lineup." *Law and Human Behavior* 3 (1979); 285–94.

———; Lindsay, R. C. L.; and Tousignant, J. P. "Effects of Expert Psychological Advice on Human Performance in Judging the Validity of Eyewitness Testimony." *Law and Human Behavior* 4 (1980): 275–85.

Wigmore, J. H. *The Science of Judicial Proof*, 3rd ed. Boston: Little, Brown, 1937.

Williams, G. *The Proof of Guilt*, 3rd ed. London: Stevens, 1963.

Wong Sun v. United States, 371 U.S. 471 (1963).

Woocher, F. D. "Did Your Eyes Deceive You? Expert Psychological Testimony on the Unreliability of Eyewitness Identification." *Stanford Law Review* 29 (1977): 969–1030.

Wright v. Smith, 434 F. Supp. 339 (W.D. N.Y. 1977).

Yarmey, A. D. "The Psychology of Eyewitness Testimony." New York: Free Press, 1979.

Yuille, J. "A Critical Examination of the Psychological and Practical Implications of Eyewitness Research." *Law and Human Behavior* 4 (1980): 335–46.

Zeisel, H., and Diamond, S. "Convincing Empirical Evidence on the Six-Member Jury." *University of Chicago Law Review* 41 (1974): 281–95.

PART IV

AFTERWORD: PERSPECTIVES ON
THE FOCUS

CHAPTER 11

Historical and Conceptual Perspectives on Psycholegal Research

11.1. INTRODUCTION AND OVERVIEW

The 1970s saw an explosive growth in social psychological research on the judicial process that continues unabated today. By the start of the 1980s, various institutional developments seemed to auger the "coming of age" of the field (Loh 1979). These developments included an outpouring of articles and books, more in a few years than had been published in the preceding three-quarters of a century (see Chapter 1, section 1.2, for a listing of recent books); the appearance of specialized journals (for example, *Law and Psychology Review; Law and Human Behavior*); the establishment of joint-degree training programs and interdisciplinary courses (Grisso, Sales, and Bayless 1979; Melton 1983) and professional societies (for example, Division 41 on "Psychology and Law" of the American Psychological Association, which has grown to over 1,000 members within three or four years of its establishment).

Despite a long tradition and the current developments, there have been few historical analyses (Sporer 1982) or theoretical assessments of the field as a whole (Tapp 1980; Monahan and Loftus 1982). The psycholegal literature is a gallimaufry of empirical studies and conceptual integration is "weak or non-existent" (Bartol 1983, p. 323; an exception is Horowitz and Willging 1984). This chapter consists of a critical overview of the field as seen from the bridge between the two disciplines. Section 11.2 sketches an intellectual history of the relations between psychology and law in order to place contemporary scholarship in perspective. Then, section 11.3 presents conceptual, legal, and methodological critiques of two areas that traditionally have been and still remain the principal foci of attention of research psychologists: eyewitness testimony and the criminal trial process. The final section (11.4)

This section and the following section were published (in another form) as part of an article by Wallace Loh, "Perspectives on Law and Psychology." *Journal of Applied Social Psychology* 11 (1981): 314–55. Reprinted by permission of the publisher. Copyright ©1981 by V. H. Winston & Sons.

concludes with some themes culled from past and present experience that capture the mood, difficulties, and prospects of applying social research to law.

The purpose of this chapter is to pull together some of the materials of the book—research findings, jurisprudential ideas, legal issues, analytical approaches—in order to provide a panoramic view of the field and to suggest some insights into two recurrent questions: What has been the policy impact of psychological research on the judicial process? What can be done to enhance it in the future?

11.2.   A LOOK AT THE PAST

The interest in psychology and law dates back to the early days of experimental psychology. The intellectual history unfolds in four stages.

Pioneering Stage (1900s): "Yellow Psychology"

The first area of psycholegal research, as well as the oldest area of applied psychology generally, was the study of the reliability of witness testimony. At the turn of the century, European psychologists proposed the creation of a "practical science of testimony" (Binet 1905). The most active expositor became William Stern (1903) of Breslau, who developed the *Aussage* or remembrance experiments. Laboratory subjects were presented with pictures and subsequently asked to recall the details under different forms of questioning and suggestive contexts. Inaccurate recollection was the norm, and this finding was generalized to the unreliability of courtroom witnesses. This procedure was later replaced by "reality experiments" designed to simulate more realistically the observation and reporting of events (Stern 1939). In a typical scenario, a quarrel between two students suddenly erupts in the midst of a class session and one of them draws a revolver. The instructor then stops the staged incident and asks for reports from the rest of the class. The results uniformly show substantial errors in the recall of almost every facet of the event (words spoken, weapon used, and so forth), with inaccuracy rising when the report is elicited by leading questions and with increasing lapse of time since the initial observation (Whipple 1909). These *Aussage* experiments were used by Stern to evaluate the trustworthiness of particular witnesses in German courts, as well as to train police officers and judicial officials in the fallibility of cognitive processes. They have also become the paradigm for current research on eyewitness identification and are repeated so often that the findings are no longer considered novel.

There was initially no indigenous psychology of *Aussage* in this country. That the evaluation of witnesses originated and was better received on the Continent than here is explainable in part by the differences in adjudication procedures. In an inquisitorial system, the judge takes the initiative in summoning and questioning witnesses, whereas in the adversarial system that task is left to the party litigants. Deciding without a jury, the continental judge is more likely to call on psychological experts for aid in examining the trustworthiness of witnesses. Most of the work here consisted in descriptions or replications of the European studies. The first book on the subject in English that introduced American psychologists and lawyers to the continental developments was written in 1908 by Hugo Münsterberg, director of the psychological laboratory at Harvard. He summarized the experimental literature bearing on the unreliability of perception and memory and proposed the use of word-association tests to aid in the determination of guilt of the accused in criminal trials. Moreover, he made sweeping claims about the superiority of psychological methods to those of law. The adversary system of adjudication was scorned as a museum of irrational procedures. With missionary zeal, Münsterberg castigated the legal profession for not embracing the new science: "The time for Applied Psychology is surely near. . . . The lawyer alone is obdurate. The lawyer and the judge and the juryman are sure that they do not need the experimental psychologist. . . . They go on thinking that their legal instinct and their common sense supplies them with all that is needed and somewhat more" (p. 9).

Lawyers promptly lambasted the "presumptuous little book" (Cairns 1935, p. 169) as "yellow psychology" (Moore 1907). In a mercilessly satiric libel suit against Münsterberg brought by the legal profession for injury to its good name, Wigmore (1909)—the leading authority on evidence law—cross-examined him on each of his assertions and found them wanting. Even some German psychologists argued that Stern's results were "overhasty" and the the "use of psychological experiments in trials must be rejected" (pp. 412–13). The article concluded with the judge finding for the plaintiff and determining that psychology had nothing to offer to the law at that time. Beneath some of the rhetorical excesses were perceptive criticisms of the *Aussage* experiments that are still applicable to current research on eyewitness testimony. Wigmore pointed out that the results on testimonial accuracy were based on group averages. In a courtroom, it is the reliability of a specific witness that is in question, and "the new psychology cannot [assess] error of individual witnesses" (p. 423). More importantly, the experiments failed to address the crux of the situation from the viewpoint of the law: "[w]hether the alleged percentages of testimonial error do really produce misleading results in the verdicts" (p. 426). The ultimate issue is not the frequency of testimonial errors of witnesses but the prejudicial impact, if any, upon the trial outcome.

Wigmore (1937, p. 698) proceeded to conduct his own reality tests in which witnesses testified about the staged incident before a jury. The results confirmed his hunch that a jury, in the course of deliberation, succeeds in finding facts that reflect more accurately what happened than would be expected from the testimonial errors. Since the time of Stern and Münsterberg, the reliability of witnesses has been "the central theme of psychology of testimony" and has "received by far the lion's share of research attention" (Fishman 1957, p. 60). However, with one notable exception (Marston 1924), every subsequent study to the present continues to regard the reliability of testimony—rather than of the verdict—as the key adjudicative issue.

After Wigmore's rejoinder, American psychologists "left the law rather severely alone" (Hutchins 1927, p. 678). Some disavowed Münsterberg's "extravagances" as "not benefit[ing] science or truth" (Morse 1913, p. 795); others disparaged as "opportunist" any undertaking in applied psychology in contrast to scientific psychology (Titchener 1914, p. 39). There followed a period of silence and inaction lasting about fifteen years, broken only by some annual reviews of *Aussage* studies and their forensic applications in Europe (Whipple 1910, 1911, 1912, 1913, 1914, 1915, 1917).

Legal Realist Stage (1930s): Psychologism in the Law

The end of the 1920s and the 1930s saw a revival of interest in psychology and law, this time initiated and borne mostly by lawyers. The interest was manifested in two directions: one was the application of psychology to selected aspects of legal practice and the other was a radical critique of substantive legal doctrines and appellate court decision-making based on psychology.

Books appeared written by and for attorneys for the purpose of presenting in a practical way the psychological factors involved in the practice of law. In *Psychology for the Lawyer* (McCarty 1929), for example, there were chapters on lie detection, covert suggestion, identification of facial and bodily expressions, and the traditional subject of testimonial certitude. Another volume on legal psychology consisted, according to its subtitle, of "psychology applied to the trial of cases, to crime and its treatment, and to mental states and processes" (Brown 1926). In an overview of law and the social sciences generally, an English lawyer observed that psychology at that time had attracted far more attention from the legal profession than the other social sciences (Cairns 1935). Then as now, the contributions were centered on two broad domains, the psychology of cognitive processes as related to witness testimony, and the psychology of crime and criminal personality. There was as much reliance then on popular psychology as on research data in the search for information useful in lawyering. Only one book in this genre was written by a psychologist during this time. In addition to covering the conventional subjects, it introduced a new topic for study in the measurement of public confusion between similar trade names (Burtt 1931).

Some legal scholars and psychologists sought to revamp the whole of legal theory and methodology with the aid of psychology. One of the most ambitious and controversial undertakings was by Edward Robinson (1935), a psychology professor and law lecturer at Yale. In *Law and the Lawyers,* he advocated the use of the method and viewpoint of science, particularly behaviorist psychology, in salvaging jurisprudence from the doldrums of its outdated conceptualism. "[I]t will be a fundamental principle of the new philosophy of law," he proposed, "that every legal problem is at bottom a psychological problem and that every one of the many traditions about human nature which are to be found in legal learning needs to be gone over from the standpoint of modern psychological knowledge" (p. 51). He urged the substitution of "plain psychological facts" for such legal concepts as intent, reasonable person, and precedent—only then would law cease to be "an unscientific science" (p. 1).

Predictably, Robinson—like Münsterberg—did not make friends and influence people in the legal community. In a scathing review entitled "The Jurisprudence of Despair," Mechem (1936) complained that Robinson had criticized a straw man of his own making, namely, the unreasonable lawyer who inhabits a world of legal fictions and is out of touch with reality. Furthermore, most of the "scientific" psychology relied upon by Robinson consisted of unverified theories and unsubstantiated generalizations. If law had to wait until psychology acquired the necessary knowledge before managing human affairs, this promise filled Mechem with despair.

The rebuff of Mechem and others (Goodrich 1936) glossed over an important contribution of Robinson to the analysis of the role of psychology in law. He perceived that the strategy of seeking one-to-one linkages between psychological findings and legal problems, characteristic of studies on witness testimony, was bound to end in disappointment. Laboratory results on the fallibility of perception and memory simply do not transfer wholesale to the practical task of evaluating witness reliability. Knowledge about these psychological processes does not readily translate into concrete guidelines for courtroom decisions. Hence, he "rejected the notion that jurisprudence can wait for a collection of psychological laws so definite and reliable as to be directly applicable to the solution of practical legal problems" (p. 118). This represented a shift in the way the relations between the two disciplines had been viewed. Up to then, psychologists began by combing through their inventory of information and then applying whatever seemed relevant to law and lawyering. Robinson cast doubt on the immediate utility of available psychological learning. He suggested instead a two-step approach. First, psychologists should begin with substantive issues of importance to law— "[i]n the existing legal materials there is a mine of data for psychological investigation" (p. 120). Then, the "interrogatory attitude of psychology" can be brought to bear on the behavioral premises implicit in legal doctrines (p. 119). The value of psychology, as he saw it, lay not in providing "ready-made" answers but in bringing to jurisprudence an attitude or point of view about the place of empirical inquiry in law (p. 115). This modest and sensible proposition, embedded as it was in his more impassioned diatribes against the conservatism of the law, was lost to his legal critics.

Some of Robinson's law colleagues at Yale actually heeded the call to apply the psychological viewpoint to specific doctrinal issues. Underhill Moore (1929) sought to explain different judicial decisions in a banking law problem as arising not from different interpretations of legal rules, but from differences in "institutional patterns of behavior" of bankers in the various jurisdictions. Principles of banking practices were thought to be discoverable by simply observing the day-to-day actions of bank employees and their responses to hypothetical problem situations. A series of elaborate observational and interview studies yielded, according to one critic, only "inconclusive" results (Fuller 1934, p. 433). Subsequently, with an experimental psychologist, he studied parking behavior of drivers in relation to changing traffic ordinances (Moore and Callahan 1943). It was again a heroic effort to apply the approach and method of psychology—in this instance, Hull's stimulus-response theory of learning—to one tiny corner of the law. This time, Moore's effort to assess the law from a rigidly behavioristic approach met with only silence from the legal community, though Hull (1944) himself expressed satisfaction at the undertaking.

Another series of studies by Robinson's colleagues during this period were critiques of evidence rules by Robert Hutchins, a lawyer, and Donald Slesinger, a psychologist. Their aim, "preliminary to experimental attack, [was to analyze] the law of evidence [so as] to make explicit its psychological assumptions and criticize them in the light of modern psychology" (1929, p. 1). These assumptions included rough-and-ready notions about the memory and mental competency of witnesses, the reliability of excited utterances made under stress (thereby rendering them admissible as an exception to hearsay), and the validity of the concept of consciousness of guilt (Hutchins and Slesinger 1928a, 1928b, 1929).

Although these essays may be among the "best informed and most intelligent analyses" (Cairns 1935, p. 219) of the psychology of evidence, their substantive impact on evidence law and psychological research has been negligible. Their proposed changes have not been incorporated in the Federal Rules of Evidence, which is followed in most jurisdictions today. The "modern psychology" they relied upon for proposing reforms of existing rules consisted as much of "fireside inductions" (Meehl

1971)—that is, untested generalizations and informed conjecture about human behavior, no more unimpeachable than the common-sense assumptions they sought to
replace—as of scientific findings. For example, they urged that hearsay consisting of
excited utterances or dying declarations be excluded (rather than admitted, as they
normally are as exceptions to the hearsay ban), on the grounds that nothing in the
psychological research literature supported the assumption of the reliability of such
statements. The experimental studies they cited were not originally designed to address evidentiary questions, so their extrapolation of the results to the courtroom
represented a big and arguably unjustified leap. As one commentator put it, they
"appropriated, not the facts of psychology, but the psychological approach in contemplating problems of law" (Redmount 1961, p. 45). Their essays were essentially policy
analyses of law based upon tenuous propositions purported to be the rigorous de-
liverances of psychology. As Justice Frankfurter (1939) cautioned, "So we have to be
constantly on our guard lest psychology be more unequivocal in her wisdom when she
speaks to lawyers than when she speaks to psychologists" (p. 297).

    Their legacy, which has been all but forgotten today, lay in how they sought to
integrate both disciplines rather than in the substance of their scholarship. In articulating this approach, Slesinger and Pilpel (1929) appeared to agree with Robinson
that it "is a naive assumption on the part of psychologists and lawyers that . . . results
exist that can be readily applied" to legal issues. They went on to propose:

> [T]he first step in the development of legal psychology should be a logical and psychological
> analysis of legal institutions. . . . The preliminary analysis is the job of the lawyer and the
> logician, and the result will not be scientific fact, but hypotheses, which, when scientifically
> tested, may become facts. When the analysis is made the student of behavior may step in, and
> not, as in the past, to coordinate the results of his study with that of the legal student, but to
> devise methods of investigating the behavioral hypotheses elaborated in a different field. [p.
> 680]

The starting point for the application of psychology are problems posed by and
central to the law. One does not begin with the corpus of psychological knowledge.
The initial question is not, "What is known in psychology that can be carried over to
the legal process?" Instead, after analyzing the legal dimensions, the question becomes, "What kinds of new research can be done by psychology to illuminate the
factual aspects of the legal problem?" In this view, rapprochement between the disciplines does not come about by coordinating existing psychological findings and legal
issues, but by conducting afresh investigations tailored to these legal concerns. In
their essays on evidence, Hutchins and Slesinger did not respond to their own call to
go beyond "coordinating" results to "experimental attack." The task was left to a later
generation.

THE CONTEXT OF LEGAL REALISM

    The developments in this period need to be seen against the background of the
legal realist movement in jurisprudence. It carried forth the revolt against formalism
in law that was sparked by Justice Holmes in 1898 when he penned the now classic
"The life of the law has not been logic, it has been experience" (p. 1). Formalist
jurisprudence conceived of law as a closed, deductive body of logically ordered rules.

In such a view, there was little room for empirical inquiry in law. Justice Holmes pierced this logical veil to consider the role that extralegal influences such as social-economic factors, judicial attitudes, and community values play in the shaping of judicial decision-making. He saw law as part of the processes of society, not as an autonomous logical system. The legal realists of the 1930s, concentrated at the Yale and Columbia law schools, went further in portraying law not as a code but as an ongoing institution, so that it opens itself to inquiry by the nontechnician (Llewellyn 1940, p. 1355). It was in this climate that some legal scholars began foraging the psychological thickets for applications to their craft and social scientists began to be appointed to law faculties (Schlegel 1979).

Not all realists, however, marched under one flag. The radical faction of the movement called for a complete overhaul of formalism. It denied that legal precepts and logical reasoning had any effect on case law except as a "basic myth" (Frank 1930, p. 3) or as after-the-fact rationalizations of decisions (Hutcheson 1929); it elevated emotional experiences and personal history to first causes of judicial conduct (Yntema 1928); it repudiated "the heaven of legal concepts" based on abstractions and embraced "such positive sciences as . . . psychology" (Cohen 1931, p. 827); it urged revamping the entire legal machinery in light of behavioral psychology because "by controlling the individual's environment you can control his character and predict his future actions" (Beutel 1931, p. 175). The middle-of-the-road faction also recognized that judicial decisions were shaped by societal and personal influences, but nonetheless believed that rules played an effective though limited role in the totality of law (Fuller 1934; Llewellyn 1930; Pound 1931).

A major difference between the two groups was in the extent of their acceptance of the curative powers of psychology. At the time, it was not an integrated discipline. This was an "era of 'psychologies,'" each of which laid claim to the title of "'the new psychology'" (Dunlap 1925, p. 309). Some radical realists chose one school, behaviorism, and accorded it a dominant place in the reform of the judicial process. These included Robinson and Moore. Others opted for the Freudian psychoanalytic school (Frank 1930), and still others adopted a melange of viewpoints (Arnold 1937). The moderates such as Hutchins and Slesinger made use of experimental findings and methods for the betterment of legal doctrines, but they did not join the bandwagon of any particular psychological school.

It is curious that the radical followers of a jurisprudence that taught the importance of keeping close to empirical facts exhibited such cavalier acceptance of debatable theories. It is also ironic that the two principal theories they subscribed to were diametrically opposed in their explanations of the springs of conduct. Behaviorism was positivist, acknowledging only observable acts as determined by external stimuli; Freudianism was subjectivist, focusing on the interplay of unconscious drives and conscious restraints. Both were mechanistic conceptions that made no accommodation for purposive action and ratiocination as movers of behavior. It was this denial of rationalism that appealed to realists intent on exposing the nonrationality of the law. They relied on psychology perhaps not so much as a science, but as an ideology for their judicial reform. The authoritarianism of precedents and rules which they reproached was replaced by dogmatic generalizations from psychological theories. They espoused not psychology, but psychologism, in the law (Kennedy 1940). Except for some greater legal sophistication, they did exactly what their law colleagues rebuked Münsterberg for doing twenty years earlier.

If what psychologists do is to be of relevance to lawyers, it needs to be marshaled and organized around issues of legal significance. This implies a conception or working hypothesis of law to guide the choice of issues for investigation and to establish a method of analysis. Realism offered a conceptual alternative to formalism. By emphasizing the factual underpinning of rules, the behavioral impact of judicial decisions, and the social policies served by law, it invited empirical inquiry into law. Such empirical studies as were carried out, however, dealt with narrowly circumscribed rules of evidence and banking law, or with relatively trivial problems such as parking behavior and, later, the writing of bad checks (Beutel 1957; for a rebuttal, see Cavers 1957). The manifestos and discussions on methodology were kept, for the most part, at a respectful distance from actual fact-gathering. The bequest of realist jurisprudence was the promise rather than the application of its social-legal approach to law. Realism did have some impact on legal education by opening up the traditional curriculum to reflect the interrelation of law and the social sciences. Thus, courses on "the social psychology of law" were designed (Britt 1940a; Llewellyn 1935).

All was quiet on the psychology-law front during the 1940s. There were scattered studies on the usual topics of witness testimony (Snee and Lush 1941), evidence rules (Britt 1940b), and criminal behavior (Schmideberg 1947); and simulations of jury decision-making were introduced (Weld and Danzig 1940). These studies were mostly gleanings from ancestral sowings. On the whole, they did not add significantly to what had been done before, and none provoked any response from the legal profession.

Forensic Stage (1950s): Psychologists on the Stand

Up to this time, legal psychology had been an applied endeavor in name only. It had made little direct impact on litigation or judicial decision-making. Although psychologists in Europe had served as expert witnesses since the turn of the century and Münsterberg had long exhorted the American judiciary to bestir itself and follow suit, here it was not until "1950 that psychologists began to make an appreciable contribution in this role" (Anastasi 1957, p. 548). The contribution, however, was not by experimental psychologists testifying on witness reliability. The era of forensic psychology was ushered in by clinical and social psychologists testifying in the areas of mental disorders, pretrial publicity, and civil rights. Their initial experiences lay the foundation for the present-day role of experimental psychologists in eyewitness identification cases.

In the 1940s and 1950s, modern legal authority was established for the proposition that clinical psychologists who are qualified in terms of their education and experience could offer expert opinion on a mental disorder and its causal connection to criminal or tortious conduct (*People* v. *Hawthorne*, 1940; *Hidden* v. *Mutual Life Insurance Co.*, 1954). The broadening of admissibility of expert psychological testimony came with increased professionalization (for example, state certification and licensure), the rapid growth of mental health professions during this period, and the formulation of legal doctrines of insanity consistent with modern psychiatry (*Durham* v. *United States*, 1954). There suddenly mushroomed an extensive literature on the professional and legal aspects of the role of psychologists in court (for example, Louisell 1955; McCary 1956; Schofield 1956; Louisell 1957; McCary 1960).

Developments in survey research and sampling methodology at this time led to their applications in litigation, particularly to assessing the extent of community bias toward a defendant due to prejudicial, pretrial publicity (Woodward 1952). However, the survey results introduced by expert testimony in support of a motion for venue change were usually excluded at first on grounds of hearsay. The original respondents, as well as the survey researcher, were expected to be present for cross-examination (Zeisel 1960). Trial courts did not reach the real issue underlying admissibility—namely, the methodological competence of the survey—until over a decade later when the Supreme Court broke precedent and reversed a conviction because of pretrial publicity (*Irvin* v. *Dowd*, 1961) and then endorsed the liberal granting of venue change requests as a judicial cure for unfavorable media impact (*Sheppard* v. *Maxwell*, 1966).

The landmark School Desegregation Cases in 1954 (*Brown* v. *Board of Education*) saw the participation of social psychologists and other social scientists in their most visible and controversial forensic role to date. Kenneth Clark (1953), as plaintiff's leading psychological expert, testified in several of the lower court proceedings on studies purporting to show the harmful effects of segregation on children's personality and learning. On the appeal to the Supreme Court, he was joined by some thirty other distinguished social scientists in appending "A Social Science Statement" to appellant's brief that summarized the available research data on the effects of segregation and the probable consequences of desegregation (Appendix to Appellant's Brief 1953). The Court, in holding that "separate educational facilities are inherently unequal," found that segregation of school children "solely because of their race generates a feeling of inferiority" and "[retards their] educational and mental development" (pp. 494, 495). The "modern authority" for these findings were the writings of Clark and others, cited in the now celebrated footnote 11. Social scientists read the opinion as an acknowledgement of their impact on constitutional adjudication. "Proof [of wrongfulness of segregation]," said Clark (1953, p. 3), "had to come from the social psychologists."

The reaction from the legal community was swift and caustic. Edmond Cahn (1955) rightly criticized the methodological shortcomings and unjustified inferences of Clark's doll-preference experiments (see also Kluger 1977, pp. 330–31). Moreover, he feared that if reliable data were tendered on the issue, the merits would be thought to stand or fall with them, so that a change in scientific conclusions would force a change in the constitutional finding regarding segregation. He argued, "I would not have the constitutional rights of Negroes—or of other Americans—rest on any such flimsy foundation as some of the scientific demonstrations in these records" (p. 157). He also dismissed a poll, cited in footnote 11, showing the nearly unanimous but undocumented opinions of social scientists on the harmful effects of segregation as "literary psychology" (p. 161). Other noted legal scholars, too, described the behavioral evidence presented in the "Brandeis brief"-like "Statement" as "more social than scientific" (Karst 1960, p. 106) and "merely corroboratory of common sense" (Black 1960, p. 430). The footnote was seen as no more than a consolation gesture to Clark and company for their fidelity to the cause.

The debate served to ventilate the issues about the possibilities and limits of the social sciences in constitutional adjudication. It helped to set the stage for contemporary applications in other areas of constitutional lawmaking. The legal critics undoubtedly had the better part of the argument in disclaiming any direct impact of the empirical findings on the decision itself. If, as the Court said, segregation is "inherently unequal," then its wrongfulness is self-evident. The holding represents a moral judgment not grounded on factual proof. This is not to say, however, that the data may not have exerted an indirect effect on the shaping of the final outcome. Even normative conclusions are generated by an awareness of the facts; research results can illuminate and sharpen the factual premises of constitutional decision-making. What was said to have been common knowledge about the psychological consequences of segregation was the product, at least in part, of the substantial corpus of research information accumulated over the years that had worked its way into popular learning and then into the living law.

The imprimatur of "modern authority" served other functions as well. It added legitimacy to the overruling of the separate-but-equal doctrine that was itself rationalized in terms of the "psychological knowledge" of its time (*Brown*, p. 495), namely, the nineteenth-century Social Darwinist ideas about the biological bases of racial attitudes and their imperviousness to change by legislation (Bernstein 1963). The united front of the social scientists, in contrast to that of other scholars, reinforced the image of broadly based agreement on the evil of segregation that the Court sought to convey in its own unanimous opinion. Another indirect use of the empirical contribution was to show merely the possibility of harm resulting from racially discriminatory legislation, thereby shifting the burden to the state to come forward and prove that its actions were not presumptively unconstitutional (Freund 1963, pp. 151–52). For this procedural objective, the Court was wholly justified in accepting the findings with an uncritical eye.

The experiences of the forensic stage suggest two ways that psychology can be used in adjudication. One is in law application, as an aid to judicial fact-finding. In resolving a dispute, a court is called upon to apply a rule of law (the major premise) to its findings of fact (the minor premise) in order to reach a decision. When the rule itself is uncontested and only the facts are in dispute, as in cases involving a defendant's mental competency to stand trial or the extent of community prejudice that renders unlikely an unbiased venire, psychological testimony about these evidentiary issues can aid in the determination of the applicability of the rule. The other use is in law creation, as an aid to judicial legislation. When both the applicable law and the facts are at issue, as they were in the desegregation problem, the presentation of behavioral data on the disputed facts can help shape judge-made law, either directly or indirectly. It is a central feature of the nature and growth of law that "the issues of fact arise out of the law, but at the point of application of law, the issue of law also arises out of the facts" (Hart and McNaughton 1959, p. 61). There is a "chicken-and-egg relationship" between law and facts that makes possible the use of empirical research in the judicial process. Existing legal rules give facts their legal significance, but facts, in turn, can also beget new legal rules.

The Cahn-Clark exchange chilled further enthusiasm by psychologists in research on law for about a decade. Each group went its separate way, and such work as was done—mostly by lawyers—simply retread old ground. A 1929 book, *Psychology for the Lawyer*, reappeared in a retitled and slightly revised version (McCarty 1960). Another attorney urged, as Hutchins and Slesinger had a generation earlier, "a complete reconsideration of the rules of evidence to conform them . . . to what we know of the human condition," but his book offered no reform proposals (Marshall 1966, p. viii). A volume on case law on eyewitness identification alluded to psychological conditions of suggestiveness, but no empirical research was described or undertaken (Wall 1965). The first psychology text since realist days appeared, entitled *Legal and Criminal Psychology* (Toch 1961). It dealt far more with "criminal" matters (psychopathic personality, drug addiction, corrections, and so forth) than with "legal" ones (for example, trial tactics and psychology of judges). This literature shows that psychology and law "mingled only at the peripheries"; the relations were marked by "high defensiveness on both sides" (Riesman 1951, p. 32). In contrast, "genuine cross-disciplinary research" between lawyers and other social scientists, notably sociologists and political scientists, came to full flower during this period (Ladinsky 1975; Skolnick 1965). Some of the studies—especially on jury decision-making (for example, Strodtbeck, James, and Hawkins 1957), legal socialization (for example, Cohen, Robson, and Bates 1958), and legal impact of school prayer and insanity decisions (for example, Muir 1967; Simon 1967)—dealt with social psychological subject matter and even relied expressly on social psychological theories and methods. The irony is that the empirical approach to law advocated by Robinson and other realists began to take hold at the time when psychologists withdrew from the field.

Coming of Age Stage (1970s and 1980s): New Research on Procedural Justice

In a 1973 conference, a legal scholar said with remarkable prescience that psychology and law would be one of the two "growth stocks" in law and social sciences generally (Friedman 1974, p. 1071). Since then, there have been more psychologists doing more empirical research on law-related matters than in all the preceding years combined. Psycholegal research has indeed become a "growth industry" in the 1980s (Melton 1983, p. 1). The interest was revived in part by the social-political activism of the 1960s, which helped shape a generation of social scientists who sought to reconcile their training in scientific research with the call of social action by engaging in studies that had, in the overused term of its day, "social relevance." The judiciary spearheaded changes in civil, criminal, and political rights, so that the courts became again a highly visible target of applied research. Three score years after the publication of Münsterberg's book, it could be said that the field was finally coming into its own.

The scope of contemporary empirical inquiry has expanded beyond the traditional confines of witness testimony and evidence rules to encompass a variety of topics not examined before. There are some common emphases in this extensive literature that help place the field as a whole in perspective. Most, though by no means all, of the research undertaken today deals with criminal justice rather than civil justice, with the judicial rather than the legislative or administrative sectors of the legal system, and with procedural rather than substantive law—in essence, the main focus is on the criminal trial process (for example, Saks and Hastie 1978; Cohn and Udolf 1979; Toch 1979; Ellison and Buckhout 1981; Greenberg and Ruback 1982). Psycholegal research, as Tapp (1980) notes, is "overcriminalized."

For the purpose of establishing a framework for the present analysis, it may be useful to think of this process as comprising four sequential phases: pretrial influences (for example, pretrial publicity and pretrial identifications) on the jury; selection of the jury; presentations of testimony (filtered through evidence rules) and of law (via judicial instructions) to the jury; and finally, decision-making by the jury. The complex of legal rules that governs each of these phases and the values the rules implicate constitute procedural justice. The organizational centerpiece of this framework of procedural justice is the jury. It is the one subject that has commanded the most research attention of psychologists in the past fifteen years (Penrod 1979, n. 5, found that 90% of jury studies were done within this period). The emphasis is conceptually justifiable. Although only a minority of criminal cases go to trial and fewer yet are heard by a jury, the ideal of using lay members to find facts, to interpose the conscience of the community, and to legitimate official action lies at the bedrock of our system of justice.

Much of procedural law can be understood only in relation to, and in the context of, the jury institution. On the one hand, jurors are regarded as "the nerve center of the fact-finding process" (*Estes* v. *Texas*, 1965, p. 545). On the other, there has been a historical distrust in the judgment of amateurs, untutored in legal subtleties and inexperienced in evaluating evidence. Consequently, an elaborate web of procedural rules has evolved to shield the jury at each phase of the fact-finding process from extraneous influences that might bias its decision. Evidence law, Thayer (1898, p. 47) noted, is "the child of the jury." The jury is the hub that holds together the spokes of procedural justice. Directly or indirectly, the jury provides the backdrop for empirical study of the criminal trial process.

11.3. AN OVERVIEW OF THE PRESENT

The contemporary literature covers so much ground that the sensible approach, for the purpose of a short but systematic overview, is to take a leaf from the case method and examine in detail selected instances of psycholegal research pertaining to the different phases of the criminal process. This section encompasses the pretrial stage (eyewitness identifications) and the trial stage (jury selection and decision-making, and presentations to the jury). It provides a fairly representative sample of the quality and emphasis of current research and suggest insights into the possibilities and limits of this research in the judicial process.

Psychology of Eyewitness Identification

Two books on eyewitness testimony (Yarmey 1979; Loftus 1979) are representative of the genre. Yarmey asserts that this is the "most advanced" area of psycholegal research and the "most able to make a significant contribution to the legal system" (p. 228). To assess how the literature measures up to these claims, it is necessary to begin by locating the research problem in its legal and historical context.

The principal message that emerges from the long history of research is the general fallibility of eyewitnesses: "We have emphasized the unreliability of eyewitness testimony" (Saks and Hastie 1978, p. 190). "What still needs emphasis and discussion . . . is the unwarranted trust that police officers, jurors, and the courts persist in giving to lineups and eyewitness identifications" (Yarmey 1979, p. 153); based not on any direct studies but on extrapolation from cognitive research generally, it is further asserted that "mistaken identity from lineups is often the rule and not the exception" (Yarmey 1979, p. 159).

In this as in any other applied endeavor, the bottom line question is the practical or policy impact of the research. Psychologists in this area concede that "the research has not had a great impact" on the judicial process (Wells 1978, p. 1547). The law has not excluded from evidence eyewitness testimony. If the testimony is as unreliable as the researchers claim it to be, the clear implication is that it should be barred, although they have seldom explicitly drawn that conclusion probably because they recognize it is a drastic and unrealistic remedy. Indeed, the trend of modern evidence law is to admit rather than exclude all relevant evidence (Weinstein and Berger 1976, pp. 105–10). The law has not adopted a requirement of corroboration because, like an exclusionary rule, it would transform an issue of weight into one of admissibility (Comment 1977). The law has not required delivery of cautionary instructions to the jury regarding the possible fallibility of such testimony, absent a specific request by counsel to do so (*United States* v. *Telfaire*, 1972). The law has rejected, far more often than it has permitted, the discretionary admission by the trial judge of expert psychological testimony on the unreliability of eyewitness evidence, relying on such makeshift reasons as trespassing on the province of the jury (*United States* v. *Amaral*, 1973; *United States* v. *Thevis*, 1982). More than a generation ago, Robinson (1935) also noted that "psychologists have not been called in any numbers to assess the credibility of witnesses" (p. 98). Thus, despite the advances of experimental psychology, its applications to courtroom testimony seem to have remained unchanged.

Various reasons have been put forth by psychologists to account for this lack of impact, none of which is wholly persuasive. One has to do with professional rivalry and misunderstanding. Yarmey (1979) believes that lawyers are "indifferent or even hostile" to psychology, guarding the courts as their private preserve and "subconsciously resent[ing] the entry of experts" (pp. 6, 32). On the other hand, he cites approvingly Paul Meehl's view (1971) that psychologists are "'ideologically tendentious and often completely uninformed with respect to the law'" (p. 16). There is nothing new in these reproaches. Even during the height of interdisciplinary collaboration of the realist period, some psychologists perceived no real meeting of the minds: "The lawyer is not convinced that the psychologist has any comprehension of legal problems; the psychologist sees the lawyer fumbling blindly . . . and rebukes him for not drawing freely upon the body of knowledge he has so carefully and laboriously built up" (Powers 1937, p. 274). Others today attribute the lack of impact to the "reactionary and closed-minded" nature of the legal system (Buckhout, in Wells 1978, p. 1547), which suggests that the chapter on yellow psychology is not over. Finally, still others point to the unavailability of published summaries of research for the legal community as a reason (Loftus 1980). "The most important contribution that psychology can make to legal decision-making is to provide scientific information that would not ordinarily be available to the law" (Yarmey 1979, p. 35).

However, it is not enough, as Slesinger and Pilpel (1929) reminded in the realist days, to simply come forward with basic psychological knowledge and hope that lawyers will grasp its legal significance. Understanding of how cognitive processes function does not readily translate into practical decision-making, any more than knowledge of the physical and chemical properties of clay would enable a sculptor to do better modeling. Beyond educating lawyers and judges about the fallibility of the senses, assuming that they are uninformed about this fact of human experience in the first instance, there remain two basic issues which have not been satisfactorily addressed to date. First, why has there not been greater judicial acceptance of the testimony of experimental psychologists on eyewitness fallibility? No such problem of admissibility was raised in the 1950s when clinical psychologists began to testify on mental disorders or when social psychologists first appeared to describe the debilitating personality consequences of segregation. Second, what can and should be done to mitigate the risk of error in eyewitness identifications, other than to continue reiterating their unreliability? It is necessary to delve into the difficulty of applying psychology to the law in order to respond to these interrelated issues. The arguments to be made here are that psychological research has not dealt with issues of policy relevance to law and that there are fundamental differences between the two disciplines in the kinds of information they gather and in the methods by which they are gathered that place limits on their rapprochement.

LEVEL OF ANALYSIS IN EYEWITNESS IDENTIFICATION

The subject of eyewitness identification can be approached from three cognate levels of analysis. The first is the psychological level: the sources, nature, and magnitude of the unreliability inherent in identifications. The second is the social psychological level of communication and influence: the impact of the testimony on the jury's verdict. And the third is the system level: the institutional procedures designed by the law to safeguard the jury against these biasing effects. Psychology and law have each given primary attention to different levels of the subject, and this is a main reason why the legal applications of psychological research have been limited.

Reality experiments have focused on the psychological level, demonstrating the fallibility of observation and recall. The history of the research is one of "show and tell"—show the existence of bias of subjects in the laboratory and tell about it to the legal community, with the inference that eyewitnesses in the real world are unreliable.

But the legal community has not been preoccupied with this level of analysis. One reason is that the law requires particularized proof rather than general proof in adjudication. "[I]t is not enough," Wigmore (1937) said, "to realize empirically that there are possibilities of error in testimonial evidence, and to adopt an attitude of caution. It is desirable to learn, if we can, how extensive are the possibilities of error. . . ." Even if such measurements of error were possible, they "would be true in general only, and would still not be usable to diagnose the individual witness" (p. 692). The law cannot assume that because eyewitnesses in general are fallible, a particular eyewitness is probably mistaken, too. At present, expert psychological testimony can only point to factors that are known to be potentially biasing. Loftus (1980) admits that "any psychologist who attempted to offer an exact probability for the likelihood that a witness was accurate would be going far beyond what is possible" (p. 200). Yet, this is precisely the judgment that the fact-finder is called upon to make, and expert testimony is of little assistance in this regard.

The real point of contention between psychology and law is not with the fact of eyewitness fallibility as such, but with the purported impact of the supposedly fallible testimony upon the ultimate outcome of the trial—that is, at the social psychological level of analysis. Psychologists assume that this testimony fatally taints the verdict. However, as early as 1909, Wigmore questioned whether the testimonial errors found in laboratory experiments produced misleading results in the verdicts. He proposed that "the way to answer this is to include a jury (or judge of fact) in the experiment, and observe whether the findings of fact follow the testimonial errors or whether they succeed in avoiding them and in reaching the actual facts" (p. 426). Of the dozens of eyewitness identification studies conducted since then, only Wigmore's own reality experiments (1937, pp. 698–701) and a major study by a psychologist-lawyer (Marston 1924) have assessed the impact on the fact-finder. In general, these results showed that "the findings . . . tend[ed] to have a lower rate of errors than the average testimonial rate; i.e., somehow the testimonial errors [were] correctly adjusted (in part) by the judge's or jury's reflection" (Wigmore 1937, p. 720). None of the current psychological writings on this subject even mention these studies. These early results are not inconsistent with the principal conclusion of Kalven and Zeisel's classic study (1966, p. 56) on the jury, which was that it is not the incompetent and unreliable fact-finder that it has been feared to be. The burden rests with the psychologists who assume that eyewitness evidence, because of its demonstrated fallibility in the laboratory, has a greater distorting effect on the jury's decision than other kinds of evidence of suspect reliability.

Otherwise stated, psychological writings equate potential bias (general fallibility) with actual bias (mistaken verdict). The law distinguishes these two elements. The due process test for evaluating eyewitness identifications states the two elements in the conjunctive: The identification set has to be suggestive and it has to result in misidentification (*Manson* v. *Brathwaite*, 1977). The law's reluctance to assume categorically a one-to-one correspondence between the potential unreliability (which is conceded) and its actual impact in a particular trial (which must be proven) is one reason that the courts have not rushed to embrace expert psychological testimony.

Since the law can do little about the fallibility of the senses as such (other than to recognize it), its attention has turned to devising institutional means of counteracting the possible effects of fallible testimony on the jury's decision. It has required the presence of counsel at postindictment lineups; it has reiterated its trust in cross-examination as an instrument to expose bias; it has recommended the drafting of legislation and regulations to govern identification procedures; it has proposed model cautionary instructions; and so on. In contrast, psychological research has largely neglected the system level where its applications would be of greatest use to law. Instead of continuing to demonstrate in the laboratory the inaccuracy of perception and recall and to bewail the futility of eyewitness testimony, psychologists need to concentrate on system level research. Otherwise, they are unlikely to attain the "integra[tion] . . . of the psychological and legal aspects of eyewitness identification" or "show the relevance and implications for the criminal justice system of the scientific literature," their common aspirations in undertaking this applied research in the first place (Yarmey 1979, p. xiii).

Yarmey's book on eyewitness testimony is a case in point. Targeted for psychologists and lawyers, it is a fine exposition of modern cognitive research. But a legal reader may be left wondering about the implications of this assemblage of data and theories for the policy issues in eyewitness identification. A meager eight pages (pp. 152–59, or 3% of the entire volume) is given to an attempt to join psychological research with the legal questions. For example, after a review of the 1967 trilogy of

Supreme Court cases, Yarmey states that there has been subsequently considerable legislative reform of lineup procedures, but then dismisses them as "beyond our scope of interest" (p. 153). Since the Court itself has declared that legislation or police regulations which eliminate the risks of suggestions at lineups might "remove the basis for regarding the stage as 'critical,'" and hence dispense with the need for counsel, one would have thought that empirical evaluation of these new procedures would be one of the most legally significant areas of applied research.

This neglect of system-level problems is not unique to Yarmey's otherwise valuable contribution, but permeates the entire psycholegal literature (Wells 1978). There has been virtually no inquiry on the adequacy of the police regulations on lineups now in effect (Read 1969; Comment 1978; American Law Institute 1975), though they represent lay efforts at behavioral control. There has been little research on the impact of cautionary instructions on eyewitness unreliability that are now in use in several jurisdictions (Greene 1983), though this has not restrained even empirically minded psychologists from professing doubts as to their effectiveness (Loftus 1979, pp. 189–90). There has been no attempt to assess the impact of different kinds of eyewitness identification (for example, pure identification versus identification plus) upon the jury, though it is nonetheless asserted that "[there is] ample justification for regarding *all* eyewitness identifications with skepticism" (Levine and Tapp 1973, p. 1124; emphasis added). Systematic evaluation studies have yet to be done on the effectiveness of available legislative and police regulations of lineups. Assessments of the impact of expert testimony at trial (Hosch 1980; Loftus 1980) or of the fairness of actual lineup regulations are the kind of system-level research that holds promise for legal policy.

THE METHODS OF EXPERIMENTAL PSYCHOLOGY AND OF LAW

The difference in levels of analysis is related to a basic difference in the methods of inquiry of psychology and law. Experimental research gathers aggregate data and uses statistical measures of central tendency and variation. This approach is suitable for dealing with large numbers of cases. Trial adjudication is adapted to the investigation and determination of the facts of a specific case. It is a "clinical" procedure that seeks particularized information of a single instance. The experimental method is designed to secure "legislative facts"—facts about broad social, economic, or behavioral phenomena that can be relied upon in the creation of new law and policy. The trial process is intended to gather "adjudicative facts"—facts that explain who did what, when, where, how, and with what motive in a given case (Davis 1958, §15.03).

Since the 1950s, the expert testimony of clinical psychologists regarding the presence or absence of a mental disorder or the testimonial competence of a defendant has been an issue only of weight, not of admissibility. The clinician does not testify about the conditions that bring about mental disorder in general. He gives his opinion about the sanity or competence of the particular defendant or witness at the trial. The experimental psychologist, in contrast, does not have the wherewithal to test the reliability of any particular eyewitness. In testifying about human fallibility in general, he is offering legislative facts to a fact-finder charged with an adjudicative task.

Expert testimony by social psychologists in the School Desegregation Cases did not raise admissibility issues. Although the subject of their testimony—the effects of segregation on the personality and learning of black children in general, not of the particular children in the lawsuit—also rested on legislative facts, they were treated by the courts more like the clinical psychologists than the experimental psychologists. The issue of school desegregation had societal implications that transcended the immediate interests of the party litigants; the courts were engaged not only in adjudication but also in judicial legislation. When matters of broad social policy are at stake, the experimental data and generalizations presented by Kenneth Clark and others at least suggested the direction the law should take and helped clarify the factual basis of the normative issues. No such legislative-type determinations are involved in evaluating the testimonal certitude of any given eyewitness. Expert testimony about general results is unhelpful in purely adjudicative cases (Robbins 1975), and this may be why experimental psychologists have found the courts less receptive to them than to their other psychological brethren.

Social Psychology of the Criminal Trial Process

Among the research topics that have seen the most effective integration of law and psychology, and consequently have elicited the greatest interest of the legal community, are those on jury decision-making.

PRESENTATIONS OF EVIDENCE AND LAW TO THE JURY

The major subject of research and debate today in the psychology of evidence law pertains to the impact of communications to the jury, specifically, to the impact of judicial instruction on the limited admissibility of evidence. A critical assessment of this research is due because the different studies yield conflicting results, thereby bearing conflicting implications for judicial policy. It also serves to illustrate a broader conceptual issue in psycholegal research, namely, the risks inherent in conducting empirical studies of legal rules without appreciation of the policies behind these rules.

In the typical experimental design, mock jurors listen to a taped criminal trial. Half of them are informed about the defendant's past record and half of them are not. A judge delivers limiting instructions to the first group. Several studies have found the instructions "futile" (Hans and Doob 1976, p. 253; Doob and Kirshenbaum 1972; Wolf and Montgomery 1977) because more convictions are rendered when record evidence is introduced. On this basis, researchers have proposed a blanket exclusion on the admissibility of prior criminality. Some reviewers conclude that "the disturbing implication [of these studies is] that jurors will typically ignore or misunderstand instructions from the bench" and that in the area of evidence, "once again legal practice and scientific psychology are in conflict" (Saks and Hastie 1978, pp. 39, 163). Others, similarly, say that the findings are proof of "uncontrolled variables affecting the impact of a trial's structure on the jury" (Cohn and Udolf 1979, p. 254). However, there are other experiments that show the opposite result: Mock jurors who are given the limiting instruction render fewer convictions than those not so instructed (Cornish and Sealy 1973). Thus, still other reviewers, noting these "conflicting results," state that the effectiveness of the instruction is "uncertain" (Davis, Bray, and Holt 1977, p. 337).

An analysis of the policy of the rule suggests that both positions are not inconsistent with each other. Here, as in other evidence rules, a balancing of competing values inherent in the fact-finding process is involved: full disclosure to aid truth determination versus fairness in the manner in which guilt is adjudicated. On the one hand, as an actuarial matter there is a strong association between past conduct and future propensity; wholesale exclusion of the record "would probably have as its principal consequence a lessening of the reliability of jury verdicts" (Weinstein and Berger 1976, pp. 105–36). On the other, it is contrary to the ideals of presumption of innocence and reformation of offenders to saddle an accused forever with the burden of his past misdeeds; unfettered admission could prejudice a jury and cause it to use a lower standard of proof with presumed incorrigibles. What the law does, then, is to strike a compromise between the two extremes. If the limiting instruction is seen as a means for harmonizing competing values, one would expect convictions to be highest under unlimited admission, lowest under total exclusion, and in between under limited admission. This, of course, is precisely what the seemingly conflicting results show. The instructions are effective in achieving the desired procedural equilibrium.

Thus, unless researchers are informed about the legal dimensions of their psycholegal studies, they run the risk of drawing wrong conclusions from the findings. In this instance, they have approached the problem solely on utilitarian grounds and neglected to consider that other social values, extrinsic to accurate fact-finding, are implicated in a trial.

The analogy of some courts of the limiting instruction to a judicial "placebo" (*United States* v. *Grunewald,* 1956, p. 574) reinforces the foregoing analysis. By definition, sometimes the pretended cure works, sometimes not. The research question is not only whether these instructions are effective, but also under what circumstances are they likely to be more or less effective. In this instance, the judicial literature is a trove of research ideas about possible determinants of effectiveness (for example, *Delli Paoli* v. *United States,* 1957)—such as the length of the prior record, the amount of other incriminating evidence, the timing of the instructions, the manner in which they are delivered—that has yet to be exploited by psychologists.

ASSESSMENT OF THE LEGAL IMPACT OF SOCIAL PSYCHOLOGICAL RESEARCH ON THE CRIMINAL TRIAL PROCESS

Except for research on jury selection, size, and decision rules, current investigations on other topics in the criminal trial process have not left a distinctive mark on the law. The potential for making a significant contribution is there, however, if two principal shortcomings are remedied.

One limitation is the lack of generalizability of simulation experiments to the legal world. Most of the courtroom studies conducted today typically have high internal validity but low external validity. Compared with the early reality experiments, for example, current social psychological studies are much more rigorous in terms of ensuring the results are due to the manipulated (rather than to uncontrolled or unknown) variables, but are no better in terms of the generality of these results. "[R]esults of most laboratory-based studies [of jury trials] are of unknown and generally unknowable generality" (Bermant et al. 1974, p. 225). This is because simulated procedures often are not the functional equivalent of actual processes. Some of the most common sources that detract from the verisimilitude of laboratory studies include, briefly, the following:

• selection of college students rather than real jurors in mock juries (real juries have been found less likely to convict; Zeisel and Diamond 1974, p. 281)
• recording of individual juror decisions rather than the group verdict (the financial and temporal advantages of this shortcut are true economies only if individual decisions are predictive of the group verdict, an assumption on which there are opposing views; Gerbasi, Zuckerman, and Reis 1977; Davis, Bray, and Holt 1977)
• presentation of a short, written transcript or audiotape of a trial rather than a more realistic audiovisual film (the greater the verisimilitude, the lower the guilty rate in jury simulations; Bermant et al. 1974)
• introduction of experimental variables in ways that are disproportionate to their actual role in litigation, thereby artificially magnifying their impact (for example, expert psychological testimony on eyewitness identification composing one-fourth of all the information given to the mock jury; Loftus 1980)
• major procedural omissions in simulated trials that, had they occurred in an actual proceeding, would have been grounds for automatic reversal (for example, many jury decision-making studies do not include any instructions on the burden or standard of proof; Loftus 1980; Wolf and Montgomery 1977; Hans and Doob 1976)
• major procedural errors in simulated trials (a not uncommon instruction to the jury is to return a verdict of "innocent or guilty" or to give verdicts expressed in degrees of guilt; Wolf and Montgomery 1977; Sue, Smith, and Caldwell 1973; Yarmey 1979, p. 24)
• "simulations" of entire court procedures that have no correspondence to the reality that purportedly is being simulated (for example, Walker, Thibaut, and Andreoli 1972)

A clear lesson from the long history of eyewitness research is that the legal community is reluctant to embrace laboratory findings of suspect generalizability. Moreover, even when that methodological feature is unimpeachable, another condition must be met to assure the legal applicability of the research—it has to be directed toward questions of significance to law. As Macaulay (1983) reminds us, "The research may be impeccable, but a rigorous answer to a silly question is still a silly answer" (p. 17). A second limitation, then, is a conceptual one. Unless researchers take into account the legal dimensions of the problem under study, they may run the risk of drawing conclusions from the data that are not legally relevant or are even possibly erroneous, as illustrated in the experiments on judicial instructions.

Conclusion

Some themes culled from the history of law and psychology can help place in perspective the current problems and future prospects of psycholegal research.

The history is characterized by a succession of dialectical interchanges. At first, with simplistic optimism, psychologists (at times joined by lawyers) propose that their methods and knowledge can be applied to the redemption of law. The overselling of psychology prompts the legal community to snap back and put psychologists in their place. This dampens further interest in interdisciplinary collaboration and for a decade or so the law is left to muddle along in its own way. The lessons are later forgotten and a new cycle of approach-rebuff-withdrawal is repeated. The debates during the different periods of this history—between Münsterberg and Wigmore, Robinson and Mechem, Clark and Cahn—illustrate this contrapuntal pattern. In the best of times, an uneasy partnership has prevailed; in the worst of times, there has been outright hostility; in between and most of the time, each side carried on "as though the other did not exist" (Fahr 1961). During the present boom period of psycholegal research, there has not been any instance of outright rejection by the legal profession. Indeed, some legal scholars have viewed favorably (Friedman 1974, p. 1070), though with a critical methodological eye (Damaška 1975), this research revival. So long as psychologists do not overshoot their mark and are sophisticated about the role and limitations of empirical inquiry in the legal process, they are unlikely to visit upon themselves the kind of legal reproach experienced in the past. The field has now come of age, and in several key respects.

First, there is increasing consciousness that psycholegal studies require, as psychologists of the realist period indicated, more "sensitivity to the lawyer's point of view" (Powers 1937, p. 274). "The first step in the development of legal psychology should be a[n] . . . analysis of legal situations" (Slesinger and Pilpel 1929, p. 680). Without a conception of the legal parameters of a problem, there is no assurance that the particular aspect being studied has any special importance, or even relevance, to the policy concerns of lawyers. This is the risk of "applied" studies on evidence or juries that ostensibly analyze a given legal problem, but in reality use the legal paradigm principally to test hypotheses regarding basic psychological processes.

In an applied endeavor, it is of higher priority to produce answers that are meaningful to law than to ask questions that advance psychological theory. On the whole, psychologists today are not insensitive to it. If there is one feature that distinguishes current books (for example, Cohn and Udolf 1979; Bartol 1983; Horowitz and Willging 1984) from those of earlier years, it is that now there are deliberate efforts to integrate the research into a legal framework. Arguably some of these efforts have not always or wholly been successful so far, but from a long-range viewpoint, the fact that they are being undertaken is in itself promising for the future.

Second, a critical mass of specialists in psycholegal studies is now forming, something that did not exist before and is needed for the development of any discipline. In the past, even as recently as the early 1970s, most of the persons writing on psychology and law did not have that subject as their principal professional interest (Saks 1979). They tended to be recognized authorities in traditional areas of legal or psychological scholarship who forayed into this interdisciplinary area as a collateral or one-time undertaking. None of the sources cited in the historical overview—not even Münsterberg (Moskowitz 1977)—can be said to have achieved his primary distinction in psycholegal research. These psychologists were not, and had no incentive to be, sufficiently sophisticated in the law so that their research would be meaningful to lawyers. Some acquaintance with the intellectual culture of law—with how law defines, analyzes, and manages problems—is needed in undertaking applied research on law. Psychologists, in general, are socialized in the scientific method; they are trained to think in terms of the formulation and empirical testing of theories, not in terms of social action. Professional recognition is seldom gained by attending to policy applications of basic research. It is not surprising, then, that until recently, most of the law-related writings of psychologists were not usually adapted to practical decision-making. Lawyers, on the other hand, are essentially applied social scientists. They are trained in those skills and sensitivities needed for the regulation—rather than the understanding—of human conduct (Ohlin, 1970). The different mind sets have created obstacles to rapprochement between psychologists and lawyers.

Psycholegal research books of the 1980s are representative of current trends not only in terms of their content but also of their authorship. They are all by younger scholars who are now establishing their reputations and establishing them principally in law and psychology. They should be joined increasingly by others who have dual credentials (graduates of the various programs recently formed) or are otherwise sufficiently informed in the methods and intellectual perspectives of both disciplines, so that they are likely to identify themselves with psycholegal research as a distinct professional specialty. With more and full-time workers expected in the vineyard, perhaps a more bounteous harvest may be reaped in the future.

Finally, the nature of psycholegal research is undergoing change. The research had consisted mainly of collating available psychological information and the legal problem. In the early writings on witness testimony or on the behavioral premises of evidence rules, psychologists and lawyers would search through the inventory of psychology to see what could be pulled out and generalized to the legal context. The limitation on this approach was that psychology did not then, and does not now, possess a corpus of reliable information that can be directly transferred to particular legal issues. Moreover, even though some basic research might have implications for a legal problem, the applicability might not be immediately obvious. A good example is given by Kalven (1968). In research that led to *The American Jury* (1966), Kalven and Zeisel were familiar with Asch's classic experiments on social conformity but did not initially sense their applicability to the problem of hung juries. These experiments had found that a subject was more likely to resist majority influence if he had at least one other ally who disagreed with the majority. It was not until they had done research directly on the legal problem, finding that juries initially split 11-to-1 would not hang but those split 10-to-2 would be stalemated, that they realized there was congruence between their jury data and the previously reported studies on conformity.

The present trend is not merely to extrapolate from existing knowledge but to engage afresh in research specifically tailored to given issues, as exemplified in the jury size studies. The coming of age signals a change in the approach to psycholegal research: from "psychology *and* law" to "psychology *in* law" and "psychology *of* law."

11.4.   REFLECTIONS ON THE FUTURE

[Conference presentation on] THE FUTURE OF LAW AND SOCIAL SCIENCES RESEARCH

Marc Galanter

I would like to begin this exercise in futurology by addressing what I think is our intellectual problem. When we talk about the "Future of Law and Social Sciences Research," we tend to talk about

institutional problems. I would like to address what I consider to be the conceptual or the theoretical aspects of this research. . .

[A] very central problem is the relation of . . . social scientific study of law to the received perspectives that come to us from so-called classical legal scholarship. . .

I speak of that set of implicit presuppositions about the nature of the legal system that informs most legal scholarship: views about the centrality of courts and adjudication to the whole process; the importance, the overwhelming importance of rules; the congruence of behavior with authoritative prescription, and so on. . . .

These presuppositions are there underlying most legal research. Legal research reflects them with its very heavy emphasis on the judicial as opposed to other legal agencies; in its concern with doctrine as opposed to other features in the legal process; . . . and in the assumption that for the most part rules reflect and control behavior. . . .

The point is that the ghost of doctrinal research and the assumptions it embodies still haunts our efforts in social research in law; and that these same presuppositions that underlie doctrinal research are still around and influence what gets studied and how it gets studied. They shape the kind of questions that we bring to material, the way we interpret it, and lead us to ignore some fruitful subjects for study. . . .

The discrepancy between law on the books and the law in action has been discovered innumerable times since Roscoe Pound used the phrase in 1910. I think it is an embarrassment that we have gone so little beyond that formulation, which is still with us today. This gap has been discovered innumerable times. The question is: What do we do with the discovery? . . .

These received views seem to have a great tenacity. They are very powerfully supported by the training and intellectual orientation of the legal profession, training which provides very elaborate categories for organizing and classifying, and remembering rules, but few conceptual tools for perceiving and keeping in view the non-rule features of the legal process. . . . This tendency is reinforced by the practical orientation of the profession: We are in the "doing something about it" business. When we discover a gap between norm and practice, this is taken not as a cause for reflection on theoretical models but as a spur to action. . . .

What I am suggesting is that the received cognitive map tends to inhibit . . . us from asking some of the large questions about the legal process and the gross relationships between law and other social phenomena.

Instead, we concentrate on this problem of the law on the books and law in action, the failure of practice to conform to the stated objectives of particular institutions or rules. This law on the books versus law in action formulation *appears* to challenge the received view, or at least come to terms with and incorporate all that departs from it; but I submit that in subtle ways, it gives expression to the received view of the legal system and inhibits the development of alternative theoretical formulations. To say, "there is a gap between the law on the books and the law in action," expresses an expectation of harmony and congruence between the authoritative, normative learning on the one hand and patterns of practice on the other. . . . It prevents us from entertaining the possibility that other relationships than harmony and congruence between law and behavior are expectable, normal, and natural. That is, [it] obstructs any attempt to build more complex models of the interaction of law and behavior that depart from this notion of one-to-one correspondence that lies in the background of that law on the books–law in action formulation. . . .

We need more from the research enterprise than merely complementing legal learning as it exists by adding an empirical dimension. Instead, we should be interested in the task of theoretical construction or reconstruction of ways of looking at the legal system—of expanding our conceptual apparatus to encompass features and relationships which lie beyond the boundaries of received legal scholarship.

I say this not in any way to denigrate research which attempts to go out and measure the existence of these discrepancies or the scientist who sees his task as the addition of an empirical dimension. . . .

I want to emphasize that most inquiry about law should and will continue to be linked to the policy concerns of lawyers.

But the question that we are going to be facing in coming years is whether there is a case for some kind of autonomous inquiry as well; that is, an inquiry that explicitly strives for general theory about the relationship between legal and other social phenomenon, which includes both empirical studies and theoretical explorations, which is concerned with cross-cultural verification of hypotheses, and which selects its subject matter and methods not with an eye to solving pressing problems of the day but out of a commitment to the attainment of universal, scientific generalizations about law in society.

The case for such autonomous social research on law need not and should not rest on its practicality. . . .

[T]he case has to rest on its theoretical interest, on the sense of obligation to pursue understanding of a pervasive aspect of human action. The claim is not unlike that to be made for the social-scientific study of religion. Presumably, there is room in the world for a sociology of religion in addition to studies by various votaries interested in reformulating and enriching their particular creeds. . . . One need not argue that the sociology of religion will contribute to salvation, spiritual elevation, or even building up church attendance.

If one is attracted by the notion of relatively autonomous (I don't like the term, but I don't have a better one at the moment) kind of social research in law, the question is: How do we get there from here? . . .

[O]ne priority for research should be its promise for conceptual development. This in turn suggests to me that we should give priority to studies that attempt to take the "givens" in the received view of the legal system and make them into variables to be explained. That is we should be looking for studies that take courts, rules, enforcement, compliance—all of the background assumptions of our everyday views of how the legal system works—and seek to explain their presence and character. This might be done by beginning with studies of the discrepancies and gaps, the so-called anomalies that don't quite fit our view of the normal, typical legal system at work. . . . They should be treated not as something marginal and abnormal but should be moved to the center of our field of vision and treated as central and pervasive features of the legal process. . . .

[L]et me close by expressing some puzzlement as to where this is going to take place; there is a real problem of institutional setting. Although the professionally oriented American law school may be opening up to empirical research, it may find social research of the kind that I have been talking about uncongenial. . . . One possibility is the development of an undergraduate program, which would provide a base for having faculty with a major commitment to non-professional studies. Autonomous research institutes within law schools are another possibility, and yet a third is that this isn't going to take place in law schools at all but over in the social science departments or elsewhere.

NOTES AND QUESTIONS

1. This volume deals with applied social research. Its purpose is to evaluate empirically the factual predicates and the social consequences of law and to stimulate reflection on more and better research of this kind. Its driving focus is the deployment of data in the service of improving law and lawyering. One of the chief tools of lawyering is rhetoric, and since our culture accords special weight to arguments based on scientific authority, advocacy gains an edge when clothed in valid scientific attire. Galanter's article provides a counterpoint to this orientation. He squarely challenges the notion that social research should be linked to the policy concerns of law. Others, too, argue that such scholarship is "derivative" and "shallow" (Priest 1983, p. 439). Galanter proposes that attention in the future should turn to "autonomous social research on law." In effect, he argues that social scientists should not borrow most of their research questions from the immediate subject of their study (the legal process) and from those who are its principal students (legal scholars), but they should frame their own issues and approaches in order to break away from the received intellectual traditions. Is this a viable future course for social-legal research in light of its past history? Can the distinction between autonomous (or basic) research and applied research be drawn as readily in the field of law as in other fields (for example, medicine)? The implications of emphasizing basic or applied social-legal research will be discussed in Chapter 13, section 13.5.

2.   Much of social-legal research consists of impact studies—that is, studies of the instrumental efficacy of law in achieving its stated objectives. Today, we know in advance that most decisions and legislation are ineffective by this instrumentalist criterion, though we continue to feign amazement at the gap between the ideal and the real, between the positive law and the operative law (Abel 1980). Impact research exposes the inadequacies and unmasks the pretensions of law (Katz 1971; Haney 1980); it is part of the American tradition of muckraking. The implication is that law can be reformed, thereby strengthening and confirming the ideology of the effectiveness of law as an instrument of social control. Galanter says that it is an "embarrassment" that we have not gone beyond the mere fact of disclosing this duality. He questions the ideology itself and wonders aloud about "alternative theoretical formulations" in which law and conduct are not expected to be in harmony.

In an essay that takes stock of social-legal research, Macaulay (1983) expands on Galanter's theme. Macaulay observes that "most researchers carry in their heads a high school civics model of the American legal system" in which the gap between promise and performance can and should be closed. The "mindless empiricism" that characterizes much of the research is actually guided by covert values of political liberalism which seep into the framing of the hypotheses and the collection and interpretation of data. The excess attention paid to the instrumentalist purposes of law has impoverished social-legal studies. He suggests that structural-functionalist theories (which look at the compromises between competing interests that produce social stability) and varieties of Marxist theories (which focus on issues of power, class, and social consciousness) could point to questions that empirical researchers have overlooked and could help explain why legal doctrines and institutions do not necessarily operate the way they should (pp. 32, 26).

If impact studies show, for example, that the exclusionary rule does not deter police misconduct, or that school desegregation does not raise the academic performance of minority students, what further inquiry would you pursue? What social functions—and whose social-economic interests—are served by maintaining (or exposing) the dichotomy between the law-in-the-book and the law-in-action?

3.   Basic research, in Galanter's vision, should strive for "the attainment of universal, scientific generalizations about law in society." It is an open question whether the state of the art in social science permits anything more than highly stylized and simplified models of reality. There are too many variables and too little information to enable us to establish lawlike relationships about complex social phenomena. Some even argue that "social science cannot be a science" because it "cannot develop a secure understanding of causal relationships which will permit it to predict important social events" (Rein 1976, p. 70). " 'Those who wait for a Newton' of the social sciences 'are not only waiting for a train that won't arrive, they're in the wrong station altogether' " (Yudof 1978, p. 101). Indeed, because of the uncertainties of social science in unraveling the complex relationships involved in social issues, some judges have turned to noninstrumentalist grounds of decision-making. If there are limits to the capability of both autonomous and applied social research to attain universal generalizations, what are other, more modest and viable roles for social-legal inquiry?

REFERENCES

Abel, R. L. "Redirecting Social Studies of Law." *Law and Society Review* 14 (1980): 805–29.

American Law Institute. *A Model Code of Pre-arraignment Procedure.* Proposed official draft. Philadelphia: American Law Institute, 1975.

Anastasi, A. *Fields of Applied Psychology.* New York: McGraw-Hill, 1957.

Appendix to Appellant's Brief. "The Effects of

Segregation and the Consequences of Desegregation: A Social Science Statement." *Minnesota Law Review* 37 (1953): 427–39.

Arnold, T. *The Folklore of Capitalism*. New Haven: Yale University Press, 1937.

Bartol, C. R. *Psychology and American Law*. Belmont, Ca.: Wadsworth, 1983.

Bermant, G.; McGuire, M.; McKinley, W.; and Salo, C. "The Logic of Simulation in Jury Research." *Criminal Justice and Behavior* 1 (1974): 224–33.

Bernstein, B. J. "Plessy v. Ferguson: Conservative Sociological Jurisprudence." *Journal of Negro History* 48 (1963): 196–210.

Beutel, F. K. "Some Implications of Experimental Jurisprudence." *Harvard Law Review* 48 (1931): 169–97.

———. *Some Potentialities of Experimental Jurisprudence as a New Branch of Social Science*. Lincoln: University of Nebraska Press, 1957.

Binet, A. "La Science du Témoignage." *L'Année Psychologique* 11 (1905): 128–37.

Black, C. L., Jr. "The Lawfulness of the Segregation Decisions." *Yale Law Journal* 64 (1960): 421–30.

Britt, S. H. "The Rules of Evidence—An Empirical Study in Psychology and Law." *Cornell Law Quarterly* 25 (1940a): 556–80.

———. "The Social Psychology of Law." *Illinois Law Review* 24 (1940b): 802–11.

Brown, M. *Legal Psychology*. Indianapolis: Bobbs-Merrill, 1926.

Brown v. Board of Education, 347 U.S. 483 (1954).

Burtt, H. *Legal Psychology*. Englewood Cliffs, N.J.: Prentice-Hall, 1931.

Cahn, E. "Jurisprudence." *New York University Law Review* 30 (1955): 150–69.

Cairns, H. *Law and the Social Sciences*. New York: Harcourt, Brace, 1935.

Cavers, D. F. "Science, Research and the Law: Beutel's 'Experimental Jurisprudence.'" *Journal of Legal Education* 10 (1957): 162–88.

Clark, K. B. "Desegregation: An Appraisal of the Evidence." *Journal of Social Issues* 9 (1953): 1–77.

Cohen, J.; Robson, R. A.; and Bates, A. P. *Parental Authority: The Community and the Law*. New Brunswick, N.J.: Rutgers University Press, 1958.

Cohen, M. R. "Justice Holmes and the Nature of Law." *Columbia Law Review* 31 (1931): 352–67.

Cohn, A., and Udolf, R. *The Criminal Justice System and Its Psychology*. New York: Van Nostrand Reinhold, 1979.

Comment. "Did Your Eyes Deceive You? Expert Psychological Testimony on the Unreliability of Eyewitness Identification." *Stanford Law Review* 29 (1977): 969–1030.

Comment. "Expert Testimony on Eyewitness Perceptions." *Dickinson Law Review* 82 (1978): 465–85.

Comment. "The Psychologist as Expert Witness: Science in the Courtroom?" *Maryland Law Review* 38 (1979): 539–621.

Cornish, W. R., and Sealy, A. P. "Juries and Rules of Evidence." *Criminal Law Review* 17 (1973): 208–30.

Damaška, M. "Presentation of Evidence and Factfinding Precision." *University of Pennsylvania Law Review* 123 (1975): 1083–1106.

Davis, K. C. *Administrative Law Treatise*. St. Paul, Minn.: West, 1958.

Davis, J. H.; Bray, R. M.; and Holt, R. W. "The Empirical Study of Decision Processes in Juries: A Critical Review." In *Law, Justice, and the Individual in Society: Psychological and Legal Issues*, edited by J. Tapp and F. Levine. New York: Holt, Rinehart & Winston, 1977.

Delli Paoli v. United States, 352 U.S. 232 (1957).

Doob, A. N., and Kirshenbaum, H. M. "Some Empirical Evidence on the Effect of S.12 of the Canada Evidence Act on the Accused." *Criminal Law Quarterly* 15 (1972): 88–96.

Dunlap, K. "The Theoretical Aspect of Psychology." In *Psychologies of 1925*, edited by C. Murchison. Worcester, Mass.: Clark University Press, 1925.

Durham v. United States, 214 F.2d 862 (D.C. Cir. 1954).

Ellison, K. W., and Buckhout, R. *Psychology and Criminal Justice*. New York: Harper & Row, 1981.

Estes v. Texas, 381 U.S. 532, 545 (1965).

Fahr, S. M. "Why Lawyers Are Dissatisfied with the Social Sciences." *Washburn Law Journal* 1 (1961): 161–75.

Fishman, J. A. "Some Current Research Needs in the Psychology of Testimony." *Journal of Social Issues* 13 (1957): 60–67.

Frank, J. *Law and the Modern Mind*. New York: Tudor, 1930.

Frankfurter, F. *Law and Politics*. New York: Harcourt, Brace, 1939.

Freund, P. *The Supreme Court of the United States:*

Its Business, Purposes, and Performance. Cleveland: World, 1963.

Friedman, L. M. "Presentation on 'the Future of Law and Social Sciences Research.'" *North Carolina Law Review* 52 (1974): 1068–73.

Fuller, L. "American Legal Realism." *University of Pennsylvania Law Review* 82 (1934): 429–62.

Galanter, M. [Conference presentation on] "The Future of Law and Social Sciences Research." *North Carolina Law Review* 52 (1974): 1060–67.

Gerbasi, K. C.; Zuckerman, M.; and Reis, H. T. "Justice Needs a New Blindfold: A Review of Mock Jury Research." *Psychology Bulletin* 84 (1977): 323–45.

Goodrich, H. F. "Institute Bards and Yale Reviewers." *University of Pennsylvania Law Review* 84 (1936): 449–66.

Greenberg, J. "Social Scientists Take the Stand: A Review and Appraisal of Their Testimony in Litigation." *Michigan Law Review* 54 (1956): 953–70.

Greenberg, M. S., and Ruback, R. B. *Social Psychology of the Criminal Justice System.* Monterey, Ca.: Brooks/Cole Publishing Co., 1982.

Greene, E. L. "Judges' Instruction on Eyewitness Testimony: Evaluation and Revision." Unpublished doctoral dissertation, University of Washington, 1983.

Grisso, T.; Sales, B.; and Bayless, S. "Law-Related Graduate Courses and Programs in Psychology Departments." Paper presented at the meeting of the American Psychology-Law Society, Baltimore, October 1979.

Haney, C. "Psychology and Legal Change: On the Limits of Factual Jurisprudence." *Law and Human Behavior* 4 (1980): 147–99.

Hans, V. P., and Doob, A. N. "Section 12 of the Canada Evidence Act and the Deliberations of Simulated Jurors." *Criminal Law Quarterly* 18 (1976): 235–53.

Hart, H. M., and McNaughton, J. T. "Evidence and Inference in Law." In *Evidence and Inference*, edited by D. Lerner. Glencoe, Ill.: Free Press, 1959.

Hidden v. Mutual Life Insurance Co., 217 F.2d 818 (4th Cir. 1954).

Holmes, O. W. *The Common Law.* Boston: Little, Brown, 1898.

Horowitz, I. A., and Willging, T. E. *The Psychology of Law: Integrations and Applications.* Boston: Little, Brown, 1984.

Hosch, H. M. "Commentary: A Comparison of Three Studies of the Influence of Expert Testimony on Jurors." *Law and Human Behavior* 4 (1980): 287–96.

Hull, C. L. "Moore and Callahan's 'Law and Learning Theory': A Psychologist's Impression." *Yale Law Journal* 53 (1944): 330–37.

Hutcheson, J. C., Jr. "The Judgment Intuitive: The Function of the 'Hunch' in Judicial Decision." *Cornell Law Quarterly* 14 (1929): 274–88.

Hutchins, R. M. "The Law and the Psychologists." *Yale Review* 16 (1927): 678–90.

———, and Slesinger, D. "Legal Psychology." *Psychology Review* 36 (1929): 13–26.

———. "Some Observations on the Law of Evidence—The Competency of Witnesses." *Yale Law Journal* 37 (1928a): 1017–28.

———; Adler, M.; and Michael, J. "Some Observations on the Law of Evidence—Spontaneous Exclamation." *Columbia Law Review* 28 (1928b): 432–40.

Irvin v. Dowd, 366 U.S. 717 (1961).

Kalven, H. "The Quest for the Middle Range: Empirical Inquiry and Legal Policy." In *Law in a Changing America*, edited by G. Hazard. Englewood Cliffs, N.J.: Prentice-Hall, 1968.

———, and Zeisel, H. *The American Jury.* Boston: Little, Brown, 1966.

Karst, K. "Legislative Facts in Constitutional Litigation." In *The Supreme Court Review*, edited by P. Kurland. Chicago: University of Chicago Press, 1960.

Katz, M. "The Unmasking of Dishonest Pretensions: Toward an Interpretation of the Role of Social Science in Constitutional Litigation." *American Sociologist* 6 (1971): 54–58.

———, and Burchard, J. D. "Psychology and the Legal Enterprise." *Kansas Law Review* 19 (1970): 197–210.

Kennedy, W. B. "Psychologism in the Law." *Georgetown Law Journal* 29 (1940): 139–64.

Kerr, N. L., and Bray, R. M. *The Psychology of the Courtroom.* New York: Academic Press, 1982.

Kluger, R. *Simple Justice.* New York: Alfred A. Knopf, 1977.

Ladinsky, J. "The Teaching of Law and Social Science Courses in the United States." Working paper no. 11. Center for Law and Behavioral Science, University of Wisconsin, 1975.

Levine, F. J., and Tapp, J. L. "The Psychology

of Criminal Identification: The Gap from Wade to Kirby." *University of Pennsylvania Law Review* 121 (1973): 1079–1131.

Llewellyn, K. N. "A Realistic Jurisprudence—The Next Step." *Columbia Law Review* 30 (1930): 431–65.

———. "On What Is Wrong with So-Called Legal Education." *Columbia Law Review* 35 (1935): 651–78.

———. "The Normative, the Legal, and the Law-Jobs: The Problem of Juristic Method." *Yale Law Journal* 49 (1940): 1355–1400.

Loftus, E. F. *Eyewitness Testimony.* Cambridge, Mass.: Harvard University Press, 1979.

———. "The Impact of Expert Psychological Testimony on the Unreliability of Eyewitness Identification." *Journal of Applied Psychology* 65 (1980): 9–15.

Loh, W. D. "Psychology and Law: A Coming of Age." *Contemporary Psychology* 24 (1979): 164–66.

Louisell, D. W. "The Psychologist in Today's Legal World: Part I." *Minnesota Law Review* 39 (1955): 235–72.

———. "The Psychologist in Today's Legal World: Part II." *Minnesota Law Review* 41 (1957): 731–50.

Macaulay, S. "Law and the Behavioral Sciences: Is There any There There?" Disputes Processing Research Program Working Paper 1983-16, University of Wisconsin Law School (1983).

Manson v. Brathwaite, 432 U.S. 98 (1977).

Marshall, J. *Law and Psychology in Conflict.* New York: Bobbs-Merrill, 1966.

Marston, W. M. "Studies in Testimony." *Journal of Criminal Law, Criminology, and Police Science* 15 (1924): 5–31.

McCarty, D. G. *Psychology for the Lawyer.* New York: Prentice-Hall, 1929; rev. ed. 1960.

McCary, J. L. "The Psychologist as an Expert Witness in Court." *American Psychologist* 11 (1956): 8–13.

———. "A Psychologist Testifies in Court." *American Psychologist* 15 (1960): 53–57.

Mechem, P. "The Jurisprudence of Despair." *Iowa Law Review* 21 (1936): 669–92.

Meehl, P. E. "Law and the Fireside Induction." *Journal of Social Issues* 27 (1971): 65–100.

Melton, G. "Training in Psychology and Law: A Directory." *Newsletter* [of the Division of Psychology and Law] 3 (1983): 1–5.

Monahan, J., and Loftus, E. R. "The Psychology of Law." *Annual Review of Psychology* 33 (1982): 441–75.

Moore, C. "Yellow Psychology." *Law Notes* 11 (1907): 125–27.

Moore, U. "An Institutional Approach to the Law of Commercial Banking." *Yale Law Journal* 38 (1929): 703–19.

———, and Callahan, C. C. "Law and Learning Theory: A Study of Legal Control." *Yale Law Journal* 53 (1943): 1–136.

Morse, J. "The Value of Psychology to the Lawyer." *Case and Comment* 19 (1913): 795–99.

Moskowitz, M. J. "Hugo Münsterberg: A Study in the History of Applied Psychology." *American Psychologist* 32 (1977): 824–42.

Münsterberg, H. *On the Witness Stand: Essays on Psychology and Crime.* New York: Clark Boardman, 1908.

Muir, W., Jr. *Prayer in the Public Schools: Law and Attitude Change.* Chicago: University of Chicago Press, 1967.

Note. "Other Crimes Evidence at Trial: Of Balancing and Other Matters." *Yale Law Journal* 70 (1961): 763–88.

Ohlin, L. "Partnership with the Social Sciences." *Journal of Legal Education* 23 (1970): 204–8.

Penrod, S. "A Study of Attorney and 'Scientific' Jury Selection Models." Unpublished doctoral dissertation, Harvard University, 1979.

People v. Hawthorne, 293 Michigan 15, 291 N.W. 205 (1940).

Pound, R. "The Call for a Realist Jurisprudence." *Harvard Law Review* 44 (1931): 697–711.

Powers, E. "Psychology and Law." *Journal of Abnormal Social Psychology* 32 (1937): 258–74.

Priest, G. L. "Social Science Theory and Legal Education: The Law School as University." *Journal of Legal Education* 33 (1983): 437–41.

Read, F. T. "Lawyers at Line-ups: Constitutional Necessity an Avoidable Extravagance?" *UCLA Law Review* 17 (1969): 337–407.

Redmount, R. S. "Psychology and Law." In *Legal and Criminal Psychology*, edited by H. Toch. New York: Holt, Rinehart & Winston, 1961.

Rein, M. *Social Science and Public Policy.* New York: Penguin Books, 1976.

Riesman, D. "Some Observations on Law and Psychology." *University of Chicago Law Review* 19 (1951): 30–44.

Robbins, I. P. "The Admissibility of Social Science Evidence in Person-Oriented Legal Adjudication." *Indiana Law Journal* 50 (1975): 493–516.

Robinson, E. *Law and the Lawyers*. New York: Macmillan, 1935.

Saks, M. J. "On Tapp (and Levine)." *Michigan Law Review* 77 (1979): 892–98.

———, and Hastie, R. *Social Psychology in Court*. New York: Van Nostrand Reinhold, 1978.

Schlegel, J. H. "American Legal Realism and Empirical Social Science: From the Yale Experience." *Buffalo Law Review* 28 (1979): 459–588.

Schmideberg, D. "Psychological Factors Underlying Criminal Behavior." *Journal of Criminal Law and Criminology* 32 (1947): 458–76.

Schofield, W. "Psychology, Law, and the Expert Witness." *American Psychologist* 11 (1956): 1–7.

Shaver, K. F.; Gilbert, M. A.; and Williams, M. C. "Social Psychology, Criminal Justice, and the Principle of Discretion: A Selective Review." *Personality and Social Psychology Bulletin* 1 (1975): 471–84.

Sheppard v. Maxwell, 384 U.S. 333 (1966).

Simon, R. *The Jury and the Defense of Insanity*. Boston: Little, Brown, 1967.

Skolnick, J. "The Sociology of Law in America." *Social Problems*. Special Summer Supplement, 1965.

Slesinger, D., and Pilpel, M. E. "Legal Psychology: A Bibliography and a Suggestion." *Psychology Bulletin* 26 (1929): 677–92.

Snee, T. J., and Lush, D. E. "Interaction of the Narrative and Interrogatory Methods of Obtaining Testimony." *Journal of Psychology* 11 (1941): 229–36.

Sporer, S. L. "A Brief History of the Psychology of Testimony." *Current Psychological Reviews* 2 (1982): 323–40.

Stern, W. *Beiträge zur psychologie der Aussage*. Leipzig: Verlag Barth, 1903.

———. "The Psychology of Testimony." *Journal of Abnormal and Social Psychology* 34 (1939): 3–20.

Stewart, I. D. "Perception, Memory, and Hearsay: A Criticism of Present Law and the Proposed Federal Rules of Evidence." *Utah Law Review* 1970 (1970): 1–39.

Strodtbeck, F. L.; James. R. M.; and Hawkins, C. "Social Status in Jury Deliberation." *American Sociological Review* 22 (1957): 713–19.

Sue, S.; Smith, R. E.; and Caldwell, C. "Effects of Inadmissable Evidence on the Deci-

sions of Simulated Jurors: A Moral Dilemma." *Journal of Applied Social Psychology* 3 (1973): 344–53.

Tapp, J. L. "Psychology and the Law: An Overture." *Annual Review of Psychology* 27 (1976): 359–404.

———. "Psychological and Policy Perspectives on the Law: Reflections on a Decade." *Journal of Social Issues* 36 (1980): 165–92.

Thayer, J. *A Preliminary Treatise on Evidence at the Common Law*. Boston: Little, Brown, 1898.

Thibaut, J., and Walker, L. *Procedural Justice: A Psychological Analysis*. Hillsdale, N.J.: Lawrence Erlbaum, 1975.

Titchener, E. "Psychology: Science or Technology." *Popular Science Monthly* 84 (1914): 39–44.

Toch, H., ed. *Legal and Criminal Psychology*. New York: Holt, Rinehart & Winston, 1961.

———. *Psychology of Crime and Criminal Justice*. New York: Holt, Rinehart & Winston, 1979.

United States v. Amaral, 488 F.2d 1148 (9th Cir. 1973).

United States v. Grunewald, 233 F.2d 556 (2d Cir. 1956).

United States v. Telfaire, 469 F.2d 552 (D.C. Cir. 1972).

United States v. Thevis, 665 F.2d 616 (5th Cir. 1982).

Walker, L.; Thibaut, J.; and Andreoli, V. "Order of Presentation at Trial." *Yale Law Journal* 82 (1972): 216–26.

Wall, P. *Eyewitness Identification of Criminal Cases*. Springfield, Ill.: Charles C. Thomas, 1965.

Weinstein, J. B., and Berger, M. A. *Weinstein's Evidence*. New York: Matthew Bender, 1976.

Weld, H. P., and Danzig, E. R. "A Study of the Way in Which a Verdict Is Reached by a Jury." *American Journal of Psychology* 53 (1940): 518–36.

Wells, G. L. "Applied Eyewitness-Testimony Research: System Variables and Estimator Variables." *Journal of Personality Social Psychology* 12 (1978): 1546–57.

Whipple, G. M. "The Observer as Reporter: A Survey of the 'Psychology of Testimony.'" *Psychology Bulletin* 6 (1909): 153–70.

———. "Recent Literature on the Psychology of Testimony." *Psychology Bulletin* 7 (1910): 365–68.

———. "Psychology of Testimony." *Psychology Bulletin* 8 (1911): 307–9.

———. "Psychology of Testimony and Report." *Psychology Bulletin* 9 (1912): 264–69.

———. "Psychology of Testimony and Report." *Psychology Bulletin* 10 (1913): 264–68.

———. "Psychology of Testimony and Report." *Psychology Bulletin* 11 (1914): 245–50.

———. "Psychology of Testimony." *Psychology Bulletin* 12 (1915): 221–24.

———. "Psychology of Testimony." *Psychology Bulletin* 14 (1917): 234–36.

Wigmore, J. "Professor Münsterberg and the Psychology of Testimony: Being a Report of the Case of Cokestone v. Münsterberg." *Illinois Law Review* 3 (1909): 399–445.

———. *The Science of Judicial Proof*, 3rd ed. Boston: Little, Brown, 1937.

Wolf, S., and Montgomery, D. A. "Effects of Inadmissable Evidence and Level of Judicial Admonishment to Disregard on the Judgments of Mock Jurors." *Journal of Applied Social Psychology* 7 (1977): 205–19.

Woodward, J. "A Scientific Attempt to Provide Evidence for a Decision on Change of Venue." *American Sociological Review* 17 (1952): 447–52.

Yarmey, A. D. *The Psychology of Eyewitness Testimony*. New York: Free Press, 1979.

Yntema, H. E. "The Hornbook Method and the Conflict of Law." *Yale Law Journal* 37 (1928): 468–83.

Yudof, M. G. "School Desegregation: Legal Realism, Reasoned Elaboration, and Social Science Research in the Supreme Court." *Law and Contemporary Problems* 42 (1978): 57–110.

Zeisel, H. "The Uniqueness of Survey Evidence." *Cornell Law Quarterly* 45 (1960): 322–46.

———. "Presentation on 'the Selection of Topics and Methods for Law and Social Sciences Research.'" *University of North Carolina Law Review* 52 (1974): 974–81.

———, and Diamond, S. "'Convincing Empirical Evidence' on the Six-Member Jury." *University of Chicago Law Review* 41 (1974): 281–95.

CHAPTER 12

Jurisprudential Perspectives
on the Judicial Process

12.1. INTRODUCTION

The concept of law is obviously too sweeping and complex a topic to be quickly canvassed. As one legal philosopher put it, "[W]hat is law? This is a question upon which whole libraries have been written and written, as their very existence shows, without definite results being attained" (Kantorowicz 1958, p. 1). Social-legal researchers have also noted that "reviews of the literature . . . indicate that there are almost as many definitions of law as there are theorists" (Vago 1981, p. 7). Nonetheless, for our purposes, boundaries have to be drawn and a working concept of law presented in order to focus our inquiry. In Chapter 2 we described law as a system of authoritative and prescriptive rules of conduct and as a process of dispute resolution via the application of these rules in adjudication. In the ensuing chapters, we sought to illustrate the workings of the law in its substantive and procedural components by means of judicial opinions and empirical studies on issues of social policy. Our expectation is that a student, after working through Parts II and III, will begin to acquire a "feel" for the intellectual culture of the law—that is, an informed sense of how lawyers define and analyze policy issues, how judges reason in adjudicating these issues, and how empirical research findings can be used in the process of legal ratiocination.

It is now time to try to articulate what this "feel" for the law is. Lawyers are not necessarily handicapped in their practice for want of a formal conception of law. By immersion in their daily professional activities, they acquire an understanding of law even when they might be hard-pressed to define it. For social scientists approaching the law from the outside, however, without the socialization experiences provided by law school and law practice, some articulated conception of law is useful to provide a point of reference for study. This is because under different legal rules and methods of judicial decision-making lies a substratum of legal philosophy or jurisprudence. Jurisprudence is the body of systematic, speculative thought about basic issues of law, including the nature of rules, principles, rights and duties, the sources of legitimacy or validity of law, the relation of law to morality and social values, the bases of legal compliance, the dynamics of legal renewal, and the role of human judgment in the workings of law. A particular theory or conception of law gives direction, contour, and scope to the legal enterprise. It also illuminates the role of social research in law. "Theory," Justice Holmes (1897) wrote, "is the most important part of the dogma of the law, as the architect is the most important man who takes part in the building of a house. . . . It is not to be feared as impractical, for . . . it simply means going to the bottom of the subject" (p. 477).

In this chapter we shall expand on the jurisprudential ideas that were briefly introduced in the beginning of the book. Three interrelated themes that have implications for social-legal inquiry will be explored. First, we shall briefly dwell upon three classical philosophical traditions in law: natural law, positivism, and historical/ sociological jurisprudence. Each offers a different view on the nature of law and on how fidelity to law is achieved. If law is essentially "the enterprise of subjecting human conduct to the governance of rules" (Fuller 1964, p. 106), then these schools of thought must account for the origin of legal rules and the sources of public compliance. Second, we shall devote most of our attention to one aspect of the jurisprudential literature: the nature of judicial decision-making. We shall focus on three models or styles of adjudication, applicable to common law and constitutional cases, whereby judges apply, create, interpret, or modify legal rules for the governance of human conduct. They are formalism, realism, and purposivism, and each is rooted in one or more of the foregoing philosophical traditions. And third, we shall examine in this chapter and again in Chapter 13 the role of social science in the formulation and justification of judicial decisions. The various theories of law and styles of judicial reasoning bear different implications for this role.

Classical Theories of Law

The multitude of definitions of law can be categorized into three major theories, which have vied for primacy at different periods in the history of Western jurisprudence. There is, inevitably, some overlap in this broad classification because no theory is exclusively interested in one line of inquiry alone. But it is a useful way of structuring the diverse conceptions of law since they all stress one or another aspect of these theories.

NATURAL LAW

Natural law theory finds the origin and ultimate sanction of law in right reason. In this approach, law is inextricably tied to morals, ethics, and justice. Its central premise is that law, in order to be recognized as such, must be morally justified, although different theorists have disagreed on particular, substantive moral positions. In the Middle Ages, canonical lawyers viewed human law as derived from a higher law called natural law which, in turn, was thought to reflect divine law. St. Thomas Aquinas in the *Summa Theologica* proposed that law is but the application of right reason for the common good of the community. The premise is that humans are moral and rational creatures made in the image of their Creator. Therefore, human rules derive their ultimate sanction from higher principles via the exercise of reason and the articulation of moral justice.

In the eighteenth century, English common law was thoroughly colored by natural law thinking. Sir William Blackstone (1723–1780) in his *Commentaries* declared that all human laws derive their force from the laws of God, and that any laws that contradict the Divine original are invalid (in Hart 1958, p. 596). In the United States, the overarching principles of rightness said to lie behind or above the given or positive law were also expressed in terms of secular morality and basic human freedoms, in addition to or in lieu of providential morality. Thus, the American Republic was founded on Lockian ideas of universal natural rights. The language of the Declaration of Independence—"We hold these truths to be self-evident; that all men are created equal; that they are endowed by their Creator with certain inalienable rights; . . . that to secure these rights, governments are instituted among men"—expresses a secular version of the divine law origins of Thomistic natural law.

The reason that this theory insists that legal norms pass moral muster is to preserve a sense of unqualified fidelity to law and to maintain the primacy of moral reasons for conduct. A practical consequence for adjudication of the conflation of law and morals is that when the rules to be applied in deciding a case are indeterminate or in conflict, there is always existing (natural) law somewhere that judges can and should rely upon.

LEGAL POSITIVISM

A second major theory is legal positivism. The term, however, is beset by ambiguity because it is used to designate several different contentions (Summers 1966, p. 889; Hart 1961, pp. 253–54).

One meaning of positivism associates the term with the command or imperative theory of law. Law is the command of political (including judicial) authorities backed by coercive sanctions. The source of law and the basis of fidelity to law lie in the will of state officials. This view, which emerged with the rise of secular nation states in the sixteenth century, stresses the political authoritativeness of established rules. Thomas Hobbes (1588–1679) wrote in the *Leviathan* that "law is the word of him that by right hath command over others" (1935, p. 109). In the nineteenth century, John Austin (1885) in England expanded on the notion of law as the "command of the sovereign," and in this country Justice Holmes (1897), in a like vein, conceived of law as the application of public force brought to bear through the instrumentality of the courts. Modern positivists in England (for example, Hart 1961) and the Continent (for example, Kelsen 1945) have oppugned the command element (in every society, people can enter into legal relations without the threat of sanctions) and proposed the idea of authoritative norms or rules as the essence of law.

A second contention of positivism is that the methodology of jurisprudence should be analytical—hence, this approach is also known as analytical jurisprudence or analytical positivism. By analytical is meant the conceptual exegesis of the meaning of basic legal concepts such as right, duty, and sovereignty (the focus of classical analysts such as Austin), and discretion, justice, rules, and responsibility (the focus of modern analysts such as Hart). It is to be distinguished from historical, sociological, and evaluational methods for studying law. Defining, classifying, interpreting, and chartering the implications of these terms is more than high-grade lexicography. Sharpened awareness of their meanings can lead to a better understanding of the reality behind the concepts: "[H]e who knows names knows also the things that are expressed by them" (Plato 1937, p. 224).

A third—and the principal—dimension of positivism is its insistence on what natural law theorists deny: the absence of any connection between law and the morals. This separation is the common denominator of analytical theorists, though they may differ on the reasons for distinguishing the law-as-is and the law-as-ought-to-be. English utilitarian thinkers in the nineteenth century such as John Austin (1790–1859), Jeremy Bentham (1748–1839), and John Stuart Mill (1806–1873) argued that law need not be morally justified in order to be recognized as valid law. They acknowledged that moral opinion influences legal standards but emphasized that law is morally neutral. If a legal rule violates the sense of right, it is still authoritative law; conversely, if a rule is just, that in itself does not qualify it as valid law.

The separation thesis—called the "Cape Horn of jurisprudence" because many a jurisprudential navigator has met shipwreck there (Summers 1982, p. 176)—is not dry, analytical fiddling. Practical concerns of the age have shaped the debate. The legal positivism of Jeremy Bentham was in part a reaction to the American and French revolutions. In his view, natural law theory, exemplified by Locke's and Rousseau's ideas of natural rights, provided an intellectual rationale for political upheaval. His recipe for political life was "to obey punctually, to censure freely" (in Hart 1958, p. 597). The confounding of law and morals justifies a revolutionary's civil disobedience because unjust law is not law. It also justifies a reactionary's blind compliance merely because it is the law. By distinguishing the factual and the normative, he sought to facilitate moral criticism of established law. The legal positivism of John Austin (and Bentham, too) was to some extent a reaction against the conservative view that the common law was the self-validated law of nature. They advocated liberal reforms in law and government (abolition of slavery, freedom of speech and press, and so forth) and argued that their positivist approach enabled individuals to see the issues posed by morally bad laws. Their utilitarian calculus (the greatest good for the greatest number at the lowest cost) fostered an instrumentalist view of law, and invited empirical inquiry into social needs and the consequences of law designed to meet those needs. The separation thesis makes possible the scientific study of law. Contemporary analytical positivists have thus described their writings as "descriptive sociology" (Hart 1961, p. vii).

HISTORICAL AND SOCIOLOGICAL JURISPRUDENCE

The third main theory of law emphasizes its social and historical origins. Law is found in the historical development of a community, in the traditions, customs, and national character of a people. The German legal philosopher Savigny (1831) proposed that law "is developed first by custom and popular faith, next by jurisprudence—everywhere, therefore, by internal silently-operating powers, not by the arbitrary will of the law-giver" (p. 30). Law arises out of and reflects societal values; it expresses the consciousness of the public at a given time and place. This approach emphasizes popular consent and compliance as the basis of fidelity to law. The English legal anthropologist Henry Maine (1906) then suggested that the evolution of law in all societies follows certain regular stages and patterns.

The historical tradition, by broadening the conception of law to encompass elements of the social order, laid the groundwork for the sociological theories of law formulated at the turn of this century (for example, Pound 1911; Ehrlich 1936). Sociological jurisprudence is not a comprehensive theory of law. Instead, it attends principally to the functions of judicial adjudication. It draws from the utilitarian heritage of positivism and conceives of legal rules as the product of a balancing of competing social interests. Decisions are thus viewed as the result of weighing the social utility of alternatives.

Styles of Judicial Reasoning

Associated with the foregoing conceptions of law are different styles of judicial reasoning—that is, different approaches to the process by which a decision-maker infers from authoritative sources (precedents, statutes, constitution, and so forth) the standards applicable to deciding a particular dispute. In adjudicating a case, a judge's substantive preoccupations will be merged with his implicit theory of law and his reasoning style, so that both will impose patterns on his perception and resolution of the problem. A judge's idea of what law is and how decisions should be reached is bound to have an impact on the substantive outcome, as well as on his receptivity to the introduction of research data as an aid in reaching or justifying the outcome.

Almost since the dawn of law in civilization, there has been a continuing debate over the proper approach to dispute resolution. Should the arbiter follow strictly pre-existing, well-defined rules in order to ensure consistency and predictability in decision-making? Or should the arbiter possess the freedom to tailor a result to the particular circumstances of each situation in order to ensure individualized justice? This is the dilemma of law versus equity or legal adjudication versus discretionary adjudication.

In ancient China, the legalist tradition emphasized *fa* or positive law, and the Confucian tradition emphasized justice according to *li*, a flexible set of moral principles and social customs. The Confucian ideal prevailed and, since then, informal mediational justice has predominated in Chinese culture over formalized adjudication (Needham 1956, pp. 202–5). In the West, however, the reverse has occurred. Aristotle (1900) declared the rule of law preferable to the reign of discretion, although the introduction of equity was allowed on special occasions when an injustice might otherwise result. In the eighteenth and nineteenth centuries, British and continental legal philosophers rejected equitable dispensation from law. Blackstone (1821) in his *Commentaries* cautioned that "the liberty of considering all cases in an equitable light must not be indulged too far, lest we destroy all law" (p. 62). He preferred law without equity to equity without law. Montesquieu (1878) in *The Spirit of Laws* proposed that the national judges are no more than the mouthpiece of the law. The distrust of equity was founded in part on the fear that personalized justice could lead to arbitrariness and abuse of power. Leading thinkers of the age believed that impersonal application of the laws would be a better safeguard of equal treatment and individual liberties. Consequently, they conceived of a law as a closed, autonomous system, divorced from social, political, and economic forces, and they viewed adjudication as the application of pre-existing norms to the given facts of a case.

In the United States, jurisprudential thought on how adjudication is and should be conducted has oscillated between the two extremes, with various intermediate stops. There are three principal models of judicial reasoning styles: formalism, dominant in the late nineteenth century and known also as conceptualism or mechanical jurisprudence; legal realism, which achieved primacy in the 1930s as a reaction against formalism; and purposive analysis, also denominated policy analysis, reasoned elaboration, or normative argumentation, which combined elements of formalism and realism to become, since the 1950s, the principal emerging methodology of contemporary jurisprudence. All three styles have had a profound impact on American law, and their influence on current legal thinking is still very much in evidence.

Formalism viewed law as an abstract system of rules, neatly and logically dovetailed. The task of judges was to apply the correct rule to the particular facts of the case at issue in order to reach a logically correct decision. As Chief Justice Marshall put it, "Courts are the mere instruments of the law, and can will nothing." The role of judges is only to "[give] effect to the will of the legislature; or, in other words, the will of the law" (*Osborne* v. *United States Bank,* 1824, p. 868). The conceptual fit of the decision with the existing system of rules was of greater importance in formalist thinking than the social consequences of the decision or the utility of that decision in advancing social and economic ends.

A new way of viewing the decisional process was called legal realism by its proponents because, like the realist movement in art and literature, they sought to lay bare the ostensibly "real" or "true" nature of law and legal reasoning. They considered any given rule or judicial decision not as a product of "logical parthenogenesis born of pre-existing legal principles," but as a social event "with social causes and consequences," born of human judgment (Cohen 1935, p. 847). Formalism provided a static "snapshot" of law as a fixed body of rules; realism offered a "movie camera" view of law as a dynamic process of rule creation and change. Realists described judicial decisions as ad hoc, discretionary responses to the unique facts and equities of specific instances. Legal rules are used as after-the-fact justifications or rationalizations that mask the real bases of decisions.

We have overstated somewhat these two styles in order to make clear the point that they represent polar models of judicial decision-making. Formalism tends to be more closely associated with natural law theory. Results should be and are foreordained by deductive syllogism, but when precedents are unavailable or indeterminate, a judge cannot push aside the law books and exercise the "sovereign prerogative of choice" (Holmes 1920, p. 239). Instead, he must derive the result from "higher law" rooted in American experience: the broad legal principles, moral standards, and societal values that provide the context of adjudication. American formalism invoked not universal natural law or divinely inspired rights as did European natural law theory, but relied on the political values and ends pursued by the American legal system. Realism, on the other hand, is associated with positivist jurisprudence. In its extreme form, adjudication is uncontrolled lawmaking. Courts act like a third legislative chamber and judicial decisions have an imperative and predictive character.

Whereas formalism conceives of adjudication as if it were primarily logical deduction and realism sees it as if it were mainly discretionary judgment, purposive or policy-oriented methodology considers the judicial function as essentially a self-conscious weighing of competing value alternatives and a principled articulation of the grounds for that normative choice. Like realism, it acknowledges the active role of a judge in choosing and making (rather than merely applying) legal rules. Like formalism, it recognizes the obligation of providing a logically consistent and rigorously reasoned (rather than merely ad hoc) justification for the decision. This teleological style of decision-making is rooted in natural law, in that cases are adjudged in ways that further the attainment of certain social ideals and values. It partakes, too, of the sociological and historical approaches to law, in that it also entails a consideration of the societal impact or consequences of the value choices.

In this chapter, we shall devote more attention to these models of decision-making than to other jurisprudential problems. Indeed, American jurisprudence as a whole "is marked by a concentration, almost to the point of obsession, on the judicial process, that is, with what courts do and should do, how judges reason and should reason, in deciding particular cases" (Hart 1977, p. 969). This preoccupation with the nature and function of the courts arises in part because of the distinctive American institution of judicial supremacy in the interpretation of the Constitution. Early on, Alexis de Tocqueville (1969) observed that "scarcely any political question arises in the United States that is not resolved, sooner or later, into a judicial question" (p. 280). American courts have the power and duty to invalidate federal and state legislation that violates constitutional rights, and they also play a dominant role in the development of common law. This function of judicial legislation, which is so unconventional in other countries (including England), accounts for our "obsession" with judicial decision-making.

The Place of Jurisprudence in Social-Legal Inquiry

The materials of this chapter pull together and bring out the different perspectives on law and the judicial process that were implicit in the court opinions and research studies of Parts II and III. For the social science student, this is useful for several reasons.

First, acquaintance with theories of law aids the understanding of judicial methods of analysis which, in turn, is necessary in considering the role and impact of social research in adjudication. Justice Frankfurter noted that "every decision is a function of some juristic philosophy" (in Berman and Greiner 1980, p. 37). If, according to formalist jurisprudence, law is conceived of as a system of logically ordered rules, then the appropriate method is deductive reasoning. So long as law is viewed as an autonomous logical enterprise, there is little room for the use of the insights and tools of the social sciences. If, however, according to purposive and legal realist jurisprudence, law is thought of as a social process for governing human conduct and legal rules are seen as a means of achieving desired ends, then policy analysis is a more appropriate method of decision-making than solely logical deduction. This utilitarian conception also opens law to inquiry by social scientists. Every use or nonuse of empirical research in judicial decisions is likewise a function of some juristic philosophy.

Second, if the law-related research of social scientists is to deal with issues that are of central importance to law, the research needs to be marshaled and organized around problems which confront lawyers. We have seen instances in this book of studies—for example, in areas of the jury and evidence rules—that address matters of virtually no policy significance to lawyers and, indeed, are sometimes premised on incorrect assumptions of law. To develop a sense of the kind of research that is policy relevant and could be applied in adjudication presupposes some notion of law as it is understood by lawyers. As Bartol (1983) cautions, "Without some guiding idea for determining what is relevant and what is not, the advancement of our knowledge [in social-legal research] will be severely restricted" (p. 323). Jurisprudential ideas of law and judicial decision-making offer the needed guidance.

Third, in addition to the foregoing conceptual reasons for turning to legal philosophy, there is a substantive consideration as well: It is a fertile source of material for the fashioning of research hypothesis (for example, Thibaut et al. 1974). Long before the social sciences came into existence, legal philosophers were wrestling with the kinds of issues that are only now being addressed by empirical inquiry. As Jones (1965) suggests:

> The literature of jurisprudence is a largely unworked mine of questions that have to be asked about the functioning of any legal order. Consider, as examples, a few of the recurring themes in the legal philosophy of the West. To what extent is law observance maintained in a society by the threat of coercive sanctions, and to what extent by widely dispersed feelings of moral obligation to abide by prescribed legal norms? . . . Should law enforce only minimum standards of social morality, or is law's educative force great enough to justify the deliberate use of law as an instrument for raising the community moral standards?
>
> Questions like those just given are, of course, far too sweeping for application as ready-made postulates for social science inquiry, but they are top priority material for [formulating hypotheses]. . . . There may be more for social science in the literature of jurisprudence than most social scientists have yet dreamed of. [pp. 41–42]

OVERVIEW

We begin in section 12.2 with an allegorical case, in which the opinions of the justices clearly illustrate and contrast the competing viewpoints on the nature and methods of the judicial process. After studying this case, you may want to reread some of the actual opinions presented in the preceding two parts of the book and subject them to jurisprudential analysis: What theory of law underlies a particular opinion and how does it manifest itself in that judge's reasoning process?

Following this overview, two classic essays in jurisprudence are presented in sections 12.3 and 12.4. They place in juxtaposition the formalist and realist styles and explicate them by argument and counterargument. Then follows a third, more recent essay in section 12.5 that describes the tenets of "reasoned elaboration," a normative style of adjudication that attempts to integrate elements of formalism and realism. The editorial comments that accompany these readings describe the social, economic, and historical context of these three methods and raise questions about their implications for applying social science in law. Finally, section 12.6 draws parallels between the jurisprudential theories and psychological theories.

12.2. SOURCES OF LAW

THE CASE OF THE SPELUNCEAN EXPLORERS
Lon L. Fuller

IN THE SUPREME COURT OF
NEWGARTH, 4300

The defendants, having been indicted for the crime of murder, were convicted and sentenced to be hanged by the Court of General Instances of the County of Stowfield. They bring a petition of error before this Court. The facts sufficiently appear in the opinion of the Chief Justice.

Truepenny, C. J. [Five speluncean explorers—the four defendants and Roger Whetmore—were trapped in a remote cave by a landslide. On the twenty-third day of their imprisonent, when they were near death by starvation, Whetmore proposed that they might survive a few days longer while awaiting rescue if they consumed the flesh of one of their number. After much discussion, the group reluctantly ageed on Whetmore's plan and proceeded to cast a pair of dice to determine the sacrificial member. The throw went against Whetmore and he was put to death and eaten by his companions. A few days later, the defendants were rescued and indicted for the murder of Whetmore. In the rescue itself, ten workers were killed by fresh landslides. At trial, the jury found the foregoing facts as stated and pronounced the defendants guilty. The trial judge sentenced them to be hanged. Jury and judge then joined in a petition to the Chief Executive asking that the sentence be commuted to an imprisonment of six months. The Chief Executive has taken no action while awaiting the decision of the Supreme Court. Ed.'s note.]

. . .

It seems to me that in dealing with this extraordinary case the jury and the trial judge followed a course that was not only fair and wise, but the only course that was open to them under the law. The language of our statute is well known: "Whoever shall willfully take the life of another shall be punished by death." N. C. S. A. (N. S.) §12-A. This statute permits of no exception applicable to this case, however our sympathies may incline us to make allowance for the tragic situation in which these men found themselves.

In a case like this the principle of executive clemency seems admirably suited to mitigate the rigors of the law, and I propose to my colleagues that we follow the example of the jury and the trial judge by joining in the communications they have addressed to the Chief Executive. . . .

Foster, J. I am shocked that the Chief Justice, in an effort to escape the embarrassments of this tragic case, should have adopted, and should have proposed to his colleagues, an expedient at once so sordid and so obvious. I believe something more is on trial in this case than the fate of these unfortunate explorers; that is the law of our Commonwealth. . . .

For myself, I do not believe that our law compels the monstrous conclusion that these men are murderers. I believe, on the contrary, that it declares them to be innocent of any crime. I rest this conclusion on two independent grounds, either of which is of itself sufficient to justify the acquittal of these defendants.

The first of these grounds rests on a premise that may arouse opposition until it has been examined candidly. I take the view that the enacted or positive law of this Commonwealth, including all of its statutes and precedents, is inapplicable to this case, and that the case is governed instead by what ancient writers in Europe and America called "the law of nature."

This conclusion rests on the proposition that our positive law is predicated on the possibility of men's coexistence in society. When a situation arises in which the coexistence of men becomes impossible, then a condition that underlies all of our precedents and statutes has ceased to exist. When that condition disappears, then it is my opinion that the force of our positive law disappears with it. . . .

The proposition that all positive law is based on the possibility of men's coexistence . . . is a truth so obvious and pervasive that we seldom have occasion to give words to it. . . .

I conclude, therefore, that at the time Roger Whetmore's life was ended by these defendants, they were, to use the quaint language of nineteenth-century writers, not in a "state of civil society" but in a "state of nature." This has the consequence that the law applicable to them is not the enacted and established law of this Commonwealth, but the law derived from those principles that were appropriate to their condition. I have no hesitancy in saying that under those principles they were guiltless of any crime.

What these men did was done in pursuance of an agreement accepted by all of them and first proposed by Whetmore himself. Since it was apparent that their extraordinary predicament made inapplicable the usual principles that regulate men's relations with one another, it was necessary for them to draw, as it were, a new charter of government appropriate to the situation in which they found themselves.

It has from antiquity been recognized that the most basic principle of law or government is to be found in the notion of contract or agreement. Ancient thinkers, especially during the period from 1600 to 1900, used to base government itself on a supposed original social compact. . . . The powers of government can only be justified morally on the ground that these are powers that reasonable men would agree upon and accept if they were faced with the necessity of constructing anew some order to make their life in common possible. . . .

This concludes the exposition of the first ground of my decision. My second ground proceeds by rejecting hypothetically all the premises on which I have so far proceeded. I concede for purposes of argument that I am wrong in saying that the situation of these men removed them of the effect of our positive law, and I assume that the Consolidated Statutes have the power to penetrate five hundred feet of rock and to impose themselves upon these starving men huddled in their underground prison.

Now it is, of course, prefectly clear that these men did an act that violates the literal wording of the statute which declares that he who "shall willfully take the life of another" is a murderer. But one of the most ancient bits of legal wisdom is the saying that a man may break the letter of the law without breaking the law itself. Every proposition of positive law, whether contained in a statute or a judicial precedent, is to be interpreted reasonably, in the light of its evident purpose. . . .

The statute before us for interpretation has never been applied literally. Centuries ago it was established that a killing in self-defense is excused. There is nothing in the wording of the statute that suggests this exception. Various attempts have been made to reconcile the legal treatment of self-defense with the words of the statute, but in my opinion these are all merely ingenious sophistries. The truth is that the exception in favor of self-defense cannot be reconciled with the *words* of the statute, but only with its *purpose*.

The true reconciliation of the excuse of self-defense with the statute making it a crime to kill another is to be found in the following line of reasoning. One of the principal objects underlying any criminal legislation is that of deterring men from crime. Now it is apparent that if it were declared to be the law that a killing in self-defense is murder such a rule could not operate in a deterrent manner. A man whose life is threatened will repel his aggressor, whatever the law may say. Looking therefore to the broad purposes of criminal legislation, we may safely declare that this statute was not intended to apply to cases of self-defense.

When the rationale of the excuse of self-defense is thus explained, it becomes apparent that precisely the same reasoning is applicable to the case at bar. If in the future any group of men ever find themselves in the tragic predicament of these defendants, we may be sure that their decision whether to live or die will not be controlled by the contents of our criminal code. Accordingly, if we read this statute intelligently it is apparent that it does not apply to this case. The withdrawal of this situation from the effect of the statute is justified by precisely the same considerations that were applied to our predecessors in office centuries ago to the case of self-defense.

There are those who raise the cry of judicial usurpation whenever a court, after analyzing the purpose of a statute, gives to its words a meaning that is not at once apparent to the casual reader who has not studied the statute closely or examined the objectives it seeks to attain. Let me say emphatically that I accept without reservation the proposition that this Court is bound by the statutes of our Commonwealth and that it exercises its powers in subservience to the duly expressed will of the Chamber of Representatives. The line of reasoning I have applied above raises no question of fidelity to enacted law, though it may possibly raise a question of the distinction between intelligent and unintelligent fidelity.

No superior wants a servant who lacks the capacity to read between the lines. . . .

I therefore conclude that on any aspect under which this case may be viewed these defendants are innocent of the crime of murdering Roger Whetmore, and that the conviction should be set aside.

Tatting, J. . . . As I analyze the opinion just rendered by my brother Foster, I find that it is shot through with contradictions and fallacies. Let us begin with his first proposition: these men were not subject to our law because they were not in a "state of civil society" but in a "state of nature." I am not clear why this is so, whether it is because of the thickness of the rock that imprisoned them, or because they were hungry, or because they had set up a "new charter of government" by which the usual rules of law were to be supplanted by a throw of the dice. Other difficulties intrude themselves. If these men passed from the jurisdiction of our law to that of "the law of nature," at what moment did this occur? . . .

I can neither accept his notion that these men were under a code of nature which this Court was bound to apply to them, nor can I accept the odious and perverted rules that he would read into that code. I come now to the second part of my brother's opinion, in which he seeks to show that the defendants did not violate the provisions of N. C. S. A. (N. S.) §12-A. . . .

It is true that a statute should be applied in the light of its purpose, and that *one* of the purposes of criminal legislation is recognized to be deterrence. The difficulty is that other purposes are also ascribed to the law of crimes. It has been said that one of its objects is to provide an orderly outlet for the instinctive human demand for retribution. *Commonwealth v. Scape.* It has also been said that its object is the rehabilitation of the wrongdoer. *Commonwealth v. Makeover.* Other theories have been propounded. Assuming that we must interpret a statute in the light of its purpose, what are we to do when it has many purposes or when its purposes are disputed?

A similar difficulty is presented by the fact that although there is authority for my brother's interpretation of the excuse of self-defense, there is other authority which assigned to that excuse a different rationale. . . . The taught doctrine of our law schools, memorized by generations of law students, runs in the following terms: The statute concerning murder requires a "willful" act. The man who acts to repel an aggressive threat to his own life does not act "willfully," but in response to an impulse deeply ingrained in human nature. I suspect that there is hardly a lawyer in this Commonwealth who is not familiar with this line of reasoning, especially since the point is a great favorite of the bar examiners.

Now the familiar explanation for the excuse of self-defense just expounded obviously cannot be applied by analogy to the facts of this case. These men acted not only "willfully" but with great deliberation and after hours of discussing what they should do. Again we encounter a forked path, with one line of reasoning leading us in one direction and another in a direction that is exactly the opposite. . . .

Since I have been wholly unable to resolve the doubts that beset me about the law of this case, I am with regret announcing a step that is, I believe, unprecedented in the history of this tribunal. I declare my withdrawl from the decision of this case.

Keen, J. . . . [The question] that I wish to put to one side is that of deciding whether what these men did was "right" or "wrong," "wicked" or "good." [That is] a question that is irrelevant to the discharge of my office as a judge sworn to apply, not my conceptions of morality, but the law of the land. . . .

The sole question before us for decision is whether these defendants did, within the meaning of N. C. S. A. (N. S.)

§ 12-A, willfully take the life of Roger Whetmore. . . .

Whence arise all the difficulties of the case, then, and the necessity for so many pages of discussion about what ought to be so obvious? The difficulties, in whatever tortured form they may present themselves, all trace back to a single source, and that is a failure to distinguish the legal from the moral aspects of this case. To put it bluntly, my brothers do not like the fact that the written law requires the conviction of these defendants. Neither do I, but unlike my brothers I respect the obligations of an office that requires me to put my personal predilections out of my mind when I come to interpret and apply the law of this Commonwealth. . . .

There was a time in this Commonwealth when judges did in fact legislate very freely, and all of us know that during that period some of our statutes were rather thoroughly made over by the judiciary. . . . It is enough to observe that those days are behind us, and that in place of the uncertainty that then reigned we now have a clear-cut principle, which is the supremacy of the legislative branch of our government. From that principle flows the obligation of the judiciary to enforce faithfully the written law, and to interpret that law in accordance with its plain meaning without reference to our personal desires or our individual conceptions of justice. . . .

Yet though the principle of the supremacy of the legislature has been accepted in theory for centuries, such is the tenacity of professional tradition and the force of fixed habits of thought that many of the judiciary have still not accommodated themselves to the restricted role which the new order imposes on them. My brother Foster is one of that group. . . .

The process of judicial reform requires three steps. The first of these is to divine some single "purpose" which the statute serves. This is done although not one statute in a hundred has any such single purpose, and although the objectives of nearly every statute are differently interpreted by the different classes of its sponsors. The second step is to discover that a mythical being called "the legislator," in the pursuit of this imagined "purpose," overlooked something or left some gap or imperfection in his work. Then comes the final and most refreshing part of the task, which is, of course, to fill in the blank thus created. . . .

[I]t remains abundantly clear that neither I nor my brother Foster knows what the "purpose" of §12-A is. . . .

You simply cannot apply a statute as it is written and remake it to meet your own wishes at the same time. . . .

A hard decision is never a popular decision. . . . But I believe that judicial dispensation does more harm in the long run than hard decisions. Hard cases may even have a certain moral value by bringing home to the people their own responsibilities toward the law that is ultimately their creation, and by reminding them that there is no principle of personal grace that can relieve the mistakes of their representatives. . . .

I conclude that the conviction should be affirmed.

Handy, J. I have listened with amazement to the tortured ratiocinations to which this simple case has given rise. I never cease to wonder at my colleagues' ability to throw an obscuring curtain of legalisms about every issue presented to them for decision. We have heard this afternoon learned disquisitions on the distinction between positive law and the law of nature, the language of the statute and the purpose of the statute, judicial functions and executive functions, judicial legislation and legislative legislation. . . .

What have all these things to do with the case? The problem before us is what we, as officers of the government, ought to do with these defendants. That is a question of practical wisdom, to be exercised in a context, not of abstract theory, but of human realities. When the case is approached in this light, it becomes, I think, one of the easiest to decide that has ever been argued before this Court.

Before stating my own conclusions about the merits of the case, I should like to discuss briefly some of the more fundamental issues involved—issues on which my colleagues and I have been divided ever since I have been on the bench.

I have never been able to make my brothers see that government is a human affair, and that men are ruled, not by words on paper or by abstract theories, but by other men. They are ruled well when their rulers understand the feelings and conceptions of the masses. They are ruled badly when that understanding is lacking. . . .

[I] believe that all government officials, including judges, will do their jobs best if they treat forms and abstract concepts as instruments. We should take as our model, I think, the good administrator, who accommodates procedures and principles to the case at hand, selecting from among the available forms those most suited to reach the proper result.

The most obvious advantage of this method of government is that it permits us to go about our daily tasks with efficiency and common sense. My adherence to this philosophy has, however, deeper roots. I believe that it is only with the insight that philosophy gives that we can preserve the flexibility essential if we are to keep our actions in reasonable accord with the sentiments of those subject to our rule. . . .

Now when these conceptions are applied to the case before us, its decision becomes, as I have said, perfectly easy. In order to demonstrate this I shall have to introduce certain realities that my brothers in their coy decorum have seen fit to pass over in silence, although they are just as acutely aware of them as I am.

The first of these is that this case has aroused an enormous public interest, both here and abroad. Almost every newspaper and magazine has carried articles about it; columnists have shared with their readers confidential information as to the next governmental move; hundreds of letters-to-the-editor have been printed. One of the great newspaper chains made a poll of public opinion on the question, "What do you think the Supreme Court should do with the Spelencean explorers?" About ninety per cent expressed a belief that the defendants should be pardoned or let off with a kind of token punishment. It is perfectly clear, then, how the public feels about the case. . . .

Now I know that my brothers will be horrified by my suggestion that this Court should take account of public opinion. They will tell you that public opinion is emotional and capricious, that it is based on half-truths and listens to witnesses who are not subject to cross-examination. . . .

But let us look candidly at some of the realities of the administration of our criminal law. When a man is accused of a crime, there are, speaking generally, four ways in which he may escape punishment. One of these is a determination by a judge that under the applicable law he has committed no crime. This is, of course, a determination that takes place in a rather formal and abstract atmosphere. But look at the other three ways in which he may escape punishment. These are: (1) a decision by the Prosecutor not to ask for an indictment; (2) an acquittal by the jury; (3) a pardon or commutation of sentence by the executive. Can anyone pretend that these

decisions are held within a rigid and formal framework of rules that prevents factual error, excludes emotional and personal factors, and guarantees that all the forms of the law will be observed? . . .

I come now to the most crucial fact in this case, a fact known to all of us on this Court, though one that my brothers have seen fit to keep under the cover of their judicial robes. This is the frightening likelihood that if the issue is left to him, the Chief Executive will refuse to pardon these men or commute their sentence. As we all know, our Chief Executive is a man now well advanced in years, of very stiff notions. Public clamor usually operates on him with the reverse of the effect intended. As I have told my brothers, it happens that my wife's niece is an intimate friend of his secretary. I have learned in this indirect, but, I think, wholly reliable way, that he is firmly determined not to commute the sentence if these men are found to have violated the law. . . .

I conclude that the defendants are innocent of the crime charged, and that the conviction and sentence should be set aside. . . .

The Supreme Court being evenly divided, the conviction and sentence of the Court of General Instances is *affirmed*. It is ordered that the execution of the sentence shall occur at 6 A.M., Friday, April 2, 4300, at which time the Public Executioner is directed to proceed with all convenient dispatch to hang each of the defendants by the neck until he is dead. . . .

NOTES AND QUESTIONS

The various opinions bring into focus the divergent jurisprudential theories and touch upon some enduring questions regarding the judicial process and human choice. Our discussion will be limited to only two broad themes addressed in these opinions, the relation of law and morals and the relation of law and society.

1.   The first half of Justice Foster's opinion is a classic example of formalist reasoning based upon natural law philosophy. Beginning with the Lockian premise that the defendants had established a new

social compact among themselves that superseded the reach of the enacted law, he deduces the conclusion that they were not guilty of murder. The starting point of one's reasoning determines in part the outcome. The question is how one chooses the initial premises—how did Justice Foster determine that the defendants were in a state of nature in the first place? Are there articulable principles that guide the selection of premises?

2.   The second half of Justice Foster's opinion exemplifies a kind of purposive analysis which is also characteristic of natural law theory. According to this methodology, to adjudicate is to be morally judgmental, to do the right thing. However, a decision is supposed to involve more than just the expression of private preferences of the judge. There are institutional constraints built into his role. He has to give an opinion that explains and justifies the result, and it must include the general principles or bases of decision-making that transcend the particulars of the case. The hallmarks of *legal* decision-making are consistent and predictable—not ad hoc and discretionary—outcomes. The opinion has to link up with the past and provide guidelines for the future. One such general basis for adjudication is the purpose of the law. As Justice Foster says, every statute or judicial precedent is to be interpreted reasonably, in the light of its evident purpose." Law consists not only of given rules (statutes, precedents) but also of received ideals and social purposes which are acknowledged or inferred from the existence of specific rules. Adjudication is not foreordained by deductive reasoning in vacuo, but proceeds against a background of higher levels of law: the social ends served by the rules.

What is really meant by legislative "purpose"? Is Justice Foster seeking to discern and implement the original purpose of the statute? Or is he remaking the law—under the guise of "intelligent fidelity" to the legislative will—according to his own conceptions of what is right and proper?

3.   Justice Tatting raises a basic question about analysis-of-purpose adjudication. "What are we to do," he asks, "when [the law] has many purposes, or when its purposes are disputed?" Is there a calculus for making value choices or is it purely a matter of individual discretion?

Return to some of the cases of this book that present competing social values—for example, the goals of deterrence and retribution in the death penalty cases (Chapter 5); racial equality and associational rights in the *School Segregation Cases* (Chapter 3); free press and fair trial in the pretrial publicity cases (Chapter 9); and so on. How did the Court weigh and choose between these alternative policies?

4.   Do you find Justice Foster's argument—that the killing of Whetmore is analogous to killing in self-defense—persuasive? Normally, self-defense is engaged in by those whose lives are threatened, but in this instance Whetmore did not place the defendants' lives in peril. Suppose Whetmore had defended himself when his companions sought to kill him, and he succeeded instead in killing one of them. Everyone, then, including Whetmore, proceeded to eat the unexpected victim. Is the excuse of self-defense available to them?

5.   Toward the end of his opinion, Justice Foster protests that he is not engaging in "judicial usurpation" by analyzing statutory purpose. He explains that he is only interpreting, not making, law. Why the pretended modesty about judicial legislation?

6.   Justice Keen's opinion also is one of logical deduction, but his first premises reflect the influence of the positivist theory of law. Although the defendants might be morally blameless, legally they are guilty. What larger implications are at stake for law, the judicial process, and the relations between the courts and other branches of government in his insistence on separating law and morality?

Suppose that a clearly unjust and inhumane law was enacted—for example, that all persons of certain racial or religious backgrounds are to be sent to concentration camps. If the essence of law is the command of the sovereign, and "the obligation of the judiciary [is] to enforce faithfully the written law," is the positivist theory necessarily a prescription for a totalitarian creed?

7.   As in the mythical Commonwealth "when judges did in fact legislate very freely," so, too, did the Supreme Court function as a super-legislature by striking down social and economic regulatory legislation under "substantive due process" from the turn of the century to the mid-1930s (see Chapter 3, section 3.6).

Chastened by historical experience and recognizing "the supremacy of the legislative branch," Justice Keen seeks to "interpret" the law "in accordance with its plain meaning without reference to our personal desires." Since the meaning of a legal concept (for example, "due process") is anything but plain, how can a judge perform the function of interpretation and still be faithful to the supremacy principle? Moreover, Justice Keen says that interpretation is either according to "plain meaning" or "personal desires." Are there no other bases or criteria for judicial decision-making than these two? Is his criticism of Justice Foster—that the latter "remake[s]" the statute to meet his "own wishes"—a justified one?

8.   This is, according to Justice Keen, a "hard case." A hard or penumbral case is one which is not clearly covered by the existing statute or legal rule. Although he eschews consulting the underlying purposes of §12-A, modern analytical positivists argue that their philosophy is not inconsistent with such purposive analysis. This is because positivism maintains only that the purposes of law are not, as a matter of logic or meaning, necessarily moral purposes. The purposes may be moral, nonmoral, or immoral. In this view, decisions at the penumbra of a statute are not necessarily dictated by its purposes but represent a kind of interstitial legislation that judges have implied discretion to formulate (Hart 1961, Ch. 7). Thus, Justice Keen's opinion represents only one version of positivist jurisprudence.

9.   Is Justice Keen consistent throughout his own opinion in his value-free approach to deciding this case?

10.   Consider the legal and moral issues posed by postwar prosecutions of "grudge informers" (Hart 1958; Fuller 1958). Nazi legislation required citizens to inform authorities of any acts against the state, including defamation. Under this statute, an unfaithful wife secured the imprisonment of her husband by informing the police of unfavorable remarks that he had made to her regarding the Third Reich. After the war, the wife was prosecuted under a new, retroactive statute that made grudge informing under the previous regime a criminal offense. Her defense was that she could not legally be convicted and punished for engaging in conduct that, at the time it was performed, was valid because the governing law required it. How would Justice Foster rule on the appeal of her conviction? And Chief Justice Truepenny and Justice Keen?

11.   The relation between law and society—does law shape society or vice versa?—is an enduring theme in jurisprudential inquiry. "Law" and "society" are polar categories, though each implies recognition of the other. The formalist method tends to emphasize law as an active principle in establishing social order. The realist method focuses more on the influence of social conditions and experience in determining conduct. The purposive method concentrates on the reciprocal relationship between law and its underlying social values, on the one hand, and their consequences on society and behavior, on the other.

12.   Justice Handy's opinion exemplifies realist reasoning (albeit somewhat in caricature). For example:

> • Law consists of judicial decisions, not rules or social norms or purposes. "The problem before us is what we . . . ought to *do* . . ." (emphasis added).
> • The basis of the decision is not "abstract theory" but "human realities." These realities include *inter alia* the "feelings and conceptions of the masses." The realist judge considers the possible impact of his decisions on society; he is consequence-oriented in his reasoning.
> • Legal rules are merely "instruments" or means, not ends in themselves. A judicial decision-maker "accommodates" and "select[s]" between available rules in order "to reach the proper result." This is a policy-oriented or result-oriented approach to law.

13.   A central feature of law is that it is a means of settling disputes according to an orderly, predictable system of rules. So long as adjudication is based on these rules, persons can generally anticipate the legal consequences of their conduct by knowing what the law is. Justice Handy, however, freely acknowledges the influence of personal emotions, public opinion, and other nonlegal considerations in his decision-making. Does his approach undermine certainty and stability in the law?

14.   Reread some of the cases of the preceding chapters. Which opinions rely on a decision-making style similar to that of Justice Foster? Of Justice Keen? Of Justice Handy? Which opinions use a combination of different styles?

12.3.   FORMALIST REASONING

THE PATH OF THE LAW

Oliver W. Holmes

When we study law we are not studying a mystery but a well known profession. We are studying what we shall want in order to appear before judges, or to advise people in such a way as to keep them out of court. The reason why it is a profession, why people will pay lawyers to argue for them or to advise them, is that in societies like ours the command of the public force is entrusted to the judges in certain cases, and the whole power of the state will be put forth, if necessary, to carry out their judgments and decrees. . . . The object of our study, then, is prediction, the prediction of the incidence of the public force through the instrumentality of the courts.

The means of the study are a body of reports, of treatises, and of statutes, in this country and in England, extending back for six hundred years, and now increasing annually by hundreds. In these sibylline leaves are gathered the scattered prophecies of the past upon the cases in which the axe will fall. These are what properly have been called the oracles of the law. Far the most important and pretty nearly the whole meaning of every new effort of legal thought is to make these prophecies more precise, and to generalize them into a thoroughly connected system. . . .

The first thing for a business-like understanding of the matter is to understand its limits, and therefore I think it desirable at once to point out and dispel a confusion between morality and law, which sometimes rises to the height of conscious theory, and more often and indeed

constantly is making trouble in detail without reaching the point of consciousness. You can see very plainly that a bad man has as much reason as a good one for wishing to avoid an encounter with the public force, and therefore you can see the practical importance of the distinction between morality and law. A man who cares nothing for an ethical rule which is believed and practised by his neighbors is likely nevertheless to care a good deal to avoid being made to pay money, and will want to keep out of jail if he can.

I take it for granted that no hearer of mine will misinterpret what I have to say as the language of cynicism. The law is the witness and external deposit of our moral life. Its history is the history of the moral development of the race. The practice of it, in spite of popular jests, tends to make good citizens and good men. When I emphasize the difference between law and morals I do so with reference to a single end, that of learning and understanding the law. . . .

If you want to know the law and nothing else, you must look at it as a bad man, who cares only for the material consequences which such knowledge enables him to predict, not as a good one, who finds his reasons for conduct, whether inside the law or outside of it, in the vaguer sanctions of conscience. The theoretical importance of the distinction is no less, if you would reason on your subject aright. The law is full of phraseology drawn from morals, and by the mere force of language continually invites us to pass from one domain to the other without perceiving it, as we are sure to do unless we have the boundary constantly before our minds. The law talks about rights, and duties, and malice, and intent, and negligence, and so forth, and nothing is easier, or, I may say, more common in legal reasoning, than to take these words in their moral sense, at some stage of the argument, and so to drop into fallacy. For instance, when we speak of the rights of man in a moral sense, we mean to mark the limits of interference with individual freedom which we think are prescribed by conscience, or by our ideal, however reached. Yet it is certain that many laws have been enforced in the past, and it is likely that some are enforced now, which are condemned by the most enlightened opinion of the time, or which at all events pass the limits of interference as many consciences would draw it. Manifestly, therefore, nothing but confusion of thought can result from assuming that the rights of man in a moral sense are equally rights in the sense of the Constitution and the law. . . .

In the law of contract the use of moral phraseology has led to equal confusion, as I have shown in part already, but only in part. Morals deal with the actual internal state of the individual's mind, what he actually intends. From the time of the Romans down to now, this mode of dealing has affected the language of the law as to contract, and the language used has reacted upon the thought. We talk about a contract as a meeting of the minds of the parties, and thence it is inferred in various cases that there is no contract because their minds have not met; that is, because they have intended different things or because one party has not known of the assent of the other. Yet nothing is more certain than that parties may be bound by a contract to things which neither of them intended, and when one does not know of the other's assent. Suppose a contract is executed in due form and in writing to deliver a lecture, mentioning no time. One of the parties thinks that the promise will be construed to mean at once, within a week. The other thinks that it means when he is ready. The court says that it means within a reasonable time. The parties are bound by the contract as it is interpreted by the court, yet neither of

them meant what the court declares that they have said. In my opinion no one will understand the true theory of contract or be able even to discuss some fundamental questions intelligently until he has understood that . . . the making of a contract depends not . . . on the parties' having *meant* the same thing but on the their having *said* the same thing. . . .

The confusion with which I am dealing besets confessedly legal conceptions. Take the fundamental question, What constitutes the law? You will find some text writers telling you that it is something different from what is decided by the courts of Massachusetts or England, that it is a system of reason, that it is a deduction from principles of ethics or admitted axioms or what not, which may or may not coincide with the decision. But if we take the view of our friend the bad man we shall find that he does not care two straws for the axioms or deductions, but that he does want to know what the Massachusetts or English courts are likely to do in fact. I am much of his mind. The prophecies of what the courts will do in fact, and nothing more pretentious, are what I mean by the law. . . .

The next thing which I wish to consider is what are the forces which determine its content and its growth. You may assume, with Hobbes and Bentham and Austin, that all law emanates from the sovereign, even when the first human beings to enunciate it are the judges, or you may think that law is the voice of the Zeitgeist, or what you like. It is all one to my present purpose. Even if every decision required the sanction of an emperor with despotic power and a whimsical turn of mind, we should be interested none the less, still with a view to prediction, in discovering some order, some rational explanation, and some principle of growth for the rules which he laid down. In every system there are such explanations and principles to be found. It is with regard to them that a second fallacy comes in, which I think it important to expose.

The fallacy to which I refer is the notion that the only force at work in the development of the law is logic. In the broadest sense, indeed, that notion would be true. . . . The condition of our thinking about the universe is that it is capable of being thought about rationally, or, in other words, that every part of it is effect and cause in the same sense in which those parts are with which we are most familiar. So in the broadest sense it is true that the law is a logical development, like everything else. The danger of which I speak is not the admission that the principles governing other phenomena also govern the law, but the notion that a given system, ours, for instance, can be worked out like mathematics from some general axioms of conduct. . . .

This mode of thinking is entirely natural. The training of lawyers is a training in logic. The processes of analogy, discrimination, and deduction are those in which they are most at home. The language of judicial decision is mainly the language of logic. And the logical method and form flatter that longing for certainty and for repose which is in every human mind. But certainty generally is illusion, and repose is not the destiny of man. Behind the logical form lies a judgment as to the relative worth and importance of competing legislative grounds, often an inarticulate and unconscious judgment, it is true, and yet the very root and nerve of the whole proceeding. You can give any conclusion a logical form. You always can imply a condition in a contract, but why do you imply it? It is because of some belief as to the practice of the community or of a class, or because of some opinion as to policy, or, in short, because of some attitude of yours upon a matter not capable of exact quantitative measurement, and therefore not capable of founding exact logical conclusions. Such matters really are battle

grounds where the means do not exist for determinations that shall be good for all time, where the decision can do no more than embody the preference of a given body in a given time and place. We do not realize how large a part of our law is open to reconsideration upon a slight change in the habit of the public mind. No concrete proposition is self-evident, no matter how ready we may be to accept it, not even Mr. Herbert Spencer's Every man has a right to do what he wills, provided he interferes not with a like right on the part of his neighbors. . . .

I think that the judges themselves have failed adequately to recognize their duty of weighing considerations of social advantage. The duty is inevitable, and the result of the often proclaimed judicial aversion to deal with such considerations is simply to leave the very ground and foundation of judgments inarticulate, and often unconscious, as I have said. . . .

So much for the fallacy of logical form. Now let us consider the present condition of the law as a subject for study, and the ideal toward which it tends. We still are far from the point of view which I desire to see reached. No one has reached it or can reach it as yet. We are only at the beginning of a philosophical reaction, and of a reconsideration of the worth of doctrines which for the most part still are taken for granted without any deliberate, conscious, and systematic questioning of their grounds. The development of our law has gone on for nearly a thousand years, like the development of a plant, each generation taking the inevitable next step, mind, like matter, simply obeying a law of spontaneous growth. . . . Most of the things we do, we do for no better reason than that our fathers have done them or that our neighbors do them, and the same is true of a larger part than we suspect of what we think. . . . Still it is true that a body of law is more rational and more civilized when every rule it contains is referred articulately and definitely to an end which it subserves, and when the grounds for desiring that end are stated or are ready to be stated in words.

At present, in very many cases, if we want to know why a rule of law has taken its particular shape, and more or less if we want to know why it exists at all, we go to tradition. . . . The rational study of law is still to a large extent the study of history. . . . For the rational study of the law the black-letter man may be the man of the present, but the man of the future is the man of statistics and the master of economics. . . .

I have been speaking about the study of the law, and I have said next to nothing of what commonly is talked about in that connection—text-books and the case system, and all the machinery with which a student comes most immediately in contact. Nor shall I say anything about them. Theory is my subject, not practical details. . . . Theory is the most important part of the dogma of the law, as the architect is the most important man who takes part in the building of a house. The most important improvements of the last twenty-five years are improvements in theory. It is not to be feared as unpractical, for, to the competent, it simply means going to the bottom of the subject. . . . The remoter and more general aspects of the law are those which give it universal interest. It is through them that you not only become a great master in your calling, but connect your subject with the universe and catch an echo of the infinite, a glimpse of its unfathomable process, a hint of the universal law.

●

NOTES AND QUESTIONS

1.   The shadow of Justice Holmes looms large in both the judicial and the jurisprudential literature. By the time of his retirement, he had emerged a "deity . . . an Olympian [whose] opinions were norms by which to measure the departure of his Court from the true path of law. . . . For the Court, but especially in dissent, thus spake Holmes and the subject was closed" (Hamilton 1941, p. 1). Justice Cardozo (1931) described him as "the greatest of our age in the domain of jurisprudence and one of the greatest of the ages" (p. 684). Few are those who are privileged to hear such encomiums during their lifetime. He was also a man of great popular appeal, whose life was the subject of a Broadway play, *The Magnificent Yankee*, in 1951.

In this classic essay, graced with aphoristic richness and vatic pronouncements, Holmes introduced a fresh way of looking at law that was almost revolutionary for his day. He laid the foundation for modern jurisprudential thinking about law (Kaplan 1983, p. 1835). The fact that many of the ideas in this essay no longer seem novel to us is a testimony to their influence on our approach to law— unknowingly, perhaps, we have already been socialized to some extent in the Holmesian philosophy. Our appropriation of his vision of law would have pleased him, because as he once mused, it is "the secret isolated joy of the thinker, who knows that, a hundred years after he is dead and forgotten, men who never heard of him will be moving to the measure of his thought" (Holmes 1920, p. 32). In the first half of the essay, he argues for the separation of law and morals and he equates law with what courts actually do—consequently, he has been described as the American father of legal positivism (Fuller 1940). In the second half, he critiques the formalist method of decision-making and proposes an alternative approach, one that anticipates the realist method of the 1930s and also foreshadows the "present trend to integrate law with the social sciences" (Woodard 1968, p. 721).

2.   Holmes begins (as Justice Keen did) by distinguishing between law as it is and law as morality would require it to be. He expounded English ideas of positivism in American legal writing.

Natural law philosophers in the nineteenth century saw nothing shameful in tolerating confusion between law-as-is and law-as-ought-to-be. To them, law was coextensive with morality. "Ethical considerations can no more be excluded from the administration of justice . . . than one can exclude the vital air from his room and live" (Dillon 1895, p. 19). The difficulty with this position is that unreasonable and unjust laws exist, and they cannot simply be defined away as not being "law." It is because of the problem posed by immoral laws that positivism sought a sharp distinction between the two.

On the one hand, if the people felt a law was bad and therefore did not view it as binding, the result would be noncompliance leading eventually to anarchy. This is the risk of identifying personal moral values with the law. On the other hand, if the people felt that a law, merely by being the law of the land, is also what it ought to be, law would supplant morality as the final test of conduct. Law escapes criticism when it is equated with the prevailing morality. Holmes, therefore, urged that we see law as a bad man sees it, caring not for its ethical content but only for its consequences.

3.   For Holmes, according to some critics, "the essence of law is physical force. Might makes legal right. The law is to be divorced of all morality" (Ford 1942, p. 275; see also Palmer 1945). Is this criticism justified? Does Holmes say that law must be cut loose from the ethical considerations that shaped it?

4.   Holmes conceives of law as the prediction of the application of physical force via court decisions. People comply with law because they anticipate the possibility of sanctions for certain conduct. He identifies the legal order with compulsion.

Some legal rules are indeed of this nature. The criminal law, for example, requires persons to act or forbear from acting in prescribed ways whether they want to or not. Other legal rules, however, do not compel but facilitate conduct. The laws of contracts, of wills, and of trusts help facilitate the attainment of individual choices. The rules of contract law, for example, do not say that a person must or must not enter into a contract. They do not command in the same way that the criminal law forbids killing. Instead, they say that "if you wish to enter into a contract, this is how you should do it in order for it to be legally enforceable." Such rules put law at the disposition of individuals; they serve to confer rights and duties, and they do so without sanction or compulsion.

How would Holmes account for the fact that people comply with legal rules that are not backed by "the incidence of the public force"? Are there different bases for fidelity to law depending on the type of legal rule in question?

5.   The second half of Holmes's essay is an elaboration of the entrancing opening paragraph of his earlier book, *The Common Law* (1881):

> The life of the law has not been logic; it has been experience. The felt necessities of the time, the prevalent moral and political theories, intuitions of public policy, avowed or unconscious, even the prejudices which judges share with their fellow-men, have had a good deal more to do than the syllogism in determining the rules by which men should be governed. [p. 1]

Because of his pragmatic and utilitarian view of the judicial process, Holmes has been "often heralded as the first legal realist" (Note, *Harvard Law Review* 1982, p. 1672, n. 22).

6.   Examine carefully the elements and implications of Holmes's conception of law and of judicial decision-making. If legal certainty is an "illusion," and if merely knowing existing doctrinal rules does not enable us to reliably predict the outcome of future cases, then how can there be order and stability in law?

If judges "can give any conclusion a logical form," thereby implying that opinions may be post-hoc rationalizations of the decision, what then are the "true" bases of judicial decisions?

If there are no "determinations that shall be good for all time," that is, there are no eternal, absolute values and principles, what standards are to guide a judge in making value determinations?

How are courts to go about "weighing considerations of social advantage"? Are they better fitted for this task than legislatures?

What role is there for social research and empirical analysis in Holmes's philosophy?

Formalism: Deductive Reasoning and Inductive Science

Holmes helped spark "the revolt against formalism" (White 1972). Also called "classical legal thought" because it stressed rationalistic ordering in thinking, formalism flourished betweeen the last quarter of the nineteenth century and the first quarter of this century (Kennedy 1980, p. 3). We will examine the nature of this style of reasoning and the social context in which it developed.

The formalist method of adjudication, allied with the natural law philosophy, consisted of reaching decisions by deduction from first principles based on moral justice or precedents. It has been characterized as "mechanical jurisprudence" (Pound 1908), because it "clung to the belief that justice must be administered in accordance with fixed rules [major premise], which can be applied by a rather mechanical process of logical reasoning to a given state of facts [minor premise], and can be made to produce an inevitable result" (Haines 1951, pp. 461–62). By clothing their decisions in the language of formal deduction, formalist judges sought to make legal reasoning seem like mathematics. If they differed on a certain conclusion, it meant simply that the disputing parties were not doing their sums right, and, if they were to add correctly, agreement inevitably would come (Holmes 1881).

Formalism was unconcerned with whether a decision was just, or workable, or conducive to the attainment of desired ends. During its heyday in the late nineteenth century, judges believed that they ought not shape "their decisions with reference to predicted consequences" (*Thorne* v. *Cramer,* 1851, p. 120). Instead, the emphasis was on harmonizing decisions with precedent. Judges worried more about preserving the orderly structure, internal symmetry, and logical consistency of the decisions that composed the body of law than about their impact upon behavior and society. In the formalist view, judges did not decide cases; legal rules decided cases. A judge did not make law; he applied the law. As Sir William Blackstone (1821), an early exponent of formalism noted in his *Commentaries,* law "depends not upon the arbitrary will of any judge, but is permanent, fixed, and unchangeable, unless changed by authority of Parliament" (p. 151). Formalism is to law as fundamentalism is to religion. A judge is only a conduit or "phonograph" through which the law is expressed to the people. Like the revival preacher, the formalist judge says, in effect, that "it is not I who speaks, but the law that speaks through me."

Formalism rested not only on a syllogistic method of reasoning but also on a conception of law as an inductive science. In the second half of the nineteenth century, Charles Langdell of Harvard began to apply for the first time the scientific method to law. In 1879, he proposed:

> Law, considered as a science, consists of certain principles or doctrines . . . [the] growth [of which] is to be traced in the main through a series of cases. . . . [The task is] to select, classify, and arrange all of the cases which had contributed in any important degree to the growth, development, or establishment of any of its essential doctrines. [p. viii]

Thus, "adjudged cases [were] to juridical science what ascertained facts and experiments [were] to the natural sciences" (Hoover 1895, p. 73). The legal scientist's laboratory was the law library; his data were decided cases. His role was to read all the reported opinions in a given area and then organize them into some orderly and logical pattern, because "all of the available materials of that science are contained in printed books (in Stevens 1971, p. 436, n. 50). By this inductive process, the true principles would emerge. Of course, Langdell's notion of "science" as descriptive classification bears little resemblance to the modern conception of science as a hypothesis-testing method.

In the formalist view, cases were not the law itself, but only evidence of the principles of law. Just as a falling apple is evidence of the law of gravity, so a case is evidence of the law that underlies it. Law exists "out there"—it was thought to exist independently of a given case or a given judge. The task of legal scientists was to discover these principles. And the task of judges was to apply these principles—which constitute the major premises in their syllogistic reasoning—to the facts of cases in adjudication. In this way, future cases can be decided on empirically based propositions, and law is made into a scientific enterprise.

Some of the greatest names in American legal scholarship at the turn of the century adopted in varying measure this approach to law. The highwater mark came in 1920 with the founding of the American Law Institute, a reform-minded group of lawyers, legal scholars, and judges dedicated to "restating" the case law in clear, logical form, so that its "true" principles would be evident to all.

The Social-Intellectual Context of Formalism

Formalism did not blossom in a vacuum. It was the product of two social and ideological movements in the late nineteenth century: the ascendancy of science as a new cultural standard of rationality and the pervasiveness of *laissez faire* and Social Darwinist ideas in American thought.

A SCIENTIFIC (OR SCIENTISTIC) ERA

Within a few years of the publication of Darwin's *Origin of Species* in 1859, the scientific method had become a dominant force in intellectual circles. The nineteenth-century conception of science, however, was not the same as that of today. The modern view is of a continuing, personal process of hypothesis formulation, experimentation to test the hypothesis, and reformulation of the hypothesis or theory (Kuhn 1962). The last century's view of science was of a procedure for data gathering, classification of the data, and the formulation thereupon of general laws (Pearson 1895, p. 7). This view of the scientific method permeated not only the sciences but also history, belles-lettres, and law. Science became the measure of all things. It was a "scientistic" era—a time of "blind faith in science," when science was viewed as "the only useful way of knowing things" (Dauer 1980–81, p. 16).

The conception of law as an inductive science was born of two circumstances of the period: the scientistic temper and the academic needs of legal education. Until the mid-nineteenth century, the majority of lawyers were trained by reading law on their own under the tutelage of a practicing attorney. Legal education took place for the most part in law offices. Then the universities, with the support of the bar, began taking over in earnest the job of training new lawyers. However, there was no tradition or established model for this undertaking. Initially, the university law schools were trade-oriented and lacking in academic stature. The schooling consisted of lectures (usually by retired judges) on rules of law that students learned by rote. Langdell, who later became dean of the Harvard Law School, changed all of that. His insight was to add a scientific patina to the study of law. He matched the scientific method, which was the dominant mode of thought of the time, with the need of law schools for intellectual respectability—the result: law as science.

The chief impetus for the development of legal science was Langdell's invention of the case method. It revolutionalized both legal education and legal philosophy. He prepared the first legal casebook (in the area of contracts). Of the thousands of reported cases, he selected those that would serve to illustrate the basic principles that underlay them. "To have such a mastery of these [principles] as to be able to apply them with constant facility and certainty to the ever-tangled skein of human affairs, is what constitutes a true lawyer" (Langdell 1879, p. viii)—and, according to him, what constitutes the business of law training.

His casebook, unlike a textbook, contained no original writing. And unlike modern law casebooks, it contained no editorial comments and nonlegal materials to guide the student. The case method was used with the so-called Socratic technique in the classroom. By blistering questions and hypothetical problems, the professor led the student to "discover" the "real" meaning or principles behind the decisions. To this end, he chose as faculty members not retired judges or practitioners but young graduates, fresh out of law school. They might never have practiced law but they were expert in a given field because they had analyzed every reported case and discovered their underlying principles. For Langdell, to invert Holmes's famous saying, the life of the law was logic, not experience.

In one stroke, Langdell placed law on the same footing in the academic world with the physical and social sciences of its day, rather than with the moral philosophy with which it had been previously associated. It has been seen by some as the single most creative American contribution to the educational process. Lord James Bryce (1888) wrote, "I do not know if there is anything in which America has advanced more beyond the mother country than in the provisions she makes for legal education" (p. 487).

Holmes was more muted in his appraisal of Langdell's contribution, since to him Langdell was the embodiment of formalism. Commenting on his contracts casebook, he wrote: "A more misspent piece of marvelous ingenuity I never read. . . . I have referred to Langdell several times in dealing with contracts because to my mind he represents the power of darkness. He is all for logic and hates any reference to anything outside of it" (in Fuller and Eisenberg 1972, p. 284). He complained that Langdell conveniently ignored "wrongly" decided cases, that is, evidence that was in conflict with the "discovered" principle. How cases can be "right" or "wrong" when the law exists "out there," independently of the cases and of the legal scientist who organizes them, is a paradox that Langdell never explained. In any event, Langdell simply relied on some cases and discarded others without ever articulating the grounds of sorting and selection. He ignored variances in the data. For the next half a century or so, the history of legal education was a struggle between Langdellians, who conceived of law study exclusively as doctrinal analysis, and anti-formalists (such as Holmes), who sought admixture of law study with other subjects.

LAISSEZ FAIRE AND SOCIAL DARWINISM

The post–Civil War years saw the surge of economic expansion. The nation began industrializing rapidly on a continental scale. Enormous strides were made in technology, production, and interstate transportation. The economic watchword during this period was *laissez faire*. There was a general belief in the wisdom of not tampering with the "natural" laws of the marketplace. Economic regulation by government intervention was generally looked upon with disfavor.

Courts, consequently, tended to decide cases in ways that promoted the development of industrial capitalism. The natural law philosophy and its associated method of formalist decision-making were adapted to this economic purpose. Formalist judges began with certain first principles, and then reasoned downward to the inevitable result. These principles, arrived at inductively from all the past decisions, found their origins in a higher law. One such fundamental principle was the right to acquire and hold property. It was a right deemed "fully recognized as inherent and indefeasible in man, . . . which human government can neither grant nor abolish, alter nor abridge" (*People* v. *Gallagher*, 1856, p. 266). Private property was "the gift of the Creator; which the law does not confer, but only recognizes" (*Slaughter-House Cases*, 1873, p. 105); it was "founded in natural equity and . . . laid down by jurists as a principle of universal law. Indeed, in a free government, almost all other rights would become worthless if the government possessed an uncontrollable power over the private fortune of every citizen" (*Chicago B. & Q. R. R.* v. *Chicago*, 1897, p. 236).

One result of the belief in the absolute right of private property, free from government interference, was the judicial defense of that right at the cost of aid to the disadvantaged. From about the turn of the century to the New Deal, the courts frequently struck down progressive welfare and economic legislation promulgated by the states to ameliorate the social ills of industrialization (including, for example, laws setting minimum wages and maximum hours). They bootlegged surreptitiously into the law their own economic preferences and erected a Magna Carta for big business under the guise of impartial application of clear, neutral rules supposedly latent in the phrase substantive due process (see Chapter 3, section 3.6).

For example, in the celebrated case of *Lochner* v. *New York* (1905), the Supreme Court invalidated a state law regulating the maximum number of hours that bakers could be compelled to work, on the grounds that such legislation infringed upon their property right to sell their services at whatever terms they wished. Since the terms were largely dictated by employers, the decision actually protected employers' right to require their bakers to work sixty hours a week. In dissent, Justice Holmes repudiated the formalist style of announcing general propositions as truths (in this instance, the right of freedom of contract as an integral feature of the sanctity of private property), and then deducing from them the inevitable conclusions. "General propositions do not decide concrete cases," he argued. Judges ought not use their office to expound their own *laissez-faire* views in the guise of formulating legal principles. He stressed instead the reasonableness of the beliefs of the state legislators that excessive working hours were deleterious to employees' health and welfare, without passing on the merits of the law itself.

The reasoning in cases such as *Lochner*, which Langdell's "legal science" method tended to foster, prompted Holmes (1920) to write, "I sometimes tell students that the law students pursue an inspirational combined with a logical method, that is, the postulates are taken for granted upon authority and without inquiry into their worth, and then logic is used as the only tool to develop the results" (p. 238).

What the *laissez-faire* theory was to economic affairs, Social Darwinism was to social relations in the late nineteenth century. Herbert Spencer in his *Social Statics* proposed that the development of individual liberty decreased as state regulatory power increased. Social problems arising from *laissez-faire* economic policies were not matters for concern, because they would solve themselves. Human nature adapts to the environment, and any artificial attempt to change is deleterious to society and the human species. The popularization of Spencer's ideas after the Civil War affected all forms of social thought and provided the framework for the social sciences of the day (Hofstadter 1966).

The doctrine of "separate but equal" treatment of the races, announced in *Plessy* v. *Ferguson* (1896) (see Chapter 3, section 3.3), exemplifies the influence of Social Darwinism in judicial thinking. The Supreme Court in that case began with the premise that it is impossible and undesirable to change "racial instinct" by legislation or judicial decision. From this truth, it then reasoned downward to the conclusion that the statute providing for separate but equal railway accommodations was not invalid. So pervasive was their ideology that Holmes remarked, "I doubt if any writer of English except Darwin has done so much to affect our whole way of thinking about the universe" (Howe 1961, p. 58). The main practical triumph of Social Darwinism and *laissez-faire* economics was attained in the courts. The Supreme Court, in particular, was an ardent sponsor of these ideas and translated them into legal policy via the formalist style of decision-making.

THE DECLINE OF FORMALISM

The excessive abstractions of the case method and its unconcern with normative concerns, or the practical workings of law, or the nonlegal influences that shape decision-making, resulted in a jurisprudence and an educational system that increasingly lost touch with reality. These characteristics of formalism prompted Holmes, and later the legal realists, to launch their assault and present an alternative jurisprudential methodology. The rise of modern, empirical social science and the onset of the Depression in the 1920s resulted in the undermining, respectively, of Social Darwinist and *laissez-faire* premises of formalism. Although formalism has long since lost its monopoly over American jurisprudence, and few if any lawyers today would characterize themselves as formalists in the Langdellian sense, nonetheless the deductive style of reasoning and the case method remain very much a part of the modern lawyer's intellectual equipment. The method of extracting principles from past cases and applying them to adjudicate new cases is still the bedrock of their education and thinking.

12.4. REALIST REASONING

A REALISTIC JURISPRUDENCE—
THE NEXT STEP

Karl N. Llewellyn

THE PROBLEM OF DEFINING LAW;
FOCUS VERSUS CONFINES

The difficulty in framing any concept of "law" is that there are so many things to be included, and the things to be included are so unbelievably different from each other. . . .

So that I am not going to attempt a definition of law. Not anybody's definition; much less my own. A definition both excludes and includes. It marks out a field. . . . I shall instead devote my attention to the *focus* of matters legal. I shall try to discuss a *point of reference*; a point of reference to which I believe all matters legal can most usefully be referred, if they are to be seen with intelligence and with appreciation of their bearings. A focus, a core, a center—

Reprinted by permission of Soia M. Llewellyn and the publisher. Copyright ©1930 by the Columbia Law Review [30 (1930): 431–65].

with the bearings and boundaries outward unlimited. . . .

PRECEPTS AS THE HEART AND CORE OF MOST THINKING ABOUT LAW

When men talk or think about law, they talk and think about *rules*. "Precepts" as used by Pound,[1] for instance, I take to be roughly synonymous with rules and principles, the principles being wider in scope and proportionately vaguer in connotation, with a tendency toward idealization of some portion of the *status quo* at any given time. And I think you will find as you read Pound that the precepts are *central* to his thinking about law. . . . But Pound mentions more as law than precepts. . . . [H]e stresses *also* ideals as to "the end" of law. These I take to be in substance standards on a peculiarly vague and majestic scale; standards, perhaps, to be applied to rules rather than to individual transactions. Finally, he stresses—and we meet here a very different order of phenomena—"the traditional techniques of developing and applying" precepts. Only a man gifted with insight would have added to the verbal formulae and verbalized (though vague) conceptual pictures thus far catalogued, such an element *of practices*, of habits and techniques of action, of *behavior*. . . .

REMEDIES, RIGHTS AND INTERESTS: A DEVELOPING INSIGHT

In the earlier stages the rules were thought of almost exclusively as rules of remedies. Remedies were few and specific. There were a few certain ways to lug a man into court and a few certain things that you or the court could do with him when you got him there. . . . And the rules of law

---

[1]*Law and Morals* (1924).

were rules about that. They clustered around each remedy. In those terms people thought. They thought about what they could see and do. Their crude minds dealt only with what they could observe. What they observed, they described.

To later writers this seemed primitive. The later thinkers find a different kind of order in the field of law. Remedies seem to them to have a *purpose*, to be protections of something else. They could imagine these somethings and give them a name: *rights*, substantive rights. Thus the important, the substantial rules of law become rules defining rights. Remedies are relegated to the periphery of attention. They are "adjective law" merely—devices more or less imperfect for giving effect to the important things, the substantive rights which make up the substance of the law. The relation of rights to rules is fairly clear: the two are aspects of the same thing. When a rule runs in favor of a person, he has a right, as measured by the rule. Or, if he has a right, that can be phrased by setting out a rule ascribing to him and persons in like situation with him the benefits connoted by the rights. Rights are thus precise counterparts of rules. . . . Rights and rules are therefore for present purposes pretty much interchangeable; the right is a shorthand symbol for the rule. . . .

The term *interests* comes in to focus attention on the presence of social factors, and to urge that substantive rights themselves, like remedies, exist only for a purpose. Their purpose is now perceived to be the protection of the interests. . . .

At this stage of the development, then, one arrives at a double chain of purposes. One starts with the interest. That is a social fact or factor of some kind, existing independent of the law. And it has value independent of the law. Indeed, its protection is the purpose of substantive legal rights, of legal rules, or precepts of substantive law. "Security of transactions" is such an interest. The rules and rights of contract law exist to protect and effectuate it. The rules and rights are not ends, but means. . . .

[T]he use of precepts, or rules, or of rights which are logical counterparts of rules—of *words,* in a word—as the *center* of reference in thinking about law, is a block to clear thinking about matters legal. I want again to make sure that I am not misunderstood. I am not arguing that "rules of substantive law" are without importance. . . . Least of all, am I attempting to urge the exclusion of substantive rights and rules from the field of "law." Instead of these things, I am arguing that rules of substantive law are of far less importance than most legal theorizers have assumed in most of their thinking and writing, and that they are *not* the most useful center of reference for discussions of law; . . . that substantive rights and rules should be removed from their present position at the *focal point* of legal discussion, in favor the *area of contact* between judicial (or official) *behavior* and the *behavior* of laymen; that the substantive rights and rules should be studied not as self-existent, nor as a major point of reference, but themselves with constant reference to that area of behavior-contacts. . . .

I see no value to be gained from the interests-rights and rules-remedies set up except to bring out, to underscore, that law is not all, nor yet the major part of, society; and to force attention to the relations and interactions of law and the rest of society; and as a matter of method, to provide words which keep legal and non-legal aspects of the situation and the interactions distinct. And it would seem to go without demonstration that *the most significant* (I do *not* say the *only* significant) aspects of the relations of law and society lie in the field of behavior, and that words take on importance either because and insofar as they are behavior, or because and insofar as they demonstrably reflect or influence other behavior.

. . .

MEANING OF RULES AND RIGHTS UNDER THE BEHAVIOR ANALYSIS

What now, is the place of rules and rights, under such an approach? To attempt their excision from the field of law would be to fly in the face of fact. I should like to begin by distinguishing real "rules" and rights from paper rules and rights. The former are conceived in terms of behavior; they are but other names, convenient shorthand symbols, for the remedies, the actions of the courts. They are descriptive, not prescriptive, except in so far as there may occasionally be implied that courts *ought to* continue in their practices. "Real rules," then, if I had my way with words, would by legal scientists be called the practices of the courts, and not "rules" at all. And statements of "rights" would be statements of likelihood that in a given situation a certain type of court action loomed in the offing. . . . This concept of "real rule" has been gaining favor since it was first put into clarity by Holmes. "Paper rules" are what have been treated, traditionally, as rules of law: the accepted *doctrine* of the time and place—what the books there say "the law" is. The "real rules" and rights—"what the courts will do in a given case, and nothing more pretentious"—are then predictions. They are, I repeat, on the level of isness and not of oughtness. . . .

THE PLACE AND TREATMENT OF PAPER RULES

Are "rules of law" in the accepted sense eliminated in such a course of thought? Somewhat obviously not. . . .

First, as to formulations already present, already existent: the accepted doctrine. There, I repeat, one lifts an eye canny and skeptical as to whether judicial behavior is in fact what the paper rule purports (implicitly) to state. One seeks the real practice on the subject, by study of how the cases do in fact eventuate. One seeks to determine how far the paper rule is real, how far *merely* paper. One seeks an understanding of *actual* judicial behavior, in that comparison of rule with practice; one follows also the use made of the paper rule in argument by judges and by counsel, and the apparent influence of its official presence on decisions. One seeks to determine when it is stated, but ignored; when it is stated and followed; when and why it is *expressly* narrowed or extended or modified, so that a new paper rule is created. One observes the level of *silent* application or modification or escape, in the "interpretation" of the facts of a case, in contrast to that other and quite distinct level of express wrestling with the language of the paper rule. One observes how strongly ingrained is the tradition of requiring a good paper justification, in terms of officially accepted paper rules, before any decision, however appealing on the facts, can be regarded as likely of acceptance. And by the same token, one observes the importance of the official formulae as tools of argument and persuasion; one observes both the stimuli to be derived from, and the imitations set by, their language. Very rapidly, too, one perceives that neither are all official formulae alike in these regards, nor are all courts, nor are all times and circumstances for the same formula in the same court. The *handling* of the official formulae to influence court behavior then comes to appear as an art, capable only to a limited extent of routinization or (to date) of accurate and satisfying description. And the discrepancy, great or small, between the official formula and what actually results, obtains the limelight attention it deserves. . . .

BACKGROUND OF THE BEHAVIOR APPROACH

All this is nothing new in social science. It is of a piece with the work of the modern ethnographer. He substitutes painstaking objective description of practice, for local *report* of what the practice is. . . . It is of a piece with the development of objective method in psychology. It fits into the pragmatic and instrumental developments in logic. . . . The only novel feature is the application to that most conventionalized and fiction-ridden of disciplines, the law. In essence the historical school of jurists from the one side, and Bentham . . . from the other, were approaching the lines of theorizing here put forth. Holmes' mind had travelled most of the road two generations back. What has been done in the last decades that has some touch of novelty, is for theorizers to go beyond theorizing, to move, along such lines as these, into the gathering and interpretation of facts about legal behavior. . . .

LAYMEN'S BEHAVIOR AS A PART OF LAW

[I] should like to glance at a few further implications of the approach. Three of them appear together. . . .

Interactions between official behavior and laymen's behavior, first; and second, the recognition of official behavior of all officials as part of the core of law. Third, and an immediate part of both, the recognition . . . that the word "official" tacitly presupposes, connotes, reaches out to include, all those patterns of action (ordering, initiative) and obedience (including passivity) on the part both of the official and of all laymen affected which *make up* the official's position and authority as such. Something of this sort is the idea underlying "consent of the governed," "ultimate dependence upon public opinion," and the like. . . . In a passing it is well to note that here, too, Max Weber's method of formulation becomes classic: the official exists as such precisely *insofar as* such patterns of action are an essential part of any phenomena we call law. . . .

CONCLUSION

In conclusion, then, may I repeat that I have been concerned not at all with marking a periphery of law. . . . I have argued that the focus of study, the point of reference for all things legal has been shifting, and should now be consciously shifted to the area of contact, of interaction, between official regulatory behavior and the behavior of those affecting or affected by official regulatory behavior; and that the rules and precepts and principles which have hitherto tended to keep the limelight should be displaced, and treated with severe reference to their bearing

upon that area of contact—in order that paper rules may be revealed for what they are, and rules with real behavior correspondences come into due importance. . . .

Included in the field of law under such an approach is everything currently included, and a vast deal more. At the very heart, I suspect, is the behavior of judges. . . . At first hand contact with officials' behavior, from another angle, lies the social set-up where the official's acts impinge directly on it. . . . Part of law, in many aspects, is all of society, and all of man in society. But that is a question of periphery and not of center, of the reach of a specific problem in hand, not of a general discussion. As to the overlapping of the field as thus sketched with that of other social sciences. I should be sorry if no overlapping were observable. The social sciences are not staked out like real estate. Even in law the sanctions for harmless trespass are not heavy.

NOTES AND QUESTIONS

1. Legal realists were a heterodox lot; they differed from as much as they resembled each other. The diversity of their doctrinal positions makes generalizations subject to qualifications and exceptions. There was no single "school" of realism; there was a "movement" consisting of "individual men, working and thinking over law and its place in society" (Llewellyn 1931, p. 1234). The common fighting faith that brought them together was "fidelity to the realities of the judicial process, unclouded by myth or preconception" (Hall 1947, p. 10). Realism means an attempt to represent things as they are. Beyond this common point of departure, there was a divergence of viewpoints. The left wing repudiated the efficacy of legal rules and attended, instead, to extralegal factors as determinants of judicial decisions. The moderates, however, did not totally deny the possibility of norms and rules, but felt that they played only a small and peripheral part in the totality of law.

An attempt to canvass these different approaches to realism within the limits to this chapter is impractical and unnecessary for our purposes. Instead, we have chosen to center attention on the work of one person, which can then serve as a point of orientation from which the entire movement can be surveyed. Karl Llewellyn, whose realism is "distinctly of the middle-of-the-road variety," is often "regarded as the man most representative of the movement as a whole" (Fuller 1934, p. 430). The essay reproduced above represents a more or less comprehensive, though succinct, exposition of his philosophy.

2. Llewellyn begins with a tripartite conception of law (derived from Pound's formulation in *Law and Morals*). The three elements of law that he identifies are legal *rules*, which include substantive rights; *social interests*, which are normative considerations independent of law; and *remedies*, or observable behavior in law. They compose the three levels of analysis in law that are generally used today: the verbal or *doctrinal* level of legal rules which constitute the instrumentalities of law; the *normative* level of social values, or the policy objectives of law; and the *behavioral* level of judicial decisions and public compliance with those decisions. The first two levels concern the "ought" in law; the last pertains to the "is." He subscribed to the positivist thesis of the separation of law and morals.

3.   There are three principal and interrelated features to the realist style of decision-making.

First, the repudiation of the deductive method of formalism. Llewellyn sought to distinguish "paper" or formal rules and "real" rules or the actual bases of decisions. Other realists, such as Frank (1930), treated legal rules even more cavalierly. He explained them as merely legal pegs on which judges hung a decision reached on nonlegal grounds.

Second, an emphasis on behavior, not legal rules, as the essence of law. Realists attended to the decision of the judge and the impact of that decision on people and institutions, not to the legal rules that served as after-the-fact rationalizations for the decision. Theirs was a version of the imperative theory of law. Consequently, they called for social science studies on how legal officials act and how law can be made more responsive to societal needs.

Third, a relativistic approach to social values and ethics. Realists disavowed absolute moral principles, especially those espoused by formalism, and called attention to the creative role of the judge in choosing between value alternatives and shaping the normative direction of the law.

4.   In a section of the essay entitled "The Place and Treatment of Paper Rules," Llewellyn provides a terse but highly illuminating exegesis of the realist style of adjudication. It can also be seen as a nutshell explanation of how to read and analyze a judicial opinion. For the student learning the techniques of case analysis, this section merits thoughtful attention.

At the outset, Llewellyn emphasizes, in reading cases one must seek to ascertain the "real rule" underlying the decision, that is, how a judge actually reached the conclusion, as distinguished from the "paper rule" that merely dresses up and justifies the conclusion in terms of the accepted paper doctrines. Specifically, he enumerates a few common techniques of decision-making. One seeks to determine:

- "when it [the paper rule] is stated but ignored"
- "when it is stated and followed"
- "when and why it is expressly narrowed or extended or modified, so that a new paper rule is created"
- "silent application or modification . . . in the 'interpretation' of the facts of a case, in contrast to . . . express wrestling with the language of the paper rule"

Review the cases presented in the preceding chapters. Which cases illustrate the application of each of the foregoing techniques?

5.   Llewellyn concludes that "the *handling* of the official formulae to influence court behavior then comes to appear as an art, capable only to a limited extent of routinization or (to date) of accurate and satisfying description." The task of the common law lawyer, then, is to learn how to handle or manipulate paper rules for the purpose of reaching a particular result. These paper formulae are the "tools of argument and persuasion," even though they may not be the "real" bases for "how the cases do in fact eventuate." Case analysis is not principally a logical operation (of applying paper rules to facts to arrive at decisions). It is an "art" that cannot be fully verbalized or described. In this sense legal reasoning is not something that can be learned by reading a textbook or listening to a few lectures. If legal reasoning is, as the formalists claimed, solely deductive reasoning from first premises, then it is an analytical skill that can be acquired relatively easily. But, Llewellyn suggests, legal reasoning involves more than logic—it is also a process of making value or policy judgments. This process is an "art" that, for a student, is honed and developed by immersion in the study of one case after another. Gradually and imperceptibly, almost as if by osmosis, the student begins to acquire a "feel" for the "real practice" of the courts and an ability to give "a good paper justification" for the results.

If judicial decision-making is essentially an "art," is the use of social science in adjudication also an "art"—that is, a matter that is "capable only to a limited extent of routinization or (to date) of accurate and satisfying description"?

6.   So skeptical were the realists about the centrality of rules in actually influencing decisions that their movement was also known as rule-skepticism. They pointed out that the notion that rules decide cases has fooled lawyers and judges for nearly one century. The realists, presumably, were not fooled, and they delighted in contrasting the positive law (or the law-in-the-books) with the operative law (or the law-in-action). We shall consider some of the reasons for their rule-skepticism. These reasons shed further insight into the "art" of case analysis.

7.   The staggering number of precedents belie the formalist notion that judges simply apply the appropriate past principle to compel any specific result in a litigated case. As Justice Douglas (1963) noted, "There are usually plenty of precedents to go around; and with the accumulation of decisions, it is no great problem for the lawyer to find legal authority for most propositions" (p. 19).

An important contribution of realism was to make explicit the role of discretion of the judge in choosing which rule or major premise to apply. If there are competing but equally authoritative premises that lead to different conclusions, there is a choice in the case. This choice, according to realists, can be justified only as a question of policy.

If policy considerations provide the basis for choice of paper rules, what criteria guide the selection of competing policies? Is the problem of choice simply pushed back from the doctrinal level to the normative level?

Langdell and his contemporaries did not face this problem of choice. Until about the mid-nineteenth century, lawyers could and sometimes did master *all* the case law in England and America on a given subject. The multiplication of cases began toward the end of the century, when economic expansion on a continental scale brought increased litigation. In the 1870s, a national Reporter System was established that systematically published and cross-referenced all the opinions by the federal courts, the state supreme courts, and the lower state courts. A formalistic, precedent-based case law method depends upon a comfortable number of precedents. However, once the number of printed cases became like the number of grains of sand, the formalist method begins to show signs of strain. One can no longer predict the course of judicial decision-making relying solely on precedents.

8.   Judges not only select and apply precedents—they also interpret them. One technique for evading the implications of prior decisions and to whittle away at their precedential value is to confine them to their own particular facts. For example, in *Brown* v. *Board of Education* (1954) the Court limited *Plessy*'s doctrine to its facts (railway accommodations), saying that it had "no place" in public schools. It did not expressly overrule *Plessy*. On the other hand, a device for capitalizing desired precedents is to interpret past decisions as broadly as possible, relying on the language of the opinion without reference to the facts of the case that called forth the language in the first place. For example, the Court desegregated public parks, restaurants, and buses, in per curiam decisions that relied on *Brown*, without regard to the educational context of that landmark opinion.

What other techniques are commonly used for the interpretation of precedents that are favorable or unfavorable to the adjudicated case?

9.   Another source of skepticism of the efficacy of rules in determining outcomes is the ambiguity of language. By design or inadvertence, words can imply different meanings, so that the same rule could be relied upon as authority by the opposite sides in a given dispute. For example, the order that school desegregation proceed with "all deliberate speed" was interpreted to emphasize either "speed" or "deliberate" by the proponents and opponents of the order, respectively. The language of law often contains "weasel words" or "safety valve concepts," as Judge Frank (1930, p. 30) liked to call them. These words are not self-interpreting; they are used by lawyers and judges who infuse them with particular meaning.

10.   Judge Jerome Frank (1930),* another major realist theoretician, followed a somewhat different approach from Llewellyn in repudiating the formalist method. He wrote:

> The process of judging, so the psychologists tell us, seldom begins with a premise from which a conclusion is subsequently worked out. Judging begins rather the other way around—with a conclusion more or less vaguely formed; a man ordinarily starts with such a conclusion and afterwards tries to find premises which will substantiate it. [p. 100]

---

*Reprinted by permission of the publisher. Copyright ©1930 by the Tudor Publishing Company.

He goes on to describe how decisions are "really" made:

> The judge really decides by feeling and not by judgment, by hunching and not by ratiocination, such ratiocination appearing only in the opinion. The vital motivating impulse for the decision is an intuitive sense of what is right or wrong in the particular case. . . . [pp. 103–4]

But what are the sources of the hunches that create law? Legal rules and precedents play a role, he concedes, but only a minor one. The real sources lie buried in the "political, economic, and moral prejudices" that judges share with their fellow human beings (p. 105).

Thus, one of the "chief uses" of legal rules is "to enable the judges to give formal justifications—rationalizations—of the conclusions at which they otherwise arrive" (p. 130). "But," he stresses, "it is surely mistaken to deem law merely the equivalent of rules and principles." "They may be the formal clothes in which [the judge] dresses up his thoughts. But they do not and cannot completely control his mental operations . . ." (p. 131). "The law, therefore, consists of *decisions*, not of rules. If so, then *whenever a judge decides a case he is making law*" (p. 128).

The realist distinction between judging and rationalizing the judgment finds a parallel in the distinction made in the philosophy of science between discovery and justification. The process of discovery involves the conception or invention of a scientific theory. The process of justification consists of elaborating a line of reasoning to support the new theory. Discovery emphasizes the discoverer; the genesis of insights and ideas may not be susceptible to logical analysis or logical reconstruction. Justification concentrates primarily on the discovery itself; the explication of inarticulate intuition requires the operation of logic. The discovery phase corresponds roughly to the judicial hunches described by the realists. The written opinion then provides an account of the decision to others who demand a reason. In the formalist model, a judge would adjudicate a dispute by considering all the relevant precedents and principles and derive therefrom a logical conclusion. He would not know the conclusion until the entire justificatory process was complete. The teaching of Judge Frank was that judges in the real world do not decide in that manner. Judges commonly decide without first clearly working out all the reasons for the decision. Only a superhuman judge would be able to discover and justify the result at the same time.

11.   If Langdell envisioned law as a "pure science," Llewellyn took "applied social science" as his model. He sought an approach to law that was more result-oriented. "The major tenet of the 'functional approach' which they [the American legal realists] have so vigorously espoused, is that law is instrumental only, a means to an end, and is to be appraised only in the light of the ends it achieves" (McDougal 1941, p. 834). Realism represents a "rediscovery of the utilitarian views of David Hume and Jeremy Bentham" in the late eighteenth century (Fuller and Eisenberg 1972, p. 287; see also Horowitz 1971; Nelson 1974; Summers 1982).

The Social-Intellectual Context of Realism

A number of social-intellectual currents shaped the climate of jurisprudential opinion in the 1930s that nurtured the birth of realism. These included sociological jurisprudence, the rise of psychology, pragmatism, and the New Deal ideology.

Sociological jurisprudence. In his essay, Llewellyn acknowledged his debt to the writings of Holmes and Roscoe Pound. Pound, dean of the Harvard Law School, and Holmes were the foremost critics at the turn of the century of Langdell and his formalist method. Both called upon judges to abandon the procedure of deducing conclusions from predetermined conceptions, and thereby laid the foundations for legal realism. Pound, however, went a step beyond Holmes and developed a jurisprudence based upon social science.

In a series of essays around 1910, Pound announced the emergence of sociological jurisprudence as a distinct legal philosophy and pronounced some of

Holmes's opinions—especially his dissent in *Lochner* v. *New York* (1905)—as among "the best exposition[s]" of this viewpoint (Pound 1909, p. 464). He elaborated an approach to law that emphasized the behavioral consequences of judicial decisions and the achievement of social purposes through law, rather than the formulation of abstract principles. He urged the "scientific apprehension of the relations of law to society and of the needs and interests and opinions of society" (1907, p. 611). "Let us not become legal monks," he pleaded, because jurisprudence cannot be self-sufficient (1910, p. 36). "The entire separation of jurisprudence from the other social sciences . . . was not merely unfortunate for the science of law . . . but was in large part to be charged with the backwardness of law in meeting social ends" (1912, p. 510). He eschewed the illusory certainty of legal rules for fair solutions in specific cases: "[W]ithin wide limits, [the judge] should be free to deal with the individual case, so as to meet the demands of justice" (1912, p. 515). Later, Pound was to describe this approach as "legal social engineering," which was but "a part of the whole process of social control" (1923, p. 958). The technological metaphors that filled his writings reflected the scientific ethos and the rapid technical advances of the time (for example, the development of the automobile, electrical light, telephone, airplane). They also disclosed Pound's own scientific bent—he acquired a Ph.D. in biology before going to law school.

Many of the proposals put forth by the realists—studying the social effects of legal rules; individualized applications of law to reach equitable solutions in particular cases; reliance on the social sciences—were propagated two decades earlier by Pound. Llewellyn (1960) credited Pound with providing "half of the commonplace equipment on and with which our work since has builded" (p. 496). Realism arose, according to its proponents, because Pound failed to deliver what he advocated—his proposals did "not come to fruition" (Llewellyn 1960, p. 7, note 3). Sociological jurisprudence remained "in large part a pious program rather than a record of achievement" (Cohen 1933, p. 1150). Query, of course, whether the same criticism can be made of realism.

Psychology. The prestige of science in the 1920s and 1930s was "colossal," and "of all the sciences it was the youngest and least scientific that most captivated the general public. . . . Psychology was king" (Allen 1959, p. 140). Legal realists, too, were deeply influenced by psychological thinking of the day. "A large literature on legal psychology grew during the twenties, with behaviorism, Freudianism, and abnormal psychology all playing a role" (Purcell 1973, p. 87). The formalist slogan "law is a science" became, under realism, "law is a social science," particularly a psychological science. It is ironic that the realists espoused two schools of psychology that were diametrically opposed in their explanations of the springs of conduct. Behaviorism was positivist, recognizing only observable acts as determined by external stimuli; Freudianism was subjectivist, focusing on the interplay of unconscious drives and conscious restraints. Both were mechanistic conceptions that made no accommodation for purposive action and ratiocination as movers of behavior. The link between these two schools and rule-skepticism was the denial of rationalism—and the realists, of course, were intent on exposing the nonrationality of the law.

Thus, Llewellyn stressed the behavior of judges—what is important is what they do (the real rule), not what they say they do (the paper rule). More radical realists went so far as to view legal institutions as "complex aggregates of many specific group habits" (Moore 1923, p. 613) or to propose revamping the entire legal machinery in light of behavioral psychology because "by controlling the individual's environment you can control his character and predict his future actions" (Beutel 1931, p. 175).

Other realists, opting for psychoanalytic theory, elevated emotional experiences to first causes of judicial conduct. The confessions of several noted federal judges (including Frank, who underwent psychoanalysis to gain self-insight) about how they decide cases capture this theme:

> I . . . give my imagination play, and brooding over the cause, wait for the feeling, the hunch—that intuitive flash of understanding which makes the jump-spark connection between question and decision. [Hutcheson 1929, p. 278]

> When I first became a student . . . I held to the idea that the judge did not create or change, but merely applied [rules]. . . . My dismay when, as a law student, I first realized that law was not an exact science founded on immutable principles, but to a great extent, constitutes premises from which other deductions must be drawn, was as nothing to the dismay I felt as a judge when I first realized that in many cases there were no premises from which any deductions could be drawn with logical certainty. [Lehman, quoted in Frank 1930, pp. 144–45]*

Even Llewellyn, the legal behaviorist, adopted some psychoanalytic ideas. He proposed the "adoption of the theory of rationalization for . . . the study of opinions" (1962, p. 56). In language that would have raised the hair of Langdell, he argued that opinions are the formal clothes in which a judge dresses up his thinking. But rationalization is more than just a means "to make decisions seem legally decent" and to cover up the real bases of decisions. Judges themselves may be unaware of the "true" bases of their conclusions. The opinions serve the further function of expressing the ideals of what the decision should represent. In any event, Llewellyn felt that self-analysis was not a precondition for judging, though Frank (1930) recommended that judges be trained in "the best available methods of psychology" so as to be cognizant of their own motives and biases (p. 147).

This reliance on psychology should be placed in perspective. The realists did not attend primarily to the application of the research methods and data of psychology to law. They accepted instead the curative powers of psychological theory. Psychology did not so much inform legal decisions as it was in some sense part and parcel of the law itself. Indeed, at that time, psychology was not an integrated discipline—it was an "era of 'psychologies'" (Dunlap 1925, p. 309). Otherwise stated, the realists relied on psychology not so much as a science, but as an ideology for their judicial reform. The authoritarianism of precedents and rules which they reproached was replaced by dogmatic generalizations from psychological theories. They espoused not psychology but psychologism in the law (Kennedy 1940). Psychology, as one of the dominant intellectual currents of the period, merely reinforced their a priori belief that judicial decision-making was not deductive reasoning alone.

Pragmatism. The principal philosophical school of the time was pragmatism. Its features—distaste for formal categories, embrace of the scientific method, emphasis on results—folded in well with realism. "Realism," according to Rumble (1968), "is pragmatism in law" (p. 6). Realists, however, were not philosophers, any more than

---

they were psychologists. They were lawyers first and foremost—lawyers who had read what philosophers (and psychologists) had to say and used their ideas for their own legal purposes.

The realists drew comfort and strength from John Dewey's writings. "[T]he trouble [with deductive reasoning]," he said, "is that while the syllogism sets forth the results of thinking, it has nothing to do with the operation of thinking" (1960, p. 118). He went on to add:

> [M]en do not begin thinking with premises. They begin with some complicated and confused case, apparently admitting of alternative modes of treatment and solution. Premises only gradually emerge from analysis of the total situation. The problem is not to draw a conclusion from given premises. . . . The problem is to find statements, of general principles and of particular fact, which are worthy to serve as premises. [p. 122]

Political movements. Jurisprudential ideas are outgrowths of, or are associated with, contemporaneous political ideas. What formalism was to *laissez faire*, sociological jurisprudence was to the progressive movement and realism was to the New Deal (White 1972; Summers 1982, p. 29).

In the early twentieth century, there was increasing recognition of the social costs of unregulated industrial capitalism among politicians and social theorists. The *laissez-faire* policies of the previous decades had resulted in extremes of wealth and poverty, nurtured the growth of trusts and monopolies, discriminated against the working class, and encouraged judges not to intervene in redressing social and economic inequities. The political framework for the critique of *laissez faire* was Progressivism (1890–1920). It rationalized "the Age of Reform" (Hofstadter 1955). Its chief tenet was social progress by experimentation; it believed in the continuing improvement of society by a government of experts responsible to the public. The result was the expansion of regulatory agencies (for example, the creation of the Federal Trade Commission, the Federal Reserve Board) and the enactment of social welfare legislation to relieve the hardships of the poor, the elderly, and the industrial workers. Antiformalism and the rise of sociological jurisprudence were manifestations of this broader ideological movement: social amelioration via the instrumentality of law and of scientific planning. The First World War and the Depression shattered progressivist assumptions of the perfectibility of man and society. But other beliefs—the value of social experimentation, the expansion of government regulation, the importance of problem-solving over theorizing—continued into the New Deal era. The architects of the New Deal were political "realists," and it was no coincidence that many prominent legal realists served in high positions in the Roosevelt Administration.

NOTES AND QUESTIONS

---

1.   Realism enlarged the scope of legally relevant considerations in the judicial process and invested them with respectability. It brought extralegal influences into the open. Llewellyn argued that the focal point of law is the "area of contact between judicial behavior and the behavior of laymen"—that is to say, what we today call legal impact studies. However, its achievements in applying social science to law did not measure up to its pretensions. "At the root of this failure" was "the lack of any definite criterion of importance which will dictate which of the infinite consequences of any legal rule or decision deserve to be investigated" (Cohen 1933, pp. 1150–51). In part, too, the research tools of social science were at the time quite rudimentary.

It was not until the 1960s that systematic studies of legal impact (see Chapter 6) were carried out (for example, Schubert, 1963). Despite its uncompromisingly empiricist flavor, realism failed to initiate the empirical research it advocated. Its enduring legacy is the point of view or sensitivity that it created in the law toward the use of social research.

2. In addition to its contributions to elucidating the judicial process, "the most important immediate consequences of legal realism were in the field of legal education" (Patterson 1962, p. 554). Nonlegal materials, drawn primarily from the social sciences, began to be included in casebooks and courses starting in the late 1920s (Currie 1951). Law schools that were hotbeds of legal realism led the way in appointing social scientists to their faculties. Courses on "psychology and law" (Robinson 1935) and "social psychology of law" (Britt 1940) were offered in law schools. The functional and interdisciplinary perspectives commonly found in law teaching today have their original inspiration in realist jurisprudence.

3. Evaluate rule-skepticism in light of the cases and materials in the preceding chapters and your understanding of the judicial process. Did the realists exaggerate the degree of uncertainty and unpredictability in adjudication based on precedent? That is, did they overestimate the freedom of judicial choice in selecting or interpreting past rules?

4. Llewellyn always insisted that "realism is not a philosophy, but a technology"; "what realism was, and is, is a method, nothing more" (1960, pp. 510, 509). Not only did he deny an interest in formulating a theory of law, he also disclaimed any ethical pretensions: "When the matter of program [of realism] in the normative aspect is raised, the answer is: there is none" (1931, p. 1254). He purported to have been interested only in methodology—on an accurate (realistic) description of the style of judicial reasoning. His reluctance to give theory its due is typical of the antitheoretical streak in American pragmatism.

Do you agree that realism is merely a method and not a normative system? Consider the cleavage between law and morals, between the "is" (real rule) and the "ought" (paper rule): How, according to realism, is the gap between the two to be eliminated? Can conduct be compelled to conform to what ought to be? If not, does the normative element have to surrender to how things are? Does Llewellyn's treatment of this basic discrepancy rest on ethical presuppositions?

5. Holmes (1881) proposed that "the first requirement of a sound body of law is that it should correspond with the actual feelings and demands of the community, whether right or wrong" (p. 41). Llewellyn in the reprinted article emphasized "consent of the governed" and "dependence upon public opinion" as essential to law. These passages suggest a political theory that dovetails with and reinforces the values of majoritarian democracy, namely, to satisfy the interests of the many at the least cost. Does this mean that policy choices of judges should be settled or be strongly influenced by popular vote? Should policy-makers not distinguish between what the citizenry wants to pursue and what it ought to pursue?

6. One result of realism, whether seen as a method or as a normative philosophy, is to challenge the legitimacy of the judicial process. If law is "made" and not "found"—that is, if law is what judges decide it to be, by relatively unconstrained exercise of discretion—then are judges not usurping the function of democratically elected representative bodies? This issue is particularly acute when it arises in the context of judicial review of the constitutionality of legislation. The conventional justification for judicial review is that judges are constrained by constitutional text, legislative history, and judicial precedents. How would you reconcile the unfettered power of unelected judges to fashion law (which may contain the seeds of judicial despotism and authoritarianism) with judicial review in a democratic government?

7. Of the constituent elements of law—policies, rules, facts, decisions, and social impact of decision— as a method of problem-solving, realists were preoccupied mainly with rules and decisions, especially with the distressing gap between real and paper rules.

The other elements were mostly neglected. There was much talk but little empirical action on the social impact of law. It was not until a generation later that social scientists began examining this aspect of law.

Realism (and formalism, too) remained indifferent to the reliability of fact-finding in the courts. This is somewhat ironic, given the relationship between facts and rules. The application or interpretation of a rule depends, in the first instance, on the nature of the facts that call forth the rule. Yet, nobody seemed particularly concerned about the liabilities in the legal methods of fact determinations. Frank (1949) later shifted attention from rule-skepticism to fact-skepticism. Realists, he argued, suffered from "appellate-court-itis." They never examined trial court ways. The chief cause of legal uncertainty derived not from uncertain legal rules of appellate judges, but from unreliable facts found by trial judges and juries. There is no assurance that the determination of fact-finders at trial coincide with the actual sequence of events. Again, it was not until the 1960s that social scientists began to conduct systematically empirical research on what we have called "procedural justice."

Finally, realism also neglected to develop a coherent approach to the analysis of the social interests or values that underlie rules. Llewellyn turned to policy as a basis for choosing between competing rules, but did not elucidate how competing policies are chosen or accommodated. It was left to a later generation of normatively oriented legal philosophers to attempt to confront this question.

8.   Summers (1982) proposes that legal realism coalesced with sociological jurisprudence and philosophical pragmatism to form America's only indigenous theory of law, namely, "pragmatic instrumentalism" (p. 19). It exerted "a colossal influence in America" and it represents "a fourth great tradition in Western legal theory" (pp. 275, 19). The other traditions attend mainly to the internal dimension of law. Positivism focuses on the analysis of concepts basic to any legal system; natural law concentrates on ideals of good and justice realized via law; historical jurisprudence dwells on modes of legal evolution and change. All tend to "neglect the instrumentalist and pragmatic aspects of legal phenomena" (p. 11). Legal realism, though it did not formally set forth a general theory and though it left a lot of unfinished jurisprudential business, is nonetheless the most sustained effort at addressing the external aspect of law: the practical uses of legal doctrine by officials in order to secure desired ends, or the law-in-action.

The Decline of Realism and the Rise of Purposive Jurisprudence

Realism came to the fore during the Depression years. Its skepticism about social and economic truths associated with natural law, and its empirical and result-oriented approach to problem-solving, made it a jurisprudence that harmonized with the experimenting spirit of the New Deal. By the 1940s, however, realism as a formal school of thought came to a "premature standstill" (Summers 1982, p. 281). The rise of the Axis powers challenged the ideals of civilization and justice. If law is simply what judges decide, and one saw what Nazi judges were doing in the name of law, then the realist method could be seen as providing an intellectual basis for authoritarianism. Law becomes simply compulsion by state officials. "Democracy versus the Absolute State means Natural Law versus Realism," cried the critics (Lucey 1942, p. 533; Palmer 1945).

American intellectuals began to disavow moral relativism and to search, once again, for unalterable moral principles. "We have begun to ask ourselves whether . . . there are not some standards of decency so fundamental and so permanent they may properly be described as absolute" (Howe 1951, p. 545). Unlike the natural law theorists of the late nineteenth century, the new, postwar generation of normatively oriented scholars was not concerned with economic values such as the sanctity of private property or with social values such as the desirability of unbridled individualism. They were more concerned with values of the political culture. They sought to identify what made American civilization unique and distinguishable from totali-

REALIST REASONING   675

tarian cultures. They attempted to redeem the ideal of the rule of law and to construct a new conception of the judicial process that could withstand the realist criticisms. The result was the emergence of a jurisprudence aimed at using law as an instrument for attaining the democratic ideals for which this nation stood and for which it had fought on two continents—the ideals of liberty and equality.

Again, the development of legal philosophy was closely intertwined with the restructuring of the curricula of legal education. The war and postwar years saw much ferment and debate in law school circles on how to refashion educational practices to serve contemporary needs and goals. Langdell had criticized the legal training of his day as being unscientific and unintellectual. Then the realists came on the scene and scorned Langdell's method as "blind, inept, factory-ridden, wasteful, defective, and empty" (Llewellyn 1935, p. 653). Now, normatively oriented scholars began to dismiss the realists' "heroic, but random, efforts to integrate 'law' and 'the other social sciences,'" because they were said to have failed to articulate "*how* and *for what purposes*" this integration was sought (Lasswell and McDougal 1943, p. 204).

The function of law and of law schools in a democratic society was the overriding theme in the 1940s and early 1950s (Clark 1942; Gellhorn 1942). Harold Lasswell, a political scientist, and Myres McDougal, a lawyer, both on the Yale Law School faculty, stated this theme as follows:

> [I]f legal education in the contemporary world is adequately to serve the needs of a free and productive commonwealth, it must be conscious, efficient, and systematic training for policy making. The proper function of our law school is, in short, to contribute to the training of policy-makers for the ever more complete achievement of the democratic values that constitute the professed ends of American policy. [1943, p. 206]

To implement this philosophy, they proposed that training in law schools include skills of thought useful in policy-making such as "goal-thinking" (the clarification of basic democratic values), "trend-thinking," and "scientific-thinking," in addition to the conventional education in "legal technicality" (logical deduction) (p. 216).

It was in this jurisprudential climate that milestone opinions dedicated to the ideal of egalitarianism in American society were delivered by the Warren Court: equality for racial minorities in education (*Brown* v. *Board of Education*, 1954) and in public life (the per curiam desegregation decisions); equality for the politically powerless (*Baker* v. *Carr*, 1962: one-person, one-vote reapportionment); equality for indigent criminal defendants (*Gideon* v. *Wainwright*, 1963: right to appointed counsel). Many of the social-legal movements of the 1950s and 1960s—civil rights, consumerism, environmentalism, women's rights—had their intellectual underpinning in the view of law-as-policy. Each of them was "the result of law in the service of a politically predetermined cause" (Dauer 1980–81, p. 19). Faced with an unresponsive majoritarian political process, disadvantaged minority groups turned to the judicial process to seek social reform. And with the forging of the link between social science and jurisprudence, the Supreme Court increasingly turned to social science evidence to justify its decisions. Thus, jurisprudential styles of decision-making are associated with important practical consequences.

It has been said that today "a good many lawyers have adopted a point of view midway between traditional legal formalism and rule-skepticism" (Rumble 1968, p. 54). However, there was not initially and there is not now a single midway point of view. There is a more or less identifiable movement consisting of different individuals examining the normative purposes of law in society. Although there is no one "school" of purposive jurisprudence as such, there are certain common tenets that distinguish it from the received traditions of formalism and realism. These tenets and their variations are described in the following article by White.

12.5.   PURPOSIVE REASONING

THE EVOLUTION OF REASONED ELABORATION: JURISPRUDENTIAL CRITICISM AND SOCIAL CHANGE

G. Edward White

. . .

FROM REALISM TO REASONED ELABORATION

. . .

In attempting to modify Realism to respond to [the criticisms directed toward it], postwar legal scholars came upon what they regarded as a significant insight. Although the Realists had observed that judges "made" law rather than merely "found" it, they had failed sufficiently to explore the implications of that observation. In their rush to show that judges were human beings, motivated in their decisions more by their own values than by legal "rules," the Realists had unduly minimized the place of institutional constraints in judicial decision-making. For to speak, as some Realists had, of institutional "personalities" meant not only that the decisions of governing bodies were affected by their personnel; it meant that the decision-makers were in turn affected by their institutional roles. And this insight generally true of officeholders, applied most particularly to judges, who were required to make public the justifications for their de-

cisions, thus inviting comment on their performance.

In emphasizing the disingenuous aspects of the use of precedent, rule, and doctrine, the Realists had made too simplistic an appraisal of the function of the rationalization process in judicial opinions. They had failed to grant due respect to the fact that a judge's use of these devices was itself constrained by the expectations of others. A new set of questions about judicial decision-making emerged, revolving around the reasoning of opinions. Had the courts adequately articulated reasons for its result? What assumptions lay behind the reasoning process? To what extent did the judge appeal to technical considerations, social policies philosophical principles, and moral values? . . .

THE TENETS OF REASONED ELABORATION

As legal scholars of the 1950's grew increasingly convinced of the importance of judicial rationalization, they came to criticize its contemporary manifestations and to formulate a new set of ideals and standards for judicial decision-making. Reasoned Elaboration, a catch phrase coined by Henry Hart and Albert Sacks in 1958,[25] came to summarize those ideals and standards. The phrase, as applied to

[25] Hart and Sacks felt that "[t]he gradual spread of the obligation of reasoned decision and elaboration" was "one of the major phenomena of contemporary law." H. Hart & A. Sacks, [*The Legal Process: Basic Problems in the Making and Application of Law* (tent. ed. 1958), at 170. Ed.'s note].

the Supreme Court, demanded, first, that judges give reasons for their decisions; second, that the reasons be set forth in a detailed and coherent manner; third, that they exemplify what Hart called "the maturing of collective thought";[26] and fourth, that the Court adequately demonstrate that its decisions, in the area of constitutional law, were vehicles for the expression of the ultimate social preferences of contemporary society.

Beginning in 1951, the *Harvard Law Review* initiated the practice of inviting legal scholars to write Forewords to its analysis of the Supreme Court's work for the preceding term. These Forewords came to serve as the major forum of Reasoned Elaborationist jurisprudence in the 1950's. Building on the observations and assumptions of their predecessors, the authors of successive Forewords gradually expanded and sharpened the focus of their critique until it came to encompass each of the above demands. . . .

In an article in the *Harvard Law Review* in 1957, Alexander Bickel and Harry Wellington implored the court not only to give reasons, but to set forth their reasoning process fully. Bickel and Wellington argued that the Court's opinions had shown an increasing incidence of "the sweeping dogmatic statement, of the formulation of results accompanied by little or no effort to support them in reason, in sum, of opinions that do not opine and of per curiam orders that quite frankly fail to build the bridge between the authorities they cite and the results they decree."[29] A decision that did not attempt to gain reasoned acceptance for the result, asserted the authors, did not make law "in the sense

which the term 'law' must have in a democratic society." A necessary prerequisite of opinion-writing, in their view, was rationally articulated grounds of decision.

Henry Hart, in his Foreword to the 1958 term, set forth the third criterion of Reasoned Elaboration, making a marked departure from Realism by assuming that, given adequate time and discussion, the thinking of judges about particular cases, perhaps initially a product of their idiosyncratic presuppositions, could mature into something more synonymous with "reason," a suprapersonal construct. This view freed the judiciary from the Realist prison of inevitable human bias. It assumed that for every judicial problem there was ultimately a "reasonable" solution—reasonable in terms of the value preference of American society at a particular point in time. This solution could be reached, despite human frailties, if judges would take the time and effort to discuss openly their views of cases, compare them with the views of their colleagues, and articulate as fully as possible the general areas of ultimate concordance. . . .

This dimension of the reasoning process proved attractive but elusive for scholars as Reasoned Elaboration matured. A case in point was Herbert Wechsler's 1959 Holmes Lectures, where he proposed that constitutional issues be decided in accordance with "neutral principles."[39] Wechsler begain by assuming that courts, especially in constitutional law cases, faced issues that involved choice among competing values or needs. Neutrality for Wechsler did not mean that judges should refrain altogether from taking positions on social issues: they were, in fact, fated to condemn or condone the activities of the other branches of government. He did, however, imply that judges

---

[26] Hart, *The Supreme Court, 1958 Term—Foreword: The Time Chart of the Justices*, 73 Harv. L. Rev. 84, 100 (1959).

[29] Bickel & Wellington, *Legislative Purpose and the Judicial Process: The Lincoln Mills Case*, 71 Harv. L. Rev. 1, 3 (1957).

[39] Wechsler, *Toward Neutral Principles of Constitutional Law*, 73 Harv. L. Rev. 1 (1959). . . .

were required to support their choices by a "type of reasoned explanation," which involved reaching judgment on analysis and reasons transcending the immediate result. Only decision-making that rested "on grounds of adequate neutrality and generality" was for Wechsler "genuinely principled." The critical point of the decision-making process, for Wechsler, came when a judge sought to relate the case before him to myriad past and future cases presenting potentially similar issues. Generalizing a result in such a manner meant invoking principles of law covering a variety of fact situations. But it meant more than that, because the legal principles themselves represented a society's value choices with regard to the regulation of social conduct. Inevitably, therefore, a judge, in resting his decision on any more than an ad hoc basis, was making a statement about the social values of his age.

In the area of constitutional law, particularly, the close connection between general principles of law and social values could be seen. As a judge reached beyond the facts of the case for a broader rationale on which to decide it, there would come a moment, Wechsler felt, when he should be aware that the case ultimately presented a "conflict in human claims of high dimension"—the conflict in *Brown v. Board of Education,* for example, between equality regardless of color and freedom of association. A "principled" decision, for Wechsler, would be one where this ultimate conflict was perceived, articulated, and resolved in a manner that gave guidance for the subsequent resolution of similar conflicts. Unprincipled decisions, by contrast, were those where this level of the adjudication process was not perceived or not articulated. Neutrality in this context meant that judges should subordinate their personal predelictions to the competing values cases presented.

With the advent of Wechsler's thesis Reasoned Elaboration reached its maturity. Its standards for judicial competence, if followed, met the overriding needs of postwar American jurists, for they presupposed a judiciary involved with the management of a complex contemporary society, mindful of the need to meet high standards of clarity and competence in its rationalization process, and dedicated to the articulation and maintenance of the general moral principles that bound Americans together. In the world of the Reasoned Elaborationists judges neither found law in the old-fashioned sense nor made it in the sense of the Realists; they reasoned toward it and then articulated their reasoning processes.

At its maturity, Reasoned Elaboration appears to have embraced certain policy goals. . . . [I]t favored institutional conservatism in the judiciary. Since principled decision-making required a full understanding of the competing social values at stake in a case, judicial intervention was premature where those values were dimly perceived or articulated.[46] In the context of the 1950's, institutional conservatism was the equivalent of political conservatism, for in emerging areas of social conflict, such as race relations, the executive and legislative branches of government had largely remained indifferent to change.

EMERGING SOCIAL PHENOMENA

It is possible to identify at least three characteristics of American society in the 1970's that have immediate relevance to discussions of the proper function of the Supreme Court. The first is the emergence of new, fragmented, vocal "minorities" who lack power and status, who perceive

---

[46] Wechsler, for example, concluded that a number of Vinson and Warren Court race relations decisions, including . . . most conspicuously, Brown v. Board of Educ., 347 U.S. 483 (1954), could not be justified on grounds that could be deemed "neutral principles."

discrimination directed at them on a variety of grounds, and who are anxious to air their grievances publicly and impatient to have those grievances resolved. Unlike the minorities whose concerns received national attention in the 1960's, these groups are not primarily racial or ethnic in composition. Racial and ethnic groups continue to articulate their concerns, but many of the techniques that they pioneered are now being adopted by groups who perceive their disadvantaged position to rest on economic considerations (consumers or environmental organizations), sexual attitudes (women and homosexuals), or a combination or moral assumptions and bureacratic imperatives (prisoners). . . .

A second feature of contemporary life in the United States revolves around the relationship of American citizens to the different branches of their government. There is an acknowledged gap between the goals of officeholders and those of their constituents, as well as a widespread judgment that those same officeholders are furthering their own goals while merely paying lipservice to their constituents' needs. . . .

A final and possibly the most significant aspect of American culture in the 1970's is the disintegration of common values or goals. In the place of consensual values around which members of American society can cohere stand sets of polar alternatives—permissiveness and regimentation, militancy and fatalism, cynicism and fantasy.

The interaction of these features of contemporary American society suggests a serious problem. A combination of the continuing emergence of new minorities, the loss of confidence in the notion of public service on which officeholders base their authority, and the residue of expectations engendered by the Warren Court appears to make vital the continued presence of the Supreme Court as a guarantor of the credibility and stature of the governmental process. The Court gave dignity to the grievances of racial and ethnic minority groups in the 1960's by grappling with their complaints, thereby giving them recognition and easing their eventual entry to the political arena; it now comes to consider a similar function with respect to the newly emerging minorities of the seventies. But how can the Court perform this function in the face of a disintegration of consensual values? How can it meet the "felt necessities of the times" if Americans cannot agree on what these necessities are? . . .

THE DIALECTIC OF ADJUDICATION

In interpreting constitutional language, the Court should not merely search for the collective wisdom of the nation. That search would be fruitless at a time marked by the absence of collective values. Rather, the Court must attempt to assist in the creation of that wisdom by calling to mind the existence or non-existence of a relationship between the asserted rights of current minorities and constitutional principles. That is precisely what the Warren Court did in *Brown,* suggesting that the quest on the part of black school children for access to public schools of their choice embodied values of fairness and equality that were endemic to American society. It urged the affirmation of those values in the context of public education, despite the inconveniences and anxieties that such an affirmation caused and despite the preference of many Americans not to give the value a high priority in the educational context.

Once the Supreme Court has attempted to influence the public in this fashion, a majority of the public has several options in response. It may applaud the decision and comply with it; it may protest the decision or its implementation in varying degrees, but stop short of taking affirmative legal action to repeal it; it may take affirmative action through its legislative representatives, thereby inviting the Court to scrutinize the action's constitutionality; or, it may take affirmative action in the form of a constitutional amendment. . . .

The Court's initial decision that asserted minority rights deserve the status of constitutional protection, then, is an *authoritative* one but one that has not yet been legitimated. It is authoritative because it rests on the generally acknowledged status of the Court as a viable and respectable governmental institution, but it is not legitimated because the Court's attempt to influence popular opinion has not yet met with a response. The process of influence and response is a *dialectical* one. The Court makes an initial judgment that some minority claims rise to the level of constitutionally protected rights, and other do not. The public responds to that judgment. The court may take note of the public's response. At some point in time, the initial judgment is legitimated or revised.

The source of legitimacy, in this formulation, is not merely the consensual values of American society at a point in time, nor is it simply majoritarian sentiment. The source is rather the dialectical process itself—the interaction of the Court's authority with the needs of its constituents. . . .

Legitimacy comes, then, when the dialectical process reveals that the Court is generally perceived as having made a "right" decision, not necessarily one that is popular in an ephemeral, immediate sense, but one that embodies values—equality and liberty conspicuous among them—that have over time emerged as endemic to American civilization, at least as it is currently perceived. "Rightness," like the dialectical process itself, is ultimately a function of history.

A NEW LOOK AT REASONED ELABORATION

. . .

If the Reasoned Elaborationist ideal of judicial performance is at least partially obsolete, what alternative jurisprudential standards shall the Court follow? The emergent social forces previously described and their jurisprudential implications seem congenial with certain guidelines for decision-making. The pressure to resolve minority grievances and the assumed absence of any consensus as to how they should be resolved suggest, for example, that the Court will have to make a number of intuitive judgments.

The discovery of intuition in the judicial process caused great excitement among the Realists, but this element has always been part of judging: it is a necessary technique of a profession charged with the responsibility of making "fair" and "just" decisions on the basis of less than complete information. The dangerous aspect of judicial intuition in the American system of government, of course, is that it can result in the tentative imposition of the subjective biases of a small group of persons on the public at large. But there is a traditional means of protecting the public from judicial fiat: the requirement, underscored by the Reasoned Elaborationists, that judges give reasons for their results, and the consequent disqualification of certain types of reasons as nothing more than illegitimate statements of personal prejudice.

The requirement of reasoning and the distinction between legitimate and illegitimate reasons can harmonize with a dialectical theory of constitutional adjudication. In articulating the basis for his intuitive judgment, a Justice should reach for arguments which make use of reasons that apply to deeply embedded cultural values and thereby transcend his own biases.

That process of reaching was associated by Reasoned Elaboration with the concept of neutral principles. But, unlike that solution, under this formulation the Court does not wait until it perceives that a social consensus exists with regard to a particular issue; Justices decide cases intuitively and then search to justify their intuitions by making arguments directed at a wide audience. The effectiveness of their arguments ultimately turns on the extent to which they can demonstrate that a given result furthers values which American society has traditionally considered of high importance, and is in that sense "right" and "just." Over time, the rightness of a result may be called into question; just as the Constitution is capable of changing interpretations, the collective insights of Justices are capable of being repudiated. But the possibility of repudiation should not deter the Court from deciding difficult cases in emerging areas of social controversy. . . .

NOTES AND QUESTIONS

1.   If formalism was a "logical science" and realism an "empirical science," then reasoned elaboration is a "normative science." It involves the conscious pursuit of explicitly defined social ends and an exegesis of the means for attaining these ends through the instrumentality of the courts. This pursuit is done on qualitative (principled, reasoned) rather than quantitative (instrumentalist, utilitarian) grounds. Although reasoned elaboration, as a species of purposive jurisprudence, developed in the context of Supreme Court decision-making, its methodology is also applicable to value choices faced by lower appellate courts in matters of nonconstitutional stature.

In this normative approach, it is not enough for law to be logically consistent, nor is it enough for it to be whatever a judge pronounces law to be. Law also has to be morally right, to be directed toward some social good. Normative analysis consists of developing arguments that are ethically persuasive and analytically reasoned and of marshaling evidence (legal and/or extralegal) to support them. In other words, law emerges from forensic argument. This perspective emerged, as White notes, in the postwar years as scholars sought to construct a new conception of the judicial process that would address the realist criticisms.

2.   An insistent critic of realism was Fuller (1964). He rejected the separation of law and morals which was espoused by legal positivists (and within which group he located the realists). He argued that law had an "inner morality" of its own that was a morality of process. He viewed law as a set of processes (for example, of adjudication, legislation, mediation) designed to order social relationships according to societal purposes. The adjudicative process consists of resolving disputes by the application of proofs and reasoned arguments. These arguments are made in terms of moral principles which are rooted in the shared purposes of the community. If disputants lacked consensual values, adjudication would fail for want of the necessary sources of principles for decision-making. The limits of adjudication would also be reached if disputes dealt with such widely ramified social issues that decisions could not be derived from arguments based on principles. Such disputes are best settled by means other than judicial adjudication. Thus, the distinguishing mark of law is procedural morality. Public compliance with law ultimately rests on how a decision is formulated, not on what the decision says. There is "morality that makes law possible" when there are no ad hoc decisions, when there is consistency and reasonableness in the way decisions are rendered (p. 39).

Fuller's ideas were presented in a different form by Hart and Sacks in *The Legal Process* (see footnote 25 in White's article), a collection of teaching materials that has remained unfinished and unpublished. Nonetheless, since 1958, it has been widely used in law schools in mimeographed form. Hart and Sacks presented a process jurisprudence. Like Fuller, they viewed adjudication as a process of rational explication of shared moral principles. This means that the test of a decision lies not so much in its outcomes as in the quality of the normative arguments used to justify it. The process approach successfully responded to the realist criticism that decisions are often arbitrary or partisan; it "redeemed the ideal of the rule of law by sponsoring an explicitly policy-guided style of argument capable of preserving reliability and neutrality . . ." (Vetter 1983, pp. 416–17).

3.   Formalists were preoccupied with discovering absolute substantive law—that is, principles of law that transcend the cases in which they arise and the judges who decide them. Process-oriented scholars (or reasoned elaborationists) are formalists, too, to the extent that they are searching for absolute procedural law, that is, "neutral principles" for decision-making which are independent of the subject matter for decision and of the personal values of the decision-maker. Consequently, these scholars were troubled by the reasoning of the landmark decisions of the Warren Court. In the postwar years, the decisions striking down racial segregation, expanding the rights of the criminally accused, reapportioning state legislatures, and banning prayer in public schools caused political controversy and rekindled debate on the role of the judiciary in American government.

According to process jurisprudence, judicial review is justifiable only if conducted by reasoned application of impersonal principles. Its advocates faulted the Court for not adhering to these standards. Thus, Wechsler (1959) could find no neutral principles to justify the school segregation cases. A court cannot function as "a naked power organ," he charged. It is "obliged to be entirely principled." A principled decision is "one that rests on reasons with respect to all the issues in the case, reasons that in their generality and their neutrality transcend any immediate result that is involved" (p. 27). Bickel (1970) acknowledged that the Court, in these decisions, "may for a time have been an institution seized of a great vision, that it may have glimpsed the future, and gained it" (p. 100). However, he was disenchanted with the alleged failure of the Court to produce reasoned justifications for these results. The opinions revealed "subjectivity of judgment," " analytical laxness," and "intellectual incoherence" (p. 45). The justices "relied on events for vindication more than on the method of reason for contemporary vindication" (p. 12). Like Fuller, he doubted that adjudication was the proper method of dealing with large-scale social problems. Problems of "great magnitude and pervasive ramifications, problems with complex roots and unpredictably multiplying offshoots," are not easily susceptible to resolution by rational derivation from principles implicit in consensual values (p. 175).

4.   Does the neutrality that process-oriented scholars speak of refer to the value-free thought processes of the decision-making? Are they urging that judges put aside their own values and attitudes in order to render decisions dispassionately? This conception of neutrality would seem to flow naturally from the judges' sworn oath of impartiality.

In the physical and social sciences, the role of human agency in the decision process is recognized:

> In our choice of areas for research, in our selection of data, in our method of investigation, in our organization of materials, not to speak of the formulation of our hypotheses and conclusions, there is always manifest some more or less clear, explicit or implicit assumption or scheme of evaluation. [Wirth 1936, p. xx]

> A "disinterested social science" is . . . pure nonsense. It never existed and it will never exist. We can strive to make our thinking rational in spite of this, but only by facing the valuations, not by evading them. [Myrdal, in Miller and Howell 1960, p. 669]

> The ideal of a knowledge embodied in strictly impersonal statements now appears self-contradictory, meaningless. . . . We must learn to accept as our ideal a knowledge that is manifestly personal. [Polanyi 1958, p. 27]

Is the process of legal decision-making so unique, so different from other forms of human thought and choice, that judicial neutrality can be attained?

5.   Or does the idea of neutrality refer to the intellectual concepts and tools of decision-making rather than to the mind set of the decision-maker himself? If reasoned elaborationists mean that the principles themselves must be impartial (that is, the principles cannot favor either side), the idea is obvious because it is inherent in the definition of a principle. But choices are made by people, not by ethereal "principles" floating in some ethical vacuum. Are neutral principles a kind of reification?

6.   In what other respects does reasoned elaboration appear to be a reincarnation of formalist decision-making?

7.   The main teaching of realism was that law consisted of what judges *did,* and what they did was to choose between competing rules of law and to create new laws. What realism failed to answer satisfactorily was *how* judges exercised their discretionary judgment and yet not indulge in arbitrary, idiosyncratic, or authoritarian decisions. To say, as Judge Frank (1930) did, that decisions are based on feelings and hunches and no more is to substitute the rule of the judge for the rule of law. When value choices of broad social significance are at stake—for example, crime control versus individual liberty; freedom of the press versus fair trial; equal rights versus private property rights; business expansion versus social welfare—surely more than emotional hunches animate the decision-making process.

These value choices are, at bottom, political issues. In our system of government, some of the most vexing policy problems are often converted into the form and language of a lawsuit. Although a case appears before a court in the guise of a private dispute, it is a contrived vehicle for framing a policy choice for authoritative judgment by decision-makers who, in theory, are above the whims and passions of the electorate.

This is precisely what troubled reasoned elaborationists. They worried about the political ramifications of the nonrepresentative branch of government deciding what are essentially questions of political choice. This is the problem of legitimacy in constitutional adjudication. (Issues of legitimacy also arise, of course, in common law adjudication when judges exercise quasi-legislative discretion in making policy choices in cases not governed by determinate precedents.) A justification for the making of these choices by appointed judges in a democratic society rests on the requirement of written opinions. The judiciary is the only branch of government that must give reasons for its decisions. This is what legitimizes and distinguishes the judicial function from the legislative role. By having judges lay bare for public scrutiny the whys and wherefores of their decision-making, an institutional check is built into the judicial process. The requirement that judges (but not legislators) be subject to a discipline of reasoning acts as a constraint on the exercise of judicial power. The elaborate reasons or rationalizations articulated in the opinion provide the basis for public reaction to the decision as legitimate or not. These reasons, as White indicates, constitute a "suprapersonal construct"; they transcend private preferences. The opinion explains how the present decision was arrived at, places it in relation to past decisions on similar questions, and looks into the future in terms of its effect in furthering societal ideals.

At this point, disagreement arises among normatively oriented scholars as to the nature of these reasons. The "formalist" wing of reasoned elaboration sought to anchor the rationalization on neutral principles. This approach, premised upon a postwar optimism in American institutions and a faith in the consensual character of American political culture, is cautious about large-scale social reforms engineered by the courts. The "realist" wing, however, as represented by White, makes no pretense at value neutrality and proposes instead that ethical considerations be expressly and coherently stated. This perspective was forged by the experience of social conflicts during the 1960s. At a time when most institutions of American government were widely perceived as unresponsive or even oppressive, the Supreme Court was the least damaged. "This was due to just those decisions that were faulted as inadequately justified; the decisions more or less matched the moral judgments of those who advocated large-scale change" (Vetter 1983, p. 420). A younger generation of normatively oriented scholars proceeded to develop a model of adjudication that would justify judicial intervention in social problems and, in particular, the actions of the Warren Court.

Both wings of reasoned elaboration must be seen as a response to the question of the soundness of judicial supremacy—that in reviewing the validity of legislation, courts improperly act as a third legislative chamber, thereby negating the will of the representatives of the people. Whether it rests on disinterested criteria or on an explication of the values at stake, the requirement that judges give reasons forecloses or minimizes the risk of ad hoc judgments that merely express transient or personal feelings of what is right.

8.   Consider some of the ways in which competing values are chosen or accommodated in adjudication.

(a) One way is for the decision to articulate the consensual values of society (for example, *Plessy* v. *Ferguson* and *Lochner* v. *New York;* see Chapter 3). The difficult question, as White points out, is, "[H]ow can the Court perform this [value decision] function in the face of a disintegration of consensual values?" Or, as Justice Tatting put it in the spelunkers' case, "[W]hat are we to do when [law] has many purposes or when its purposes are disputed?"

(b) In the absence—and without awaiting for the emergence—of social consensus, White suggests that courts create social values (not just legal rules) via "judicial intuition." What cases in the preceding chapters could be said to exemplify the intuiting of a new normative order? Are you convinced that reasoned elaboration provides a sufficient safeguard against the imposition of biases of unelected officials upon society at large?

(c) White talks about a dialectical relationship between judicial decisions and their impact upon the public. In other words, another basis of decision-making is impact-thinking. To think teleologically is to think in terms of anticipated results. Justice Cardozo (1924) noted that "some of the errors of courts have their origin in imperfect knowledge of the economic and social consequences of a decision, or of the economic and social needs to which a decision will respond" (pp. 116–17). A jurisprudence of purposes is intertwined with a jurisprudence of consequences. One convergence point of jurisprudence and social science, then, is research on the effect of law on life (see Chapter 6).

(d) Sometimes judges do not choose between competing values or policies: instead, they try to accommodate these values or compromise between them. They seek a Solomonic, split-the-baby solution. Give examples of decisions illustrating this approach.

(e) At other times, judges opt to not decide or to postpone the decision by asserting that the issue presented is not yet "ripe" for adjudication or that the party who raises it lacks "standing" to do so. These procedural devices, which Bickel (1962) called "passive virtues," enable a court to circumvent the dilemma of choosing between principle and expediency: either yielding to expediency by constitutionally validating a politically necessary compromise or rigidly insisting on principle and thereby provoking political conflict. The per curiam decision (for example, *Furman* v. *Georgia*, in Chapter 5, section 5.4) also represents a temporizing measure: There is a summary decision that disposes of the case but provides no coherent rationale for how the broader issue ought to be decided in the future.

(f) Articulating shared values, intuiting new values, assessing the impact of value choices, compromising between competing values, avoiding or postponing value choices—these are some of the means of normative analysis. What are other means, or combinations of means, of deciding disputed value questions?

Other Postrealist Models of Adjudication

The age-old dilemma between equity and law in adjudication has been manifested in recent years in a debate between H. L. A. Hart, a modern analytical positivist, and Ronald Dworkin, a rejuvenated natural law theorist. A brief and necessarily oversimplified exposition of this debate can help pull together and place in contemporary jurisprudential perspective the classical ideas discussed in this chapter. An appreciation of their contrasting theories of judicial decision-making can also shed light on the correlative debate between proponents and opponents of the use of social science in constitutional adjudication (see Chapter 13, section 13.2).

Since midcentury, the writings of Hart have permanently and beneficiently transformed legal philosophy. In *The Concept of Law* (1961), a landmark contribution to analytical jurisprudence, he defends the separability thesis and identifies those features that distinguish the legal system from other social and moral institutions. In the course of developing a theory of law as authoritative rules, validated by the manner in which they come into being, he also articulates a model of decision-making. This model (which is *via media* between formalism and realism) and Dworkin's countermodel (which combines tenets of formalism and purposivism) are the subject of our focus.

HART'S POSITIVIST MODEL

Legal rules have the quality of "open texture"; they possess both "a core of certainty and a penumbra of doubt" when particular facts are brought within their scope (Hart 1961, pp. 120, 119). When the settled law is determinate, a judge is able to justify his decision as a deduction from precedential rules. To the extent that much of the business of adjudication consists of straightforward application of unambiguous rules, formalism is true and realism is false.

However, when there is indeterminacy as to the applicability of existing rules to a given set of facts, a judge exercises discretion to make "a choice between open alternatives" and thus engages in "creative or legislative activity" (pp. 124, 131). This discretion "often involves a choice between moral values," but "it is folly to believe that where the meaning of the law is in doubt, morality always has a clear answer to offer" (p. 200). Once created and sustained by practice, the new rule exists independently of the moral (or any other) ground invoked by the judge. In these penumbral cases, realism is correct in teaching that judges should and do go beyond the boundaries of the positive law and that their quasi-legislative actions are binding law. Hart, then, seeks to preserve the partial truth of each of the two traditional approaches to adjudication.

DWORKIN'S NATURAL LAW MODEL

Dworkin, an American who succeeded Hart as holder of the chair of jurisprudence at Oxford, has challenged Hart's theory of adjudication. In a series of articles (1963, 1967, 1975, 1977, 1981, 1982) he develops a neo-natural law view—one that fuses "classical Natural Law theory and positivism," according to Hart (1976, p. 546)—that judges are never free to exercise discretion, even when no legal rule dictates a clear result. Every developed legal system is rich enough (a "seemless web," 1975, pp. 1093–96) to provide a single, correct answer to every legal issue. If there is no discretion to choose, there is one uniquely right answer to be discovered in the legal principles, political ideas, and moral standards that lie behind indeterminate legal rules. Even in the penumbra of law, judges should not and do not create law but merely "enforce existing political rights" (1975, p. 1063). To do so, judges should and do decide cases based on "principle" and not "policy."

Adjudicatory principles and legislative policies. Dworkin's theory of decision-making rests upon a sharp demarcation between judicial and legislative functions in a democratic society. He is troubled by the unfairness of retroactive adjudication when judges create new law and impose obligations ex post facto on the losing party. He is also concerned about the distinctively American problem of the legitimacy of judicial supremacy in the constitutional system: the incoherence of placing final determination of the validity of statutes on judges who are not popularly elected or responsible.

This demarcation is made by distinguishing between policies and principles. The former involve collective goals of the community and are weighed in a utilitarian calculus. It may be desirable under a policy to offer less benefit to an individual if the result is greater benefit to the community as a whole. The latter involve individual or group rights. By definition, rights bestow entitlements on individuals; they possess threshold weight and are less amenable to balancing.

Dworkin proposes that judges should and do rely on "arguments of principle" to justify decisions which secure or respect rights and not on "arguments of policy" that advance the general social welfare (1975, p. 1059). Judges are confined to deciding the rights that people are entitled to as a matter of distributive justice. They are not to evaluate the costs/benefits and social impact of decisions, because to do so is to tread on forbidden ground reserved for elected government officials. In short, judges are to decide what the law is, not what it ought to be. If, as he postulates, law is a gapless system of rights that people are entitled to, then in every case there is a uniquely correct solution that merely awaits discovery by the judge. Judges have no discretion to create law because every decision is foreordained by pre-existing rights. When law appears uncertain, it is only because of limited human powers of discernment, not because law has a truly "open texture."

Under this theory, the losing party in a case cannot be heard to complain of unfair surprise. The winning party had a predetermined right to win, which is "a generic political right" (1975, p. 1066). As one of Dworkin's colleagues puts it, "[A] litigant before a court of law is not in the position of one begging a favor from a potential benefactor, but rather in that of one demanding a particular decision as a matter of right, as something to which the law entitles him" (Sartorious 1971, p. 153). By finding and applying the one and only correct result, judges are thereby shielded from charges of undemocratic lawmaking. Hence, the title of Dworkin's book, *Taking Rights Seriously* (1977), captures this (pre-existing) "rights thesis."

Rules and principles in hard cases. Not since William Blackstone and the heyday of formalism has a jurisprudential scholar preached so insistently that judges merely discover law. A crucial issue, of course, is how the law—the pre-existing rights—are identified. To this end, Dworkin distinguishes between legal rules and principles. Rules command a specific decision; they are either applicable or not to a given case. If the facts stipulated by a rule exist, that rule provides a definitive solution. When two rules conflict, one supersedes the other only if another rule specifies precedence. Principles do not dictate a result. They state a general justification but are equally binding as rules. Principles are "requirement[s] of justice or fairness or some other dimension of morality" (1967, p. 31). They often appear as legal maxims and adages (for example, due process, human dignity, no man may profit from his own wrong); they are the higher law behind specific legal rules. Rules that violate these principles are immoral rules and hence are not (valid) law.

In an "easy case" at the core of law, where the relevant rules are determinate, a judge simply deduces the result from the established precedents. There is no need to inquire into the content of the rules or their underlying principles. In this type of a case, Dworkin's model is undistinguishable from that of Hart. In the "hard case" at the penumbra of law (whether statutory, constitutional, or common law), where extant rules are ambiguous and their language and purpose are equivocal guides to action, a judge must turn to principles. For Dworkin, they are the ultimate standards of decisional justification. Hart, however, dichotomized the adjudication process and neglected to cover the rich middle ground found between rule deduction (emphasized by formalists) and untrammeled discretion (emphasized by some realists)—he did not give adequate attention to the principles in which rules are claimed to be explicitly or implicitly embedded.

As an example of "hard case" adjudication, Dworkin cites *Riggs* v. *Palmer* (1889). The court held that a murderer could not inherit under his victim's valid will despite an inheritance statute that did not provide an exception for a homicidal legatee. Hart would describe the result as discretionary lawmaking at the interstices of the statute. Such a view, according to Dworkin, means that the judge has overstepped the legal bounds of his authority. Instead, the decision should be seen as the application of a broader principle inherent in our legal system—the maxim that "no man should profit from his own wrong" (*Riggs*, p. 509). Thus, the judge gave effect to a pre-existing just solution by considering the legal system as a whole and did not usurp the legislative prerogative. Hard cases show that legal principles cannot be divorced from moral norms of the community, as positivists are wont to do.

The Herculean political theory. Dworkin's "rights thesis" also suggests an answer to the harder case where principles are in conflict. Principles, like rules, may be subject to debate; the principle of not profiting from one's wrong may compete, for example, with the principle that a testator's wishes are always respected. Again, a judge is not at liberty to choose between them based upon his own values or policy reasons. He must fall back on something else as a guide to adjudication. That something else is an overarching "political theory," which he must construct. It consists of a complex "set of principles" that "best justifies" or fits existing legal institutions and legal doctrines relevant to the case (1975, pp. 1086, 1093). If there are several competing theories, the soundest one is the one that coheres best with the moral and political traditions of the community. These traditions are not ascertained by opinion polls of popular views, but by reflection on the principles that underlie social institutions.

This is a Herculean task, so Dworkin invokes the help of "Hercules," an ideal judge of "superhuman skill, learning, patience and acumen" to construct the best political theory (1975, p. 1083). Obviously, this is a thoroughly normative model. In reality, different judges, with different backgrounds, construct different theories. Human judges, lacking the perspicacity of Hercules, do not always know which putative political theory is the soundest or which is the one correct result to be derived therefrom. Nonetheless, judges must decide as if there is one single best theory and one single correct solution in order to avoid the pitfalls of judicial legislation. In this way, their decisions will be "as close to the correct ideals of a just legal system as possible" (1982, p. 168).

Dworkin's model of adjudication is an attempt to curb the common temptation, inspired by legal realism, to view controversial decisions as nothing more than personal rationalizations of the judge. It is also a defense of a particular natural law theory that is specifically opposed to Hart's positivism. This theory teaches that judicial reasoning in hard cases depends on moral and political reasoning as well as rule reasoning. The claimed inseparability of these forms of reasoning reflects Dworkin's devout faith in the congruence of law, morality, and rationality.

A nonjudicial example. The application of Dworkin's decision-making model can be illustrated by a simple example from a nonjudicial setting (adapted from Greenawalt 1977). Suppose that a new sport, soccer, is invented. Elected representatives of a soccer federation establish a league of teams and promulgate a basic set of rules for play. A commissioner oversees the day-to-day management of league affairs and appoints a group of referees who are responsible for applying the federation rules in league games. Each decision by a referee is subsequently publicized and influences the actions of players and other referees in future games.

In one game, a defender tackles an opposing forward. This is the first time in the history of the sport that any player has performed this move. The established rules say nothing about tackles and the referee must decide whether it is valid. In the absence of prior decisions and directly applicable rules, an "activist" referee would evaluate utility considerations: Will tackles result in more injuries? Will it make the game more exciting to the fans and thereby boost sagging attendance at games? If the interests of the players are not harmed and the long-term collective good is advanced by tackles, there would be strong arguments of policy for declaring it legal. In so doing, the referee has created a new rule.

A "principled" referee would not consider instrumentalist reasons cast in terms of future effects. Those considerations belong to the rule-makers of the soccer federation. He will also certainly not decide according to his own likes or dislikes of tackles. Instead, he constructs a theory that justifies the sport as it now exists in order to help him determine whether tackling is congruent with this conception of soccer. The referee evaluates tackling in the broader context of soccer as a sport of speed and finesse. It is more akin to other semicontact sports (such as basketball) than to sports where brute force prevails (such as football). The referee also examines the rationales behind various rules that govern related actions (for example, a rule prohibiting pushing a player). Arguments of principle that draw on the generally accepted norms of the organization of sports in society would narrowly lead him to disallow this disputed action. He would conclude that the forward has a right not to be tackled.

NOTES AND QUESTIONS

1. Dworkin's model is more normative than descriptive. Judges in fact do rely on policy considerations, if only because they lack Herculean theory-building capacities. The question is whether they ought to rely on arguments of policy. If the answer, perhaps unexciting, is that sometimes they should (and do) and sometimes they shouldn't (and don't), it is of no small moment to ascertain when and how they should (and do) do one or the other. What is needed is an approach to decision-making that reconciles features of the Hart and Dworkin models. Is a halfway house model feasible?

2. A hard case, by definition, is one in which neither side is sure of its rights ahead of time. When the tackle was made, the validity of the maneuver was unclear. That is why it must be ruled upon by a third party arbiter. Do you agree that there is no unfairness from the retroactive effect of adjudication if a decision is justified on grounds of principle rather than policy? Are decisions less likely to be uniform—an essential characteristic of principled decision-making—if a referee considers the future good of soccer rather than the existing overall norms of the sport? Is it possible, in practice, to separate neatly considerations of utility and of principle? If not, what is the significance of the distinction?

3. There are times when claims of right and reasons of policy are in conflict. For example, a given claim to desegregated schooling might be counterbalanced by opposing reasons based upon the community upheaval that would ensue. The Bill of Rights recognizes the possibility of conflict and therefore institutionalizes certain individual liberties versus claims of collective welfare. Does Dworkin's approach mean, simply, that when opposing arguments of principle and policy are in equipose, judges ought to give more weight to the former?

4. What are the similarities and differences between Dworkin's approach and the purposive reasoning of G. Edward White? The "neutral principles" method of Wechsler? The classical natural law style of Justice Foster in the speluncean case?

5. Hart (1976) remains unmoved by Dworkin's challenge. Hart is troubled by the issue of where one draws "the line of distinction between what is to be taken as settled law from which the guiding justificatory principles are to be derived and what is to be taken as unsettled law which provides the hard cases to be decided by reference to the principles so derived" (p. 549). More important, even assuming the line can be drawn, he—and other commentators (for example, Soper 1977; Munzer 1977)—finds it "difficult to believe" that any one set of principles can be demonstrated to fit a situation better than another, thereby yielding only one uniquely correct answer (p. 550).

6.   Justice Cardozo (1924) estimated the number of (easy) cases whose outcomes were predestined by adherence to precedent at "nine-tenths, perhaps more" (p. 60). In the few hard cases, deductive reasoning is at its weakest and other methods are needed. Judge Coffin (1980), too, asserts that only in a small fraction of the total number of appeals are judges obliged to choose among competing values (p. 196 et seq.). If, in reality, principles are not as unequivocally determinative of results when applied by nonomniscient judges, can it be said that social science provides more consistent and predictable guidance in hard cases?

7.   Utilitarian ideas underlie positivist theories of law and of the judicial process. Dworkin's jurisprudence is hostile to utilitarianism. It has greater affinity with eighteenth century ideas of inalienable rights. To the extent that the positivist theories, dominant in this country since Justice Holmes, are now being challenged, if not overshadowed, by theories based upon individual moral rights, what are the broader ramifications of this trend for political philosophy? For the receptivity of law to social science?

12.6.   A SUMMING UP

Jurisprudential Theories and Psychological Theories

"Logic and history, and custom and utility, and the accepted standards of right conduct," wrote Justice Cardozo (1921), "are the forces which singly or in combination shape the progress of the law" (p. 112). These three "forces" (logical deduction, discretionary judgment, and purposive argumentation, respectively) can be seen as generalized mind sets that are also found in—and have shaped the development of—other fields of intellectual endeavor. In psychology, for example, there are also three major theoretical systems that define the subject matter and the method of inquiry of the discipline: structuralism, behaviorism and Freudianism, and cognitive psychology (purposive behaviorism and Gestalt psychology).

The psychological analogue to formalism was structuralism. Scientific psychology is usually said to have begun in 1879 with the establishment of the first psychological laboratory in Leipzig by Wilhelm Wundt. To divorce psychology from metaphysics and place it on a scientific basis, he had to redefine its subject and approach. According to Wundt (1910), psychology was the study of the basic units of consciousness, such as "sensations," "feelings," and "images." The method consisted of introspection or self-observation by trained individuals who would rigorously record and classify their impressions. One of his students, Edward Titchener (1898), called it structural psychology. The science of psychology consisted of describing and organizing the structure of the mind in order to unravel its component elements. While formalists sought principles underlying cases, structuralists spoke of the "apperceptive mass"—the focal point of consciousness—underlying sensations and feelings. Like a closed, logically ordered system of rules that was formalist jurisprudence, structural psychology also envisioned mental life as the totality of associations between its constitutive parts.

As formalism led to realism and both, in turn, to purposivism, so all of the great "father systems of contemporary psychology" are reactions to, or adaptations of, structuralism (Wolman 1960, p. 21). Two major theoretical systems grew out of the revolt against the introspectionist approach to the conscious mind. One system was behaviorism. An early exponent, John Watson (1913), urged the elimination of states of consciousness as a proper subject for investigation. He proposed focusing only on outer experience or observable conduct. All behavior is simply a chain of sensory-motor responses to stimuli. The other system was psychoanalytic theory. Freud probed beneath the surface of overt behavior and of the conscious mind, seeking to disclose the unconscious springs of conduct. What Watson and Freud had in common, notwithstanding their diametrically opposed conceptions of behavior, was a rejection of ratiocination and purposive action in animating human action. This denial of rationality in individuals appealed to realists who proclaimed the nonrationality of law.

The third major theoretical system revolves around a functionalist perspective. Early on, William James (1890) proposed that psychology must deal not only with the structure but also the function of the mind. He viewed psychological functioning as part of the process of adaptation to the environment. Others later introduced the organism as the missing link between stimulus and response (S-O-R theory). Edward Tolman (1932) proposed the notion of "purposive behaviorism": Conduct is a series of means-end relationships, leading to an intended objective. Even rats, in learning situations, were said to possess "cognitive maps" and to respond as if they were following "signs" and "expecting" to reach a goal. Finally, Gestalt psychology also rejected the mechanistic view of humans implicit in the other psychological theories. It emphasized, instead, the goal-directedness of thinking, the volitional nature of conduct, and the role of insight and intuition in learning (Koffka 1935).

In intellectual thought as in the arts, there are thus alternating rhythms of classicism and romanticism. During the classical period, there are formal rules of organization and structure. The conceptual edifice is like the model of Euclidean geometry: neat, tidy, logical. It is surrounded by a traditional and stately air. In time, however, the formulation becomes rigid and eventually falls.

During the romantic period, the old formal rules are discarded. The Young Turks improvise and experiment; they deny the existence of the mind and spurn deductive reasoning. Everything is formless, chaotic, but exciting. Their new proposals tend to be trendy, sprightly, and avant-garde—law is social science; behavior is S-R connections.

Once the romantic energy has spent itself, a new classicism emerges that seeks to synthesize elements of both earlier traditions. But this, too, eventually gives way and the cycle begins anew. At present, law as a normative enterprise is "an unstable creature," according to Dauer (1980–81). He concludes:

> As realism nudged aside Langdellianism and as normative argument began to repel realism, so normative argument too has begun to crumble. No one, at least not I, knows what's going to replace it. . . . The future, to say the least, is tantalizingly unformed. [pp. 19–20]

Law: A House with Many Mansions

The diversity of methods of adjudication suggests that there is no single, correct view of what law is and how cases are decided. Indeed, "law is not a single discipline" (Dauer 1980–81, p. 20), and legal scholarship is not a single process. The contemporary legal literature reveals a medley of approaches to studying, practicing, and deciding law. There is law and social science, law and history, law and economics; there is also traditional logical analysis, value-oriented policy analysis, value-free conceptual analysis, law as social engineering. Law is like a cubist painting: It can be looked at from several different points of view, none of which is inherently less worthy than another, and all of which add to the appreciation of the rich variety that is the life of the law.

Figure 12-1 is a schematic summary of the judicial decision-making process. At what stage of this process is formalism dominant? Realism? Purposive analysis? At what stage(s) of this process has social science been used?

FIGURE 12.1

Diagram of the Appellate Decision-making Process

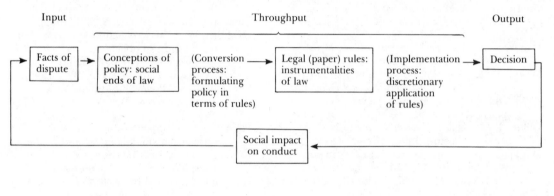

REFERENCES

Allen, F. L. *Only Yesterday.* New York: Bantam Books, 1959.

Aristotle. *The Politics of Aristotle,* Book III. Translated by B. Jowett. New York: P. F. Collier, 1900.

Austin, J. *The Province of Jurisprudence Determined.* Students' edition. London: J. Murray, 1873.

———. *Lectures on Jurisprudence, or the Philosophy of Positive Law,* 5th ed. Revised and edited by R. Campbell. London: J. Murray, 1885.

Baker V. Carr, 369 U.S. 186 (1962).

Ballew v. Georgia, 435 U.S. 223 (1978).

Bartol, C. R. *Psychology and American Law.* Belmont, Ca.: Wadsworth, 1983.

Berman, H. J., and Greiner, W. R. *The Nature and Function of Law,* 4th ed. Mineola, N.Y.: Foundation Press, 1980.

Beutel, F. K. "Some Implications of Experimental Jurisprudence." *Harvard Law Review* 48 (1931): 169–97.

Bickel, A. M. *The Least Dangerous Branch.* Indianapolis: Bobbs-Merrill, 1962.

———. *The Supreme Court and the Idea of Progress.* New York: Harper & Row, 1970.

Blackstone, W. *Commentaries on the Laws of England,* vol. 1. London: Sweet & Milliken, 1821.

Britt, S. H. "The Social Psychology of Law." *Illinois Law Review* 24 (1940): 802–11.

Brown v. Board of Education, 347 U.S. 483 (1954).

Bryce, J. *The American Commonwealth,* vol. 2. New York: Macmillan, 1888.

Cardozo, B. N. *The Nature of the Judicial Process.* New Haven: Yale University Press, 1921.

———. *The Growth of the Law.* New Haven: Yale University Press, 1924.

———. "Mr. Justice Holmes." *Harvard Law Review* 44 (1931): 682–92.

Chicago B. & Q. R. R. v. Chicago, 166 U.S. 226 (1897).

Clark, C. E. "The Function of Law in a Democratic Society." *University of Chicago Law Review* 9 (1942): 393–405.

Coffin, F. M. *The Ways of a Judge: Reflections From the Appellate Bench.* Boston: Houghton Mifflin, 1980.

Cohen, F. S. "Justice Holmes and the Nature of Law." *Columbia Law Review* 31 (1931): 352–67.

———. "Review of Bentham's Theory of Fictions by C. K. Ogden." *Yale Law Journal* 42 (1933): 1149–52.

———. "Transcendental Nonsense and the Functional Approach." *Columbia Law Review* 35 (1935): 809–49.

Currie, B. "The Materials of Law Study." *Journal of Legal Education* 3 (1951): 331–83.

Dauer, E. A. "Law and the Life of the Mind." *Yale Law Report* 27 (1980–81): 13–21.

Dewey, J. "Logical Method and Law." In *Landmarks of Law: Highlights of Legal Opinion*, edited by R. D. Henson. New York: Harper & Row, 1960.

Dillon, J. *Laws and Jurisprudence of England and America.* Boston: Little, Brown, 1895.

Douglas, W. O. "Stare decisis." In *Essays in jurisprudence from the Columbia Law Review.* New York: Columbia University Press, 1963.

Dunlap, R. "The Theoretical Aspect of Psychology." In *Psychologies of 1925*, edited by C. Murchison. Worcester, Mass.: Clark University Press, 1925.

Dworkin, R. "Judicial Discretion." *Journal of Philosophy* 60 (1963): 624–38.

———. "Model of Rules." *University of Chicago Law Review* 35 (1967): 14–46.

———. "Hard Cases." *Harvard Law Review* 88 (1975): 1057–1109.

———. *Taking Rights Seriously.* Cambridge, Mass.: Harvard University Press, 1977.

———. "The Forum of Principle." *New York University Law Review* 56 (1981): 469–524.

———. " 'Natural' Law Revisited." *University of Florida Law Review* 34 (1982): 165–88.

Ehrlich, E. *Fundamental Principles of the Sociology of Law.* Translated by W. Moll. Cambridge, Mass.: Harvard University Press. 1936.

Ford, J. "The Fundamentals of Holmes' Juristic Philosophy." *Fordham Law Review* 11 (1942): 255–78.

Frank, J. *Law and the Modern Mind.* Garden City, N.Y.: Doubleday, 1930.

———. *Courts on Trial: Myth and Reality in American Justice.* Princeton, N.J.: Princeton University Press, 1949.

Fuller, L. "American Legal Realism." *University of Pennsylvania Law Review* 82 (1934): 429–62.

———. *The Law in Quest of Itself.* Chicago: Foundation Press, 1940.

———. "The Case of the Speluncean Explorers." *Harvard Law Review* 62 (1949): 615–45.

———. "Positivism and Fidelity to Law—A Reply to Professor Hart." *Harvard Law Review* 71 (1958): 630–72.

———. *The Morality of Law.* New Haven: Yale University Press, 1964.

———, and Eisenberg, M. *Basic Contract Law*, 3rd ed. St. Paul, Minn.: West, 1972.

Furman v. Georgia, 408 U.S. 238 (1972).

Gellhorn, W. "The Law School's Responsibility for Training Public Servants." *University of Chicago Law Review* 9 (1942): 469–76.

Gideon v. Wainwright, 372 U.S. 335 (1963).

Greenawalt, K. "Policy, Rights, and Judicial Decision." *Georgia Law Review* 11 (1977): 991–1054.

Haines, C. G. "General Observations on the Effects of Personal, Political, and Economic Influences in the Decisions of Judges." In *Readings in Jurisprudence and Legal Philosophy*, edited by M. R. Cohen and F. S. Cohen. Boston: Little, Brown, 1951.

Hall, M. E., ed. *The Selected Writings of Benjamin Nathan Cardozo.* New York: Fallon, 1947.

Hamilton, W. H. "On Dating Justice Holmes." *University of Chicago Law Review* 9 (1941): 1–29.

Hart, H. L. A. "Positivism and the Separation of Law and Morals." *Harvard Law Review* 71 (1958): 593–629.

———. *The Concept of Law.* Oxford, England: Oxford University Press, 1961.

———. "Law in the Perspective of Philosophy: 1776–1976." *New York University Law Review* 51 (1976): 538–51.

———. "American Jurisprudence Through English Eyes: The Nightmare and the Noble Dream." *Georgia Law Review* 11 (1977): 969–89.

Hobbes, T. *Leviathan.* Cambridge, England: Cambridge University Press, 1935.

Hofstadter, R. *The Age of Reform; from Bryan to FDR.* New York: Alfred A. Knopf, 1955.

———. *Social Darwinism in American Thought.* Boston: Beacon Press, 1966.

Holmes, O. W. *The Common Law.* Boston: Little, Brown, 1881.

———. "The Path of the Law." *Harvard Law Review* 10 (1897): 457–78.

———. *Collected Legal Papers.* New York: Harcourt, Brace & Howe, 1920.

Hoover, C. "Stare Decisis." *Albany Law Journal* 52 (1895): 73–75.

Horowitz, M. "The Emergence of an Instrumental Conception of American Law, 1780–1820." *Perspectives in American History* 5 (1971): 285–331.

Howe, M. D. "The Positivism of Mr. Justice Holmes." *Harvard Law Review* 64 (1951): 529–46.

———, ed. *Holmes-Pollock Letters*. Cambridge, Mass.: Belknap Press, 1961.

Hutcheson, J. "The Judgment Intuitive: The Function of the "Hunch" in Judicial Decisions." *Cornell Law Quarterly* 14 (1929): 274–88.

James, W. *Principles of Psychology*. New York: Henry Holt, 1890.

Jones, H. W. "A View from the Bridge." *Law and Society: A Supplement to the Summer Issue of Social Problems* (1965): 39–46.

Kalven, H., Jr. "The Quest for the Middle Range: Empirical Inquiry and Legal Policy." In *Law in a Changing America*, edited by G. Hazard. Englewood Cliffs, N.J.: Prentice-Hall, 1968.

Kantorowicz, H. *The Definition of Law*. Cambridge, England: Cambridge University Press, 1958.

Kaplan, B. "Encounters with O. W. Holmes, Jr." *Harvard Law Review* 96 (1983): 1828–52.

Kelsen, H. *General Theory of Law and State*. Translated by A. Wedberg. Cambridge, Mass.: Harvard University Press, 1945.

Kennedy, D. "Toward an Understanding of Legal Consciousness: The Case of Classical Legal Thought in America, 1850–1940." *Research in Law and Sociology* 3 (1980): 3–24.

Kennedy, W. B. "Psychologism in the Law." *Georgetown Law Journal* 29 (1940): 139–64.

Koffka, K. *Principles of Gestalt Psychology*. New York: Harcourt Brace & Howe, 1935.

Kuhn, T. *The Structure of Scientific Revolutions*, 2nd ed. Chicago: University of Chicago Press, 1962.

Langdell, C. *A Selection of Cases on the Law of Contracts*. Boston: Little, Brown, 1879.

Lasswell, H. D., and McDougal, M. S. "Legal Education and Public Policy: Professional Training in the Public Interest." *Yale Law Journal* 52 (1943): 203–95.

Llewellyn, K. N. *The Bramble Bush: On Our Law and Its Study*. Dobbs Ferry, N.Y.: Oceana, 1930.

———. "A Realistic Jurisprudence—The Next Step." *Columbia Law Review* 30 (1930b): 431–65.

———. "Some Realism About Realism—Responding to Dean Pound." *Harvard Law Review* 44 (1931): 1222–64.

———. "On What Is Wrong with So-Called Legal Education." *Columbia Law Review* 35 (1935): 651–68.

———. *The Common Law Tradition: Deciding Appeals*. Boston: Little, Brown, 1960.

———. *Jurisprudence: Realism in Theory and Practice*. Chicago: University of Chicago Press, 1962.

Lochner v. New York, 198 U.S. 45 (1905).

Lucey, F. E. "Natural Law and American Legal Realism." *Georgetown Law Journal* 30 (1942): 493–533.

Maine, H. *Ancient Law: Its Connection with the Early History of Society and Its Relation to Modern Ideas*. New York: Henry Holt, 1906.

McDougal, M. S. "Fuller v. the American Legal Realist: An Intervention." *Yale Law Journal* 50 (1941): 827–40.

Miller, A. S., and Howell, R. F. "The Myth of Neutrality in Constitutional Adjudication." *University of Chicago Law Review* 27 (1960): 661–95.

Montesquieu, C. *The Spirit of Laws*. Translated by T. Nugent. London: William Clowes, 1878.

Moore, U. "Rational Basis of Legal Institutions." *Columbia Law Review* 23 (1923): 609–25.

Munzer, S. R. "Right Answers, Preexisting Rights, and Fairness." *Georgia Law Review* 11 (1977): 1055–68.

Needham, J. *Science and Civilisation in China*. Cambridge, England: Cambridge University Press, 1956.

Nelson, W. E. "The Impact of the Antislavery Movement upon Styles of Judicial Reasoning in Nineteeth Century America." *Harvard Law Review* 87 (1974): 513–66.

Note. " 'Round and 'Round the Bramble Bush: From Legal Realism to Critical Legal Scholarship." *Harvard Law Review* 95 (1982): 1669–90.

Osborne v. United States Bank, 22 U.S. (9 Wheat.) 738 (1824).

Palmer, B. W. "Hobbes, Holmes, and Hitler." *American Bar Association Journal* 31 (1945): 569–73.

Patterson, E. W. *Jurisprudence: Men and Ideas in Theory and Practice*. Chicago: University of Chicago Press, 1962.

Pearson, K. *The Grammar of Science*. London: W. Scott, 1895.

People v. Gallagher, 4 Mich. 244 (1856).

Plato. *Dialogues of Plato,* vol. 1. Translated by B. Jowett. New York: Random House, 1937.

Plessy v. Ferguson, 163 U.S. 537 (1896).

Polanyi, M. *The Study of Man.* Chicago: University of Chicago Press, 1958.

Pound, R. "The Need for a Sociological Jurisprudence." *Green Bag* 19 (1907): 606–15.

———. "Mechanical Jurisprudence." *Columbia Law Review* 8 (1908): 605–23.

———. "Liberty of Contract." *Yale Law Journal* 18 (1909): 454–87.

———. "Law in Books and Law in Action." *American Law Review* 44 (1910): 30–41.

———. "The Scope and Purpose of Sociological Jurisprudence." *Harvard Law Review* 24 (1911): 591–619.

———. "The Scope and Purpose of Sociological Jurisprudence." *Harvard Law Review* 25 (1912): 489–516.

———. "The Theory of Judicial Decision." *Harvard Law Review* 36 (1923): 940–59.

Purcell, E. *The Crisis of Democratic Theory.* Lexington: University of Kentucky Press, 1973.

Riggs v. Palmer, 115 N.Y. 506 (1889).

Robinson, E. *Law and the Lawyers.* New Haven: Yale University Press, 1935.

Rumble, W. E., Jr. *American Legal Realism.* Ithaca, N.Y.: Cornell University Press, 1968.

Sartorious, R. "Social Policy and Judicial Legislation." *American Philosophical Quarterly* 8 (1971): 151–60.

Savigny, F. K. *Of the Vocation of Our Age for Legislation and Jurisprudence.* Translated by A. Hayward. London: Littlewood, 1831.

Schubert, G., ed. *Judicial Decision-Making.* Glencoe, Ill.: Free Press, 1963.

Slaughter-House Cases, 83 U.S. 394 (16 Wall. 36) (1873).

Soper, E. P. "Legal Theory—The Obligation of a Judge: The Hart/Dworkin Dispute." *Michigan Law Review* 75 (1977): 473–519.

Stevens, R. "Two Cheers for 1870: The American Law School." In *Perspectives in American History,* vol. 5, edited by D. Fleming and B. Bailyn. Cambridge, Mass.: Harvard University Press, 1971.

Summers, R. S. "The New Analytical Jurists." *New York University Law Review* 41 (1966): 861–96.

———. *Instrumentalism and American Legal Theory.* Ithaca, N.Y.: Cornell University Press, 1982.

Thibaut, J.; Walker, L.; LaTour, S.; and Houlden, P. "Procedural Justice as Fairness." *Stanford Law Review* 26 (1974): 1271–89.

Thorne v. Cramer, 15 Barb. 112 (N.Y. Sup. Ct. 1851).

Titchener, E. B. "The Postulates of a Structural Psychology." *Psychological Review* 7 (1898): 449–65.

Tocqueville, A. de. *Democracy in America,* vol. 1. Garden City, N.Y.: Doubleday, 1969.

Tolman, E. C. *Purposive Behavior in Animals and Men.* New York: Appleton-Century, 1932.

Vago, S. *Law and Society.* Englewood Cliffs, N.J.: Prentice-Hall, 1981.

Vetter, J. "Postwar Legal Scholarship on Judicial Decision Making." *Journal of Legal Education* 33 (1983): 412–23.

Watson, J. B. "Psychology as the Behaviorist Sees It." *Psychology Review* 20 (1913): 158–73.

Wechsler, H. "Toward Neutral Principles of Constitutional Law." *Harvard Law Review* 73 (1959): 1–35.

White, G. E. "From Sociological Jurisprudence to Realism: Jurisprudence and Social Change in Early Twentieth-Century America." *Virginia Law Review* 58 (1972): 999–1028.

———. "The Evolution of Reasoned Elaboration: Jurisprudential Criticism and Social Change." *Virginia Law Review* 59 (1973): 279–302.

Williams v. Florida, 399 U.S. 78 (1970).

Wirth, L. Preface to *Ideology and Utopia,* by K. Mannheim. New York: Harcourt, Brace & Howe, 1936.

Wolman, B. B. *Contemporary Theories and Systems in Psychology.* New York: Harper, 1960.

Woodard, C. "The Limits of Legal Realism: An Historical Perspective." *Virginia Law Review* 54 (1968): 689–739.

Wundt, W. *Principles of Physiological Psychology.* New York: Macmillan, 1910.

CHAPTER 13

Conceptual and Jurisprudential Perspectives on the Uses of Social Research in the Judicial Process

13.1. INTRODUCTION AND OVERVIEW

"How to inform the judicial mind" of legal and social science information, which Justice Frankfurter once described as "one of the most complicated problems" (in Friedman 1969, p. 63), has been the leitmotif of this book. In the chapters of Parts II and III, we sought to gain insights into the application of empirical data in judicial decision-making by looking in rigorous detail at some specific examples. The various case studies served as springboards for examining the broader subject of the role of social science in law. In this final chapter, we shall try to pull together some of these insights and delineate in a more systematic way the scope and contours of this role.

There is, of course, no single, graceful, consensual bridge between social research (the realm of social facts) and judicial lawmaking (the realm of social values). There are those in the legal community who deny that there is any significant overlap between the two endeavors. Judge Doyle (1977) asserts that "social science data and other evidence are less important in judicial decisionmaking in the field of constitutional law than most people think" (p. 10). "[M]y impression," says Yudof (1978), "is that, with few notable exceptions, there has been a marked decline in the willingness of the Supreme Court to embrace social science evidence as the basis for constitutional decisions." Moreover, "for every judge who relies on policy research, there is another (or occasionally the same judge in a different case) who decries reliance on the vagaries of social science research in constitutional adjudication" (p. 70). However, there are others in the legal and social science communities who are of the opposite view. Judge McMillan (1975) believes that social science is "a source of enlightenment" and that it "can add valuable information and opinion to responsible judging—pragmatic, principled, or otherwise" (pp. 157, 163; see also Judge Craven 1975, p. 151). A lawyer-social psychologist writes that "with few exceptions, most scholars in law and behavioral science agree that there exists some role of greater or lesser importance to be played by disciplines like psychology in the formulation of legal policy and the rendering of judicial decisions" (Haney 1980, p. 182).

There is dissensus among experts not only on whether empirical research has an influence at all in deciding matters of constitutional dimension. Even when the answer is affirmative, there is also uncertainty about when and how it can be used in judicial lawmaking. In part, this is because "[t]here exists no authoritative body of learning or generally agreed upon ideas on the subject of how legal decisions are actually arrived at, to say nothing of how they ought to be arrived at" (Cowan 1963, p. 507). Courts have not announced the criteria they employ in deciding whether to rely on empirical evidence, nor have they indicated the general conditions under which such evidence would be deemed essential or irrelevant (Katz 1971, p. 55). Thus, it is difficult to formulate a generalized account of the relationship between social facts and social values. A study by Rosenblum (1978) sheds some light on the Supreme Court's reliance on social science. He examined the citations to the social science literature in opinions decided every fifth year, from 1954 to 1974. The frequency of citations was cyclical, but the trend overall was upward: In 1954, five cases alluded to social science references; two decades later, twenty-one cases. Works from psychology and sociology accounted for nearly 30% of the cited materials. The remainder were drawn from economics, political science, and other social science disciplines. The briefs of the parties appeared to inform the Court's response. In about two-thirds of the cases where social science was mentioned, one or both of the briefs also contained similar information. Institutional parties involved in continuing litigation (for example, the NAACP and the ACLU) made frequent use of nonlegal sources. The topics most likely to trigger citation of social science involved equal protection and due process claims in connection with the rights of criminal defendants and of racial minorities—a scope of coverage that is mirrored in the contents of this book. However, it is incumbent upon us to go beyond this recitation of the number and types of cases in which social science and law have commingled. We should attempt to build a conceptual bridge.

We begin in section 13.2 with a debate between two social scientists on the use of social science evidence in the courts. One represents a latter-day realist viewpoint and the other subscribes to a jurisprudence of reasoned elaboration. Their arguments help to identify some of the key issues. The realist position assumes that social science is indispensable to responsible decision-making and focuses on *how* the courts are to obtain and evaluate such information. The main argument is that the adversary process distorts scientific fact-finding, so that new methods of establishing social facts—for example, via independent boards of scientific experts or a science court— need to be employed. The purposive analysis approach is preoccupied, instead, with the question of *whether* the courts should predicate their decisions on social science findings in the first instance. Doubts about the legitimacy of the judiciary's use of empirical research forestalls further discussion of its competence in using it. At bottom, this debate reflects a more basic disagreement over the proper function of the courts: should they have an activist or a restrained role in making social policy?

Neither side in this debate gives sustained attention to the issue of *when* the courts rely on social science evidence, assuming that such reliance is legitimate. The essay that follows in section 13.3 faces this issue squarely. It proposes that empirical analysis is most productive when it is applied to problems in "the middle range" of the fact-value continuum. However, it does not articulate the parameters of this mid-range.

There are numerous reasons for the underutilization or nonutilization of empirical data by the courts. These include diffidence in dealing with unfamiliar material, unaccessibility of the evidence, skepticism about its reliability, and the like. In sections 13.4 and 13.5, we concentrate on two other—and possibly more significant—limits to the widespread application of social research in law. The first deals with the differences in the subject matter and in the methods of reasoning and proof in law and in science. Some of the issues of applicability and relevance are rooted in epistemology. The second concerns the differences in the professional socialization and professional values of lawyers and social scientists which create difficulties for interdisciplinary collaboration. A brief history of the rise and decline of empirical research in law schools—which has reverberating effects on the profession as a whole—helps to explain why legal policy analysis today is mostly value-laden and data-free.

The question of the role of social research in the courts involves, essentially, the question of how information about social reality contributes to shaping the way society should be ordered. It involves the integration of the objectively true with the morally right. Section 13.6 discusses three paradigmatic uses of empirical evidence by the courts: for adjudicating facts, creating new law, and rationalizing decisions. These uses reflect the influence, respectively, of three jurisprudential approaches to decision-making: formalism, realism, and reasoned elaboration. We conclude that social science serves a heuristic rather than a determinative role in social policy. It can inform and make more responsible the exercise of normative judgments upon which judicial lawmaking is predicated, even though it does not and cannot displace the act of judging itself.

13.2.   WHETHER AND HOW TO USE SOCIAL RESEARCH

Framing the Issues

SOCIAL SCIENCE EVIDENCE AND THE COURTS: REACHING BEYOND THE ADVERSARY PROCESS*

Peter W. Sperlich

. . .

[I] will argue that (1) courts cannot responsibly discharge their duties in isolation from the work and findings of the scientific disciplines; (2) courts cannot rely on briefs and records to obtain relevant social facts, but must take the initiative to go beyond; (3) better procedures must be developed to enable the courts to deal competently with technical social fact materials; (4) the testing mechanisms of the adversary process cannot be relied upon exclusively to establish the validity of social fact assertions: new methods are needed for the clarification and/or resolution of social fact disputes.

IGNORING SCIENTIFIC FINDINGS

The U.S. Supreme Court, as other American courts, often shows reluctance

*[This is one of two companion articles by the same author. The other is ". . . And Then There Were Six: The Decline of the American Jury" (*Judicature* 63 [1980]: 262–79), regarding the use of social science in the jury size cases. Ed's note.]
Reprinted by permission of the author. Copyright © 1980 by Peter W. Sperlich [*Judicature* 63 (1980): 280–89].

to take cognizance of scientific findings. Involved is not only the traditional preference for judicial passivity and full reliance on the record as brought to the Court, but an almost instinctive disdain when scientific evidence is offered. If social facts are needed to decide a particular case, judges tend to prefer to take judicial notice of "common knowledge" or to rely on personal experience, rather than to use the findings of scientific investigations. . . . [Rosenblum notes] that there is a "judicial proclivity to make observations or behavioral predictions with eloquence, intensity, and a cavalier sense of certainty without empirical support."[3] . . .

THE MAJOR OBSTACLES

It it likely that the most important obstacles to the legal profession's use of scientific findings are lack of scientific training and difficulty in obtaining evidence. . . .

Attorneys and judges need a knowledge of science, at least enough to understand how scientific research is done, to have a basic acquaintance with scientific terminology, and to know when science is relevant. Law schools must accept the major blame for the fact that many lawyers do not possess this minimum understanding. To the detriment of their clients, many lawyers are so unacquainted with "science and its methods that they are neither able to distinguish problems which can properly be studied empirically from those which cannot, nor to formulate questions and designs for empiric investigation of appropriate problems." . . .

While closest to the concerns of the law, the social sciences tend to meet with the strongest resistance. . . .

No science . . . generates absolute knowledge. But the social sciences in particular are subject to charges of inconsistency and instability.[14] To some degree the charges are true, but what are the implications? Do these characteristics make (social) science useless? . . .

LETTING SCIENCE SERVE

It would be a mistake, however, for the legal profession to wait for complete agreement and stability. These are not the attributes of science. To use scientific knowledge necessarily means using knowledge in transformation. Except when instability is caused by error, it is a virtue rather than a failing. . . .

Social science knowledge must reflect the inconsistencies and changes found in the social world if it is to serve the law properly, that is, provide the most accurate knowledge possible about current reality. And one function of science is the evaluation of methods and findings. Courts need not be left at the mercy of instability. It should not be overlooked in this context that the law itself is neither stable nor uniform. . . .

Whatever the imperfections of science—real or imagined—the courts must come to terms with the methods and findings of the scientific disciplines for at least two reasons. First, case facts (adjudicative facts) generally are not adequate even to decide the factual issues of the particular case. Case facts must be understood in the context of general scientific propositions. . . .

Second, courts, particularly appellate courts, have legislative functions. They

---

[3]Victor G. Rosenblum, A Place for Social Science Along the Judiciary's Constitutional Law Frontier, 66 *Northwestern University Law Review*, 455, 459, (1971).

[14]An additional objection is that of bias. . . . There is no doubt that social scientists as citizens have policy preferences (biases), and that some social scientists permit these preferences to influence their science. This, however, represents a *failure* of scientific work, not its normal operation. What distinguishes science from ideology and partisan journalism is precisely its *Wertfreiheit*, that is, that the results of the investigation are not determined by the preferences of the investigator. . . .

not only find law, they make it. Courts must take into account the policy consequences of their decisions. Policy consequences cannot be known by case facts. The information must come from somewhere else. Judicial intuition and personal experience are not dependable guides to social facts. And even the self-evident can be wrong. The earth *does* revolve around the sun. The question is not *whether* to rely on scientific knowledge, but *when* and *how*.

The *when* presents fewer difficulties than the *how*. If it can be agreed that the task of the courts is to determine a variety of issues—definitional, normative, empirical, etc.—and to join these determinations in a decision, then the question can be answered by saying that scientific findings should be taken into account whenever empirical issues must be decided. . . . Focusing specifically on the social sciences, Rosenblum gives a similar answer:

I would propose a simple criterion: [the social sciences] should be applied in judicial decision-making when the courts themselves formulate or invoke propositions or norms conditioned upon knowledge within the competence of the social sciences. This criterion would not require their utilization, for example, when grounds for decision are found exclusively in moral precepts, past precedent, or interpretations of language of statutes or constitutions. . . .

Regarding the *how*, two aspects require separate attention: how are courts to obtain scientific data, and how are the data to be evaluated and tested? The first is a problem in part because attorneys often fail to introduce important evidence during trial. As noted earlier, many attorneys do not recognize needs and opportunities for scientific assistance. . . .

Of course, courts have long relied on information not subjected to adversary proceedings. By the device of judicial notice, judges take into account "common knowledge," requiring neither formal

proof nor adversary testing. Judges have taken judicial notice of such materials at their own initiative as well as at the urging of counsel.[31] The judicial notice technique, however, is not easily extended to scientific evidence regarding social facts. Scientific knowledge is common knowledge only at a trivial level, and scientific knowledge hardly ever is free of disputes. . . .

MODIFYING THE RULES

Scientific findings are not simply there to be noticed. They must be assembled and they must be evaluated. The question is by *whom* and *how*. The answer should be such that the essential fairness of the adversary process is preserved, even if the traditional procedures and rules have to be modified. . . .

Some modifications require only minor changes in current procedures:

The Court can make it known to the bar that it expects counsel to present complete and responsible treatments of social fact issues, which must include all relevant scientific evidence. . . . At present,

[t]he adversary system almost induces opposing counsel to misrepresent or manipulate facts before the Court. The primary goal of the advocate is, after all, to achieve a favorable legal decision even at the expense of empirical truth. For that matter, the courtroom setting, with its ringing tones of partisanship, is not the ideal place to examine social science findings.

Scientific truth is served best when the discourse is cooperative and dispassionate. The standard adversary proceeding "helps

---

[31]The Brandeis brief is a well-known technique for asking the court to take judicial notice of social facts. . . . "But the utility of the Brandeis brief can be questioned because the Court has no guarantee that the brief will always contribute to the integrity of the fact-finding process. . . . no formal tests are prescribed for the materials that may be included in the brief. Any kind of extra-legal material—from astrology to social science—can go into a Brandeis brief." . . .

to clarify many issues. It only seems to obfuscate behavioral issues." . . .

It can be argued in any case that social fact determinations should not be made at the trial court level. High appellate courts are more likely to have the broad perspective needed for judicial lawmaking; they also can provide the desirable uniformity in judicial legislation. The matter is important all the more because fact determinations of trial courts are strongly shielded from review on appeal unless they can be shown to be "clearly erroneous." Horowitz comments:

Findings of social fact, however, whether based on testimony or documentation, should not be similarly insulated from review. The credibility of an expert witness is not really measured by his demeanor; it is measured by comparing his assertions with the scholarly literature and his own data that purport to support the assertion. An appellate court can do this every bit as well as a trial court, and the inexperience of judges in evaluating such material argues for the widest latitude for correcting errors. . . .

A MORE ACTIVE ROLE

[T]hese limited modifications assign to the adversary process a task it was not designed to handle and which, most likely, it will not be able to discharge satisfactorily. Not only is the bar unprepared to adopt the style of dispassionate scientific inquiry, the bench is not prepared to sit in judgment of conflicting scientific evidence, and standard trial court procedure is not congenial to social fact determination. . . . It does not seem that the Court can avoid going beyond the record generated by the adversary process in the trial courts and the briefs of counsel which supplement the record. The Court, it appears, must play an active role in the determination of social fact issues. . . .

The court can delegate the social factfinding task to a body of scientific experts, representing the discipline(s) relevant to the issue. Such a body should provide the Court with a complete account of existing evidence (or lack thereof), indicate the relative coherence or inconsistency of various parts of the evidence, assess the soundness of the research underlying the various findings, report on the relative support of the findings in the scholarly community, assess the relative stability of the findings, and render a balanced appraisal of the substance (meaning), validity, and reliability of the current evidence. The task of such a body would *not* be to render a verdict. The final social fact decision cannot be made by any agency other than the Court.

ORGANIZING THE EXPERTS

The body of experts can take form in at least four ways:

First, it can be organized as a permanent or ad hoc advisory board of independent experts, similar to the National Institute of Health the National Science Foundation review boards, assembling and working only as required. . . .

Second, the body of experts could be organized as a "science court," that is, as a group in full-time service. A science court would have a regular budget; its members would have employee status. It would not be part of the regular court structure. . . . Given that a science court is likely to develop a bureaucratic structure and a variety or organizational goals, strict litigational neutrality may be more difficult to achieve than for an independent advisory board.

Third, the experts can be organized as the research office of the Court, the scientist-members being regular employees of the Court and paid for out of the Court's budget. . . . While such an office will be more quickly responsive to the needs of the court, it is not likely to inspire the same confidence in its neutrality or have the same prestige as an advisory board or science court.

Finally, the experts can be organized as an office of a governmental agency other than the Court, such as the Department of Justice. . . .

In my judgment, the four organizational forms are listed in the order of their general desirability. But this is a tentative conclusion. Much more analysis and, if possible, some experimentation will be required to make firm recommendations.

THE QUESTION OF FAIRNESS

. . . Even when the Court reaches beyond the normal adversary process—as it must—the basic principles of fairness associated with that process still require satisfaction.

For reasons developed earlier, it does not seem fruitful to submit the scientific social fact evidence to a trial court adversary procedure, nor should the Supreme Court import such procedures for its own actions. But at least this must be provided to the parties: notice and the opportunity to challenge and rebut. . . .

Under the present theory of fairness, however, the Court is *not* required to let counsel voir dire and cross-examine the outside experts who produced the Court's empirical evidence. It is precisely the suspension of cross-examination that distinguishes the "modified procedures" from regular trial court proceedings.

The Court will base its decision on the evidence provided by the experts and on whatever comments, challenges, contrary interpretations, and contrary evidence have been submitted by counsel. It is important to emphasize that the Court decides how the outside evidence is to be used. The "modified procedures" will not enable scientists to become judges. . . .

The point of the modifications discussed is not to substitute science for law, but to enable the Court to make better use

of science. Constitutionally valid decisions require valid social facts, and scientific investigations are vastly more dependable guides to such facts than judicial intuition or common knowledge. . . .

SOCIAL SCIENCE AND THE COURTS: THE SEDUCTION OF THE JUDICIARY

David M. O'Brien

. . .

[The seduction of law by the social sciences] . . . raises serious issues for constitutional adjudication. In what ways for example, are the social sciences necessary and capable of contributing to judicial decision-making? To what degree do judges have the capacity to use social science and to what extent may judges legitimately base their rulings on social science? . . .

Sperlich argues that judges are culpable in adopting realist premises for their decisions and then relying on "common knowledge" instead of supplying empirical data or, even worse, incompetently using scientific findings.

Diagnosis of the intersection of social science and constitutional adjudication leads to innovative and Promethean prescriptions. Because the adversary system perpetuates the rivalry between science and law, and thereby forecloses the possibility that courts will obtain the necessary "social fact materials" essential to their "legislative functions," Sperlich recommends "moving beyond the adversary process" and "letting science serve.". . .

With science as a suitor, the seduction of the judiciary appears complete: if judges are to render competent decisions, they must get and stay on top of social science research, and, therefore, they need to keep experts on tap.

THE PROPRIETY OF SPERLICH'S PRESCRIPTIONS

Undoubtedly, many students of law and social science will embrace Sperlich's prescriptions. Perhaps only social science skeptics, political and fiscal conservatives, jurisprudes, and civil libertarians will question the benefits and propriety of "letting science serve." Social science skeptics, for example, may well find Sperlich's prescriptions premature and imprudent, while political and fiscal conservatives may doubt the legitimacy and cost-effectiveness of such institutional and organizational rearrangements. Jurisprudes understandably will recoil at the professed infidelity to "the life of the law," and civil libertarians may object to rendering constitutional rights contingent upon social science and fundamentally utilitarian calculations. Still, these four objections to Sperlich's prescriptions appear worthy of consideration by lawyers and laity. . . .

THE TRANSFORMATION OF THE JUDICIARY

The attractiveness of invitations for judicial use of social science, as much as the growing literature cautioning against the rise of an "imperial judiciary," reflects the changing role of courts in contemporary society. Judges today do appear less like abstemious 18th century legal monks or even enterprising turn-of-the-century social engineers and more like "robed legislators," inclined towards expansive policy-making. . . .

The transformation of the judiciary heralds two interrelated but distinguishable crises. Extensive judicial intervention into the affairs of a democratic polity poses, on the one hand, a *crisis of legitimacy* and, on the other hand, a *crisis of competence* in terms of the capacity of judges to assess and manage complex problems of public policy. Jurisprudes and conservatives might well find the crisis of legitimacy foremost and, indeed, they suggest that resolution of that crisis forestalls any crisis of competence. Contrariwise, Sperlich, among others, presumes that solutions to the crisis of competence concomitantly resolves the legitimacy crisis.

If judges only had the capacity to assess the empirical evidence necessary to comprehend complex litigation and prescribe as well as implement appropriate policy decrees, then they might legitimately engage in broad policy-making. The contribution of social science to judicial performance thus promises benefits in two important ways: (1) enhancing judicial perception of the nature of social problems and identifying in a reliable way the necessity for legal and social change; and (2) informing judges of the possible consequences of decisions and the prospects for compliance and effective implementation.

PRUDENCE AND SOCIAL SCIENCE

To be sure, if judges base their rulings on empirical propositions, those propositions should prove demonstrable and reliable, rather than merely expressions of judicial observation or political guesswork. A social science skeptic, however, might well caution lawyers and laity about too high expectations of improved judicial decision-making as the result of increased attention to social science data and policy analysis. . . .

Even well-intended and well-designed frameworks for policy analysis have been criticized for inherent ideological bias. . . .

[There are also] theoretical and practical problems of policy analysis. Theoretical difficulties center around the disagreements over identifying the problems and objectives of public policy, and defining the nature of "social benefits" and "social costs," as well as studying the "outcomes" and "impact" of governmental programs—whether established by legislatures, administrative agencies, or courts. In deferring to policy analysts, judges—like legislators and administrative officials—may well also confront serious practical problems in getting reliable policy analysis.

For example, judges may find that well-intended studies suffer difficulties in research design, or that those studies supplied are generated merely to "whitewash" prior judicial proclivities. In addition, there remains the problem that judges must render their decisions in relatively short order, but empirical research frequently requires considerable time and financial expenditure. Accordingly, for the social science skeptic, deference and delegation of responsibility to policy analysts presents more obstacles than opportunities for improving judicial fact-finding performance. . . .

THE SOCIAL AND POLITICAL COSTS

[Q]uite apart from the social science skeptic's concern about the capability of policy analysis to reliably predict the impact and consequences of judicial decrees, political and fiscal conservatives are likely to raise . . . [several objections]. . . .

The propriety of courts functioning like social reform agencies and the greater prospects for judges deferring to social science when justifying their decisions strikes political conservatives as unconscionable and antithetical to representative government. . . .

Rather than celebrating the use of social science by the courts, condemnation may be expected precisely because the objectives and role of judges and social scientists are divergent and often incompatible. As Senator Daniel Patrick Moynihan argues:

It is the business of the law, as it were, to order alimony payments; it is the business of social science to try [to] estimate the likelihood of their being paid, or their effect on work behavior and remarriage in male and female parties, or similar probabilities.[50]

Ponderous, too, are the managerial and bureaucratic problems of organizing the social science experts who will serve the courts. . . .

If judges rely more on empirical data for their rulings and their research staff becomes larger and more bureaucratic, they may sustain more political conflicts over the direction of judicial policies and governmental allocation of financial resources.

Bureaucratic, political and financial costs, therefore, may outweigh any anticipated benefits from judicial deference to an organized body of social science experts.

A MODEST PROPOSAL

Whereas the social science skeptic cautions jurists about the utility and reliability of social science theories and evidence, the conservative attends to the propriety and cost-effectiveness of measures to further bureaucratize and politicize the judiciary. The jurisprude remains concerned about the legitimacy of the "legislative functions" of judges that Sperlich presumes and presupposes as inevitably necessitating judicial deference to social science experts.

Jurisprudes or the judicially "modest," as Martin Shapiro calls them, reject as too cavalier and inappropriate that "political jurisprudence" and "result-oriented" *cum* "teleological jurisprudence" which depicts the judiciary as only a "naked power

[50]Moynihan, Social Science and the Courts, 54 *Pub. Interest* 12, 16 (1979).

organ." More concerned with judicial craftsmanship than "judicial statecraft," jurisprudes argue for "reasoned elaboration" and principled judicial decision-making. For the judicially modest, judges are not free to give untrammelled effect to their personal or policy preferences. . . . In disputing with Sperlich's presuppositions and prescriptions, jurisprudes do not deny certain benefits of judicial attention to social science materials, whether those materials are presented by counsel or discovered through independent judicial inquiry. Jurisprudes do deny, however, that judges should simply base their decisions and decrees on social science materials. They do so precisely because jurisprudes, unlike Sperlich, distinguish between judicial *motivation cum* orientation towards resolving a controversy and the enterprise of judicial *justification* of a ruling.

Judicial motivation and orientation toward problem-solving is crucial with respect to . . . the process of uncovering the relevant empirical evidence and legal material necessary to reaching a decision. Jurisprudes might well rejoice in greater judicial attention to social science materials insofar as those materials contribute to judicial fact-finding, further clarify legal issues and their social implications, and perhaps encourage judicial self-examination by discouraging responses to litigation based on intuitive understandings, personal preferences, or emotional reactions. Social science materials, nevertheless, remain largely inappropriate for the "process of justification" or judicial articulation of a principled decision.

FORMAL ASPECTS OF PRINCIPLED DECISIONS

. . . These are the formal distinguishing characteristics of a principled judicial decision.

First, . . . [a] judge must treat the immediate case in the same way as other instances embraced by the principle controlling the decision. If a judge treats cases differently, then a distinguishing characteristic must be specified and another general principle articulated in order to account for the "significant difference" drawn between the two cases.

Second, the decision must be *impartially rendered*. . . .

Third, the application of principles to cases and circumstances must be made with *consistency*.

For the jurisprude, these minimal requirements combine to foreclose ad hoc, egocentric decisions. . . .

SUBSTANTIVE CONDITIONS

With respect to appellate courts and especially the Supreme Court, jurisprudes typically argue that a sound judicial decision must meet not only the minimal formal criteria but also three substantive conditions.

First, a judge may not dispense with the legal concepts or primary rights and duties set forth in the Constitution. . . .

Second, the legal concepts employed must be applied with relevance to the circumstances of the case and with regard to that instant case and other similar but distinguishable cases. . . .

Third, the judge must endeavor to articulate the narrowest possible principle so as to clarify not only the decision in the instant case but also the relevant features of its broad application so as to guide the conduct of citizens and government officials.

Precisely because judicial craftsmanship requires principled articulation of substantive principles of law, the jurisprude . . . finds the legislative functions of judges considerably more circumscribed than Sperlich indicates.

JUDICIAL CRAFTSMANSHIP

Finally, jurisprudes may point out that, even if judges disagree about the demands for principled judicial decisions, it remains politically prudent for judges to pursue judicial craftsmanship. . . .

[C]ontrary to what Sperlich says, the major crisis for the judiciary may not arise with the incompetent use of empirical evidence, but rather simply because the judiciary bases its decisions on social science evidence.

As Hans Linde points out, the Supreme Court has been more often hurt rather than helped by realist premises for its rulings.[89] The Supreme Court, for example, encountered severe criticism and opposition to its rulings on the desegregation of public schools, the exclusionary rule, and the retroactivity of its decisions, precisely because the Court relied on empirical generalizations. Moreover, it may matter little whether judges find and competently use reliable empirical evidence. The factual premises of judicial decisions may be either incorrect or, more importantly, perceived by the public to be so, and, thus, provide an occasion for political conflict. For example, urging Congress to override *Miranda v. Arizona,* Senator Sam Ervin argued:

The Supreme Court has no right to make constitutional determinations based on unsound factual assumptions. . . .

In short, sharply reasoned opinions, rather than mere recital of social science evidence, will minimize the magnitude of potential political opposition to judicial rulings. The increased use of social science materials may thus prove subversive to judicial craftsmanship per se and pernicious rather than salutary for the prestige and efficacy of the judiciary.

SOCIAL SCIENCE AND CIVIL LIBERTIES

. . .

From a civil libertarian perspective, three concerns about realist premises for constitutional rulings become paramount. First, use of empirical data may not further libertarian objectives, since judges will not always agree on the data or the conclusions to be drawn. Second, the status of constitutional rights may actually become more uncertain and precarious. Third, social science materials may encourage judges to engage in "constitutional common law."

Use of social science materials guarantees neither more colleagial [sic] and unanimous decisions nor more reliable and predictable rulings. The Supreme Court's treatment of the death penalty cases illustrates that an empirical approach to understanding constitutional provisions may well further divide and frustrate decision-making.

In *Furman v. Georgia,* for example, concurring and dissenting justices took divergent views of empirical data and thereupon disputed the constitutionality of capital punishment. . . . Social science materials may not prove convincing or may simply provide opportunities for justices to dispute with each other over the nature of constitutional rights, and, thus, frustrate consensus building.

More important than the possible consequences for the internal decision-making of the Supreme Court, recent rulings on the exclusionary rule and the privilege against self-incrimination indicate that judicial deference to empirical data at times may place constitutional rights on the proverbial slippery slope of

---

[89][Judges, critics, and the realist tradition, 82 *Yale L.J.* 227, 238–244 (1972).]

utilitarian theory and social science evidence. The exclusionary rule, for example, has been construed to depend not upon judicial articulation of a theory of personal rights, but rather on whether application of the rule furthers certain policy objectives—namely, deterrence of police misconduct and preservation of judicial integrity and noncomplicity in illegal government activities. Consequently, the rule's protection extends to some but not all defendants, since its application depends on whatever empirical generalizations may be found to determine the effectiveness of the rule in different contexts of police investigation. . . .

In adopting realist premises and basing decisions on empirical generalizations the Supreme Court transforms constitutional interpretation into a kind of constitutional common law. As Justice Black understood, such a judicial enterprise remains as fundamentally opposed to our written Constitution and Bill of Rights as the rendering of constitutional rights contingent upon policy objectives and social science evidence.

JUDICIAL STATECRAFT AND CRAFTSMANSHIP

Prescriptions for increased judicial use and deference to social science may be applauded by those devotees of an active and aggressive judiciary, inasmuch as judicial statecraft has had an undoubted appeal for citizens denied access to or frustrated by the political process. Still, those prescriptions presuppose extensive alterations in the judicial process and promise mixed blessings for the judiciary and the polity. . . .

NOTES AND QUESTIONS

1.   O'Brien articulates the formal and substantive principles of decision-making according to what might be described as neo-formalist jurisprudence. Sperlich, however, does not set forth the realist predicates of instrumental decision-making. What would you deem to be the principal canons of a realist style of decision-making?

2.   In a sharp rejoinder, Sperlich (1980b) protested that O'Brien, who "worships at the temple of *Pure Law*" (p. 96), "[t]akes a large step toward the elevation of ignorance to a principle of adjudication: judicial decisions will generally be of better quality when they're not contaminated by social science findings" (p. 95). The "central tenet" of the "postrealist" viewpoint represented by O'Brien—that "*valid evidence is bunk*"—is the "stale and standard fare of generations of uninformed critics" (pp. 93, 95). Sperlich argues that scientific findings are superior to judicial guessing and do not necessarily impair civil liberties, and their use is subject to judicial control. He writes in the context of the problem of freedom of speech:

> [I]t may become necessary to determine whether . . . shouting "fire" in a crowded theater belongs to the category of "clear and present danger." . . . Only now have we reached an empirical issue. . . . To determine the true dangers of shouting "fire," the judges might ask themselves what they would do in such a situation—would they panic? Or the judges might reflect on what they think the "average person" might do. Or . . . they might refer to scientific studies. . . .
>
> It is impossible to say beforehand what scientific studies might reveal. They may find that most people do panic in such circumstances, or that they don't. The one finding may contribute to a narrowing of free speech, . . . the other to its enlargement. But judicial introspection or guessing about the average person can equally well lead to either of these findings. . . . The difference between "judicial knowledge" and scientific knowledge does not

lie in the substance . . . of the findings, but in the relative confidence that we can place in them. [p. 98]

3.   In a cross-rejoinder, O'Brien (1981) clarified his perception of their differences: "Our basic disagreement is not whether judges should be informed about social science findings, but whether judges should base their decisions on realist premises" (p. 286). He emphasized anew the distinction between "judicial motivation" and "judicial justification." The former refers to the "process of uncovering the relevant empirical evidence . . . necessary for reaching a decision," and he declared that "we neither deny or underestimate the important contributions of social science to judicial decisionmaking" (pp. 286, 287). Every decision contains factual premises which control it, whether expressly relied upon or implicit in the decisional process. Greater reliance on social science would discourage judges from expounding on the basis of their intuitions of the facts or their personal predilections. If there are any limitations to the fact-finding role of social science in the judicial process, it is in the adequacy of the evidence itself and in the sophistication of the judges in using them.

The latter refers to the *ratio decidendi* of the opinion—the articulated rationale for the ruling. Judges are expected to write down the reasons for their actions and, by disclosing them publicly, an institutional safeguard is erected against idiosyncratic judgments. The justifications also provide a basis for public evaluation of the legitimacy of the decision. O'Brien, however, reiterated his view that these justifications should be conditioned on "judicial craftsmanship" and "principled decisionmaking," not on empirical findings. "Social science plays a crucial role in the factfinding process, but a limited and subordinate role in the process of judicial justification" (p. 288). Thus, even if judges make decisions in reliance on social research, they should nonetheless explicate them on principled or nonempirical grounds.

Do you agree that the claimed benefits of such absence of candor in judicial rationalizations outweigh the asserted disadvantages of disclosing the "real" bases of decision-making?

4.   O'Brien is a representative of the growing movement of "neo-conservative" scholars both in law and in the social sciences who, since the mid-seventies, have deplored social policy-making by the courts. They have condemned it as "disaster by decree" (Graglia 1976) and "government by judiciary" (Berger 1977). The Supreme Court, as the principal target, has been portrayed as an "imperial judiciary" (Glazer 1975; see also Horowitz 1977 and Sowell 1981). Their central thesis is that the courts ought to exercise self-restraint—be "modest," in O'Brien's phrase—and not engage in the kind of policy-making that should flow from the elected representatives of the people. The courts should abide by their traditional, quietistic role of limiting the actions of other sectors of government rather than require affirmatively that the executive and legislative branches meet certain minimum standards of performance. In any event, the judiciary is seen as basically incapable of formulating effective social policies. The limits are inherent in the nature of the judicial function. Adjudication is essentially piecemeal and deals with specific historical facts. Social policy-making goes beyond individual cases and deals with events of wide-ranging scope. The incremental method of adjudication suggests that courts will never have enough information to consider all the policy alternatives prior to making a decision. It has no means for anticipating the effects of its actions and for taking the needed corrective action for unanticipated results (Horowitz 1977). The argument for judicial self-restraint is, of course, long-standing. It was well expressed by Justice Frankfurter in his dissent in *Sherrer* v. *Sherrer* (1948):

> [C]ourts are not equipped to pursue the paths for discovering wise policy. A court is confined within the bounds of a particular record, and it cannot even shape the record. Only fragments of a social problem are seen through the narrow windows of a litigation. Had we innate or acquired understanding of a social problem in its entirety, we would not have at our disposal adequate means for constructive solution. [pp. 365–66]

Thus, the debate over judicial reliance on social science implicates the broader debate over the proper function of the judiciary in policy-making. The proponents of judicial activism hark back to such hallowed epigrams as "the Constitution is what judges say it is" (Chief Justice Hughes 1928, p. 120) and "the prophecies of what the courts will do in fact, and nothing more pretentious, are what I mean by the law" (Justice Holmes 1897, p. 462). In the realist tradition, judges create law—law does not have an existence prior to the act of declaration by the judge. It is by the process of decision that opaque constitutional texts are imbued with meaning and become the living law. Conversely, proponents of strict construction in judicial review see constitutional principles as antecedent to judicial decision-making. Judgments are the product, not the cause, of law (Linde 1972). Judges, like the Hebrew prophets of old, do not make law but are merely the conduits for the expression of higher authority.

The fact that critics of judicial activism are also critics of judicial use of social science is not surprising. At least since the postwar years, social scientists as a group have subscribed to liberal social-political values. Their profession seeks to understand and predict future events; hence, they tend to recruit to their ranks those "whose interests are in shaping the future rather than preserving the past" (Moynihan 1979, p. 19). Most of the theory and research deal with "social change," not with the "status quo." The alliance between social science and liberally oriented judicial lawmaking was particularly evident during the fifties and sixties, as the activist Warren Court spearheaded far-reaching reforms in social, political, and criminal procedure rights. However, in the seventies and eighties, with the shift toward a more "modest" Supreme Court, a minority viewpoint in the social science community—popularly known as revisionism or the new conservatism—emerged (or became more vocal). Its adherents feel a philosophical kinship with the neo-formalists in the legal community. Both groups seek to preserve the social peace and the existing order by interpreting the standards of the past rather than following uncertain empirical predictions about the future. Thus, Moynihan (1979) justifies judicial nonintervention by citing lines ascribed to Sir Thomas More: "The law, Roper, the law. I know what's legal, not what's right. And I'll stick to what's legal—I'm not God" (p. 31).

5.   O'Brien disapproves of realist justifications partly because they render civil liberties "more uncertain and precarious." For example, if the police are not deterred by the *Miranda* warnings or if school desegregation does not raise the achievement scores of minority children, the instrumentalist approach that characterizes realism would counsel or justify the abandonment—or, at least, the contraction—of the constitutional entitlement.

However, judges have the power to control the role of social science evidence. As Rosen (1972) observes:

> [T]he Court alone determines the pattern of legal reasoning that goes into a given judicial opinion and thus the particular factual questions that are raised and that need to be answered. Therefore, it can hardly be doubted that the Court, and not the social scientist, retains absolute authority to determine the legal relevance of all social science findings and whether in any given instance a specific social science finding is to be used. [p. 225]

Judges can frame constitutional questions in instrumentalist or normative terms, thereby predetermining the relevance of empirical data. The right to suppress illegally obtained confessions can be grounded on the need to deter improper police interrogations or on the need to vindicate individual rights to fair process. The prohibition against cruel and unusual punishment can be framed in terms of the deterrent effect of the sanction on criminal activity or on the inherent wrongness of the state to authorize the deprivation of life. Courts, then, can formulate the issues in ways that invite a broader role for social science in constitutional adjudication, or in terms that cannot be easily explicated on empirical grounds (Yudof 1978, p. 75).

If constitutional rights become unstable when a decision rests on instrumentalist premises, why do courts continue to rely on them? Why do courts resist always writing opinions that are based exclusively on "principled" grounds?

Is the feared instability of civil liberties due to their insecure social science justifications or to the absence of widespread public support for the rights themselves? In the aftermath of *Brown*, would southern officials have been more accepting of school desegregation if footnote 11 had been omitted?

6.   Instrumentalist/realist decisions implicate "causal judgments" or empirical correlations between legally important variables (for example, death penalty and crime rates). Principled decisions involve the making of "interpretive judgments" or normative assertions about the meaning of events in society. Such judgments are guided by the wisdom of the past and are rendered in the context of prevailing social-political norms: "What do we have to assume about political rights, political goals, political morality—what do we have to assume in order to suppose that [constitutional] decisions are right as a matter of political principle?" (Dworkin 1977a, p. 24).

What political theory underlies principled decision-making? What reasons are there to suppose, as O'Brien does, that principled or interpretive judgments are more certain, consistent, and legitimate than causal or empirical judgments? Are judges necessarily any more competent at making the former than the latter?

7. O'Brien treats interpretive decisions as "principled" and instrumentalist decisions as "ad hoc." Are the two styles inconsistent and mutually exclusive? Can an opinion be justified (at least in part) in the language of causation and social science without violating the formal and substantive conditions for principled decisions? Can it be assumed that appeals to constitutional history, legal precedents, and moral aspirations are never motivated by expediency?

8. O'Brien makes the counterintuitive assertion that "the prestige and efficacy of the judiciary" would be enhanced, and potential "political opposition" to its rulings minimized, if the opinions were "sharply reasoned." A court's stature is not assessed in a social-political vacuum. What considerations in addition to judicial reasoning are necessary to gain public acceptance and legitimation of decisions?

9. The relevance of social science in the judicial process must be examined in comparative context. There are various sources of extralegal information, besides social science, which help inform judicial decision-making and justification. History, logic, philosophy, ethics, and so forth, are some of the alternative or complementary sources of knowledge. The issue, then, is: "What is the comparative advantage that will come to law from using behavioral science?" (Grundstein 1967, p. 88).

Stone (1966) has organized legal thought into three major classifications: "law and logic" (the internal realm of law: the self-enclosed system of logically ordered rules and legal reasoning), "law and justice" (the normative realm of law: the moral postulates that undergird and permeate legal rules), and "law and society" (the external realm of law: the social reality in which law operates). The application of social science is obviously most evident to matters of law and society. But how relevant is social science in this area when compared with, say, speculative notions of social utilitarianism? For example, are the issues regarding the social impact of law shaped and given content more by social philosophy or by empirical data?

Presenting Social Science Evidence

COMMUNICATION AND EVALUATION OF THE EVIDENCE

Social science evidence is usually introduced in the trial court by expert testimony and/or memoranda and in the appellate court by briefs and oral arguments. The separation between fact-determination at trial and law-determination on appeal is not, in practice, so neat and tidy with respect to legislative facts. Findings of fact may be reconsidered on appeal as fully as rulings of law if the findings are pertinent to the making of law. "Questions of fact," wrote Justice Frankfurter, "have traditionally been deemed to be the kinds of questions which ought not to be recanvassed on here [on appeal] unless they are entangled in the proper determination of constitutional or other important legal issues" (*Dick* v. *New York Life Insurance Co.*, 1959, p. 454).

The difficulties raised by the use of social science evidence at the trial or appellate levels concern not so much its admissibility as its evaluation. The usual exclusionary rules of evidence are generally inapplicable to expert testimony. So long as the expert evidence has legal relevance, it is admissible at the discretion of the trial judge. The distinct trend of modern evidence law is to admit rather than to exclude information that may be helpful in fact-finding (Weinstein and Berger 1976, pp. 105–10). In the appellate courts, of course, there are no procedural rules that screen the evidence presented.

Evaluation of expert information—that is, assessment of its sufficiency and weight—is a different matter. Commentators have long pointed out the "inadequacy of the judicial machinery" for determining such facts pertinent to lawmaking (Note, *Harvard Law Review*, 1948, p. 693). There is a "[s]trange neglect of problems of how legislative facts are to be determined by a court" (Hart and McNaughton 1959, p. 63). In the legal literature, "there fails to emerge . . . any coherent philosophy regarding the treatment of scientific knowledge in the courts" (Korn 1966, p. 1081). Decision-makers without special training find it hard to criticize an expert's methods and inferences. Experts can be fallible, and when they "help the courts make policy, they are not likely to shed their attitudes on the ultimate policy issues" (Karst 1960, p. 105).

The conventional approach is to put one's faith in the adversary process—in cross-examination and in the joining of experts and counterexperts in battle. What-ever its merits in assessing adjudicative facts, one should consider its appropriateness in evaluating legislative facts. Indeed, Sperlich asserts that adversariness simply "ob-fuscates behavioral issues." He is not alone among social scientists in faulting the method of confrontation for "distorting" scientific fact-finding (Wolf 1981; Saks and Baron 1980). The idea that partisan advocacy is incompatible with the determination of scientific truth and that, in consequence, social fact-finding should be delegated to experts operating in a nonadversarial setting merits closer scrutiny. It may be that the adversary method of law is a limitation on the application of social research in the courts.

FACTS, VALUES, AND THE ADVERSARY PROCESS

Sperlich's argument rests on the assumption that issues of fact and issues of law can be cleanly severed. In theory, the "is" can be distinguished from the "ought"; in practice, the two commingle. As Judge Bazelon (1982) observes, "Legal and policy questions are multidimensional. They involve scientific, moral, and social judg-ments" (p. 116). Values intrude in every phase of scientific inquiry: in the selection of problems for study, in the formulation of hypotheses, and in the handling and inter-pretation of data. Although some researchers claim to see a clear and "entirely proper" distinction between "ethical values" and "current scientific evidence" in social-legal studies (Wolf 1981, p. 258), the days of any serious claim to a value-free social science are behind us. "A disinterested social science is pure nonsense" (Myrdal, quoted in Miller and Howell 1960, p. 661). There is no immaculate conception of facts. Observation is a goal-directed activity and is not immune from value contamina-tion. All inquiry is selective; some facts are attended to and others are neglected. Empirical knowledge of the social order is interwoven with the beliefs and ideologies one holds. A central teaching of the sociology of knowledge is that truth is not found in facts themselves, but in the way they are organized in relation to some interpretive scheme. This scheme shapes one's perceptions of social reality and explains why things seem to be the way they are (Mannheim 1952). To recognize that descriptive and normative thought merge is not to say that scientific inquiry is impossible. Values shape scientific statements (which are subject to verification by the methods of sci-ence), but that does not render them value statements (which are empirically un-verifiable).

Liberal and neo-conservative social scientists alike have attributed the distor-tions in expert testimony not only to the influence of personal values, but also to the nature of the adversary process which pushes the experts into unaccustomed advo-cacy roles. "By bringing [psychology] into the adversarial confines of law, it is ren-dered controversial and sometimes important," and "its image [of objectivity] is tarnished" (Haney 1980, p. 183). "It is absurd" to use trial procedures to inform decision-makers of social science evidence. "There are no two sides to purely factual matters any more than there are two answers to a problem in arithmetic" (Wolf 1981, p. 262). It is against this background of opinion that Sperlich proposes alternative methods of scientific fact-finding that rely on impartial experts.

A major difficulty with these proposals is that they do not face the problem of the intrusion of values in empirical research. Confessing to "a passionate ambivalence about the behavioral sciences," Judge Bazelon (1982) has urged psychologists and other experts who enter the arena of public policy-making to be "truly open" in their pronouncements. "The main problem" is that "they often do not expose the values underlying their choice of facts" and "often operate with hidden agendas." They also do not disclose the presuppositions that underlie their research and fail to "come clean on the uncertainties and divisions of opinion that may exist about [their] findings" (pp. 115–7). The ethical standards of the American Psychological Association (1981) require "discussion of the limitations" of one's findings and "acknowledge[ment of] the existence of alternative hypotheses and explanations" (p. 1). However, increased self-awareness and disclosure of these values and research constraints are not always feasible. Some social scientists may not be conscious of the ideological scheme in which they operate, any more than fish are aware of the medium in which they swim. The adversary process can help expose these normative assumptions. It is precisely because there is no scientific consensus on the kinds of complex facts implicated in social policy matters—facts based upon an intricate structure of data and inference, not upon simple arithmetic—that they are at issue in litigation. Even physical science proponents of a "science court" agree that an adversary relation is "necessary for the proper resolution of scientific questions" (Martin 1977, p. 1066). It provides an institutional check on experts who might foist their preferences on policy in the guise of scientific expertise. Moreover, the processes of authority yield finality to competing claims of fact more cheaply, categorically, and immediately than the processes of science. To preserve social order, disputes must be resolved one way or another even in the absence of complete information. Science is indentured to tomorrow's evidence; faced with uncertainty, it withholds judgment. Law, however, has a device for definitive settlement. It simply allocates the loss to the party that failed to sustain the burden of proof. In addition, the confrontation inherent at trial helps bring issues to a head. Cross-examination puts to affirmative use the inevitable bias of experts by revealing the weaknesses of the other side. The adversary system, which Justice Holmes called a miniature marketplace of ideas, ensures that opposing views are raised (*Abrams* v. *United States,* 1929).

Some social scientists have even argued that "the scientific enterprise as a whole follows an adversary model," though not in the formalized manner of a trial (Levine 1974, p. 669). Rivlin's idea (1973) of "forensic social science" actually embraces an adversary approach to social fact-finding:

> [This is an approach] in which scholars or teams of scholars take on the task of writing briefs for or against particular policy positions. They state what the position is and bring together all the evidence that supports their side of the argument, leaving to the brief writers of the other side the job of picking apart the case that has been presented and detailing the counter evidence. . . . [In evaluating a brief as] an example of forensic social science, one should not ask: Is it balanced and objective? Rather, one should ask: [Did the authors] make clear the position they are trying to prove or disprove? Is their evidence convincing? [p. 61]

THE ROLE OF EXPERTS AND THE "SCIENCE COURT"

The conventional role of an expert is as a party-chosen witness. Sperlich's proposals for "organizing the experts" casts them in different roles, such as those of an impartial adviser or a neutral decision-maker. In the past, proposals similar to these have been advanced, but nothing much has come from them. For example, Judge Cardozo (1921) recommended the creation of a "Ministry of Justice" which included a research office attached to the courts. It was the judicial equivalent of a legislative reference bureau, geared toward collecting data germane to cases under consideration. Another proposal, which has been implemented on occasion, is to have court-appointed experts who testify at trial and are subject to cross-examination by both sides (Korn 1966, p. 1083). Experts also serve as neutral advisers to the court. In antitrust and patent litigation, judges have sometimes appointed experts to serve as their law clerks. In domestic relations courts, experts are often called upon to provide information to the judge on the family life and background of the parties to the case. These practices, however, have not involved social scientists on matters of broad social policy.

The idea of a "neutral" expert assumes that scientific interpretation of evidence is unequivocal. In forensically relevant disciplines such as psychology and economics, scholars may owe allegiance to particular schools of thought which color their reading of the evidence, even though they may be neutral in the sense of not receiving a fee from either side. Lempert (1981) notes that "it is probably more common for experts to be paid because of the positions that they espouse than for experts to espouse positions because they are paid" (p. 125). He suggests another role for "impartial" experts: as resource persons to educate the jury, rather than as sources of expert opinion. Such experts could describe the competing theoretical perspectives within the discipline or explain technical concepts used by the parties' experts.

A proposal that has earned substantial attention is that of a science court. There are different variations of this idea, but common to all of them are (1) separate allocation of scientific questions to scientific experts and policy questions to public officials charged with policy-making, (2) reliance on the adversary process to ensure that all conflicting factual issues are raised and considered, and (3) publication of the findings of scientific fact (Martin 1977). Consider, however, some of the unresolved issues:

How are the scientific advocates selected? In a common law court, the parties have a personal stake in the outcome, and they select their own counsel. In a science court, the advocates may represent a wider and more diffuse interest—for example, who represents the side that argues for a twelve-person jury? What incentives are there to keep them advocating devilishly?

Who are the judges and how are they selected? To whom are they accountable? Should they be naive or knowledgeable experts? A social scientist who is an authority on, say, school desegregation, may have his or her own biases that are brought to the decision-making process. A social scientist who is inexpert in this field may have to be trained before sitting in judgment on school desegregation disputes. If there is a judging panel, should there be a cross-sectional representation of viewpoints among the judges?

Who will select the scientific issues for the scientific court to consider? The selection is, itself, a political function.

What effect should be given to the findings of fact of the science court, advisory or conclusive? Some finality is needed to enable policy determination to proceed. But pronouncements by a "Supreme Court of Social Science" may live a long life and become calcified, inhibiting further inquiry.

Sperlich calls for "experimentation" to determine the effectiveness of the proposed alternatives. But how does one assess the success of a science court? Is effectiveness in this context an empirical question?

Is the separation of decision-making by scientists on issues of science and decision-making by policy-makers on issues of policy a desirable one in a democratic society? Ours is a specialized society that elevates the position of the expert. Arguably, however, social policy-making requires a different kind of expertise: the capacity to see things in perspective. Issues regarding the effect of school desegregation on minority achievement, or the effect of the exclusionary rule on police conduct, are not merely technical ones. The scientific aspects are separated from the policy aspects only by a permeable membrane.

The place and function of the judiciary is to resolve conflicting social interests. Can a one-function judiciary, that decides only issues of policy, effectively discharge that responsibility? What are the broader political ramifications of segregating fact-determination and policy-determination in specialized tribunals?

Does the concept of a science court with an expert as judge make more sense in the administrative process than in the judicial process?

JUDICIAL NOTICE

Perhaps the most common source of extralegal information relied upon in appellate adjudication is simply a judge's own knowledge, supplemented by any available testimony or briefs by experts. By using the multifaceted doctrine of judicial notice, a judge may determine legislative facts free from the constraints of trial procedures. This doctrine refers to the determination of the facts and/or to the independent acquisition of information pertinent to that determination. To say, for example, that a court judicially notices the deleterious effects of segregation on children's personalities means that a court determines that such are the facts and/or that a court may resort to informal investigation (such as reading the psychological literature) to acquire the pertinent information. Thus, a court is not restricted to the evidence presented by the parties and found in the trial record.

There is disagreement about what facts may be properly noticed—that is, what facts may be established without formal submission of evidence or what facts a court may determine by its own independent efforts. Under the traditional and narrow usage, a court may notice only matters that are commonly known within its jurisdiction. It allows a judge to give legal expression to that which is assumed to be generally familiar and indisputable. As members of the community, judges share in the common fund of social experience, and it is this shared consensus that makes judicial notice possible. For example, Justice Brewer in *Muller* v. *Oregon* (1908) wrote, "We take judicial cognizance of all matters of general knowledge [regarding the effect of long working hours on the health and welfare of women]." Of course, common knowledge may not be compatible with scientific knowledge. It can be a guise for uninformed assumptions about social reality. This common knowledge standard would certainly exclude scientific information known only to specialists.

Many courts today use the verifiable certainty standard. It permits notice of generalized knowledge that, although not commonly known, is capable of determination by examining reliable sources. It includes specialized information on which the scholarly community has reached a consensus. This standard allows a court to take into account new scientific findings when they are widely accepted within the discipline, even though they may not have yet filtered down to society at large. With this standard, a court can use judicial notice as a tool to keep abreast of the latest developments in scientific fields and bring them into the law. In practice, of course, information on the frontiers of scientific inquiry may not be readily verifiable or be accepted with a high degree of consensus.

What questions of procedural fairness and political legitimacy are raised by court decisions which are justified solely or largely on judicially noticed information?

13.3.   WHEN TO USE SOCIAL RESEARCH

THE QUEST FOR THE MIDDLE RANGE: EMPIRICAL INQUIRY AND LEGAL POLICY

Harry Kalven, Jr.

. . .

[M]y point put bluntly is that the law on the whole remains today gratuitously unscientific. Put less bluntly, we in the legal world need some literacy as to scientific method and as to the scientific idiom of exposition. Most important we need to develop some *taste*, and I use the word advisedly, in scientific inquiry. We are fond of talking about getting "the feel" of a rule of law; we need also to get "a feel" for empirical inquiry in law. . . .

THE MIDDLE RANGE

. . .

It seems clear the law does, and should, embody value judgments that are beyond the reach of factual impeachment. When these profound premises are involved, there will necessarily be an embar-

Reprinted from Harry Kalven, Jr., "The Quest for the Middle Range: Empirical Inquiry and Legal Policy," in The American Assembly, *Law in a Changing America*, ed. G. Hazard, pp. 56–74. Copyright ©1968 by The American Assembly.

rassing distance between the premise and any facts modern social science can offer in its support. Perhaps this means . . . that social science cannot after all play much of a role in lawmaking at the constitutional level. The values at that level are too fundamental.

The image of high level premises which are beyond the reach of fact suggests the converse phenomenon, premises so mundane and commonplace as not to need any systematic confirmation. There is a considerable domain in law where common experience and amateur factfinding provide the knowledge that is needed; professional social science inquiry in such areas will be viewed as an expensive way of telling us what we already knew. . . .

Robert Merton some years ago observed that in their current state the social sciences could aspire only to theories in the middle range. We can adapt his remark to the application of social science to legal problems: it can only aspire to facts in the middle range. Some premises are too deeply held for actual footnoting, and some facts are too well and accessibly known for professional inquiry. What remains then as the critical area is the middle range where the premises are not that unshakeable and where the facts are not that accessible.

It is for this reason, I suspect, that both sides in any ideological dispute about bringing social science empiricism to law tend to overshoot the mark. On the one hand, it is simplistic to urge that because law makes factual assumptions, there should be a one-to-one linking and testing of the underlying social facts, an endless dropping of empirical footnotes to points of law. On the other hand, it is nonsense to say that better documentation of fact cannot ever be relevant to law because the final business of law is not truth but political preference.

Our metaphor of the middle range does not dispose of the perplexities about facts and values which have so haunted discussions of law and science. We would note three further points. First, even when the norms or values are not the ones most deeply held, it remains true that facts do not per se resolve value issues, or, as Professor Patterson put it, that purely factual premises cannot yield a normative conclusion. Their relevance is oblique. They serve to narrow the controversy by eliminating certain points of disagreement or by suggesting unsuspected connections to other points. To take a simple example. There has been a good deal of controversy in recent years over the retention of the jury in civil cases. One point of criticism has gone to the jury's contribution toward court delay because it takes longer to try a case to a jury than to a judge alone. We were able to make an informed estimate of just how much longer a jury trial was, and the "scientific" answer was 40 per cent. This fact alone surely does not resolve the value-ridden controversy about the retention of the jury in civil cases, but it does help to focus the argument and reduce exaggerations on either side. . . .

Next, as the jury example suggests, there is the familiar point that law has a multiplicity of ends and that we can always escape the thrust of factual impeachment by shifting the grounds. The point is one most likely to dismay our social scientist

colleagues who wish to pin down a legal premise for testing. Legal rules and especially legal institutions do not have a single avowed end or purpose against which their performance can be tidily measured. We appear to say, for example, that the jury's official function is to decide issues of fact—certainly a social scientist looking at cases would find endless statements to that effect. If, then, he elects to test how well the jury finds facts, we are likely to smile and tell him its real function is to introduce equity and the community sense of justice into the legal system, or to guard against the corruption or bias of American judges, or to provide a lightning rod for community resentment in the disposition of hard cases, or to provide civic education for the juror citizen. One can almost hear the exasperated social scientist shouting, "Stand still for a minute, damnit!" But while this multiplicity of ends may be a profound point about the nature of practical action and about law in particular, it is a shallow point in the relation of science to law. At most, it is a warning against too simplistic a scientific approach. To say the purposes of law are multiple is not to say they are indeterminate or Hydra-headed. . . .

The third familiar theme is that law deals with preference, not truth, and we wish to make the policy choices ourselves and not delegate them to the scientific expert. We want the expert for his facts, not for his values. This is part of a problem larger than that of the social scientist in the democratic process. However clear the principle for the division of labor, it is, as we see with the use of the psychiatric expert in insanity pleas, awkward to apply cleanly in practice. What interests us at the moment is not so much this point as the closely related one it leads to. For social science learning to have an impact on the living law, will it first have to become *popular* learning and thus enter law via the normal political process? . . . Until they become more widely shared among the public of judges, they cannot have their impact on the law. . . . [W]e can dimly see a fascinating general topic about the role of science in forming public opinion on matters that affect law. . . .

[CONCLUSION]

. . .

We need a critical mass of empirical legal studies which are widely shared in legal culture so that a sense of the liberating possibilities of scientific inquiry into social fact can develop. . . . The "golden era" will come when such work has become routine, and is seen as simply another resource for legal scholarship and not as an applied mechanic.

It is not inappropriate to end soliloquies of this sort with a slogan for the future. I have one to offer: let us "empiricize" jurisprudence and intellectualize fact finding.

NOTES AND QUESTIONS

1.   Kalven does not specify the boundaries of the "middle range" of the fact-value continuum. What criteria would you use to determine whether a given legal issue fell in the upper, middle, or lower range? Is this a useful way of thinking about when social research can be applied effectively to judicial decision-making? Even though many problems of constitutional stature involve interpretive judgments and are not immediately responsive to empirical data, does it follow that "social science cannot after all play much of a role in lawmaking at the constitutional level"?

2.   Rosenberg (1971) gives a "homely test" of whether a problem falls in what Kalven might term the upper range: "Can you visualize evidence concerning the impact of your preferred version upon human behavior or conditions that would lead you to reject that choice for an alternative one? If not, the choice is animated by value considerations" (p. 202). For example, if reliable evidence clearly showed that the death penalty deterred criminal activity but some people remain unmoved in their opposition to this sanction, then for them this issue would be beyond the reach of factual determination. Critique this test.

3.   Law is inextricably linked to political processes and to public acceptance. If "the final business of law is not truth but political preference," is the use of social science in judicial decision-making and justification also, ultimately, a matter of political choice?

4.   "[T]he most suitable model of social scientific involvement in constitutional litigation is a model by means of which scholars may direct themselves explicitly toward the investigation of the empirical and logical foundations alleged to justify the causal inferences and assumptions that underlie the official policy under investigation" (Katz 1971, p. 56). Do you agree that this is the "most suitable" use?

13.4.   LIMITS TO RAPPROCHEMENT: DIFFERENCES IN METHODOLOGY

Since the introduction of the Brandeis brief, the use of social research in the courts has been somewhat common but not ubiquitous. Commentators have puzzled over "why lawyers do not offer, nor courts invite, such testimony more often" (Hart and McNaughton 1959, p. 64). Even in the halcyon days of realism, there has always been a residual doubt and a lingering dissatisfaction regarding the yield of the social sciences for law (Cohen 1959, p. 67; Fahr and Ojemann 1962, p. 60). In the postrealist period, the "patterns of conflict" between the two fields have been drawn more sharply (Katz and Burchard 1970, p. 198), and "a profound skepticism" about their eventual rapprochement has been voiced by normatively oriented scholars (Yudof 1978, p. 71).

There are various reasons for this state of affairs. In both the legal and social science communities, some advocates for increased collaboration have blamed the "inertia" and "negative attitudes" of the legal profession toward empirical research (Lochner 1974, p. 1035). "[L]awyers and law professors are generally so ignorant of science and its methods that they are neither able to distinguish problems which can properly be studied empirically from those which cannot, nor to formulate questions and designs for empiric investigation of appropriate problems" (Loevinger 1966, p. 540). Since the turn of the century to the present, some psychologists have perceived lawyers as "obdurate" (Münsterberg 1908, p. 9), "reactionary," and "close-minded" (quoted in Wells 1978, p. 1547), who "resent the entry of experts" into their domain (Yarmey 1979, p. 32). As additional reasons, others have pointed to the opacity of social science concepts, the seeming impenetrability of statistical reasoning, and the absence of published summaries of research findings in a format accessible to lawyers.

Explanations motivated by professional rivalry and ideological tendentiousness add little to an understanding of the problem. Lawyers and judges have been inventive in various fields—for example, they have applied economic principles to antitrust cases and mastered technological subjects for patent litigation. Thus, with effort and assistance, they could also become informed consumers of social science knowledge. The reasons for their underutilization of social research cannot be attributed mainly to the inaccessibility of that research or to their ignorance of it. One must turn, instead, to more basic reasons that have to do with epistemology and professional socialization. In this section, we will look at limits to rapprochement that arise from differences in the subject matter and in the methods of inquiry of science and law. In the next section, we will focus on the differences in occupational training and rewards that shape the different professional values of social scientists and lawyers. These materials may offer some insights into why there never has been and probably never will be "interdisciplinary bliss" (Katz and Burchard 1970, p. 197). They also suggest that a lasting *entente cordiale* is not beyond reach.

PSYCHOLOGY AND LEGAL CHANGE: ON THE LIMITS OF A FACTUAL JURISPRUDENCE

Craig Haney

. . .

PARADIGMS IN CONFLICT: THE DIVERGENT METHODS AND STYLES OF PSYCHOLOGY AND LAW

. . .

Substantial differences exist between the styles and methods of reasoning, proof, and justification used in psychology and law. To identify some of them may help us locate potential areas where psychological categories translate imperfectly, if at all, into legal forms. They suggest possible limitations in the practical ability of psychology to effect renovations in the law and legal system. . . .

A. In academic psychology, as in other social sciences, a premium is placed upon the *creative*. From early in their graduate careers, academic psychologists are rewarded for thinking thoughts and rendering interpretations that are different and innovative. There is thus a strong emphasis on the new, the novel and unique solution. . . .

In contrast, our legal system operates on a precedential or *stare decisis* model in which past decisions control current cases. Indeed, a truly unique idea or argument is likely to lose in a court of law. In a system in which legal decisions in the present are made on the basis of legal decisions in the past, lawyers are forced to adopt a more intellectually *conservative* stance than that of social scientists. . . .

B. Judges typically base their decisions upon the earlier rulings of some prior court. . . . Thus the impact of a decision often depends less upon the wisdom or cogency of its analysis than on the authority or legal status of the court that issued it. In this sense, the epistemology of law is largely *authoritarian*. . . .

On the other hand, psychology and other social sciences are largely *empirical* enterprises whose principles and propositions depend for their confirmation upon the collection of consistent and supporting data. . . .

C. Epistemology implies methodology. The methodology employed by empirical psychology to arrive at its version of "truth" is primarily *experimental*. . . .

In marked contrast, the law commonly uncovers truth through an adversarial process—contending positions or points of view confront one another in litigation, and truth is tested and refined through this "combative" method. . . .

D. The pronouncements of the law are primarily *prescriptive*—they tell people how they should behave (and provide for certain consequences if they do not). In contrast, psychology is essentially a *descriptive* discipline, seeking to describe behavior as it actually occurs. . . .

On the surface, at least, psychology is concerned with "what is," the law with "what should be." In fact, however, values permeate behavioral science and "shoulds" occupy priority positions in the hidden agendas of most researchers. . . .

E. The focus of the judicial lawmaking is primarily *idiographic*—it concentrates upon the single case. Legal cases are adjudicated on an individual basis and the idiosyncratic facts of a particular case form the basis for decision in that case. . . . Empirical psychology, on the other hand, seeks to be *nomothetic* in scope—concentrating upon general principles, relationships, and patterns that transcend the single instance. For the most part it eschews case studies and principles generated from single cases. In this sense, the data of psychology are more akin to "legislative" than "adjudicatory" facts in the law. . . .

Several consequences follow from this clash of idiographic and nomothetic perspectives. For one, courts are reluctant to admit social science generalizations into evidence. . . . And it also limits the kind of information they acquire about the broader structural context of the controversies themselves. . . . The emphasis on individual cases means that courts are poorly situated to uncover and assess patterns. Thus the significance of the patterns or nomothetic configurations that are presented via social science data may elude them as well.

F. Perhaps because the consequences of legal decisions are so often irrevocable, decisionmaking is rendered more palatable by the appearance of *certainty*. . . . The legal emphasis on certainty—or predictability and finality—has a long history. Indeed, some suggest that it underpins the primacy of the legal form in modern society. . . .

Empirical psychology, on the other hand, deals in explicitly *probabilistic* terms. Psychologists are accustomed to attaching qualifiers and conditionals to statements of relationships they uncover. Indeed, their most unequivocal statement—that a relationship is "statistically significant"—is in terms of explicit probabilities. . . .

G.   Psychology is a *proactive* enterprise in that its issues, problems, and concerns are initiated primarily by its practitioners. It is academic psychologists who decide what is important or interesting and worthy of psychological study. Influenced, of course, by the socioeconomic and intellectual contexts in which they function, they select and define the problems on which they work. The law, on the other hand, is primarily *reactive*—its mechanisms respond to issues and conflicts brought to its attention by persons *outside* the system—clients. . . .

H.   Finally, and in a related vein, the brand of psychology most often employed in legal change efforts remains largely *academic* in nature. Its "issues" are commonly determined by the intellectual curiosities of psychologists and the practical reality of having to publish in order to prosper. For this reason, its concerns can and often do get far out of contact with the "real world." . . . [Psychologists] typically avoid—and are therefore often naive about—the power struggles that precede policy change. Even so-called "applied" psychological research is conducted most often by persons untrained in the nature and process of application.

The law, however, is primarily an *operational* discipline—its concerns are those of the real world and its problem solving is geared to application. . . .

I have tried to highlight potentially conflicting elements of the psychological and legal perspective as they typically intersect in legal change efforts. Like all such caricatures, these contain imperfections and apparent exceptions that range in importance. But the distinctions I have drawn between characteristic modes of thought and action in psychology and law represent potential areas of friction that

can retard the use of psychology to effect legal change. . . .

PROSPECTS AND PESSIMISM: SOME REALISM ABOUT LEGALISM

. . .

A.   SOME TACTICAL CONSIDERATIONS: CONFRONTING AND NEGOTIATING PROFESSIONAL DIFFERENCES. Let me be more specific and explicit now about some of the implications of divergent professional styles and methods for "psychology and law." . . .

The adversarial nature of much legal process means that psychological data-as-evidence is susceptible to distortion. Precautions against this may include the active and extended participation of psychologists in the litigation process itself, so that they can more actively shape the manner in which their data are presented and received. . . .

Adversary settings, in addition, are not designed to facilitate implementation of outcomes. To prevail acrimoniously at trial may ensure defeat at a later implementation stage. Psychological input should be structured with this later, ultimate goal in mind. . . . Although it has not been generally recognized as such, the implementation of such judicial decrees is largely a matter of applied social psychology and may be an especially productive area for participation by psychologists committed to legal and social change. . . .

The tension between prescription and description is in some ways related to the idiographic bias of the law. Put simply, while psychologists are most skilled at providing data on how people generally *do* behave, the courts are most concerned with how *this* defendant *should have* behaved. Thus, psychologists might more selectively present evidence in legal forums where decisionmakers can consider data that extend beyond the facts of a single case—to a certain extent appellate courts and to a greater degree legislative and administrative bodies. . . . The growing use of psychology to challenge the validity of eyewitness identification provides some concrete examples. . . . But the importance of such testimony is limited by its highly idiographic, single-case focus. Little widespread or lasting legal change occurs as a result. . . .

[E]xpressions of uncertainty or probability [in law] breed a lack of confidence. The legal system must come to see decisions as more tentative so that probabilistic data become more tolerated. . . . [Donald] Campbell has advocated instead ". . . an experimental approach to social reform." . . . This same logic can be applied generally to legal decisions and policies. Although impractical in certain instances, court decrees and implementation orders might be given more of an experimental tone with periodic evaluation and reassessment structured into the decisions themselves, to facilitate their modification and eliminate the need for false certainty in factual records.

The largely reactive nature of legal practice may mean that in many instances legal change is simply a poor vehicle for social change. Legal cases are often unrepresentative of social problems. . . . There is thus no guarantee that legal resources are allocated in proportion to the moral or social importance of the problem addressed. . . .

Under these conditions, psychologists might adopt a more proactive stance in the legal process itself. Typically, . . . [l]awyers decide when an area of law needs changing, when they have an appropriate case in which to attempt it, and when psychologists might have something to contribute to the effort. But by adopting a more proactive stance here, psychologists might reverse this process somewhat. *They* are best positioned to assess the state of psychological knowledge on particular

legal issues. . . . [P]sychologists can sensitize change-oriented attorneys about what to look for and where. . . .

[T]he clear implication of my contrast between psychology and law is that there are numerous ways in which the nature and form of psychological data grate against the legalistic perspective, giving judges a motive to reject it. But there has been little systematic study that would allow us to predict conditions under which judges would give social science evidence a more or less favorable reception. . . .

D.   A FINAL NOTE ON LEGALISM. In the dichotomy between law and psychology, I have suggested that law represents a powerful and entrenched structure and that psychological methods and data are for the most part *assimilated* into it. But at the basis of much of the preceding discussion has also been the implicit suggestion that psychologists press for the *accommodation* of the legal structure itself to the psychological data that are brought to it.[58] . . .

[There is] a final impediment to the use of psychology in effecting legal change. In a sense, psychological analysis "rationalizes" the legal system and makes it more predictable. By acknowledging and gathering data on a fuller range of determinants in legal decisionmaking, we render the outcomes of legal processes more predictable. Legal consequences can be more accurately anticipated. Yet, lawyers may have a vested interest in preserving— in image or reality—a legal system that is somewhat "irrational," arcane, and difficult to negotiate. As the system becomes

---

[58]The metaphor is psychological. Piaget uses the term "assimilation" to suggest that information that is taken in by an organism is changed or transformed to better conform to the organism's preexisting cognitive structure or schema. He uses "accommodation" to suggest that in this process of incorporating information an organism's cognitive structure is altered by the nature of the information itself. . . .

more predictable lawyers are rendered correspondingly less necessary. . . . Individual differences between attorneys will have less impact on decisions. . . .

[P]sychologists who intervene in this system are taking power from the powerful, from persons expert in its use. To do so will not be easy. . . .

NOTES AND QUESTIONS

Haney's description of the differences in fact-finding and reasoning between law and psychology (or social science generally) goes far in explaining why their respective practitioners appear to be marching to different drummers. We shall examine some of these differences.

1.   Law is indeed "intellectually conservative," if by that is meant that stability and predictability in social norms are valued. However, some of the most significant innovations in American society in recent years—for example, in civil rights and women's rights—were wrought or spearheaded by the courts. What are some of the means by which judges hide their creative light under a doctrinal bush? Why do they strive to make things appear unchanged when, in fact, they are changing them?

2.   The social impact of a decision is said to depend less upon its "wisdom" than the "authority" of the court. What is the basis for public recognition of and acquiescence in the authority of the judiciary, an institution which, in the words of Alexander Hamilton, possesses neither purse nor sword? Scientific findings are no doubt more satisfying to the modern mind than conclusions simply declared to be so by a judge. What is there to recommend to the processes of authority over an empirical epistemology as a means of resolving social disputes? Will advances in social science knowledge diminish the "continuing attractions in the Delphic Oracle" (Hazard 1967a, p. 77)?

3.   Important implications flow from the descriptive orientation of science and the prescriptive tenor of law. The purposive and imperative character of law colors its fact-finding and decision-making processes. This is why decisions cannot always be deduced solely from the particulars to which legal rules are applied, in the same manner that scientific conclusions are derived from the application of theory to data. In adjudication, facts can be bent to serve ulterior purposes (Hart and McNaughton 1959). Although the manipulation of facts may be intellectually dishonest in other fields, in law it enjoys underground respectability. For example, considerations of fairness may affect the wisdom of scientific determinations of paternity in different contexts. Blood-grouping tests showing nonpaternity can be made conclusive in filiation proceedings. The same result might be unacceptable in a custody proceeding where the child was sired by a stranger but raised by the "social" father. A jury can thwart the law and find "inaccurate" facts, even in the face of scientific evidence, in order to inject its notions of community justice. The power of the jury to render a general verdict without any supporting reasons or explanation is an instance of the institutionalization of the practice of bending facts. In short, the law often consciously sacrifices truth to other social values. Evidentiary privileges (confidentiality of communications between attorney and client, priest and penitent, husband and wife, and other valued relationships) are an example in point. Science makes no such concessions to competing values. When the main purpose of an inquiry is peaceful resolution of a social dispute rather than acquisition of knowledge, more than "truth" is at stake. Legal fact-finding is not only an untrammeled cognitive exercise of determining what "is"; it is also a judgmental process of determining what "ought" to be.

4.   The "idiographic" character of adjudication is a clinical method of data gathering which is appropriate for the determination of individual, historical facts. The "nomothetic" approach, based on measurements of central tendency and dispersion, is better adapted to securing group data. Loevinger (1966) argues that "[t]he empiric and the dialectic methods are not rivals or alternatives but complementary methods adapted to different problems and applicable to different situations" (p. 541). In what kinds of situations are the two methods complementary or competitive?

5.   Another distinction between the legal and scientific methods is the degree of conclusiveness that each accords to disputed facts. Law satisfies itself with less than absolute certainty and finality in fact-finding. Indeed, it even preserves erroneous fact determinations via such doctrines as res judicata and collateral estoppel. Science, on the other hand, withholds judgments when the data are incomplete. How does the law resolve factual disputes in the presence of uncertainty? What are the implications of this difference for the application of the scientific method to improve or enrich legal inquiry?

6.   Haney asserts that social research "rationalizes" law and makes it "more predictable." Legal realists have always exhorted judges, with scant success, to give their decisions a more "experimental tone," so that "legal consequences can be more accurately anticipated." Is there wisdom in the courts' instinctive wariness of resting their decisions on the "rationality" of impact research?

7.   Scientific inquiry presupposes voluntary acceptance of its findings. New findings are appraised in the community of scientists by the reliability and validity of the procedures by which they are obtained and by their statistical significance. Scientific conclusions are objectively and independently verifiable. Legal conclusions, in comparison, lack this autonomy and are linked instead to the political process and to public acceptance. From this difference, do you agree that this conclusion follows: "To the extent that a problem has ripened to the stage where the legal process is required for its resolution, so also to that extent has it ripened beyond resolution by scientific procedures" (Hazard 1967a, p. 75).

8.   There is always a level of particularity at which two things can be distinguished and a level of generality at which they can be said to be analogous. These two approaches can be found among methodologists of law and of science. There are those who maximize differences and minimize similarities (the "splitters") and those who find that every turn in the methodology of one has its counterpart in the other (the "lumpers") (Scriven 1971, p. 189). The question is not who is correct, since neither one may be wrong, but which approach is more enlightening.

For purposes of analysis, two aspects of legal inquiry can be separated: the fact-finding process (the "empirical" component) and the decision-making process (the "thinking" component: reasoning, inference, justification). Scientific inquiry is more readily "lumped" with legal fact-finding than with legal decision-making.

Figure 13.1 sketches the processes of factual proof in law and science. In science, the event under

FIGURE 13.1

Fact-finding in Science and Law

Scientific proof

Present event	→	Method: Controlled observation subject to rules of reliability and validity	→	Data about the event	→	Research hypothesis or theory about the event	→	Statistical standards of proof of hypothesis or theory

Legal proof

Historical event	→	Method: Witness testimony subject to rules of evidence	→	Evidence about the event	→	Legal theory about the event	→	Judicial standards of proof of the theory

study is observed systematically, subject to established criteria of reliability and validity. The data so obtained are used to test a research hypothesis or theory concerning the event. The hypothesis is then evaluated in terms of generally accepted standards of statistical significance. In law, there is a parallel logic of proof. Information regarding a past event is secured by witness testimony. To assure its reliability, the testimony is filtered through layers of exclusionary rules of evidence. The evidence is used to support or rebut a legal theory, under the applicable substantive law, regarding the event. Finally, the sufficiency of the theory is evaluated by the fact-finder according to judicial standards of proof.

The decision-making process of law—applying the major premise of rules to the minor premise of facts—is sufficiently unique that it should be "split" from its scientific counterpart. Legal reasoning contemplates subsuming the particular facts found at trial under previously established general rules. The application of rules always involves the simultaneous processes of determining (deductively) which rule should be applied to the facts and selecting (inductively) the particular facts that call into play the rule (Hart and McNaughton 1959). This kind of circular reasoning is uncommon in scientific thinking. Scientific generalizations are derived from data and are controlled by them. For example, from various studies, a researcher could arrive at the empirical generalization that certain forms of school segregation could be harmful to minority students. In contrast, the generalizations of law are normative as well as descriptive. The assertion of the inequality of segregated schools does not arise wholly from the facts but implicates a value judgment, too. Judicial conclusions cannot be deduced ineluctably from the particulars to which general rules are applied.

13.5.   LIMITS TO RAPPROCHEMENT: DIFFERENCES IN PROFESSIONAL SOCIALIZATION AND CULTURE

PARTNERSHIP WITH THE SOCIAL SCIENCES

Lloyd E. Ohlin

. . . [T]here are significant differences in the intellectual interests of social scientists and lawyers in addressing matters of public policy, theory or research. While thinking about these differences I found myself contrasting impressions I had acquired from research and teaching in a sociology department, a school of social work and a law school. I would like to describe briefly a few of the more striking contrasts that may illustrate both the challenges and frustrations of interdisciplinary work.

Obviously these three educational systems are preparing students for very different occupational careers. It should not be surprising therefore that they use different educational criteria and measures of excellence in recruiting and training students and judging their professional competence. Similar tests are applied to faculty members.

In social science disciplines and surely in sociology, where I am more certain of my ground, prestige is accorded those who display theoretical imagination and research ingenuity. Major professional rewards are given to sociologists who publish treatises describing persuasive conceptual frameworks for studying various aspects of social life, and also to those who have acquired the skills and inventiveness to undertake significant empirical inquiries. On the other hand professional prestige is rarely won by sociologists primarily preoccupied with the policy of programmatic implications of social science theory and research results. [See also Gerard (1983): "The culture in the typical psychology department offers no reward for . . . the study of real-world problems" (p. 876). Ed.'s note.]

This stands in marked contrast to

the system of rewards employed in professional schools of social work and law. In schools of social work the qualities most admired in students and faculty are a capacity for empathy and identification with the personal problems of client groups. They also value skills not only in identifying these problems, but in forming relationships leading to a significant therapeutic interchange. . . .

In law schools, on the other hand, great stress is placed on the ability to analyze and order facts so as to invoke legal principles of decision favorable to a client's case. In public roles it is the ability to mobilize facts supporting particular policies and programs as solutions to public problems that is most valued.

Thus these systems of education sort out and reward rather different abilities according to what are regarded as the significant intellectual capacities and skills required for successful performance of the profession's task. . . . As one listens to students interacting formally in these different settings it becomes clear that they live in very different educational subcultures and that the student's environment and his learning experience train capacities of a different intellectual order. They are all, of course, highly competitive environments. The difference really lies in the criteria by which achievements are evaluated, and such differences necessarily train certain intellectual capacities and sensitivities at the expense of others.

It is immediately apparent that these differences in educational objective will pose somewhat different crucial tests of the student in the course of his training. In sociology the doctoral dissertation has been traditionally the critical index of achievement. It is the quality of research skill and theoretical inventiveness displayed in the doctoral dissertation which in large part determines his subsequent career possibilities. One unfortunate consequence of this fact is the creation of a group of very able but insecure "perennial" graduate students who experience enormous difficulty in completing their doctoral dissertations. The requirement of an "original contribution to knowledge" produces for many a lengthy apprenticeship in research and considerable personal trauma before this hurdle is overcome.

The profession of social work rewards excellence in field-work rather than academic work in selecting graduating students for the most prized career opportunities. To the extent that excellence in field-work involves great sensitivity in the use of oneself in inter-personal relationships with client groups, it encourages students to achieve greater personal insight through some type of disciplined self-analysis. . . .

Law schools on the other hand place enormous stress on the display of reasoning and analytic ability. The reward system and learning experience is focused with great intensity on the first year of law school training. Such rewards as membership on the Law Review and subsequent occupation preferments, including desirable court clerkships, are thus largely won or lost when the professional training is only one-third completed. This intense focus on the training of analytical ability as the central intellectual capacity clearly stimulates a brilliant growth in this ability among some students while producing in others enormous anxiety, self-doubts and personal conflicts. . . .

In the foregoing comments I have tried to highlight contrasts in these three systems of education. I think these differences are real to the student despite the fact that all of these educational settings value intellectual capacities for conceptualizing, empathizing and analyzing. The difference lies in the order of priority given to these different intellectual capacities and their related technical skills. I suspect this difference is likely to become less rather than greater in the future. Sociologists are becoming more action oriented than they have been in the past. Social work education stresses more the potential contribution of theory and research in the design of effective social action programs and policies. Similarly law schools are making greater use of other disciplines on the one hand to challenge fundamental assumptions about social problems and on the other to bring to bear new types of empirical data on the choice of policy and program alternatives.

These differences in the training and professional orientation of sociologists, social workers and lawyers suggest some of the difficulties a sociologist may expect to encounter in . . . carrying on research in a law school. Law students are most interested in discussions relating to the solution of social problems and the grounds for choosing among public policy alternatives. They tend to be impatient with the theorizing interests of social scientists, the complications of research design and the detailed development of proof for different hypothetical propositions. For example, law students are much less interested in the conceptual distinctions and empirical evidence for different explanations of deviant conduct than they are in the question "what difference will it make for either action or policy if one or the other theory is correct?" I have found that student interest is sustained better if some of the alternative policy and program implications are dealt with at the outset, followed by an examination of the theoretical or factual support in favor of one or the other. One of the problems in this approach, of course, is that the social science literature is not written in this fashion. It is only rarely that one encounters social science material organized to address alternative policy and action implications.

There is another type of problem which the social scientist encounters in . . . the law school setting. It is possible to develop a body of theory and research findings to increase understanding of the sources of various types of social problems with which lawyers are concerned, such problems for example as crime. . . . However, explanations of the sources of social problems do not necessarily provide clear guidelines to the solution of those problems. Development of such [solutions] offers an appropriate area for interdisciplinary collaboration and cooperative contributions by social scientists and lawyers.

If interdisciplinary collaboration is to bear fruit it will become increasingly important to define what each discipline might bring to the study of a particular problem and what each in turn may get out of it. [One must accept] the fact that social scientists and lawyers must have different career commitments and colleague groups to which they must be responsive. In collaborative work there is a common area of activity and concern which they can share but each must then be free to address the specialized audience toward which his own career and professional identifications are oriented. Thus in addition to the shared product emerging from their work it should also be possible to develop ideas and research findings which address specialized interests of their own respective disciplines. . . .

Social Science (and Economics) in Law Schools

If lawyers are to become more receptive to and better informed consumers of social science, the foundation for this change has to be laid in the law school years. Ohlin's article points out how the socialization experiences of law school help shape professional attitudes and interests. Thus, changes in the curriculum of legal education can have reverberating effects on the profession as a whole. Empirical inquiry first came into the law on a systematic basis as a result of the endeavors of a small coterie of professors in major law schools, together with some scholarly minded judges and attorneys. A brief sketch of the erratic history of social research in law schools may shed some light on the difficulties and prospects of trying to "empiricize jurisprudence" (Kalven 1968, p. 70).

Legal education in the colonial period was more or less haphazard, consisting of law office apprenticeships and proprietary law schools. It later underwent three major periods of reform, coincident with the emergence of the three major jurisprudential approaches to law.

LAW SCHOOLS AND FORMALISM

The first change was associated with formalism. By the mid-nineteenth century, the country had entered a phase of rapid geographic and economic expansion. A deanglicized, native common law blossomed as the courts were called upon to regulate this growth. These developments precipitated the need for more and better trained lawyers, so that by the turn of the century, a number of university-affiliated law schools had been established. The Harvard Law School was the first and most prominent of them. Its Dean, Charles Langdell (1871), invented the case method of instruction for searching and analyzing the enduring principles of law. Over the next fifty years or so, this technique and its formalist premises became the orthodoxy of legal education. The legal profession was ripe for this new religion. The formalist conception of law as a closed system of rules, that was applied to the given facts to produce an inevitable result, embodied hidden ideas drawn from the dominant ideologies of the day, such as *laissez faire*. Langdell's approach made law into a "science" and gave it academic respectability. At the same time, it served the needs of an industrializing nation by justifying a quietistic role of judges in social and economic change.

LAW SCHOOLS AND REALISM

The law schools' courtship of the social sciences began in earnest in the 1920s and 1930s, in connection with attempts at wholesale reform of their pedagogical curriculum. These changes were manifestations of that state of mind known as legal realism. A rising generation of young academics rejected the philosophy and methods of Langdell and pioneered a broader vision of law and of legal education that took into account extralegal influences.

The Columbia Law School was at the forefront of these developments. It saw law as "a form of social control intimately related to those social functions which are the subject matter of economics and the social sciences generally" (Currie 1955, pp. 10–11). It proposed a radical reorganization of the curriculum—one of the most important ever made in legal education—to convert a professionally oriented school into a scholarly, research-oriented institution. This grand design was hotly debated but never implemented, as the traditionalists on the faculty prevailed to keep the school a training ground for future members of the bar. Responsibility to the profession triumphed over commitment to empirical scholarship partly because of the high cost of the graduate school model of legal education and partly because of the realization that the social sciences at that time were of "far less help to the legal scholar than had been expected" (Stevens 1971, pp. 475–76). There simply was no sufficient corpus of reliable data of direct applicability to legal inquiry. The reformers resigned from Columbia; some went to Yale and others to the Johns Hopkins Institute for the Study of Law (a center for nonprofessional, empirically oriented studies).

The great stock market crash ended the funding largesse of foundations and the Johns Hopkins Institute folded permanently. In the late twenties and in the thirties, the lamp of reform passed to Yale Law School and catapulted the institution to pre-eminence. Several social scientists were appointed as lecturers and research associates, and they collaborated with the law faculty on a wide range of projects, including the psychology of evidence law, bankruptcy administration, surveys of the bar, legal sanctions, and legal procedure (Schlegel 1979, 1980). Interdisciplinary courses and seminars were created. One jointly taught offering, "The Judicial Process from the Point of View of Social Psychology," was highly successful and led to the publication of two books (Robinson 1935; Arnold 1935). The law school was instrumental in establishing the Yale Institute of Human Relations for the purpose of undertaking collaborative studies with the medical school and with social science departments. Of course, not all faculty members were enraptured by these goings-on (Frey 1934), but social-legal scholarship was the dominant theme and this was what made Yale a special place. These visionary academics led American lawyers out of the Langdellian bondage of fixed legal rules and into the new realist wilderness of empiricism and changing law. In the end, the courtship of the social sciences turned out to be short-lived. The reasons for the termination, as recounted by Schlegel (1979; 1980), shed light on the problems of merging the two fields.

The realists yoked the reformist politics of Progressivism and the New Deal (White 1972) with the emerging quantitative approach of the social sciences in the 1930s (Haskell 1977). Their objective was to bring about social amelioration via legal change and scientific fact-finding. As Dean Charles Clark of Yale put it, "We regard facts as the prerequisite of reform" (in Schlegel 1979, p. 468). Thus, social science and legal realism were offshoots of the same historical root, namely, social reform (Furner 1975).

However, by the 1930s, they were branching out in different directions. Social scientists aspired to academic respectability and political neutrality—as law professors had half a century earlier—by severing their ties to social action and by adopting the language and methods of the "hard" sciences. The process of fragmentation of the unified "social science" of the late nineteenth century into the various "social sciences" as we know them today was nearing completion. The specialist disciplines were institutionalized in separate academic departments. For example, sociology split off from political science and psychology from philosophy. A precondition for recognition by the university community of their scientific status was the divorce of research from policy prescription (Haskell 1977). Social scientists became preoccupied with counting and the niceties of experimental design. Statistics began to assume a dominant role in social research.

Realist lawyers, however, soon found that the quantitatively oriented disciplines could not be easily hitched to the bandwagon of reform. They disliked being hobbled by the methods of science and the constraints of data. The exigencies of change shaped the nature and scope of their investigations. For them, reliable data were less important than effective data. They used findings to buttress a priori reform goals. The experience with empirical research of Professor (later Justice) William O. Douglas at Yale was typical. With a social scientist, he studied the causes of business failures and the efficiency of bankruptcy administration, a subject that then commanded widespread attention. To the dismay of his social science colleague, he constantly drew causal inferences and reached conclusions which were unwarranted by the data but which supported his reform expectations. "[N]ot only did he not follow the appropriate methodological rules, he reverted to the kind of arm-chair theorizing that methodological rules were designed to foreclose" (Schlegel 1979, p. 543).

In addition, social science did not turn out to be immediately relevant to the policy concerns of law. For example, Dean Robert Hutchins (1934) of Yale, who with a psychologist (Donald Slesinger) pioneered the classic studies on the psychology of evidence, concluded that "what we have discovered was that psychology had dealt with very few points raised by the law of evidence" and that many of the basic issues "had not been touched at all" by psychology (p. 511). In short, "The social sciences had been oversold" (Stevens 1971, p. 435). Much of the research was simply not intended to deal with policy concerns. Slesinger quickly recognized the importance of starting with the legal side of social-legal research, if the study was to have practical utility: "[T]he first step in the development of legal psychology should be an . . . analysis of legal situations, and then the student of behavior may step in . . . to investiga[te] the behavioral hypothesis . . ." (Slesinger and Pilpel 1929, p. 677).

In the end, the tension between the legal and scientific methods could not be overcome without each compromising its respective norms. The social scientists at Yale gradually drifted away from law-related studies. At a time when they were striving for methodological rigor, they were bewildered by the lawyers' preference for bad data over good data and disenchanted with their attitude that research which did not advance a reform objective was not worth pursuing. Some realists continued with mindless collection of data and suffered the unsympathetic reviews of their more traditional legal colleagues ("There is such a thing as getting so scientific that one forgets what [one's] scientific about"; in Schlegel 1980, p. 284, n. 549). Most realists, however, turned to other pursuits when they discovered to their disappointment that scientific knowledge did not translate directly into reform. William O. Douglas lamented, "All the facts that we worked so hard to get don't seem to help a hell of a lot" (in Schlegel 1979, p. 543). As the 1930s progressed, disenchantment with empirical studies spread throughout the law school world (Dawson 1983, p. 407). At Yale, the diminution of funds led to cutbacks in the educational and research programs. The empirically oriented ones, as the most recent and most expensive, were the first to be trimmed. And so it was that of the two facets of legal realism, the philosophical and the scientific, the former—which gave the movement its name and fame—flourished, while the latter—like an old soldier—did not die but simply faded away.

LAW SCHOOLS AND POSTREALISM

Efforts to integrate law and social science continued in the immediate post war years, but little progress was made. Lasswell and McDougal (1943) observed that the "heroic, but random, efforts [of the realists] to integrate 'law' and 'other social sciences' fail through lack of clarity about *what* is being integrated, and *how*, and for *what purposes*" (p. 204). They sought to meet the quandary of moral relativism, posed and unanswered by the realists, by proposing a comprehensive policy science scheme to guide law and legal education. This scheme welded various intellectual themes of the day: empirical inquiry, rule-deductive reasoning, and value analysis. The "proper function of our law schools," they declared, is "to contribute to the training of policy-makers" in order to implement "democratic values" (p. 206). This approach, however, was never implemented. It rested on a dated empirical foundation that assumed a value-free social science. It also assumed an omnicompetent role for the attorney as a maker of policy or an adviser to policy-makers. In reality, the bulk of the legal profession performs traditional practice roles. Very few law students anticipate a career that places them in influential policy positions. The "las-douglian" model was simply too elitist and removed from the reality of the law school, which has always had as its primary mission—even in the heyday of realism—the training of future members of the bar. "[T]he historical roots of legal education prevented the American law school from ever becoming a center for the study of policy-making" (Stevens 1971, p. 532)—or, one might add, a center for social-legal research.

Succeeding generations of postrealist academic lawyers have sought to address the legacy of moral nihilism of the 1930s. Some engaged in normative analysis of law, relying on history, moral philosophy, and political philosophy. Others turned to positive analysis of law, based upon the concepts and methods of the social sciences, or to an admixture of normative and positive analysis.

Postrealism and Normative Analysis of Law

There is a rich diversity of philosophies in the normative analysis of law (Chapter 12, section 12.5). On the one hand, there is the latter-day "formalist" jurisprudence that emphasizes "neutral principles" in constitutional decision-making (Wechsler 1959), and the new natural law model of common law and constitutional adjudication based upon "arguments of principle" rather than "arguments of policy" (Dworkin 1977b). On the other hand, there is the latter-day "realist" jurisprudence that justifies the Supreme Court's activism in terms of judicial intuition and articulation of the fundamental values of American culture (White 1973). Many of the popular movements of the fifties and sixties which the courts helped launch—civil rights for minorities; procedural rights for the criminally accused; consumer protection; environmentalism—had their intellectual underpinning in the view of law as an instrument of social policy.

Common to the different normative approaches is the belief that social science is not sufficient or even necessary for responsible decision-making. In contrast to the thirties, the positions of social scientists and legal scholars have been partly reversed. Many social scientists, liberal and neo-conservative alike, are now actively engaged in policy-related research. Some (for example, Wolf 1981) are contemporary realists attired in empirical clothes. Their selective use and manipulation of data to support preconceived values is reminiscent of the realists' commitment of expediency to social science. But normatively oriented legal scholars, unlike their realist predecessors, are skeptical that the answer to the problem of the legitimacy of the judiciary's role in formulating social policy is found in instrumentalist-empirical analysis. This is the jurisprudential outlook that informs the legal critique of social research in constitutional adjudication, from Cahn's reaction to Clark's dolls studies in the fifties to O'Brien's response to Sperlich's proposals in the eighties. The attitude of these legal academics is that the social science is all very interesting and has a (modest) place in the scheme of legal things (for example, applicability to "middle range" problems), but is not very relevant to deciding issues of constitutional stature. For them, teaching and research in law schools remain, as they always have been, mostly value-laden and largely data-free.

The uneasy marriage of formalism and realism led to reappraisals of legal scholarship. In the late 1970s, a small group of scholars was self-identified with the "critical legal studies movement" (Unger 1983, p. 561). This movement has no definitive methodology. It relies, instead, on an amalgam of approaches, including historiography (Gordon 1981), Marxist dialectics (Gabel 1980: "Legal reasoning is an inherently repressive form of interpretive thought . . . [that] originates, of course, within the consciousness of the dominant class . . ."; pp. 25–6), analytical philosophy, and structuralism (that is, the use of overarching conceptual models to explain how legal categories legitimate the existing social order; Kennedy 1979). It is "critical" because it calls into question legal rules, legal institutions, and all other forms of legal scholarship. It seeks to demystify the law by exposing legal rules as the products of historical circumstances and historically specific modes of reasoning, and by showing how legal thought contributes to maintaining the status quo. Critical legal scholars assert that all scholarship is shaped by political preferences, so they self-consciously embrace a vision of radical change based on participatory democracy or decentralized socialism. They are heirs of realism's iconoclastic skepticism, but they reject the tradition of social engineering and liberal reform. They debunk the research in law and economics (Kelman 1983), resting as it does on conservative assumptions such as the superiority of market forces over government regulation. Whereas other (nonradical) normative scholars consider social research as merely not relevant to constitutional issues, critical legal scholars appear to distrust it. They deem "empirical conclusions unpersuasive—products of a closed cultural system" (Note, *Harvard Law Review* 1982, p. 1682, n. 85). Much of social-legal research—from the questions asked to the conclusions drawn—is, in fact, colored (usually covertly) by liberal ideology. Whether this radical philosophy will have a lasting influence on scholarship and politics remains to be seen. It should, for now, prompt empirical researchers to be more critical of the assumptions that undergird their work.

Postrealism and "Law and Social Science"

While many legal scholars turned to normative analysis, some focused again on the social sciences. In the cyclical history of the relations between law and social science in law schools, different disciplines have been favored. In the 1930s, law and social science meant primarily law and psychology (including psychoanalytic theory). The realists talked about applying economics to law, but they never engaged in much economic analysis. In the 1960s, law and social science meant primarily law and sociology. This decade, in fact, resembled the thirties on a modest scale. By this time, the efforts to raise and increase the uniformity of academic standards in legal education, begun in the postwar period, were coming to fruition. Many state university law schools began to achieve prominence and compete with the elite, private institutions.

The realist innovations—research seminars, interdisciplinary courses, appointments of social scientists and economists to the faculty—trickled down to a wide range of schools. "Law and . . ." courses sprouted in almost every law school and it became fashionable to include "policy" in the title of new offerings. Private sources such as the Russell Sage Foundation supported the establishment of training and research programs in law and social science in various law schools. The overall climate was one of receptivity to empirical inquiry (Zeisel 1974, p. 1051).

By the mid-seventies and into the eighties, the pendulum swung away from social research. In the law schools, law and social science became identified primarily (but not exclusively) with law and economics. The sociology of law remained safe and sound in sociology departments. "Law and economics scholarship," as distinct from "straight economics scholarship" and "straight legal scholarship," deals with the self-conscious application of economic analysis to legal rules and institutions that govern economic behavior. Outside the fields of antitrust and regulated industries, it is "a fairly new body of work, having developed . . . largely within the past decade [1970s]" (Hansmann 1983, p. 218). It is written mostly by and for legal scholars, and therefore it has had its principal impact on the legal profession rather than the economics profession. Even those not identified with this field recognize that economics has been "a major factor" in shaping the "overall quality of American scholarship on law" at this time (Summers 1983, p. 337).

The 1980s also saw the implosion of law and psychology scholarship. However, it was initiated in and is being carried forward mainly in psychology departments (where it is a "growth industry"; Melton 1983, p. 1), not in law schools. To be sure, there are psychologists and psychologist-lawyers on law school faculties, courses on law and psychology for law students, and joint-degree programs at several institutions. But as in the 1930s, and unlike law and economics scholarship today, psycholegal studies have not yet become part of the active consciousness of most legal scholars, nor has it been fully assimilated into the mainstream of legal scholarship. At best, most legal academics have remained on the sidelines as interested observers.

Economics has a long and distinguished history. It has widely shared paradigms (for example, rational utility maximization) and widely accepted laws (for example, supply and demand) that are applicable to legal decision-making in areas involving economic behavior. It may well be that economics is "the most promising [for law] simply because economics is the most advanced social science" (Posner 1981, p. 1121). Its relative success compared to the "soft" social sciences is one of degree rather than kind. The main contribution of all of the social sciences to law is a functional one. They help illuminate two basic questions. One question is about impact: What effect do legal rules and institutions have upon (economic and social) behavior? The other question is about context: How do (economic and social) forces shape the law? For the most part, neither law and economics scholarship nor law and social science scholarship has provided definitive answers to these questions when they have been raised with respect to specific topics. For example, there is a substantial literature on the economic analysis of liability rules in tort law. But after two decades of writing on the topic, one still does not know for certain whether negligence or strict liability is the more economically efficient rule in various areas of accident law (Hansmann 1983, p. 226). And after three decades of research by social scientists, one still cannot say with certainty how much improvement in achievement test scores of minority students can be expected as a result of school desegregation.

The utility of economic analysis or of social research does not lie in providing conclusive answers to positive and normative questions in law. It lies in the questions that they raise and in the viewpoints that they offer. "[Legal] decision-making," Judge Bazelon (1982) reminds us, "does not need governing paradigms or universal causal laws. It needs facts, insights, and perspectives" (p. 116). These disciplines are relevant for law primarily because they provide a methodology for thinking about legal issues, rather than because they have accumulated particular knowledge. They are traditions of inquiry and analysis. They question reigning behavioral or economic assumptions in law. Their educational purposes are to help the legal community to understand the consequences of existing rules, to ascertain the ways in which these rules are or are not socially effective or economically efficient, and to recommend ways to facilitate the attainment of their objectives. They force legal thinking to go beyond doctrinal analysis and become more functionally oriented—that is, to take into account considerations of impact and context. Although law is often framed in consequential terms, these disciplines can improve the sophistication of the analysis by clarifying the terms and the factual predicates. "Economics," Hansmann (1983) says, "provides us with a more powerful syntax and semantics for legal argumentation" (p. 227). This has been shown in areas of law that deal primarily with economic activity, such as antitrust, contracts, insurance, and torts. The analytical tools of social science are not as refined as those of economics. But in areas that deal with social behavior, such as in civil rights law and criminal procedure law, empirical analysis has helped focus the legal issue and added clarity to legal thinking.

Although law can be informed by economic and/or empirical analysis, it is not about to lose its distinctiveness by folding into economics or any of the other social sciences. Despite ringing calls for incorporating these disciplines in law school teaching and research—"[W]e ignore the social sciences at our peril," warned Bok (1983, p. 45), the president of Harvard and former dean of its Law School—there has been little large-scale mobilization of resources toward this goal (Margolick 1983). Even with the most promising of the social sciences, "Economic analysis of law in the classroom is more embryonic than real" (Gellhorn and Robinson 1983, p. 268). We shall examine some of the obstacles to and possibilities for rapprochement. There are certain institutional realities that set limits to the increased involvement by law schools in interdisciplinary teaching and research. These observations are relevant to any social science, but apply with particular force to psychology and sociology.

IMPLICATIONS FOR RAPPROCHEMENT

Dominance of Case Analysis

Case analysis, or the clarification of doctrine developed in opinions, is the traditional and dominant mode of legal scholarship. The teaching of legal doctrine and of case analysis skills constitutes the bedrock of legal education. Case analysis involves the comparison of appellate decisions in order to reconcile or distinguish opposing results, clarify ambiguities in reasoning, and pull together diverse lines of cases into a coherent whole. In evaluating opinions, lawyers consider not only whether they are intellectually sound and consistent with other authorities such as precedents and the Constitution, but also whether they accord with social values, notions of rightness, and practicality. The tools of case analysis are analogical reasoning, commonsense intuition, and rhetorical argumentation. The brunt of case analysis performed in the classroom and in legal publications is "formalist" in emphasis, in the sense that the analysis does not go much beyond the logical or doctrinal structure of the opinions. Arguments are made or defeated by determining whether the facts of one case are similar to or different from the facts of another case. The criteria for these comparisons of facts, from which legal conclusions are drawn, are often vague. Case analysis is largely a self-contained analysis; it need not make use of other fields of learning.

One reason for the popularity of economic analysis in law schools is that it folds in well with case analysis. It is essentially a form of doctrinal analysis using the language and analytical tools of microeconomic theory. Legal economists, like conventional legal scholars, typically begin with a group of cases. Their purpose is to expose and critique the inner logic of the law. They evaluate the rationales for the decisions given by the courts and other (doctrinal) commentators. Then they propose alternative criteria for the decisions—after postulating certain simplified assumptions about, say, transaction costs and information availability—based upon considerations of efficiency. Legal economists are neorealists in that they seek to disclose the "real" (economic) rule behind the "paper" (doctrinal) rule. There is both a positive and a normative component to economic analysis of law. It describes how cases are decided (for example, the court's choice of rule X rather than rule Y creates efficient incentives) and it also prescribes, explicitly or implicitly, how cases should be decided (for example, the no-fault rule is superior to the negligence rule in allocating liability in accident cases). Thus, economic analysis is attractive to legal scholars because it deals with the clarification of legal doctrine. As Posner (1981) points out, "doctrinal analysts and economic analysts are no longer, as a practical matter, easily separable" (p. 1115). Moreover, it provides a normative framework for assessing the law, which also meshes well with the normative character of legal scholarship. Indeed, much of the law and economics literature is "written to prove a normative point rather than simply being a dispassionate exercise of objective social science" (Hansmann 1983, p. 233).

The relative success of economic analysis suggests lessons for the other "law and" disciplines. Interdisciplinary research has to be adapted to the concerns of lawyers if it is to command interest, as Ohlin argued. These concerns are about legal doctrine and legal policy on the one hand, and about legal practice on the other. One reason why the sociology of law, the main "law and" discipline of the 1960s, faded from the law school scene is because it did not address either of these two concerns. For the most part, it involved what Galanter called "autonomous social research on law" (Chapter 11, section 11.4). Sociological concepts and methods were used to arrive at scientific generalizations about the interrelationships between law and society. For example, Durkheim (1947) observed that increased division of labor in society led to an increased ratio of cooperative legal rules to penal and repressive rules. This kind of positive analysis contributes to basic knowledge about the legal system. In the long run, scientific understanding can provide a firm foundation for legal reform and policy. But given the overriding preoccupation with legal doctrine and the law schools' vocational entrustment, it is unlikely that research aimed at theory building will attract or retain the attention of most law students or law professors. The pursuit of fundamental inquiry, important as it is, is more appropriately carried out in an academic department.

In contrast, the resurgence of psycholegal research in the late 1970s and 1980s is due in large measure to its explicitly applied orientation. Its impact to date has been primarily on the practicing bar rather than the academic bar. For example, psychologists have participated in jury selection, served as expert witnesses in a variety of areas, and conducted surveys for use in trademark infringement litigation and in criminal proceedings. They have deployed their empirical skills in the service of lawyering. They have been less prominently involved in the clarification of legal doctrine.

As already indicated, the analysis of the social consequences and context of legal rules can help inform doctrinal thinking by providing an instrumentalist perspective on law. Social research does not possess the conceptual edifice of economics; therefore, it cannot readily provide the vocabulary and the analytical tools that can be employed in legal argumentation. But it does contribute to legal scholarship in one important way that economic analysis does not—it gathers information about reality. Economic analysis of law is largely a priori reasoning. It is armchair analysis like doctrinal analysis, though it uses a different language. In evaluating existing rules or in proposing alternative rules with the aid of economic theory, the "data" consist of reported opinions and commonsense observations. Economic reasoning in law is not tested against empirical reality. Facts about the social or behavioral impact of law do not yield normative conclusions, but they help narrow the range of choices and refine the analysis. Thus, social research can serve a heuristic role in legal scholarship, in addition to its technical role in legal practice. The impact of social research in law schools will increase as the use of empirical analysis in doctrinal analysis increases.

Despite the current prominence of the law and economics movement, there is no risk that traditional case analysis is going to be reduced to economic analysis. There are about 6,000 legal academics in the country, and about 300 are involved in teaching and research that make use of economic analysis. Of these, it is estimated that only a handful would advocate reorganizing the legal curriculum to give primacy to economic analysis over the traditional doctrinal analysis (Summers 1983, p. 348). The number of legal academics actively involved in enriching their teaching and research with empirical analysis is surely much smaller. The directory of law teachers lists about 100 persons who teach or have an interest in the area of law and social science. Interdisciplinary work is not likely to replace case analysis as the intellectual mainstay of the law school, but it could shape its direction and contours.

Professional Orientation of Law Students

"Most law schools," Gellhorn and Robinson (1983) observe, "are still, in major part, trade schools for which economic, or any form of nonlegal, analysis is perceived by instructors and students alike as . . . superfluous" (p. 271). The content of professional training is shaped directly or indirectly by the preoccupations of attorneys. As members of accrediting agencies or as influential alumni, they exert continuing pressure to make legal education more practice-oriented and thus more removed from the scholarly tradition. When a law school community turns primarily to the university for professional identification, status, ideas, and criticism, it weakens the "symbiotic relationship" between the academic bar and the practicing bar (Allen 1983, p. 404). Moreover, one professor observed, law schools have become "an adjunct to the hiring hall" (in Margolick 1983, p. 36). Any change in receptivity toward empirical inquiry needs to start with the curriculum, but law schools are resistant to change because of their ties to the profession. There is a continuing tug between the obligations to train students for the workaday world and to contribute to scholarship.

Law students as a group are not particularly interested in pure knowledge. They want doctrinal exposition and skills acquisition which will be useful for future practice. They tolerate intellectual study of law in much the same way that many engineering students view the humanities: such courses are fine so long as they remain elective adornments. By temperament and training, they are oriented toward solving specific problems. They have little pride in constructing elegant theories and testing them empirically. The curriculum of the first year, designed to teach neophytes how to "think like a lawyer" (that is, how to engage in case analysis), has a powerful effect in molding a sense of vocation. Most aspire to career in practice rather than in research or policy-making. This atheoretical, problem-solving mental set, systematically cultivated in the classroom, permeates the lawyer's perception and thinking. Professional education and interdisciplinary study are seen as antithetical to each other, although this view presumes a rather narrow conception of professional education. In any event, as Ohlin stresses in his article, if social research is to capture the interest of lawyers, it has to be designed and written to address their practical concerns.

It is not too much of an oversimplification to say that "the curriculum and the teaching method we now employ [in law school] were basically designed in the nineteenth century as an undergraduate program for non-college trained students" (Stevens 1983, p. 443). As in a liberal arts program, law students take a wide sampling of (doctrinal) courses in order to be exposed to different areas of the law. There is little intensive study of a particular subject. Rarely is there a one-to-one working relationship between student and professor as is typical of graduate education in the arts and sciences. The academic apprenticeship model, whereby research skills are honed and scholarly traditions are passed from one generation to the next, is not a part of the law school environment. In essence, law study "is a kind of post-baccalaureate baccalaureate" (Riesman 1982, p. 117).

The pedagogical foundation of this vocational training is the modern adaptation of Langdell's case method. Doctrinal analysis has lingered on, even after the formalist theory has faded away, because it develops case reasoning skills. The process of extracting principles from past cases and applying them to decide new ones is central to the craft of lawyering. Another reason it has lasted this long is that it is an inexpensive method of education. So long as law study consists of reading appellate decisions, all one needs is a casebook, a professor, and a classroom. The case method is well suited to large classes—a 1-to-25 faculty-student ratio is not uncommon at the best law schools, compared with about a 1-to-6 ratio in graduate schools. Likewise, if legal research consists of analyzing and synthesizing doctrinal developments, all one needs is a law library. Lawyers, unlike social scientists, need not go out and collect data. They receive reams of information consisting of published opinions on an almost daily basis, all superbly indexed and accessible by computerized retrieval. This kind of library research is far cheaper than field research or even laboratory experimentation. Hence, law schools are usually financially self-sufficient units within universities—sometimes profitable enough so as to support other units on campus—and have not had to turn to private and governmental sources for research finding.

To the extent that doctrinal study of law is carried on as an autonomous enterprise, there is really no need for the infusion of insights from other learned professions. Moreover, the very method of doctrinal instruction, the so-called Socratic technique, may inhibit the learning and teaching of empirical analysis. The dialectical give and take characteristic of the law school classroom nurtures (or reinforces) a relentless and willful individualism in students. Since the time of Langdell, professors have taught students to regard every case decision with skepticism. It is part of the process of sharpening critical faculties. By forensic tradition, students are encouraged to argue with professors with a verve not often seen elsewhere in the academy. They are given the responsibility of editing the learned journals of the profession, including editing the writings submitted by their professors. They are recognized for writing "notes" and "comments" that evaluate critically the opinions of judges in leading cases. Nonrefereed and nonpeer-edited publications exist nowhere else in the academy. All of this shapes in lawyers "what is, at its worst, a kind of omnicompetent arrogance that there is no problem which they cannot master in a two-week period . . ." (Riesman 1982, p. 116). Part of the conception of the lawyer as a generalist is the notion that a good lawyer can handle virtually any task. This mythology persists in the face of studies that show that the legal profession is not unitary, that it is stratified and specialized in its functions, and that not all lawyers are cut from the same Langdellian mold (Heinz and Laumann 1983).

The self-confidence of lawyers may come across as a cocky attitude. It is a style that may serve useful professional purposes. It may help counter the same individualism manifested by clients; it may provide the psychological resilience needed to engage in adversarial roles. However, it can also impede interdisciplinary work. Most law students do not take advantage of the opportunities to enroll in legally relevant courses in other departments on campus. The existing system of student-edited law journals, while unmatched as a means of perfecting skills in doctrinal analysis, makes it difficult for social-legal research to flourish in law schools. Students selected as editors have demonstrated competency in case analysis and therefore are capable of evaluating traditional legal scholarship. But they may not necessarily be capable of— or even interested in—evaluating nondoctrinal work. This screening process affects the quantity and quality of empirical research contained in the publication of the profession. Some law professors, interested in broadening the scope of legal scholarship, have urged that law faculties assume editorship of interdisciplinary journals (Cramton 1982, p. 330).

Professional Orientation of Law Professors

Students who master case analysis get high grades on examinations. Those with high grades are selected for editorship of the school's law journal. Those who excel in editing are recruited for the professoriat, after a clerkship with an appellate judge which allows them to sharpen further their doctrinal-analytical skills to a fine edge. With this process of student evaluation and faculty recruitment, it is not surprising that the teaching and analysis of legal doctrine is firmly established in law schools. What is surprising is that nondoctrinal learning has been able to make as much headway as it has into this relatively closed system.

The dominance of case analysis fosters excellence in teaching but retards empirical legal studies. Law schools, unlike graduate schools, are primarily teaching schools, not research schools. Law professors have dual roles, as "Hessian trainers" and "true academics." "The time they must give over to the preparation of their Hessian-trainer roles makes it literally impossible to produce serious works of [non-doctrinal] scholarship" (Bergin 1968, p. 645). New professors, or experienced ones who are offering a new course, typically invest six to ten hours or more in preparation for each hour of class. As a group, law professors enjoy talking about different methods and philosophies of teaching. They hold conferences on the subject and they even have a journal devoted largely to matters related to teaching. Most social scientists, in contrast, view teaching as ancillary to their research commitment. If they were as preoccupied about teaching as their law school colleagues, their scholarly productivity would be compromised. Even in the elite law schools, Friedman (1974) says, with only a touch of overstatement, "the emphasis is not on research but on classroom performance. It is not only possible but common to find endowed professors at the most prestigious law schools who have produced nothing beyond a handful of articles and a casebook. It is hard to think of another field where one can make so tremendous a reputation by editing materials to serve up to students. . . . [T]his order of prestige discourages research on law and society . . ." (p. 1069). To the extent that law professors have engaged in substantial scholarship, it has tended to be multivolume treatises on doctrinal subjects. Their writings strive for *elegantia juris*, the coherent ordering of rules in a logical structure, interwoven with normative analysis and, at most, a nodding reference to empirical information. As one legal academic conceded, "[R]esearch in legal processes is impeded by the intractability of inside professional conceits in the law school. We are so good at doctrinal analysis that we are resistant to the idea that brilliance of intuition ought in any way to be qualified by going out and finding out what really happens. It is kind of cheating to find facts" (Hazard 1967b, p. 307). "Empirical research," Friedman adds, "involves a lot of very grubby, hard slogging that law professors aren't trained for and don't want to do." Hence, "the vast bulk of this research is . . . not even treated in class by law professors" (in Margolick 1983, p. 30).

Academic lawyers, like practicing lawyers, propagate the image of the "omnicompetent" generalist. The law school remains the only unit in a university that is not divided into departments. Specialized programs are the exception rather than the rule. Most professors pride themselves as capable of teaching almost any subject in the legal curriculum, a boast that would not be seen as a virtue in nonlegal fields. According to the dean of the Yale Law School, "today's young academic" is expected to be "enormously sophisticated in humanistic and social science studies. To get a grip on the limits of law, an academic must work in political philosophy; so, too, if he is interested in distributive justice. Nor can he fail to know economics, and he is delinquent if he ignores history" (in Posner 1981, p. 1118). The (Yale) image of the academic lawyer is that of a Renaissance scholar, one who is expected to meet the prodigious challenge of mastering the whole of social thought in addition, of course, to the usual doctrinal analysis. Omnicompetence, whether imagined or real, can impede interdisciplinary activity. Absent from the preceding decanal vision is collaboration with colleagues in relevant branches of learning. This is because law professors, generally, resist intellectual teamwork. When they write in fields such as legal history and legal philosophy, they often do so with no interchange with their counterparts in the academic departments. Co-authorship of articles in legal periodicals is less common than in the journals of the arts and sciences. In law and social science, there have been some notable instances of joint ventures between social scientists and legal academics—for example, Schlesinger and Hutchins in the 1930s on the psychology of evidence; Thibaut and Walker on the psychology of legal procedure (Chapter 9, section 9.2); Horowitz and Willging (1984) co-authoring a textbook on psychology and law. On the whole, however, there have been few official bridges between law schools and other departments.

Historically, most law professors interested in empirical legal studies have been self-instructed in the methods and theories of social science. This process of learning can be unsystematic and inefficient. At its best, the result can be imaginative applications to new problems; at its worst, "the law professor reinvents the wheel but gets it wrong" (Zimring 1983, p. 455). There are horror stories from the realist era when lawyers taught themselves statistics and the rudiments of experimental methodology but never understood the theory behind them (Schlegel 1980, p. 317). So long as each generation has to reinvent the wheel, there will be phoenix-like cycles of rediscovery of social science by legal scholars.

In the past decade or two, a number of institutional developments have helped raise legal academics' consciousness of empirical analysis and economic analysis. An increasing number of law schools have appointed social scientists and economists as fulltime faculty members. The results, however, have been mixed. In-house experts can serve as resource persons and role models for empirical legal scholarship. But they can also find themselves removed from the mainstream of their own discipline and of doctrinal scholarship. "In the sociometrics of the law school, the non-law-trained expert is frequently regarded as a second-class citizen" (Zimring 1983, p. 457). Formal training for law faculty has been introduced. In the late 1960s and early 1970s, there were summer institutes on social research methods for law professors. Currently, there are similar institutes on microeconomics, amply funded by private enterprise. There are now attempts to establish "research residencies on the installment plan," whereby legal scholars can come to a research center to undertake social-legal studies with on-site specialists (Zimring 1983, p. 443). Other means of bridging the gap include producing scholars with double doctorates. Within the past few years, about half a dozen institutions have started joint-degree programs in law and psychology alone. The benefits of this approach need to be balanced against the diseconomies. The opportunity costs of acquiring a second degree are high. Law graduates have little financial incentive to do so. Social scientists run the risk of co-optation. Many budding empirical researchers have been lost to blue chip law firms. Moreover, for the purpose of gaining competence to undertake empirical legal study, a law graduate does not require four or five years of doctoral training, and a social scientist with a Ph.D. likewise should not have to endure three years of case analysis. As an alternative, some law schools have created special programs that allow graduate and postgraduate students to spend a year studying law with a view toward scholarship rather than practice.

All of these ways of altering the professional orientation of law professors—self-instruction; short-term training institutes and research residencies; collaborative studies; recruitment of nonlegal experts to the faculty; combined J.D.-Ph.D. programs—are bound to have a collective impact upon legal education and legal scholarship over the long haul. The extent of that impact will depend upon how successfully the role of empirical scholarship can be accommodated to the constraints of professional education and the tradition of doctrinal analysis. In the next section, we will suggest that the influence of empirical analysis on legal doctrine will likely be oblique rather than direct, and heuristic rather than determinative.

13.6   A SUMMING UP: MAPPING THE ROLE OF SOCIAL RESEARCH IN LAW*

The role of social research in the courts is part of the broader subject of how information about social reality ("what has already become") contributes to shaping the way society should be ordered ("what is in the process of becoming") (Mannheim 1936, p. 112). It deals with the integration of the objectively true and the morally right.

There is no definitive, elegant, and consensual link between the realms of fact and value. One way to map this role is in terms of judicial functions. If decisions reflect some underlying jurisprudential philosophy, then so do the applications of social research in decision-making. There are three paradigmatic uses of social research—in judicial adjudication, judicial legislation, and judicial rationalization—which reflect, respectively, the influence of three jurisprudential approaches to judicial decisions: formalism, realism, and reasoned elaboration.

Law "consists of decisions, not rules" (Frank 1930, p. 128). It is a method of problem-solving that consists of applying a legal rule (a kind of prescriptive major premise) to the facts of the case (minor premise) in order to reach a conclusion. The rule or the facts may be certain or disputed. There are four possible categories of decision-making based on the foregoing combinations: certain rule/certain facts, disputed rule/certain facts, certain rule/disputed facts, and disputed rule/disputed facts. When the facts are certain, empirical inquiry is unlikely to have any role. In the first category, litigation may not even arise; the dispute would be settled by application of precedent. The second category would involve nonfactual, doctrinal interpretation and textual exegesis. Social science is relevant, then, only in the last two types of decision-making.

Judicial Adjudication

When the rule itself is uncontested and only the facts are at issue, social science evidence aids in determining the applicability of the rule—that is, in judicial adjudication. For example, if an attitude survey shows that most of the eligible jurors in a community are highly biased against a defendant, the rule requiring an impartial jury might lead to a decree of a change of venue. It is a kind of programmed or prefabricated decision-making—a jurisprudence of antecedents, associated with formalism. Once the "adjudicative facts" are ascertained, the judge reasons from the governing rule to the inescapable conclusion. The use of social research here is not problematic—it does not lead to any change in legal doctrine or policy. Social research is employed in a technical capacity.

*This section consists of revised excerpts from W. Loh, "In Quest of *Brown*'s Promise: Social Research and Social Values in School Desegregation," *Washington Law Review* 58 (1982): 129–74. Reprinted by permission of the publisher. Copyright ©1982 by the Washington Law Review Association.

Judicial Legislation

A second and more unsettled role of social research is in the creation of law—that is, in judicial legislation. When both the applicable law and the facts are at issue, as they were in *Brown,* a court must resolve conflicting claims of "legislative fact" and decide between opposing interests. It is a kind of unprogrammed decision-making, used in original, first-impression types of cases—a jurisprudence of discretion, associated with realism. The presentation of empirical data on the disputed facts can influence judge-made law either directly or indirectly.

A *direct* or *instrumental* role of social research is in ascertaining the impact of decisions (Miller and Howell 1960). One ground for choosing between different legal premises is an evaluation of their anticipated social and behavioral effects. Decision implies choice, and choice implies prediction. Impact research can help shape decisions because of the reciprocal relationship between issues of fact and law. It is a central feature of the nature and growth of law that "[the] issues of fact arise out of the law but at the point of application of law, the issues of law also arise out of the facts" (Hart and McNaughton 1959, p. 22). Existing legal rules give facts their legal significance, but facts, in turn, can also beget new legal rules; *ex facto jus oritur* (out of facts springs the law). This result-oriented method of decision-making is not unique to law. It has parallels in "rational-comprehensive" and "scientific" decision-making in public administration (Lindblom 1959) and organizational behavior (Simon 1957). Empirical evaluation and informed commentary on the decisional products of a court are part of the lawmaking processes of the judiciary.

Nonetheless, as indicated in the introduction to this chapter, many in the legal community deny that social research has any real effect on constitutional decision-making (for example, Doyle 1977, p. 10; Yudof 1978, p. 107). Critics of judicial reliance on social science are also, unsurprisingly, critics of judicial activism in social policy-making. This is because social scientists, as a group, have subscribed to a liberal ideology and, historically, they have joined forces with proponents of social reform. These critics argue inter alia that the increased use of social science would provide a "rationale for non-compliance and for open political attack on constitutional guarantees" (Linde 1972, p. 240). If the exclusionary rule does not deter police misconduct or if desegregation does not raise achievement scores of minority children, the rights are undercut by studies that challenge the factual predicates. Social research findings are also said to be inconclusive, subjective, and labile; therefore, constitutional principles should not be made to rest on the latest empirical generalizations (O'Brien 1980). Normatively oriented scholars assert that judges should and in fact do "make interpretive rather than causal judgments" (Yudof 1978, p. 77). Interpretive or value judgments are based on shared understandings and political morality. They do not imply quantitative, causal relationships, but they locate "a particular phenomenon within a particular category of phenomena by specifying its meaning within the society in which it occurs" (Dworkin 1977a, p. 21).

However, judges have the power to control the influence of social science evidence; at the outset, they can frame the right in question in instrumentalist or normative terms. The right to desegregated education can be premised on its purported academic benefits or on the imperative of vindicating the interest in equality and fairness. Since the days of realism, we all know that rarely are judicial decisions wholly or largely effective in achieving their stated objectives, even though we continue to fake amazement at the gap between the ideal and the real (Abel 1980). How the issue is posed loads the dice. In any event, when judges have turned to social facts, they have been careful not to place constitutional rulings exclusively on the proverbial slippery slope of instrumentalist reasoning. They have treaded a middle ground, relying on both causal premises and normative judgments. For example, in *Brown,* the Court stressed the "inherent" inequality of segregated schools, an assertion which bespeaks a value judgment, in addition to citing the social psychological studies in footnote 11. In *Miranda* v. *Arizona* (1966), the Court repeatedly pronounced custodial interrogation to be permeated by "inherent compulsion," in addition to relying on empirical texts that described the coercive methods of police interrogation.

The difficult issue, then, is not whether social science has a role but when it can be used. Kalven (1968) proposed that empirical inquiry is most productive when it is applied to issues "in the middle range" of the fact-value continuum (p. 66). These are issues which do not involve deeply held values and inaccessible facts (for example, the wrongfulness of segregation) or, conversely, problems which involve facts too well known to warrant empirical footnoting (for example, the unreliability of hearsay). Of course, holdings embodying a moral judgment are not grounded on factual proof. If, as *Brown* said, segregation is "inherently unequal," its wrongfulness represents an axiomatic claim. Instrumental analysis becomes less relevant as the questions become more aspirational.

It does not follow, however, that data may not have an *indirect* or *heuristic* effect on shaping the outcome. What was claimed by legal critics of footnote 11 to have been but common knowledge about the consequences of segregation was the product, at least in part, of the substantial body of research that had accumulated over the years and worked its way into popular culture and then into the living law. Even normative conclusions are generated by an awareness of facts. Research results can illuminate or sharpen the factual premises of constitutional decision-making. Empirical reality defines what purposes are realizable and thereby sharpens the focus of moral debate (Homans 1978). Whether intended or not, the use of social science can frame or redefine the policy issue. In school finance litigation, for example, both sides disagreed on the impact of greater expenditures on educational quality, but implicitly they (and the court) agreed that educational quality was measured by performance on standardized achievement tests (Levin 1975; Coons 1977). Social research channeled thinking about the issue as a technical matter of improving test scores of low-income minority children rather than as a moral dilemma posed by economic inequality. In the Detroit school case of *Milliken* v. *Bradley,* expert testimony was a factor in persuading the judge that improved achievement scores made school desegregation worth the candle. The indoctrination hypothesis (Wolf 1981) is another instance of the heuristic role of social science.

In brief, there is both a chasm and a bridge between the realms of fact and value. Without the chasm, there would be no place for purposive analysis—normative issues would surrender to empirical inquiry. Without the bridge, social research would have nothing to contribute to the moral choices that preoccupy the law. The role of empirical inquiry in judicial lawmaking is not an either-or matter. Both instrumentalist and interpretive judgments are implicated because the empirical and the normative are interwoven. In the short run, values organize facts. Empirical inquiry cannot be conducted independently of a normative framework. In the long run, however, facts can organize values. Over the course of time, as reality unfolds into history, values can also arise out of facts. Data, not from any single study but from the totality of established knowledge, can become a source of authority for social action.

Judicial Rationalization

The requirement that judges elaborate in writing the justifications for their rulings serves as an institutional safeguard against idiosyncratic decision-making. A third role of social research, then, is in the legitimation of judicial lawmaking—that is, in judicial rationalization.

Although in substance the growth of the law is legislative, judges are reluctant to engage openly in the function of creating law. In order to preserve the appearance of continuity and certainty in the law, unprogrammed decisions are dressed in formalist attire. Landmark decisions are said not to constitute "an abrupt break" with the past but merely a "return to . . . old precedents" (*Gideon* v. *Wainwright*, 1963, p. 344); new holdings are described as "not an innovation in our jurisprudence" (*Miranda* v. *Arizona*, 1966, p. 442). Reform-minded judges, according to the jurisprudence of reasoned elaboration, "decide cases intuitively and then search to justify their intuitions by making arguments directed at a wide audience" (White 1973, p. 300). They intuit the values endemic to American society at a particular time and then give elaborate reasons in order to persuade the public of the legitimacy of the judgment.

Impact-thinking can be a form of rationalization in that it sets forth the results—rather than the actual processes—of decision-making. To consider in advance all the possible consequences of alternative courses of action prior to a decision assumes a degree of rationality and information availability that is exaggerated. In law and in public administration generally, there is often no agreement on desired ends, and decision-makers are reduced to choosing without first clarifying the goals sought. Decision-making is incremental—a "muddling through" process in which each step produces only a marginal change, and each decision is a successive approximation to the objective, even as the objective itself continues to change under reconsideration (Lindblom 1959; Shapiro 1965). However, since decision-makers are expected to justify their actions, they discharge their responsibility by pretending to engage in "rational-comprehensive" analysis.

Some proponents of principled judicial decisions, while acknowledging that social research has some impact on adjudicative and legislative functions, nonetheless object to instrumentalist justifications of decisions. They insist that decisions be premised on "impartial, consistent, and neutral application of legal principles," rather than on social science materials (O'Brien 1981, p. 28). Courts often do use empirical findings the way a drunk uses a lamppost: for support rather than illumination. The findings serve to ornament decisions reached on other grounds. Social research can be used for purposes of "judicial statecraft," that is, for the "calculation of the political consequences" of decisions (Linde 1972, p. 23). Judges have been known to cite studies the way they cite cases, treating scientific conclusions as highly malleable holdings that can be assimilated into an existing normative scheme.

However, instrumentalist justifications need not necessarily be ad hoc, any more than normative justifications are by definition "principled." Decisions can be conditioned, at least in part, on well-established facts, and done so in a consistent and coherent fashion. Indeed, if social research influenced judicial thinking—for example, by helping to diagnose the nature of the social problem, to anticipate the possible consequences of alternative choices, or to inform on the prospects of public compliance—it would be unjustifiable to pretend that such considerations never entered into the decision-making. The "ought" cannot be derived from the "is," but accurate knowledge of social reality can discipline or condition thinking so as to make possible the normative leap. The explication of these factual predicates is not incompatible with purposive analysis, unless one posits an unbridgeable gap between facts and values.

Thus, the imprimatur of "modern authority" in *Brown* helped to justify the avoidance of the *Plessy* doctrine which was itself rationalized in terms of the "psychological knowledge" of its time. The united front of the social scientists, documented in footnote 11, served the statecraft purpose of reinforcing the image of broadly based agreement on the evil of segregation that the Court sought to convey with its own unanimous opinion. Judges are more likely to use social research for rationalization when the experts agree on the evidence, it clearly supports or refutes the legal matter at issue, and it implies a solution that is within the court's control. Absent these attributes, as in the northern school desegregation cases, judges avoid any overt justification based upon social research and rely instead on flexible legal fictions such as de jure violations.

Conclusion

A theme that runs through the various case studies of this volume is that the subject of the role of social research in the judicial process is one in which questions arise more readily than enduring answers. The kinds of legal issues that prompt scientific fact-finding are usually complex, indeterminate, and unresponsive to conclusive resolution. The empirical research brought to bear on these issues is also characterized more by dissensus than consensus. Judge Wisdom (1975) observed that there is "a vast amount of social research" on certain constitutional issues, yet "there is little agreement on methodology or conclusions, even when the data relied on are the same" (p. 136). It seems that the more sophisticated the research becomes and the more information is gained, the more visible are the gaps in knowledge and the more contradictory the explanations. Hence, postrealist scholars have expressed doubts about the objectivity, maturity, and relevance of social research as applied to major issues of social policy. They assert that it is "suffering from a crisis of legitimacy, one that perhaps runs deeper than that in the law" (Yudof 1978, p. 71). Constitutional decisions, they say, cannot be made to rest on such uncertain factual grounds.

Implicit in this view is the expectation that increased knowledge should lead to improved recommendations for policy. This expectation reflects a misapprehension about social research. Thorstein Veblen pointed out that "the outcome of any serious research can only be to make two questions grow where one question grew before" (in Weinberg 1975, p. 241). In the physical sciences, research advances lead to greater clarity about the phenomena and to convergence of conceptual paradigms (Kuhn 1970). In the social sciences, the result is sometimes the opposite, especially when the facts at issue are intertwined in a seamless web with normative considerations. As Cohen and Weiss (1977) observe, "[I]mproved knowledge does not always lead to more effective action" (p. 92). Uncertainty in research conclusions exists not only because of the epistemological limitations of the discipline (Nagel 1961), but also because of the values that precondition empirical inquiry and the uncertainty surrounding the social purposes of the issue under consideration.

The fact that social science at this time cannot provide lawlike, predictive generalizations of complex social phenomena does not necessarily mean that it is wholly irrelevant for constitutional decision-making. So long as one expects social science to provide guidance in policy decisions, that is, to serve a deterministic role in the judicial process, one is bound to be disillusioned and to want to cast (as some judges had done) a pox on both liberal and revisionist houses of social science (for example, Judge Wright, *Hobson* v. *Hansen,* 1967, p. 859). However, if one sees that social science plays mainly an oblique and heuristic role in policy matters, educating the courts and society at large about the factual dimensions of the issue at stake, one begins to appreciate its uses and limits in judicial decision-making. It can expose the varied facets of social problems and stimulate further reflection on the adequacy of one's preconceptions. It might prompt a different view of the issue and expand the range of alternative solutions. In short, it can inform and make more responsible the exercise of judgment, even though it should not and cannot displace the act of judging itself.

In a pluralistic world with competing social values, it is not unexpected and certainly no disgrace to find dissensus among the experts on social facts. These uncertainties stimulate debate about societal purposes. If there were no dilemmas because data resolved ethical issues, there would be no opportunity for moral discourse on human affairs. The capitulation of ethics to science is "at war with the very purpose and the principal *modus operandi* of a free society" (Hart and McNaughton 1959, p. 72). "How to inform the judicial mind" of social science yields no easy solutions. One can, however, take comfort in the fact that although social science might not answer all the questions posed by issues of legal policy, it could make us wiser about the mysteries.

REFERENCES

Abel, R. L. "Redirecting Social Studies of Law." *Law and Society Review* 14 (1980): 805–29.

Abrams v. United States, 250 U.S. 616 (1929).

Allen, F. A. "Legal Scholarship: Present Status and Future Prospects." *Journal of Legal Education* 33 (1983): 403–5.

American Psychological Association. *Ethical Principles of Psychologists.* Wash., D.C.: American Psychological Association, 1981.

Arnold, T. *The Symbols of Government.* New Haven: Yale University Press, 1935.

Bazelon, D. L. "Veils, Values, and Social Responsibility." *American Psychologist* 37 (1982): 115–21.

Bergin, T. "The Law Teacher: A Man Divided Against Himself." *Virginia Law Review* 54 (1968): 637–57.

Berger, R. *Government by Judiciary: The Transformation of the Fourteenth Amendment.* Cambridge, Mass.: Harvard University Press, 1977.

Bok, D. C. "A Flawed System." *Harvard Magazine,* May–June 1983, p. 30.

Cardozo, B. N. "A Ministry of Justice." *Harvard Law Review* 35 (1921): 113–26.

Cohen, J. "Factors of Resistance to the Resources of the Behavioral Sciences." *Journal of Legal Education* 12 (1959): 67–70.

Cohen, D. K., and Weiss, J. A. "Social Science and Social Policy: School and Race." In

Education, Social Science and the Judicial Process, edited by R. Rist and R. Anson. New York: Teachers College Press, 1977.

Coons, J. E. "Recent Trends in Science Fiction: *Serrano* Among the People of Number." In *Education, Social Science and the Judicial Process,* edited by R. Rist and R. Anson. New York: Teachers College Press, 1977.

Cowan, T. A. "Decision Theory in Law, Science, and Technology." *Rutgers Law Review* 17 (1963): 499–530.

Cramton, R. C. "The Current State of the Law Curriculum." *Journal of Legal Education* 32 (1982): 321–35.

Craven, J. B., Jr. "The Impact of Social Science Evidence on the Judge: A Personal Comment." *Law and Contemporary Problems* 39 (1975): 150–56.

Currie, B. "The Materials of Law Study." *Journal of Legal Education* 8 (1955): 1–78.

Dawson, J. P. "Legal Realism and Legal Scholarship." *Journal of Legal Education* 33 (1983): 406–11.

Dick v. New York Life Insurance Co., 359 U.S. 437 (1959).

Doyle, W. E. "Social Science in Constitutional Cases." In *Education, Social Science and the Judicial Process,* edited by R. Rist and R. Anson. New York: Teachers College Press, 1977.

Durkheim, E. *The Division of Labor in Society.* New York: Free Press, 1947.

Dworkin, R. "Social Sciences and Constitutional Rights—The Consequences of Uncertainty." In *Education, Social Science and the Judicial Process,* edited by R. Rist and R. Anson. New York: Teachers College Press, 1977a.

———. *Taking Rights Seriously.* Cambridge, Mass.: Harvard University Press, 1977b.

Fahr, S., and Ojemann, R. "The Case of Social and Behavioral Science Knowledge in Law." *Iowa Law Review* 48 (1962): 59–75.

Frank, J. *Law and the Modern Mind.* New York: Tudor, 1930.

Frey, A. H. "Some Thoughts on Law Teaching and the Social Sciences." *University of Pennsylvania Law Review,* 82 (1934): 463–71.

Fried, C. "The Artificial Reason of the Law or: What Lawyers Know." *Texas Law Review* 60 (1981): 35–58.

Friedman, L., ed. *Argument: The Oral Argument Before the Supreme Court in Brown v. Board of Education of Topeka, 1952–55.* New York: Chelsea House, 1969.

Friedman, L. [Presentation on] "The Future of Law and Social Sciences Research." *North Carolina Law Review* 52 (1974): 1068–73.

Furner, M. *Advocacy and Objectivity: A Crisis in the Professionalization of American Social Science.* Lexington: University of Kentucky Press, 1975.

Gabel, P. "Reification in Legal Reasoning." *Research in Law and Sociology* 3 (1980): 25–51.

Gellhorn, E., and Robinson, G. O. "The Role of Economic Analysis in Legal Education." *Journal of Legal Education* 33 (1983): 247–73.

Gerard, H. B. "School Desegregation: The Social Science Role." *American Psychologist* 38 (1983): 869–77.

Gideon v. Wainwright, 372 U.S. 335 (1963).

Glazer, N. "Towards an Imperial Judiciary." *Public Interest* 41 (1975): 104–23.

Gordon, R. W. "Historicism in Legal Scholarship." *Yale Law Journal* 90 (1981): 1017–56.

Gouldner, A. "Anti-Minotaur: The Myth of a Value-Free Sociology." *Social Problems* 9 (1962): 199–216.

Graglia, L. *Disaster by Decree.* Ithaca, N.Y.: Cornell University Press, 1976.

Grundstein, N. D. "The Relevance of Behavioral Science for Law." *Case Western Reserve Law Review* 19 (1967): 87–97.

Haney, C. "Psychology and Legal Change: On the Limits of a Factual Jurisprudence." *Law and Human Behavior* 4 (1980): 147–99.

Hansmann, H. "The Current State of Law-and-Economics Scholarship." *Journal of Legal Education* 33 (1983): 217–36.

Hart, H. M., and McNaughton, J. T. "Evidence and Inference in Law." In *Evidence and Inference,* edited by D. Lerner. Glencoe, Ill.: Free Press, 1959.

———, and Sacks, A. "The Legal Process: Basic Problems in the Making and Application of Law." Mimeographed. Cambridge, Mass.: Harvard Law School, 1958.

Haskell, T. *The Emergence of Professional Social Science: The American Social Science Association and the Nineteenth Century Crisis of Authority.* Urbana: University of Illinois Press, 1977.

Hazard, G. C., Jr. "Limitations on the Uses of Behavioral Science in the Law." *Case Western Reserve Law Review* 19 (1967a): 71–77.

———. Hearings Before the Subcommittee on Governmental Research of the Committee on Government Operations, National

Foundation or Social Sciences. U.S. Senate, 90 Cong., 1 Sess. (1967b).

Heinz, J. P., and Laumann, E. D. *Chicago Lawyers: The Social Structure of the Bar.* New York: Russell Sage Foundation, 1983.

Hobson v. Hansen, 327 F. Supp. 844 (D.D.C. 1967).

Holmes, O. W. "The Path of the Law." *Harvard Law Review* 10 (1897): 457–78.

Homans, G. "What Kind of Myth Is the Myth of a Value-Free Social Science?" *Social Science Quarterly* 58 (1978): 530–41.

Horowitz, D. *The Courts and Social Policy.* Washington, D.C.: Brookings Institution, 1977.

Horowitz, I. A., and Willging, T. E. *The Psychology of Law: Integrations and Applications.* Boston: Little, Brown, 1984.

Hughes, C. *The Supreme Court of the United States.* New York: Columbia University Press, 1928.

Hutchins, R. "The Autobiography of an Ex-Law Student." *University of Chicago Law Review* 1 (1934): 511–18.

Kalven, H., Jr. "The Quest for the Middle Range: Empirical Inquiry and Legal Policy." In *Law in a Changing America,* edited by G. Hazard. Englewood Cliffs, N.J.: Prentice-Hall, 1968.

Kaplan, A. *The Conduct of Inquiry.* San Francisco: Chandler, 1964.

Karst, K. L. "Legislative Facts in Constitutional Litigation." In *The Supreme Court Review,* edited by P. Kurland. Chicago: University of Chicago Press, 1960.

Katz, M. "The Unmasking of Dishonest Pretensions: Toward an Interpretation of the Role of Social Science in Constitutional Litigation." *American Sociologist* 6 (1971): 54–58.

———, and Burchard, J. M. "Psychology and the Legal Enterprise." *Kansas Law Review* 19 (1970): 197–210.

Kelman, M. G. "Misunderstanding Social Life: A Critique of the Core Premises of 'Law and Economics.'" *Journal of Legal Education* 33 (1983): 274–84.

Kennedy, D. "The Structure of Blackstone's Commentaries." *Buffalo Law Review* 28 (1979): 205–382.

Korn, H. L. "Law, Fact, and Science in the Courts." *Columbia Law Review* 66 (1966): 1080–1116.

Kuhn, T. *The Structure of Scientific Revolutions,* 2nd ed. Chicago: University of Chicago Press, 1970.

Langdell, C. C. *A Selection of Cases on the Law of Contracts.* Boston: Little, Brown, 1871.

Lasswell, H., and McDougal, M. S. "Legal Education and Public Policy: Professional Training in the Public Interest." *Yale Law Journal* 52 (1943): 203–95.

Lempert, R. O. "Civil Juries and Complex Cases: Let's Not Rush to Judgment." *Michigan Law Review* 80 (1981): 68–132.

Levin, H. M. "Education Chances, and the Courts: The Role of Social Science Evidence." *Law and Contemporary Problems* 39 (1975): 217–40.

Levine, J. P. "Scientific Method and the Adversary Model: Some Preliminary Thoughts." *American Psychologist* 28 (1974): 661–77.

Lindblom, C. "The Science of Muddling Through." *Public Administration Review* 19 (1959): 79–88.

Linde, H. "Judges, Critics, and the Realist Tradition." *Yale Law Journal* 82 (1972): 227–56.

Lochner, P. R., Jr. "Some Limits on the Application of Social Science Research in the Legal Process." *Law and the Social Order* 1972 (1972): 815–48.

———. [Presentation on] "Evaluation, Dissemination, and Application of Law and Social Sciences Research." *North Carolina Law Review* 52 (1974): 1033–38.

Loevinger, L. "Law and Science as Rival Systems." *University of Florida Law Review* 19 (1966): 530–51.

Loh, W. D. "In Quest of *Brown*'s Promise: Social Research and Social Values in School Desegregation." *Washington Law Review* 58 (1982): 129–74.

Mannheim, K. *Ideology and Utopia.* New York: Harcourt, Brace, 1936.

———. *Essays on the Sociology of Knowledge.* London: Routledge & Kegan Paul, 1952.

Margolick, D. "The Trouble with America's Law Schools." *New York Times Magazine,* May 22, 1983, p 36.

Martin, J. A. "The Proposed 'Science Court.'" *Michigan Law Review* 75 (1977): 1058–91.

Melton, G. "Training in Psychology and Law: A Directory." *Division of Psychology and Law Newsletter* 3 (1983): 1–5.

McMillan, J. B. "Social Science and the District Court: The Observations of a Journeyman Trial Judge." *Law and Contemporary Problems* 39 (1975): 157–63.

Miller, A. S., and Howell, R. F. "The Myth of Neutrality in Constitutional Adjudication." *University of Chicago Law Review* 27 (1960): 661–95.

Miranda v. Arizona, 384 U.S. 486 (1966).

Moynihan, D. P. "Social Science and the Courts." *Public Interest* 54 (1979): 12–31.

Muller v. Oregon, 208 U.S. 412 (1908).

Münsterberg, H. *On the Witness Stand: Essays on Psychology and Crime*. New York: Clark Boardman, 1908.

Nagel, E. *The Structure of Science: Problems in the Logic of Scientific Explanation*. New York: Harcourt, Brace & World, 1961.

Note. "Social and Economic Facts: Appraisal of Suggested Techniques for Presenting Them to the Courts." *Harvard Law Review* 61 (1948): 692–702.

Note. "'Round and 'Round the Bramble Bush: From Legal Realism to Critical Legal Scholarship." *Harvard Law Review* 95 (1982): 1669–90.

O'Brien, D. M. "Social Science and the Courts: The Seduction of the Judiciary." *Judicature* 64 (1980): 9–21.

———. "Of Judicial Myths, Motivations and Justifications: A Postscript on Social Science and the Law." *Judicature* 64 (1981): 285–89.

Ohlin, L. E. "Partnership with the Social Sciences." *Journal of Legal Education* 23 (1970): 204–8.

Posner, R. "The Present Situation in Legal Scholarship." *Yale Law Journal* 90 (1981): 1113–30.

Rein, M. *Social Science and Public Policy*. New York: Penguin Books, 1976.

Riesman, D. "The Law School: Critical Scholarship vs. Professional Education." *Journal of Legal Education* 32 (1982): 110–19.

Rivlin, A. M. "Forensic Social Science." *Harvard Educational Review* 43 (1973): 61–75.

Robinson, E. S. *The Law and the Lawyers*. New Haven: Yale University Press, 1935.

Rosen, P. L. *The Supreme Court and Social Science*. Urbana: University of Illinois Press, 1972.

Rosenberg, M. "Comments." *Journal of Legal Education* 23 (1971): 199–204.

Rosenblum, V. G. "A Place for Social Science Along the Judiciary's Constitutional Law Frontier." *Northwestern University Law Review* 66 (1971): 455–80.

———. Report on the Uses of Social Science in Judicial Decision Making. Unpublished report to the National Science Foundation, 1978.

Rostow, E. "The Democratic Character of Judicial Review." In *Judicial Review and the Supreme Court*, edited by L. Levy. New York: Harper & Row, 1967.

Saks, M., and Baron, C., eds. *The Use/Nonuse/ Misuse of Applied Social Research in the Courts*. Cambridge, Mass.: Abt Books, 1980.

Schlegel, J. H. "American Legal Realism and Empirical Social Science: From the Yale Experience." *Buffalo Law Review* 28 (1979): 459–588.

———. "American Legal Realism and Empirical Social Science: The Singular Case of Underhill Moore. *Buffalo Law Review* 29 (1980): 195–324.

Scriven, M. "Methods of Reasoning and Justification in Social Science and Law." *Journal of Legal Education* 23 (1971): 189–99.

Shapiro, M. "Stability and Change in Judicial Decisions: Incrementalism or Stare Decisis?" *Law in Transition Quarterly* 2 (1965): 134–57.

Sherrer v. Sherrer, 334 U.S. 343 (1948).

Simon, H. *Administrative Behavior*, 2nd ed. New York: Macmillan, 1957.

Slesinger, D., and Pilpel, M. E. "Legal Psychology: A Bibliography and a Suggestion." *Psychological Bulletin* 26 (1929): 677–92.

Sowell, T. *Ethnic America*. New York: Basic Books, 1981.

Sperlich, P. W. "Social Science Evidence and the Courts: Beyond the Adversary Process." *Judicature* 63 (1980a): 280–89.

———. "Postrealism: Should Ignorance Be Elevated to a Principle of Adjudication." *Judicature* 64 (1980b): 93–98.

Stevens, R. "Two Cheers for 1870: The American Law School." In *Law in American History*, edited by D. Fleming and B. Bailyn. Boston: Little, Brown, 1971.

———. "American Legal Scholarship: Structural Constraints and Intellectual Conceptualism." *Journal of Legal Education* 33 (1983): 442–48.

Stone, J. *The Province and Function of Law*. Cambridge, Mass.: Harvard University Press, 1966.

Summers, R. S. "The Future of Economics in Legal Education: Limits and Constraints." *Journal of Legal Education* 33 (1983): 337–58.

Tapp, J. L. "Psychological and Policy Perspectives on the Law: Reflections on a Decade." *Journal of Social Issues* 36 (1980): 165–92.

Unger, R. M. "The Critical Legal Studies Movement." *Harvard Law Review* 96 (1983): 561–676.

Wechsler, H. "Toward Neutral Principles of Constitutional Law." *Harvard Law Review* 73 (1959): 1–35.

Weinberg, M. "The Relationship Between

School Desegregation and Academic Achievement: A Review of the Research." *Law and Contemporary Problems* 39 (1975): 240–70.

Weinstein, J. B., and Berger, M. A. *Weinstein's Evidence*. New York: Matthew Bender, 1976.

Wells, G. L. "Applied Eyewitness Testimony Research: System Variables and Estimator Variables." *Journal of Personality and Social Psychology* 12 (1978): 1546–57.

White, G. E. "From Sociological Jurisprudence to Realism: Jurisprudence and Social Change in Early Twentieth-Century America." *Virginia Law Review* 58 (1972): 999–1028.

———. "The Evolution of Reasoned Elaboration: Jurisprudential Criticism and Social Change." *Virginia Law Review* 59 (1973): 279–302.

Williams, D. A. "Go to the Head of the Class." *Newsweek*, October 4, 1982, pp. 64–65.

Wisdom, J. M. "Random Remarks on the Role of the Social Sciences in the Judicial Decisionmaking Process in School Desegregation Cases." *Law and Contemporary Problems* 39 (1975): 134–49.

Wolf, E. *Trial and Error: The Detroit School Segregation Case*. Detroit, Mich.: Wayne University Press, 1981.

Yarmey, A. D. *The Psychology of Eyewitness Testimony*. New York: Free Press, 1979.

Yudof, M. G. "School Desegregation: Legal Realism, Reasoned Elaboration and Social Science Research in the Supreme Court." *Law and Contemporary Problems* 42 (1978): 57–110.

Zeisel, H. [Comments on] "Developments in Law and Social Sciences Research." *North Carolina Law Review* 52 (1974): 1050–52.

Zimring, F. E. "Where Do the New Scholars Learn New Scholarship?" *Journal of Legal Education* 33 (1983): 453–58.

INDEX OF CASES

Italics indicate major extracts.

Abrams v. United States, 711, 744

Adams v. Texas (1980), 228, 269

Adams, United States ex rel. McCann v., 429, 475

Adams v. United States, 600

Addington v. Texas, 523, 544

Albemarle Paper Co. v. Moody, 177–178, 180, 186

Aldridge v. United States, 388, 420

Alexander v. Holmes County Board of Education, 117, 186

Alexander v. Louisiana, 363, 364, 420

Allegeyer v. Louisiana, 165 U.S. 578 (1897), 86, 91, 103, 361

Allen v. United States, 446, 473

Amaral, United States v., 554, *589–590,* 590, 603, 619, 634

Anderson, People v., 232, 271

Anti-Monopoly, Inc. v. General Mills Fun Group, Inc., 411, 420

Apodaca v. Oregon, 432, 442–444, 452, 473

Arizona v. Chapple, 590

Ash, United States v., 559, 603

Ashcraft v. Tennessee, 280, 345

Ashe v. Swenson, 518, 544

Atlas Roofing Co. v. Occupational Safety and Health Review Commission, 469, 473

Baker v. Carr, 675, 691

Ballew v. Georgia, 218, 219, 228, 342, *437–441,* 451, 452, 473, 691

Baltimore v. Dawson, 68, 103

Barbier v. Connolly, 90, 103

Barclay v. Florida, 261, 268, 269

Barefoot v. Estelle, 262, 269

Barefoot v. State, 592, 601

Barron v. Baltimore, 46, 103

Beacon Theatres, Inc. v. Westover, 465, 473

Beck v. Washington, 387

Bell v. Patterson, 216, 269

Bell v. School City, 122, 187

Berea College v. Kentucky, 48, 105

Bernstein v. Universal Pictures, Inc., 471, 473

Board of School Commissioners (1971), United States v., 140, 190

Board of School Commissioners (1974), United States v., 190

Boise Cascade Securities Litigation, In re, 466, 474

Bolling v. Sharpe, 62, 80, 81, 103

Boyd v. United States, 346

Bradley v. Milliken (1971), 123, 135, 187

Bradley v. Milliken (1975), 187

Brewer v. School Board, 187

Bridges v. California, 412, 415, 421

Briggs v. Elliott, 59, 62, 71, 76, 103, 115, 187

Brooks v. Beto, 421

Brooks v. Tennessee, 480, *485–487,* 487, 488, 496, 544

Brown v. Allen, 209, 269

Brown v. Board of Education of Topeka, 347 U.S. 483 (1954), 26, 39, 43–44, 45, 50, 54, 55, 56, 59, *62–66,* 66, 67, 68, 69, 76, 77, 80, 81, 96, 99, 100, 102, 103, 107, *109,* 110–113, 121, 144, 151, 153, 157–160, 181, 187, 300, 320, 437, 615, 616, 631, 668, 675, 691, 741, 743

Brown v. Board of Education of Topeka, 349 U.S. 294 (1955), 26, 39, 107, 108, 110, 113, 115, 187, 300

Brown v. Mississippi, 231, 269, 280, 346

Brown, United States v., 603

Brunson v. Board of Trustees, 139–140, 187

Bruton v. United States, 481, 515, 516, 544

Burch v. Louisiana, 442, 445, 473

Burr, Aaron, United States v., 413, 423

Bushell's Case, 428, 473, 479, 537, 544

Bustamante, People v., 558, 562, 602

Byrne v. Boadle, 528, 544

Cagle, People v., 522, 546

Calandra, United States v., 310, 349

Calhoun v. Cook, 133, 187

California v. Prysock, 288, 346

Carolene Products Co., United States v., 95, 105

Castaneda v. Partida, 356, *364–368,* 369, 370, 382, 421

Chandler v. Florida, 508–509, 544

Chapple, State v., 591, 592, 593–594, 602

Chicago B. & Q. R.R. v. Chicago, 661, 691

City of Mobile v. Bolden, 384, 421

Civil Rights Cases, 47, 51, 103

Coker v. Georgia, 262, 267, 269

Colgrove v. Battin, 425, 431, 437, 473

Collins, People v., 481, *524–527,* 527, 546

Collins, United States v., 603

Columbus Board of Education v. Penick, 132, 187
Commonwealth v. Roane, 299, 346
Commonwealth v. Soares, 390, 421
Commonwealth v. Webster, 522, 544
Contreras, United States v., 288, 349
Cook, State v., 591, 602
Cooper v. Aaron, 116
Coppedge v. Franklin County Board of Education, 116, 187
Craig v. County of Los Angeles, 179, 187
Crampton v. Ohio, 217, 256, 269
Crawford v. Board of Education, 140, 188
Crews, United States v., 559, 603
Crowe, People v., 388, 422
Cumming v. County Board of Education, 48, 56, 64, 103

Dairy Queen, Inc. v. Wood, 465, 474
Davis v. County School Board, 59, 62, 74, 77, 103, 107, 110
Dayton Board of Education v. Brinkman, 132, 154, 188
Deal v. Cincinnati Board of Education, 122, 188
Defore, People v., 275, 348
Delli Paoli v. United States, 624, 631
Dick v. New York Life Insurance Co., 709, 745
Dougherty, United States v., 428, 447–450, 475, 599
Downs v. Board of Education, 122, 188
Drew v. United States, 517, 545
Duncan v. Louisiana, 214, 270, 429, 435, 436, 452, 474
Dunn v. Blumstein, 95, 104
Duren v. Missouri, 218, 229, 270, 370, 421
Durham v. United States, 614, 631

Elkins v. United States, 310, 346
Escobedo v. Illinois, 281, 282, 346
Estelle v. Smith, 288, 346
Estes v. Texas, 19, 21, 353, 421, 508, 545, 618, 631

Fane v. Michael C., 288, 299, 346
Fay v. Noia, 209, 269
Fay, United States v., 277, 349
Federated Publications v. Swedberg, 415, 421
Ferguson v. Skrupa, 93, 104
Fosher, United States v., 529, 603
Frank v. Mangum, 270

Frazier, United States v., 288, 349
Furman v. Georgia, 193, 199, 232, 234–241. 256, 262, 265, 266, 267, 270, 684, 692

Gaitor, State v., 559, 602
Gallagher, People v., 52, 661, 694
Galloway, State v., 591, 592, 593, 602
Gannett Co., Inc. v. DePasquale, 418, 421
Gardner v. Florida, 211, 270
Gault, In re, 299
Gay v. Waiters' and Dairy Lunchmen's Union, 356, 379–383, 383, 421
Gayle v. Browder, 67, 68, 104, 108, 188
Gebhart v. Belton, 62, 77, 104
Georgia v. Brailsford, 537, 545
Gideon v. Wainwright, 346, 601, 675, 692, 742, 745
Gilbert v. California, 549–550, 601
Gillebeau, People v., 568, 602
Godfrey v. Georgia, 255, 270
Gong Lum v. Rice, 64
Green v. County School Board, 116–117, 118, 188
Greene, State v., 562, 602
Gregg v. Georgia, 193, 200, 251–254, 255, 256, 259, 260, 261, 265, 267, 270
Griggs v. Duke Power Co., 174, 175, 176–177, 188
Grisby v. Mabry, 229, 230
Grunewald, United States v., 516, 547, 624, 634
Guardians Association of New York City v. Civil Service Commission, 180, 188
Guinn v. United States, 68, 104
Guster, State v., 599, 602

Hall v. State, 262, 276
Hamilton v. State, 450, 474, 601
Hampton v. State, 450, 591, 601
Harris v. New York, 516, 545
Havens, United States v., 310, 349
Hawthorne, People v., 614, 633
Hazelwood School District v. United States, 356, 376–378, 382, 422
Hart v. Community School Board, 133, 188
Hearst, United States v., 603
Hidden v. Mutual Life Insurance Co., 614, 632
Hobson v. Hansen, 9, 21, 160, 161–162, 182, 188, 744, 746
Hodges, United States v., 603
Holden v. Hardy, 86

Holmes v. Atlanta, 68, 104
Hopkins v. State, 592, 601
Horning v. District of Columbia, 474, 492
Hovey v. The Superior Court of Alameda County,
199, *217–227*, 227, 270

ILC Peripherals Leasing Corp. (Memorex) v.
International Business Machines Corp., 466,
474
Illinois v. Gates, 311, 347
Ingraham v. Wright, 270
In re Boise Cascade Securities Litigation, 466,
474
In re Gault, 299
In re Japanese Electronic Products Antitrust
Litigation, 432, 466, 474
In re Kemmler, 270
In re U.S. Financial Securities Litigation, 463,
469, 474
In re Winship, 522, 529, 545
Irvin v. Dowd, 387, 414, 422, 615, 632

Jackson v. Denno, 515, 545, 591, 602
Janis, United States v., 310, 349
Japanese Electronic Products Antitrust Litiga-
tion, In re, 432, 466, 474
Jefferson County Board of Education (1966),
United States v., 190
Jefferson County Board of Education (1967),
United States v., 116, 190
Johnson v. Louisiana, 445, 474
Jordan, State v., 599, 602
Jurek v. Texas, 255, 260, 261, 270

Kelley v. Metropolitan County Board of Edu-
cation, 133, 189
Kemmler, In re, 233, 270
Keyes v. School District No. 1 (1970), 189
Keyes v. School District No. 1 (1973), 121,
122, 123, 189, 384, 422
King v. Warickshall, The, 280, 349
Kirby v. Illinois, 599, 602
Korematsu v. United States, 95, 104
Krulewitch v. United States, 511, 545
Kusley v. State, 561, 602

Lakeside v. Oregon, 545
Lampe v. Franklin American, 523, 545
Larry P. v. Riles, *162–170*, 173, 174, 175, 189
Lau v. Nichols, 189
Lawrence, People v., 559, 602
Lawton v. Steele, 91, 104

Lochner v. New York, 57, 85, 86, 87, 88, 90,
92, 104, 661, 670, 683, 693
Lockett v. Ohio, 262, 265, 270
Lockett, State v., 271
Louisiana ex rel. Francis v. Resweber, 233,
271

McCann, United States ex rel. v. Adams, 429,
475
McGautha v. California, 231, 243, 271
McGowan v. Maryland, 94, 104
McLaurin v. Oklahoma State Regents for
Higher Education, 49, 64, 65, 104
McNabb v. United States, 274, 347
Manson v. Brathwaite, 553, *559–561*, 561, 562,
602, 621, 633
Mapp v. Ohio, 275, 301, 303, 305, 308, 310,
316, 318, 319, 343, 347, 549, 602
Marbury v. Madison, 93, 104
Maskeny, United States v., 370, 423
Matter of Storar, 319, 347
Maxwell v. Bishop (1968), 201, *205–209*, 210,
231, 263, 264, 271, 368, 378
Maxwell v. Bishop (1970), 210, 271, 422
Maxwell v. State, 271
Maxwell v. Stephens, 271
Michelson v. United States, 519, 546
Michigan v. DeFillippo, 310, 347
Michigan v. Mosley, 288, 347
Milliken v. Bradley (1973), 189
Milliken v. Bradley (1974), 108–109, *123–126*,
131–132, 158, 189, 741
Milliken v. Bradley (1977), 132, 158, 159, 189,
741
Miranda v. Arizona, 278, 286–287, 288, 319,
347, 452, 474, 546, 549, 558, 562, 602, 741,
742, 746
Missouri ex rel. Gaines v. Canada, 48, 64, 104
Moore v. Illinois, 271, 559, 602
Morgan v. Kerrigan, 137, 138, 140, 189
Muller v. Oregon, 45, *85–87*, 88–90, 92, 96,
104, 747
Muller, State v., 85

Nash v. United States, 511, 546
Nebraska Press Association v. Stuart, 357, *415–
417*, 422
New Orleans Parks Association v. Detiege, 68,
105
Nobles, United States v., 590, 603
Norris v. Alabama, 360, 422

Olmstead v. United States, 310, 348
Oregon v. Bradshaw, 288, 348
Oregon v. Mathiason, 288, 348
Osborne v. United States Bank, 642

Palm Beach Newspapers, Inc., State v., 509, 547
Parent Association of Andrew Jackson High
    School v. Ambach, 140, 189
Parents in Action on Special Education v.
    Hannon, 171, 189
Parsons v. Bedford, 441, 464, 475
Patton v. United States, 434, 475
Payner, United States v., 310, 349
Pearce v. Commissioner, 442, 475
People v. Anderson, 232, 271
People v. Bustamante, 558, 562, 602
People v. Cagle, 522, 546
People v. Collins, 481, 524–527, 527, 546
People v. Crowe, 388, 422
People v. Defore, 275, 348
People v. Gallagher, 52, 661, 694
People v. Gillebeau, 568, 602
People v. Hawthorne, 614, 633
People v. Lawrence, 559, 602
People v. Powell, 356, 371–373, 373, 422
People v. Shapiro, 517, 546
People v. Speck, 216, 271
People v. Wheeler, 390, 422
Pittman v. State, 216, 271
Plessy v. Ferguson, 44, 47, 48, 49, 50–54, 56,
    63, 64, 67, 70, 83, 105, 108, 158, 190, 342,
    348, 683, 694
Pointer v. United States, 386
Powell v. Alabama, 231, 271, 452, 475, 602
Powell, People v., 356, 371–373, 373, 422
Processed Plastic Company v. Warner Com-
    munications, 411, 422
Proffitt v. Florida, 255, 260, 271
Pulley v. Harris, 262, 264, 268, 271

R. v. Edmonds, 471, 475
Reynolds v. United States, 214, 271
Rhode Island v. Innis, 288, 348
Richmond Newspapers, Inc. v. Virginia, 418,
    422
Rideau v. Louisiana, 414, 423
Riggs v. Palmer, 686–687, 694
Ristiano v. Ross, 406, 423
Roberts v. City of Boston, 51, 55, 64, 67, 105
Roberts v. Louisiana, 255, 260, 271
Robinson v. California, 232, 271
Rochin v. California, 275, 348

Rosales-Lopez v. United States, 406, 423
Ross v. Bernhard, 463, 465, 475

San Antonio Independent School District v.
    Rodriguez, 95, 105, 154, 159, 190
Santa Clara County v. Southern Pacific Rail-
    road Co., 91, 105
Sauer, State v., 522, 547
SCM Corp. v. Xerox Corp., 473, 475
Shapiro, People v., 517, 546
Shelley v. Kraemer, 49, 68, 69, 105
Sheppard v. Maxwell, 407, 414, 415, 423, 615,
    634
Sherrer v. Sherrer, 707, 747
Sims, United States v., 591, 603
Sipuel v. Oklahoma, 64
Skidmore v. Baltimore and Ohio R.R., 429,
    475
Slaughter-House Cases, 47, 64, 105, 661, 694
Smith v. Allwright, 68, 105
Smith v. Rapid Transit, Inc., 528, 547
Smuck v. Hobson, 162
Sneed, State v., 527, 547
South Carolina, United States v., 180, 190
South Dakota v. Neville, 288, 348
Spano v. New York, 281, 348, 562, 602
Sparf and Hansen v. United States, 538, 547
Speck, People v., 216, 271
Spencer v. Texas, 516, 547
Spinkellink v. Wainwright, 263, 271
State v. Chapple, 591, 592, 593–594, 602
State v. Cook, 591, 602
State v. Gaitor, 559, 602
State v. Galloway, 591, 592, 593, 602
State v. Greene, 562, 602
State v. Guster, 599, 602
State v. Jordan, 599, 602
State v. Lockett, 271
State v. Muller, 85
State v. Palm Beach Newspapers, Inc., 509,
    547
State v. Sauer, 522, 547
State v. Sneed, 527, 547
State v. Warren, 591, 599, 602
State v. Williams, 271
State v. Wright, 564, 602
Stell v. Savannah-Chatham County Board of
    Education (1963), 121, 190
Stell v. Savannah-Chatham County Board of
    Education (1964), 190
Stettler v. O'Hara, 96

Strauder v. West Virginia, 64, 67, 105, 271, 360, 423

Stroble v. California, 410

Stovall v. Denno, 549–550, 603

Swain v. Alabama, 356, 357–358, 360, 361, 362, 363, 364, 385–386, 388, 389–390, 423, 603

Swann v. Charlotte-Mecklenburg Board of Education, 108, 117–120, 121, 122, 154, 190

Sweatt v. Painter, 49, 64, 65, 69, 105

Sweezy v. New Hampshire, 243, 271

Tague v. Louisiana, 218, 288, 349, 359

Tasby v. Wright, 133, 182, 190

Taylor v. Louisiana, 229, 271, 375, 423

Telfaire, United States v., 554, 577, 596–599, 603, 619, 634

Thevis, United States v., 590, 592, 593, 603, 619, 634

Thiel v. Southern Pacific Co., 271

Thorne v. Cramer, 658, 694

Triangle Publications v. Rohrlick, 411, 423

Trop v. Dulles, 233, 271

Turner v. United States, 528, 547

United States v. Amaral, 554, 589–590, 603, 619, 634

United States v. Aaron Burr, 413, 423

United States v. Ash, 559, 603

United States v. Board of School Commissioners (1971), 140, 190

United States v. Board of School Commissioners (1974), 190

United States v. Brown, 603

United States v. Calandra, 310, 349

United States v. Carolene Products Co., 95, 105

United States v. Collins, 603

United States v. Contreras, 288, 349

United States v. Crews, 559, 603

United States v. Dougherty, 428, 447–450, 475, 599

United States v. Fay, 277, 349

United States v. Fosher, 592, 603

United States v. Frazier, 288, 349

United States v. Grunewald, 516, 547, 624, 634

United States v. Havens, 310, 349

United States v. Hearst, 603

United States v. Hodges, 603

United States v. Janis, 310, 349

United States v. Jefferson County Board of Education (1966), 190

United States v. Jefferson County Board of Education (1967), 116, 190

United States v. Nobles, 590, 603

United States v. Maskeny, 370, 423

United States ex rel. McCann v. Adams, 429, 475

United States v. Payner, 310, 349

United States v. Scotland Neck Board of Education, 140, 190

United States v. Sims, 591, 603

United States v. South Carolina, 180, 190

United States v. Telfaire, 554, 577, 596–599, 603, 619, 634

United States v. Thevis, 590, 592, 593, 603, 619, 634

United States v. Wade, 275, 349, 452, 475, 549–550, 551, 553, 554–557, 558, 561, 562, 599, 603

United States v. Watson, 592, 603

United States v. Williams, 311, 349

U. S. Financial Securities Litigation, In re, 466, 469, 474

University of California Regents v. Bakke, 68, 108

Village of Arlington Heights v. Metropolitan Housing Development Corp. 190–191, 384, 420

Wade, United States v., 275, 349, 452, 475, 549–550, 551, 553, 554–557, 558, 561, 562, 599, 603

Wainwright v. Goode, 268, 272

Warren, State v., 591, 599, 602

Washington v. Davis, 178–179, 180, 191, 384, 423

Watkins v. Sowders, 591, 603

Watson, United States v., 592, 603

Watts v. Indiana, 299, 349

Weeks v. United States, 301, 349

Weems v. United States, 233, 272

Wheeler, People v., 390, 422

Whitus v. Georgia, 363, 364, 423

Wilkerson v. Utah, 233, 272

Williams v. Florida, 214, 272, 432–434, 437, 441, 442, 452, 469, 475, 694

Williams v. Mississippi, 47, 105

Williams, State v., 271
Williams v. State, 211, 272
Williams, United States v., 311, 349
Winship, In re, 522, 529, 545
Witherspoon v. Illinois, 199, 210, *211–213*, 214, 215, 216, 218, 219, 256, 272, 390, 423
Wolf v. Colorado, 308, 349

Woodson v. North Carolina, 255, 261, 265, 272
Wong Sun v. United States, 558, 603
Wright v. Smith, 565, 603
Wright, State v., 564, 602
Wylie v. Warden, 450, 475
Wyrick v. Fields, 288, 349

NAME INDEX

Italics indicate major extracts.

Aaron, H., 128
Abel, R.L., 630, 741, 744
Abram, T.G., 383, 423
Abt, L.E., 8, 20, 422, 546
Adams, T.F., 324, 345
Adler, M., 632
Ajzen, I., 403, 420
Alexander, P., 298, 299, 347
Alfini, J.J., 539, 543, 545
Allen, F.A., 734, 744
Allen, F.L., 670, 691
Allman, T.D., 311, 345
Allport, F.H., 59
Allport, G.W., 59, 143, 147, 152, 160, 186,
   246, 269, 569
Alprin, G.M., 329, 336
Amir, Y., 152, 186
Amsterdam, A.G., 216, 269, 281, 332, 336,
   345
Anastasi, A., 44, 103, 171, 186, 614, 630
Andenaes, J., 29, 39
Anderson, J.K., 500, 545
Andreoli, V., 488, *492–495,* 499, 547, 625, 634
Anson, R., 187, 745
Antunes, G., 257, 269
Aquinas, T., 638–639
Aristotle, 641, 691
Armor, D.J., 143–147, 148, 149, 150, 182, 186
Armstrong, S., 66, 105
Arnold, M.S., 464
Arnold, T.W., 29, 39, 340, 345, 613, 631,
   727, 744
Aronson, R.H., 478, 544
Asch, S., 392, 420, 436, 569
Ashurst, D.E., 173, 186
Austin, J., 500, 544, 639, 640, 691
Avakian, S., 544
Ayres, R., 289

Babcock, B.A., 387, 389, 420
Bailyn, B., 694, 747
Balch, R., 325, 345
Balch, R.W., 387, 420
Baldus, D.C., 255, 256, 269, 376, 378, 420
Baldwin, J., 8, 20
Baldwin, James, 325, 345
Banks, W.C., 152, 186
Banton, M., 327, 345

Barksdale, H., 408, 420
Barnes, D.W., 15, 20, 369, 375, 420
Baron, C.H., 8, 22, 269, 710, 747
Bartlett, F.C., 568
Bartol, C.R., 8, 10, 20, 324, 326, 345, 402,
   420, 445, 447, 461, 491, 544, 574, 577, 580,
   607, 626, 631, 644, 691
Barton, A., 420, 422
Barzun, J., 193, 269
Bates, A.P., 617, 631
Batey, R., 337, 338, 339, 345
Bayes, T., 530–531
Bayless, S., 607, 632
Bazelon, D.L., 581, 710, 711, 732, 744
Beccari, C., 195
Bedau, H.A., 195, 197, 269, 272
Bell, D., 133, 139, 151, 181, 182, 187, 190
Bender, D.C., 504–507, 546
Bentham, J., 640, 669
Berberich, J., 326, 349
Bergin, T., 737, 744
Berger, M.A., 509, 519, 547, 619, 624, 634,
   709, 748
Berger, R., 707, 744
Berk, R., 399, 420
Berkowitz, L., 422
Berliner, D.C., 190
Berman, H.J., 12, 21, 23, 24, 28, 39, 643, 691
Berman, J.J., 404, 422
Bermant, G., 8, 21, 388, 391, 420, 421, 460,
   508, 544, 575, 624, 625, 631
Bernard, V.W., 59
Berns, W., 242, 269
Bernstein, B.J., 55, 103, 616, 631
Bersoff, D.N., 161, 171, 172, 187
Beutel, F.K., 343, 346, 613, 614, 631, 671,
   691
Bice, S.H., 243, 269
Bickel, A.M., 55, 103, 682, 684, 691
Binet, A., 608, 631
Bittner, E., 327, 346
Black, C., Jr., 256, 269
Black, C.L., Jr., 54, 55, 69, 83, 103, 615, 631
Blackstone, W., 639, 641, 658, 691
Blalock, H., 379
Blumstein, A., 259, 269, 270
Boas, F., 58, 103
Bobbitt, P., 428
Bok, D.C., 13, 21, 732, 744
Bonora, B., 400, 420

Borchard, E., 551
Bordua, D., 348
Boster, F., 504–507, 546
Bowers, W., 194, 196, 200, 201, 263, 264, 269
Bowles, S., 150, 187
Bradley, C.M., 311, 346
Brandeis, L.D., 44–45, 56, 83, 84, 87–90, 92–93, 96, 103, 310
Brandis, P., 394
Bray, R.M., 8, 11, 21, 402, 421, 431, 460, 461, 474, 546, 623, 625, 631, 632
Brigham, J.C., 567, 574, 577, 580, 595
Brilmayer, L., 529, 532, 544
Britt, S.H., 614, 631, 673, 691
Broderick, J.J., 323, 329, 346
Brodsky, S.L., 8, 21
Broeder, D.W., 355, 387, 389, 390, 421, 426
Bronson, E., 229
Brown, M., 610, 631
Brown, M.K., 322, 323, 326, 327, 346
Bruner, J.S., 59, 569
Bryan, W., Jr., 399, 421
Bryce, J., 660, 691
Buckhout, R., 8, 21, 402, 421, 574, 579, 593, 617, 619, 631
Bull, R., 8, 21, 568, 577
Burchard, J.D., 10, 21, 632, 716–717, 746
Burger, W.E., 209, 268, 269, 307, 308, 331, 346
Burke, E., 27
Burns, H.J., 576
Burtt, H., 631
Byrne, D., 402, 422
Byrnes, J.F., 84, 103

Cahn, E., 71, 75, 77, *78–81*, 82, 83, 103, 121, 136, 183, 187, 404, 421, 437, 615, 631
Cairns, H., 609, 610, 611, 631
Calabresi, G., 428
Caldwell, C., 625, 634
Callahan, C.C., 611, 633
Campbell, D., 490, 546
Campbell, D.T., 297, 298, 318, 346
Campbell, E.Q., 187
Canon, B.C., 319, 320, 346
Cantril, H., 59
Caplan, G., 346
Cardozo, B.N., 101, 102, 103, 303, 344, 346, 656, 684, 689, 691, 712, 744
Carter, R., 70
Cavers, D.F., 614, 631
Charrow, R.P., 539, 544

Charrow, V., 539, 544
Chein, I., 59, 61, 73
Chesler, M., 190
Chevigny, P., 311, 327, 340, 346
Christie, R., 397, 399, 421, 423
Clark, C., 343, 346, 727
Clark, C.E., 675, 691–692
Clark, K.B., 44, 59, 60, 65, 70–73, 77, 78, 79, 81–83, 110, 112, 143, 182, 183, 187, 188, 615, 623, 631
Clark, M.P., 59, 70, 77, 103, 128, 143
Clark, T.C., 501, 544
Cleary, E.W., 477, 544
Clifford, B.R., 8, 21, 568, 577
Clotfelter, C.J., 138, 187
Cobb, T., 200, 269
Coffin, F.M., 689, 692
Cohen, D.K., 150, 187, 743–744
Cohen, E.G., 153, 187
Cohen, F.S., 642, 670, 673, 692
Cohen, J., 259, 269, 509, 544, 617, 631, 716, 744
Cohen, L., 529, 536, 544
Cohen, M.R., 613, 631, 692
Cohn, A., 8, 21, 484, 544, 617, 623, 626, 631
Cohn, R.M., 378, 421
Cole, J., 376, 378, 420
Coleman, J.S., 137, 138, 139, 141–143, 149, 182, 187
Collins, B.E., 269, 569, 601
Collins, M.E., 143
Collins, R.K.L., 84, 85, 103
Colman, R., 423
Conrad, A.F., 375, 421
Constantini, E., 407, 421
Cook, S.W., 59, 152
Cooke, G., 8, 21
Cooley, C.H., 58, 103
Coons, J.E., 745
Cornish, W.R., 514, 515, 519, 544, 623, 631
Costner, H.L., 348
Cowan, C.L., 221, 269
Cowan, T.A., 342, 346, 696, 745
Crain, R.L., 150, 188
Cramton, R.C., 736, 745
Craven, J.B., 140, 188, 695, 745
Critchlow, B., 193
Cromwell, H., 488, 489, 544
Cronbach, L., 173, 188
Cundrick, B.P., 547
Currie, B., 673, 692, 726, 745
Curtis, W., 375, 421

Dai, B., 59
Damaška, M., 185, 188, 500, 544, 626, 631
Dane, F.C., 460
Danet, B., 538, 544
Daniels, S., 267, 270
Danzig, E.R., 535, 547, 614, 634
Dauer, E.A., 659, 675, 690, 692
Davidow, R.P., 247, 270
Davies, T.Y., 216, 270, 346
Davis, A., 59
Davis, J.H., 78, 402, 421, 446, 460, 474, 631
Davis, K.C., 96, 103, 324, 337, 341, 346, 622,
    623, 625, 631
Dawson, J.P., 728, 745
Deffenbacher, K.A., 567, 576–577, 579, 595
Deutsch, M., 143
Deutscher, M., 61, 65, 73, 103
Devine, P.G., 564, 575, 579
Devlin, P.A., 276, 346, 353, 354, 390, 421,
    425, 434, 464, 471, 552, 592, 600, 601
Dewey, J., 343, 346, 672, 692
Diamond, S.S., 391, 399, 423, 437, 453–456,
    460, 461, 470, 475, 625, 635
Dillehay, R.C., 406, 409, 410, 422, 461
Dillon, J., 657, 692
Dittenhoffer, T., 251, 272
Dix, G.E., 487, 544
Dollard, J., 58, 103, 143, 188
Doret, D.N., 503, 544
Doro, M.E., 87–90, 96, 103
Doob, A.N., 512–514, 515, 519, 545, 564, 623,
    625, 631, 632
Douglas, W.O., 668, 692, 728
Douglass, F., 69
Doyle, W.E., 695, 740, 745
Driver, E.D., 297, 346
Dunlap, K., 613, 631
Dunlap, R., 671, 692
Durkheim, E., 12, 733, 745
Dworkin, R., 685–688, 689, 692, 708,
    729, 740, 745

Ebbesen, E.B., 7, 8, 21, 460, 461, 462
Egeth, H.E., 577, 578, 581, 595
Ehrlich, E., 258, 259, 641, 692
Eisenberg, M., 660, 669
Eisenhower, D.D., 67–68
Elfenbein, D., 250, 270
Ellison, K.W., 8, 21, 402, 421, 574, 617, 631
Ellman, I.M., 536, 545
Ellsworth, P.C., 221–222, 223, 244–246, 247,
    259, 269, 270, 272

Elwork, A., 3, 8, 21, 460, 539, 543, 545
Emerson, C.D., 402,421
Emrich, B., 423
Epps, E.G., 152, 188
Erikson, K.T., 194, 270
Erlanger, H.A., 460
Etzioni, A., 399, 404, 421

Fahr, S.M., 10, 21, 626, 631, 716, 745
Fairley, W.B., 527, 532, 533, 545
Faris, R.E., 58, 104
Farley, R., 188
Farmer, L.C., 547
Filler, J., 270
Fink, C.J., 431
Finkelstein, M.O., 362, 403, 421, 530, 532,
    533, 545
Fishbein, M., 269, 403, 420
Fisher, J., 152, 188
Fisher, R.A., 530
Fishman, J.A., 609, 631
Fiss, O., 121, 154, 188
Fitzgerald, R., 270
Flaugher, R., 170, 171, 188
Fleming, D., 694, 747
Florence, B.T., 504–507, 546
Flynn, L.J., 436
Fontes, N., 504–507, 546
Ford, J., 657, 692
Fraenkel, O.K., 96, 104
Frank, J., 21, 27, 39, 89, 545, 613, 631, 667,
    668–669, 671, 674, 683, 692, 739, 745
Frankel, M.E., 498, 545
Frenkel-Brunswik, E., 59
Frankfurter, F., 3, 24, 26, 39, 56, 66, 92,
    104, 198, 243, 274, 344, 346, 410, 612,
    631, 643
Franklin, J.H., 46, 47, 55, 104
Frederick, J., 392–399, 422
Freud, S., 690
Freund, P.A., 92, 96, 104, 616, 631
Frey, A.H., 727, 745
Fried, C., 745
Friedman, L., 3, 8, 9, 13, 21, 66, 78, 104, 216,
    270, 617, 626, 632, 695, 737, 745
Friesen, J., 84, 85, 103
Fuller, L., 498, 545, 611, 613, 632, 638, 645–
    650, 652, 656, 660, 669, 681, 692
Furner, M., 727, 745

Gabel, P., 730, 745
Galanter, M., 6, 21, 627–629, 629–630, 632

Garner, W.R., 178, 191
Garrett, H., 74, 121
Geller, W.A., 311, 319, 321, 346
Gellhorn, E., 675, 692
Gellhorn, W., 732, 734
Gerard, H.B., 151, 152, 153, 160, 188, 723, 745
Gerbasi, K.C., 402, 421, 460, 461, 625, 632
Gewin, W., 374, 421
Gibson, J.L., 209–210, 270
Giffiths, L.T., 420
Gilbert, M.A., 634
Gilmore, G., 266
Gillespie, M., 421
Girsh, F.G., 270
Gist, N.P., 59
Glazer, N., 182, 188, 707, 745
Goldberg, F.J., 212
Goldman, R., 172, 188
Goldstein, A., 497, 545
Goldstein, H., 322, 323, 327, 328, 346
Goldstein, S.R., 276, 348
Goodman, F.I., 135, 188
Goodrich, H.F., 610–611, 632
Gordon, R.W., 730, 745
Gotcher, E., 84
Gottlieb, G.H., 198, 270
Gottlieb, J., 173, 190
Gouldner, A., 745
Graber, D., 420, 421
Graglia, L., 707, 745
Graham, H., 55, 104
Grant, W.R., 131, 134, 136, 188
Granucci, A.F., 232, 270
Green, R., 137–138, 190
Green, W., 270
Greenawalt, K., 687, 692
Greenberg, J., 104, 632
Greenberg, M.S., 8, 21, 402, 403, 421, 617, 632
Greene, E., 518, 543, 545, 546
Greene, E.L., 599, 601, 622, 632
Greer, D.S., 580
Gregor, A.J., 77, 104
Greiner, W.R., 12, 21, 23, 24, 28, 39, 643, 691
Grisso, T., 299, 346, 607
Gross, S., 263
Grossman, H., 172, 188
Grundstein, N.D., 709, 745
Gunther, G., 174, 188
Gurin, P., 190
Gutman, S.M., 389, 421

Hahn, H., 322, 324, 326, 347
Haines, C.G., 658, 692
Hall, C., 307
Hall, E.O., 420
Hall, M.E., 666, 692
Hamilton, A., 43, 104, 463, 721
Hamilton, W.H., 656, 692
Hand, L., 96, 104
Haney, C., 175, 178, 188, 226, 228, 229, 270, 403, 421, 630, 632, 696, 710, 711, 717–721, 721, 722, 745
Hans, V.P., 409, 421, 512–514, 515, 519, 545, 623, 625, 632
Hansmann, H., 731, 732, 733, 745
Harring, S., 401, 422
Harris, R.N., 323, 347
Hart, H.L.A., 5, 21, 639, 641, 681, 684–685, 686, 687, 688, 692
Hart, H.M., 21, 24, 25, 26, 40, 99, 104, 185, 188, 616, 632, 640, 652, 710, 716, 721, 723, 740, 744, 745
Hart, R., 320, 347
Hartig, L., 172, 188
Hartley, E., 420
Haskell, T., 6, 21, 727, 745
Hassett, J.N., 413, 421
Hastie, R.H., 8, 21, 229, 402, 403, 423, 431, 446, 447, 460, 491, 546, 617, 618, 623, 634
Hauser, P., 128
Hawkins, C., 431, 446, 474, 617, 634
Hawkins, G., 256, 272
Hayden, R.M., 500, 545
Hayward, A., 694
Hazard, G.C., Jr., 35, 40, 104, 537, 546, 632, 714, 721, 722, 737, 745, 746
Hedblom, J.H., 271
Hegland, K., 16, 21
Heinz, J.P., 736, 745
Heller, K.A., 173, 188
Hepburn, J.R., 402, 422
Herbsled, J.P., 404, 422
Hess, D.W., 289
Heyman, I., 69, 104
Higginbotham, P.E., 473, 474
Hobbes, T., 639, 692
Hobson, C.J., 187
Hocking, J., 504–507, 546
Hofstadter, R., 56, 104, 661, 672, 692
Hogarth, R.M., 535, 545
Holmes, O.W., 9, 21, 27, 29, 40, 57, 92, 96, 104, 343, 347, 422, 613–614, 632, 638, 639, 642, 653–656, 656–657, 658, 661, 662, 669–670, 673, 692, 707, 711, 746

Holt, L., 75–76
Holt, R.W., 402, 421, 460, 474, 623, 625, 631
Holtzman, W.H., 173
Homans, G., 741, 746
Hook, L.H., 431
Hoover, C., 658, 693
Hornum, F., 265, 270
Horowitz, D., 707, 746
Horowitz, I.A., 8, 21, 401, 422, 450, 607, 626, 632, 738, 746
Horowitz, M., 669, 693
Hosch, H.M., 595, 622, 632
Houlden, P., 694
Houts, M., 582–588, 588–589
Hovland, C.I., 489, 490–491, 545, 546
Howe, M.D., 57, 104, 661, 674, 693
Howell, R.F., 547, 682, 693, 710, 740, 746
Howley, W.D., 189
Hudson, J.R., 327, 347
Hughes, C., 707, 746
Hughes, G., 13, 21
Hull, C.L., 611, 632
Hume, D., 669
Hunt, A.L., 257, 269
Hunt, M., 399, 403, 404, 422
Hutcheson, J.C., Jr., 632, 671, 693
Hutchins, R.M., 568, 609, 611, 612, 632, 728, 738, 746
Hyman, E.M., 338, 347

Inger, M., 116, 188
Israel, J.H., 270, 389, 422

Jacoby, J.E., 263, 270
Jacoubovitch, M.D., 508
Jaffe, L.L., 92, 104
James, R.M., 431, 617, 634
James, W., 690, 693
Janis, I.L., 490–491, 545
Jay, J., 43, 104
Jeffrey, C.R., 258, 270
Jensen, A.R., 188
Jensen, D.L., 320, 347
Johnson, A., 45
Johnson, J.G., 177, 188
Johnson, R., 501, 545
Jonakait, R.N., 562
Jones, E.M., 344, 347
Jones, H.W., 21, 644, 693
Judson, J., 408, 423
Jurow, G.L., 220–221, 270

Kadane, J.V., 229, 270, 360, 422
Kadish, S., 257, 270
Kahn, R.L., 321, 327, 338, 339, 347
Kairys, O., 360, 400, 401, 422
Kalmuss, D., 190
Kalven, H., 3, 4, 6, 21, 104, 391, 403, 419, 422, 426, 427, 429, 430, 431, 436, 446, 460, 462, 463, 469, 470, 536, 539, 545, 621, 627, 632, 693, *714–716,* 716, 726, 741, 746,
Kamisar, Y., 270, *306–309,* 310, 320, 347, 389, 422, 551, 602
Kantorowicz, H., 637, 693
Kaplan, A., 34, 40, 296, 297, 347, 746
Kaplan, B., 656, 693
Kaplan, J., 255, 270, 347, 387, 422
Kaplan, M.F., 447
Karst, K.L., 56, 104, 615, 632, 710, 746
Kassin, S.M., 517, 545
Katz, D., 59, 321, 327, 338, 339
Katz, I., 190
Katz, M., 10, 21, 630, 632, 696, 711, 716–717, 746
Katz, P., 152, 186, 189
Kaye, D.H., 375, 378, 379, 422, 437, 441, 528, 530, 532, 533, 536, 545
Keeton, R., 487, 545
Kelley, H.H., 490–491, 545
Kelly, A.H., 55, 67, 104, 435
Kelly, S., 137, 182, 187
Kelman, M.G., 730, 746
Kelsen, H., 639, 693
Kennedy, D., 658, 693, 730
Kennedy, W.B., 613, 632, 671, 746
Kerr, N.L., 8, 11, 21, 402, 422, 431, 460, 461, 546, 632
Kidd, R.F., 530, 534, 535, 536, 546
Killian, L.M., 111–113, 189
King, J., 407, 421
King, M.L., Jr., 108
Kirp, D.L., 162, 173, 189
Kirshenbaum, H.M., 564, 623, 631
Klineberg, O., 58, 59, 104
Kluger, R., 44, 49, 66, 70, 72, 73, 75, 78, 99, 104, 107, 110, 189, 270, 615, 632
Koeninger, R.L., 201, 270
Koffka, K., 690, 693
Kohlberg, L., 250, 270, 271
Kohn, J., 69, 74, 84, 104
Konečni, V.J., 7, 8, 21, 460, 461, 462
Konefsky, S.J., 92, 104
Korn, H.L., 710, 712, 746
Kornblum, G., 501, 545
Kornhauser, L., 529, 532, 544

Kotinsky, 65
Krauss, E., 400, 420
Krech, D., 59
Kuhn, T., 659, 693, 743, 746
Kurland, P., 632, 746
Kyle, F.D., 269

Ladinsky, J., 617, 632
LaFave, W.R., 270, 277, 330, 331, 347, 389, 422
Lamm, H., 446
Lambert, N., 172, 173, 189
Lana, R.E., 489–490, 545
Langdell, C.C., 658, 659–660, 668, 669, 675, 693, 726, 746
LaPierre, 246–247
Lasswell, H.D., 343, 347, 675, 693, 728, 729, 746
LaTour, S., 694
Laumann, E.D., 736, 745
Lawson, R.G., 483, 489, 490, 491, 545
Lee, A.M., 59
Lee, R.E., 547
Lehoczky, J.P., 360, 422
Leiken, L.S., 299, 347
Leippe, M.R., 564–565
Lempert, R.O., 34, 242, 257, 258, 259, 270, 297, 347, 355, 403, 422, 431, 435, 436, 437, *456–460*, 460, 462, 470, 480, 485, 518, 545, 712, 746
Lepper, M.R., 251, 270
Lerner, D., 21, 40, 104, 188, 632, 745
Levi, E.H., 183, 185, 186, 189
Levin, B., 137, 154, 189
Levin, H.M., 150, 187, 189, 741, 746
Levine, F.J., 8, 22, 271, 421, 551, 622, 631, 632
Levine, J.P., 327, 338, 347, 711, 746
Lewis, P.W., 287, 347
Lightfoot, S.L., 151, 189
Lincoln, A., 45
Lind, E.A., 500, 546, 547
Lindblom, C., 267, 270, 344, 345, 347, 740, 742, 746
Linde, H., 708, 740, 742, 746
Lindsay, R.C.L., 565, 566, 567, 595
Lipset, S.M., 326, 328, 347
Lipsitt, P.D., 8, 21
Llewellyn, K.N., 16, 18, 22, 24, 26, 27, 40, 100, 101, 102, 104, 480, 546, 613, 614, 633, *661–666*, 666–669, 669, 670, 671, 672, 673, 675, 693

Lochner, P.R., Jr., 717, 746
Loevinger, L., 717, 721, 746
Loewenthal, M., 320, 347
Loftus, E.F., 8, 22, 461, 518, *539–543*, 543, 545, 546, 568, 574, 576, 577, 578, 579, 589, 591, 593, 595, 596, 607, 618, 619, 620, 622, 625, 633
Loh, W.D., 29, 40, 157, 189, 529, 546, 607, 633, 738, 746
Lord, C.G., 251, 270
Louisell, D.W., 35, 40, 511, 537, 546, 615, 633
Lowe, G.D., 247, 270
Lucey, F.E., 674, 693
Luchins, A.S., 489, 492, 546
Lund, F.H., 488, 489, 491, 498, 546
Lundman, R.J., 326, 347
Luneborg, W.V., 471
Lush, D.E., 614, 634

McBarnet, D., 216, 271
McCarty, D.G., 610, 616, 633
McCary, J.L., 615, 633
McCloskey, M., 577, 578, 581, 595
McConahay, J.B., 139, 152, 153, 189, *392–399*, 401, 422
McConville, M., 8, 20
McCormick, C.T., 515, 523, 546, 590, 591
McCrystal, J.L., 501, 502, 546
McDougal, M.S., 343, 347, 675, 693, 728, 729, 746
McDougall, W., 57, 104
McGowan, C., 335, 341, 347
McGuire, M., 631
MacIver, R.N., 59, 65
McKinley, W., 63
McLuhan, M., 501–502, 546
MacMillan, D.C., 171, 172, 173, 189
McMillan, J.B., 695, 746
McNaughton, J.T., 21–26, 40, 99, 185, 616, 632, 710, 716, 721, 723, 740, 744, 745
McPartland, J., 150, 187, 189
Macaulay, S., 8, 9, 21, 625, 630, 633
Maccoby, E., 420
Madden, P.B., 173, 189
Madison, J., 43, 104
Mahan, L., 523, 547
Mahard, R.E., 150, 188
Mahon, A., 149, 189
Mahon, T., 149, 189
Maine, H., 479, 641, 693
Malpass, R.S., 564, 565, 575, 579

Mandell, W., 489, 545
Mannheim, K., 4, 22, 710, 739, 746
Manning, P.K., 326, 347
March, J.G., 344, 347
Margolick, D., 13, 22, 732, 735, 737, 746
Marshall, J., 617, 633
Marshall, T., 46, 49, 70, 104, 107, 131, 248, 249, 642
Marston, W.M., 609, 621, 633
Martin, A.W., 535, 536, 546, 746
Martin, J.A., 711, 712
Maschari, A.B., 501
Maurs, R., 263
Mayo, L.H., 344, 347
Mead, G.H., 58, 104
Mechem, P., 610, 633
Medalie, R.J., 298, 299, 347
Meehl, P.E., 611–612, 619, 633
Melton, G., 607, 633, 746
Meltsner, M., 198, 199, 210, 215, 231, 242, 271, 617, 731
Merryman, J.H., 22, 32
Mertens, W.J., 320, 337, 347
Merton, R.K., 59
Messick, S., 173
Meyers, C.E., 171, 172, 173, 186, 189
Michael, J., 632
Mill, J.S., 640
Miller, A.S., 342, 343, 347, 682, 693, 710, 740, 746
Miller, D.G., 576
Miller, D.T., 251, 259, 271
Miller, G.R., 504–507, 507, 546
Miller, N., 151, 152, 153, 188, 490, 546
Mischel, W., 403, 422
Mitchell, H.E., 402, 422
Moise, P., 154, 189
Moll, W., 692
Monahan, J., 8, 22, 262, 271, 607, 633
Montesquieu, C., 641, 693
Montgomery, D.A., 623, 625, 634
Mood, A.M., 187
Moore, C., 609, 633
Moore, H., 399, 422
Moore, J., 137, 182, 187
Moore, U., 611, 633, 670, 693
More, T., 708
Morrill, A.E., 501, 546
Morris, A., 198, 271
Morris, A.A., 66, 93, 104
Morris, A.M., 320, 347
Morse, J., 609, 633

Moskowitz, M.J., 626, 633
Mosteller, F., 150, 186, 187, 189, 377, 527, 545
Moynihan, D.P., 150, 186, 187, 189, 708, 747
Moynihan, J., 149, 189
Muir, W., Jr., 617, 633
Mulcahy, E.M., 461
Muller, C., 84
Mullin, C.J., 392–399, 422
Münsterberg, H., 8, 10, 12, 22, 44, 105, 568, 569, 609, 614, 626, 633, 717, 747
Munsterman, G.T., 471, 473, 475
Munzer, S.R., 688, 693
Murchison, C., 631, 692
Murchison, K.M., 200, 265, 266, 271
Murphy, G., 59
Murphy, M.J., 301, 348
Murphy, W.F., 66, 105
Murray, J.R., 185, 189, 575
Muse, B., 69, 105
Myers, D.G., 446
Myrdal, G., 58, 65, 105, 143, 189, 682, 710

Nagel, E., 744, 747
Nagin, D., 259, 269, 270
Needham, J., 641, 693
Nelson, W., 537, 546
Nelson, W.E., 669, 693
Nemeth, C., 8, 21, 402, 420, 421, 422
Nesson, C.R., 529, 530, 532, 546
Newby, I.A., 57, 105, 121, 189
Newcomb, T., 59, 420
Nicholson, H., 504–507, 546
Niederhoffer, A., 323, 325, 326, 348
Nieland, R., 538, 546
Nietzel, M.T., 406, 409, 410, 422, 461
Noble, A.M., 402, 421
Nordenberg, M.A., 471
Normand, C., 147–149, 190

Oaks, D.H., 302, 307, 308, 309, 313–314, 315, 320, 321, 327, 348
Oberer, W., 198, 211, 271
O'Brien, D.M., 701–706, 706, 707, 709, 740, 742, 747
Ohlin, L.E., 11, 22, 626, 633, *723–725,* 747
Ojemann, R., 716, 745
Okun, J., 405, 422
Orfield, G., 133, 137, 189
Orne, M.T., 251, 271
Osborne, R.T., 121
Ostrom, T.M., 564–565

Packer, H.L., 274, 348
Padawer-Singer, A., 420, 422
Palmer, B.W., 657, 693
Parker, L.C., 8, 22
Parsons, T., 128, 188
Partington, D.H., 201, 271
Paternoster, R., 263, 270
Patterson, E.W., 673, 693
Paulsen, M., 257, 270
Pearson, E., 530
Pearson, K., 659, 683
Peel, R., 276
Pennington, N., 8, 21, 447, 496, 546
Penrod, S.D., 8, 21, 402, 422, 447, 460, 517, 518, 547, 618, 633
Peoples, K.D., 287, 347
Percival, R.V., 216, 270
Pettigrew, T.F., 137–138, 139, *147–149*, 149, 150, 151, 160, 189
Pierce, C.M., 272
Pierce, G.L., 263, 264, 269
Pilpel, M.E., 612, 619, 626, 634, 728, 747
Plato, 640, 694
Polanyi, M., 682, 694
Pollak, L.H., 69, 96, 105
Pollock, A., 422
Posner, R.A., 311, 348, 731, 733, 737, 747
Pound, R., 24, 40, 342, 348, 613, 633, 641, 658, 669–670, 694
Powers, E., 10, 22, 619, 626, 633
Priest, G.L., 9, 22, 40, 629, 633
Pritchard, J.L., 194, 271
Pulaski, C.A., Jr., 269
Purcell, E., 670, 694
Pyszczynski, T.A., 496, 546

Quick, A.T., 328, 338, 348
Quinn, J.R., 348

Radin, M.J., 243, 265, 271
Radke, M.T., 77, 105
Rankin-Widgeon, B., 190
Raven, B., 569
Ravitch, D., 136, 137, 138, 182–183, 190
Read, F.T., 190, 562, 622, 633
Redfield, R., 59
Redmount, R.S., 612, 633
Reichert, W.O., 198, 271
Reid, I.D., 59
Reidel, M., 209, 272
Rein, M., 630, 633, 747

Reis, H.T., 402, 421, 460, 461, 625, 632
Reiss, A.J., Jr., 295, 298, 327, 348
Remington, F., 331, 347
Reschly, D.J., 170, 171, 172, 174, 190
Reston, J., 78
Riesman, D., 617, 633, 735, 736, 747
Riley, R.T., 150, 187
Rist, R.C., 151, 187, 190, 745
Rivlin, A.M., 576, 711, 747
Robbins, I.P., 623, 633
Robinson, C.D., 348
Robinson, D.N., 8, 22
Robinson, E.S., 610, 611, 620, 633, 673, 694, 727, 747
Robinson, G.O., 732, 734, 745
Robinson, H., 170, 190
Robinson, N.M., 170, 173, 190
Robson, R.A., 617, 631
Rooker, C.K., 547
Roper, R., 436, 437
Rose, L., 251, 270
Rose, M., 59
Rosen, P.L., 57, 78, 84, 93, 96, 105, 708, 747
Rosenberg, M., 716, 747
Rosenblatt, A.M., 436
Rosenblatt, J.C., 436
Rosenblum, V.G., 3, 22, 696, 747
Rossell, C.H., 138, 139, 190
Rostow, E., 747
Rourke, R., 377
Ruback, R.B., 8, 21, 402, 403, 421, 617, 632
Rubinstein, J., 329, 348
Rumble, W.E., Jr., 671, 675, 694
Rush, B., 195, 197

Sacks, A., 681, 745
Saenger, G., 59
Sage, W., 399, 423
Saks, M.J., 8, 22, 269, 401, 402, 403, 423, 431, 446, 460, 491, 530, 534, 535, 536, 546, 617, 618, 623, 626, 634, 710, 747
Sales, B.D., 3, 8, 10, 21, 22, 387, 392, 404, 420, 422, 423, 460, 539, 543, 545, 607, 632
Salo, C., 631
Saltzburg, S., 480, 518, 545
Sanders, J., 136, 155, 190
Sandoval, J., 171, 190
Sanford, R.N., 59
Sarat, A., *247–250*, 251, 271
Sargent, S.S., 59
Sarratt, R., 107, 190

Sartorious, R., 686, 694
Savigny, F.K., 640, 694
Schantz, M., 289
Scheflin A., 429, 450, 451
Schlag, P.J., 311, 348
Schlegel, J.H., 613, 634, 727, 728, 738, 747
Schlesinger, S.R., 303–304, 308–309, 320, 327, 348, 738
Schmideberg, D., 614, 634
Schmidt, B.C., 419, 423
Schofield, W., 615, 634
Schubert, G., 673, 694
Schulman, J., 399, 400, 401, 422, 423
Schum, D.A., 535, 536, 546
Schwartz, L.B., 276, 322, 323, 348
Schwartz, R.D., 8, 22
Schwarzer, W.W., 537, 538, 546
Schwitzgebel, R.K., 8, 22
Schwitzgebel, R.L., 8, 22
Scriven, M., 722, 747
Sealy, A.P., 514, 515, 519, 544, 523, 623, 631
Sebille, C., 425
Seeburger, R.H., 297, 348
Sellin, T., 195, 198, 257, 270, 271
Selye, H., 326, 348
Semmel, M.I., 173, 190
Severance, L., 539–543, 543, 546
Shapard, J., 388, 391, 420
Shapiro, M., 742, 747
Shaver, K.F., 634
Shaver, P., 423
Sherif, M., 569
Siegel, B., 507, 546
Siegel, D., 544
Simon, H., 345, 348, 740, 747
Simon, H.A., 344, 347
Simon, R., 523, 547, 617, 634
Simon, R.J., 419, 420, 422, 423
Simson, G., 429
Skolnick, J., 22, 311, 318, 324, 326, 328, 329, 348, 617, 634
Slavin, R.E., 160, 190
Slesinger, D., 568, 611, 612, 619, 626, 632, 634, 728, 747
Smith, A.B., Jr., 383, 423
Smith, B., Sr., 73, 348
Smith, M.B., 59
Smith, M.S., 147–149, 190
Smith, R.E., 625, 634
Snee, T.J., 614, 634
Sobel, N.R., 551, 552, 561, 562

Soper, E.P., 688, 694
Sowell, T., 707, 747
Specter, A., 348
Spencer, H., 56, 661
Sperlich, P.W., 441, 466, 697–701, 702, 706–707, 710, 711, 712, 713, 747
Spiotto, J.E., 313, 314, 315, 316, 318, 319, 320, 348
Sporer, S.L., 607, 634
Stampp, K., 194, 271
Stanley, J.C., 297, 346
Stasser, G., 431, 446
Stephan, W.G., 150, 153, 190
Stern, W., 568, 608, 634
Stevens, R., 658, 694, 727, 728, 747
Steward, P., 423
Stewart, I.D., 634
St. John, N., 150, 152, 153, 190
Stone, J., 709, 747
Stotland, E., 326, 349
Stouffer, S.A., 59, 143
Strawn, D.U., 471, 473, 475
Strodtbeck, F.L., 431, 617, 634
Stuart, I.R., 8, 20, 422, 546
Sue, S., 625, 634
Suggs, D., 3, 8, 21, 387, 392, 398, 423, 460
Summers, R.S., 639, 640, 669, 672, 674, 694, 731, 734, 747
Sumner, W.G., 57, 105
Swisher, C.B., 105

Taeuber, K.E., 134, 190
Tanke, E.D., 441
Tanke, T.J., 441
Tapp, J.L., 8, 22, 271, 421, 551, 607, 617, 622, 631, 632, 634, 747
Taylor, W.L., 135, 190
Teeters, N.K., 271
Terris, B.J., 349
Thayer, J.B., 356, 423, 480, 509, 521, 547, 618, 634
Thibaut, J., 8, 22, 484, 488, 492–495, 497, 498, 499, 500, 501, 547, 625, 634, 644, 694, 738
Thomas, E.J., 431
Thomas, G., 377
Thompson, W.C., 221, 269
Tiffany, L.P., 349
Titchener, E.B., 609, 634, 689, 694
Tivnan, E., 423
Toch, H., 8, 22, 349, 617, 633, 634

Tocqueville, A. de, 5, 22, 43, 105, 197, 643, 644
Tolman, E.C., 690, 694
Tousignant, J.P., 595
Trager, H.G., 77
Tribe, L.H., 528, 529, 532, 535, 547
Trubek, D., 343, 346

Udolf, F., 8, 21, 484, 544, 617, 623, 626, 631
Underwood, B., 536, 547
Unger, R.M., 730, 747
Useem, E.L., 147–149, 190

Vago, S., 8, 22, 637, 694
van den Haag, E., 77, 105, 121
Van Dyke, J., 405, 423, 429, 450, 451
Veblen, T., 743
Vetter, J., 682, 683, 694
Vidmar, N., 8, 21, 193, *244–246,* 247, *247–250,* 251, 259, 271, 272, 399, 401, 408, 409, 420, 421, 423, 461
Vorenberg, J., 306
Vose, C.E., 69, 105

Wald, M., 289
Walker, L., 8, 22, 484, 488, *492–495,* 497, 498, 499, 500, 501, 546, 547, 625, 634, 694, 738
Wall, P., 617, 634
Waltz, J., 387, 422
Warner, W., 59
Warren, E., 59, 67, 79, 110, 154
Wasserstrom, S., 320, 337, 347
Watson, J.B., 689, 690, 694
Weber, M., 12
Wechsler, H., 68–69, 105, 265, 272, 682, 694, 729, 747
Weinberg, M., 132, 150, 152, 191, 743, 747, 748
Weinstein, J.B., 509, 519, 547, 619, 624, 634, 709, 748
Weiss, J.A., 187, 743–744
Weiten, W., 460
Weld, H.P., 535, 547, 614, 634
Wells, G.L., 488, 547, 563, 564–565, 566, 567, 569, 574, 575, 580, 619, 622, 634, 748
Wentzel, A.A., 544
Westen, P., 488, 547
Westin, A., 40
Wettick, R.S., Jr., 297, 348
Whipple, G.M., 608, 609, 634–635
White, G.E., 267, 272, 657, 672, *676–681,* 683–684, 688, 694, 727, 729, 741, 748

White, W., 215, 272
White, W.S., 287, 349
Whitebread, C.H., II, 289
Widgidor, A.K., 178, 191
Wigmore, J.H., 10, 22, 28, 40, 320, 349, 477, 478, 479, 498, 535, 547, 609, 620, 621, 635
Wilkey, M.R., 302–306, 307, 308, 311, 329, 349
Wilkinson, J.H., III, 66, 105, 115, 133, 181, 191, 376, 423
Willging, T.E., 8–9, 21, 450, 607, 626, 632, 738, 746
Williams, D.A., 748
Williams, G.R., 507, 547, 552
Williams, H., 511, 546
Williams, M.C., 634
Williams, R., 394
Williams, R.M., 59
Williams, T.A., 544
Wilson, J.Q., 191, 317, 324, 328, 349
Wilson, J.V., 329, 336, 349
Wilson, L., 375, 421
Wilson, O., 349
Wilson, W.C., 212
Winfield, F.D., 187
Winick, B.J., 390, 423
Winter, R.K., 521, 547
Wirth, L., 682, 694
Wisdom, J.M., 182, 191, 743, 748
Witt, J.W., 349
Wolf, E.P., 126–131, 132, 133, 134, 135, 136, 150, 154, 155, 158, 182, 183, 191, 625, 710, 711, 729, 741, 748
Wolf, S., 623, 634
Wolfgang, M.E., 201–202, 209, 264, 272
Wolfram, C.W., 463
Wolman, B.B., 689, 694
Woocher, F.D., 552, *569–573,* 577
Woodard, C., 656, 694
Woodward, B., 66, 105
Woodward, C.V., 55, 105
Woodward, J., 407, 423, 615, 635
Woodworth, G., 269
Worchel, S., 544
Wright, S., 9, 161, 162, 413, 423
Wrightsman, L.A., 460, 496, 517, 545, 546
Wundt, W., 689, 694

Yarmey, A.D., 8, 22, 568, 579, 618, 619, 621, 622, 625, 635, 717, 748
Yntema, H.E., 613, 635

York, R.L., 187
Young, J., 504
Yudof, M.G., 132, 133, 161, 191, 630, 635, 695, 708, 717, 740, 743, 748
Yuille, J., 574, 575, 576, 577, 580, 581

Zeisel, H., 22, 210, 219, 222, 256, 257, 258, 263, 272, 391, 399, 403, 408, 419, 422, 423, 426, 427, 429, 430, 431, 436, 437, 445, 446, *453–456*, 461, 462, 463, 469, 470, 536, 539, 545, 575, 615, 621, 625, 627, 632, 635, 731, 748
Zeitz, J., 298, 299, 347
Zimbardo, P., 297, 349
Zimring, R., 256, 272, 738, 748
Zuckerman, M., 402, 421, 460, 461, 625, 632

ABA Commission on Standards for Judicial Administration, 389

ABA Report, 415, 418–419

Academic achievement within various racial and ethnic groups, 142–143; standards of measurement, 148

Adjudicating disputes as court function, 96

Administrative Procedure Act, 337

Adversarial method of fact-finding, 498, 499–500, 500–501

Adversary system, 33–34

Advisory Committee on Fair Trial and Free Press, 415

Allen instruction, 446

American Law Institute, 659

American Psychological Association: ethical standards, 711

Analytical jurisprudence, 639

Analytical positivism, 639

Anglo-American common law approach to cases, 34

Answer, 35

Antiformalism, 672

Antiformalists, 660

Anti-Monopoly surveys, 411–412

Appellant, 37

Appellate brief, 98

Appellate court functions, 30–31

Appellate process, 37–38; steps in decision-making, 691

Appellate review function, 30

Appellee, 38

Applied eyewitness testimony research, 569

Atlanta school system, 133

Attitude: concept of, 246, 247

Attitudes and (moral) values, distinction between, 251

Aussage experiments, 568, 608, 609

Authoritarianism and propensity to convict, 397, 402

Authoritarian personality theory, 397

Automatic death penalty jurors, 224, 225, 229

Automatic life imprisonment jurors, 217, 227, 229, 230

Bayes' Theorem, 531, 535, 536; application to identification evidence, 532–534; application to school admissions, 531–532

Behavioral level of judicial decisions, 667

Behaviorism, 670, 689–690

Bench-Bar-Press Guidelines, 415

Bench trial, 36

Bennett Mechanical Comprehension Test, 176

Beta Examination, 177

Beyond a reasonable doubt, 521, 522, 529

Biased lineup, 564

Bifurcated verdict trial, 216

Bill of Rights, 38–39, 413, 451, 452, 688; and capital punishment, 232; and guarantee of jury trial, 427; purpose of, 246

Binomial distribution, 362

Binomial formula, 362; vs. use of Chi square test, 374

Biracial schooling, effects on children, 137–138, 139, 141–143, 149–154, 157, 160; *see also* School desegregation

Black Coalition to Maximize Education, 133

Black Codes, 45

Black Intelligence Test for Cultural Homogeneity (BITCH), 171

Blank lineup, 564

Body language: used in jury selection, 398

Brandeis Brief, 84–90, 96, 108; due process and, 92–93

Brand name, 411

"Brand-name Survey," 411

Briefing, 97–98, 101–102

Burden of going forward with the evidence, *see* Burden of production

Burden of persuasion, 521–522

Burden of production, 521

Burden of proof, 478, 521

Busing to achieve school integration, 121, 133, 139, 143–149, 182; black opposition, 157

California death-qualification procedure, 224, 227

California death-qualified jurors, 224, 225

Canadian exclusionary rule, 309

Cape Horn of jurisprudence, 640

Capital punishment: attempts to restrict or abolish, 199, 266, 268; attitudes toward, 214, 219–224, 228, 230, 244–246, 249–250, 266; case examples, 205–209, 211–213, 217–227, 234–241; deterrent effect of, 256–260, 343; history, 194–195; issues regarding, 265; judicial challenges, 197–199, 231; legality, 198–199, 232, 243, 259, 266–

Capital punishment (cont.)
267; and predictors of future criminality,
262; public opinion polls used to assess attitudes toward, 224, 229, 230, 244–246,
247–250; and racial inequality in execu-
tions, 200, 201, 205, 210, 263, 264; Su-
preme Court on, 210, 215–216, 229, 231–
233, 255, 265, 266, 267, 268, 549
Case analysis, 667, 732–734, 735, 736–737;
and economic analysis, 733
Case-brief, 97–98, 102
Case complexity: effect on jury functioning,
462–471; and Federal Rules of Civil Proce-
dure, 471, 473
Case-in-chief, 36, 482
Case-in-rebuttal, 483
Case-in-rejoinder, 483
Case-in-reply, 483
Case method, 659–660, 726
Cause of action, 35
Change of venue, 393–394, 407–409
Charter of Rights and Freedoms (Canadian),
309
Chicago Jury Project, 426, 427, 431
Chicanos, see Mexican-Americans
Chi square test, 356, 374, 383; vs. use of bi-
nomial formula for standard deviation, 374
Chi square value formula, 374
Civil action, 34
Civil cases, standard of proof in, 522–523
Civil jury preservation, 462–466
Civil lawsuit, 34
Civil Rights Act of 1866, 45
Civil Rights Act of 1875, 46, 47
Civil Rights Act of 1964, 108, 149, 175; Title
VII, 175–176
Civil Rights Movement, 108
Civil War Amendments, 38–39, 45, 46, 47
Cluster sampling, 410
Coleman Report of 1966, 137–138, 139, 141–
143, 149–150, 152
Columbia Law School, 726
Communication order, see Gross order of pre-
sentation; Internal order of presentation;
Opinion change; Primacy effect
Community scouts, 400
Compelling interest standard, 94–95
Composite sketches, 561
Conceptualism, 642, see also Formalism
Confession: voluntariness of, 591
Confession resulting from police interroga-
tions: impact of warnings on, 289–295,

297–300; motions to exclude improper con-
fessions from evidence, 301–302
Confrontation by witness, 550; pretrial
identification, 550–552, 557–558, 561–563;
Sixth Amendment right, 550
Constitutional decision-making, 56, 68
Construct validity, 296, 297
Contact theory, 143–144, 147
Continental civil law approach to a case, 34
Conviction, and relationship to authoritarian-
ism, 397, 402
County court, 31
Court-packing plan, 93
Court system: appellate process, 37–38; fed-
eral courts, 31–32; state courts, 31; struc-
ture, 29–33; trial process, 34–37
Creating law, as function of court, 96
Criminal act, 29
Criminal conviction, standard of proof for,
522
Criminal court, 31
Criminal defendant rights, and Warren
Court, 198
Criminal prosecution, 34
Criminal trial process, 482, 618; legal impact
of social psychological research on, 624–
625; presentation of evidence and law to
the jury, 623–624; see also Evidence presen-
tation order
Cross-examination, 483

Death penalty, see Capital punishment
Death-qualification process, 211, 226, 227,
229, 230, 231
Death-qualification of prospective jurors, 211,
212; case example, 211–213
Death-qualified jurors, 211, 214, 215, 216,
222, 224, 226, 230
Decision-making, appellate: deductive syllo-
gistic method, 342–343; impact analysis
method, 343–344
Decision-making process of law, 722, 723
Declaration of Independence, 639
Deductive syllogistic method of appellate
decision-making, 342–343
De facto segregation, 108, 120, 122, 134, 153,
154, 181, 384
De jure segregation, 108, 122, 134, 135, 140,
153, 384
Deposition, 35
Desegregation: consequences, 59–62; defined,
147; effects, 78; housing, 68; school, 68,

69–70; *see also* Integration; School desegregation

Deterrence, 256, 257, 258, 259, 320

Deterrent effect of death penalty, 256–260

Detroit public school system desegregation, 131, 136, 154, 158–159

Direct deterrence, 320

Discovery stage of trial process, 35

Discrimination: employment, 175–181, 376–384, 385; in jury selection, 356–358, 360, 362, 363–368, 370, 371–375, 385–386, 435–446; *see also* Employment discrimination; Racial discrimination; Segregation

Discrimination litigation, and role of statistician, 375–376

Discrimination, racial, *see* Racial discrimination

District court, 31

Diversity jurisdiction, 31–32

Doctrinal level of legal rules, 666

Dolls test, 70–71, 77, 96, 143, 152, 615

Due process, 90–93

Due process adjudication, rule of reason in, 91–92

Due Process Clause, 46, 54, 65, 90, 91, 94, 214, 231, 360, 562

Due process principles, 216

Due process revolution, 198

Due process test to determine validity of confessions, 562

Due process/voluntariness, and police interrogation, 280–281, 287

Economic analysis studied in law schools, 731–732, 733; and case analysis, 733

Eighth Amendment: and capital punishment, 242, 243, 255, 259, 261, 262, 263; challenges to, 232–233; early adjudication, 232–233

Electric chair, 196

Elementary and Secondary Education Act of 1965, 132

Ellsworth Attitude Survey, 223

Ellsworth Conviction-Proneness Study, 221–222, 225

Emancipation Proclamation, 69

Empirical research: relevance to law, 7; use of, 4, 25

Employment discrimination, 378–379, 383–384, 385; case examples, 376–377, 379–383; use of testing as form of, 175–181

Employment testing, 175–181

E.M.R., 161, 162, 172

E.M.R. programs, 161, 162, 166–167, 171, 172–173, 175; case example, 162–170

Equal Employment Opportunity Commission (EEOC), 176

Equal Protection Clause, 54, 94, 360, 361

Evidence: admissibility of, 509–520; burden of production and burden of persuasion, 521–523; effective presentation and jury competence, 473; instructions to jurors on evaluating, 537–544; presentation mode, 501–508; presentation order, 481–501; psychology, 611; quantification of, 523; role of, on jury verdicts, 431; sufficiency of, 520–537

Evidence evaluation instructions for jurors, 537, 543; historical background, 537–538, research on comprehensibility, 538–543

Evidence illegally obtained by police, 301, 303; *see also* Fourth Amendment, exclusionary rule

Evidence-in-chief, 482

Evidence-in-defense, 483

Evidence law, 519, 568, 611, 618, 619

Evidence presentation, 501–502; applications to judicial process, 502; use of videotape technology, 501, 502–507; *see also* Testimony; Videotape technology in judicial process

Evidence presentation order: case example, 485–487; gross order and internal order, 484–485, 487, 488; stages, 481–484

Evidence psychology, 728

Evidentiary privileges, 721

Evidentiary relevance, 509

Exclusionary rule, 275; and expert testimony, 709; and police enforcement practices, 275–276, 301–310, 311, 312–318, 319, 320; in West Germany, 311; *see also* Fourth Amendment; Fifth Amendment; Sixth Amendment; Fourteenth Amendment

Exclusionary zoning, 384

Executions and homicides, relationship between, 258

Executions, moratorium on, 266

Execution statistics in United States, 268

Expert psychological testimony: admissibility, 614–615; regarding mental disorder, 622; regarding testimonial competence of a defendant, 622

Expert psychological testimony on eyewitness fallibility, 582–589; examples of admissibility, 593–595; general principles of admissi-

Expert psychological testimony on eyewitness
   fallibility (cont.)
   bility, 591–593; procedure, 590–591; research pertinent to, 595–596
Expert testimony: evaluation of, 709, 710;
   role of experts, 712
External validity, 460
Extrinsic rewards as form of motivation applied to police force, 338
Eyewitness identification, 550–600; case examples, 554–557, 559–561, 589–590, 596–
   599; dangers of, 550, 551–553, 618–619;
   level of analysis in, 620–622; safeguards
   against fallible, 581–582; sources of bias,
   553; sources of erroneous pretrial, 552;
   stages, 553; unreliability, 569–573, 574,
   618–619, 620; see also Fallible eyewitness
   identification safeguards; Lineup identification; Lineup identification safeguards
Eyewitness identification studies, 569–573,
   609, 618–622; conditions of accuracy, 579;
   deceiving the memory of observers, 576;
   ideological premise of the research, 580–
   581; inconsistent results, 576–577; level of
   analysis in, 620–622; self-selection of subjects, 574–575; standard of accuracy, 579–
   580; unreality of simulation, 575–576;
   wrongful convictions, 577–579, 621
Eyewitness testimony: effects of, in court, 550;
   and jurors' views, 574; unreliability, 569–
   573, 574–581; see also Eyewitness identification; Lineup identification; Pretrial
   identification

Fact-finding process in science and law, 722–
   723
Fair trial and free press, 412
Fallible eyewitness identification safeguards,
   581; cautionary instructions by judge,
   596–600, 619; exclusion of eyewitness testimony, 582; expert psychological testimony, 582–596, 620
FBI, and investigation of prospective jurors'
   backgrounds, 405
Federal courts, 31–33
Federal question jurisdiction, 32
Federal Rules of Civil Procedure (FRCP), 465,
   471, 473, 544
Federal Rules of Criminal Procedure (FRCrP),
   517, 544
Federal Rules of Evidence (FRE), 480, 509,
   510, 511, 611

Field interrogation, 279, 298
Fifth Amendment: due process clause, 463,
   466, 470; exclusionary rule, 275, 277–278,
   287, 341; origin of, 287; right to counsel,
   282, 288; right to silence, 487, 549; Supreme Court and, 278, 286
Findings of Fact, 98
First Amendment, guarantee of free flow of
   information, 421, 413
Forensic psychology, 614–617
Forensic social science, 711
Formalism, 612–614, 638, 642, 643, 657–659,
   672, 682, 683; decline of, 662; in law
   schools, 726; repudiating, 668; social-
   intellectual context of, 659–662
Formalist reasoning, 653–656, 658, 661
Fourteenth Amendment, 46, 47, 54, 159, 384,
   389; and Brown v. Board of Education (1954),
   63–64, 65, 66, 67; Due Process Clause, 46,
   54, 65, 90, 91, 94, 214, 231, 360; Equal
   Protection Clause, 54, 94, 360, 361; and exclusionary rule, 275; and Plessy v. Ferguson,
   51, 52, 54; right to confront one's accusers,
   483; and school segregation, 67, 153, 174;
   underrepresentation in venire as violation,
   389
Fourth Amendment: alternatives to, 305–306,
   307–308, 309; criticisms of, 304–305; decisional history, 301; deterrent effectiveness,
   317–318, 319, 320, 321; effects of, 303–
   304, 316–318; exclusionary rule, 275, 278,
   310, 339, 340, 341; exclusion procedure,
   301–302, 549; impact on police enforcement practices, 312–318; purpose, 302,
   310; and Supreme Court, 303, 310; violation by police officers, 328–330
Free press and fair trail, 412–415
Freudianism, 670

Gambling charges: and exclusionary rule,
   340; suppression motions for, 313, 314, 315
General deterrence, 256, 257, 320
General Mills surveys, 411–412
Goal-thinking, 675
Grand jury, 356
Gross order of presentation, 484–485, 488,
   492, 493, 494, 495, 496; see also Evidence
   presentation order; Opinion charge; Pri-
   macy effect
Group polarization phenomenon, 446
Guilty verdicts: and impact of peremptory
   challenges, 391

Habeas corpus petition, 209
Harvard Law School, 726
Hearsay evidence rule, 478, 515
Historical/sociological jurisprudence, 638, 640–641
Homicides and executions, relationship between, 258
Hung jury, 436, 446; and jury size, 436; in majority jurisdictions, 446; in unanimous jurisdictions, 446

Idiographic character of adjudication, 721
Illegally obtained evidence, suppression of, 301, 303–304, 313–316, 318, 319
Impact analysis method of appellate decision-making, 343–344, 345; steps in, 344
Impact research, 630
Impression formation studies, 489–490
Incommunicado interrogation, 279
Indirect and long-term deterrence, 320
Inequality of races, 68; see also Racial discrimination; Segregation
Inferential statistics used in discrimination litigation, 375
Informal questioning, 279
Informal suspect identification in field, 552
Inquisitorial method of fact-finding, 497–498, 499–500, 500–501
Integration, 182–183; distinction between desegregation and, 139, 147, 151; in education, effects, 137–138, 139, 141–143, 149–150; induced, 144; natural, 144; role of, and reduction of white prejudice toward blacks, 143–144; see also Desegregation; School desegregation
Integration policy model, 143–148
Intelligence as a function of heredity, 57
Intelligence testing in schools, 57, 58; bias, 170–172, 173, 174; cultural influences on, 171–172; evaluation, 109; used for E.M.R. placement, 161, 162–170, 172, 173
Intergroup contact theory, see Contact theory
Internalized motivation, applied to police force, 338–339
Internal order of presentation, 484, 485, 492, 493, 494; see also Evidence presentation order
Internal validity, 297, 460
Interracial attitudes and desegregation, 153
Interrogation: custodial, 279, 286; field, 279, 298; incommunicado, 279; informal questioning, 279; see also Police interrogation

Invisible discrimination, 181, 356, 376; see also Discrimination; Racial discrimination; Racial underrepresentation
I.Q. testing, see Intelligence testing

Japanese-American relocation cases, 95
Job performance and employment testing, 176, 177, 178, 179, 180
Job relatedness, 177–178, 179
Johns Hopkins Institute for the Study of Law, 727
Joinder of charges, 517
Joined trial, 517–518
Joint Committee of Reconstruction, 45
Judge: as creator of law, 278, 707–708; as decision-maker, 34; role in determining admissibility, 509–510; role in excluding illegally obtained evidence, 335
Judicial bias in inquisitorial and adversarial methods, 499–500
Judicial decision-making, 96–97
Judicial instructions: empirical and normative justification of, 518–520
Judicial notice, 713–714
Judicial opinion: case synthesis, 101–103; elements of, 97, 98–101
Judicial opinions, reading, 97–98; structure and analysis of case, 98–101; synthesis of case, 101–103
Judicial process: nature and methods, 644–650; and social research, 4, 5–6
Judicial reasoning styles, 641–643
Judicial review, 266, 682; concept of, 93–94; reasonable standard, 94; strict scrutiny or compelling interest standard, 94–95
Jurisdiction: of federal courts, 31–32; of state courts, 31
Jurisdiction over controversies to which the United States is a party, 32
Jurisprudence, defined, 637–638
Juror "black lists" maintained by local prosecutors, 405
Juror characteristics and prediction of verdicts, 401–403
Juror partiality, 392–399
Juror partiality and pretrial publicity, 407–419; case example, 415–417; change of venue, 407–409; free press/fair trial controversy, 412–415, 418; research, 418–420
Jurors: view of eyewitness testimony, 574; women, on rape cases, 403
Jurow Study, 220–221, 227

Jury, 36; hung, 436; nullification power of, 450–451; origins, 353–356; overview, 356–357; right to unbiased, 214, 215; size, 430–431, 432, 434–436, 441–442, 451, 453–460; as subject for research, 618

Jury deliberation phases, 446

Jury functioning, 425–473; in civil trials, 428–429; competence, 426–427; constitutional dimensions, 430–431; in criminal trials, 428, 429; effects of case complexity on, 462–471; effects of decision rules on, 442–453; methodological issues in jury research, 453–462; size and, 430–442, 451, 453–460; sovereignty, 427–430; see also Jury selection; Jury size

Jury nullification instructions, 450–451

Jury selection: abuses in, 404; authoritarian personality theory used in, 397; body language used in, 398; discrimination, 356–358, 360, 362, 363–368, 369, 370–375, 386, 389, 435; grounds for challenging, 360–361; mathematical model used in, 395–397, 402; mechanics, 359–360; peremptory challenges, 385–392; racial-neutral, 356; racial underrepresentation, 356, 363–364, 386, 389, 435, 446; scientific, 357, 399; and Supreme Court, 356, 375, 406; survey research, 400; systematic, 399–401, 402, 403, 404; voir dire process, 386–389, 389

Jury Selection and Service Act of 1968, 359

Jury simulation, 460–462

Jury size, 340–431, 432, 434–436, 441–442, 451, 453–460; case examples, 432–434, 437–441; studies conducted regarding, 453–460; Supreme Court and, 431, 435, 436, 441–442; underrepresentation and, 435, 441

Jury wheel, 359, 360

Justice courts, 31

Juvenile court proceedings: and right to counsel and silence, 299

Juveniles, and Miranda rights, 299

Kinesics and paralinguistics: used in jury selection, 398

Laissez-faire economic policies, 661, 662, 672
Laissez-faire philosophy, 92
Laissez-faire theory, and formulation of legal principles, 661

Landellians, 660

Lanham Act, 410, 411

Law: concept of, 23–24; function of, 28–29; as inductive science, 659–660; levels of analysis, 666–667; as process of solving disputes, 26–28; as system of rules, 24–26

Lawmaking process, 183–186

Law of Primacy in Persuasion, 488

Law professors, professional orientation, 736–739

Law schools: economics in, 731–732, 733; educational criteria and socialization experiences in, 723–725; and formalism, 726; and postrealism, 728–729; and realism, 728–729; social science in, 725–731

Law students, professional orientation, 734–736

Lawsuits by or against the federal government, 32

Legal and social science communities: collaboration between, 716–717; in conflict, 717–719; confronting and negotiating professional differences, 719–721; degree of conclusiveness between, 722; differences in professional socialization and culture, 721, 723–725

Legal compliance and punishment, as form of motivation applied to police force, 338

Legal Defense Fund of the NAACP, 199, 201; and capital punishment, 212, 215, 231

Legal economics, 733

Legal education, 659–660, 673, 723–725; and case analysis skills, 732–734; and role of economics, 731–732; and role of social science, 725–731

Legal impact studies, 672, 673

Legalist tradition in ancient China, 641

Legally significant facts, identifying, 27

Legal positivism, 638, 639–640

Legal realism, 610–614, 638, 642, 643, 666–669, 670, 672–674, 683; critics, 681; decline, 674–676; and law schools, 726–728; social-intellectual context of, 669–672; see also Realist reasoning

Legal realist movement, 612–614

Legal realists, 666

Legal reasoning, 10–13, 27, 183–186; segregation used as example in, 184–185; as social process of problem solving, 186

Legal rules, 24–26; choosing appropriate rule to apply to facts, 27

Legal social engineering, 670

Legal technicality, 675

Limiting instruction, 511, 512–514, 514–518, 519–520

Lineup identification, 550–551; procedure reform, 622; proposals for conducting, 562–563; research on, 563–568; right to counsel during, 557–558; and use of composite drawings, 561; see also Lineup identification studies

Lineup identification studies, 563–564, 567, 568; biased instructions, 564; lineup similarity, 565–567; lineup size, 564–565; witness confidence, 567

Lynchings, 201

Magna Carta, 90

Magnet school, 133

Mainstreaming, 173

Mathematical model used in jury selection, 395–397

Maximum work hours, 91

Mechanical jurisprudence, 642; see also Formalism

Mental retardation, 172

METCO program (Boston), 144–145, 148

Methodological quality of studies, 153

Mexican-Americans: case example, 364–368; and discrimination in jury selection, 368, 369–370

Minority group children: effect of prejudice, discrimination, and segregation on, 59–62

Minority relations and police force, 325, 326

Miranda warnings, 275, 287, 288; impact on police interrogation, 289–295, 297–300

Misidentification, see Expert psychological testimony on eyewitness fallibility; Eyewitness identification; Fallible eyewitness identification

Mock jurors, 460–461

Morals legislation, 340

Motivational bases of organizational functioning applied to policemen, 338

Motivation Survey, 412

Mug shots, see Photographic identification of suspects

Multiple regression analysis, used to examine relationship between frequency of executions and capital homicide rate, 258

Municipal courts, 31

Municipal elections and racial underrepresentation, 384

Narcotics proceedings: accounts of police actions in, 329; and exclusionary rule, 340; suppression hearings in, 302

National Association for the Advancement of Colored People (NAACP), 48, 59, 69, 78, 110, 121; local Atlanta chapter, 133

National Consumers' League, 84

National Jury Project, 403

Natural law, 638–639

Natural law model (Dworkin), 685–688

Natural law theory, 640; and formalism, 642, 650–651

New conservatism, 708

Nomothetic approach to adjudication, 721

Normative analysis of law, 681; and postrealism, 729–730

Normative argumentation, 642; see also Purposive analysis

Normative level of social values, 666–667

Nullification power of jury, 450–451

Objective probability, 530

Opinion change: order of communication and, 488–492, 495, 496; see also Evidence presentation order; Gross order of case presentation; Witness presentation sequence

Opinion, concept of, 246, 247

Opinion evidence, 36

Opinion evidence rule, 478

Organizational behavior modification, applied to police force, 338

Original jurisdiction, 32

"Other crimes evidence" rule, 510–511

Panel on Research on Deterrent and Incapacitative Efforts of the National Research Council, 358

Parker Doctrine, 115–116, 158, 215

Peer Review Panel, 339

Peremptory challenges to jury selection, 389–392; case example, 385–386

Persuasion research, 488–495

Petit jury, 356, 406

Photographic identification of suspects, 552, 561

Plain English Movement, 538

Plaintiff's role in lawsuit, 36–37

Pleadings, 35

Police: attitudes toward, and compliance with legality, 328–329; efficiency vs. legality, 328; efforts to regulate, 275–276, 277, 280–282, 288, 297–298; function, 273–276; history of, 276–277; individual and organizational characteristics, 322–330; interrogation by, 279–282, 301–302; limitations on effectiveness of, 273–275, 304–305; minority relations and, 325, 326; organization and functions, 323; personal characteristics of, 324–326; as policymaking agency, 333–334; prosecutors and, 331; regulation, 341–342, 331–337; self-regulation, 278, 305–306, 332–335, 336, 337, 339–340, 341; social-economic background of, 322; socialization and training, 322–323; solidarity, 326–327

Police as policymaking agency, 333–334; obtaining motivation to comply with policy developed, 338–339; policy formulation process, 334–335, 336, 337; policy and judicial review, 339

Police brutality, extraction of confessions through, 280

Police discipline, creating an effective system for, 338–339

Police enforcement practices: in Canada, 309; in Europe, 309; evaluating legality of, at pretrial hearings, 302; and exclusionary rule, 275–276, 301–310, 311, 312–318, 319, 320; in Great Britain, 311; judicial regulation, 275–276, 277, 280–282, 288, 297–298, 301–312, 335; judicial review, 339; and lineup standards, 562, 563; observations on, 316–318; policy formulation process, 337; prosecutors and, 331; role of court in, 336; Supreme Court and, 278, 335, 336; see also Fourth Amendment; Fifth Amendment; Sixth Amendment; Fourteenth Amendment

Police identification practices, 552, 591

Police Intelligence Ordinance, 336–337

Police interrogation: aspects of warning on, 298–300; and brutality, 280; case example, 282–286; determinant in adversarial fact-finding trial, 551; due process/voluntariness, 280–281; and Fifth Amendment, 275, 278; and Fourth Amendment, 275, 278; impact of Miranda on, 289–295, 297; impact of warning on confessions, 297–298; judicial regulation of, 280–282; protection against, 287; and psychological coercion, 280; purpose of, 287; role of, 279–280; Supreme Court and, 280, 281, 282, 286, 287, 299

Police power, 90

Policy analysis, 642; see also Purposive analysis

Policy judgments, 28

Positivism, 629–640, 674

Positivist jurisprudence, 642, 651, 652, 656–657

Positivist model (Hart), 684–685

Postconviction proceedings of capital convicts, 209, 268

Postrealism: and law and social science, 730–732; and normative analysis of law, 729–730

Pragmatic instrumentalism, 674

Pragmatism, 671–672

Predictive validity, 296, 400

Pre-indictment right to counsel, 282, 298–299

Preponderance, 523

Preponderance of the evidence, 521, 522–523

President's Commission on Law Enforcement and the Administration of Justice, 198, 274, 277, 280, 322, 330, 331, 332, 335, 337, 338, 339–340, 341

Presumption, 528

Pretrial conference, 35

Pretrial criminal process, 551

Pretrial identification: composite sketches and, 561; in lineup, 550–551; photo identification, 561; right to counsel during, 557–558; sources of erroneous, 552; see also Eyewitness identification

Pretrial publicity and juror partiality, 407; case example, 415–417; change of venue, 407–409; free press/fair trial controversy, 412–415, 418; research on, 418–420

Primacy effect, 488–489, 491–492, 496; anticipation of opposing communication, 490–491; delay between opposing communications, 490; and prior familiarity with communication, 489–490; see also Evidence presentation order; Gross order of presentation; Internal order of presentation; Opinion change

Primacy experiments, 488–492

Prima facie case, 361

Private school and white flight, 137, 138

Privileged evidence, 478

Probability theory: used in litigation, 523–537; see also Objective probability; Subjective probability

Probate court, 31

Procedural justice, 19, 674
Process of judgment, 27–28
Progressivism, 672
Proof methods, 497; adversarial and inquisitorial, 497–500, 500, 501
Property, right to acquire and hold, 661
Prosecution, and order of communication, 496
Psychoanalysis, used by judges to gain self-insight, 671
Psycholegal research history: coming of age stage (1970s and 1980s), 617–618; forensic stage (1950s), 614–617; legal realist stage (1930s), 610–614; pioneering stage (1900s), 608–609
Psychological research; problems and prospects of, 625–629
Public accomodations and racial discrimination, 46, 47
Public opinion surveys: used to assess attitudes on capital punishment, 224, 229, 230, 244–246, 247–250; used to determine possibility of fair trial, 408; see also Survey research
Punishment, arbitrariness in, 242
Purposive analysis, 642, 643, 651
Purposive behaviorism, 690
Purposive jurisprudence, 643, 674–681
Purposivism, 638

Quantification of probative value of evidence, 523, 529

Racial discrimination, 50–54; and capital punishment, 198, 199, 200, 201–205, 210, 263, 264–265; creation of Civil War Amendments and Reconstruction legislation and dismantling, 45–47; in early framework of U.S. government, 43; in employment, 376–385; and executions for rape, 200, 201, 210; and imposition of death penalty, 200, 201–205, 263, 264–265; intelligence testing and, 57; and jury selection, 356–357, 360, 362, 363–364, 369, 370, 373–375, 386, 435, 446; and limiting of questioning at voir dire, 406; and lynchings, 201; movement against, 57–59; rise of Jim Crow legislation, 47–48, 55; and school segregation, 44, 46, 48–50; in sentencing, 209; and Social Darwinism, 56–57, 58
Racial discrimination law: and reinterpretation of Brown, 157–160

Racial separation, see Segregation
Racial underrepresentation: in employment, 384; in exclusionary zoning, 384; in jury selection, 356, 363–364, 386, 389, 435, 446; in municipal elections, 384; in Northern school segregation, 384; see also Discrimination; Racial discrimination
Radical Reconstruction legislation, 45
Random sampling, 410
Rape: as capital crime, 200, 201–205, 210, 262, 267; racial inequality in executions for, 200, 201–205, 210, 263
Rape cases, women jurors on, 403
Rape legislation, 29
Ratio decidendi, 100
Rational-comprehensive decision-making, 344
Rationalization and study of opinions, 671
Realism, see Legal realism
Realist reasoning, 662–666; see also Legal realism
Realist style of decision-making, 667
Reality experiment, 568, 608, 620
Reasonableness, 93–94
Reasoned elaboration, 642, 676–681; see also Purposive analysis
Rebuttal brief, 38
Recorder's court, 31
Regression analysis, 258; used in juror verdict prediction, 402; see also Multiple regression analysis
Relevance (evidence) rule, 478
Relevance of evidence, 515; and joinder, 517; vs. sufficiency of evidence, 510
Remembrance experiments, 568
Resegregation, 140; within classrooms, 161
Residential segregation, 48, 49, 69, 122, 123, 127, 128, 134–136, 143
Retributive justice, 259
Revisionism, 708
Robberies, and use of eyewitness identification, 551
Royal Commission on Capital Punishment, 196
Russell Sage Foundation, 731

Sampling methodology: applications to litigation, 615
School desegregation, 107, 175, 181, 623; benefits, 157; and busing, 113–114, 117–120, 121, 123–126, 133, 139, 143–149; community control movement, 133; court-ordered, and white flight, 139; differences

School desegregation (cont.)
  between schools attended by whites and blacks, 141–142; effects on residential segregation, 135–136; implementation of *Brown*, 109–115; mandatory vs. voluntary, 151; Northern school desegregation, 121–123; post-*Brown* Southern school desegregation, 115–121; research on, 182; and self-esteem of minority children, 152; and Supreme Court, 150; and white flight, 137–140; *see also* Biracial schooling; School segregation
School desegregation cases, 3
School segregation, 44, 46, 48–50, 62–66, 67, 107; consequences of, 68; drive against, 69–70; effects of, 59–62, 77, 79, 129–130, 615, 623; and racial discrimination, 44, 46, 48–50; and residential segregation, 134–135; social scientists involved in legal process related to, 78–83, 615; white flight and, 137–140; *see also* School desegregation; Segregation
Science court, 712–713
"Scientific" decision-making, 344
Scientific jury selection, 357, 399
Scientific psychology, 689
Scientific thinking, 675
Search and seizure laws, 321, 328, 329; *see also* Fourth Amendment
Segregation, 107; case example, 62–66; effects of, 59–62, 70–77, 78, 133, 143, 158; and Northern migration of blacks, 122; in public areas, 68; residential, 48, 49, 69, 122, 123, 127, 128, 134–136, 143; school, 44, 46, 48–50, 63–66, 67, 129–130; Social Darwinism and, 57; social and personality effects of, 160; social science evidence used in court, 78–83; and suburbanization, 122; *see also* Biracial schooling; School segregation
Segregation laws, 47–48, 55; case example, 50–54
Selective migration theory, 58, 61
Self-esteem of minority children, 152
Sentencing, and racial discrimination, 209
Separate-but-equal doctrine, 48, 63, 67, 68, 70, 77, 79, 662; case example, 50–54
Sequestration of jury, 407; impact, 405
Seventh Amendment: case complexity and, 462–466, 469; right to a jury in civil cases, 355, 431, 437
Sexual assault, *see* Rape

Sexual underrepresentation, on jury panels, 360, 370
Shadow jury technique, 404
Showup, 552
Simple random sampling, 410
Single verdict trial, 216
Sixth Amendment, 275, 384; right to confront one's accuser, 483, 487–488, 550; right to an impartial jury, 412; right to a jury in criminal cases, 335, 431, 434, 435; right to a public trial, 508; underrepresentation in venire as violation of, 389
Slavery: and capital offenses, 194–195; and Thirteenth Amendment, 45
Social Darwinism, 69; formalism as product of, 659; influence on judicial thinking, 662; racial discrimination and, 56–57; reaction against, 58
Social-legal inquiry: place of jurisprudence in, 643–644
Social-legal research: approaches to, 6; introduction to, 8–10; trends in, 5
Social science: role in law creation, 78–81; use in legal processes related to desegregation, 78–83, 130–131; use in legal processes related to social welfare programs, 84–85; use in trials with political and racial overtones, 392–399; used in jury selection, 399–401, 402, 403, 404; used in post-*Brown* school desegregation, 133–157
Social science disciplines, educational criteria, 723–725
Social science evidence in desegregation cases, 154–155
Social science evidence presentation: communication and evaluation of evidence, 709–710; facts, values, and adversary process, 710–711
Social science in law school curriculum, 725–726; and formalism, 726; and realism, 726–728
Social science research: and bridge to judicial decision-making, 5–6; and judicial adjudication, 739; and judicial legislation, 740–742; and judicial rationalization, 742–743; role in court, 3; whether to use and how to use in court, 696–709, 714–716
Sociological jurisprudence, 669–670, 672, 674
Socio-pedagogic purpose of law, 29
S-O-R theory, 690
Southern Manifesto, 107

Special deterrence, 256, 320
Split verdict trial, 216, 231
Standard of reasonable doubt, 522
Stanford-Binet test, 171
State courts, 31
State courts of appeals, 31
State criminal processes, 451–452
Stationhouse lineup, 552; *see also* Lineup identification
Stratified sampling, 410
Stress, effect on eyewitness identification, 577
Strict scrutiny standard, 94–95
Struck jury, 388
Subjective probability, 530–531, 536; Bayes' Theorem, 531–534
Substantive due process, 91; demise of, 93; and *laissez-faire* philosophy, 92; as tool for blocking social and economic regulations, 92
Suburbanization and racial imbalance, 122
Sufficiency of evidence: vs. relevance of evidence, 510
Summary judgment, 35
Summation at trial, 483–484
Superior court, 31
Suppression decisions, 339; inconsistency in decisions by judges, 332
Suppression hearings, 301–302, 330–331; description by police of actions that were taken during, 329, 339; in narcotics proceedings, 302
Suppression motions, 301–302, 313–316, 318, 319; for gambling charges, 313, 314, 315; for narcotics charges, 313, 314, 315; for weapons charges, 313, 314, 315
Supreme Court: as arbiter of constitutionality, 93; capital punishment and, 210, 215–216, 229, 231–233, 255, 265, 266, 267, 268, 549; decision-making process, 66; and early Civil Rights cases, 47; and employment discrimination, 382; and eyewitness identification evidence safeguards, 549–550; and Fifth Amendment, 278, 286; and Fourteenth Amendment, 47; and Fourth Amendment, 303, 310, 549; and identification cases, 552; and jury selection; 356–357, 406; and jury size, 431, 435, 436, 441–442; and jury verdicts, 431; and municipal elections, 384; organization and duties, 32; police enforcement practices and, 278, 335, 336; police interrogation and, 280, 281, 282, 286, 287,

299; and pretrial publicity/juror partiality, 413–414, 418, 615; right to counsel at pretrial phase, 557–558; and Seventh Amendment right to jury trial in civil cases, 464–465; and school desegregation, 150, 615, 616; and standard of proof, 529; and trademark infringement, 411; and use of social science evidence, 675, 695, 696, 697–698; and use of television equipment at trial, 508–509
Survey research: applications in litigation, 615; to establish community bias, 409–410; to establish trademark infringement, 410–412; in jury selection, 400
Systematic deterrence, 320
Systematic jury selection, 399–401, 402, 403, 404, 405, 406

Television cameras in courtroom, 508–509
Test, 21, 178
Test bias, 170–174
Testimony: controversy over prerecording by videotape, 502, 504; deletion of inadmissible testimony by use of videotape, 503, 506–507
Test validation in employment testing, 176, 177–178, 180
"Thermos survey," 411–412
"Tide Survey," 412
Totality of the circumstances test, 561–562
Tracking system within schools, 161–162
Trademark, 410
Trademark infringement, 410–412
Trend-thinking, 675
Trial by jury: litigants' opposition to, 470; Seventh Amendment right to, 355; Sixth Amendment right to, 355; Supreme Court and, 355; *see also* Jury
Trial courts, 30; separation of functions in, 37; in state court system, 31
Trial process, 34–37
Twenty-fourth Amendment, 108

Underrepresentation, *see* Discrimination; Racial discrimination; Racial underrepresentation
United States Constitution: ambiguity in language, 56; capital punishment and, 232; Eighth Amendment, 232–233; Fifteenth Amendment, 46; Fifth Amendment, 232; Fourteenth Amendment, 46, 47, 51, 52, 54,

United States Constitution (cont.)
63–64, 232; provisions from, 38–39; Thirteenth Amendment, 45, 46, 51
United States Court of Appeals, 32
United States District Courts, 31–32
University of Chicago Project, *see* Chicago Jury Project

Validity: construct, 296, 297; internal, 297, 460; in measurement theory, 296; predictive, 296
Values (moral) and attitudes, distinction between, 251
Venirepersons, 35
Verdicts by jury, 428–431, 432; agreement between judge and jury, 426–427, 429–430; and impact of peremptory challenges, 391; majority decision rule, 445; in majority jurisdictions, 446; predicting from juror's characteristics, 401–403; role of evidence on, 431; in unanimous jurisdictions, 446
Verifiable certainty standard, 714
Victimless crimes, 340
Videotape technology in judicial process, 501, 502, 507–508; economics and efficiencies, 503–504; impact on jury, 504–507; potential for editorializing, 503; technical aspects, 503; *see also* Evidence presentation; Testimony
Voir dire, 35, 228, 357; objectives, 386–387, 490; procedure, 387–392; *see also* Jury selection
Voting Rights Act, 108

Warren Commission, 414–415
Washington Pattern Jury Instructions, 523
Weapons charges, 340; and exclusionary rule, 340; suppression motions for, 313, 314, 315
White flight: forms of, 138; judicial responses to, 139–140; measurement differences, 138–139; social science debate on, 137–139
White House Conference Report of 1950, 70, 72
White suburbanization trend, 138
Wickersham Commission, 277, 280
WISC (Wechsler Intelligence Scale for Children), 164, 171, 172
Witherspoon-qualified persons, 222, 223, 224, 225, 227, 228, 229
Witness presentation sequence, 484–485, 487, 488; case example, 485–487
Women, underrepresentation on jury panels, 360, 370, 446
Women jurors on rape cases, 403
Wonderlic Personnel Test, 176, 177
Workhours: maximum for women, 84–85; case example, 85–87
Writ of certiorari, 32
Wrongful convictions and eyewitness testimony, 574, 577–579

Yale Institute of Human Relations, 727
Yale Law School, 727, 728
Yellow psychology, 609

Zoning, exclusionary, 384
Z statistic, 382
Z test, 356, 382, 383